DICTIONARY
OF
SCIENTIFIC BIOGRAPHY

PUBLISHED UNDER THE AUSPICES OF
THE AMERICAN COUNCIL OF LEARNED SOCIETIES

The American Council of Learned Societies, organized in 1919 for the purpose of advancing the study of the humanities and of the humanistic aspects of the social sciences, is a nonprofit federation comprising forty-six national scholarly groups. The Council represents the humanities in the United States in the International Union of Academies, provides fellowships and grants-in-aid, supports research-and-planning conferences and symposia, and sponsors special projects and scholarly publications.

MEMBER ORGANIZATIONS
AMERICAN PHILOSOPHICAL SOCIETY, 1743
AMERICAN ACADEMY OF ARTS AND SCIENCES, 1780
AMERICAN ANTIQUARIAN SOCIETY, 1812
AMERICAN ORIENTAL SOCIETY, 1842
AMERICAN NUMISMATIC SOCIETY, 1858
AMERICAN PHILOLOGICAL ASSOCIATION, 1869
ARCHAEOLOGICAL INSTITUTE OF AMERICA, 1879
SOCIETY OF BIBLICAL LITERATURE, 1880
MODERN LANGUAGE ASSOCIATION OF AMERICA, 1883
AMERICAN HISTORICAL ASSOCIATION, 1884
AMERICAN ECONOMIC ASSOCIATION, 1885
AMERICAN FOLKLORE SOCIETY, 1888
AMERICAN DIALECT SOCIETY, 1889
AMERICAN PSYCHOLOGICAL ASSOCIATION, 1892
ASSOCIATION OF AMERICAN LAW SCHOOLS, 1900
AMERICAN PHILOSOPHICAL ASSOCIATION, 1901
AMERICAN ANTHROPOLOGICAL ASSOCIATION, 1902
AMERICAN POLITICAL SCIENCE ASSOCIATION, 1903
BIBLIOGRAPHICAL SOCIETY OF AMERICA, 1904
ASSOCIATION OF AMERICAN GEOGRAPHERS, 1904
HISPANIC SOCIETY OF AMERICA, 1904
AMERICAN SOCIOLOGICAL ASSOCIATION, 1905
AMERICAN SOCIETY OF INTERNATIONAL LAW, 1906
ORGANIZATION OF AMERICAN HISTORIANS, 1907
AMERICAN ACADEMY OF RELIGION, 1909
COLLEGE ART ASSOCIATION OF AMERICA, 1912
HISTORY OF SCIENCE SOCIETY, 1924
LINGUISTIC SOCIETY OF AMERICA, 1924
MEDIAEVAL ACADEMY OF AMERICA, 1925
AMERICAN MUSICOLOGICAL SOCIETY, 1934
SOCIETY OF ARCHITECTURAL HISTORIANS, 1940
ECONOMIC HISTORY ASSOCIATION, 1940
ASSOCIATION FOR ASIAN STUDIES, 1941
AMERICAN SOCIETY FOR AESTHETICS, 1942
AMERICAN ASSOCIATION FOR THE ADVANCEMENT OF SLAVIC STUDIES, 1948
METAPHYSICAL SOCIETY OF AMERICA, 1950
AMERICAN STUDIES ASSOCIATION, 1950
RENAISSANCE SOCIETY OF AMERICA, 1954
SOCIETY FOR ETHNOMUSICOLOGY, 1955
AMERICAN SOCIETY FOR LEGAL HISTORY, 1956
AMERICAN SOCIETY FOR THEATRE RESEARCH, 1956
SOCIETY FOR THE HISTORY OF TECHNOLOGY, 1958
AMERICAN COMPARATIVE LITERATURE ASSOCIATION, 1960
MIDDLE EAST STUDIES ASSOCIATION OF NORTH AMERICA, 1966
AMERICAN SOCIETY FOR EIGHTEENTH-CENTURY STUDIES, 1969
ASSOCIATION FOR JEWISH STUDIES, 1969

DICTIONARY
OF
SCIENTIFIC BIOGRAPHY

FREDERIC L. HOLMES

Yale University

EDITOR IN CHIEF

Volume 18

Supplement II

ALEKSANDR NIKOLAEVICH LEBEDEV–FRITZ ZWICKY

CHARLES SCRIBNER'S SONS · NEW YORK

Copyright © 1970, 1971, 1972, 1973, 1974, 1975, 1976, 1978, 1980, 1990
American Council of Learned Societies.
First publication in an eight-volume edition 1981.

Library of Congress Cataloging in Publication Data

Main entry under title:

Dictionary of scientific biography.

''Published under the auspices of the American Council
of Learned Societies.''
Includes bibliographies and index.
1. Scientists—Biography. I. Gillispie, Charles Coulston.
II. American Council of Learned Societies
Devoted to Humanistic Studies.
Q141.D5 1981   509'.2'2 [B]   80-27830
ISBN 0-684-

ISBN 0-684-16963-0 Vols. 1 & 2   ISBN 0-684-16968-1 Vols. 11 & 12
ISBN 0-684-16964-9 Vols. 3 & 4   ISBN 0-684-16969-X Vols. 13 & 14
ISBN 0-684-16965-7 Vols. 5 & 6   ISBN 0-684-16970-3 Vols. 15 & 16
ISBN 0-684-16966-5 Vols. 7 & 8   ISBN 0-684-19177-6 Vol. 17
ISBN 0-684-16967-3 Vols. 9 & 10   ISBN 0-684-19178-4 Vol. 18

Published simultaneously in Canada
by Collier Macmillan Canada, Inc.
Copyright under the Berne Convention.

1 3 5 7 9 11 13 15 17 19   20 18 16 14 12 10 8 6 4 2

Printed in the United States of America.

Editorial Board

DICTIONARY
OF
SCIENTIFIC BIOGRAPHY

LEBEDEV, ALEKSANDR NIKOLAEVICH (*b.* Moscow, Russia, 21 May 1881; *d.* Moscow, 3 June 1938), *biochemistry.*

After graduating from a classical gymnasium in Moscow, Lebedev entered the Faculty of Natural Sciences at Moscow University in 1897. Upon receiving his bachelor's degree in 1901, he became an assistant in the chemical laboratory of N. D. Zelinsky at the university. There he became interested in catalysis and the occurrence of catalytic phenomena in living forms.

Already possessing an exceptional chemical background, Lebedev decided to expand his biological and agronomical education while continuing his work at Zelinsky's laboratory by enrolling in the Petrov-Rasumov (today the Timiriazev) Agricultural Institute, from which he received a master's degree in agronomy (1904).

Lebedev was sent abroad in the year 1905–1906 to train for the professorship. He worked with Georg Bredig in Heidelberg, where he conducted his first research on the influence of a high-frequency current on hydrogen peroxide. In 1907 he went to Berlin, where he worked in the laboratory of Eduard Buchner at the University of Berlin. For a few months in 1910 he worked with Emil Fischer at his Institute of Organic Chemistry, also at the University of Berlin.

In Buchner's laboratory Lebedev began his lengthy research on the chemical nature of alcohol fermentation. At that time the discussions resulting from contradictions in the opinions of Louis Pasteur, Marcellin Berthelot, and Moritz Traube had not been forgotten, and the conception that the chemical metabolic processes in the cell could be represented as a chain of connected biocatalytic reactions was being increasingly affirmed. Lebedev studied the kinetics of alcoholic fermentation, then began to search for intermediate products of the conversions of sugar in the process of alcohol fermentation. He was seeking to determine a general scheme of these processes, something that Adolf von Baeyer and Eduard Vohl had already attempted to do, but unsuccessfully and only speculatively. Lebedev's intense work in the laboratory led to a hemorrhage in his eye and an exacerbation of existing tuberculosis. He discontinued his work in the laboratory and went to Palermo, Sicily, where he began to summarize the data he had collected.

In 1911 Lebedev continued his research on fermentation at the Pasteur Institute's biochemical section, headed by Gabriel Bertrand. Here he developed a method for obtaining the enzyme of fermentation, zymase, from dry yeast. (More precisely, zymase is an enzyme complex inducing extracellular fermentation of sugars.) This method of maceration became the classical one, displacing Buchner's method. Lebedev read a paper on this work before the Paris Chemical Society, which awarded him its prize for it.

Upon his return to Russia, Lebedev was given a teaching position at the Don Polytechnical Institute in Novocherkassk. While there, he published his most important articles on the chemical nature of fermentation, and he summarized his research in *Khimicheskie issledovaniia nad vnekletochnym spirtovhym brozheniem* (Chemical research on extracellular alcohol fermentation, 1913), which he presented to Moscow University for the doctorate in chemistry. This work received the University Award, and in 1914 Lebedev elected professor of the highest order at the Don Polytechnical Institute.

In 1911 Lebedev showed that dihydroxyacetone is fermented by yeast juice; and in 1912, with N. Griaznov, he established that for fermentation to occur, the enzyme reductase was required, the activity of which was induced by a thermostable coenzyme. This coenzyme could be separated from zymase by means of dialysis, and the addition of the dialysate or a small quantity of boiled yeast juice restored the initial activity of zymase that was lost during dialysis. Lebedev obtained osazones of intermediate products of fermentation, and he identified them as hexose-phosphorus ethers.

In 1909 Lebedev proposed the first scheme of alcohol fermentation, with the main role in this process being played by trioses: glyceraldehyde and dihydroxyacetone. In 1912 Lebedev clarified this scheme, including in it triose phosphates as indispensable intermediate products of the anaerobic decomposition of carbohydrates. This scheme was confirmed by Otto Meyerhof and Gustav Embden.

In 1921 Lebedev moved to Moscow as professor of agronomy at Moscow University (where he worked until his death). At the same time he became a member of the Scientific Research Institute of the university. From 1930 he headed the biochemical laboratory of the Central Scientific Research Food Institute, and from 1935 he headed the biochemistry laboratory of the All-Union Institute of Experimental Medicine in Moscow.

BIBLIOGRAPHY

I. ORIGINAL WORKS. "Über Hexosephosphorsäureester," in *Biochemische Zeitschrift*, **28** (1910), 213–229; "Extraction de la zymase par simple macération," in *Comptes rendus de l'Académie des sciences* (Paris), **152** (1911), 49–51; "Über den Mechanismus der alkoholischen

Gärung," in *Biochemische Zeitschrift*, **46** (1912), 483–489; and *Khimicheskie issledovaniia nad vnekletochnym spirtovnym brozheniem* (Chemical research on extracellular alcohol fermentation; Novocherkassk, 1913).

II. SECONDARY LITERATURE. Anatoly Bezkorovainy, "Contributions of Some Early Russian Scientists to the Understanding of Glycolysis," in *Journal of the History of Medicine*, **28**, no. 4 (1973), 388–392.

A. N. SHAMIN

LEFSCHETZ, SOLOMON (*b*. Moscow, Russia, 3 September 1884; *d*. Princeton, New Jersey, 5 October 1972), *mathematics*.

Lefschetz was the son of Alexander Lefschetz, an importer, and his wife, Vera, who were Turkish citizens. Shortly after his birth the family moved to Paris, where he grew up with five brothers and one sister. French was his native tongue, but he learned Russian and other languages in later years. From 1902 to 1905 Lefschetz studied at the École Centrale, Paris, graduating as *ingenieur des arts et manufactures*. In November 1905 he emigrated to the United States and found a job at the Baldwin Locomotive Works near Philadelphia. In early 1907 he joined the engineering staff of the Westinghouse Electric and Manufacturing Company in Pittsburgh. In November of that year he lost his hands and forearms in a tragic accident.

Lefschetz soon realized that his true bent was mathematics, not engineering. Among his professors at the École Centrale had been Émile Picard and Paul Appell, authors of famous treatises on analysis and analytic mechanics that he now read. In 1910, while teaching apprentices at Westinghouse, Lefschetz determined to make his career in mathematics. He enrolled as a graduate student at Clark University, Worcester, Massachusetts, and obtained the Ph.D. in just one year with a dissertation on a problem in algebraic geometry proposed by W. E. Story. On 17 June 1912 Lefschetz became an American citizen, and on 3 July 1913 he married Alice Berg Hayes, a fellow student at Clark who had received a master's degree in mathematics. She helped him to overcome his handicap, encouraging him in his work and moderating his combative ebullience. They had no children.

From 1911 to 1913 Lefschetz was an instructor at the University of Nebraska, Lincoln, where he taught a heavy load of beginning courses but found ample time to pursue his own work in algebraic geometry. In 1913 he moved to a slightly better position at the University of Kansas in Lawrence. As his work became known in America and Europe, he rose through the ranks to become full professor

in 1923. In 1919 he was awarded the Prix Bordin by the Académie des Sciences of Paris and in 1923 the Bôcher Memorial Prize of the American Mathematical Society.

In 1924 Lefschetz accepted a post at Princeton University, where he spent the rest of his life. He had prized the opportunity for solitary research at Nebraska and Kansas, but he welcomed the new world that opened up to him at Princeton. He acquired distinguished geometers as colleagues—James W. Alexander, Luther P. Eisenhart, Oswald Veblen—and met stimulating visitors from abroad, such as Pavel Aleksandrov, Heinz Hopf, M. H. A. Newman, and Hermann Weyl. His first (1926) of some thirty doctoral students was the topologist-to-be Paul A. Smith, who had followed him to Princeton from Kansas.

From his Ph.D. to his appointment to the faculty of Princeton, Lefschetz worked mainly in algebraic geometry, his most important results being presented in his 1921 paper "On Certain Numerical Invariants of Algebraic Varieties with Application to Abelian Varieties" and in his 1924 monograph *L'analysis situs et la géométrie algébrique*. The study of the properties of families of algebraic curves and surfaces began in the nineteenth century as part of the theory of algebraic functions of complex variables. For Lefschetz, too, curves and surfaces—and, more generally, algebraic varieties—were significant representations of the corresponding functions. He was able to solve some of the problems encountered by his predecessors and to enlarge the scope of the subject by the use of new methods. As he put it, "It was my lot to plant the harpoon of algebraic topology into the body of the whale of algebraic geometry."

In the 1850's G. F. B. Riemann founded the modern theory of complex algebraic curves by considering, for each curve, an associated surface now called the Riemann surface. The theory was further developed by Guido Castelnuovo, Federigo Enriques, Francesco Severi, and especially Émile Picard. (Lefschetz, while at the École Central, had taken Picard's demanding course.) Riemann and these later mathematicians recognized that it is the topological properties of the Riemann surface (the connectedness properties of the surface as a whole rather than its metrical and local properties) that are significant, yet at the time there was no theory of such properties. In the 1890's Henri Poincaré established such a theory (under the name "analysis situs"), and Lefschetz used Poincaré's results to extend the work of Riemann and his successors.

Riemann had used a series of cuts to turn the

Riemann surface into an open 2-cell (and the correspondence between the function and the 2-cell then gave the desired results); Lefschetz used a series of cuts to turn a nonsingular algebraic variety of complex dimension d into an open $2d$-cell. This allowed him to answer many questions (for example, he showed that not all orientable manifolds of even dimension are the carrier manifolds of algebraic varieties) and to extend the theory of integrals of the second kind to double and triple integrals on an algebraic variety of any dimension.

Lefschetz took up Poincaré's study of curves on a surface, which he generalized to the study of subvarieties of an algebraic variety. He found necessary and sufficient conditions for an integral ($2d$-2)-dimensional homology class of variety V of complex dimension d to contain the cycle of a divisor on V. This result and others allowed Lefschetz to make important contributions to the theory of correspondences between curves and to the theory of Abelian varieties. (A much more detailed review by W. V. D. Hodge of Lefschetz's work and influence in algebraic geometry appears in the volume *Algebraic Geometry and Topology*.)

According to Hodge, "Our greatest debt to Lefschetz lies in the fact that he showed us that a study of topology was essential for all algebraic geometers." Lefschetz' work in algebraic geometry also gave great impetus to the study of topology, since its value to other areas of mathematics had been demonstrated. In 1923 Lefschetz turned to the development of Poincaré's topology, calling it algebraic topology to distinguish it from the abstract topology of sets of points.

Almost all of Lefschetz' topology resulted from his desire to prove certain fixed-point theorems. Around 1910 L. E. J. Brouwer proved a basic fixed-point theorem: Every continuous transformation of an n-simplex into itself has at least one fixed point. In a series of papers Lefschetz obtained a much more general result: For any continuous transformation f of a topological space X into itself, there is a number $L(f)$, often called the Lefschetz number, such that if $L(f) \neq 0$, then the transformation f has a fixed point. $L(f)$ is defined as follows: f induces a transformation f_p of the pth homology group H_p of the space X into itself; consider H_p as a vector space over the rational numbers and let $\mathrm{Tr}(f_p)$ be the trace of f_p; then $L(f) = \Sigma (-1)^p \mathrm{Tr}(f_p)$. For $L(f)$ to be well defined, certain restrictions must be placed on X; Lefschetz succeeded in progressively weakening these restrictions.

Lefschetz used the following simple example to explain his fixed-point theorem. Let f be a continuous transformation of the interval $0 \leq x \leq 1$ into itself. The curve consisting of the points $(x, f(x))$ represents f. (See Figure 1.) The diagonal $0 \leq x = y \leq 1$ represents the identity transformation i, that is, the transformation that sends each point of the interval to itself. The points of intersection (called the coincidences) of f and i are the fixed points of f. We want a number that is the same for all continuous transformations of the interval $0 \leq x \leq 1$. The number of coincidences is not constant; f and g, for example, differ in this respect. But if, for a particular transformation, we count the number of crossings from *above* to below (marked a in the figure) and the number of crossings from *below* to above (marked b in the figure), and if we subtract the latter from the former, we get a number (here, 1) that is the same for all continuous transformations of an interval into itself. That is, for this space (the interval $0 \leq x \leq 1$), the Lefschetz number $L(f)$ is 1. Since $L(f)$ is not zero, any continuous transformation of $0 \leq x \leq 1$ into itself has a fixed point. (It is intuitively clear that any continuous curve passing from the left side of the square to the right side must intersect the diagonal.)

In 1923 Lefschetz proved this fixed-point theorem for compact orientable manifolds. Since an n-cell is not a manifold, this result did not include the Brouwer fixed-point theorem. By introducing the concept of relative homology groups, Lefschetz in 1927 extended his theorem to manifolds with boundary; his theorem then included Brouwer's. He continued to seek generalizations of the theorem; in 1927 he proved it for any finite complex, and in 1936 for any locally connected space. Lefschetz studied fixed points as part of a more general study of coincidences. If f and g are transformations of space X into space Y, the points x of X such that $f(x) = g(x)$ are called the coincidences of f and g. One can prove that under certain conditions two transformations must have coincidences—for example, in Figure 1, if f and g are continuous and f is above g at 0 and below g at 1, then the number of times f crosses g from above to below (marked α) minus the number of times f crosses g from below to above (marked β) is necessarily 1.

In the course of this work Lefschetz invented many of the basic tools of algebraic topology. He made extensive use of product spaces; he developed intersection theory, including the theory of the intersection ring of a manifold; and he made essential contributions to various kinds of homology theory, notably relative homology, singular homology, and cohomology.

A by-product of Lefschetz' work on fixed points

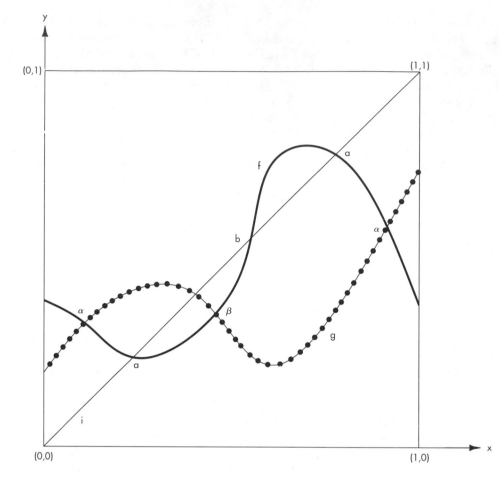

FIGURE 1.

was his duality theorem, which provided a bridge between the classical duality theorems of Poincaré and of Alexander. The Lefschetz duality theorem states that the p-dimensional Betti number of an orientable n-dimensional manifold M with regular boundary L equals the $(n-p)$-dimensional Betti number of M modulo L (that is, without L). Figure 2 shows an oriented 2-manifold M with regular boundary L in three parts, one exterior and two interior. The absolute 1-cycles c_1 and c_2 generate the 1-dimensional Betti group of M with boundary L, and the relative 1-cycles d_1 and d_2 generate the relative 1-dimensional Betti group of M modulo L. Thus the 1-dimensional Betti numbers of M and M modulo L are both 2. Cuts along d_1 and d_2 turn the 2-manifold into a 2-cell. (A full exposition of Lefschetz' fixed-point theorem and his duality theorem is in his *Introduction to Topology*, 1949.)

During his years as professor at Princeton (1924–1953), Lefschetz was the center of an active group of topologists. His *Topology* (1930) and his *Algebraic Topology* (1942) presented comprehensive accounts of the field and were extremely influential. Indeed,

these books firmly established the use of the terms "topology" (rather than "analysis situs") and "algebraic topology" (rather than "combinatorial topology"). (A thorough review by Norman Steenrod of Lefschetz' work and influence in algebraic topology appears in *Algebraic Geometry and Topology*, 1957.)

Lefschetz was an editor of *Annals of Mathematics* from 1928 to 1958, and it was primarily his efforts—insisting on the highest standards, soliciting manuscripts, and securing rapid publication of the most important papers—that made the *Annals* one of the world's foremost mathematical journals. As Steenrod put it, "The importance to American mathematicians of a first-class journal is that it sets high standards for them to aim at. In this somewhat indirect manner, Lefschetz profoundly affected the development of mathematics in the United States."

There was another way in which Lefschetz contributed to the beginning of the publication of advanced mathematics in the United States. As late as the 1930's the American Mathematical Society, whose Colloquium Publications included books by

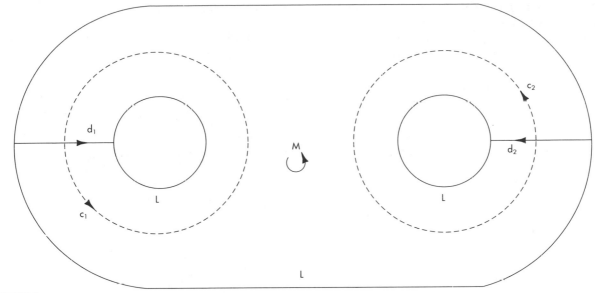

FIGURE 2.

Lefschetz in 1930 and 1942, was almost the only U.S. publisher of advanced mathematics books. However, two important series of advanced mathematics monographs and textbooks began in 1938 and 1940: the Princeton Mathematical Series and the Annals of Mathematics Studies, both initiated by A. W. Tucker, student and colleague of Lefschetz. Lefschetz wrote two important books for the former series (1949, 1953) and wrote or edited six books for the latter.

In 1943 Lefschetz was asked to consult for the U.S. Navy at the David Taylor Model Basin near Washington, D.C. Working with Nicholas Minorsky, he studied guidance systems and the stability of ships, and became acquainted with the work of Soviet mathematicians on nonlinear mechanics and control theory. Lefschetz recognized that the geometric theory of differential equations, which had begun with the work of Poincaré and A. M. Liapunov, could be fruitfully applied, and his background in algebraic geometry and topology proved useful. From 1943 to the end of his life, Lefschetz gave most of his attention to differential equations, doing research and encouraging others.

Lefschetz was almost sixty years old when he turned to differential equations, yet he did important original work. He studied the solutions of analytic differential equations near singular points and gave a complete characterization, for a two-dimensional system, of the solution curves passing through an isolated critical point in the neighborhood of the critical point. Much of his work focused on nonlinear differential equations and on dissipative (as distinct

from conservative) dynamic systems. This work contributed to the theory of nonlinear controls and to the study of structural stability of systems. The Russian topologist L. S. Pontriagin, who was a good friend of Lefschetz' both before and after the war, also turned to control theory as a result of his wartime work. (Lawrence Markus' "Solomon Lefschetz: An Appreciation in Memoriam" contains a more detailed account of Lefschetz' work and influence on differential equations.)

In 1946 the newly established Office of Naval Research provided the funding for a differential equations project, directed by Lefschetz, at Princeton. This soon became a leading center for the study of ordinary differential equations, and the project continued at Princeton for five years after Lefschetz' retirement in 1953. In 1957 he established a mathematics center under the auspices of the Research Institute for Advanced Study (RIAS), a branch of the Glen L. Martin Company of Baltimore (now Martin-Marietta). In 1964 Lefschetz and many of the other mathematicians in his group at RIAS moved to Brown University to form the Center for Dynamical Systems (later named the Lefschetz Center for Dynamical Systems). J. P. LaSalle, who had spent the year 1946–1947 with the differential equations project at Princeton and who was Lefschetz' second in command at RIAS, became director at the Brown center. Lefschetz helped to found the *Journal of Differential Equations* and served as an editor for some fifteen years. He continued his work at Brown until 1970.

Lefschetz translated two Russian books on differential equations into English, and he edited several volumes on nonlinear oscillations. He gave constant encouragement to his younger colleagues, in some cases cajoling them into proving important theorems. His work in differential equations showed the usefulness of geometric and topological methods and helped to raise the intellectual stature of applied mathematics.

Throughout his life Lefschetz loved to travel. In the 1920's and 1930's he made many trips to Europe, especially to France, Italy, and the Soviet Union. During World War II, European travel was impractical, so Lefschetz was visiting professor at the National University of Mexico (1944). Although he did not know Spanish when he arrived there, several weeks later he was giving his lectures in that language. He returned for several months in the academic year 1945–1946, and in the following two decades made many trips to Mexico City, spending most winters there from 1953 to 1966. He helped to build a lively school of mathematics at the National University of Mexico, and in recognition of his efforts the Mexican government in 1964 awarded him the Order of the Aztec Eagle, rarely presented to a foreigner.

Lefschetz was Henry Burchard Fine (research) professor of mathematics at Princeton (1933–1953), succeeding Oswald Veblen, the first holder of the chair (1926–1932). He was chairman of the department of mathematics at Princeton from 1945 until his retirement in 1953. Lefschetz served as president of the American Mathematical Society (1935–1936). The Accademia Nazionale dei Lincei of Rome awarded him the Antonio Feltrinelli International Prize, one of the world's highest mathematical honors, in 1956. In 1964 he was awarded the National Medal of Science by President Johnson "for indomitable leadership in developing mathematics and training mathematicians, for fundamental publications in algebraic geometry and topology, and for stimulating needed research in nonlinear control processes." He was granted honorary degrees by Paris, Prague, Mexico, Clark, Brown, and Princeton. He was a member of the American Philosophical Society and of the National Academy of Sciences, and a foreign member of the Royal Society of London, of the Académie des Sciences of Paris, of the Academia Real de Ciencias of Madrid, and of the Reale Instituto Lombardo of Milan.

BIBLIOGRAPHY

I. ORIGINAL WORKS. Lefschetz' doctoral dissertation (Clark University, 1911), "On the Existence of Loci with

Given Singularities," was published in *Transactions of the American Mathematical Society,* **14** (1913), 23–41. Major works include *L'analysis situs et la géométrie algébrique* (Paris, 1924; repr. 1950); *Topology* (New York, 1930; 2nd ed., 1956); *Algebraic Topology* (New York, 1942); *Introduction to Topology* (Princeton, 1949); *Algebraic Geometry* (Princeton, 1953); *Differential Equations: Geometric Theory* (New York, 1957; 2nd ed., 1962); *Stability by Liapunov's Direct Method* (New York, 1961), written with Joseph P. LaSalle; *Stability of Nonlinear Automatic Control Systems* (New York, 1964); and *Applications of Algebraic Topology* (New York, 1975). A vivid self-portrait of Lefschetz is "Reminiscences of a Mathematical Immigrant in the United States," in *American Mathematical Monthly,* **77** (1970), 344–350.

Selected Papers (New York, 1971) brings together "A Page of Mathematical Autobiography," in *Bulletin of the American Mathematical Society,* **74** (1968), 854–879, awarded the society's 1970 Leroy P. Steele Prize; "On Certain Numerical Invariants of Algebraic Varieties with Application to Abelian Varieties," in *Transactions of the American Mathematical Society,* **22** (1921), 327–482, awarded the society's 1924 Bôcher Memorial Prize and, in its original French version, the 1919 Prix Bordin of the Paris Academy of Sciences; the 1924 monograph cited above; 16 other principal papers; and a bibliography (to 1970). The paper "The Early Development of Algebraic Topology," in *Boletim da Sociedade brasiliera de matematica,* **1** (1971), 1–48, summarizes Lefschetz' view of the development of algebraic topology.

Lefschetz' works are listed in Poggendorff, V, 723; VI, 1488; VIIb, 2802–2804.

II. SECONDARY LITERATURE. On Lefschetz and his work see Raymond C. Archibald, *A Semicentennial History of the American Mathematical Society* (New York, 1938), 236–240; R. H. Fox, D. C. Spencer, and A. W. Tucker, eds., *Algebraic Geometry and Topology* (Princeton, 1957), 1–49; Philip Griffiths, Donald C. Spencer, and George W. Whitehead, "Solomon Lefschetz," in *Biographical Memoirs, National Academy of Sciences,* **61** (1990); Sir William Hodge, "Solomon Lefschetz, 1884–1972," in *Biographical Memoirs of Fellows of the Royal Society,* **19** (1973), 433–453, repr. in *Bulletin of the London Mathematical Society,* **6** (1974), 198–217, and in *The Lefschetz Centennial Conference,* pt. I, *Proceedings on Algebraic Geometry,* D. Sundararaman, ed. (Providence, R.I., 1986), 27–46; and Lawrence Markus, "Solomon Lefschetz: An Appreciation in Memoriam," in *Bulletin of the American Mathematical Society,* **79** (1973), 663–680. These memoirs all contain bibliographies; Markus also cites the reviews of Lefschetz' publications in *Mathematical Reviews.* Other memoirs are Sir William Hodge, "Solomon Lefschetz, 1884–1972," in *American Philosophical Society Year Book, 1974* (1975), 186–193; and Joseph P. LaSalle, "Memorial to Solomon Lefschetz," in *IEEE Transactions on Automatic Control,* **AC-18** (1973), 89–90, and "Solomon Lefschetz: A Memorial Address," in *Dynamical Systems,* I, Lamberto Cesari, Jack K. Hale, and Joseph P. LaSalle, eds. (New York, 1976), xvii–xxi. Also see *National Cyclopedia of American Biography*, LVI (Clifton, N.J., 1975), 503–504.

ALBERT W. TUCKER
FREDERIK NEBEKER

LEHMAN, JEAN-PIERRE (*b.* Caen, France, 10 August 1914; *d.* Paris, France, 26 February 1981), *vertebrate paleontology.*

Jean-Pierre was the second child of Madeleine Auvray and Gaston Lehman, a civil engineer descended from old Parisian stock. He studied at the Lycée Carnot, and later at the Sorbonne, then the seat of the Faculty of Sciences, escaping for only a year to Grenoble, where chemistry instruction (then required for a *licence* in natural sciences) was of a higher standard. In Grenoble he met Ingegärd Eneström, a Swedish doctor's daughter, who was finishing her higher education in French. They married and lived in Paris most of their lives, with an annual trip to Sweden; they had one son and two daughters. Although educated as a Catholic, Lehman professed a serene atheism. He was an officer of the Légion d'honneur and of the Palmes académiques and was elected in 1979 to the Académie des sciences.

Lehman taught at the Lycée de Nice from 1940 to 1945, then at the Laboratoire de géologie de la faculté des sciences de Paris from 1950 to 1955, and finally at the École normale supérieure de Saint-Cloud and the Muséum national d'histoire naturelle, as the holder of the chair in paleontology, from 1956 to 1981. He attracted a large number of students and founded a school of paleoanatomy that soon became officially recognized as the Institut de paléontologie, now one of the world's most important centers of paleontology. He also organized international colloquia (1961, 1966, 1973), gave conferences in many foreign countries, and served as secretary, then vice president, of the Société géologique de France. His tireless efforts in promoting the cause of paleontology led him to become editor of the journal *Les annales de paléontologie*, then to found the *Cahiers de paléontologie*, where several of his disciples have published anatomical monographs. He was also a member of the scientific committee of the Fondation Singer Polignac, which published, thanks to his influence, several paleontological works.

Lehman contributed to the *Traité de zoologie* of P. P. Grassé (vol. XIII, fasc. 3) and the *Traité de paléontologie* of Jean Piveteau (vols. III, IV, and V). He translated many paleontological works from Swedish, German, and English. Not content to publish in his specialized field of research alone, he addressed the major problems of paleontology and evolution in four thoughtful books and many papers. Finally, he oversaw the renovation of the Galerie de paléontologie, established the Galerie de paléobotanique, and organized public paleontological exhibitions in the Parc de Vincennes and in the museum.

The driving power behind all these activities was Lehman's tenacity and enthusiasm for research. His *Diplôme d'études supérieures* (1937), a prelude to the *Agrégation* degree (1939), influenced his whole career: it concerned the fishes of the Upper Devonian of Scania and was prepared at the Museum of Natural History of Stockholm. He later dedicated all his scientific activity to the study of lower vertebrates and to work directly or indirectly carried out with the Swedish team; Erik A. Stensiö had made Stockholm the heart of such research. Lehman began with a study of Agnatha (jawless vertebrates), and the knowledge he acquired on this group allowed him later to discuss the problem of the origin of vertebrates. But very rapidly the fish of North Africa and Madagascar became a main focus of his research, with the material coming essentially from his own excavations (in 1950, 1952, 1954, 1961, 1964, 1966, 1969, 1974, and 1979). His 1969 expedition to Spitzbergen, for which he obtained much financial and material support, produced twenty-three tons of fossils that are still under study. The Arthrodires from the Upper Devonian of Morocco were known previously only by isolated plates. Lehman's new material brought not only the knowledge of new taxa of giant size, but also that of the endocranium, the thoracic shield, and the head-thorax link.

On the other hand, the presence in Africa of species of an otherwise American genus allowed him to draw paleogeographic conclusions. The Actinopterygians from Madagascar (Paleonisciformes, Parasemionotiformes) were the subject of his doctoral thesis. Before his studies, reconstructions of the endocranium were rare; he made some with such great precision that they are now "better known than those of many genera of extant Teleostomes." He also followed the evolution of the dermal cephalic skeleton, showing that bone fusions or dissociations are frequent in Actinopterygians. He confirmed moreover the morphogenetic role of the pit lines and established the precocity of bone regression in these fishes. Finally he showed that the Actinopterygian *Cheirolepis* was not an intermediate form between Crossopterygians and Actinopterygians and that "Chondrichthyens" and "Holosteens" were not valid systematic units. Lehman was still studying Actinopterygian fishes when he died.

For the Crossopterygians and Dipnoans, Lehman used the same methodology: the search for fossils, careful anatomical study, establishment of bone homologies (for example, between the squamosal of Crossopterygians and the propercular of Actinopterygians), and phyletic considerations (for example, the heterogeneity of the Crossopterygians, the origin of Urodeles).

The Triassic stegocephalians constitute the second center of his research. Those from Madagascar had rarely been studied. After finding well-preserved skulls of néorachitomes, bentosuchids, rhinosuchoids, and Trematosauria, he described them, followed growth series, and recognized new taxa, including the most ancient members of the Brachypodoids. The presence of freshwater Bentosuchids in marine formations led him to reconstruct local paleoecology and to recognize continental relations between Madagascar and the Northern Hemisphere in the Eotriassic, as well as a separation between Madagascar and Africa as early as that epoch. Concerning the Moroccan stegocephalians, they were virtually unknown until the work of Lehman. They appear to be quite varied, but their study mainly demonstrated the insufficient systematic value of the vertebral criterion in Stegocephalia; the existence of two separate lineages, batracomorphs and reptiliomorphs; the evolution of the otic notch in this group; and the state of specialization of Embolomers. It also clarified the composition of the Ichthyostegalia.

These numerous and various analyses were underlined by Lehman's constant preoccupation "to consider each fossil as a vestige of a once living animal" and "to revive these ancient groups whose comparison with extant forms gives less evident results than do Tertiary vertebrates." Lehman was one of the first paleontologists to examine lower vertebrates from a functional as well as an anatomical point of view, relying heavily on comparative anatomy.

BIBLIOGRAPHY

I. ORIGINAL WORKS. "Etude complémentaire des poissons de l'Eotrias de Madagascar," in *Kungl. Svenska Vetenskapsak. Handlingar*, 4th ser., **2**, no. 6 (1952); "Généralités sur les amphibiens: Les embolomères et les seymouriamorphes, Les rachitomes, Les phyllospondyles," in Jean Piveteau, ed., *Traité de paléontologie*, V (Paris, 1952–), 3–52, 67–125, 173–224, 227–249; "Les arthrodires du Dévonien supérieur du Tafilalet,"

in *Notes et mémoires, serv. géol. Maroc* (Rabat, 1956), 1–70; "Compléments à l'étude des genres *Escrinesomus* et *Bobasatrania*," in *Annales de paléontologie*, **42** (1956), 1–28; "Sous classe des actinopterygii: Généralités et évolution, superordre des chondrostéens," in Pierre Paul Grassé, ed., *Traité de zoologie*, XIII, fasc. 3 (Paris); *L'évolution des vertébrés inférieurs* (Paris, 1959); "Les dipneustes du Dévonien supérieur du Groenland," in *Meddelelser om Grönland*, **160** (1959); "Les stégocéphales du Trias de Madagascar," in *Annales de paléontologie*, **47** (1962).

"Actinopterygii, dipnoi et crossopterygii, brachiopterygii," in Jean Piveteau, ed., *Traité de paléontologie*, IV, fasc. 3 (Paris, 1952–); "Nouveaux stégocéphales de Madagascar," in *Annales de paléontologie (vertébrés)*, **52**, fasc. 2 (1966), 117–139; *Précis de géologie*, 2 vols. (Paris, 1967–1968), written with Jean Auboin and P. Brousse; "Nouveaux vertébrés fossiles du Trias de la série de Zarzaïtine," in *Annales de paléontologie (vertébrés)*, **57**, fasc. 1 (1971), 71–93; "Quelques réflexions sur la phylogénèse des vertébrés inférieurs," in *Colloque Internat. du CNRS*, no. 218 (1975); "Nouveaux poissons fossiles du Dévonien du Maroc," in *Annales de paléontologie (vertébrés)*, **62** fasc. 1 (1976), 1–34; *Les preuves paléontologiques de l'évolution* (Paris, 1973), trans. by Patricia Crampton as *The Proofs of Evolution* (New York and London, 1977); "Nouveaux trématosaures de Madagascar: Les stégocéphales malgaches et leur paléoécologie," in *Annales de paléontologie (vertébrés)*, **65**, fasc. 1 (1979), 35–54.

II. SECONDARY LITERATURE. For obituaries, see Z. Rocek, *Vesmir, Prirod. Casopsis Ceskosl. Akad. Ved.*, **60**, no. 3 (1981), 272; and Donald and Denise Russell, *News Bulletin of the Society of Vertebrate Paleontologists*, **122** (1981), 65–66.

D. SIGOGNEAU-RUSSELL

LEIPUNSKII, ALEKSANDR IL'ICH (*b.* Dragli, Grodnenskaia guberniia, Russia [now Poland], 7 December 1903; *d.* Obninsk, Kaluzhskaia oblast, U.S.S.R., 14 August 1972), *physics.*

Leipunskii's father, Il'ia Isaakovich Leipunskii, was a construction and road technician; his mother, Sophia Naumovna, was a housewife.

Leipunskii started working in 1918; before he entered the Petrograd Polytechnical Institute (1921) he had served as an unskilled laborer and as a foreman's assistant at a chemical factory in Rybinsk (now Andropov). He graduated from the Faculty of Physics and Mechanics at the Petrograd Polytechnical Institute (PTI) in 1926. When he was still a student, he started work at the PTI in the laboratory of N. N. Semenov (1924–1928). After a year of preparation, Leipunskii moved to the Ukrainian PTI in Kharkov, where he worked from 1929 to 1941 (with two interruptions when he was at the Cavendish Laboratory, Cambridge [1934–1935], and in Leningrad as head of a department at the Radium Institute). At the Ukrainian PTI, Leipunskii advanced from senior physicist to director. From 1941 to 1952 he was head of the department of physics, deputy director, and director of the Institute of Physics of the Ukrainian Academy of Sciences (Kiev). In 1952 he moved to the Institute of Energy Physics in Obninsk and from 1959 to 1972 was its scientific head.

At the Leningrad PTI, Leipunskii was involved with chemical physics and electronic chemistry. The main results are concerned with the experimental investigation of nonelastic collisions when the excited atoms (molecules) transfer their energy to slow electrons by the radiation-free mechanism; this reaction is inverse to that of excitation of atoms by electrons due to elastic collisions. With G. D. Latishev, Leipunskii conducted a classical experiment that demonstrated the existence of such processes for excited atoms of mercury. He also investigated dissociation and recombination of halogen molecules and the formation of the negative ions.

After moving to Kharkov, Leipunskii shifted his attention to nuclear physics and worked on the design of linear (and in the late 1930's cyclic) accelerators. With his colleagues he carried out an experiment on splitting the nuclei of lithium by artificially accelerated protons (this experiment, the first of its kind in the Soviet Union, was a modification of a classical experiment by J. D. Cockroft and E. T. S. Walton). In a series of experiments on absorption of neutrons within a wide temperature range (20–463 K), Leipunskii was the first to discover the resonance effects on light nuclei during neutron scattering.

While at the Cavendish Laboratory in Cambridge (1934–1935), directed by Rutherford, Leipunskii carried out important research on β-decay and on the physics of the neutrino. He developed the experimental technique for demonstrating the existence of the neutrino that was based on the investigation of energy distribution of recoil nuclei of the C 11 isotope released in the course of β-decay associated with the "flight" of a neutrino. This experiment (realized in part) may be thought of as a prototype of the research carried out in 1938 at A. I. Alikhanov's laboratory at the Leningrad PTI and of the decisive result achieved by James Allen in 1942 in his investigation of an energy spectrum of recoil nuclei arising from the decay of Be 7.

Leipunskii devoted the last twenty-five years of his life to the development of reactor engineering.

In 1947, during his study of nuclear processes involving fast neutrons, Leipunskii developed the idea of breeding the nuclear fuel in fast-neutron reactors following the formation of plutonium from U 238. In 1949 he started working on the practical realization of this idea. At the Institute of Energy Physics in Obninsk, he developed the procedure of designing breeder fast-neutron reactors, having solved many problems associated not only with the nuclear processes but also with some purely engineering problems, particularly the choice of a heat-transfer fluid, for which he suggested using liquid metals (sodium).

As a result of these efforts, the first fast-neutron reactor in the Soviet Union started operating in 1955. By the end of the 1950's, the possibility of breeding the nuclear fuel and the reliability of the reactors' design had been demonstrated by experiments on their laboratory prototypes, built by Leipunskii's group. In 1959 the 5,000-kw fast-neutron reactor went into operation, and work had started on design and construction of an industrial power station with fast-neutron reactors, its electrical power being equal to 350,000 kw. The station and reactor, located at Shevchenko, on the coast of the Caspian Sea, would solve three problems at once: production of nuclear fuel, production of electric energy, and distillation of water (the last saving power). The importance of this plant increased with time because the fast-neutron breeders solved the problem of supply of a nuclear fuel.

Leipunskii's achievements are not limited to those already mentioned. He was chief editor of the journal *Physikalische Zeitschrift der Sowjetunion*, which was published in the Soviet Union from 1932 to 1937 and received international recognition. He also was among the founders of the Moscow Institute of Engineering Physics, where he taught and served as head of a department.

In 1924 Leipunskii was elected a full member of the Ukrainian Academy of Sciences. In 1960 he and his colleagues O. D. Kasachkovskii, I. I. Bondarenko, and L. N. Usachev were awarded the Lenin Prize for their work on fast-neutron reactor physics. In 1963 Leipunskii was awarded the title of Hero of Socialist Labor.

BIBLIOGRAPHY

I. ORIGINAL WORKS. "Stösse zweiter Art zwischen Elektronen und angeregten Molekülen," in *Zeitschrift für Physik*, **58** (1929), 104–128, written with E. Strauff; "Dissoziation durch Stoss positiver Ionen," *ibid.*, **59** (1929), 857–863, written with A. Schechter; "The Disintegration of Lithium by High Velocity Protons," in *Physikalische*

Zeitschrift der Sowjetunion, **2**, no. 3 (1932), 285, written with G. D. Latyshev, K. D. Sinelnikov, and A. K. Walter; "Slowing Down of Neutrons in Liquid Hydrogen," *ibid.*, **9**, no. 6 (1936), 696–698, written with V. Fomin, F. G. Houtermans, and L. V. Schubnikov; "Determination of the Energy Distribution of Recoil Atoms During β Decay and the Existence of the Neutrino," in *Proceedings of the Cambridge Philosophical Society*, **32** (1936), 301–302; "Issledovanie po fizike reaktorov na bystrykh neitronakh" (Investigation of physics of fast-neutron reactors), in *Atomnaia energiia*, **5**, no. 3 (1959), 277–293; "Budushchee bystrykh reactorov" (The future of fast reactors), *ibid.*, **11**, no. 4 (1961), 370–378, written with O. D. Kasachkovskii and M. S. Pinkhasik; "Bystrye reactory BN-350 i BOR" (Fast reactors BN-350 and BOR), *ibid.*, **21**, no. 1 (1966), 450–462, written with 17 co-authors; "Razvitie iadernoi energetiki v SSSR s reaktorami na bystrykh neitronakh" (Development in the U.S.S.R. of reactor energetics with fast-neutron reactors), *ibid.*, **25**, no. 5 (1968), 380–387; and "Opit pusko-naladochnikh rabot i energo-pusk reaktora BN-350" (Experience of starting and adjustment, and the beginning of energy supply of reactor BN-350), *ibid.*, **36**, no. 2 (1974), 91–97, written with 21 coauthors.

II. SECONDARY LITERATURE. A. P. Alexandrov, I. K. Kikoin, and Iu. B. Chariton, "Pamiati Aleksandra Il'icha Leipunskogo" (In memory of Aleksandr Il'ich Leipunskii) in *Atomnaia energiia*, **35**, no. 4 (1973), paste-in page; and O. D. Kasachkovskii, "A. I. Leipunskii i razvitie atomnoi nauki i tekhniki v SSSR" (A. I. Leipunskii and the development of atomic science and technology in the U.S.S.R.), in *Ukrainskii fizicheskii zhurnal*, **24**, no. 3 (1979), 420–422.

V. J. FRENKEL

LEMAÎTRE, GEORGES (*b.* Charleroi, Belgium, 17 July 1894; *d.* Louvain, Belgium, 20 June 1966), *astrophysics, cosmology.*

Georges Lemaître was the oldest son of Joseph Lemaître, a factory owner, and Marguerite Lannoy, the daughter of a brewer. His parents were devout Catholics and in 1904 sent him to a Jesuit school in Louvain, where he received education in religion, humanities, and classical languages. Attracted by the exact sciences, he enrolled at the Catholic University of Louvain in 1911, where he studied engineering. Lemaître served as a soldier in the Belgian army during World War I and received several military honors. After the war he returned to the University of Louvain, where he changed from engineering to mathematics and physics. He received his doctorate in 1920. In 1927 he was appointed professor at the university, a position he kept until his retirement in 1964.

Parallel with his scientific career, Lemaître had an ecclesiastical career in the Catholic church. After theological studies he was ordained as an abbé in 1923 and later he obtained the rank of monseigneur. From 1960 until his death he served as president of the Pontifical Academy of Sciences in Rome. Lemaître published several theological works. He believed that religion and science should not be mixed, although they would ultimately lead to the same truth. Lemaître believed that God would hide nothing from the human mind, not even the physical nature of the very early universe. This epistemic optimism, derived from his Christian belief, may have helped him in formulating the first scientific creation cosmology.

Lemaître's scientific career began in 1923, when he received a traveling fellowship. He went to Cambridge and studied under Eddington, under whose influence he specialized in the theory of general relativity. In 1924 and 1925 he continued his postgraduate studies in the United States, at Harvard and MIT. During his stay in the United States, he attended the American Astronomical Society conference in Washington, at which Hubble's discovery of the Cepheid variables in the Andromeda nebula was announced. He became increasingly occupied with cosmology and, while at MIT in 1925, suggested a modification of de Sitter's cosmological theory. Lemaître's model was nonstatic and included a red shift caused by the Doppler effect. After his return to Louvain, he developed his theory further, and in 1927 he published a new cosmological theory that combined the advantages of the earlier theories of Einstein and de Sitter. Lemaître showed that the field equations of general relativity allowed an expanding universe and derived a velocity-distance relation. Although Lemaître's universe was expanding, in 1927 Lemaître's theory did not involve a creation or a definite age. The basic equation of Lemaître's theory was nearly the same as the one found by Alexander A. Friedmann in 1922, but Lemaître had been unaware of Friedmann's work.

Lemaître's paper went unnoticed until 1930, when he called Eddington's attention to it. Eddington strongly endorsed Lemaître's work and had it translated into English. In 1931 Lemaître moved from obscurity to fame. He suggested that the world might have originated from just one quantum of enormous energy and later the same year he developed this scenario into the hypothesis of the primeval atom. According to Lemaître's "fireworks theory of evolution" the world started as a super-radioactive disintegration of the primeval atom. During the 1930's he published several expositions of this idea, the first example of a big bang cosmology. He believed that it could be put to observational tests and that the cosmic rays were remnants of the original super-radioactive disintegration.

In order to decide whether the cosmic radiation is of cosmogonic origin, Lemaître engaged in the 1930's in an extensive examination of the orbits of charged particles in the geomagnetic field. This work, done in collaboration with Manuel Sandoval Vallarta, was seriously criticized by Fredrik Störmer, the dean of the field. The idea of the primeval atom also had consequences regarding the formation of galaxies and clusters of galaxies. Lemaître studied these consequences in several papers and believed that they were supported by astronomical observations.

Lemaître's work was primarily in cosmology and astrophysics, but he also worked in other fields. He was an able mathematician who liked to deal with classical mathematical problems such as the three-body problem, and he was very interested in the computational problems of astronomy.

Lemaître favored a simple and direct approach to the study of the universe and emphasized physical ideas rather than mathematics. He did not believe that cosmology could be made a deductive science and disliked tendencies of mysticism or apriorism. During the 1930's Eddington, Edward Milne, and others developed cosmological theories which were based upon a priori principles and rational thought. Lemaître was opposed to these rationalist cosmologies and also to the later steady state theory, which he criticized for being founded on philosophical rather than scientific reasoning.

Lemaître received many awards and honors. In 1934 he received the Osborne Mendel Medal (U.S.A.) and the Prix Franqui (Belgium) and in 1953 the first Eddington Medal (England).

BIBLIOGRAPHY

I. ORIGINAL WORKS. Papers and notes left by Lemaître are kept at the Catholic University of Louvain-la-Neuve. Published works include: "The Motion of a Rigid Solid According to the Relativity Principle," in *Philosophical Magazine*, 6th ser., **48** (1924), 164–176; "Note on de Sitter's Universe," in *Journal of Mathematics and Physics*, **4** (1925), 188–192; "Un univers homogène de masse constante et de rayon croissant," in *Annales de la Société Scientifique de Bruxelles*, **47** (1927), 49–56, translated as "A Homogeneous Universe of Constant Mass and Increasing Radius Accounting for the Radial Velocity of Extra-Galactic Nebulae," in *Monthly Notices of the Royal Astronomical Society*, **91** (1931), 483–501; "The Beginning of the World from the Point of View of Quantum Theory," in *Nature*, **127** (1931), 706; "On Compton's Latitude Effect of Cosmic Radiation," *Physical Review*, 2nd ser., **43**

(1933), 87–91, written with M. S. Vallarta; "La formation des nébuleuses dans l'univers en expansion," in *Comptes rendus hebdomadaire des séances de l'Académie des sciences*, **196** (1933), 1085–1087; "Evolution of the Expanding Universe," in *Proceedings of the National Academy of Sciences*, **20** (1934), 12–17; "On the Geomagnetic Analysis of Cosmic Radiation," in *Physical Review*, 2nd ser., **49** (1936), 719–726, written with M. S. Vallarta; *L'hypothèse de l'atome primitif* (Neuchâtel, 1946), translated by Betty H. Korff and Serge A. Korff as *The Primeval Atom* (New York, 1950); and "Cosmological Application of Relativity," in *Reviews of Modern Physics*, **21** (1949), 357–366.

II. SECONDARY LITERATURE. A. Berger, ed., *The Big Bang and Georges Lemaître* (Dordecht, 1984); P. A. M. Dirac, "The Scientific Work of Georges Lemaître," in *Pontificia accademia delle scienze: Commentarii*, **2**, no. 11 (1968), 1–20; O. Godart, "Mgr Lemaître et son oeuvre," in *Ciel et terre*, **83** (1967), 57–86; O. Godart and M. Heller, *Cosmology of Lemaître* (Tucson, Arizona, 1985); H. Kragh, "The Beginning of the World: Georges Lemaître and the Expanding Universe," in *Centaurus*, **32** (1987), 114–139; C. Manneback, "Georges Lemaître, le savant et l'homme," in *L'académie pontificale des sciences en mémoire de son second président Georges Lemaître à l'occasion du cinquième anniversaire de sa mort* (Rome, 1972); and *Revue des questions scientifiques*, **155**, no. 2 (1984), 139–224.

HELGE KRAGH

LEVERETT, FRANK (*b.* Denmark, Iowa, 10 March 1859; *d.* Ann Arbor, Michigan, 15 November 1943), *glacial geology.*

Leverett was the eldest child of Ebenezer Turner Leverett and Rowena Houston Leverett, descendants of English emigrants who settled in the Massachusetts Bay Colony in the mid seventeenth century. He was educated in Denmark, Iowa, first in the public schools and later at the Denmark Academy. Upon completion of these studies in 1878, at age nineteen, he took a teaching position in the public schools in Denmark. From 1880 to 1883 he served as instructor in natural sciences at the Denmark Academy. This appointment proved to be a turning point in Leverett's career, for during these years he became interested in geology, frequently leading his students to fossiliferous localities in nearby Pennsylvanian strata. During this time he also fulfilled college language requirements in Latin and Greek that would permit him to continue his education.

Though he never again engaged in full-time teaching, Leverett maintained close ties with the academic community through his position as staff lecturer at the University of Michigan. He spent the academic year 1883–1884 at Colorado College, Colorado

Springs, where he further developed his interest in geology, particularly mineralogy. In September 1884 he entered Iowa State College of Agriculture and Mechanic Arts at Ames and received the B.S. in 1885. During this relatively brief stay at Iowa State the pattern of his professional career began to unfold. He wrote, for example, a senior thesis on an artesian well near Des Moines; and his first scientific paper, "Drainage Changes in Eastern Iowa," was published in 1885 in *Aurora*, the college monthly. Water wells and drainage changes induced by continental glaciation were subjects that held his interest throughout his professional career.

On 22 December 1887 Leverett married Frances E. Gibson, who died in 1892. He married Dorothy Christina Park on 18 December 1895. There were no children from either marriage.

Leverett was elected to the American Philosophical Society in 1924 and to the National Academy of Sciences in 1939. He was a fellow of the Geological Society of America and the American Association for the Advancement of Science, serving as vice president of the latter in 1928. He was president of the Michigan Academy of Science, Arts, and Letters in 1910. Leverett was a member of the academies of science of Iowa, Wisconsin, and Washington, D.C., and the Geological Society of Washington; a corresponding member of the National Geographic Society; and a member of the American Geophysical Union, Phi Kappa Phi, and Sigma Xi. He was awarded an honorary D.Sc. by the University of Michigan in 1930.

Leverett's professional career began in 1886, when he was hired as a field assistant by Thomas C. Chamberlin, who was in charge of the Division of Glacial Geology of the U.S. Geological Survey. Leverett remained a field assistant until 1890, at which time he was appointed an assistant geologist with the survey. In 1901 he advanced to geologist, and in 1928 to senior geologist, the position he held at the time of his retirement in 1929. From 1909 until 1929 he was staff lecturer in glacial geology at the University of Michigan.

Leverett was first and foremost a field geologist. Although he traveled extensively in Canada and Europe as well as in the United States, his published work deals almost exclusively with the glacial geology of the north-central United States. Working at a time and in areas where few topographic base maps existed, Leverett mapped glacial deposits and landforms with a precision and attention to detail previously unknown. Most of his fieldwork was done on foot and alone. He estimated that in the course of his work he had walked the equivalent of four

times around the globe. His detailed mapping extends from the eastern Dakotas to Pennsylvania and is meticulously documented in more than 300 field notebooks on file with the U.S. Geological Survey. It has been estimated that these contain more than 45,000 pages of notes.

Leverett described his field technique in some detail, stating, according to Rieck and Winters (1981), that an "effective field party" should include people who, collectively, possess the following skills: the ability to recognize, map, photograph, and sketch all classes of glacial features; sufficient familiarity with the region to "work out the directions of ice movement and to discriminate superposed drift sheets of different constitution and age"; the ability to survey and make topographic maps; and familiarity "with plant communities and their relations to various soils," including buried soils. Leverett thought that a party of four was necessary to encompass all these specialties. That he worked alone is an indication of the breadth of his knowledge and understanding.

Leverett's published work is monumental; at the time of his death he ranked first among the members of the U.S. Geological Survey in terms of the number of reports published—some 170 titles. Though, by virtue of his training and temperament, he was ideally suited to engage in the detailed but broad-ranging studies that these reports represent, the early influence of Chamberlin is nevertheless clearly evident. In 1884 Chamberlin had published his report on the terminal moraine of the second glacial epoch and recognized the overall continuity of these deposits from the Dakotas to the Atlantic. This work provided a broad outline; Leverett contributed detailed descriptions and interpretations, tasks for which Chamberlin offered encouragement and counsel, but that he had neither the time nor the inclination to undertake himself. Leverett's work documented multiple glaciation, implying climatic change. Aside from his detailed maps, Leverett's greatest contribution to glacial geology was the historical framework and the evidence of multiple glaciation that emerged from his work.

BIBLIOGRAPHY

I. ORIGINAL WORKS. A small selection of Leverett's published works includes: "On the Correlation of Moraines with Raised Beaches of Lake Erie," in *Transactions of the Wisconsin Academy of Sciences, Arts, and Letters*, **8** (1892), 233–240; *The Illinois Glacial Lobe*, U.S. Geological Survey Monograph 38 (1899); *Glacial Formations and Drainage Features of the Erie and Ohio Basins*, U.S.

Geological Survey Monograph 41 (1902); and *The Pleistocene of Indiana and Michigan and the History of the Great Lakes*, U.S. Geological Survey Monograph 53 (1915), written with Frank B. Taylor, as well as numerous other monographs published by the U.S. Geological Survey. The department of geography at Michigan State University in East Lansing and the U.S. Geological Survey Library at Denver, Colorado, have numerous letters, field notebooks, and other prime source material on file.

II. SECONDARY LITERATURE. Stanard G. Bergquist, "Memorial to Frank Leverett," in *Science*, **99** (1944), 312–313; William H. Hobbs, "Biographical Memoir of Frank Leverett, 1859–1943," in *Biographical Memoirs, National Academy of Sciences*, **23** (1944), 203–215, and "Memorial to Frank Leverett," in *Proceedings of the Geological Society of America* (1943), 183–193, with bibliography; Richard L. Rieck and Harold A. Winters, "Frank Leverett, Pleistocene Scholar and Field Worker," in *Journal of Geological Education*, **29** (1981), 222–227; George M. Stanley, "Memorial to Frank Leverett," in *Forty-Sixth Annual Report: The Michigan Academy of Science, Arts, and Letters* (1945), 49–53, and "Frank Leverett," in *Dictionary of American Biography*, supp. 3 (1973), 455–456; and Harold A. Winters and Richard L. Rieck, "Frank Leverett: Michigan's Master Geologist," in *Michigan History*, **64** (1980), 11–13.

RICHARD C. ANDERSON

LEVINSON, NORMAN (*b.* Boston, Massachusetts, 11 August 1912; *d.* Boston, 10 October 1975), *mathematics*.

Levinson entered the Massachusetts Institute of Technology in 1929, having graduated from Revere High School earlier that year. In June 1934 he received the B.S. and M.S. degrees in electrical engineering. At that time he had completed practically every graduate course offered by the department of mathematics and had obtained results that H. B. Phillips, head of the department, described as "sufficient for a doctor's thesis of unusual excellence." Among these courses was Fourier series and integrals, given in the fall of 1933–1934 by Norbert Wiener. Wiener had given Levinson a copy of the unpublished manuscript "Fourier Transforms in the Complex Domain," by R. E. A. C. Paley and Wiener, for revision. When Levinson found a gap in a proof and was able to prove a lemma that corrected it, Wiener typed the proof, affixed Levinson's name to the paper, and submitted it to a journal for him.

This incident began a friendship that lasted the rest of their lives. Wiener and Phillips arranged an MIT Redfield traveling fellowship for Levinson for the year 1934–1935, which Levinson spent at Cambridge University, where he studied under the distinguished mathematical analyst G. H. Hardy. In June 1935 he received the doctorate in mathematics from MIT. Levinson was then awarded a National Research Council fellowship for the years 1935–1937, which he spent at the Institute for Advanced Study and Princeton University under the supervision of John von Neumann. Upon being offered an instructorship in mathematics at MIT, Levinson was released from his fellowship, went to MIT in February 1937, and remained there for the rest of his life, except for periods on leave. In February 1938 he married Zipporah Wallman.

Levinson's early work centers on results related to the Paley-Wiener book (published in 1934). Levinson sharpened many results and obtained significant new ones. In 1940 the American Mathematical Society published his work in this area as *Gap and Density Theorems*. After its appearance Levinson decided to shift his field to nonlinear differential equations. He soon obtained substantial mathematical results, and his outstanding contributions to differential equations were recognized by the American Mathematical Society in 1954 when it awarded him the Bôcher Prize. In addition, Levinson's work touched many areas of mathematical analysis and its applications. In the period 1946–1947 he wrote two papers that simplified and explained Wiener's work on stationary time series, which had a significant impact on random signal theory in general and on geophysical signal processing in particular. His work contributed to some of the improved petroleum prospecting methods that made possible the discovery of virtually all the offshore oil fields found since 1960, as well as most of the onshore discoveries.

Levinson did work in probability, quantum mechanics, complex programming, and analytic number theory. In 1967 he became the fortieth mathematician to be elected to the National Academy of Sciences, and in 1971 he was appointed Institute professor at MIT. Also in 1971 he was awarded the Chauvenet Prize of the Mathematical Association of America. The paper for which he received this prize was in analytical number theory and served as a precursor to the papers he wrote on the Riemann hypothesis. Levinson greatly advanced this theory and was on the threshold of perhaps his greatest achievement in mathematics at the time of his death.

BIBLIOGRAPHY

I. ORIGINAL WORKS. "A Heuristic Exposition of Wiener's Mathematical Theory of Prediction and Filtering," in *Journal of Mathematics and Physics*, **26** (1947), 110–

119; "The Wiener RMS (Root Mean Square) Error Criterion in Filter Design and Prediction," in *J. Math. Phys.*, **25** (1947), 261–278; and *Gap and Density Theorems* (New York, 1940).

II. Secondary Literature. E. A. Robinson, "A Historical Perspective of Spectrum Estimation," in *Proceedings of the IEEE*, **70**, no. 9 (1982), 885–907.

Enders A. Robinson

LEVIT, SOLOMON GRIGOREVICH (*b*. Vilkomir [modern Ukmerge], Lithuania, 6 July 1894; *d*. time and place unknown, probably in the Lubianka prison, Moscow, on or about 17 May 1938), *medical genetics.*

Levit was the youngest of four sons born into a poor Baltic Jewish family. His invalid father worked as a night watchman. The only member of his family to receive an education, Levit worked his way through public school and subsequently the Vilkomir gymnasium by coaching and tutoring. He remained at home supporting his parents until the Germans attacked Lithuania in 1915, then moved to Petrograd to study law, and finally to Moscow after less than a year to study medicine.

Levit entered the Moscow University medical school in 1916. With the outbreak of civil war in 1918, he was drafted into the Red Army as a medic, but after falling ill with typhus he was demobilized and returned to his medical studies. Upon earning his degree in January 1921, he worked in the university clinic (1921–1928) and in D. D. Pletnev's department of clinical therapy, first as an intern and then as a research assistant, and served on the university's administrative board (1922–1925). In 1925 Levit was posted to Germany and worked under P. Rona (1871–1945) in his laboratory of physical and colloidal chemistry. In 1928 he was appointed docent. In his studies of clinical medicine, Levit devoted most of his attention to blood diseases and published a monograph in 1929 on hemorrhagic diathesis.

Levit joined the Communist Party in 1919 or 1920. In October 1924, together with a group of young research assistants, he set up the Circle of Materialist Physicians at the Moscow medical school and became its permanent chairman. In November 1926 the group was renamed the Society of Materialist Physicians and subsequently came under the auspices of the Communist Academy's natural and exact sciences section, of which Levit was scientific secretary from 1 February 1926 until 16 April 1930.

In the mid 1920's Levit was a strident advocate of Lamarckism and strongly supported it in his administrative work. In 1924 he called for a synthesis of Darwinism and Lamarckism, claiming that only two factors—the influence of the external environment and the inheritance of acquired characteristics—were capable of explaining the origin of new variations. In 1926 he suggested that opposition to Lamarckism was motivated by bourgeois political sympathies. His support for Lamarckism apparently stemmed from his conviction that if the human constitution was determined by an unchanging genotype impervious to environmental influence, the physician would be rendered therapeutically impotent.

By late 1927 Levit had reversed himself. One of the main reasons appears to have been H. J. Muller's findings on X-ray mutagenesis, published in *Science* in July 1927. For Levit and other Marxists, what was most unappealing about the classic gene was its apparently abstract, immutable, immortal character; for them, Muller's discovery demonstrated that the gene was material and might be subject to human control. Levit devoted himself to the study of genetics under A. S. Serebrovskii's direction, joining in work on mutations in the scute region of the X chromosome of *Drosophila melanogaster* and contributing to the "step-allelism" theory of gene structure. In the discussions at the Communist Academy in April 1929, Levit spoke with the enthusiasm of a recent convert, calling for an end to Lamarckian dominance over that academy's biological research.

In late 1928 Levit left the Moscow University clinic and joined the staff of the Medico-Biological Institute (MBI) of the Commissariat of Public Health (Narkomzdrav), which had been formed in 1924 under the direction of V. F. Zelenin, a specialist in internal medicine. On 21 December, together with N. N. Malkova, Levit and Serebrovskii established at the MBI a *kabinet* (office) of human heredity and constitution directed by Levit. In a brief note in its first volume of research papers, published in 1929, Levit declared that the *kabinet* would study human chromosomes, human population genetics, and human pathological forms by using case histories, genealogies, and twin studies. The volume's lead article, however, was a piece by Serebrovskii that made the case for a socialist eugenics and advocated the application to human beings of the techniques of mass artificial insemination used in cattle and sheep breeding. Understandably, this article provoked criticism and ridicule in Marxist circles and among the wider public.

At the time of the first Five-Year Plan (1929–1932), there were widespread institutional reorganizations, ideological attacks on "bourgeois" experts, and their replacement by Communists. In March 1930 Levit replaced Zelenin as director of the Medico-Biological Institute. His *kabinet* of human heredity and constitution was expanded into the institute's new Genetics Division, and it published a second volume (1930) that reflected the new ideological tenor of the times. Comprising fourteen research papers, the volume opened with an editorial by Levit that drew a sharp distinction between eugenics and anthropogenetics (the science of human heredity), and concluded with a long letter by Serebrovskii apologizing for some of the statements in his 1929 article.

In May 1930 the agency of the Commissariat of Education in charge of science, Glavnauka, nominated Levit for a Rockefeller Foundation grant to study in the United States. He left for New York on 19 December 1930, arrived a month later, and spent 1931 working in the laboratory of H. J. Muller in the zoology department of the University of Texas at Austin. Also working there was I. I. Agol, another party member who had won a Rockefeller grant through Glavnauka to study with Muller. Meanwhile, in connection with the imposition of a new party line in the Soviet Union, Levit, Agol, and Serebrovskii were under increasing ideological attack as "Menshevizing idealists."

In January 1932, while Levit was en route home from Texas, he was replaced as director of the MBI by the acting director, B. B. Kogan, who suspended genetics research at the institute and turned it to purely clinical pursuits. Upon Levit's arrival in Moscow on 22 February, he was informed that he had lost his job. For the next six months he found work in the department of pathological physiology of the Second Moscow Medical Institute. We do not know what went on behind the scenes during those months. Levit published an article that year strongly critical of racism, fascism, and social Darwinism, which may have brought him back into official favor. V. P. Efroimson reports that when Levit recruited him to work on human genetics at the MBI in mid 1932, Levit said that the party central committee had instructed him to create an institute of human genetics.

In any event, on 15 August 1932 the MBI was reopened and Levit was once again its director. The institute's new mission was to study problems of human biology, pathology, and psychology from a genetic viewpoint, and it included new divisions of cytology, internal secretions, and neurology, and offices of roentgenology, anthropometrics, and psychology. Levit organized a genetics course for physicians, first offered at the MBI during the academic year 1933–1934, which included lectures on Mendelism, Morganism, sex determination, mutations, population and evolutionary genetics, twin studies, human genetics, and medical cytology, and four lectures on "bourgeois eugenics and its class character." By 1934 the institute had been given the name of Maxim Gorky, and seemed productive and secure.

Although Levit's research program had emerged intact from the ideological disruptions of the early 1930's, the rise of nazism in Germany created problems in Stalinist Russia for an enterprise historically tied to eugenics. An institute conference held on 15 March 1934 seemed to settle on the right language and approach. A series of programmatic papers by Levit and others called for the establishment and expansion of a new discipline in the Soviet Union, to be called "medical genetics," as a way of improving human health and combating fascist pseudoscience. The final resolution of the conference called for the creation of academic and clinical departments, teaching materials, and courses to retrain physicians.

In March 1935 the institute was renamed the Maxim Gorky Scientific Research Institute of Medical Genetics (MGI). In July its impressive fourth volume of research was sent to press, presenting the work of some thirty staff members or affiliates of the institute during 1934 and early 1935. The 543-page tome opened with an important review article by Levit that analyzed the genetic component of a host of diseases and critiqued international findings on the genetics of human traits and illnesses. The twenty-five original research papers included studies of hereditary factors in asthma, allergies, pernicious anemia, diabetes, stomach ulcers, and breast cancer. In addition, a remarkable series of papers on pairs of identical twins analyzed their electrocardiograms (107 pairs), height and weight (129 pairs), and fingerprints (234 pairs). One paper, reporting attempts to train identical twins to perceive differently, was co-authored by the head of the institute's new psychology division, A. R. Luria, now considered by many to have been one of this century's greatest psychologists. When it was published in 1936, the volume was arguably the best single collection of original research on human heredity that had appeared anywhere.

Much of this work was developed in close consultation with H. J. Muller, who had come to Leningrad in late 1933 at Nikolai Vavilov's invitation to head a laboratory at the new Institute of Genetics of the U.S.S.R. Academy of Sciences. In 1934 Muller was a featured speaker at the conference convened by Levit's institute to inaugurate "medical genetics."

Later that year both the academy and Vavilov's institute were moved to Moscow. The shortage of suitable space in the city forced the Levit institute to move to more cramped quarters, but Muller's presence in the capital opened new possibilities for collaboration.

Muller had come to the Soviet Union in the hopes of creating a socialist eugenic society along the lines described by Serebrovskii in 1929. In *Out of the Night*, published in Britain and the United States in 1935, Muller proposed a large-scale program of human artificial insemination, using the sperm of eugenically selected male donors. In the spring of 1936, perhaps on Levit's suggestion, he sent a copy of the book to Stalin, together with a long letter proposing that the Soviet Union adopt such a plan. Muller also played a central role in organizing the Seventh International Congress of Genetics, scheduled for Moscow in 1937. Against the opposition of important political authorities, he hoped to give human genetics a central role at the congress, confronting the German delegation over nazi race biology and highlighting the excellent Soviet work of the Levit institute. With this in mind, Muller saw to it that Levit was on the organizing committee of the congress, nominated him as its general secretary, and gave Levit his proxy when he was out of Moscow.

Muller's behavior may inadvertently have helped make Levit and his institute vulnerable. In late 1936, as a new wave of purges was gaining momentum, party members who had been accused of "Menshevizing idealism" and had spent time abroad were especially at risk. On 13 November 1936 the party official in charge of science in Moscow, Ernst Kol'-man, staged a public meeting to denounce Levit as an abettor of nazi doctrines. At the session of the Lenin All-Union Academy of Agricultural Sciences held 19–27 December 1936, Muller raised the issue of human heredity despite explicit political instructions that he was not to do so. This indiscretion led Lysenko's supporters to attack genetics as a fascist pseudoscience, and one ominously remarked that Levit had already been "unmasked." At the time of the purges, such language had dangerous implications. Informed by Vavilov that he might be arrested, Muller hastily left the Soviet Union in March 1937. That month Stalin delivered a speech calling for "the liquidation of Trotskyites and other double-dealers," and shortly thereafter Lysenko's closest aide published a commentary declaring Levit to be such a person.

On 5 July 1937 Levit was removed as director of the MGI. That fall his internal passport was sus-

pended, and he remained in Moscow awaiting his arrest. It finally came during the night of 11 January 1938, when agents of the secret police (NKVD) seized him at his apartment and took him to the Lubianka prison. Subsequent communications from Levit to his family indicated that he was accused of being an American spy. That spring all communication ceased. In May and June a Narkomzdrav commission investigated his institute, concluding that it should continue to exist, but it was instead demoted to the status of a laboratory of medical genetics and finally liquidated in autumn 1939. As a result of these events, much of the research done by the institute from 1935 through 1937 was never published, the world's premier center of medical genetics was abolished, and the Soviet Union permanently lost its leadership in the field.

As is the case with many purge victims of the late 1930's, the date and place of Levit's death are difficult to establish with precision. An official NKVD notice to his family dated 17 May 1938 indicated that Levit had been denied the right of correspondence. More than five years later, during World War II, his family was officially notified that he had died on 21 December 1943 of a "brain hemorrhage" (the usual cause of death given for those who had been shot in the head, a standard form of NKVD execution). For a number of reasons, however, this later date is unlikely, and it is probable that Levit was executed on or about 17 May 1938 at the Lubianka prison in Moscow.

During Nikita Khrushchev's de-Stalinization campaign of the mid 1950's, Levit's family and several of his former colleagues petitioned to have his name cleared, and he was officially rehabilitated on 13 September 1956. Since the mid 1960's, when Soviet genetics was reborn, Levit has gradually come to be recognized in the Soviet Union as a founder of medical genetics.

BIBLIOGRAPHY

I. ORIGINAL WORKS. For Levit's work in the 1920's, see "Evoliutsionnye teorii v biologii i marksizm" (Marxism and theories of biological evolution), in *Vestnik sovremennoi meditsiny*, 1925, no. 9; *Problema konstitutsii v meditsine i dialekticheskii materializm* (Dialectical materialism and the problem of constitution in medicine), Trudy kruzhka Vrachei-materialistov I-ogo MGU za 1925–1926 gg., no. 2 (Moscow, 1927); *Gemorragicheskie diatezi* (Hemorrhagic diathesis; Moscow, 1929); and "O poniatii bolezni" (On the concept of disease), in *Estestvoznanie i marksizm*, 1929, no. 1, 93–105. For his research on *Drosophila* under Serebrovskii's direction, see "Stupenchatyi allelomorfizm u *Drosophila melanogaster*, V, Mutatsiia scute[9] i vopros ob allelomorfakh-analizatorakh'' (Step-allelomorphism in *Drosophila melanogaster*, 5, The scute[9] mutation and the question of allelomorph analyzers), *Zhurnal eksperimental'noi biologii*, ser. A, **6**, no. 4 (1930), 287–299.

Levit's principal publications on human genetics appeared in four volumes, which he edited or coedited, issued by his institute. In *Trudy Kabineta nasledstvennosti i konstitutsii cheloveka pri Mediko-biologicheskom institute* (Works of the Office of Human Heredity and Constitution of the Medico-Biological Institute), I (Moscow, 1929), co-edited by A. S. Serebrovskii, see especially "Genetika i patologiia (v sviazi s sovremennym krizisom meditsiny)'' (Genetics and pathology in relation to the current crisis in medicine), 20–39; and "Materialy k voprosu o stseplenii genov u cheloveka'' (Material on gene linkage in humans), 40–50. In *Trudy Geneticheskogo otdeleniia (b. kabineta nasledstvennosti i konstitutsii cheloveka) pri Mediko-biologicheskom institute* (Works of the Genetic Division [Formerly the Office of Human Heredity and Constitution] of the Medico-Biological Institute), II, co-edited by A. S. Serebrovskii, issued as *Mediko-biologicheskii zhurnal*, no. 4–5 (Moscow, 1930), see especially "Chelovek kak geneticheskii ob'ekt i izuchenie bliznetsov kak metod antropogenetiki'' (The human as a genetic object and the study of twins as a method of anthropogenetics), 273–287.

In *Trudy Mediko-biologicheskogo nauchno-issledovatel'skogo Instituta imeni M. Gor'kogo* ("Works of the Maxim Gorky Medico-Biological Research Institute''), III (Moscow and Leningrad, 1934), see "Nekotorye itogi i perspektivy bliznetsovykh issledovanii'' (Some results and prospects of twin studies), 5–17; "Genetika sakharnogo diabeta'' (The genetics of diabetes mellitus), 132–147, written with L. N. Pesikova; and "Kriticheskie zamechaniia po povodu raboty Goldena 'O khromosomnykh aberratsiiakh u cheloveka' '' (Critical comments on Haldane's "On Cytological Abnormalities in Man''), 235–238. Finally, in *Trudy Mediko-geneticheskogo nauchno-issledovatel'skogo instituta imeni M. Gor'kogo* (Works of the Maxim Gorky Scientific Research Institute of Medical Genetics), IV (Moscow and Leningrad, 1936), see "Predislovie'' (Preface), 5–16; "Problema dominantnosti u cheloveka'' (The problem of dominance in humans), 17–40; and "Obuslovlen li diabetes insipidus 'khoroshim' dominantnym genom?'' (Is diabetes insipidus caused by a "good'' dominant gene?), 149–158, written with L. N. Pesikova.

Levit published other articles in the 1930's, notably "Darvinizm, rasovyi shovinizm, sotsial-fashizm'' (Darwinism, racial chauvinism, and social fascism), in P. I. Valeskaln and B. P. Tokin, eds., *Uchenie Darvina i marksizm-leninizm* (Darwinism and Marxism-Leninism; Moscow, 1932), 107–125; "Antropogenetika i meditsina'' ("Anthropogenetics and Medicine''), in *Konferentsiia po meditsinskoi genetike: Doklady i preniia* (Conference on Medical Genetics: papers and proceedings), issued as a supplement to *Sovetskaia klinika*, **20**, no. 7–8 (1934), 3–

16; "Tsitologiia i meditsina'' (Cytology and medicine), in *Uspekhi sovremennoi biologii*, **3**, no. 1 (1934), 50–57; and "Sovremennoe sostoianie problemy dominantnosti'' (The current status of the problem of dominance), *ibid.*, **3**, no. 2 (1934), 208–228.

II. SECONDARY LITERATURE. In English, see Mark B. Adams, "Eugenics in Russia, 1900–1940,'' in Mark B. Adams, ed., *The Wellborn Science: Eugenics in Germany, France, Brazil, and Russia* (New York, 1990), 153–216; A. E. Gaissinovitch, "The Origins of Soviet Genetics and the Struggle with Lamarckism, 1922–1929,'' Mark B. Adams, trans., in *Journal of the History of Biology*, **13**, no. 1 (1980), 15–18, 49–51; and occasional references to Levit in Elof Axel Carlson, *Genes, Radiation, and Society* (Ithaca, N.Y., 1981); David Joravsky, *Soviet Marxism and Natural Science 1917–1932* (New York, 1961) and *The Lysenko Affair* (Cambridge, Mass., 1979); and Zhores A. Medvedev, *The Rise and Fall of T. D. Lysenko*, I. Michael Lerner, trans. (New York, 1969).

In Russian, see V. P. Efroimson, "K istorii izucheniia genetiki cheloveka v SSSR'' (On the history of the study of human genetics in the USSR), in *Genetika*, 1967, no. 10, 114–127; A. E. Gaissinovich, *Zarozhdenie i razvitie genetiki* (The birth and development of genetics; Moscow, 1988), 293–322; and E. K. Ginter, "Nachal'nye etapy razvitiia sovetskoi meditsinskoi genetiki'' (Early stages of the development of medical genetics), in *Meditsinskii referativnyi zhurnal*, sec. XXI, 1985, no. 10, 1–7.

MARK B. ADAMS

LEVITSKII, GRIGORII ANDREEVICH (*b*. Belki, Ukraine, 19 November 1878; *d*. in prison, Zlatoust, Cheliabinsk province, U.S.S.R., 20 May 1942), *botany, cytology, cytogenetics*.

Levitskii was born into the family of a Russian Orthodox priest. He received his early education at a primary school in Kiev and his secondary education at the collegium of P. Galagan. In 1897 he entered the natural sciences division of the physicomathematical faculty of the University of St. Vladimir (Kiev University). There he specialized in botany, working under the direction of N. V. Tsinger and the renowned cytologist S. G. Navashin (1857–1930), discoverer of double fertilization in plants (1898). After his graduation in 1902 he worked as an assistant in the botanical laboratory of the Kiev Polytechnic Institute. In May 1907, however, he was arrested for his involvement with the All-Russian Union of Peasants and his participation in political demonstrations. After a brief incarceration at the Butyrka prison in Moscow, he was sent into exile abroad for four years.

During his first two years in Europe (1907–1909) Levitskii traveled to Austria, Germany, England,

and France, absorbed European culture, picked grapes in French vineyards, and studied cytology in the libraries of Paris and London. In March and April of 1909 he worked at the Russian marine biological station at Villefranche. Later that year he found a post at the Botanical Institute of the University of Bonn, working as a privatdocent under the plant cytologist Eduard Strasburger (1844–1912). During the next two years Levitskii studied the chondriosomes (mitochondria) of plant cells, developing fixative techniques, working out their microscopic organization, and observing their continuity through cell division. His findings appeared in a series of papers, published in German scientific periodicals (1910–1913), that established his reputation in plant cytology.

Upon his return to Kiev in 1911, Levitskii resumed his studies at the Kiev Polytechnic Institute. With the outbreak of war in 1914, he was mobilized into the Russian Army. Following his demobilization in 1915, he transferred to the physico-mathematical faculty at the University of St. Vladimir, where he soon passed his examination for the master's degree in botany. In the fall of 1917 he became a privatdocent in botany at the university and opened his own course, called "The Structure and Organization of Protoplasm."

During the civil war (1918–1921), Kiev was taken and retaken many times by opposing armies, and normal scientific life was disrupted. In 1918 Levitskii became a docent at the Kiev Commercial Institute and a lecturer at the People's University associated with the Kiev Polytechnic Institute, which served as his academic base. In 1920 and 1921 the Reds finally established control of the city, and the Kosianenko brothers were appointed Red director and political commissar of the polytechnic institute. Following a falling out with Levitskii, they dismissed him from the institute on the false charge that he was a Ukrainian nationalist. In subsequent years he supported himself by teaching botany at the Kiev Economic Institute (1920–1925) and the Kiev Agricultural Institute (1921–1923), where he chaired a department.

However, Levitskii soon managed to get an excellent post with the Sugar Trust, which had been established to manage the Ukrainian sugar beet industry. Beginning in 1920 he taught courses for the trust on general biology and biometrics. In 1922, together with a number of other botanists, he was invited to organize the trust's Scientific Institute of Selection. There he created an excellent cytological laboratory, which he directed from April 1922 until October 1925.

Foreign scientific journals had not been received in Kiev since around 1915 because of war. In 1921–1922 N. I. Vavilov was sent abroad to reestablish scientific contact and obtain recent scientific books and journals. Around 1922 Levitskii spent several weeks in Petrograd poring over the new materials and acquainting himself with the spectacular results of recent research, particularly the chromosomal theory of heredity developed by T. H. Morgan's group. According to the testimony of Theodosius Dobzhansky, who was sharing an apartment with him at the time, Levitskii returned to Kiev a changed man. On the basis of his extensive notes, he began teaching cytogenetics to a small group at the university and wrote one of the first textbooks in the field, entitled *Material'nye osnovy nasledstvennosti* (The material basis of heredity; 1924).

The term *karyotype* was first coined in 1922 by L. N. Delone (another of Navashin's Kiev students) to signify a genus, in his view the systematic taxon whose constituent species share a uniform "typical" chromosome complement. In 1924 Levitskii used the term to signify the sum of the specific characteristics of a cell nucleus, including chromosome number, form, size, and points of spindle fiber attachment. On the basis of his extensive comparative cytological analysis of varieties, species, and higher taxa of domesticated and natural plants, Levitskii demonstrated that Delone's conception of the genus as karyotypically uniform was mistaken, since quite different genera can have very similar karyotypes, whereas various species within a single genus can exhibit quite different karyotypes. For Levitskii the karyotype was a mediator between phenotype and genotype, since the chromosomes are not only observable physical structures, but are also the material basis of heredity and the genes. The term *idiogram* had been coined by Levitskii's teacher S. G. Navashin to mean the totality of structures of the cell nucleus (in particular the complement of metaphase chromosomes) that typify a species and can serve as its symbol. Levitskii later adapted the term to mean the diagrammatic representation of a karyotype. He was thus the first to deploy these two terms in essentially their modern meanings.

Levitskii's work brought him to the attention of Vavilov, who in 1925 was made director of the new All-Union Institute of Applied Botany and New Cultures in Leningrad (renamed the All-Union Institute of Plant Industry [VIR] in 1930). Vavilov invited Levitskii to create the institute's Laboratory of Cytology. He accepted and moved to Leningrad, serving officially as laboratory director from 1 September 1925, although the laboratory itself was created only in 1927 outside the city at Detskoe Selo (renamed Pushkin in 1937). Concurrently he served as a professor of botany in the Institute of Domestic Farming (1930–1933) at Detskoe Selo.

At the VIR, Levitskii occupied one of the best research positions in plant cytology in the world. After 1929 the institute became the hub of the Lenin All-Union Academy of Agricultural Sciences (VASKhNIL) and was in charge of dozens of plant breeding stations and hundreds of thousands of seeds, plants, and specimens sent back from all over the world by the institute's many collecting expeditions. Levitskii was in charge of all the cytological investigations on this material, which included agriculturally important plants such as rye, barley, wheat, peas, legumes, beets, and tea, as well as Muscari, yucca, and other plants of more theoretical interest.

A 1931 volume of the VIR journal was devoted to the work of Levitskii's laboratory during its first four years (1927–1931) and contains his 156-page review, "Morfologiia khromosom" (The morphology of chromosomes). After surveying the history of cytology, Levitskii described special techniques he had devised for measuring chromosome length, surveyed the karyotypes of various plants, and concluded with a theoretical discussion of chromosome morphology, primary and secondary constriction, karyosystematics, and cytogenetics. In a 1933 article on the importance of cytology for plant breeding, he emphasized its role in producing polyploids, in hybridizing distant forms where infertility may result from disrupted meiosis, and in analyzing the effects of mutagens. In the 1930's he investigated the cytological effects of X rays and other mutagens, and described the chromosomal fragmentation, deletions, duplications, and translocations they produced in the karyotypes of various species.

Levitskii also considered the implications of karyosystematics and cytogenetics for evolution. Noting that the karyotypes of distantly related plants can be quite similar, he acknowledged that much evolution takes place by natural selection acting on small genetic variations without any major alteration of chromosome structure. However, he knew that closely related plants can have remarkably different karyotypes. Increasingly impressed by the data on natural and artificially produced polyploid species, he became convinced that new species can arise quite suddenly in the plant kingdom through changes in karyotype that establish reproductive isolation.

On 29 March 1932, because of his prominence at the VIR as the country's leading plant cytogeneticist, Levitskii was elected a corresponding member of the division of mathematical and natural sciences of the USSR Academy of Sciences in cytology and genetics. However, with the advent of Stalinism in the early 1930's, repression became increasingly widespread and indiscriminate. In January 1933 Levitskii and several of his colleagues at the Detskoe Selo branch of the VIR were arrested on the absurd charge that they had organized a terrorist group. Levitskii refused to confess, and after months of fruitless investigation he was sentenced to three years of exile. He was first sent to Achinsk, then to Biriliussy, then into the countryside some ten kilometers from the town. By the fall of 1933, through the efforts of Vavilov, H. J. Muller, and Doncho Kostov, Levitskii was permitted to live in Saratov, where he resumed his scientific work at an agricultural experimental station. In February or March of 1934 he was allowed to return to Detskoe Selo and resumed his former post. The same year he was invited by G. D. Karpechenko to join the Department of Plant Genetics of Leningrad University, where he served as a professor until 1941.

As the Soviet Union's leading plant cytogeneticist, Levitskii came into increasing conflict with T. D. Lysenko and his philosophical ally I. I. Prezent, who also taught at Leningrad University. Beginning in 1935 Prezent attacked Levitskii's conception of the karyotype, the chromosome, and the gene as "metaphysical," claiming that they played no special hereditary role and were subject to constant alteration by a plant's normal metabolic processes. At the VASKhNIL session of December 1936, Levitskii suggested that Prezent's view was inconsistent with Darwinism and declared that thanks to the recent discovery of the giant salivary gland chromosomes in *Drosophila*, genes could actually be seen under the microscope.

In the spring of 1937 the university newspaper *Leningradskii Universitet* published articles attacking Levitskii and questioning his loyalty, but his position at the university apparently remained secure. He was arrested once again, but was released a day later. At the VIR, however, his situation gradually deteriorated. Lysenko became president of VASKhNIL in 1938 and used that position to harass Vavilov and his protégés, refusing to allow Levitskii's work to be displayed at agricultural and academy exhibitions. Supporters of Lysenko were appointed to the VIR staff, including an officer of the secret police (NKVD) without scientific qualifications who was made Vavilov's assistant director.

In August 1940 Vavilov was arrested by NKVD agents while on a collecting trip in the western Ukraine. During the preparation of the case against him, several of his closest colleagues were also seized. On 28 June 1941 Levitskii was arrested and was not heard from again. At the end of World War II, all members of the U.S.S.R. Academy of Sciences were given honorary awards in connection with its 220th anniversary, and the 14 June 1945 issue of *Izvestiia* announced that Levitskii had won the Order of the Red Banner of Labor. Taking this to mean that he was still alive and exonerated, Levitskii's wife turned to the authorities for information. As a result of this inquiry Levitskii's wife and daughter were arrested; his wife died shortly thereafter; his daughter, N. G. Levitskaia, survived. Apparently Levitskii's award had been the result of a bureaucratic mistake.

Shortly after her release, Levitskaia petitioned the office of the chief prosecutor on 6 January 1956 to reconsider her father's case. On 14 September she was informed that on 17 December 1955—even before her petition—all charges against her father relating to his 1941 arrest had been dropped for lack of evidence. Four months later she received a similar notice concerning his 1933 arrest. Thus Levitskii was formally rehabilitated in the mid 1950's.

In the mid 1960's his works began to be republished, but for many years the date and circumstances of his death remained uncertain. As recently as 1974, an official academy source indicated that he died "no earlier than July 1945." Only in mid 1988 were the details of his various arrests published in the Soviet Union. According to this account, written by A. A. Prokof'eva-Bel'govskaia in the 1970's, Levitskii was arrested 28 June 1941 on charges of counterrevolutionary "wrecking" and was evacuated to a prison in Zlatousk in early July, where he died on 20 May 1942. The cause of his death and the place of his burial remain unknown.

BIBLIOGRAPHY

I. Original Works. Many of his publications have been reissued in G. A. Levitskii, *Tsitologiia rastenii: Izbrannye trudy* (Plant cytology: selected works; Moscow, 1976), and *Tsitogenetiki rastenii: Izbrannye trudy* (Plant cytogenetics: selected works; Moscow, 1978). Two of his papers appear in the anthology *Klassiki sovetskoi genetiki* (Classics of Soviet genetics; Leningrad, 1968), 171–244.

Transliterating his name as "Lewitsky," he published a number of works in German, including "Über die Chondriosomen in pflanzlichen Zellen," in *Berichte der Deutschen botanischen Gesellschaft*, **28** (1910), 538–546; "Vergleichende Untersuchung über die Chondriosomen in lebenden und fixierten Pflanzenzellen," ibid., **29** (1911), 697–703; "Über die Chondriosomen bei den Myxomyzeten," in *Zeitschrift für Botanik*, **16**, no. 2 (1924), 65–89; and "Zur Frage der karyotypischen Evolution der

Gattung Muscari Mill.," in *Planta*, **9**, no. 4 (1930), 760–775, written with E. Tron.

Levitskii's two texts are *Elementy biometriki: Obshchedostupnoe posobie dlia naturalistov i agronomov, Chast' 1, Statisticheskii analiz iavlenii izmenchivosti* (Elements of biometrics: a general handbook for naturalists and agronomists, Part 1, The statistical analysis of variation phenomena; Kiev, 1922); and *Material'nye osnovy nasledstvennosti* (The material basis of heredity; Kiev, 1924).

After 1925 most of his major works were published in the VIR periodical, *Trudy po prikladnoi botanike, genetike i selektsii*. See "Kario- i genotipicheskie izmeneniia v protsesse evoliutsii" (Karyotypic and genotypic changes in the evolutionary process), **15**, no. 5 (1925), 3–28; and "Kariologicheskii metod v sistematike i filogenetike roda *Festuca* (podrod *Eufestuca*)" (The karyological method in the systematics and phylogenetics of the genus *Festuca* [subgenus *Eufestuca*]), **17**, no. 3 (1927), 1–36; written with N. Kuz'mina. In *Trudy*, **27**, no. 1 (1931), see "Obzor rabot tsitologicheskoi laboratorii Vsesoiuznogo instituta rastenievodstva" (Survey of the work of the Cytological Laboratory of the All-Union Institute of Plant Breeding), 9–17; "Morfologiia khromosom: istoriia, metodika, fakty, teoriia." (The morphology of chromosomes: History, methodology, facts, theory), 19–174; "Morfologiia khromosom i poniatie 'kariotipa' v sistematike" (The morphology of chromosomes and the concept of "karyotype" in systematics), 187–240; "Tsitologiia pshenichno-rzhanykh amfidiploidov" (The cytology of wheat-rye amphidiploids), 241–264, written with G. Benetskaia; and "Preobrazovaniia khromosom pod vliianiem rentgenovykh luchei" (Transformations of chromosomes under the influence of Roentgen rays), 265–303, written with A. Araratian.

See his chapter "Ocherk geneticheskoi tsitologii" (Essay on genetic cytology) in *Posobie po selektsii* (Handbook on selection; Moscow, 1936), I, 81–174. See also his notes in *Doklady Akademii nauk SSSR*, "O zakonomernostiiakh i preobrazovaniiakh khromosom, vyzyvaemykh X-luchami" (On regularities and transformations of chromosomes caused by X rays), **4**, no. 1–2 (1934), 84–87, written with M. A. Sizova; "Novye dannye po zakonomernostiiam v preobrazovaniiakh khromosom, vyzyvaemykh X-luchami u *Crepis capillaris* Wallr." (New data on regularities in chromosome transformations caused by X rays in *Crepis capillaris* Wallr.), **4** (9), no. 1–2 (70–71) (1935), 67–70, written with M. A. Sizova; "O genotipicheskoi obuslovlennosti strukturnykh preobrazovanii khromosom" (On genotypic conditioning of structural transformations of chromosomes), **15**, no. 9 (1937), 551–554; and "Sravnitel'naia morfologiia khromosom pshenits" (Comparative morphology of wheat chromosomes), **25**, no. 2 (1939), 144–147, written with M. A. Sizova and V. A. Poddubnaia-Arnol'di.

See his comments in *Spornye voprosy genetiki i selektsii* (Issues in genetics and selection), O. M. Targul'ian, ed. (Moscow and Leningrad, 1937), 153–155. Finally, Levitskii published some important popular articles, notably "Tsitologicheskii metod v selektsii" (The cytological method in selection), in *Sotsialisticheskoe rastenievodstvo*, 1933, no. 5–6, 30–47; and "Tsitologicheskie osnovy evoliutsii" (The cytological basis of evolution), in *Priroda*, 1939, no. 5, 33–44.

II. Secondary Literature. The most complete biography is P. K. Shkvarnikov and N. I. Savchenko, "Grigorii Andreevich Levitskii," in *Biulleten' Vsesoiuznogo instituta rastenievodstva*, no. 83 (1978), 9–15. The most complete bibliography is N. G. Levitskaia, "Bibliografiia rabot G. A. Levitskogo" (Bibliography of the works of G. A. Levitskii), *ibid.*, 15–21. On Levitskii's cytological work see A. A. Prokof'eva-Bel'govskaia, "Grigorii Andreevich Levitskii," in *Vydaiushchiesia sovetskie genetiki* (Outstanding Soviet geneticists; Moscow, 1980), 24–36.

See also the following studies by Z. M. Rubtsova: "Razvitie evoliutsionnoi tsitogenetiki rastenii G. A. Levitskim i ego shkoloi" (The development of the evolutionary cytogenetics of plants by G. A. Levitskii and his school), in *Istoriia i teoriia evoliutsionnogo ucheniia* (Evolutionary theory and its history; Leningrad, 1973), 101–112; and *Razvitie evoliutsionnoi tsitogenetiki rastenii v SSSR (1920–1940-e gody)* (The development of the evolutionary cytogenetics of plants in the USSR [1920's–1940's]; Leningrad, 1975).

On the date of Levitskii's death, see also *Akademiia nauk SSSR: personal'nyi sostav* (Personnel of the U.S.S.R. Academy of Sciences; Moscow, 1974), II, 171; *Biologi: Biograficheskii spravochnik* (Biologists: biographical handbook; Kiev, 1984), 363; and "Stranitsy istorii sovetskoi genetiki v literature poslednikh let" (Pages of the history of Soviet genetics from the literature of recent years), in *Voprosy istorii estestvoznaniia i tekhniki*, 1988, no. 2, 109–110.

Mark B. Adams

LI SIGUANG (*b.* Hubei, China, 26 October 1889; *d.* Beijing, China, 29 April 1971), *geology, paleontology.*

Li Siguang, formerly J. S. Lee (Jonquei Ssu-kuang Lee), was one of the most distinguished geologists in China. His father, Li Zhuohou, was a teacher at a private country school. At the age of fourteen, Li was sent by the provincial government to study shipbuilding in Japan. He returned to China in 1910 and taught at the Hubei Technical College at Wuchang.

Li Siguang was admitted to Birmingham University (England) in 1913. His interests were mathematics, astronomy, physics, and especially geology. In 1917 he received the B.Sc. degree, and the M.Sc. in 1918. He married Xu Shubin in 1921; they had one daughter.

In 1922 Cai Yuanpei, the president of the National University of Peking, offered Li the post of deputy professor of geology at the university, which he accepted. He joined Zhang Hongzhao (H. T. Chang), Ding Wenjiang (V. K. Ting), Weng Wenhao (W. H. Wong), and others in establishing the Geological Society of China in 1922 and always took an active part in the society; he was elected vice president (1922–1925), secretary general (1928), and president (1932–1933, 1939, 1945, 1949–1951, 1953–1971). In 1929 Li was elected a foreign member of the Geological Society of London, and in 1939 the Council of the Geological Society of China appointed him to the Council of the International Paleontological Union.

During a vacation in 1923, Li and his assistant, Zhao Yazeng (Y. T. Chao), investigated the geology of the Yangtze Valley from Ichang to Tzekwei, which subsequent geologists have classified as belonging to the Paleozoic stratigraphy of central China. Li published "Geology of the Gorge District of the Yangtze" in 1924, a valuable paper in which he proposed a highly improved stratigraphic classification.

Li conducted research on the fusulinids of north China that shed much light on the development of the Carboniferous and Permian rocks over a wide area of Eurasia, and on the life history of those highly specialized Foraminifera. For his monograph *Fusulinidae of North China*, Birmingham University awarded him the D.Sc. in 1927. From 1928 to 1949 he was director of the National Research Institute of Geology, Academia Sinica. In the year 1934–1935 Li was invited by the Universities' China Committee in London to deliver a series of lectures at British universities. Some of the lectures were included in his book *The Geology of China* (1939).

Li conducted research on glaciation for many years, obtaining evidence in several localities, especially in the Lushan area of central China. Although he declared the existence of Quaternary glaciation in China, he was unable to persuade some scientists with different views. It remains a scientific controversy.

During World War II, beginning in 1937, Li continued his research work on the tectonic types in southern China and concluded that the epsilon type, denominated by him, is the most important type and was widely distributed not only in China but also in many other parts of the world. In 1945 he received an honorary Ph.D. from the University of Oslo. He represented the Geological Society of China at the 1948 International Geological Congress held in London, where he presented the paper "The Myth of the Neocathaysian Seas."

In 1949, soon after the founding of the People's

Republic of China, Li was appointed vice president of the Chinese Academy of Sciences. In 1950 he returned to China, where he was appointed minister of geology in 1952. In 1958 he was elected corresponding academician of the U.S.S.R. Academy of Sciences.

Under Li's supervision the Research Institute of Geomechanics was established in 1956. He applied mechanics and his field experiences to research on geological structure. His important book *An Introduction to Geomechanics*, (in Chinese) was published in 1962. The theory of geomechanics has proved valuable in geothermal and earthquake studies, in the search for metallic and nonmetallic ores, and in confirming that China would have to import oil in order to survive.

BIBLIOGRAPHY

I. ORIGINAL WORKS. Li's writings include "Geology of the Gorge District of the Yangtze," in *Bulletin of the Geological Society of China*, **3** (1924), 351–391; "The Fundamental Cause of Evolution of the Earth's Surface Features," *ibid.*, **5** (1926), 209–262, also published separately (Peking, 1927); *Fusulinidae of North China* (Peking, 1927), in Chinese and English; *The Canon of Marine Transgression in Post-Paleozoic Times*, National Research Institute of China, Institute of Geology, memoir no. 6 (Shanghai, 1928), in Chinese and English, the English version also in *Bulletin of the Geological Society of China*, **7** (1928), 81–128; *Geological Guide to the Lungtan District, Nanking* (Nanking, 1932), written with S. Chu, in English and Chinese; *The Geology of China* (London, 1939); and *Quaternary Glaciation in the Lushan Area, Central China* (Nanking, 1947), in Chinese and English.

II. SECONDARY LITERATURE. See Xia Xiangrong, *History of the Geological Society of China* (Beijing, 1982), in Chinese; and C. C. Yu, "Professor Jonquei Ssu-kuang Lee (Biographical Note)," in *Contributions of the National Research Institute of Geology, Academia Sinica*, no. 8 (1948), i–vii (no. 8 is a special number titled "In Commemoration of the Sixtieth Birthday of J. S. Lee, M.Sc., D.Sc.").

XIA XIANGRONG

LIFSHITS, IL'IA MIKHAILOVICH (*b*. Kharkov, Russia, 13 January 1917; *d*. Moscow, U.S.S.R., 23 October 1982), *physics*.

Lifshits' father, Mikhail Il'ich Lifshits, was a physician and a professor at the Kharkov Medical Institute; his mother, Bertha Evsorovna, was a housewife. In his youth Il'ia was greatly influenced by his elder brother Evgenii, who also became a physicist.

Most of Lifshits' life was associated with Kharkov. After graduating from the university there in 1936, he started to work in the theoretical department founded by Lev Davidovich Landau at the Ukrainian Physico-Technical Institute. In 1939 Lifshits defended his candidate thesis, and in 1941 his doctoral dissertation, both of which dealt with the quantum mechanics of the condensed state. Then, at the age of twenty-four, he became the head of one of the two theoretical groups at the Ukrainian Physico-Technical Institute (the other one was headed by A. I. Akhiezer).

In the vast range of Lifshits' research interests, the leading place belonged to solid state physics. He was also involved in various applied problems, however, including the theory of diffusion pumps, zone-refining of metals, and the physics of powder sintering. Soon after he had joined the Ukrainian institute, Lifshits had a short, unsuccessful period of experimental work at I. V. Obreimov's laboratory. For most of his professional life, however, he was a "pure" theoretician with a fine physical sense who was able to uncover physics in many applied problems arising in engineering and technology.

The first, prewar series of Lifshits' works was associated with the scattering of X rays by crystals. In this theory he took into account the presence of isotopes, of holes, and of other defects characteristic of real crystals. He worked out a matrix method of analysis of phenomena associated with oscillations of the crystal lattice that enabled him to investigate the phonon spectrum.

In the late 1920's, Felix Bloch and Archibald Wilson demonstrated the fundamental importance of the structure of the energy spectrum of crystals for the description of their various properties. The states of electrons whose energy is close to the Fermi energy are crucial for the properties of metals. Lifshits stated and completely solved an important problem of reconstruction (reproduction) of the energy spectrum from the experimental data. The characteristic of the nonelastic scattering of neutrons, together with the resonance experiments, enabled Lifshits to reconstruct the Bose branch of the energy spectrum, and the effects observed in the presence of a magnetic field (for instance, the de Haas–van Alfven effect or that of de Haas–Shubnikov) made it possible for him to restore the Fermi branches. Combined efforts of Soviet theoreticians (most of them belonging to Lifshits' school) and experimentalists have led to the determination of the topology of the Fermi surfaces practically for all metals. The shape of these surfaces has turned out to be fairly fantastic for a number of metals, and therefore they began to be called *"monstres."*

Lifshits obtained important results related to the energy spectrum and quantum excitation of disordered media (amorphous bodies, disordered alloys). He made a great contribution to the formation of the notion of quantum crystals and studied the singularities of behavior of defects within this type of crystal. Lifshits also described these defects in terms of the quasiparticles able to move at absolute zero. With A. F. Andreev, Lifshits predicted the phenomenon of quantum diffusion in such crystals (which is something like tunneling through the interlattice barriers).

The physics of quasiparticles, founded in the Soviet Union by I. E. Tamm, Ia. I. Frenkel, L. D. Landau, S. I. Pekar, and others, was significantly enriched by Lifshits' investigations.

The following series of Lifshits' papers is related to the theory of phase transitions. He introduced a phase transition associated with reconstruction of the Fermi surface (the so-called 2½ or Lifshits transition). He also described in detail the kinetics of the second-order phase transition and the transition from a superconducting to an ordinary state under the influence of a magnetic field. These results were complemented by investigations of phase transformation of macromolecules, which is a subject equally relevant for physicists, chemists, and biologists. Lifshits and his collaborators formulated the criteria for that type of transformation and built up their quantitative theory for single-chain molecules. These problems attracted Lifshits' attention during the last years of his life.

The scientific activity of Lifshits received a wide recognition. In 1948 he was elected corresponding member, and in 1967 full member, of the Ukrainian Academy of Sciences; the Soviet Academy also elected him corresponding (1960) and full (1970) member. The leading position of Lifshits in Soviet physics was confirmed when he was invited in 1969 by P. L. Kapitsa to head the theoretical department at the Institute of Physical Problems in Moscow (a position earlier occupied by Landau). In 1967 Lifshits was awarded the Lenin Prize.

Lifshits suffered from heart disease and died after a short period of illness, as the result of a second heart attack. He was, however, active in science and teaching until the last weeks of his life.

BIBLIOGRAPHY

I. ORIGINAL WORKS. A bibliography is in M. Ia. Azbel and M. I. Kaganov, "Ilia Mikhailovich Lifshits," in *Us-*
pekhi fizicheskikh nauk, **91**, no. 3 (1967), 560–561. Selected works are "Optical Behaviour of Non-ideal Crystal Lattices in the Infra-red," in *Journal of Physics (USSR)*, **7**, no. 5 (1943), 215–228, no. 6 (1943), 249–251, and **8**, no. 2 (1944), 89–105; "O vyrozhdennykh reguliarnykh vozmushcheniiakh" (On degenerate regular perturbations), in *Zhurnal eksperimentalnoi i teoreticheskoi fiziki*, **17**, no. 11 (1947), 1017–1025, and no. 12 (1947), 1076–1089; "Some Considerations on the Twinning of Calcite Crystals," in *Journal of Physics (USSR)*, **11**, no. 2 (1947), 121–130, written with V. I. Obreimov; "Ob opredelenii energeticheskogo spektra boze-sistemy po ee teploemkosti" (On the determination of the Bose-system spectrum on the basis of its heat capacity), in *Zhurnal eksperimentalnoi i teoreticheskoi fiziki*, **26**, no. 5 (1954), 551–556; "Ob opredelenii poverkhnosti Fermi i skorostei v metalle po ostsilliatsii magnitnoi vospriimchivosti metallov pri nizkikh temperaturakh" (On the determination of Fermi surface and of a metal on the basis of magnetic susceptibility oscillations at low temperatures), in *Doklady Akademii nauk SSSR*, **96**, no. 1 (1954), 6, written with A. V. Pogorelov; "O strukture energeticheskogo spektra i kvantovykh sostoianiiakh neuporiadochennykh kondensirovannykh sistem" (On the structure of an energetical spectrum and on quantum states of disordered condensed systems), in *Uspekhi fizicheskikh nauk*, **83**, no. 4 (1964), 617–663; "Elektronnaia teoriia metallov i geometriia" (Electron theory of metals and geometry), *ibid.*, **129**, no. 3 (1979), 487–529, written with M. I. Kaganov; *Elektronnaia teoriia metallov* (Moscow, 1971), written with M. Ia. Azbel and M. I. Kaganov, translated by Albin Tubulewicz as *Electron Theory of Metals* (New York, 1973); *Kvazichastitsy* (Moscow, 1976), written with M. I. Kaganov, translated by V. Kissin as *Quasiparticles* (Moscow, 1979); and *Vvedenie v teoriiu neuporiadochennykh sistem* (Introduction to the theory of disordered systems; Moscow, 1982), written with S. A. Gredeskul and L. A. Pastur.

II. SECONDARY LITERATURE. M. Ia. Azbel and M. I. Kaganov, "Ilia Mikhailovich Lifshits: K piatidesiatiletiiu so dnia rozhdenia" (For his fiftieth birthday), in *Uspekhi fizicheskikh nauk*, **91**, no. 3 (1967), 559–561. Obituaries are *ibid.*, **140**, no. 3 (1983), 521–522; and in *Physics Today*, no. 3 (1983), 83–84.

V. J. FRENKEL

LINDERSTRØM-LANG, KAJ ULRIK (*b.* Frederiksberg, Copenhagen, Denmark, 29 November 1896; *d.* Copenhagen, 25 May 1959), *biochemistry, protein chemistry.*

Linderstrøm-Lang was a leader in protein chemistry, both theoretical and experimental. His power of mathematical analysis and his grasp of modern physical chemistry enabled him to develop new approaches to the chemistry of proteins. He was also a highly skilled and imaginative experimentalist who developed new microchemical techniques that permitted studies on the metabolism of individual living cells and tissues. These talents, and Lang's remarkable personal qualities, made the chemical department of the Carlsberg Laboratory in Copenhagen, under his directorship, one of the greatest centers in the world for research in protein chemistry and related fields; it attracted gifted investigators from many parts of the world. Although Lang traveled widely and spent a year in the United States, his life was centered at the Carlsberg Laboratory from the time he received his university degree until his death.

His father, Carl Frederik Linderstrøm-Lang, a teacher of German and Latin at the Frederiksberg Gymnasium, was the son of the cantor at Vemmetofte, a home for unmarried ladies of rank. The cantor's second wife (Lang's grandmother), Johanna Ulrica Linderstrøm, was the daughter of a cavalry officer and lighthouse inspector; from her the family acquired the name Linderstrøm. Teaching had long been a vocation in the Lang family and was part of the atmosphere in which young Lang grew up. His mother, born Ellen Hedvig Bach, was the daughter of P. J. Bach, a banker in Svendborg. Most of the men of the family had been fishermen, and it was primarily because of a leg injury that P. J. Bach became a banker instead. Ellen Linderstrøm-Lang was musical and artistic and had wanted to be a music teacher; her brother was an architect. Lang considered that his strong artistic bent was inherited from his mother, to whom he was always close. Lang was the youngest child; he had two sisters, both of whom became schoolteachers.

The friends of the family were largely in academic circles. At dinner parties there were lively discussions of cultural and artistic subjects; humorous after-dinner speeches, verses, and recitals played an important part on these occasions. Such diversions were later characteristic of Lang's own social gatherings; as a host he was memorable for his liveliness and charm.

As a boy he drew, painted, modeled, played the violin, wrote poetry, and was a good carpenter. In spite of his diverse talents, he was self-conscious and considered himself to be hopelessly ugly. The family situation suffered a change after his father died of cancer when Lang was fifteen. Their house had to be sold, and their way of life was altered. Nine years later his mother died of tongue cancer, for which she had had an operation some ten years earlier.

At the age of seventeen Lang began the study of chemistry at the Technical University in Copenhagen. His fellow students held him in high esteem for his talents as a playwright in their annual theatricals and for his other gifts, but his academic work in chemistry was not distinguished. His major interests were artistic and literary; he was bold enough to send one of his plays to the eminent critic Georg Brandes, who replied that the play was "not boring" but that Lang would have to decide whether he really had the necessary talent to continue. He found no publishers for his writings and experienced what was apparently a rather serious emotional crisis. However, he graduated in 1919 from the university with a respectable record.

Soon afterward an event occurred that was decisive for his future career. Lang had obtained a temporary job at the National Research Institute on Animal Husbandry in Copenhagen. His supervisor, A. C. Andersen, who had previously worked at the Carlsberg Laboratory, recognized the young man's talents and recommended him to Søren P. L. Sørensen, the great protein chemist who was head of the chemical department at Carlsberg. Lang applied for a job as assistant there and was appointed in August 1919.

Sørensen was then at the height of his career, but there was a grave shortage of chemicals and supplies, which had been cut off during the war. He set Lang to preparative and analytical work, demanding high purity in the products and accuracy in the analyses. Lang performed thousands of Kjeldahl nitrogen analyses during this period. This discipline, under the guidance of a demanding but kindly master deeply devoted to science, was a turning point in Lang's life. He wrote later in his obituary of Sørensen: "Science and its employment in the service of mankind was his only passion; it was the principle on which he built his life. I never came across any scientific question that did not interest him and which he was not willing to hear about, however busy he might be. Therefore he was the most encouraging chief imaginable."[1] Soon Lang was Sørensen's most trusted assistant, and he became dedicated to science without losing his keen interest in art, music, and literature.

In March 1922 Lang married Gerda Kyndby, a schoolteacher who was a close friend of his sister's. They had two daughters and a son. She kept her interest in teaching while her life became increasingly busy with the activities of the laboratory and its numerous visitors. When Lang succeeded Sørensen as director in 1939, the family moved into the director's quarters in the laboratory building, so that their home life was closely interwoven with that of the laboratory.

Lang went deeply into the study of what were then frontiers of physical chemistry. With much help from personal discussions with Niels Bjerrum and Jens A. Christiansen, he mastered the work of Willard Gibbs and others, as well as the newer knowledge of electrolyte solutions, molecular structure, and intermolecular and interionic forces. His first independent paper (1924), on the "salting out" of polar and nonpolar molecules by electrolytes in water, was an extensive experimental study combined with a thoughtful theoretical discussion of intermolecular forces in solution.

In "On the Ionization of Proteins" (1924) Lang applied the interionic attraction theory of Debye and Hückel—published the previous year—to the analysis of the influence of electrostatic forces on acid-base equilibria in proteins. All proteins contain many acid and basic groups, so that the net charge, Z (in proton units), on a protein molecule can assume a wide range of values, both positive and negative, as the pH is varied by adding acids or bases. As Z increases in either direction, electrostatic repulsion makes the addition of more charges of the same sign increasingly difficult. However, the addition of neutral salts, which in water are completely ionized, diminishes this repulsion, since the electrostatic field around the protein ion is partly counterbalanced by a preferential clustering of small ions of opposite charge in its neighborhood, as explained in detail by the Debye-Hückel theory.

As a model for the protein Lang chose a sphere of radius b, and the net charge Z was assumed to be spread uniformly over its surface. This was the simplest working assumption available at the time, and it worked well when applied to experimental data. The ionic strength $I = 1/2 \sum c_i z_i^2$, where c_i is the molar concentration of the i'th ion of the salt, and z_i is its valence. The electrical free energy (Gibbs energy) of the protein ion is:

$$G_e = \frac{Z^2 \varepsilon^2}{2D}\left(\frac{1}{b} - \frac{\kappa}{1 + \kappa a}\right) = Z^2 kTw \qquad (1)$$

where ε is the proton charge, D is the dielectric constant of the solvent, k is Boltzmann's constant, and κ is the reciprocal mean distance of the ion atmosphere around the central protein ion in the Debye-Hückel theory. In water near 25°C, $\kappa = 0.33 \times 10^8 \sqrt{I}$ cm^{-1}. The first term in parentheses gives the G_e value for the protein ion at zero ionic strength; the second term, which increases with the square root of the ionic strength, partly counterbalances the first. The distance a represents the

distance of closest approach between the centers of the protein ion and the small ions; approximately $a = b + 2$ (values in Ångström units). The parameter w, as defined here, was introduced by Linderstrøm-Lang. It is a measure of the shift in the form of the titration curve that arises from electrostatic repulsions. It decreases as the square root of the ionic strength increases but is always positive, since $a > b$. If one is titrating a protein (or other macromolecule) containing a set of n equivalent acid or basic groups, the slope of the titration curve $d\bar{Z}/dpH$ at the midpoint, when half the groups have been titrated, is given by

$$\left(\frac{d\bar{Z}}{dpH}\right)_{mid} = -\frac{2.303\,n}{2(wn + 2)}. \qquad (2)$$

Here $\bar{Z}$ is the mean value of Z, averaged over all protein molecules in the system.

Actually the slope, as defined by this equation, remains essentially constant for a considerable distance on either side of the midpoint. R. K. Cannan[2] showed later that the data for a set of equivalent acid groups, all with the same intrinsic pK value, reduce to a simplified form of Lang's equations:

$$pH = pK_{int} + \log[\alpha/(1 - \alpha)] - 2w\bar{Z}/2.303. \qquad (3)$$

Here α represents the fraction of the groups in the set from which protons have been removed.

Lang recognized from the beginning that the distribution of charges in such an assembly of macromolecules must be statistical. At a given moment a particular molecule may carry a net charge Z; but all the molecules are constantly exchanging protons with the solvent, and the value of Z for any individual molecule is constantly fluctuating. Hence the charge as measured from the titration curve is a mean value, $\bar{Z}$, averaged over all the molecules in the system. Later Lang showed, in his Dunham lectures at Harvard Medical School (1939), that the standard deviation of $\bar{Z}$ is directly related to the steepness of the titration curve, which gives $\bar{Z}$ as a function of pH at any point:

$$d\bar{Z}/d\ln(H^+) = -d\bar{Z}/2.3pH = \bar{Z}^2 - (\bar{Z})^2. \qquad (4)$$

This simple and elegant relation is applicable to any system involving the binding of ligands, in which the binding can be defined by a sequence of dissociation (or association) constants, such as the combination of oxygen molecules with the four heme groups of hemoglobin.

In 1926 Lang applied the analysis developed in this 1924 paper to the titration of egg albumin at various ionic strengths previously carried out by Sørensen and Ellen Lund. The form of the curves accorded well with the predictions of the theory, and it was possible, from the observed values of w, to calculate the radius b of the protein molecule, taking $a = b + 2$ (values in Ångströms), which is a reasonable estimate for the closest distance of approach of the small ions to the protein surface. The resulting value of b was 22 Å, in close agreement with that derived from the molecular weight deduced by Sørensen from osmotic pressure measurements.

Lang never lost interest in these electrostatic interactions of macromolecules. In a much later paper (1953) he calculated the activity coefficients of large multipolar ions of various shapes and charge distributions, taking account of and extending the studies in this field by John G. Kirkwood and others.

In the same paper of 1926 Lang also introduced an important distinction, for proteins and other ampholytes, between two quantities, which he termed the isoelectric point and the isoionic point. The isoelectric point may be defined as the pH value at which the mean net charge of the protein, arising from all bound ions, including H^+ and OH^-, is zero. To define the isoionic point, consider a protein in its state of maximum positive charge Z_{max} when all potential cationic groups in the molecule are charged, and then remove Z_{max} protons per molecule by addition of hydroxyl ion. The resulting protein is then isoionic by definition. If the protein combines only with H^+ and OH^-, the isoelectric and isoionic points coincide; but if it combines with other ions as well, the two may be significantly different. To determine the isoionic point, one needs isoionic protein, which may be prepared by electrodialysis or (better) by treatment with a mixed-bed ion-exchange resin.

Lang proposed that either procedure removes essentially all small ions, other than H^+ or OH^-, from the system. Two experimental methods for determination of the isoionic point were proposed: according to one, it is the pH of the protein solution that does not change on the addition of more isoionic protein; according to the other, it is the pH of a solution of the isoionic protein in water, or in a solution of another solute that does not produce H^+ or OH^- ions when dissolved in water alone. These definitions are based on a much later discussion in one of Lang's last papers, written with Sigurd O. Nielsen (1959), in which he gave the most mature formulation of his concepts in this field; it appeared in *Electrophoresis*, edited by Milan Bier.

Lang's doctoral dissertation (1929), on the fractionation of the milk protein casein, reflected Sørensen's concerns with the purification and separation of proteins from the complex mixtures found in nature. He demonstrated clearly, by laborious fractionations, that casein, then widely supposed to be a pure protein, was actually a mixture of several closely related constituents—a conclusion later fully confirmed by the simpler and more powerful techniques that had become available in the meantime. He did not pursue further studies in this area but turned in other directions.

Lang worked in the United States from 1931 to 1932 as a Rockefeller research fellow at the California Institute of Technology. He broadened his primarily chemical background by studying general biology with Thomas Hunt Morgan and worked on biochemical problems with Linus Pauling and Henry Borsook. This year was important in his life, and he established close and lasting relations with many American friends.

Lang had early developed a strong interest in enzymes, especially proteolytic enzymes, and in 1926 he spent two months in the laboratory of Richard Willstätter in Munich, which was then the most famous center of enzyme chemistry. He was not, however, converted to Willstätter's view that enzymes were not proteins and pursued his independent path upon returning to Copenhagen. He concentrated his investigations on the peptidases, enzymes that hydrolyzed rather small peptides. He showed in the period 1929 to 1930 that two dipeptides, leucylglycine and alanylglycine, were attacked by two different enzymes from the mucous membrane of the intestine; one of them could break down longer peptide chains, provided they contained a terminal leucine. Some members of Willstätter's school sharply criticized these conclusions, and it was several years before it was definitely established that Lang's views were correct.

A major influence on Lang's research was the arrival in 1930 of a young Austrian, Heinz Holter, in the laboratory. Holter was eager to trace the biological role of enzymes by relating their activity to the structure of the cells and tissues in which they occur. Lang pointed out that it was essential to work quantitatively and to be able to measure extremely small amounts of material in a well-defined region of a tissue—ideally, to work with individual cells. This required the development of micromethods of a totally new sort. These studies on enzymatic histochemistry lasted for twenty years. Lang and Holter developed a wide array of sensitive and precise ultramicro methods for the study of the distribution of a great variety of enzymes and other constituents of cells and tissues; the work was widely influential in other laboratories. Lang's remarkable versatility was evident in his ability to apply physical principles to new analytical methods. The use of the Cartesian diver for the measurement of oxygen consumption or of specific enzyme activity, in single microscopic sections of tissue or even in individual cells, is an outstanding example. Lang not only developed the experimental technique but also treated the theory of the method in great detail, considering all sources of error and the means of correcting them. Another major contribution was the use of mixtures of components of different densities in such a way as to form a density gradient column. This could be used to determine the density of very small droplets by determining the position at which they came to rest in the column. For this it was essential that the material in the droplets be insoluble in the column.

Holter stayed at the Carlsberg Laboratory for the rest of his career. In 1942 he became head of the new subdepartment of cytochemistry within the chemical department. In 1956 he became head of the physiological department of the Carlsberg Laboratory, as successor to Øjvind Winge.

Though his work with Holter on cytochemistry absorbed much of Lang's time and energy during the 1930's, he continued to work on protein chemistry. There was much debate over the nature of native proteins, partly inspired by the cyclol theory of Dorothy Wrinch, which for a few years aroused much interest. For a time Lang considered it possible that native proteins might not contain peptide bonds, and that these bonds might appear, by an intramolecular rearrangement, only after the protein had become denatured. He pictured the attack of proteolytic enzymes on the protein as involving a process that, in its simplest form, could be written as

$$\text{native protein} \rightleftharpoons \text{denatured protein}$$
$$\xrightarrow{\text{enzyme}} \text{split products.}$$

If the native and denatured proteins were in a reversible equilibrium, the attack of the enzyme on the latter would constantly shift the equilibrium to the right, and hydrolysis would proceed.

In pursuing this problem, Lang, with C. F. Jacobsen (1941), studied the volume changes accompanying the enzymatic breakdown of proteins. For simple peptides, the breakage of a peptide linkage in neutral solution is accompanied by a volume decrease, of the order of 15–22 cm^3 per mole. Denoting a peptide by the simplified formula $R \cdot NH \cdot CO \cdot R$, the process may be written thus:

$$R \cdot NH \cdot COR' + H_2O \rightleftharpoons R \cdot NH_3^+ + R'COO^- ; \Delta V = -15 \text{ to } -20 \text{ cm}^3/\text{mol.}$$

This shrinkage in volume is due primarily to electrostriction; the electric field around the ions produced by the hydrolysis causes the surrounding polar water molecules to become oriented around the ions and to pack more tightly together. Using dilatometers, Lang and Jacobsen followed the volume change that occurred with β-lactoglobulin hydrolyzed by trypsin or chymotrypsin, correlating the volume change with the number of bonds broken by the enzyme. In the early stages of hydrolysis the volume change, ΔV, was -50 cm^3/mol of bonds broken, far higher than for simple peptides. As hydrolysis proceeded, the bonds broken at a later stage gave lower ΔV values, like those of simple peptides. Lactoglobulin is a compact globular protein molecule that readily forms excellent crystals. They found that another protein, the histone clupein, with a more open flexible structure, behaved much like simple peptides; ΔV was near -15 cm^3/mole throughout the course of its hydrolysis. Lang and Jacobsen inferred that the native lactoglobulin, with its highly folded structure, was initially undergoing a partial collapse of the native structure, involving volume changes that could not be explained simply in terms of breakage of peptide linkages.

Nearly a decade later, in his Lane lectures at Stanford University (published in 1952), Lang elaborated these ideas into a more general picture of the structure of native proteins. By that time Frederick Sanger's work on insulin at Cambridge had provided decisive evidence that amino acid residues in proteins are indeed linked by peptide bonds. Lang pictured the structure of native proteins as being describable in terms of three levels of order: (1) primary structure, defined by the sequence of amino acid residues in the peptide chain; (2) secondary structure, consisting of segments of the peptide chain that are arranged in a definite repeating spatial order, such as the α-helix or the pleated sheets described by Linus Pauling; (3) tertiary structure, involving the additional folds and turns that completed the formation of the structure of the native protein. Lang's conceptual scheme and his terminology have found general acceptance among biochemists as a convenient basis for describing the structures of native globular proteins, consisting of a single peptide chain or subunits of proteins containing several such chains. J. D. Bernal later extended the scheme for globular proteins composed of several peptide chains by the concept of "quaternary structure," which involves the packing together of the individual folded chains to form a compact structure of higher order.

Lang's researches on the action of proteolytic

enzymes became directed, especially after 1945, to the use of such enzymes as tools for exploring the secondary and tertiary structure of proteins by following changes in volume, optical rotation, and other properties, and correlating them with the number of peptide bonds broken as hydrolysis proceeded. The addition of denaturing agents, such as urea, could be used to shift the balance between native and reversibly denatured protein to probe further the effects of breaking peptide bonds that were important for maintaining the native structure. L. Korsgaard Christensen (1952) studied in great detail the enzymatic hydrolysis of β-lactoglobulin, with some additional important experiments on egg albumin. As in many other cases, Lang's name does not appear on this long paper, but his thinking is apparent throughout. A year later (1953) Lang gave a detailed exposition of his ideas on the modes of degradation of proteins by enzymes, and their implications for protein structure, at the Ninth Solvay Congress. His discussion was inevitably tentative; the direct evidence from X-ray diffraction for the three-dimensional structures of proteins did not become available until several years later, but the general picture, as he envisaged it, was to be borne out by later developments.

Also in his Lane lectures, Lang considered the problem of protein biosynthesis, about which little was then known. His thinking was in several respects ahead of his time. He emphasized the thermodynamic considerations that must impose constraints on any biosynthetic scheme and pointed out the likelihood that the phosphorylation of amino acids, probably by adenosine triphosphate (ATP), could, in the presence of suitable catalysts, provide a higher level of free energy that could be expended in the formation of peptide bonds. It seemed to him highly unlikely that the biosynthesis of proteins could be brought about by the same enzymes that hydrolyzed them, acting in reverse; rather, it seemed necessary that a different set of enzymes must be involved, drawing upon the free energy reserves provided by ATP (or some other free energy source) to make the process go. To a significant extent his thinking foreshadowed the extraordinary advances in this field that began a few years later. Indeed, Paul C. Zamecnik, who became one of the leaders in those developments, had worked earlier in Lang's laboratory (1939), although on different problems.

Lang's last major line of research introduced a new and powerful approach to the study of the forces responsible for maintaining secondary and tertiary structure. This was the study of hydrogen-deuterium exchange between proteins and the water

around them. By infrared spectroscopy H. Lenormant and E. R. Blout (1953) had shown that proteins contained at least two different kinds of peptide linkages; one kind was easily deuterated with D_2O at room temperature, whereas the others exchanged H for D only at high temperature or at high or low pH. Lang decided to study such exchanges by measuring the rate of change in the density of the water surrounding the protein, since the mass of deuterium (D) is twice that of hydrogen (H). The density gradient systems that he had developed much earlier permitted rapid and accurate density determinations on very small drops of water in the gradient tubes. Hydrogen bound to carbon was essentially nonexchangeable, but in small molecules, including simple peptides, H-D exchange was generally very rapid for hydrogens attached to oxygen, nitrogen, or sulfur. For proteins, however—Lang studied insulin, pancreatic ribonuclease, and β-lactoglobulin—there was a wide range of exchange rates from virtually instantaneous to extremely slow. Indeed, at temperatures near 0°C some peptide hydrogens showed virtually no exchange over several days. Rise of temperature to 38°C or above greatly increased the rates for some of these peptides, as did change of pH to more acid or more alkaline values, or the addition of denaturing agents, such as urea or guanidinium chloride.

Lang proposed models to interpret the data, but these were necessarily tentative; it was only later that detailed structural data became available for correlation. He had, however, opened up a new and powerful approach to the dynamics of protein structures that could reveal the character and frequency of fluctuations in the native structure that would permit exchange of hydrogens as portions of the native structure opened up momentarily and exposed normally buried hydrogens to contact with the solvent. Lang led the way in introducing these methods. His death in 1959, preceded by a year of illness, cut off the further progress of his work. Other workers, using a variety of techniques—nuclear magnetic resonance, tritium-hydrogen exchange followed by radioactivity measurements, and neutron diffraction studies on protein crystals, among other methods—have carried such studies much further; but Lang was certainly the pioneer in this field.

During World War II, Denmark had been largely cut off from the outside world, especially during the long German occupation. Lang was active in the resistance movement and aided many Jews and other refugees to escape to Sweden. As the country recovered from the war, the Carlsberg Laboratory became a great center of attraction, especially to protein chemists, from foreign lands. Among them were Christian B. Anfinsen, William F. Harrington, Frederic M. Richards, John A. Schellman, and Harold A. Scheraga from the United States, and Sidney J. Leach from Australia, along with many others. These visitors worked largely as independent investigators, although they published joint papers with Lang on some occasions; there was constant free discussion and interchange of ideas. The enthusiasm and intellectual stimulus that Lang provided were pervasive, and his influence was far more than intellectual.

The range of Lang's talents was immense: He was a painter of considerable talent, a gifted writer, a musician, a delightful conversationalist and raconteur. There was a strong element of gaiety in his nature, together with sensitiveness to human difficulties and suffering. His scientific gifts, great as they were, do not fully account for the remarkable flowering of the Carlsberg Laboratory under his directorship. He traveled widely to scientific meetings and other events and took a deep interest in the international relations of science. In addition to many other honors, he was elected president of the International Union of Biochemistry, succeeding Marcel Florkin, in 1958. He never took office, however; he had suffered for some years from a mild diabetes that became greatly exacerbated after the removal of a benign intestinal tumor in 1958. He spent the last year of his life mostly in the hospital and died in 1959 at the age of sixty-two.

NOTES

1. K. Linderstrøm-Lang, "S. P. L. Sørensen 1868–1939," in *Comptes rendus des travaux du Laboratoire Carlsberg, série chimique*, **23** (1939), i–xxi; see xi.
2. For later developments in this field, derived from Linderstrøm-Lang's work, see R. Keith Cannan, "The Acid-Base Titration of Proteins," in *Chemical Reviews*, **30** (1942), 395–412; and Charles Tanford, "The Interpretation of Hydrogen Ion Titration Curves of Proteins," in *Advances in Protein Chemistry*, **17** (1962), 69–165. As the three-dimensional structure of many proteins has become known in detail, correspondingly elaborate calculations of electrostatic forces around protein ions have been developed, notably by F. R. N. Gurd and his associates.

BIBLIOGRAPHY

I. ORIGINAL WORKS. Listings of Linderstrøm-Lang's works are in Poggendorff, VI, 1535, and VIIb, 2283–2287. Most of his papers appeared (in English) in *Comptes rendus des travaux du Laboratoire Carlsberg, série chimique (CRLC)*; others were in diverse journals, conference proceedings, and treatises. He never published a book. The biographical article by Heinz Holter (see below) lists 154 publications to which his name is attached, but many other papers from the laboratory reflect his influence. A

very useful collection is *Kai Linderstrøm-Lang: Selected Papers*, Heinz Holter, Hans Neurath, and Martin Ottesen, eds. (Copenhagen, New York, and London, 1962); the twenty-five papers in this volume include the complete texts of his Lane Medical Lectures at Stanford, which originally appeared as *Proteins and Enzymes*, Stanford University Publications, University Series, Medical Sciences, 6 (1952).

His writings include "On the Salting-out Effect," in *CRLC*, **15**, no. 4 (1924); "On the Ionization of Proteins," *ibid.*, **15**, no. 7 (1924); "On Peptide Bonds in Globular Proteins," in *Nature*, **142** (1938), 996, with R. D. Hotchkiss and G. Johansen; "The Contraction Accompanying Enzymatic Breakdown of Proteins," in *CRLC*, **24**, no. 1 (1941), 1–48, with C. F. Jacobsen; "On the Cartesian Diver Microrespirometer," *ibid.*, **24**, no. 17 (1943), 333–398; "Degradation of Proteins by Enzymes," in *Rapport et discussion . . . Institute International Chimique Solvay, 9 Congrès* (1953), 247–296; and "Deuterium Exchange Between Peptides and Water," in *Special Publications of the Chemical Society (London)*, no. 2 (1955), 1–20. The *Selected Papers* also contains a jeu d'esprit "The Thermodynamic Activity of the Male Housefly," with the imaginary F. Fizz-Loony. Two important reviews, written near the end of his life, are "Acid-Base Equilibria in Proteins," in Milan Bier, ed., *Electrophoresis*, I (New York, 1959), 35–89, with Sigurd O. Nielsen; and "Protein Structure and Enzyme Activity," in Paul D. Boyer, Henry Lardy, and Karl Myrbäck, eds., *The Enzymes*, 2nd ed., rev. (New York, 1959), 443–510, with John A. Schellman. These are more than reviews; they contain original ideas not previously discussed elsewhere.

II. SECONDARY LITERATURE. The most important biographical article on Lang is Heinz Holter, "K. U. Linderstrøm-Lang, 1896–1959," in *CRLC*, **32** (1960/1962), i–xxxiii, including a portrait and a bibliography. This is reprinted, without the bibliography but with several additional photographs and illustrations of apparatus, in Heinz Holter and K. Max Møller, eds., *The Carlsberg Laboratory, 1876–1976* (Copenhagen, 1976), 88–117. Other articles in this book provide important background, especially Lang's article on Sørensen, 63–81.

Other useful articles on Lang include K. Bailey, in *Proceedings of the Chemical Society (London)* (1960), 92–93; F. Duspiva, in *Ergebnissen der Physiologie* **51** (1961), 1–20; John T. Edsall, in *Advances in Protein Chemistry*, **14** (1959), xiii–xxiii, with portrait; Herman M. Kalckar, "Kaj Ulrik Linderstrøm-Lang, Scientist, Man, Artist," in *Science*, **131** (1960), 1420–1425; Hans Neurath, in *Archives of Biochemistry and Biophysics*, **86** (1960), i–iv; Martin Ottesen, in *American Philosophical Society: Year Book 1959* (1960), 133–138; and A. Tiselius, in *Biographical Memoirs of Fellows of the Royal Society*, **6** (1960), 157–168.

JOHN T. EDSALL

LINNIK, IURII VLADIMIROVICH (*b.* Belaia Tserkov', Ukraine, Russia, 21 January 1915; *d.* Leningrad, U.S.S.R., 30 June 1972), *mathematics*.

Linnik's parents, Vladimir Pavlovitch Linnik and Maria Abramovna Yakerina, were schoolteachers. His father later became a famous scientist in the field of optics and a member of the U.S.S.R. Academy of Sciences. After graduation from secondary school in 1931, Linnik, having worked for a year as a laboratory assistant, entered Leningrad University, where he studied theoretical physics and mathematics. He graduated from the university in 1938 and received the doctorate in mathematics in 1940, joining the staff of the Leningrad branch of the V. A. Steklov Institute of Mathematics of the U.S.S.R. Academy of Sciences. From 1944 he was simultaneously a professor in the Mathematics Department of Leningrad University. Linnik organized the chair of probability theory and mathematical statistics and founded the Leningrad school of probability and statistics.

Linnik's principal fields of endeavor were number theory, probability theory, and mathematical statistics. A characteristic feature of his work was the use of very advanced analytical techniques. His early works were devoted to analytic number theory. He began with the problem of the representation of an integer by positive ternary quadratic forms. Linnik next developed a powerful new method of investigating similar problems, the so-called ergodic method in number theory. A short paper (1941) served as a beginning of another powerful method now known as the large sieve method. In the 1950's Linnik developed a new strong method of analytic number theory. This method made it possible to solve some problems of additive number theory that cannot be treated by earlier methods. This method, which also uses some ideas of probability theory, is known as the dispersion method in number theory.

In the late 1940's Linnik began to work in probability theory and statistics. He immediately became famous because of his papers on probability limit theorems. Most important here was his work on probability of large deviations, where he found a new understanding of the problem. In the 1950's Linnik advanced the arithmetic of probability distributions, which had ceased to develop at the end of the 1930's. He did very important research in mathematical statistics and was one of the first to use the powerful analytical apparatus of the modern function theory for the solution of statistical problems. In a sense he created analytical statistics. He solved such difficult problems of statistics as characterization problems, the Behrens-Fisher problem, and the minimax property of the Hotelling T^2 test. Linnik was elected a member of the U.S.S.R. Academy of Sciences in 1964. He was also a member

of the Swedish Academy and of many other societies and held an honorary doctorate from the University of Paris. For many years he was president of the Leningrad Mathematical Society.

BIBLIOGRAPHY

I. ORIGINAL WORKS. Works by Linnik that are available in English are *Method of Least Squares and Principles of the Theory of Observations*, Regina C. Erlandt, trans., N. L. Johnson, ed. (New York, 1961); *The Dispersion Method in Binary Additive Problems*, S. Schur, trans. (Providence, R.I., 1963); *The Decomposition of Probability Distributions*, S. J. Taylor, ed. (New York, 1964); *Elementary Methods in Analytic Number Theory*, A. Feinstein, trans., rev. and ed. by L. J. Mordell (Chicago, 1965), written with A. Gelfond; "Characterization of Tests of the Bartlett-Schaffé Type" and "On the Construction of Optimal . . . Solutions of the Behrens-Fischer Problem," in *Articles on Mathematical Statistics and the Theory of Probability*, Proceedings of the Steklov Institute of Mathematics no. 79 (1966); *Ergodic Properties of Algebraic Fields*, M. S. Keane, trans. (New York, 1968); *Statistical Problems with Nuisance Parameters* (Providence, R.I., 1968); *Independent and Stationary Sequences of Random Variables*, J. F. C. Kingman, ed. (Groningen, 1971), written with I. A. Ibragimov; "Nonlinear Statistics and Random Linear Forms," written with A. A. Zinger, and "Gamma Distribution and Partial Sufficiency of Polynomials," written with A. L. Ruhin and S. I. Strelic, in *Theoretical Problems in Mathematical Statistics*, Proceedings of the Steklov Institute of Mathematics no. 111 (1972); *Characterization Problems in Mathematical Statistics*, B. Ramachandran, trans. (New York, 1973), written with A. M. Kagan and C. Radhakrishna Rao; and *Decomposition of Random Variables and Vectors*, Judah Rosenblatt, ed. (Providence, R.I., 1977), written with I. V. Ostrovskii.

II. SECONDARY LITERATURE. Bibliographies are in *Uspekhi matematicheskikh nauk*, **20**, no. 2 (1965), 229–236, and **28**, no. 2 (1973), 210–213.

I. A. IBRAGIMOV

LITTLE, CLARENCE COOK (*b*. Brookline, Massachusetts, 6 October 1888; *d*. Ellsworth, Maine, 22 December 1971), *mammalian genetics*.

Little was the son of James Lovell Little and Mary Robbins Revere Little, a descendant of Paul Revere. He was educated at Harvard (B.A. 1910; Ph.D. 1914), taking his doctorate under William Castle, the first mammalian geneticist in the United States. He married Katharine Day Andrews on 27 May 1911; they had two sons and a daughter and were divorced in 1929. The following year he married Beatrice W. Johnson; they had a son and a daughter.

He was a member of the American Academy of Arts and Sciences and of the National Academy of Sciences and received numerous honorary degrees.

In 1922, at the age of thirty-three, he became president of the University of Maine. Three years later he accepted the presidency of the University of Michigan, where he remained until 1929. In that year he founded the Jackson Laboratory in Bar Harbor, Maine. The original staff of the laboratory consisted of seven investigators, all of whom had been associated with him during his years as college president, and about an equal number of animal caretakers. During his twenty-seven years as active head of the laboratory, it grew in size and became a world-renowned center for research in mammalian genetics and cancer.

From 1929 to 1945, besides his work as director of the Jackson Laboratory, Little was managing director of the American Cancer Society, twice president of the American Association for Cancer Research, and an original member of the National Advisory Cancer Council created by Congress in 1937 to help establish policies for the National Cancer Institute.

Little's research was dominated by two interests: mammalian (especially mouse) genetics, and a search for the causes of cancer, with emphasis on genetic factors in its etiology. His most lasting contribution to mammalian genetics was his development of two of the earliest inbred strains of mice. Prior to 1914, while he was still in graduate school, the potential of inbreeding for the production of uniform strains of plants and animals had gained general recognition among geneticists. It also was common knowledge, however, that inbreeding could cause loss of fertility and vigor. Despite the problems that this raised, Little started the inbreeding of one strain, subsequently known as DBA, while at Harvard, and a second, C57BL, a few years later. The mice were mated, brother with sister, for generation after generation. By the use of a sufficient number of animals and careful selection, he succeeded in establishing two healthy strains. While the two strains were obviously different from each other, in coat color and the incidence of cancer, the mice within each strain were strikingly alike. Throughout his career, Little insisted that his role as administrator should not stand in the way of the steps necessary to ensure that these strains were maintained.

The genetic uniformity of these and other inbred strains has made them an indispensable tool in a great variety of research. In biology, they serve a function analogous to that of purified compounds in chemistry. Experiments can be repeated with the assurance that the experimental material will remain the same. The strains are widely and extensively used in laboratories throughout the world.

Another of Little's major contributions to science also was initiated while he was in graduate school. It concerned the genetics of tissue transplantation. In 1909, E. E. Tyzzer of the Harvard Medical School had reported on the growth of a transplantable tumor indigenous to one strain of mice when it was transplanted to a second, quite unrelated strain, and to hybrid generations derived from crosses between the two strains. He concluded that the genetics of susceptibility to the transplants did not conform to Mendelian principles. In 1914, Little published a paper in *Science* showing that a Mendelian interpretation was possible. In collaboration with Tyzzer, he carried out a second study that tended to confirm his interpretations.

When the Jackson Laboratory was founded, the first project undertaken by the staff was a continuation of experiments on the genetics of transplantation. The availability of inbred strains greatly enhanced the precision of the results. The results showed that susceptibility and resistance are determined by at least twelve loci, with susceptibility being dominant. This work became the foundation of all subsequent studies in the genetics of transplantation.

Little's third major contribution was the demonstration that, in strains of mice with a high incidence of mammary tumors, the development of the tumors requires an agent present in the mother's milk. The indication of this agent first came from genetic studies. The tumor incidence in hybrids between high-cancer and low-cancer strains seemed to be determined by the cancer incidence of the strain providing the maternal parent. The role of the mother was further established by foster-nursing experiments, which definitely proved transmission through the milk. While most of the experiments in this study were carried out by the staff of the Jackson Laboratory, Little played an important guiding role. Subsequent work performed elsewhere showed the milk agent to be a virus. These studies were thus an early step toward the recognition that viruses play a role in the etiology of many animal cancers.

A fourth research undertaking to which Little contributed, though almost entirely as an initiator, was a pioneering study in the genetics of behavior. The research at first was based on the use of four very dissimilar breeds of dogs but subsequently was shifted to mice. Once again, the great uniformity of inbred strains was proved to be an invaluable resource.

To an unusual degree Little combined the talents of an administrator with those of an innovative scientist. His considerable energies, his talent as a public speaker, and his ability to enlist the support of others made it possible for him to contribute significantly in both areas.

BIBLIOGRAPHY

I. ORIGINAL WORKS. A complete bibliography of Little's publications appears in George D. Snell, "Clarence Cook Little," in *Biographical Memoirs. National Academy of Sciences*, **46** (1975), 240–263.

II. SECONDARY LITERATURE. Jean Holstein, *The First Fifty Years at the Jackson Laboratory*, William L. Dupuy, ed. (Bar Harbor, Me., 1979); Herbert C. Morse III, ed., *Origins of Inbred Mice* (New York, 1978); and George D. Snell, ed., *The Biology of the Laboratory Mouse* (Philadelphia, 1941).

GEORGE D. SNELL

LITTLEWOOD, JOHN EDENSOR (*b*. Rochester, England, 9 June 1885; *d*. Cambridge, England, 6 September 1977), *mathematics.*

Littlewood was the eldest son of Edward Thornton Littlewood and Sylvia Ackland. His father, a graduate of Peterhouse, Cambridge, took his family to South Africa in 1892 when he became headmaster of a school at Wynberg, near Cape Town. John spent the years 1900 to 1903 at St. Paul's School in London, where his mathematics master was Francis Sowerby Macaulay, himself a creative mathematician.

Littlewood went to Cambridge as a scholar at Trinity College in October 1903. At this time the physical sciences were in a very strong position in Cambridge. As a result mathematics was looked upon as ancillary to physical science, which meant that the emphasis was on special functions and differential equations, where the treatment was far from rigorous. Moreover, great emphasis was put on manipulative skill. All this was not to Littlewood's taste: "I wasted my time except for rare interludes for the first two academic years." He did, however, value lectures given by Alfred North Whitehead on the foundations of mechanics.

Littlewood's research began during the long vacation of 1906. His tutor and director of studies was E. W. Barnes, who later left Cambridge for a career in the Anglican church and became better known as bishop of Birmingham. In 1907 Littlewood ac-

cepted the post of lecturer at Manchester University. He returned to Cambridge in 1910 and succeeded Whitehead as college lecturer at Trinity College.

It would be wrong to give the impression that Littlewood was concerned solely with mathematics; he had very wide interests. He was strong, somewhat shorter than average, and a very able athlete. He rowed for his college in Cambridge and later was very active in rock climbing and skiing. He also had a strong interest in music and was a good raconteur. However, his absorbing passion was mathematics, and although he was by no means averse to applied mathematics (indeed, he made important contributions to ballistics; *Collected Papers*, p. 21), his real interest was in analysis. Thus any account of Littlewood must be largely occupied with his contributions to pure mathematics. The mathematically inclined reader will find an excellent account in J. C. Burkill et al. (1978).

At the time Littlewood began his research, Barnes had studied entire functions of nonzero order, but his methods did not extend to functions of zero order, so he suggested that Littlewood might work on those functions. Littlewood later said, "I rather luckily struck oil at once (by switching to more elementary methods) and after that never looked back." In fact the "switch" was a big leap forward. He was able to establish for general functions a relation between the maximum and minimum moduli of these functions on large circles extending to infinity. Barnes had worked with special functions. There was a curious sequel that reveals much about analysis in Cambridge at the time. Barnes now suggested a problem on the zero of a certain analytic function. This was the notorious Riemann zeta function, which is very important in prime number theory. In 1859 Georg Friedrich Riemann had conjectured that all its complex zeros have real part 1/2. This is the famous Riemann hypothesis, which has never been proved. That Barnes should suggest this problem even to a very brilliant pupil shows that he could have had no idea of what was involved. Although Littlewood failed to prove the Riemann hypothesis, his investigations bore fruit. His work on the Riemann zeta function had great permanent value and led to his maxim "Never be afraid to tackle a difficult problem, however difficult it may appear. You may not solve it, but it could lead you on to something else."

Littlewood's second achievement about this time was the discovery of his famous Tauberian theorem (*Collected Papers*, p. 757). Sometime before, an earlier but less deep Tauberian theorem had been proved by G. H. Hardy, and the common interest of these two mathematicians in Tauberian theory was an important factor in initiating their lifelong collaboration. Hardy and Littlewood had very different personalities—indeed, they had little in common apart from the fact that they were both mathematicians working in Cambridge. Their joint work was collected in the papers of Hardy, and some three-quarters of the papers in the first three volumes of his papers were written jointly with Littlewood. During some of the most fruitful years, Littlewood was in Cambridge and Hardy in Oxford; they worked by correspondence. However, after Hardy's return to Cambridge, they still preferred to work in this way even though they were both at Trinity College. This remarkable collaboration between two equally outstanding scientists was probably the greatest ever between two mathematicians. Harald Bohr states that it was not started without misgivings. It was important to them that their collaboration not cramp either of their styles or encroach on their freedom:

> Therefore as a safety measure . . . they amused themselves by formulating some so-called axioms . . . . The first of them said that, when one wrote to the other it was completely indifferent whether what they wrote was right or wrong. As Hardy put it, otherwise they could not write completely as they pleased, but would have to feel a certain responsibility thereby. The second axiom was to the effect that, when one received a letter from the other he was under no obligation whatsoever to read it, let alone to answer it, . . . it might be that the recipient . . . would prefer not to work at that particular time, or perhaps he was just interested in other problems. The third axiom was to the effect that, although it did not really matter if they both simultaneously thought about the same detail, still it was preferable that they should not do so. And finally, the fourth and perhaps the most important axiom, stated that it was quite indifferent if one of them had not contributed the least bit to the contents of a paper under their common names; otherwise . . . now one and then the other, would oppose being named as co-author. *(Collected Works, I, p. xxviii)*

The contribution of Hardy and Littlewood to analysis was enormous. It extended over a vast range including Diophantine approximation, additive number theory, Waring's problem, the Riemann zeta function, prime number theory, inequalities, and Fourier series. In many cases their results are the best known to date, and work is still being done on many of their problems. Much of this is dealt with adequately by Titchmarsh et al., so we mention only the work on the rearrangement of functions and the Hardy-Littlewood maximal function, which has become fundamental in harmonic analysis (Stein and Weiss, p. 53).

Littlewood's work on the Riemann zeta function was outstanding and of great permanent value. An account of it and the subsequent developments is given by Montgomery in the Royal Society biographical memoir. Littlewood did not approve the Riemann hypothesis and became increasingly skeptical about it. Indeed, he privately expressed the opinion that it was false, but that the first zero in the critical script not on the critical line would be so far removed as to be beyond computation even by the most sophisticated methods, thereby rendering the problem unsolvable in the foreseeable future. This view was partly the result of his work on the functions $\pi(x)$ and $\text{li}(x)$ discussed by Montgomery.

Littlewood collaborated with other mathematicians besides Hardy. He and Harald Bohr prepared a book on the Riemann zeta function, but when it was completed, they were too exhausted to send it to the publisher. The manuscript was passed on to Ingham and Edward Charles Titchmarsh, and later incorporated in their larger works. Littlewood collaborated with Dame Mary Cartwright on differential equations, with A. C. Offord on random equations and entire functions, and with R. E. A. C. Paley on Fourier analysis. The differential equations considered in the work with Cartwright arose in the study of electric circuits. A brief account with further developments is given by Peter Swinnerton-Dyer in Littlewood's *Collected Papers* (p. 295) and by Cartwright (1974). Following the work with Offord, there is now a considerable literature on zeros of polynomials and related matters. There is a brief account of the developments by Bollobas in Littlewood's *Collected Papers* (pp. 1343, 1421) and further development by Kleitman.

Littlewood's work with Paley represents one of the most far-reaching advances in Fourier analysis. In terms of its one-dimensional Fourier series, they define the dyactic decomposition of a function and, by employing the Poisson integral, a certain nonlinear operator they called the *g*-function. The Littlewood-Paley theory was based on complex variable methods and thus was limited to one dimension. It was later realized that an *n*-dimensional result could be deduced from the one-dimensional theory, and this led in turn to some of the most exciting developments in analysis. There is a brief account by Brannan in Littlewood's *Collected Papers* (p. 664) and also by E. M. Stein in *Singular Integrals* (pp. 81–94) and *Topics in Harmonic Analysis.*

At the age of eighty-two, Littlewood gave a lecture at Rockefeller University entitled "The Mathematician's Art of Work." After reading this and *A*

Mathematician's Miscellany, it seems fair to say that few mathematicians have told us so much about themselves and their style of work as has Littlewood.

BIBLIOGRAPHY

I. ORIGINAL WORKS. Littlewood's writings are brought together in his *Collected Papers* (Oxford, 1982) and in G. H. Hardy, *Collected Papers*, 7 vols. (Oxford, 1966–1979). See also Littlewood's *A Mathematician's Miscellany* (London, 1953); and "The Mathematician's Work of Art," in *Rockefeller University Review*, **5** (1967), 1–7.

II. SECONDARY LITERATURE. Harald Bohr, *Collected Mathematical Works*, I (Copenhagen, 1952); J. C. Burkill, W. K. Hayman, H. L. Montgomery, A. Zygmund, and A. C. Offord, "John Edensor Littlewood," in *Biographical Memoirs of Fellows of the Royal Society*, **24** (1978), 323–367; Mary L. Cartwright, in *Bulletin of the Institute of Mathematics and Its Applications*, **10** (1974), 329; D. J. Kleitman, "Some New Results on the Littlewood-Offord Problem," in *Journal of Combinatorial Theory*, **A20** (1976), 89–113; Elias M. Stein, *Singular Integrals and Differentiability Properties of Functions* (Princeton, 1970), *Topics in Harmonic Analysis Related to the Littlewood-Paley Theory* (Princeton, 1970), and *Introduction to Fourier Analysis on Euclidean Spaces* (Princeton, 1971), with Guido Weiss; and E. C. Titchmarsh et al., "Godfrey Harold Hardy," in *Journal of the London Mathematical Society*, **25** (1950), 81–138.

A. C. OFFORD

LONG, CYRIL NORMAN HUGH (*b.* Nettleton, Wiltshire, England, 19 June 1901; *d.* Pemaquid Beach, Maine, 6 July 1970), *biochemistry, endocrinology.*

Long was the elder son of John Edward and Rose Fanny Langdill Long. His father, a tax surveyor, had strong interests in history, literature, collecting rare books, and a variety of handicraft hobbies. The parents encouraged their children to participate in intellectual and cultural matters. Long attended the Wigan Grammar School until 1918, and then the University of Manchester, which awarded him the B.Sc. in chemistry with first-class honors in 1921 and the M.Sc. in physiology in 1923, under the tutelage of Archibald Vivian Hill, who had received the Nobel Prize in physiology or medicine for 1922.

From 1923 to 1925 Long was demonstrator in physiology at University College, London, and from 1925 to 1932, lecturer and assistant professor of medical research at McGill University, Montreal. During this period he received the M.D., C.M. from McGill (1928) and the D.Sc. from Manchester (1932).

He was director of the George S. Cox Medical Research Institute and assistant professor of medicine at the University of Pennsylvania from 1932 to 1936. In 1936 Long moved to Yale University, where he served as professor and chairman of the department of physiological chemistry until 1951, and simultaneously was chairman of the department of pharmacology (1939–1941) and dean of the medical school (1947–1952). He was chairman of the department of physiology from 1951 to 1964. From his retirement in 1969 until his death, he was a fellow of the John B. Pierce Foundation Laboratory, New Haven.

In 1928 Long married Hilda Gertrude Jarman; they had two daughters, Barbara Rosemary and Diana Elizabeth. He became a U.S. citizen in 1942.

Long was appointed Sterling professor of physiological chemistry and in physiology at Yale. He was a fellow of Calhoun College, Yale, and received many honorary degrees, including the M.A. (Yale), Sc.D. (Princeton, McGill), and M.D. (University of Venezuela). He also received the Squibb Award of the Endocrine Society, the Banting Memorial Medal of the American Diabetes Association, the Schering Scholarship of the Endocrine Society, the Modern Medicine Award, the Scientific Award of the Pharmaceutical Manufacturers Association, the Medal of Hiroshima University, the Army-Navy Certificate of Appreciation, and a plaque from the Faculty of Medicine, Tokyo University. In 1966 Yale established the C. N. H. Long professorship in his honor. He was a fellow of the John S. Guggenheim Memorial Foundation (1955–1956) and was elected to membership in the National Academy of Sciences and the American Philosophical Society, and to fellowship in the American Academy of Arts and Sciences.

Long was a member of the American Diabetes Association, the American Physiological Society, the American Society for Clinical Investigation (elected president, 1945), the Argentine Society of Biology, the Association of American Physicians, the Biochemical Society (Great Britain), the British Diabetic Association, the Endocrine Society (elected president, 1947), the Fulton Society, the Horseshoe Club (London), the International Brain Research Association, the Peripatetic Club, the Physiological Society (Great Britain), and the Society for Experimental Biology and Medicine. He also served as a member of the editorial boards of *American Journal of Physiology, Endocrinology, Journal of Applied Physiology, Physiological Reviews, Proceedings of the Society for Experimental Biology and Medicine*, and *Yale Journal of Biology and Medicine*.

In the summer of 1950, Long traveled to Japan

to head an advisory group of the Atomic Bomb Casualty Commission, whose goal was the rebuilding of the medical schools there after World War II. He was consultant or member of the Armed Forces Institute of Pathology, the Atomic Energy Commission, the Armed Forces Quartermaster's Food and Container Institute, the Department of Health, Education, and Welfare, the Institute for Defense Analyses, the National Research Council, the National Science Foundation, the Office of Scientific Research and Development, the President's Scientific Advisory Committee for the United States Army, and the United States Public Health Service.

Several factors probably influenced Long's development into a scientist. His father's hobby of experimenting with making jams, soaps, and perfumes induced an interest in laboratory manipulations that was encouraged by his father, who hoped young Hugh would become a serious scholar and scientist. As a schoolboy Long was interested in photography and in other hobbies that he followed into his adult life, such as stamp collecting. He did well in school, both scholastically and in athletics, participating actively in cricket, soccer, and camping. During his final year at Wigan School, Long was first exposed to chemistry. Under the tutelage of an enthusiastic, effective science master he rose immediately to the top of his class, and became infected with the interest he followed for the remainder of his life.

Because of the eminence of its Honors School of Chemistry, Long selected Manchester as his university. His undergraduate studies centered on organic chemistry, especially of the carbohydrates, but after graduation he volunteered or was persuaded (the recollections of Hill and Long differ) to join A. V. Hill in studies of the mechanism of muscle contraction. It was recognized at that time that during muscle activity, the concentration of muscle glycogen fell and that of lactic acid increased. One hypothesis about the mechanism of contraction was that the increased intracellular acidity associated with formation of lactic acid might somehow cause a shortening of the protein fibers that make up the active machinery of the muscle cell. Hill's approach to studying this possibility involved following the changes in concentration of glycogen and lactic acid during the course of muscle activity in animals, and of glucose and lactate in the blood plasma of exercising human subjects.

At first Long was not enthusiastic about working with biological systems. In his own words, he was "used to dealing with substances that could be crystallized, whose physical constants and chemical properties were predictable. The heterogeneous,

messy and unknown properties of extracts of cells or of blood which this investigation required me to analyze seemed to offer nothing but a struggle against large odds" (Smith and Hardy, 270). Yet he entered into the research, providing both the analytical expertise and a good deal of the exercise and blood required for the human part of the investigation. From this research Long published, alone or jointly with Hill, H. Lupton, L. N. Katz, and others, some fifteen papers concerned with lactic acid, oxygen, and hydrogen ion metabolism in resting and exercising skeletal and heart muscle. With K. S. Hetzel he published a paper on the metabolism of a diabetic individual during and after exercise (1926), his first study in the field that was to become the major interest of his scientific life.

Long's early researches on lactate production, first in conjunction with Hill and his colleagues and later with Jonathan Meakins (1927) and others in Montreal, involved him in a study of the mechanisms controlling glycogen synthesis, the level of glucose in the blood, and the conversion of precursors such as lactate and, more important, protein into carbohydrate. By the early 1930's it had become apparent from the work of Carl and Gerty Cori and others that the lactate released from muscles during exercise is converted into glycogen in the liver and released into the blood as glucose to replenish the muscle glycogen. Epinephrine stimulates breakdown of liver glycogen and promotes this process, but does not produce the pattern of diabetes mellitus. It raises the blood glucose concentration and lowers the liver glycogen level, but it does not increase conversion of protein to carbohydrate (gluconeogenesis) or cause increased production of partially oxidized fatty acids (ketone bodies), nor does chronic administration of epinephrine lead to established diabetes mellitus. Nevertheless, the idea of diabetogenic hormone(s) causing overproduction of glucose as a cause of diabetes mellitus continued to be prominent, though the exact endocrine mechanism was not known.

In 1921, at about the time Long became interested in carbohydrate metabolism, Frederick Banting, Charles Best, and John James MacLeod first isolated an extract (insulin) from pancreatic islets that corrects the metabolic abnormality of diabetic animals and human beings. At about the same time Bernardo Houssay, in Argentina, reintroduced the importance of nonpancreatic endocrine secretion in the pathogenesis of diabetes mellitus by demonstrating that removal of the pituitary gland of diabetic toads and dogs ameliorates many of the metabolic abnormalities of the disease. In Long's words, "The diabetes was not entirely obliterated, but was transformed from a rapidly fatal condition into one of mild degree'' (''Recent Advances in Carbohydrate Metabolism,'' 169). In 1932 Houssay, Biasotti, and Rietti showed that administering an alkaline aqueous extract of the pituitary gland to diabetic hypophysectomized dogs restores the severity of diabetes, and that the same extract produces hyperglycemia and glycosuria in normal dogs.

At this time Long had moved from McGill to become director of the George S. Cox Medical Research Institute of the University of Pennsylvania, where a plaque on the wall instructed him that the purpose of the institute was ''to find a cure for diabetes,'' a task not accomplished even fifty years later! Long immediately recognized the importance of Houssay's findings in pursuing this mission, and set about trying to discover how the pituitary gland exerts its effects on carbohydrate metabolism. He appreciated that ''in the absence of these (pituitary) hormones, sugar production from protein is decreased and . . . a greater portion of glucose formed from protein is utilized'' (''Recent Advances in Carbohydrate Metabolism,'' 169). Of the target glands controlled by the anterior pituitary, the thyroid and the gonads were dismissed as unlikely candidates for a role in diabetogenesis. The adrenal cortex, however, was an attractive candidate. Hypophysectomy causes atrophy of the adrenal cortex (but not of the medulla, the source of epinephrine); adrenalectomy of normal animals results in low fasting blood glucose and liver glycogen levels; extracts of the adrenal cortex raise the blood glucose and liver glycogen concentrations. In human Addison's disease, where adrenal cortical function is defective, the blood glucose is low.

Using this rationale, Long, with Francis D. W. Lukens, attempted the difficult task of removing the adrenal glands from cats with diabetes mellitus (1936). After a successful technique had been developed, they published a series of important papers demonstrating that adrenalectomy reduced the high blood glucose and urinary glucose excretion, reduced the loss of nitrogen into the urine (a reflection of protein breakdown), prevented accumulation of ketone bodies and the acidosis associated with them, and extended the survival of untreated animals from four days to several weeks. Moreover, although pituitary extract restored diabetes in hypophysectomized diabetic animals, it did not have this effect in adrenalectomized animals with diabetes mellitus.

On the other hand, adrenal corticosteroids such as corticosterone both restored the severity of the diabetes in adrenalectomized pancreatectomized animals and caused hyperglycemia and glycosuria in normal animals. Long concluded that ''these experiments strongly suggest that the ketogenic (and diabetogenic) activity of anterior pituitary extracts may be mediated through the adrenal cortex'' (''Recent Advances in Carbohydrate Metabolism,'' 172). This judgment was somewhat premature, since it incorrectly overlooked the contribution of hypophyseal growth hormone to the control of carbohydrate metabolism. In his later work Long recognized this factor.

An important basic question remained to be answered: Where does the increased carbohydrate associated with adrenocortical activity come from? A series of elegant experiments performed after Long's move to Yale, with B. Katzin and Edith Fry, proved that the glucose and glycogen produced by adrenal cortical hormones could be accounted for quantitatively by increased breakdown of protein to glucose (1940).

These studies stimulated Long, Jay Tepperman, and F. L. Engel to explore intensively the nature of the hormones of the pituitary and their relationship to adrenal function (1943). With Abraham White he had succeeded in purifying prolactin (1942); and with White and George and Marion Sayers a purified preparation of adrenocorticotropic hormone (ACTH) was isolated (1943). The key to this isolation and purification was the development of a simple assay for corticotropic activity. This was provided first by the demonstration by the Sayerses, White, and Long that ACTH reduces the concentration of cholesterol in the adrenal of the rat (1943). Later the Sayerses provided simpler assay, measuring the ability of ACTH to reduce the content of adrenal ascorbic acid, that was widely used (1946). Studies of the effects of ACTH explained why pituitary extracts did not affect carbohydrate metabolism in adrenalectomized animals, since ACTH is ineffective unless the adrenal cortex is present. Alfred Wilhelmi, Jane Russell, and Jack Fishman, from the Yale laboratory, later prepared the first crystalline pituitary growth hormone (somatotropin). All of these hormones proved to have important direct or indirect effects on carbohydrate metabolism.

The most common form of diabetes mellitus is associated with obesity. In 1940 Long, with John R. Brobeck and Jay Tepperman, began a series of experiments to study the effects of inducing obesity in diabetic rats (published 1943). The method most deeply studied involved producing electrolytic (and later chemical) lesions in the hypothalamus. This induces uncontrolled hyperphagia, which leads to obesity and aggravation of pancreatic diabetes. With

Brobeck and others, an important contribution was made to the functional anatomy of the hypothalamus. The presence and encouragement of the eminent neurophysiologist John F. Fulton, chairman of the department of physiology, was of great importance in this work.

After America's entry into World War II in 1941, much attention was paid to research on the metabolic nature of traumatic shock. Frank L. Engel, Jay Tepperman, Helen Harrison, Jane Russell, Alfred Wilhelmi, and Long studied this problem for several years, demonstrating that reduced blood flow and oxygen supply to the liver is the most important single contributor to the metabolic derangements (1944).

Two major themes occupied Long's research interest for the remainder of his life. With Ora K. Smith, W. W. Winternitz, and others, he pursued in detail the mechanisms controlling the metabolism of the tissue amino acids and gluconeogenesis, especially in muscle, liver, and kidneys. In addition, with A. Brodish, W. V. McDermott, H. Gershberg, and Fry he studied the regulation of ACTH secretion (1950, 1956, 1962), its effects on the adrenal cortex, and, with F. Ulrich and Denis M. Abelson, the metabolism of the corticosteroids. He and his team were leaders in working out the way in which the anterior pituitary and the adrenal cortex modulate the metabolic interrelationships of carbohydrate, protein, and fat. He also enunciated perhaps the most basic principle of endocrinology: hormones modulate existing pathways but do not engender new reactions.

In 1936, when Long left the Cox Institute to become chairman of the department of physiological chemistry at Yale, he replaced the eminent biochemical nutritionist Lafayette Mendel. At that time the department was composed almost entirely of scientists studying the chemistry of the diet and the requirements for adequate nutrition. This group continued to make contributions under the leadership of George R. Cowgill, in a separate laboratory of nutrition that was a subdivision of the department. Hubert B. Vickery, who was director of the Connecticut Agriculture Station and an adjunct professor in the department, was especially important in his studies of the chemistry of amino acids. However, the main body of the department took a new direction reflecting Long's interests in endocrinology, intermediary metabolism, and the physiological factors controlling the mixture of metabolic substrates. He had brought with him from Philadelphia the most consistently helpful and loyal of his colleagues, Edith Fry and Gerald Evans. In addition he recruited

outstanding physiologists such as Jane Russell, Clara M. Szego, and Daniel L. Kline; Ralph I. Dorfman, a steroid chemist; Philip P. Cohen, an enzymologist; and protein chemists such as Abraham White and Alfred E. Wilhelmi. A collaboration with the Sheffield Scientific School of Yale added biochemists such as Joseph S. Fruton, Sofia Simmonds, Henry D. Hoberman, and Jacob B. Fishman.

Long never forgot his roots as a physician, and welcomed many postdoctoral M.D. trainees, including Philip K. Bondy (later chairman of the department of medicine at Yale and professor of medicine at Royal Marsden Hospital, London), William V. McDermott, Jr. (who became chairman of the department of surgery at Harvard), Sheila P. V. Sherlock (later professor of medicine at the Royal Free Hospital, London, and president of the Royal College of physicians of London), James A. F. Stevenson (who became chairman of the department of physiology and dean of the Faculty of Graduate Studies, University of Western Ontario), and Jay Tepperman (later professor of experimental medicine, State University of New York Upstate Medical Center).

As a result of these changes, the department evolved into three separate but integrated groups: a team concerned mainly with endocrinology and the physiology of metabolic processes, led by Long; a separate nutrition laboratory led by Cowgill; and a team of basic biochemists and enzymologists led by Fruton. This diversity provided the wide-ranging interests essential for the ultimate evolution into a general department of biochemistry. When Long left to head the department of physiology, he took with him the group interested in physiological interactions. The nutritional group had, by this time, retired or moved elsewhere; and the residue, under Fruton, evolved into a leading department of biochemistry.

Although he became increasingly involved in political and committee work on the national and international scene, Long was not an "absentee chairman" of his department of physiological chemistry. He was an outstanding lecturer and carried other formal teaching responsibilities, but he was most at home wandering around the research and teaching laboratories, lounging against the desk with his crooked smile, asking questions, making suggestions, and providing a framework on which to hang research results. He did not hector his young colleagues, but he had little patience with bluffing or hazy comprehension. When he found soft thinking, he would probe relentlessly until the student reached a solid base of understanding. When he was pleased, he was generous in his praise. But his visits to the laboratory were not always concerned with science. He had a good sense of humor and an intense interest in the questions of the day, including sports. He was especially taken by new equipment, interesting gadgets, and unconventional ways of thought.

As an educator Long embraced the Yale system enthusiastically. This philosophy, first introduced in the 1920's by Dean Milton W. Winternitz, assumes that medical students are adults and as capable as other graduate students of taking responsibility for their education. Thus, evidence of scholarship is required in the form of a thesis; examinations are used to test comprehension rather than to estimate class standings; and students are expected to regulate their attendance at classes, laboratories, and conferences so as to obtain the maximum benefit from the opportunities provided them. Long supported the emphasis on the unity of science and felt that the most important consideration was to teach ways of thinking about science rather than details of facts and techniques. This is especially important since, as he said, "independence of thought and a capacity to form judgments will be required of the physician all his life, while techniques and the interpretation of information are always changing."

Long also felt that an excessive amount of time was spent in formal education for the M.D. degree. He crusaded for integrating college and medical school into a single course in the European style, to be completed within five years after graduating from high school. His sponsorship of this reform was not successful at Yale, though other universities, such as Brown and Johns Hopkins, later worked out a schedule similar to that proposed by Long.

Hugh Long was the last part-time dean at Yale. The burden of handling the administrative chores of the deanship increasingly competed with the time necessary for building and running an effective medical school department. As a result, Long and the administration at Yale became convinced that the deanship should be held by a professional educational administrator on a full-time basis. Thus Long's experience helped to prepare the way for appointment of his successor, Vernon W. Lippard, the first full-time dean at Yale. In spite of the pressures, however, Long achieved a good deal as dean. Perhaps the most important developments during his tenure were the amalgamation of New Haven Hospital with the Grace Hospital to form Grace-New Haven Hospital (now Yale-New Haven Hospital). He was also involved in establishing the valuable affiliation with the West Haven Veterans Administration Medical Center.

Not the least of the special qualities of Long's interaction with his department and with the medical school was the warm interest he and his wife, Hilda, had in the students and young faculty. They provided a social atmosphere that encouraged friendship, and provided help for the newcomer and support for the troubled. Long was ready to give advice and counsel that was direct, honest, and realistic.

After his retirement, Long continued to work with Ora Smith at the John B. Pierce Foundation; his last paper, on renal gluconeogenesis, was published with her (1971). He died suddenly, apparently of a heart attack, while on holiday in Maine.

BIBLIOGRAPHY

I. Original Works. "The Metabolism of the Diabetic Individual During and After Muscular Exercise," in *Proceedings of the Royal Society of London*, **B99** (1926), 279–306, with K. S. Hetzel; "Oxygen Consumption, Oxygen Debt and Lactic Acid in Circulatory Failure," in *Journal of Clinical Investigation*, **4** (1927), 273–293, with Jonathan Meakins; "Recent Advances in Carbohydrate Metabolism with Particular Reference to Diabetes Mellitus," in *Annals of Internal Medicine*, **9** (1935), 166–174; "The Effects of Adrenalectomy and Hypophysectomy upon Experimental Diabetes in the Cat," in *Journal of Experimental Medicine*, **63** (1936), 465–490, with Francis D. W. Lukens; "The Adrenal Cortex and Carbohydrate Metabolism," in *Endocrinology*, **26** (1940), 309–344, with B. Katzin and E. G. Fry; "Prolactin," in *Journal of Biological Chemistry*, **143** (1942), 447–464, with A. White and R. W. Bonsnes; "The Effect of Experimental Obesity upon Carbohydrate Metabolism," in *Yale Journal of Biology and Medicine*, **15** (1943), 893–904, with J. R. Brobeck and J. Tepperman; "Preparation of Pituitary Adrenotropic Hormone," in *Proceedings of the Society of Experimental Biology and Medicine*, **52** (1943), 199–200, with G. Sayers, M. A. Sayers, and A. White; "A Review of Adrenal Cortical Hypertrophy," in *Endocrinology*, **32** (1943), 373–402, with J. Tepperman and F. L. Engel; "Biochemical Studies on Shock. III. The Role of the Liver and the Hepatic Circulation in the Metabolic Changes During Hemorrhagic Shock in the Rat and the Cat," in *Journal of Experimental Medicine*, **79** (1944), 9–22, with F. L. Engel and H. C. Harrison; "The Effect of Pituitary Adrenotrophic Hormone on the Cholesterol and Ascorbic Acid Content of the Adrenal of the Rat and the Guinea Pig," in *Endocrinology*, **39** (1946), 1–9, with G. Sayers, M. A. Sayers, and T.-Y. Liang; "Mechanism of Control of Adrenocorticotrophic Hormone," in *Yale Journal of Biology and Medicine*, **23** (1950), 52–66, with W. V. McDermott, E. G. Fry, and J. R. Brobeck; "Changes in Blood ACTH Under Various Experimental Conditions by Means of a Cross-Circulation Technique," in *Endocrinology*, **59** (1956), 666–676, with A. Brodish; and "ACTH-Releasing Hypothalamic

Neurohumor in Peripheral Blood," *ibid.*, **71** (1962), 298–306, with A. Brodish.

II. SECONDARY LITERATURE. P. K. Bondy, obituary, in *Endocrinology*, **88** (1971), 537–539; Joseph Fruton, "Cyril Norman Hugh Long (1901–1970)," in *American Philosophical Society Year Book 1970* (1971), 143–145; and O. L. K. Smith and J. D. Hardy, "Cyril Norman Hugh Long," in *Biographical Memoirs. National Academy of Sciences*, **46** (1975), 265–309.

PHILIP K. BONDY

LÖWENHEIM, LEOPOLD (*b.* Krefeld, Germany, 26 June 1878; *d.* East Berlin, German Democratic Republic, 5 May 1957), *mathematical logic*.

The son of Elise Röhn, a writer, and Detmold Louis (Ludwig) Löwenheim, a mathematics teacher at the Krefeld Polytechnic until 1881 and a private scholar thereafter, Lowenheim received his secondary education in Berlin at the Königliche Luisen-Gymnasium, from which he graduated in 1896. That same year he showed inclinations to philosophical and social thought by joining the Deutsche Gesellschaft für Ethische Kultur (to which his father had belonged). He studied mathematics and natural science from 1896 to 1900 at Friedrich Wilhelm University in Berlin and at the Technische Hochschule in Charlottenburg (then an autonomous neighboring city of Berlin). Having qualified in 1901 as a teacher of mathematics and physics in the upper grades, and of chemistry and mineralogy in the middle grades, Löwenheim was appointed *Oberlehrer* at the Jahn-Realgymnasium in Berlin in 1904, after a year of postgraduate training and a year as a probationary teacher. In 1915 he was given the title *professor*, and in 1919 he became *Studienrat*.

Although in subsequent years much of his time was taken up by teaching obligations, Löwenheim not only managed to revise and edit his father's unfinished work on Democritus (it was published in 1914) but also began his most fruitful period of study and research in mathematical logic, a field with which he had become acquainted through review articles and Ernst Schröder's *Vorlesungen über die Algebra der Logik* (1890–1905). In 1906 Löwenheim joined the Berlin Mathematical Society, to which he read his first paper in 1907, and became a member of the reviewers' staff of the *Jahrbuch über die Fortschritte der Mathematik*. In spite of World War I, during which Löwenheim served in France, Hungary, and Serbia from August 1915 to December 1916 (after which he returned to teaching in Berlin), it was between 1908 and 1919 that he published his most important papers on the algebra of logic,

continuing and adding to the work of C. S. Peirce, Schröder, and Alfred North Whitehead.

In papers of 1908 and 1910, Löwenheim analyzed and improved upon the customary methods for solving equations in the calculus of classes or domains (that is, set theory in its Peirce-Schröderian setting) and proved what is now known as Löwenheim's general development theorem for functions of functions. The techniques employed admit of extension to the Peirce-Schröder calculus of relatives, a form of the logic of relations shown by Löwenheim, in a paper of 1913, to be expandable into a calculus of $m \times n$ "matrices of domains" similar to the now customary theory of matrices, especially regarding the representation of transformations by matrices. Löwenheim greatly simplified some of Whitehead's results on substitutions and proved that every theorem about transformations of any arbitrary object is valid if its validity can be shown for transformations of domains.

In his 1915 paper "Über Möglichkeiten im Relativkalkül," Löwenheim reported three results considered classic today. He proved that in classic first-order quantificational logic (with equality, but this is an unnecessary restriction), every formula without free individual variables that is satisfiable at all is already satisfiable in a denumerable (a finite or denumerably infinite) domain. The importance of this theorem of Löwenheim lies in its demonstration that one cannot "implicitly define" the domain of objects satisfying an axiom system formulated in first-order logic, or even the structure of such domains. For example, an axiom system for the real numbers (a nondenumerable domain, as Georg Cantor had shown in 1874) also has a denumerable model, and therefore at least two nonisomorphic models: the intended "standard" one consisting of the reals and the denumerable, "nonstandard" model shown to exist by Löwenheim's theorem.

This situation has been called the Löwenheim-Skolem paradox, but Thoralf Skolem, who extended Löwenheim's theorem in 1920 and 1923, and developed general methods for constructing nonstandard models, pointed out that the result was not paradoxical; rather, it indicated a limit to the characterizability of structures by formal systems and revealed the relativity of (for example, set-theoretical) concepts defined within them. Besides this result, the 1915 paper contained a decision procedure for monadic quantificational logic (that is, with only one-place predicates) and a reduction of the decision problem for full quantificational logic (that is, of finding an algorithmic procedure that effectively decides between satisfiability or nonsatisfiability of an arbitrary formula of the theory) to the decision problem for the subtheory with one- and two-place predicates.

Löwenheim's later papers in mathematical logic have not so far proved to be of equal importance, and in fact his interests broadened to a more philosophical and existential outlook in which questions of mathematical education maintained a prominent place.

In 1931 Löwenheim married Johanna Rassmussen Teichert. His professional life came to an abrupt (but temporary) end in 1934, when he had to accept forced retirement as a 25 percent non-Aryan. He subsequently supported himself by teaching eurythmy and geometry at the Anthroposophic School of Eurythmy in Berlin. A further blow was the loss of all his belongings, including 1,100 geometrical drawings and some geometrical models, and unpublished manuscripts on logic, geometry, music, and the history of art, in the bombing of Berlin on 23 August 1943. Löwenheim managed to survive, however, and again taught mathematics at the Pestalozzi-Schule and the Franz-Mehring-Schule, both in Berlin-Lichtenberg, from 1946 to 1949. Professional logicians (among whom Paul Bernays, Heinrich Scholz, and Alfred Tarski had visited Löwenheim in the 1930's) were convinced that he had not survived the war.

It seems that Löwenheim did not know of the publication of his paper "On Making Indirect Proofs Direct" (translated from the German by Willard Van Orman Quine) in 1946. He left to his stepson, Johannes Teichert, some manuscripts to be used for instruction in schools of eurythmy and for the training of teachers in Waldorf schools, some autobiographical notes, and the sheet proofs of an unpublished sequel to his paper of 1915, written for publication in the 1939 volume of *Fundamenta mathematicae*.

BIBLIOGRAPHY

I. ORIGINAL WORKS. "Über das Auflösungsproblem im logischen Klassenkalkül," in *Sitzungsberichte der Berliner mathematischen Gesellschaft*, **7** (1908), 89–94; "Über die Auflösung von Gleichungen im logischen Gebietekalkül," in *Mathematische Annalen*, **68** (1910), 169–207; "Über Transformationen im Gebietekalkül," *ibid.*, **73** (1913), 245–272; "Über eine Erweiterung des Gebietekalküls, welche auch die gewöhnliche Algebra umfasst," in *Archiv für systematische Philosophie und Soziologie*, **21** (1915), 137–148; "Über Möglichkeiten im Relativkalkül," in *Mathematische Annalen*, **76** (1916), 447–470, translated by Stefan Bauer-Mengelberg as "On Possibilities in the Calculus of Relatives," in Jean van Heijenoort, ed., *From Frege to Gödel: A Source Book in Mathematical Logic, 1879–1931* (Cambridge, Mass., 1967), 228–251; "Einkleidung der Mathematik in Schröderschen Relativkalkül," in *Journal of Symbolic Logic*, **5** (1940), 1–15; and "On Making Indirect Proofs Direct," Willard V. Quine, trans., in *Scripta mathematica*, **12**, no. 2 (1946), 125–147.

II. SECONDARY LITERATURE. Gottlob Frege, *Wissenschaftlicher Briefwechsel*, Felix Meiner, Gottfried Gabriel, et al., eds. (Hamburg, 1976), 157–161; Thoralf Skolem, "Sur la portée du théorème de Löwenheim-Skolem," in Ferdinand Gonseth, ed., *Les entretiens de Zurich sur les fondaments et la méthode des sciences mathématiques, 6–9 décembre 1938* (Zurich, 1941), 25–52; and Christian Thiel, "Leben und Werk Leopold Löwenheims (1878–1957): Teil I, Biographisches und Bibliographisches," in *Jahresbericht der Deutschen Mathematiker-Vereinigung*, **77** (1975), 1–9, with portrait; "Leopold Löwenheim: Life, Work, and Early Influence," in R. O. Gandy and J. M. E. Hyland, eds., *Logic Colloquium 76* (Amsterdam, 1977), 235–252, with bibliography; "Gedanken zum hundertsten Geburtstag Leopold Löwenheims," in *Teorema*, **8** (1978), 263–267, with portrait; and "Löwenheim, Leopold," in Jürgen Mittelstrass, ed., *Enzyklopädie Philosophie und Wissenschaftstheorie*, II (Mannheim, 1984), 715f.

CHRISTIAN THIEL

LUKIRSKII, PETR IVANOVICH (*b*. Orenburg, Russia, 13 December 1894; *d*. Leningrad, U.S.S.R., 16 November 1954), *physics*.

Lukirskii's father, Ivan Egorovich Lukirskii, was a land surveyor; his mother, Evdokia Stepanovna, was a housewife. In 1903 the family moved to Novgorod, where Lukirskii graduated from the gymnasium in 1912 (with a gold medal) and in the same year entered the Faculty of Mathematics and Physics of Petersburg University. In 1915 he graduated from the university but remained there to prepare for the professorship. Approximately at the same time, along with his university activities, Lukirskii joined the seminar on modern physics headed by A. F. Ioffe, which met at the Polytechnic Institute. (From this seminar came such outstanding physicists as I. G. Dorfman, P. L. Kapitsa, N. N. Semenov, and Y. I. Frenkel.) In 1918 Lukirskii became one of the first fellows of the Physical-Technical Institute (PTI), founded by Ioffe, where he concentrated on problems of electron physics. He is rightfully considered to have initiated this field in the U.S.S.R. In one of his first experimental works (with Semenov, 1923), he investigated the scattering of electrons from the surface of liquid mercury. At that time there were no satisfactory metallic monocrystals; mercury, with its ideally smooth surface (from which it was easy to remove the layers of absorbed substances), was a happy choice for the determination of the work function of secondary electrons and their angular and energy distributions.

Another of Lukirskii's fields was X-ray physics (he was the head of that department at PTI). Being interested in soft X-rays (10–150 Å), which are difficult to study with optical and crystal lattices, he suggested using maximum values of the energy of photoelectrons knocked from the surface of a sphere to determine, via Einstein's relation, the wavelength of the incident X-rays. (The sphere served as one electrode of a spherical condenser). The spherical condenser method resulted in substantially more accurate measurements and became standard for Lukirskii's investigations. With its aid he demonstrated the effect of polarization of X rays in Compton scattering and investigated the normal photoeffect from the surface of pure metals; he also determined the Planck constant with great accuracy.

Lukirskii next turned to further investigations of the photoeffect. Using the method of mote in Millikan's condenser (employed by Millikan in measuring the electron charge), he determined the value of the photoeffect threshold for a number of crystals. He also studied the selective photoeffect and the influence of absorption of impurities on the metal's surface on the value of the electron work function. These investigations had considerable applied importance. Lukirskii was scientific head and consultant of research laboratories of the "Svetlana" plant, the largest producer of vacuum tubes in the Soviet Union in the early 1930's.

In the mid 1930's Lukirskii and his collaborators developed the first antimony-cesium photoelement. Its cathode demonstrated the greatest sensitivity then recorded in the violet and ultraviolet spectral regions, and the spectral characteristics were stable over time and not very sensitive to variations in the technology of cathode production. Lukirskii's antimony-cesium cathode has played a significant role in the Soviet Union not only in engineering, electronics, automation, and astrophysics, but also in sound cinematography. Lukurskii initiated research work on autoemission electronics in the Soviet Union (1944–1950); the points of the emitters he investigated were also covered by antimony-cesium layers.

In 1944 Lukirskii carried out the classic experiment related to the problem of the equilibrium form of crystals. Heating a sphere of rocksalt, he showed that the equilibrium figure is a polyhedron with curved ribs. (A rough demonstration of this phenomenon was that the sphere, which had been freely rolling along the smooth surface, started "jumping" on it after being heated.) These works stimulated theoretical investigations of equilibrium forms of crystals (L. D. Landau, Frenkel) and the mechanism of natural roughness of crystals.

Lukirskii also studied problems of nuclear physics. From 1943 until the end of his life he headed the physics department at the Radium Institute of the Academy of Sciences of the U.S.S.R. Even earlier, in 1936, he had already begun experiments on elastic scattering of neutrons. A number of his researches involved nuclear reactions in thick-layered emulsions. For example, he investigated the reaction $Be^9 + \pi \rightarrow Li^7 + 2n$, in which both neutrons go off in the same direction (bineutron). In collaboration with Zhdanov he investigated nuclear reactions caused by a heavy meson (the negative K-meson).

Lukirskii devoted great attention to teaching, and was a good lecturer. From 1919 to 1938 he taught at Leningrad University; for a number of years, he occupied a chair at the Leningrad Institute of Cinematographic Engineers; and from 1945 until his death, he served as professor and head of the department of physical electronics at the Leningrad Polytechnic Institute. Lukirskii was elected a corresponding member of the Academy of Sciences of the U.S.S.R. in 1933 and a full member in 1946. He was an excellent sportsman, especially absorbed by yachting and tennis. He was married to Elizaveta Nikolaevna, with whom he had one daughter and two sons.

BIBLIOGRAPHY

I. ORIGINAL WORKS. Monographs include *Osnovi elektronnoi teorii* (Fundamentals of electron theory; 2nd ed., Moscow and Leningrad, 1929); *O fotoeffekte* (On the photoeffect; Leningrad and Moscow, 1933); *Neitron* (Neutron; Leningrad and Moscow, 1935); *Stroenie veshchestva* (The structure of matter; Leningrad, 1938), pts. 1–3. Papers include "Rasseyanie elektronov zhidkoi rtutiyu" (Electron scattering on liquid mercury surface), in *Zhurnal Russkogo fiziko-khimicheskogo obshchestva, chast fizicheskaia*, **55**, nos. 1–3 (1923), 107–119; "Photoeffect an Kristallen," in *Zeitschrift für Physik*, **37**, nos. 4–5 (1926), 308–318; "Issledovanie skorostei fotoelektronov" (The study of photoelectron velocities), in *Zhurnal Russkogo fiziko-khimicheskogo obshchestva, chast fizicheskaia*, **58**, no. 2 (1926), 319–328, written with S. S. Prilezhaev; "Über den normalen Photoeffekt," in *Zeitschrift für Physik*, **49**, nos. 3–4 (1928), 236–258; "The Compton Effect and Polarisation," in *Nature*, **122** (1928), 275–276; "Versuche über die Eigenschaften der Atomschichten" in *Zeitschrift für Physik*, **71**, nos. 5–6 (1931), 306–324; "Abhängigkeit der lichtelektrischen Emission des Kaliums von der Anordnung von atomaren Wasserstoff- und Kaliumschichten auf ihrer Oberfläche,'' *ibid.*, **75**, nos. 3–4 (1932), 249–252; ''Slow Neutrons,'' in *Nature,* **136** (1935), 681–682, written with T. Tsareva; ''On the Complex Photocathode Mechanism,'' in *Techn. Phys. URSS,* **3**, no. 8 (1936), 685–699; ''Experiments with Rock-Salt Crystals,'' in *Comptes-rendus del'Académie des sciences de l'URSS,* **46**, no. 7 (1945), 274–276; ''The Negative Meson and Its Mass,'' *ibid.*, **54**, no. 3 (1946), 219–222; ''Opiti po izucheniiu avtoelektronnoi emissii pri zazlichnikh temperaturakh'' (Experiments on autoelectronic [field] emission at various temperatures), in *Sbornik posvyashchennii 70-letiiu akademika A. F. Ioffe* (Moscow, 1950), 109–112, written with T. V. Tsareva; ''Iadernoe rasshcheplenie tyazhelim mesonom'' (Nuclear splitting by heavy mesons), in *Doklady Akademii nauk SSSR,* **94**, no. 5 (1954), 843–844, written with Iu. G. Degitariev and A. P. Zhdanov.

II. SECONDARY LITERATURE. Obituaries are in *Uspekhi fizicheskikh nauk,* **55**, no. 3 (1955), 289–295; *Vestnik LGU, ser. mat. i fiz.,* no. 2 (1955), 203–204; and *Zhurnal tekhnicheskoi fiziki,* **25**, no. 3 (1955), 367–376. See also *Piotr Ivanovich Lukirskii (1894–1954)* (Moscow, 1959).

V. J. FRENKEL

LYSENKO, TROFIM DENISOVICH (*b*. Karlovka, now in Poltava Province, Russia [now Ukrainian S.S.R.], 29 September 1898; *d*. Moscow, U.S.S.R., 20 November 1976, *plant physiology, agrobiology.*

A Soviet agronomist and head of the ''Michurinist'' trend in Soviet biology, Lysenko was one of the most controversial figures in twentieth-century science. Beginning in 1935, his opposition to genetics on theoretical, practical, and ideological grounds gained the support of Soviet agricultural and political authorities, culminating in 1948 in the official condemnation of genetics and approval of Lysenko's biology by Stalin and the Central Committee of the Communist Party. Lysenko's dominance of Soviet biology ended only in 1965.

The son of a peasant, Lysenko attended horticultural schools in Poltava (1913) and Uman (1917–1920). In 1921 he took courses offered by the Sugar Trust and worked in its experimental stations at Verkhniachka, Khristinov region, Kiev oblast (1921) and Belaia Tserkov (1922–1925). Concurrently, he studied agronomy at the Kiev Agricultural Institute (1921–1925) and published two brief articles (1923) on tomato breeding and sugar beet grafting.

Lysenko first rose to national prominence while posted in Azerbaidzhan (1925–1929). During its dry summers, all the water was needed for the cotton monoculture; other crops had to be grown during the mild, moist winters. As head of legume selection at an experimental station in Gandzha (now Kirovabad), Lysenko introduced pea varieties from Kiev that were early ripeners, but he noticed that some became late ripeners in Gandzha and concluded that this plant characteristic depends less on the breed than on the conditions under which it is grown. In his first major article, ''Vliianie termicheskogo faktora na prodolzhitel'nost' faz razvitiia rastenii'' (1928), Lysenko argued that cold temperature was related to late ripening. This work suggested that it was possible to produce desirable characteristics by manipulating growing conditions.

Lysenko made such an attempt on his father's Ukrainian farm in 1928 and 1929. In order to make winter wheat sowable in the spring, he suggested that germinating seeds be buried in snow before planting, and this reportedly led to greatly increased yields. Lysenko termed this procedure ''vernalization'' *(iarovizatsiia),* and its apparent success brought his work to the attention of agricultural officials. In 1929 he was given a laboratory in the physiology division of the All-Union Institute of Genetics and Selection in Odessa. To popularize his work, in 1931 the Ministry of Agriculture created the journal *Bulleten' iarovizatsii* (renamed *Iarovizatsiia* in 1935, *Agrobiologiia* in 1946).

Although Nikolai I. Vavilov, Boris A. Keller, and a few other plant scientists apparently found Lysenko's results interesting and helped him to gain scientific legitimacy, his meteoric rise to prominence during the First Five-Year Plan (1929–1933) derived principally from the concerted support of agricultural and political authorities. At a time when bourgeois technical specialists came under increasing attack, Lysenko's peasant background gave him an important advantage. His techniques may have seemed an immediate way of overcoming the food shortage occasioned by the collectivization of agriculture; their implementation fit the social organization of the kolkhoz and the sovkhoz.

During the heyday of Soviet ''vernalization'' (1929–1935), Lysenko devised and applied similar techniques to a wide range of vegetables, fruits, and grains, and the term itself came to include almost anything done to a crop before planting in order to alter its development to suit local growing conditions—for example, the sprouting of potato tubers before planting. However, there is no doubt that his techniques were not properly tested; for example, Lysenko's ''study'' of the conversion of ''Kooperatorka'' winter wheat into spring wheat involved only two plants, one of which died in the process. Nonetheless, Lysenko and his supporters made extravagant claims for the efficacy of his techniques, and in the early 1930's ''vernalization'' was reportedly applied to many millions of hectares of crops. For this work, in 1934 Lysenko became the scientific director of the Odessa institute and a full member of the Ukrainian Academy of Sciences.

Throughout the remainder of his career, Lysenko maintained his political support by replicating the essence of his vernalization experience. He led analogous campaigns for the summer planting of potatoes (1935); grafting or "vegetative hybridization" (late 1930's); the "grassland system" of planting (1939–1952); the "cluster method" of forestation (1948–1952); the cultivation of maize (1956); and methods for increasing the butterfat content of milk (1958–1962). All were inexpensive nostrums designed by Lysenko and his followers to fulfill expressed State agricultural policy needs; all were touted as promising immediate and spectacular improvements in agricultural production; all were introduced into widescale practice by government order without proper testing; most were quietly phased out when they proved unsuccessful. These techniques and campaigns have been well described by Medvedev (1969), Joravsky (1970), and Roll-Hansen (1985).

The year 1935 marked a turning point in Lysenko's career. Linking up with the Leningrad lawyer and philosopher I. I. Prezent, he began to elaborate his agronomic practices into a theoretical framework with heavy ideological content. In two 1935 pamphlets (*Teoreticheskie osnovy iarovizatsii* and *Selektsiia i teoriia stadiinogo razvitiia rastenii*), Lysenko and Prezent propounded the theory that every plant goes through distinct developmental stages or phases, each characterized by certain "requirements" for development; by altering conditions at the end of a developmental stage, they asserted, the heredity of the plant could be destabilized or "cracked," making it plastic and malleable. This soon led to a definition of heredity as "the property of a living body to require definite conditions for its life and development and to respond in a definite way to various conditions."

In the early 1930's, propaganda about the elder plant breeder Ivan V. Michurin elevated him to heroic proportions in the public mind. Following Michurin's death in 1935, Lysenko declared himself the heir to Michurin's tradition and named his own approach "Michurinist biology," contrasting it with genetics, a "capitalist," "bourgeois" science based on the "metaphysical" views of the Austrian monk Gregor Mendel and the "idealist" germ plasm theory of August Weismann. This position had explicit political implications. Lysenko and his followers were portrayed as agricultural Stakhanovites. He was made a member of the government's Central Executive Committee from 1935 to 1937 and was as-

sistant to the president of the council of the Supreme Soviet from 1937 to 1950. During the late 1930's Lysenko claimed that geneticists had sabotaged Soviet agriculture, and he resurrected their earlier, relatively mild eugenic views to argue that his opponents were tied to fascism and Nazi ideology. At the time of the great purges, such accusations invited repression.

In 1935 Lysenko was elected a full member of the Lenin All-Union Academy of Agricultural Sciences (VASKhNIL) and the next year was put in charge of its Odessa institute. Also in 1935, Vavilov was removed as president of VASKhNIL; its two subsequent presidents (A. I. Muralov and G. K. Meister) were arrested in the purges, and in 1938 Lysenko assumed the presidency himself and held it until 1956. With the help of the NKVD, he used his new position to harass and undermine Vavilov's supporters. In the 1939 elections to the U.S.S.R. Academy of Sciences, Lysenko was elected a full academician and appointed a member of its governing presidium. In August 1940 Vavilov was arrested, and in subsequent months G. D. Karpechenko, G. A. Levitskii, and other Vavilovites disappeared; all died in prisons or camps in the early 1940's. Recent evidence provided by Popovsky and Soyfer indicates that Lysenko and his followers were directly or indirectly involved in these arrests. In late 1940, immediately following Vavilov's arrest, Lysenko left Odessa to replace him as director of the academy's Institute of Genetics in Moscow, a post he held until 1965.

Despite these events, Lysenko was not yet in control of Soviet biology. After World War II, genetics was resurgent, attempts were made by the U.S.S.R. Academy of Sciences to create a new institute of genetics, and there was widespread public criticism of many of Lysenko's views. But in mid 1948, at Stalin's order, a large number of Lysenko's supporters became members of VASKhNIL by fiat, and in a surprise August session of the academy Lysenko announced, "The Central Committee has read my report and approved it." Later Lysenko confirmed that Stalin had personally gone over his text. It portrayed Michurinist biology as a socialist, materialist, proletarian science, a kind of "creative Darwinism" deriving from Darwin, Kliment Timiriazev, and Michurin that united theory and practice, and had mastered the control of heredity. By contrast, genetics was depicted as a capitalist, idealist, bourgeois enterprise linked to fascism, deriving from Malthus, Mendel, and Weismann, and incapable of aiding agricultural production. The report asserted that heredity was a malleable property of the whole organism and that one species could be transformed into another in one generation. It categorically denied the reality of intraspecific competition and the existence of genes, characterizing the search for any hereditary material as a hopeless philosophical mistake.

In the edicts that followed the August 1948 VASKhNIL session, most Soviet geneticists were fired from their jobs, laboratories and institutions were disbanded or reorganized, degree certification and curricula in the biological sciences fell under Lysenkoist control, and "Michurinist biology" became officially sanctioned government policy. By 1952 Lysenko had embraced a number of extreme theories purporting to have the same philosophical basis as his own, including Ol'ga Borisovna Lepeshinskaia's doctrine that living cells form spontaneously from nonliving matter (thus denying the classic cell theory according to which all cells are produced by other cells) and G. M. Bosh'ian's analogous doctrine of viruses. The 1953 elections to the U.S.S.R. Academy of Sciences packed its biological sciences division with supporters of Michurinism. In the following years Lysenko's prominent allies included botanists N. V. Tsitsin and V. N. Stoletov, "geneticists" I. E. Glushchenko and N. I. Nuzhdin, biochemists A. I. Oparin and N. M. Sisakian, paleontologist L. Sh. Davitashvili, and philosopher G. V. Platonov.

In 1948 and 1949 the massive Soviet reforestation program employed Lysenko's cluster method of planting; the extensive losses of seedlings that resulted made Lysenko vulnerable, and the first critical articles began to appear in late 1952 in *Botanicheskii zhurnal* with the support of its editor, botanist and forest ecologist Vladimir N. Sukachev. In 1953 the publication of the Watson-Crick model for the structure of DNA aroused interest in genetics among leading figures in the U.S.S.R. Academy of Sciences, including such chemists as Academy president Aleksandr N. Nesmeianov, Nobelist (1956) Nikolai N. Semenov, and Ivan L. Knuniants; physicists Petr Kapitsa, Igor Tamm, Igor Kurchatov, and Andrei D. Sakharov; and mathematicians A. N. Kolmogorov, S. L. Sobolev, A. A. Liapunov, and M. A. Lavrentev. These scientists had gained great prestige and influence as a result of their work in Soviet nuclear, space, and weapons research, and over the next decade they proved to be effective opponents of Lysenkoism.

With Stalin's death in 1953 and the subsequent de-Stalinization, Lysenko was forced to resign as president of VASKhNIL in 1956, and it appeared for a time that his hegemony over Soviet biology was ending. With the strong support of biochemist Vladimir A. Engel'hardt and other academy leaders, molecular genetics began to develop under a variety of institutional and disciplinary rubrics despite Lysenko's opposition.

By late 1958, however, Lysenko had succeeded in solidifying his relationship with Nikita Khrushchev by appealing to their common Ukrainian rural background, embracing Khrushchev's agricultural policy, and convincing him that its lack of success was due to the opposition of powerful bureaucrats in the academies and ministries. In subsequent years, Khrushchev's agricultural program became linked with various Lysenkoist nostrums, and in 1961 and 1962 Lysenko briefly resumed the presidency of VASKhNIL.

Scientific opposition to Lysenko continued to mount, however, and by 1963 Khrushchev was in open conflict with the U.S.S.R. Academy of Sciences over Lysenkoism. Khrushchev's ouster in October 1964 produced a convergence of interests between an academy leadership determined to see genetics reborn and a new political leadership anxious to legitimate Khrushchev's removal. Many press articles critical of Lysenko began to appear even before Khrushchev's ouster was officially announced. In early 1965, without political instructions, the Ministry of Agriculture and the two academies established a joint commission to investigate Lysenko's Lenin Hills experimental farm. Its report filled the entire November 1965 issue of the journal *Vestnik Akademii nauk SSSR* and demonstrated that Lysenko's experimental work was improperly carried out and tested, and that all of his agricultural techniques were either ineffective or harmful.

In 1965 Lysenko was removed as director of the Institute of Genetics. It was officially disbanded and reconstituted as the Institute of General Genetics under the direction of geneticist N. P. Dubinin. However, a number of Lysenkoists were kept on at the institute, and Lysenko's former allies continued to occupy important posts within academy and ministry structures. After a period of relatively candid and open revelation of past errors, public discussion of the history of Lysenkoism ceased in the Soviet Union in the early 1970's. Lysenko continued as a full academician and kept control of his Lenin Hills farm, where he worked from 1966 until his death. During his long career he won eight Orders of Lenin, three State Prizes, and numerous medals and awards.

Lysenko's influence did not end with his death, however. Implanted in Soviet institutions and ideology under Stalinism, Michurinist biology survived within the powerful bureaucracies of the Brezhnev period. There was a mild resurgence of Lysenkoism in the mid-1970s, and its sometime supporters have continued to occupy important posts in Soviet agriculture. Since 1987, with the opening of free expression under Gorbachev, the Soviet past has been publicly reexamined and old controversies have resurfaced. Understandably, one of the central preoccupations of this *glasnost'* literature has been Lysenkoism: articles detailing the repression of genetics have appeared in *Ogonek, Moscow News*, and other periodicals, but there have also been many articles defending Lysenko and his ideas. For Soviets, Lysenko's career continues to raise troubling questions about the role of Marxist-Leninist ideology, the Communist Party, and the Soviet government in the scientific and cultural life of the country.

Nor was Lysenko's effect limited to the U.S.S.R. His rise to power provoked dissent in western Marxist circles, alienating J. B. S. Haldane and other prominent Communist biologists in Britain and elsewhere from party and profession alike. In the late 1940's and early 1950's Lysenkoism followed Soviet influence into Eastern Europe and China, leading to considerable difficulty for their agricultural scientists, biologists, and geneticists. Lysenkoism also played an important role in western cold war rhetoric, serving for many years as a prime example of the perversion of truth under totalitarianism and the necessity of freedom and autonomy for science.

Scholars continue to disagree about many aspects of Lysenko's career, including the legitimacy of his early work on vernalization and plant physiology; the relationship of dialectical materialism and Marxist ideology to his evolving views; the collaboration of legitimate scientists in his rise to power; his role in the purges; the degree of Stalin's personal involvement in supporting him and shaping his views; his actual effect on Soviet agricultural production and practice; and the reasons for the remarkable longevity of his influence. Opinions differ over whether Lysenko was a true believer or merely a charlatan—and even over whether he belongs in the history of science. There is no doubt, however, that his career poses abiding issues about the sociopolitical dimensions of science and the complex interactions between theory, philosophy, ideology, and practice.

BIBLIOGRAPHY

I. ORIGINAL WORKS. Most of Lysenko's works before 1950 have been reprinted in the various editions of his *Agrobiologiia: Raboty po voprosam genetiki, selektsii, i semenovodstva* (Agrobiology: Works on genetics, selec-

tion, and seed breeding, Moscow, 1943; 6th ed., 1952). His pamphlet *O nasledstvennosti i ee izmenchivosti* (Moscow 1943; repr. 1944) was translated into English by Theodosius Dobzhansky and published as *Heredity and Its Variability* (New York, 1946; 3rd ed., 1953). His speech at the 1936 session of the Lenin All-Union Academy of Agricultural Sciences is published in O. M. Targul'ian, ed., *Spornye voprosy genetiki i selektsii* (Moscow, 1937); his long summary of his views at the 1948 session is available in English in *The Science of Biology Today* (New York, 1948) and in *The Situation in Biological Science: Proceedings of the Lenin Academy of Agricultural Sciences of the U.S.S.R., Session: July 31–August 7, 1948* (Moscow 1948, 1949; New York, 1949).

A complete bibliography of his works published prior to 1952, compiled by A. P. Epifanova, together with a brief biography by I. E. Glushchenko, is in *Trofim Denisovich Lysenko* (Moscow 1953), issued in the bibliographic pamphlet series on leading Soviet scientists published by the U.S.S.R. Academy of Sciences (Materialy k biobibliografii uchenykh SSSR, Seriia biologicheskikh nauk, Agrobiologiia, no. 1).

Most of Lysenko's publications after 1950 appeared in the central press. See, for example, "Ob agronomicheskom uchenii V. P. Vil'iamsa" (On V. R. Viliams's agronomic teachings), in *Pravda*, 15 July 1950; "Novoe v nauke o biologicheskom vide" (What is new in science concerning the biological species), *ibid.*, 3 November 1950, repr. in *Botanicheskii zhurnal* 1953, no. 1, 44–56, and in *Bol'shaia sovetskaia entsiklopediia*, 2nd ed., s.v. "Vid"; "K voprosu o pod'eme urozhainosti v nechernozemnoi polose" (On increasing crop yields in the non-black earth belt), in *Pravda*, 21 May 1953; "Ob obrabotke tselinnykh i zalezhnykh zemel'" (On the cultivation of virgin and idle lands), in *Izvestiia*, 20 February 1954; "Pretvorim v zhizn' resheniia ianvarskogo Plenuma TsK KPSS" (We will implement resolutions of the January plenary session of the Central Committee of the Communist Party of the Soviet Union), in *Pravda*, 27 April 1955; "Interesnye raboty po zhivotnovodstvu v Gorkakh leninskikh:Beseda s akademikom T. D. Lysenko" (Interesting work in animal husbandry at Lenin Hills: Interview with academician T. D. Lysenko), *ibid.*, 17 July 1957; "Teoreticheskie uspekhi agronomicheskoi biologii" (Theoretical successes of agronomic biology), in *Izvestiia*, 8 December 1957; "Nekotorye vazhneishie voprosy zemledeliia tselinnykh raionov" (Some of the most important questions of farming in virgin land areas), in *Pravda*, 5 August 1960; and "Teoreticheskie osnovy napravlennogo izmeneniia nasledstvennosti sel'skokhoziaistvennykh rastenii" (Theoretical foundations of the directed alteration of the heredity of agricultural plants), in *Pravda* and *Izvestiia*, 29 January 1963.

Articles published elsewhere include "Za materializm v biologii" (For materialism in biology), in *Voprosy filosofii*, 1958, no. 2, 102–111; "O zakone zhizni biologicheskikh vidov i ego znachenii dlia praktiki" (On the law of the life of biological species and its significance for practice),

in *Nasledstvennost' i izmenchivost'*, I (Moscow, 1959),
212–235; and "K voprosu o vzaimootnosheniiakh biologii
s khimiei i fizikoi" (On the question of interrelationships
of biology with chemistry and physics), in *Voprosy filosofii*
1959, no. 10, 103–106. See also his speeches in the proceedings of the Twentieth Party Congress, *XX S''ezd
KPSS, 14–25 fevralia 1956 goda*, II (Moscow, 1956), 348–
353; and of the plenary sessions of the Central Committee
of the Communist Party of the Soviet Union (TsK KPSS)
in *Plenum TsK KPSS, 15–19 dekabria 1958 goda* (Moscow,
1959), 234–240; *Plenum TsK KPSS, 22–25 dekabria 1959
goda* (Moscow, 1960), 327–332; and *Plenum TsK KPSS,
10–18 ianvaria 1961 goda* (Moscow, 1961), 337–345.

II. SECONDARY LITERATURE. The secondary literature
on Lysenko and Lysenkoism is vast. After 1948, a spate
of articles were published in the *Journal of Heredity* and
many popular periodicals, and several books appeared,
notably Conway Zirkle, ed., *Death of a Science in Russia*
(Philadelphia, 1949), a collection of translated Soviet articles; Julian Huxley, *Heredity East and West* (New York,
1949); a heroic Soviet account by V. Safonov, *Land in
Bloom* (Moscow, 1951); and Zirkle's *Evolution, Marxian
Biology, and the Social Scene* (Philadelphia, 1959). In
the decade after 1964, a number of general histories appeared, of which the most reliable are David Joravsky,
The Lysenko Affair (Cambridge, Mass., 1970); and Zhores
A. Medvedev, *The Rise and Fall of T. D. Lysenko* (New
York, 1969).

Recent works dealing with the relationship between
Lysenko's views and Marxist philosophy include those
by Loren Graham, *Science and Philosophy in the Soviet
Union* (New York, 1972; 2nd ed., New York, 1987); Ivan
T. Frolov, *Genetika i dialektika* (Genetics and dialectics;
Moscow, 1968); Dominique Lecourt, *Lyssenko: Histoire
réelle d'une "science prolétarienne"* (Paris, 1976), available
in English as *Proletarian Science? The Case of Lysenko*,
trans. Ben Brewster (London, 1977); and Denis Buican,
L'éternel retour de Lyssenko (Paris, 1978). Archival information on Lysenko's role in the purge of geneticists
is provided in Mark Popovsky, *The Vavilov Affair* (Ham-
den, Conn., 1984). Recent reevaluations of the history
of Lysenkoism and Soviet genetics include Mark B. Adams, "Biology After Stalin," in *Survey*, **23**, no. 102 (1977/
1978), 53–80; Raissa L. Berg, *Acquired Traits: Memoirs
of a Geneticist from the Soviet Union*, trans. David Lowe
(New York, 1988); Johann-Peter Regelmann, *Die Geschichte des Lyssenkoismus* (Frankfurt am Main, 1980);
and Nils Roll-Hansen, *Ønsketenkning som vitenskap:
Lysenkos innmarsji sovjetisk biologii 1927–37* (Oslo, 1985),
and "A New Perspective on Lysenko?" in *Annals of
Science*, **42** (1985), 261–278. See also, by Valery Soyfer,
"Gor'kii plod" (Bitter harvest), in *Ogonek*, 1988, no. 1,
pp. 26–29 and no. 2, pp. 4–7, 31; and *Vlast' i nauka:
Istoriia razgroma genetiki v SSSR* (Science and power:
A history of the rout of Soviet genetics; Tenafly, N.J.:
Hermitage, 1989. Recent Soviet novels dealing with Ly-
senkoism are Daniil Granin, *Zubr* (Bison; Leningrad, 1987;

New York, 1989); and Vladimir Dudintsev, *Belye odezhdy*
(White robes; Moscow, 1988).

MARK B. ADAMS

MACARTHUR, ROBERT HELMER (*b.* Toronto,
Ontario, Canada, 7 April 1930; *d.* Princeton, New
Jersey, 1 November 1972), *ecology*.

"In November 1972 a brief but remarkable era
in the development of ecology came to a tragic,
premature close with the death of Robert MacArthur
at the age of 42." So wrote Martin Cody and Jared
Diamond in the 1975 memorial volume *Ecology and
Evolution of Communities*.

MacArthur will be remembered as one of the
founders of evolutionary ecology. It is his distinction
to have brought population and community ecology
within the reach of genetics. By reformulating many
of the parameters of ecology, biogeography, and
genetics into a common framework of fundamental
theory, MacArthur, more than any other person
who worked during the decisive decade of the 1960's,
set the stage for the unification of population biology.

MacArthur was the youngest son of John Wood
MacArthur, a professor of genetics at the University
of Toronto and Marlboro College in Vermont. After
completing his undergraduate education at the latter
institution and the requirements for a master's degree
in mathematics at Brown University, Robert
MacArthur took a Ph.D. in 1957 at Yale University
under the direction of G. Evelyn Hutchinson. He
spent the academic year 1957–1958 with David Lack
at Oxford University in order to receive additional
training in field ornithology. Hutchinson, Lack, and
an older brother of Robert's, the physicist John W.
MacArthur, Jr., were dominant influences in shaping
MacArthur's unique blend of mathematical and
ecological interests. From 1958 to 1965 MacArthur
advanced from assistant professor to full professor
at the University of Pennsylvania; he then moved
to Princeton University, where he ended his career
as Henry Fairfield Osborn Professor of Biology. In
1952 he married Elizabeth Bayles Whittemore; they
had four children (Duncan, Alan, Elizabeth, and
Donald). He died of renal cancer.

MacArthur began his career with three articles
that revealed an unusual power and originality of
approach. The first (1955) was the proposal of a
measure of community stability taken from information theory, formalizing for the first time a concept
that previously had been the subject of simple verbal
description. MacArthur employed entropy, the sum

of the product of the frequencies of occurrence of species and the logarithms of the frequencies, a very general and intuitively satisfying way of condensing a large amount of complex data. Soon afterward (1957) came the celebrated "broken-stick" model of the relative abundance of bird species.

MacArthur proposed that the relative abundance of mutiple related species living in the same community (such as the songbirds of an island) can often be generally approximated by comparison with a stick broken into segments of randomly selected lengths, each segment representing the abundance of a particular species. The rationale was that when species compete, they divide the environment randomly and in a mutually exclusive fashion, like a stick divided into segments.

Although the specific hypothesis of competition embodied in the broken-stick distribution has been disputed, and the approach was later dismissed as obsolete by MacArthur himself, we should not overlook the real significance of this contribution. In three pages MacArthur audaciously confronted a central problem of community ecology that had scarcely been put into words by previous writers. He characterized the issue in such a way as to suggest that the deepest remaining mysteries of natural history can be reached by leaps of the imagination, so long as such efforts are disciplined by the postulational-deductive method.

Reviewers sometimes forget that the broken-stick hypothesis was only one of three frequency distributions presented in the article, each derived from a different, competing set of biological hypotheses. The method of multiple working hypotheses was thereby introduced to this branch of ecological theory. The 1957 article set the tone for all of MacArthur's later work. Inevitably, his approach was condemned by some ecologists as oversimplification, but right or wrong in particular applications, it energized a generation of young population biologists and transformed a large part of ecology.

MacArthur's third early contribution was an elegant analysis of niche division in warblers (1958). For this somewhat more conventional study, he received the Mercer Award of the Ecological Society of America. In a sense the warbler study revealed the real secret of MacArthur's success, his almost unique status as a mathematician-naturalist. He was a mathematician of professional grade, having been trained in the discipline before commencing the formal study of ecology. He had the convictions of a pure mathematician, which, according to G. H. Hardy (whom he resembled very much in temperament and philosophy), are simply "that a mathematician was a maker of patterns of ideas, and that beauty and seriousness were the criteria by which his patterns should be judged." MacArthur would say in conversation that the best science comes to a great extent from the creation of de novo and heuristic classification of natural phenomena. "Art," he enjoyed quoting Picasso, "is the lie that helps us to see the truth."

But MacArthur was also a born naturalist. He watched birds with the patience and skill of a professional ornithologist, visited the tropics as often as he could, and delighted in the endless facts of natural history, which were temporarily exempted from his Cartesian scalpel. The store of random information thus accumulated and the shadowy play of its many patterns were the real inspiration of his theoretical work.

The 1960's was a period of intense activity for MacArthur. While serving on the faculty of the University of Pennsylvania and then at Princeton, he began a parallel series of investigations, many in collaboration with colleagues and students, that touched on a wide range of topics around the central problem of species diversity. Part of his special genius was an ability to work closely with persons of widely varying talents and interests, turn them into fast friends, and bring out the best in their scientific labors. MacArthur and his coworkers analyzed the evolution of the demographic parameters, established the environmental correlates of bird diversity, and formulated and partly solved the species packing problem, in which the relation of niche breadth is correlated with the number of species crowding into the same area. One of his most influential works was *The Theory of Island Biogeography* (1967), with E. O. Wilson, which created species equilibrium theory. In this approach, consideration is given to the numbers of species belonging to a particular group of organisms (such as birds or ants) found on a given island or isolated patch of habitat. The numbers are seen as the result of the balance between the immigration rates of new species and the extinction rates of species already present. The rates in turn vary with the size of the islands and their distance from other islands.

As time passed, MacArthur spoke of himself increasingly as a biogeographer, and he made the subject the focus of his teaching at Princeton. In 1971, when he learned he had only a year or two left to live, he quickly brought the many threads of his work together in the book *Geographical Ecology: Patterns in the Distribution of Species.* The clarity and incisiveness of this synthesis show him at the height of his powers. *Geographical Ecology* is both the reflective memoir of a senior scientist and the prospectus of a young man whose creative effort ended at the point of its steepest trajectory.

BIBLIOGRAPHY

I. ORIGINAL WORKS. A complete bibliography of MacArthur's writings is provided by Martin L. Cody and Jared M. Diamond in the volume they edited, *Ecology and Evolution of Communities* (Cambridge, Mass., 1975), 13–14. MacArthur presented many of his successful ideas, either originally or in review, in *The Theory of Island Biogeography* (Princeton, 1967), written with Edward O. Wilson; and in *Geographical Ecology: Patterns in the Distribution of Species* (New York, 1972; repr. Princeton, 1984).

II. SECONDARY LITERATURE. An evaluation of much of MacArthur's work is provided by the multiple authors of *Ecology and Evolution of Communities* (see above), and by many textbooks of the 1970's and 1980's, among which Mark H. Williamson, *Island Populations* (Oxford and New York, 1981); and James H. Brown and Arthur C. Gibson, *Biogeography* (St. Louis, 1983), are perhaps the most thorough. A brief personal portrait of MacArthur, with a firsthand account of the development of the theory of island biogeography, is provided by Edward O. Wilson in *Biophilia* (Cambridge, Mass., 1984), 68–71, 73–74.

EDWARD O. WILSON

McATEE, WALDO LEE (*b*. Jalapa, Indiana, 21 January 1883; *d*. Chapel Hill, North Carolina, 7 January 1962), *ecology, ornithology.*

McAtee was the first child of Anna Morris and John Henry McAtee, a carpenter, who subsequently moved the family of three boys and three girls to industrial Marion, Indiana. Assisted by loans, McAtee attended Indiana University, taking an A.B. (1904) and an A.M. (1906). He married Fannie E. Lawson of Oxford, Indiana, on 13 September 1906; they had two sons, one of whom died in infancy, and a daughter. McAtee joined the U.S. Bureau of Biological Survey in 1904 and remained a government scientist, in Washington, D.C., for his entire career. A pioneer in studies of the food habits of common farmland birds, he directed the Biological Survey's economic ornithology research. He was a competent taxonomist and acting custodian of hemiptera at the U.S. National Museum from 1920 to 1942. Possessed of rugged health and a love of the outdoors, McAtee was active in fieldwork; he also wrote and edited numerous bulletins and agricultural pamphlets. After retirement he moved in 1950 to Chapel Hill, turning to the study of dialect and "Hoosier" pioneer literature. Indiana University granted him an honorary D.Sc. in 1961.

McAtee indulged his philosophical and literary bent with a holiday custom of privately printed booklets of his short poems, epigrams, and parables, expressing his philosophy of honesty, equality, and fairness. Reacting to a fundamentalist church upbringing, he was a professed agnostic and critic of the hypocrisy he saw in organized religion. He opposed what he called "kowtowing" and considered himself unsociable, resisting the mixing and politicking inherent in a government position. Nonetheless, he belonged to more than thirty organizations. His religion was a love of nature and conservation, expressed in part in active membership in various ornithological, entomological, botanical, and scientific societies. He also joined three societies of folklore and dialect, and the Freethinkers of America. He was most active in the American Ornithologists' Union (AOU), serving as treasurer from 1920 to 1938. An organizer and charter member of the Wildlife Society, he was founding editor, in 1937, of its *Journal of Wildlife Management*. His critical and forthright personality made professional relationships often prickly, but these same traits engendered widespread respect for his honesty and integrity. Not one to compromise, he inevitably became embroiled in vitriolic scientific controversy.

McAtee's serious scientific interests were sparked in 1899 by a series of lectures given in Marion by the famous ornithologist Frank M. Chapman. Immediately McAtee began to keep careful field notes on the local fauna, and then he entered zoology studies at university. While a student he worked as curator of birds at the Indiana University Museum. Chapman was a great proselytizer for not only the pleasures of bird study but also the value of birds, and McAtee followed his lead in early research. The thesis he submitted in 1906 to Indiana University had already been published as Bulletin 23 of the Biological Survey, *Horned Larks and Their Relation to Agriculture*. This marked the beginning of his prolific research and publication in economic ornithology, a subject for which he was the recognized authority from the 1920's to the 1940's.

In the 1880's Stephen A. Forbes in Illinois and Francis E. L. Beal in Iowa had begun the analysis of the stomach contents of birds, to determine their food habits systematically. Important to both was showing the economic impact on agriculture of insectivorous birds. Applied ecology was appearing all over the United States with various state agricultural and entomological commissions, and within the federal Department of Agriculture (USDA). Economic ornithology became a USDA division in 1886, largely as a result of pressure from influential members of the AOU; C. Hart Merriam moved from heading the AOU research committee to the new USDA post, as did Beal, who initiated a massive program of bird stomach contents analysis. The Division of Economic Ornithology and Mammalogy was reorganized into the USDA Bureau of Biological Survey in 1905, at which time McAtee was assistant biologist to Beal. McAtee eventually headed the food habits research from 1916 to 1934, becoming head of his own new division, Food Habits Research, in 1921. With the food of most American birds poorly known, the researches of Beal and McAtee, published in a long series of jointly and singly authored USDA bulletins, were basic advances in ecology.

Bird insectivory was a contentious theoretical point because the debates about Darwinian natural selection so often depended on the evidence drawn from the phenomenon of protective coloration in insects. The theory that selection by birds created camouflage or protective mimicry in their prey was used by Edward B. Poulton of Oxford to vigorously defend Darwinism at the turn of the century, but the trouble was that naturalists were not agreed that birds ate butterflies, the standard example, or avoided supposedly protected insects. Poulton and G. A. K. Marshall instigated the collating of evidence from naturalists all over the world and claimed great support for their contentions that predators avoided the protectively colored insects.

McAtee meanwhile had been reviewing the Biological Survey data, and in 1912 he published an attack on the selectionist theory; his significant claim was that naturalists' conclusions about food preferences drawn from anecdotes were worthless and that experiments with captive birds were misleading. Thus his stomach analyses provided the only rigorous data, and they appeared to deny the protective value of coloration. The debate simmered for twenty years only to blow up in 1932, with the publication of McAtee's major work, based on 80,000 stomach analyses.

McAtee engaged Poulton and other British zoologists in a long-running and at times acrimonious exchange. He agreed that the effectiveness of protective coloration was a crucial support for Darwinism. Long an opponent of excesses and contradictions and a lack of rigor within Darwinism, he thought he had demonstrated the nonexistence of selection for protective coloring in nature. He argued that birds took their prey on the basis of the abundance of the insects. His opponents pointed out that from his aggregate lists of insect species found in bird species, nothing could be concluded about preferences without actual data on insect abundances. It was remarkable that such a massive quantitative research effort, however useful for agriculture, had been statistically naive and was useless for the biological question of selection in nature. McAtee's distrust of mathematics and statistics, despite his quantitative approach and versatility as a nauralist, left him out of the mainstream of ecology after the 1930's.

Nonetheless, the economic ornithology research program, including McAtee's steady promotion of wildlife conservation and the widely disseminated government publications, had lasting importance by promoting the value of birds. These efforts were directly influential in the passage of a succession of bird and wildlife protection laws in the United States between 1900 and 1930.

BIBLIOGRAPHY

I. ORIGINAL WORKS. McAtee wrote nearly 1,000 scientific papers, of which many were USDA bulletins on food habits and conservation. His major work was "Effectiveness in Nature of the So-called Protective Adaptations in the Animal Kingdom, Chiefly as Illustrated by the Food Habits of Nearctic Birds," in *Smithsonian Miscellaneous Collections*, **85**, no. 7 (1932). Never published were two book-length manuscripts, a critique of Darwinism and a compilation of folk taxonomy of American birds.

McAtee left a complete set of his diverse publications and autobiographical material at the University of North Carolina, Chapel Hill. There are correspondence and reminiscences of the Biological Survey in the Library of Congress Manuscripts Division, and a set of papers concerning his research in the American Philosophical Society Library, Philadelphia. His records and letters on AOU business are in the Witmer Stone Papers, Academy of Natural Sciences, Philadelphia.

II. SECONDARY LITERATURE. An obituary drawing on McAtee's autobiographical fragments is E. R. Kalmbach, "In Memoriam: W. L. McAtee," in *Auk*, **80** (1963), 474–485.

WILLIAM C. KIMLER

MACHATSCHKI, FELIX KARL LUDWIG (*b.* Arnfels, Styria, Austria, 22 September 1895; *d.* Vienna, Austria, 17 February 1970), *mineralogy, crystal chemistry.*

Felix Karl Ludwig Machatschki was the third child of adjunct judge Felix Machatschki and his wife, Christine, née Schalmun. He was baptized a Roman Catholic. After attending primary school in Greifenburg (Carinthia) and Feldbach (Styria), Machatschki spent eight years at the classical secondary school I. Staatsgymnasium in Graz, where he graduated in 1914 with distinction. At this institution he acquired a good knowledge of classical languages, a subject he was very interested in.

In the winter term 1914–1915 he enrolled at the University of Graz to study natural sciences, intending to become a secondary school teacher. But because of World War I his studies were far from regular. From March 1915 to November 1918 he was in the military, serving in the south and at the eastern front. He was slightly wounded several times and was awarded military decorations. He left the army as a lieutenant. During his military service Machatschki had only one three-month leave for studies. Even the end of the war did not bring a normal student life; up to the end of 1919 he took part in the defense of territory in Styria and Carinthia against Yugoslavia.

But since he was gifted with intelligence and energy, he was able to finish his studies very quickly. In 1920 he passed the state examination for secondary school teachers, with natural sciences as the main subject and mathematics and physics as subsidiary subjects. He intended to specialize in botany and had begun preliminary work for a thesis in this field when in 1920 R. Scharizer offered him a job as assistant at the Institute for Mineralogy and Petrography at the University of Graz. Machatschki accepted, and though he never regretted this decision, a love for botany remained with him all his life. In 1921 he married Dr. Bertha Josepha Laurich, a botanist; their only child, Kurt, was born in 1923.

On 12 April 1922 Machatschki submitted a thesis on the chloritoid schists of the glein-alpe, and, having passed examinations in mineralogy, petrography, chemistry, and philosophy, the Ph.D. was conferred on him by the University of Graz on 2 June 1922.

He continued as Scharizer's assistant until 1927, although initially, he claimed, not with much enthusiasm for mineralogy. But he acquired an excellent knowledge of classical mineralogy and petrography, crystallography, and mineral and rock analysis. Eventually he became interested in this field of science, especially in mineral chemistry. In 1925 he qualified as lecturer in mineralogy and petrography. His early publications show him to have been a very good and diligent young scientist, but they do not hint at his later scientific excellence.

The great break in Machatschki's career occurred in 1927 when he obtained a Rockefeller scholarship

to work in Oslo with V. M. Goldschmidt, one of the most famous mineralogists and petrographers of his time and a founder of modern geochemistry and crystal chemistry.

In 1928 Machatschki published what was probably his most important paper, even though it was only eight pages long, "Zur Frage der Struktur und Konstitution der Feldspate (Gleichzeitig vorläufige Mitteilung über die Prinzipien des Baues der Silikate)". To be able to appreciate the importance of this work it is necessary briefly to recall the situation of silicate mineralogy and crystal chemistry in 1927. At that time the chemical bulk composition of the more common silicate minerals was already rather well known, but the transformation of the analytical results into chemical formulas was often difficult. For example, scientists observed continuous series between end-members containing chemically quite different elements, for one, the olivine group, the composition of which was known to vary continuously from Mg_2SiO_4 to Fe_2SiO_4. More serious were cases where a continuous transition was observed between end-members that seemed to be salts of quite different silicic acids. A famous example was the plagioclases, one of the most common mineral groups in the earth's crust, the chemical composition of which was known to vary from $NaAlSi_3O_8$ to $CaAl_2Si_2O_8$. In such cases it was often assumed that the corresponding silicic acids had, in spite of their different chemical formula, a similar shape on a molecular basis. In a number of cases it was almost impossible to derive for a mineral a reasonable chemical formula; this was the case for the tourmalines.

As for the crystal structure, the atomic arrangement was known of the SiO_2 polymorphs quartz, tridymite, and cristobalite; olivine (Mg_2SiO_4), zircon ($ZrSiO_4$), garnet ($Ca_3Al_2[SiO_4]_3$), beryl ($Be_3Al_2[Si_6O_{18}]$), and essentially also of phenakite (Be_2SiO_4). All these minerals contained SiO_4 tetrahedra, that is, units in which four oxygen atoms occupy the corners of a (possibly slightly distorted) tetrahedron that houses a silicon atom at its center. The edge length of the tetrahedron is about 2.70 Å (angstroms), the distance Si–O about 1.65 Å. The SiO_4 tetrahedra were known to occur isolated in olivine, zircon, and garnet, polymerized via each two oxygen corners to Si_6O_{18} rings in beryl and polymerized via all four oxygen corners in the SiO_2 polymorphs quartz, tridymite, and cristobalite.

In the field of crystal chemistry generally, the atomic arrangement in quite a number of chemically simple compounds was known, due largely to the pioneering work of the Braggs. The concept of effective ionic radii was well developed. Goldschmidt and his co-workers were active in this field and, based on Wasastjerna's value $r(O^{-2}) = 1.32$ Å, systematically derived the effective ionic radii of a large number of elements in their different states of valency. Goldschmidt's aim was to obtain a better insight into the laws governing the distribution of the elements in the earth.

The general building principles of the silicates beyond the state discussed above were, however, unknown. Even a scientist of the rank of Goldschmidt wrote in 1926, when dealing with the silicates in his *Geochemische Verteilungsgesetze der Elemente. VII. Die Gesetze der Krystallochemie:*

> The so-called metasilicates $MgSiO_3$ (enstatite and polymorphous modifications) and $CaSiO_3$ (wollastonite) correspond in crystal chemistry to none of the structure types of compounds ABX_3.
>
> Therefore, the so-called magnesium metasilicate $MgSiO_3$ is evidently magnesium orthosilicate + "crystal silicon dioxide," that is, $Mg_2SiO_4 \cdot 1SiO_2$, corresponding to a formula already used by P. Niggli in his textbook. The incongruent melting behavior of enstatite with its decomposition into orthosilicate and silicic acid does indeed remind one of the decomposition of a salt containing water of crystallization. (p. 111)

And, some few lines further:

> One could interpret orthoclase, which like anstatite has an incongruent melting point, as leucite + crystal silicon dioxide, or $KAlSi_2O_6 \cdot 1SiO_2$; leucite as kaliophilite plus crystal silicon dioxide, or $KAlSiO_4 \cdot 1SiO_4$; and consequently orthoclase as $KAlSiO_4 \cdot 2SiO_2$.
>
> Such dissections of formulas may in many cases be mere idle play. However, in connection with what I have said on the analogy between the ions SiO_4 and SO_4, the new formulas seem to offer a means to study the constitution of silicates. That is to say, it should be possible to prepare, so to speak, "structural models" of these silicates that are sulfates.

Machatschki's 1928 paper contains two pioneering concepts on the constitution of crystallized silicates. First, with the exception of some simple cases like the orthosilicates with their SiO_4 tetrahedra, he broke from the concept that crystallized silicates contain finite radicals of silicic acids; second, he postulated that Si can be substituted by Al^{+3} in the silicates.

Considering the silicates as salts of silicic acids of finite size was a widespread view at that time, and a publication of W. Wahl in 1927 along these lines was the immediate motivation for Machatschki's paper. Wahl drew analogies between organic acids and silicic acids and, for example, formulated orthoclase ($KAlSi_3O_8$) as

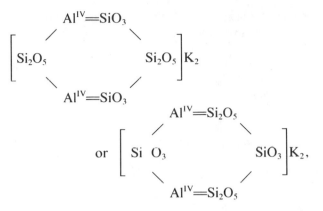

where SiO_3 and Si_2O_5 are finite radicals and the expressions in the square brackets symbolize complex but finite radicals (in which aluminum is fourfold coordinated). Machatschki, however, argued that "as a rule it is useless to speak of a molecule in connection with silicates."

The next important item he addressed in this paper is the coordination number of oxygens around aluminum in silicates. Evidently, only crystal structures in which Al is coordinated to six oxygens were known at the time. But it was well known that the effective ionic radius of Al^{+3} is larger than that of Si^{+4}, although smaller than that of Mg^{+2}. Goldschmidt considered the following values to be the most reliable: $r(Si^{+4}) = 0.39$ Å, $r(Al^{+3}) = 0.57$ Å, and $r(Mg^{+2}) = 0.78$ Å. The brilliant idea of Machatschki was to assume that Al^{+3} could also be 4coordinated in the silicates:

> For the structure of silicate crystals it is of further importance that the ion Al^{+3}, as a consequence of its size relative to that of O^{-2}, is on the borderline between 4 and 6 as to its coordination number toward O^{-2} and, therefore, is likely to occur in silicates with both coordination numbers toward O^{-2}. Where it has coordination number 4, it replaces Si^{+4} at the centers of O^{-2} tetrahedra, whereby these should expand somewhat.

This theory allowed Machatschki to postulate that the arrangement of the building units in the feldspars must correspond principally to a pure SiO_2 structure with part of the silicon ions replaced by Al^{+3} and with the ions K^+, Na^+, Ca^{+2}, and Ba^{+2} in the interstices. He further recognized from the effective ionic radii $r(Na^+) = 0.98$ Å, $r(Ca^{+2}) = 1.06$ Å, $r(K^+) = 1.33$ Å, and $r(Ba^{+2}) = 1.43$ Å that complete solid solutions are to be expected between albite ($NaAlSi_3O_8$) and anorthite ($CaAl_2Si_2O_8$) on the one side, and between potassium feldspar ($KAlSi_3O_8$) and barium feldspar ($BaAl_2Si_2O_8$) on the other side. He gave to this main type of silicate the preliminary name "feldspar type"; later he spoke of *Geruest-silikate* (framework silicates). H. Strunz introduced the expression *Tektosilikate* (tectosilicates).

In his 1928 paper Machatschki also presented the essential building principles of the metasilicates, the pyroxenes, of which a chemically simple representative is enstatite ($MgSi_3$). He predicted that in this class of silicates each SiO_4 tetrahedron has to share two oxygen ions with neighboring tetrahedra, probably to form chains.

Machatschki's postulates were later confirmed by crystal structure determinations: on the feldspars by W. H. Taylor (1933), W. H. Taylor, J. A. Darbyshire, and H. Strunz (1934), and others; on the pyroxenes by B. Warren and W. L. Bragg (1928) and others.

Machatschki was always fully aware of how much he owed to others, especially to Goldschmidt and to Bragg. In his speech accepting the Roebling Medal, he said:

> I became acquainted [in Graz] with the work of V. M. Goldschmidt and his co-workers on the crystal structure of simple compounds. By means of a Rockefeller fellowship I was able to go to the laboratory of Goldschmidt in Oslo. Here I studied the early publications of Sir William L. Bragg and his co-workers on the crystal structure of some silicates. Now it was merely a synthesis of all these results which made it inevitable to abandon the assumption of discrete molecules in the silicates and other groups of inorganic compounds. Instead, the replacement of tetravalent Si by trivalent Al was assumed, as well as other non-isovalent substitutions.

In 1928 Machatschki published two important papers on the crystal structure of the fahlores, a group of chemically complex minerals essentially consisting of copper, antimony (or arsenic), and sulphur. At that time the atomic arrangement in several simple crystallized sulfides was known: galena (PbS), sphalerite (cubic ZnS), wurtzite (hexagonal ZnS), pyrite (cubic FeS_2), and a few others. But the atomic arrangement was not known on anything with the chemical complexity of the fahlores. The chemical formulas given for the antimony fahlore, tetrahedrite, varied between Cu_3SbS_3 and Cu_3SbS_4.

The essential clue for the determination of structure was the similarity of the X-ray powder diagrams of the fahlores and of sphalerite. It was known that the atomic arrangement of sphalerite can be described by a unit cell in the form of a small cube with edge length (= lattice constant) 5.41 Å, containing four Zn and four S atoms in such a way that when the cell is continued, each Zn atom is tetrahedrally surrounded by four S atoms, and vice versa.

The unit cell of tetrahedrite also has the shape of a cube, but, as a consequence of weak reflections, with the lattice constant doubled in comparison to sphalerite; in sphalerite such a cell would contain twenty-four Zn and twenty-four S atoms (being three-fourths of $4 \times Z^3$).

For tetrahedrite Machatschki assumed first the idealized formula Cu_3SbS_3, of which the cell contains eight units, that is, it contains twenty-four Cu, eight Sb, and twenty-four S atoms. He showed that the essential relationship between the sphalerite and the tetrahedrite structure can be described as follows: of the thirty-two Zn atoms in the sphalerite, twenty-four are replaced in tetrahedrite by Cu and the remaining eight by Sb (in an ordered way); of the thirty-two atoms in sphalerite, only twenty-four are occupied (again by S), and the rest are vacancies. He further showed that the antimony atoms are not exactly at the same locations as the corresponding Zn atoms in sphalerite but are shifted by ~ 0.5 Å. All this results in Sb forming a SbS_3 pyramid with three S neighbors; eight pyramids are contained in the unit cell. One half of the Cu atoms have a tetrahedral coordination of S atoms, the other half has a one-sided coordination of only two S atoms.

Machatschki was fully aware that reliable analyses of tetrahedrite indicated a somewhat higher S content than required by the formula Cu_3SbS_3. He recognized that the formula given by G. Tschermak in 1903, $SbS_3Cu_3 \cdot SbS_4CuZn_2$, fits the analyses best. It can be rewritten $Cu_{10}Zn_2Sb_4S_{13}$, of which the cell contains two units, that is, the cell contains twenty-four Cu, Zn; eight Sb; and twenty-six S atoms (instead of the twenty-four in Machatschki's idealized structure). In his first paper he gives a possible location for the two excess S atoms in an ordered structure, while in the second he writes: "The excess sulphur atoms can enter the structure at those places where in the fahlore the S atoms are missing in comparison with the sphalerite structure." This would require a statistical distribution of these two S atoms. An experimental decision between the two models would have been impossible with the only roughly estimated intensities.

L. Pauling and E. W. Neuman, working on arsenic fahlore in 1934, became convinced that Machatschki's first proposal was the correct one. The final experimental proof of this view was given for tetrahedrite by B. Wuensch in 1964.

In 1928 and 1929 Machatschki worked with Sir William L. Bragg in Manchester, and from this laboratory in 1929 he published another paper, "Die Formeleinheit des Turmalins." The tourmalines are the most widespread borosilicates in nature, but their chemical composition is so complex that no agreement on a chemical formula had yet been reached, and the proposals varied widely. By putting ions of similar size (independent of their valence state and chemical properties) into groups, he proposed the formula $XY_9Si_6B_3H_xO_{31}$ for this mineral, with X for large ions (mainly Na^+ and Ca^{+2}) and Y for medium-size ions that were expected to have an octahedral oxygen coordination (mainly Al^{+3}, Mg^{+2}, Fe^{+3}, Fe^{+2}, and Li^+). His suggestion was first confirmed by a structure determination of tourmaline by G. E. Hamburger and M. J. Buerger in 1948.

In Manchester Machatschki also worked on the experimental determination of the structure of danburite ($CaB_2Si_2O_8$), which, according to his principles, should belong to the feldspar type, that is, the framework structure. But according to Bragg (1965), "it proved to be a refractory structure to analyze, and Machatschki's usually high spirits were sometimes replaced by intervals of deepest despair when the crystal just would not 'come out.'" The structure was published by C. Dunbar and F. Machatschki in 1931 and showed the expected features, although the B atom seemed to be rather strongly displaced from the center of the oxygen tetrahedron. A much later structure refinement by G. Johansson (1959) showed, however, that the BO_4 tetrahedron in danburite is quite normal.

Machatschki spent the winter term 1929–1930 in Göttingen, where Goldschmidt was now professor. His suggestion that the arsenate mineral berzeliite has the same structure type as the garnets dates from this time. In 1930 he received invitations to the university of Graz and also to Tübingen. Because Graz could not afford the X-ray equipment he required, he went to Tübingen, where he was full professor of mineralogy and petrology until 1941 and dean from 1931 to 1933. He had now found his style of work, and his institute developed into an international center of research. He continued to work on minerals with complicated chemical compositions, while maintaining an interest in analogies of silicates with phosphates and arsenates and in other fields of mineralogy and petrography.

In 1941 he moved to Munich, but his home and institute were soon destroyed by air attacks. In 1944 Machatschki went to Vienna to succeed the late A. Himmelbauer as professor of mineralogy and petrography at the university. Soon this institute was also damaged, although work continued until the early spring of 1945. Machatschki spent the very end of the war in Styria, but he soon returned to Vienna, and in 1945 resumed his teaching and re-

search. He went on to build the institute's international reputation. He wrote three books covering the whole field of mineralogy, including raw materials, and served as editor of *Tschermaks Mineralogische und Petrographische Mitteilung* until his retirement in 1967.

Machatschki received many honors. The Bavarian Academy of Sciences elected him a member in 1943, followed by the academies in Austria, Sweden, Italy, Göttingen, the Deutsche Akademie der Naturforscher Leopoldina, and the academies in Norway and Yugoslavia. He was elected honorary member or correspondent of several scientific societies. In 1958 he received the Schrödinger Prize of the Austrian Academy of Science, in 1959 the Roebling Medal of the Mineralogical Society of America, and in 1965 the Becke Medal of the Mineralogical Society of Austria. In the same year a special Machatschki volume of *Tschermaks Mineralogische und Petrographische Mitteilungen* appeared. In 1961 he was awarded the Österreichisches Ehrenzeichen für Wissenschaft und Kunst, and in 1962 he became honorary citizen of his native town, Arnfels.

In spite of all the honors, Machatschki remained a modest man to the end. He liked company and a glass of wine. During his time in Vienna he had little to do with his wife and son. For years he lived in the institute. His death was a great loss for mineralogists and solid-state chemists all over the world.

In 1977 K. Walenta named a secondary arsenate mineral in his honor, and on 11 May 1984 a commemorative bronze tablet was unveiled at the Institute for Mineralogy and Crystallography and at the University of Vienna.

BIBLIOGRAPHY

I. ORIGINAL WORKS. "Zur Frage der Struktur und Konstitution der Feldspate (Gleichzeitig vorläufige Mitteilung über die Prinzipien des Baues der Silikate)," in *Zentralblatts für Mineralogie, Geologie und Paläontologie,* sec. A (1928), 97–104; "Formel und Kristallstruktur des Tetraedrites," in *Norsk geologisk tidsskrift,* **10** (1928), 23–32; "Präzisionsmessungen der Gitterkonstanten verschiedener Fahlerze. Formel und Struktur derselben," in *Zeitschrift für Kristallographie,* **68** (1928), 204–222; "Die Formeleinheit des Turmalins," *ibid.,* **70** (1929), 211–233; "Berzeliit, ein Arsenat vom Formel- und Strukturtypus Granat $(X_3Y_2Z_3O_{12})$," *ibid.,* **73** (1930), 123–140; "Structure of Danburite, $CaB_2Si_2O_8$," *ibid.,* **76** (1931), 133–146, written with C. Dunbar; "Acceptance of the Roebling Medal of the Mineralogical Society of America," in *American Mineralogist,* **45** (1960), 411–412.

II. SECONDARY LITERATURE. Obituaries, with bibliographies, are by H. Heritsch in *Almanach. Österrei-*

chische Akademie der Wissenschaften. Wien, **120** (1970), 330–344; and by J. Zemann in *Tschermaks Mineralogische und Petrographische Mitteilungen*, 3rd ser. **15** (1971), 1–13, and in *American Mineralogist*, **56** (1971), 698–706.

See also W. L. Bragg, "Introduction," in *Tschermaks Mineralogische und Petrographische Mitteilungen*, 3rd ser. **10** (1965); I. Campbell, "Presentation of the Roebling Medal to Felix Machatschki," in *American Mineralogist*, **45** (1960), 407–410; V. M. Goldschmidt, *Geochemische Verteilungsgesetze der Elemente. VII. Die Gesetze der Krystallochemie* (Oslo, 1926); G. E. Hamburger and M. J. Buerger, "The Structure of Tourmaline," in *American Mineralogist*, **33** (1948), 532–540; G. Johansson, "A Refinement of the Crystal Structure of Danburite," in *Acta Crystallographica*, **12** (1959), 522–525; L. Pauling and E. W. Neuman, "The Crystal Structure of Binnite, (Cu, Fe)$_{12}$As$_4$S$_{13}$, and the Chemical Composition and Structure of Minerals of the Tetrahedrite Group," in *Zeitschrift für Kristallographie*, **88** (1934), 54–62.

W. H. Taylor, "The Structure of Sanidine and Other Feldspars," *ibid.*, **85** (1933), 425–442; W. H. Taylor, J. A. Darbyshire, and H. Strunz, "An X-ray Investigation of the Felspars," *ibid.*, **87** (1934), 464–498; W. Wahl, "Über die Konstitution der Silikate," *ibid.*, **66** (1927), 33–72; K. Walenta, "Machatschkiit, ein neues Arsenat aus der Grube Anton im Heubachtal bei Schiltach (Schwarzwald, Bundesrepublik Deutschland), in *Tschermaks Mineralogische und Petrographische Mitteilungen*, 3rd ser. **24** (1977), 125–132; B. Warren and W. L. Bragg, "The Structure of Diopside, CaMg(SiO$_3$)$_2$," in *Zeitschrift für Kristallographie*, **69** (1928), 168–193; B. J. Wuensch, "The Crystal Structure of Tetrahedrite, Cu$_{12}$Sb$_4$S$_{13}$," *ibid.*, **119** (1964), 437–453.

JOSEF ZEMANN

MCLENNAN, JOHN CUNNINGHAM (*b.* Ingersoll, Ontario, 14 April 1867; *d.* near Abbeville, France, 9 October 1935), *physics*.

McLennan's father, David, arrived in Canada from Scotland, in 1865, and was joined in 1866 by his wife, Barbara Cunningham, and their infant daughter. After having established himself as a miller and flour dealer, David McLennan relocated the family in Clinton, Ontario, in order to send his children to the local secondary school, the Collegiate Institute; when the family finally settled in Stratford, young John remained as a boarder in Clinton. In 1883, at age sixteen, he passed the Junior Matriculation Examination of the University of Toronto, which served as a secondary-school leaving certificate. McLennan then applied to work with the Grand Trunk Railway but failed to be hired. After a year living at home and working in his father's office, he declared his intention to pursue a four-year arts degree at the University of Toronto. Since his father's business was then foundering, McLennan had to earn money for his studies by teaching school.

At the end of a three-year pedagogical commitment, McLennan decided on a career in exact sciences. He took private lessons at home in preparation for the Senior Matriculation Examination at Toronto, the successful passing of which exempted a student from first-year studies. McLennan accomplished the task, and in 1889, at age twenty-two, he arrived in Toronto as a second-year student of mathematics and physics. Allowing himself few diversions, he received a B.A. degree in 1892, first in his class.

McLennan arrived at Toronto just when physics had become a separate institutional discipline. His physics professor, James Loudon, an undistinguished researcher who excelled at political maneuvering, had risen from classics tutor to physicist to, in 1892, president of the university. Since President Loudon retained his chair of physics, he required subordinates to carry out the routine tasks of teaching. Three men presented themselves for the posts: William James Loudon (who may have been related to James), Clarence Augustus Chant, and McLennan. The first two advanced up the academic ladder in mechanics and astrophysics while McLennan stayed on as President Loudon's assistant. His progress, in scientific and professional terms, was painfully slow; his assistant demonstratorship of 1892 was converted into a demonstratorship only in 1899.

As assistant demonstrator, McLennan sensed that advancement in the world of physics depended on being initiated into its deeper mysteries in Europe, so he toured a number of laboratories in Great Britain and on the Continent during the summer of 1896. The experience fired his interest for research, but he did not know where to begin. Like English-speaking men the world over, he resolved to study with J. J. Thomson at Cambridge. But in 1897 his father died. He pleaded with his mother for the year in England; she consented, and he left in June 1898. He stayed at the Cavendish for a year, but funds were insufficient to allow him the second year of residence required for a Cambridge B.A.

Upon his return to Toronto, McLennan began research in radioactivity. A paper on electrical conductivity in gases traversed by cathode rays appeared in the *Philosophical Transactions of the Royal Society*; Wilhelm Ostwald had it translated for his *Zeitschrift für physikalische Chemie*. Another minor piece was published in Canada. These articles were sufficient for the University of Toronto to award McLennan a Ph.D.—the doctorate then generally being reserved by Canadian universities as a reward for assiduous faculty members. A few more short publications followed until, in 1903, McLennan and Eli Franklin Burton observed radiation in the atmosphere. They, like other researchers who noticed the phenomenon, did not identify it as penetrating radiation—the cosmic rays of Viktor Hess and Jacob Clay.

McLennan came to direct physics at Canada's premier twentieth-century university through the offices of his patron, President Loudon. Around 1900, at Loudon's behest, McLennan took command of the university's alumni association. The university was controlled by the provincial government; McLennan guided the alumni to pressure the government to take over the financing of four science departments and to construct new buildings, among them an impressive physics laboratory, during the next seven years. McLennan rode the crest of Loudon's wave: in 1902 he became associate professor, and in 1904 he advanced to direct the physics laboratory. When Loudon finally retired in 1906, his chair went, as expected, to McLennan, in 1907.

Once in charge of his own destiny, McLennan began to produce research articles on radioactivity, spectroscopy, and cryogenics. His principal investigations concerned extracting helium from natural gas, low-temperature superconductivity, and demonstrating that the auroral green line was due to excited oxygen. Most of his research was undertaken with students, some of whom later made their mark in the field: Gordon Merritt Shrum, who worked with McLennan on liquid helium and on the aurora; Charles Seymour Wright, who accompanied Robert Falcon Scott to the South Pole; physicist David Arnold Keys at McGill; and McLennan's successor at Toronto, E. F. Burton. McLennan's style did not endear him to his students—for instance, he cabled the first news of the auroral green line to *Nature* without indicating Shrum as a coauthor. It is questionable whether he had a hand in all the research that appeared under his name or, indeed, whether much of the research had permanent value. Nevertheless, the results propelled him to become, in the 1920's, the most visible and productive physicist outside Europe and the United States.

Toronto was where McLennan felt at home. His family lived in Stratford, close at hand; in 1901 his sister Jean married William Arthur Parks, a geology instructor at Toronto. (He had no close relationship with his brother, an unsuccessful entrepreneur.) In 1910 McLennan married Elsie Monro Ramsay, the daughter of a wealthy merchant. By 1914 he was beginning to receive calls to British universities: Birmingham, Sheffield, Newcastle, Aberdeen, Glasgow, Belfast, and Bristol. He was tempted by John Henry Poynting's chair at Birmingham and, later, by one at Bristol, but in the end he declined to leave Toronto, where his scientific reputation and his political position seemed unassailable, and his research facilities were all that he could ask for. The usual imperial honors came his way: fellow of the Royal Society in 1915; Order of the British Empire in 1917 for antisubmarine and dirigible research during the war.

McLennan's success was crowned in 1930 by his being named dean of the Graduate School at Toronto. He set out to invest his school with central authority for research and research funding. The various departments rebelled and forced his resignation as dean two years later. McLennan took the occasion to retire to private life in England the same year. He was suffering from heart trouble, and his wife's health was not robust. He and his wife (they had no children) built a house in Surrey, and McLennan commuted to London, where he worked on cancer therapy at the Radium Institute. The pleasures of McLennan's new life were cut short in 1933 with the death of his wife. In 1935 he was knighted—a distinction then conferred on Canadians if they resided in England. Sir John savored his title for four months. He died on a train in France while returning from a meeting of the International Bureau of Weights and Measures, on whose council he sat as the representative of the British Empire.

BIBLIOGRAPHY

I. ORIGINAL WORKS. A list of McLennan's publications is in the biography by Langton (see below). Papers collected by McLennan's sister, Janet, are in the archives of the University of Toronto. Letters are in the Rutherford scientific correspondence (Cambridge and Montreal) and in the archives of McGill University, Montreal.

II. SECONDARY LITERATURE. The standard biography is Hugh Hornby Langton, *Sir John Cunningham McLennan: A Memoir* (Toronto, 1939), by a former librarian at the University of Toronto; it includes a short discussion by E. F. Burton as well as the list of publications mentioned above. Obituaries are in publications of the Royal Societies of London and of Canada. See also Lewis Pyenson and Milan Singh, "Physics on the Periphery: A World Survey, 1920–1929," in *Scientometrics*, **6** (1984), 279–306.

LEWIS PYENSON

MACLEOD, COLIN MUNRO (*b.* Port Hastings, Nova Scotia, Canada, 28 February 1909; *d.* London, England, 11 February 1972), *microbiology, medicine.*

The son of a Presbyterian minister, MacLeod

spent his youth in Canada, where the family lived a rather unsettled life moving between Nova Scotia, Saskatchewan, and Quebec. As a child prodigy he left secondary school in Richmond, Quebec, at the age of fifteen, but returned to teach there until he was old enough to enter medical school. At the age of twenty-three he received his medical degree at McGill University. Two years later, in 1934, he began medical research in New York City, where he was attached to the Pneumonia Service directed by Rufus Cole and O. T. Avery in the Rockefeller Institute Hospital. In 1938 he married Elizabeth Randol; they had one daughter.

Possibly MacLeod had been attracted to the idea of research at the Rockefeller Institute by his old friend Martin Henry Dawson, who worked there on bacterial transformation in 1928 and 1929. Certainly MacLeod had read F. Griffith's famous paper describing bacterial transformation while he was a medical student at McGill.[1] On his arrival in New York he quickly settled to the task of repeating the experiments of Dawson and of J. L. Alloway. The former had achieved in vitro transformation, but with dead intact cells; the latter successfully substituted cell extracts for entire cells.

After three years devoted to this topic MacLeod had greatly improved the experimental procedures but had not made sufficient progress toward characterizing the transforming principle to justify publication. Discouraged, he dropped this research in order to collaborate with Frank Horsfall and Kenneth Goodner in their development of the antiserum treatment of pneumococcal pneumonia. No sooner had MacLeod switched to serum therapy than the superiority of chemotherapy over serum therapy began to emerge with the introduction of the sulfonamides. He promptly turned to the testing of sulfapyridine against pneumococcal infections and reported on the unpleasant side effects of this drug, which included nausea, vomiting, and the appearance of skin rashes. He also reported the development of drug resistance both in the host and in the test tube. Type I pneumococcus, he said,

> can be adapted to growth in increasing concentrations of sulfapyridine until finally it will multiply freely in concentrations of the drug which inhibit the growth of organisms not so accustomed. Throughout the procedure of adaptation the pneumococcus retains not only its type-specific capsule but its virulence as well. This "drug-fast" strain, unlike the parent strain from which it was derived, does not respond to the therapeutic effect of sulfapyridine in experimental infections.[2]

MacLeod was describing this phenomenon in the language of the 1930's, which assumed that bacteria acquire new adaptive characters in a Lamarckian fashion.

These studies were followed by an attempt, in collaboration with Avery, to identify the mysterious substance produced in the blood of patients with acute pneumonia infections. They called it the "C-reactive protein," but why it is produced and what function it serves have remained an enigma. At this stage (1940) Avery and MacLeod judged it was time to return to bacterial transformation. Although in 1941 MacLeod left the Rockefeller Institute Hospital to become chairman of the Department of Microbiology at the New York University School of Medicine, he continued to follow the research that Maclyn McCarty took over on his arrival at the institute that year, and MacLeod's name appeared as a coauthor on the world-famous paper (1944) describing the identification of the transforming principle.

The phenomenon of bacterial transformation was something of an oddity. Strains of pneumococcus had been grouped into a number of "types" based on their immunological reactions and the differing constitutions of their sugary protective coats or capsules. They could lose their coats to become "rough" (on account of the appearance of their colonies), and they could revert to the capsular form that produced "smooth" colonies. Such spontaneous reversion from R to S was always to the same capsular type. However, cultured with the dead cells of an S pneumococcus of another type, R cells could acquire the capsules of the dead type; they could be "transformed."

Before MacLeod entered the field, the process of transformation, although in vitro, was erratic, and quantitative estimates of transforming activity were unreliable. MacLeod isolated a particular R strain of the type II pneumococcus ($R36$) that had no tendency to spontaneous reversion to S and was very susceptible to transformation by other pneumococcal types. He also improved the medium, heating the chest fluid to inactivate enzymes that destroyed the transforming principle, and adapted the operations for achieving transformation on a large scale. As Walsh McDermott remarked, MacLeod "had taken an almost formless, erratic phenomenon and made it into something predictable and measurable."[3] He had also achieved a scale of production sufficient for the isolation and chemical identification of the transforming principle.

MacLeod left the institute reluctantly. His appointment as an assistant resident physician and assistant in medicine had not been a tenured one. When the offer from New York University came, the institute's director, Thomas Rivers, urged MacLeod to accept, for, as McCarty discovered later, Rivers was about to bring Frank Horsfall back to the institute as a full member to succeed Avery as director of the Pneumonia Service. Hence it was with some secret chagrin that MacLeod saw the transformation work taken up by McCarty in his place.

At the time of MacLeod's departure from the institute, Avery had come to the conclusion that RNA, or yeast nucleic acid as it was then called, though a prominent component of pneumococcal cells, was not necessary for transformation, but that the active extract contained a little DNA. MacLeod, however, made no mention of DNA in his 1941 report to the board of science directors of the institute. Instead he pursued the alleged need for some of the specific soluble substance (the polysaccharide of the donor cell capsule) to be present to "prime" the enzyme produced as a result of transformation. Moreover, the success of transformation was still very variable due to the many factors influencing the process. After MacLeod left the institute, McCarty showed conclusively that carbohydrate was necessary for transformation, and gradually during 1942, together with Avery and MacLeod, he came to the conclusion that the active substance was DNA. They described it in 1944 as a "highly polymerized and viscous form of sodium desoxyribonucleate."[4]

During the fifteen years MacLeod spent at New York University he established an effective program of basic research in the medical school. In 1956 he became John Herr Musser Professor of Research Medicine at the University of Pennsylvania, and in 1960 he returned to New York University as professor of medicine. Finally, MacLeod became vice president for medical affairs of the Commonwealth Fund.

From the entry of the United States into World War II, MacLeod served as a science adviser to the U.S. War Department, becoming president of the Army Epidemiology Board in 1945 and of the subsequently enlarged board for all the armed forces from 1949 until 1955. He also advised the National Institutes of Health, the president's Science Advisory Committee, and the executive office of presidents Kennedy and Johnson. Among his many tasks as a science adviser were his direction of the U.S.–Japan cooperative program in the medical sciences and his chairmanship of the technical committee of the Cholera Research Laboratory in Dacca, India, which had been set up by the South East Asia

Treaty Organization. It was while on his way to Dacca in 1972 that he died.

NOTES

1. F. Griffith, "The Significance of Pneumococcal Types," in *Journal of Hygiene*, **27** (1928), 113–159.
2. MacLeod, "Chemotherapy of Pneumococcic Pneumonia," in *Journal of the American Medical Association*, **113** (1939), 1405.
3. McDermott, "Colin Munro MacLeod," in *Biographical Memoirs. National Academy of Sciences*, **54** (1983), 187.
4. Avery, MacLeod, and McCarty, "Studies on the Chemical Nature of the Substance Inducing Transformation of Pneumococcal Types," in *Journal of Experimental Medicine*, **79** (1944), 152.

BIBLIOGRAPHY

I. ORIGINAL WORKS. In his biographical memoir given below Walsh McDermott lists forty-five papers. Seventeen of these appeared in the *Journal of Experimental Medicine* and five in the *Proceedings of the Society for Experimental Biology and Medicine*. The remainder were scattered among a number of medical journals.

II. SECONDARY LITERATURE. The most detailed obituary is by Walsh McDermott in *Biographical Memoirs. National Academy of Sciences*, **54** (1983), 183–219. Maclyn McCarty wrote two obituaries, to be found in the *Yearbook of the American Philosophical Society*, (1972), 222–230, and in the *Transactions of the Association of American Physicians*, **85** (1972), 31–34. MacLeod's lifelong friend and collaborator, R. Austrian, wrote an obituary in *Journal of Infectious Diseases*, **127** (1973), 211–214. MacLeod's contribution to the work on bacterial transformation is discussed in René J. Dubos, *The Professor, the Institute, and DNA* (New York, 1976), and in Maclyn McCarty, *Transforming Principle: Discovering that Genes are Made of DNA* (New York, 1985).

ROBERT OLBY

MAGNUS-LEVY, ADOLF (*b.* Berlin, Germany, 9 September 1865; *d.* New York City, 5 February 1955), *medicine, physiology.*

Magnus-Levy pioneered the study of human metabolism and its relation to such diseases as diabetes, goiter, and multiple myeloma, and applied studies of energy exchange to clinical medicine. An early interest in history was abandoned in order to pursue medical studies at Berlin, Tübingen, Leipzig, Heidelberg, and Freiburg, but he was disappointed at the heavy emphasis on morphology and pathology at these schools. He ultimately concluded that anatomy dealt only with the sites of physiological processes, without seeking an understanding of the role of those processes in health and disease. Only the physiology lectures of Carl Ludwig at Leipzig from 1886 to 1888 stimulated Magnus-Levy to realize that he sought enlightenment through the understanding of physiological processes.

After receiving the M.D. at Heidelberg in 1890, Magnus-Levy sought to study analytical methods, first with Nathan Zuntz at Berlin, where he gained experience in gas analysis and the study of energy exchange. At Freiburg, with Eugen Baumann, he participated in the chemical analysis of thyroid extract. He completed his studies at Erlangen, where he was awarded the Ph.D. in 1893.

Magnus-Levy spent most of the next decade as a clinical assistant, first at the Urban Hospital in Berlin, where he worked in association with Albert Fränkel, who by 1884 had discovered the pneumococcus (*Diplococcus pneumoniae*). Here he gained valuable clinical experience while focusing on metabolic problems. After two years he moved to Frankfurt-am-Main to join Carl von Noorden, who investigated nutritional problems, particularly those connected with diabetes. At this time Magnus-Levy equipped a personal laboratory and initiated studies on energy relationships in patients with diabetes, with myxedema, and with obesity problems. Pursuing suggestions made by others in connection with exophthalmic goiter, he showed that to treat goiter, metabolism must be increased, and that the weight reduction produced in obese patients when they were given thyroid extract was attributable to the increased use of energy. A paper on respiratory metabolism under the influence of the thyroid and in various pathological conditions, published in 1895, brought him an offer to further his studies at the Strassburg Clinic.

The clinic, under the leadership of Bernard Naunyn, was doing important studies on diabetes and gallstones. It was there, in 1889, that Oscar Minkowski and Joseph von Mering had demonstrated the importance of the pancreas in carbohydrate metabolism.

At Strassburg, Magnus-Levy focused on the extreme diabetic condition known as acidosis and associated with acetone on the breath an almost acidic reaction of the blood. He was successful in isolating beta-hydroxybutyric acid as a principal component of diabetic blood under conditions of acidosis. Along with a number of investigators he concluded that fatty acid oxidation is incomplete in diabetes, stopping with the formation of modified butyric acids instead of continuing to conversion into carbon dioxide and water. His *Habilitationsschrift,* "Oxybutyric Acid and Its Relation to the Diabetic

Coma," led to his promotion to *Privatdozent* in 1899.

In 1901 Magnus-Levy returned to Berlin, where he established a limited private practice that supported the continuation of his metabolic studies. He was granted a titular professorship at the University of Berlin Medical School in 1905; this involved no time-consuming obligations, however, so he was able to restrict his activities primarily to research in his private laboratory. In 1910 he was made chief of medical service of Urban Hospital in Berlin. In 1921 he was married; soon after his marriage, he resigned the hospital post in order to have more time for private practice and research and for his wife and two daughters.

Magnus-Levy's research included a broad spectrum of metabolic problems. In his early work he used the concept of basal metabolic rate (BMR) to deal with fundamental metabolic conditions free of extraordinary stress conditions. This was extended to metabolic changes in normal health and in various disease states.

Magnus-Levy was one of the first physiologists to give careful attention to the metabolism of electrolytes present in human organs: carbonate, chloride, sodium, potassium, magnesium, calcium, and iron ions. Attention was also given to the metabolic role of water and proteins. He had a strong interest in the behavior of Bence-Jones proteins, especially in connection with multiple myeloma, a form of cancer of the bone marrow.

Except for the period with Naunyn at Strassburg, Magnus-Levy's research was carried out independently, without university support and without collaborators. In Berlin his friend Wilhelm His, Jr., director of the Charité Clinic, provided space in a small laboratory where he continued metabolic studies into the 1930's.

Magnus-Levy prized his independence and was critical of the departure of younger medical investigators from the traditions of earlier physiologists who had worked in what he considered to be the heroic age of medical research. He was an uncompromising critic of physicians who were content to ignore the emerging science of medicine, continuing to look upon medicine as an art.

Because the family was Jewish, their lives were placed in serious jeopardy as a result of the rise to power of the Nazis in Germany. Magnus-Levy lost the use of the hospital laboratory and his titular professorship at the university. Although he continued his research privately, he was denied the right to publish in German medical journals. His classical research on multiple myeloma was published in *Acta medica scandinavica* in 1938. In 1940 he and his family went to America. John Fulton provided a position for him in the Physiology and History of Medicine Departments at Yale University. After five years he retired to New York City, where he pursued his lifelong interest in German literature until his death in his ninetieth year. He was survived by his two daughters.

BIBLIOGRAPHY

I. ORIGINAL WORKS. The limited numbers of Magnus-Levy's published papers are well-crafted descriptions of his laboratory and clinical research. His first paper, written with his teacher Nathan Zuntz, was "Beiträge zur Kenntniss der Verdaulichkeit und des Nährwerthes des Brodes," in *Archiv für die gesamte Physiologie des Menschen und der Tiere*, 49 (1891), 438–459. Other early papers were "Über die Grösse des respiratorischen Gaswechsels unter dem Einfluss der Nahrungsaufnahme," *ibid.*, 52 (1892), 475–479; 55 (1893), 1–126. His interest in the thyroid gland and goiter developed early; principal papers were "Über den respiratorischen Gaswechsel unter dem Einfluss der Thyroiden sowie unter verschiedenen physiologischen Zuständen," in *Berliner klinische Wochenschrift*, 32 (1895), 650–652; "Gaswechsel und Fettumsatz bei Myxödem und Schilddrüsenfütterung," in *Verhandlungen des Kongresses für innere Medizin* (Wiesbaden), 14 (1896), 137–165; "Versuche mit Thyreoantitoxin und Thyrojodin," in *Deutsche medizinische Wochenschrift*," 22 (1896), 393–396; "Über Organtherapie beim endemischen Kretismus," in *Berliner klinische Wochenschrift*, 40 (1903), 733–735; "Über Myxödem," in *Zeitschrift für klinische Medizin*, 52 (1904), 201–256. Gout was investigated in "Beiträge zum Stoffwechsel bei Gicht," in *Berliner klinische Wochenschrift*, 33 (1896), 416–418; "Über Aufgaben und Bedeutung von Respirationsversuchen für die Pathologie des Stoffwechsels," in *Zeitschrift für klinische Medizin*, 33 (1897), 258–268; "Über Gicht. klinische Beobachtungen, chemische Blutuntersuchungen und Stoffwechselversuche," *ibid.*, 36 (1898–1899), 353–416; "Harnsäuregehalt und Alkaleszenz des Blutes in der Gicht," in *Verhandlungen des Kongresses für innere Medizin*, (Wiesbaden), 16 (1898), 266–270. In 1910 Magnus-Levy was invited to the United States to deliver the Harvey Lecture, which was subsequently published by the Harvey Society, "Uric Acid in Gout," *The Harvey Lectures* 5th series (Philadelphia, 1910), 251–276.

His early interst in energy and mineral metabolism and composition of body fluids led him to pursue investigations relevant to diseases associated with hormone-related illness. Among these are "Untersuchungen zur Schilddrüsenfrage und Stoffwechseluntersuchungenfrage bei Schilddrüsenfütterung," *ibid.*, 33 (1897), 269–314; "Über den Stoffwechsel bei akuter und chronischer Leukämie," in *Archiv für pathologische Anatomie und Physiologie und für klinische Medizin*, 152 (1898), 107–130; "Der Einfluss von Krankheiten auf den Energiehaushalt im Ruhestand," in *Zeitschrift für klinische Medizin*, 60 (1906), 177–224; "Über Paarung der Glukuronsäure mit optischen Antipoden," in *Biochemische Zeitschrift*, 2 (1907), 319–331; "Der Mineralstoffwechsel in der klinischen Pathologie," in *Verhandlung des Kongresses für innere Medizin* (Wiesbaden) (1909), 15–42; "Über den Gehalt normaler menschlicher Organe an Chlor, Calcium, Magnesium, und Eisen sowie an Wasser, Eiweiss und Fett," in *Biochemische Zeitschrift*, 24 (1910), 363–380; "Über den Mineralstoffgehalt einiger Exsudate und Transsudate," in *Zeitschrift für klinische Medizin*, 88 (1919), 1–8.

An early interest in proteins, particularly in their modification in multiple myeloma (a tumor of bone marrow), led him to pursue specific studies. Noteworthy is "Über den Bence-Jones' schern Eiweisskörper," in *Zeitschrift für physiologische Chemie*, 30 (1900), 200–240; slightly peripheral were his studies on the role of amino acids in the elimination of benzoic acid in the urine as hippuric acid: "Über die Herkunft des Glykokols in der Hippursäure; ein Beitrag zur Frage des Eiweissabbaues im Organismus," in *Münchner medizinische Wochenschrift*, 52 (1905), 2168–2170; "Über das Auftreten einer Benzoesäure-Glukuronsäureverbindung im Hammelharn nach Benzoesäure-Fütterung," in *Biochemische Zeitschrift*, 6 (1907), 502–522; "Über die Neubildung von Glykokoll. Studien zur Hippursäurefrage," *ibid.*, 523–540; "Über das Verhalten benzoylierter Aminosäuren im Organismus," *ibid.*, 541–554; "Über das Verhalten formulierter Aminosäuren im Organismus," *ibid.*, 555–558.

Magnus-Levy's interests in diabetes spanned much of his career. Among his publications on this topic are "Untersuchungen über die Acidosis im Diabetes mellitus und die Säureintoxication im Coma diabeticum," in *Archiv für experimentelle Pathologie und Pharmakologie*, 45 (1901), 389–434; "Über ätherlösliche Säuren im normalen Urin," in *Beiträge zur wissenschaftlichen Medizin und Chemie. Festschrift . . . Ernst Salkowski* (Berlin, 1904), 253–262; "Respirationsversuche an diabetischen Menschen," in *Zeitschrift für klinische Medizin*, 56 (1905), 89–99; "Chylurie und Diabetes," in *Zeitschrift für klinische Medizin*, 66 (1908–1909), 524–526; "Über Diabetiken-Gebäcke des Handels. Zusammensetzung und Anwendung," in *Berliner klinische Wochenschrift*, 47 (1910), 233–238; "On Diabetic Acidosis," *Johns Hopkins Medical Bulletin*, 22 (1911), 46–52; "Über den Diabetes im Krieg," *ibid.*, 1150; "Über Haferkuren bei Diabetes mellitus," *ibid.*, 48 (1911), 213–217; "Das Insulinproblem und die Theorie des Diabetes," *Deutsche medizinische Wochenschrift*, 50 (1924), 494–496. Much of his later career focused on body fluids and multiple myeloma; see "Von Basen und Säuren beim kranken Menschen," in *Deutsche medizinische Wochenschrift*, 56 (1930), 571, 609; "Ein neuer Typus der Phosphaturie mit hoher Ammoniakaustreibung," in *Zeitschrift für klinische Medizin*, 115 (1930), 1–12; "Bence-Jones-Eiweiss und Amyloid," *ibid.*, 116 (1931), 501–531; "Über die Myelomkrankheit, vom Stoffwechsel der Bence-Jones-Proteinurie," in *Zeitschrift für klinische Medizin,* **119** (1932), 307–362; "Multiple Myeloma, der Stoffwechsel ausserhalb der Proteinurie," *ibid.,* **120** (1932), 313–320; "Über die Myelomkrankheit: Beiträge zur Klinik und Pathologie," *ibid.,* **121** (1932), 533–562; "Multiple Myeloma," *Acta medica Scandinavica,* **95** (1938), 217–280.

While Magnus-Levy was at Yale he prepared a historical study, "Energy Metabolism in Health and Disease," in *Journal of the History of Medicine and Allied Sciences,* **2** (1947), 307–320.

II. SECONDARY LITERATURE. The principal obituaries are Martin G. Goldner, "Adolf Magnus-Levy, 1865–1955," in *Diabetes,* **4** (1955), 422–424; G. Haller, *Deutsche medizinische Wochenschrift,* **80** (1955), 729; I. Zadek, *Münchener medizinische Wochenschrift,* **79** (1955), 834–835.

AARON J. IHDE

MARRACK, JOHN RICHARDSON (*b.* Clevedon, Somerset, England, 26 November 1886; *d.* Houston, Texas, 13 June 1976), *immunology, chemical pathology, nutrition.*

Marrack, the second son of the three sons and one daughter of John Read Marrack, a mathematics teacher, and of Mary Saunders, was educated at Blundell's School in Tiverton, Devon. The school left a lasting impression on him, for it was there that his interest in the chemistry of biological phenomena began—sparked, so he said, when he heard of Friedrich Wöhler's synthesis of urea. He decided to study medicine in order to make a living from this interest. Marrack went up to St. John's College, Cambridge, on a mathematics scholarship and took a first in part I of the natural sciences tripos and a second in part II. He went on to the London Hospital Medical College as a Price Scholar for the clinical part of his studies.

A tough and vigorous man, Marrack played rugby for the hospital for about ten years, and represented it in wrestling and boxing. He was runner-up in the interhospital competition as a middleweight in 1910 and won the welterweight championship in 1912, holding it for the next seven years. His boxing came in handy when, at about the age of fifty, he was attacked by a gang that, it was said, had to be taken to the hospital in an ambulance. Throughout his life he loved cycling and walking.

Marrack completed his medical studies at Cambridge in 1912 with an M.A. and an M.D. Postgraduate honors included the John Lucas Walker Studentship, which supported his first research project, on rheumatoid arthritis, a disease from which his father had suffered. He also held the Beit Memorial Fellowship for Medical Research, which enabled him to work in the laboratories of the Cambridge Research Hospital (now the Strangeways Laboratory).

Marrack joined the Royal Army Medical Corps during World War I, serving as battalion medical officer and bearer officer. He suffered a fractured femur at Ypres, was twice mentioned in dispatches, and was awarded the Distinguished Service Order and the Military Cross. In 1917 he transferred to work on the military uses of poison gases, and he ended the war in charge of a mobile pathology laboratory specializing in gas warfare.

After the war Marrack returned to Cambridge as lecturer in chemical pathology, but soon resigned to accept a post at London Hospital Medical College as lecturer and chemical pathologist. He was appointed professor in 1934. Marrack remained at the Hale Clinical Laboratories of London Hospital until his retirement in 1952.

In 1913 Marrack married Bertha Ada Fitzgerald Whiddington, whom he divorced in 1921; they had one son. His second marriage, in 1922, was to Alice May Swaffield Milward. Their three sons followed their father into medicine, starting, as he had done, from the London Hospital.

Marrack's first years as lecturer were taken up with teaching and organizing routine services for the hospital. At the same time he collaborated with hospital clinicians and with the hospital's morbid anatomist, Dorothy Russell, on problems such as the chemical changes in nephritis. His superior, Philip Noel Panton, director of the hospital's laboratories, was the author of a textbook of clinical pathology that had appeared in 1913, and it was among Marrack's duties to help him update it for successive editions. For the historian of immunology, the chapter "Immunity" of the (fourth) 1939 edition is a neat compendium of practical immunology or serology of the period. "Panton & Marrack," as it was known, gives details of vaccines for localized infections using *Staphylococci* and *Gonococci,* chronic nasal discharge, and even Robert Koch's tuberculin preparation. Koch's treatment is usually supposed by historians to have been discredited about 1900, soon after its introduction; Panton & Marrack says in 1939 that its use is "declining." Much space is given to technical details of the Wassermann and Kahn tests for syphilis and their interpretation. Indeed, the word serology was often used to mean just those tests.

Clinical pathology in the early part of the century, under the voluntary hospital system, suffered from a lack of status and funding compared with clinical medicine. The London Hospital was unusually lucky in that it had been given an anonymous gift of £50,000 for medical research. Marrack therefore had the opportunity to do research as well as teaching and routine work. After some preliminary work on the physical chemistry of proteins, he began the series of papers on the antigen-antibody reaction that was to be his main interest.

The immunochemistry of the first half of the twentieth century derived from the practical problems with the assay of the diphtheria antiserum, introduced into medical practice in 1894. Much of the work centered on the reaction of diphtheria toxin and antitoxin. Conflicting views of this reaction had been proposed by Paul Ehrlich and by Jules Bordet around the turn of the century. Ehrlich's theory claimed that the reaction was a purely chemical one, and Bordet's that it was a physical adsorption of one component upon the other. Physical adsorption meant that the reaction was one of those typical of colloid chemistry, dependent on surface phenomena rather than on the chemical nature of the reactants. Bordet himself, and also Svante Arrhenius and Thorvald Madsen, later suggested a reversible acid-base neutralization as a model for the reaction. The work of Karl Landsteiner started from an opposition to Ehrlich's point of view. By 1918 he had found evidence that antigenic specificity depends on the charge outline of an antigen, thus implicating both surface phenomena and the chemical nature of the antigen.

Marrack's work on immunochemistry began in the late 1920's, and focused on the antigen-antibody reaction and its interpretation. His first series of experiments showed that the precipitate formed by diphtheria toxin and antitoxin is mostly antitoxin, and that the antitoxin is composed of serum globulin. Quantitative tests showed that increasing amounts of antigen resulted in an increase in the proportion of antigen in the complexes. Similar findings were made by Michael Heidelberger and Frank Kendall in New York. In 1934 Marrack summed up existing knowledge of the problem in *The Chemistry of Antigens and Antibodies*. Here he proposed a new model for the reaction, that of a crystal lattice, the relationship between antigen and antibody being like that between the molecules in a crystal. They were linked not by true chemical valencies, as Ehrlich's theory had it, but by the short-range forces that surround a molecule, the same forces that determine the specific selection of molecules built into a crystal. The reaction was less specific than crystal formation, however, because the fit had to cover only a small depression and not a whole molecule. Marrack suggested that if the antibody, like the antigen, had more than one binding site, the antigen-

antibody complexes would bind together in the form of a lattice. The theory accounted for immune precipitation in that the polar groups of the globulin, on which its solubility depended, attracted each other instead of water, and so allowed the formation of an aggregate that came out of solution. Heidelberger and Kendall followed this up with a more fully worked out quantitative version of the lattice concept, summarized in a review of 1939.

Marrack continued to work on the antigen-antibody reaction, designing experiments with various junior collaborators to answer questions on the conditions affecting the precipitin reaction and the phenomena, such as that known as zoning, connected with it, which he explained by means of the lattice theory. His year of greatest productivity was 1938, when four of his substantial papers appeared in *British Journal of Experimental Pathology*, and he published the second edition of *Antigens and Antibodies* as well as a review.

Marrack's suggestion that there were two binding sites on precipitating antibodies received support in 1940 when A. M. Pappenheimer found a nonprecipitating antibody that nevertheless bound to its antigen. He called this "incomplete" antibody. Based upon the lattice theory, Pappenheimer, and Heidelberger and Kendall, proposed that this type of antibody was probably monovalent. Marrack himself resisted this interpretation. He preferred, he said, to make no assumptions about valency, but to regard antibodies of different types as having different biological functions. He continued to feel that the failure to precipitate was caused by the antigen-antibody complex's not having lost its attraction for water. As Marrack wrote in 1951, the incomplete antibodies remained a nuisance in practice and no more than an academic interest in theory, until the early 1940's, when they were shown to be produced by immunization to the Rhesus blood groups, and to be responsible for *Erythroblastosis foetalis*, hemolytic disease of the newborn. The relation of incompleteness to the nature of the antibody and to its biological function began to be resolved in the 1960's, when Rodney Porter's models elucidated the chain structure of the globulin molecule. Incomplete antibody was not monovalent; it had two binding sites.

The 1930's was a period of political activism for Marrack. He belonged to the well-known group of left-wing scientists that included Lancelot Hogben, J. B. S. Haldane, J. D. Bernal, and J. G. Crowther. At first a Liberal, he joined the Communist party in the early 1930's, at about the same time that many of his colleagues and friends became Marxists, but he resigned in 1937 over a question of policy, just before Haldane became a member. Even after the break, he remained a close friend of Harry Pollitt, the party secretary. During the Spanish Civil War he was secretary of the Spanish Medical Aid Committee and was with the International Brigade at the siege of Barcelona.

Marrack also became concerned with food and welfare, at a time when nutrition and food supply were matters of growing interest in scientific and political circles. Reports on nutrition were brought out by both the Medical Research Council and the British Medical Association. The scientists of the left, including Marrack, began to agitate for a national food distribution policy. He was in touch with the Cambridge group led by L. J. Harris, whose program of nutrition surveys, started in the early 1930's, used Marrack's expertise as a chemical pathologist in the design of urine tests that would detect the partial nutritional deficiency the group felt was very common among the less well-off. Along with Hogben, Marrack began in the mid 1930's to prepare in a practical way for food shortages in what they both felt was the coming war against fascism. He and his family dug up their large garden to grow vegetables.

The outbreak of World War II made state control of food distribution an urgent necessity in Britain. Marrack's *Food and Planning* (1942) discusses not only the dietary requirements but also the history of food planning and the nutrition of populations during World War I in Britain and Europe, and it proposes postwar "planning for plenty," a phrase that echoes Hogben's "planning for an age of plenty." Marrack argued for state control of food production and distribution under the direction of a supranational authority. In 1943 he was appointed director of the Bureau of Nutrition surveys, and he continued to work along these lines for some years after the war. His contributions in this field were aimed at organizing and explaining the data on food requirements from a policymaking point of view.

Marrack's immunochemistry work was interrupted during World War II—again his knowledge of gas warfare was called upon—but in 1950 he resumed his work on the physicochemical parameters of the antigen-antibody reaction with young collaborators.

In 1958, at the age of seventy-two, Marrack undertook the founding editorship of *Immunology*, the official organ of the British Society for Immunology; he resigned five years later. When he retired, the new editor shared some of his editorial functions among a group of editorial advisers, experts in different fields. His last paper, the fruit of a visiting professorship at the University of Texas M. D. Anderson Hospital and Tumor Institute in Houston, published in 1972, concerned the application of a new physical method to the problem of the formation of the antigen-antibody complex.

In 1971, at the First International Congress of Immunology, Marrack was one of five senior workers to receive a Distinguished Service Award. His citation read: "For revolutionary ideas that have become commonplace in his lifetime, and for pioneering work in the physicochemical interpretation of antigen-antibody interactions." Marrack's work, however, was not really revolutionary. His thinking remained within the perimeter marked out by Landsteiner's conception of the physicochemical nature of specificity. His experimental work was well regarded and often cited, but it was perhaps his reviews that had most influence on the field. *Antigens and Antibodies* was an organized account of a new and complex subject, difficult to grasp from the primary literature. It was the introduction to the field for many who later became leading immunologists, thereby contributing to the acceptance of Landsteiner's view on the nature of specificity. Marrack noted in a 1942 review that immunochemistry was changing. In the years between the wars, it had been concerned mainly with the relation of specificity to chemical structure, and the nature of the antigen-antibody reaction. In 1942 he saw that it had begun to focus more on protein chemistry and the nature of the antibody molecule. Marrack changed with the times: some of his papers of the 1950's and 1960's did deal with molecular fragments. But *Antigens and Antibodies* had appeared at just the right moment to summarize the thinking of its era. Up to now, little of that thinking has been superseded: fifty years after its last edition, it still is often cited.

BIBLIOGRAPHY

I. ORIGINAL WORKS. Marrack published nearly ninety articles and three books. The most important book was *The Chemistry of Antigens and Antibodies* (London, 1934; 2nd ed., 1938). His main papers include "The Composition of Diphtheria Toxin-Antitoxin Floccules," in *Proceedings of the Royal Society*, **B106** (1930), 1–19, with Frank C. Smith; "Diphtheria Toxin-Antitoxin Floccules," in *British Journal of Experimental Pathology*, **11** (1930), 492–494, with Frank C. Smith; "Quantitative Aspects of Immunity Reactions: The Precipitin Reaction," *ibid.*, **12** (1931), 30–35, with Frank C. Smith; "Quantitative Aspects of Immunity Reactions: The Combination of Antibodies with Simple Haptens," *ibid.*, **13** (1932), 394–402, with Frank C. Smith; and "Derived Antigens as a Means of Studying the Relation of Specific Combination to Chemical Structure," in *Proceedings of the Royal Medical Society*, **27** (1934), 1063–1065, with Frank C. Smith. In 1938 he produced "Cross-reactions of Vegetable Gums with Type II Anti-*Pneumococcus* Serum," in *British Journal of Experimental Pathology*, **19** (1938), 53–65, with Blanche R. Carpenter; "Immunological Behaviour of Fractions of Serum Globulin," *ibid.*, 171–178, with Dora A. Duff; "Surface Films of Antigens and Antibodies. I. The Effect of Spreading on a Water Surface on the Specific Properties of Pneumococcal (Type II) Antibody and Horse Serum Globulin," *ibid.*, 393–396, with J. F. Danielli and Mary Danielli; "Effects of Increased Salt Concentration on the Amount of Precipitate Formed by Antisera with Specific Precipitant," *ibid.*, 424–433, with Helga F. Hollering; and "Immunochemistry and Its Relation to Enzymes," in *Ergebnisse der Enzymeforschung*, **7** (1938), 281–300.

Marrack also wrote a number of shorter reviews on subjects connected with the antigen-antibody reaction. They include "Immunochemistry," in *Annual Review of Biochemistry*, **11** (1942), 629–658; "The Biological Significance of Complete and Incomplete Antibodies," in *International Archives of Allergy and Immunology*, **2** (1951), 264–273; "Forty Years of Immunochemistry," *ibid.*, **5** (1954), 192–197; and "Structure of Antigen-Antibody Aggregates and Complement Fixation," in *Annual Review of Microbiology*, **9** (1955), 369–386.

Marrack's work on nutrition includes "A National Food Policy," in *Labour Monthly*, **20** (1938), 502–507; "Food in Wartime: Free Basic Ration—or Higher Wages," in *Medicine Today & Tomorrow*, **2** (1940), 2–9; *Food and Planning* (London, 1942; 2nd ed., 1944); "Modern Views on Diet," in *Practitioner*, **151** (1943), 277–290; "Standards for Food Requirements," *ibid.*, **155** (1945), 129–153; and "Laboratory Investigations into the State of Nutrition," part of "Proceedings of the Nutrition Society: Forty-fifth Scientific Meeting: Results of Recent Investigations of Nutritional Status in Great Britain," in *British Journal of Nutrition*, **2** (1948), 147–158.

Most of Marrack's papers, which include an unfinished manuscript on the history and philosophy of immunology, are in the possession of his son, Dr. David Marrack, 420 Mulberry Lane, Bellaire, Texas 77401.

II. SECONDARY LITERATURE. No study of Marrack's work has yet appeared, nor is there a full bibliography in print. His lattice theory is discussed in Debra J. Bibel, *Milestones in Immunology: A Historical Exploration* (Madison, Wis., 1988), 91–94, with an excerpt from *Antigens and Antibodies*. Obituaries and short biographical articles include Rosa Augustin, "Editorial: Professor J. R. Marrack, M.D., D.S.O., M.C.," in *Immunology*, **6** (1963), 1–2; J. H. Humphrey, "Obituary," in *Nature*, **263** (1976), 535; F. C. O. V. and E. R. H., "Professor Marrack," in *London Hospital Gazette*, **55** (1952), 153–154; and R. G. W(hite), "John Richardson Marrack," in *Lancet* (1976), **ii**, 378.

PAULINE M. H. MAZUMDAR

MARSDEN, ERNEST (*b*. Rishton, near Blackburn, Lancashire, England, 19 February 1889; *d*. Lowry Bay, New Zealand, 15 December 1970), *atomic physics, administration.*

Ernest was the second of the five children, including four sons, of Phoebe (Holden) and Thomas Marsden, a weaver, later a draper and hardware dealer. He won scholarships to Queen Elizabeth's Grammar School in Blackburn and in 1906 to the University of Manchester, where he took the honors course in physics under Arthur Schuster and supplemented his scholarship by teaching.

In 1907, under Ernest Rutherford's influence, Marsden became interested in radioactivity. His most important research work was done as an undergraduate in Rutherford's department at the University of Manchester. Assisting Hans Geiger by counting α-particles fired down a glass tube, he found that they were diffusely reflected from the tube walls. On Rutherford's suggestion he found that α particles are scattered through large angles from a metal surface, the scattering varying with the atomic weight of the metal. From these results (1909) Rutherford conceived the nuclear theory of atomic structure (1911). Marsden completed his B.Sc. in 1909 with first-class honors, became a Hatfield Scholar at Manchester, and was then appointed lecturer in physics at East London College (1910). Returning to Manchester as John Harling Fellow (1911–1912), he continued with Geiger experiments that tested Rutherford's predictions and confirmed his conception. Marsden took part in this series of experiments, since recognized as some of the most beautiful ever performed, when he was only twenty-four years old. He succeeded Geiger as lecturer and research assistant (1912–1914) and was awarded the degree of D.Sc. in 1914.

In 1913 Marsden married Margaret Sutcliffe of Colne, Lancashire (*d*. 1957); they had a daughter and a son. In 1914, on Rutherford's recommendation, he was appointed professor of physics at Victoria University College, Wellington, New Zealand, succeeding T. H. Laby. Soon after arriving in New Zealand early in 1915, he joined the territorial forces and volunteered for overseas service with the Divisional Signals, but was transferred to the Royal Engineers sound-ranging unit in France, perfecting techniques for directing artillery fire on enemy batteries. He was twice mentioned in dispatches and awarded the Military Cross (1919).

After the war Marsden resumed his university post, showing his gift for getting what he wanted by obtaining a new physics building, and always pursuing many extramural enthusiasms. "The exhilaration and excitement," he claimed, "are always in the chase—the conclusion is invariably an anticlimax." He believed the secret of staying enthusiastic about one's work was to change jobs every decade. In 1922 he became assistant director of the New Zealand Education Department, pursuing his scientific interests in his spare time. In 1926 he assisted Sir Frank Heath, who was invited to advise the New Zealand government on the application of science to industry.

As a result of the Heath Report (1926), the government established a Department of Scientific and Industrial Research (DSIR) with Marsden as permanent secretary. He tackled the new job with enthusiasm, informality, impatience of red tape, and a warm feeling for people. The new department was created by consolidating physical science units from other state departments (Dominion Observatory, Dominion Laboratory, Geological Survey, Meteorological Service), but New Zealand's most urgent needs were biological, to serve agriculture and pastoral farming. Marsden persuaded the wheat, dairy, wool, tobacco, and hops industries that cooperative research was worthwhile and practical, establishing, with their financial support, research associations to serve their needs and interests. Plant research and soil bureaus were established; other units worked on entomology, fats research, plant chemistry, geophysical exploration, and physical testing. Marsden played a very personal role in promoting these agencies.

Although set back by economic depression in the 1930's, Marsden remained to experience the challenge of the first Labour government (1935), which increased science funding. The DSIR played a vital part in World War II in the areas of munitions production, import substitutes, dehydrated foods, and submarine detection. Marsden trained in radar production at Bawdsey Manor, England, returning to New Zealand to promote the local manufacture of radar sets used in the Pacific before United States production took over. In 1943 a chance meeting with James Chadwick and Mark Oliphant in Washington led to ten young New Zealand physicists' participating in the early years of atomic energy development.

Marsden was the right man to establish New Zealand's DSIR on a liberal basis of both basic and applied research, but for the postwar period he believed he was not the right man. Retiring from DSIR, he became scientific liaison officer in London (1947–1954), representing New Zealand at conferences and promoting renewal of oil prospecting and an iron industry from magnetic irons and ores. He delivered the Rutherford Lecture in South Africa just prior to retiring in June 1954. He continued to work for science in retirement, promoting New Zealand's participation in International Geophysical Year (IGY), Antarctic exploration, use of geothermal energy, and petroleum investigations that led to a gas-condensate industry. His main interest was in the health hazards of radiation, both natural and man made activities. In 1958 he married Joyce Winifred Chote of Wellington, who became his constant companion and assistant in such retirement interests. They traveled widely for meetings and research, and visited Taiwan, where Marsden advised on scientific development. In 1966 he suffered a stroke, but retained an interest in science although confined to a wheelchair.

Rather short in stature, Marsden had a neat, brisk figure, expressive eyes, and a penetrating mind. His voice retained a Lancashire intonation. He enjoyed good health, was genial, puckish, and full of fun, and had a zest for life and for science. His contagious enthusiasm inspired others, who were stimulated to do their best. He could readily communicate with laymen, children, and the media. He liked routine in his life, claiming that this saved the mental energy of constantly making unimportant decisions. He was gregarious and became an active member of the Rotary Club.

Ernest Marsden was appointed CBE (1935) and CMG (1946) and was knighted in 1958. His contribution to the Allied war effort won him the United States Medal of Freedom (Bronze Palms). He was a Fellow of the Royal Society of New Zealand (1921) and of the Royal Society of London (1946) and received honorary degrees from Oxford and Manchester universities and from Victoria University of Wellington.

BIBLIOGRAPHY

I. ORIGINAL WORKS. Marsden owes his reputation as an atomic physicist to about twenty papers, the majority dealing with α particles, mostly written jointly with H. Geiger, T. Barratt, C. G. Darwin, and others, between 1909 and 1915. These and other publications are listed in the memoir by C. A. Fleming in *Biographical Memoirs of Fellows of the Royal Society*, **17** (1971), 463–496. His later papers, reports, articles, and lectures cover a wide interdisciplinary spectrum, reflecting the busy life of a scientific leader and administrator whose interest in Rutherford and in radioactivity persisted. His letters and other papers are in the Alexander Turnbull Library, Wellington.

II. SECONDARY LITERATURE. *Sir Ernest Marsden, 80th Birthday Book*, P. Van Asch *et al.*, eds. (Wellington, New Zealand, 1969), includes personal anecdotes and tributes to his career and achievement. See also the biographical memoir by F. R. Callaghan in *Proceedings of the Royal Society of New Zealand*, **99** (1971), 111–125. For background on the history of experiments that supported the nuclear atom, see J. L. Heilbron, "The Scattering of Alpha and Beta Particles and Rutherford's Atom," in *Archive for History of Exact Science*, **4** (1968), 247–307.

C. A. FLEMING

MARTIN, CHARLES JAMES (*b.* Hackney, England, 9 January 1866; *d.* Chesterton, near Cambridge, England, 15 February 1955), *physiology, physiological chemistry, microbiology, nutrition.*

Following preliminary education at a boarding school in Hastings, in 1881 Martin became a junior clerk in a London life insurance company where his father worked as an actuary. Martin's growing interest in science and his admiration for his uncle, Francis Buckell, a country practitioner in Hampshire, soon led him to seek medical training. At the age of seventeen, after passing his matriculation, he began medical studies at St. Thomas's Hospital, London.

Some of Martin's courses were given at Guy's Hospital, where he met and developed a special affection for fellow student Ernest H. Starling. Frederick Gowland Hopkins, five years Martin's senior, was working as an assistant chemist in Thomas Stevenson's laboratory at Guy's Hospital at the time and took a special interest in Martin, who was allowed to work in the laboratory as well. When the University of London granted Martin the B.Sc. degree in 1886, he won honors in physiology and the University Gold Medal.

Following in the footsteps of other British medical graduates who sought careers in physiology or related disciplines, Martin went to study with Carl Ludwig at the world-renowned Leipzig Physiological Institute. He was soon invited to be a demonstrator in Gerald F. Yeo's department of physiology at King's College, London. While holding this position, Martin completed his medical studies and was awarded the M.B. degree by London University in 1890. When he was twenty-five, Martin accepted the position of demonstrator in physiology at the medical school of the University of Sydney, Australia, where he succeeded Almroth Wright. Shortly before his departure for Australia, Martin married Edythe Cross, the daughter of a Hastings architect.

During the second half of the nineteenth century, there was growing interest in the chemistry and physiological effects of snake venom. Australia provided the snakes, and Martin's sophistication in biochemical techniques learned from Hopkins, Ludwig, and Yeo enabled him to study the physiological actions of the various components of snake venom that he separated.

An innovative investigator and resourceful inventor, Martin designed some of the apparatus he used in these experiments. One of the most important pieces of equipment he developed was the gelatin ultrafilter, produced by pouring melted gelatin into the pores of a Pasteur filter. This enabled him to separate heat-coagulable from uncoagulable protein elements. In a series of sophisticated experiments that represents one of his most enduring scientific contributions, Martin separated the venom of the black snake (*Notechis Pseudechis*) into three components: a neurotoxin, a cytolytic substance, and an enzyme that triggered intravascular coagulation.

These experiments, designed to identify the various components of black snake venom, were widely heralded. Especially important was the series of studies Martin conducted to characterize the local and systemic effects of the protein constituents of the venom. Combining many sophisticated techniques and using various animals, Martin demonstrated that the effects on the animal varied dramatically, depending upon the dose and route of administration of the different protein components of the venom.

Carefully planned experiments revealed that the substance that caused death by intravascular coagulation was heat labile. Moreover, when this substance was injected subcutaneously, intravascular coagulation was not the cause of death; the animal succumbed to asphyxiation through suppression of the respiratory center of the brain. Martin's premise that variations in the substance's diffusibility in the animal accounted for this difference in the mode of death was supported by results derived from the use of his gelatin filter in an additional series of experiments. Practical application of these discoveries in the treatment of snake bites became possible as Martin and others laid the scientific foundations for serum therapy based upon their research into toxicology and immunology. Martin viewed his work on various aspects of snake venom as his most important scientific contribution.

In 1897 Martin left Sydney to accept the position of lecturer in physiology at the medical school of the University of Melbourne. There he studied the immunology of snake venom and undertook investigations of the metabolism and heat regulation of marsupials. A productive investigator, Martin had published more than two dozen papers, mainly dealing with snake venom, by 1901, when he was elected a fellow of the Royal Society.

In 1903 Martin returned to London as director of the Lister Institute of Preventive Medicine. In acknowledgment of his success as an investigator and teacher, he was selected over eight other candidates for the position. Incorporated in 1891 as the British Institute of Preventive Medicine, the institute was organized to support basic scientific research into the etiology, prevention, and treatment of disease and to develop specific substances, such as vaccines and antitoxins, for the prevention and cure of disease. The Lister Institute flourished under Martin's direction; becoming a productive research center of international stature. There, the scope of Martin's own research effort expanded to include the biochemistry of proteins, the role of protein and vitamins in nutrition, mammalian thermal regulation, and tropical diseases. In 1905 the Lister Institute was incorporated into London University, and departments of protozoology, statistics, and entomology were soon added.

Concern about the increasing incidence of bubonic plague in India led to the establishment in 1904 of the Commission for Investigation of Plague in India. Martin spent several months in India in 1905 and organized studies into the cause and prevention of plague at the Lister Institute that ultimately demonstrated the role of fleas in transmitting the disease from rats infected with a specific bacterium (*Yersinia pestis*).

During World War I, Martin's research shifted to the infectious diseases encountered by military personnel. He undertook investigations into various types of dysentery, jaundice, and meningitis. The war effort strained the resources of Britain to feed its troops and people, and led to increased emphasis at the institute on the scientific aspects of nutrition and the treatment of nutritional disorders. Nutrition had been a subject of research there for more than a decade, and it was under Martin's direction that Casimir Funk undertook his classic studies on nutritional deficiency and vitamins.

Martin resigned as director of the Lister Institute in 1930 and returned to Australia as director of the Division of Animal Nutrition at the University of Adelaide. He arrived in Adelaide in April 1931 but remained in Australia for only two years, retiring at the age of sixty-seven to a pleasant estate, Roebuck House, at Chestertown, near Cambridge, England. Unable to give up his scientific interests and activity, Martin soon became affiliated with the department of animal pathology at Cambridge, where, in conjunction with scientists at the Lister Institute, he continued his experiments on nutrition.

Like most London-based organizations, the Lister Institute found its activities severely disrupted by World War II. Martin invited the Division of Nutrition to transfer its apparatus and activities to his estate. Nutritional research once again took on strategic importance during World War II. By this time, Martin's role was largely that of elder statesman. To his younger colleagues he brought his broad experience in the biochemistry and the pathophysiology of nutrition, and his ability to define problems and direct research with wisdom and generosity. Like his teacher Carl Ludwig, Martin was intimately involved in the conception of research projects, the performance of experiments, and the interpretation of data from dozens of studies, the results of which were reported under the names of his pupils alone. Martin was generous with his time and ideas, and was greatly admired by his pupils and colleagues for his unselfishness and lack of concern regarding recognition of his contributions to their work.

Following a long and productive career, Martin died at the age of eighty-nine. His accomplishments were acknowledged by fellowships in King's College, London, the Royal College of Physicians, and the Royal Society; the latter awarded him a Royal Medal in 1923. He received honorary degrees from the universities of Sheffield, Dublin, Edinburgh, Adelaide, and Cambridge. Martin was knighted in 1927 for his many contributions to medical science.

BIBLIOGRAPHY

I. Original Works. Among Martin's more important publications representing his diverse interests are "A Rapid Method of Separating Colloids from Crystalloids in Solutions Containing Both," in *Journal of Physiology*, **20** (1896), 364–371; "The Contribution of Experiments with Snake Venom to the Development of Our Knowledge of Immunity. Discussion on Immunity," in *British Medical Journal* (1904), **2**, 574–577; "Snake Poison and Snakebite," in [T.] C. Allbutt and H. D. Rolleston, eds., *A System of Medicine by Many Writers*, II, pt. 2 (London, 1907), 783–821, written with G. Lamb; "Observations on the Mechanism of the Transmission of Plague by Fleas," in *Journal of Hygiene*, supp. 3 (1914), 423–439, written with Arthur W. Bacot; "Notes on the Etiology of Dysentery. I. Types of Dysentery Bacilli Isolated at No. 3 Australian General Hospital, Cairo, March–August 1916, With Observations on the Variability of the Mannite-Fermenting Group," in *British Medical Journal* (1917), **1**, 479–480, written with F. E. Williams; "Thermal Adjustment of Man and Animals to External Conditions. Croonian Lectures," in *Lancet* (1930), **2**, 561–566, 617–

620, 673–678; and "Curative Action of Nicotinic Acid on Pigs Suffering from the Effects of a Diet Consisting Largely of Maize," in *Biochemical Journal*, **32** (1938), 10–12, written with H. Chick, T. F. Macrae, and A. J. P. Martin.

II. SECONDARY LITERATURE. The most comprehensive biographical sketch (which includes a complete bibliography of Martin's more than 100 papers) is Harriette Chick, "Charles James Martin," in *Biographical Memoirs of Fellows of the Royal Society*, **2** (1956), 173–208. Brief obituaries include S. P. Bedson, "Sir Charles James Martin, 1866–1955," in *Journal of General Microbiology*, **14** (1956), 487–493; and Muriel Robertson, "Charles James Martin," in *Journal of Pathology and Bacteriology*, **71** (1956), 519–533. See also A[lbert] Calmette, *Venoms. Venomous Animals and Antivenomous Serum-Therapeutics* (London, 1908); and Harriette Chick, Margaret Hume, and Marjorie Macfarlane, *War on Disease: A History of the Lister Institute* (London, 1971).

W. BRUCE FYE

MARTYN, DAVID FORBES (*b*. Cambuslang, near Glasgow, Scotland, 27 June 1906; *d*. Camden, New South Wales, Australia, 5 March 1970), *ionospheric physics*.

Martyn was the eldest child of Harry Somerville Martyn, an ophthalmic surgeon, and his wife, Elizabeth Craig Allan, née Thom. He grew up in comfortable middle-class circumstances on the outskirts of Glasgow, where his father had his practice. Graduating B.Sc. from the Royal College of Science, London, in 1926 with a major in physics, he then took up a research studentship at the University of Glasgow, investigating the triode oscillator circuit both experimentally and theoretically; he successfully traced the instability in frequency that had puzzled many observers to a hitherto neglected flow of current to the valve's grid. For this work he was awarded a Ph.D. by the University of London in October 1928.

Martyn remained at Glasgow for a further year before accepting an appointment as a research officer—one of four notable new appointments made at this time—with the Australian Radio Research Board (RRB). His ensuing move to Australia and into the burgeoning field of upper atmosphere research was of fundamental importance to his future career. Martyn's early work for the board was largely experimental. It soon became evident, however, that his real strength was as a theorist with a quite remarkable command of the behavior of systems of charged particles in electromagnetic fields.

Martyn was initially attached to the RRB group working in T. H. Laby's laboratory at the University of Melbourne, where he undertook a systematic investigation, with R. O. Cherry, of the fading of signals from local radio stations. Following his transfer to the Sydney group under the direction of J. P. V. Madsen, this work evolved into a more general investigation of sky waves reflected from the ionosphere and hence into the properties of the ionosphere itself.

Martyn also continued, however, to work directly on radio propagation. In late 1932 the Australian government initiated a major inquiry into the nation's broadcasting services, and Martyn made significant technical contributions to the debate that resulted over the use of long-wave versus medium-wave carriers. Soon afterward, in the course of surveying available data on the propagation of medium waves in the ionosphere, he developed a very useful theorem, now known as Martyn's theorem, by which expressions relating to waves incident obliquely on the ionosphere could be obtained from those for vertical incidence.

In addition, with V. A. Bailey, Martyn developed in full quantitative detail a theory to explain the newly discovered "Luxembourg effect," in which signals from a long-wave broadcasting station in Luxembourg had been found to interact with the carrier wave of other European stations. The initial idea almost certainly came from Bailey, who had been a student of J. S. Townsend at Oxford, and later a collaborator in his authoritative studies on the motions of electrons in gases. Their explanation amounted to an application of Townsend's methods and data to the ionosphere. A powerful signal such as the Luxembourg one would, they argued, affect the mean velocity of agitation of electrons in the ionosphere in the vicinity of the station, and hence their collision frequency. The absorbing power of that region of the ionosphere would thus vary with the modulation level of the station, and the resulting modulation would be impressed on any other carrier wave traversing the region.

By mid 1935 Martyn's colleague O. O. Pulley had successfully commissioned a new semiautomatic pulse-echo recorder of his own design that provided both a continuous display of ionospheric layer heights and ionization densities at frequent intervals. The data so obtained formed the basis of an influential paper by Martyn and Pulley on conditions in the upper atmosphere. Perhaps their most striking conclusion was that the temperature of the F_2 layer was 1000° C or more. In addition they provided a stimulating discussion, drawing on evidence from a wide range of sources, of possible processes of electron detachment and loss that might explain the persistence of high electron concentrations in the *F* region even at night.

Shortly afterward Martyn, in collaboration with Pulley and J. H. Piddington, perfected a "pulse-phase" technique for probing the ionosphere that combined the advantages of E. V. Appleton's frequency-change method and the pulse-echo method invented by Gregory Breit and Merle A. Tuve. The new technique yielded continuous data on the state of polarization of reflected waves and hence on changes taking place in the reflecting layers of the ionosphere. Martyn was at once able to take advantage of it in a debate with other leading workers in the field over the validity of the "Lorentz" polarization term in relation to ionospheric reflections, concluding that Sellmeier's rather than Lorentz's dispersion formula was applicable in this case.

During this same period Martyn also became interested in the connections between ionospheric disturbances, as detected on the continuous recorders now available to him, and events occurring on the sun. This marked his introduction to questions of solar physics and the beginning of his long association with workers at Australia's Mount Stromlo Observatory.

As early as 1930 Martyn, in an unpublished RRB report, had pointed out the advantages of using ultra-high frequencies for both long-distance communications (suggesting the use of the moon as a reflector) and obtaining information about objects from which the beam was reflected. During a visit to Britain in 1936 he at once guessed the nature of the secret work on radiolocation being done by R. A. Watson Watt and his colleagues, and on his return to Australia successfully urged that UHF work be initiated there too. He was the natural choice when, in February 1939, the British government invited Australia, along with the other dominions, to send a scientist to England to learn the secrets of radar. Later in the same year he was appointed head of Australia's new Radiophysics Laboratory, charged with developing an independent Australian radar capability.

Unfortunately, Martyn's period in this post was an unhappy one. He chafed under a peculiar administrative arrangement that had him sharing responsibility for the running of the laboratory with his former mentor, Madsen, and he alienated officials with whom he was required to deal. During 1941 his duties were more and more assumed by F. W. G. White, and Martyn subsequently transferred to the armed services to head a newly established operational research group with special responsibilities for problems associated with radar. He married

Margot Adams of Sydney in 1944. They had no children.

By the war's end Martyn had found a new scientific home at the Mount Stromlo Observatory, where he remained until appointed in 1956 as officer in charge of the RRB station at Camden, New South Wales, a station that two years later became an independent Upper Atmosphere Section specially created for him within Australia's Commonwealth Scientific and Industrial Research Organization.

Soon after arriving at Mount Stromlo Martyn developed a theory of temperature radiation at radio frequencies from the sun. This led him to predict coronal radiation corresponding to a black body at 1,000,000° C at wavelengths of about 1 meter, and also significant limb brightening at centimeter wavelengths. Both predictions were quickly confirmed, the former by Martyn's one-time Radiophysics Laboratory colleague J. L. Pawsey.

The ionosphere, however, remained Martyn's chief preoccupation, and in four major papers in 1947 and 1948 he developed a modified "dynamo" theory, based on the identification of large solar and lunar atmospheric tides, to account for marked deviations of the experimentally determined values of the ionization in the F_2 region from that predicted by Sydney Chapman's classical (and essentially static) theory. Horizontal winds due to these tides would give rise, he argued, to motions of electrons along the lines of the earth's magnetic field that would in general have a vertical component that could account for the observed semidiurnal variations in both the ionization of the upper atmosphere and the earth's magnetic field itself. Evidence for the existence of the tides was derived from long runs of data that had by then been recorded at various ionospheric observatories, especially those at Mount Stromlo and the Carnegie Institution of Washington's observatory at Huancayo, Peru.

A serious difficulty remained for the dynamo theory, however, in accounting for variations in the earth's magnetic field, namely, that the conductivity of the upper atmosphere appeared to be too low to explain the observed changes. In 1948 Martyn suggested that inhibition of the transverse (Hall) current by polarization of the medium might allow a higher-than-expected conductivity. Though the idea was criticized initially, Martyn and his one-time RRB colleague W. G. Baker worked out the theory in detail and showed that it would account most satisfactorily for the unexpectedly high conductivity. They also showed that the conductivity should be greater still in a narrow zone near the magnetic equator, giving rise to an intense equatorial electrojet.

This would explain quantitatively the then recently discovered strong enhancement of the daily magnetic variations near the magnetic equator. Such an electrojet was at about the same time observed directly using a rocket-borne magnetometer. As a result of this work the dynamo theory, first proposed by Balfour Stewart in 1882, came at last to be regarded as securely established.

During the 1950's Martyn also attempted to extend his analysis of the upper atmosphere to account for some of the features of auroras and the magnetic "storms" associated with them. In particular, he tried to explain on electrodynamic grounds how the streams of charged particles responsible for the aurorae penetrated the atmosphere to the level at which aurorae were observed to occur—their speed appeared to be much too low to permit this—and why aurorae occurred mainly in particular high-latitude zones. Subsequent observational work, however, indicated that the mechanism he suggested was less important than he had supposed.

Martyn was elected a fellow of the Royal Society of London in 1950. Together with M. L. E. Oliphant he was the driving force behind the formation of the Australian Academy of Science in 1954. He was the academy's first secretary (physical sciences) and was its president from 1969 until the time that, in poor and deteriorating health, he took his own life. He was also very active in various international scientific bodies, most notably the International Union of Radio Science (URSI) and, in his later years, the United Nations Scientific and Technical Committee on the Peaceful Uses of Outer Space, of which he was chairman from 1962 until his death.

BIBLIOGRAPHY

I. ORIGINAL WORKS. A complete list of scientific publications accompanies the memorial essays by H. S. W. Massey in *Biographical Memoirs of Fellows of the Royal Society of London*, **17** (1971), 497–510, and J. H. Piddington and M. L. Oliphant in *Records of the Australian Academy of Science*, **2**, no. 2 (1971), 47–60. See also Martyn's "Personal Notes of the Early Days of Our Academy," *ibid.*, **1**, no. 2 (1967), 53–72. There is a small collection of his papers, chiefly administrative, at the Australian Academy of Science, and a considerably larger one, including extensive files of correspondence with G. H. Munro and others, at the CSIRO Archives, Canberra. Files from his period at the Radiophysics Laboratory are at the CSIRO Division of Radiophysics, Sydney.

II. SECONDARY LITERATURE. Martyn's work with the Radiophysics Laboratory and the Radio Research Board are discussed in two books by W. F. Evans, *History of the Radiophysics Advisory Board, 1939–1945* (Melbourne, 1970), and *History of the Radio Research Board, 1926–1945* (Melbourne, 1973). His role in the formation of the Australian Academy of Science is recorded in the academy's silver jubilee volume, *The First Twenty-five Years* (Canberra, 1980).

R. W. HOME

MARVEL, CARL SHIPP ("SPEED") (*b.* Waynesville, Illinois, 11 September 1894; *d.* Tucson, Arizona, 4 January 1988), *organic chemistry, polymer science.*

The son of John Thomas Marvel and Mary Lucy Wasson Marvel, Carl was born on a farm and expected to be a farmer. He later said that his uncle, who had been a high school teacher, urged him to study science "because the next generation of farmers was going to need scientific knowledge to get the most out of their work." In 1911 Marvel entered Illinois Wesleyan University, where he studied chemistry under Alfred W. Homberger. As a junior, Marvel found what he really enjoyed doing—synthesizing organic compounds.

After receiving the B.A. and M.S. degrees in 1915, Marvel accepted a $250 scholarship to the University of Illinois at Urbana to study chemistry, though he still expected to return to the family farm. Unimpressed by Marvel's transcript from Illinois Wesleyan, David Kinley, dean of the graduate school, told him, "You apparently do not know very much chemistry, so I'll have to give you an overload of work to catch up." As a result, Marvel's dormitory colleagues gave him the nickname "Speed," which he used throughout his career, even in official correspondence, because of his ability to work late in the laboratory, sleep until the last moment in the morning, and still get to breakfast before the dining hall closed at 7:30 A.M.

In the summer of 1916, the year in which Marvel received his A.M. degree, Clarence Derick established a production unit at Illinois called Organic Chemical Manufactures, to produce organic chemicals that had been imported from Germany before World War I. During the academic year 1917–1918 Marvel worked in this unit, but in 1919 he returned to full-time graduate studies, working under department head William Albert Noyes and receiving the Ph.D. in 1920.

Since industrial jobs were then scarce, Marvel stayed at Illinois, becoming successively instructor (1920–1921), associate (1921–1923), assistant professor (1923–1927), associate professor (1927–1930), professor of organic chemistry (1930–1953), and research professor of organic chemistry (1953–1961). With Roger Adams and Reynold C. Fuson, he was instrumental in making the organic chemistry program at Illinois preeminent in the United States. After his retirement in 1961 he became professor of chemistry at the University of Arizona (1961–1978). Following his second retirement he continued research with a small group of postdoctoral fellows, working almost daily in his laboratory until the summer before his death of renal failure at the age of ninety-three.

On 26 December 1933 Marvel married Alberta Hughes, a librarian and former high school English teacher. They had one son and one daughter. Despite his voluminous research Marvel considered teaching his greatest contribution; 176 students earned their doctorates under his tutelage, and 150 postdoctoral fellows worked with him. It is difficult to find organic polymer chemists anywhere in the world who have not had some relationship to Marvel.

Marvel worked primarily on the structure and synthesis of polymers—the large, high-molecular-weight molecules comprising plastics, elastomers, and fibers. His first sixty to seventy articles dealt largely with preparative organic chemistry, including syntheses of amino acids and organometallic compounds. While trying to synthesize bromoalkyl diethylamines for possible use in drug manufacture, Marvel obtained low polymers in the form of polyalkyl ammonium salts. By measuring the ratio of ionic to nonionic bromine in these polymers, he was able to calculate the molecular weights.

Marvel became more involved with polymers after he became a consultant for DuPont in 1928. (In his sixty years with DuPont he gave 19,000 individual consultations.) Asked to investigate the claim of English chemist F. E. Matthews that polymers could be formed by the reaction of sulfur dioxide (SO_2) and ethylene, by using the more convenient cyclohexene, Marvel confirmed the formation of polysulfones, from which poker chips could be made but which was not stable enough for commercial use. Beginning in 1933, he studied copolymers of SO_2 and α-olefins, determining their structure and developing initiators (such as peroxide or ultraviolet light) for the polymerization reactions involved in their preparation. In 1937 Marvel began to investigate the mechanism of the polymerization and structure of vinyl polymers. He proved that the repeating units in most polymers prepared from polyvinyl chloride are formed with the chlorine atoms on alternate carbon atoms (head-to-tail), as Hermann Staudinger had suggested, rather than on adjacent carbon atoms (head-to-head). This work led to the preparation and polymerization of new monomers.

Between 1942 and 1945 Marvel headed a group of chemists, numbering a hundred at its peak, who worked as part of the U.S. government's synthetic rubber program. He and his team investigated the synthesis and polymerization of numerous butadiene derivatives, showing that the thiol used in the polymerization of synthetic rubber controlled the final molecular weight of the butadiene-styrene copolymer and developing the redox systems that proved to be effective in the emulsion polymerization of butadiene and styrene.

They also found that polyunsaturated fatty acids present in some of the soaps, used to emulsify the insoluble monomers with water, interfered with polymerization and that when the soap was hydrogenated, the inhibition ceased. In addition, they studied the relationship between the structure and physical properties of butadiene copolymers by use of free-radical initiators and alkali metal catalysts. In their search for new synthetic rubbers, they prepared polysulfides from diolefins and dimercaptans. During the next decade they synthesized many new polymers.

In 1946 Marvel was a member of a technical intelligence team that went to Germany. They found that the Germans had been working on a new polymerization process that could produce a better synthetic rubber by operating at 5° C (41° F), in contrast with the earlier process, which was at 70° C (158° F). Marvel's group took up this research and developed the cold rubber process for American industry.

Beginning in 1956, high-temperature–resistant synthetic materials became important in the government's space program. In his syntheses of these polymers, Marvel developed cyclopolymerization. In what is regarded as one of the most significant advances in the chemistry of high-temperature polymers during the 1960's, he prepared polymers with repeating rigid heterocyclic or benzenoid groups in the main chain, and he synthesized polymers with repeating benzimidazole units (polybenzimidazoles, or PBI's), heat-resistant (to as high as 600° C [1,112° F]) macromolecules of high molecular weight. In 1980 PBI became the first new man-made fiber to be produced commercially in nearly a decade. It is a substitute for fiberglass and asbestos (no longer used for health reasons), and because of its exceptional resistance to fire, it is used in suits for astronauts and fire fighters. Marvel continued his work on heat-resistant polymers at the University of Arizona until his death.

Marvel was active in the American Chemical Society, in which he held many offices, including president in 1945. A member of numerous domestic and foreign scientific societies, he was elected to the National Academy of Sciences in 1938 (chairman of the Section of Chemistry, 1944–1947). He received honorary D.Sc. degrees from Illinois Wesleyan University (1946), the University of Illinois (1963), and the New York Polytechnic Institute (1983), and a doctoral honoris causa degree from the University of Louvain (1970). Marvel's American Chemical Society honors include the Nichols Medal (1944), the Willard Gibbs Medal (1950), the Priestley Medal (the society's highest honor, 1956), the Witco Award of the Division of Polymer Chemistry (1964), the Polymer Division Education Award (1984), and the Chemical Education Award (1984). His other awards include the American Institute of Chemists' Gold Medal (1955) and the Chemical Pioneer Award (1967), the Society of Plastics Engineers' International Award (1964), the Society of Chemical Industry's Perkin Medal (1965), and the U.S. government's National Medal of Science (1986). The Carl Shipp Marvel Laboratories of Chemistry at the University of Arizona and Marvel Hall at the American Chemical Society's headquarters in Washington, D.C., were named in his honor.

BIBLIOGRAPHY

I. ORIGINAL WORKS. During his long research career Marvel wrote more than 500 articles and 4 books, and he held 52 patents. For personal accounts of his life and career, as well as of the history of organic and polymer chemistry in the United States, see "Autobiography," in R. D. Ulrich, ed., *Contemporary Topics in Polymer Science*, I, *Macromolecular Science: Retrospect and Prospect* (New York, 1978), 133–141; "My 69 Years of Chemistry," in *CHEMTECH*, **10** (1980), 8–11; "The Development of Polymer Chemistry in America—The Early Days," in *Journal of Chemical Education*, **58** (1981), 535–539. During his career Marvel accumulated ninety-three boxes of manuscripts, letters, research reports, books, photographs, and awards, which his family donated in 1988 to the National Library of Chemical History, associated with the Arnold & Mabel Beckman Center for the History of Chemistry, located at the University of Pennsylvania in Philadelphia.

II. SECONDARY LITERATURE. Burton C. Anderson, " 'Speed' Marvel at DuPont," in *Journal of Macromolecular Science—Chemistry*, **A21** (1984), 1665–1687; Burton C. Anderson and Robert D. Lipscomb, "Carl Shipp Marvel: 'Speed at 90,' " in *Macromolecules*, **17** (1984), 1641–1643; Herman Mark, "The Contribution of Carl (Speed) Marvel to Polymer Science," in *Journal of Macromolecular Science—Chemistry*, **A21** (1984), 1567–1606; "Marvel, Carl Shipp," in *McGraw-Hill Modern Scientists and Engineers*, II (New York, 1980), 282–283; Peter J. T. Morris, *Polymer Pioneers: A Popular History of the Science and Technology of Large Molecules* (Philadelphia, 1986), 61–63; J. E. Mulvaney, "Interview with Carl S. Marvel," in *Journal of Chemical Education*, **53** (1976), 609–613; Raymond B. Seymour, "Polymer Science Pioneers: Carl Shipp Marvel," in *Polymer News*, **5** (1979), 216–217; and Ward Worthy, "Carl Marvel: An Extraordinary Influence on American Chemistry," in *Chemical & Engineering News*, **66**, no. 17 (25 April 1988), 20–22.

GEORGE B. KAUFFMAN

MATHER, KIRTLEY FLETCHER (*b*. Chicago, Illinois, 13 February 1888; *d*. Albuquerque, New Mexico, 7 May 1978), *geology*.

Kirtley Mather was descended from the Puritan Mathers of New England. William Green Mather, a railroad agent, and Julia (King) Mather, Kirtley's parents, were not college educated, but taught their children to value education and a nondoctrinaire Baptist faith. Mather's interest turned to geology in high school, was deepened at Denison University (B.S., 1909), and was honed at the University of Chicago (Ph.D., 1915). In June 1912 Mather married his college sweetheart, Marie Porter. He left graduate school to teach at the University of Arkansas (1911–1914), but he returned to Chicago to finish his dissertation on Morrowan fossils of Arkansas and Oklahoma. From 1915 until 1918 Mather taught at Queen's University, Kingston, Ontario. For the next six years he taught at Denison University, moving to Harvard University in 1924, where he remained on the active faculty until 1954.

Political activism and a desire to demonstrate the mutual relevance of science and religion are hallmarks of Kirtley Mather's life. He appeared at the Scopes trial, on Darrow's defense team, arguing that evolution was true but need not undermine Christian faith. He fought vigorously against teachers' oaths and all infringements on academic freedom. Mather's gentlemanly but determined style earned applause from liberals but led to criticism from some quarters during the McCarthy era of the 1950's. In March 1953 he was subpoenaed by the Jenner Subcommittee to discuss subversion in higher education, but was not personally charged with any misconduct. The scientific community elected Mather president of the American Association for the Advancement of Science (1951), and he served four terms as president of the American Academy of Arts and Sciences (1957–1961). Marie, with whom Kirtley raised three daughters, died in 1971; he married Muriel S. Williams in 1977. Mather was a driving force in adult education, the civil liberties movement, the American Association of University Professors, the YMCA, peace organizations, and many groups that fostered a dialogue between science and religion.

Field observation was a strength of Mather's geologic research. That was evident in his first professional article, written while an undergraduate, on the genesis of a gorge in central Ohio. During and after graduate school, Mather conducted geomorphic research with Wallace W. Atwood in the San Juan Mountains of Colorado. Petroleum exploration in Kentucky and Oklahoma occupied his summers of 1917 and 1918, and he investigated oil potential in the mountains and jungles of Bolivia in 1919 and 1920. His reports of that work earned him an invitation to Harvard University as visiting professor for 1923. Field exploration in Alaska, Nova Scotia, Mexico, and California, where Mather consulted for the United States government in the Elk Hills Reservoir case of 1926, rounded out his firsthand involvement with petroleum geology. In the 1930's Mather and Harvard graduate students investigated the geomorphology of Cape Cod. Mather's last research article, coauthored in 1965 with his son-in-law, Sherman A. Wengerd, concerned the age of the Ridgway Till of Colorado.

Mather considered himself to be a generalist and a liberally educated scientist. The breadth of his publication record bears out that assessment. Research interests included geomorphology, paleontology, petroleum geology, and resource-distribution analysis. But Mather's research-related publications were a small part of his total output of books, reviews, and over 250 published articles. He was more a communicator, educator, and popularizer than a researcher. Professors such as Kirtley Mather often contribute to science in ways that do not fit the simplistic equation that merit equals the number of research papers. Teaching, reviewing books, pioneering the use of media in science education, and defending academic freedom were among the activities that Mather pursued throughout his career. His Denison students included Carey Croneis, Howard Jefferson, L. Don Leet, Alonzo Quinn, A. Nelson Sayre, and C. Langdon White, all of whom became well-known earth scientists. At Harvard, Mather was appreciated for his eloquence, clarity, and range of interests. Few graduate students had him as their prime research adviser, but he served on doctoral committees of many who were to become leading geologists.

Mather's Harvard and Radcliffe lectures in introductory geology were widely regarded as responsible for influencing an entire generation of geologists in the choice of their careers. They also provided a training ground for his teaching assistants,

whose numbers include many leading figures in geology, among them senior officers of the United States Geological Survey (including at least one head, H. W. Menard), senior professors at American and foreign universities, and the officers of geological societies and commissions. He was a gifted photographer who incorporated slides and movies of geologic features into his teaching. Today's scientific documentaries descend from the pioneering efforts of Mather and others in the 1920's and 1930's.

In that same era he chaired the editorial board of the *Scientific Book Club Review*. Board colleagues included Arthur Compton, Robert Millikan, Harlan Stetson, and Edward Thorndike. From 1943 to 1954 Mather served as editor of "The Scientist's Bookshelf" in the *American Scientist*, and he was the science reviewer from 1946 through 1975 for the *Key Reporter* of Phi Beta Kappa. His reviews, of more than twelve hundred books, transcended mere listings of contents as he informed the reader of the essence of the author's message. Civil rights and civil liberties were important to Mather, whether the issue was education for blacks and women, the right of political dissent, or the value of communication among scientists around the world. Along with his close friend Harlow Shapley, Mather was a respected scientist who was vocal about civil liberties in the McCarthy era of the 1950's. That political activism did not dissuade scientists from electing him president for 1951 of the American Association for the Advancement of Science. The social implications of science, antiscientific trends, the responsibility of scientists to inform the public, and the need for improved science education were among the issues that Mather addressed. His effectiveness as a leader of the scientific community, and of many organizations, was due to his warmth, charm, humor, and integrity.

BIBLIOGRAPHY

I. Original Works. Mather followed his own advice about the need for scientists to communicate with the public. His early books, such as *Old Mother Earth* (Cambridge, Mass., 1928), *Science in Search of God* (New York, 1928), and *Sons of the Earth* (New York, 1930), were aimed at enlightening the reader about the wonders of geology and the interactions of science and religion. He developed the same topics in extensive lecture tours and the innovative use of radio as an educational tool. Texts for many of his speeches may be found in the Harvard University Archives. One well-received geological publication was the Wallace Atwood and Mather United States Geological Survey *Professional Paper 166* (Washington, D.C., 1932) on the geomorphology of the San

Juan Mountains of Colorado. *Adult Education: A Dynamic for Democracy* (New York, 1937), written with Dorothy Hewitt, was widely recognized as a fundamental contribution to the field.

Geology students were served by the laboratory manuals (1934, 1950, 1952) that Mather developed with his students C. J. Roy and L. R. Thiesmeyer. *Enough and to Spare* (New York, 1944) contended that science, good planning, and international cooperation should combine to allow worldwide prosperity based on well-managed resources. Study of the history of geology was furthered by publication of *A Source Book in Geology* (New York, 1939), written with S. L. Mason, and *Source Book in Geology, 1900–1950* (Cambridge, Mass., 1967). Mather was instrumental in the genesis of the journal *Daedalus*, sponsored by the American Academy of Arts and Sciences. *The Earth Beneath Us* (New York, 1964), won prizes for the best popular science book of the year. Mather authored the *Dictionary of Scientific Biography* articles on T. C. Chamberlin, Reginald Daly, August Foerste, Rollin Salisbury, and others.

II. SECONDARY LITERATURE. Valuable accounts include Sherman Wengerd's memorial in the *American Association of Petroleum Geologists Bulletin*, **62** (1978), 2337–2340, and the commentary of Harvard colleagues in *Harvard Gazette* (11 July 1980), 6. Kennard Bork has written a biographic article, ''Kirtley Fletcher Mather's Life in Science and Society,'' in *Ohio Journal of Science*, **82** (1982), 74–95. Important archival materials, by and about Mather, exist at Harvard University, Denison University, and the University of Chicago.

KENNARD B. BORK

MAYER, MARIA GOEPPERT (*b.* Kattowicz, Upper Silesia [now Katowice, Poland], 28 June 1906; *d.* La Jolla, California, 20 February 1972), *physics.*

Mayer was a mathematical physicist with a facility for the matrix manipulations of group theory and quantum mechanics and a chemist's appreciation for the accumulation and analysis of large quantities of physical data. She is best known for the work in nuclear physics that won her the Nobel Prize, but this was done relatively late in her career, when she had recently come to the field of nuclear physics from atomic and chemical physics. Her earlier work, which is not as well known, demonstrates Mayer's unusual physical intuition. Much of this work has remained unchanged since the 1930's and provides theoretical bases for several important developments in laser physics, laser isotope separation, double-beta decay, and molecular orbital calculation.

Maria Gertrud Käte Goeppert was the only child of Maria Wolff Goeppert and Friedrich Goeppert, both from old German professional families that included several university professors. Friedrich

Goeppert was professor of pediatrics at Georgia Augusta University in Göttingen, the sixth generation of his family to be a university professor. He actively encouraged his daughter to develop her scientific curiosity. Maria Goeppert attended public elementary school and a private girls' school for college preparation before entering Georgia Augusta University in 1924, with the intention of studying mathematics.

Goeppert studied mathematics for three years at Göttingen before she was attracted by quantum mechanics and decided to take her degree in physics instead. The physics department at Göttingen was led by James Franck and Max Born; Goeppert developed close relationships with both of them, particularly Born. From them she learned to apply the mathematical techniques of quantum mechanics to the interpretation of spectra. The strict mathematical formalism of the Göttingen style of physics, which did not appeal to some of Born's students, was well suited to Goeppert's tastes. Of his many talented students, Born later described Goeppert as one of the best.

Goeppert was young enough when she first encountered quantum mechanics to find it easy to accept. Her first systematic exposure to the theory came through reading proofs for Born and Pascual Jordan's *Elementare Quantenmechanik*. She also wrote the section in the book on P. A. M. Dirac's theory of radiation.

Goeppert's doctoral dissertation (1930) was an extension of Dirac's theory of radiation and matter to the case of two-photon processes, which required calculating the second-order time-dependent perturbation in addition to the first. Goeppert recognized that double-photon emission and absorption are analogous to the Raman effect; the dispersion formula of Kramers and Heisenberg could be applied to this process, but with only qualitative results. She estimated from it that the transition probabilities for such processes would be very low. Since the Raman effect can be analyzed as a case of dispersion, Goeppert used Dirac's theory for dispersion to calculate the transition probabilities. Using a suggestion made by Tatiana Ehrenfest, she added a term to the Lagrangian that is a total differential with respect to time, and derived a Hamiltonian in which the second-order term is much smaller than the first. That made the second-order perturbation a feasible calculation. The probability of double-photon emission or absorption came out so low that it seemed to have no physical significance. As Eugene Wigner pointed out forty years later, however, her doctoral thesis was clear and mathematically elegant.

While completing her work at Göttingen, Goeppert

met and married Joseph Edward Mayer, an American chemist who had taken a degree with Gilbert Newton Lewis at Berkeley and who was in Göttingen on a Rockefeller International Education Board fellowship for the years 1929 and 1930. Joseph Mayer was trained as an experimentalist but, in part owing to his wife's influence, came to be known for the application of theoretical physics, particularly quantum mechanics and statistical mechanics, to chemistry. After their marriage in January 1930, Mayer completed her doctoral degree. Then she and her husband moved to America, where Joseph Mayer took up a position as associate professor of chemistry at Johns Hopkins University. While in Baltimore, the Mayers had a daughter and a son. Maria Mayer became an American citizen in 1933.

Maria Mayer had no regular academic appointment at Johns Hopkins for the nine years she was there. She taught occasional courses, particularly in the chemistry department, and collaborated with her husband and the theoretical chemical physicist Karl F. Herzfeld. Most of her research during the years 1930 to 1939 was therefore in the fields of chemical physics and physical chemistry. The common thread that runs through Herzfeld and Mayer's joint work is the problem of explaining the existence of a stable phase (a liquid) between a state of complete disorder (the gas) and a state of complete geometrical order (the crystal). Mayer and Herzfeld wrote several articles in which they attempted to analyze the liquid phase in terms of the energetics of the transition from a liquid to a solid. By examining the pressure-volume curve for the equation of state for a simple lattice, they were able to show that there is a temperature at which every crystal breaks down (melts), resulting in a stable liquid phase.

Maria Mayer's work with Joseph Mayer centered on the application of quantum mechanics to chemistry. In one paper they developed a general method for determining the entropy of a polyatomic molecule from spectroscopic data. By generalizing a method for diatomic molecules and determining the number of rotational states from the symmetry number of a molecule, they described a method that is generally valid for polyatomic molecules, applying it in particular to the calculation of the entropy of ethane. In a second paper the Mayers looked at methods of calculating the polarizability of ions from spectral data. While considering several different methods, they demonstrated the general validity of the Born-Heisenberg relation for polarizability, derived in 1924 on the basis of the old quantum theory. These collaborations exposed Mayer to the use of exper-

imental data in theory, and taught her to apply her talents with theory to specific physical situations.

The research for which Mayer was best known before 1949 was a paper she wrote with Alfred Lee Sklar, a student of Herzfeld's at the Catholic University of America, where Herzfeld taught after 1936. Herzfeld was interested in how chemical structure determines optical properties such as color and suggested this as a thesis topic for Sklar. Because of the complexity of the mathematical techniques involved, Mayer assisted Sklar in the analysis. In calculating molecular energy levels, they used the Heitler-London-Slater-Pauling approximation and the Hund-Mulliken method. The first involves constructing wave functions for the molecule from linear combinations of orbitals of its individual constituent atoms. Sklar used this method in his dissertation, published in 1937.

About a year later Sklar and Mayer published a paper on the spectrum of benzene based on the Hund-Mulliken approximation. They built their Hamiltonian for the molecule by summing the contributions of the individual atoms and added the interaction energy between atoms as a correction. This was one of the first calculations of energy levels for a complex molecule from strictly theoretical principles. The only empirical parameter used in the calculation was the carbon-carbon distance in benzene. This work was elaborated in 1939 when Sklar collaborated with Hertha Sponer, Lothar Nordheim, and Edward Teller on a systematic analysis of the benzene spectrum. This was subsequently the method most commonly used in the construction of molecular orbitals for conjugated systems, and the primary reason that Mayer was generally regarded, between 1939 and 1949, as a specialist in the analysis of the spectra of complex systems.

Mayer also applied the techniques developed in her doctoral dissertation to a problem in nuclear physics. Wigner suggested that she calculate the probability of double-beta decay, since Enrico Fermi had recently demonstrated that beta decay can be treated in the same way that Dirac had treated radiation: the emission of an electron and its accompanying neutrino is analogous to the emission of light by an excited atom. Mayer determined how likely it would be that a nucleus would emit two electrons accompanied by two neutrinos. She set up an expression for the probability that came directly from the one she derived for double-photon emission. Using a Thomas-Fermi potential to describe the nuclear potential, she found that a nucleus of atomic number 31 would have a half-life greater than 10^{17} years for double-beta disintegration. This result, like her calculation of the probability of double-photon decay, was regarded as a clear and competent analysis of a situation with little likelihood of ever being tested.

During their last years at Johns Hopkins, Mayer and her husband completed the textbook *Statistical Mechanics,* which grew out of their collaboration in teaching the quantum mechanical basis of statistical mechanics to chemists. The book, published in 1940, became a standard; it went through ten printings by 1963; a second edition, with few changes, appeared in 1977.

In 1939, when Joseph Mayer's contract at Johns Hopkins was not renewed, the Mayers went to Columbia University, where Joseph Mayer was hired as associate professor of chemistry. Maria Mayer again had no official appointment, although she was asked by Harold Urey to give lectures in the chemistry department, and after the beginning of the Manhattan Project in 1941, she was asked, on twenty-four hours' notice, to take over Fermi's class in the physics department.

Mayer's first research project at Columbia was a problem suggested by Fermi. In 1939 Emilio Segrè had shown that the chemical behavior of one of the radioactive decay products of uranium indicated that it was one of the rare earths. A year later, however, Edwin McMillan and Philip Abelson suggested that the element was instead a transuranic element. Fermi recommended that Mayer test this hypothesis by calculating the expected energy levels for several of the rare earth elements and for the transuranic elements, in order to determine if the expected chemical behaviors were similar. Using a statistical (Thomas-Fermi) potential, Mayer calculated the energy and spatial extension of the $4f$ eigenfunctions for the rare earth elements and the $5f$ eigenfunctions for the transuranic elements. In both cases she found that the binding energy increased dramatically and the radii of the orbitals decreased abruptly at the beginning of each series, supporting the hypothesis that the transuranic elements would have chemical behavior similar to the rare earths.

After the outbreak of World War II, Mayer was asked to join Harold Urey's group, the Substitute Alloy Materials Laboratory (SAM), devoted to solving the problem of isotope separation for the Manhattan Project. Since Urey considered several alternatives to the gaseous diffusion method of separation, Mayer's work during the war was not all directed toward a single method. In fact, the first method she examined was photochemical separation. This required a thorough understanding of the differences between the spectra of U^{235} and U^{238}. The problem was ideal for Mayer, since her primary expertise was in spectroscopy. She compiled all available data on the spectra of the uranium compounds and then determined where further measurement was needed; the chemists in the experimental group then filled in the gaps. The results of this work were published in 1949 by Gerhard Dieke and Albert Duncan, who edited *Spectroscopic Properties of Uranium Compounds.* Mayer found that she could account for the high number of closely spaced electronic states in the uranyl ion by assuming that it has three fundamental vibrations: a symmetric stretching, an asymmetric stretching, and a bending vibration. The analysis showed that photochemical separation of uranium was not promising, and the project was phased out.

Mayer moved on to study chemical separation. With Jacob Bigeleisen she found a function describing the separability of two compounds of uranium that was related to the partition-function ratio. Again the outcome of the analysis was that the method would not be effective for uranium, and the possibility was dropped. Mayer did, however, make a contribution to a successful method, gaseous diffusion. She analyzed the structure of uranium hexafluoride (UF_6) from measurements of the Raman spectrum carried out by Bigeleisen.

Mayer's work at the SAM Laboratory marked a turning point in her career. She was working for the first time without her husband's emotional support (Joseph Mayer was working for the Naval Ordnance Laboratory at Aberdeen, Maryland, throughout most of the war, and was home in New York only one day each week), and was responsible for the first time for the work of other people. Later she regarded this period as the beginning of her career as an independent professional scientist.

In 1945 Joseph and Maria Mayer were offered positions at the University of Chicago, she as voluntary associate professor. They were also both invited to join the new Institute for Nuclear Studies, and in 1946 Maria Mayer was offered a half-time position as research physicist in the theoretical division of the new Argonne National Laboratory. Mayer at this time knew very little about the physics of the nucleus; she developed her knowledge of the field not from books but from discussions with colleagues about current problems. She did not gain a comprehensive background in the subject, and so had what proved to be the advantage of unfamiliarity with many of the traditional beliefs of nuclear physics.

In 1945 the common understanding of nuclear

structure was based on Niels Bohr's compound-nucleus interpretation of nuclear reactions and the assumption that the nucleus behaves like a liquid drop. In Bohr's view, it was impossible to assign different energy and momentum values to individual nucleons because of the intensity and short range of the nuclear force. Bohr's authority and the success of the liquid-drop model in accounting for such phenomena as nuclear fission combined to discourage attempts to explain the nucleus as a collection of discrete particles. In addition, Hans Bethe, in his very influential review articles of 1936 and 1937, which served as the primary textbook of nuclear physics for more than a decade, argued against treating nucleons as discrete particles.

Early in 1947 Mayer began to look carefully at data for isotopic abundances in conjunction with a theory she and Teller were proposing to explain the origin of the elements. Mayer noticed that nuclei with fifty and eighty-two neutrons were particularly abundant. This phenomenon could not be explained by the liquid-drop model, which predicted an essentially smooth curve for the binding energy as a function of neutron number. The discrepancy prompted Mayer to look even more closely at abundances, and she found that a marked pattern emerged. Nuclei having 2, 8, 20, 50, or 82 neutrons or protons or 126 neutrons were unusually stable. This conclusion was borne out not only by isotopic abundances but also by delayed-neutron emission and neutron-absorption cross sections. Mayer was convinced that these numbers indicated something special about the structure of the nucleus, and soon took to calling them "magic numbers," a phrase she had picked up from Wigner, who thought the whole idea was charming nonsense.

Pronounced periodicities in the abundance and stability of various nuclei obviously suggested a corresponding periodic structure in the nucleus, and an analogy to the electronic shell structure was almost inevitable. Mayer recognized this analogy and published her results in 1948, in a paper entitled "On Closed Shells in Nuclei," in which she summarized all of the data leading to the conclusion that nucleons occupy discrete energy levels in the nucleus. This paper contained no theory to account for the phenomenon, however, because quantum theory applied to a standard central potential, either harmonic oscillator or square well, did not predict the same numbers of nucleons in closed shells as those indicated by experimental data.

This difficulty had been noted much earlier by Walter Elsasser and Karl Guggenheimer, who discovered the phenomenon of the magic numbers in data similar to Mayer's. In 1933 and 1934 they pointed out the evidence for some sort of nuclear shell structure and attempted to account for shell closure at particular numbers of nucleons. No theory proposed, however, could adequately predict the magic numbers above nucleon number 20. Many physicists were aware of the failure of the older nuclear shell models, which Bethe had discussed at length in the "Bethe Bible." Mayer was unaware of this history until Bethe pointed it out to her in 1948, but she felt that the more recent evidence for nuclear shells was sufficiently compelling to warrant publishing in spite of the view held by the majority of nuclear physicists.

The publication of Mayer's paper on closed shells in nuclei, which included much new evidence, prompted several other physicists to try their hands at new shell models. From preprints of such papers by Eugene Feenberg and Lothar Nordheim, Mayer learned about Theodore Schmidt's technique of assigning an angular momentum value to the last (odd) nucleon in a nucleus, based on the measured spin and the total nuclear magnetic moment j. For Mayer, this method for determining nucleon spins supplied one of the missing pieces of the puzzle.

Sometime early in 1949 Mayer was discussing this question with Fermi when he asked, "Is there any evidence of spin-orbit coupling?" She immediately recognized that there was, and by taking it into account, she found that the energy-level splitting occurred at exactly the magic numbers. For a fermion with a given value of l, there are two possible total angular-momentum values, $j = l + \frac{1}{2}$ and $j = l - \frac{1}{2}$. For electrons, the energy difference between these two levels is small compared with the energy difference between adjacent l-values, and it had been assumed for several reasons that the same was true for nucleons. Mayer saw that if she used Schmidt's technique for spin assignments to nucleons, then the $j = l + \frac{1}{2}$ level must actually lie below the $j = l - \frac{1}{2}$ level (an inverted doublet), and if the energy due to spin-orbit coupling was proportional to a $(l \cdot s)$ term, then the magnitude of the splitting would be greater for greater l-values. This immediately explained why the square-well potential yields correct energy-level spacings for nuclei up to a neutron or proton number equal to 20, but not above. For low l-values the spin-orbit splitting is not large enough to alter the standard square-well spacing, but for high l-values, the magnitude of the separation is at least as large as the separation between adjacent l-levels. Mayer's postulation of this nuclear spin-orbit interaction was strictly phenomenological. The effect was clearly

TABLE I. This corrected table from Mayer's first nuclear shell model paper (*Physical Review*, **75** [1949], 1969) shows how nuclear spin-orbit coupling can account for the magic numbers. For example, the total occupation number at the close of the fourth oscillator group is 70. However, the spin-orbit splitting of the $1h$ level lowers the energy of the $1h_{11/2}$ state enough that it falls in the fourth oscillator group rather than the fifth, giving an additional twelve nucleons in that group, and shell closure at eighty-two nucleons.

Osc. No.	Square well	Spect. term	Spin term	No. of states	Shells	Total No.
0	$1s$	$1s$	$1s_{1/2}$	2	2	2
1	$1p$	$2p$	$1p_{1/2}$	4	6	8
			$1p_{3/2}$	2		
2	$1d$	$3d$	$1d_{5/2}$	6	12	
			$1d_{3/2}$	4		
	$2s$	$2s$	$2s_{1/2}$	2		20
			$1f_{7/2}$	8	8?	28?
3	$1f$	$4f$				
			$1f_{5/2}$	6	22	
	$2p$	$3p$	$2p_{3/2}$	4		
			$2p_{1/2}$	2		
			$1g_{9/2}$	10		50
4	$1g$	$5g$				
			$1g_{7/2}$	8	32	
			$2d_{5/2}$	6		
	$2d$	$4d$				
			$2d_{3/2}$	4		
	$3s$	$3s$	$3s_{1/2}$	2		
			$1h_{11/2}$	12		82
5	$1h$	$6h$				
			$1h_{9/2}$	10	44	
	2	$5f$	$2f_{7/2}$	8		
			$2f_{5/2}$	6		
	$3p$	$4p$	$3p_{3/2}$	4		
			$3p_{1/2}$	2		
			$1i_{13/2}$	14		126
6	$1i$	$7i$				
			$1i_{11/2}$			
	$2g$	$6g$				
	$3d$	$5d$				
	$4s$	$4s$				

not electromagnetic in origin because the magnitude of the spin-orbit energy level separation had to be much greater for nucleons than for electrons and was of the opposite sign.

The remarkable simplicity of the scheme immediately convinced Mayer that she had found the solution to her problem. With the assumption of strong spin-orbit coupling, a simple square well gave level spacings at exactly the right places without the need to assume ad hoc crossing of energy levels (see Table I). Mayer first published her theory in a brief letter to *Physical Review* that appeared in the same issue as Feenberg's and Nordheim's papers on the same subject. Her note was so brief that it convinced almost no one, and appeared to be simply another alternative shell model. By the time she published a longer exposition in April 1950, however, Mayer's model had gained a large number of influential adherents. It had great value to experimental nuclear physicists because it could account for nuclear spins and magnetic moments, for which there was a tremendous amount of new data in the 1950's. In spite of this phenomenological success, however, there remained some problems with the shell model. There was no direct experimental evidence that spin-orbit coupling is a strong effect for nucleons until 1952, when George Freier and M. Heusinkveld at the University of Minnesota demonstrated that the widely spaced $p_{3/2}$-$p_{1/2}$ doublet in Li^5 was inverted, as Mayer had assumed. There was also no good explanation of how nuclear shells could exist separately in the strong nuclear potential. This problem was not adequately addressed until the mid 1960's, when a strict shell model of the nucleus had given way to the collective model.

One possible reason that Mayer's model was accepted so readily by physicists who had recently believed that discrete particles could not exist in the nucleus was that the same model was proposed simultaneously and independently by Otto Haxel, J. Hans D. Jensen, and Hans Suess in Germany. Jensen was the nuclear theorist of the group. He and Mayer formed a close friendship when they met in 1951. Mayer and Jensen worked together to develop various theoretical aspects of the shell model. (Mayer also worked with Nordheim and Steven Moszkowski on a shell-model analysis of beta-decay.) The ultimate result of Mayer's friendship with Jensen was their collaboration on the first textbook devoted entirely to the nuclear shell model, *Elementary Theory of Nuclear Shell Structure*, published in 1955.

Mayer remained at the University of Chicago and Argonne Laboratory for five years after the publication of *Elementary Theory of Nuclear Shell Structure*. She published little during those years but was active in the physics department. In 1959 the University of California established a new graduate research program at San Diego and offered both Mayers full (paid) professorships. Although the University of Chicago countered by offering Maria Mayer a salary, the Mayers preferred California, and moved to La Jolla in September 1960. Less than a month after they arrived, Mayer suffered a stroke. Although she continued her work, her health was never good again, and she channeled her diminished energies into teaching until her death in 1972. In 1963 Mayer and Jensen shared half the Nobel Prize for physics for their work on the nuclear shell model.

Mayer's approach to physical problems changed considerably during her career. Her early work was extremely mathematical, but her later work was much more physical in character. She learned to approach data in the manner of a chemist—to compile and collate large amounts of information in search of patterns. This step was one of the keys to her success with the shell model—the extensive experimental evidence convinced her to continue searching for a theoretical explanation. This same step was taken in Germany by a chemist (Suess) and not a physicist. The role of the physicist (Jensen) became important only after the pattern had been established on the basis of the experimental data. Mayer's great strength was in her ability to assume both roles.

The single most remarkable aspect of Mayer's work is the way that her mathematically derived theories retained their physical validity and, in many cases, were far ahead of their time. The theory of double-photon decay could not be tested experimentally until the 1960's. With lasers to provide a sufficiently high intensity source of radiation, however, Mayer's predictions were verified. This led to the development in the 1970's of the double-photon absorption technique in laser spectroscopy as a means of eliminating the Doppler broadening of an absorption line. Mayer's prediction of the half-life for double beta-decay served as a guide for its eventual detection in 1987. The theoretical model most commonly used in describing the rare earth elements derives from the work of Fermi and Mayer. With the development of very-high-resolution lasers, photochemical isotope separation has become a standard technique, even for uranium compounds. In all of these cases, Mayer's early work served as a solid theoretical basis for later developments.

Mayer was remembered by her students as a de-

manding teacher. She was not a particularly good lecturer, since she spoke very softly and expected students to supply many of the logical connections. She was known at the University of Chicago for keeping the attention of her audience, though, because of her habit of chain-smoking while lecturing. No matter how often she switched chalk and cigarette from hand to hand, no student ever saw her smoke the chalk or write with the cigarette. Mayer had only a few graduate students during her career, but they included some very talented physicists: Robert Sachs (at Johns Hopkins) and Steven Moszkowski and Dieter Kurath (at the University of Chicago) received their doctorates under Mayer's direction.

Joseph and Maria Mayer were known for their gracious life-style. They entertained frequently and lavishly, and were particularly famous for their New Year's Eve parties. Mayer traveled extensively throughout her life. From 1930 until her mother's death in 1937, she spent most of every summer in Germany. After World War II, and as a result of her connection with the Manhattan Project, she and her family traveled frequently in the American Southwest. On these trips Mayer pursued her strong interest in Native American pottery and archaeology. By the mid 1950's she and Joseph were again traveling abroad: in 1953 they spent six months going around the world, giving lectures and attending conferences. These trips did not stop after Mayer's stroke; in 1965 she was guest of honor at Women's Week in Japan, and in 1966 and 1967 she was a visiting lecturer in India.

Unlike most of the scientific refugees arriving in the United States in the 1930's, Mayer came voluntarily and not as a result of the Nazi racial laws. She was active in an organization formed to give aid to displaced German scientists in the 1930's, but she still had family and close friends living in Germany during the war, and her feelings about celebrating V-E Day were ambivalent. In the same way, although she worked willingly on the Manhattan Project, she was also active in 1945 and 1946 in the campaign against military control of nuclear energy.

By the end of her life, Mayer was a highly respected member of the physics community. In addition to receiving the Nobel Prize, she was elected a member of the National Academy of Sciences and the American Philosophical Society and a fellow of the American Physical Society and the American Academy of Arts and Sciences. She was awarded five honorary D.Sc. degrees.

BIBLIOGRAPHY

I. ORIGINAL WORKS. The most complete bibliography of Mayer's publications is in Robert G. Sachs, "Maria

Goeppert Mayer," in *Biographical Memoirs National Academy of Sciences*, **50** (1979), 311–328. Publications resulting from her doctoral dissertation are "Über die Wahrscheinlichkeit des Zusammenwirkens zweier Lichtquanten in einem Elementarakt," in *Die Naturwissenschaften*, **17** (1929), 932; and "Über Elementarakte mit zwei Quantensprüngen," in *Annalen der Physik*, **9** (1931), 273–294.

Mayer published five papers with Karl F. Herzfeld; among them are "On the Theory of Fusion," in *Physical Review*, 2nd ser., **46** (1934), 995–1001; "On the States of Aggregation," in *Journal of Chemical Physics*, **2** (1934), 38–45; and "On the Theory of Dispersion," in *Physical Review*, 2nd ser., **49** (1936), 332–339. During the same period she wrote "The Entropy of Polyatomic Molecules and the Symmetry Number," in *Journal of the American Chemical Society*, **55** (1933), 37–53, with Joseph E. Mayer and Stephen Brunauer; "The Polarizability of Ions from Spectra," in *Physical Review*, 2nd ser., **43** (1933), 605–611, written with Joseph E. Mayer; "Double Beta-Disintegration," *ibid.*, 2nd ser., **48** (1935), 512–516; and "Calculations of the Lower Excited Levels of Benzene," in *Journal of Chemical Physics*, **6** (1938), 645–652, written with Alfred L. Sklar. *Statistical Mechanics* (New York, 1940; 2nd ed., 1977) was written with Joseph E. Mayer.

Between 1940 and 1945 Mayer wrote "Rare Earth and Transuranic Elements," in *Physical Review*, 2nd ser., **60** (1941), 184–187; "Calculation of Equilibrium Constants for Isotopic Exchange Reactions," in *Journal of Chemical Physics*, **15** (1947), 261–267, written with Jacob Bigeleisen; and "Vibrational Spectrum and Thermodynamic Properties of Uranium Hexafluoride Gas," *ibid.*, **16** (1948), 442–445, written with Jacob Bigeleisen, Peter C. Stevenson, and John Turkevich. See also Gerhard H. Dieke and A. B. F. Duncan, *Spectroscopic Properties of Uranium Compounds* (New York, 1949).

At the University of Chicago Mayer wrote two papers with Edward Teller: "On the Origin of the Elements," in *Physical Review*, 2nd ser., **76** (1949), 1226–1231; and "On the Abundance and Origin of Elements," in *Les particules élémentaires: Institut International de Chimie Solvay: Huitieme Conseil de Physique, 1948* (Paris, 1950), 59–88.

Mayer's development of the nuclear shell model is summarized in "On Closed Shells in Nuclei," in *Physical Review*, 2nd ser., **74** (1948), 235–239; "On Closed Shells in Nuclei. II," *ibid.*, 2nd ser., **75** (1949), 1969–1970; "Nuclear Configurations in the Spin-Orbit Coupling Model. I. Empirical Evidence," *ibid.*, 2nd ser., **78** (1950), 16–21; "Nuclear Configurations in the Spin-Orbit Coupling Model. II. Theoretical Considerations," *ibid.*, 22–23; and *Elementary Theory of Nuclear Shell Structure* (New York, 1955), written with J. Hans D. Jensen. Mayer applied the shell model in a series of papers written between 1951 and 1965: "Nuclear Shell Structure and Beta Decay. I. Odd *A* Nuclei," in *Reviews of Modern Physics*, **23** (1951), 315–321, written with Steven A. Moszkowski and Lothar Nordheim; "Electromagnetic Effects Due to Spin-Orbit

Coupling," in *Physical Review*, 2nd ser., **85** (1952), 1040–1041, written with J. Hans D. Jensen; "Classifications of β-Transitions," in Kai Siegbahn, ed., *Beta- and Gamma-ray Spectroscopy* (New York, 1955), 433–452; "Statistical Theory of Asymmetric Fission," in Ilya Prigogene, ed., *Proceedings of the International Symposium on Transport Processes in Statistical Mechanics* (New York, 1958), 187–191; and "The Shell Model: Shell Closure and *jj* Coupling," in Kai Siegbahn, ed., *Alpha-, Beta- and Gamma-Ray Spectroscopy*, I (Amsterdam, 1965), 557–582, with J. Hans D. Jensen.

Mayer's more general accounts of the nuclear shell model include "The Structure of the Nucleus," in *Scientific American*, **184**, no. 3 (1951), 22–26, 72; and "The Shell Model," in *Nobel Lectures: Physics*, IV (Amsterdam, 1972), 20–37.

Mayer's papers and correspondence, along with those of Joseph E. Mayer, are deposited in the Special Collections of Mandeville Library, University of California at San Diego.

II. SECONDARY LITERATURE. For the most complete account of Mayer's life and career, see Joan Dash, *A Life of One's Own: Three Gifted Women and the Men They Married* (New York, 1973). See also Mary Harrington Hall, "The Nobel Genius," in *San Diego*, **16** (1964), 64–69, 108–111; and Robert G. Sachs, "Maria Goeppert Mayer—Two-fold Pioneer," in *Physics Today*, **35**, no. 2 (1982), 46–51.

For discussions of Mayer's scientific contributions, see Karen E. Johnson, "Maria Goeppert Mayer and the Development of the Nuclear Shell Model" (Ph.D. diss., University of Minnesota, 1986), and "Maria Goeppert Mayer: Atoms, Molecules and Nuclear Shells," in *Physics Today*, **39** no. 9 (1986), 44–49; Robert G. Sachs, in *Biographical Memoirs. National Academy of Sciences* (above); Harold C. Urcy, "Maria Goeppert Mayer (1906–1972)," in *American Philosophical Society Year Book 1972* (1973), 234–236; and Eugene Wigner, "Maria Goeppert Mayer," in *Physics Today*, **25**, no. 5 (1972), 77, 79. See also J. Hans D. Jensen, "Glimpses at the History of the Nuclear Structure Theory," in *Nobel Lectures: Physics*, IV (Amsterdam, 1972), 40–50; and Peter Zacharias, "Zur Entstehung des Einteilchen-Schalenmodells," in *Annals of Science*, **28** (1972), 401–411.

KAREN E. JOHNSON

MEHL, ROBERT FRANKLIN (*b.* Lancaster, Pennsylvania, 30 March 1898; *d.* Pittsburgh, Pennsylvania, 29 January 1976), *metallurgy, chemistry*.

As teacher, academic administrator, and researcher, Mehl played a major role in the broadening of metallurgical science in the mid twentieth century. The son of George H. Mehl and Sarah Ward Mehl, he received a B.S. in chemistry from Franklin and Marshall College in 1919. In 1922, after three years of teaching chemistry in small colleges, he entered

Princeton University, where he earned a Ph.D. in 1924. On 27 December 1923 Mehl married Helen Charles; they had a son and two daughters. After heading the chemistry department at Juniata College (1923–1925), he spent the years 1925–1927 at Harvard University as a National Research Council fellow, working on compressibility and chemical affinity in alloys. At Harvard he came under the influence of Theodore W. Richards, Percy W. Bridgman, and Albert Sauveur, the last inspiring his lifelong interest in the relation between the physical properties and the structure of metals.

Most of Mehl's mentors had studied in Germany, and as a result he became a disciple of the Göttingen chemist Gustav Tammann, one of whose books, *Aggregatzustände, die Änderung der Materie in Abhängigkeit von Druck und Temperatur*, he translated into English in 1925. From 1927 to 1931 he was superintendent of the Division of Physical Metallurgy at the Naval Research Laboratory in Washington, D.C. There he developed gamma-ray radiography for the detection of defects in large steel castings and, in association with Charles S. Barrett, commenced studies of the mechanisms of phase change in alloys, a topic that interested him throughout his life. In 1932, after a brief period in industry, he went to Carnegie Institute of Technology (now Carnegie-Mellon University) as professor of metallurgy and director of the Metals Research Laboratory.

An ambitious and energetic man, Mehl effectively combined research with administration and teaching. His associates and students were prominent in the development of the new metallurgy. At one time they constituted 25 percent of the heads of all academic departments of metallurgy in the United States and Canada.

Mehl regarded it as essential for a scientist to have sensory contact with the materials studied. This belief began in a little laboratory in his home when he was twelve. He maintained close contact with industrial operations throughout his life, once remarking, "An industrial plant is a veritable museum of fascinating phenomena."

Most of Mehl's research was on quantitative structural and kinetic aspects of transformations in solids. The lamellar morphology (known as the Widmannstätten structure, after its popularizer, Alois Beck von Widmannstätten) that results from oriented growth within a crystal of a second phase—the solubility of which decreases with temperature—had been observed in the huge crystals of metallic meteorites by William Thompson in 1804. By 1900 it was an accepted feature in the microstructure of man-made steel, usually attributed to mechanical cleavage planes in the parent lattice. In 1926 the English physicist J. Young first used X-ray diffraction to determine the orientation relations between the two crystalline components in a meteorite. Mehl saw the basic importance of the phenomenon and commenced a long research program based on the central belief that the character of the interface between the two phases was more important than the structure or orientation of either. Seven papers on the relations in many different alloys that emanated from Mehl's laboratory in the years 1931 to 1935 formed a potent nucleus for the studies of intermediate levels of structure that soon thereafter came to characterize solid-state physics.

Next Mehl and his students worked on diffusion and reaction kinetics in general, studying the epitaxy of corrosion-product layers, with particular attention to distinguishing quantitatively between stages of nucleation and growth during phase change and also during the recrystallization of cold-worked metals and alloys. They also investigated the strength and ductility of steels and were pioneers in the application of statistics in scientific studies and as a means of quality control in industry. Virtually all of Mehl's research was done in collaboration, usually with his students. Though his students regarded him as rather stern and authoritarian, they valued the experience of interactively exploring with him fruitful areas for research. The exploration was usually followed by Mehl's benign neglect and an occasional unwillingness to accept experimental results that did not support his initial theory.

Like most metallurgists at the time, Mehl was not an especially talented mathematician, though he strongly encouraged advanced mathematical treatment on the part of his students. Nevertheless, despite his strong mental inclination toward physics, his pride in metallurgy as a profession encompassing everything from the smelting of ores to the treatment of the final product made him somewhat unsympathetic to the trends that have matured into materials science, which encompasses the nature and properties of all materials, regardless of their origin or composition.

Mehl took a keen interest in the broadest aspects of the metallurgical profession and especially of education. The curriculum that he developed at Carnegie Institute of Technology became the model for those at many other institutions. He received many medals and other honors from scientific societies throughout the world. His *Brief History of the Science of Metals*, published in 1948, was the first historical account to reflect the broadening of the profession beyond its traditional concern with the chemistry of smelting and refining.

In 1944 Mehl made the first of many visits to Brazil to advise on both industrial and educational aspects of metallurgy. He became dean of graduate studies at Carnegie Institute in 1953 but resigned in 1960 and moved to Zurich, where he was consultant to the U.S. Steel Corporation. Returning to the United States in 1966, he served briefly as visiting professor at the University of Delaware and Syracuse University before returning to Pittsburgh in 1968, where he died after a long illness.

BIBLIOGRAPHY

I. Original Works. Mehl's works include *The States of Aggregation* (New York, 1925), a translation of the 2nd ed. of Gustav Tammann, *Aggregatzustände, die Änderung der Materie in Abhängigkeit von Druck und Temperatur* (Leipzig, 1922; 2nd ed., 1923); *Metalurgia do ferro e do aço* (The metallurgy of iron and steel), Vicente Chiaverini *et al.*, trans. (São Paulo, Brazil, 1945), lectures Mehl delivered at the Polytechnic of the University of São Paulo in 1944; and *A Brief History of the Science of Metals* (New York, 1948). Most of his scientific contributions are published in *Transactions of the American Institute of Mining and Metallurgical Engineers* from 1931 to 1960. "Commentary on Metallurgy," in *Transactions of the Metallurgical Society of AIME*, **218** (1960), 386–395, consists of general remarks on the history and current state of the field; "A Department and a Research Laboratory," in *Annual Review of Materials Science*, **5** (1975), 1–26, is a semiautobiographical account that gives a good picture both of his own research philosophy and of the state of the field.

Cyril Stanley Smith

MEISSNER, WALTHER (*b*. Berlin, Germany, 16 December 1882; *d*. Munich, Germany, 15 November 1974), *physics.*

Walther Meissner was the son of a chief engineer, Waldemar Meissner, and of his wife, Johanna Greger. He was educated in Königsberg and in Berlin-Charlottenburg, where he graduated from high school in 1901. He studied engineering at the Charlottenburg Technical University and passed the preliminary examination in mechanical engineering in 1906. Since he had attended lectures in mathematics, philosophy, and physics at the University of Berlin for several semesters, Meissner decided to study physics a short time before his final examination. He wanted to write an experimental doctoral dissertation under Paul Drude on the internal forces associated with

semiconductors, a proposal that was rejected because the subject did not conform to the university's program. Since Meissner had successfully completed the six-semester cycle of lectures and practical courses under Max Planck, he decided to study for his doctorate under him. He submitted a theoretical work on thermoelectricity, intending to use it in expanded form as his dissertation. Planck thought it contained too much criticism of other works and turned it down. But he suggested another subject, radiation pressure on moving bodies, for a dissertation on which Meissner received his doctorate in 1906.

In the following year Meissner worked with his father on engineering problems, after which, through Planck's mediation, he entered the pyrometry laboratory of the engineering department of the Physikalisch-Technische Reichsanstalt (PTR) in 1908. There, besides taking his engineering examinations, he wrote several works, among them those on thermometry and viscosity.

In 1912, after one year of marriage, Meissner's wife died while giving birth to a daughter. He sought consolation in research. With great ambition and hard work, that same year he succeeded in entering the electricity subdivision in the science department of the PTR, where, at the request of its president, Emil Warburg, he introduced the liquefaction of hydrogen. In the same year he put into operation a Nernst-type liquefaction apparatus manufactured by the Hoenow Company in Berlin. His first works were based on the study of the optical characteristics of liquid hydrogen and the measurements of the electrical and thermal conductivity of copper at temperatures between 20 and 375K.

In early 1915 Meissner interrupted his scientific activity to serve in World War I as a volunteer. During his service with the air force he worked on problems of measurement of distance and altitude, rose to the rank of commissioned officer, and was decorated with the Iron Cross (second class). In 1921 Meissner married Johanna Galinert; they had two sons. At the PTR he continued his low-temperature studies with the measurement of the thermal and electrical conductivity of metals such as lithium. In collaboration with the Linde Company (Munich) and with the support of the Emergency Association of German Science, he prepared the installation of helium liquefaction equipment in accordance with the Leiden method using precooled hydrogen. On 7 March 1925 Meissner succeeded in liquefying about 200 cc of helium that he had separated from a helium-neon mixture produced by Linde. Thus, besides the laboratories in Leiden (Kamerlingh Onnes, since

1908) and Toronto (John C. McLennan, since 1923), there was now a third laboratory where temperatures as low as about 1.5K were available for experiments. Meissner wanted to find out whether all metals could become superconductive simply by being at a low enough temperature and in a pure enough state. He studied monocrystalline filaments of gold, zinc, and cadmium, as well as polycrystalline iron, platinum, nickel, silver, and cadmium. Neither a high degree of purity nor the most uniform crystal structure led to superconductivity at temperatures as low as 1.3K.

According to the plans of the Ministry of the Interior and the Emergency Association of German Science, a large cryogenics institute was to be built in Germany in the mid 1920's; the nation's major centers for physics, Berlin and Göttingen, were being discussed as possible sites. Finally Berlin was chosen, not only because Meissner had already built a hydrogen liquefaction unit at the PTR and was just about to install a helium liquefier there, but also because of Max Planck's influence. In 1927 the new cryogenics laboratory, which was directly under the control of the president of the PTR, was inaugurated. The possibility of numerous openings for guest researchers was welcomed by scientists at the university and in industry alike.

In the new cryogenics laboratory Meissner and his colleagues studied a great number of elements for superconductivity; in 1928 they discovered the sixth superconductive element known at that time: tantalum, used in the filaments of incandescent light bulbs. It was the first superconducting element in group V of the periodic system. Further elements that Meissner discovered to be superconductive were thorium, titanium, and vanadium. Copper sulfate was also found to lose its resistance at low enough temperatures. It was the first time that a chemical compound had become superconductive; moreover, one of its components was an insulator. This result led to systematic studies on further compounds and alloys, among which carbides, especially niobium carbide, displayed superconductive properties even at about 10K—that is, at a temperature scientists had already been able to achieve using solid-state hydrogen.

Meissner conducted further experiments to shed light on the nature of superconductivity, studying currents in superconductive metals. On this subject, which to him was closely related to the magnetic behavior of superconductors, he remained in close contact with Max von Laue, who had been a theoretical physicist at the PTR since 1925 and was available to experimenters for consultation half a day per week. In order to answer the question discussed by many physicists—whether a current in a superconductor fills the entire cross section or flows on the surface—Laue suggested that the magnetic field be studied between two superconductors placed very close to each other, both with a current running through. In the spring of 1933, in the course of these measurements Meissner and his colleague Robert Ochsenfeld observed a new phenomenon that contributed greatly to the understanding of superconductivity. The magnitude of the magnetic field measured between conductors was a function of the direction of the current, which could be explained by the role played by the earth's magnetic field. Therefore, Meissner and Ochsenfeld carried out the measurements of changes in the magnetic field close to the conductors when these were subject only to the earth's field, that is, without any current running through them. Before superconductivity set in, the magnetic lines of force penetrated the crystals with almost no resistance because of their low susceptibility. From what was known about superconductivity at that time, it was expected that the distribution of the lines of force would remain unchanged if the temperature were lowered below the threshold level. However, Meissner and Ochsenfeld observed an increase in the lines of force in close proximity to the superconductors. Meissner interpreted this result as follows: the magnetic field flux was displaced from the crystals when superconductivity set in (see Figure 1). The magnetic field flux that previously flowed inside the conductors was now flowing between the crystals.

The Meissner-Ochsenfeld effect showed that, contrary to previous assumptions, the transition from the state of normal conductivity to that of superconductivity was completely reversible. As long as only ideal conductivity was considered to be the characteristic feature of superconductivity, according to Maxwell's theory the state of a superconductive sample should depend on its prior state. When a sample was first made superconductive by cooling and then an outside magnetic field was applied, the sample should remain without a field, since ideal conductivity should prevent the entry of a field. In the reverse case, when the cooling followed the application of a magnetic field, a magnetic field should remain, as if frozen, inside the superconductor, even after the removal of the field. Meissner and Ochsenfeld proved that the sample in the latter case also lost its inner field through the displacement of the lines of force, which meant that the final state was independent of the means by which it was

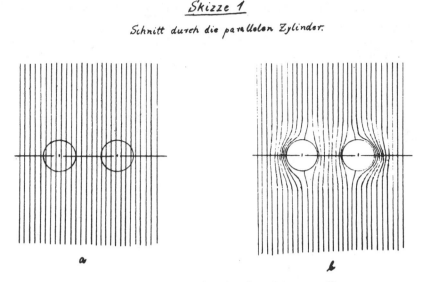

Skizze 1

Schnitt durch die parallelen Zylinder.

a

b

FIGURE 1. Meissner's first drawing of the new effect.

attained. This finding immediately led to the development of thermodynamic theories on superconductivity and became the starting point for Fritz and Heinz London's phenomenological theory of superconductivity.

Cryogenics was not the only field that captured Meissner's interest. At the same time he directed the laboratory for "electrical-atomic" research, where precise measurements of the magnetic moments of, among other elements, potassium and lithium were carried out using atomic radiation. Among Meissner's numerous scientific studies were his measurements of the susceptibilities of gases, the change in the electrical conductivity of the purest metals in magnetic fields, contact resistance, and the plasticity of metal crystals.

It seemed that with Planck's and Laue's support Meissner had a chance to expand his research activity. He expected to assume an honorary professorship at Berlin University, where he had qualified as a lecturer in 1930. However, Meissner perceived the new director of the PTR, Johannes Stark (a National Socialist supporter), as a threat to his work. Stark was opposed to his being concurrently active at the PTR and at the university, especially because Max von Laue, one of the few people to speak out against the National Socialist government, was teaching there. When Meissner was offered a chair at Munich's Technical University in 1934, his conflicts with Stark were one of the major reasons why he left the unique cryogenics laboratory in Germany for a chair in engineering physics despite his interest in pure physics.

Once in Munich, Meissner immediately started making plans to build a new cryogenics laboratory. In collaboration with the Linde Company, he developed a helium liquefier that worked without precooled hydrogen, in accordance with a method of Peter Kapitza's. But it was not completed until 1941, during the war. In 1943 Meissner moved his institute to Herrsching on the Ammersee, southwest of Munich, in order to escape bomb attacks.

After World War II, Meissner worked hard for scientific recovery. Since he had not been a National Socialist supporter, he was offered numerous positions in science administration. He was concurrently the director of both institutes for experimental physics at the Technical University as well as dean of the Faculty of Sciences, director of the government's testing bureau, president of the Bavarian Academy of Sciences (1946–1950) (of which he had been a member since 1938), president of the Bavarian Physical Society, and member of the board of directors of the Deutsches Museum. Within the Bavarian Academy of Sciences he established the Commission for Cryogenics Research. After becoming professor emeritus in 1952, Meissner continued to do cryogenics research. His guidance resulted not only in studies on curves of hysteresis in superconductors and the transition of the superconducting into the normal state, on the electrostatic effects in superconductors, and on the design of new helium liquefiers, but also on the critical Reynolds number for flow in pipes, the discovery of the paramagnetic effect, and the development of highly sensitive galvanometers. At a session of the

Bavarian Academy of Sciences in 1962, Meissner, by then almost eighty years old, reported on studies conducted by two students, R. Doll and M. Näbauer, who had proven that the magnetic flux in a superconductive ring is quantized.

Meissner was coeditor of *Zeitschrift für angewandte Physik, Kältetechnik,* and *Technische Physik in Einzeldarstellungen.* Besides numerous scientific honors, he received the German Federal Republic's Distinguished Service Cross.

BIBLIOGRAPHY

I. ORIGINAL WORKS. Meissner's scientific work has been recorded in over 200 publications. No comprehensive edition of his works exists, but some are listed in Poggendorff, V, 830–831. A list of his works between 1907 and 1952 was published by G. U. Schubert (see below). His writings include "Erzeugung tiefer Temperaturen und Gasverflüssigung," H. Geiger and K. Scheel, eds., *Handbuch der Physik,* XI (1926), 272–399; "Telephon und Mikrophon," *ibid.,* XVI (1927), 167–200; *Elektronenleitung. Galvanomagnetische, thermoelektrische und verwandte Effekte,* XI, pt. 2 of W. Wien and F. Harms, eds., *Handbuch der Experimentalphysik* (Leipzig, 1935), with M. Kohler and H. Reddemann; "Wärmeleitung in festen Körpern," in G. Joos, ed., *Naturforschung und Medizin in Deutschland 1939–1946,* VIII (Wiesbaden, 1947), 212–221, with G. U. Schubert; "Supraleitung," *ibid.,* IX (Wiesbaden, 1948), 143–162, with G. U. Schubert. The first mention of the Meissner-Ochsenfeld effect is in "Ein neuer Effekt bei Eintritt der Supraleitfähigkeit," in *Die Naturwissenschaften,* 21 (1933), 787–788, with R. Ochsenfeld. There is a detailed discussion in "Über die Änderung der Stromverteilung und der magnetischen Induktion beim Eintritt der Supraleitfähigkeit," in *Physikalische Zeitschrift,* 37 (1936), 499–470, with F. Heidenreich.

Most of Meissner's extensive scientific correspondence is at the Deutsches Museum. A small portion of it is in various archives, as indicated in Thomas S. Kuhn *et al., Sources for History of Quantum Physics* (Philadelphia, 1967).

II. SECONDARY LITERATURE. No biography of Meissner exists, only some laudatory articles on his birthdays and obituaries. They include F. X. Eder, "Walther Meissner zum 80. Geburtstag," in *Zeitschrift für angewandte Physik,* 14 (1962), 697–698; H. Meier-Leibnitz, "Walther Meissner," in *Jahrbuch der Bayerischen Akademie der Wissenschaften,* 1975, 232–236; and G. U. Schubert, "Zum 70. Geburtstag von Walther Meissner," in *Allgemeine Wärmetechnik,* 3 (1952), 252–254, with a bibliography of 156 works.

HELMUT SCHUBERT

MELDOLA, RAPHAEL (*b.* London, England, 19 July 1849; *d.* London, 16 November 1915), *chemistry, biology, science administration.*

Raphael Meldola was the son of Samuel Meldola and grandson of Raphael Meldola, the chief rabbi of London during the first half of the nineteenth century. Of Sephardic lineage, the family traced its ancestry back through sixteen generations to Toledo in the late thirteenth century. According to family tradition, the Meldola surname was derived from a town near Ravenna, Italy.

Meldola's early education took place at Gloucester House School in Kew, which in the early 1860's was still a rural village on the outskirts of London, and at a boarding school kept by a relative, Rev. A. P. Mendes, at Northwick College, Maida Vale. In 1866 Meldola entered the Royal College of Chemistry, where for a while he was an assistant in the laboratory of John Stenhouse. Despite his deep interest in natural history, Meldola earned his living as a chemist. In 1868 he became chemical adviser to W. & W. H. Stead, Seed Crushers and Oil Refiners, of Liverpool. For more than two years, beginning in 1870, Meldola tried his hand full-time in industrial chemistry at Williams, Thomas and Dower, color manufacturers, at the Star Chemical Works in Brentford. The position offered him limited scope for his own research interests, so in 1873 Meldola returned to the Royal College of Chemistry at its new home in South Kensington to work as a private assistant in Edward Frankland's laboratory. In 1874 Meldola joined Joseph Norman Lockyer's laboratory for a three-year period, during which he studied problems relating to spectral analysis and the chemistry of photography. As Lockyer's assistant he took charge of the Royal Society eclipse expedition to Camorta in the Nicobar Islands when his chief was unable to go. The eclipse occurred on 6 April 1875, and although clouds prevented the party from observing the brief moment of complete occlusion, it was able to collect a mass of data for publication.

During this academic interlude Meldola also taught organic chemistry as a lecturer at St. Mark's College in Chelsea and general science at the Ratcliff School of the Cooper's Company. In 1877 he again turned to the industrial side of chemistry when he took the position of "scientific chemist" in the laboratory of Brooke, Simpson, and Spiller at the Atlas Colour Works of Hackney Wick. During the ensuing eight years he was given free reign to explore and to publish his research. It was here that Meldola began working on the chemistry of coal tar and initiated the lines of investigation that he developed throughout his career. He returned to an academic setting in 1885 when he joined Finsbury Technical College, an institution sponsored by the City and Guilds of London Institute, to occupy its chair of chemistry. That same year Silvanus P. Thompson, who had been a fellow student at the Royal College of Science during the mid 1870's, became principal of the college and professor of physics. The association rekindled a lifelong friendship. In 1886 Meldola married Ella Fredcrica Davis. Children are mentioned in various biographical accounts, but not by name.

Meldola was particularly active as a member of the Chemical Society of London. From 1883 to 1886 and again in 1890, he served as a member of its council; in 1901 and 1902 he performed the function of foreign secretary; between 1902 and 1905 he served as vice president; and from 1905 to 1907 he held the office of president. During much of that period Meldola also served the Institute of Chemistry of Great Britain and Ireland. Founded in 1877, this organization was intended to oversee the areas where professional chemists and analysts performed public services. Meldola was vice president of the institute between 1909 and 1912 and its president from 1912 until his death. While president, Meldola particularly advanced the interests of the teachers of chemistry and successfully brought about the move of the institute to new quarters. In 1908 and 1909 he also was president of the Society of Chemical Industry, an institution founded to strengthen the bonds between academic and industrial chemists. In all, he was clearly an effective and respected leader in the management of science. The Chemical Society's historians best capture these talents by describing Meldola as "a good man of affairs—clear, judicious, tactful, and good-humoured."[1]

Throughout his life as a chemist, Meldola remained an ardent enthusiast of natural history. As a young man he was personally encouraged in this avocation by John Keast Lord, author of *At Home in the Wilderness* (1867). He maintained an eleven-year friendship with Charles Darwin. He corresponded extensively with the great German naturalist Fritz Müller, and he was a good friend of Alfred Russcl Wallace. He joined the Entomological Society of London in 1872, served as its secretary between 1876 and 1880, and was president in 1895 and 1896. On the basis of his work in entomology, Meldola was proposed by Darwin for membership in the Royal Society. He was elected a fellow in 1886 and served on its council from 1896 to 1898 and again in 1914 and 1915. In 1914 he was appointed a vice president of the society. In 1880 he became a founding member of the Essex Field Club, an organization devoted to natural history, archaeology, and the preservation of wild areas.

Meldola received many honors for his work in chemistry and natural history. In 1910 Oxford University awarded him an honorary D.Sc.; on that occasion Meldola delivered the Herbert Spencer Lecture. In 1911 he received an LL.D. from St. Andrew's; in 1913 the Royal Society awarded him the Davy Medal; and both in 1901 and 1913 he received the Albert Medal of the Society of Arts for papers on industrial chemistry. In 1911 the French Chemical Society presented him with its Jubilee Award, and the Italian city of Turin honored him with a gold medal. In 1900 and in 1907 the French government invited Meldola to receive the Legion of Honor, but on both occasions the British Foreign Office forbade him to accept the award.

Meldola died while actively engaged in Britain's wartime efforts. He had been a founding member and, from 1911 on, president of the Maccabaeans, a London-based society that promoted the affairs of British Jews in the professional world. Meldola was buried on 18 November 1915 in the Spanish-Portuguese (Sephardic) Cemetery at Golder's Green. He bequeathed his entomological collection and cabinets to the Hope Museum at Oxford. Among his other bequests was the sum of £200 to Sutherland Technical College for awards for swimming and lifesaving, which became known as Meldola badges.

Chemistry. As a result of the enormous success of the coal-gas industry, organic chemistry in the second half of the nineteenth century went through a dramatic revolution. One of the major by-products of the destructive distillation of gas from coal was coal tar, which by the 1850's chemists, such as August Wilhelm von Hofmann and William Henry Perkin, began to analyze systematically. Meldola concentrated his own research entirely on the chemistry of coal tar and on a limited number of problems closely associated with the production of synthetic dyes. He had no graduate students at Finsbury whom he could set on a range of related projects; he had to rely instead upon a single paid assistant and the cooperation of a line of willing collaborators. The chemist Arthur G. Green wrote in retrospect that "Meldola's technical researches were in great measure of a pioneer character; they opened up new ground, but were not always capable of bearing immediate fruit."[2] His former collaborator John V. Eyre and Ernest Harry Rodd gave further perspective on Meldola's chemical career by noting that the Finsbury phase was ". . . not characterized by the earlier originality, but rather by dogged perseverance in selected lines of investigation."[3]

Nevertheless, his peers and students recognized Meldola as a craftsman who paid meticulous attention to details, who had a vast knowledge of the chemical literature, and who was a dextrous performer at the laboratory bench.

One major line of Meldola's work, begun in 1878 and the subject of eleven memoirs over a twenty-year period, entailed the discovery and analysis of many derivatives of naphthalene, a product of a fraction of coal tar known as "carbolic oil." This work helped unravel the complexities of isomerism of naphthalene compounds and established the patterns of substitutions of radicals. A second line of his research resulted in the development of the first oxazine dye, which became known as Meldola's blue (1879). Otto Witt had demonstrated that a dye could be produced by the heating of nitrosodimethylaniline hydrochloride with m-tolylenediamine; Meldola substituted a phenol for the m-diamine and discovered a dye that colored silk a dull violet and wool a deep indigo. He published a description of the process in 1879 without his or the firm of Brooke, Simpson, and Spiller's having taken out a patent on the process. German chemists later discovered the chemical's value as a dye for mordanted cotton and produced the chemical commercially under the names of Neublau, Naphthalenblau, Echtblau, and Baumwollblau. Meldola's firm, however, did take out a patent on his discovery of the first alkali green, which they exhibited at the Paris Exhibition in 1878 under the name of viridine. This became the forerunner of many sulfonated dyes of the malachite green variety.

Over an extended period commencing in 1882, Meldola also pursued research into the many complexities of azo compounds and developed a particularly novel method for reducing the nitro radicals of nitroazo compounds without reducing the azo radicals in the process. His procedures resulted in the discovery of a range of new dyes. Between 1886 and 1895 Meldola and his colleague Frederick William Streatfeild at Finsbury College wrestled, only partly successfully, with the little-understood problems of isomerism of diazoamine compounds. Toward the end of his career, he turned to the chemistry of nitro compounds and to aromatic substances, "which contributed considerably to our knowledge of the conditions governing the displacement of groups in aromatic compounds."[4]

Natural History. Meldola's first publications were in the area of natural history. As an avid collector of *Lepidoptera* and other insects, Meldola shared the joys of outings with his wife. Even at the outset, however, his interests were much broader than tax-onomic. He saw the value of experimentation and of observations of insect behavior. In later life he deplored the lack of a field station in Great Britain where experimental and ethological studies could be carried out. More important, Meldola took a deep interest in the contemporary controversies over the mechanism of evolution. Although he did not subscribe to the neo-Darwinian extreme promoted by August Weismann and Alfred Russel Wallace, he was an ardent supporter of the mechanism of natural selection.

It was natural, given his interest in entomology and evolution theory, that Meldola should become an active participant in the discussions over protective coloration, warning colors, and mimicry. Although one cannot credit Meldola with any major contribution in these areas, his formal publications and frequent letters to the editor of *Nature* were distinguished by their analytic acumen. In 1873 he wrote a valuable analysis of protective coloration, in which he distinguished five classes of this phenomenon. Between 1871 and 1882 he exchanged over thirty letters with Charles Darwin on these and related issues. It was Darwin who encouraged Meldola to translate from the original German Weismann's *Studies in the Theory of Descent*, to which Darwin added a brief preface and which Meldola embellished with numerous scholarly comments. Darwin also made him aware of Fritz Müller's paper "*Ituna* and *Thyridia*," which Meldola also translated and thereby introduced English naturalists to the Müllerian form of mimicry. The paper issued in an extended controversy between Darwin's supporters and those, such as William Lucas Distant, who sought other mechanisms of evolution. Meldola sided with Wallace in finding Müllerian mimicry a powerful argument in favor of the action of natural selection. He added further support to Müller's theory by calculating how two distasteful species might converge in pattern and by pointing out that the practice of mimicry tended to concentrate in groups of such "protected" butterflies as the danaids and heliconids. Edward B. Poulton, who also worked extensively on these problems and who became a close friend of and coworker with Meldola, later remarked that Meldola's elaboration of Müller's theory of mimicry "opened up a new and fruitful field in which much research is still being carried on."[5]

Between 1886 and 1891 Meldola crossed swords with George J. Romanes on the issue of coadaptation and particularly on Romanes' "physiological" theory of selection. On that occasion Meldola again strongly supported the pure Darwinian explanation. In 1896, in the form of letters to the editor of *Nature*, Meldola reflected favorably on the Darwinian implications of Walter F. R. Weldon's biometrical experiments on the dimensions of crab carapaces. Finally, in 1895 and 1896 he took the opportunity of his two presidential addresses before the Entomological Society of London to lecture his entomological friends against extreme empiricism and to argue for bringing physiology and chemistry to bear upon the general problems of the appearance and utility of variations.

Popularizer and Publicist. From the accounts of his students, one cannot conclude that Meldola was a master lecturer in an age that had become used to Thomas H. Huxley and John Tyndall. Nevertheless, he was admired for the clarity and forcefulness of his presentations. His lively wit and ability to tell anecdotes made him a popular after-dinner speaker. Meldola also possessed the talent to popularize chemistry in straightforward and lucid prose. He lectured to general audiences at Finsbury College, at the London Institution, and elsewhere. Some of these lectures later appeared in book form. He wrote a volume for Henry Holt's Home Universal Library titled *Chemistry*, which contained no formulas but offered in an elegant fashion a complete elementary survey of the science. A lecture series at Finsbury Technical College, given to practical photographers as well as chemistry students in the spring of 1888, was later published in Macmillan's Nature Series as *The Chemistry of Photography* (1889). Meldola's best-known popular science work grew out of a lecture given at the London Institution on 20 January 1890 and published by the Society for Promoting Christian Knowledge. *Coal and What We Get from It. A Romance of Applied Science* (1891) was both historical and descriptive of the contemporary knowledge of coal tar chemistry. It did not spare the reader the names of many of the complex organic derivatives but presented the technical material in such a captivating manner that the volume went through four editions. From 1897 to 1898 Meldola also served as the editor of Arnold's Practical Science Manuals.

By the end of the century, Meldola had become a harsh critic of the lack of a governmental policy toward science and of industry's indifference to research. This combination of attitudes had allowed Germany to capitalize upon the chemistry of coal tar in a way that Great Britain, the natural beneficiary of recent chemical discoveries, had not done. Beginning in 1886, in an address to the Society of Arts, Meldola assumed the role of gadfly to the English dye industry. By 1910, in a talk before the Society of Dyers and Colourists titled "Tinctorial Chemistry, Ancient and Modern," he unhesitatingly fingered the cause of the decline of the nation's lead in industrial chemistry in the face of excuses put forth by the dye industry:

> It is amazing that there should have ever been any cause suggested than the true cause, which is RESEARCH, writ large! The foreign manufacturers knew what it meant and realised its importance, and they tapped the universities and technical high schools and they added research departments and research chemists to their factories, while our manufacturers were taking no steps at all, or were calmly hugging themselves into a state of false security, based on the belief that the old order under which they had been prosperous was imperishable.[6]

Despite the fact that he had spoken on the authority of his experience in industrial and academic chemistry, Meldola remained an unappreciated prophet of the decline of Great Britain's chemical industry. Only with the arrival of World War I did the country shake loose its apathy and recognize the great lead that Germany had assumed in this area of science. As he told his colleagues in March 1914, in his presidential address to the Institute of Chemistry, his feeling about the situation was "one of humiliation."[7] Nevertheless, Meldola threw himself with characteristic vigor into the war effort. The Board of Trade appointed him to the Chemical Products Committee and to the Council of the "Scheme for the Organisation and Development of Scientific and Industrial Research." In July 1915 he assumed the chairmanship of the Advisory Council of British Dyes, Ltd. As a member of the council of the Institute of Chemistry, Meldola served on a number of its wartime committees and was chairman of its important Glass Research Committee. It was during this flurry of patriotic activity that Meldola overtaxed his health and died at his home on Brunswick Square at the age of sixty-six.

NOTES:

1. Tom Sidney Moore and James Charles Phillip, *The Chemical Society*, 95.
2. James Marchant, ed., *Raphael Meldola* . . . , 47.
3. John V. Eyre and E. H. Rodd, in Alexander Findlay and William Hobson Mills, eds., *British Chemists*, 111.
4. *Ibid.*, 122.
5. Edward B. Poulton, "Raphael Meldola, 1849–1915," in *Proceedings of the Royal Society*, **A93** (1916–1917), 35.
6. Quoted in Marchant, ed., 59–60.
7. Quoted in *ibid.*, 61.

BIBLIOGRAPHY

I. ORIGINAL WORKS. Meldola's complete bibliography (in Marchant) contains 453 separate listings of books, articles, and published reports. These cover a wide range of subjects from chemistry and natural history to miscellaneous accounts in archaeology, geology, astronomy, and science education and organization. The most important items have been annotated by the compilers. The overwhelming majority of Meldola's chemical papers appeared in *Chemical News, Journal of the Chemical Society,* and *Berichte der deutschen chemischen Gesellschaft.* The first description of "Meldola's blue" appears in "Einwirkung von Nitrosodimethylanilin auf Phenole, welche die Methylgruppe enthalten," in *Berichte,* **12** (1879), 2065–2066; the first description of viridine appears in "Ueber die Einwirkung des Benzylchlorids auf Diphenylamin," in *Berichte,* **14** (1881), 1385–1386. Meldola's translation of Fritz Müller, "*Ituna* and *Thyridia*; a Remarkable Case of Mimicry in Butterflies," is in *Proceedings of the Entomological Society* (1879), 20; his extension of Müller's theory is "Mimicry Between Butterflies of Protected Genera," in *Annual Magazine of Natural History,* 5 ser., **10** (1882), 417–425. Other important writings on the evolution of protective coloration and mimicry include "On a Certain Class of Cases of Variable Protective Colouring in Insects," in *Proceedings of the Zoological Society* (1873), 153–162; and "Entomological Notes Bearing on Evolution," in *Annual Magazine of Natural History,* 5 ser., **1** (1878), 155–161. Meldola's two presidential addresses to the Entomological Society include the formal papers "Speculative Method of Entomology" and "The Utility of Specific Characters and Physiological Correlation," which appear in the *Proceedings* of the society (1895), xlviii–lxviii, and (1896), lxii–xcii, respectively.

The translation and annotations of August Weismann's important work on evolution appeared as *Studies in the Theory of Descent,* Raphael Meldola, trans. and ed., prefatory notice by Charles Darwin, 2 vols. (London, 1882; repr. New York, 1975). Meldola's Oxford address, "Evolution, Darwinian and Spencerian," first published in 1910 by the university, has become more accessible in *Herbert Spencer Lectures. Decennial Issue 1905–1914* (Oxford, 1916). Meldola's popular works include *The Chemistry of Photography* (London, 1889; repr. 1891, 1901); *Coal and What We Get from It. A Romance of Applied Science* (London, 1891); and *Chemistry* (New York, 1912; 2nd rev. ed., London, 1937). Darwin's letters to Meldola are in Edward B. Poulton, *Charles Darwin and the Theory of Natural Selection* (London, 1896, repr. New York, 1902) 199–218.

II. SECONDARY LITERATURE. The most useful obituaries of Meldola are Sir William A. Tilden and Edward B. Poulton, "Raphael Meldola, 1849–1915," in *Proceedings of the Royal Society,* A**93** (1916–1917), 29–37, with portrait. Both obituaries are reprinted, without the portrait, in *Journal of the Chemical Society,* **111,** Transactions (1917), 349–359. Shorter versions of these obituaries appear in *Nature,* **96** (1915), 345–347. The most detailed account of Meldola's chemical achievements, by John V. Eyre and E. H. Rodd, is in Alexander Findlay and William Hobson Mills, eds., *British Chemists* (London, 1947), 96–

125. This essay includes a photograph taken around 1907. Twenty-three of Meldola's former colleagues, students, and friends wrote memorial accounts of various aspects of Meldola's life, which appear in James Marchant, ed., *Raphael Meldola . . . Reminiscences of His Worth and Work by Those Who Knew Him, Together with a Chronological List of His Publications . . .* (London, 1916). This volume also contains resolutions of sympathy sent to Mrs. Meldola by the many organizations and institutions with which her husband had been associated. Finally, this work also contains a complete bibliography of Meldola's writings, arranged both chronologically and by subject.

For an extended discussion of Meldola's involvement in controversies over the significance of Müllerian mimicry and on the evolutionary debates in the Entomological Society of London, see Muriel L. Blaisdell, "Darwinism and Its Data: The Adaptive Coloration of Animals" (Ph.D. diss., Harvard University, 1976), 186–241, 281–302. Information about Meldola's activities in various chemical societies may be gleaned from Tom Sidney Moore and James Charles Philip, *The Chemical Society 1841–1941. A Historical Review* (London, 1947), *passim;* and Richard B. Pilcher, comp., *The Institute of Chemistry of Great Britain and Ireland . . . History of the Institute: 1877–1914* (London, 1914), 249–282. A third portrait of Meldola is included in this latter work.

FREDERICK B. CHURCHILL

MICHAELIS, LEONOR (*b.* Berlin, Germany, 16 January 1875; *d.* New York City, 8 October 1949), *biochemistry.*

Few twentieth-century scientists have contributed significantly in as many different areas of scientific endeavor as Michaelis. His contributions range from embryology to magnetochemistry and bespeak the extraordinary fertility of his mind. Although a central figure in the development of modern biochemistry, especially in the application of physical-chemical principles to biological problems, Michaelis did not attain a permanent academic post with adequate facilities for his work until he was appointed at the age of fifty-four to the staff of the Rockefeller Institute of Medical Research in New York. Even before the rise of Hitler, anti-Semitism was a fact of German university life, and Michaelis, a man who had already demonstrated his remarkable ability as a teacher and as an investigator, was denied the opportunity to participate fully in the education of future German scientists and physicians.

He was the son of Moriz Michaelis, who ran a small business; his mother's maiden name was Hulda Rosenbaum. The educational program of the Berlin Koellnisches Gymnasium, from which he graduated in 1893, was directed to the liberal arts but offered to selected students the use of a chemical and physical laboratory for additional work. Michaelis thus acquired proficiency in Latin and Greek, modern languages, literature, and history, along with a desire to become a scientist. The broad scope of his cultural interests, especially his love of linguistics and music, may be traced to his school days. He chose to enter science through the study of medicine at the University of Berlin and received the M.D. degree there in 1897. Among his teachers were Wilhelm von Waldeyer in anatomy, Oskar Hertwig in histology and embryology, Emil du Bois-Reymond in physiology, and Emil Fischer in chemistry. Although Michaelis passed the premedical examination (*Physikum*) in 1895 with distinction in all subjects, his performance in the examination for a medical license (especially in surgery and gynecology) was only satisfactory; the latter was taken at Freiburg im Breisgau, where he spent the final semester of medical training in 1897.

Michaelis began his scientific research as a medical student and spent his free time in Hertwig's laboratory. An investigation of the histology of milk secretion won Michaelis a prize awarded by the medical faculty, and his first publication (1896) dealt with the fertilization of the egg of the amphibian *Triton taoniatus*. For his M.D. thesis he studied the direction of the first cleavage in the frog's egg and showed that the point at which the sperm fertilizes the egg does not determine the first cleavage furrow. His enthusiasm for communicating new knowledge to students, evident throughout his later life, led him to prepare the small book *Kompendium der Entwicklungsgeschichte des Menschen, mit Berücksichtigung der Wirbeltiere*, published in 1898. It was well received and went through many editions; the ninth appeared in 1921. By that time his scientific interests were far removed from embryology. Three further editions appeared between 1927 and 1931 under the authorship of Richard Weissenberg.

After completing his medical studies in Freiburg, Michaelis resumed work in Hertwig's laboratory, where he observed that eosinophilic cells accumulate in the lactic gland of the guinea pig during the colostrum period. Paul Ehrlich happened to learn of this, asked Michaelis to show him the histological preparations, and thereupon offered him an appointment as his private assistant in his Institut für Serumforschung und Serumprüfung in Steglitz, a Berlin suburb. Michaelis' assignment was to continue Ehrlich's work on histological staining, which Ehrlich could not pursue because of his immunological research. This obliged Michaelis to delve deeply into the organic chemistry of the dyes that had been developed for the textile industry. He also studied intensively the new physical chemistry and the mathematics underlying its principles, in order to understand better the interaction of dyes with the chemical constituents of tissues. He remained an omnivorous student of these subjects the rest of his life. During his brief association with Ehrlich, Michaelis made the important histological discovery of the specific staining by Janus green of cellular granules later to be called mitochondria; this method of vital staining was widely employed, especially by Edmund Vincent Cowdry. Michaelis also wrote the book *Einführung in die Farbstoffchemie für Histologen*, published in 1902.

According to Michaelis' personal account, his agreement with Ehrlich was that after one year in the latter's laboratory, Michaelis would enter clinical medicine since, in Ehrlich's view, "only a man of sufficient wealth should stay permanently in fundamental scientific research."[1] Consequently, in 1900 Michaelis joined the staff of Moritz Litten, the physician in chief of the Berlin municipal hospital. During the four years of his clinical service there, Michaelis managed to continue research on histological staining and also began to publish papers on immunology.

In 1903 Michaelis was appointed *Privatdozent* at the University of Berlin; his *Habilitationsschrift* dealt with protein precipitins. Among his findings was the observation that brief digestion (with pepsin) of serum albumin markedly altered its immunological properties. Later he entered the arena of controversy between Ehrlich and Svante Arrhenius regarding the application of the mass-action law to immunology. Michaelis' other immunological contributions included the demonstration that aqueous extracts of normal livers can be used for the Wassermann test and that the complement-fixation test in the Wassermann reaction can be replaced by a direct precipitation test through the use of high-potency extracts of syphilitic fetuses.

Among his other publications from Litten's medical division was one on iron-containing inclusions in tumors of the urinary bladder. This paper led Ernst von Leyden to invite Michaelis in 1904 to become a research assistant at the newly created section for cancer research in the First Medical Clinic (headed by Leyden) at the Charité Hospital in Berlin. Michaelis' contributions to cancer research were not striking, but his finding that various strains of mice differ in their susceptibility to transplantation with Jensen's mouse carcinoma merits mention. For his later work, of greater impact was his introduction in 1904 to the ultramicroscope invented by Henry Siedentopf and Richard Zsigmondy and made commercially available by the Zeiss Optical Works. This instrument figured in the subsequent development of colloid chemistry, a field in which Michaelis became active shortly afterward.

Michaelis married Hedwig Philipsthal in 1905; they had two daughters. The same year he married, Michaelis received the title of *ausserordentlicher Professor* at the University of Berlin, a post without salary, laboratory, or funds for research. This dubious distinction convinced him that his chances for an established academic post were negligible, and in that year he accepted a newly created position of bacteriologist at the Berlin municipal hospital "am Urban." Except for the years of World War I, when Michaelis served in various hospitals (tuberculosis, gastrointestinal diseases, infectious diseases), he remained at "am Urban" until 1921, and there made many of his most distinguished contributions to biochemistry. Together with his friend Peter Rona, the chemist at the hospital, he established a small laboratory from which there emerged over the years a series of studies on physical-chemical aspects of biology. The following account of Michaelis' achievements during the period 1905–1921 is not given in chronological order, but rather in relation to the various fundamental problems that he attacked, often concurrently. These problems included (1) the role of the hydrogen ion concentration in determining the properties of solutions of proteins and enzymes; (2) the mode of enzyme-substrate interaction in catalysis; (3) the adsorption of small molecules by colloidal substances.

Priority for some of Michaelis' work on hydrogen ion concentration belongs to the Danish chemist Søren P. L. Sørensen, whose memorable 1909 paper[2] presented a detailed description of the electrometric method for the determination of the hydrogen-ion concentration, the introduction of the term pH (negative logarithm of the hydrogen ion concentration), the preparation of buffer solutions of fixed pH, the use of dyes for the colorimetric determination of pH, and studies on the effect of pH on the catalytic activity of several enzymes.

According to Michaelis, Sørensen's paper appeared when his own work on the use of the hydrogen electrode to determine the effect of hydrogen-ion concentration on enzyme activity was nearing completion. Michaelis extended the scope of these studies, notably by showing in 1911 (with Heinrich Davidsohn) that the pH dependence of enzymatic catalysis resembles that of the dissociation of a weak acid. Moreover, he developed the theory of the dissociation of amphoteric electrolytes, such as amino acids and proteins, and gave quantitative

formulation to the concept of the isoelectric point, introduced in 1900 by William Bate Hardy. In a series of experimental papers Michaelis demonstrated that the isoelectric point of proteins is not only an index of change in electrical charge but also a minimum or maximum for other properties, such as solubility or viscosity. For the determination of the isoelectric point of proteins, he developed an electrophoretic method in which the pH was kept constant during the flow of the current; data on the isoelectric points of many proteins were obtained and were found to agree with the results on the effect of pH on their solubility properties. In 1914 Michaelis published his influential book *Die Wasserstoffionenkonzentration: Ihre Bedeutung für die Biologie und ihre Messung*; there was a second edition in 1923 and an English translation (by William A. Perlzweig) in 1926.

The studies by Sørensen and Michaelis on the role of pH in the catalytic activity of enzymes led to important work in Michaelis' laboratory on the effect of substrate concentration on the initial rates of enzyme action. Such measurements, but without control of pH, had been made earlier by several investigators, notably in 1903 by Victor Henri, who proposed that an intermediate enzyme-substrate complex is formed in the catalytic process. The validity of Henri's data and his theory were questioned, however, in particular by William Maddock Bayliss.[3] Michaelis' work, initially conducted with the help of a Canadian guest, Maud Leonora Menten, began with the enzyme invertase, which catalyzes the hydrolysis of sucrose. Their 1913 paper not only removed many of the objections to Henri's data but also provided the definition of a constant for the affinity of an enzyme for its substrate. Later authors termed this dissociation constant of the assumed enzyme-substrate complex the Michaelis constant (or Michaelis-Menten constant), and the symbol K_M to denote it has become a permanent component of the language of modern biochemistry. It should be noted, however, that this did not come about at once. Until about 1930 many biochemists denied the protein nature of enzymes, and relatively little importance was assigned to Michaelis' mathematical treatment of enzyme kinetics. The climate of opinion began to change only after the crystallization of pepsin by John Howard Northrop and the appearance of the valuable book by J. B. S. Haldane.[4]

In addition to studies on the dependence of initial rates on substrate concentration for enzymes other than invertase, Michaelis also extended Henri's treatment of the inhibition of enzyme action and made a clear distinction between inhibitors that act by competition with the substrate for the free enzyme and those that affect the rate at which the enzyme-substrate complex decomposes to form reaction products and to regenerate the free enzyme. After World War II the mathematical treatment of this aspect of enzymology was greatly refined because of its importance in the study of enzyme mechanisms and in the development of new chemotherapeutic agents.

To the above achievements of the period between 1905 and 1921 may be added studies on the adsorption of ions and small molecules by such surface-active materials as charcoal and cellulose. This work, largely conducted in association with Rona, reflected the then-current preoccupation of biologists with the colloidal state of living matter. In his typical fashion Michaelis wrote a book on the subject, entitled *Dynamik der Oberflächen*, published in 1909; an English translation (by W. H. Perkins) appeared in 1914. He also wrote an introductory textbook in mathematics for biologists and chemists, published in 1912, with later editions in 1922 and 1927, and *Praktikum der physikalischen Chemie, insbesondere der Kolloidchemie für Mediziner und Biologen*. The latter appeared in 1921 (subsequent editions were published in 1922, 1926, and 1930), and an English translation (by T. R. Parsons) of the second edition was published in 1925. French and Spanish translations soon followed. Michaelis' collaboration with Rona included a series of studies (1908) on the estimation of blood sugar. As an outgrowth of their interest in adsorption phenomena, methods were devised for the removal of serum proteins by means of kaolin or ferric hydroxide. In addition, Michaelis published experimental papers on bacterial agglutination and pH indicators, as well as on various clinical topics.

In 1921 the post-Wilhelmine government gave Michaelis the title of *Professor extraordinarius* for physical chemistry applied to medicine and biology at the University of Berlin, but without salary or facilities for research. By that time he had acquired worldwide recognition, and his modest laboratory at the "am Urban" hospital had attracted many young German physicians and postdoctoral guests from abroad. The city administration, however, had not changed its policy of discouraging basic research in the Berlin municipal hospitals. Michaelis therefore accepted an appointment with the Berlin firm Vereinigte Fabriken für Laboratoriumsbedarf, where he was given a research laboratory and served as a consultant in the manufacture of scientific apparatus. This association was brief, for in 1922 he was invited to become a visiting full professor at the Aichi Prefectural Medical School (in Nagoya, Japan), whose status had just been raised to that of a university; it later became part of the University of Nagoya.

Michaelis remained in Japan until 1925. He later wrote enthusiastically about his experience there, for he was given a good laboratory and had many research students, with whom he published numerous papers. He continued work on many of the problems studied in his Berlin laboratory, in particular adsorption phenomena and electrochemistry, and also embarked on a sustained investigation of semipermeable membranes. Michaelis also learned to speak Japanese and studied Chinese.

Among Michaelis' American admirers was Jacques Loeb, whose remarkable career as an experimental biologist was nearing its close with his studies on the physical chemistry of proteins at the Rockefeller Institute for Medical Research.[5] In 1923 Loeb wrote to Michaelis in Japan, inviting him to come to the United States for a lecture tour, which Michaelis undertook in May and June 1924. The tour was carefully arranged by Loeb and proceeded according to schedule, but Michaelis' pleasure at this recognition was dimmed by his distress at Loeb's sudden death that February. The lectures were collected in his book *The Effects of Ions in Colloidal Systems*, published in 1925, and dealt with Michaelis' studies on the adsorption of ions, electrical double layers, and other aspects of biophysical chemistry. One of the stops on the lecture tour was the Johns Hopkins School of Medicine, and on that occasion Michaelis was invited to come there as a resident lecturer for three years, after the expiration of his appointment in Japan. He accepted and began work in Baltimore in the spring of 1926.

After settling in the United States, Michaelis continued his research on semipermeable membranes, but by 1928 he had begun to shift his attention to the electrometric study of oxidation-reduction processes. His first efforts in this field (with Louis B. Flexner and E. S. G. Barron) were not notably successful because they dealt with the cysteine-cystine system, which responds sluggishly at metallic electrodes. Also, as was his wont, he wrote a book, *Oxidations-Reduktions-Potentiale, mit besondere Berücksichtigung ihrer physiologischen Bedeutung* (Berlin, 1929); an English translation (by Louis B. Flexner) appeared a year later, and a second German edition was published in 1933. In connection with this shift in Michaelis' scientific interests, it is noteworthy that in 1927 William Mansfield Clark was appointed professor of physiological chemistry at the Johns Hopkins School of Medicine. Beginning in 1920, Clark had conducted studies on the oxidation-reduction potentials of organic dyes (for instance, methylene blue), and he continued to make decisive contributions to this field in Baltimore.[6]

Michaelis finally attained his hope of securing a permanent position in 1929, when he was appointed a member of the Rockefeller Institute for Medical Research. He remained there until his death, and his research was not interrupted by transfer to emeritus status in 1941. Shortly after moving to New York, Michaelis made his most significant contribution to the study of the reversible oxidation-reduction of organic substances. At that time, largely owing to the work of Clark, it was accepted that in the reduction of the oxidized form of an organic dye (for instance, methylene blue) to its reduced form (leucomethylene blue), two electrons are transferred from the reductant, and it was considered that this electron transfer occurs without intermediate steps. In 1931, however, Michaelis (with Ernst Friedheim) reported that in the electrometric oxidation-reduction titration of the natural pigment pyocyanine, the titration curve in alkaline solution was consistent with simultaneous two-electron transfer, but at acidic pH values there was a stepwise one-electron transfer, with the intermediate formation of a free radical that Michaelis termed a "semiquinone." It should be noted that this discovery was made independently at about the same time by Bene Elema when he was a graduate student at Delft.

At first Michaelis' interpretation of his data was greeted with skepticism, but he soon produced massive evidence in support of his conclusions. Apart from potentiometric studies showing that the principle of stepwise univalent oxidation-reduction applied to other organic substances, he also used the methods of magnetochemistry to demonstrate that the semiquinones are paramagnetic, owing to the presence of an unpaired electron. In the latter work he enlisted the aid of experimental physicists but also contributed to the methodology by modifying the magnetic balance for the purpose of his studies. Moreover, Michaelis proceeded to acquaint himself thoroughly with the quantum theory underlying the principles of magnetochemistry. His enthusiasm as a teacher was again evident in the series of lectures he gave on quantum mechanics at the Rockefeller Institute during the 1930's. To this should be added the words of Clark: "As one whose work occasionally overlapped that of Dr. Michaelis, I wish to say that he taught me much and that true to the instincts of a good teacher he generously ignored the fact that I had had an opportunity to find what he later discovered."[7]

Other problems were also investigated in Michaelis' laboratory at the Rockefeller Institute. The stability of semiquinones in acid solutions permitted an extension of the pH scale for aqueous solutions up to 11 molar sulfuric acid; this complemented the "acidity scale" developed by Louis Plack Hammett. Also, the dimerization of organic radicals derived from dyes led Michaelis to study the relation of this process to metachromatic effects in histological staining. In addition, there was a series of studies on cysteine, especially the mechanism of its iron-catalyzed oxidation and its reaction with iodoacetic acid. Related to this work was the finding, in association with David Goddard, that the reduction of the cystine-rich hair keratin by means of thioglycolate gives a soluble form of the protein, digestible by proteolytic enzymes; this observation was later adopted in the cosmetic industry to produce a "cold" permanent wave.

Another area of investigation, largely developed by Michaelis' associate Sam Granick, was the study of the iron-containing protein ferritin. In addition to Granick, Michaelis' chief research associates at the Rockefeller Institute were Maxwell Schubert, Carl Smythe, and Edgar Smith Hill. Among the numerous guest investigators, apart from Goddard, were James Baumberger, Jannik Bjerrum, John Runnström, Kurt Salomon, Gerold Schwarzenbach, and Kurt G. Stern.

Michaelis was a short man of stocky stature and unprepossessing appearance. Although kindly toward younger scientists, he was not always tactful with senior colleagues. In times of relaxation, as at the Woods Hole Marine Biological Laboratory, where he spent many summers, he was a lively conversationalist. A talented pianist, he delighted in entertaining his friends with musical improvisations. He did not seek honors and received few: his election to the National Academy of Sciences came in 1943, and he was awarded an honorary degree by the University of California at Los Angeles in 1945.

NOTES

1. L. Michaelis, *Biographical Memoirs. National Academy of Sciences*, **31** (1958), 284.
2. S. P. L. Sørensen, "Enzymstudien II. Über die Messung und die Bedeutung der Wasserstoffionenkonzentration bei enzymatischen Prozessen," in *Biochemische Zeitschrift*, **21** (1908), 131–200.
3. W. M. Bayliss, *The Nature of Enzyme Action* (London, 1908).
4. J. B. S. Haldane, *Enzymes* (London, 1930); see also T. R. C. Boyde, *Foundation Stones of Biochemistry* (Hong Kong, 1980).
5. Jacques Loeb, *Proteins and the Theory of Colloidal Behavior* (New York, 1922).

6. William Mansfield Clark, *Oxidation-Reduction Potentials of Organic Systems* (Baltimore, 1960); "Notes on a Half-Century of Research, Teaching and Administration," in *Annual Review of Biochemistry*, **31** (1962), 1–24.

7. William Mansfield Clark, "Leonor Michaelis 1875–1949," in *Science*, **111** (1950), 55.

BIBLIOGRAPHY

I. ORIGINAL WORKS. A list of Michaelis' publications, appended to his autobiographical sketch in *Biographical Memoirs. National Academy of Sciences*, **31** (1958), 282–321, includes 484 items. Regrettably, the list is riddled with errors. The books he wrote are listed in the text. Among his more important articles in scientific journals are the following: "Die vitale Färbung, eine Darstellungsmethode der Zellgranula," in *Archiv für mikroskopische Anatomie und Entwicklungsgeschichte*, **55** (1900), 558–575; "Über die Adsorption der Neutralsälze," in *Zeitschrift für Elektrochemie*, **17** (1911), 1–5, 917–919, with H. Lachs; "Die Wirkung der Wasserstoffionen auf das Invertin," in *Biochemische Zeitschrift*, **35** (1911), 386–412, with Heinrich Davidsohn; "Die Kinetik der Invertinwirkung," ibid., **49** (1913), 333–369, with M. L. Menten; "Über die verschiedenartige Natur der Hemmungen der Invertasewirkung," ibid., **60** (1914), 79–90, with H. Pechstein; "Potentiometric Study of Pyocyanine," in *Journal of Biological Chemistry*, **91** (1931), 355–368, with E. Friedheim; "A Study on Keratin," ibid., **106** (1934), 605–614, with David R. Goddard; "The Paramagnetism of the Semiquinone of Phenanthrenequinone-3-sulfonate," in *Journal of the American Chemical Society*, **60** (1938), 202–204, with G. F. Boeker and R. K. Reber; "Ferritin and Apoferritin," in *Science*, **95** (1942), 439–440, with Sam Granick; and "The Semiquinone Radical of Tocopherol," ibid., **109** (1949), 313–314, with S. A. Wollman. Michaelis contributed to the history of science in "Zur Erinnerung an Paul Ehrlich: Seine wiedergefundene Doktor-Dissertation," in *Die Naturwissenschaften*, **7** (1919), 165–168.

II. SECONDARY LITERATURE. There is no adequate biography of Michaelis, and most of the obituary notices on him are based on his autobiographical sketch (with brief addendum by D. A. MacInnes and Sam Granick) in *Biographical Memoirs. National Academy of Sciences* (see above). Among them are those by E. S. G. Barron in *Biological Bulletin*, **101** (1951), 13–16; William Mansfield Clark, in *Science*, **111** (1950), 55; and Sam Granick, in *Nature*, **165** (1950), 299–300. See also George W. Corner, *A History of the Rockefeller Institute, 1901–1953* (New York, 1964), 178–181.

JOSEPH S. FRUTON

MICHAELIS, PETER (*b*. Munich, Germany, 28 May 1900; *d*. Cologne, Germany, 3 August 1975), *botany, genetics.*

Michaelis was the only son of Oskar Michaelis, a portrait painter, and his wife, Thusnelda Jaeger, the daughter of a professor of philosophy at Tübingen. His parents' home was a place where artists and other prominent persons met in his mother's salon; many of them had their portraits painted by his father. Meeting these people considerably influenced Michaelis' education. He was talented in music and drawing, and very interested in living things. By the age of seventeen he had an extensive knowledge of the flora around Munich, including algae, mosses, ferns, and fungi.

Michaelis' education at the Realgymnasium was interrupted when he entered the army as a cadet in May 1918. He was discharged in January 1919 without having seen action. In October 1919 Michaelis enrolled at the University of Munich to study botany, geology, geography, and zoology. He received a Ph.D. in July 1923. His dissertation, done under Karl von Goebel, dealt with the flower morphology of the Euphorbiaceae with special regard to the angiospermous flower's phylogeny. This work, based on the investigation of 130 genera out of nearly 300, was awarded a prize by the university.

In April 1923 Otto Renner had appointed Michaelis his assistant at Jena. Michaelis remembered this period with ambivalence. Not only did he have to share the position with a colleague, he also fell ill, and an extended stay in the hospital toppled him into financial ruin. On the other hand, at Jena he began his lifelong genetic work on cytoplasmic inheritance in *Epilobium* (the willow herb), which in some ways paralleled Renner's work on plastid inheritance in *Oenothera*. The phenotypic difference of reciprocal hybrids in *Epilobium*, which earlier had attracted the attention of other geneticists, could be attributed to genetic differences in the cytoplasm apart from the chromosomes. Fritz von Wettstein, Correns' former assistant, created the term "plasmone" for them. At that time the debate on the role of the genome and the plasmone in heredity and their bearing upon development was in full swing. Michaelis' first contribution to this question was published in 1929.

In 1927 Michaelis moved to Stuttgart, where he was chief assistant to Richard Harder until 1933. He lectured and taught courses on various botanical subjects. During the winters of 1931 to 1932 and 1932 to 1933, he carried out ecological research in the Alps, connecting this work with his hobbies of mountain climbing and skiing. Assisted by his fiancée, Gertrud Aichele, he studied the influence of wintry climatic conditions on the timberline. They were married in 1932 and had two daughters and one son.

The departure of Harder, whose field was cryptogamic botany, to become professor at the University of Göttingen (1933) influenced Michaelis' career. His consequent pursuit of the experiments on plasmic inheritance in *Epilobium*, documented by a series of publications, had brought him a reputation in the field of non-Mendelian genetics. Thereupon Erwin Baur, director of the Kaiser Wilhelm Institute for Breeding Research in Müncheberg/Mark (not far from Berlin), offered him a staff position, which Michaelis accepted. From April 1933 on, he could concentrate on his work on *Epilobium*. Baur, who supported him personally and professionally, died in the fall of 1933. His successor, Wilhelm Rudorf, gave Michaelis his own department of plasmic inheritance research. In 1941 he was appointed a scientist member of the Kaiser-Wilhelm-Gesellschaft. In 1944 the prosperous period of Müncheberg eventually was ended. The approaching eastern battlefront necessitated the transfer of equipment, livestock, and seed material to various locations in the interior of Germany.

From 1946 through 1955 the Kaiser Wilhelm Institut—now a part of the Max-Planck-Gesellschaft—was provisionally reestablished at Voldagsen, near Hameln (not far from Hannover), and in 1956 it was moved to Cologne. In both places Michaelis continued his work on cytoplasmic inheritance, until he retired in 1968. He became an internationally known geneticist in the still controversial field of plasmic inheritance, to which he contributed more than 100 publications. He had shown that the plasmone may differ not only between different species but also between races of the same species. By 1947 he had investigated about 500 strains from 25 species of *Epilobium*. In most cases plasmone differences appeared as an absence of the necessary cooperation between nucleus and cytoplasm, resulting in flower malformation or inhibition of vegetative development and growth. In general these disturbances were nonspecific.

When it was observed that the inhibited plants produce phenotypic alterations with the tendency to better growth and eventual normalization in certain areas, Michaelis tried to use these alterations as a tool in the analysis of the plasmone. Altered shoots could be propagated vegetatively and regenerated to whole plants. In part Michaelis recognized similarities with dauermodifications; on the other hand, the alterations showed maternal inheritance. Michaelis regarded them as different plasmotypes. He created the hypothesis of intraindividual recombination of the plasmone constituents under certain conditions by segregation and selective multiplication of these genetic elements, a great number of which should be present in the cytoplasm. In order to test this new hypothesis, he elaborated the method of variegation pattern analysis. Even though the method could be applied successfully to the plastid segregation, the cytological difficulties concerning the plasmotypes could not be overcome. It was not yet possible to solve the problems of localization and of the mode of action of the cytoplasmic determinants.

At the end of his scientific career Michaelis was invited by the Japan Society for the Promotion of Science to lecture for two months in Japanese universities and research institutes. In November 1967 the University of Strasbourg awarded him an honorary doctorate.

BIBLIOGRAPHY

I. ORIGINAL WORKS. Michaelis' dissertation, "Blütenmorphologische Untersuchungen an den Euphorbiaceen unter besonderer Berücksichtigung der Phylogenie der Angiospermenblüte," is in *Botanische Abhandlungen*, **3** (1924), 1–150. His ecological work yielded five publications, the last being "Ökologische Studien an der alpinen Baumgrenze. V. Osmotischer Wert und Wassergehalt während des Winters in den verschiedenen Höhenlagen," in *Jahrbücher für wissenschaftliche Botanik*, **80** (1934), 337–362. A comprehensive review of his genetic work on *Epilobium* is "Cytoplasmic Inheritance in *Epilobium* and Its Theoretical Significance," in *Advances in Genetics*, **6** (1954), 287–401, with a detailed bibliography. Of Michaelis' later publications the following are noteworthy: "Über Gesetzmässigkeiten der Plasmon-Umkombination und über eine Methode zur Trennung einer Plastiden-, Chrondriosomen-, resp. Sphaerosomen-, (Mikrosomen)- und einer Zytoplasmavererbung," in *Cytologia*, **20** (1955), 315–338; "Cytoplasmic Inheritance on *Epilobium* (a Survey)," in *Nucleus*, **8** (1966), 83–92; and "Über Plastiden-Restitutionen (Rückmutationen)," in *Cytologia*, **34** supp. no. (1969), 1–115.

WILFRIED STUBBE

MINKOWSKI, OSKAR (*b*. Aleksotas, near Kaunas, Russia [now Lithuanian S.S.S.R.], 13 January 1858; *d*. Fürstenberg, Germany, 18 June 1931), *internal medicine, clinical-experimental pathology.*

Minkowski, best known for his discovery and exploration of the role of the pancreas in diabetes, was the son of a wealthy German-Jewish grain trader. His brother Hermann (1864–1909) was a distinguished mathematician who developed the theory of quadratic forms in *n*-variables, worked on the mathematical physics of space and time, and taught Albert Einstein at Zurich. Another brother was a successful businessman and art collector. Oskar attended school in Kaunas and Königsberg, then studied medicine at Strassburg and Freiburg before qualifying as a doctor of medicine at the University of Königsberg in 1881 under Bernhard Naunyn's supervision.

Naunyn's influence determined the direction of Minkowski's medical career in several ways. First, Naunyn passed on to Minkowski an orientation to medical problems inspired by Johannes Peter Müller, a pioneer of the classical period in nineteenth-century German physiology. Müller had instigated the transition of German medicine from the romantic idealism of its heritage of *Naturphilosophie* to a more empirical approach. The new empiricism eschewed strictly vitalistic interpretations of physiological phenomena in favor of direct observation and the analysis of mechanical and chemical aspects of physical processes. The approach continued to emphasize physiological processes as a systemic whole, however, rather than particular organs or mechanisms.

Second, Naunyn's research interests came to form the matrix of Minkowski's medical preoccupations. A key concept formulated by Justus von Liebig, that of *Stoffwechsel*, encouraged the investigation of physiological processes by viewing the body as an "economy." Not quite equivalent to "metabolism," *Stoffwechsel* was tinged with vitalism in its principal idea that each living thing needed continually to transform matter in order to maintain its own form. Naunyn's attention had turned to *Stoffwechsel* in the laboratory of Friedrich Theodor von Frerichs, an experimental pathologist. Frerichs interested Naunyn in metabolic pathology and passed on to him the study of the liver and related organs as the great chemical laboratory of the body. Naunyn opened a laboratory for experimental pathology at Königsberg, the first of its kind in connection with a medical clinic in Germany. He explored five broad areas in a path-breaking combination of clinical and experimental research: diabetes mellitus, liver function, the pathology of urinary ammonia and acid, hepatogenous jaundice, spinal injuries and fever.

Third, Naunyn impressed upon Minkowski the priority of the clinical aspect of medicine. At Naunyn's Königsberg clinic, experimental pathology and pharmacology were united with clinical work in a conscious effort to help the patients. This natural science approach to clinical medicine did much to define both the horizons and the limitations of Minkowski's work. He belonged to a generation of medical pioneers trained to integrate experimental with clinical pathology in an age still fearful of systematic medical experimentation.

Minkowski's rare combination of talents made him an ideal disciple of Naunyn. He demonstrated an unusual capacity to analyze problems critically and then synthesize new solutions. Added to a razor-sharp intelligence were the intuition and dexterity of a gifted surgeon. At a time when surgery was only beginning to benefit from antiseptics and other improved techniques, Minkowski proved a virtuoso and an innovator in the operating theater. His skills and versatility led to major contributions to medical knowledge on a wide range of diagnostic and therapeutic problems.

Minkowski's dissertation was a study of the relationship between electrical stimulation of the brain and blood circulation. His abilities won him an immediate assistantship in Naunyn's clinic. Ernst Stadelmann, Minkowski's predecessor, had been analyzing diabetic urine and had isolated an anomalous unknown acid as one of its components. In 1884 Minkowski correctly identified this substance as β-hydroxybutyric acid and related its production to the faulty metabolism of fats. Further study enabled Minkowski to help confirm the role of acidosis in diabetic coma. He attempted to forestall this dreaded final stage of the disease by using a blood gas pump to compensate for depleted alkali reserves and obtained some favorable results. Until the discovery of insulin, alkali therapy remained a last treatment for diabetics showing severe keto acidosis.

Naunyn's laboratory was also investigating the role of the liver in metabolism. In 1885 Naunyn proposed to observe the effects of total hepatectomy on a dove and chose Minkowski to attempt the intricate and difficult procedure. Unlike some of his colleagues, Minkowski was interested in animal experiments, and he succeeded brilliantly where others had failed. He hepatectomized a series of larger birds such as geese years before others mastered the technique. For anatomical reasons these birds, unlike mammals, survived hepatectomy long enough to measure its effects. Naunyn and Minkowski were mainly interested in determining the origins of bile pigments; in 1886 the hepatectomies allowed Minkowski to demonstrate the liver's role in hemolytic jaundice.

Minkowski characteristically pursued his researches within the traditional physiological and medical context that accorded the liver a central role in the bodily "economy." Yet despite the classic experiments of Claude Bernard on the glycogen function of the liver, little about this process was then understood, and pathological investigations into hepatrophy and phosphorism had not been much help. Minkowski sought a key in the waste products of metabolism, and chose to investigate the liver's function in the production of urine. It was known that neither muscles nor kidneys were responsible for ureapoiesis, the chemical synthesis of ammonia and carbonic acid to form urea. Hepatectomy allowed Naunyn and Minkowski to study several stages of this process, including the formation of ammonia from the decomposition of complex molecules. Minkowski inferred the intermediary stages of carbohydrate metabolism from the presence of lactic and amino acids, and theorized that these recombined in the liver to produce uric acid. While this theory was later disproven, it nevertheless formed the starting point for further investigations of the problem.

Minkowski took special pride in two of his early achievements. In his first contribution to endocrinology he drew upon Rudolf Virchow's analogy of the pituitary and thyroid glands to suggest in 1887 that pituitary malfunction was the cause of acromegaly. Three years later the theory was verified by Pierre Marie. In 1888 Minkowski contradicted prevalent views on the effects of polyneuritis by demonstrating that severe functional and psychic disturbances to the central nervous system resulted from the disorder.

In 1889 Minkowski followed Naunyn to the medical clinic at Strassburg. Here Naunyn's experimental pathology was cross-fertilized by the experimental pharmacology of his friend Oswald Schmiedeberg, whose institute was at Strassburg. In this creative atmosphere Minkowski began to make the major contributions of his career.

In April 1889, while visiting the library at Hoppe-Seyler's institute in Strassburg, Minkowski met Joseph von Mering, who in 1886 had produced experimental diabetes in animals by means of phlorizin, and was now studying the use of certain fats in nutritional therapy. These studies, von Mering told Minkowski, assumed that functional defects of the pancreas rendered the body incapable of splitting fats in digestion. After his own work on the liver, Minkowski's natural reaction was to challenge von Mering to prove his assumption experimentally by excising the pancreas. Fired by his recent surgical triumphs and, as he later admitted, by the "naive overconfidence of youth," Minkowski could not resist the counterchallenge of von Mering's reply that total pancreatectomy was impossible. That same day, according to Minkowski, von Mering assisted him at Naunyn's clinic in performing a total pancreatectomy on one of Hoppe-Seyler's laboratory dogs.

A family illness that called him out of town prevented von Mering from moving the depancreatized dog to his own laboratory to study fat resorption. The dog recovered from surgery at Naunyn's laboratory and was being trained to empty its bladder and bowels into special containers, the usual procedure when metabolic investigations were being conducted. The dog instead urinated repeatedly and frequently on the laboratory floor. Minkowski reprimanded the laboratory attendant. The attendant replied that he had taken the dog out regularly, but that the animal had developed constant polyuria. Minkowski's experience and training led him to test the urine for sugar, which he measured at more than 10 percent. After pancreatectomizing several more dogs, Minkowski concluded with astonishment that total extirpation of the pancreas invariably induced diabetes mellitus in the dogs. The literature contains no references to a later story that the attraction of flies to the dog's urine prompted the first test for glycosuria—a story Minkowski later denied.

When von Mering returned a week later, Minkowski informed him of the discovery. But von Mering possessed neither the surgical skills nor a particular interest in following up its implications. Minkowski, on the other hand, characteristically resolved to pursue both the original problem of fat resorption and the new problem of pancreatic diabetes. He shared with von Mering the authorship of the report "Diabetes mellitus nach Pankreas-exstirpation," which appeared in *Zentralblatt für klinische Medizin* in 1889 and in *Archiv für experimentelle Pathologie und Pharmakologie* in 1890. There was no further collaboration. When a colleague suggested that the true discoverer was actually the laboratory attendant who noticed the dog's polyuria, Minkowski replied that if that was so, then the cleaning woman who left a dust rag on Röntgen's cathode tubes discovered X rays. Not only was it Minkowski who had grasped the significance of the polyuria, but he alone pursued the far-reaching implications of the initial discovery. Von Mering, who had contributed little more than the lab attendant, was not involved in any further aspect of the work.[1]

Minkowski correctly argued that the major achievement in the discovery of pancreatic diabetes was less the surgery or the recognition of its consequence than his grasp of the significance of the discovery for the theory of carbohydrate metabolism. The report of his experiments, published with variations in several journals in 1889 and 1890, was a classic exposition setting the problem of pancreatic diabetes in dogs in the context of medical literature in which pancreatic dysfunction had been seen to accompany, but had never been recognized as a cause of, diabetes in humans. Minkowski detailed his own investigations of pancreatic diabetes and discussed the theoretical and research implications of the possible explanations of the condition.

The most immediate question for Minkowski was whether pancreatic diabetes resulted directly from the removal of some specific pancreatic function or indirectly from some internal trauma induced by the pancreatectomy. The observation that partial pancreatectomy did not lead to diabetes weighed heavily in favor of the former. Next, two possible scenarios suggested themselves to explain the interruption of intermediary metabolic processes caused by pancreatectomy: extirpation of the pancreas might permit the accumulation of some abnormal substance in the metabolic system, or the operation might remove some normal function of the pancreas that enabled the body to metabolize sugar (and the absence of which caused diabetes). Minkowski rejected the first assumption for two reasons. First, his experiments showed that blood transfusions from a diabetic to a normal dog caused no diabetes in the recipient. Second, tying off the pancreatic ducts while the pancreas remained in place did not cause diabetes. Since only total excision had this result, Minkowski concluded that the removal of some pancreatic function necessary for carbohydrate metabolism caused diabetes.

Minkowski realized that further research was needed to uncover this metabolic function of the pancreas. He wondered whether the function was unique to the pancreas, that is, whether total pancreatectomy merely hindered or fully prevented the utilization of sugar. One step would be to undertake more exact quantitative analyses. Meanwhile, however, Minkowski's study of experimentally induced diabetes led him to consider the role of the pancreas as exclusive. He argued that common theories explaining diabetes as originating in disorders of the nerves, liver, or muscles had no experimental basis. He realized, on the other hand, that the pancreatic function he sought to isolate might well constitute one link in a metabolic chain that could easily be broken at other links. Far from forming a clear hypothesis about an internal secretion of the pancreas, in an 1890 paper, "Diabetes mellitus und Pankreasaffection," Minkowski used the analogy of proteinuria, a result of kidney disease, to conceptualize the relationship between glycosuria and the pancreas. He had already experimented with oral administration of fresh pancreas and interpreted the extracts' failure to reduce glycosuria as evidence that it was the metabolic rather than the digestive system that required the mysterious pancreatic function.

The discovery of pancreatic diabetes by von Mering and Minkowski in 1889 encouraged many researchers to seek explanations of the relationship. Minkowski spent much of the next four years following up the clues he had amassed. In 1892 and 1893 he published a second series of reports, including "Weitere Mitteilungen über den Diabetes mellitus nach Pankreasexstirpation" (1892) and "Untersuchungen über den Diabetes mellitus nach Exstirpation des Pankreas" (1893). Minkowski pancreatectomized cats, rabbits, pigs, birds, and frogs to compare the results with those he had achieved on dogs (known to researchers as "Minkowski dogs"). He was able to induce and observe many degrees of diabetes mellitus and came to believe, somewhat erroneously, that in the most advanced stage of diabetes after pancreatectomy, no sugar at all could be metabolized. Against the suggestions of other researchers, he correctly denied any analogous metabolic function between the pancreas and organs such as the intestines or the salivary glands. He reiterated that no other organ shared the role of the pancreas in carbohydrate metabolism.

More important, Minkowski reported the results of transplantation experiments on dogs, confirmed by E. Hédon at Montpellier, in which he removed the greater part of the pancreas and attached the small remaining piece, with its blood supply intact, subcutaneously to the wall of the abdomen. No diabetes resulted until after this remnant was removed. This result strengthened Minkowski's suspicion that the pancreas "produced something" indispensable for carbohydrate metabolism elsewhere in the body, and the lack of it caused diabetes. Many years later, in a letter of 12 January 1923 to J. J. R. Macleod and in a 1929 paper, he insisted that both this "something" and his earlier references to a "pancreatic function" were meant to denote an internal secretion of the pancreas, and that the only reason for his transplantation experiments had been to demonstrate that the pancreas functioned analogously to other endocrine glands. At the time, he referred only to a "substance," and in 1906 to an "internally directed secretion." In the context of the impossibility of isolating such a hypothetical secretion, his terminology remained flexible until the exact function of the substance could be established.

If such a secretion did exist, it had to possess certain properties. Against the view of J.-R. Lépine in France that the pancreas produced an enzyme or other glycolytic substance that entered the bloodstream by way of the lymphatic system, Minkowski contended that sugar was decomposed not in the blood but (more likely) in muscles and tissues. From this and several other factors he argued that the mysterious "something" was not likely to be an enzyme. First, depancreatized dogs showed a rapid decline of glycogen stored in the liver. Second, carbohydrate feedings were followed by carbohydrates in the urine, but pure meat and protein feedings resulted in severe glycosuria. Minkowski theorized that animals manufactured sugar from protein in the ratio D:N, that is, the amount of dextrose eliminated was proportional to the amount of urinary nitrogen. This "Minkowski quotient" became widely used in studies of protein metabolism. Third, Minkowski noted that levorotary sugars were metabolized much more easily than dextrorotary. On the basis of this data he correctly hypothesized that the metabolic role of the pancreas was to create a chemical affinity between sugar molecules circulating in the bloodstream and the organs that normally utilized sugar.

Yet Minkowski reluctantly acknowledged in 1893 that he was no closer to a therapy for diabetes. Pancreas transplantations were impossible because of blood supply problems. He now visualized the pancreatic substance he sought as an analogue to the thyroid preparations that had recently proved a therapeutic marvel against myxedema. As a result, he experimented further with both oral and subcutaneous administration of pancreatic extracts, but to no avail. Subcutaneous injections did lead to reduced glycosuria, but their side effects were so severe that not only were the extracts unusable therapeutically but their positive effectiveness remained in doubt. True to his training as a clinician, Minkowski abhorred premature experimental therapies.

In 1905 and 1906 Minkowski was forced to defend his theories on pancreatic diabetes in the face of criticism from Eduard Pflüger, a respected physiologist at Bonn. Pflüger disputed both the relationship between total pancreatectomy and diabetes and the probable existence of an internal secretion of the pancreas. Minkowski attributed Pflüger's attacks to a personal vendetta and masterfully demolished his opponent's main argument. He disproved Pflüger's theory of nerve stimulation in the duodenum as the cause of glycosuria by totally removing the duodenum in dogs with no resulting glycosuria.

But Pflüger's claim that extirpation experiments were insufficient to prove the existence of an internal pancreatic secretion that could alleviate diabetic symptoms was not as easily refuted.[2] In 1906 Minkowski admitted the possibility that his theory of an internal secretion might not fit the puzzle of pancreatic diabetes. Two years later his student Joseph Forschbach performed parabiotic experiments that strongly reinforced the contested theory. Forschbach connected the blood supply of a normal dog to that of a diabetic dog, whose glycosuria diminished dramatically. He also introduced into Minkowski's laboratory Georg Zuelzer, a Berlin physician who had carried out promising experiments with pancreatic extracts to reduce glycosuria and acidosis. But once again severe toxic effects led Minkowski the clinician to condemn Zuelzer's extracts as therapeutically impracticable. Minkowski the theorist also disagreed with Zuelzer's hypothesis that the pancreas worked mainly to modify the effects of adrenalin in the liver. Despite isolated reports to the contrary, the brilliant results expected of organotherapy in pancreatic diabetes remained conspicuously absent. Until such results could be achieved, the doubts raised by Pflüger and others about the internal secretion hypothesis had to be acknowledged.

Minkowski received the news of the discovery of insulin in Toronto by J. J. R. Macleod, F. G. Banting, J. B. Collip, and C. H. Best in the year 1921–1922 as a vindication of his theories about the role of the pancreas in metabolism. To Zuelzer's claim for recognition as the father of the new pancreatic hormone, Minkowski replied that he, too, regretted that he had not chemically isolated insulin. The Toronto group sent Minkowski some of the first insulin to be used in Germany, and he served as chairman of the committee established to organize German production of the new hormone. He told his students that while he had hoped to be the father of insulin, he was content with the Canadians' designation of him as its grandfather.

Minkowski later blamed himself for not having tried harder, both in his own researches and after Zuelzer's researches, to eliminate the side effects of pancreatic extracts he had known could lower glycosuria. For several reasons, he felt, the time and place had been wrong for him or Zuelzer to discover insulin. First, microanalytical methods for measuring minute fluctuations in blood sugar levels had only recently been mastered. Second, endocrinology had just developed to the point where internal secretions were sufficiently understood. Third, the talents of the Toronto researchers had been supplemented by limitless amounts of raw materials available to them in North America for both research and the actual production of insulin.

Minkowski's sensible retrospective analysis of why three decades passed between the discovery of the role of the pancreas in diabetes and the discovery of insulin did not take into account the influence of his own character and training. The very circumspection that his students and colleagues so admired in his approach to experimental and clinical pathology tempted him to pursue medical knowledge more broadly than deeply. The pattern of his researches reinforced his belief that every new fact raised more questions and every new solution contained new puzzles. His theoretical preconceptions led in the same direction—to wide-ranging, almost limitless inquiry. Some remarks in Naunyn's memoirs suggest, as well, that Minkowski was not passionately ambitious and tended to be content with his routine of medical explorations and teaching.

In practice this meant that Minkowski occupied his time with many problems in addition to pancreatic diabetes. His clinical work took him to Cologne in 1900 to direct the municipal hospital and in 1904 to teach at the Academy for Practical Medicine. From 1905 he headed the medical clinic at Greifswald, and from 1909 he directed the medical clinic and was full professor of internal medicine at the University of Breslau (now Wrocław, Poland), where he remained until 1926. Students remembered him as a reserved but friendly teacher, at once modest and intellectually formidable.

Minkowski's clinical work was accompanied by many publications on therapeutic themes and by experimental researches on a wide range of problems. Among his most important contributions in clinical and experimental pathology were continued researches on liver function. He filled out the etiological picture of hemolytic jaundice as originating in disturbances of blood pigments and introduced the idea of the excretion of liver cells into the bloodstream. In a classic article contributed to Naunyn's *Festschrift* in 1904, Minkowski theorized correctly that these disturbances resulted from primary changes in the spleen and suggested that splenectomy provided the most effective therapy for the condition.

Minkowski also made important contributions to knowledge of the chemical and pathological role of uric acid. Throughout his career he published often on such topics as purine and nuclein metabolism, fermentation in the stomach, and the role of the esophagus in digestion. His masterpiece in this area involved him as one of the first to identify an excess of uric acid as the cause of gout. The monograph, published in 1930, included a photograph of Minkowski's own eye to illustrate symptoms of gout.

A third area of deep interest to Minkowski was the pathology of respiration. In 1912 he published several papers on emphysema and a masterful, comprehensive study of the breathing process. These works proved useful during World War I, when Minkowski served as a consulting internist for the German Ninth Army. The War Ministry asked him to study the pathology of gas poisoning. The resulting monograph interwove chemical, physiological, pathological, and therapeutic aspects of this new medical problem. It was not published until 1921, after the issue had largely ceased to interest the German medical community.

Few aspects of internal medicine escaped Minkowski's critical attention. By the same token, he did not deviate from, but rather brought to fruition, the teachings of Bernhard Naunyn. In both clinical and experimental pathology, Minkowski was primarily a first-rate diagnostician who excelled in discovering the broad patterns of pathological and physiological processes, often using techniques of comparison and analogy. His emphasis on logical reasoning was deeply rooted in traditional approaches harking back to Liebig and Müller. The synthesis of old and new techniques in the laboratories of Naunyn, Minkowski, and their associates contributed substantially to the medical understanding of carbohydrate metabolism and pancreatic diabetes, giving enormous impetus to German experimental pathology. But Minkowski's approach proved insufficient to unravel the peculiar complexities of the pancreas as an endocrine gland. "No one of us should regret," he wrote in 1899, "that he might be able to plant only for the next generation. Meanwhile, we can satisfy our own hunger for effective therapies quite nicely on the wild fruits of the old empiricism."

Despite his outstanding abilities, Minkowski did not accede to the rank of full professor until he was fifty years old. Veiled remarks by Naunyn and other colleagues allude to the tacit anti-Semitism of German government policy as the main reason for his delayed promotion. Nevertheless, he was an influential member of the German Association for Internal Medicine and was internationally recognized as the foremost expert on pancreatic diabetes before the discovery of insulin. In 1923 Minkowski joined a team of physicians called to Moscow to attend Lenin after his final stroke. After retiring to Wiesbaden in 1926, Minkowski longed to return to Berlin, where his married daughter resided. When he finally undertook the move in 1931, his health broke down. He died that year of pneumonia and secondary thrombosis, leaving also a son who inherited the mathematical skills of his uncle Hermann. During World War II, Minkowski's widow, the former Marie Siegel, moved to Argentina, where she spent her remaining years.

NOTES

1. See Minkowski, "Die Lehre vom Pankreas-Diabetes in ihrer geschichtlichen Entwicklung," in *Münchener medizinische Wochenschrift*, **76**, no. 8 (22 February 1929), 310–315. Although this narration of the events surrounding the discovery of pancreatic diabetes follows Minkowski's and Naunyn's version, von Mering never contradicted it in any way. British pathologists tended to give more credit to von Mering (and still do!—see V. C. Medvei, *A History of Endocrinology* [Lancaster, England, 1982]), whose earlier discovery of phlorizin diabetes inspired them to seek an extract that could cure diabetes; German pathologists seem to have leaned the other way, especially after Minkowski's death, urging that von Mering's name be removed from the 1890 article. As late as 1913, Mering and Krehl's *Lehrbuch der inneren Medizin* included work by Minkowski on the liver and the pancreas, but did not include the pancreas in the chapter on endocrine glands by F. Kraus. Kraus's section on *Stoffwechsel* does, however, mention Georg Zuelzer's attempts to find a workable pancreatic extract.

2. To follow the exchange discussed in this paragraph, see Pflüger, "Über die im tierischen Körper sich vollziehende Bildung von Zucker aus Eiweiss und Fett," in *Archiv für die gesamte Physiologie*, **103** (1904), 66–70; Minkowski, "Bemerkungen über den Pankreasdiabetes. Zur Abwehr gegen Eduard Pflüger," in *Archiv für experimentelle Pathologie und Pharmakologie*, **53** (1905), 331–338; Minkowski, "Über die Zuckerbildung im Organismus beim Pankreasdiabetes. Zugleich eine Entgegnung auf die wiederholten Angriffe von Eduard Pflüger," in *Archiv für die gesamte Physiologie*, **111** (1906), 13–60; Minkowski, "Die Totalexstirpation des Duodenums," in *Archiv für experimentelle Pathologie und Pharmakologie*, **58** (1908), 271–288; Roy G. Hoskins, *The Tides of Life* (New York, 1933), 311; Minkowski, "Die Lehre vom Pankreas-Diabetes in ihrer geschichtlichen Entwicklung," in *Münchener medizinishe Wochenschrift*, **76**, no. 8 (22 February 1929), 310–315; Georg Zuelzer, "Diskussion," appended to Minkowski, "Über die bisherigen Erfahrungen mit der Insulinbehandlung des Diabetes," in Deutsches Gesellschaft für Innere Medizin, *Verhandlungen*, 36th Congress (Kissingen, 1924), 91–108, 136; Minkowski, "Das alte und das neue in der Diabetestherapie," *ibid.*, 33rd Congress (Wiesbaden, 1921), 225–233; and Karl Loenig, "Organotherapie des Diabetes mellitus," *ibid.*, 297–302.

BIBLIOGRAPHY

I. Original Works. Virtually none of Minkowski's personal correspondence survived World War II; a few letters to the discoverers of insulin are in the Insulin Committee records at the University of Toronto Library. The most complete available list of Minkowski's 14 monographs and over 170 articles was assembled by his student Martin Nothmann and appended to L. Krehl's obituary as "Oskar Minkowskis Arbeiten," in *Archiv für experimentelle Pathologie und Pharmakologie* (hereafter *Naunyn-Schmiedebergs Archive*), **163** (1931–1932), 626–635. Many of Minkowski's works were published in that journal. Included here are only his key works and others referred to in this article.

"Über das Vorkommen von Oxybuttersäure im Harn bei Diabetes mellitus," in *Naunyn-Schmiedebergs Archive*, **18** (1884), 35–55; "Untersuchungen über den Einfluss der Leberexstirpation auf den Stoffwechsel," *ibid.*, **21** (1886), 41–88; "Diabetes mellitus nach Pankreasexstirpation," in *Zentralblatt für klinische Medizin* (1889), no. 23, and in *Naunyn-Schmiedebergs Archive*, **26** (1890), 371–387, written with Joseph von Mering; "Diabetes mellitus und Pankreasaffection," in *Berliner klinische Wochenschrift*, **27**, no. 8 (24 February 1890), 167–169; "Weitere Mitteilungen über den Diabetes mellitus nach Exstirpation des Pankreas," in *Berliner klinische Wochenschrift* (1892), no. 5, 90–94; "Untersuchungen über den Diabetes mellitus nach Exstirpation des Pankreas," in *Naunyn-Schmiedebergs Archiv*, **31** (1892–1893), 85–189; "Über experimentelle Therapie," in *Die Therapie der Gegenwart*, **40** (1899), 95–96; "Zur Pathogenese des Ikterus," in *Zeitschrift für klinische Medizin*, **55** (1904), 34ff.; "Über die Zuckerbildung im Organismus beim Pankreasdiabetes. Zugleich eine Entgegnung auf die wiederholten Angriffe von Eduard Pflueger," in *Archiv für die gesamte Physiologie*, **111** (1906), 13–60; "Über die bisherigen Erfahrungen mit der Insulinbehandlung des Diabetes," Deutsche Gesellschaft für Innere Medizin, *Verhandlungen*, 36th Congress (Kissingen, 1924), 91–40; "Die Lehre vom Pankreas-Diabetes in ihrer geschichtlichen Entwicklung," in *Münchener medizinische Wochenschrift*, **76**, no. 8 (22 February 1929), 311–315; and "Gicht," in Georg and Felix Klemperer, eds., *Die neue deutsche Klinik* (Berlin, 1930).

II. Secondary Literature. For biographical and bibliographical information, see the following obituaries: E. Frank, "Oskar Minkowski zum Gedächtnis!" in *Klinische Wochenschrift*, **10**, no. 29 (28 July 1931), 1381–1383; G. Klemperer, "Zur Erinnerung an Oskar Minkowski," in *Die Therapie der Gegenwart*, **572** (July 1931), 335–336; and L. Krehl, "Oskar Minkowski," in *Naunyn-Schmiedebergs Archiv*, **163** (1931–1932), 621–635. See also Frederick M. Allen, *Studies Concerning Glycosuria and Diabetes* (Boston, 1913); Michael Bliss, *The Discovery of Insulin* (Toronto and Chicago, 1982); Erich Frank, *Pathologie des Kohlehydratstoffwechsels* (Basel, 1949); B. A. Houssay, "The Discovery of Pancreatic Diabetes: The Role of Oscar Minkowski," in *Diabetes*, **1**, no. 2 (March–April 1952), 112–116; Victor Cornelius Medvei, *A History of Endocrinology* (Lancaster, England, and Boston, 1982); Joseph von Mering and Ludolf von Krehl, eds., *Lehrbuch der inneren Medizin*, 8th ed. (Jena, 1911); John Theodore Merz, *A History of European Thought in the Nineteenth Century*, II (Edinburgh and London, 1903); Hans M. Meyer, "Schmiedebergs Werk," in *Naunyn-Schmiedebergs Archiv*, **92** (1922), 1–17; Bernhard Naunyn, "Oswald Schmiedeberg," in *Naunyn-Schmiedebergs Archiv*, **90** (1921), 1–7, and *Erinnerungen, Gedanken und Meinungen* (Munich, 1925); Karl Oppenheimer, ed.,

Handbuch der Biochemie des Menschen und der Tiere, III, pt. 1 (Jena, 1910); Karl E. Rothschuh, *History of Physiology*, Guenter B. Risse, trans. and ed. (Huntington, N.Y., 1973); Hans Peter Schönwetter, *Zur Vorgeschichte der Endokrinologie* (Zurich, 1968); Swale Vincent, *Internal Secretion and the Ductless Glands* (London, 1912; 2nd ed., 1922); and F. G. Young, "The Evolution of Ideas about Animal Hormones," in Joseph Needham, ed., *The Chemistry of Life* (Cambridge, 1970), 125–155.

SUZANNE ZELLER
MICHAEL BLISS

MIRSKY, ALFRED EZRA (*b*. Flushing, New York, 17 October 1900; *d*. New York City, 19 June 1974), *biochemistry, cell biology.*

Mirsky, son of Michael David Mirsky and Frieda Ittelson Mirsky, graduated from the Ethical Culture School in New York City and from Harvard College, obtaining a B.A. degree in 1922. He studied at the College of Physicians and Surgeons of Columbia University for two years. On receipt of a fellowship from the National Research Council in 1924, he worked at Cambridge University under Joseph Barcroft during the academic year 1924–1925, and completed his graduate studies under Lawrence J. Henderson at Harvard. He wrote a dissertation titled "The Haemoglobin Molecule" and received a Ph.D. from Cambridge in 1926.

The molecularity of hemoglobin and the molecular weight of the protein were established by Theodor Svedberg and Gilbert Adair in 1925. Their results demonstrated that proteins are rigorously definable species of large molecules, and were important in showing that proteins, despite their size, should be described in the molecular terms of the chemist. The initial postulates of protoplasmic components as being essentially undefinable, dispersible, and colloidal aggregates were eventually replaced by the view that the major constituents of protoplasm contain protein molecules whose shape, charge, and state of aggregation are markedly affected by the response of their ionizable groups to the hydrogen ion concentration (pH). Mirsky's early papers demonstrate that he had adopted a rigorously chemical orientation from the beginning of his career.

In 1924 and 1925 Mirsky published eight papers on hemoglobin with Mortimer L. Anson, of which the first two had Barcroft as coauthor. Anson was a fellow student in Barcroft's laboratory, as well as a later colleague at the Biophysics Laboratory of the Cancer Commission at Harvard. The collaboration of Mirsky and Anson on hemoglobin continued until 1935. As presented in preliminary form in Mirsky's dissertation, the disruption of protein organization and precipitation (denaturation) had been observed to be reversible. The mechanisms of these phenomena were the major problems studied by these young investigators for the next decade.

On 25 May 1926 Mirsky married Reba Paeff; they had a daughter and a son. In 1927 Mirsky was appointed an assistant in the laboratory of Alfred E. Cohn at the hospital of the Rockefeller Institute for Medical Research. Anson was appointed to the laboratory of John Howard Northrop at the Princeton branch of the institute. Cohn was engaged in the quantitation of activities of the human heart. Mirsky began his work in Cohn's laboratory with studies of pH in the blood of developing chicks, using a glass electrode developed with Anson. The increase in pH simulated the curve of decrease in oxygen consumption during development. The resulting paper marked the end of Mirsky's association with Cohn's research program, since Cohn had become more interested in humanistic studies than in those of laboratory science.

Mirsky and Anson resumed the study of hemoglobin and its denaturation and renaturation. In a second series of papers written between 1929 and 1935, they showed that protein coagulation takes place in two steps, in which unfolding can be separated from precipitation. Horse hemoglobin, coagulated by various methods, including heat or acid, can be solubilized and its unfolded state converted by a cyanide solution to a state indistinguishable from native hemoglobin; this product can then be crystallized to a denaturable hemoglobin. The denaturable portion of the hemoglobin was shown to be the globin; it was found that other denaturable proteins, such as serum albumin, can be renatured. These results were extended to the formation of an active trypsin from an inactive denatured enzyme.

Free sulfhydryl groups appeared in the denaturation of egg albumin and serum albumin. Although other researchers had proposed that such groups are generated from disulfide bonds during denaturation, another hypothesis was formulated in 1936, during Mirsky's sabbatical year at the California Institute of Technology. Mirsky and Linus Pauling then proposed that native proteins are coiled in specific configurations whose parts are stabilized largely by hydrogen bonds, and that unfolding and denaturation reveal groups previously obscured and protected by the originally folded chains. This paper was an important early statement of now-current views of protein structure and of the mechanism of denaturation and renaturation. Both views of the appearance of sulfhydryl groups are now believed to be correct, since in many proteins native structure is also maintained by disulfides whose reduction generates sulfhydryls and opens the structure.

In 1937 Mirsky studied changes in muscle proteins in an attempt to correlate them with functional alterations in the muscle as a result of elevated temperature. An irreversible muscle shortening, known as thermal rigor, was associated with the appearance of sulfhydryl groups, and he concluded that this phenomenon was due to a denaturation. He also believed that denaturation was part of muscle contraction generally, although he realized that not enough was known about muscle proteins at the time.

An interest in structural proteins led Mirsky to attempt the isolation of a protein complex that had been described in 1938 as derived from the cytoplasm. The fibrous material was found to contain large amounts of deoxyribonucleic acid (DNA) and was clearly nuclear in origin. He then began a new line of investigation, attempting to understand the structural and functional significance of nuclear nucleoproteins. In the mid 1930's the discovery that the plant viruses are ribonucleoproteins and that ribonucleic acid (RNA) is present in cytoplasmic particulates had begun the growth of biochemical interest in the nucleic acids, culminating in the 1944 discovery by O. T. Avery and his colleagues that DNA is the pneumococcal transforming agent. By 1941 enough was known of the relation of genes to chromosomes to pose the problem of the chemical nature of the hereditary determinants. In approaching this question, Mirsky, who in 1940 had become an associate member of the Rockefeller Institute, established a collaboration with the cytochemist Arthur W. Pollister, of the department of zoology at Columbia Unversity. For the next decade Mirsky's laboratory at Rockefeller Institute was a leading center for structural and functional studies of cell nuclei.

Mirsky's first formal paper with Pollister describes the extraction of nucleoproteins from a wide variety of animal cells. Their major approach was the differential use of neutral sodium chloride solutions of varying concentrations: physiological saline removed protein and cytoplasmic constituents; concentrated saline (1 M to 2 M) extracted DNA and other proteins that were precipitated in physiological saline. (It was shown later that concentrated saline dissociated DNA and proteins.) These soluble components reassociated and reprecipitated at lower salt concentrations. Hence, the mild procedure, often suitable for the isolation of DNA, nevertheless introduced restructuring of the original cellular com-

plex. Some thirty years later it was shown that chromosomal subunits of DNA and various proteins, known as nucleosomes, are isolable without dissociation, and hence represent a better approach to the isolation of a more native DNA-protein complex. Nevertheless, the DNA-protein complexes isolated in 1941 were shown to come from cell nuclei and were believed to be components of chromosomes. Mirsky's review of the status of this field in 1943 is a useful summary of this early period of the biochemistry of genetic material. Mirsky did not speculate as to the specific chemical nature of the gene; he suggested that the newly isolated DNA proteins were either "the genes themselves or were intimately related to genes."

Mirsky and Pollister then attempted to isolate chromatin from the nuclei of certain types of animal cells and thought that they had obtained threads of this material, which might even have been intact chromosomes. From 1946 to 1951 these efforts were extended with the collaboration of Hans Ris. Threads possessing the main cytological features of chromosomes were isolated from calf thymus lymphocytes and analyzed. Over 90 percent were found to consist of nucleohistone containing DNA. An insoluble residue contained protein determining the form of the "chromosome" as well as some RNA and DNA. These studies were extended to the isolation of similar "chromosomes" from many kinds of cells, including more voluminous structures from interphase nuclei. In his last papers, however, Mirsky became more circumspect about problems of isolating active chromatin.

In 1948 Mirsky became a member of the Rockefeller Institute; occupying new laboratories, he enlarged his group, which in addition to Ris included Vincent Allfrey, Marie Daly, and Herbert Stern. Foreign visitors such as Alberto Monroy began to work on problems of chemical embryology. With Ris, Mirsky showed that diploid somatic cells of an organism contain identical amounts of DNA, twice that of haploid germ cells. In 1950 Hermann J. Muller congratulated Mirsky and referred to the "grand discovery" of DNA constancy, which supported the concept of DNA as the hereditary material.

In 1950, in a symposium commemorating the fiftieth anniversary of the rediscovery of Mendel's work, Mirsky presented a paper titled "Some Chemical Aspects of the Cell Nucleus." Noting the constancy of DNA, in contrast with the variability of RNA, he concluded that DNA is part of the gene substance. Nevertheless, some six years after Avery's discovery, he was still unconvinced that DNA itself was the sole genetic material, pointing out the insensitivity of the assay and the difficulty of assuring that minute quantities of protein are not attached to the DNA. As noted by Norman W. Pirie, who had similar reservations in later years concerning the infectivity of viral RNA, "Scepticism and objectivity are near neighbors." The chemical evidence of the purity of transforming DNA or of an infectious RNA was little better in the late 1980's than it was in the 1950's. Nevertheless, new bodies of data demonstrate the validity of the views that certain nucleic acids themselves may determine genetic continuity, and that sequences of bases in these polymeric nucleates determine the specificity of the genetic units.

In the early 1950's Mirsky and his colleagues turned to the problems of the regulation of gene expression and other metabolic activities of cell nuclei. Much work was done on the enzymatic content of nuclei and on their capacity to generate energy and to effect various syntheses. They demonstrated glycolytic systems in nuclei, as well as the nuclei's ability to synthesize and utilize adenosine triphosphate (ATP) in the synthesis of RNA. As it became clear that nuclei contain many proteins and enzymatic functions, many laboratories joined in this work, which had now merged with the broad front of the advance of knowledge of cellular and organelle structure and metabolic function. By the end of the 1960's the concluding work of the laboratory was concerned with problems of embryological development (with H. Naora and E. Davidson), observations on the modification of histones by acetylation and methylation, and on the effects of such substitutions on gene expression (with Vincent Allfrey and B. G. T. Pogo), and many other aspects of the contents and activities of cell nuclei. Mirsky's last papers, published in the early 1970's, were on the role of the histones in the structure of chromatin and in its replication and transcription.

In 1954, when the institute became the Rockefeller University, Mirsky's title was "professor." He became quite active in university affairs, particularly on committees concerned with the graduate program. In 1959 Mirsky initiated a series of lectures for high school students, now named in his honor. Following retirement from his laboratory in 1964, he served as librarian of the Rockefeller University from 1965 until 1972. His wife died in 1966, and he married Sonia Wohl in 1967. Mirsky became professor emeritus in 1971, after forty-four years at the Rockefeller Institute and University.

Mirsky's most active laboratory investigations occurred in the first thirty years at the Rockefeller Institute. His early studies on protein structure had enabled him to develop a new line of work that both pioneered in an understanding of cell organization and genetic chemistry and merged with the major biochemical advances of the period. The significant accomplishments of his laboratory led to his election to the National Academy of Sciences in 1954.

From 1951 to 1961 Mirsky served as an editor of the *Journal of General Physiology*. From 1959 to 1965 he was a coeditor, with Jean Brachet, of the compendium *The Cell*. Between 1954 and 1964, he was awarded honorary degrees by the University of Gothenburg, the University of Santiago de Chile, and the University of Palermo. The breadth of his interests and accomplishments, and his extensive writings of reviews and historical essays, led to his election in 1964 to the American Philosophical Society. Mirsky traveled widely and was quite knowledgeable in archaeology and art history; his fine collection of art and historical objects is at the Rockefeller University.

BIBLIOGRAPHY

I. Original Works. A chronological list of Mirsky's publications is available from the Rockefeller University archives. Key publications include "On the Correlation Between the Spectra of Various Haemoglobins and Their Relative Affinities for Oxygen and Carbon Monoxide," in *Proceedings of the Royal Society of London*, **B97** (1924), 61–83, with Mortimer L. Anson, Joseph Barcroft, and S. Oinuma; "On Some General Properties of Proteins," in *Journal of General Physiology*, **9** (1925), 169–179, with Mortimer L. Anson; "A Description of the Glass Electrode and Its Use in Measuring Hydrogen Ion Concentration," in *Journal of Biological Chemistry*, **81** (1929), 581–587, with Mortimer L. Anson; "Protein Coagulation and Its Reversal: The Reversal of the Coagulation of Hemoglobin," in *Journal of General Physiology*, **13** (1929), 133–143, with Mortimer L. Anson; "Protein Coagulation and Its Reversal: Serum Albumin," *ibid.*, **14** (1931), 725–732, with Mortimer L. Anson; "The Equilibrium Between Active Native Trypsin and Inactive Denatured Trypsin," *ibid.*, **17** (1934), 393–398, with Mortimer L. Anson; "Sulfhydryl and Disulfide Groups of Proteins: II. The Relation Between Number of SH and S-S Groups and Quantity of Insolable Protein in Denaturation and in Reversal of Denaturation," *ibid.*, **19** (1935), 427–438, with Mortimer L. Anson.

"On the Structure of Native, Denatured, and Coagulated Proteins," in *Proceedings of the National Academy of Sciences*, **22** (1936), 439–447, with Linus Pauling; "Protein Denaturation," in *Cold Spring Harbor Symposia on Quantitative Biology*, **6** (1938), 150–163; "Nucleoproteins of Cell Nuclei," in *Proceedings of the National Academy* *of Sciences*, **28** (1942), with Arthur W. Pollister; "Fibrous Nucleoproteins of Chromatin," in *Biological Symposia*, **10** (1943), 247–260, with Arthur W. Pollister; "Chromosomes and Nucleoproteins," in *Advances in Enzymology*, **3** (1943), 1–34; "The Chemical Composition of Isolated Chromosomes," in *Journal of General Physiology*, **31** (1947), 7–18, with Hans Ris; "The State of the Chromosomes in the Interphase Nucleus," *ibid.*, **32** (1949), 489–502, with Hans Ris; "The Desoxyribonucleic Acid Content of Animal Cells and Its Evolutionary Significance," *ibid.*, **34** (1951), 451–462, with Hans Ris; "Some Chemical Aspects of the Cell Nucleus," in Leslie C. Dunn, ed., *Genetics in the 20th Century* (New York, 1951), 127–153; "Some Enzymes of Isolated Nuclei," in *Journal of General Physiology*, **35** (1952), 559–578, with Herbert Stern, Vincent G. Allfrey, and Hans Saetren; "The Chemistry of the Cell Nucleus," in *Advances in Enzymology*, **16** (1955), 411–500, with Vincent G. Allfrey and Herbert Stern; "Protein Synthesis in Isolated Cell Nuclei," in *Journal of General Physiology*, **40** (1957), 451–490, with Vincent G. Allfrey and Syozo Osawa; "Mechanisms of Synthesis and Control of Protein and Ribonucleic Acid Synthesis in the Cell Nucleus," in *Cold Spring Harbor Symposia on Quantitative Biology*, **28** (1963), 247–262, with Vincent G. Allfrey; "Changing Patterns of Histone Acetylation and RNA Synthesis in Regeneration of the Liver," in *Proceedings of the National Academy of Sciences*, **59** (1968), 1337–1344, with B. G. T. Pogo, A. O. Pogo, and Vincent G. Allfrey; "The Structure of Chromatin," *ibid.*, **68** (1971), 2945–2948; and, with Jean Brachet as coeditor, *The Cell: Biochemistry, Physiology, Morphology*, 6 vols. (New York, 1959–1964).

The Rockefeller University archives have extensive holdings of Mirsky's notebooks, correspondence, and other documents, and supplies a curriculum vitae.

II. SECONDARY LITERATURE. See George Washington Corner, *A History of the Rockefeller Institute (1901–1953): Origins and Growth* (New York, 1965); Carolyn Kopp, "The Alfred E. Mirsky Papers at the Rockefeller University Archives," in *The Mendel Newsletter*, no. 23 (November 1983), 1–5; and Bruce S. McEwen, "Alfred Ezra Mirsky (1900–1974)," in *American Philosophical Society. Year Book 1976* (1977), 100–103.

SEYMOUR S. COHEN

MONOD, JACQUES LUCIEN (*b*. Paris, France, 9 February 1910; *d*. Cannes, France, 31 May 1976), *molecular biology*.

A highly complex personality, Jacques Monod was most of all a scientist, and the totality of the scientific ideas and experimental results of his careeer form an immense theoretical edifice. But he was also a musician, a military officer, a sportsman, a writer, an administrator and politician, and a philosopher. He was a man of action and a gifted organizer, but his domain of choice was the de-

velopment of theory. His ideal was knowledge: for him that was the highest goal of human activity; it was the thing that made man special and was the destiny of humankind.

Life. The Monod family was descended from a Swiss Huguenot pastor who came to France from Geneva in 1808. Jacques's father, Lucien Hector Monod, was an artist and art historian, an anomaly in a family of government officials, pastors, and doctors. His mother, Charlotte Todd McGregor, was American. Both parents had an important influence on young Jacques's education.

Lucien Monod was a sensitive artist, but also a humanist and a positivist. He had a special admiration for the work of Darwin and Ernst Haeckel, and young Jacques showed an early interest in biology, collecting beetles and tadpoles. Lucien Monod was also interested in music, and Jacques learned to play the cello as a young child. Music and biology were his two intellectual loves, and he hesitated between them for many years before finally choosing his profession.

When Jacques was seven years old, the family moved to Cannes; the house they built there, "Clos Saint-Jacques," remained his favorite residence ever after.

Studies. As a pupil at the Collège de Cannes, Monod was fortunate to find several important mentors, in particular his professor of Greek, M. Dor de la Souchère. After graduating in the summer of 1928, Monod enrolled in the Faculté des Sciences in Paris, where he lived with his older brother Philippe, a lawyer who later became a diplomat and played an important role in Jacques's life, discreetly helping him in his career and suggesting the right professional chores. Monod received his degree in 1931 but he was dissatisfied with his university education, which, he later noted, "lagged behind contemporary biological science by nearly twenty years or more." Only one of his professors had any real impact on him: Georges Urbain, who taught thermodynamics. Like many other students of biology, after graduation Monod went to the Roscoff marine biology station, where he became acquainted with four scientists who shaped his conception of science and his scientific practice: Georges Teissier, who gave him the taste for quantitative description; André Lwoff, who introduced him to microbiology; Boris Ephrussi, in physiological genetics; and Louis Rapkine, who taught him that only chemical and molecular descriptions could provide a complete interpretation of how living beings functioned.

In the autumn of 1931 Monod won a fellowship to study at the University of Strasbourg, in the laboratory of Edouard Chatton, the leading French protistologist of the time. Here he became familiar with the techniques of microbiology, learning, among other things, to cultivate pure cultures of ciliates. It was during this period that, in collaboration with Chatton and André and Marguerite Lwoff, he published his first scientific articles, on the stomatogenesis of infusorians. In October 1932 Monod won the Commercy Scholarship and returned to Paris, where he spent two years in the Laboratory on the Evolution of Organized Beings, directed by Maurice Caullery.

In 1934 Monod became an assistant in the zoology laboratory of the Sorbonne. That summer he took part in a scientific expedition to Greenland on the *Pourquoi pas?* In the spring of 1936 he was about to embark on a new expedition of the *Pourquoi pas?* when Boris Ephrussi invited him to go along on a trip to America. That invitation was a turning point in Monod's life, in two senses: the *Pourquoi pas?* and its entire company were lost off the coast of Greenland, and Monod's stay in America was decisive in setting the course of his scientific career.

Having obtained a Rockefeller Fellowship, Monod spent a year at the California Institute of Technology, where the "*Drosophila* group" directed by T. H. Morgan was working. Here he learned not only genetics but also another way of doing science, a new scientific style based on collective effort, ease of personal relations between scientists, and freedom of critical discussion.

When Monod returned to Paris, Louis Rapkine and Boris Ephrussi convinced him that he lacked the basic knowledge he needed to make music his career, and he opted definitively for biology. Monod returned to the Sorbonne to prepare a doctoral dissertation (defended in 1941) on the subject he had finally chosen under the influence of Georges Teissier: bacterial growth.

Monod also continued his activity as an amateur musician. He formed a Bach choir, La Cantate, which he directed until 1948. It was there that he met Odette Bruhl, an archaeologist and orientalist who specialized in the art of Nepal and Tibet and later became curator of the Guimet Museum. They married in 1938, and Odette brought him the enrichment of a visual culture and sensibility complementary to his own. They had twin sons, Olivier and Philippe, who both became scientists, the former a geologist and the latter a physicist.

The War and the Resistance. Monod was exempted from military service because of a minor physical handicap (the consequence of polio), but he joined a Resistance group after the German army

occupied France. His Sorbonne laboratory became a meeting place and an underground print shop for propaganda bulletins. Many armed Resistance groups were formed after the Allied invasion of Normandy in 1944, and Monod decided to join the Franc-Tireurs Partisans (FTP). The year before, he had joined the French Communist Party (PCF), the only political party with significant weight in the Resistance leadership. He resigned from the PCF in 1945 because he disagreed with the party's postwar policy and, with his spirit of independence, he was unable to accept the organization's rigid discipline.

Assigned to coordinate resistance actions as the head of the Troisième Bureau, Monod organized the general strike that led to the liberation of Paris. After the liberation, he became an officer in the Free French Forces and a member of General de Lattre de Tassigny's general staff. For his military activity Monod was awarded the Croix de Guerre, the Legion of Honor, and the American Bronze Star.

The Pasteur Institute. In late 1945 Monod joined the Pasteur Institute as laboratory director in the department headed by André Lwoff. He spent the rest of his scientific career in this prestigious institution. The National Center of Scientific Research allowed him a post of technical aide, and he hired Madeleine Jolit, who worked as the main technician in his laboratory until 1971. In collaboration with Alice Audureau, Monod continued his research on bacterial growth and enzyme adaptation, in particular studying the enzyme that became the classic subject of his later research, β-galactosidase.

During his days in the military, Monod had come across an issue of the journal *Genetics* in a mobile library of the American army. In it he read an article by Salvador Luria and Max Delbrück demonstrating the spontaneous character of bacterial mutations. In 1946 he attended the Cold Spring Harbor symposium at which Alfred Hershey demonstrated genetic recombination among viruses and Joshua Lederberg and Edward Tatum announced the discovery of bacterial sexuality. All the biologists at this symposium realized that bacteria, and even crystallizable viruses, really did have mutable genes capable of sexual recombination and replication, just like the genes of animals and plants. It was also at this symposium that Monod made contact with the small group of researchers gathered around Max Delbrück who later detailed the mechanisms of transference of genetic information by studying the system constituted by *Escherichia coli* bacterium and its series-T viruses.

Upon his return to Paris, Monod joined with Elie

Wollman in experiments on growth inhibition among bacteria infected with bacteriophages, and he was strongly tempted to continue working on bacteriophages. But in the end he decided not to opt for this shift in research program, and instead continued working on various other subjects until 1947, when he was invited to present a general report on enzyme adaptation at the Growth Symposium. Examining the existing literature, including his own earlier research, Monod realized the importance and scope of this phenomenon, recognized yet still unexplained, in which a genetic and a chemical determinant were linked. It became clear to Monod that the fundamental problem of enzyme adaptation lay in assessing the respective roles of the hereditary and environmental factors (the substratum) in enzyme synthesis. This became the point of departure of his research program.

The "Grenier." Lwoff's department, in which Monod worked, became a place of truly mythic proportions in the history of molecular biology. There were two research groups, housed at opposite ends of a long, narrow corridor in the famous *grenier,* an attic of the biological chemistry building: Monod's group on enzyme adaptation and Lwoff's, which in 1949 began a fresh approach to the study of lysogeny. That same year another major protagonist of French molecular biology joined the *grenier*: François Jacob, who collaborated very closely with Elie Wollman.

There was a constant and ever-changing flow of trainees through the *grenier,* especially foreigners. The department was part of a narrow network of advanced biological research centers for the members of the small scientific community that was then in the process of creating a new discipline: molecular biology. Despite the cosmopolitan atmosphere, the science conducted in the *grenier* retained a typically French character, not only in the subjects chosen and in the tendency to emphasize the more strictly physiological aspects, but above all in a scientific style that combined extreme experimental rigor with the boldest speculation. The elegance and deductive clarity of demonstration were considered just as important as the results achieved.

From 1948 on, a fundamental contribution to the implementation of the research program on enzyme adaptation was made by the American immunologist Melvin Cohn, who spent five years in Paris. Collaboration (and debate) with his colleagues, and later with his students, was of great importance to Monod, for his own thinking was stimulated by confrontation with the ideas of others, and his theories were refined in the course of discussion and debate. This challenge was essential in the rethinking of his own ideas, and in the constant proposal of new ones.

Department Director. In 1953, after the death of Michel Macheboeuf, Monod was assigned to create and direct the department of cellular biochemistry (Service de Biocheme Cellulaire). The establishment of this department was the result of a carefully theorized project based on the definition of a clear research program. Monod believed that fundamental chemical organization would be revealed at the level of cellular constituents rather than at the level of tissue or differentiated organs. Modern biochemistry had been oriented to the study of the processes of biosynthesis, and Monod possessed a powerful tool for this study: the investigation of bacterial growth. Biochemistry would thus become cellular, microbial biochemistry. Monod managed to obtain the funds necessary for a complete and modern department partly from the National Center for Scientific Research but also, to a large extent, from donations from Mmes. Edouard de Rothschild and Bethsabée de Rothschild and grants from American institutions such as the Rockefeller Foundation, the National Science Foundation, and the National Institutes of Health. In 1955 the department moved into new headquarters on the ground floor of the same building in which the *grenier* had been housed.

The new department finally had sufficient space, and many students began to arrive, primarily (and this was Monod's choice) specialists in the physical and mathematical sciences. His characteristic combination of powerful self-assertion and great sensitivity and generosity made him an ideal mentor. He had the capacity to delineate both problems to be studied and techniques that could maximize everyone's potential. Himself an excellent experimenter, Monod was able to predict theoretically the results of an experiment and to draw all the requisite consequences. A skilled architect of advanced research programs, he had the characteristic of a true master thinker: the ability to pick out the most important elements of a problem or a theory. His implacable Cartesian deductive logic, which always seemed to isolate the weak points in an argument or an experimental procedure, enabled him to eliminate all that was secondary in logical reasoning, such that everything seemed to fall into a coherent, inevitable, and therefore comprehensible framework.

At the end of 1958, Monod was invited to become professor of biochemistry at the Faculty of Sciences of the University of Paris. After long consideration, he decided to accept, provided he would be able to continue working at the Pasteur Institute. The post he took up in 1959 was originally called chair of the chemistry of metabolism, but in April 1966 the name was changed to chair of molecular biology. In 1967 Monod was elected to the Collège de France and named chair of molecular biology. His inaugural lecture in November 1967 was a solemn occasion for raising the philosophical implications of modern biology.

The Great Collaboration. Beginning in 1957, Monod and François Jacob established a very close collaboration. At the time, the development of research on inductible systems required the methods of crossing bacteria and of zygotic induction developed by Jacob in collaboration with Elie Wollman. Whereas Cohn played a major role in the initial, biochemical phase of Monod's study of the relations between genes and enzymes, Jacob's participation was essential during the second, genetic and regulatory phase. But the consequences of what Francis Crick called "the great collaboration" went well beyond the solution to the problem of enzyme adaptation, uncovering the general mechanism of the regulation of protein synthesis and its genetic determination. The constant exchange of ideas and experimental results, and the interminable conversations between Jacob and Monod, were decisive in this.

The great collaboration produced three theoretical models that proved fundamental in the development of molecular biology: operon, messenger RNA, and allosteric interactions.

The Nobel Prize. In 1965 Jacob and Monod were awarded the Nobel Prize in physiology or medicine for all this research, together with André Lwoff, who had laid the scientific and institutional groundwork that made it possible. This honor for the three French biologists was not unexpected. Lwoff and Monod had been brought to the Nobel Committee's attention in the 1950's, and after the triumph of the operon model in the early 1960's, proposals to award the prize to Jacob, Monod, and Wollman had come from various quarters.

The Nobel Prize entailed fresh responsibilities for Monod. He was suddenly a celebrity, and his ideas and statements carried great weight in public opinion. He used his fame to demand university reform and to fight for the advancement of French science. During May 1968 Monod supported the student movement against the academic establishment, which he had always considered one of the major causes of France's cultural and scientific backwardness. He took part in student assemblies, but soon had to acknowledge a deep division between himself and the students. They considered him a member of the establishment against which they were rebelling, and he criticized the irrational and purely destructive aspects of the student movement.

Monod had always been an ardent defender of human rights, never shirking commitment when it was necessary. In the early 1950's he publicly protested the repression of intellectuals in America and any restriction of the free circulation of people and ideas. In 1960, after a difficult campaign that included a trip to Budapest, he succeeded in getting Agnès Ullmann and her husband out of Hungary. He came out against the French Secret Army Organization, met in 1966 with the Reverend Martin Luther King, Jr., in Paris, and condemned the treatment of Jews in the Soviet Union, as well as assaults on freedom in various other countries. He supported the activities of the French family planning movement, fighting for the legalization of abortion, and signed in 1974 a plea in favor of beneficent euthanasia. The value and dignity of the individual was his fundamental ethical guideline.

Director of the Pasteur Institute. In 1965, during a broad movement for the renovation of the Pasteur Institute, Monod and his colleagues had proposed thoroughgoing changes in the management of the institution. It was felt that the combination of financial difficulties and an accumulated lag in scientific progress had made such changes long overdue.

It was therefore no surprise when Monod was offered the post of director of the institute in 1970; after lengthy consideration, he accepted the appointment. His decision reflected both his sense of duty (sharpened by his Protestant sense of responsibility) and his deep gratitude to the institution that had permitted him to pursue his research in complete freedom. In 1971 the institute's financial situation was so catastrophic that its very existence seemed threatened. Monod wanted to infuse the prestigious institution with fresh vitality, and he felt that he alone would be able to accomplish that. Moreover, to lead the Pasteur Institute at that time was an extraordinary challenge, and Monod loved challenges. Risk excited him, a trait that had made him a rock climber in his youth and later an expert sailing skipper.

On 15 April 1971 Monod became the director general of the Pasteur Institute. He assumed the post with a fully developed plan and with clear ideas—perhaps even dreams—of what an institution of biomedical research should be like. He completely restructured the institute, creating a subsidiary company—Institut Pasteur Production—for the revitalization of industrial activities. Monod improved the financial situation, which was definitively stabilized when a permanent state subsidy was won. When necessary, he reorganized research, eliminating or recasting many departments and creating others. Authoritarian and inflexible, he made decisions firmly and courageously, though sometimes without sufficient consultation. This gave rise to resentment and opposition, and many friendships were broken.

Monod's years as head of the Pasteur Institute were difficult for personal reasons as well. In 1972 he suffered a six-month bout of viral hepatitis, and that same year his wife died after a long illness. His administrative tasks made it impossible for him to continue his scientific activity, and he was compelled to resign his chair at the Collège de France and to cede his post as director of the cellular biochemistry department to Georges Cohen.

Because of the urgency of the administrative and financial reforms, Monod was unable to elaborate any real plan of scientific development, and the difficulties he faced undermined his hope of turning the Pasteur Institute into a model research center. Only in 1975 did he sketch out a medium-term policy of scientific development for the institute, centered on what he considered his fundamental vocation: the advance of the biological sciences in the service of humankind.

But Monod had no time to implement this project. In October 1975 an incurable disease, aplastic anemia, was diagnosed. Though well aware of the prognosis, he continued to serve as director of the Pasteur Institute. From time to time he left to rest at his home in Cannes, where he died on 31 May 1976.

Scientific Work. Monod divided his research into four periods corresponding to different phases of a single scientific trajectory. Despite the apparent diversity of these phases, they unfolded with remarkable continuity, each as a necessary and inevitable consequence of its predecessors.

Kinetics and Physiology of Bacterial Growth (1935–1947). In 1935 Monod became interested in the quantitative aspects of the growth of bacterial cultures, demonstrating in particular that the growth rate relative to the concentration of available food was not linear but asymptotically approached a value representing the maximum rate of cell division. This function turned out to be identical to the kinetic equation describing the speed of an enzyme reaction relative to the concentration of substratum. The growth rate was therefore determined by an enzyme-type reaction. The growth of bacterial cultures obeys simple quantitative laws. By measuring the growth in the presence of various sugars, Monod showed

that the growth yield relative to energy source was independent of the growth rate. This suggested that there was no such thing as a "maintenance concentration" and that nearly all of the available energy was used in biosynthesis.

During a study of the interaction of two carbon sources, Monod noted a new phenomenon of growth of cultures of *Escherichia coli*. When two carbohydrates instead of one are placed in the milieu as food sources, it is normally observed that the total growth yield equals the sum of the yields of each sugar. However, certain mixtures of sugars show quite different curves, indicating two clearly distinct phases of exponential growth separated by a phase of latency in which there is most often no growth or even a decrease of the cultures. Monod called this phenomenon "diauxy," or double growth. The study of the phenomenon showed that it was a result of a variation in the enzyme constitution of the bacteria caused by the presence of the different substrata.

In December 1940 Monod asked André Lwoff's opinion of this new phenomenon; Lwoff replied that it could be considered an instance of bacterial "enzyme adaptation." This phenomenon—in which the formation of certain enzymes is selectively stimulated by the specific substratum of the enzyme—had been noted by Émile Duclaux and Frédéric Dienert in 1901, and in 1926 Hans von Euler-Chelpin had clearly shown that the phenomenon had to do with protein synthesis. In the 1930's the Finnish researcher Henning Karström called this "enzyme adaptation," distinguishing between constitutive and adaptive enzymes. Later, Marjory Stephenson had noted that the appearance of new enzyme activity in a bacterial population in process of multiplication could result either from a chemical stimulus (induction) exercised by a substratum on the totality of individuals in the population or from a gradual selection of spontaneous genetic variants.

During the war, Monod was forced to leave his laboratory at the Sorbonne, and Lwoff brought him into his department of microbial physiology at the Pasteur Institute, where Monod was able to continue his research, showing that enzyme adaptation corresponded to the synthesis of a particular protein. In collaboration with Alice Audureau, he worked on the genetic determination of enzyme adaptation in bacteria. The problem was to isolate the cellular mechanisms by which the presence of a given substratum, lactose, could "stimulate" the synthesis of a specific enzyme that would permit the assimilation of this substratum. The research on β-galactosidase also concerned the explanation of the mutation that brought a bacterial strain from a state in which the synthesis of the enzyme was inductible to one in which the synthesis occurred continuously (constitutivity). The problem of the apparent duality of the particular determinism of the biosynthesis of enzymes—genetic determinism on the one hand, chemical on the other—was therefore clearly posed.

The importance of this research was that enzyme adaptation seemed to be the only phenomenon that allowed direct experimentation on the construction— or ontogeny, as it was then called—of enzymes. There were also hopes of developing an explanation of cell differentiation, in particular of the synthesis of antibodies. Most of all, this problem was considered an aspect of the more general problem of biological specificity and offered an ideal experimental system for understanding the "physical basis of specificity" (1947). The analysis of the genetic determination of enzyme specificity showed that it was linked to the enzyme's configuration, which was controlled by a single gene. Enzyme induction thus constituted a model system for the study of protein synthesis and of the relations between genetics and cellular physiology.

Enzyme adaptation (1947–1957). In the late 1940's the problem was to understand why the addition of a substratum could provoke either an increase in the rate of enzyme synthesis (adaptation) or a diauxic inhibition. This latter phenomenon was also called the "glucose effect": the synthesis of a large number of enzymes was sometimes completely inhibited when the growth of the organisms occurred in the presence of certain glucides, more particularly glucose.

Explaining this effect (in *Growth Symposium*, 1947), Monod revived a simple model proposed by John Yudkin in 1938. According to this model, the enzyme was formed from a precursor, through an equilibrium reaction. The inductive action of a substratum could then be interpreted by assuming that the formation of the enzyme-substratum complex shifted the balance in favor of the formation of the enzyme. The hypothesis was that "different enzymes can be issued by a common precursor," the specificity of the enzyme being determined by "a preexisting self-replicating entity (the gene)." The particular configuration of an enzyme was thus determined by a master pattern, which could be the enzyme itself, another molecule formed by the cell independently of the presence of the substratum, or even the substratum. The immunological methods developed by Cohn and Monod and applied to the study of β-galactosidase (in collaboration with Annamaria Torriani, a young Italian biologist who came

to Paris in February 1948) permitted the exploration of lines of descent and kinship between protein molecules. Indeed, if one protein is derived from another through differentiation, then we ought to expect that these molecules must inevitably have very close antigenic structures, which could be brought out by crossed serological reactions. The results showed that bacteria induced by galactose contained two distinct antigens, called Gz and Pz, Gz being β-galactosidase and Pz an enzymatically inactive protein. The noninduced bacteria seemed to contain only Pz. The very closely related antigenic structures of Gz and Pz showed that Pz could be a precursor of the enzyme:

$$Pz \xrightarrow{\text{inductor}} Gz.$$

In 1950, in order to be able to study bacterial growth in the most stable and controlled conditions possible, Monod developed a method of continuous culture of bacteria (*bactogène*) through which a physiologically stable state could be maintained indefinitely. If a "continuous dilution at constant volume" is maintained, the growth rate is limited by the concentration of food, which can be controlled by the rate of dilution. By using this method—which had been independently developed and published by Leo Szilard and Aaron Novick—the growth rate could be considered an independent variable and the speed of the process of synthesis could be studied as a function of different variables.

Three hypotheses had been advanced to explain the mechanism of enzyme induction: (1) the functional hypothesis, which held that the synthesis of the enzyme was related to its activity and that the inductor acted as a substratum; (2) the hypothesis that synthesis was limited by a dynamic equilibrium that was broken when the enzyme was exposed to a specific complex (this was proposed by Monod in 1947 and 1949); (3) the organizing or formation hypothesis, which held that the inductor played an organizing role in the synthesis of the enzyme, through its action (whether direct or not) on a "forming system." This last hypothesis was the model proposed by Monod in 1943 and 1945.

Since it was impossible to obtain the enzyme in crystalline form, Monod and Cohn undertook the study of a series of substitutions in the molecule of the glactosides, determining the inductive power of each analogue and its properties as substratum of the enzyme. The β-thiogalactosides, in which the oxygen of the galactosidic group is replaced by sulfur, proved highly useful for the study of β-galactosidose induction. The results showed that, contrary to theories current at the time, the inductive power was not related to the enzyme's action on the inductor, or even on its affinity for it. The induction of an enzyme is independent of its activity, and the activity of the inductor therefore could not be due to a combination with the enzyme. Consequently, neither the functional nor the equilibrium hypothesis could be accepted. The inductor must act as an organizer, and Monod revived the hypothesis of a catalytic action at the level of the formation center of the enzyme in the cell. The basic idea, borrowed from immunology, was that the inductor served as a model in the formation "matrix" of the protein. Melvin Cohn called this paradoxical situation a "theatre of the absurd," since the bacteria produce a useless enzyme, β-galactosidase, in response to a substance, such as thiomethylgalactoside, that they cannot metabolize. To explain these results, Monod introduced the notion of "gratuitous" induction: since the inductor had no necessary affinity for the protein that it induced, certain distinct cellular sites of the protein itself must be capable of forming a specific combination with it.

One consequence of this "theatre of the absurd" was that the expression "enzyme adaptation" seemed ill suited to describe an effect that in certain cases was not at all functionally adaptive. Monod therefore proposed to abandon the expression in favor of "induced biosynthesis of enzymes." This proposal was accepted by all the major researchers working in the field, who signed a sort of encyclical published by *Nature* in 1953.

Since the physical, chemical, and immunochemical properties of the "constitutive" enzyme were identical to those of the "induced" enzyme, it was natural to suppose that the underlying mechanism of synthesis must be the same. In 1953 Monod and Cohn formulated the hypothesis that the synthesis of all enzymes was subject to a like mechanism of specific control. A simple hypothesis was that the constitutive systems could be induced by endogenous inductors (the theory of generalized induction, known by its French initials, TIG).

The essential problem posed by the phenomenon of the induced biosynthesis of enzymes was to find out whether it consisted of the activation of a pre-existing protein or whether, on the contrary, it was a question of the synthesis of a new protein. The model Monod accepted until 1952 supposed that the intervention of the inductor was reflected not in the synthesis of a protein de novo but rather in the transformation of the precursor Pz into the enzyme Gz.

With Alvin Pappenheimer and Germaine Cohen-Bazire, Monod showed that the induced formation of the enzyme required the simultaneous presence of each of the essential amino acids, which itself indicated that the process involved the complete biosynthesis of a protein. On the other hand, the kinetics of this biosynthesis obeyed a remarkably simple law:

$$\delta z = p\delta x$$

or

$$\delta z/\delta x = p,$$

in which δz is the increase of the enzyme, δx the growth of the total bacterial mass from the point of addition of the inductor, and p (the differential synthesis rate) the coefficient expressing the speed of enzyme synthesis.

This linear kinetics ("Monod's plot"), which stated that the synthesis of the enzyme after the addition of the inductor is a constant fraction of the rate of total protein synthesis, was incompatible with the hypothesis of the conversion of an accumulated precursor, which implied an autocatalytic mechanism, and supported "complete synthesis," the formation de novo of a protein entirely new not only in its specific structure but also in the origin of its elements. The study of the incorporation of the radioactive isotope sulfur 35 into the protein in the course of its induced synthesis confirmed this indirect reasoning, showing that the formation of β-galactosidase corresponded to the total synthesis of the protein on the basis of its elements, without the formation of precursors or intermediaries. This result definitively eliminated the idea of any conversion of Pz into Gz. The immunological similarity of two proteins therefore proved to be a false track.

One of the consequences of this research was that it challenged the theory of the "dynamic state" of intracellular proteins, proposed by Rudolf Schoenheimer in 1941. This theory held that proteins continually exchange radicals with other cellular chemical constituents. Monod's results, on the contrary, showed a practically complete (and surprising) stability of proteins among multiplying bacteria: the synthesis of proteins is the result not of a dynamic equilibrium but of a series of irreversible parallel processes.

Factors of Specific Permeation (1953–1957). Concurrently with the research on induction, Monod's laboratory was interested in the phenomenon of certain *Lac⁻* (lactose-negative) mutants called "cryptics." These mutants cannot develop on lactose, even when they have large quantities of β-

galactosidase. Kinetic measurements had shown a difference in the behavior of cellular extracts and intact cells.

To explain this phenomenon, Georges Cohen, who joined Monod's laboratory in 1954, had proposed the hypothesis that there were specific permeation factors in bacteria. At first Monod rejected this suggestion, but he soon changed his mind and made a fundamental contribution to the understanding of the phenomenon. Cohen had proposed a model based on stoichiometric receptors that absorbed the substratum on stereospecific acceptors, but Monod, after converting the radioactivity measured in milligrams into number of molecules, concluded that there had to be some catalytic action. This soon led to the isolation of a functionally specialized factor, distinct from metabolic enzymes. This factor—first considered an enzyme, called ε, then called system y and later galactoside-permease—is an inductible protein quite similar to an enzyme in its kinetic action and in its narrow specificity. The permease concentrates the galactosides in the cell without modifying the cell chemically. The cryptic mutants had clearly lost their system y.

It must be remembered that at this point permease was only a theoretical construct (the first of many) that was ill received by biochemists and enzymologists, who were accustomed to isolating enzymes first and then deducing their function. Though inferred theoretically in 1956, β-galactoside-permease was not isolated until 1965, by Eugene P. Kennedy.

The discovery of permeases had important, unforeseen consequences. Since galactosidase and permease appeared more or less simultaneously after induction, there had to be a functional relationship between the enzyme and the corresponding permeation factor. Moreover, the two systems were genetically linked. The analysis of constitutive mutants showed that the constitutive mutation affects the two systems simultaneously. Studying the genetic determination as a whole, Monod and his collaborators classed the mutants into three elementary types, on the basis of (a) their capacity (y^+) or incapacity (y^-) to synthesize permease; (b) their capacity (z^+) or incapacity (z^-) to synthesize β-galactosidase; (c) the inductible (i^+) or constitutive (i^-) character of the synthesis of the two systems.

Once Monod's program had reached this point, toward the beginning of 1957, he had to find methods suitable for genetic exploration of the kinetics of genetic expression and for studying the structure of the loci. Such a study presupposed an analysis of the genetic determination of constitutive mutations and of the relations between the determinants governing constitutivity and those governing the structure of the synthesized protein.

Genetic Regulation (1957–1961). New methods of studying the genetics of the synthesis of bacterial enzymes had been formulated in the framework of another research program, which had been developed in a "parallel universe" (Cohn) to the one inhabited by Monod and his group, a universe initially housed at the other end of the *grenier*'s corridor. This research program was focused on lysogeny and the mechanisms of bacterial sexuality.

In 1950 Lwoff and his collaborators discovered that lysis could be induced in lysogenic bacteria by exposing them to ultraviolet radiation. In 1953 François Jacob and Elie Wollman undertook the systematic study of genetic and biochemical mechanisms concerning the localization, latency, induction, and expression of the genetic determinant of the phage, the prophage. They used the technique of genetic recombination established by Tatum and Lederberg in *Escherichia coli* K12 and the discovery, achieved independently by Luigi L. Cavalli-Sforza in 1950 and William Hayes in 1953, of bacterial strains exhibiting a high frequency of recombination (*Hfr*).

Jacob and Wollman's experiments on the conjugation of bacteria soon produced evidence of the phenomenon that would later be called "zygotic induction": the chromosome of a donor bacterium bearing a prophage penetrates a nonlysogenic receptive cell and there stimulates the expression of phages and bacterial lysis. The essential event in the conjugation of bacteria is the transfer of a segment of the genetic material and the donor bacterium to the receptor. This transfer occurs in only one direction and at a constant rate. Proof of this was given in an elegant experiment conducted by Wollman and Jacob in 1955, known as the "spaghetti experiment" because the explanatory model depicted the female swallowing the male chromosome like a strand of spaghetti. The conjugating pairs of bacteria were separated by means of a high-speed homogenizer that pulled the bacteria apart and broke the chromosome. By applying this treatment at varying times, the length of the chromosome segment penetrating the female could be selected at will, the expression of the penetrated genes could be studied, and a genetic map could be drawn up in units of time. With this system it became possible to analyze the bacterial chromosome not merely by classical genetic methods but also by physical and chemical measures.

In a conjugation between *Hfr* bacteria bearing the prophage and nonlysogenic female bacteria, the prophages that enter the cytoplasm of the receptor bacterium are immediately induced. The zygotic induction shows that the transferred genes can be expressed immediately after their entry into the host cytoplasm, quite apart from any genetic recombination. Moreover, for some amount of time the receptor bacterium possesses two copies of a sequence of genes, which permits the study, in bacteria, of genetic phenomena (such as dominance) peculiar to sexually reproductive organisms. That was exactly the technical and theoretical instrument needed by the research program on enzyme induction.

The experimental problem Monod was interested in was to verify the hypothesis of generalized induction, which could be tested by using methods of zygotic induction, in order to determine dominance. The development of this program was the result of collaboration between Monod and Jacob, which began in the spring of 1957 and was not immediately and deliberately applied to the core of the two programs. Together, Jacob and Monod conceived the famous Pa-Ja-Mo experiment, conducted in collaboration with Arthur Pardee, an American biochemist spending a sabbatical year in Paris. The experiment bore a name formed of the initial syllables of the names of its three designers, and later came to be called, for obvious reasons, the Pyjama experiment. The aim of this series of experiments (1957–1958) was to study the biosynthesis of β-galactosidase during the crossing

$$Hfr\ lac^+ \times F^-\ lac^-.$$

An experiment conducted in December 1957 was designed to use the complementary crossings

$$Hfr\ z^-i^- \times F^-\ z^+i^+ \qquad (1)$$

and

$$Hfr\ z^+i^+ \times F^-\ z^-i^- \qquad (2)$$

to clarify the mechanism of transfer and the kinetics of the expression of the gene for β-galactosidase. None of the initial bacterial strains was capable of synthesizing β-galactosidase, for in the case of z^-i^- there was no gene for the enzyme, and in the case of z^+i^+ the synthesis did not take place in the absence of the inductor.

The results of the first experiment confirmed the theory of generalized induction: in crossing (1), there is no synthesis of β-galactosidase among the merozygotes, while in a type (2) crossing this synthesis almost immediately follows the gene's entry into the host cytoplasm, which according to the theory contains the internal inductor.

The second phase of the experiment was conducted three months later, to examine the kinetics of the enzyme synthesis over a period of several hours after conjugation. This phase produced a genuine "surprise," according to Jacob. After a certain time lapse, enzyme synthesis was blocked and would restart only after the addition of the inductor. The cell had therefore passed from the state of constitutivity to the state of inductivity. This suggested, contrary to all expectations, that of the two alleles i^- and i^+ the dominant one was not the constitutive but the inductible. This dominance dictated the inevitable conclusion that the i gene was responsible for the synthesis of a "repressor" that blocks the synthesis of β-galactosidase and permease at the same time.

The most important conclusion to be drawn from the Pyjama experiment was the existence of a double genetic determinism in protein synthesis. Two distinct genes intervened, one determining the structure of the synthesized molecule and the other controlling the expression of the first, either permitting it or preventing it. Another conclusion was that different genes determining the structure of distinct proteins were subject to the same regulation system and that this functional association was correlated with their genetic association.

The elaboration of a unified model of cell regulation was not merely the consequence of linear deductive reasoning based on the Pyjama experiment, but was also the result of a kind of assembly process at the insight of which lay a bold theoretical beginning by François Jacob. As he was preparing his 1958 Harvey Lecture, Jacob had the idea of driving the parallel between the genetic determinism of lysogeny and of the lactose system to its ultimate consequences. He draws three conclusions: (1) the regulation must be located at the level of genes, and not in the cytoplasm; (2) the regulating action must be exercised on a structure common to several genes at once; (3) this locking together must occur through a simple switch—in other words, a yes-or-no principle.

These conjectures by Jacob were at first categorically rejected by Monod, who was shocked by the idea of genetic localization of the control of protein synthesis and by the notion of a simple binary interrupter, a switch that either sets in motion or blocks a complex chemical machinery. Although Monod alone among the members of the group had studied classical genetics (or perhaps exactly because he had), he could not accept this kind of direct action on genes, which geneticists considered distant and inaccessible objects, "like the material of galaxies," as Monod put it. In the end, however, the link that Monod had long ago established between genetic determinism and protein biosynthesis, and his capacity to grasp the consequences of an unorthodox idea rigorously and creatively, enabled him to contribute decisively to the full exploitation of the parallel between lysogeny and enzyme induction.

In a preliminary note presented to the Académie des Sciences in October 1959, an analogical interpretation of the observations of the two systems paved the way for the distinction between the structural genes responsible for the structure of proteins and the regulator genes that govern their expression through the intermediary of a cytoplasmic repressor. The existence of groupings of genes whose expression is subject to a single repressor suggested to Jacob and Monod the hypothesis that there might be a single structure sensitive to the repressor and controlling the activity of the entire group of genes. A theoretical note presented to the Académie des Sciences in 1960 introduced the concept of operon, a unit of coordinated expression made up of an operator and the group of structural genes that it coordinates.

The operon model posed three problems. The first was the nature of the repressor, another theoretical entity whose chemical nature was wholly unknown. The second was the mechanism of the repressor's chemical action and its relation to the target and the inductor. The third concerned the molecular mechanisms of the transfer of genetic information for protein synthesis, a problem that lay at the root of the idea of the messenger.

Monod did not participate in the "search for the repressor," which was completed only in 1966 by Benno Müller-Hill and Walter Gilbert, or in the development of the messenger idea. After elaborating the theory of the messenger (in collaboration with François Jacob and with Francis Crick and Sydney Brenner) and proposing that the role was played by very short-lived RNA capable of linking up with the ribosomes, he left the task of isolating this new theoretically deduced chemical substance to others: his collaborator François Gros, François Jacob, and British and American molecular biologists.

Monod concentrated instead on the action mechanisms of the repressor and its chemical interactions with the target and the inductor, a problem that enabled him to turn again to models of stereospecific interactions, a constant theme throughout his scientific career.

In the original operon model, the repressor was considered a ribonucleic acid, probably because an RNA could have interacted more easily, owing to its complementarity, with genes, which are themselves made up of nucleic acid. But in 1960, theoretical considerations, as well as experimental results principally obtained by Agnès Ullmann in Monod's laboratory, made it clear that the repressor had to be a protein. The major reason for this was that the repressor had to recognize very different chemical structures, such as the inductor (a small metabolite) and the operator (a genetic structure). Only proteins could have this property.

Regulatory Interactions in the Control of Cell Metabolism (1961–1976). Monod and his pupil J.-P. Changeux elaborated a mechanism based on an interaction between two distinct and separate ("nonoverlapping") sites of protein structure, one for the substratum and the other for the regulatory ligand, or "effector." The interactions of the ligands are completely indirect, transferred by the protein. The attachment or detachment of effectors governs the conformation of the enzyme, and therefore its catalytic action. The model for this mechanism was hemoglobin, in which the binding of oxygen entails a concerted conformational alteration that exhibits "coordinative" properties.

Jacob and Monod generalized the concept of allosteric transition in the conclusions of the Cold Spring Harbor symposium in 1961, and the first systematization of the concept was presented in an article drafted by Monod in 1962 and published in 1963 under the signatures of Changeux, Jacob, and Monod.

The basic notions derived from the operon model were (1) the repressor is only a transductor of controlling signals; (2) the effect of the substrate on the synthesis of the enzyme is indirect, and the repressor must be therefore an allosteric protein; (3) there is no necessary chemical or metabolic relation between the fact that β-galactosidase hydrolyzes β-galactosides and the fact that its biosynthesis is induced by the same chemical compounds. The relation is gratuitous, chemically arbitrary. The allosteric interactions allow complete freedom in the choice of chemical mechanisms, escaping all chemical constraints and obeying only the physiological constraints imposed by the system's consistency and submitted to the action of natural selection. Monod therefore considered the concept of allosteric interaction "the second secret of life," the first being the double helix and the genetic code.

In 1965 Monod elaborated a formalized model of allosteric transitions based on the idea of interaction between equivalent subunits in a regulatory protein. The work was done in collaboration with Changeux and Jeffries Wyman, who between 1948 and 1960 had published articles on the correlation between symmetry and binding cooperativity. The central idea, a purely formal one, was of the conformational transition of an oligomeric protein that conserves structural symmetry. The concerted transition of subunits entails a concerted transition of affinity of sites. A modification of quaternary structure thus explains function.

This model, considered excessively philosophical, was not well received in scientific circles. Francis Crick, for instance, with whom Monod exchanged a long series of letters on the subject, could not see the logical necessity or experimental basis of the postulate of conservation of symmetry, which for Monod was central.

This model was counterposed to the hypothesis suggested by Daniel Koshland—that conformational change was induced by interaction with the ligand ("induced fit"), which led to a multiplicity of varied structural states. For Koshland, structural cooperativity was the consequence of the distortions induced by the ligands, which altered the energy relations between subunits, whereas Monod regarded conservation of symmetry as a basic principle.

Symmetry allowed for regularity and structural order of molecular sequences, and this order corresponded to the specific and unique functions of living systems. Monod wondered about the role and forms of globular proteins, seeking to establish the rules governing the folding and stability of a protein. He had always been fascinated by the symmetrical, formal beauty of organisms, especially the simplest ones, the beauty that had fascinated all the great morphologists of the nineteenth century, from Cuvier to Haeckel. Monod considered symmetry a fundamental natural constant, for "without invariants, without order and symmetry, science would be not merely boring, but impossible." Order, symmetry, and beauty were part of the foundation of the scientific method: "A beautiful model or theory may not be right, but an ugly one must be wrong."

An Ethics of Knowledge. At the beginning of the 1960's, Monod had started to ponder the general problems raised by the development of molecular biology. Life seemed finally to be yielding its secrets, and in view of the upheaval in the conception of life, evolution, and humanity itself, Monod felt an ethical duty to place science in modern culture as a whole.

During a conference at the University of Oregon at Eugene in October 1960, Monod expounded his idea that modern biology stood in contradiction to any anthropomorphic interpretation of the universe or of life. The old ethical values no longer applied, and new ones had to be discerned. In a world in which science had demonstrated that human existence itself was contingent, acquisition of knowledge had to become the supreme value. Monod dealt with this same question of the social responsibilities of scientists in the face of political power in *Le puits de Syène*, a play he wrote in 1964.

Monod presented these long-pondered themes to the general public on a number of occasions: his inaugural lecture at the Collège de France (1967), the Robbins Lectures of 1969, a course he taught at the Collège de France in the year 1969–1970, and most of all his best-selling book, *Le hasard et la nécessité* (1970). This essay on "natural philosophy"—often considered no more than a popular exposition of the ideas of molecular biology or even a conceited attempt to invade uncharted territory—is actually an effort to examine the problem of existence itself on the basis of the scientific experience. Monod believed that the sense of alienation from scientific culture exhibited by a number of trends in contemporary philosophy and literature was the result of a distrust of science; the book is also a response to the irrationalism that underlies such positions. The deep malady of our society, which gives rise to the constant existential anguish of modern man, is our awareness of being alone in the universe.

The book's title is taken from a quotation that is attributed to Democritus but in fact exists nowhere in the Greek philosophical texts that have come down to us and was probably an invention of Monod himself: "All that exists in the universe is the product of chance and necessity." Monod considered this conclusion to be the quintessence of the molecular theory of the genetic code, of cell regulation, and of evolution by natural selection.

By interpreting the essential properties of organisms in terms of molecular structures, molecular biology had wrought a new definition of life, one that Monod summarized in three basic characteristics of biological objects: teleonomy, the existence of an "internal program"; independent morphogenesis; and reproductive invariance.

By the very nature of these mechanisms, evolution constructs unique objects, products of the interplay of chance and necessity. Each organism is the latest link in a four-million-year-old chain. Chance alone lies at the source of every novelty, of every creation in the biosphere. The "noise" that creeps into the perfect mechanism of invariant reproduction—noise that is preserved with the music—stands at the origin of our universe and of our lives.

This position, a kind of scientific existentialism, is quite close to French philosophical and literary existentialism, but with one big difference: for Monod, communication between the world of knowledge and the world of values is not only possible but also necessary.

The basis of Monod's position is the "objectivity postulate": the exclusion of any interpretation in terms of ultimate causes. This was also a reflection of his scientific trajectory and his philosophical battles against any instructive theory in biology (including that of Lysenko). For Monod, to build knowledge on the basis of a postulate is a choice—or, more precisely, an ethical choice: "To accept the objectivity postulate is therefore to state the basic proposition of an ethic: the ethic of knowledge." In the end man must realize that he is alone in the universe, "from which he emerged by chance." He alone is aware of his position and his destiny; and it is here, too, that the essence of man lies, in the dualism between biology and knowledge and between nature and ethics, "that rending dualism that is expressed in art, in poetry, and in human love."

Scientific Honors. In addition to the Nobel Prize, Monod received numerous scientific honors, including the Prix Montyon de Physiologie (Académie des Sciences, 1955), the Louis Rapkine Medal (1958), the Prix Charles Léopold Mayer (Académie des Sciences, 1962). He was also named chevalier of the Ordre des Palmes Académiques (1961) and officer of the Legion of Honor (1963). He was an honorary foreign member of the Deutsche Akademie der Naturforscher Leopoldina (1965) and foreign member of the Czechoslovakian Academy of Sciences (1965), the Royal Society (1968), the National Academy of Sciences of the United States (1968), the American Philosophical Society (1969), the American Society for Microbiology (1970), the Institute of Medicine and Medical Research of New Delhi (1970) and the Accademia dei XL (1975). He was awarded honorary doctorates by the University of Chicago (1965), Rockefeller University (1970), Oxford University (1973), and the Free University of Brussels (1975).

BIBLIOGRAPHY

I. ORIGINAL WORKS. Monod published only one book, *Le hasard et la nécessité. Essai sur la philosophie naturelle de la biologie moderne* (Paris, 1970), trans. by Austryn Wainhouse as *Chance and Necessity* (New York, 1971). He published 131 scientific papers, of which a complete bibliography is given by Lwoff (1977; see below), who also gives a selected list of other publications. A large selection of Monod's scientific papers has been collected in André Lwoff and Agnès Ullmann, eds., *Selected Papers in Molecular Biology by Jacques Monod* (New York,

1978). The more important scientific papers are *Recherches sur la croissance des cultures bactériennes* (Paris, 1941); "Sur un phénomène nouveau de croissance complexe dans les cultures bactériennes," in *Comptes rendus de l'Académie des sciences, Paris*, **212** (1941), 934–936; "Sur la nature du phénomène de la diauxie," in *Annales de l'Institut Pasteur*, **71** (1945), 37–40; "Mutation et adaptation enzymatique chez *Escherichia coli-mutabile*," ibid., **72** (1946), 868–878, with A. Audureau; "The Phenomenon of Enzymatic Adaptation and Its Bearing on Problems of Genetics and Cellular Differentiation," in *Growth Symposium*, **11** (1947), 223–289; "La technique de culture continue. Théorie et applications," in *Annales de l'Institut Pasteur*, **79** (1950), 390–410; "Sur la biosynthèse de la β-galactosidase (lactase) chez *Escherichia coli*. La spécificité de l'induction," in *Biochimica et Biophysica Acta*, **7** (1951), 585–599, with G. Cohen-Bazire and M. Cohn; "La biosynthèse induite des enzymes (adaptation enzymatique)," in *Advances in Enzymology*, **13** (1952), 67–119, with M. Cohn; "Specific Inhibition and Induction of Enzyme Biosynthesis," in R. Davies and E. F. Gale, eds., *Adaptation in Micro-Organisms* (Cambridge, 1953), 132–149, with M. Cohn; "Terminology of Enzyme Formation," in *Nature*, **172** (1953), 1096, with M. Cohn, M. R. Pollock, S. Spiegelman, and R. Y. Stanier; "Studies on the Induced Synthesis of β-galactosidase in *Escherichia coli*: The Kinetics and Mechanism of Sulfur Incorporation," in *Biochimica et Biophysica Acta*, **16** (1955), 99–116, with D. S. Hogness and M. Cohn; "Remarks on the Mechanism of Enzyme Induction," in Oliver H. Gaebler, ed., *Enzymes: Units of Biological Structure and Function* (New York, 1956), 7–28; "La galactoside-perméase d'*Escherichia coli*," in *Annales de l'Institut Pasteur*, **91** (1956), 829–857, with M. V. Rickenberg, G. N. Cohen, and G. Buttin; and "Bacterial Permeases," in *Bacteriological Reviews*, **21** (1957), 169–194, with G. N. Cohen.

After the beginning of the collaboration with F. Jacob, the more important papers published by Monod are "Sur l'expression et le rôle des allèles 'inductible' et 'constitutif' dans la synthèse de la β-galactosidase chez des zygotes d'*Escherichia coli*," in *Comptes rendus de l'Académie des sciences, Paris*, **246** (1958), 3125–3128, written with A. B. Pardee and F. Jacob; "The Genetic Control and Cytoplasmic Expression of 'Inducibility' in the Synthesis of β-galactosidase by *Escherichia coli*," in *Journal of Molecular Biology*, **1** (1959), 165–178, with A. B. Pardee and F. Jacob; "Gènes de structure et gènes de régulation dans la biosynthèse des protéines," in *Comptes rendus de l'Académie des sciences, Paris*, **249** (1959), 1282–1284, with F. Jacob; "L'opéron: Groupe de gènes à expression coordonnée par un opérateur," in *Comptes rendus de l'Académie des sciences, Paris*, **250** (1960), 1727–1729, with F. Jacob, D. Perrin, and C. Sanchez.

Three classic papers, written with F. Jacob, constitute the synthesis of the work on the operon model and outline its main consequences: "Genetic Regulatory Mechanisms in the Synthesis of Proteins," in *Journal of Molecular Biology*, **3** (1961), 318–356; "On the Regulation of Gene

Activity," in *Cold Spring Harbor Symposium on Quantitative Biology*, **26** (1961), 193–211; and "General Conclusions: Teleonomic Mechanisms in Cellular Metabolism, Growth and Differentiation," *ibid.*, 389–401.

After 1961, other important scientific papers are "Summary of the Columbia Symposium," in Alfred Gellhorn, ed., *Basic Problems in Neoplastic Disease* (New York, 1962), 218–237; "Genetic Repression, Allosteric Inhibition, and Cellular Differentiation," in Michael Locke, ed., *Cytodifferentiation and Macromolecular Synthesis* (New York, 1963), 30–64, with F. Jacob; "Allosteric Proteins and Cellular Control Systems," in *Journal of Molecular Biology*, **6** (1963), 306–329, with F. Jacob and J.-P. Changeux; "Quelques réflexions sur les relations entre structures et fonctions dans les protéines globulaires," in *L'année biologique*, **4**, fasc. 3–4 (1965), 231–240; "On the Nature of Allosteric Transitions: A Plausible Model," in *Journal of Molecular Biology*, **12** (1965), 88–118, with J. Wyman and J.-P. Changeux; "The Operon: A Unit of Coordinated Gene Action," in Royal A. Brink and E. Derek Styles, eds., *Heritage from Mendel*, (Madison, 1967), 155–177, with G. Buttin and F. Jacob; and "Introduction," in Jonathan R. Beckwith and David Zipser, eds., *The Lactose Operon*, (Cold Spring Harbor, N.Y., 1970), 1–14, with F. Jacob.

After 1965 most of Monod's writings were devoted to general reflections on science, its history, and its bearings on culture and society. Among them are "De l'adaptation enzymatique aux transitions allostériques," in *Les Prix Nobel en 1965* (Stockolm, 1966), English version "From Enzymatic Adaptation to Allosteric Transitions," in *Science*, **154** (1966), 475–483, repr. in David Baltimore, ed., *Nobel Lectures in Molecular Biology 1933–1975* (New York, 1977), 259–280; *De la biologie moléculaire à l'éthique de la connaissance*, his inaugural lecture at the Collège de France (Paris, 1967); "On Symmetry and Functions in Biological Systems," in A. Engstrom and B. Strandberg, eds., *Symmetry and Function of Biological Systems at the Macromolecular Level* (Stockholm, 1968), 15–27; "On Values in the Age of Science," in Arne Tiselius and Sam Nilsson, eds., *The Place of Value in a World of Facts* (Stockholm, 1971), 19–27; and "On the Molecular Theory of Evolution," in Rom Harré, ed., *Problems of Scientific Revolution* (Oxford, 1975), 11–24.

Monod left a large quantity of manuscripts, collected with his correspondence, notebooks, photos, and other documents, in the Monod Papers, Service des Archives, Institut Pasteur. The more important manuscripts are the drafts of two unpublished books, "Enzymatic Cybernetics" (1958), to be published with M. Cohn, and "Principes de biochimie," a tutorial for the Sorbonne course (1963); the Jessup Lectures, the Harvey Lecture, and the Robbins Lectures; and the preliminary versions of *Le hasard et la nécessité*.

II. SECONDARY LITERATURE. The main source of information on Monod's life, work and personality is André Lwoff and Agnès Ullmann, eds., *Les origines de la biologie moléculaire. Un hommage à Jacques Monod* (Paris and Montreal, 1980), English ed., *Origins of Molecular Biology: A Tribute to Jacques Monod* (New York, 1979). See also some of the papers in Ernesto Quagliariello, Giorgio Bernardi, and Agnès Ullmann, eds., *From Enzyme Adaptation to Natural Philosophy: Heritage from Jacques Monod* (Amsterdam and New York, 1987). Horace F. Judson, *The Eighth Day of Creation: Makers of the Revolution in Biology* (London, 1979), contains many details of Monod's work and thought, the result of a series of interviews with the author, and much material on the history of molecular biology. F. Jacob's autobiography, *La statue intérieure* (Paris, 1987), contains many insights on Monod's personality and on the history of the operon model. A short autobiography was written by Monod for McGraw-Hill's *Modern Men of Science*, I (New York, 1968), and for *Scienziati e tecnologi contemporanei* (Milan, 1974), 258–262.

For an account of Monod's life, see Melvin Cohn, "In Memoriam," in Jeffrey H. Miller and William S. Reznikoff, eds., *The Operon* (Cold Spring Harbor, N.Y., 1978), 1–9; F. H. C. Crick, "Jacques Monod, 1910–1976," in *Nature*, **262** (1976), 429–430; Bernardino Fantini, "Jacques Monod, 9 febbraio 1910–31 maggio 1976," in *Scientia*, **110** (1975, published 1976), 899–905; André Lwoff, "Jacques Monod, 1910–1976," in *Nouvelle presse médicale*, 1976, 2002–2004, and "Jacques Monod," in *Biographical Memoirs of Fellows of the Royal Society*, **23** (1977), 385–412; M. R. Pollock, "Obituary: Jacques Monod," in *Trends in Biochemical Sciences*, **1** (1976), N208; M. Rouzé, *Les Nobel scientifiques français* (Paris, 1988); R. Y. Stanier, "Jacques Monod, 1910–1976," in *Journal of General Microbiology*, **101** (1977), 1–12. For a recent biography that takes into account the documents preserved in the archives of the Pasteur Institute, see *Pour une éthique de la connaissance. Textes choisis et présentés par Bernardino Fantini* (Paris, 1988).

More material for the history of the French contribution to the development of molecular biology is in Pnina G. Abir-Am, "How Scientists View Their Heroes: Some Remarks on the Mechanism of Myth Construction," in *Journal of the History of Biology*, **15** (1982), 281–315; Georges N. Cohen, "Four Decades of Franco-American Collaboration in Biochemistry and Molecular Biology," in *Perspectives in Biology & Medicine*, **29** (1986), S141–S148; A. Danchin, *Ordre et dynamique du vivant: Chemins de la biologie moléculaire* (Paris, 1978); Claude Debru, *Philosophie moléculaire. Monod, Wyman, Changeux* (Paris, 1987); Bernardino Fantini, "Les origines de la biologie moléculaire" (book review), in *Revue d'histoire des sciences*, **35** (1982), 178–180; C. Galperin, "Le bactériophage, la lysogénie et son déterminisme génétique," in *History and Philosophy of the Life Sciences*, **9** (1988), 175–224; M. D. Grmek and B. Fantini, "Le rôle du hasard dans la naissance du modèle de l'opéron," in *Revue d'histoire des sciences*, **35** (1982), 193–215; F. Gros, *Les secrets du gène* (Paris, 1986); Jacques Monod and Ernest Borek, eds., *Of Microbes and Life* (New York, 1971); K. F. Schaffner, "Logic of Discovery and Justification in Regulatory Genetics," in *Studies in the History and Philosophy of Science*, **4** (1974), 349–385; and Gunther S. Stent, "The Operon: On Its Third Anniversary," in *Science*, **144** (1964), 816–820.

BERNARDINO FANTINI

MONTEL, PAUL (*b*. Nice, France, 29 April 1876; *d*. Paris, France, 22 January 1975), *mathematics*.

Paul Montel was the son of Aristide and Anaïs (Magiolo) Montel. His father was a photographer. He was educated in the Lycée of Nice, and in 1894 he was admitted to the École Normale Supérieure in Paris. After graduation in 1897 he taught classes in several provincial lycées preparing students for the competitive entrance examinations to the École Polytechnique and other engineering schools. He enjoyed teaching and liked a quiet life with plenty of leisure to devote to literature and travel, and he might have remained all his life a lycée professor if his friends had not urged him not to waste his talents and to start writing a thesis. He therefore returned to Paris to work on a doctorate, which he obtained in 1907. He did not become a university professor in Paris until 1918, occupying in the interim several teaching jobs in lycées and technical schools. During the German occupation he was dean of the Faculty of Science, and he was able to uphold the dignity of the French university in spite of the arrogance of the occupiers and the servility of their collaborators. Montel retired in 1946. He married late in life and had no children.

Most of Montel's mathematical papers are concerned with the theory of analytic functions of one complex variable, a very active field among French mathematicians between 1880 and 1940. The idea of compactness had emerged as a fundamental concept in analysis during the nineteenth century: provided a set is bounded in $\mathbf{R}^n$, it is possible to define for any sequence (x_n) of points of the set a subsequence (x_{n_k}) which converges to a point of $\mathbf{R}^n$ (the Bolzano-Weierstrass theorem). Riemann had sought to extend this extremely useful property to sets E of functions of real variables, but it soon appeared that boundedness of E was not sufficient.

Around 1880 G. Ascoli introduced the additional condition of equicontinuity of E, which implies that E has again the Bolzano-Weierstrass property. But at the beginning of the twentieth century Ascoli's theorem had very few applications, and it was Montel who made it popular by showing how useful it could be for analytic functions of a complex variable. His fundamental concept is what he called a *normal family*, which is a set H of functions defined in a domain $D \subset C$, taking their values in the Riemann sphere S and meromorphic in D, and satisfying the following condition: from any sequence of functions of H it is possible to extract a subsequence that, in every compact subset of D, converges uniformly either to a holomorphic function or to the point ∞ of S.

Montel's central observation is that if H consists of uniformly bounded holomorphic functions in D, it is a normal family; this is a consequence of the Cauchy integral and of Ascoli's theorem. From this criterion follow many others; for instance, if the values of the functions of a set H belong to a domain Δ that can be mapped conformally on a bounded domain, then H is a normal family. This is the case in particular when Δ is the complement of a set of two points in the complex plane $\mathbf{C}$.

Montel showed how the introduction of normal families may bring substantial simplifications in the proofs of many classical results of function theory, such as the mapping theorem of Riemann and Hadamard's characterization of entire functions of finite order. An ingenious application is to the proof of Picard's theorem on essential singularities: suppose O is an essential singularity of a function f holomorphic in $\Delta: O < |z| \leq 1$. Then Picard's theorem asserts that $f(z)$ takes on all finite complex values, with one possible exception, as z ranges through Δ. It can be proved by observing that if there are two values that f does not take in Δ, then the family of functions $f_n(z) = f(z/2^n)$ in the ring $\Gamma : \frac{1}{2} \leq |z| \leq 1$ would be a normal family, and there would be either a subsequence (f_{n_k}) with $|f_{n_k}(z)| \leq M$ in Γ, or a subsequence with $|f_{n_k}(z)| \geq 1/M$ in Γ, contradicting the assumption that O is an essential singularity of f.

Other applications made by Montel and his students concern univalent and multivalent functions and algebroid functions. He also investigated what he called quasi-normal families H, which are such that in the domain of definition D each point has a neighborhood in which H is a normal family, with the exception of a finite number of "irregular" points; the consideration of quasi-normal families leads to other applications to complex function theory.

Montel was also interested in the relations between the coefficients of a polynomial and the location of its zeros in the complex plane. For instance, if in a polynomial

$$1 + a_1 x + \cdots + a_{p-1} x^{p-1} + x^p + a_{n_1} x^{n_1} + \cdots + a_{n_k} x^{n_k}$$

the number p and the number k are given (but the

a_j and the n_i are arbitrary), then the polynomial always has a root of absolute value at most

$$\binom{k+p}{p}^{1/p}$$

Montel often was invited to lecture in countries where most mathematicians understood French, such as Belgium and Egypt, and in South America. He was especially honored in Rumania, which he visited often and where he had several students. He was the recipient of many honors and was elected a member of the French Academy of Sciences in 1937.

BIBLIOGRAPHY

Selecta, 1897–1947: *Cinquantenaire scientifique* (Paris, 1947); F. J. Beer, ed., *Paul Montel, mathématicien niçois* (Nice, 1966).

JEAN DIEUDONNÉ

MOORE, RAYMOND CECIL (*b.* Roslyn, Washington, 20 February 1892; *d.* Lawrence, Kansas, 16 April 1974), *geology, paleontology.*

Moore was the son of Bernard Harding Moore, a Baptist minister, and of Winifred Denney Moore. He graduated with honors from Denison University in 1913 and received a Ph.D. from the University of Chicago in 1916.

Moore joined the faculty of the University of Kansas in 1916 as an assistant professor of geology, becoming a full professor in 1919. This institution remained his base throughout his career. Also in 1916 he was appointed as state geologist, serving until 1937. From 1937 to 1945 he was both co–state geologist and director of the Kansas Geological Survey; Moore reassumed the office of state geologist in 1945 and held that position until 1954. In 1917 Moore married Georgine Watters; they had one daughter. Following a divorce from his first wife, Moore married Lilian Botts in 1936. He was head of the Department of Geology at Kansas three times: 1920–1933, 1940–1941, and 1952–1954. In 1958 he was appointed the first Solen E. Summerfield distinguished professor of the university. He retired in 1970.

Moore was known early in his career for his work on the Mississippian and Pennsylvanian stratigraphy of the midcontinent, particularly in Missouri and Kansas. His research in physical stratigraphy emphasized the cyclic nature of the sedimentary record and produced increasingly refined stratigraphic studies, eventually tracing some units one centimeter in thickness for several hundred kilometers. He was the first to recognize and name the Nemaha Anticline, a buried mountain range extending north-south from Nebraska to Oklahoma.

In 1923 Moore was the geologist of the U.S. Geological Survey expedition that surveyed the Grand Canyon, the first scientific expedition through the canyon since the voyages of John Wesley Powell in 1869 and 1871–1872. Because of a flash flood, all the expedition members were reported drowned. For many years Moore had Powell's obituary notice framed and hanging on his office wall.

Moore was a superb editor. He was a charter member of the American Association of Petroleum Geologists and editor of its *Bulletin* from 1920 to 1926. He was an organizer of the Society of Economic Paleontologists and Mineralogists, and editor of the *Journal of Paleontology* from 1930 to 1939. He helped establish the *Journal of Sedimentary Petrology* and edited it from 1931 to 1939. Moore was the founder (1946) and for many years the editor of the *Paleontological Contributions* of the University of Kansas.

During the early part of World War II, as a contribution to the oil and gas investigations of the U.S. Geological Survey, Moore mapped strata in north-central Texas, extending fieldwork he had done twenty years before in that region for the Texas Geological Survey. From 1929, Moore was a captain in the U.S. Army Corps of Engineers reserves. During World War II, from 1943 to 1945, he was on active duty with the rank of major, as assistant chief of the planning branch, Fuels and Lubricants Division, in the Office of the Quartermaster General. In 1949, Moore served as a civilian consultant to Gen. Douglas MacArthur and evaluated the coal resources of Japan.

Although he was a skilled field geologist, Moore is best known as a paleontologist who described a variety of fossil invertebrate groups, concerned with both their paleobiology and their utility as indicators of stratigraphic age. His principal works concerned the class Crinoidea (echinoderms growing on a stem and popularly known as fossil sea lilies), and he became an expert at identifying the age of rock strata from isolated fragments of these multiplated animals. Moore also wrote monographic works on corals and bryozoans. His geological and paleontological studies resulted in more than three hundred published papers.

Moore's greatest contribution to earth science and to biology was the *Treatise on Invertebrate Paleontology*, which he initiated in 1948. This multivolume work, an international effort to summarize and revise all the described invertebrate fossil animals, is published by the Geological Society of America. For more than two decades (1953–1974) Moore was editor of this project; Curt Teichert joined him as the editor, with special responsibility for the revised volumes, and served from 1964 to 1975. Moore enlisted hundreds of specialists on fossil invertebrates from dozens of countries to prepare sections of this work. When it was impossible to find a specialist, Moore, alone or in conjunction with a colleague, would undertake the necessary descriptions and classification. Although it was originally designed only as a compilation, the *Treatise* led to major classification of many fossil organisms and has exceeded the thirty-six volumes originally planned. During Moore's tenure as editor almost twenty volumes were published. This work ranks as one of the standard references of invertebrate paleontology and zoology.

Moore was foreign correspondent or honorary member of six European organizations. He received numerous awards and eight medals, including the first Paleontological Society Medal in 1963. He was president of the Society of Economic Paleontologists and Mineralogists (1928), the Paleontological Society (1947), the Geological Society of America (1957–1958), and the American Geological Institute (1960). Moore was active in the Association of State Geologists; he was vice president from 1934 to 1937 and again from 1939 to 1941, both coeditor and secretary-treasurer from 1937 to 1939, and president from 1941 to 1942. He also was chairman of the American Commission on Stratigraphic Nomenclature and a charter member of the Association of State Geologists. The building housing the Kansas Geological Survey is named for him. His monument, however, remains the *Treatise*, supported in part by an endowment he willed to the University of Kansas.

BIBLIOGRAPHY

I. Original Works. Moore's works include *Geology of Salt Dome Oil Fields* (Chicago, 1926); *Historical Geology* (New York and London, 1933); *Evolution and Classification of Paleozoic Crinoids* (New York, 1943), written with Lowell R. Laudon; *Introduction to Historical Geology* (New York, 1949; 2nd ed., 1958); and *Invertebrate Fossils* (New York, 1952).

The following parts of the *Treatise on Invertebrate Paleontology* were directed and edited by R. C. Moore: C, Protista 2, I and II (1964); D, Protista 3 (1954); E, Archaeocyatha and Porifera (1955); F, Coelenterata (1956); G, Bryozoa (1953); H, Brachiopoda, I and II (1965); I, Mollusca 1 (1960); K, Mollusca 3 (1964); L, Mollusca 4 (1957); N, Mollusca 6, I and II (1969), III (1971); O, Arthropoda 1 (1959); P, Arthropoda 2 (1955); Q, Arthropoda 3 (1961); R, Arthropoda 4 (1969); S, Echinodermata 1 (1967); U, Echinodermata 3, I and II (1966); V, Graptolithina (1955); W, Miscellanea (1962). Part T, Echinodermata 2 (1978), is edited by Moore and Teichert. Part A, Introduction (1979), is dedicated to Moore as founder and contains a pen-and-ink sketch of him. Volumes through 1966 were published by the Geological Society of America and the University of Kansas Press; subsequent volumes were published by the Geological Society and the University of Kansas.

II. Secondary Literature. Carl O. Dunbar, "Raymond Cecil Moore," in Curt Teichert and Ellis L. Yochelson, eds., *Essays in Paleontology and Stratigraphy, R. C. Moore Commemorative Volume* (Lawrence, Kans., 1967), with portrait and extensive bibliography; D. F. Merriam, "Raymond Cecil Moore," in *Geological Society of London, Annual Report for 1974* (1975), 42–43.

Ellis L. Yochelson

MOORE, ROBERT LEE (*b.* Dallas, Texas, 14 November 1882; *d.* Austin, Texas, 4 October 1974), *mathematics.*

Moore was the fifth of the six children of Charles Jonathan and Louisa Ann (Moore) Moore. His father had moved to the southern United States from Connecticut to fight on the side of the South during the Civil War and eventually settled in Dallas, where he established a hardware and feed store. Moore attended a private school in Dallas and the University of Texas (now the University of Texas at Austin), where he spent most of his professional life. In 1910 he married Margaret MacLelland Key of Brenham, Texas; they had no children.

According to the registrar's records, while Moore was at the University of Texas (1898–1902), he did very well in mathematics courses under George Bruce Halsted and Leonard Eugene Dickson. He obtained both the B.S. and the M.A. in 1901. He continued at the university as a fellow for the year 1901–1902. In one of his classes Halsted posed a problem that resulted in Moore's proving that one of the axioms in David Hilbert's *Grundlagen der Geometrie* (1899) was not independent of the other axioms. This was brought to the attention of Eliakim Hastings Moore (no direct relation), the leading professor of mathematics at the University of Chicago, who was able to provide R. L. Moore with a scholarship for graduate work at Chicago beginning in 1903. R. L. Moore was taking courses under Halsted in 1902, but when the university regents refused, over Halsted's protests, to renew Moore's teaching fellowship, Moore went to teach for a year

(1902–1903) at a high school in Marshall, Texas. Halsted was himself fired by the regents in December 1902 for reasons that remain unclear.

In 1905 Moore received his doctoral degree at Chicago with a dissertation entitled "Sets of Metrical Hypotheses for Geometry" and supervised by Oswald Veblen. After Chicago, Moore held teaching positions at the University of Tennessee (1905–1906), Princeton University (1906–1908), Northwestern University (1908–1911), and the University of Pennsylvania (1911–1920). In 1914 he became an associate editor of *Transactions of the American Mathematical Society* and continued in this position to 1927. In 1920 Moore returned to the University of Texas as associate professor of mathematics and three years later was appointed professor.

By 1920 Moore had published seventeen papers making use of the axiomatic procedures then being developed by mathematicians under the influence principally of Veblen, E. H. Moore, and others at Chicago. He had, however, his own distinctive approach and took little interest in such topics as the logical status of the Axiom of Choice, a problem in the foundations of mathematics that interested many mathematicians during most of Moore's career. He seemed more interested in using axiomatics as a tool in developing a unique approach within set-theoretic topology or, as he termed it, point-set topology.

The first edition of Moore's only book, *Foundations of Point Set Theory* (1932), represented the culmination of the major part of his research to date. It also formed the basis of his subsequent work, which was expressed more through his teaching and his students than through publications: fifty of his total of sixty-eight publications appeared before 1932, and forty-one of his fifty doctoral students were awarded their degrees in the period 1932 to 1969. A revised edition of his book (1962) incorporated many of the results of his students and others in the field during the previous thirty years.

In his book Moore gradually reveals a collection of axioms and develops at each stage the consequences of the axioms admitted thus far. For example, chapter 2 is entitled "Consequences of Axioms 0, 1 and 2"; Euclidean space of any finite dimension and Hilbert space are examples that satisfy these axioms. By chapter 4, axioms 3, 4, and 5 have been added and, as Moore states in his preface, from these six axioms "it is possible to prove a very considerable portion of the well known topological propositions of the plane." The fruitfulness of Moore's axioms lies in the fact that, however close they may appear to determine the Euclidean plane, a space satisfying them need not be metric and indeed may depart rather wildly from Euclidean space.

Though his courses followed his book in subject and axiomatic style, Moore told his graduate students not to read it or any other mathematically relevant literature, and he strongly discouraged any mathematical communication between students outside of class. He regarded his classes as research sessions in which students learned by presenting their work at the blackboard and by critically evaluating others' presentations. Moore presented possible definitions, axioms, and theorems, and the ground rules for the class, but otherwise took the role of a researcher himself. His technique has been much analyzed and imitated because, though its basic idea may not be original with him, in his hands it resulted in what is regarded by many mathematicians outside the Moore school as the most distinguished group of mathematicians in the United States to have been taught by the same person.

Most of Moore's students became research mathematicians and professors at universities and used some version of his teaching method. Some continued to make use of his axiom system in the study of abstract spaces and the structure of continua (F. Burton Jones, for example) or in the related area of set-theoretic topology (Mary E. Estill Rudin). Others entered related branches, such as algebraic topology (Raymond L. Wilder), analytic topology (Gordon T. Whyburn), and topology of manifolds (R. H. Bing).

The University of Texas regulations in 1953 allowed Moore to continue to teach beyond the usual retirement age of seventy, and he taught until he was eighty-six. Although willing to continue, he was then retired. His last official contact with the university occurred in 1973, when he sent his appreciation to the regents for naming the new building housing the departments of mathematics, physics, and astronomy after him.

Moore's career spanned the period of rapid growth in American mathematics that began at the turn of the century. He contributed a branch of topology and created an influential method of teaching mathematics. His honors included election to the National Academy of Sciences (1931); visiting lecturer of the American Mathematical Society, the first American to be so honored (1931–1932); and the presidency of the American Mathematical Society (1937–1938).

BIBLIOGRAPHY

I. ORIGINAL WORKS. Moore's principal work, *Foundations of Point Set Theory*, appeared as volume 13 of the American Mathematical Society Colloquium Publications. The first edition (New York, 1932) was brought up to date in many details in a revised edition (Providence, R.I., 1962) that included a much more extensive bibliography. It was reprinted with corrections in 1970. A complete bibliography of Moore's articles can be found in Raymond L. Wilder's biographical article (see below).

The R. L. Moore Collection in the Archives of American Mathematics, University Archives, University of Texas at Austin, contains Moore's correspondence, personal papers, library, and other items from his home.

II. SECONDARY LITERATURE. General biographical articles on Moore include R. E. Greenwood, "In Memoriam—Robert Lee Moore," in *Documents and Minutes of the General Faculty* (Austin, Tex., 1974–1975), 11653–11665, and "The Kinship of E. H. Moore and R. L. Moore," in *Historia Mathematica*, **4** (1977), 153–155; and Raymond L. Wilder, "Robert Lee Moore, 1882–1974," in *Bulletin of the American Mathematical Society*, **82** (1976), 417–427, which includes a bibliography of Moore's publications. D. Reginald Traylor, William Bane, and Madeline Jones, *Creative Teaching: Heritage of R. L. Moore* (Houston, 1972) includes the names and publications of Moore's doctoral students and of each successive generation of their students; it is reviewed by P. R. Halmos in *Historia Mathematica*, **1** (1974), 188–192. Moore's work is treated in Raymond L. Wilder, "The Mathematical Work of R. L. Moore: Its Background, Nature and Influence," in *Archive for History of Exact Sciences*, **26** (1982), 73–97.

Studies of Moore's teaching method include F. Burton Jones, "The Moore Method," in *American Mathematical Monthly*, **84** (1977), 273–278; Lucille E. Whyburn, "Student-Oriented Teaching—The Moore Method," *ibid.*, **77** (1970), 351–359; and the fifty-five-minute motion picture *Challenge in the Classroom: The Method of R. L. Moore*, produced by the Mathematical Association of America in 1965.

ALBERT C. LEWIS

MORDELL, LOUIS JOEL (*b.* Philadelphia, Pennsylvania, 28 January 1888; *d.* Cambridge, England, 12 March 1972), *mathematics*.

Mordell was the third child of Phineas Mordell, who later became a noted Hebrew scholar, and of Annie Feller Mordell. Both were poor Jewish immigrants from Lithuania. At a young age he went to England, where he spent the rest of his life, and became a British subject in 1929. In May 1916 he married Mabel Elizabeth Cambridge; they had a daughter and a son.

At the age of fourteen, when he entered Central High School in Philadelphia, Mordell was already fascinated with mathematics learned from used books he had bought for five or ten cents at a well-known

Philadelphia bookstore. Many of the examples in these books were taken from Cambridge scholarship or tripos papers, a fact that gave Mordell the desire to attend Cambridge. Having demonstrated his mathematical abilities by completing the four-year high school mathematics course in two years and earning a very high grade on a test administered by a friend of his father's, he scraped together the fare to Cambridge. In 1907 he placed first on the scholarship examination and received a scholarship to St. John's College. He took part I of the mathematical tripos in 1909 and was third wrangler (after P. J. Daniell and E. H. Neville). On completing the tripos he began research in the theory of numbers, in which there was then little interest in England; he regarded himself as self-taught in the subject.

Mordell's work was a systematic study of the integral solutions (x,y) of the Diophantine equation

$$y^2 = x^3 + k. \tag{1}$$

This equation has a long history, going back to Pierre de Fermat (1601–1665) for some values of k, but Mordell decided the solubility for many new values of k and in some cases gave complete solutions. He also showed that the determination of the solutions was equivalent to solving the set of equations $f(u,v) = 1$, where f runs through representatives of the equivalence classes of integral cubic forms of discriminant $-4k$. This won him a Smith's Prize, but he failed to obtain a college fellowship. He went on to show that the determination of the integral solutions (x,y) of an equation

$$y^2 = ax^3 + bx^2 + cx + d \tag{2}$$

is equivalent to determining the solutions of $f(u, v) = 1$, where f now runs through representatives of a class of quartic forms with given invariants. Axel Thue had already shown that equations of the type $f(u, v) = 1$ have only finitely many solutions, which implies that this is also the case for (1) and (2); but Mordell learned of Thue's work only later, and at the time believed that some equations (1) or (2) could have infinitely many integral solutions.

From 1913 to 1920 Mordell was a lecturer at Birkbeck College, London. His main interest was in modular forms, and he made two important advances, both anticipating approaches that remain central in the theory. One of these concerned the tau function, introduced by Srinivasa Ramanujan, who had conjectured that it has the property of multiplicativity. This Mordell proved. The central argument (the Hecke operator) was rediscovered by Erich Hecke in 1937. The tau function is the set of coefficients of a certain modular form, and Hecke showed that Mordell's theorem is a special case of a general and important phenomenon. Mordell's other advance was to systematize the theory of the representation of integers as the sum of a fixed number n of squares of integers. Many special results were known. Mordell showed how to deduce those results and to obtain new ones by using the finite dimensionality of the space of modular forms of a given type. In the hands of Hecke and others, this idea was exploited with great effect in the study of representation by positive definite quadratic forms in general.

During the period from 1920 to 1922, when he was lecturer at Manchester College of Technology, Mordell worked out the result for which he is most widely known, his "finite basis theorem." Henri Poincaré had shown that the determination of all the rational points on a given curve of genus 1 defined over the rationals is equivalent, once one rational point has been given, to the determination of the rational points on a curve

$$y^2 = 4x^3 - g_2 x - g_3, \qquad (3)$$

where g_2, g_3 are given rational numbers (depending on the given curve). The rational points on (3) have a natural structure as an abelian group, and Poincaré conjectured that this group is finitely generated. In the course of an investigation with another aim, Mordell found a proof of this conjecture. The curve (3) is an abelian variety of dimension 1. The finite basis theorem was extended by André Weil to abelian varieties of any dimension and to any algebraic number field as ground field, and there are further generalizations. The theorem plays a key role in many aspects of Diophantine analysis. Mordell, however, played no part in these later developments.

Toward the end of the paper just discussed, Mordell conjectures that there are only finitely many rational points on any curve of genus greater than unity. This acquired notoriety as "Mordell's conjecture" and was proved by Gerd Faltings in 1983.

In 1922 Mordell moved to the University of Manchester, where from 1923 to 1945 he was Fielden professor of pure mathematics and head of the mathematics department; in 1924 he was elected to the Royal Society—while still an American citizen. There was already a fine tradition of mathematics at Manchester, and during Mordell's tenure it became a leading center. He gave great attention both to teaching and to research and built up a strong team that attracted many visitors. He was extremely active in assisting refugees from continental tyrannies, and for some of them he found temporary or even permanent positions. Mordell's own research ranged widely within the theory of numbers. One problem (suggested by Harold Davenport) was the estimation of trigonometric sums and of the number of points on curves and other varieties defined over finite fields. Mordell devised an averaging argument that gave stronger results than those already known. The results were largely superseded by the Riemann hypothesis for function fields of Hasse and Weil, but Mordell's argument suggested to Ivan Vinogradov his technique for estimating more general sums. In the late 1930's, with Harold Davenport and Kurt Mahler (both then at Manchester), Mordell initiated a period of great advances in the geometry of numbers.

In 1945 Mordell succeeded Godfrey Harold Hardy as Sadleirian professor of pure mathematics at Cambridge, and became a fellow of St. John's. He rapidly built up a strong research school. After his retirement in 1953 he continued to live in Cambridge but traveled widely. He retained his passionate interest in mathematics and did much to foster that interest in others, particularly beginners. He published many papers; perhaps none were of the first rank, but some nevertheless display an extraordinary virtuosity with comparatively elementary techniques. Mordell was a problem solver, not a system builder. Even when his work revealed a system waiting to be built (as, for example, with modular forms or the finite basis theorem) he turned to other work after solving the problem of interest to him.

Mordell enjoyed robust health throughout his life. After a very brief period of ill health, he slipped into unconsciousness and died five days later.

BIBLIOGRAPHY

I. ORIGINAL WORKS. Mordell gives an entertaining account of his early career in "Reminiscences of an Octogenarian Mathematician," in *American Mathematical Monthly*, **78** (1971), 952–961.

Mordell wrote only one book: *Diophantine Equations* (London, 1969). Significant papers include "The Diophantine Equation $y^2 - k = x^3$," in *Proceedings of the London Mathematical Society*, 2nd ser., **13** (1913), 60–80; "Indeterminate Equations of the Third and Fourth Degrees," in *Quarterly Journal of Pure and Applied Mathematics*, **45** (1914), 170–186; "On Mr. Ramanujan's Empirical Expansion of Modular Functions," in *Proceedings of the Cambridge Philosophical Society*, **19** (1917), 117–124; "On the Representation of a Number as a Sum of an Odd Number of Squares," in *Transactions of the Cambridge Philosophical Society*, **22** (1919), 361–372; "On the Rational Solutions of the Indeterminate Equations of the 3rd and 4th Degrees," in *Proceedings of the Cambridge Philosophical Society*, **21** (1922), 179–

192; "A Theorem of Khintchine on Linear Diophantine Approximation," in *Journal of the London Mathematical Society*, **12** (1937), 166–167; "On Numbers Represented by Binary Cubics," in *Proceedings of the London Mathematical Society*, 2nd ser., **48** (1943), 198–228; and "Observations on the Minimum of a Positive Quadratic Form in Eight Variables," in *Journal of the London Mathematical Society*, **19** (1944), 3–6.

II. SECONDARY LITERATURE. There is an account of Mordell's life and work by John W. S. Cassels in *Biographical Memoirs of Fellows of the Royal Society*, **19** (1973), 493–520, with a complete bibliography. A slightly different version of this account is in *Bulletin of the London Mathematical Society*, **6** (1974), 69–96, also with a complete list of his publications. A short biographical memoir by Harold Davenport is in *Acta arithmetica*, **9** (1964), 1–22, with a bibliography and a portrait.

JOHN W. S. CASSELS

MORET, LÉON (*b.* Haute-Savoie, France, 4 July 1890; *d.* Isère, France, 22 November 1972), *geology, paleontology.*

The son of a notary at Annecy, Moret studied medicine. As he was interested in natural history, he also took courses in geology (with a special interest in paleontology) at the University of Lyons. During World War I he served as a military doctor, temporarily interrupting his studies. But his passion for geology remained, and in 1919 he left the medical profession and became an assistant at the recently reconstituted University of Strasbourg in the Department of Geology, the first chairman of which was Maurice Gignoux. Moret married Elizabeth Denarié; they had two sons and two daughters.

Moret began his academic career under the direction of the great master Gignoux, who soon also became a friend. They met again in 1925, when Moret was named lecturer in geology at the University of Grenoble, where in 1926 Gignoux became chairman of the department of geology, succeeding Wilfrid Kilian. Thirty years later Moret succeeded Gignoux as departmental chairman and, like his predecessor, received many honors and rose through the ranks to become dean of the Faculty of Sciences. In 1957 he became a member of the Academy of Sciences. He was also a commander in the Legion of Honor.

Moret's scientific works are extensive. Although a paleontologist by training, he remained a generalist, as can be seen in the variety of topics covered in his more than 350 publications. In the field of paleontology, his name was first linked with the fossil Spongia, mainly of the Upper Cretaceous, which was the subject of his doctoral thesis. But it was through his *Manuel de paléontologie animale* (1939),

followed by *Paléontologie végétale* (1942), that his name came to be internationally known among geologists.

Moret was above all an Alpine geologist. His first works in this area dealt with the Savoic Alps, especially with the ranges located north of the Annecy Lake (Bornes massif). It is there that folded units of the Alpine edge (subalpine zone) are juxtaposed with allochthonous outliers (klippen) coming from the east, that is, from the more internal Alpine zones, after a thrust of some tens of kilometers. In addition to its geological interest, his memoir, "Geologie du massif des Bornes" (1934), was an innovation in Alpine geological literature because of the quality of its illustrations and because it introduced the concept of "geological landscapes" and their deciphering. All previous publications, at least in France, had confined themselves to the description of stratigraphic sequences and of tectonics along transverse sections.

In the second part of his Alpine career, Moret extended his activities to the entire French Alps. Among his numerous published works in this field, three merit mention. *Description géologique du bassin supérieur de la Durance* (1938), written with Gignoux, is the first clear approach to the internal Alpine zones along the Gap-Briançon transverse. The originality of this work lies in the relationship it maintains among stratigraphy, paleogeography, and tectonics. The study of such relationships soon became an important field of geology called structural geology. *Géologie dauphinoise; ou, Initiation à la géologie par l'étude des environs de Grenoble* (1944), also written with Gignoux, is a masterpiece, still unequaled for its mixture of geological precision and clear, simple presentation of geological data. This book became quite popular with the general public and stimulated many geological careers.

Moret's third work on the French Alps was a film depicting the rise of the Alpine range over the past 200 million years. Not only was the pedagogic value of this movie obvious, but it also illustrated in a striking way the mechanics of gravity tectonics, a theory developed by Gignoux. This theory maintains that rocks, because they are susceptible to deformation, are more or less plastic, given a sufficient period of time. On a suitable scale (millions of years), any rock mass can acquire plastic properties and thus flow, like a mudslide, down a slope, even a gentle one, solely as a result of gravity. Even if modern studies have not generalized this concept to all nappe structures, it still remains suitable for the interpretation of many of them.

Besides his Alpine activities Moret worked in

Morocco and Cyrenaica. He sought to apply geological knowledge to landslides in mountainous areas, to dam foundations, and to hydrogeology and thermal springs. This last topic was the subject of a handbook he published in 1946.

After retiring, Moret led an active life, seeing to the successive editions of his books and remaining attentive to new developments in Alpine geology. Having more time at his disposal, he was able to demonstrate his artistic talent, painting Dauphiné and Savoie landscapes in watercolors that have formed the basis of several public exhibitions. Moret also wrote biographies of many of the pioneers of Alpine geology. Of special note is that of Dieudonné (Déodat) Dolomieu, for whom the mineral dolomite was named.

BIBLIOGRAPHY

I. ORIGINAL WORKS. "Geologie du massif des Bornes (Savoie)," in *Mémoires de la Société geologique de France* (1934); *Les sources thermominerales* (Paris, 1946); *Géologie dauphinoise* (2nd ed., Paris, 1952), written with Maurice Gignoux; *La genèse des Alpes françaises*, a color film (1961); *Paléontologie végétale* (3rd ed., Paris, 1964); *Manuel de paléontologie animale* (5th ed., Paris, 1966); and *Précis de géologie* (5th ed., Paris, 1967).

II. SECONDARY LITERATURE. Reynold Barbier, "L'oeuvre scientifique de Léon Moret (1890–1972)," in *Bulletin de la Société géologique de France*, 7th ser., **16** (1974), 10–22.

JACQUES DEBELMAS

MOSTOWSKI, ANDRZEJ (*b.* Lvov, Poland, 1 November 1913; *d.* Vancouver, Canada, 22 August 1975), *set theory, mathematical logic.*

Mostowski belonged to the first generation of mathematical logicians who investigated foundational questions from a purely mathematical (rather than a philosophical) viewpoint and who also transformed axiomatic set theory into a branch of logic. For three decades after World War II he was the leader of mathematical logic in Poland. A man of considerable talent, energy, and charm, he was known for his personal and scientific generosity. Philosophically, he was a realist concerning the real numbers and, after Cohen's 1963 independence results, a formalist concerning set theory.

His father, Stanislaw Mostowski, an assistant in the department of physical chemistry at the University of Lvov, joined the army in 1914 and died a year after his son was born. Mostowski's mother, Zofia Mostowska, whose maiden name was Kram-

styk, worked in a bank. During the winter of 1914 the family went to Zakopane for a vacation; World War I forced them to stay until 1920, when they moved to Warsaw. There, from 1923 to 1931, Mostowski attended the Stefan Batory Gymnasium. A good student, he was interested in both mathematics and physics. When he was sixteen, he fell seriously ill, and this later kept him from serving in the army.

In 1931 Mostowski entered the University of Warsaw, where he was attracted to logic, set theory, and the foundations of mathematics. His teachers in these subjects were eminent researchers—Kuratowski, Leśniewski, Lukasiewicz, Sierpiński, and the two who influenced him most: Lindenbaum and, above all, Tarski.

After Mostowski received a master's degree in 1936 and wrote his doctoral dissertation, he went abroad to study. During the summer semester of 1937, at the University of Vienna, he attended Gödel's course on constructible sets, where the relative consistency of the axiom of choice was first established. In Zurich, convinced that he needed a practical skill in order to find a job in Poland (where positions in mathematics were scarce), Mostowski studied statistics in order to become an actuary. Bored with that subject, he enjoyed lectures by Polya and by Hermann Weyl as well as a seminar by Bernays. He did research on recursion theory and on the axiom of choice.

In 1938 Mostowski returned to Warsaw, where, in February 1939, he defended his doctoral dissertation, showing that various definitions of finiteness are not provably equivalent in logic without the axiom of choice. Tarski, who was then a *Privatdozent*, directed the dissertation, but the official supervisor was Kuratowski. Unable to find a position at the University of Warsaw, Mostowski worked at the National Meteorological Institute.

A year after the Nazis invaded Poland in September 1939, Mostowski became an accountant in a small plant that manufactured roofing and remained there until 1944. From 1942 to 1944 he also taught analytic geometry and Galois theory at the Underground University of Warsaw. One of the students there was Maria Matuszewska, whom he married in September 1944; they had a daughter and two sons, one of whom became a mathematician. Sierpiński, a colleague at the Underground University, remarked in 1945 that Mostowski was very close to being habilitated there in July 1944. Then came the Warsaw uprising of August 1944, when the Nazis devastated the city. Afterward, as he was about to be sent to a concentration camp, some Polish nurses helped Mostowski to escape, spiriting him through the German lines to a hospital.

Many of Mostowski's wartime results—on the hierarchy of projective sets, on arithmetically definable sets of natural numbers, and on consequences of the axiom of constructibility in descriptive set theory—were lost when his apartment was destroyed during the uprising. He had to choose whether to flee with a thick notebook containing those results or with bread. He chose bread.

Later Mostowski was able to reconstruct just a fraction of his discoveries, such as the decidability of the theory of well-ordering (a result obtained in 1941 but only announced, jointly with Tarski, in 1949 and only published in 1978).

In January 1945 the unemployed Mostowski tried to make a living by giving private lessons, then had to pawn his few possessions. For a few months shortly after the war he held a position as a research fellow at the Silesian Polytechnic (temporarily housed in Cracow). Then he taught briefly at the Jagellonian University in Cracow, where his *Habilitationsschrift* was approved in 1945. From January to September 1946 he was an acting professor at Lodz University.

Nevertheless, Mostowski's career was to be in Warsaw. In 1946 he returned to the University of Warsaw as an acting professor, becoming an extraordinary professor the following year and ordinary (full) professor in 1951. He occupied the chair of philosophy of mathematics, then the chair of algebra, and finally the chair of foundations of mathematics. In 1952 he served as dean of the Faculty of Mathematics and Physics. From 1948 to 1968 he was also head of the division of the foundations of mathematics at the National Institute of Mathematics (which became the Mathematics Institute of the Polish Academy of Sciences). From 1968 until his death he headed the section on the foundations of mathematics at the University of Warsaw.

When he returned to Warsaw in 1946, Mostowski was the only logician there left from the vigorous group that before the war had included Leśniewski, Lukasiewicz, and Tarski. Although Mostowski had little previous experience as an organizer and disliked administrative duties, he threw himself into rebuilding Warsaw as a major center for mathematical logic. In this effort he was quite successful. He also considered it important to strengthen algebra as an adjunct to logic. In this spirit he wrote for a Polish audience a number of textbooks in algebra, logic, and set theory. As early as 1946 he attracted excellent graduate students, the first of whom (Andrzej Grzegorczyk and Helena Rasiowa) received doctorates in 1950. Among his students were also Henry Hiz,

Antoni Janiczak, and Andrzej Ehrenfeucht. After 1965 the number of his students increased and he conducted a large seminar on the foundations of mathematics.

A variety of honors came to Mostowski, beginning with a Polish state prize in 1952 (and another in 1966). In 1956 he was elected an associate member of the Polish Academy of Sciences and became a full member seven years later. In 1972 he received a Jurzykowski Foundation prize and also became president of the division of logic, methodology, and philosophy of science of the International Union for the History and Philosophy of Science. Internationally he was highly respected by his fellow logicians.

Mostowski did much editorial work, serving on the editorial boards of *Fundamenta Mathematicae* and *Journal of Symbolic Logic*, as well as *Annals of Mathematical Logic*, which he helped to found. Moreover, he coedited the series for mathematics, physics, and astronomy of the *Bulletin* of the Polish Academy of Sciences. Beginning in 1966, he also served as an editor of the series "Studies in Logic and the Foundations of Mathematics" published by North-Holland.

Mostowski traveled abroad repeatedly, spending the academic years 1948–1949 at the Institute for Advanced Study in Princeton, 1958–1959 at the University of California at Berkeley, and 1969–1970 at All Souls College, Oxford. In addition, he participated in many congresses and conferences in Europe and America. After spending the summer of 1975 at Berkeley and Stanford, he was on his way to a conference in Ontario when he stopped at Simon Fraser University in Vancouver to deliver a lecture. There he died suddenly.

Mostowski's earliest publications prior to World War II, on Boolean algebras and on Fraenkel-Mostowski (FM) models for set theory, illustrate two major themes of his work: algebra applied to logic, and the semantics of set theory. His early research on recursion theory and undecidability, a third theme, did not appear in print until after the war.

His work on FM models was stimulated in 1935 when Lindenbaum posed the problem of how to formulate Fraenkel's independence results on the axiom of choice in a logically unobjectionable way. Lindenbaum and Mostowski did so, developing the theory of FM models and carefully distinguishing the object language and the metalanguage in the manner of Tarski. In 1939 Mostowski published a rigorous proof that the axiom of choice cannot be deduced from the ordering principle; Fraenkel's earlier argument had not been adequate. He went beyond Fraenkel by showing that Tarski's five notions of finiteness were nonequivalent, both in the theory of types and in Bernays-Gödel set theory with urelements. In 1948 Mostowski proved that the principle of dependent choices does not imply the axiom of choice. This result used an uncountable set of urelements, while all earlier independence results relied on a countable set. Mostowski's *Habilitationsschrift* (1945) established necessary and sufficient conditions for the axiom of choice restricted to families of *m*-element sets to imply the axiom for *n*-element sets. His isomorphism theorem (1949) on transitive models was fundamental to later research on models of set theory. Finally, during the 1970's he worked on Kelley-Morse set theory and its models.

During World War II, Mostowski began investigating recursion theory and undecidability. He developed the analytical hierarchy of sets of integers, as Kleene did independently. In 1939 Mostowski, working with Tarski, reduced Gödel's incompleteness theorems to a form that depended only on finitely many first-order arithmetic axioms, thus enabling many theories to be proved undecidable. They prepared their results for publication a decade later with R. M. Robinson. At that time Mostowski also developed an algebraic method for proving nondeducibility results in intuitionistic logic. In 1959 he introduced β-models for second-order arithmetic (models that make well-orderings absolute). He showed that some ω-models are not β-models and was one of those to establish the existence of a minimal β-model.

Much of Mostowski's postwar work in logic concerned extensions of first-order logic. Thus, in a 1957 paper he introduced the notion of generalized quantifiers and, in particular, quantifiers such as "there exist uncountably many." He showed that many logics with generalized quantifiers do not have a recursively enumerable set of valid sentences and posed the completeness problem for the remaining such logics: Does there exist a recursively enumerable set of axioms and rules of inference such that a sentence is provable if and only if it is valid? In the same paper he also established that in any logic with a generalized quantifier not definable from "for all" and "there exists," the Löwenheim-Skolem-Tarski theorem fails; this result helped lead to Lindstrom's characterization of first-order logic in terms of the Löwenheim-Skolem theorem and the compactness theorem. With Grzegorczyk and Ryll-Nardzewski, Mostowski extended Gödel's incompleteness results to second-order arithmetic supplemented by the ω-rule. In 1961, solving a problem of Tarski's, he showed that the theory of real numbers cannot be axiomatized in weak second-order logic. Finally, in 1962 he proved that the completeness problem has a positive solution for some very general kinds of many-valued first-order logic.

Several of Mostowski's papers from the 1950's involve model theory. In 1952 he studied the conditions under which the truth of a sentence is preserved by a finite direct product of models, thereby stimulating more general work by Vaught and by Feferman. Three years later he exhibited a first-order theory (a form of set theory) with no recursively enumerable models. But Mostowski's most important model-theoretic research, done jointly with Ehrenfeucht (1956), introduced the notion of indiscernible elements and of models generated by such elements, giving conditions under which a theory has a model with many such elements. These ideas proved very fruitful in model theory and set theory.

BIBLIOGRAPHY

I. ORIGINAL WORKS. A bibliography of Mostowski's works is in *Foundational Studies: Selected Works*, Kazimierz Kuratowski et al., eds., 2 vols. (Amsterdam, 1979), containing about half of his published and unpublished works (translated into English when originally in another language, since Mostowski published in English, French, German, and Polish). His monograph *Thirty Years of Foundational Studies* (New York, 1966) remains the best historical introduction to logic during the seminal years 1930 to 1964.

II. SECONDARY LITERATURE. The best biography is Stanislaw Krajewski and Marian Srebrny, in *Wiadomości matematyczne*, **22** (1979), 53–64. *Foundational Studies* contains a short biography by Wiktor Marek as well as essays on Mostowski's contributions to recursion theory (by Andrzej Grzegorczyk), model theory (by Leszek Pacholski), logical calculi (by Cecylia Rauszer), second-order arithmetic (by Pawel Zbierski), and set theory (by Wojciech Guzicki and Wiktor Marek). A biography by Helena Rasiowa appears in Robin O. Gandy and J. M. E. Hyland, eds., *Logic Colloquium 76* (Amsterdam, 1977), 139–144. See also Wiktor Marek et al., eds., *Set Theory and Hierarchy Theory: A Memorial Tribute to Andrzej Mostowski*, Springer Lecture Notes, no. 537 (Berlin, 1976), for a brief biography, bibliography, and an unpublished paper. Fragmentary autobiographical reminiscences are in John N. Crossley, ed., *Algebra and Logic*, Springer Lecture Notes, no. 450 (Berlin, 1975), 7–47.

GREGORY H. MOORE

MOUFANG, RUTH (*b.* Darmstadt, Germany, 10 January 1905; *d.* Frankfurt, Germany, 26 November 1977), *mathematics.*

Ruth Moufang was the younger daughter of Dr. Eduard Moufang, an industrial chemist, and his wife, Else Fecht Moufang. Her interest in mathematics was first stimulated at the Realgymnasium in Bad Kreuznach, which she attended from 1921 to 1924. From 1925 to 1930 she studied mathematics at the University of Frankfurt. In 1929 she took her teacher's examination, and in October 1931 she received her Ph.D. with a dissertation on projective geometry supervised by Max Dehn. She held a fellowship in Rome during 1931 and 1932, and the following academic year a teaching assignment at the University of Königsberg.

Moufang then returned to Frankfurt, where she held teaching assignments from 1934 to 1936. During this period she continued working on the geometry of the projective plane, and in 1936 she completed her habilitation thesis to qualify as a university lecturer. By this time, however, the Nazi government had made a distinction between the habilitation and the *venia legendi* (which conferred the right to teach). On 9 February 1937 Moufang became the third woman in Germany to receive the habilitation in mathematics. A month later, however, the Ministry of Education informed her that she could not receive a *Dozentur.* A *Dozent* had to qualify as a leader of an almost exclusively male student body, argued the ministry, and "in the future the preconditions for the fruitful activity of a female *Dozent* are lacking."

With the help of a friend, Moufang found employment as an industrial mathematician at the Krupp research laboratories in Essen; she worked there from November 1937 to August 1946, during which time she authored and coauthored several papers, most of them on applied elasticity theory. In 1946 Moufang was asked to return to the University of Frankfurt, where she was given the *venia legendi.* There she held a lecturer's position until her appointment as associate professor in December 1947; she became full professor in February 1957. In the years after the war she published almost nothing, although she was a successful teacher.

Moufang's work from 1931 to 1937 was the main starting point for a new specialty in mathematics, the study of projective planes, in which geometrical and algebraical structures are closely interrelated. At the turn of the century David Hilbert had shown the existence of non-Desarguian planes. With her dissertation of 1931 Moufang started the systemic study of such planes. Her adviser, Max Dehn, had posed the problem of surveying the interdependence of closure theorems like Desargues's in planes. Such theorems state the closure of a geometric configuration if certain incidences of points and lines are given. In the case of a plane generated by four points, Moufang showed that all closure theorems can be derived from one special case of Desargues's theorem in which the vertices of one of the perspective triangles lie on the sides of the other.

In 1932 Moufang studied the plane generated by five points and showed the equivalence of the above theorem, which she called D_9, with the theorem of the complete quadrilateral. The latter can be used in coordinatization to deduce all algebraic laws for a field except associativity. This is a special case of what is now called a "Moufang plane." In two further papers (1933, 1934) she took up the concept of an alternative division ring (introduced by Max Zorn in 1930), an algebraic structure in which all laws for a field hold except the associative law, for which a weaker "alternation law" is valid. Moufang proved the fundamental theorem for Moufang planes: that if D_9 or, equivalently, the theorem of the complete quadrilateral holds in a projective plane, then and only then can it be coordinatized by an alternative division ring (of characteristic not 2). The main theorem in this field was then proved by Skornjakov (1950) and by Bruck and Kleinfeld (1951): that any alternative division ring of characteristic other than 2 is either associative or a Cayley-Dickson algebra over its center. In 1934 Moufang also studied the multiplicative structure of alternative division rings, which led to what today is called a "Moufang loop."

BIBLIOGRAPHY

I. ORIGINAL WORKS. Important papers are "Zur Struktur der projektiven Geometrie der Ebene," in *Mathematische Annalen,* **105** (1931), 536–601; "Die Schnittpunktsätze des projektiven speziellen Fünfecksnetzes in ihrer Abhängigkeit voneinander," *ibid.,* **106** (1932), 755–795; "Alternativkörper und der Satz vom vollständigen Vierseit (D_9)," in *Abhandlungen aus dem Mathematischen Seminar der Hamburgischen Universität,* **9** (1933), 207–222; and "Zur Struktur von Alternativkörpern," in *Mathematische Annalen,* **110** (1934), 416–430.

II. SECONDARY LITERATURE. A brief biography and description of Moufang's work, including a list of publications (incomplete in applied mathematics), is in Bhama Srinivasan, "Ruth Moufang 1905–1977," in *Mathematical Intelligencer,* **6,** no. 2 (1984), 51–55.

H. MEHRTENS

NAIMARK, MARK ARONOVICH (*b*. Odessa, Russia, 5 December 1909; *d*. Moscow, U.S.S.R., 30 December 1978), *mathematics*.

Naimark was the son of Aron Iakovlevich Naimark, a professional artist, and of Zefir Moiseevna Naimark. He showed his mathematical talents at an early age; and from 1924 to 1928, studying independently, he completed a university course in mathematical analysis. In 1929 he enrolled at the Odessa Institute of National Education, and four years later was admitted to graduate study (*aspirantura*) at Odessa State University, under the direction of Mark G. Krein. On 1 June 1932 he married Larisa Petrovna Shcherbakova; they had two sons.

Naimark defended his candidate's thesis (roughly corresponding to the U.S. doctoral dissertation) in 1936. Two years later he moved to Moscow. In 1941 he received the doctorate (often called the "big" doctorate) from the Steklov Mathematical Institute and was immediately appointed professor at the Seismological Institute of the U.S.S.R. Academy of Sciences. When the Soviet Union entered World War II, Naimark embarked upon military work, spending eighteen months in Tashkent with the evacuated Seismological Institute. He worked at a number of institutes, including the Institute of Chemical Physics and the U.S.S.R. Academy for the Arms Industry, after returning to Moscow when the war was over. In 1954 Naimark became a professor at the Moscow Physical-Technical Institute, and in 1962 he was appointed professor at the Steklov Mathematical Institute, a post he held until his death.

Naimark's life was governed by total dedication to science that led to a large scientific output. Nevertheless, he found time to read Western writers in their original languages and to follow developments in the fine arts. He was a skillful painter and knew a great deal about music.

During his early career Naimark carried a heavy load of classroom teaching. In later years he taught only graduate courses and guided the research of his many students. In the 1960's he traveled widely; in 1967 he made a lecture tour through Canada that did much to further contacts between Soviet and Western mathematicians. During his last ten years Naimark suffered from heart disease but bore his affliction with grace and humor. When too ill to sit up, he dictated mathematics to his wife.

Naimark's first mathematical writings were joint papers with Krein, mostly on the separation of roots of algebraic equations. After his arrival in Moscow, he was at the forefront of functional analysis and group representations, two fields that were in a state of rapid ferment in the Soviet Union and else-

where. (He is, in fact, justly considered one of the founders of functional analysis and group representations.) His most famous early contribution was the elaboration of the classical Gelfand-Naimark theorem (1943), which showed that norm-closed self-adjoint algebras of operators in Hilbert space can be described by a few simple axioms that in the commutative case serve to characterize the algebras of all continuous complex-valued functions on compacta. Also in 1943 he published his generalization to locally compact abelian groups of John von Neumann's spectral theorem. In 1950 Izrail M. Gelfand and Naimark published their important treatise on irreducible unitary representations of the classical matrix groups. In this work they explicitly obtained a large number of these representations—enough, in fact, for Plancherel's theorem for these groups. Their results strongly influenced J. Michael G. Fell's work on group representations done in the 1950's and 1960's, and opened the way for Harish-Chandra's definitive work on Plancherel's theorem, done from about 1953 to about 1970. (But the irreducible unitary representations have not yet been obtained explicitly.)

Naimark also made fundamental contributions to the theory of non-self-adjoint operators in Hilbert spaces, to the theory of Banach algebras with involution, and to the theory of representations of groups and algebras in inner product spaces bearing an indefinite metric. His scientific oeuvre consists of 123 research papers and 5 books.

Naimark's books are models of lucidity, completeness, and scholarship. His *Normirovannye koltsa* (Normed rings, 1956) has gone through three editions and has been translated into German, French, and English. His *Lineinye differentsialnye operatory* (Linear differential operators, 1954) also has gone through several editions and translations. His last work, written with A. I. Shtern while he was gravely ill, is *Teoriya predstavlenii grupp* (Theory of group representations, 1976). This book, which also appeared in French and English, is both a textbook and a vade mecum on the theory of Lie groups and their finite-dimensional representations.

BIBLIOGRAPHY

I. Original Works. Naimark's works are listed in *Uspekhi matematicheskikh nauk*, **15**, no. 2 (1960), 233–236; *Matematika v SSSR, 1958–1967*, II (1970), 949–950; and *Uspekhi matematicheskikh nauk*, **35**, no. 4 (1980), 139–140. His most important works include "On the Imbedding of Normed Rings into the Ring of Operators in Hilbert Space," in *Matematicheskii sbornik (Recueil* *mathématique)*, n.s. **12**, no. 54 (1943), 197–219, written with Izrail Gelfand (his name is misspelled as Neumark); "Polozhitelno-opredelennye operatornye funktsii na kommutativnoi gruppe" (Positive definitive operator functions on a commutative group), in *Izvestiia Akademii nauk SSSR, seriia matematicheskaia*, **7** (1943), 237–244; *Unitarnye predstavleniya klassicheskikh grupp* (Unitary representations of classical groups), in *Trudy Matematicheskogo instituta imeni V. A. Steklova*, **36** (1950), 1–288, written with Gelfand; *Lineinye differentsialnye operatory* (Moscow, 1952), trans. by E. R. Dawson and edited by W. N. Everitt as *Linear Differential Operators*, 2 vols. (New York, 1967–1968); *Normirovannye koltsa* (Moscow, 1956), trans. by Leo F. Boron as *Normed Rings* (Groningen, 1959; rev. ed., 1970); and *Teoriya predstavlenii grupp* (Moscow, 1975), trans. by Elizabeth Hewitt and edited by Edwin Hewitt as *Theory of Group Representations* (New York, 1982), written with A. I. Shtern.

II. SECONDARY LITERATURE. An obituary by Izrail M. Gelfand and others appeared in *Uspekhi matematicheskikh nauk*, **35**, no. 4 (1980), 135–139, English trans. in *Russian Mathematical Surveys*, **35**, no. 4 (1980), 157–164. See also the article in honor of Naimark's fiftieth birthday in *Uspekhi matematicheskikh nauk*, **15**, no. 2 (1960), 231–236, English trans. by W. F. Lunnon in *Russian Mathematical Surveys*, **15**, no. 2 (1960), 169–174.

EDWIN HEWITT

NATTA, GIULIO (*b*. Porto Maurizio [now Imperia], Italy, 26 February 1903; *d*. Milan, Italy, 2 May 1979), *chemistry*.

Natta was the son of Francesco Natta, a judge, and of Elena Crespi Natta. The traditional profession in the Natta family was that of law, but after completing secondary school at the age of sixteen, Natta enrolled in the two-year engineering preparatory course at the University of Genoa, and in 1921 he entered the Milan Polytechnic Institute, from which he graduated with a degree in chemical engineering in 1924. As a student he worked in the first Italian center for X-ray crystallography, directed by Giuseppe Bruni and Giorgio Renato Levi.

Natta became *libero docènte* at twenty-four. He taught analytical chemistry from 1925 until 1933 at the Milan Polytechnic and physical chemistry from 1931 until 1933 at Milan University. In 1932 he went to Freiburg, where he studied the techniques of electron interference in the laboratory of the physicist H. Seemann. At Freiburg he also became acquainted with Hermann Staudinger and his important work on macromolecules. In 1933 Natta was appointed to the chair of general chemistry at the University of Pavia; in the academic years 1935–1936 and 1936–1937 he was professor of physical chemistry at Rome

University; in the years 1937 to 1938 and 1938 to 1939 he worked at the Turin Polytechnic Institute as professor of industrial chemistry. In 1939 he returned to Milan Polytechnic, where he was professor of industrial chemistry until his retirement in 1973.

In 1935 Natta married Rosita Beati; they had two sons. His wife died in 1968. Natta was a nature lover, fond of outdoor activities; in his youth he was a mountain climber. During long walks he collected fossils and mushrooms. These activities ceased with the onset of Parkinson's disease in 1959.

Natta was elected a member of the Accademia dei Lincei in 1955 and belonged to many Italian and foreign academies and chemical societies. In 1942 he received the Royal Award of the Reale Accademia d'Italia for his achievements in X-ray crystallography and industrial catalysis. In 1963 he and Karl Ziegler shared the Nobel Prize for chemistry, Natta for his studies on stereospecific polymerization and macromolecular chemistry.

Natta's scientific activity may be divided into three periods: roughly until he went to Pavia University (1933); the two decades until the discovery of stereospecific polymerization (1954); and from 1954 until his retirement (1973). In the first period Natta published many X-ray studies on alloys and other inorganic substances (fifty-six papers in seven years), including important studies on spinels, ionic radii, and solid hydride structures. The use of fast electron diffraction was crowned in 1936 with a study on cellulose. At the same time Natta applied the most advanced structural knowledge of the crystalline texture of catalysts to the formidable task of selecting a catalyst for the synthesis of methanol.

Thus he succeeded in breaking the monopoly of Badische Anilin und Soda Fabrik of the synthetic production of methanol, and from the end of the 1920's his work was increasingly directed toward the solution of key problems of the chemical industry. Most of these were solved in connection with leading Italian chemical firms: coal gasification, the synthesis of formaldehyde, and the polymerization of formaldehyde with Montecatini SpA. (later Montedison) in 1932; the preparation of butadiene and its separation from butenes with Società per Azioni Pirelli in 1942; and oxosynthesis (reaction of carbon monoxide and hydrogen with olefins) with Bombrini Parodi Delfino in 1945.

After World War II, Natta developed close ties with the top management of Montecatini, and he was able to provide Milan Polytechnic with advanced instrumentation and brilliant young scientists. From the beginning of the 1950's, Natta became fascinated with the problems of the polymer solid state. In 1952 he attended K. Ziegler's lecture at Frankfurt on his recently discovered Aufbau reaction and was greatly impressed. The Aufbau (literally "buildup") reaction employs aluminum triethyl to link ethylene molecules end to end to form higher alkyls. At the time, Ziegler had obtained only molecules of low molecular weight, but with a very important feature: the chains were unbranched, a fundamental step toward the synthesis of ordered polymers that are crystallizable into high-strength solids. That feature did not elude Natta and was instrumental in bringing him into contact with the German scientists working for Montecatini. The discovery of linear polyethylene in Ziegler's laboratory with a titanium/aluminum alkyl system as catalyst (fall of 1953) was quickly followed in Natta's laboratory by the synthesis of linear polypropylene in March 1954.

If Ziegler opened the path, Natta realized where it led. The staff of his institute was put to work in research, and in December 1954 a letter titled "Crystalline High Polymers of α-Olefins" was sent to the editor of the *Journal of the American Chemical Society*. In this seminal paper, signed by Natta and his principal co-workers, a threefold (three monomeric units) helical structure of polypropylene was proposed, and the isotactic concepts of poly(α-olefin) structures were defined. The authors wrote in a footnote: "We propose to designate as 'isotactical chains,' from the Greek words $\iota\sigma o\sigma$ = equal, and $\tau\alpha\tau\tau\omega$ = to set up, the polymer chains having such exceptionally regular structure, containing series of asymmetric carbon atoms with the same steric configuration ('isotactical' asymmetric carbon atoms)." The impact of Natta's proposal on the scientific community was strengthened by a continous flow of discoveries from Milan. Several classes of monomers, from styrenes to cycloolefins, were studied. For every monomer the best stereospecific catalyst was found, and the properties of both the polymer and the catalyst were fully investigated if the reaction appeared to have industrial and economic uses.

On the purely scientific side, Natta's interpretation of the structure of the stereospecific polymers had a major consequence in the search for a way to produce an optically active polymer from a nonchiral (that is, that can be superimposed upon its mirror image) monomer. Such a process had (and has) important theoretical implications because of the light it can throw on the ubiquitous presence of optically active biopolymers in living organisms. The first definite results were obtained by the Milan school in 1960, and Natta showed his intense interest in the field by recalling the problem in his Nobel Prize lecture, "Macromolecular Chemistry: From the Stereospecific Polymerization to the Asymmetric Autocatalytic Synthesis of Macromolecules."

Under Natta's leadership the Milan school published over 1,200 papers; he himself signed 540 papers and nearly 500 patents. Since Stanislau Cannizzaro's time the Italian school of chemistry had nourished the ideal of a German-style relationship between advanced academic science and the chemical industry; a scientist in the German mold, Natta converted the ideal into fact.

BIBLIOGRAPHY

I. ORIGINAL WORKS. Natta's important papers in the field of X-ray and fast-electron structure determinations are those on spinels, "Spinelli del cobalto bivalente: Alluminato, cromito, ferrito e cobaltito cobaltosi," in *Gazzetta chimica italiana*, **59** (1929), 280–288, with Luigi Passerini; on ionic radii, "Dimensioni degli atomi e degli ioni monovalenti nei reticoli dei cristalli," in *Memorie della Classe di scienze fisiche, matematiche e naturali della R. accademia d'Italia*, **2**, no. 3 (1931), 365–379; and on cellulose, "Esame della cellulosa coi raggi di elettroni," in *Atti dell'Accademia nazionale dei Lincei*, **23** (1936), 444–447, with Mario Baccaredda. Natta discusses his research on the catalytic synthesis of methanol in Paul H. Emmett, ed., *Catalysis* (New York, 1955), III, 349–411.

Natta's seminal paper on the crystalline high polymers of α-olefins, cited in the text of this article, is "Crystalline High Polymers of α-Olefins," in *Journal of the American Chemical Society*, **77** (1955), 1708–1710, with Piero Pino as coauthor and five of Natta's colleagues supplying special discussions on X-ray structure determinations, infrared spectra, physical determinations, and the polymerization of α-olefins. A more complete treatment, with an extensive list of co-workers, is "Une nouvelle classe de polymères d'α-olefines ayant une régularité de structure exceptionnelle," in *Journal of Polymer Science*, **16** (1955), 143–154, with a brief English synopsis. The English text of Natta's Nobel Prize lecture, "Macromolecular Chemistry," is in *Science*, **147** (1965), 261–272.

Natta's major works on polymer chemistry were collected by Natta in *Stereoregular Polymers and Stereospecific Polymerizations*, edited with Ferdinando Danusso, Luisa M. Vaccaroni, trans., 2 vols. (Oxford, 1967).

Natta's constant interest in "the grand organic synthesis" is demonstrated in "Le nuove grandi sintesi organiche," in *La chimica e l'industria* (Rome), **20** (1938), 187–198; and "Orientamenti nel campo delle grandi sintesi organiche negli Stati Uniti," *ibid.*, **30** (1948), 63–72.

II. SECONDARY LITERATURE. An excellent comparative study of Natta and Ziegler is F. M. McMillan, *The Chain Straighteners* (London, 1979). Important studies on Natta's life and work are in Sergio Carrà, Federico Parisi, Italo

Pasquon, and Piero Pino, eds., *Giulio Natta. Present Significance of His Scientific Contribution* (Milan, 1982). Papers having to do with Natta's contributions that were given at a symposium on the history of polyolefins (held at Miami Beach in 1985) are in Raymond B. Seymour and Tai Cheng, eds., *History of Polyolefins* (Dordrecht and Boston, 1986).

LUIGI CERRUTI

NEUBAUER, OTTO (*b.* Karlsbad, Germany, 8 April 1874; *d.* Oxford, England, 24 November 1957), *biochemistry, metabolic pathology.*

The son of Wolfgang Neubauer, a general practitioner in Karlsbad, Neubauer studied medicine at the German University in Prague from 1892 to 1898. He remained there after graduation as an assistant in the Pharmacology Institute and worked with the chemist and physiologist Karl H. Huppert. During this period he acquired (largely on his own) the strong knowledge of chemistry that provided the foundation for much of his later research. In 1901 Neubauer accepted a position as assistant to Friedrich von Müller at the Medical Clinic in Basel; in 1902 he followed Müller to the Second Medical Clinic in Munich. In 1909 he was appointed instructor of internal medicine and in 1917 was promoted to assistant professor. During World War I he was drafted and served in the German army as an internist. In 1918 Neubauer, who was Jewish, was appointed head physician of the Munich Schwabinger Hospital, a position he held until he was forced to resign in 1933 with the rise of the Nazi regime. In 1939 he left Germany and immigrated to England.

Throughout his career, Neubauer worked as a physician and performed his research in the context of his clinical activity. Thus, many of his contributions were directed toward specific pathological conditions or served a clinical function. For example, in 1903 Neubauer developed a test for uribilogen using Paul Ehrlich's aldehyde reaction. Although he soon realized that this reaction was not a specific test, it became an important clinical-diagnostic tool after Hans Fischer discovered the reaction sequence from bilirubin to uribilogen. In 1914 Neubauer developed a test that used the quantity of creatinine in the blood to evaluate kidney function.

While he was an assistant to Müller, Neubauer made his most significant contributions to basic biochemical science. Müller was much concerned with pathologies of metabolism, and under his influence Neubauer turned his attention to the chemical foundations of metabolic disorders, particularly those concerned with aromatic amino acids. One of these disorders was alkaptonuria, the primary symptom of which is a blackening of the urine upon exposure to air due to the presence of homogentisic acid. It had been established previously that the amino acid tyrosine could give rise to homogentisic acid in alkaptonuria patients, but the effect had been attributed to bacterial action. Two researchers in Müller's unit, Leo Langstein and Wilhelm Falta, showed that phenylalanine also gave rise to homogentisic acid. With Falta, Neubauer tested a number of aromatic amino acids and showed that all of them were precursors of homogentisic acid. Neubauer interpreted the problem not as due to bacteria but as resulting from the disruption of amino acid metabolism—from the failure to metabolize homogentisate.

Neubauer extended this work into a broader set of liver perfusion studies directed at developing a general schema for amino acid metabolism. In the course of this, he produced evidence that the first step in the catabolism of α-amino acids is not the formation of an α-hydroxy acid, as then thought, but an oxidative deamination to form an α-keto acid. He proposed a schema for the catabolism of phenylaminoacetic acid according to which phenylglyoxylic acid was first produced by an oxidative deamination, and then the hydroxy acid mandelic acid was produced as a side product by a reduction reaction. Neubauer further proposed that phenylglyoxylic acid, but not mandelic acid, was metabolized to yield acetone. He found confirming evidence for this scheme in liver perfusion studies that he conducted with Walter Gross and Hans Fischer.

As a result of further studies on yeast, Neubauer and Konrad Fromherz suggested that pyruvic acid could be formed from the deamination of alanine and that ethanol was produced through a subsequent decarboxylation and reduction. They found that yeast could metabolize pyruvic acid, and therefore proposed that it might be an intermediary not only in amino acid metabolism but also in alcohol fermentation. Until that time pyruvic acid was not thought to figure in fermentation because it was at a higher oxidation level than the end product, ethyl alcohol, but Neubauer used the evidence that it was readily fermented in the process of alanine oxidation to argue for a more general role. Neubauer's hypothesis may have played a role in the development of Carl Neuberg's work, for shortly thereafter Neuberg identified an enzyme responsible for the decarboxylation of pyruvic acid. Two years later Neuberg and Johannes Kerb proposed their model of fermentation, which gave a central place to pyruvic acid.

After becoming head physician at Munich Schwabinger Hospital, Neubauer had little time for basic research. He did, however, write two important papers, one on techniques for studying intermediary metabolism and the other on intermediary stages in protein metabolism. In addition, he developed a number of instruments for clinical use. In 1920 he developed an aneroid device for measuring blood pressure. He later devised a slide for counting red and white blood cells. In 1930, with Heinrich Lampert, he invented a blood transfusion device that prevented the coagulation of the blood without adding anticoagulants. A related device allowed for the counting of blood platelets and for easier determination of blood coagulation time.

BIBLIOGRAPHY

I. ORIGINAL WORKS. "Über das Schicksal einiger aromatischen Säuren bei der Alkaptonurie," in *Zeitschrift für physiologische Chemie*, **42** (1904), 81–101, written with Wilhelm Falta; "Über den Abbau der Aminosäuren im genunden und kranken Organismus," in *Deutsches Archiv für klinische Medizin*, **95** (1909), 211–256; "Zur Kenntnis des Tyrosinabbaus in der künstlich durchbluteten Leber," in *Zeitschrift für physiologische Chemie*, **67** (1910), 219–229, written with Walter Gross; "Beiträge zur Kenntnis der Leberfunktionen," *ibid.*, 230–240, written with Hans Fischer; "Über den Abbau der Aminosäuren bei der Hefegärung," *ibid.*, **70** (1910/1911), 326–350, written with Konrad Fromherz; "Verwendung des Kreatinins zur Prüfung der Nierenfunktion," in *Münchener medizinische Wochenschrift*, **61** (1914), 857–859; *Methoden zur Untersuchung des intermediären Stoffwechsels: Abderhaldenschen Handbuch der biologischen Arbeitsmethoden*, pt. 4, sec. 9 (Berlin, 1925); and "Über den intermediären Eiweissstoffwechsel," in Albrecht T. Bethe, Gustav von Bergmann, Gustav Embden, and Alexander Ellinger, eds., *Handbuch der normalen und pathologischen Physiologie*, V (Berlin, 1928), 670–989.

II. SECONDARY LITERATURE. Frederich Valentin, "Nachruf für Prof. Otto Neubauer," in *Münchener medizinische Wochenschrift*, **100** (1958), 354–355.

WILLIAM BECHTEL

NEVANLINNA, ROLF HERMAN (*b*. Joensuu, Finland, 22 October 1895; *d*. Helsinki, Finland, 28 May 1980), *mathematics*.

Nevanlinna came from a Swedish-speaking Finnish family. His father, Otto Wilhelm Nevanlinna, was a noted mathematician and teacher; his mother was Margarete Romberg Nevanlinna. Rolf was the second of their four children.

Nevanlinna could already read and write when he entered primary school. Apparently he was so advanced over his classmates that he grew bored and left school for a year and a half. In 1904 the family moved to Helsinki, where school was more challenging and he learned German and French, starting the development of his superb gift for languages. Perhaps his best teacher was his father, who taught him mathematics and physics in secondary school.

When Nevanlinna graduated from secondary school in 1913, his chief interests were classics and mathematics. Between graduation and enrolling at university, he read the *Introduction to Higher Analysis* of Ernst Lindelöf, a cousin of his father and the outstanding scientist at Helsinki University. It kindled in him the enthusiasm for analysis that led to his life's work.

On 4 June 1919, after receiving the doctorate, Nevanlinna married his cousin Mary Elise Selin; they had four children. In 1918 he had been exempted from conscription for Mannerheim's war of liberation because of his low weight of 110 pounds, and instead served as a clerk.

In 1945, while helping to organize a chamber music society, Nevanlinna met Sinikka Kallio-Visapää, an author and translator (particularly of the works of Thomas Mann). His marriage was dissolved, and he and Sinikka were married in 1958. They had one daughter.

In 1919 Nevanlinna became a schoolteacher, since there were no jobs in the Finnish universities, and for a time joined the Salama Insurance Company, for which his brother Frithiof worked, while continuing to teach eighteen classes a week. He became a docent at the University of Helsinki in 1922 and professor in 1926.

During the 1920's Nevanlinna developed the theory of value distribution that bears his name. It is concerned with the distribution of roots of equations $f(z) = a$, or a-values. Here $f(z)$ is a function of the complex variable z, which is everywhere either differentiable or takes the value infinity so that $1/f(z)$ is differentiable. Such functions are called meromorphic. In 1880 Charles Émile Picard had proved that a-values exist except for at most two values of a. For instance, $f(z) = e^z$ is never 0 or infinite, and so has no 0 values or ∞ values.

Nevanlinna turned this quantitative statement into a theory of unprecedented precision. He introduced a characteristic function $T(r, f)$, which refers to the behavior of f in a circle $|z| \leq r$. For any a, Nevanlinna's first fundamental theorem states that as $r \rightarrow \infty$,

$$N(r, a) + m(r, a) = T(r) + \text{a bounded term,}$$

where $N(r, a)$ measures the number of a-values in $|z| < r$ and $m(r, a)$ measures the closeness of $f(z)$ to a on $|z| = r$. The second fundamental theorem says that for any q values a_1 to a_q,

$$m(r, a_1) + m(r, a_2) + \cdots + m(r, a_v) < 2T(r) + S(r),$$

where $S(r)$ is in general small compared with $T(r)$. In particular $N(r, a)$ is never much larger than $T(r)$ and is much smaller than $\frac{1}{3}T(r)$ for at most two values of a. Nevanlinna's original result was for $q = 3$. The extension to general q was suggested by J. E. Littlewood and E. F. Collingwood in 1924.

The characteristic function $T(r)$ has allowed a much closer study of analytic functions, and it has also been useful in the study of many other situations. An analysis of multiple roots of equations $f(z) = a$ and of linear combinations of meromorphic functions with few zeros and poles has proved very fruitful.

Another concept that has been very valuable is Nevanlinna's invention of harmonic measure in 1935. The theory of harmonic measure, originally published in a series of papers, was also presented in two books, *Le théorème de Picard-Borel et la théorie des fonctions méromorphes* (1929) and *Eindeutige analytische Funktionen* (1936). Although Nevanlinna continued to write books and papers throughout his life, his reputation rests on these two works. The German book in particular contains many important concepts derived from such authors as Lars Ahlfors, Élie Cartan, and O. Frostman, as well as the Nevanlinna theory proper.

Nevanlinna traveled extensively after the age of thirty and was warmly received by mathematicians in many countries. He was visiting professor at Göttingen in 1936 and 1937 and guest professor at the Eidgenössische Technische Hochschule in Zurich from 1946 to 1973. He was rector of Helsinki University from 1941 to 1945 and president of the International Mathematical Union from 1959 to 1962. In 1948 he became one of the twelve members of the newly established Finnish Academy. He held honorary doctorates from eight universities and was an honorary or foreign member of more than a dozen scientific societies, including the Institut de France.

BIBLIOGRAPHY

I. Original Works. Important works by Nevanlinna include *Le théorème de Picard-Borel et la théorie des fonctions méromorphes* (Paris, 1929); *Eindeutige analytische Funktionen* (Berlin, 1936; 2nd ed., 1953), translated by Phillip Emig as *Analytic Functions* (New York, 1970); and *Absolute Analysis*, Phillip Emig, trans. (Berlin and New York, 1973), written with Frithiof Nevanlinna.

II. Secondary Literature. Walter K. Hayman, "Rolf Nevanlinna," in *Bulletin of the London Mathematical Society*, **14** (1982), 419–436, has a list of Nevanlinna's published books and papers.

Walter K. Hayman

NEWMAN, HORATIO HACKETT (*b.* near Seale, Alabama, 19 March 1875; *d.* Clearwater, Florida, 29 August 1957), *genetics*.

Newman was the first of four children born to Albert Henry Newman, a distinguished professor of theology, and Mary Augusta Ware Newman. He grew up in a highly literate, middle-class household. When Newman was six, the family moved to Toronto, where his father became professor of church history at Toronto Baptist College (now McMaster University, in Hamilton, Ontario). Newman's mother was active in the Baptist church and in missionary work. Despite his strong Baptist upbringing, Newman's scientific work shows no religious influence—for instance, he soundly rejected vitalism.

Newman received a B.A. from Toronto Baptist College in 1896 and was a special student at the University of Toronto for one year before teaching biology and Latin at Des Moines College for one year (1897–1898). He entered the University of Chicago in 1898 and received a Ph.D. in zoology in 1905, having taken off four years to teach biology and chemistry at Culver Military Academy in Indiana (1900–1904). After teaching at the University of Michigan (1905–1908) and heading the department of zoology at the University of Texas (1908–1911), Newman was appointed associate professor of zoology and embryology at the University of Chicago in 1911 and professor of zoology in 1917. With Frank R. Lillie and Charles M. Child, he was responsible for raising the zoology department at Chicago to the first rank. Following his retirement in 1940, he ceased active research and divided his time between Clearwater, Florida, and Go Home Lake on Georgian Bay, Ontario.

Newman married Isobel Currie Marshall in 1907; they had a daughter and a son. Following the death of his wife, he married Marie E. Heald on 5 June 1954. A robust man, he prided himself on his athletic prowess and remained physically active until his final illness.

While at Toronto Baptist College, Newman received honors in the classics but primarily studied natural science, writing a series of entomological sketches for the college magazine. He worked under

Charles O. Whitman, William M. Wheeler, and Lillie at Chicago. He was most influenced by Whitman, and throughout his professional life continued to advocate the latter's views supporting orthogenesis and de Vriesian mutation as the mechanism of the origin of species.

Newman's dissertation was on the meaning of variations in the armor of *Chelydridae*, the land tortoise. He viewed the supernumerary scutes that always occurred in the same locations as reversions to ancestral conditions, examples of systematic atavism in the sense of Hugo de Vries. In focusing on how the number of scutes had been reduced over the evolutionary development of the most generalized family of land tortoises, he hoped to throw some light on the phylogeny of *Chelonia* and arrive at the hypothetical ancestral type.

From 1907 to 1923 Newman used the nine-banded armadillo and teleost hybrids to probe the crucial questions puzzling embryologists at the turn of the century: What are the relative contributions of heredity and epigenesis to the character of the individual? What is the precise role of the spermatozoon in early embryonic development? What are the relative contributions of the maternal and paternal germ plasms?

Newman rejected Edwin G. Conklin's theory that differentiation of the embryo is determined by the egg cytoplasm rather than by the nucleus. He found in 1910 that the developmental rhythm of the young embryo of a *Fundulus* hybrid was distinctly influenced by the spermatozoon as early as fourteen hours after fertilization. However, by 1914 he admitted that early cleavage was not controlled by the nucleus. He distinguished between heredity and embryonic development. In work on teleost hybrids Newman concluded that although foreign sperm may materially alter the rate of early development, they play no role in the heredity of the organism until embryonic differentiation is well under way.

In later hybridizing experiments on teleosts, Newman's results did not support the hypothesis of Jacques Loeb that heterogenic hybrids are purely maternal in all their hereditary characters and that sperm only initiate development. Newman found unmistakable cases of paternal heredity even in suborder crosses. He maintained that the modes of inheritance in teleost hybrids support Mendelian particulate inheritance.

In 1909, while at the University of Texas, Newman made a fortunate choice of research animal when he chose to study the natural history of the ubiquitous *Dasypus novemcinctus texanus*, the nine-banded armadillo. When Newman and J. Thomas Patterson

discovered that this armadillo species always bears quadruplets from a single zygote, Newman began to concentrate on a causal theory of twinning. Their findings comprised the first direct embryological evidence that one-egg twinning occurs among mammals. Newman and Patterson dissected hundreds of armadillo uteri, studying various stages of fetal development from the late cleavage stage, in which there were only eleven embryonic cells, to a full-term armadillo egg. In later studies Newman confirmed that members of a litter are as closely similar to one another as are the right and left sides of a single individual.

Newman advanced his first theory of twinning in 1913. Although he would refine it over the next ten years, he consistently argued that twinning is only a variation of symmetrical division, like the development of the right and left sides of a single individual. He saw the whole process as quantitative.

The traditional view of twinning as advanced by William Bateson was that twins resulted from physiological isolation of the two-cell stage of cleavage. Newman argued that twinning could occur at varying stages of embryonic development. In armadillos twinning does not occur until three weeks after ovulation, when gastrulation is complete. This three-week period of inhibited growth disorganizes the integrational relations of the embryo, Newman wrote in 1923, weakening the polarity of the egg so that all parts of the embryo are left on parity.

Newman elaborated on his twinning theory in *The Biology of Twins*, an important book published in 1917 that focused attention on human twins and their possible uses as research materials. Not since Francis Galton compared the differences between monozygotic and dizygotic twins in 1875 had significant work been done on human twins. Newman's work, along with a keen interest in eugenics in the United States and western Europe, initiated a spate of nature-nurture studies during the period between the two world wars.

In *The Physiology of Twinning* (1923) Newman brought together for the first time all previously published data on one-egg twinning in the animal kingdom and noted that twinning is especially common in the vertebrates and echinoderms because early cleavage cells appear to be totipotent, that is, each cell is able, if isolated, to produce a whole new individual.

Newman's primary interest from 1913 to 1940 was how to account for differences between genetically identical individuals. Because of this interest, Newman studied the inheritance of variation in armadillo armor. He assumed that the degree of difference among the quadruplets should indicate the potency of epigenetic factors, while degree of similarity would serve as a criterion for the relative strength of predeterminative factors. After analyzing the armors of nearly 200 sets of quadruplets and their mothers, Newman found that epigenetic disturbances effect alterations in the end result ranging from 2 to 8 percent. Although at first he attributed this inequality among quadruplets to some profound inaccuracy in mitosis during early cleavage, he later viewed all epigenetic effects as the results of asymmetry reversal.

Newman wrote extensively on the effects of asymmetry reversal in human identical twins. While studying armadillos he frequently noticed that an asymmetrical peculiarity inherited from the mother would appear on the left side of one twin, the right side of another, and sometimes on both sides of a third. In human twins, Newman noted similar inequalities: one twin was right-handed, the other left-handed; one twin had a clockwise hair whorl, the other a counterclockwise whorl. He published several studies on the reversals in palm print, fingerprint, and toe print patterns in monozygotic twins. He explained these inequalities by noting that one twin had been derived from a partially differentiated left side, the other from a partially differentiated right side of a single embryo.

Newman studied twins with varying degrees of asymmetry reversals from identical identicals to conjoined twins who were significantly different in physiology, temperament, shape and size of head, height, and weight. He assumed that monozygotic twins are products of the division of a single bilateral embryo that, if not separated, would form the right and left sides of a single individual. The most similar monozygotic twins represented a separation very early in embryonic development, perhaps at the four-cell cleavage stage. By contrast, conjoined twins separated after gastrulation was complete and the two sides of the embryo had become asymmetrically differentiated.

Newman predicted that identical twins with many asymmetry reversals would show more intrapair differences in mental and physical characters than those with few asymmetry reversals. This was not borne out in studies of sixty-nine sets of identical twins. There was no greater degree of difference between twins with extensive asymmetry reversals than between more identical twins.

In 1926 Newman began an extensive study of fifty pairs of identical twins and fifty pairs of fraternal twins reared together. Working with his University of Chicago colleagues Frank N. Freeman, a psychologist, and Karl J. Holzinger, a statistician, he examined the physical characters and administered a battery of intelligence and personality tests. They extended the study to nineteen pairs of identical twins reared apart. Their results were published in *Twins: A Study of Heredity and Environment* (1937). They compared the physiological, mental, and personality differences of these pairs of twins, the first time such a study had been done. They concluded that identical twins reared together are more alike in physical dimensions, intelligence, and educational achievement than fraternal twins reared together, but not much more alike than fraternal twins in personality and temperament.

Newman wished to attribute all differences not only in physical characters but also in mental and personality traits in identical twins reared together to prenatal influences such as asymmetry reversals and unequal blood supply and nutrition to the two fetuses. Holzinger and Freeman, on the other hand, recognized that identical twins in the same family can have slightly different postnatal environments and that mutual association can actually cause them to exaggerate their differences.

In their study of monozygotic twins reared apart, the authors noted that differences in the twins correlated with differences in their environment. The closest correlation was between schooling and educational achievement, the next closest between schooling and intelligence. They concluded that environmental differences that are real and large have a marked effect and that differences in mental ability are brought about by different social environments. They did not find a correlation between environmental differences and personality differences. Personality traits offered the most contrast between identical twins reared apart. Individual interviews revealed even greater personality differences between them than did the tests. They concluded that some features of the personality are more modifiable by environment than are others. The authors were equivocal on the results of the overall study. They could offer no definite solution or simple formula on the nature-nurture problem and stated that what heredity can do, environment can do also.

This twin study is recognized as a classic in the field, and the statistical methods developed are still considered valid. However, in the individual case studies of twins reared apart, the authors gave only superficial treatment to such crucial factors as psychological environment, parent-child relationships, neuroses, and sexual behavior. Moreover, the twins raised apart had a mean age of twenty-six years, whereas the twins reared together had a mean age of thirteen years. With such an age discrepancy between the two groups, it is hard to determine the nature or the degree of any environmental influence other than age. The sample of identical twins reared apart was biased in favor of twins who were extremely similar. Newman advertised and sought any information about twins who were remarkably similar and who lived apart. He rejected at least one pair of possible monozygotic twins because they wrote him that they were very different in some respects, and he feared they might be fraternal.

The book shows the basic disagreement between Newman and his colleagues over the relative influence of environment and heredity on intelligence and personality traits. In 1932 Newman warned against placing an extreme environmentalist interpretation on the data already collected, noting that the tests were biased toward measuring mental achievement rather than innate mental ability. He found the data pointing to a marked environmental influence disconcerting, and stated his deep-seated conviction that hereditary differences are perhaps twice as influential in determining mental ability as differences in environment.

In 1940 Newman revealed that he had given in to the environmentalist interpretation of his colleagues because most twin studies prior to theirs had overemphasized the force of heredity. Newman said he had always been much more impressed by the very great intrapair similarities after the identical twins had been exposed to marked environmental differences. He believed that environment could have a marked effect only during early embryonic development.

Newman did not confine his scientific activity to the laboratory. He was committed to educating the public and the average university student about the basic principles of evolution and genetics. In 1920 he offered a general course on evolution, genetics, and eugenics that drew large numbers of Chicago students from outside the field of biology. Newman's *Evolution, Genetics and Eugenics* was written as a text for the course, and its three editions went into numerous printings. He also edited *The Nature of the World and of Man* as a text for a general course, by the same name, required of all freshmen and sophomores at Chicago.

Newman journeyed to Dayton, Tennessee, in 1925 to testify at the trial of John T. Scopes. Although the judge did not allow expert scientific witnesses to testify in court, Newman was one of seven scientists whose statements were placed in the trial record. He found no conflict between science and religion, and noted that most major theologians were evolutionists. Newman wrote *The Gist of Evolution* in 1926 to explain the principle of evolution to the general public. In it he urged readers not to equate Darwinism and evolution. Like many biologists of his time, Newman rejected natural selection acting on minute variations as the major mechanism of evolutionary change.

BIBLIOGRAPHY

I. ORIGINAL WORKS. Works by Newman include "The Process of Heredity as Exhibited by the Development of *Fundulus* Hybrids," in *Journal of Experimental Zoology*, **5** (1908), 504–561; "A Case of Normal Identical Quadruplets in the Nine-Banded Armadillo, and Its Bearing on the Problems of Identical Twins and of Sex Determination," in *Biological Bulletin*, **17** (1909), 181–187, written with J. Thomas Patterson; "The Development of the Nine-Banded Armadillo from the Primitive Streak Stage to Birth; with Especial Reference to the Question of Specific Polyembryony," in *Journal of Morphology*, **21** (1910), 360–423, written with J. Thomas Patterson; "The Limits of Hereditary Control in Armadillo Quadruplets: A Study of Blastogenic Variation," *ibid.*, **22** (1911), 855–926, written with J. Thomas Patterson; "The Modes of Inheritance of Aggregates of Meristic (Integral) Variates in the Polyembryonic Offspring of the Nine-Banded Armadillo," in *Journal of Experimental Zoology*, **15** (August 1913), 145–192; "Modes of Inheritance in Teleost Hybrids," *ibid.*, **16** (February 1914), 447–499; "Heredity and Organic Symmetry in Armadillo Quadruplets," in *Biological Bulletin*, **29** (July 1915), 1–32; "Development and Heredity in Heterogenic Teleost Hybrids," in *Journal of Experimental Zoology*, **18** (May 1915), 511–576.

The Biology of Twins (Chicago, 1917); "Hybrids Between *Fundulus* and Mackerel: A Study of Paternal Heredity in Heterogenic Hybrids," in *Journal of Experimental Zoology*, **26** (August 1918), 391–421; *Vertebrate Zoology* (New York, 1920; repr. 1926); *The Physiology of Twinning* (Chicago, 1923); "Studies of Human Twins. II. Asymmetry Reversal, or Mirror Imaging in Identical Twins," in *Biological Bulletin*, **55** (October 1928), 298–315; "Differences Between Conjoined Twins," in *Journal of Heredity*, **22** (July 1931), 201–215; *Twins: A Study in Heredity and Environment* (Chicago, 1937), written with Frank H. Freeman and Karl J. Holzinger; and *Multiple Human Births* (New York, 1940).

Correspondence between Newman and Frank R. Lillie is in the library of the Marine Biological Laboratory, Woods Hole, Massachusetts.

II. SECONDARY LITERATURE. A brief biographical memoir is Herulf H. Strandskov, "Horatio Hackett Newman, Pioneer in Human Genetics," in *Science*, **127** (1958), 74.

MARY MORRICE BOGIN

NEYMAN, JERZY (*b.* Bendery, Russia, 16 April 1894; *d.* Berkeley, California, 5 August 1981), *statistics.*

Early Years. Jerzy Neyman was born in Bendery, Russia, to parents of Polish ancestry. His full name with title, Spława-Neyman, the first part of which he dropped at age thirty, reflects membership in the Polish nobility. Neyman's father, Czesław, who died when Jerzy was twelve, was a lawyer and later a judge, and an enthusiastic amateur archaeologist. Since the family had been prohibited by the Russian authorities from living in central Poland, then under Russian domination, Neyman grew up in Russia: in Kherson, Melitopol, Simferopol, and (after his father's death) in Kharkov, where in 1912 he entered the university.

At Kharkov, Neyman was first interested in physics, but because of his clumsiness in the laboratory abandoned it in favor of mathematics. He was greatly struck by Henri Lebesgue's *Leçons sur l'intégration et la recherche des fonctions primitives,* "the most beautiful monograph that I ever read," as he called it many years later. A manuscript on Lebesgue integration (530 pages, handwritten) that he submitted to a prize competition won a gold medal.

One of his mentors at Kharkov was Sergei Bernstein, who lectured on probability theory and statistics (including application of the latter to agriculture), subjects that did not particularly interest Neyman. Nevertheless, he later acknowledged the influence of Bernstein, from whom he "tried to acquire his tendency of concentrating on some 'big problem.'" It was also Bernstein who introduced him to Karl Pearson's *The Grammar of Science,* which made a deep impression.

After World War I, Poland regained its independence but soon became embroiled in a war with Russia over borders. Neyman, still in Kharkov, was jailed as an enemy alien. In 1921, in an exchange of prisoners, he finally went to Poland for the first time, at the age of twenty-seven.

In Warsaw he established contact with Wacław Sierpiński, one of the founders of the journal *Fundamenta Mathematicae,* which published one of Neyman's gold medal results (**5** [1923], 328–330). Although Neyman's heart was in pure mathematics, the statistics he had learned from Bernstein was more marketable and enabled him to obtain a position as (the only) statistician at the agricultural institute in Bydgoszcz (formerly Bromberg). There, during 1921 and 1922, he produced several papers on the application of probabilistic ideas to agricultural experimentation. In the light of Neyman's later development, this work is of interest because of its introduction of probability models for the phenomena being studied, more particularly a randomization model for the case of a completely randomized experiment. (For more details of Neyman's treatment, see Scheffé, *Annals of Mathematical Statistics,* **27** [1956], 269.) He had learned the philosophy of such an approach from Pearson's book, which laid great stress on models as mental constructs whose formulation constitutes the essence of science.

In December 1922 Neyman gave up his job in Bydgoszcz to take up a position at the State Meteorological Institute, a change that enabled him to move to Warsaw. He did not like the work—being in charge of equipment and observations—and soon left this position to become an assistant at the University of Warsaw and special lecturer in mathematics and statistics at the Central College of Agriculture; he also gave regular lectures at the University of Kraków. In 1924 he obtained his doctorate from the University of Warsaw with a thesis based on the papers he had written at Bydgoszcz.

Since no one in Poland was able to gauge the importance of his statistical work (he was "sui generis," as he later described his situation), the Polish authorities provided an opportunity for Neyman to establish his credibility through publication in British journals. For this purpose they gave him a fellowship to work with Karl Pearson in London. He did publish three papers in *Biometrika* (based in part on his earlier work), but scientifically the academic year (1925–1926) spent in Pearson's laboratory was a disappointment. He found the work of the laboratory old-fashioned and Pearson himself surprisingly ignorant of modern mathematics. (The fact that Pearson did not understand the difference between independence and lack of correlation led to a misunderstanding that nearly terminated Neyman's stay at the laboratory.) So when, with the help of Pearson and Sierpiński, he received a Rockefeller fellowship that made it possible for him to stay in the West for another year, he decided to spend it in Paris rather than in London.

In Paris, Neyman attended the lectures of Lebesgue and a seminar of Jacques Hadamard. "I felt that this was real mathematics worth studying," he wrote later, "and, were it not for Egon Pearson [Karl's son], I would have probably drifted to my earlier passion for sets, measure and integration, and returned to Poland as a faithful member of the Warsaw school and a steady contributor to *Fundamenta Mathematicae.*"

The Neyman-Pearson Theory. What pulled Neyman back into statistics was a letter he received in the fall of 1925 from Egon Pearson, with whom he had had little contact in London. Egon had begun to question the rationale underlying some of the current work in statistics, and the letter outlined his concerns. A correspondence developed and, reinforced by occasional joint holidays, continued even after the end of the Rockefeller year, when Neyman returned to a hectic and difficult life in Warsaw. He again took up his lectures at the university (as docent after his habilitation in 1928), at the Central College of Agriculture, and at the University of Kraków. In addition, he founded a small statistical laboratory at the Nencki Institute for Experimental Biology. To supplement his meager academic income, and to provide financial support for the students and young co-workers in his laboratory, Neyman took on a variety of consulting jobs. These involved different areas of application, with the majority coming from agriculture and from the Institute for Social Problems, the latter work being concerned with Polish census data.

Neyman felt harassed, and his financial situation was always precarious. The bright spot in this difficult period was his work with the younger Pearson. Trying to find a unifying, logical basis that would lead systematically to the various statistical tests that had been proposed by William S. Gossett (also "Student") and Ronald A. Fisher was a "big problem" of the kind for which he had hoped since his student days with Bernstein.

In 1933 Karl Pearson retired from his chair at University College, London, and his position was divided between Fisher and Egon Pearson. The latter lost no time and, as soon as it became available in the spring of 1934, offered Neyman a temporary position in his laboratory. Neyman was enthusiastic. This would greatly facilitate their joint work and bring relief to his Warsaw difficulties.

The set of issues addressed in the joint work of Neyman and Pearson between 1926 and 1933 turned out indeed to be a "big problem," and their treatment of it established a new paradigm that changed the statistical landscape. What concerned Pearson when he first approached Neyman in 1926 was the ad hoc nature of the small sample tests being studied by Fisher and "Student." In his search for a general principle from which such tests could be derived, he had written to "Student." In his reply "Student" had suggested that one would be inclined to reject a hypothesis under which the observed sample is very improbable "if there is an alternative hypothesis which will explain the occurrence of the sample with a more reasonable probability" (E. S. Pearson, in David, ed., 1966). This comment led Pearson to

propose to Neyman the likelihood ratio criterion, in which the maximum likelihood of the observed sample under the alternatives under consideration is compared with its value under the hypothesis. During the next year Neyman and Pearson studied this and other approaches, and worked out likelihood ratio tests for some important examples. They published their results in 1928 in a fundamental two-part paper, "On the Use and Interpretation of Certain Test Criteria for Purposes of Statistical Inference." The paper contained many of the basic concepts of what was to become the Neyman-Pearson theory of hypothesis testing, such as the two types of error, the idea of power, and the distinction between simple and composite hypotheses.

Although Pearson felt that the likelihood ratio provided the unified approach for which he had been looking, Neyman was not yet satisfied. It seemed to him that the likelihood principle itself was somewhat ad hoc and had no fully logical basis. However, in February 1930, he was able to write Pearson that he had found "a rigorous argument in favour of the likelihood method." His new approach consisted of maximizing the power of the test, subject to the condition that under the hypothesis (assumed to be simple), the rejection probability has a preassigned value (the level of the test). He reassured Pearson that in all cases he had examined so far, this logically convincing test coincided with the likelihood ratio test. A month later Neyman announced to Pearson that he now had a general solution to the problem of testing a simple hypothesis against a simple alternative. The result in question is the fundamental lemma, which plays such a crucial role in the Neyman-Pearson theory.

The next step was to realize that in the case of more than one alternative, there might exist a uniformly most powerful test that would simultaneously maximize the power for all of them. If such a test exists, Neyman found, it coincides with the likelihood ratio test, but in the contrary case—alas—the likelihood ratio test may be biased. These results, together with many examples and elaborations, were published in 1933 under the title "On the Problem of the Most Efficient Tests of Statistical Hypotheses." While in the 1928 paper the initiative and insights had been those of Pearson, who had had to explain to Neyman what he was doing, the situation was now reversed, with the leadership having passed to Neyman, leaving Pearson a somewhat reluctant follower.

The 1933 work is the fundamental paper in the theory of hypothesis testing. It established a framework for this theory and stated the problem of finding the best test as a clearly formulated, logically convincing mathematical problem that one can then proceed to solve. Its importance transcends the theory of hypothesis testing since it also provided the inspiration for Abraham Wald's later, much more general statistical decision theory.

Survey Sampling and Confidence Estimation. In the following year Neyman published another landmark paper. An elaboration of work on survey sampling he had done earlier for the Warsaw Institute for Social Problems, it was directed toward bringing clarity into a somewhat muddled discussion about the relative merits of two different sampling methods. His treatment, described by Fisher as "luminous," introduced many important concepts and results, and may be said to have initiated the modern theory of survey sampling.

The year 1935 brought two noteworthy events. The first was Neyman's appointment to a permanent position as reader (associate professor) in Pearson's department. Although at the time he was still hoping eventually to return to Poland, he in fact never did, except for brief visits. The second event was the presentation at a meeting of the Royal Statistical Society of an important paper on agricultural experimentation in which he raised some questions concerning Fisher's Latin Square design. This caused a break in their hitherto friendly relationship and was the beginning of lifelong disputes.

Neyman remained in England for four years (1934 to 1938). During this time he continued his collaboration with Egon Pearson on the theory and applications of optimal tests, efforts that also included contributions from graduate and postdoctoral students. To facilitate publication and to emphasize the unified point of view underlying this work, Neyman and Pearson set up a series, Statistical Research Memoirs, published by University College and restricted to work done in the department of statistics. A first volume appeared in 1936, and a second in 1938.

Another central problem occupying Neyman during his London years was the theory of estimation: not point estimation, in which a parameter is estimated by a unique number, but estimation by means of an interval or more general set in which the unknown parameter can be said to lie with specified confidence (probability). Such confidence sets are easily obtained under the Bayesian assumption that the parameter is itself random with a known probability distribution, but Neyman's aim was to dispense with such an assumption, which he considered arbitrary and unwarranted.

Neyman published brief accounts of his solution to this problem in 1934 and 1935, and the theory in full generality in 1937, in "Outline of a Theory of Statistical Estimation Based on the Classical Theory of Probability."

Neyman's approach was based on the idea of obtaining confidence sets $S(X)$ for a parameter Θ from acceptance regions for the hypotheses that $\Theta = \Theta_0$ by taking for $S(X)$ the set of all parameter values Θ_0 that would be accepted at the given level. This formulation established an equivalence between confidence sets and families of tests, and enabled him to transfer in entirety the test theory of the 1933 paper—lock, stock, and barrel—to the theory of estimation. (Unbeknown to Neyman, the idea of obtaining confidence sets by inverting an acceptance rule had already been used in special cases by Pierre-Simon de Laplace—in a large-sample binomial setting—and by Harold Hotelling.)

In his paper on survey sampling, Neyman had referred to the relationship of his confidence intervals to Fisher's fiducial limits, which appeared to give the same results although derived from a somewhat different point of view. In the discussion of the paper, Fisher welcomed Neyman as an ally in the effort to free statistics from unwarranted Bayesian assumptions, but then proceeded to indicate the disadvantages he saw in Neyman's formulation. The debate between the two men over their respective approaches continued for many years, usually in less friendly terms; it is reviewed by Neyman in "Silver Jubilee of My Dispute with Fisher" (*Journal of the Operations Research Society of Japan*, **3** [1961], 145–154).

Statistical Philosophy. During the period of his work with Pearson, Neyman's attitude toward probability and hypothesis testing gradually underwent a radical change. In 1926 he tended to favor a Bayesian approach in the belief that any theory would have to involve statements about the probabilities of various alternative hypotheses, and hence an assumption of prior probabilities. In the face of Pearson's (and perhaps also Fisher's) strongly anti-Bayesian position, he became less certain, and in his papers of the late 1920's (both alone and with Pearson), he presented Bayesian and non-Bayesian approaches side by side. A decisive influence was Richard von Mises's book *Wahrscheinlichkeit, Statistik und Wahrheit* (1928), about which he later wrote (*A Selection of Early Statistical Papers of J. Neyman*, 1967; author's note) that it "confirmed him as a radical 'frequentist' intent on probability as a mathematical idealization of relative frequency." He remained an avowed frequentist and opposed any subjective approach to science for the rest of his life.

A second basic aspect of Neyman's work from the 1930's on is a point of view that he formulated clearly in the closing pages of his presentation at the 1937 Geneva conference, "L'estimation statistique traitée comme un problème classique de probabilité" (*Actualités scientifiques et industrielles*, no. 739, 25–57). He states that his approach is based on the concept of "comportement inductif," or inductive behavior, instead of on inductive reasoning. That is, statistics is to use experience not to extract "beliefs" but as a guide to appropriate action.

In other writings (for example, in *Review of the International Statistical Institute*, 25 [1957], 7–22), Neyman acknowledges that a very similar point of view was advocated by Carl F. Gauss and Laplace. It is of course also that of Wald's later general statistical decision theory. This view was strongly attacked by Fisher (for example, in *Journal of the Royal Statistical Society*, B17 [1955], 69–78), who maintained that decision making has no role in scientific inference, and that his fiducial argument provides exactly the mechanism required for scientific inference.

Move to the United States. By 1937 Neyman's work was becoming known not only in England and Poland but also in other parts of Europe and in the United States. He gave an invited talk about the theory of estimation at the International Congress of Probability held in 1937 at Geneva, and in the spring of 1937 he spent six weeks in the United States on a lecture tour organized by S. S. Wilks. The visit included a week at the graduate school of the Department of Agriculture in Washington, arranged by W. E. Deming. There he gave three lectures and six conferences on the relevance of probability theory to statistics, and on his work in hypothesis testing, estimation, sampling, and agricultural experimentation as illustrations of this approach. These *Lectures and Conferences on Mathematical Statistics,* which provided a coherent statement of the new paradigm he had developed and exhibited its successful application to a number of substantive problems, were a tremendous success. A mimeographed version appeared in 1938 and was soon sold out. Neyman published an augmented second edition in 1952.

After his return from the United States, Neyman debated whether to remain in England, where he had a permanent position but little prospect of promotion and independence, or to return to Poland. Then, in the fall of 1937, he received an unexpected letter from G. C. Evans, chairman of the department of mathematics at Berkeley, offering him a position in his department. Neyman hesitated for some time. California and its university were completely unknown quantities, while the situation in England—although not ideal—was reasonably satisfactory and offered stability. An attractive aspect of the Berkeley offer was the nonexistence there of any systematic program in statistics, so that he would be free to follow his own ideas. What finally tipped the balance in favor of Berkeley was the threat of war in Europe. Thus in April 1938 he decided to accept the Berkeley offer and immigrate to America, with his wife Olga (from whom he later separated) and his two-year-old son, Michael. He had just turned forty-four and he would remain in Berkeley for the rest of his long life.

The Berkeley Department of Statistics. Neyman's top priority after his arrival in Berkeley was the development of a statistics program, that is, a systematic set of courses and a faculty to teach them. He quickly organized a number of core courses and began to train some graduate students and one temporary instructor in his own approach to statistics. Administratively, he set up a statistical laboratory as a semiautonomous unit within the mathematics department. However, America's entry into World War II in 1941 soon put all further academic development on hold. Neyman took on war work, and for the next years this became the laboratory's central and all-consuming activity.

The building of a faculty began in earnest after the war, and by 1956 Neyman had established a permanent staff of twelve members, many his own students but also including three senior appointments from outside (Michel Loève, Miriam Scheffé, and David Blackwell). Development of a substantial faculty, with the attendant problems of space, clerical staff, summer support, and so on, represented a major, sustained administrative effort. A crucial issue in the growth of the program concerned the course offerings in basic statistics by other departments. Although these involved major vested interests, Neyman gradually concentrated the teaching of statistics within his program, at least at the lower division level. This was an important achievement both in establishing the identity of the program and in obtaining the student base, which alone could justify the ongoing expansion of the faculty. In his negotiations with the administration, Neyman was strengthened by the growing international reputation of his laboratory and by the increasing postwar importance of the field of statistics itself.

An important factor in the laboratory's reputation was the series of international symposia on mathematical statistics and probability that Neyman organized at five-year intervals between 1945 and 1970, and the subsequent publication of their proceedings. The first symposium was held in August 1945 to celebrate the end of the war and "the return to theoretical research" after years of war work. The meeting, although rather modest compared with the later symposia, was such a success that Neyman soon began to plan another one for 1950. In later years the symposia grew in size, scope, and importance, and did much to establish Berkeley as a major statistical center.

The spectacular growth Neyman achieved for his group required a constant struggle with various administrative authorities, including those of the mathematics department. To decrease the number of obstacles, and also to provide greater visibility for the statistics program, Neyman soon after his arrival in Berkeley began a long effort to obtain independent status for his group as a department of statistics. A separate department finally became a reality in 1955, with Neyman as its chair. He resigned the chairmanship the following year (but retained the directorship of the laboratory to the end of his life). He felt, he wrote in his letter of resignation, that "the transformation of the old Statistical Laboratory into a Department of Statistics closed a period of development . . . and opened a new phase." In these circumstances, he stated, "it is only natural to have a new and younger man take over."

There was perhaps another reason. Much of Neyman's energy during the nearly twenty years he had been at Berkeley had gone into administration. His efforts had been enormously successful: a first-rate department, the symposia, a large number of grants providing summer support for faculty and students. It was a great accomplishment and his personal creation, but now it was time to get back more fully into research.

Applied Statistics. Neyman's research in Berkeley was largely motivated by his consulting work, one of the purposes for which the university had appointed him and through which he made himself useful to the campus at large. Problems in astronomy, for example, led to the interesting insight (1948, with Scott) that maximum likelihood estimates may cease to be consistent if the number of nuisance parameters tends to infinity with increasing sample size. Also, to simplify maximum likelihood computations, which in applications frequently became very cumbersome, he developed linearized, asymptotically equivalent methods—his BAN (best

asymptotically normal) estimates (1949)—that have proved enormously useful.

Neyman's major research efforts at Berkeley were devoted to several large-scale applied projects. These included questions regarding competition of species (with T. Park), accident proneness (with G. Bates), the distribution of galaxies and the expansion of the universe (with C. D. Shane and particularly Elizabeth Scott, who became a steady collaborator and close companion), the effectiveness of cloud seeding, and a model for carcinogenesis. Of these, perhaps the most important was the work in astronomy, where the introduction of the Neyman-Scott clustering model brought new methods into the field.

Neyman's applicational work, although it extends over many different areas, exhibits certain common features, which he made explicit in some of his writings and which combine into a philosophy for applied statistics. The following are some of the principal aspects.

1. The studies are indeterministic. Neyman has pointed out that the distinction between deterministic and indeterministic studies lies not so much in the nature of the phenomena as in the treatment accorded to them ("Indeterminism in Science and New Demands on Statisticians," in *Journal of the American Statistical Association,* **55** [1960], 625–639). In fact, many subjects that traditionally were treated as deterministic are now being viewed stochastically. Neyman himself has contributed to this change in several areas.

2. An indeterministic study of a scientific phenomenon involves the construction of a stochastic model. In this connection Neyman introduced the important distinction between models that are interpolatory devices and those that embody genuine explanatory theories. The latter he describes as "a set of reasonable assumptions regarding the mechanism of the phenomena studied," while the former "by contrast consist of the selection of a relatively ad hoc family of functions, not deduced from underlying assumptions, and indexed by a set of parameters" ("Stochastic Models and Their Application to Social Phenomena," presented at a joint session of the Institute of Mathematical Statistics, the American Statistical Association, and the American Sociological Society, September 1956; written with W. Kruskal). The distinction is discussed earlier, and again later in Neyman's papers (*Annals of Mathematical Statistics,* **10** [1939], 372–373; and *Reliability and Biometry,* [Philadelphia, 1974], 183–201).

Most actual modeling, Neyman points out, is intermediate between these two extremes, often exhibiting features of both kinds. Related is the realization that investigators will tend to use as building blocks models that, "partly through experience and partly through imagination, appear to us familiar and, therefore, simple" ("Stochastic Models of Population Dynamics").

3. To develop a "genuine explanatory Theory" requires substantial knowledge of the scientific background of the problem. When the investigation concerns a branch of science with which the statistician is unfamiliar, this may require a considerable amount of work. For his collaboration with Scott in astronomy, Neyman studied the astrophysical literature, joined the American Astronomical Society, and became a member of the Commission on Galaxies of the International Astronomical Union. When he developed an interest in carcinogenesis, he spent three months at the National Institutes of Health to learn more about the biological background of the problem.

An avenue for learning about the state of the art in a field and bringing together diverse points of view that Neyman enjoyed and repeatedly used was to arrange a conference. Two of these (on weather modification in 1965 and on molecular biology in 1970) became parts of the then-current symposia. In addition, in 1961, jointly with Scott, he arranged a conference on the instability of systems of galaxies, and in July 1981, with Lucien Le Cam and on very short notice, an interdisciplinary cancer conference.

Epilogue. A month after the cancer conference, Neyman died of heart failure at age eighty-seven. He had been in reasonable health until two weeks earlier, and on the day before his death was still working in the hospital, on a book on weather modification.

Neyman is recognized as one of the founders of the modern theory of statistics whose work on hypothesis testing, confidence intervals, and survey sampling has revolutionized both theory and practice. His enormous influence on the development of statistics is further greatly enhanced through the large number of his Ph.D. students.

His achievements were recognized by honorary degrees from the universities of Chicago, California, Stockholm, and Warsaw, and from the Indian Statistical Institute. He was elected to the United States National Academy of Sciences and to foreign membership in the Royal Society, the Royal Swedish Academy, and the Polish National Academy. In addition he received many awards, including the United States National Medal of Science and the Guy Medal in Gold of the Royal Statistical Society.

Neyman was completely and enthusiastically dedicated to his work, which filled his life; there was not time for hobbies. Work, however, included not only research and teaching but also social aspects, such as traveling to meetings and organizing conferences. Pleasing his guests was an avocation; his hospitality had an international reputation. In his laboratory he created a family atmosphere that included students, colleagues, and visitors, with himself as paterfamilias.

As an administrator Neyman was indomitable. He would not take no for an answer, and was quite capable of resorting to unilateral actions. He firmly believed in the righteousness of his causes and found it difficult to understand how a reasonable person could disagree with him. At the same time, he had great charm that often was hard to resist.

The characteristic that perhaps remains most in mind is his generosity: furthering the careers of his students, giving credit and doing more than his share in collaboration, and extending his help (including financial assistance out of his own pocket) to anyone who needed it.

BIBLIOGRAPHY

I. ORIGINAL WORKS. A complete bibliography of Neyman's work is given at the end of David Kendall's memoir, in *Biographical Memoirs of Fellows of the Royal Society* (see below). Some of the early papers are reprinted in *A Selection of Early Statistical Papers of J. Neyman* and *Joint Statistical Papers of J. Neyman and E. S. Pearson* (Berkeley, 1967). Neyman's letters to E. S. Pearson from 1926 to 1933 (but not Pearson's replies) are preserved in Pearson's estate.

An overall impression of Neyman's ideas and style can be gained from his *Lectures and Conferences on Mathematical Statistics and Probability*, 2nd. ed., rev. and enl. (Washington, D.C., 1952). The following partial list provides a more detailed view of his major paradigmatic papers: "On the Use and Interpretation of Certain Test Criteria for Purposes of Statistical Inference," in *Biometrika*, **20A** (1928), 175–240, 263–294, written with E. S. Pearson; "On the Problem of the Most Efficient Tests of Statistical Hypotheses," in *Philosophical Transactions of the Royal Society of London*, **A 231** (1933), 289–337, written with E. S. Pearson; "On the Two Different Aspects of the Representative Method," in *Journal of the Royal Statistical Society*, **97** (1934), 558–625 (a Spanish version of this paper appeared in *Estadística*, **17** [1959], 587–651); "Outline of a Theory of Statistical Estimation Based on the Classical Theory of Probability," in *Philosophical Transactions of the Royal Society of London*, **A 236** (1937), 333–380.

Neyman's other theoretical contributions include "'Smooth' Test for Goodness of Fit," in *Skandinavisk aktuarietidskrift*, **20** (1937), 149–199; "On a New Class of 'Contagious' Distributions, Applicable in Entomology and Bacteriology,'' in *Annals of Mathematical Statistics*, **10** (1939), 35–57; ''Consistent Estimates Based on Partially Consistent Observations,'' in *Econometrica*, **16** (1948), 1–32, written with E. L. Scott; ''Contribution to the Theory of the Chi-Square Test,'' in J. Neyman, ed., *Proceedings of the Berkeley Symposium on Mathematical Statistics and Probability* (Berkeley, 1949); ''Optimal Asymptotic Tests of Composite Statistical Hypotheses,'' in U. Granander, ed., *Probability and Statistics* (Uppsala, Sweden, 1959), 213–234; ''Outlier Proneness of Phenomena and of Related Distributions,'' in J. S. Rustagi, ed., *Optimizing Methods in Statistics* (New York and London, 1971), 413–430, written with E. L. Scott.

Neyman's position regarding the role of statistics in science can be obtained from the following more philosophical and sometimes autobiographical articles: ''Foundation of the General Theory of Statistical Estimation, in *Actualités Scientifiques et industrielles*, no. 1146 (1951), 83–95; ''The Problem of Inductive Inference,'' in *Communications in Pure and Applied Mathematics*, **8** (1955), 13–45; '' 'Inductive Behavior' as a Basic Concept of Philosophy of Science,'' in *Review of the International Statistical Institute*, **25** (1957), 7–22; ''Stochastic Models of Population Dynamics,'' in *Science* (New York), **130** (1959), 303–308, written with E. L. Scott; ''A Glance at Some of My Personal Experiences in the Process of Research,'' in T. Dalenius, G. Karlsson, and S. Malmquist, eds., *Scientists at Work* (Uppsala, Sweden, 1970), 148–164; and ''Frequentist Probability and Frequentist Statistics,'' in *Synthèse*, **36** (1977), 97–131.

II. SECONDARY LITERATURE. The most important source for Neyman's life and personality is Constance Reid, *Neyman—from Life* (New York, 1982), which is based on Neyman's own recollections (obtained during weekly meetings over a period of more than a year) and those of his colleagues and former students, and on many original documents. A useful account of his collaboration with E. S. Pearson was written by Pearson for the Neyman festschrift, F. N. David, ed., *Research Papers in Statistics* (New York, 1966). Additional accounts of his life and work are provided by the following: D. G. Kendall, M. S. Bartlett, and T. L. Page, ''Jerzy Neyman, 1894–1981,'' in *Biographical Memoirs of Fellows of the Royal Society*, **28** (1982), 379–412; L. Le Cam and E. L. Lehmann, ''J. Neyman—on the Occasion of his 80-th Birthday,'' in *Annals of Statistics*, **2** (1974), vii–xiii; E. L. Lehmann and Constance Reid, ''In Memoriam—Jerzy Neyman, 1894–1981,'' in *American Statistician*, **36** (1982) 161–162; and E. L. Scott, ''Neyman, Jerzy,'' in *Encyclopedia of Statistical Sciences*, VI (1985) 215–223.

E. L. LEHMANN

NIEUWENKAMP, WILLEM (*b*. Lunteren, Netherlands, 1 January 1903; *d*. Bilthoven, Netherlands, 12 November 1979), *geology*.

Willem Nieuwenkamp was the second of four children (and the only son) born to Anna Wilbrink, daughter of an old Dutch landed family, and Wijnand Otto Jan Nieuwenkamp, a painter and engraver. A large part of his early life was spent on the water in the family's elegantly appointed houseboat, *de Zwerver*, a full 100 feet long, wintering on the Dutch canals and cruising up the Rhine to Basel and back in summer. His quick intelligence showed itself in primary school, where, on finishing his assigned work before the other children, he would ask and receive the teacher's permission to do somersaults up and down the aisle that divided the schoolroom.

In 1922 the Nieuwenkamps moved to Rome, and in 1926 they settled in San Domenico di Fiesole, outside Florence, in the villa Riposo de' Vescovi. Nieuwenkamp had entered the University of Utrecht in 1919, and remained in Holland to complete his studies, spending vacations in Italy with the rest of the family. Despite an early interest in astronomy (which he never lost), he chose to study geology, seeing behind its then preponderantly descriptive and systematic character a future opportunity for exciting theoretical advances. His formal studies ended with the *doctoraal* examination in 1926, and he received the D.Sc. degree (cum laude) in 1932 for a dissertation on the crystal structures of lead bromide and lead fluorobromide. In 1947 he was appointed professor of mineralogy, crystallography, and petrology (later of geochemistry) at Utrecht, and held this post until his retirement in 1968. In 1965 he was elected to the Royal Netherlands Academy of Sciences.

Nieuwenkamp's early experiences were varied and practical. After a year in Patagonia with an oil company, he went in 1933 to Göttingen as assistant to V. M. Goldschmidt, and later worked on gravity measurements, first with F. A. Vening Meinesz in submarines and then, with the onset of war, on land with a bicycle. But his thoughts were never far from the large-scale theoretical problems of geology that were waiting for solutions. His voyage to South America may have sparked an interest in global tectonics; a map drawn by him in this period shows the Atlantic continents assembled with their major tectonic lineaments restored. In these prewar years (1932–1937), he followed up his dissertation with ten papers on crystallographic subjects that included structure determinations on several halogen salts and on cristobalite. However, his abiding preoccupation was with the need for a satisfactory theory of the origin of rocks. Quick to see the logical flaws in classical magmatism (then still the orthodox view of petrogenesis), he traced it back to its origins in the neptunist-plutonist debate of 150 years before, looking for where it had gone wrong. This notorious controversy had ended in a posthumous victory for James Hutton in which, ironically, his cyclic picture of the earth's metabolism was all but blotted out by the magma that had defeated Abraham G. Werner's neptunists. On this magmatic tide Justus Roth then floated a new school of geology in Germany; it prospered and developed under Harry Rosenbusch into what is now called classical magmatism.

Classical magmatism postulated that the primitive crust of the earth had been made of magmatic rocks congealed from the supposedly molten globe. These igneous rocks were then weathered to produce sediments, which accumulated at the surface, and soluble cations (among them sodium), which accumulated in the sea. The loss of igneous rocks to weathering was made good by fresh eruptions, from the still molten interior, of what became known to the later magmatists as "juvenile" magma, that is, magma fresh from the mantle, never before having seen the light of day. This contrasted with the Huttonian view, according to which the magma, being made of melted sediments, was resurgent. Classical magmatism admitted, however, that buried sediments could be subjected to heat and stress and converted into metamorphic rocks recognizable by their foliated or banded appearance. This could happen to igneous rocks, too, so that sedimentary and igneous rocks could become indistinguishable when metamorphosed. There was orthogneiss from granite, and paragneiss from mud. But magma was paramount. Hundreds of different kinds of igneous rocks were discovered, examined, and classified with materialistic zeal.

Sedimentation was thus viewed as an essentially secular process. Estimates of the earth's age based on this view, whether derived from the supposed mass of the sedimentary rocks (T. M. Reade) or the amount of sodium released on their formation from igneous rocks and now in the sea (J. Joly), had agreed faily well with Lord Kelvin's result from the supposed cooling history of the earth. But they did not accord with the radiometric dates that began appearing on the geologic time scale a decade or two later and that by Nieuwenkamp's day indicated that all of the sodium now in the sea could have accumulated, at the present rate, since some time in the Cretaceous Period. F. W. Clarke in 1908 calculated the mass of sediment that should correspond to the sodium now in the sea, and V. M. Goldschmidt repeated the calculation, with some refinements, in 1933. Their results were essentially the same: enough to spread an even layer 2,000 meters thick over the land surface of the earth. At the time, no one seemed troubled by this outcome, which was so paltry in contrast with the observed mass of sediments of the earth's crust.

The confining war years extended Nieuwenkamp's command of the literature and ripened his ideas. Exhaustive reading of Hutton and John Playfair, and of their opponents in the Wernerian Society, and careful study of field observations, especially those of the great Scandinavian geologists, such as Pentti E. Eskola and Johannes J. Sederholm, drew Nieuwenkamp to the neo-Huttonian viewpoint from which he later created the "persedimentary hypothesis" that came to be associated with his name. After the war he was able to travel and see for himself. Detailed studies of granitic bodies and their field relations in Spain and in the Massif Central of France made it clear that many granites had originated from sedimentary rocks, an idea that is commonplace today but was still controversial in 1950. These field studies formed the subject of a number of doctoral dissertations at Utrecht, and the sedimentary heritage of granite made it the starting point for a new approach to petrogenesis through the "continuous rock series." No rock can be defined in a natural way; each grades imperceptibly in character into its neighbors, and all together form a continuum. In an article published in 1968 he wrote: "We need only suppose that the rocks have been formed somehow in order to get convinced that it will be hard to ascribe two diametrically opposed derivations to two rocks . . . lying close together in the series" (p. 367). If orthoamphibolite was formed by metamorphism of basalt erupted from the mantle, what of paraamphibolite derived from marl, if one could not tell the difference between them?

Nieuwenkamp developed his ideas in a sporadic series of papers and in conversations with European geologists who, like himself, saw the difficulties of classical magmatism and welcomed "persedimentarism" as an alternative working hypothesis. Prominent among these were T. F. W. Barth, A. Holmes, E. Raguin, and H. G. F. Winkler, all of whom were strongly influenced by Nieuwenkamp and carried his influence into the general current of European geologic thought. He drew attention to the sodium problem at the International Geological Congress at London in 1948. Until then, nobody had seriously questioned Clarke's and Goldschmidt's poor sediment yield from the sodium calculation, although some (including Holmes, a pioneer in radiometric age measurement) had begun to suspect the reason why Joly, using the same argument before them, had failed to get a reasonable age for earth.

The chief significance of this paper, "Geochemistry of Sodium," was that it brought the "sodium problem" into juxtaposition with another question that had been recognized more recently by the Scandinavians and others working on granitic terrains that were clearly of sedimentary origin: What was the source of the sodium that had created these rocks out of mudstones and shales? The answer of classical magmatism was unsatisfying: It was brought in a hypothetical "ichor" of (juvenile) magmatic origin that arose from the earth's interior and pervaded the sediments. A few years earlier S. J. Shand had criticized this ad hoc invention and suggested that the sodium had been there all the time, in connate pore water. For Nieuwenkamp, the possibility that these two problems might be solvable at one stroke by closing a loop in the sodium cycle between the ocean (losing sodium) and the metasediments (gaining it) through marine sediments carrying entrapped sodium opened a line of thought whose destination was not yet clear:

In the original plutonism of Hutton, the magma consisted of melted sediments. It would be an interesting historical study to see how it came about that this origin has been rejected. . . . The whole interest which could be derived from such an investigation depends on whether anything more definite can be postulated, than merely that every rock or lava once has been a sediment (1948).

The idea is developed further in "Géochimie classique et transformiste" (1956), which begins with the calculation of a geochemical balance between igneous rocks on the one hand and sediments and seawater on the other. Uncertainty about the proportions of shale, sandstone, and limestone in the sedimentary reservoir is ingeniously sidestepped by expressing the abundance of each element (as its lowest oxide) in terms of alumina, whose virtually exclusive occurrence in the clay fraction of sediments (of whatever kind) reduces the problem to comparison of the average igneous rock with the average clay. Among the seven major elements, the only significant discrepancies are in magnesium, calcium, and sodium. The missing calcium and magnesium are inadequate to account for any reasonable estimate of the proportion of carbonate rocks to shales unless the Precambrian sediments and metasediments (poor in carbonates) are included; but this makes the case of sodium much worse than before: The amount found in the sea is far too small, and the earth's sedimentary cover is far too thick, to agree with classical magmatism.

Next, the continuous rock series is examined at the convergence of gneiss and granite. Here is a dilemma: If a granite and a gneiss of similar composition are found side by side, no one will readily admit that their origins have nothing in common. Either most of the granite comes from a juvenile magma whose alkaline exhalations have transformed the adjoining sediments into gneiss and, eventually, granite (classical magmatism), or the gneiss is entirely of sedimentary origin (the sodium congeneric, having been held in pore water and on clay minerals). Then what are the odds that a granitic magma of the same composition happened to arrive from the depths of the earth and congeal just beside it? Surely the odds are much longer than that some of the gneiss melted and congealed to form granite.

Once on [that] road, there's no stopping. If the granite was formed entirely from sediments, it seems absurd to postulate a juvenile source for rhyolite. There is no sharp line between granite, diorite and gabbro. If granite is made from sandy clay, marly clays make more basic rocks. Associations of amphibolites, basic [eruptive] rocks and metamorphic limestones are common too. Amphibolites and gabbros pose the same problem as gneisses and granites (1956, pp. 419–420).

Nieuwenkamp stops short of denying altogether the existence of juvenile magmas; instead he advances the persedimentary hypothesis as a "clear, unequivocal starting point for petrogenetic and geochemical interpretations," an antithesis to classical magmatism, so that the two can be compared in regard to their predictions concerning geochemical and petrologic data.

As an example, the distribution of some refractory elements (such as aluminum) and some mobile ones (such as boron) between different geologic reservoirs (igneous rocks, metamorphic rocks, sediments, hydrosphere, atmosphere) is examined from each viewpoint. For both, the refractory elements should be distributed in essentially the same manner: more or less equally among the three rock reservoirs, scarce or absent in the hydrosphere and atmosphere. With the volatile elements it is otherwise. They should be scarce in igneous and metamorphic rocks (depending on their mobility), and distributed instead among sediments, hydrosphere, and atmosphere according to their individual propensities. But here the two models diverge. Classical magmatism, with its secular scheme of sedimentation, limits the amount of sediment produced in geologic time so severely that it cannot even account for the observed mass of Phanerozoic sediments, let alone the Precambrian ones. According to it, the volume of these latter (whose existence we cannot doubt) must be minuscule. Whatever mobile elements in seawater (for example, boron) are concentrated in insoluble sedimentary minerals ought to be much more abundant in the scarce Precambrian sediments than in the much larger mass of Phanerozoic ones.

The persedimentary model, on the other hand, imposes no such restrictions. The sediments are recycled again and again; there is no reason to suppose that the Precambrian ones, when laid down, were any less abundant than those of today, or that the concentration of boron in them should be any different. The persedimentary prediction, not too easily verified in 1956, was later thoroughly vindicated by R. C. Reynolds, Jr. (1965), who measured the boron content of thirty-one Precambrian marine illites ranging in age from 1.0 to 1.7 billion years. Twenty-three of the measurements lay inside the 95 percent confidence limits for seventy samples from Phanerozoic rocks. Classical magmatism was unable to account for (1) the distribution of sodium among igneous rocks, sediments, and the ocean; (2) the sodium added in metamorphism of sediments to paragneiss; (3) the observed proportion of limestone in the Phanerozoic sedimentary reservoir; and (4) the observed age distribution in sediments of some mobile minor elements, among them boron.

The basalt-amphibolite-marl problem still had to be confronted. Nieuwenkamp dealt with it in "Oceanic and Continental Basalts in the Geochemical Cycle" (1968). This paper begins with a thorough examination of the terms *juvenile* and *resurgent* in which almost no possibility is left unexplored, no stone (one might also say) unturned. The looming bulk of the earth's mantle is considered as though possibly by some stretch it could be called resurgent in an emergency. (Meteorites on arrival are definitely not resurgent; but they become surface rocks at the moment of impact, might even be weathered before becoming part of the growing mantle. Then, if they should ever come to the surface again, they would technically qualify as resurgent.)

The importance of magma has been further attenuated by seismology, which has looked in vain for great reservoirs of it under the crust: whatever comes up must once have been solid rock and then melted for the occasion. With so limited a supply on hand, making large amounts of granite by differentiation would be more difficult than getting it by melting sediments. Winkler's famous experiments in Bonn (1958–1961) have shown that this can be done. In this paper Nieuwenkamp displays the continuous rock series in its definitive, three-dimensional form (Figure 1, p. 679), with both the rocks them-

selves and the pathways by which they cycle around. Everything is resurgent; nothing is juvenile.

Making granite from shale poses no "space problem"; the transformation can be isovolumetric (more or less). In fact, it solves the problem posed by large granite bodies in former times: if they are intrusive, how did they find room? The case of marl and basalt is quite different: "Derivation of all basalts from marly sediments can hardly be seriously entertained because of the disproportion between the enormous volumes of basalt and the scarce occurrences of metamorphic limestones" (1968, p. 369). Nieuwenkamp proposes the following solution: juvenile basic magma formed a primeval crust of lava that was weathered wherever it rose above the sea.

$$\text{silicates} + CO_2 = \text{quartz} + \text{carbonates}$$

(Clays, of course, would be formed as well.) The quartz (solid) accumulated on the spot and was reincorporated in the crust there, making it gradually more siliceous and lighter, so that it came to ride high on the mantle as emergent granitic masses. The carbonate (dissolved) went to the ocean, accompanied by calcium, magnesium, iron, and perhaps some clay, where it was precipitated with them on the floor. Lava that remained submerged was not weathered but formed a basaltic crust to which was added the sedimentary material derived from the emergent (protocontinental) crust. Subduction under continental margins converted these sediments to amphibolite (with release of volatiles and excess calcium), and eventually to basalt that was plated onto the subducted oceanic basement. Each realm, continental and oceanic, developed its own metabolism, the one granitic and the other basaltic, separate but interacting. Some basalt erupted onto the continents, which in turn supplied sediment of like composition to the ocean floor. (Material exchange in subduction zones does not seem to have been envisaged.)

In this scheme, the disproportion between basalt and "metamorphic limestone" was no longer cause for worry. The six-kilometer oceanic crust must have been subducted and recycled several times in four billion years, enough to have incorporated a considerable thickness of deep-sea sediment, and so "tuned" the convergence of ortho- and paraamphibolite. Nieuwenkamp points out some snags, among which he mentions the high potassium content of granitic rocks that "can hardly be derived from basic volcanics." This does not seem too great a difficulty, granted the affinity of potassium for clay, which presumably would remain largely in the continental domain. More serious, perhaps, would be

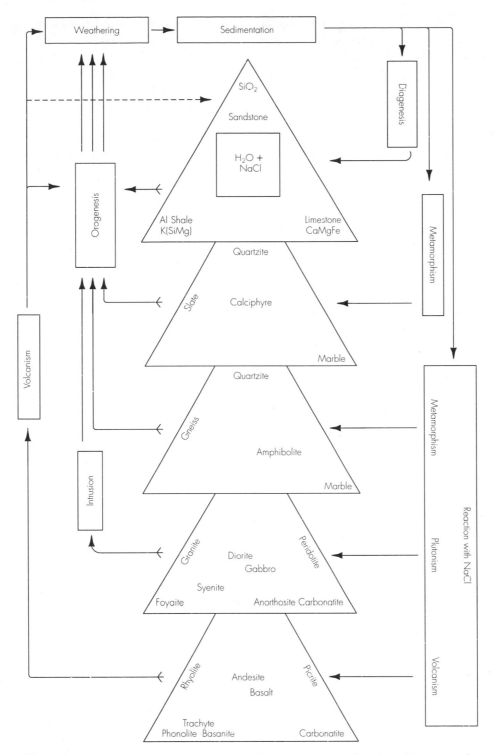

FIGURE 1. Three-dimensional representation of the continuous rock series with attempted neo-Huttonian interpretation. From Nieuwenkamp, "Oceanic and Continental Basalts in the Geochemical Cycle," in *Geologísche Rundschau*, **57** (1968), 362–372.

the disproportion not between basalt and "metamorphic limestone" but between the latter and the earth's mantle (especially as the proportion of lime in deep-sea sediments may have been quite low until Mesozoic times).

It was not very well known, in 1968, what became of the slabs of oceanic crust that were subducted under the leading edges of drifting plates. Nieuwenkamp supposed that the continents perhaps rode over them in the fashion of an icebreaker, but was not sure: "Leaving aside detailed guesses, the general conclusion seems unavoidable that parts of the basaltic ocean floor disappear downwards at or somewhere before the prow, and are reconstituted in the wake of a drifting continent." If this were anything like the case, one could imagine the ocean floor, perhaps, as an entity somehow confined to the uppermost zone of the earth and effectively sealed off from the mantle beneath. From later work, however, it became apparent that subducted tectonic plates descended into the mantle or sank even deeper, perhaps to equilibrate with the mantle as a whole. In that case the influence of the sediment they carried with them must, even over four billion years, be negligible. "Once on [that] road, there's no stopping."

The persedimentary hypothesis had no alternative but to dive bravely into the mantle, that vast source of almost undeniably juvenile magma. If the mantle were well mixed, there would be faint hope of its ever coming back. Against the odds, it did. B. L. Weaver, D. A. Wood, J. Tarney, and J. L. Joron, after analyzing basaltic lavas from the South Atlantic, wrote in 1986: "The trace-element of Pb isotopic geochemistry of these lavas is explicable by contamination of the ocean-island basalt source that gave rise to Ascension, Bouvet and St. Helena lavas by variable, but small (about 1 percent) amounts of ancient (1.5–2.0 Ga) pelagic sediment." Thus the influence of sediments was seen to extend even into the mantle, which was not well mixed enough to eradicate it.

The persedimentary hypothesis, developed before geophysics and geochemistry had revealed the detailed workings of subduction zones, could not foresee the full extent of interplay between the continental and oceanic regimes. It regarded the more silicic igneous rocks (granite-diorite and the volcanic equivalents) as little more than melted sediments. For a few of these rocks (such as dacites on St. Lucia, Windward Islands), this view seems valid; but the majority appear to have originated from remelted oceanic crust with or without an admixture of sediment. Thus some granitic magmas do seem

to have risen from the depths, bringing with them heat to granitize sediments. And if they bring back, too, the conundrum of compositional convergence in rocks of different provenance, perhaps at the same time they bridge a gap between the continental and oceanic metabolisms that would otherwise make it difficult to understand the continuity between granite and gabbro.

Nieuwenkamp set out by inquiring in 1948 whether anything more definite could be postulated than merely that every rock or lava once had been a sediment. This postulate itself was an extreme one antithetical to that of classical magmatism, and chosen for that reason. It was the starting position, not the goal. Time (and improved analytical techniques) ultimately showed the pervasive influence of sediments in the earth's metabolism, and at least vindicated the statement that every "rock or lava" appearing at the surface is likely to have had some prior experience, however dim or tenuous, of the exogenic environment. But the answer that influenced the course of geochemistry was the same Hutton had given in 1785 and James Croll had given again in 1871: the sediments are recycled again and again, and their mass remains more or less the same ("Géochimie classique et transformiste," 1956). This time something was perceived that had been missed on the two previous occasions. A few people were becoming interested in modeling geologic processes mathematically; but although many small-scale processes were understood well enough to be modeled successfully, there was no satisfactory physical basis for modeling global phenomena such as the "rock cycle" (a mere textbook platitude) or the chemistry of the ocean.

The idea in "Geochemistry of Sodium" (1948) of an essentially steady-state ocean with cyclic fluxes was taken up by Harald Carstens (a student of Barth) in 1949. He translated it mathematically into a steady-state reservoir with constant input and an output regulated by first-order, feed-forward control, and showed that the steady state would have been attained (more or less) within the first few hundred million years of the ocean's existence, so far as sodium was concerned. Barth later worked out residence times for several other elements; all were short compared with the lifetime of the ocean. Carstens' model became the archetype of countless others that were applied in the succeeding decades, with varying degrees of complexity, to all sorts of geologic systems ranging from the continental crust to the global climate. The era of geochemical cycles had begun, preparing the way for a true synthesis

680

in the 1980's (Veizer and Jansen, 1985) of cyclic and secular influences in the history of the earth.

Nieuwenkamp left no voluminous literature behind him, nor did his soft, conversational voice carry far in the great lecture halls of Europe's scientific societies. He never visited the United States. His considerable influence was felt instead at small colloquiums, at roadside stops by his favorite outcrops, in quiet bars and restaurants, in his comfortable and elegant room at the old geological institute on the Oude Gracht in Utrecht, and, by a lucky few, at his house in Bilthoven, where he and his wife, Sienie (Essienie Nannenga, also a geologist), and their three children kept a table justly reputed for its cuisine, wines, and conversation. His ideas were spread by his friends, most of all Barth, who restated and augmented them in his well-known textbook (*Theoretical Petrology,* 2nd. ed., 1962) and in a number of papers written in the early 1960's. One of these (Barth, 1961) has practically the same title as one of Nieuwenkamp's ("Korrelation von Sediment und Eruptivgesteine," 1956).

It has been mainly through the assimilation of his ideas into the writings of Barth and others (with all of whom he was on the most cordial terms) that Nieuwenkamp's cyclic views of geochemistry and petrology have achieved the wide (but still largely anonymous) currency that they enjoy today. Recognition came in the United States in 1972 with the founding of the Work Group on Geochemical Cycles (incorporated into the Geochemical Society in 1983), which has held a series of symposia attended by leading North American geochemists as well as by distinguished visitors from other continents. In 1980 the National Science Foundation sponsored a five-day conference with the theme "Chemical Cycles in the Evolution of the Earth," the proceedings of which (Gregor *et al.,* 1988) were published in a volume commemorating Nieuwenkamp's contributions to geochemistry. Nieuwenkamp's lifetime interest in the origins of geology led him to participate in the founding of the International Committee for the History of the Geological Sciences at the inaugural convocation at Yerevan, Armenia, in 1967; he remained active in this committee until his death.

In the last decade of his life, Nieuwenkamp turned his attention to scientific biography, writing articles on M. van Marum and (for the *Dictionary of Scientific Biography*) C. L. von Buch, C. R. T. Krayenhoff, and F. A. Vening Meinesz. But his interest in the cycles never flagged, and at the time of his death he had begun a manuscript entitled (with characteristic modesty) "The New Petrology of Tom F. W. Barth." Nieuwenkamp's extraordinary eru-

dition allowed him to view a subject from many vantage points, and a wide command of languages (both modern and classical) gave him access to a range of literature beyond the reach of most of his contemporaries. His underlying attitude was one of benign skepticism, and nothing amused him more than to discover in some dogma of the day an inconspicuous but pregnant inconsistency.

On his retirement from the chair of geochemistry, his colleagues at Utrecht gave Nieuwenkamp a beer mug engraved with the motto "Who sows doubt shall reap insight" ("Wie twijfel zaait zal inzicht oogsten"). Always urbane and good-natured, he made many friends among scientific supporters and opponents alike. His wit was mordant but never cruel. He was a delightful companion, and traveling with him was a continual series of digressions rewarded by unusual discoveries, arresting views, unexpected meetings, and memorable meals. He had little patience with stupidity, but was never unkind to simple ignorance. His towering intellect was half hidden by an irrepressible sense of fun that made him approachable. On hearing that a student using pyknometers thought they must have something to do with pigs, he got a glassblower to make some shaped like pigs and surreptitiously substituted them for the real ones. Unfailingly courteous, he would meet visitors at the little railway station in Bilthoven and walk or drive with them the half mile or so to his house in the Tenkatelaan. He continued this practice even after his health began to fail in 1978, and one would step from the train to see his slight, stooped figure stand tall for a moment with pleasure at the prospect of an approaching guest.

BIBLIOGRAPHY

I. ORIGINAL WORKS. A comprehensive bibliography of Nieuwenkamp's articles is in R. D. Schuiling, "In Memoriam W. Nieuwenkamp (1903–1979)," in *Geologie en mijnbouw,* **59** (1980), 183–186. Among them are "Geochemistry of Sodium," in *Report of the International Geological Congress, 18th Session,* II (London, 1948), 96–100; "Géochimie classique et transformiste," in *Bulletin de la Société géologique de France,* 6th ser., **6** (1956), 407–429; "Korrelation von Sediment und Eruptivgesteine," in *Gedenkboek H. A. Brouwer, Verhandelingen van het K. nederlandsch geologisch-mijnbouwkundig genootschap,* **16** (1956), 309–316; and "Oceanic and Continental Basalts in the Geochemical Cycle," in *Geologische Rundschau,* **57** (1968), 362–372.

II. SECONDARY LITERATURE. T. F. W. Barth, "Ideas on the Interrelation Between Igneous and Sedimentary Rocks," in *Bulletin de la Commission géologique de Finlande,* **196** (1961), 321–326, and *Theoretical Petrology*

(New York, 1952; 2nd ed., 1962); H. Carstens, "Et nytt prinsipp ved kvantitative geokimiske bereginger," in *Norsk geologisk tidskrift*, **28** (1949), 47–50; F. W. Clarke, *The Data of Geochemistry* (Washington, D.C., 1908); J. Croll, "On a Method of Determining the Mean Thickness of the Sedimentary Rocks of the Globe," in *Geological Magazine*, **8** (1871), 97–102, 285–287; V. M. Goldschmidt, "Grundlagen der quantitativen Geochemie," in *Fortschritte der Mineralogie, Kristallographie und Petrographie*, **17** (1933), 112–156; C. B. Gregor, R. M. Garrels, F. T. Mackenzie, and J. B. Maynard, eds., *Chemical Cycles in the Evolution of the Earth* (New York, 1988); J. Hutton, *Abstract of a Dissertation Read in the Royal Society of Edinburgh . . . Concerning the System of the Earth, Its Duration and Stability* (Edinburgh, 1785); J. Poly, "An Estimate of the Geological Age of the Earth," in *Scientific Transactions of the Royal Dublin Society*, 2nd ser., **7** (1899), 23–66; T. M. Reade, "Measurement of Geological Time," in *Geological Magazine*, 3rd ser., **10** (1893), 97–100; R. C. Reynolds, Jr., "The Concentration of Boron in Precambrian Seas," in *Geochimica et Cosmochimica Acta*, **29** (1965), 1–16; S. J. Shand, *Eruptive Rocks* (London, 1943); E. den Tex, "Willem Nieuwenkamp," in *Jaarboek van het K. nederlandsch akademie van wetenschappen* (1979); J. Veizer and S. L. Jansen, "Basement and Sedimentary Recycling—2: Time Dimension to Global Tectonics," in *Journal of Geology*, **93** (1985), 625–643; Barry L. Weaver, David A. Wood, John Tarney, and Jean Louis Joron, "Role of Subducted Sediment in the Genesis of Ocean-Island Basalts: Geochemical Evidence from South Atlantic Ocean Islands," in *Geology*, **14** (1986), 275–278; H. G. F. Winkler, "La Genèse du granite et des migmatites par anatexie expérimentale," in *Revue de géographie physique et géologie dynamique*, **3** (1960), 67–76; and H. G. F. Winkler and H. van Platen, "Experimentelle Gesteinsmetamorphose—II: Bildung von anatektischen granitischen Schmelzen bei der Metamorphose von NaCl-führenden kalkfreien Tonen," in *Geochimica et Cosmochimica Acta*, **15** (1958), 91–112, "Experimentelle Gesteinsmetamorphose—III: Anatektische Ultrametamorphose kalkhaltiger Tone," *ibid.*, **18** (1960), 293–316, and "Experimentelle Gesteinsmetamorphose—IV: Bildung anatektischer Schmelzen aus metamorphisierten Grauwacken," *ibid.*, **24** (1961), 48–69.

Grateful acknowledgement is made to John Wiley & Sons for permission to use material from "W. Nieuwenkamp, a Biographical Note," in C. B. Gregor, R. M. Garrels, F. T. Mackenzie, and J. B. Maynard, eds., *Chemical Cycles in the Evolution of the Earth* (New York, 1988).

BRYAN GREGOR

NIKOLAEV, VIKTOR ARSENIEVICH (*b*. 6 December 1893, Nizhnii Novgorod (now Gorky), Russia; *d*. 25 September 1960, Leningrad, U.S.S.R.), *petrology*.

Nikolaev's father, Arsenii Ivanovich, was a shop assistant; he died in 1910. His mother, Ekaterina Petrovna Nikolaeva, survived her husband by twelve years. In 1911 Viktor Nikolaev finished technical school with honors and then left for Petersburg, where he easily passed entrance exams to the Faculty of Geology and Exploration at the Mining Institute. The institute was very popular with young people and only one in twenty applicants was admitted. Nikolaev's interest in nature, shown already in his childhood, became pronounced in his college years when he concentrated on natural sciences, particularly geology. The leading professors at the Mining Institute, including E. S. Fedorov, petrographer and crystallographer; Ivan Vasilievich Mushketov, author of a major textbook in physical geology; and Karl Ivanovich Bogdanovich, a prominent specialist in the theory of mineral deposits, noticed the talented student and paid special attention to him.

Nikolaev graduated from the Mining Institute in 1918 with the diploma of the first degree, having completed the eight-year program at the institute in seven years, and got the degree of mining engineer. During his studies Nikolaev had to earn his living. In 1914 he applied for a job as technician-hydrogeologist at the Department of Soil Improvement of the Ministry of Agriculture. The next summer, attracted by the romance of geological trips, he took part in the geological expedition to a largely unexplored eastern part of the northern Tien Shan. There he studied Paleozoic volcanics, and afterward used the data obtained in his senior thesis, which contained the first detailed petrographic description of these rocks. A year later, in the same expedition, Nikolaev studied previously unknown glaciers of the Dzhungar Alatau river basins. In 1917 he worked in the north of the country, along the Murmansk railroad, studying the magmatic and metamorphic rocks. He paid special attention to alkaline rocks, in which he remained interested for many more years.

After graduating from the Mining Institute, Nikolaev worked for the first two years (1918–1919) in the Urals, in the Zlatoust mines region. In 1919 and 1920 he was at the administration of the Kemerovo mines of the Kuznets coal basin, and in 1920 he joined the Geological Committee in Petrograd, with which he remained associated until 1949. He was married and had four children, two sons and two daughters.

In addition to his work at the Geological Committee, which later became the All-Union Scientific Research Geological Institute (VSEGEI), and at the Laboratory of the Precambrian of the Soviet Academy of Sciences (1951–1960), Nikolaev devoted much of his energy to teaching. Between 1925 and 1932, he read the course of petrography at the Leningrad Mining Institute and between 1947 and 1960 he was head of a department there. From 1933 till 1945 he also lectured at the Central Asian Industrial Institute in Tashkent. In 1935 Nikolaev became professor and in 1937 he received the degree of doctor of science, geology, and mineralogy. In 1946 he was elected corresponding member of the Soviet Academy of Sciences.

Nikolaev's research concerned mostly regional geology, magmatism, tectonics, and metallogeny of Central Asia. In his early works on magmatic rocks of the Tien Shan he classified them on the structural and mineralogical basis and provided evidence of processes leading to their secondary alteration. In his research he rejected the prevailing view that the rock alteration was caused by weathering and proved that it was induced by postvolcanic factors.

At the start of his activity at the Geological Committee, Nikolaev was working at the geological mapping of Turkestan, with the scale of 1:420,000. He compiled the hydrogeological map for the bigger part of this region over the right bank of the Zeravsham River. He was, however, increasingly attracted by high mountainous regions, which he had visited as a student, and so, in the early 1930's, he went to the Pamirs to examine exposures of magmatic rocks.

Owing to this research, by the end of the 1930's Nikolaev had become a leading expert in the petrology and geology of this complex region. Thorough examination enabled him to establish the Paleozoic age of granitic intrusives and thus totally disprove the then prevalent idea that this region belonged to the Alpine fold zones. Most of the typical features of the magmatism of the Pamirs outlined by him were confirmed in later research by other geologists.

Nikolaev paid special attention to the tectonics of the vast Tien Shan and Pamirs area. His studies led to a number of interesting conclusions about the general structure and evolution of mobile zones of the earth's crust. Drawing from the results of his geological surveys as well as from data of other geologists, Nikolaev outlined the structural division that broke the Tien Shan into two zones—the northern and the southern. He proved that his dividing line was of primary order and traced it for 1,200 kilometers from the Khantengri massif to northwestern spurs of Karatau. He further showed the absence of transitional facies between these two distinctive zones, concluding that either such facies had never existed or they had been covered by the southern zone thrust northward over land that had

emerged there in Caledonian times. The Tien Shan structural division outlined by Nikolaev was sound evidence of a deep fault. His scheme of the Tien Shan structural-facies zonation later became the basis for the tectonic zonation throughout eastern Central Asia.

Expanding on his idea of the internal organization of the Tien Shan, Nikolaev extended his conclusions to the structure and evolution of structural-facies zones in mobile belts of the earth's crust. He distinguished inner and outer geosynclinal zones and inner and peripheral geoanticlinal zones. In addition, he discussed smaller units successively exposed to various stages of geosynclinal evolution. From his analysis of the geologic history of the earth's crustal mobile belts, Nikolaev concluded that the period of Alpine tectonogenesis was uniquely characterized by the evolution of tectonic zones.

These significant theoretical conclusions in tectonics resulted from Nikolaev's ongoing investigation of magmatic rocks. From the very start of his scientific career he won a high reputation as a keen and precise petrographer who possessed a thorough knowledge of the laboratory techniques of rock examination. He would always study samples himself, and not only his own collections made on expeditions in the Tien Shan and Pamirs. He gave no less thorough treatment to samples given to him by geologists who worked in other regions. This undoubtedly contributed to the breadth of his petrologic outlook.

In the last decades of his career Nikolaev concentrated on the theory of magmatism and metamorphism. Working on problems of physicochemical petrology he aimed at analyzing petrological processes on the basis of thermodynamic law. In particular, he expanded the theory of silicate systems with volatile components and that of petrologic systems with various phases under differential pressure.

He also showed the significance of phase equilibria studies for magmatic and metamorphic petrogenesis, and he calculated metamorphic reactions for systems including water and carbon dioxide.

The studies of the magmatic process led Nikolaev to the delineation of its major stages. He pointed out three formative factors affecting hydrothermal solutions: (1) migration of gaseous phase into the intruded rock; (2) cooling of gaseous phase left after the melt crystallization; (3) effect of the water-rich residual solution from the crystallizing melt at stages after distillation.

Prominent in Nikolaev's academic works are his ideas on the formation of granite. He disproved granitization as an explanation of the genesis of all granites because he believed that ideas of the uniformity of granite formation were invalid, as deep metasomatic granitization could not be extended to subsurface zones. Critical of the "basic front," Nikolaev argued against the idea of the formation of subsurface granitoid intrusions by *in situ* metasomatic granitization.

Nikolaev developed and disseminated his scientific beliefs not only through his own publications but also in papers and books written by a group of authors under his leadership. In this respect, the collective work *Major Problems in the Theory of Magmatogenic Ore Deposits* (1955) is of special prominence since it brought Nikolaev the Lenin Prize in 1958. In 1955 he was also elected president of the All-Union Mineralogical Society and occupied this position until his death. In 1959 Nikolaev had a myocardial infarction and exudative pleurisy and never fully recovered. After a year of serious illness he died at the age of sixty-six.

BIBLIOGRAPHY

I. ORIGINAL WORKS. "O vazhneishei strukturnoi linii Tian-Shania" ("On the Most Important Structural Line of the Tien Shan"), in *Zapiski Vserossiiskogo mineralogicheskogo obshchestva*, **62**, no. 2 (1933), 347–354; *Shchelochnye porody reki Kaindy v Talasskom Alatau* ("Alkaline Rocks of the Kainda River in Talass Alatau"; Moscow, 1935); "O nekotorykh chertakh stroeniia i razvitiia podvizhnykh poiasov zemnoi kory" ("On Some Features of the Structure and Evolution of Mobile Belts of the Earth's Crust"), in *Izvestiia Akademii nauk, Seriia geologicheskaia*, no. 2 (1953), 19–38; ed., *Osnovnye problemy v uchenii o magmatogennykh rudnykh mestorozhdeniiakh* ("Major Problems in the Theory of Magmatogene Ore Deposits"; Moscow, 1955); ed., *Metodicheskoe rukovodstvo po geologicheskomu kartirovaniiu metamorficheskikh kompleksov* ("Methodical Guidebook on Geological Mapping of Metamorphic Complexes"; Moscow, 1957); and *Osnovy teorii protsessov magmatizma i metamorfizma* ("Fundamentals of the Theory of Processes of Magmatism and Metamorphism"), written with V. V. Dolivo-Dobrovolskii (Moscow, 1961).

II. SECONDARY LITERATURE. E. N. Goretskaiia and R. V. Dolivo-Dobrovolskii, "Viktor Arsenievich Nikolaev (1893–1960)," in *Vydaiushchiesia uchenye Geologicheskogo Komiteta* (Leningrad, 1982), 190–211; and S. P. Solovev, "Tvorcheskii put V. A. Nikolaeva" ("Life and Work of V. A. Nikolaev"), in *Zapiski Vserossiiskogo mineralogicheskogo obshchestva*, **90**, no. 2 (1961), 129–135.

V. V. TIKHOMIROV

NISHINA, YOSHIO (*b.* Okayama, Japan, 6 December 1890; *d.* Tokyo, Japan, 10 January 1951), *physics, nuclear physics.*

Yoshio was the sixth son of Tsune and Arimasa Nishina. They had seven sons and two daughters. Arimasa was a rich landowner engaged in agriculture and salt making. Tsune used to make her children arrange such family events as travels and birthday parties. Yoshio's grandfather Arimoto had been famous for his handling of the finances of Aoki-fun, a feudal clan in the area. Yoshio was known as a bright boy of strong physical health and a warm heart. He liked such sports as tennis and boat racing.

After receiving his education through high school in Okayama, Nishina entered the College of Engineering at the University of Tokyo, where he majored in electrical engineering. In 1918 Nishina graduated as valedictorian, for which he received the Taisho emperor's celebrated silver watch. Having been stimulated by reading Einstein and others, Nishina went to the graduate school of the university, where he majored in physics. From 1918 to 1920 Nishina attended lectures by Hantaro Nagaoka, known for his Saturnian atomic model, and he became a Nagaoka disciple. In 1918 Nishina became a research associate at the Institute of Physical and Chemical Research (Riken), which had been established in 1917 with the financial support of the Japanese government and business interests. The institute sent him abroad (to England, Germany, Denmark) for advanced study from 1921 to 1928.

After completing the Klein-Nishina formula in Copenhagen, Nishina returned to Japan at the end of 1928 and started to work at Riken again. Nishina was invited by Kyoto University to deliver special lectures on quantum mechanics in May 1931. His lectures, which were based on Werner Heisenberg's book *Die physikalischen Prinzipien der Quantentheorie* (1930), were attended with great interest by young physics students, including Hideki Yukawa and Shinitiro Tomonaga (Nobel Prize winners in 1949 and 1965), Shoichi Sakata, and Minoru Kobayashi. From 1931 Nishina managed his own laboratory at Riken, Nishina Laboratory, which became the most important center for theoretical and experimental nuclear physics in Japan before World War II. The first generation of the Elementary Particle Theory Group of Japan was trained by Nishina.

During and after World War II Nishina played an important role as science administrator rather than research physicist. He became the president of Riken in 1946 and the vice chairperson of the Japan Science Council in 1949. Nishina was hospitalized with liver cancer just before his sixtieth birthday, and he died the following year. He was awarded the Order of Cultural Merit of Japan in 1946. Nishina had married Mie in 1929; they had two sons.

The development of physics based on quantum mechanics in Japan was greatly enhanced by what Nishina had learned in Europe. From the fall of 1921 Nishina studied experimental physics for about one year under Lord Rutherford at the Cavendish Laboratory at Cambridge University. His topic was experimental analysis on the X rays scattered by electrons. From the winter of 1922 to the spring of 1923 Nishina studied theoretical physics by attending lectures by Max Born and David Hilbert at Göttingen University. From the spring of 1923 to the fall of 1928 he remained mostly in Copenhagen. These years were a time of significant development in quantum mechanics. Nishina worked at the Institute for Theoretical Physics under Niels Bohr, around whom gathered such physicists as Hendrik Kramers, Werner Heisenberg, Wolfgang Pauli, Pascual Jordan, Oskar Klein, and Paul Dirac.

While at the Bohr Institute, Nishina published his first paper, which aimed to give experimental evidence for Bohr's atomic theory. Nishina was very interested in quantitative chemical analysis by means of X-ray spectra. He brought this approach back to Japan with him. In 1927 he published a paper in *Zeitschrift für Physik* with two Japanese chemists, Shinichi Aoyama and Kenji Kimura, who were also in Copenhagen. From Copenhagen Nishina went to Paris in the summer of 1927, and then visited Wolfgang Pauli at Hamburg University, where he met Isidor Rabi, an American physicist born in Austria. They worked together and became very good friends.

In early 1928 Nishina returned to Copenhagen and worked with Oskar Klein. As a result of their cooperation, the Klein-Nishina formula was completed in October of the same year, before Nishina's return to Japan. In 1923 the quantum (particle) nature of X rays was discovered by Arthur Compton. Nishina had once made an experimental approach to this phenomena at the Cavendish Laboratory. The relation among the increased wavelength of the scattered X rays, the energy of recoiled electrons, and the scattering angle was accounted for by the quantum nature. In 1928 Nishina and Klein calculated the cross section and intensity of the Compton scattered radiation by the use of Dirac's new relativistic quantum mechanics of electrons. They succeeded in a complicated calculation by doing this separately and checking it together. (Nishina also brought this method of calculation with a team back to Japan.)

Nishina and Klein searched for the solution of Dirac's wave equation in the case of a free electron (initially at rest) in the field of a plane electromagnetic wave. For the intensity I of the Compton scattered radiation at a distance r and in a direction making an angle $\textcircled{H}$ with the normal to the primary wave, they obtained the following expression:

$$I = I_o \frac{e^4}{m^2c^4\nu^2} \frac{sin^2\zeta}{(1 + \alpha(1 - \cos\textcircled{H}))^3} \left(1 + \alpha^2 \frac{(1 - \cos\textcircled{H})^2}{2\sin^2\zeta(1 + \alpha(1 - \cos\textcircled{H}))}\right),$$

where ζ is the angle between the observed direction and electric vector in the primary wave

$$\alpha = \frac{h\nu}{mc^2}.$$

Their result differed from the earlier relativistic quantum mechanics of Dirac and Gordon by the order α^2, while the difference between the quantum theory and classical theory had been on the order of α. The wavelength of cosmic rays that had been estimated by Dirac-Gordon called for a modification. The new result was brought to the attention of the Russian physicist Dmitri Skobelzyn, who began a scientific correspondence with Nishina.

As a continuing part of their work, Nishina and Klein calculated the polarization of Compton scattered radiation on the Dirac theory with the help of a young Danish physics student, Christian Möller. Their results were published in 1929. Pauli published results of similar work, that is, the calculation of the intensity of the scattered radiation in the case of a "moving" electron, in 1933. The Klein-Nishina formula played an important role in discussions of the applicable limits of quantum mechanics to studies of cosmic rays and nuclear physics.

In late 1928 Nishina returned to Japan with a number of useful experiences, including his close observation of the process of development in quantum mechanics and his direct participation in this development. He was particularly impressed by the productive and open-minded atmosphere among various physicists at the Bohr Institute. This so-called "Copenhagen spirit" was brought back to Japan with Nishina. One his brightest followers, Hideki Yukawa, described this "spirit" in his 1958 autobiography:

> If I were asked to describe the spirit of Copenhagen, I would not be able to do so in a few words. However, it is certain that it had much in common with the spirit of generosity. Having been liberally educated, I was especially attracted by that, but I was also attracted by Dr. Nishina himself. I could talk to him easily, although I was usually very quiet. Perhaps I recognized

in Nishina the kindly father figure that I could not find in my own father. Whatever it was, my solitary mind, or my closed mind, it began to open in the presence of Dr. Nishina (*Tabibito, The Traveler* [Singapore, 1982], 177).

Through his long experiences in Europe, Nishina was convinced that an intimate contact between theory and experimentation was necessary to carry out creative research in physics. This is the approach followed by the research program on nuclear physics at Nishina Laboratory from its birth in 1931. In the field of experimentation, Ryokichi Sagane, the fifth son of Hantaro Nagaoka, and Masa Takeuchi, new graduates from the University of Tokyo, began to construct such instruments as Geiger-Müller counters and Wilson cloud chambers. By means of Geiger-Müller counters, measurements of cosmic rays, in Shimizu tunnel for example, were carried out by members of the experimental physicists group. Investigations of tracks of cosmic rays were made by the use of a large-scale cloud chamber (40 centimeters in diameter placed in a uniform magnetic field 10,000 gauss in intensity). They succeeded in distinguishing between proton tracks and those of meson, which had been predicted by Hideki Yukawa in 1935. The paper by Nishina, Takeuchi, and Torao Ichimiya was published right after the famous one by Carl Anderson and Seth H. Neddermeyer in 1937.

In the field of theory, Shinitiro Tomonaga and Shoichi Sakata, graduates of Kyoto University, began to calculate the process of positron-electron pair creation by the use of Dirac's 1933 electron theory. In 1934 Minoru Kobayashi, a classmate of Sakata's (who went to Osaka to become Hideki Yukawa's assistant) and Hidehiko Tamaki, a new graduate from the University of Tokyo, joined this group. In the summer of 1935 in Karuizawa (a famous summer resort in Japan) they worked together to translate the newly published second edition of Dirac's book, *The Principles of Quantum Mechanics*, into Japanese. Their translation, published in 1936, played an important role among young physicists and students. At the recommendation of Nishina, Tomonaga was sent from Riken to Germany to work under Werner Heisenberg at Leipzig University from 1937 to 1939. Tomonaga later developed his famous "super-many-time" theory.

The first cyclotron in Japan was constructed by members of Nishina Laboratory between 1935 and 1937. For this construction Riken collected donations from Japanese business circles totaling about $3 million between 1936 and 1937. The Mitsui-funded foundation Mitsui Hōonkai, established in 1933, offered about $150,000 for the buildings. The main part of the machine was contributed by the Japan Wireless Telegraph Company, established with government funds in 1925. The running costs were covered by an endowment of $100,000 from the Tokyo Electric Light Company (Toshiba).

Nishina's followers noticed that his attitude toward journalists and the general public changed rapidly around this time. In his public lectures he tried to emphasize how studies in experimental nuclear physics are useful for people's daily lives. He also wrote a number of articles in popular science journals. These activities, Nishina thought, were crucial to the fundraising effort.

Nishina considered the first small cyclotron to be preliminary to a larger one like Ernest Lawrence's cyclotron at Berkeley, California. From 1938 Ryokichi Sagane and others at the Nishina Laboratory began to construct a sixty-inch cyclotron with a two-hundred-ton magnet. The main parts of this cyclotron were obtained from the United States with Lawrence's help. Construction of the larger cyclotron was more difficult than the smaller one. Sagane and others visited Lawrence to receive his technical advice on details. Their efforts are evident in their correspondence with Lawrence (carton no. 9, file no. 38, Bancroft Library, University of California, Berkeley). But despite their efforts, the cyclotron remained uncompleted and was destroyed by the American military, owing to a misunderstanding, in 1945. This experience helped Nishina to recognize the deep technological gap between Japan and the U.S.

Nishina was never appointed professor at national universities such as the University of Tokyo and Kyoto University. This was due to his having graduated from a college of "engineering" rather than "science." It was through the Institute of Physical and Chemical Research that Nishina established himself as the founder of nuclear physics in Japan. Because of Riken, Nishina was allowed to spend more years abroad than professors at national universities, who used to return after only two or three years. As part of Riken, the Nishina Laboratory rapidly increased its space, personnel, and budget from 1931 to the end of World War II. Nishina had the great fortune of developing such genius followers as the Nobelists Hideki Yukawa and Shinitiro Tomonaga. Without Nishina's return from Europe with the principles of quantum mechanics, these two physicists might never have developed their potentials to the fullest.

BIBLIOGRAPHY

I. ORIGINAL WORKS. Nishina's principal papers include "Röntgenspectroskopie. Über die Absorptionsspektren in der *L*-Serie der Element La(57) bis Hf(72)," in *Zeitschrift für Physik,* **18** (1923), 207–211, written with D. Coster and S. Werner; "On the L-absorption Spectra of the Elements from Sn(50) to W(74) and Their Relation to the Atomic Constitution," in *Philosophical Magazine,* **49** (1925), 521–537; "Die Abhängigkeit der Röntgenabsorptionsspekren von der chemischen Bindung," in *Zeitschrift für Physik,* **44** (1927), 810–833, written with S. Aoyama and K. Kimura; "Über die Streuung von Strahlung durch freie Elektonen nach der neuen relativistischen Quantendynamik von Dirac," *ibid.,* **52** (1929), 853–868, written with O. Klein; "Die Polarisation der Comptonstreuung nach der Diracschen Theorie des Elektrons," *ibid.,* 869–877; "A Note on the Interaction of the Neutron and the Proton," in *Scientific Papers of the Institute of Physical and Chemical Research,* **30** (1936), 61–69, written with S. Tomonaga and H. Tamaki; "On the Nature of Cosmic-Ray Particles," in *Physical Review,* **52** (1937), 1198–1199, written with M. Takeuchi and T. Ichimiya.

The Nishina Kinen Zaiden owns Nishina's books and manuscripts and has published *George Hevesy–Y. Nishina, Correspondence 1928–1949* (Tokyo, 1983). They are planning to publish a biography of Nishina. H. Tamaki and other members of the Zaidan have been reporting results of their research to the History of Physics Section at the annual meetings of the Physical Society of Japan. The address of the Zaidan is 2-28-45 Motokomagome, Bunkyoku, Tokyo 113, Japan.

II. SECONDARY LITERATURE. *Nishina Yoshio denki to kaisō,* S. Tomonaga and H. Tamaki, eds., (Tokyo, 1952) includes an outline of Nishina's life and work by Fumio Yamazaki, Nishina's essays from 1949 and 1950, and reminiscences by H. Yukawa, S. Tomonaga, H. Tamaki, S. Sakata, and others. Cosmic ray studies at the Nishina Laboratory are discussed in M. Takeuchi, Yataro Sekido, and Harry Elliot, eds., *Early History of Cosmic Ray Studies* (Dordrecht and Boston, 1985). The academic and social backgrounds of physics in Japan are discussed in Nakayama Shigeru, David L. Swain, and Yagi Eri, eds., *Science and Society in Modern Japan* (Cambridge, Mass., 1974) and the Physical Society of Japan, ed., *Nihon no Butsurigakushi* ("One Hundred Years of Physics in Japan"), 2 vols. (Tokyo, 1978).

ERI YAGI

NOBLE, GLADWYN KINGSLEY (*b.* Yonkers, New York, 20 September 1894; *d.* Englewood, New Jersey, 9 December 1940), *herpetology, ethology, experimental biology.*

Noble's father, Gilbert Clifford Noble, was one of the founders of the Barnes and Noble bookstore and publishing house, which, however, experienced serious reverses while Noble was in college. His mother, Elizabeth Adams, was a member of the first graduating class at Vassar. G.K. (as he was called) was their second son (of seven children).

After graduating from Yonkers High School, Noble entered Harvard, majoring in zoology. He received his A.B. in 1916 and his A.M. in 1918. He spent much of his time as student at the Museum of Comparative Zoology, working as assistant to Thomas Barbour, who greatly influenced him. In the summers from 1914 to 1916 he made field expeditions (Guadeloupe, Newfoundland, Peru) and learned under Barbour's guidance how to publish on his collections and observations. At first mostly interested in birds, Noble gradually moved to reptiles and amphibians through Barbour's influence. After one year's service in the U.S. Navy in 1918 and 1919, he entered Columbia University, selecting William K. Gregory as his supervisor. At the same time he accepted a position as assistant curator of herpetology at the American Museum of Natural History. In 1921 he married Ruth Crosby; they had two sons.

Noble's thorough training in comparative anatomy under Gregory enabled him in his dissertation to place the classification of frogs and toads on a much more secure foundation. That dissertation, "Phylogeny of the Salientia" (1922) was soon recognized as a major contribution to herpetology. The classification was mainly based on such anatomical characters as the vertebral articulation and the configuration of the thigh muscles, instead of the more superficial characters previously used.

Noble devoted the years after he received the Ph.D. (1922) to the intense study of the amphibians; this resulted in the great text *The Biology of the Amphibia* (1931), which had an enormous impact on the field and was for many decades the "bible" of herpetologists. It was perhaps the first book in any branch of biology to be a successful synthesis of natural history and experimental biology. The volume documents not only Noble's very broad competence, ranging from anatomy and physiology to ontogeny, life history, behavior, ecology, and classification, but also his mastery of the literature and in particular his familiarity with the foreign-language literature (French and German). At a time when frogs and salamanders were increasingly used in experimental embryology and other fields of laboratory biology, such a synthesis was particularly useful.

In a series of studies in the 1920's and 1930's, Noble tested the effect of thyroid, pituitary, and gonadal hormones on development and particularly on metamorphosis in various amphibians and reptiles; he also investigated the effect of hormones on life history, particularly reproduction.

Inevitably the study of hormonal effects on behavior led to a study of behavior per se and to the neural control of behavior. The study of behavior in the field and in the laboratory became Noble's dominant interest in the last decade of his life. Social dominance, peck order, sexual selection, and many other aspects of behavior were studied experimentally in organisms of all classes of vertebrates from fishes to mammals. Noble pioneered in conducting experiments with wild individuals in free-living populations. How would a male flicker react to his female if the male characters were painted on the female? How would a territory-holding male act if the dummy of a conspecific male or female were introduced into the territory? How would the behavior of a free-living immature male be changed if it was injected with male hormone?

In the case of fixed behavior patterns Noble was very much interested in whether he could locate the control center in a defined area in the brain. His experimental researches were so successful that he was able to persuade the administration to build for him a two-story department of experimental biology as part of the American Museum, a great innovation as far as any natural history museum is concerned. He became curator of this department in 1928, in part as a reward for having planned and supervised the installation of two remarkably innovative museum exhibits, the Hall of Living Reptiles and the Hall of Animal Behavior, in which the latest findings of science were made available to the public. At the same time Noble massively enlarged the museum's collections of reptiles and amphibians.

Noble was dynamic, tending to express his convictions forcefully, and thus was not always easy to deal with. His list of achievements in less than twenty years of professional life provides some indication of his almost compulsive drive. Yet his achievements were combined with such enthusiasm that Noble was able to inspire many amateurs to join him in research projects; there are thirty-seven coauthors in the list of his publications. During the depression of the 1930's Noble succeeded in putting an "army" of W.P.A. workers to work card indexing the literature, translating important papers from the foreign literature, and setting up a voluminous information storage system. In the midst of working on numerous unfinished researches and of planning several new projects, Noble, otherwise in splendid health, succumbed within forty-eight hours to a strep throat infection, at age forty-six.

BIBLIOGRAPHY

I. ORIGINAL WORKS. Noble wrote 135 papers on reptiles and amphibians, and about 50 papers on anatomy, behavior, and experimental biology. Among his works are "The Phylogeny of the Salientia," in *Bulletin of the American Museum of Natural History*, **46** (1922), 1–87, with 23 plates; "Contributions to the Herpetology of the Belgian Congo," in *Bulletin of the American Museum of Natural History*, **49** (1923–1924), 147–347; and *The Biology of the Amphibia* (New York, 1931).

II. SECONDARY LITERATURE. Lester R. Aronson, "The Case of *The Case of the Midwife Toad*," in *Behavior Genetics*, **5** (1975), 115–125 [Noble is widely known as the discoverer of one of Paul Kammerer's frauds; Aronson corrects many of the errors and insinuations in Arthur Koestler's book *The Case of the Midwife Toad*]; William K. Gregory, "Gladwyn Kingsley Noble," in American Philosophical Society, *Year Book 1941* (1942), 393–397; Walter L. Necker, "Gladwyn Kingsley Noble, 1894–1940: A Herpetological Bibliography," in *Herpetologica*, **2**, no. 2 (1940), 47–55; and Ruth Crosby Noble, *The Nature of the Beast* (Garden City, N.Y., 1945), which includes detailed accounts of Noble's behavioral studies and a bibliography of 33 of his behavioral writings.

ERNST MAYR

NOVIKOV, PETR SERGEEVICH (*b*. Moscow, Russia, 15 August 1901; *d*. Moscow, 9 January 1975), *mathematics*.

Novikov was the son of Sergei Novikov, a merchant in Moscow, and his wife Alexandra. In September 1919 the young Novikov entered the physics and mathematics department of Moscow University. After serving in the Red Army between March 1920 and July 1922, he returned to the university and was graduated in 1925. During the next four years he was a postgraduate student under Nikolai N. Luzin. Subsequently Novikov taught mathematics at the Moscow Chemical Technological Institute, and in 1934 he was invited to join the newly organized Steklov Mathematical Institute. He worked there in the department of real function theory until 1957, when he organized the department of mathematical logic and became its head. In 1935 Novikov received the doctorate in mathematics, and four years later he became a full professor. In 1953 he was elected a corresponding member, and in 1960 a full member, of the Soviet Academy of Sciences.

In 1935 Novikov married Ludmila Vsevolodovna Keldysh, a well-known mathematician specializing in topology. They had five children. One of their sons, Sergei Petrovich, is president of the Moscow Mathematical Society.

While still a student, Novikov began to work on descriptive set theory. Very soon he became one of the most active members of Luzin's school of descriptive set theory. In his paper "Sur les fonctions implicites mesurables'' (1931) Novikov investigated the problem of whether the equations $f_i(\bar{x}, \bar{y}) = 0$ and $(1 \leq i \leq q)$ with Borel functions f_i can implicitly define a Borel function $\bar{y} = f(\bar{x})$. He discovered a new method that is referred to as the index comparison principle. Using a generalization of this method, he proved, in his 1935 paper, that for the second projective class of sets the following two separability propositions hold: (1) any two CA_2-sets are separable by B_2-sets if they are disjoint; (2) there exist two disjoint A_2-sets that are nonseparable by B_2-sets. These propositions unexpectedly turned out to be dual to the known laws for the first projective class.

In his 1938 paper on mathematical physics, Novikov proved that any two solids having the same constant density must coincide if they both are star-shaped relative to a common point and have the same external gravitational potential. This pioneering result became the basis of many studies by other authors.

In the late 1930's Novikov began to study mathematical logic and the theory of algorithms. In the paper "On the Consistency of Certain Logical Calculus" (1943), he developed a method of providing the consistency based on a notion of "regularity." He also, in the same paper, proved the consistency for the formal arithmetic with recursive definitions using this method. In 1951 Novikov proved the consistency of two propositions in the Gödel system Σ of axiomatic set theory: (1) there exists a CA-set without perfect subsets; and (2) there exists a B_2-set that is not Lebesque-measurable. This proof was based on Gödel's method published in 1940.

The following word problem had been proposed by Max Dehn in 1912: Let a group G be defined by a finite number of generators and defining relations. For an arbitrary word W in the generators of G, decide in a finite number of steps whether or not W defines the identity element of G.

In 1952 Novikov constructed a finitely defined group H with an unsolvable word problem, that is, a group with no algorithm to solve the word problem for H. This result was first announced in his 1952 paper "Ob algoritmicheskoi nerazreshimosti problemy tozhdestva" ("On the Algorithmic Unsolvability of the Word Problem"). The complete proof was published three years later. In 1957 William W. Boone gave another example of a group with an unsolvable word problem, and therefore this result is called the Novikov-Boone theorem. Important corollaries derived from this theorem have suggested that there are many unsolvable algorithmic problems in fundamental branches of classical mathematics.

Novikov received the Lenin Prize for this significant achievement in 1957.

Novikov's last important result, proved jointly with S. I. Adian, was a negative solution of the Burnside problem of periodic groups, proposed in 1902. In 1959 Novikov announced the existence of infinite, finitely generated periodic groups of any given exponent $n \geq 72$. The complete proof of the result for odd exponents $n \geq 4,381$ was published in a joint article in 1968. In my book, *The Burnside Problem and Identities in Groups* (1979), there is an exposition of the Novikov-Adian method for any odd exponent $n \geq 665$ and many applications.

The exceptional influence of Novikov on the advancement of mathematics was also due to his lectures at Moscow University and at the Moscow State Teachers Training Institute, where he chaired the department of analysis from 1944 to 1972. He founded a large school in mathematical logic and its applications in the USSR; his book *Elements of Mathematical Logic* (1959) was the first original textbook on the subject in the country. His second book, *Constructive Mathematical Logic from the Point of View of Classical Logic* (1977), has exerted a considerable influence on the development of proof theory.

Novikov retired from the State Teachers Training Institute in 1972 and from the Steklov Mathematical Institute in 1973. He was ill for the last three years of his life.

BIBLIOGRAPHY

I. Original Works. Novikov's works, up to 1968, are listed in *Uspekhi matematicheskikh nauk*, **26**, no. 5 (1971), 239–241. The most important works are "Sur les fonctions implicites mesurables," in *Fundamenta Mathematicae*, **17** (1931), 8–25; "Sur la separabilité des ensembles projectifs du seconde classe," *ibid.*, **25** (1935), 459–466; "Ob edinstvennosti obratnoi zadachi potentsiala" ("On the Uniqueness of the Inverse Problem of Potential Theory), in *Doklady Akademii nauk*, **18** (1938), 165–168; "On the Consistency of Certain Logical Calculus," in *Matematicheskii sbornik (Recueil mathématique)*, n.s., **12** (1943), 231–261; "O neprotivorechivosti nekotorych polozhenii deskriptivnoi teorii mnozhestv," in *Trudy Matematicheskoro instituta imeni V. A. Steklova*, **38** (1951), 279–316, trans. by Elliott Mendelson as "On the Consistency of Some Propositions of the Descriptive Theory of Sets," in *American Mathematical Society Translations*, ser. 2, **29** (1963), 51–89; "Ob algoritmicheskoi nerazreshimosti problemy tozhdestva" ("On the Algorithmic Unsolvability of the Word Problem"), in *Doklady Akademii nauk*, **85**, no. 4 (1952), 709–712; "Ob algoritmicheskoi nerazreshimosti problemy tozhdestva slov v teorii grupp," in *Trudy*

Matematicheskogo instituta imeni V. A. Steklova, **44** (1955), 1–144, trans. by K. A. Hirsch as "On the Algorithmic Unsolvability of the Word Problem in Group Theory," in *American Mathematical Society Translations,* ser. 2, **9** (1958), 1–122; "O periodicheskikh gruppakh," in *Doklady Akademii nauk,* **127,** no. 4 (1959), 749–752, trans. by J. M. Weinstein as "On Periodic Groups," in *American Mathematical Society Translations,* ser. 2, **45** (1965), 19–22; *Elementy matematicheskoi logiki* (Moscow, 1959), trans. by Leo F. Boron as *Elements of Mathematical Logic* (Edinburgh, 1964); "O bezkonechnykh periodicheskikh gruppach" ("On Infinite Periodic Groups"), in *Izvestiia Akademii nauk, seriia matematicheskaia,* **32,** nos. 1–3 (1968), 212–244, 251–254, 709–731, with S. I. Adian; *Constructivnaia matematicheskāia logika s tochki zreniia classicheskoi* ("Constructive Mathematical Logic from the Point of View of Classical Logic"), F. A. Kabakov and B. A. Kushner, eds., preface by S. I. Adian (Moscow, 1977); and *Izbrannye trudy* ("Selected Works"; Moscow, 1979).

II. Secondary Literature. S. I. Adian, *The Burnside Problem and Identities in Groups,* John Lennox and James Wiegold, trans. (Berlin and New York, 1979); Kurt Gödel, *The Consistency of the Axiom of Choice and of the Generalized Continuum-Hypothesis with the Axioms of Set Theory,* Annals of Mathematics Studies, no. 3 (1940). See also "Petr Sergeevich Novikov," in *Uspekhi matematidheskikh nauk,* **26,** no. 5 (1971), 231–241; and *Matematicheskaia logika, teoriia algoritmov i teoriia mnozhestv* ("Mathematical Logic, the Theory of Algorithms and Set Theory"), S. I. Adian, ed., in *Trudy Matematicheskogo instituta imeni V. A. Steklova,* **133** (1973), 5–32.

S. I. Adian

ONSAGER, LARS (*b.* Oslo, Norway, 27 November 1903; *d.* Coral Gables, Florida, 5 October 1976), *chemistry, physics.*

In 1968, when the news arrived that Lars Onsager had been awarded the Nobel Prize, the natural question was, "In physics or in chemistry?" Was it for his solution of the two-dimensional Ising model[1]? Was it for explaining the electrical conductivity of ice[2]? Was it for flux quantization in superconductors[3]? Was it for his theory of electrolytes[4]? As it happened, it was for what was called the Onsager Reciprocal Relations, developed in two papers published in *Physical Review* in 1931[6], and it was in chemistry.

Other major research for which Onsager is known includes the formula for the dielectric constant of polar liquids[7], isotope separation by thermal diffusion[8], the energy spectrum of turbulence[9], the statistical-mechanical description of vortices in two dimensions (negative absolute temperatures when they roll up)[5], quantization of the circulation of vortices in superfluid helium[10], an explanation of the Wien effect[11], electron-ion recombination statistics[12], interpretation of the De Haas-Van Alphen effect[13], the statistical interpretation of the dissipation function[14], and a new definition of the Bose-Einstein condensation for interacting particles applicable to the lambda-point transition to superfluidity of liquid helium[15].

Life. The son of Erling Onsager, a barrister, and of Ingrid Kirkeby Onsager, Lars was brought up in Oslo and graduated from secondary school there. He then studied chemical engineering at the Norges Tekniske Hogskole at Trondheim. While there, he worked through most of the problems in Whittaker and Watson's *Modern Analysis*[16]—a difficult mathematics book with very challenging problems. At age twenty he discovered a correction to the just-published Debye-Hückel theory of electrolytes. In 1925, Onsager traveled to Zurich and told Debye about it in person. Debye took him on as a research assistant at the Eidgenössische Technische Hochschule, where he worked from 1926 to 1928. Years later, he told proudly of rowing in crew races on the Zürchersee.

In 1928 Onsager accepted a position as teaching associate in the chemistry department at Johns Hopkins University. His assignment was freshman chemistry. The students, however, complained that what he said in class was over their heads. Indeed, those who have heard Onsager lecture would agree that Onsager and freshmen were a mismatch. The challenges in his lectures, even to the expert, were formidable. In mathematical derivations, intermediate steps would be omitted. Onsager didn't need them and preferred to overestimate his audience's ability rather than to assume his listeners were less intelligent than he. The job ended after one term. During that spring he formulated the prize-winning Reciprocal Relations.

Later that same year Onsager moved to Brown University as an instructor in the chemistry department, but with no undergraduate teaching duties. He taught the graduate course in statistical mechanics and began a collaboration with Raymond M. Fuoss, a graduate student who made measurements on electrolytes, that was to last for over thirty years. During his first year in Providence, Onsager submitted an abstract (in Norwegian) for a meeting of the Scandinavian Physical Society, on simultaneous irreversible processes, that announced the Reciprocal Relations.

A couple of years later Onsager sent Debye a manuscript for publication in *Physikalische Zeit-*

schrift, of which Debye was an editor. It was another correction to a Debye formula, the one for the dielectric constant of a substance whose molecules have a permanent electric dipole moment. This time Debye did not yield so readily, and the "Onsager formula" was not published until 1936, when J. G. Kirkwood persuaded Onsager to rewrite the paper in English and send it to the *Journal of the American Chemical Society*[7].

Another line of research that began during Onsager's five years at Brown was thermal diffusion as a means of isotope separation. The Soret effect—a solution placed in a temperature gradient develops a concentration gradient—had been discovered in the nineteenth century. This is the kind of "coupled-flows" situation that the Reciprocal Relations are about. But it is also a practical application of abstract ideas in the kinetic theory of gases to the separation of an isotopic gas mixture. The influence of five years as a chemical engineering student appeared to be showing. Later, during World War II, separating the isotopes of uranium became a crucial step in the production of atomic-bomb material.

In 1933 Brown University, financially strapped, did not renew Onsager's appointment. The distinguished electrochemist Herbert Harned wanted to bring him to Yale, which offered him a Sterling Fellowship, a prestigious postdoctoral appointment that could be held without teaching duties. Thus began a career at Yale that was to last until his retirement. The summer before Yale he spent in Europe. He had been corresponding about questions in electrochemistry with Hans Falkenhagen, then at the University of Cologne, and they spent some weeks together. During this time Onsager met Falkenhagen's sister-in-law, Margarethe Arledter. They were married on 7 September 1933, before Onsager returned to the United States. They had three sons and a daughter.

Shortly after Onsager's arrival in New Haven, there was an administrative snag. His appointment was to a postdoctoral fellowship, but he had no doctorate. Actually, he had submitted a version of the Reciprocal Relations to his alma mater, the Norges Tekniske Hogskole in Trondheim, as a doctoral dissertation, but apparently it had not been in the proper form. Harned hit on the obvious solution: Yale could award Onsager a Ph.D. Course requirements could be waived, but a dissertation was necessary. Onsager, the story goes, pulled a stack of papers out of a file, smiled, and asked, "Will this do?" The work, "Solutions of the Mathieu Equation of Period 4π and Certain Related Functions," looked more like a mathematics than a chemistry disser-

tation. In fact, it seemed to be built on some of the densest parts of Whittaker and Watson. The local expert on that branch of mathematics, Einar Hille of the mathematics department, read it and suggested a Ph.D. in mathematics.

Apparently the chemists insisted on awarding the Ph.D. themselves. This was appropriate, since the problem had arisen in the chemical context of electrolytes[4] as well as of ionized gases[12], where one must deal with Brownian motion. In working out the theory of random thermal motion of clusters of ions, Onsager obtained the Mathieu equation, which he knew from Whittaker and Watson. He used the results in the 1938 paper "Initial Recombination of Ions." He never published the dissertation.

Onsager's thirty-nine years at Yale included twenty-seven years as the J. Willard Gibbs professor of theoretical chemistry. Gibbs had been America's first great theoretical physicist. He spent his working life as professor at Yale and is generally considered the father of statistical mechanics. That the Gibbs chair should be held by Onsager, the great twentieth-century practitioner of statistical mechanics, seems appropriate indeed. The appointment to that professorship followed what many consider Onsager's spectacular achievement: the solution of the two-dimensional Ising model. Onsager also held guest professorships at other universities. The sabbatical year 1951 to 1952 was spent as Fulbright professor at Cambridge University. His host was David Shoenberg, director of the Royal Society Mond Laboratory, the part of the Cavendish Laboratory dedicated to low-temperature physics. Onsager had been spending time with the low-temperature physicists at Yale, and in 1949 he had announced the quantization of hydrodynamic circulation in liquid helium. Shoenberg's experimental research was on the De Haas-Van Alphen effect, the oscillations of magnetic susceptibility as magnetic field is varied. He knew that Onsager had been thinking about electrons in metals. Those thoughts culminated in a quantitative interpretation of the "susceptibility oscillations" in terms of the dimensions of the Fermi surface of the metal. Through a mixture of friendship, gamesmanship, and nagging, Shoenberg persuaded Onsager to write it down for publication shortly before leaving England—in three pages[13].

Other visiting professorships came in 1961, at the then very new La Jolla campus of the University of California at San Diego; in the years 1967 to 1968, at the Rockefeller University in New York; and in 1968, at Göttingen. During the spring of 1970,

Onsager was Lorentz professor at the University of Leiden.

The 1960's saw the development of a theory of proton motion in ice. Threads from earlier work came together: conduction in electrolytes; dielectric properties; semiconductors; lattice combinatorics. Ice is a solid, so how can its protons move around? There is enough room in the crystal for molecular rotation, but a proton jump requires a defect. Onsager seized on Bjerrum faults[17]: "The positive ion moves by donating a proton, the negative by stealing one." Ice doped with ions of an impurity becomes a protonic semiconductor.

In 1971 he turned 68, Yale's official retirement age. Onsager had seven honorary doctorates; he had been awarded the Rumford Medal of the American Academy of Arts and Sciences (1953); the Lorentz Medal of the Royal Netherlands Academy of Sciences (1958); the American Chemical Society's G. N. Lewis Medal (1962), J. G. Kirkwood Medal (1962), J. W. Gibbs Medal (1962), T. W. Richards Medal (1964), P. W. Debye Medal (1965); Yeshiva University's Belfer Award in Pure Science (1966); the President's National Medal of Science (1968); and the Nobel Prize in chemistry (1968). He had no intention of leaving New Haven. He had research grants and knew he could count on continued government research support, including a salary, past retirement. The chemistry department assured him an office in the Sterling Laboratory of Chemistry.

But Yale had a rule that an emeritus faculty member could not be principal investigator on a research grant. Onsager suggested that the rule be waived. The administration turned him down.

Onsager gave Yale several months to reconsider. He was too offended to enter into negotiations. When Yale did not change its position, he accepted an offer from the University of Miami's Center for Theoretical Studies as Distinguished University Professor. He took along the research grants, which allowed him a group of postdoctoral research fellows and a secretary. The four years in Coral Gables saw the flowering of a number of seeds started earlier. The work on proton movement in ice, begun a decade earlier, was a natural sequel to over four decades of work on conduction of electrolytes. Were there analogues to transport mechanisms in membranes? At the Conference on Physical Principles of Biological Membranes (1968), Onsager's "Possible Mechanisms of Ion Transit"[18] revealed his considerable knowledge of biology as well as his legendary command of organic chemistry. Later he became an associate of the Neurosciences Research Program and attended its meetings.

For Onsager's seventieth birthday the University of Miami Center for Theoretical Studies mounted a symposium of invited speakers, including many of his former students and postdoctoral fellows. His own contribution[27], "Life in the Early Days," is a speculative paper on the origins of life on earth.

Reciprocal Relations and Fluctuation Statistics. Why did the Nobel committee choose the Reciprocal Relations for the award of the Prize? It might well have been because of their enormous reach into such a great diversity of phenomena. Wherever there are coupled flows—of matter, of energy, of electricity—reciprocal relations arise. In the first of his two 1931 papers, Onsager chose heat conduction in an anisotropic crystal as his example: coupled heat flows. He may well have made this choice because it illustrated a difficulty in defining macroscopic variables of state in terms of which the entropy would turn out to be a quadratic form. He overcame the difficulty by choosing the x, y, and z coordinates of the "center of mass" of the heat as the variables of state. No one had discussed heat conduction in those terms before; measurements are made in steady-state situations. Onsager needed a description of an irreversible process in terms of the relaxation of a nonequilibrium state to an equilibrium state. To define the rate constants (kinetic coefficients), he assumed a linear relationship between the relaxation rate and the departure from equilibrium. For small departures, linearity would be assured. The trick was in measuring the departure from equilibrium. Onsager's "α-type" variables were a suitable measure of "how far away from equilibrium" a system was. Having the entropy function quadratic in the α's made possible a very general definition of "thermodynamic forces" tending toward equilibrium: the derivatives of the entropy function with respect to the α's. If the relation between the α's and their time derivatives is linear, then the relation between the thermodynamic forces and the corresponding "fluxes" (the $d\alpha/dt$'s, also called J's) is automatically linear. The coefficients in those linear relationships—the kinetic coefficients—are what the experimenter measures. They form a square matrix. Onsager's theorem is that the matrix is symmetric.

In his Nobel address[17] Onsager tells how his proof was born. He had been working on electrical conduction in electrolytes. The flows of the different species of ion interact because of the Coulomb forces between ions. The flow rates of the different ions (the fluxes) are linearly related to the gradients of their chemical potentials (the forces). The coefficients (he calls them L_{ij}) are essentially conductivities.

The coefficient L_{11} is the conductivity of ion species 1. It relates the current density of those ions to their chemical potential gradient, essentially a field. Similarly, L_{22} is the conductivity of ion species 2. The coefficient L_{12} measures how much a concentration gradient of species 2 affects the current of species 1, and L_{21} measures how much a concentration gradient of species 1 affects the current of species 2. According to Onsager's theorem, those two cross-coefficients have to be equal: $L_{12} = L_{21}$.

Onsager called the reciprocal of the L_{ij} matrix the R_{ij} matrix. It is essentially a matrix of resistivity coefficients. The quadratic form in the fluxes $\Sigma R_{ij} J_i J_j$ is called the dissipation function. It measures the rate at which entropy is produced in the system and tells how quickly free energy is degraded by the irreversible flows. Helmholtz had defined an analogous dissipation function in the nineteenth century, as had Rayleigh and Kelvin. They had recognized that for stationary flow—the steady state—the dissipation function is a minimum. Onsager's insight was the recognition that this "principle of least dissipation" was equivalent to symmetry in past and future. He speaks of "the principle of detailed balancing," and in the proof of the theorem he very carefully defines and uses the somewhat more general "principle of microscopic reversibility."

One of Onsager's professors at Trondheim had been C. N. Riiber, who made optical-rotation measurements on sugar solutions and discovered that there were at least three modifications of galactose. Onsager writes:[17]

> The possibility that any one of these might transform into either of the others gave rise to a little problem in mathematics. In analyzing it I assumed, as any sensible chemist would, that in the state of equilibrium the reaction $1 \rightarrow 2$ would occur just as often as $2 \rightarrow 1$, etc., even though this is not a necessary condition for equilibrium, which might be maintained by a cyclic reaction—as far as the mathematics goes; the physics did not seem reasonable. Now if we look at the condition of detailed balancing from the thermodynamic point of view, it is quite analogous to the principle of least dissipation.

The term "cyclic reaction" means that the rate of $1 \rightarrow 2 \rightarrow 3 \rightarrow 1$ reactions is faster or slower than the rate of $1 \rightarrow 3 \rightarrow 2 \rightarrow 1$ reactions—exactly what detailed balancing forbids.

Reciprocal relations had been known well before Onsager's proof. Perhaps best known is the Kelvin relation between the Seebeck e.m.f.[19] and the Peltier heat[20]. The Seebeck e.m.f. is the voltage developed in a circuit containing two junctions between dissimilar metals kept at different temperatures. The Peltier heat is the heat per unit charge transported from one junction to the other when a current flows in the circuit. Kelvin had proved his "second relation" fifty years before Onsager, using what is today called a pseudo thermodynamic argument.

Onsager's proof rests on a postulate that connects irreversible behavior with fluctuation behavior: that the system does not remember its history, that it does not care whether it arrived at a given state as a result of a thermal fluctuation or as a result of an experimenter's interference. Formally stated, the regression of fluctuations (the expected path from a nonequilibrium state "back" to equilibrium) is that predicted by the linear relation between the forces and the fluxes. In the language of stochastic processes, the postulate is that the fluctuations are linear Markov processes characterized by the kinetic coefficients that describe the system's irreversible behavior.

Toward the end of the second 1931 paper, Onsager writes: "It is worth pointing out that the dissipation function has a direct statistical significance." The hint lay untouched for twenty years. The statistical interpretation of the entropy function given by Einstein in 1910: the probability of a system's being in a state α as a result of a spontaneous thermal fluctuation is proportional to exp $S(\alpha)/k$, where S is the entropy and k is Boltzmann's constant. But what of the probability of a particular time sequence of states, a particular "path" $\alpha(t)$? Onsager's Ph.D. student Stefan Machlup derived[14] a probability functional for fluctuations about the equilibrium state. It is the exponential of a time integral of the function

$$-(1/2k)[\Sigma R_{ij} d\alpha_i/dt \, d\alpha_j/dt + \Sigma L_{ij} X_i X_j],$$

where the "thermodynamic forces" X_i are the derivatives of the entropy function with respect to the α_i. The integral is defined by specifying the value of the α's at discrete points in time and choosing the minimum value consistent with those constraints. This is now called the Onsager-Machlup functional. The "slalom gate" definition of the integral is made complete by taking the minimum value of the integral subject to a constraint at each gate, that is, each specified point in time. The corresponding theorem in the frequency domain is known as the fluctuation-dissipation theorem.

Solution of the Ising Model. Ordered systems are most easily described in terms of a lattice model. The phase transition between the states of magnetic order and disorder (Curie point) in a crystal is typical of second-order phase transitions in general. The

Ising model is a primitive attempt to find a mathematical model that will show such an order-disorder transition. Lattice points (atoms) are in one of two possible states. The usual convention is to call the states "up" and "down," as for spin ½. Interactions are between nearest neighbors only. Though primitive, the hope was that the model would be mathematically tractable, that one could calculate thermodynamic functions for it. The real-life transition does occur at a well-defined temperature, called the critical temperature (T_c). In one dimension—a long chain of elementary magnets—the Ising model shows no phase transition; T_c is absolute zero.

In 1940, Wannier[21] used the idea of the transfer matrix for an approximate treatment of the two-dimensional Ising lattice, showing a nonzero T_c. In 1942 Onsager presented a contributed paper[22] announcing that he had calculated the partition function for the two-dimensional (square) Ising lattice exactly. It had a second-order transition.

Onsager writes[23]:

> It was a sort of investigation where you got a good lead, and certainly you had to pursue that; and before you reached the end of that lead, up opened another, and this was, if anything, even more fascinating. . . . It took a few months, though, to verify the guess, but it was doable. . . . Well, after I got out a paper on that Ising model, there was a young lady, Bruria Kaufman. . . . First of all, she insisted on working with me. . . . Secondly, she insisted on working on the Ising model. Now, that was the kind of a task that I would never want to impose on a student.

He continues[24]:

> Unable to talk her out of the idea, I suggested that she explore the structure of W as well as the effect of joining crystal ends on a torus with a twist, etc. She made good progress; but as she got her bearings she was more intrigued by the ubiquitous trigonometric relations and decided to look for a possible connection with spinor theory. Why not? . . . By the summer of 1946 she had a beautifully compact computation of the partition function, bypassing all tedious detail.

So the thermodynamic properties of the Ising model were solved for zero magnetic field. But what of the spontaneous magnetization? What followed in the next two years involves terms like spinor algebra, the Milne integral equation, the Wiener-Hopf technique, elliptic integrals, and finally the evaluation of Toeplitz (infinite) determinants. The result was that the spontaneous magnetization near T_c is proved to be proportional to $(T-T_c)^{1/8}$. The approximate theories had given an exponent ½;

the critical exponent ⅛ was novel indeed. Onsager announced that result at a conference at Cornell in the summer of 1948, and again during a discussion period at a conference of the Italian Physical Society held in March 1949 at Florence. It appeared in the printed "proceedings" of the conference[25], but he never published the calculation. C. N. Yang published the result in 1952[26].

The "critical exponent" ⅛ is quite close to experimental values for a number of real systems that have transitions of an essentially two-dimensional type. The three-dimensional Ising model has never been solved exactly. Thus Onsager's solution stands as a monument.

Style. His colleagues were fond of saying Onsager was thirty years ahead of his time. "Irreversible thermodynamics"—the heart of the 1931 reciprocal relations—became fashionable only in the 1960's. Critical exponents for phase transitions came in the late 1960's. Negative absolute temperatures, first discussed by Onsager in 1949[5], were not talked about until the invention of optical pumping and lasers[28].

Onsager published on the order of one journal article per year. A number of his discoveries were announced in the discussion periods at scientific meetings, sometimes cryptically; some he never tried to publish. For example, a complete manuscript exists of the band theory of electrons in metals, written just before the publication of the Bloch theory.

Onsager's graduate students, who were never numerous, tended to come from physics rather than chemistry. His interests were so wide that students were often in entirely different scientific areas. There was never a "group," and Onsager did not found a "school."

With students and colleagues Onsager generally talked about what he was working on at the time, always in very few words. Questions were welcome and were patiently answered. He preferred working things out himself to reading other people's solutions and urged students to do the same. His erudition was phenomenal, though occasionally exasperating. The low-temperature physicist C. T. Lane once said to him, "Lars, you don't know everything." Onsager answered, "But I'm learning."

NOTES

1. L. Onsager, "Crystal Statistics I. A Two-Dimensional Model with an Order-Disorder Transition," in *Physical Review*, **65** (1944), 117–149; Bruria Kaufman, "Crystal Statistics II. Partition Function Evaluated by Spinor Analysis," *ibid.*, **76** (1949), 1232–1243; Bruria Kaufman and Lars Onsager, "Crystal Statistics III. Short-Range Order in a Binary Ising

Lattice," *ibid.*, 1244–1252. See also Elliott W. Montroll, Renfrey B. Potts, and John C. Ward, "Correlations and Spontaneous Magnetization of the Two-Dimensional Ising Model," in *Journal of Mathematical Physics*, **4** (1962), 308–322.

2. L. Onsager and M. Dupuis, "Electrical Properties of Ice," in *Rendiconti S.I.F. "Enrico Fermi," corso* X, Varenna, *Electrolytes*, supp. to *Nuovo Cimento* (1960), 294–315; L. Onsager, "The Electrical Properties of Ice," in *Vortex*, **23** (1962), 138–141; L. Onsager and L. K. Runnels, "Mechanism for Self-diffusion in Ice," in *Proceedings of the National Academy of Sciences*, **50** (1963), 208–210; Lars Onsager, Mou-shan Chen, Jill C. Bonner, and J. F. Nagle, "Hopping of Ions in Ice," in *Journal of Chemical Physics*, **60** (1974), 405–419.

3. L. Onsager, "Magnetic Flux Through a Superconducting Ring," in *Physical Review Letters*, **7** (1961), 50.

4. L. Onsager, "Zur Theorie der Electrolyte I," in *Physikalische Zeitschrift*, **27** (1926), 388–392, and ". . . II," *ibid.*, **28** (1927), 277–298; L. Onsager and R. M. Fuoss, "Irreversible Processes in Electrolytes," in *Journal of Physical Chemistry*, **36** (1932), 2689–2778.

5. L. Onsager, "Statistical Hydrodynamics," in supp. to *Nuovo Cimento*, 9th ser., **6** (1949), 279–287.

6. L. Onsager, "Reciprocal Relations in Irreversible Processes I," in *Physical Review*, **37** (1931), 405–426, and ". . . II," *ibid.*, **38** (1931), 2265–2279.

7. L. Onsager, "Electric Moments of Molecules in Liquids," in *Journal of the American Chemical Society*, **58** (1936), 1486–1493.

8. W. H. Furry, R. Clark Jones, and L. Onsager, "On the Theory of Isotope Separation by Thermal Diffusion," in *Physical Review*, **55** (1939), 1083–1095; W. W. Watson, L. Onsager, and A. Zucker, "Apparatus for Isotope Separation by Thermal Diffusion," in *Review of Scientific Instruments*, **20** (1949), 924–927.

9. L. Onsager, "The Distribution of Energy in Turbulence" (abstract), in *Physical Review*, **68** (1945), 286. This was independently discovered by A. N. Komogorov, C.R. Acad. Sci. USSR, **30** (1941), 301–305, and **32** (1941), 16–18.

10. Remark in the discussion following a paper by C. J. Gorter on the two-fluid model of liquid helium, Supp. to *Nuovo Cimento*, 9th ser., **6** (1949), 249–250.

11. L. Onsager, "Deviations from Ohm's Law in Weak Electrolytes," in *Journal of Chemical Physics*, **2** (1934), 599–615.

12. L. Onsager, "Initial Recombination of Ions," in *Physical Review*, **54** (1938), 554–557.

13. L. Onsager, "Interpretation of the de Haas-Van Alphen Effect," in *Philosophical Magazine*, 7th ser., **43** (1952), 1006–1008.

14. L. Onsager and S. Machlup, "Fluctuations and Irreversible Processes," in *Physical Review*, **91** (1953), 1505–1512; S. Machlup and L. Onsager, "Fluctuations and Irreversible Processes II. Systems with Kinetic Energy," *ibid.*, 1512–1515.

15. O. Penrose and L. Onsager, "Bose-Einstein Condensation and Liquid Helium," in *Physical Review*, **104** (1956), 576–584.

16. E. T. Whittaker and G. N. Watson, *A Course of Modern Analysis*, 2nd ed. (Cambridge, 1915).

17. Lars Onsager, "The Motion of Ions: Principles and Concepts," in *Science*, **166** (1969), 1359–1364. See also *Les Prix Nobel en 1968* (Stockholm, 1969), 169–182.

18. Lars Onsager, "Possible Mechanisms of Ion Transit," in F. Snell *et al.*, eds., *Physical Principles of Biological Membranes* (New York, 1970), 137–141.

19. T. J. Seebeck in *Annalen der Physik und Chemie*, **6** (1826), 133, 263.

20. A. Peltier, "Nouvelles expériences sur la caloricité des courants électriques," in *Annales de chimie*, **56** (1834), 371–

386; *Comptes rendus . . . de l'Académie des sciences*, **1** (1835), 360.

21. H. A. Kramers and G. H. Wannier, "Statistics of the Two-Dimensional Ferromagnet. Part I," in *Physical Review*, **60** (1941), 252–262. See Stephen G. Brush, "History of the Lenz-Ising Model," in *Review of Modern Physics*, **39** (1967), 883–893 and T. Shedlovsky and E. Montroll, *J.Math.Phys.*, **4** (1963), the introduction to the "Proceedings of Conference on Irreversible Thermodynamics and the Statistical Mechanics of Phase Transitions," a conference to celebrate the thirtieth anniversary of the Reciprocal Relations.

22. L. Onsager, "Crystal Statistics" (abstract), in *Physical Review*, **62** (1942), 559.

23. Lars Onsager, "Autobiographical Commentary of Lars Onsager," in R. E. Mills *et al.*, eds, *Critical Phenomena in Alloys, Magnets and Superconductors* (New York, 1971), xxi.

24. Lars Onsager, "The Ising Model in Two Dimensions," in R. E. Mills *et al.*, eds., *Critical Phenomena in Alloys, Magnets and Superconductors* (New York, 1971), 3–12.

25. Remark in the discussion following a paper by G. S. Rushbrooke, in supp. to *Nuovo Cimento*, 9th ser., **6** (1949), 261. Further along in the same discussion period Onsager talks about the phenomenon of critical slowing down—that it takes a long time to reach equilibrium near a critical point. Perhaps this is the earliest announcement of a now familiar kind of "divergence."

26. C. N. Yang, "The Spontaneous Magnetization of a Two-Dimensional Ising Model," in *Physical Review*, **85** (1952), 808–816.

27. Lars Onsager, "Life in the Early Days," in S. L. Mintz and S. M. Widmayer, eds., *Quantum Statistical Mechanics in the Natural Sciences* (New York, 1974), 1–14.

28. E. M. Purcell and R. V. Pound, "A Nuclear Spin System at Negative Temperature," in *Physical Review*, **81** (1951), 279–280; N. F. Ramsey, "Thermodynamics and Statistical Mechanics at Negative Absolute Temperatures," *ibid.*, **103** (1956), 20–28.

BIBLIOGRAPHY

H. Christopher Longuet-Higgins and Michael E. Fisher, "Lars Onsager," *Biographical Memoirs of Fellows of the Royal Society*, **24** (1978), 443–471, is a detailed biography containing a complete list of Onsager's publications as well as a bibliography of (numerous shorter) biographies.

Microfilms of Onsager's letters, research notes, and papers are archived at the Sterling Library of Yale University.

STEFAN MACHLUP

OPARIN, ALEKSANDR IVANOVICH (*b.* Uglich, Iaroslav Province, Russia, 2 March 1894; *d.* Moscow, U.S.S.R., 21 April 1980), *biochemistry, origin of life.*

The youngest child of Ivan Dmitrievich Oparin and his wife, Aleksandra Aleksandrovna, Oparin was born in the family home in the village of Uglich. The eldest sibling, his sister Aleksandra, worked as a nurse at the front during World War I. His older brother, Dmitrii, graduated from the Petrograd

Polytechnical Institute as an economist in 1915. Oparin graduated from the Second Moscow Gymnasium in 1912 and entered Moscow University, supporting himself by working in a pharmaceutical factory.

Career. After graduating from the natural sciences division of the physicomathematical faculty of Moscow University in 1917, Oparin was accepted as a graduate student in its department of plant physiology, where he subsequently worked as a teaching assistant (1921–1925). The university sent him abroad in 1922 to study in the laboratory of Albrecht Kossel at Heidelberg, and he subsequently visited Austria and Italy (1924) and France (1925). Upon his return in 1925, he was permitted to teach his own course, "Chemical Bases of Living Processes," at Moscow University. In 1931 he began teaching a course there in technical biochemistry.

Although Oparin studied and taught various courses at Moscow University over the years, he apparently never earned a regular graduate degree; in 1934 the presidium of the U.S.S.R. Academy of Sciences awarded him a doctorate in biological sciences without his having defended a dissertation. As to his university position, Soviet sources are curiously inconsistent. One source indicates that he became a professor of biochemistry in 1929 and chaired the biochemistry department from 1937 to 1960 (*Biologi*, Kiev, 1984). However, an earlier and more authoritative source (*A. I. Oparin*, Moscow, 1964) states that he chaired the department of plant biochemistry from 1942 through 1960. This inconsistency may reflect the uncertain academic status of biochemistry as that discipline gradually became established in the Soviet Union, but it also highlights the fact that Oparin's career developed largely outside of the university setting.

Oparin's role in Soviet biochemistry owed much to the influence of his mentor and patron, Aleksei N. Bach (Bakh). Bach had belonged to a revolutionary party in tsarist days and left Russia in 1885 to work in Paris. In 1894 he settled in Geneva, where he gained an international reputation for his research in medical and agricultural chemistry, returning to Russia only in 1917. After the October Revolution, he helped to organize the chemical section of the National Economic Planning Council (VSNKh), which was responsible for organizing the Russian chemical industry, and in 1918 he became the founder and director of its Central Chemical Laboratory (renamed the L. Ia. Karpov Chemical Institute in 1922), charged with working out new production methods.

In 1918 Oparin asked to be sent to Geneva to work with Bach on plant chemistry, only to be informed that Bach had returned to Moscow. The two met and Oparin soon became the sixty-year-old chemist's protégé. Oparin brought to the relationship both a research interest in Bach's specialty and practical industrial experience. As the pharmaceutical factory's delegate to the first convention of the All-Russian Union of Chemical Industry Workers in 1918, Oparin was elected to its central committee. He subsequently served under Bach in the chemical division of VSNKh (1919–1922) and at the Central Chemical Laboratory (1921–1925).

A prominent scientific supporter of the Bolshevik government, Bach joined the Communist Party in 1927 and rapidly rose in administrative power, serving as a member of the government's Central Executive Committee (from 1927), an organizer of the All-Union Association of Scientists and Technicians (1928), and the perpetual president of the All-Union Chemical Society (from 1932). In the late 1920's Bach took an active role in organizing research in the food industry, and his protégé was appointed to a series of appropriate posts. From 1927 through 1934 Oparin worked at the Central Institute of the Sugar Industry in Moscow as assistant director in charge of science and as head of the biochemical laboratory. Concurrently he was a professor of technical biochemistry at the D. I. Mendeleev Institute of Chemical Technology in Moscow (1929–1931) and at the Moscow Institute of Grain and Flour (1930–1931). During this period Oparin conducted biochemical research on tea, sugar, flour, and grains. He continued this practical work as professor at the Moscow Technical Institute of Food Production (1937–1949), where he also studied nutrition and vitamins.

In 1929 Bach became one of the first Communists elected to the U.S.S.R. Academy of Sciences. When Bach headed the academy's Laboratory of Biochemistry (1931–1935), he put Oparin in charge of scientific research; when he was director of the academy's Institute of Biochemistry (1935–1946), Oparin was his associate director. Bach was academician-secretary of the chemical sciences division of the academy from 1939 through 1945; Oparin was elected a corresponding member of the academy's mathematical and natural science division on 29 January 1939, in plant biochemistry. When Bach died in May 1946, his institute was renamed the A. N. Bach Institute of Biochemistry and Oparin was appointed its director, a post he held for the rest of his life. On 30 November 1946 Oparin was elevated to full academy membership in the division of biological sciences.

Origin of Life. Oparin's first publication (1917) dealt with free amino groups in plants, and over the next two decades he published a number of scientific and popular articles on plant ferments (enzymes) and their role in metabolism. In addition to such research, however, propaganda, teaching, and administration took much of his time, and many of his publications were popular articles for newspapers or industrial magazines. Both lines of work came together in the central intellectual concern of his career, the problem of the origin of life.

In the early 1920's many tracts were published as part of the government's campaign to support materialism and undermine religion, and popular pamphlets on Darwinism, human evolution, and experimental biology abounded. Several dealt with the especially telling issue of the ultimate origin of life itself, but here materialists faced a vexing problem: Louis Pasteur, a hero of scientific medicine, had apparently disproved spontaneous generation in the nineteenth century; without it, however, there seemed no philosophically acceptable way to account for the origin of the primitive forms from which later life evolved. Oparin's original treatment of the problem came out of this context.

In 1922, at a meeting of the Moscow Botanical Society, Oparin presented his first paper on the origin of life, but it has never been published and may no longer exist. In 1924, however, a reworked version was issued as a 71-page pamphlet by the propaganda outlet Moscow Worker. Opening with a history of the problem of spontaneous generation, Oparin's brochure attacked vitalism. He dwelt on the similarity of protoplasm and colloidal gels, asserting that there is no difference between the living and the nonliving that cannot be fully accounted for by physicochemical laws. As regards spontaneous generation, Oparin found a way out of the apparent dilemma. He argued that the gradual accumulation and coagulation of hydrocarbons in the earth's early history could have led to the spontaneous generation of colloidal gels with the basic properties of life, but once this life had appeared, further spontaneous generation was precluded because such organic materials would be consumed by the life that already existed.

Although hailed decades later by J. D. Bernal and J. B. S. Haldane, Oparin's 1924 work went largely unnoticed at the time. He subsequently published brief accounts in *Herald of the Communist Academy* (1927), *Under the Banner of Marxism* (1928), and elsewhere, but he apparently did not resume serious work on the subject until around 1934 or 1935. By then, however, the Soviet ideological context had changed. During the period 1929–1933 a party line had been imposed on Soviet philosophy, resulting in a "dialectical materialism" that embraced certain general laws of natural development and castigated "mechanistic materialists" who reduced living phenomena to physics and chemistry. In 1936 Oparin published a 159-page book entitled *Vozniknovenie zhizni na zemle* ("The Origin of Life on Earth") that reflected these ideological changes. The work appeared in English translation in 1938 under a slightly misleading title, *The Origin of Life*, and almost immediately thereafter was translated into Japanese, Spanish, and several other languages.

Oparin's 1936 book expanded and modified his earlier views in several important ways. First, he drew more heavily on the current international literature in astronomy, geochemistry, organic chemistry, and plant enzymology, citing recent works by Vladimir I. Vernadskii on the chemical evolution of the biosphere. Second, he expressed his views in the form of a dialectical materialist analysis that explicitly cited Friedrich Engels and attacked spontaneous generation. He now saw life as a naturally emergent stage in the evolution of matter, one in which physicochemical laws had been supplemented by the "purely biological" laws of natural selection and metabolism. Finally, he drew upon H. G. Bungenberg de Jong's work of the early 1930's on colloidal coacervation, arguing that the formation of coacervate droplets by the electrostatic attraction of organic sols in the early seas provided a key requirement for the emergence of life: chemical pools separated by a membrane from the surrounding medium. Such droplets could selectively assimilate materials, and collect and accumulate catalysts and promoters that would accelerate chemical reactions. Although most such coacervates were short-lived, Oparin believed that those with the fastest rates of reaction, the most stable internal configurations, and the ability to grow and divide most rapidly would begin to undergo natural selection leading to more organized forms and eventually to primitive living systems.

The book's second Russian edition (1941) added more than 100 pages of material, and its third edition (1957) added almost 200 more. Although these subsequent versions updated and amended Oparin's theory, they all embodied the view that the central characteristic of life is metabolism, which gradually emerged in coacervates as a natural stage in the evolution of matter. The language of dialectical materialism became more prominent over time, and Oparin began to allude explicitly to such dialectical laws as the interaction and unity of opposites (for instance, the droplet or organism versus its surroundings; anabolism versus catabolism) and the transition from quantitative to qualitative change (as when physicochemical laws become gradually supplemented by biological laws in the evolution of coacervates). Oparin also became increasingly hostile to genetics, berating it as "mechanistic," and denied the growing claims that genes, viruses, and nucleic acids played a privileged role in the origin and evolution of life on the grounds that they require the existence of complex living systems to function. After World War II he declared Erwin Schrödinger's *What Is Life?* to be "ideologically dangerous," and became increasingly sympathetic to the views of Lysenko and other Michurinists.

A number of investigators in both the Soviet Union and the West have had difficulty replicating Oparin's laboratory work on coacervate droplets, and recent international research on the origin of life has developed independently of Oparin's specific biochemical findings and procedures, and along different lines. Nonetheless, his 1936 book is an enduring contribution to world science. By proposing a hypothetical but plausible scenario whereby metabolizing entities could gradually have emerged on a lifeless earth, he helped to make the origin of life a modern scientific problem.

Science, Politics, and Lysenkoism. It is not clear when and why Oparin became a supporter of Lysenko and his so-called Michurinist biology. In many ways the two had remarkably parallel careers: both rose in administrative importance after 1929 through their practical work; both developed theories in the 1920's that were greatly expanded and popularized in the mid 1930's; both infused their writings with ideological language and hewed to the Communist Party line in all matters, although neither was ever a party member; both were first elected to the U.S.S.R. Academy of Sciences in 1939 (the same year Stalin was elected); both gained enormous influence in 1948 and shared dominance over Soviet biology until 1955; both were rewarded with important political posts; both were hostile to genetics and molecular biology, and castigated them as mechanistic; both lost influence in Soviet science in the early 1960's.

The available evidence suggests that philosophical, scientific, and political factors all may have played a role in shaping Oparin's support for Lysenko. In the mid 1930's Oparin took part in the ideological quickening of debate on which Lysenko's support relied: dialectical materialist philosophy played a major role in Oparin's expositions on science in general and his views on the origin of life in particular.

His scientific work on plant physiology, enzymes, proteins, and the origin of life emphasized dynamic changes of metabolic chemical pools, which may have led to his hostility toward genetics and his sympathy with Lysenko's metabolic concept of heredity. Finally, like his mentor and patron Bach, Oparin learned to survive and prosper by subordinating himself to political authorities. In the late 1930's Bach signed newspaper articles supporting Lysenko and castigating Soviet geneticists for links with fascism, and Oparin may have followed Bach's lead in this matter as he did in most others. Indeed, it is even possible that Oparin's support was mere lip service motivated by fear or careerism. It is difficult to sort out the roles played by philosophy, science, politics, and ambition in Oparin's support for Lysenko, however, because he was able to state that support with more scientific plausibility and philosophical sophistication than any other major Soviet scientist.

At a special session of the presidium of the U.S.S.R. Academy of Sciences held on 24 August 1948, in the wake of Lysenko's triumph at the Lenin All-Union Academy of Agricultural Sciences earlier that month, Oparin was one of Lysenko's strongest, most prestigious, and probably most sincere advocates. Noting his own long-standing opposition to the views of T. H. Morgan, H. J. Muller, C. B. Bridges, and Erwin Schrödinger, and their Soviet supporters N. K. Kol'tsov, V. L. Ryzhkov, A. A. Malinovskii, and N. P. Dubinin, Oparin was able to brag, with some justice, that Michurinist biology prospered more in his Institute of Biochemistry than in any other institution within the academy's division of biological sciences except Lysenko's own Institute of Genetics. As a result of the session, Oparin replaced Pavlov's student L. A. Orbeli as the division's academician-secretary.

As the academy's chief administrator of biology from late 1948 through 1955, Oparin oversaw the implementation of policies aimed at the liquidation of Soviet genetics in the U.S.S.R. Academy of Sciences. During that period he wrote widely in support of Lysenko and Michurinism, and against genetics. He was also the chief public supporter of the cytological theories of Ol'ga Borisovna Lepeshinskaia, who had claimed that cells can form spontaneously from organic noncellular "living matter." Following Stalin's death in 1953, moves were under way to weaken Lysenko's stranglehold on Soviet biology. By the end of 1955 more than 300 scientists had signed a petition demanding Oparin's removal as academician-secretary of the academy's biology division. He was replaced in early 1956 by Vladimir

A. Engelhardt, a world-renowned muscle biochemist and a leading Soviet advocate of molecular biology.

Oparin greeted the explosive international growth of molecular biology in the 1950's ambivalently and without enthusiasm. Although he had worked in the laboratory of Kossel, a pioneer in the study of nucleic acid structure, and although one might think that a rapid development of DNA research would be welcomed by a biochemist, Oparin severely criticized the "central dogma" and the idea of a "genetic code" as mechanistic reductionism. Even when it would have been ideologically acceptable and tactically useful to support molecular biology and genetics, he did not do so. As president and chairman of the Fifth International Congress of Biochemistry, held at Moscow in 1961, Oparin refused to permit the term "molecular biology" to be used in the title of any of its sections or publications. However, within his own institute, he did support the work of A. N. Belozerskii on plant nucleic acids (apparently interpreting it as a refutation of the idea of a genetic code), and during the 1950's and 1960's he coauthored papers on the behavior of DNA and RNA in coacervate droplets. Perhaps sensing a change in the politics of Soviet science, Oparin was reportedly neutral in the debates that finally led to Lysenko's fall from dominance in 1964–1965.

Oparin's international reputation for his work on the origin of life led to increased prestige and power at home, and his political reliability made him a suitable Soviet representative abroad. He was appointed to the Supreme Soviet of the RSFSR (1951–1959) and served on its presidium (1955–1959). After 1948, at a time when foreign travel by Soviet scientists was a highly restricted political privilege, he traveled on official business not only to North Korea, Rumania, East Germany, Poland, Bulgaria, Hungary, and China, but also to Finland, Austria, France, Sweden, Britain, Japan, Belgium, Italy, Switzerland, and the United States. He became an active Soviet representative in various international scientific and political organizations, notably the World Peace Council (1950–1959) and the World Federation of Scientists, of which he was vice president from 1952 to 1966.

For his work Oparin won various Soviet awards, including the Order of the Red Banner of Labor (1944), the Bach Prize (1950), the Mechnikov Medal (1960), the Order of Lenin (1964), Hero of Socialist Labor (1969), the Lenin Prize (1974), and the Lomonosov Gold Medal (1979). He became president of the International Biochemical Society in 1959, presided over its Moscow congress in 1961, and continued as vice president after 1962. In 1970 he became the first president of the International Society for the Study of the Origin of Life. Oparin was awarded honorary degrees from Jena (1958), Rome (1961), and Poitiers (1963), and was elected a foreign member of the Finnish Chemical Society and of the national science academies of Bulgaria (1952), Czechoslovakia (1952), East Germany (1956), and, after 1964, Cuba, Spain, and Italy.

From 1965 through 1980, when the Soviet Union was striving to rebuild genetics and to create molecular biology, the Bach Institute remained the bastion of an older style of biochemistry and was soon eclipsed by other, newer research centers. Oparin continued as its director, although he was widely disliked by many Soviet scientists because of his involvement with Lysenkoism. Troubled by ill health, obesity, and growing deafness in his final years, he died, probably of a heart attack, shortly after being denied permission to attend a meeting in Israel.

BIBLIOGRAPHY

I. ORIGINAL WORKS. Oparin's earliest statement on the origin of life is *Proiskhozhdenie zhizni* (Moscow, 1924), trans. by Ann Synge as "The Origin of Life," in J. D. Bernal, *The Origin of Life* (London, 1967), 199–234. His subsequent articles on the subject include "Khimicheskaia teoriia proiskhozhdeniia zhizni" (The chemical theory of the origin of life), in *Vestnik Kommunisticheskoi akademii*, 1927, no. 1, 229–243; and "Die Entstehung des Lebens vom chemischen Standpunkt," in *Unter dem Banner des Marxismus*, 1928, no. 3, 331–345.

Oparin's classic book is *Vozniknovenie zhizni na zemle* (The origin of life on earth; Moscow and Leningrad, 1936 [159 pp.]; 2nd ed., 1941 [268 pp.]; 3rd ed., 1957 [459 pp.]). The first edition appeared in English as *The Origin of Life*, Sergius Morgulis, trans. (New York, 1938; 2nd ed., 1953); it also appeared in Japanese (Tokyo, 1939), and in Spanish as *El origen de la vida* (Buenos Aires, 1940). The reworked and much enlarged third Russian edition appeared in English as *The Origin of Life on the Earth*, Ann Synge, trans. (Edinburgh, 1957). See also *Vozniknovenie zhizni na zemle: Trudy mezhdunarodnogo simpoziuma, 19–24 avgusta 1957 goda, Moskva* (Moscow, 1959), and its Western edition, as *Proceedings of the First International Symposium on the Origin of Life on the Earth, Held at Moscow 19–24 August 1957*, International Union of Biochemistry, Symposium series, I (New York, 1959).

Oparin subsequently wrote three more popular books on the subject: *Zhizn', ee priroda, proiskhozhdenie i razvitie* (Moscow, 1960; 2nd ed., 1968), trans. by Ann Synge as *Life: Its Nature, Origin, and Development* (Edinburgh, 1962; New York, 1964); *The Chemical Origin of Life*, Ann Synge, trans. (Springfield, Ill., 1964); and *Vozniknovenie i nachal'noe razvitie zhizni* (Moscow, 1966), trans. by Eleanor Maass as *Genesis and Evolutionary Development of Life* (New York, 1968). For his strongest statement supporting Lysenko, see his remarks in *Vestnik Akademii nauk SSSR*, 1948, no. 9, 38–44.

II. SECONDARY LITERATURE. For a list of Oparin's publications and a brief scientific biography, see *Aleksandr Ivanovich Oparin*, O. V. Isakova, comp., Akademiia nauk SSSR, Materialy k biobibliografii uchenykh SSSR, ser. biokhimii, no. 6 (2nd ed., Moscow, 1964; 3rd ed., 1979). For a popular biography, see V. M. Mikhailov, *Put' k istine* (Path to the truth; Moscow, 1984). See also the discussions of Oparin in Mark B. Adams, "Genetics and Molecular Biology in Khrushchev's Russia" (Harvard University, 1973); J. D. Bernal, *The Origin of Life* (London, 1967); John Farley, *The Spontaneous Generation Controversy from Descartes to Oparin* (Baltimore, 1977), 163–187; Loren R. Graham, *Science and Philosophy in the Soviet Union* (New York, 1972), 257–296, and its 2nd ed., *Science, Philosophy, and Human Behavior in the Soviet Union* (New York, 1987), 68–101; Valery Soyler, Vlast' i nauka (Tenafly, 1989); and Gustav A. Wetter, *Dialectical Materialism*, Peter Heath, trans. (New York, 1958, 442–451.

MARK B. ADAMS

ORCEL, JEAN (*b.* Paris, France, 3 May 1896; *d.* Paris, 27 March 1978), *mineralogy*.

Orcel's father, Edouard, an engineer in public works, and his mother, Pauline Lesuisse, a teacher, gave him a taste for exact, methodical, and thorough work. He was finishing his studies at the Lycée Henri IV when World War I began. Nevertheless, he was able to continue his studies at the Sorbonne, having been exempted from military service because of poor health. A few years later he married Jeanne Bianconi; they had four children.

Orcel's primary interest was in chemistry. While working toward a degree in science (1917), he was noticed by F. Wallerant, professor of mineralogy, who took him into his laboratory at the Faculty of Science as a research assistant.

In 1920 Alfred Lacroix, *secrétaire perpétuel* of the Académie des Sciences in Paris and professor of mineralogy, offered Orcel a post as teaching assistant in his department at the Muséum National d'Histoire Naturelle, where Orcel was to spend the rest of his career. He became professor in 1937, succeeding Lacroix when the latter retired.

Orcel's work can be divided into several stages, each characterized by a special orientation of his research, often imposed by the functions entrusted to him. From 1917 to 1927 he studied complex hydrated phyllosilicates, chlorites, which were the subject of his doctoral dissertation. This accurate and detailed study, which contains more than three

hundred chemical analyses, was made possible by his improvements in methods of analyzing silicates. The fact that chlorites contain a notable quantity of water in their structure led him to test this element quantitatively and to note the temperature at which OH leaves the lattice. He thought this test was essential to define the different species. He used a new technical method found by Saladin and Le Châtelier, differential thermal analysis, and demonstrated that chlorites lose their water in two stages. This easy and swift method is now used universally in geological sciences, chemistry, metallurgy, and the ceramic industry. It was by using X rays and Orcel's chemical analysis of chlorites that Charles Mauguin established the first model of atomic order in the structure of these minerals.

Orcel made field trips to collect specimens; at Matra in Corsica, he found beautiful crystals of realgar. In 1920, working in collaboration with the Service de la Carte Géologique de France, he reviewed two geological maps. While working on the revision of the St. Jean de Maurienne map, he discovered, in the Comberousse Valley, a rare aluminous chlorite, sheridanite. The revision of the Roanne map enabled him to collect many specimens from the Charrier mine (Allier) for microscopic study.

This work marked the beginning of a study (1927–1937) of the optic properties of opaque minerals, which cannot be studied by transmitting light through them and which are the principal constituent of metallic ores. Orcel not only observed the color and brightness but also devised a measuring apparatus. He put a photoelectric cellule at the upper part of the microscope in reflected light. The cellule was connected to a galvanometer, which measured the reflecting power of the minerals. These optical results led him to identify oxides, sulfides, and other opaque species. Using a polarized microscope in reflected light, Orcel established the order of succession of the different minerals in complex ores and reconstructed the genesis of the ore deposit.

From 1937 until 1944 Orcel devoted his time to teaching and to preserving the finest and most precious specimens of the museum's collection. He was also active in the French Resistance. After the war, Frédéric Joliot asked Orcel to draw up an inventory of uranium deposits in France and in its overseas possessions. With his colleague L. Barrabé he also trained young prospectors. This was the most exciting period of his career, for he was very happy among his students and passed on to them his passion for well-done work and careful research. Results came rapidly, and a very rich uranium mineral, pitchblende, was discovered at Grury (Saône et Loire) and at La Crouzille (Haute Vienne).

In 1947, with a group he had formed in his laboratory for the purpose of continuing his research on phyllosilicates, Orcel established the Groupe Français des Argiles and served as its president for many years. He also contributed to forming the Commission Internationale pour l'Étude des Argiles (CIPEA), later the Association Internationale pour l'Étude des Argiles (AIPEA).

During his last active years Orcel became interested in philosophical reflections. He also extended the subjects he taught to include geochemistry and cosmochemistry. This, in turn, led to the study of meteorites. He was fascinated by the explorations made on the moon and by the study of specimens collected on it. Meteorites can vary from a one-microgram particle of dust to a block of several tons. Orcel studied the chemical composition of meteorites very thoroughly. He observed that the most common chondrites (stony meteorites) are chemically similar to earthly rocks such as dunites, basic rocks formed by the anhydrous magnesium silicate olivine. Among the chondrites he studied particularly carbon meteorites that contain not only carbon but also hydrated phyllosilicates. Because of this research, Orcel was the French delegate to the permanent international committee established to coordinate investigations and research on meteorites.

In 1968, immediately after he retired, Orcel organized remarkable expositions of meteorites, or *messagères du cosmos*, as he liked to call them. His purpose was to demonstrate that the history of meteorites reveals a long voyage through the cosmos.

Orcel was very courteous and easy to approach. He devoted his final efforts to his students and to the Académie des Sciences of Paris, of which he had been a member since 1963. His colleagues and students remember him as an untiring worker, fond of innovation in the field of mineralogy, and a remarkable experimenter gifted with a curious and sharp mind.

BIBLIOGRAPHY

I. ORIGINAL WORKS. A bibliography is in Poggendorff, VIIb, 3759–3761. Orcel published two books: *Les minerais* (Paris, 1930), written with C. Berthelot, and *Les volcans* (Paris, 1953), written with E. Blanquet. Among the most important of his 165 articles are "L'examen microscopique des minéraux opaques des roches et des minerais métalliques" and "Emploi de l'analyse thermique et des diagrammes de diffraction des rayons X dans l'étude des roches argileuses," in F. Rinne, ed., *La science des roches*, rev. ed., L. Bertrand, ed. (Paris, 1949), and "Météorites et météores," in Encyclopédie de la Pléiade, *Astronomie* (Paris, 1962), 1239–1263.

II. SECONDARY LITERATURE. Simonne Caillère, "Jean Orcel, 1896–1978," in *Bulletin de minéralogie*, **102** (1979), 303–305, with portrait, and Jean Wyart, "Notice nécrologique sur Jean Orcel, membre de la section des sciences de l'univers," in *Comptes rendus de l'Académie des sciences de Paris*, **286** (19 June 1978), 139–143.

SIMONNE CAILLÈRE

ORLOV, YURI ALEKSANDROVICH (*b.* Tomyshevo, Russia, 13 June 1893; *d.* Moscow, U.S.S.R., 2 October 1966), *histology, vertebrate paleontology.*

Orlov was the son of Alexander Fyodorovich Orlov, an employee of the Forest Department. In 1911 he entered the Physical-Mathematical Faculty at Petersburg University. He specialized in histology under A. S. Dogel. In 1916 he was invited by A. A. Zavarzin to hold the post of assistant in the Faculty of Histology and Embryology of the newly opened University of Perm. From 1925 to 1935 Orlov worked in the department of histology and embryology, headed by Zavarzin, of the Military Medical Academy in Leningrad, where his renewed love of paleontology led him to take part in paleontological field researches. His first field work, in 1925, was at the excavations of Neocene and Quaternary mammals in western Siberia and northwestern Kazakhstan.

In 1930 Orlov began scientific work at the new Paleontological Institute of the U.S.S.R. Academy of Sciences. In 1936 the institute moved to Moscow, and after that time Orlov's career was completely dedicated to paleontology. Orlov became the first manager of the institute's museum. In 1939 he was named head of the department of paleontology at Moscow University, and in 1945, after A. A. Borissiak's death, he was made director of the Paleontological Institute. Orlov's scientific organizing activity was quite successful and many-sided. He was one of the organizers of the Mongolian paleontological expedition of the U.S.S.R. Academy of Sciences (1946–1949) and of the joint Soviet-Chinese paleontological expedition (1959–1960).

In 1953 Orlov was elected a corresponding member of the U.S.S.R. Academy of Sciences, and in 1953 he became a full member. He was the editor in chief of the fifteen-volume *Fundamentals of Paleontology*. He visited many foreign countries, participating in international congresses and symposia. Orlov was an honorary member of the Moscow

Society of Naturalists, the All-Union Paleontological Society, the Associación Paleontológica Argentina, the American Society of Vertebrate Paleontology, the Geological Society of London, and many others. He promoted the consolidation of relationships between many scientists in different countries, as was acknowledged in an honorary diploma from the Soviet Peace Committee. He was awarded the gold medal of the Paleontological Society of India.

Orlov's scientific activity can be divided into two main periods. In the first period, up to the end of the 1920's, he conducted his research mainly on comparative invertebrate systematics; in the second period he concentrated on paleontology. Orlov made a valuable contribution to the problem of neuron organization of the nervous system of arthropods. He established an important parallel between the structures of the nervous systems in arthropods and vertebrates, expressed particularly in the presence of a detachable third neuron between the sensory and motor neurons of the reflex arc. Orlov's paleontological researches focused mainly on Neocene mammals. In his first such works, published between 1927 and 1930, he describes fossil camels of northwestern Kazakhstan.

Orlov also wrote a series of works on fossil carnivores: saber-toothed cats, ichthyosaurs, hyenas, badgers, martens, and otters. These works raised the study of fossil mammals in the Soviet Union to a new level and have retained their essential importance. Among Orlov's works on carnivores are those on the giant marten, which he named *Perunium*, from the Meotian of Moldavia (Grebenniki village), and on the otterlike carnivorous *Semantor* from the hipparion fauna of Pavlodar. Orlov classified the *Semantor*, known only from posterior parts of the skeleton and the shoulder bone, as a connecting link between otters and seals. He categorized it as Pinnipedia, within which he distinguished a new family, Semantoridae, more primitive than Otariidae. *Semantor* is now classified not as Pinnipedia but directly as martens (Mustelidae); the recent seals (Phocidae) are known from more ancient deposits than *Semantor* (the middle Miocene).

Semantor's adaptations show the course of formation of specialized pinniped aquatic carnivores. In Orlov's opinion *Perunium*, described from a skull 20 centimeters long, demonstrated the combination of some adaptations of the largest mustelids—gluttons *(Gulo)* and bears. This conception was reflected in the species denomination for *Perunium—P. ursogulo*—offered by Orlov, who classified it as a special subfamily of mustelids, to which he related the large fossil honey eaters of the genus *Eomellivora*. This placement was unsuccessful, and *Perunium* is now classified as an ordinary mustelid, related to the genus *Plesiogulo*, known from the Pliocene of China and North America. Orlov's detailed biological analysis of the cerebral structure of *Perunium* was of great importance; the external morphology was described in details from the cast of the skull cavity.

Orlov's last major work of paleontology, published in 1958, addressed Upper Permian carnivorous deinocephalian fauna from the Ishejev locality (Middle Volga). This work is one of the best ever on the descriptive morphology of deinocephalians. Orlov also published many articles of a general character, including one on the tasks of studies in the field of paleoneurology of vertebrates (1949). He was interested in history of science and published articles on the lives and activities of Russian scientists, such as A. A. Inostrantsev, V. P. Amalitskii, A. A. Borissiak, V. A. Obruchev, and A. P. Bystrov.

During the last years of his life, Orlov paid much attention to the popularization of science. His book *In the World of Ancient Animals*, illustrated by K. K. Flerov, was published twice in the Soviet Union (1961 and 1968). Orlov wrote about two hundred publications.

BIBLIOGRAPHY

Orlov's important works include "*Semantor macrurus* (ordo Pinnipedia, fam. Semantoridae fam. nov.) aus den Neogen-Ablagerungen Westsibiriens," in *Trudy Paleontologicheskikh instituta Akademiia nauk SSSR* **2** (1933), 165–268 (in Russian); "Fundort der Hipparion-Fauna am Irtysch in der Stadt Pavlodar (W. Sibiriens)," *ibid.*, **5** (1936), 155–169 (in Russian); "Tertiäre Raubtiere des westlichen Sibiriens. 1. Machairodontidae," *ibid.*, **5**, 111–152 (in Russian); "*Peruniinae*, novoje podsemeistvo kunitz iz neogena Evrazii (k filogenii kunitz)," *ibid.*, **8**, no. 2 (1941); "Tretichnie hischniki Zapadnoi Sibiri. 2. Barsuki. 3. Kunitzi. 4. Gieni. 5. Iktiterii," *ibid.*, no. 3; "Hischnie deinotzefali fauni Isheeva (titanozuhi)," *ibid.*, **72** (1958); and *V mire drevnih zivotnih* (Moscow, 1968).

L<small>EONID</small> T<small>ATARINOV</small>

OSTERHOUT, WINTHROP JOHN VANLEUVEN (*b*. Brooklyn, New York, 2 August 1871; *d*. New York City, 9 April 1964), *botany, general physiology.*

Osterhout was the only surviving child of John Vanleuven Osterhout, an idealistic, financially unsuccessful Baptist minister of old New York Dutch ancestry, and Annie Loranthe Beman, a daughter of English immigrants, who died when her son was two. Osterhout studied at Brown University, the

University of Bonn, and the University of California. A dedicated academic, with few interests outside science, he held positions at Berkeley, Harvard, and the Rockefeller Institute for Medical Research. He was a member of the National Academy of Sciences (elected in 1919) and cofounder of the *Journal of General Physiology* (with Jacques Loeb in 1918). Osterhout married Anna Maria Landstrom in 1899; they had two daughters and were divorced in 1932. The following year he married his research associate, Marian Irwin. Blinded soon afterward as the result of glaucoma, he grew dependent on her both personally and scientifically. Nevertheless, he continued research until he was over eighty.

Osterhout was a significant participant (and one of the few botanists) in the network of American academic biologists who oriented their science at the beginning of the twentieth century around laboratory research and methods drawn from the physical sciences. A solitary and bookish child raised in Baltimore and in Providence, Rhode Island, Osterhout was first drawn to the life sciences in 1891 as an advanced undergraduate by the young Brown University professor H. C. Bumpus. The next summer he studied at the Marine Biological Laboratory in Woods Hole, Massachusetts, where W. A. Setchell guided him toward the study of algae. After receiving his undergraduate degree in 1893, Osterhout taught botany at Brown for two years and summered as an instructor at the Marine Biological Laboratory. He obtained an M.A. from Brown in 1894. In the academic year 1895–1896 he studied at Bonn with the plant cytologist Eduard Strasburger, working on the reproduction of the alga *Batrachospermum*. He then followed Setchell to the University of California at Berkeley as an instructor, obtaining a Ph.D. from that institution in 1899.

At Berkeley, Osterhout sought to relate academic botany to agricultural advancement, both by developing an elementary course and textbook in plant physiology and by acting as a liaison between the university and the horticultural "wizard" Luther Burbank. His interests took a more specific direction in 1903, when the innovative general physiologist Jacques Loeb arrived from the University of Chicago. Loeb had shown that slight changes in the ionic composition of protoplasm could have major physiological consequences; Osterhout recognized that such "salt effects" were important both for marine algae and for flowering plants, and he began to investigate the influences of both simple and complex salt solutions on plant growth. He was encouraged in this work by Hugo de Vries and Svante Arrhenius,

for whom he was a host on their visits to Berkeley in the summer of 1904.

Osterhout's involvement with the application of the new physical chemistry to biology, as well as his teaching ability, resulted in a call to Harvard in 1909 to become assistant professor of botany, in spite of a lack of enthusiasm for his research on the part of leading American botanists. In the next years he improved his command of both mathematics and electrochemistry and began an extensive project on the permeability of cells to ions. Working primarily at Woods Hole, Osterhout applied to plants the standard techniques for measuring the conductivity of electrolytes, devising an apparatus in which a current passed through a large number of disks of the brown kelp *Laminaria*. By measuring changes in permeability of plant tissues bathed in different ionic media, he was able to interpret injury and death as quantifiable electrochemical processes and, more speculatively, as problems in reaction kinetics.

As a mild-mannered Harvard scholar (he became a full professor in 1913) Osterhout took the lead in promoting general physiology as an academic discipline in America, a role for which his mentor Loeb, who left Berkeley for the Rockefeller Institute in 1910, was temperamentally unsuited. He maintained his ties with Arrhenius and established good relations with leading Harvard chemists, including T. W. Richards, A. B. Lamb, and G. P. Baxter. In addition to teaching elementary botany, Osterhout worked closely with the zoologist G. H. Parker to promote graduate work in physicochemically oriented biology at Harvard; his students included L. R. Blinks and W. O. Fenn, and he supported the work of such younger zoologists as Selig Hecht and W. J. Crozier. Osterhout joined Loeb in establishing the *Journal of General Physiology* in 1918, and he collaborated with Loeb and T. H. Morgan in editing the influential series Monographs on Experimental Biology. In 1920 he became a member of the Rockefeller Institute's Board of Scientific Directors.

A year after Loeb's death in 1924, Osterhout became the Rockefeller Institute's chief general physiologist. Until his retirement in 1939 he led a research group that investigated the electrical properties of giant algal cells. As early as 1923 he measured directly the electrical potential across an algal cell membrane, and by the end of the decade he was arguing that the selective permeability of the membrane for different cations was the basis for the membrane potential. As an advocate of general physiology at a medical research center, Osterhout hoped that these projects would provide the foundations for work on more complex and delicate animal tissues. This hope was justified with regard to problems and methods; Osterhout provided a model and guide for the early work of Kenneth Cole and Detlev Bronk. But the properties of algae were sufficiently complex to keep Osterhout's small research group from making the fundamental discoveries they sought. With the recognition in the mid 1930's that the squid axon could be studied in the same way as the giant algae, the center of research on bioelectricity shifted to the direct investigation of nerve.

BIBLIOGRAPHY

I. ORIGINAL WORKS. Osterhout was the author or coauthor of five books and over 260 scientific papers; a bibliography is in L. R. Blinks, "Winthrop John Vanleuven Osterhout," in *Biographical Memoirs, National Academy of Sciences*, **44** (1974), 213–249. His books include *Experiments with Plants* (New York, 1905), an elementary text; *Injury, Recovery and Death in Relation to Conductivity and Permeability* (Philadelphia, 1923), a synthesis of the work on *Laminaria*; and *The Nature of Life* (New York, 1923), a short presentation of his general views. Osterhout provided a brief résumé of his research in "The Use of Aquatic Plants in the Study of Some Fundamental Problems," in *Annual Review of Plant Physiology*, **8** (1957), 1–10. A collection of his correspondence and manuscripts (approximately 2,500 items) is in the American Philosophical Society Library, Philadelphia.

II. SECONDARY LITERATURE. The major source on Osterhout's life, with photograph and bibliography, is Blinks (see above). See also George W. Corner, *A History of the Rockefeller Institute, 1901–1953: Origins and Growth* (New York, 1964).

PHILIP J. PAULY

PALLADIN, ALEKSANDR VLADIMIROVICH (*b.* Moscow, Russia, 10 September 1885; *d.* Kiev, U.S.S.R., 10 December 1972), *biochemistry.*

A. V. Palladin was the son of V. I. Palladin, one of the leading Russian biochemists and plant physiologists of the turn of the century. In 1903 he entered the Faculty of Natural Sciences at St. Petersburg University. In 1905, while still a student, he became a scientific worker first at the university laboratory of I. P. Pavlov, and then in the Department of Physiology under N. E. Vvedensky. Under the latter Palladin completed his first research in 1907, "Phenomena of Excitation and Retardation in the Reflex Apparatus During Contamination by 2,3-Dimethoxystrichnine and Carbolic Acid," which was awarded a gold medal by the university.

After graduation from the university in 1908, Palladin worked in the department of physiology of the Women's Pedagogical Institute in St. Petersburg until 1916, as well as at the Higher Women's Agricultural Courses from 1914 to 1916. During these years he conducted research on the processes of the origin of creatine in an organism as well as on its role in muscle activity. Palladin came to the conclusion that a major role in the metabolism of muscles is played by creatine-phosphoric acid and also that arginine is the precursor of creatine in muscles. Palladin's work on the metabolism of creatine and creatine-phosphoric acid led to the expansion of research in the biochemistry of muscle activity. For his work "Research on the Formation and Secretion of Creatine in Animals," Palladin was granted a master's degree in physiology and comparative anatomy at St. Petersburg University. In 1916 he accepted a professorship at the Novo-Aleksandrijsky (today Kharkovsky) Institute of Agriculture and Forestry, where he worked until 1923. From 1921 to 1931 he was chairman of the Department of Physiological Chemistry at the Kharkov Medical Institute.

After the October Revolution, Palladin became active in the propaganda of scientific knowledge, striving to make it accessible to the people. In 1919 his book "The Scientific Bases of Public Nutrition" appeared; it was republished many times in the following years.

Palladin taught special courses in biochemistry at Kharkov University (1917–1921) and at the Kharkov Medical Institute (1921–1931). These courses formed the basis for one of the first Soviet textbooks on biochemistry (the first edition was published in 1924, the twelfth in 1946, and it was translated into a number of foreign languages).

From 1925 to 1969, Palladin headed the Ukrainian Biochemical Institute in Kharkov, which was the first specialized biochemical research institute in the Ukraine and the second in the Soviet Union. In 1926 he founded the first specialized biochemical journal in the Soviet Union, "Scientific Notes of the Ukrainian Biochemical Institute" (the journal was renamed the "Ukrainian Biochemical Journal" in 1934).

In 1926, without having defended a dissertation, Palladin was granted the degree of doctor of biology, and in 1929 he was elected a full member of the Academy of Sciences of the Ukrainian S.S.R.

In 1931 the Ukrainian Biochemical Institute was moved to Kiev and renamed the Institute of Biochemistry of the Academy of Sciences of the Ukrainian S.S.R. From 1934 to 1954 Palladin, in addition to working at the institute, headed the biochemistry department of Kiev University. The institute expanded significantly and became a major center of biochemical research. Under Palladin's guidance extensive research on the chemical composition and metabolism of muscles at work, at rest, and during exercise was greatly developed. The numerous experimental data and conclusions accumulated served as the basis for the development of research in the biochemical fundamentals of the theory of human physical culture.

In the war years (1941–1945) the collective at the institute did not stop its work. During evacuation in 1944 Palladin synthesized vicasol, a water-soluble analogue for the antihemorrhagic vitamin K, which found wide application in medical practice. At the institute, research on the biochemistry of the nervous system, and especially of the brain, which had been begun before the war, was continued and expanded. The concept of the "biochemical topography" of the brain was created.

In 1942 Palladin was elected a full member of the Academy of Sciences of the U.S.S.R., and in 1944 he was among the first five biochemists to be elected full members of the Academy of Medical Sciences of the U.S.S.R. (established in 1944). From 1946 to 1962 he was president of the Academy of Sciences of the Ukrainian S.S.R. From 1967 to 1969 he served as president of the All-Union Biochemical Society.

Palladin was an active and important public figure. From 1946 to 1962 he was a deputy of the Supreme Soviet of the U.S.S.R. In 1945 he participated in the United Nations Conference at San Francisco as a member of the Ukrainian S.S.R. delegation. He was involved in the first conference on the peaceful uses of atomic energy. The scientific and civic activity of Palladin was distinguished by the V. I. Lenin Prize (1929) and by the Hero of Socialist Labor Award, the highest honor in the U.S.S.R. (1955). He was elected an honorary member of the academies of sciences of Bulgaria, Hungary, Romania, and Poland, and received many Soviet and foreign awards.

BIBLIOGRAPHY

I. ORIGINAL WORKS. *Voprosy biokhimii nervnoi sistemy* (Kiev, 1965), trans. by M. Artman and ed. by S. Herschkopf as *Biochemistry of the Nervous System* (Jerusalem, 1967); *Belki golovnogo mozga i ikh obmen* (Kiev, 1972), written with V. Belik and N. M. Polyakova, trans. by Basil Haigh, trans. ed. by Abel Lajtha, as *Protein Metabolism of the Brain* (New York, 1977); and *Sobranie sochineny* (Collected works; Kiev, 1975).

II. SECONDARY LITERATURE. A. M. Utevsky, *Aleksandr Vladimirovich Palladin* (Kiev, 1975).

A. N. SHAMIN

PAPALEKSI, NIKOLAI DMITRIEVICH (*b.* Simferopol. Russia, 2 December 1880; *d.* Moscow, U.S.S.R., 3 February 1947), *radiophysics, electrotechnology*.

Papaleksi was the son of Dmitrii Konstantinovich Papaleksi, an army officer. After graduating with a gold medal from the gymnasium at Poltava in 1899, he studied physics in Berlin and then at Strasbourg University, from which he graduated in 1904. He stayed in Strasbourg until 1914, except for the year 1907, which he spent at the Cavendish Laboratory at Cambridge, where he worked on fluorescence under the direction of J. J. Thomson. At Strasbourg, Papaleksi joined the brilliant school of Ferdinand Braun, who trained a number of outstanding Russian physicists, including Aleksandr Aleksandrovich Eichenwald, Boris Borisovich Golitsin, Petr Petrovich Lasarev, Petr Nikolaevich Lebedev, and Leonid Isaakovich Mandel'stam. (Papaleksi established a long-time and fruitful friendship with Mandel'stam.) In 1904 Papaleksi defended his doctoral dissertation, "Ein Dynamometer für schnelle elektrische Schwingungen. Theorie und Versuche," and then became Braun's assistant. In 1911, after defending a dissertation for the right to lecture (*venia legendi*), he was appointed *Privatdozent* in the department of physics.

Late in July 1914 Papaleksi returned to Russia. He became a consultant to the Russian Wireless Telegraph and Telephone Company, and until 1916 he did experiments in directional radiotelegraphy, radio communication to submarines, remote control, and electron tubes. In 1918 he went to Moscow, and later to Odessa, where he and Mandel'stam participated in the organization of the Odessa Polytechnic Institute. He was named professor of theoretical electrotechnics at the institute in 1920. Also, with the assistance of Igor Evgenievich Tamm and of Mandel'stam, he helped to establish the production of electronic valves at the Polytechnic Institute and at the "Vacuum Group" in Odessa.

From 1922 to 1935 Papaleksi continued his cooperation with Mandel'stam, though at a distance. Papaleksi's activity was concentrated in Leningrad, at the Central Radio Laboratory. In 1930 he became head of the department of scientific radiotechnology at the Leningrad Electrophysical Institute (which had been part of the Physical-Technical Institute).

Papaleksi was also the head of the department of radio engineering of the Faculty of Physics and Mechanics at the Leningrad Polytechnic Institute. In 1935 he was named head of the department of oscillations at the P. N. Lebedev Physics Institute in Moscow, and an active member of the Power Institute, both parts of the U.S.S.R. Academy of Sciences.

From the early years of his cooperation with Mandel'stam, Papaleksi was primarily responsible for the translation of ideas and theories into real apparatuses. This division of labor dated from the years at Strasbourg, when the two scholars did radiometric investigations for German firms. In 1938 Mandel'stam wrote of Papaleksi:

> Our cooperation in the field of electromagnetic oscillations has lasted over thirty years. During this long period there developed such a closeness between us regarding both the initiative and the treatment of problems (theoretical and experimental) that in most cases it is difficult to say what has been done by one or the other. As to the technical realization of results, the main role has been played by Nikolai Dmitrievich (*Sobranie trudov*, p. 21).

The main result of Papaleksi's scientific activity was the formulation of the general theory of nonlinear oscillations. Mandel'stam and Papaleksi tried to implant in the minds of scholars what they called "nonlinear psychology," that is, a willingness to step out of the framework of linear problems. This transition was to a great extent associated with the development of substantially nonlinear elements of radio-engineering devices, such as electron valves (the first work of Papaleksi in this field was published in 1912).

The discovery of a new principle of self-excitation of electromagnetic oscillations due to a periodic alteration of capacity or inductance resulted from investigations of nonlinear oscillations and treatment of the corresponding mathematical theory. This research entailed a great number of technical applications, first in radio engineering. The principle of parametric excitation and amplification of oscillations was applied in the parametric filter used for suppression of hindrances to radio reception, as well as in a number of new methods of frequency transformation. New generations of parametric amplifiers built on the basis of general principles worked out by Mandel'stam and Papaleksi have found important applications in modern observatory astrophysics. Further, before World War II, Mandel'stam and (especially) Papaleksi built electrical machines working on the principle of parametric excitation.

These machines do not require excitative windings and have many other advantages compared with conventional generators and dynamos.

In the early 1930's Papaleksi and Mandel'stam developed a method of measuring the velocity of propagation of electromagnetic waves. This method, based on the phenomenon of wave interference, served as a theoretical basis for creation of radio distance meters. Their research stimulated the theoretical work of Vladimir Aleksandrovich Fock and others of the theory of propagation of radio waves around the Earth's surface. Before World War II this method found many applications in navigation. And in 1942 Mandel'stam and Papaleksi suggested using these applications for astronomical measurements: Papaleksi performed the calculations connected with the radiolocation of the moon (which was done in the United States in 1945).

After Mandel'stam's death (1944) Papaleksi concentrated on problems related to solar electromagnetic radiation. He participated in the formulation of the program investigating solar electromagnetic radiation during a solar eclipse in 1947. This eclipse, observed in Brazil by a Soviet expedition, enabled the scientists to obtain important data related to the distribution of radio brightness of the solar surface.

Although Papaleksi worked very hard all his life, he also found time for relaxation. He was an outstanding athlete, alpinist, and chess player, and he not only knew Russian poetry very well, but wrote poems himself. He and his wife, Klara Efraimovna Viller-Papaleksi, had no children.

With Mandel'stam, Papaleksi created a world-recognized school devoted to nonlinear oscillations that included many outstanding Soviet physicists, for instance, Aleksandr Aleksandrovich Andronov. Papaleksi's accomplishments were widely recognized: in 1931 he was elected corresponding member, and in 1939 full member, of the U.S.S.R. Academy of Sciences. With Mandel'stam he was awarded the Mendeleev Prize in 1936, and in 1942 he received the State Prize. A lunar crate was named for him.

Papaleksi worked at the Lebedev Physical Institute of the U.S.S.R. Academy of Sciences until a few days before his death—without respite, according to S. M. Rytov (*Sobranie trudov*, p. 36). Ten days before his death he finished the review on the theory of nonlinear oscillations and resumed work on his biography of Mandel'stam.

BIBLIOGRAPHY

I. ORIGINAL WORKS. Papaleksi's works are listed in *Izvestiia Akademii nauk SSSR, seriia fizicheskaia*, **12,** no. 1 (1948), 49–52. The most important include "Über die Vorgänge in einem Wechselstromkreis mit elektrischem Ventil," in *Annalen der Physik*, 4th ser., **39** (1912), 976–996; "Exposé des recherches récentes sur les oscillations non linéaires," in *Technical Physics of the USSR*, **2**, no. 2–3 (1935), 81–134, written with L. Mandel'stam, A. Andronov, S. Chaikin, and A. Witt; "Parametricheskoe generirovanie peremennykh tokov" (Parametrical generation of alternating currents), in *Elektrichestvo*, **11** (1938), 67–76; "O nekotorykh primeneniiakh radiointerferentsionnykh metodov" (On some applications of radio-interference methods), in *Izvestiia Akademii nauk SSSR, seriia fizicheskaiia*, **3**, no. 4 (1938), 539–550; *Radiopomekhi i borba s nimi* (Radiointerferences and a fight against them; Moscow, 1942; 2nd ed., 1944); "Razvitie ucheniia o nelineinykh kolebaniiakh i ikh primenenii" (The development of the doctrine of nonlinear oscillations and their applications), *Izvestiia Akademiia nauk SSR, seriia fizicheskaia*, **9**, no. 3 (1945), 145–160; "Kratkii ocherk zhizni i nauchnoi deiatelnosti akademika L. I. Mandel'stama" (Short sketch of L. I. Mandel'stam's life and scientific activity), *ibid.*, no. 1–2 (1945), 8–20, also published in Papaleksi's *Sorbranie trudov*; "Ob izmerenii rasstoianiia ot zemli do luny s pomoshchiu elektromagnitnykh voln" (On the measurement of the distance between the Earth and the moon by electromagnetic waves), in *Uspekhi fizicheskikh nauk*, **29**, no. 3–4 (1946), 250–268; "Nekotorye issledovaniia v oblasti nelineinykh kolebanii provedennye v SSSR, nachinaia s 1935 g." (Some investigations in the field of nonlinear oscillations performed in the USSR since 1935), *ibid.*, **33**, no. 3 (1947), 335–352, written with A. A. Andronov, G. S. Gorelik, and S. M. Rytov; and *Sobranie trudov* (Collected works), S. M. Rytov, ed. (Moscow, 1948).

Papaleksi's papers are in the archives of the U.S.S.R. Academy of Sciences.

II. SECONDARY LITERATURE. *Izvestiia Akademii nauk SSSR, seriia fizicheskaia*, **12**, no. 1 (1948), is a memorial volume dedicated to Papaleksi; see particularly the article by S. M. Rytov, which also appeared in Papaleksi's *Sobranie trudov*. A short biographical notice is in *Uspekhi fizicheskikh nauk*, **21**, no. 2 (1939), 240–241.

V. J. FRENKEL

PATTERSON, JOHN THOMAS (*b.* Piqua, Ohio, 3 November 1873; *d.* Austin, Texas, 4 December 1960), *embryology, genetics, evolution.*

Patterson was the youngest of five children of James N. Patterson, a farmer with broad interests in mathematics and astronomy, and of Anna Linn Patterson, a schoolteacher with a college education. He and his siblings grew up in a home where books and conversation were valued, and the norm was to attend and graduate from college. He was a frail teenager, his health weakened by a bout of pneumonia, and after finishing the ninth grade was given a high school education by private tutors to spare him the daily trip to the public high school several miles from home. With this preparation Patterson attended the normal school in Ada, Ohio (now Ohio Northern University), and then entered the College of Wooster (Ohio) in 1900. After graduating in 1903, he taught at Buena Vista College, Storm Lake, Iowa, for two years. There he met Alice Jane Tozer, whom he married in 1906; they had a daughter and two sons.

In 1905 Patterson entered the graduate school of the University of Chicago, where he received the Ph.D., summa cum laude, in 1908. He also was elected to Phi Beta Kappa. Patterson's research career started at the University of Chicago in 1905, while he was a doctoral candidate under the eminent zoologist and embryologist Charles O. Whitman. He was greatly influenced in the development of his scholarly interests not only by Whitman but also by the embryologist Charles M. Child, the botanist James M. Coulter, and the paleontologist Samuel W. Williston. He took as his research problem a study of the early developmental stages of the chick and the pigeon, with emphasis on the onset of gastrulation.

After receiving the Ph.D. in 1908, Patterson moved to Austin to become instructor of zoology at the University of Texas. Here he became involved in research with the chairman of the department of zoology, H. H. Newman, who was greatly interested in twinning in mammals. Together they worked on the nine-banded armadillo, *Dasypus novemcintus*, and published papers on the phenomenon of polyembryony in this Texas resident. The female armadillo always gives birth to quadruplets, and as a result of Patterson's and Newman's work it became apparent that the quadruplets are identical. Patterson proved this conclusively after Newman left the university in 1911. Beginning in 1913, he published a notable series of papers showing that the four embryos of a single fertilization derive from a single blastocyst.

After completing his work with the armadillo, Patterson turned his attention to a parasitic wasp, *Paracopidosomopsis floridans*, that lays its eggs on the Autographa moth. From one egg of this wasp several hundred larvae emerge after having developed by an extreme form of polyembryony.

Patterson became chairman of the department and professor of zoology after Newman's departure. He immediately began to build the course offerings and faculty, and initiated a doctoral program in zoology. Carl B. Hartman entered this program and in 1915 received (under Patterson) the first Ph.D.

granted by the University of Texas in any field. By 1920 the departmental faculty had grown to five, primarily owing to Patterson's efforts. Hartman was retained as a faculty member, and Theophilus S. Painter and Hermann J. Muller were recruited by Patterson. D. B. Casteel completed the quintet that in the 1920's made the department an internationally recognized center of zoological research concentrating primarily on genetics, cytogenetics, and development.

While administering the department, teaching a full load, and doing his research, Patterson found time to build up the zoological library, raise money for research, and design and see to completion a new building for the biological sciences. The biological laboratories, in a four-story building housing the departments of zoology and botany, was dedicated in 1925. Once in the new laboratories, Patterson began to shift his interest from development to genetics. Muller was beginning his studies with X rays and *Drosophila*; and Patterson, realizing that money was going to be needed to support Muller's work, set about finding it. First he wangled a considerable sum from the university administration for an X-ray machine and air conditioning equipment for the *Drosophila* laboratory, and in 1925 he was able to persuade the General Education Board of the Rockefeller Foundation to appropriate $65,000 to be "used for the development of graduate instruction and research in zoology." Further grants from the board and matching funds from the university continued until 1954, when research grants from the federal government became the primary source of funds.

Patterson collaborated with Muller in the late 1920's. He was mainly interested in demonstrating that X rays could cause mutations in somatic cells, and with Muller he showed that in *Drosophila*, at least, reverse mutations—or mutations back to the original wild type—could be induced by X rays. In addition he did extensive studies on the production of gynandromorphs by inducing X-chromosome nondisjunction with X rays. He and his students also constructed a large number of aneuploid strains that they used to study the effects of hypoploidy and hyperploidy for various regions of the second and third chromosomes.

In 1938, Patterson and a former student, Wilson S. Stone, started an ambitious program to investigate speciation in the genus *Drosophila*. This was to result in his most distinguished contribution to biology. He and his graduate students collected *Drosophila* in many parts of the United States and Mexico. They did ecological, geographical, cyto-

genetic, genetic, and physiological studies on the numerous species they collected in the wild and then reared in the laboratory. The laboratory received international recognition for this work, much of which was summarized in a book by Patterson and Stone, published in 1952. Shortly afterward Patterson retired from research and rested on his considerable laurels.

Patterson was a member and officer of the American Association for the Advancement of Science (vice president, Section F, 1941); the American Society of Zoologists (president, 1939); the International Society for the Study of Evolution (founding member and president, 1947); and the Genetics Society of America (president, 1954). He was awarded an honorary D.Sc. by the College of Wooster in 1938, and elected to the National Academy of Sciences in 1941. In 1947 he received the Daniel Giraud Medal from the National Academy of Sciences for his work on isolating mechanisms in *Drosophila*.

BIBLIOGRAPHY

I. ORIGINAL WORKS. Patterson's writings include: "A Case of Normal Identical Quadruplets in the Nine-Banded Armadillo, and Its Bearing on the Problems of Identical Twins and Sex Determination," in *Biological Bulletin*, **17** (1909), 181–187, written with H. H. Newman; "Gastrulation in the Pigeon's Egg, a Morphological and Experimental Study," in *Journal of Morphology*, **20** (1909), 65–123; "Development of the Nine-Banded Armadillo from the Primitive Streak Stage to Birth; with Especial Reference to the Question of Specific Polyembryony," *ibid.*, **21** (1910), 359–424, written with H. H. Newman; "Studies on the Early Development of the Hen's Egg. I. History of the Early Cleavage and of the Accessory Cleavage," *ibid.*, 101–134; "Polyembryonic Development in *Tatusia novemcincta*," *ibid.*, **24** (1913), 559–682; "The Development of Paracopidosomopsis," *ibid.*, **36** (1921), 1–44; "Polyembryony in Animals," in *Quarterly Review of Biology*, **2** (1927), 399–426; and "The Production of Mutations in Somatic Cells of *Drosophila melanogaster* by Means of X-rays," in *Journal of Experimental Zoology*, **53** (1929), 327–372.

"Are 'Progressive' Mutations Produced by X-rays?" in *Genetics*, **15** (1930), 495–577, written with Hermann J. Muller; "The Production of Gynandromorphs in *Drosophila melanogaster* by X-rays," in *Journal of Experimental Zoology*, **60** (1931), 173–211; "Gynandromorphs in *Drosophila melanogaster*," in University of Texas Publication no. 3825 (1938), 1–67, written with Wilson Stone; "Experimentally Produced Aneuploidy Involving the Autosomes of *Drosophila melanogaster*," University of Texas Publication no. 4032 (1940), 167–189, written with Meta S. Brown and Wilson S. Stone; "The Virilis Group of *Drosophila* in Texas," in *American Naturalist*, **75** (1941), 523–539; "Interspecific Hybridization in the

Genus *Drosophila*," University of Texas Publication no. 4228 (1942), 7–15; "The Drosophilidae of the Southwest," University of Texas Publication no. 4313 (1943), 7–216, written with Robert P. Wagner and L. T. Wharton; "The Drosophilidae of Mexico," University of Texas Publication no. 4445 (1944), 9–101, written with Gordon B. Mainland; "Incipient Reproductive Isolation Between Two Subspecies of *Drosophila pallidipennis*," in *Genetics*, **30** (1945), 429–438, written with Theodosius Dobzhansky; "The Insemination Reaction and Its Bearing on the Problem of Speciation in the Mulleri Subgroup," University of Texas Publication no. 4720 (1947), 41–77; and *Evolution in the Genus Drosophila* (New York, 1952), written with Wilson S. Stone.

II. SECONDARY LITERATURE. A memoir is Theophilus S. Painter, "John Thomas Patterson," in *Biographical Memoirs. National Academy of Sciences*, **38** (1965), 223–262.

R. P. WAGNER

PAYNE, FERNANDUS (*b.* near Shelbyville, Indiana, 13 February 1881; *d.* Frankfort, Indiana, 13 October 1977), *genetics*.

Payne, the third of six children, was born in a log cabin. His father, Daniel, was a carpenter who abandoned the family when Payne was eight years old. His mother was Alice Garlitch. The children were dispersed to foster homes, and until he was eighteen, Payne lived in three households where he was usually treated like a hired hand. He excelled in school and borrowed money to attend Valparaiso Normal School (1899) and Indiana University, where he completed his B.A. (1905) and M.A. (1907) after interrupting his studies to teach school in 1900, 1901, and 1903. In 1907 he began his doctoral studies at Columbia University and completed his Ph.D. in a record two years. He was married in 1910 to Elizabeth Janeway; they had one son. He refused a Bruce fellowship at Johns Hopkins University in order to join the faculty at Indiana University. In 1927 Payne chaired the zoology department and served as dean of the graduate school. He retired in 1951 and did full-time research in a laboratory the university provided for him. When he was ninety, he entered a home for the aged in Frankfort, Indiana, where he spent his final years writing an autobiography.

Payne's research while a student at Indiana University was morphological and behavioral. He studied blind fauna with Carl Eigenmann. His first paper (1906) was a histological study of the rudimentary eyes of the blind Cuban lizard *Amphisboena punctata*. He confirmed Eigenmann's rule that degenerate organs show a more severe alteration of their active parts (for instance, the muscles and iris of the eye) than of their inactive parts (cornea, retina, and lens). The following year Payne published a behavioral analysis of blind fish that abound in the limestone caves of southern Indiana. He demonstrated that the fish, *Amblyopsis spelaeus*, is negatively phototropic, positively geotropic, and responsive to light through its skin. He proved that its vestigial eyes play no role in these characteristics.

Payne served as curator of Eigenmann's extensive fish collection but preferred more modern work for his dissertation. He received a fellowship to attend Columbia University and quickly began projects with Thomas Hunt Morgan and Edmund Beecher Wilson. Morgan suggested that he use *Drosophila* raised in total darkness for many generations to study the effects of disuse on the flies' response to light. Morgan had not yet begun his own work on *Drosophila* in 1907, but he did use Payne's cultures later when he tried to duplicate Hugo de Vries's experiments on speciation through sudden mutations. Payne's results, based on sixty-nine generations of flies grown in the dark, showed no permanent effects of disuse other than a delayed response to positive phototropism of a few seconds that he did not believe to be significant because other factors, such as food conditions in the dark, may have played a role.

For Wilson, Payne began a series of remarkably detailed studies of the toad bug *Gelastocoris* (formerly *Galgulus*) *oculatus* and the kissing bugs (*Reduviidae*). In these hemipteran bugs the sex chromosomes are distributed in unequal sets, producing males and females with different chromosome numbers. The females produce eggs with a uniform number of sex chromosomes, but the males produce an unequal $1 + (N - 1)$ distribution. This led to fertilizations yielding, for male and female, respectively, three or four in *Fitchia*, four or six in *Prionidus*, and four or eight sex chromosomes in *Acholla* among the *Reduviidae*. For *Gelastocoris* he found a spectacular clustering of the sex chromosomes within a circle of autosomes, the sex chromosomes distributing in a $1 + 4$ pattern in spermatogenesis and in a $4 + 4$ pattern in oogenesis. The eggs (fifteen autosomes + four sex chromosomes) would thus result in diploid cells of thirty-eight ($30 + 8$) and thirty-five ($30 + 5$) for the daughter and son, respectively.

Payne's work proved that sex chromosomes are not simply XX = female, X or XY = male. He believed the multiplication of sex chromosomes arose by fragmentation of a single X from an original species having XX female and X male origin, and that the number of sex chromosomes was not the exclusive basis for sex determination.

After Payne was married and settled into his teaching and research at Indiana, he took a leave in 1912 to tour Europe. He worked at the Naples Zoological Station, where he demonstrated that U.S. and European mole crickets of the genus *Gryllotalpa* differ in chromosome number, a finding that contradicted Clarence E. McClung's belief that closely related species share a common chromosome number. At Würzburg, Payne visited Theodor Boveri, who suggested that he study the effects of radium on the fertilized eggs of the nematode *Ascaris megalocephala univalens*. Payne observed numerous chromosome fragments and unequal distributions of chromosome material in the cleavage stages. After returning to Indiana, he studied the effects of selection on scutellar bristle number in *Drosophila* and found he could increase it from 4 to a mean of 9.85 after thirty-eight generations. When he could not select back to the original four bristles, he concluded that he had begun with a heterozygous stock and ended up with a highly homozygous one that had lost most of its variability.

Payne's contributions to genetics after 1918 were not based on his further research but on his skills as an administrator. As dean of the graduate school he actively recruited outstanding scholars, especially in the life sciences, including Ralph Cleland, Tracy M. Sonneborn, and Hermann J. Muller. Payne's philosophy was to encourage scholarly research and to protect his most productive faculty from committee work and routine clerical activities. He was a person of uncommon tolerance, willing to overlook past errors and refractory personalities, as well as to bend rules to bring out the best in his colleagues and students.

BIBLIOGRAPHY

I. Original Works. "The Eyes of the Blind Vertebrates of North America. VII. The Eyes of *Amphisboena punctata* (Bell), a Blind Lizard from Cuba," in *Biological Bulletin*, **11** (1906), 60–70; "The Reactions of the Blind Fish *Amblyopsis spelaeus* to Light," ibid., **13** (1907), 317–323; "On the Sexual Differences of the Chromosome Groups in *Galgulus oculatus*," ibid., **14** (1908), 297–303; "Some New Types of Chromosome Distribution and Their Relation to Sex," ibid., **16** (1909), 119–166; "A Study of the Effect of Radium upon the Eggs of *Ascaris megalocephala univalens*," in *Archiv für Entwicklungsmechanik der Organismen*, **36** (1913), 287–293; "A Study of the Germ Cells of *Gryllotalpa borealis* and *Gryllotalpa vulgaris*," in *Journal of Morphology*, **28** (1916), 287–327; and *Memories and Reflections* (Bloomington, Ind., 1975).

Payne's papers are at Indiana University, in the Lilly Library and the Jordan Hall Biology Library.

II. Secondary Literature. For an account of Payne's role in recruiting H. J. Muller, see Elof Axel Carlson, *Genes, Radiation and Society: The Life and Work of H. J. Muller* (Ithaca, N.Y., 1981), 286–287. For Payne's account of how he recruited J. D. Watson as a graduate student and changed his interest from ornithology to genetics, see his *Memories and Reflections*, 99.

Elof Axel Carlson

PEGRAM, GEORGE BRAXTON (*b.* Trinity, North Carolina, 24 October 1876; *d.* Swarthmore, Pennsylvania, 12 August 1958), *physics, academic administration.*

Pegram was one of five children of William Howell Pegram, professor of chemistry at Trinity College (later Duke University) and Emma Craven Pegram, daughter of the college's founder. His upbringing left him with a taste for methodical work and the friendly, soft-spoken demeanor of a Southerner, a manner that served him well in the many positions of trust he came to hold. After taking his bachelor's degree at Trinity in 1895, Pegram worked as a high school teacher and then, in 1899, went to Columbia University. In 1900 he became a teaching assistant in physics and began a steady advance up the academic ladder, with a doctorate in physics in 1903 and an instructorship in 1905, achieving full professorship in 1918. Despite attractive offers he spent his entire career at Columbia.

Pegram's career was centered on administration. He became executive officer of the department of physics in 1913 and continued to head the department until 1945. In 1917 he was named acting dean, and in 1918 dean, of the Faculty of Applied Sciences. He resigned in 1930, hoping to return to research, but in 1936 was called to serve as dean of graduate faculties, a post he held until 1949. Professional organizations also claimed Pegram's time. He was treasurer (1918–1957) and president (1941) of the American Physical Society; treasurer (1917–1949) and president (1949–1951) of Sigma Xi; and both secretary (1931–1945) and treasurer (1938–1956) of the American Institute of Physics.

Pegram remained active after going into semiretirement in the mid 1950's. With all his responsibilities he had little time for scientific research; it was as a master of budgets and committees that he made an indelible mark on the American physics community.

Pegram's doctoral dissertation, "Secondary Radioactivity in the Electrolysis of Thorium Solutions," led him into the popular new field of radiation measurements, and over the next decade he and others at Columbia ran a brisk sideline business checking the radioactivity of ores, mineral waters, and supposedly therapeutic potions. Pegram's chance to learn more advanced science came in 1907, when a Tyndall fellowship enabled him to study at European physics laboratories, notably those in Cambridge and Berlin. During his travels he met Florence Bement; they were married on 3 June 1909 and had two sons.

Pegram had published little research when he moved into administration, and except for helping to organize submarine detection studies during World War I, he did no more science until the 1930–1936 hiatus in his deanships. That was a good period to return to work: the neutron had been discovered (1932), and nuclear physics had burst out of its tradition of passive radioactivity measurements. Pegram joined forces with John R. Dunning and other young members of the Physics Department, making them discuss their ideas and contributing many of his own, turning up in the laboratories at any hour of the day or night. He signed some thirty papers and short notes, always in collaboration, and participated in much other work he did not sign. The papers reported a variety of painstaking measurements on the absorption and scattering of neutrons, particularly slow neutrons, and established an important body of facts.

Columbia was becoming a world center for nuclear research, and Pegram helped to advance this reputation, not only in the area of research but also in administration. Already in 1926 he had moved the physics department into a tall new building. In the 1930's he raised funds to build a cyclotron and attracted and encouraged a brilliant group of scientists, including Harold Urey, I. I. Rabi, and Enrico Fermi.

After the discovery of uranium fission (1939), when Fermi and others launched the effort that would lead to the first nuclear reactor, they turned to Pegram for organizational help and advice. In March 1939 he sent Adm. S. C. Hooper, chairman of the Naval Research Committee, the first letter any government body received from a scientist suggesting work on the release of nuclear energy. As the work unfolded, he took a prominent role on the National Defense Research Council's Advisory Committee on Uranium, which laid the foundations for the Manhattan Project. At the same time he chaired Columbia's Committee on War Research, overseeing such work as the establishment of the U.S. Navy's Underwater Sound Research Laboratory, birthplace of a magnetic airborne detector that helped clear the Atlantic of German submarines. For a decade after the war, Pegram continued to be deeply involved in the university's relations with military research. At the same time he quietly opposed excessive reliance on nuclear weapons.

It is hard to evaluate Pegram's impact on Columbia as graduate dean, as vice president (1949–1950), and as friend and adviser to the university's presidents. But "Dean Pegram," as everyone called him, probably accomplished much behind the scenes with his ability to remain calm through divisive committee meetings, his mastery of budgets, and his talent for getting others to do what was needed.

Pegram's influence within the physics community is more obvious. By the 1930's he was one of the half-dozen elder statesmen of the American Physical Society, the men who had to be consulted before any new steps were taken and who usually initiated such steps. Most significant was Pegram's founding, with Karl T. Compton and a few others, of the American Institute of Physics (1931). The constitution, bylaws, and traditions of this federation of societies, crafted by Pegram more than anyone else, gave physics a professional administrative apparatus and a coherent public role that would become the envy of other disciplines.

Brookhaven National Laboratory was another institution born in discussions at Columbia, and again Pegram was a founding board member, serving as trustee of Brookhaven's parent organization, Associated Universities, Inc. He was also trustee of the Oak Ridge Institute of Nuclear Studies, and served the American Physical Society and Sigma Xi, as well as many other professional societies.

BIBLIOGRAPHY

I. ORIGINAL WORKS. Pegram's papers are at Columbia University.

II. SECONDARY LITERATURE. A memoir by Lee Anna Embrey is in *Biographical Memoirs. National Academy of Sciences*, **41** (1970), 357–407, with bibliography; one by Karl K. Darrow is in *Yearbook of the American Philosophical Society* (1961), 152–158.

SPENCER R. WEART

PEYER, BERNHARD (*b.* Schaffhausen, Switzerland, 25 July 1885; *d.* Zurich, Switzerland, 23 February 1963), *paleontology.*

Peyer was the son of Bernhard Peyer, a manufacturer, and Sophie Frey. In the spring of 1905 he completed his classical education at Schaffhausen. While still in secondary school, he became acquainted with the geologist Ferdinand Schalch, who was doing fieldwork in the Schaffhausen area. There had been scientists in his family for many years, the most notable being the anatomist Johann Conrad Peyer (1653–1712).

In the autumn of 1905, Peyer began his studies in general natural sciences at Tübingen, where he spent three semesters. He continued his studies in Munich, where he attended lectures on zoology given by Richard von Hertwig and on paleontology by Ferdinand Broili and Ernst Stromer von Reichenbach. In the autumn of 1907 Peyer matriculated at the University of Zurich, where he wrote his dissertation, "Die Entwicklung des Schädelskeletes von *Vipera aspis*," under the guidance of Arnold Lang, a student of the zoologist Ernst Haeckel. Peyer took part in several expeditions to Rovigno, Italy (1912), England (with Schalch, 1907), and South America (with the anatomist Hans Bluntschli, 1912–1913). The last gave him the opportunity to study and collect rich material of anthropoid monkeys.

In 1918 Peyer became qualified as *Privatdozent*. His inaugural lecture, "Wesen und Ziele der Paläontologie," represented the beginning of systematic paleontological research at the Zoological Institute in Zurich. The title of his inaugural dissertation was "Ueber die Flossenstacheln der Welse und Panzerwelse, sowie der Karpfen." This interest in fossil vertebrates was connected with the beginning of systematic excavations, in 1924, of Middle Triassic strata of Monte San Giorgio in southern Switzerland, which yielded the most comprehensive vertebrate fauna then known. Several excavations were organized by Peyer (supported by the Georges and Antoine Claraz Foundation and the director of the Zoological Institute, Karl Hescheler). The most important records of vertebrates were described in monographs by Peyer and published especially in the *Schweizerische paläontologische Abhandlungen*.

Besides his work in southern Switzerland, Peyer did research on the evolution of mammals. According to the dates of the geological fieldwork of Schalch in the Klettgau region (northern Switzerland), in 1942 Peyer discovered in Upper Triassic layers at Hallau, about seventy teeth of primitive mammals and mammal-like reptiles.

In recognition of his scientific work, Peyer was an honorary member of a great many natural science societies, including the Naturforschende Gesellschaft Schaffhausen (1932), and Basel (1953), and the Kaiserlich Leopoldinisch-Carolinische Deutsche Akademie der Naturforscher in Halle.

In 1926 Peyer married Hildegard Amsler; they had five children. The first notable record (excavation

in 1924) of a new placodont was named after her, *Cyamodus hildegardis,* and described in 1931.

In 1930 Peyer was appointed associate professor, in 1939 director of the Museum of Zoology and Anthropology at the University of Zurich (a post he held until his retirement), and in 1943 full professor at the University of Zurich. He retired in 1955. Peyer was deeply interested in the history of dentition. About 1960 he began the preparation of a volume on comparative odontology that was published posthumously. Besides his extensive paleontological research, Peyer produced numerous publications on the history of medicine and biology. Peyer died after a long illness. His work was recognized in 1967 by the community of Meride, where he had lived during the excavations at Monte San Giorgio, by the naming of a street for him.

BIBLIOGRAPHY

I. ORIGINAL WORKS. A complete bibliography of Peyer's works can be found in the obituary by H.-C. Peyer (see below).

II. SECONDARY LITERATURE. Obituaries of Peyer include H. Fischer, "Bernhard Peyer 1885–1963," in *Gesnerus,* **20** (1963), 179, and "Bernhard Peyer (1885–1963)," in *Vierteljahrsschrift der Naturforschenden Gesellschaft Zürich,* **108** (1963), 467; H.-C. Peyer, "Prof. Dr. Bernhard Peyer 1885–1963," in *Verhandlungen der schweizerischen Naturforscher Gesellschaft* (1963), 242, with bibliography by E. Kuhn-Schnyder; J. Piveteau, "Notice nécrologique sur Bernhard Peyer," in *Actes des sciences* (1963), 4087; and Rainer Zangerl, "Bernhard Peyer, 1885–1963," in *News Bulletin, Society of Vertebrate Paleontology,* no. 68 (1963).

RUDOLF SCHLATTER

PFANNENSTIEL, MAX JAKOB (*b.* Wanzenau, Alsace, Germany [now France], 25 July 1902; *d.* Freiburg im Breisgau, Federal Republic of Germany, 2 January 1976), *geology.*

Pfannenstiel, a versatile geologist whose work encompassed paleontology, Quaternary geology, marine geology, and the history of geology, was the son of Hermann and Maria Reinach Pfannenstiel. His father was a notary and senior government adviser who came from a family of lawyers. The family subsequently moved to Mainz, where he graduated from the gymnasium in 1921. Pfannenstiel then studied natural sciences, particularly geology, with W. Salomon-Calvi in Heidelberg and occasionally with H. Cloos in Breslau. He received his doctorate under Salomon-Calvi in 1926, with a dissertation on joint tectonics: "Vergleichende Untersuchung der Grund- und Deckgebirgsklüfte im südlichen Odenwald" (published 1927). In 1926 he became an assistant to W. Deecke at Freiburg im Breisgau, where he remained until 1930. Then he studied to qualify as a science librarian, completing this course at Munich in 1932. On 8 April 1933 he married Christine Hormuth; they had two daughters. On 1 August 1933, Pfannenstiel was dismissed on racial grounds from his civil service position at the University of Freiburg library. Thereafter he worked in a bookstore in Freiburg.

In this first period of scientific activity in Freiburg, Pfannenstiel made important contributions to a fossil catalog of the Upper Rhine (1931) and studied fossil amphibians. Other interests included the volcanic history of the Kaiserstuhl and the volcanic tuff of the foothills region.

From 1935 to 1938, Pfannenstiel was in Geneva as a Rockefeller scholar at the library of the Hygienics Institute of the League of Nations. Then Salomon-Calvi, who had been working in Ankara since 1934, found him a position there as director of the library of the agricultural technical school. The new environment awakened new interests: the diluvial rubble terraces of Ankara and the Old Stone Age cultures of Anatolia. Above all, being at a site that earlier had been on the coast kindled in him an enduring passion for the sea. In 1941 Pfannenstiel returned to Germany, where he was called up for military service. (His being one-quarter Jewish was of less importance than his knowledge of the eastern Mediterranean.) Doing cartographical work with the Berlin-Wannsee military geological staff and examining the hydrogeological relationships of Palestine and bordering regions, he was able to gather additional material for his Quaternary geological studies of the Levant.

In 1945 Pfannenstiel resumed his duties at the library of the University of Freiburg, and on 1 January 1947 he was named professor of geology, as successor to Wolfgang Soergel. In 1949 and 1950 Pfannenstiel served as dean of the department of mathematics and natural sciences; in 1954 and 1955 he was rector of the university.

Besides constructing the geological institute, Pfannenstiel used his mastery of the written and the spoken word to renew severed ties with Switzerland and France. And, to increase knowledge of early Tertiary vertebrates, he made systematic excavations near Oehningen (1947–1950) and at Höwenegg.

In Freiburg two interests crystallized out of Pfannenstiel's earlier involvement with coastal geology: marine geology and the Ice Age. The evidence of Ice Age mirror variations of the Mediterranean and the Black Sea shed light on the Quaternary history of those areas. With his students Pfannenstiel developed bathymetric charts of the eastern Mediterranean. In "Quartär der Levante," he addressed the coastal history of Palestine and Syria as well as the oasis depression in Egypt. As early as 1947, he devoted himself to researching the Quaternary of the Black Forest region. He and his colleague G. Rahm arrived at the view that during the Riss phase of the Ice Age, the glaciated area was substantially larger than had previously been thought.

Pfannenstiel became preoccupied with the history of geology and wrote articles on the subject. In 1970 he became emeritus. He devoted his last years to the reconstruction of the "geologists' archive," whose 45,000 manuscripts had fallen victim to wartime bombing.

Pfannenstiel was an amiable, generous man, and an enthusiastic researcher with deep roots in the tradition. Among his honors were member of the German Academy of Natural Scientists, Leopoldina (1952); honorary doctorate, University of Besançon (1961); member of the Heidelberg Academy of Sciences, Mathematics-Natural History Class (1962); officer of the Order of the Palms of the Paris Academy of Sciences (1966); and the Hans Stille Medal of the German Geological Society (1974).

BIBLIOGRAPHY

I. Original Works. A bibliography of Pfannenstiel's writings by Hugo Genser is in *Berichte der Naturforschenden Gesellschaft Freiburg im Breisgau*, **67** (1977), 13–19. His works include "Vergleichende Untersuchung der Grund- und Deckgebirgsklüfte im südlichen Odenwald," in *Berichte der Naturforschenden Gesellschaft Freiburg im Breisgau*, **27** (1927), 1–98, his dissertation; "Wirbellose und Wirbeltiere des Palaeozoikums," in *Oberrheinische Fossilienkatalog*, Lieferung 1 (Berlin, 1931), 1–25, with Wilhelm Salomon-Calvi; "Gehirnkapsel und Gehirn fossiler Amphibien," in *Monographien zur Geologie und Paläontologie*, 2nd ser., VI (Berlin, 1932), 1–85; "Die diluvialen Schotterterrassen von Ankara und ihre Einordnung in die europäische Quartärchronologie," in *Geologische Rundschau*, **31** (1940), 407–432; "Diluvialen Entwicklungsstudien und die Urgeschichte von Dardanellen, Marmarameer und Bosporus," *ibid.*, **34** (1944), 341–434; "Lorenz Oken," in *Reden der Wissenschaftliche Gesellschaft Freiburg im Breisgau*, **14** (1953), 1–24; "Die Vergletscherung des südlichen Schwarzwaldes während der Risseiszeit," in *Berichte der Naturforschenden Gesellschaft Freiburg im Breisgau*, **48** (1959), 231–272; and "Das Meer in der Geschichte der Geologie," in *Geologische Rundschau*, **60** (1970), 3–72.

II. SECONDARY LITERATURE. There is a list of secondary literature in Gilbert Rahm, "Pfannenstiel, M. J.," in *Badische Biographie*, n.s. **1** (1982), 220–221. See René Hantke and Gilbert Rahm, "Max Pfannenstiel †, 1902–1976," in *Eiszeitalter und Gegenwart*, **26** (1975), 277–279; Franz Kirchheimer, "Max Pfannenstiel," in *Nachrichten der Deutschen geologischen Gesellschaft*, **15** (1976), 34–37; Max Schwarzbach, "Max Pfannenstiel, 1902–1976," in *Geologische Rundschau*, **65** (1976), 1130–1132; and Otto Wittmann, "Max Pfannenstiel, 1902–1976," in *Jahresberichte und Mitteilungen des Oberrheinischen geologischen Vereins*, n.s. **58** (1978), 77–79.

EMIL KUHN-SCHNYDER

PLACZEK, GEORGE (*b*. Brünn, Moravia [now Brno, Czechoslovakia], 26 September 1905; *d*. Zurich, Switzerland, 16 October 1955), *molecular spectrocopy, nuclear physics*.

Placzek was the oldest of three children born to Alexander Plazcek and Marianne Pollack. His father owned a factory in Brünn, and the family was quite well-to-do. Placzek apparently attended primary and secondary schools in Brünn, displaying abilities in both science and languages. Later known for his unusual erudition, he particularly enjoyed reading Renaissance science treatises in their original languages. Placzek and his family were Jewish but did not practice the religion. His parents and sister were deported and died and his brother committed suicide during World War II. Placzek was twice married, the second time, in 1943, to Els Halban. He suffered for many years from pernicious high blood pressure, which caused considerable pain in later years. He became an American citizen in 1945.

Placzek studied physics at the universities of Prague and Vienna, receiving his doctorate under Felix Ehrenhaft in 1928. His dissertation involved an experimental study of the electrodynamics of colloidal particles. His subsequent work, pursued at the leading research centers in Europe and America, concerned the scattering of electromagnetic radiation and neutrons in matter. He was regarded as a foremost authority on both subjects.

Electromagnetic waves entering matter are reflected, refracted, or dispersed in various directions and at various frequencies. Working with H. A. Kramers and L. S. Ornstein at Utrecht (1928–1931), Placzek began applying the newly established quantum mechanics to the equally recent discovery of the Raman effect, a type of inelastic scattering of light by molecules. Unlike elastic (Rayleigh) scattering, the emitted frequency differs from the incident frequency, since the scattering molecule is left in an excited vibrational or rotational state. The frequencies of such states, which yield infrared electron spectra, appear in the Raman effect as shifts in the visible or ultraviolet spectra. Both the infrared and the Raman spectra depend on the symmetry of the molecular configuration, but in different ways. Valuable symmetry information can be extracted from a comparison of the two types of observations. This is now a standard procedure in molecular chemistry, but it relies upon relating the properties of Raman spectra to molecular symmetry.

Placzek was the founder of this important line of research. Taking a phenomenological approach, he related the amplitudes and polarizations of the observed Raman lines to the matrix elements of the polarization tensor of the scattering molecule, taken between vibrational and rotational quantum states. While the infrared spectra derive from the electric dipole moment of the molecule, the Raman spectra depend upon more complex configurations and symmetries. In 1932 Placzek wrote the then definitive treatise on the Raman effect while at Fermi's institute in Rome.

During the period 1932–1939 Placzek worked intermittently at Bohr's institute in Copenhagen and with Lev Landau in Kharkov. During the 1934–1935 academic year he taught at the Hebrew University in Jerusalem; in 1938 he worked with Hans von Halban, Jr., in Joliot's institute in Paris; and in 1939 he was appointed research associate at Cornell University. During these travels Placzek's research turned increasingly to experimental and theoretical studies of neutron absorption and neutron-induced reactions, topics inspired by the discovery of the neutron in 1932.

Placzek's work in Copenhagen rendered him a leading authority on neutron scattering and absorption in matter. In a series of experiments, Placzek and Otto Frisch demonstrated that the absorption of neutrons in matter is strongly dependent upon the atomic mass of the material and the velocity of the neutrons, but for slow neutrons and light elements, such as boron 10, the neutron-capture cross section is inversely proportional to the velocity, v. They used boron 10 as a velocity "indicator" to study neutron absorption in heavier elements, for which they observed absorption resonances. Placzek and H. A. Bethe provided a fundamental theory of neutron absorption resonances by analogy to the Raman effect, from which they derived the $1/v$ law and selection rules for various forms of inelastic scattering. Using the optical theorem and Bohr's liquid-drop model of the nucleus, Placzek, Bohr, and Peierls offered a fundamental theory of neutron-induced nuclear reactions. These works proved essential to the subsequent development of nuclear theory and to development of nuclear reactor design.

Placzek's critical skepticism of any work, including his own, sometimes hindered his publications but it stimulated others to clarify and to expand upon their ideas. This was evident after the discovery of nuclear fission late in 1938. Placzek's initial skepticism induced Frisch, then in Copenhagen, to search for fission fragments. It also encouraged Bohr's realization of the crucial isotope effect for natural uranium: uranium 235 is fissionable by slow neutrons, uranium 238 by fast; intermediate-velocity neutrons have no effect.

After conceding the existence of fission, Placzek worked at Cornell, and in collaboration with Fermi's group at Columbia University, on problems of neutron propagation in nuclear chain reactions. In 1943 Halban appointed Placzek head of the Theoretical Physics Division of the Canadian Nuclear Research Laboratory at Chalk River, near Montreal. In 1945 he joined the staff of the Los Alamos Scientific Laboratory; in 1946 he transferred to the laboratories of the General Electric Company; and in 1948 he became a member of the Institute for Advanced Study at Princeton. His research after 1942 concerned methods for the treatment of the slowing down and diffusion of neutrons in matter for application to reactor design. His lectures at Los Alamos on neutron diffusion became a standard textbook on the subject.

Much of Placzek's work during his last years remains unpublished, just as his contributions as a communicator and critic of ideas remain little appreciated. His work at Princeton, supported in part by the Atomic Energy Commission, continued to concern the relationship of neutron diffusion to material structure. His pioneering studies of the inelastic scattering of high-energy neutrons in dense crystals contributed both to crystallography and to reactor design, and opened a new field of interdisciplinary research. In the midst of this research Placzek suffered a fatal heart attack shortly after arriving in Europe to begin a Guggenheim Fellowship in Rome.

BIBLIOGRAPHY

I. ORIGINAL WORKS. Bibliographies of most of Placzek's publications may be found in Edoardo Amaldi, "George Placzek," *La ricerca scientifica*, **26** (1956), 2037–2042; and in Poggendorff, VIIb (Berlin, 1980), 4040–4041. Placzek's main treatises on the scattering of radiation and neutrons are "Rayleigh-Streuung und Raman-Effekt," in Erich Marx, ed., *Handbuch der Radiologie*, VI, pt. 2 (Leipzig, 1934), 205–374, translated by Ann Werbin as *The Rayleigh and Raman Scattering* (Berkeley, Calif., 1959); and *Introduction to the Theory of Neutron Diffusion*, I (Los Alamos, N.Mex., 1953), written with K. M. Case and F. de Hoffmann.

Manuscript sources include one box of papers at the Center for the History of Physics, American Institute of Physics, New York; correspondence in the possession of friends and colleagues; and scattered materials listed in the Inventory of Sources for History of Twentieth Century Physics, University of California, Berkeley.

II. SECONDARY LITERATURE. The most complete obituaries include those by Amaldi, cited above; and by Léon van Hove, *George Placzek 1905–1955* (Princeton, n.d.), and "George Placzek (1905–1955)," in *Nuclear Physics*, **1** (1956), 623–626. Recollections are provided by Otto R. Frisch, "Experimental Work With Nuclei: Hamburg, London, Copenhagen," in Roger H. Stuewer, ed., *Nuclear Physics in Retrospect: Proceedings of a Symposium on the 1930s* (Minneapolis, 1979), 65–75; and John A. Wheeler, "Some Men and Moments in the History of Nuclear Physics: The Interplay of Colleagues and Motivations," *ibid.*, 217–306. See also Lew Kowarski, interview by Charles Weiner, 3 May 1970, transcript at Center for History of Physics, American Institute of Physics, New York. An account of some of Placzek's wartime research activities is provided by Spencer Weart, *Scientists in Power* (Cambridge, Mass., 1979). A textbook account of the Raman effect, based in large part on Placzek's work, is Gerhard Herzberg, *Molecular Spectra and Molecular Structure*, II, *Infrared and Raman Spectra of Polyatomic Molecules*, J. W. T. Spinks, trans. (New York, 1945).

DAVID C. CASSIDY

POHL, ROBERT WICHARD (*b*. Hamburg, Germany, 10 August 1884; *d*. Göttingen, Germany, 5 June 1976), *physics*.

Pohl was the son of a shipbuilding engineer, Robert Pohl, and his wife, Martha Lange. His father's career had a major influence on his early interest in engineering and natural science. In Hamburg he attended the prestigious Johanneum, a classical gymnasium, from which he graduated in 1903. Even in his later years as a scientist, Pohl maintained a close relationship with this school, where the teaching of physics and mathematics was excellent. As a young student he was especially impressed by the worldwide excitement created by the discovery of X rays in 1895. He continued to have this enthusiasm for important but spectacular phenomena all his life.

Pohl studied physics at Heidelberg for one semester under Georg Hermann Quincke, to whom, later, he often attributed his guiding principle: "Theories come and go, facts are here to stay."

Pohl was almost notorious for his contempt for theoretical physics, though a closer look at his life reveals evidence of his high regard for it. At Heidelberg he also made the acquaintance of James Franck, studied with him at Berlin, later became his colleague at Göttingen, and eventually lost contact with him in 1933 after he resigned and left Germany because he opposed National Socialist policy against Jewish citizens. An important friendship developed between the two.

It was in Berlin (1904–1914) that Pohl's scientific personality took its definitive form. There he came to know Paul Drude, Heinrich Rubens, Emil Warburg, Walter Nernst, and their scientific work. While in the scientific colloquium, he reviewed Philipp Lenard's publications on luminescence. During his vacations he went home to Hamburg, where he conducted experiments on X-ray diffraction that were published in 1908. He had not forgotten Röntgen's discovery, the object of his childhood fascination.

But Pohl was also intrigued by the physics of gas discharge, the prerequisite of Röntgen's discovery. His first three publications, before his dissertation under Warburg in 1906, were on radiation of light caused by gas ionization. They soon gave his essential ideas for his first theses on the movement of electrons in solids. He qualified to lecture in 1911 with a research thesis, on X rays, that demonstrated that all diffraction experiments were ultimately inconclusive.

However, as early as 1904, Pohl had been working in a new field, solids. He had started with the photoelectric effect on metal surfaces, which had just gained great importance for science and metrology. With his colleague Peter Pringsheim he studied the effects of the state of polarization and the angle of incidence of light on the number of electrons emitted from surfaces of, for example, solid platinum, and also the quantum yield (electrons per light quantum). They utilized the new method of cathode sputtering to form metal surfaces. Moreover, in 1912 they developed their own experimentation technique, the evaporation of reflecting metal surfaces at pressures of 10^{-3} mm to 10^{-4} mm mercury. Their mastery of experimentation as well as their feel for important developments (such as quantum theory) brought the first major recognition for their work until 1914, just before World War I. During the war Pohl was a captain assigned to the development of radio technology.

In 1916 Pohl was offered an associate professorship of experimental physics at Göttingen University. However, he was not able to assume the post until after the war. In 1920 he became full professor and was named director of the First Physics Institute. In 1922 he married Auguste Madelung, sister of the physicist Erwin Madelung; they had two daughters and one son. With the newly appointed Franck and Max Born, Pohl started what came to be known as the splendid era of Göttingen as one of the world's centers for atomic physics; it was, however, brutally terminated by the National Socialists' accession to power in 1933 and the emigration of Franck, Born, and other Göttingen physicists.

The students at Göttingen had the choice among Pohl, the master of experimentation and demonstration; Franck, the genius at reconciling experiments with theory; and Born, the absolute theorist. The relationship among these three had its tensions; their personalities, fields of work, and opinions were too different. Franck's and Born's research met with great recognition from the beginning. Pohl's work remained virtually unknown until the 1930's.

In 1920 Pohl's interest had turned from the external to the internal photoelectric effect. From then on, he was especially interested in all phenomena related to electric processes within solids. The internal aspects of solids, however, were to many physicists, such as Wolfgang Pauli as early as 1931, only an "order-of-magnitude-physics" or simply "dirt effects." How could these lead to any major insights into nature? Indeed, one big problem was the low grade of purity of the crystals available in nature. The production of very pure alkali halides (first by Spiro Kyropoulos) in 1925 was the first major achievement of Pohl's Institute. Alkali halides as the ideal prototype then became an important object of study at Pohl's institute within the framework of a comprehensive research program pursued until World War II.

Analogous to the successful case of atomic physics, the existence of simple physical laws would be shown particularly by means of the optical and electrical characteristics of crystals. For instance, "multicolor" phenomena of light absorption would have a simple explanation, just like "multicolor" phenomena of gas discharges. The results achieved in these studies had a significance that went far beyond alkali halides as prototype, as Frederick Seitz put it in his review in 1946, which greatly influenced the future course of solid-state physics: "The properties of the alkali halides . . . have gradually provided us with a better and better understanding of some of the most interesting properties of all solids."

This was especially true of the optical and electrical explanation of a specific part of the visual spectrum, the absorption band of which was finally attributed to atomic defects joined with separable electrons, known after 1930 on as *Farbzentren* (color centers). The development of semiconductor technology and physics from 1926 on—especially with the rectifying substance copper dioxide (Cu_2O) used by the company Siemens and Halske in Berlin—was instrumental in the long discussions on the exact structure of these point defects. Based on the rejection of interstitial lattice ions being the primary carriers of current in Pohl's alkali halides, Walter Schottky developed his famous thesis of defects, named for him, stating that the number of anion and cation vacancies in a crystal lattice were equal. At an international conference in Bristol, England, in 1937, the most important feature of which was a comprehensive review lecture by Pohl on alkali halide research, the color center was definitively identified as an electron in an anion vacancy. This conference was as significant to the physics of the nearly perfect crystal as the first Solvay Conference was for quantum theory. Defects in crystals and their significant effects on many qualities of solids were becoming increasingly important as objects of research in physics and engineering.

Other studies conducted by Pohl's school were on ion conductivity, photochemical processes (in connection with silver salts), and the luminescence of alkali halides and related substances. Pohl's most important colleagues were Bernhard Gudden (even before 1925), Rudolf Hilsch, and Erich Mollwo. Pohl was the one who determined how and in which direction research was to be conducted, but the results depended largely on the others' skill. What made these results greatly significant for the subsequent development in the theoretical field were the meticulousness and creative imagination with which the institute utilized equipment and conducted experiments, Pohl's feel for broad interconnections as well as for the limitations of big programs, and the ability of his colleagues to find questions answerable through experimentation and to answer them. These results were no doubt achieved also through Pohl's persistent adherence, as much as possible, to irrefutable quantitative facts obtainable through experiments, as well as through his excellent—even though authoritarian—leadership and his knack for wise management (especially in his contacts with the university, the institutions promoting research, and industry). His institute also conducted research of an international order but of an entirely different nature, such as the first important tests leading to the discovery of vitamin D (absorption spectroscopy of cholesterol, 1926) and research on the eyes of spiders.

Many of the results also led to technologically important developments. One was already mentioned: the production of artificial crystals. The discovery of crystal luminescence, for example, led to the design of the scintillation counter; photochemistry led to a better understanding of the processes in photographic layers; the production of thin layers and the observation of the reduction in reflection led to the optical coating of lenses. The first working amplifier crystal (analogous to the three-electrode amplifier tube) was built at Pohl's institute by R. Hilsch in 1938. But it can hardly be considered the direct precursor of the transistor, since it was basically unusable for steady operation and common frequencies. Pohl was highly interested in the technological significance of scientific results, but he regarded basic research as the exclusive duty of his university institute.

Pohl's lectures, speeches, and textbooks played an instrumental role in the way the teaching of physics developed. His experimental lectures—called "Zirkus Pohl" with a mixture of respect and mockery—have been shaping university teaching for over thirty years, adding important innovations in method, such as the elimination of fixed lecture desks and the introduction of slide presentation of instruments and experiments. His university textbooks, which were even more influential, had appeared in fifty-one editions in Germany by the time of his death. They have been translated into several languages.

BIBLIOGRAPHY

I. ORIGINAL WORKS. There is no scientific bibliography or edition of Pohl's publications. There are, however, lists in Poggendorff, V, 989–990; VI, 2037–2038; and VIIa, pt. 3, 601–602.

Between 1905 and 1955 Pohl's name appeared as author or coauthor of about 170 articles. His family, in Göttingen, owns a collection of special editions in bound single volumes. The Deutsche Museum in Munich owns a copy of their catalog. There were further publications after 1955. For the period between 1905 and 1938 there is a printed list of Pohl's publications in *Jahrbuch der Deutschen Akademie der Luftfahrtforschung*, **2** (1939), 118–124. Besides his textbooks *Einführung in die Elektrizitätslehre* (Berlin, 1927); *Einführung in die Mechanik und Akustik* (Berlin, 1930); *Einführung in die Optik* (Berlin, 1940; after 1954, . . . *Optik und Atomphysik*), he published two major monographs: *Die Physik der Röntgenstrahlen* (Brunswick, 1912) and *Die lichtelektrischen Erscheinungen* (Brunswick, 1914), with Peter Pringsheim.

There are archival documents, such as letters from and to Pohl, manuscripts, and tape recordings of interviews with him, at various locations; some copies are at the

Deutsches Museum, Munich. Unfortunately, there is no longer a record of almost the entire correspondence of Pohl before 1945. For a more detailed listing, see Jürgen Teichmann, "Für Geschichte der Festkörperphysik-Farbzentrenforschung bis 1940" (Stuttgart, 1988). A tape recording of an interview with Pohl has been published: "Statement from R. Pohl to C. A. Hempstead, 25 July 1974, in Krefeld," Rosemarie Teare, trans., in Nevill F. Mott, *The Beginnings of Solid State Physics* (London, 1980), 112–115. See also Joan Warnow-Blewelt and Jürgen Teichmann, comps., *Guide to Sources for History of Solid State Physics* (New York, 1989).

II. SECONDARY LITERATURE. Ernst Caspari, "The Lectures of Professor Robert Pohl in Göttingen," in *American Journal of Physics,* **19** (1951), 61–63; Walter Gerlach, "Robert Wichard Pohl 10.8.1884–5.6.1976," in *Jahrbuch der Bayerischen Akademie der Wissenschaften,* 1978, 214–219; and Bernhard Gudden, "R. W. Pohl zum 60. Geburtstag," in *Die Naturwissenschaften,* **32** (1944), 166–169. See also Frederick Seitz, "Color Centers in Alkali Halide Crystals," in *Reviews of Modern Physics,* **18** (1946), 384–408; *R. W. Pohl, Gedächtniskolloquium* (Göttingen, 1978).

JÜRGEN TEICHMANN

POLÁNYI, MIHÁLY (MICHAEL) (*b.* Budapest, Hungary, 12 March 1891; *d.* Northampton, England, 22 February 1976), *chemistry, philosophy, sociology.*

Polányi came from a middle-class family. His father, Mihály, was a civil engineer and businessman who planned and developed railroads. His mother, Cecilia Wohl, regularly held literary gatherings that attracted the leftist intelligentsia, some of them Marxists. The children of the family—Laura, Charles, and Michael—joined left-wing youth movements at an early age.

Polányi studied medicine at the University of Budapest, graduating in 1913. At the age of nineteen, before receiving his medical degree, he published a paper entitled "Adatok a hydrocephalus polyadek kemiajahoz" (Chemistry of the hydrocephalic liquid, 1910) and in 1911 reported on his investigations concerning the chemical and physical changes in blood serum during starvation. From 1914 to 1917 Polányi served as a medical officer in the army. In 1917, besides qualifying as a physician, he earned the Ph.D. from the University of Budapest with a dissertation on the thermodynamics of adsorption of gases. Three years later he expounded this theory—at the invitation of Fritz Haber—in a public discussion at the Kaiser Wilhelm Institute of Physical Chemistry in Berlin at which Einstein was another participant. Although his theory was rejected at the time, his views began to gain acceptance in the 1930's.

During the Hungarian Republic (1919–1920) Polányi was under secretary of health. In 1920 he married Magda Kemény, a chemist; they had two sons. Polányi and his wife then immigrated to Germany, where he became *Privatdozent* at the Technical University of Karlsruhe and did physical-chemical research that produced important results. Later in 1920 Polányi was hired by the Kaiser Wilhelm Institute for Fiber Chemistry in Berlin. He worked in a novel field, research on vegetable fibers, and was the first to apply and interpret X-ray diffraction in structure investigations of fibers. With K. Weissenberg he improved the rotating crystal method of X-ray analysis developed by M. de Broglie, which proved to be of eminent importance in crystallography. In 1923 Polányi became a researcher at the Kaiser Wilhelm Institute for Physical Chemistry, working on the plasticity of solids. While there he established his well-known dislocation theory. His work with Eugene Wigner concerned the uncertainty principle for angular momentum and the absolute rate of unimolecular dissociation.

Polányi left Berlin when Hitler seized power in 1933; he immigrated to England, where he became professor of physical chemistry at the University of Manchester. His main work there was in reaction kinetics; major achievements were the theory of bimolecular activation energy (with Henry Eyring), the generalized theory of absolute rates of reaction (with Meredith Evans), and studies on ionic reactions in solution, on bond dissociation energies, and on the mechanism of polymerization.

In the meantime, Polányi's interest in the social sciences was reawakened. He started to publish on such subjects and soon became better known for these writings than for his accomplishments, by no means insignificant, in physical chemistry. In 1948 he gave up his professorship in physical chemistry for a personal chair in social studies at the University of Manchester. He retired in 1958 but continued work in sociology and philosophy of science as senior research fellow of Merton College, Oxford.

Polányi's philosophical-sociological activities spanned a very broad field. His views won him many adherents, particularly in the United States, but also gave rise to sharp criticism, rejection, and even disparagement. The historical analysis of the paths of scientific discoveries led him to make conclusions regarding the general values of human society. He attacked positivistic and postpositivistic scientific views, since they result in scientific detachment. The basis of modern science is objective knowledge, dismissing everything that cannot be proved directly. Polányi considered this a distorted ideal, in contradiction to human nature, which has personal notions and concepts always surpassing the provable scientific facts of a given period. He was opposed to reductionism, to the concept that all things can be understood only in terms of the laws of inanimate nature. Many of his critics declared Polányi's views metaphysical.

In the mid 1930's Polányi visited the Soviet Union. After his return he wrote several articles and a book criticizing Soviet economic notions, and on planning and guidance of scientific research; fundamental research, in his opinion, was being pushed into the background in favor of short-term applied research. He was a supporter of complete freedom in scientific research, not only concerning its content but also in choice of the subject. He sharply disapproved of any centralized measures in the United Kingdom that interfered with scientific research or attempted to plan research, even if such measures meant financial support. He fought for his concepts in his writings and started a movement in the interest of their success: he was a founding member of the Society for the Freedom of Science.

Polányi received invitations to several universities in the United States but accepted none. He was a member of many scientific organizations, including the Royal Society, the American Academy of Arts and Sciences, and the Kaiser Wilhelm Gesellschaft (now the Max-Planck-Gesellschaft).

BIBLIOGRAPHY

I. ORIGINAL WORKS. Books by Polányi are *Atomic Reactions* (London, 1932); *USSR Economics* (Manchester, 1936); *Full Employment and Free Trade* (Cambridge, 1945); *Science, Faith and Society* (Chicago and London, 1946); *The Logic of Liberty* (Chicago, 1951); *Personal Knowledge: Toward a Post-Critical Philosophy* (Chicago, 1958; repr. 1962); *The Study of Man* (Chicago, 1959); *Beyond Nihilism* (Cambridge, 1960); *The Tacit Dimension* (Garden City, N.Y., 1966); and *Scientific Thought and Social Reality* (New York, 1974).

II. SECONDARY LITERATURE. A good summary of Polányi's life and views is given by Richard Gelwick in *The Way of Discovery: An Introduction to the Thought of Michael Polányi* (New York, 1977). See also E. P. Wigner and R. A. Hodgkin, "Michael Polányi," in *Biographical Memoirs of Fellows of the Royal Society*, **23** (1977), 413–448.

FERENC SZABADVÁARY

POMERANCHUK, ISAAK IAKOVLEVICH (*b.* Warsaw, Poland, 20 May 1913; *d.* Moscow, U.S.S.R., 14 December 1966), *physics*.

Pomeranchuk's father, Iakov Isaakovich, was a chemical engineer; his mother, Amalia Davydovna, was a dentist.

In 1918 the family moved from Warsaw to Rostov-on-Don in southern Russia, and later to the Don coal region (Donbass). There Pomeranchuk studied at a two year "factory" school; after graduating he began to work, in 1929, in a chemical plant. In 1931 he enrolled in the Institute of Chemical Engineering at Ivanovo, and the following year transferred to the Faculty of Physics and Mechanics of the Leningrad Polytechnical Institute, from which he graduated in 1936.

In 1935 Pomeranchuk was sent to Kharkov, where he prepared his thesis at the Ukrainian Physical-Technical Institute under the guidance of Lev Davidovich Landau. Pomeranchuk's subsequent scientific activity was closely connected with Landau and his school. His first two papers, published in 1936, were written with Landau; of his some 130 papers, eight were written jointly with Landau, and many others were first discussed with him ("passed through the teacher," as their colleagues used to say).

During the first period of his scientific career, Pomeranchuk often changed his work place: the Ukrainian Physical-Technical Institute (1936–1937), Leningrad University (1938–1939), the Leningrad Physical-Technical Institute (1939–1940), the P. N. Lebedev Institute of Physics in Moscow (1940–1943), and again the Leningrad Physical-Technical Institute (1948–1949). He was also associated with the Kurchatov Institute of Atomic Energy (1943–1946) and the Alikhanov Institute of Theoretical and Experimental Physics (1946–1948); at the latter, after his return from Leningrad, he was head of the theoretical department from 1949 until his death.

In 1953 Pomeranchuk was elected corresponding member, and in 1964 full member, of the U.S.S.R. Academy of Sciences. He was awarded the State Prize in 1950 and 1952. He organized a number of theoretical groups at the Institute of Technical and Experimental Physics, at the Kurchatov Institute of Atomic Energy in Moscow, and at the Joint Institute for Nuclear Research in Dubna. For two decades he served as a professor at the Moscow Institute for Engineering Physics, in the same department as M. A. Leontovich and I. E. Tamm.

Pomeranchuk's scientific activity embraced a wide range of theoretical physics. He liked to work with his pupils and colleagues; he wrote a great number of publications jointly with A. I. Akhiezer, who was Landau's first pupil, as well as with V. B. Berestetskii, Lev Borisovich Okun' (Pomeranchuk's pupil), and Vladimir Naumovich Gribov from the Physical-Technical Institute in Leningrad (the last series of papers was written between 1962 and 1966).

During the late 1930's Pomeranchuk was mostly involved in solid state physics. In 1936 he and Landau showed that the interaction of conduction electrons leads to a quadratic law of the temperature dependence of the resistivity of pure metals at low temperatures (in contrast with the law of T^5 [$R \sim T^5$] determined by scattering from thermal oscillations of a lattice). The paper constituted his candidate thesis, defended in 1936 after a year and a half of postgraduate work with Landau's group. This work was complemented in a 1958 paper, in which Pomeranchuk took into account the role of isotopes entering the lattice of a pure (free of admixtures) crystal. Because of the differences in mass change, the lattice oscillations change, which in turn directly influences electrical resistivity of a metal at low temperatures.

In 1937 Pomeranchuk turned his attention to neutron physics and created the theory of elastic and nonelastic scattering of slow neutrons by nuclei bound in a crystal; in particular he studied in detail the case of scattering in crystal hydrogen. He returned to that problem in the late 1940's, in a paper written with Akhiezer, in which they showed that the interaction of neutrons with ferromagnetics and paramagnetics demonstrates a close analogy with common optics (the refraction coefficient and the angle of total internal reflection being dependent on the orientation of the neutron's spin).

A number of papers that formed Pomeranchuk's doctoral dissertation (defended in 1941) are devoted to the phonon theory of heat conduction of dielectrics for a wide range of temperatures. Here he took into account anharmonic effects and demonstrated the necessity of calculating multiphonon interaction (of order higher than 3). He also included in his analysis other mechanisms of phonons' scattering, such as admixtures, reflections from the crystallites' walls, and centers of elastic deformations. Pomeranchuk showed that in this "dirty" (Wolfgang Pauli's expression) science one might obtain meaningful and far-reaching results.

Of great importance for Pomeranchuk's scientific biography is a series of his applied works dealing with the physics of nuclear reactors. He began to be involved in this field in 1943, when he became the head of a research team in charge of the design of a nuclear reactor. With Igor Vasil'evich Kurchatov, Pomeranchuk developed the theory of "exponential experiments." He and Isai Izrailevich Gurevich then postulated the necessity of hetero-geneous deployment of uranium blocks within the reactor's active zone and formulated the theory of resonance absorption of neutrons in that system.

Pomeranchuk published other papers on nuclear reactors, and is rightly considered the founder of the Soviet general theory of reactors.

Several papers written with Akhiezer are devoted to the scattering of neutrons in liquid helium. In a paper on liquid helium written with Landau in 1948, it was shown that any particle—be it atom or molecule—in a superfluid helium (including isotopes of He^4) can participate in the normal, but not superfluid motion. In a 1950 paper on the theory of liquid He^3 (tritium), Pomeranchuk developed the qualitative theory of quantum liquids with Fermi energy spectrum and predicted the "Pomeranchuk effect," that is, the existence of a minimum melting point for He^3 on the pT plane (this minimum was later confirmed experimentally). In the same paper he demonstrated the theoretical possibility of reaching ultralow temperatures by adiabatic solidification of liquid He^3.

During the period 1946–1949, Pomeranchuk obtained important results (with Lev Andreevich Artsimovich and Dmitrii Dmitrievich Ivanenko) on synchrotron radiation. In particular the authors showed that this radiation determines most of the losses associated with acceleration of electrons in betatrons and synchrotrons. A paper written with Landau presented a complete theory of bremsstrahlung. Pomeranchuk also achieved significant results in papers devoted to the spectra of positronium and to the mu-meson atom.

A large number of Pomeranchuk's papers dealt with quantum field theory, the physics of strong interactions, and high-energy physics. In papers written in 1956, partly in collaboration with Okun', the equality of cross sections of elastic and nonelastic scattering of π^+, π^-, and π^0 mesons by nucleons was obtained. The analysis of dispersion relations (1958) showed that for high energies the complete effective interaction cross section of a particle and an antiparticle with the same target tends toward the same limit as the collision energy increases (Pomeranchuk theorem). This result has been confirmed in the experiments on the most powerful accelerators.

In the last series of papers, written between 1962 and 1966 in collaboration with Gribov, Pomeranchuk further developed the method of complex momenta, first suggested by Tullio Regge, for a study of asymptotic behavior of cross sections of various processes in the high-energy limit. In these papers, based on the investigation of behavior of the "Pomeranchuk poles,'' he proved important theorems concerning the relative values of cross sections for various processes of scattering and in relation to the effect of concentration of Regge poles and the branching points on the plane of complex momenta.

Despite a grave illness, Pomeranchuk continued his intensive work even after being hospitalized. His last paper (on asymptotic behavior of the complete cross section of the electron-positron annihilation in argon) was completed two days before his death. A number of papers that he discussed with his colleagues during the last month of his life were published posthumously, including a paper on weak interactions (the limitation of the rate of growth of cross sections for the $[v,e]$ process).

Pomeranchuk's friend V. B. Berestetskii said about him: "His work was his highest enjoyment. He was tireless. Physics was his life. He did not understand how one could spare time for anything else."

BIBLIOGRAPHY

I. ORIGINAL WORKS. Pomeranchuk's works are listed in *Uspekhi fizicheskikh nauk*, **92**, no. 2 (1967), 360–365, and in his *Sobranie nauchnykh trudov* (Collected scientific works), III (Moscow, 1972), 411–416. The most important papers are "O svoistvakh metallov pri ochen nizkikh temperaturakh" (On the properties of metals at very low temperatures), in *Zhurnal eksperimentalnoi i teoreticheskoi fiziki*, **7** (1937), 649, written with Lev D. Landau; "On the Thermal Conductivity of Dielectrics," in *Physical Review*, **60**, no. 11 (1941), 820–821; "On the Heat Conductivity of Salts Used in the Magnetic Cooling Method," in *Journal of Physics of the USSR*, **8**, no. 4 (1944), 216, written with A. I. Akhiezer; "O maksimalnoi energii, dostizhimoi v betatrone" (On the maximum energy reachable in the betatron), in *Doklady Akademii nauk SSSR*, **44** (1944), 343, written with Dmitrii D. Ivanenko; "Izluchenie bystrykh elektronov v magnitnom pole" (The radiation of fast electrons in the magnetic field), in *Fizicheskii zhurnal*, **9**, no. 4 (1945), 267, written with Lev A. Artsimovich; "O rasseianii neitronov s energiei neskolko gradusov v zhidkom gelii II" (On the scattering of low-energy electrons in helium-II), *ibid.*, **9**, no. 6 (1945), 461, written with A. I. Akhiezer; *Nekotorye voprosy teorii iadra* (Some problems of the nuclear theory; Moscow, 1948; 2nd ed., 1950), written with A. I. Akhiezer; "O dvizhenii postoronnikh chastits v gelii II" (On the motion of foreign particles in liquid helium-II), in *Doklady Akademii nauk SSSR*, **59** (1948), 669–670, written with Lev D. Landau; "K teorii zhidkogo ³He" (On the liquid ³He theory), in *Zhurnal eksperimentalnoi i teoreticheskoi fiziki*, **20** (1950), 919–924; "Asymptotic Behaviour of Annihilation and Elastic Scattering Processes at High Energies," in *Nuclear Physics*, **33**, no. 3 (1962), 516–523, written with Vladimir N. Gribov; "Regge Poles and Landau Singu-

larities," in *Physical Review Letters*, **9**, no. 5 (1962), 238–242, written with Vladimir N. Gribov; and *Sobranie nauchnykh trudov* (Collected scientific works), V. B. Berestetskii, ed. 3 vols. (Moscow, 1972).

II. SECONDARY LITERATURE. V. N. Berestetskii, "Isaak Iakovlevich Pomeranchuk," in *Uspekhi fizicheskikh nauk*, **92**, no. 2 (1967), 355–365; I. N. Golovin, *I. V. Kurchatov* (Moscow, 1972), 53–54, and L. I. Lapidus, "Isaak Iakovlevich Pomeranchuk," in *Priroda* (1967), no. 12, 51.

V. J. FRENKEL

POULTON, EDWARD BAGNALL (*b.* Reading, England, 27 January 1856; *d.* Oxford, England, 20 November 1943), *natural history, entomology, evolutionary biology.*

Poulton was the second of three children and only son of a successful architect, William Ford Poulton. His mother, Georgina Selina Bagnall Poulton, was author of an 800-page history of England. Poulton carried the family regard for professionalism, hard work, and close attention to voluminous detail throughout his career. The family was comfortable enough for him to be educated at a succession of boarding schools, primarily W. M. Watson's new school at Oakley House, Reading. Poulton entered Oxford in 1873 and remained there for the rest of his career, which included an honors degree in zoology (1876), various demonstratorships, a geology research scholarship, lectureships, and finally election to the Hope professorship of zoology in 1893, from which he retired in 1933. He received the D.Sc. in 1900.

A large and robust man not prone to hiding his enthusiasms, Poulton entered vigorously into the life of the university, both in his department and museum and in the wider field of university affairs. He was extremely active, and regularly held office, in the British Association for the Advancement of Science (president, 1937), the Linnean Society of London (president, 1912–1916), and especially the Entomological Society of London (president, 1903–1904 and 1925–1926), which named him honorary life president in 1933, when it became the Royal Entomological Society. He had a wide circle of colleagues, correspondents, and friends. Poulton married Emily Palmer in 1881; they had two sons and three daughters, of whom Poulton survived all but one. Of his many honors, knighthood in 1935 was the most public recognition of a long career.

That career had its inauspicious, if rather traditional, beginnings in natural history. From early childhood, Poulton was an insect collector and observer. His fledgling interests in natural science did not suit the schools' orientation to the classics, and little of his schooling was scientific. It was not unusual for Poulton to find himself defending entomological pursuits against the derision of even his masters, who questioned their utility. Having gained his scientific education from his own reading, he attempted but failed to obtain a scholarship to Oxford, and began work in his father's office in 1872.

At the time it was typical in Britain to gain a natural history education by independent study, although professorships in the biological sciences had been established at Oxford and Cambridge in the 1860's. Continued late-night study convinced Poulton's father of his serious scientific intentions, and he then was encouraged to work and study part-time at the University Museum, Oxford. The choice of Oxford was largely because of his mother's wish that he attend that university, but it proved to be a most fitting choice for a budding naturalist primed to receive the influence of some of the best of the Victorian zoologists.

In 1873 Poulton attended the lectures of George Rolleston, first Linacre professor of anatomy and physiology, and worked in his department at the University Museum three days a week. The result was success in the examinations for a Jesus College science scholarship, enabling him to attend university. He also spent the last hours of the day in the Hope department of entomology, examining specimens and talking with John Obadiah Westwood, first Hope professor and foremost entomologist in Britain, if not the world. Never converted to Darwinism, Westwood attempted to warn the young, enthusiastic entomologist against it, but the lesson had little impact; Poulton read Darwin's *Origin of Species* and was convinced by it. Westwood continued to help, nonetheless, even if his taxonomic orientation did not suit Poulton's far more ecological interests in entomology. More directly inspiring as a teacher was Rolleston, who captured Poulton's imagination and inspired him to pursue a career in zoology.

Westwood and Rolleston were typical of Oxford biologists in their emphases on taxonomy and comparative morphology, rather than on the newer experimental physiology. Under Rolleston's influence, Poulton progressed from amateur natural history to comparative morphology, with its distinctively Darwinian questions about development and phylogenetic evolution. He chose to stay at Oxford after graduating, to work under Rolleston. But as inspiring as Rolleston was, he was not skilled at directing research. Nor did Poulton find much time, after his duties as demonstrator, for original work.

Frustrated, and in a precarious financial situation, he studied for and won the Burdett-Coutts scholarship in geology in 1878, which enabled him to work with Joseph Prestwich, the professor of geology. He enthusiastically began research under his new mentor, and thus his first scientific publications were on geological topics. Not surprisingly, given his wish to return eventually to zoology, the stratigraphic results in his analysis of a Reading riverbed included detailed discussion of mammalian remains.

The opportunity to work in zoology came with the appointment of Henry N. Moseley as Linacre professor in 1881. Poulton, by then a Keble College tutor, had started a series of microscopic studies on mammalian tongues and taste organs. Moseley learned of these and immediately encouraged Poulton, aiding him by providing study material from the *Challenger* expedition. With a little prompting, Poulton's research flourished into a series of papers in the 1880's on the comparative anatomy and evolutionary origins of taste buds and other structures of the duck-billed platypus.

His researches on monotremes and marsupials had important Darwinian implications. Poulton presented a transitional sequence for these mammals, to show how complex adaptive structures of the tongue could be built gradually by the specialization of ordinary epithelial parts. He revealed in detail the origins, in a primitive group, of distinctive, higher features. The duck-billed platypus, classified as the nearest living representative of the ancestral form through which mammals evolved, seemed an evolutionary enigma as a transitional form because it lacked the teeth so characteristic of mammals. Poulton solved the problem by examining a series of young specimens and showing that the animal possesses true teeth that are lost before adulthood. Poulton's analysis of the structure and embryology of the platypus' hair led him to argue that mammalian hair is a persistence from reptilian ancestors. He used the independent persistence, loss, or development of important class features among reptiles, early mammals, and later mammals to deduce the linkages and transitions essential to the construction of phylogenies.

Well set on a course of research widely acknowledged to be the foremost task facing evolutionary morphologists, and with aid from people established in the field, Poulton at the same time began a series of rather different investigations in entomology. The taxonomical work typical of museum entomologists did not appeal to him, but Alfred Russel Wallace's *Contributions to the Theory of Natural Selection* (1870) had in 1878 aroused an interest in working on insects, especially the phenomena of coloration. As Poulton's morphological research got under way, Raphael Meldola's translation of August Weissmann's *Studies in the Theory of Descent* (1880–1882) appeared, and it directly inspired Poulton to a new kind of Darwinian research in 1883. Meldola's editorial comments were provocative suggestions for research; Poulton, starting with the question of how the cryptic green color of certain caterpillars is acquired, quickly made his morphological studies experimental and physiological, in a novel combination of field and laboratory work. Meldola promoted the work, as did Weismann, Moseley, Wallace, and E. Ray Lankester.

Thus Poulton again was elevated into the ranks of the foremost Darwinian zoologists of the day, culminating with his election to the Royal Society in 1889. Although he had been trained in classical natural history, including its taxonomical and geological emphasis, Poulton's experimental methods were nevertheless relatively novel, just as his questions about the ecological aspects of insect biology had been little investigated. The combined inspiration from the naturalist Wallace and the experimental morphologist Weismann, the leading spokesmen for Darwinism, led Poulton to the lifelong course for which he would become most famous—his ardent defense of Darwinian natural selection as the mechanism of evolution.

Poulton's transformation of research methodology in studying the colors of insects mirrors the changes in natural history research in the late 1800's. From a taxonomic and morphological base, he first investigated, from 1884 through the 1890's, such questions as how green coloration is acquired from plant chlorophyll and the causes of other correlations of insect color with the colors in the environment. Next, in 1886, he began experiments on the relations of insect colors to the selection pressures faced by the insect. Experimental demonstration of the effectiveness of cryptic colors as protection against predators was a welcome addition to the Darwinian argument, especially since Poulton's extensive, detailed experiments were innovative amid the typically observational data of natural history.

But the methods of comparative morphology did not completely disappear; Poulton created a comparable argument with comparative ecology to support Darwinism. Poulton's version of ecology, growing out of the tradition of such Darwinian naturalists as Wallace and Henry Walter Bates, continued to stress comparative studies as it concentrated on the organism's adaptations to its environment. Interest in the ecology of adaptation

was, for Poulton, tied to the provision of new, more rigorous arguments for natural selection. Indeed, the study of adaptations had become the special province of the most vocal Darwinians, even as the mechanism of natural selection was declining in popularity among physiologists, embryologists, and students of heredity.

The adaptation that had particularly captured Poulton's interest was the phenomenon of protective colors and resemblances, presented in Wallace's influential essay of 1867, which was reprinted in *Contributions to the Theory of Natural Selection*. Wallace had elaborated upon Bates's discovery of mimicry, in which one butterfly species mimics, or resembles in superficial coloration, an unrelated species, called the model. Bates had argued in 1861 that the models were protected from predators such as birds by various qualities, such as bad flavor or tough bodies; the mimics had evolved a disguise to cover their own defenselessness by taking on the color patterns of the models. Protective resemblance would be favored in the struggle for existence, in what seemed to be a proof in nature for the theory of evolution by natural selection.

Wallace made explicit the theoretical connection of this mimetic form of resemblance to other, well-known instances of protective coloration, such as camouflaged insects that look like sticks or leaves. Poulton's interest in cryptically green caterpillars started with their significance for the selectionist argument; and Weismann had in fact been arguing against competing, physiological theories that tried to eliminate the need for natural selection in the explanation of such phenomena as coloration.

This was not the only Weismann campaign to which Poulton devoted his research: he also used his insect morphology studies to attack neo-Lamarckian theories of the inheritance of acquired characteristics. Poulton also took on the task of getting Weismann's *Essays upon Heredity and Kindred Biological Problems* translated into English and published in 1889. Support for Weismann's germplasm theory as the mechanism of heredity consistent with the operation of natural selection was the theme Poulton carried on a lecture tour of America in 1894. As Darwinism was being eclipsed in the 1890's by newer evolutionary theories, Poulton joined Wallace and Weismann in leading the defense of natural selection as the predominant mechanism of evolution.

Poulton's first major foray into the battle was *The Colours of Animals* (1890), in which he extended the arguments from Bates and Wallace. Starting with a brief survey of the way in which colors are physically produced, he argued that the explanation of why an organism has its particular colors lies in the utility or significance of those colors for its survival. The entire book, devoted almost exclusively to insects—indeed, to butterflies—was one long argument that coloration demonstrates natural selection in action in nature. Drawing together a large number of studies, and emphasizing experimental results when possible, Poulton surveyed the known cases of protective resemblances, sexual dimorphisms, mimicries, and other useful coloration. By relating them to their uses in defense or otherwise, he reorganized the various phenomena of appearance into a scheme based on adaptiveness. In so doing, he introduced terminological rigor by separating and naming the varieties of defensive colors, crypticity, mimicry, warning colors, alluring colors, recognition marks, and courtship displays.

Much of Poulton's presentation merely gave details of adaptation, to convince the reader of the validity of Darwinism. In fact, his major explicitly theoretical argument was directed within the selectionist camp. He supported Darwin on sexual selection, against Wallace's view of the opposition of natural selection to sexual selection. He rejected Wallace's theory that male colors are due to a surplus of physiological vitality. Poulton briefly countered a handful of other proposed mechanisms for acquisition of coloration that explained it by internal mechanisms without regard for external selective pressures.

This would become the theme for Poulton's Darwinian arguments for the next forty years: internal mechanisms explain little of the evolutionary acquisition of adaptations, which must find their explanation in the external relations of the organism with its environment. The dichotomy between internal and external causes was the framework for his arguments against the unfolding of embryological plans, recapitulation of phylogeny, physiological orthogenesis of various coloration patterns, and the sufficiency of merely physical causes of colors in explaining their significance. He was one of the first Darwinians to make the strong distinction between these proximate causes and the ultimate evolutionary causation. Poulton's internalist-externalist dichotomy was also the framework in which he received the new Mendelian genetics after 1900, seeing it as one more inadequate analysis of the causation of adaptive form.

In many ways, *The Colours of Animals* was the prelude to Poulton's greatest body of work. It was with this survey of protective resemblances that he began research on mimicry. It was a widely noticed entry into the increasingly polemical debate over Darwinism, presenting his perennial denial of the inheritance of acquired characters and support for natural selection as the only sufficient explanation for the evolution of adaptation. In both arguments he depended more and more after 1890 on evidence from mimicry.

Poulton's enormous body of work on mimicry truly got under way, however, only with his appointment to the Hope professorship upon Westwood's death in 1893. The chair was recognized as Britain's leading entomological position, and Poulton was entrusted with the University Museum's large collection of insects. He took the opportunity to transform the Hope Collection, turning from the traditional taxonomical orientation to a more ecological one. He specialized in mimetic species, gathering specimens over broad geographical ranges and emphasizing the variation in nature. This was a radical change in museum method and purpose, and Poulton fully intended this new working collection to be a resource for the proof of natural selection. It also meant that over the forty years of his tenure he expanded the collection enormously, frequently using his own money as well as incessantly petitioning the university for more funding. He built a worldwide network of corresponding naturalists and collectors; more than one of these correspondents came to work in unofficial positions in the department. Encouragement of a number of entomologists and extremely active involvement in the Entomological Society of London gave Poulton great influence. He was a major figure in orienting the field toward ecological and evolutionary studies.

Mimicry was the vehicle of this change. Facing the attacks of non-Darwinian evolutionary theorists, Poulton devoted himself to developing the Bates-Wallace claim that mimicry is the natural experiment proving the operation of natural selection. The grand Darwinian argument that he thought was overlooked in the proposed internalist mechanisms of evolution was the biogeographical evidence. Species collected widely enough show a distribution of variation, and these small or continuous variations, he argued, are the stuff of evolution. Since only natural selection of useful variations could explain acquisition of adaptive structure, it was necessary to investigate the bionomics, or ecology, of the species involved. In his new position, Poulton continued the experiments on relations of insect color to environment, as well as a new series in 1898 and 1899 to measure the predation dangers facing insects. Most of his detailed ecological data, however, came from his growing network of naturalists, especially in Africa.

From 1897 through the 1930's, Poulton published

regularly on mimetic complexes of Africa, creating the paradigmatic case study of mimicry with the *Papilio* swallowtail butterflies and their associated species. He and his collaborators (including, at various times, Roland Trimen, Guy A. K. Marshall, W. A. Lamborn, C. A. Wiggins, Harry Eltringham, and G. D. Hale Carpenter) unraveled the often confusing and mistaken taxonomy and ecology of the several butterfly species involved in this mimicry ring. They argued that sexual dimorphism within the group revealed ancestral and derived forms, with geographical distributions providing consistent evidence. The males remained close to the ancestral condition while the females diverged into the wide range of mimetic color and form. They collected the apparent transitional forms from the predicted sites and, more important, were able to breed and rear butterflies with characters supporting their general argument for the gradual acquisition of the adaptive coloration.

Guy A. K. Marshall, of South Africa, was Poulton's most important collaborator in gathering field evidence that bird predation is a great and documentable selective pressure on butterflies. The lack of quantitative or experimental evidence was a frequent criticism of scenarios of natural selection. From observations made between 1897 and 1902, Poulton orchestrated a campaign in the pages of the *Transactions of the Entomological Society of London* to demonstrate the action of this selection in nature. Such attempts proved to be convincing only in the short run, since the same criticism, doubting the importance of predation, appeared in 1915 from the geneticist Reginald C. Punnett and again in 1932 from the ecologist Waldo L. McAtee. Each time Poulton used the pages of the *Transactions* to solicit support from naturalists in the field and to present his own voluminously detailed collection of evidence.

Although continued, the geographical and ecological data collection begun in the 1890's was augmented after 1903 with breeding experiments. In part, Poulton needed the results of crosses of different geographic races or mimetic forms to reveal the possible evolutionary pathways of transitional forms within a mimetic complex. More critically, however, after 1900 the rediscovery of Mendelism and its assimilation into antiselectionist, mutationist theory impelled Poulton to respond to the new genetics. From 1901 through the early 1920's, a dominant motif within Poulton's argument for natural selection was a reaction to the mutationist interpretation of hereditary variation. It was a heated debate in general, and Poulton responded to the strong claims of William Bateson with sharply worded papers and addresses. He gathered and edited his most substantial papers on theories of heredity, evolution, and mimicry into *Essays on Evolution: 1889–1907* (1908). In a polemical preface on mutationism and Mendelism, he complained about the claims of de Vries and Bateson that they had explained evolution with mutations and without any need for natural selection. For Poulton it was yet another example of the internalist error in explaining an externalist cause. Moreover, he resented the belittling of the contributions of the great naturalists.

The book was Poulton's most influential single work, capping the raging debate during the 1909 Darwin centennial, cogently arguing the case for natural selection, and presenting in one place many examples within his argument for mimicry as the proof for selection. He also included a 1904 address in which he redefined species, in an early statement of the modern biological species concept, in order to stress continuous variation and belittle notions of speciation by single mutation. Poulton was a highly visible spokesman for Darwinism during the Darwin centennial, writing a paper on mimicry in the Cambridge celebratory volume *Darwin and Modern Science* (1909) and writing the historical and theoretical *Charles Darwin and the Origin of Species* (1909), a sequel of sorts to his earlier *Charles Darwin and the Theory of Natural Selection* (1901). In all of these forums, he argued for the role of the naturalist able to see natural selection in action in ecological studies. The data on variation, gathered widely in the field, were to be taken as seriously as the laboratory Mendelism.

The heat of the polemic undoubtedly obscured Poulton's compromise position on genetics. Opposed to the Mendelian embracing of discontinuous variations as the raw material of evolution, he tried to demonstrate how coloration phenomena developed from continuous variation. The complexity of the adaptations also was an argument for their gradual building. Miscast as opposed to Mendelism, he actually argued that it only clarified Weismann's germ-plasm theory, and that small variations would be seen to be Mendelian. It was another decade before biologists began to accept that continuous variation is indeed Mendelian; and most geneticists were convinced from laboratory work, not from Poulton's breeding or field data from mimetic species.

For a few important contributors to the Modern Synthesis, combining the evolutionary theory of Darwinism with Mendelism, however, Poulton did have a great influence. Mimicry again was the vehicle. Through a debate with Punnett over the genetic basis of mimetic color and its evolution, Poulton attracted and collaborated with G. D. Hale Carpenter, his eventual successor in the Hope chair, and Ronald A. Fisher, a principal architect of the synthesis.

Punnett began a running debate with Poulton over the Mendelian mutationist version of mimicry, in a series of articles (1913–1914) in the pages of *Bedrock*, a short-lived journal for scientific controversy that Poulton helped to found and edit. In *Mimicry in Butterflies* (1915), Punnett recapitulated his arguments for the single large-step creation of mimetic resemblance. He also doubted the standard ecological scenario of bird predation and the geographical relationships of mimic and model, drawing on both field studies and breeding results for a swallowtail butterfly complex of southeast Asia. Poulton could belittle Punnett's knowledge of taxonomy, ecology of butterflies, and awareness of the wealth of other data, but he could not deny the genetic results that implied discontinuous mutational steps in the evolution of the mimicry.

Poulton's response was to depend more on the other cases he had built, especially the African swallowtails, for which he had breeding results supporting continuous steps of variation. Carpenter's work in Africa, directed largely by Poulton through correspondence, gave the critical biogeographical data. Poulton took it and emphasized the complexity of the complete Darwinian story, with its genetical, morphological, taxonomical, geographical, and ecological consistency. But he also attacked the mutationists on their own theoretical ground. In papers of 1914 and 1916, he called for a new definition of mutation that would reduce its size and thus make continuous variation part of the same Mendelian mechanism as Punnett's larger steps, which Poulton took to be rare and usually useless. The papers were little noticed, partly because of the war and partly because of Poulton's typical style of burying the theoretical suggestions within a mass of entomological detail.

Fisher noticed the same argument that Poulton was making in William E. Castle's results on modifier genes and the genetical nature of continuous variation, and began his series of theoretical papers in 1918. In 1927 he had Poulton's help with the mimetic examples and data to produce an influential paper on modifier genes and the Darwinian basis of mimicry, providing a new model to explain Punnett's case. As a chapter in Fisher's *Genetical Theory of Natural Selection* (1930), the mimicry case developed by Poulton and Fisher exerted great theoretical influence. Fisher's frequent collaborator Edmund B.

Ford, who had been Poulton's student at Oxford in the 1920's, elaborated, from 1933 to 1980, the ecological genetics of mimicry as the paradigmatic proof of adaptation by natural selection. He and Carpenter collaborated on *Mimicry* (1933), which briefly summed up much of the data and argument developed at the Hope department. By this time, Poulton had done much to solidify mimicry's place as a demonstration of natural selection.

Poulton, however, never produced the anticipated masterwork on mimicry, although he gathered plates and manuscript for it for years. The deaths of three of his children between 1915 and 1919, especially the loss of his younger son in World War I, slowed him considerably. By his retirement in 1933, despite colleagues' hopes for a summary work, Poulton was in his seventies. He had never been able to disengage himself from the mass of details in running the department and collections, supervising and assisting his correspondent naturalists. Perhaps most important, he hewed closely to the incredible intricacies of his research material, as often as not obscuring the impact of his theoretical discussions. For instance, his 1880's papers on insect colors contained early, yet unnoticed, versions of a concept of frequency-dependent selection, so important in the later work of Ford and others.

Poulton's tenure as Hope professor both created and constrained his work, ultimately leaving much of his work to be carried out by colleagues, protégés, and the institution he largely created. He spent his career promoting ecological studies over traditional taxonomy, in the process helping to carry ecology into university specialization in Britain. He was instrumental in aiding his protégé Marshall in the establishment of the Imperial Bureau of Entomology, an early governmental applied science institution. Foremost among these indirect influences were his constant defense of the Darwinian theory and the creation of a body of scientists developing its details.

BIBLIOGRAPHY

I. ORIGINAL WORKS. Poulton's best-known works are *The Colours of Animals* (London, 1890), and *Essays on Evolution* (Oxford, 1908), which includes many of his most important papers. A useful guide to 137 of his more than 200 publications is the scholarly bibliography, arranged by subject, in G. D. Hale Carpenter, "Edward Bagnall Poulton," in *Obituary Notices of Fellows of the Royal Society of London*, **4** (1942–1944), 655–680. Poulton included an autobiographical chapter in his memoir *John Viriamu Jones and Other Oxford Memories* (London, 1911). His papers and correspondence are in the Hope Entomological Library, University Museum, Oxford.

II. Secondary Literature. G. D. Hale Carpenter wrote several obituaries of Poulton; the most complete biographical treatment is his notice for the Royal Society of London (see above). On Poulton's views on mimicry and the genetical debates leading to the Modern Synthesis, see William C. Kimler, "Mimicry: Views of Naturalists and Ecologists Before the Modern Synthesis," and John R. G. Turner, "'The Hypothesis That Explains Mimetic Resemblance Explains Evolution': The Gradualist-Saltationist Schism," both in Marjorie Grene, ed., *Dimensions of Darwinism* (Cambridge, 1983). On Poulton's role in twentieth-century ecology, see William C. Kimler, "Advantage, Adaptiveness, and Evolutionary Ecology," in *Journal of the History of Biology*, **19** (1986), 215–233. For a detailed treatment of Poulton's mimicry research and debates, see William C. Kimler, "One Hundred Years of Mimicry: History of an Evolutionary Exemplar" (Ph.D. diss., Cornell University, 1983).

WILLIAM C. KIMLER

PRUVOST, PIERRE EUGÈNE MARIE JOSEPH (*b.* Raismes [Nord], France, 1 August 1890; *d.* Paris, France, 5 June 1967), *geology.*

Though his father, grandfather, and brother were doctors, Pruvost studied the geological sciences. At nineteen he became an assistant at the Coal Museum of the University of Lille, directed by Charles Barrois. In 1918, at the University of Lille, he defended his doctoral thesis on the continental fauna of the coal-bearing regions of northern France; it was published the following year in the collection of explanatory treatises accompanying the geological map of France.

Pruvost was named lecturer in 1919 and professor of applied geology in 1922. In 1926 he succeeded his mentor, Barrois, in the chair of geology and mineralogy at the University of Lille, a position he held for twenty-four years. From 1943 to 1950 he was dean of the Faculty of Sciences.

In 1950 Pruvost accepted the chair of general geology at the Sorbonne, in which capacity he continued his research despite his heavy administrative and teaching assignments. He devoted much of his time to the young geologists whose work he guided.

Highly esteemed in university, scientific, and industrial circles, Pruvost was twice elected president of the Geological Society of France (1948, 1963) and presided over many scientific and university institutions, such as the National Geology Committee and the geology sections of the National Council of Scientific Research and the Universities' Consultative Committee. He was elected corresponding member of the Academy of Sciences in 1947 and full member in 1954. He was also a corresponding foreign member of the Academy of Sciences of Lisbon and the Royal Academy of Belgium.

Pruvost's achievements were recognized in many awards: officer of the Legion of Honor (1949), commander of the Ordre des Palmes Académiques (1959), commander of the National Order of Merit (1966), and officer of the Crown of Belgium (1948). He was an honorary member of the geological societies of Belgium, England, Scotland, Sweden, Switzerland, and the United States, and received honorary doctorates from the universities of Louvain and Mainz. He was awarded the Prix Gosselet and Prix Gaudry of the Geological Society of France, the Prix Kuhlmann of the Lille Society of Sciences, and several medals from various European geological societies.

These honors never affected Pruvost's modesty; upon his election to the Academy of Sciences, he established a prize meant to encourage young researchers, the Pierre Pruvost Foundation Prize, awarded annually by the Geological Society of France.

Pruvost's scientific work was enormous, as evidenced by his more than 200 articles dealing with the stratigraphy of the Paleozoic, the paleontology of coal, the geology of coal basins, the relation between tectonics and sedimentation, and the geology of the Armorican Massif.

Pruvost did considerable research in the coal basins of western Europe, including those of Nord and the Pas de Calais, the Saar-Lorraine Basin, the Belgian Basin, and the St. Étienne Basin. He made a great contribution to the stratigraphy of the Upper Paleozoic, emphasizing the importance of the break between the Autunian and the Saxonian, which he related to the Saalian phase. (In Europe this coincided with the initial raising of the Urals, leading to the formation of the Eurasian bloc.) With W. J. Jongmans, Pruvost proposed to incorporate the Autunian into the Carboniferous and to adopt the term "Pennsylvanian" to define the totality of terrains ranging from the Namurian to the Autunian.

Discussing the Precambrian-Paleozoic boundary, Pruvost proposed to incorporate into the Paleozoic a sedimentary layer noted in the Anti-Atlas Mountains of Africa and in North America that, conformably distributed under the olenellus biozone of the Lower Cambrian, is strongly discordant with the Precambrian. This stratum, known as Infracambrian, a term used by Nikolai Menchikov, corresponds to a period of 130 million years. Although the term has been abandoned, the discussion that lay at its origin remains an excellent example of stratigraphic reasoning.

Pruvost's earliest work was devoted to the description of the rich and varied fauna of the coal-bearing regions of the Nord and Pas de Calais basins. He then undertook a monograph on the continental fauna of the Belgian coal-bearing region, which he compared with that of other European basins. This enabled him to forge a synthesis of the chronology of the continental fauna of the coal regions of western Europe, which was presented at international congresses held in Brussels (1922) and Heerlen (1927).

On the basis of work conducted in the coal basins of western Europe, Pruvost developed several ideas that proved fundamental in paleographic reconstruction. He conceived the notion of lateral variation of facies: The outer reaches of coal basins are marked by deposits of large detrital rock and conglomerated accumulations of vegetal debris that produce coal, as well as claylike mud formed of the remains of fish, which sometimes becomes oil shale. Veins of coal are therefore deposited in annular form, concentrically around the banks of the original basin. Pruvost also recognized that the zone of alluviation of a basin may be displaced by the rising of edges such that the sedimentary series is rarely complete along any given vertical. Yet another of his contributions was the idea of subsidence, defined as a "prolonged and continuous descending movement produced by repeated drops of slight amplitude in a submerged region of the earth's crust in which an appreciable thickness of sediments is accumulated by virtue of this phenomenon." This concept explains the rhythmic alternation of veins of coal and sterile rock several thousand meters thick in terrains whose nature suggests deposits of slight depth.

Pruvost's Armorican activity dates back to 1924, when, at the invitation of Barrois, he contributed to revising the geological map of Redon. He continued to be interested in this region, in which he conducted many geological investigations. In "Les mers et les terres de Bretagne aux temps paléozoïques" (1949) he presented a paleographic sketch of the Armorican Massif for the Paleozoic era. This sketch indicated the existence of a central east-west pit marked by the Chateaulin-Laval synclinorium median, the site of nearly continuous sedimentation during the Paleozoic, a pit bounded by two mountain ranges, Domnonée in the north and Ligeria in the south. This schema is still employed in paleographic reconstitutions of the Armorican Massif.

Pruvost was a man of great culture, gifted with a lively intelligence and devoted to his work. He was also sensitive and attentive, and his willingness to help others was legendary. Many young scientists found welcome refuge in his Sorbonne office, where his kindness put them at ease despite the solemnity of the surroundings. An opponent of dogmatism of any kind, Pruvost sought to awaken the intelligence of the young through an objective and rigorous approach, often suggesting several interpretations where it would have been easier to propose just one. He rejected the notion of schools of thought as excessively constraining. He was always careful of people's feelings, and considered his collaborators friends rather than colleagues. Pruvost was concerned that all people have the chance to be themselves, for he held that the richness of thought rests on the diversity of human nature.

BIBLIOGRAPHY

I. ORIGINAL WORKS. "Introduction à l'étude du bassin houiller du Nord et du Pas-de-Calais: La faune continentale du terrain houiller du nord de la France," in *Mémoires pour servir à l'explication de la Carte géologique détaillée de la France* (Paris, 1918); "Les divisions paléontologiques dans le terrain houiller de l'Europe occidentale, d'après les caractères de la faune limnique," in *Congrès géologique internationale, Bruxelles. Comptes-rendus de la XIIIe session*, II (Brussels, 1922), 639–654; "La faune continentale et la division stratigraphique des terrains houillers (Europe occidentale)," in *Comptes-rendus du Congrès internationale de stratigraphie et de géologie du carbonifère* (Heerlen, 1927), 519–534; "Sédimentation et subsidence," in *Livre jubilaire de la Société géologique de France . . .* , II (1930), 545–564; "Introduction à la faune continentale du terrain houiller de Belgique," in *Mémoires du Musée royal d'histoire naturelle de Bruxelles*, no. 44 (1931); "Un bassin houiller paralique de l'époque crétacée," in *Comptes-rendus hebdomadaires des séances de l'Académie des sciences*, **214** (1942), 847–848; "Les mers et les terres de Bretagne aux temps paléozoïques," in *Annales Hébert et Haug*, **7** (*Livre jubilaire Charles Jacob*) (1949), 345–362; "Les subdivisions du Carbonifère continentale," in *Bulletin de la Société géologique de France*, 5th ser., **20** (1950), 335–344, with W. J. Jongmans; and "L'Infracambrien," in *Bulletin de la Société belge de géologie, de paléontologie et d'hydrologie*, **60** (1951), 43–65.

II. SECONDARY LITERATURE. John R. Fanshawe, "Memorial to Pierre Pruvost (1890–1967)," in *Proceedings. Geological Society of America*, 1967 (1970), 243–251, with bibliography and a portrait; Jean Piveteau, "Notice nécrologique sur Pierre Pruvost (1890–1967), membre de la section de minérologie et géologie," in *Comptes-rendus hebdomadaires des séances de l'Académie des sciences*, **266** (1968), 110–114; P. Routhier and G. Waterlot, "Pierre Pruvost (1890–1967)," in *Bulletin de la Société géologique de France*, 7th ser., **10** (1968), 519–534, with a bibliography of 207 references and a portrait; and *Titres et travaux scientifiques de M. Pierre Pruvost* (Paris, 1954), with a bibliography of 168 references.

MICHEL COLCHEN

PURDIE, THOMAS (*b*. Biggar, Lanarkshire, Scotland, 27 January 1843; *d*. St. Andrews, Scotland, 14 December 1916), *chemistry*.

Purdie's father, a banker, died in Thomas's early childhood, and he was brought up by his mother, well supported by his paternal uncle, a wealthy Edinburgh businessman. He was educated at the Edinburgh Academy, and after an abortive start at a business career, Purdie and his cousin traveled to South America, where in the 1860's they purchased a farm in Argentina. After seven years a combination of bad harvests, political unrest, and Indian trouble brought the venture to a close, and Purdie returned to Britain. At the age of twenty-nine he enrolled in the Royal School of Mines in 1872. There he came under the influence of Thomas Huxley and Sir Edward Frankland. After his graduation with a B.Sc. in 1875, Frankland appointed Purdie demonstrator in the chemical laboratories of the Royal College of Science at South Kensington, a post he held for three years. In 1878 Purdie traveled to Germany to study at the University of Würzburg under Johannes Wislicenus. That same year he married Marianne Rotherham.

While studying for the Ph.D., Purdie met the Cambridge botanist Sydney Howard Vines and the chemists Percy Faraday Frankland and William Henry Perkin, Jr. After obtaining the Ph.D. at Würzburg in 1880, Purdie returned to England in 1881. Unable to obtain a university post, he taught chemistry at the grammar school of Newcastle-under-Lyme until 1884. In that year, aged forty-six, he succeeded to the chair of chemistry at St. Andrews University. Purdie was much influenced in his chemical career by the work of his mentor Wislicenus, who had led the extension and application of the stereochemical ideas of Jacobus Van't Hoff and G. Bell in German universities. Purdie is best remembered for his role in the development of research into optical activity and stereochemistry in Britain at the turn of the century, and for the manner in which he built the small University of St. Andrews into a strong center for research in organic chemistry.

With J. Wallace Waller, Purdie demonstrated a method of resolving racemic lactic acid that was based on the use of strychnine. Following Pasteur's work with tartaric acid, Purdie showed that racemic lactate can form supersaturated solutions, from which successive seeding with a trace of the optically active modification leads to the separation of the *d*- and *l*- forms in alternate crops.

In measuring the magnitude of molecular rotations in some chemical reactions, Purdie discovered an organic reaction that proved to be of great utility. He found that when a hydroxy compound such as an alcohol is treated with dry silver oxide and an alkyl iodide, alkylation of the hydroxy groups proceeds uniformly and smoothly. Purdie was quick to perceive that this "silver oxide" reaction might find extensive scope in work on the structure of sugars, and he directed the energies of his students and collaborators, most notably J. C. Irvine, into this channel. The principle underlying such constitutional studies can be expressed in general terms. By methylation, the free hydroxyl groups of the sugar complex can be protected. The estimate of the number, distribution, and stability of the hydroxyl groups gives definite evidence as to the structure of the parent substance. Walter Norman Haworth, who joined Purdie and Irving at St. Andrews in 1912, later used the methylation technique to establish the pyranose structure of methylglucose.

Purdie's scientific work was recognized by his election as fellow of the Royal Society (1895) and of the Chemical Society (1875). He was vice president of the Chemical Society in 1899. He was awarded the LL.D. from Aberdeen University in 1894 and retired from the administrative duties of his chair in 1909. Purdie died of heart failure in 1916.

BIBLIOGRAPHY

I. ORIGINAL WORKS. Among Purdie's important scientific papers are "Action of Sodic Alcoholates on Ethereal Fumarates and Maleates," in *Journal of the Chemical Society*, **47** (1885), 855–878; "The Action of Metallic Alkylates on Mixtures of Ethereal Salts with Alcohols," *ibid.*, **51** (1887), 627–634; and "Resolution of Lactic Acid into Its Optically Active Compounds," *ibid.*, **61** (1892), 754–765, with James W. Walker. A further list is in *Royal Society Catalogue of Scientific Papers*, XVII, 1047.

II. SECONDARY LITERATURE. P. F. F(rankland), "Thomas Purdie," in *Proceedings of the Royal Society*, **A101** (1922), iv–x; and J. C. Irvine, "Thomas Purdie," in *Journal of the Chemical Society*, **111** (1917), 359–369.

NEIL DAVIES MORGAN

RAMSDELL, LEWIS STEPHEN (*b*. Clinton, Michigan, 4 June 1895; *d*. Palo Alto, California, 14 June 1975), *mineralogy, crystallography*.

Ramsdell, the son of Dwight H. and Phoebe Voorhies Ramsdell, attended the University of

Michigan, where he received his bachelor's degree in 1917, his master's degree in 1919, and his doctorate in 1925. In 1920 he married Lois Ethel Calkins, who received her bachelor's degree from Michigan that year. The Ramsdells had two daughters.

From the first, Ramsdell's primary interest lay in mineralogy, and as the topic for his Ph.D. dissertation, he investigated the crystal structures of certain metallic sulfides and closely related selenides, tellurides, arsenides, and antimonides, to determine the degrees of isomorphism among members of these species. To accomplish this difficult task, Ramsdell applied X-ray diffraction techniques, using apparatus built by the General Electric Company. At that time, X-ray diffraction was a relatively new method of studying minerals, used in very few laboratories in the world. Only a handful of structures were known, but it enabled the investigator to solve the structures of crystals on an atomic scale.

Using X-ray diffraction required great ingenuity and patience. Each practitioner had to devise sample preparation and mounting techniques, to determine optimal exposure intervals (which Ramsdell found to vary between fifteen and forty hours!), and to find reproducible methods of measuring films, which were prone to different amounts of shrinkage. Since structures are not deducible directly from the diffraction pattern, high degrees of both geometrical and physicochemical insight are prerequisites for success. Despite these difficulties, Ramsdell determined the structures of nearly twenty metallic sulfides and related minerals, and classified them into isostructural groups. In the course of this work he also obtained atomic radii for selenium and tellurium.

Ramsdell was appointed instructor in the department of mineralogy at the University of Michigan when he received his master's degree in 1919. After receiving his doctorate in 1925, he was appointed an assistant professor in 1926. In 1933 he went to England to learn advanced X-ray diffraction techniques at the University of Manchester. On returning to Michigan he built his own X-ray apparatus, using a resuscitated dental transformer, and began teaching a course in which he ultimately trained generations of students in X-ray crystallography. Ramsdell was appointed associate professor in 1935 and full professor in 1944. His introduction of X-ray theory and practice into the curriculum at the University of Michigan was the outstanding accomplishment of his long career as a teacher.

Ramsdell worked out the crystal structures of numerous particularly difficult mineral species. He acted as an adviser to Newman Thibault, who completed a doctoral thesis on silicon carbide structures

in 1943. For the next ten years Ramsdell focused much of his attention on SiC, an artificial abrasive with a simple formula but an endlessly confusing array of crystalline structure types. Two polymorphic forms of SiC, with cubic and hexagonal symmetry, were already known, as were at least four different hexagonal and rhombohedral varieties—named I, II, III, and IV for the order of their discovery. Ramsdell identified several more types of SiC and then realized that they could be arranged in a series with integrally proportional axial ratios, that is, the lengths of the repeating cells making up the different types were integer multiples of the same unit.

Crystallographic structures in which identical two-dimensional sheets or layers are stacked at intervals that are multiples of one another were later named polytypes by Lester Strock. Ramsdell proposed that the polytypes of SiC be renumbered in the order of increasingly larger intervals between layers. Where he found gaps in the series of polytypes, he predicted that additional members, with appropriate stacking intervals, would be found. In due time, many more SiC polytypes were found, including those he predicted, and polytypical behavior was discovered to be common to many mineral species. Ramsdell's work on polytypism was a contribution of fundamental importance to the knowledge of crystal structure.

Ramsdell also classified some of the manganese oxide minerals on the basis of their crystal structures and minor element compositions. After x-raying more than fifty specimens of black opaque samples called psilomelane and "wad," he identified them as belonging to six separate species. In 1943, the importance of his research on the manganese oxides was recognized by the naming of a newly characterized dimorph of pyrolusite, MnO_2, "ramsdellite" in his honor.

In 1955, Ramsdell determined the crystal structure of coesite, an artificially created, high-pressure, polymorphic form of silica. This mineral was subsequently discovered in target rocks at meteorite impact sites, where it forms at shock wave pressures in excess of 300 kilobars. It is now used as one of the criteria for identifying impact scars.

Ramsdell was one of the "front five" professors who brought great renown to the department of mineralogy at the University of Michigan. In addition to his research and teaching, Ramsdell wrote a textbook of mineralogy with two of the five, Edward H. Kraus and Walter F. Hunt, and he served for many years as an editor of *American Mineralogist*, the journal that set high standards for the reporting of mineralogical research results. After a long period of aiding the chief editor, Walter F. Hunt, in an anonymous capacity, Ramsdell was appointed assistant editor (1952–1957) and editor (1957–1961). In 1951 he was appointed chairman of the department of mineralogy, a position he held until he retired from the University of Michigan in 1961. Thereafter, the department of mineralogy merged with geology, a change that had taken place in many other universities. After his retirement, the Ramsdells moved to Palo Alto, California.

BIBLIOGRAPHY

I. ORIGINAL WORKS. A list of Ramsdell's publications appears in a memorial to him written by E. William Heinrich, *American Mineralogist*, **61** (1976), 532–534. The other chief source of information is the Alumni Records Archives at the University of Michigan.

II. SECONDARY LITERATURE. No biography of Ramsdell has been written, and there are virtually no sources of information on his life aside from Heinrich's memorial and the Alumni Records Archives at the University of Michigan.

URSULA B. MARVIN

RENNER, OTTO (*b*. Neu-Ulm, Germany, 25 April 1883; *d*. Munich, Germany, 8 July 1960), *plant genetics*.

Renner was typical of late-nineteenth- and early-twentieth-century German biologists. He was greatly respected by researchers in plant physiology and plant cytogenetics, but almost unknown to other scientists. He never wrote a book or a scientific monograph that summed up his research discoveries. The topic to which he made his major contributions, the cytogenetics of the evening primrose (*Oenothera*), is removed from the mainstream of cytogenetic research. Nevertheless, his discoveries help to explain both the nature of the "mutations" upon which Hugo de Vries built his "mutation theory" of evolution and the chromosomal mechanism that permits an organism to retain a high degree of genetic heterozygosity and still produce constant, true-breeding descendants.

In his private life Renner had broad interests. He was thoroughly familiar with ancient literary classics, which he read in the original Greek. A dedicated naturalist, he knew both the flora of his native Germany and tropical floras, although floristics was more an avocation than a serious object of research for him.

The son of Ludwig Renner, a teacher, and of

Marie Kopf Renner, Renner spent his entire life in academic surroundings. After attending the gymnasium in Ulm, he studied at the University of Munich, from which he graduated in 1905. The following year he spent one semester at the University of Leipzig, where, under the direction of the plant physiologist Wilhelm Pfeffer, he acquired the first of his two major research interests, water relations in plants. The botanist Karl Goebel called him back to Munich to be his first assistant. Except for service during World War I in the German army, after which he worked as a bacteriologist at a hospital in Ulm, Renner remained at Munich until 1920. At first he combined research on plant morphology with that on water relations of growing plants, but in 1913, when he was promoted to assistant professor of plant physiology and pharmacognosy, he engaged in a scientific discussion that launched his career in plant genetics, to which he made major contributions.

Richard Goldschmidt, then a *Privatdozent* in zoology at Munich, told Renner about an apparent example of patroclinous inheritance (derived or inherited from the male parent) in the evening primrose (*Oenothera*). When Goldschmidt presented his explanation to Renner—that the plants in question contained only genes derived from the pollen of the male parent—Renner, highly skeptical, decided to test the hypothesis. He quickly obtained cytological evidence to show that Goldschmidt was wrong.

Continuing his research on *Oenothera*, Renner had shown by 1920 that in the species upon which de Vries had based his mutation theory of evolution, the independent assortment of gene differences predicted by Mendel's second law of heredity is largely or completely absent. Most plants produce two, and only two, kinds of egg or pollen nuclei, as if all of the genes were linked on a single chromosome. Furthermore, a combination of lethal genes causes embryos and seeds to die unless they are derived from pollen and egg that contain different sets of genes. As a result, many strains that have uniparental reproduction, via self-pollination, nevertheless are highly heterozygous genetically. The sets of genes that are transmitted intact, generation after generation, became known as Renner complexes.

These startling results, plus his solid research on water relations, earned Renner in 1920 the position of professor of botany and director of the botanical garden at Jena, where he remained for twenty-eight years.

In 1920 Renner married Johanna Unterbirker. They had a daughter, Hildegard, who became a physician, and a son, Erwin, who died in a climbing accident.

During the next decade, the American cytologist Ralph E. Cleland showed that Renner's unexpected results could be explained on the basis of the unusual behavior of the chromosomes during meiosis. Instead of forming seven pairs, the fourteen chromosomes become united into either a single ring or a ring of twelve and a pair. Normal eggs and pollen are formed only when chromosomes that occupy alternate positions in the ring—1, 3, 5, 7, 9, 11, 13 and/or 2, 4, 6, 8, 10, 12, 14—pass to the same pole of the spindle and are included in the same gamete. These sets of chromosomes contain the genes that make up Renner complexes.

Unusual deviation from this behavior can cause the complex to be broken up, giving rise to aberrant progeny of the sort that de Vries called "mutations." Such "mutations" do not involve any change in the genes themselves, but only in their pattern of distribution. When Renner and Cleland realized that their discoveries complemented each other, Cleland spent a year (1927–1928) in Renner's laboratory, and with the German cytologist Friedrich Oehlkers he completed the synthesis of genetic and cytological information.

Continuing his research on *Oenothera* hybrids, Renner found reciprocal differences in inheritance of chlorophyll pigmentation that could best be explained on the hypothesis that cellular organelles such as chloroplasts carry genetic information. Analyzing the behavior of a mutant, *cruciata*, that gives rise to abnormally shaped petals, he obtained evidence of gene conversion. In these respects his research on developmental genetics anticipated modern trends.

A staunch Catholic, Renner could not accept Hitler's regime, but maintained his research institute at Jena as well as he could. The institute was completely destroyed by bombing in the spring of 1945 (he barely escaped alive). He fled from Jena in 1948 and returned to Munich; he restored the buildings before he retired in 1953. He continued to work in the botany department at Munich until his death.

Renner received many honors. Among his honorary degrees were those awarded by the universities of Jena, Erlangen, and Freiburg. He was a member of German academies of sciences—Berlin, Leipzig, Göttingen, Halle, and Munich—as well as foreign member of the Genetical Society of Great Britain, the Royal Society, the Botanical Society of America, the American Academy of Arts and Sciences, the American Philosophical Society, and the U.S. National Academy of Sciences. In 1952 he was made knight of the Order pour le Mérite, the oldest, highest, and rarest award given in Germany.

Renner was an original, dynamic, and outspoken scientist. He was equally critical of Nazism and the communism that followed it in East Germany. Nevertheless, his scientific integrity and warm personality won the approval of all who knew him.

BIBLIOGRAPHY

I. ORIGINAL WORKS. "Wasserversorgung der Pflanzen," in *Handwörterbuch der Naturwissenschaften*, **10** (1915), 538–557; "Versuche über die gametrische Konstitution der Oenotheren," in *Zeitschrift für Vererbungslehre*, **18** (1917), 121–294; *Artbastarde bei Pflanzen*, vol. II, pt. A, Lieferung 7 of Erwin Baur and Max Hartmann, eds., *Handbuch der Vererbungswissenschaft* (Berlin, 1929); "Zur Genetik und Cytologie der *Oenothera chicaginensis* und ihre Abkömmlinge," in *Zeitschrift für Vererbungslehre*, **66** (1933), 275–318, written with Ralph E. Cleland; "Zur Kenntnis der Letalfaktoren und des Kopplungswechsels bei Oenotheren," in *Flora*, **127** (1934), 212–250; "Zur Kenntnis der nichtmendelnden Buntheit der Laubblätter," *ibid.*, **130** (1935–1936), 218–290; "Über *Oenothera atrovirens* Sh. et Bartl. und über somatische Konversion im Erbgang des Cruciata-Merkmals der Oenotheren," in *Zeitschrift für Vererbungslehre*, **74** (1938), 91–124; "Über die Entstehung der homozygotischen Formen aus komplexheterozygotischen Oenotheren," in *Flora*, **135** (1941), 201–238; "Über das Crossing-over bei *Oenothera*," *ibid.*, **136** (1942), 117–214; "Über den Erbgang des Cruciata-Merkmals der Oenotheren. V," in *Planta*, **48** (1957), 343–392; and "Somatic Conversion in the Heredity of the Cruciata Character in *Oenothera*," in *Heredity*, **13** (1959), 283–288.

II. SECONDARY LITERATURE. R. E. Cleland, "Otto Renner," in *Genetics*, **53** (1966), 1–6; and C. D. Darlington, "Otto Renner," in *Biographical Memoirs of Fellows of the Royal Society*, **7** (1961), 207–220, with complete bibliography.

G. L. STEBBINS

RÉNYI, ALFRÉD (*b*. Budapest, Hungary, 30 March 1921; *d*. Budapest, 1 February 1970), *mathematics*.

Rényi was the son of Artur Rényi, an engineer and linguist, and of Barbara Alexander, both of whom were Jewish. Rényi's paternal grandfather, originally named Rosenthal, left Germany and settled in Hungary under the name of Rényi after an adventurous interlude of sheep farming in Australia. In Budapest he founded a walking-stick factory and made a modest fortune. Rényi's maternal grandfather, Bernát Alexander, was professor of philosophy at the University of Budapest and a literary critic.

At school Rényi excelled in classical Greek. From early on, he was interested in astronomy, and that led him to physics, which in turn sparked his interest in mathematics. His university studies (1940–1944) were in mathematics and physics. In 1944 he was called up for forced labor service, but he managed to escape and lived in hiding. When conditions normalized, he obtained a Ph.D. in mathematics at Szeged (1945) under Frigyes (Friedrich) Riesz for work on Cauchy-Fourier series. Among his other teachers were Rózsa Péter (in high school) and Lipót Féjér (at Budapest). In 1946 he was awarded a scholarship that made it possible for him to go to Leningrad with his wife, Katalin Schulhof, whom he had married earlier that year. In Leningrad he worked with Yuri V. Linnik and made spectacular discoveries in the theory of numbers, which he expounded in his 1947 paper on the representation of an even number as the sum of a prime and an almost prime. There he also encountered the theory of probability, and he returned to Hungary already embarked on his brilliant career as a probabilist.

Rényi was the acknowledged founder of the school of probabilists centered at the Mathematical Research Institute of the Hungarian Academy of Sciences in Budapest, of which he was the director from 1950 to 1970. Among his Ph.D. students were many who subsequently made their mark in probability theory, including A. Prékopa, P. Révész, J. Mogyorodi, J. Kumlós, G. Tusnády, G. Katona, and D. Szász. His interest in the theory of numbers persisted throughout his life and (often in probabilistic contexts) found expression in his regular collaboration with Pál (Paul) Erdös and Pál (Paul) Turán. He held many important and influential positions—professor of mathematics at the universities of Debrecen (1949–1950) and of Budapest (1952–1970), general secretary of the Bolyai János Mathematical Society (1949–1955), and secretary of the Mathematical Section of the Hungarian Academy of Sciences (1949–1953)—and soon was recognized worldwide as one of the leaders in probability theory. Indications of the geographical range of this influence are his publication of a paper in Chinese and his receipt of an Overseas Fellowship from Churchill College, Cambridge, where he gave the prestigious Rouse Ball lecture in 1966. His publications and occasional writings, 355 in number, are listed in his *Selected Papers* (1976), which contains English translations of many of the most important items.

In the hands of writers like Linnik, Erdös, and Rényi, the theory of numbers is not clearly distinguished from the theory of probability. Each lends techniques to the other, and important problems lie along their common frontier. Thus, when Rényi is referred to as a great applied probabilist, this is partly because of his interest in probability applied to other parts of mathematics. A joint paper with Erdös, "On the Evolution of Random Graphs" (1960), illustrates this interest very well. A set of points called vertices is given, and "edges" joining pairs of vertices are then created by some specific time-dependent random mechanism. What results is an evolving "random graph." This is truly applied mathematics, important, for example, in studies of the spread of disease.

Another illustration is "random space-filling," which at first may be seen as a problem in stochastic geometry but turns out to be very important in chemistry, in physics, and in such applications as the design of parking lots. A careful study of the complete bibliography in Rényi's *Selected Papers* reveals (especially in the titles of the shorter notes, usually published in Hungarian) the practical origin of many of Rényi's more famous "pure" papers. An example of an explicitly practical paper is "On Two Mathematical Models of the Traffic on a Divided Highway" (1969).

Rényi was, however, an important contributor to fundamentals. In 1954, at the International Congress of Mathematicians in Amsterdam, he announced a new system of axioms for probability (for a later account, see "On a New Axiomatic Theory of Probability" [1955]), based on conditionality as a fundamental concept. The full impact of this has yet to be absorbed. He also made seminally important contributions to the foundations of information technology.

Rényi's most famous single achievement was his proof of the representability of each even number as the sum of a prime and an "almost prime"; in the best contemporary improvement (by Chen Jing-run), "almost prime" has been refined to "integer with at most two prime factors."

Rényi wrote many books; among them, *Foundations of Probability* (1970) is perhaps the most beautiful text ever written on the subject. He had an exceptionally clear and lucid style, and his longer papers are full of comments and insights that enhance their value. His great interest in the history of ideas found expression in fictitious dialogues and letters (*Dialogues on Mathematics* [1967] and *Letters on Probability* [1972]), which combine great depth with astonishing artistry. *A Diary on Information Theory* (1984), published after his death, is a natural successor to these two remarkable works.

Rényi traveled widely, especially in Europe, and did much to reunify the mathematical community after World War II. One of his sayings, now widely current, defined a mathematician as "a machine for converting coffee into theorems." (Turán improved on this by a remark, prompted by a cup that was too weak: "This coffee is fit only for lemmas.") These anecdotes show that for Rényi, mathematics was a social activity through which he generated a great number of friends.

In 1969 Rényi's wife, also a distinguished mathematician, with whom he had written "The Prüfer Code for *k*-Trees," died; and less than six months later, Rényi died at the age of forty-eight.

BIBLIOGRAPHY

I. ORIGINAL WORKS. *Selected Papers of Alfréd Rényi*, Pál Turán, ed., 3 vols. (Budapest, 1976), lists 355 publications and manuscripts, and reprints a great many of these, in English translation where necessary, together with valuable commentaries. Vol. I contains a portrait and a short biography by Turán. Bibliographies are in *Studia scientiarum mathematicarum Hungarica*, **6** (1971), 3–22, with addition in *ibid.*, **7** (1972), 477; and by B. Gyires, in *Universitatis Debreceniensis, Institum mathematicum, Publicationes mathematicae*, **17** (1970), 1–17.

Among Rényi's works are "O predstavlenii chetnvikh chisel v vide summ'e odnogo prostogo i odnogo prochti-prostogo chisla" ("On the Representation of an Even Number as the Sum of a Prime and an Almost Prime," in *Doklady Akademii nauk USSR*, **56** (1947), 455–458, English trans. in *American Mathematical Society Translations*, 2nd ser., **19** (1962), 299–321; "On a New Axiomatic Theory of Probability," in *Acta mathematica Academiae scientiarum Hungaricae*, **6** (1955), 285–335; "Egy egydimenziós véletlen térkitöltési problémáról" ("On a One-Dimensional Random Space-Filling Problem"), in *Magyar tudományos Akadémia matamatikai kutató intézetének közleményei*, **3** (1958), 109–127; "On the Dimenand Entropy of Probability Distributions," in *Acta mathematica Academiae scientiarum Hungaricae*, **10** (1959), 193–215; "On the Evolution of Random Graphs," in *Magyar tudományos Akadémia matematikai kutató intézetének közleményei*, **5** (1960), 17–61, written with Paul Erdös; "On Measures of Entropy and Information," in *Proceedings of the 4th Berkeley Symposium on Mathematical Statistics and Probability*, vol. I (1961), 547–561; "Über die konvexe Hülle von *n* zufällig gewählten Punkten," in *Zeitschrift für Wahrscheinlichkeitstheorie*, **2** (1963–1964), 75–84, and **3** (1964–1965), 138–147, and "Zufällige konvexe Polygone in einem Ringgebiet," *ibid.*, **9** (1968), 146–157, written with R. Sulanke; "On Two Mathematical Models of the Traffic on a Divided Highway," in *Journal of Applied Probability*, **1** (1964), 311–320; "On the Theory of Random Search," in *Bulletin of the American Mathematical Society*, **71** (1965), 809–828; *Dialogues on Mathematics* (San Francisco, 1967); "Applications of Probability Theory to Other Areas of Mathematics," in *12th Biennial International Seminar of the Canadian Mathematical Congress* (Vancouver, 1970), 177–295; *Foundations of Probability* (San Francisco, 1970); "The Prüfer Code for *k*-Trees," in *Combinatorial Theory and Its Applications*, vol. III (Amsterdam, 1970), 945–971, written with Kató Rényi; *Letters on Probability*, Laszló Vekerdi, trans. (Detroit, 1972); "On Some Applications of Probability Methods to Additive Number Theoretic Problems," in *Contributions to Ergodic Theory and Probability* (Berlin, 1970), 37–44, written with Paul Erdös; and *A Diary on Information Theory*, Louis Sucheston, ed. (Budapest, 1984; repr. New York, 1987).

II. SECONDARY LITERATURE. Obituaries include those by David G. Kendall in *Journal of Applied Statistics*, **7** (1970), 509–522; and by P. Révész and I. Vincze, in *Annals of Mathematical Statistics*, **43**, no. 6 (1972), i–xvi. There is a group of articles in *Matematikai lapok. Bolyai János Matematikai tórsulat*, **21** (1970): by Pál Turán, 199–210, by P. Révész, 211–231, by I. Csiszár, 233–241, by G. Katona *et al.*, 243–244, and by V. B. Mészáros, 245–248.

DAVID G. KENDALL

RICHARDS, ALFRED NEWTON (*b*. Stamford, New York, 22 March 1876; *d*. Bryn Mawr, Pennsylvania, 24 March 1976), *physiology, pharmacology*.

Richards was the youngest of three sons of Leonard E. Richards, a Presbyterian minister, and Mary Elizabeth Burbank, a schoolteacher before her marriage. Life in the Richards household was strict and austere. Reverend Richards' salary was under $1,000 annually, but the family saved enough to help support Richards and his brothers through college. Richards received his B.A. in chemistry from Yale in 1897. He remained in New Haven for another year, working under physiological chemist Russell Chittenden in the Sheffield Scientific School. Richards spent the next decade at Columbia, where he received his Ph.D. in physiological chemistry in 1901. He was an assistant and tutor in physiological chemistry until 1904, and he offered the first laboratory-based course in pharmacology at Columbia, beginning in 1904.

In 1908, the year he married Lillian L. Woody (on 26 December), Richards accepted an offer to organize a pharmacology program at Northwestern University. He remained at Northwestern until 1910, when he accepted the professorship of pharmacology at the University of Pennsylvania Medical School. Richards spent the rest of his career in Philadelphia. He was an active member of many scientific organizations, and his career as a scientific researcher and administrator earned Richards over a dozen honorary degrees from universities in the United States and abroad.

Richards' most significant contributions as a researcher concerned renal physiology, a subject to which he devoted more than twenty years. He began this work to help settle a debate, dating back to the 1840's, over the mechanism by which kidneys form urine. Scientists formulated the earliest theories of urine formation solely on the basis of anatomical structure. In 1842 William Bowman reported that the microscopic spherical bodies of the outer kidney, which Marcello Malpighi had observed in the mid-seventeenth century, were expanded ends of the urine-bearing tubules that stretched into the interior of the kidney. A tuft of capillaries projected into each of these tubule ends. Bowman believed these capillaries provided the aqueous vehicle for urine and that the tubules—themselves encircled by capillaries—eliminated the particles from the blood that made up urine.

As an alternative to this "secretory" theory, Carl Ludwig published his "filtration-reabsorption" theory of urine formation in 1844. According to Ludwig, a particularly high blood pressure within the tuft of capillaries produced a filtrate in the Malpighian spherical body, or glomerulus, of urinous and other particles that could permeate the capillary wall. The capillaries surrounding the tubules, which contained the concentrated blood, reabsorbed (by osmosis) most of the fluid and many of the vital particles filtered in the glomerulus. The remaining fluid and waste particles emerged from the tubules as urine.

Richards initiated the kidney project about 1913, shortly after he and Cecil Drinker developed a perfusion apparatus that could supply blood to an animal's kidney in much the same way as the heart did. The apparatus possessed the advantage of allowing the researchers to control the flow, velocity, and pressure of blood in the kidney. In 1922 Richards and his colleagues reported that as pressure increased within glomerular capillaries, urine output increased as well—just as the filtration-reabsorption theory predicted.

Two years later, Richards and J. T. Wearn published the first of many papers on the composition of glomerular urine in the amphibian kidney. This research required tremendously difficult techniques, such as micropuncture of glomeruli and ultramicrochemical analysis, but it was the most direct way available to learn about the formation of urine. Their simultaneous analyses of blood, glomerular fluid, and urine revealed that the glomerulus contained many of the normal constituents of blood, such as sodium chloride and glucose, which urine lacked. Also, dyes incorporated into perfusion fluid and injected into animals appeared in the glomerulus.

This provided compelling evidence for glomerular filtration, as did their quantitative comparisons of blood plasma and glomerular fluid, most of which they carried out in the early 1930's. Plasma and fluid had about the same percentage of permeative components (glucose, urea, and inulin, among others), and the two solutions had about the same pH. The investigations of the role of kidney tubules conducted in Richards' laboratory, most of which were published in 1937, suggested that reabsorptive (and some secretory) processes operated between the tubules and blood. Overall, Richards' contributions to renal physiology went a long way toward settling a century-old dispute about the nature of renal functions and laid the foundation for a better understanding of renal pathology.

Richards achieved equal prominence as an administrator of scientific research. His first major position was as vice president in charge of medical affairs at the University of Pennsylvania from 1939 to 1948. During this period he headed two scientific bodies that had a significant impact on the national and international scientific communities. From 1941 to 1947 Richards was chairman of the Committee on Medical Research, an organization that the U.S. Congress created to help meet the country's wartime medical needs. It mobilized medical researchers from universities, industry, government laboratories, and private foundations, and it recommended projects (such as research on penicillin and antimalarials) that merited the highest priority from the standpoint of national defense to its parent body, the Office of Scientific Research and Development.

Richards was president of the National Academy of Sciences from 1947 to 1950. He firmly believed that researchers in industry could contribute in a major way to the advancement of science. Thus, he helped shape the research policies of one of the leading research-oriented firms in the pharmaceutical industry, Merck and Company, which he served as a consultant from 1930 to 1960.

Richards' contributions to science, therefore, are twofold. As a researcher he shed considerable light on fundamental physiological processes in the kidney. As an administrator he guided institutions and organizations that played an important part in the broad progress of science.

BIBLIOGRAPHY

I. ORIGINAL WORKS. Richards' key summaries of his kidney research include "Kidney Function," in *American Journal of the Medical Sciences*, **163** (1922), 1–19; *Methods and Results of Direct Investigations of the Function of* *the Kidney* (Baltimore, 1929); "Urine Formation in the Amphibian Kidney," in *American Journal of the Medical Sciences*, **190** (1935), 727–746, with Arthur M. Walker; and "Processes of Urine Formation," in *Proceedings of the Royal Society of London*, **B126** (1938), 398–432. Among the relevant individual articles and groups of papers on his kidney work are three papers by Richards and Oscar Plant in *American Journal of Physiology*, **59** (1922), 144–202, which report the effect of changes in renal blood pressure on urine output; "Observations on the Composition of Glomerular Urine . . . ," *ibid.*, **71** (1924), 209–227, with J. T. Wearn, the first detailed publication of their qualitative analysis of glomerular fluid; eight articles from Richards' laboratory in *Journal of Biological Chemistry*, **101** (1933), 179–267, **107** (1934), 661–672, **110** (1935), 749–761, and **116** (1936), 735–747, on quantitative studies of glomerular fluid; and six papers by Richards and his colleagues in *American Journal of Physiology*, **118** (1937), 111–173, which discuss their investigation of renal tubule fluid.

Richards summarized the work of the Committee on Medical Research in the foreward to Edwin C. Andrus *et al.*, eds., *Advances in Military Medicine*, 2 vols. (Boston, 1948), I, xli–liv.

The most comprehensive source on Richards' professional career and personal life is the extensive collection of his personal papers in the University of Pennsylvania Archives (a total of 42 boxes). Additional documents on Richards' service to the Committee on Medical Research are in the papers of the Office of Scientific Research and Development, Record Group 227, National Archives, Washington, D.C.

II. Secondary Literature. The best biography of Richards is Carl F. Schmidt, "Alfred Newton Richards," in *Biographical Memoirs. National Academy of Sciences*, **42** (1971), 271–318. The collection of articles in Isaac Starr, ed., "Alfred Newton Richards, Scientist and Man," in *Annals of Internal Medicine*, **71**, supp. 8, no. 5, pt. 2 (1969), covers many areas of Richards' life and work, including his years as head of the Committee on Medical Research and his kidney research. David Y. Cooper, "Alfred N. Richards and the Discovery of the Mechanism of Urine Formation," in *Transactions and Studies of the College of Physicians of Philadelphia*, **6** (1984), 63–73, discusses Richards' kidney research in depth.

John Patrick Swann

RIDDLE, OSCAR (*b*. Cincinnati, Indiana, 27 September 1877; *d*. Plant City, Florida, 29 November 1968), *physiology, endocrinology*.

Oscar Riddle spent his research career studying birds to explore questions of evolution and the nongenetic physiology of reproduction and determination of sex. Best known for his isolation of the hormone prolactin, he also devoted considerable time to matters of science education and free public information about evolution.

The son of Jonathan Riddle and Amanda Emiline Carmichael, Riddle was born in a log house in Greene County, Indiana. His father was a farmer; his maternal grandfather ran a general store and flour mill in Cincinnati, Indiana. Unfortunately, when Jonathan Riddle died in 1882, he left his wife with nine children and few resources. The family managed only because the children contributed to the family economy. Oscar helped to haul drinking water from the nearby spring, store milk and vegetables, clear land, and do general farming. When he was nine and ten, Oscar worked on a farm two miles away to supplement the family income. He experienced a typical midwestern farmer's education, walking to a one-room cabin for a short school season; he later walked two miles to the village school. By age fourteen, Riddle was supporting himself and had acquired through his outdoor work a curiosity about the material world around him, including fossils. He had also begun to question religious dogma about the Flood.

According to Riddle's memoirs, a local lecture presented by a college classmate of his older brother's affected the course of Oscar's life. The young fellow was studying zoology at Indiana with Carl H. Eigenmann, who examined blind cave fish to explore questions of evolution and adaptation. The student took a collection of Eigenmann's fishes to Cincinnati and discussed evolution. Riddle was enthralled, for "nothing in a long life has equaled the release, thrill, and resolution obtained from this message, so simply delivered by a young man from a neighboring farm" (Corner, p. 430). Riddle attended high school in Bloomfield, then began at Indiana University in 1896. There he chose biology, spending his summers at the Turkey Lake biological field station.

In 1899 Eigenmann recommended Riddle for a position with the U.S. Fish Commission, collecting fish in Puerto Rico. Riddle gathered specimens there but also taught biology at the new Model and Training School in San Juan. As his Spanish improved, he received other teaching assignments throughout Puerto Rico. In 1901 he traveled to Trinidad and to the Orinoco River in Venezuela for collecting and observing. He returned to Indiana, then traveled with Eigenmann in 1902 to collect blind fish in western Cuba. After receiving his B.A. from Indiana University in 1902, Riddle rejected job offers in business and enrolled as a graduate student at the University of Chicago.

At Chicago, Riddle found Jacques Loeb's physiological ideas particularly intriguing. Unfortunately, Loeb left for California that year. In 1903, to help put his sister through college, Riddle took a position teaching physiology at Central High School in St. Louis, where he remained for five half-years, through 1906. The half-years allowed him to attend the Marine Biological Laboratory's summer session in physiology in 1903 and to hold an assistantship at Indiana for the summer of 1904 and for a longer period in 1905. In 1906 he reenrolled at Chicago, with an assistantship in zoology. As a result of personality conflicts with the physiologist G. N. Stewart, Riddle decided to concentrate instead on zoology under Charles Otis Whitman, with a minor in biochemistry under Albert Prescott Matthews.

Riddle joined in Whitman's work on pigeons and evolution. Whitman suggested that for his dissertation Riddle examine the causes of barring, the appearance of alternating light and dark bars on the feathers of pigeons and other birds. When Riddle took up the study that had become so important a part of Whitman's own career and life, Whitman virtually embraced him as a son. Thus, when Riddle completed his Ph.D. in 1907, he stayed at Chicago in joint positions in teaching, as associate in zoology and embryology, and in research, as assistant in experimental therapeutics.

In mid 1910 Riddle traveled to Europe, with Whitman's promise that he would be made assistant professor in biology upon his return. He spent several weeks in Berlin, visited Paul Ehrlich in Frankfurt, then went on to the Naples Zoological Station. Unfortunately, Whitman died unexpectedly on 6 December 1910, after caring for his pigeons during a cold spell. Riddle decided to return early to Chicago after Whitman's successor, Frank Rattray Lillie, informed Riddle that he would not be reappointed for the next year because of internal opposition. With fears about his livelihood and about the fate of Whitman's extensive unpublished, somewhat disorganized research results, and that of the research pigeons, Riddle left Naples. His decision to publish Whitman's work required a formidable commitment of time and energy. The decision determined the course of Riddle's own lifework.

Matthews obtained a six-month research appointment for Riddle in his Laboratory of Experimental Therapeutics, and Riddle acquired some money to maintain the pigeon colony still at Whitman's home. In 1912 came his first and only important move, to a position as research associate with the Carnegie Institution of Washington, which also promised to publish Whitman's papers and to maintain the pigeon colony. In 1913 Riddle moved to the Station for Experimental Evolution at Cold Spring Harbor, New York, where he continued his research even after his official retirement in 1945. He married Leona Lewis there in 1937.

At the laboratory Riddle pursued many problems of physiology and reproduction in pigeons and doves. Yet his biographer George Corner reports that Riddle's research life was not particularly happy there. The first laboratory director, Charles Benedict Davenport, did not really approve of Riddle's loyalty to Whitman's non-Mendelian and descriptive approach, which Davenport likely regarded as old-fashioned. Riddle did rather dogmatically follow Whitman's lead in his emphasis on attacking the general problems of life rather than focusing narrowly on one or another analytical problem. Thus he emphasized the way in which barring results from metabolic, and hence nongenetic changes rather than from inheritance. In fact, many of Riddle's specific conclusions have been shown to be inadequate or incorrect. His most significant research contribution was his isolation of prolactin, the pituitary hormone that stimulates the mammary gland to produce milk.

Riddle had already been among the first to use extracts of other glands, including insulin, thyroxin, adrenalin, and pituitary extract, in his explorations of pigeon metabolism. After reading a report that extracts of the anterior lobe of the pituitary gland of rabbits could stimulate milk secretion, he set out to isolate the substance responsible. By 1932, R. W. Bates, S. W. Dykshorn, and Riddle had obtained a substance that did produce lactation, but the substance remained in an impure form. They called it prolactin, continued their work, and identified prolactin as a protein. Riddle then found that the crop milk which pigeons produce is also induced by a pituitary hormone. He quickly identified it as prolactin and obtained it in a reasonably pure form. Using Riddle's correlation of crop growth and lactation, others purified the hormone further and eventually prepared it in a useful crystalline form.

Riddle had few assistants, a small laboratory, and no students because he remained at a research laboratory throughout his career. Yet perhaps his most important contribution to science lay in his public lobbying for freethinking in education, beginning with his first publication in 1906. Specifically, he became concerned that evolution be taught in high schools and colleges. His nonteaching position secured him from the attacks of antievolutionists. After a public address in 1936 attacking high schools for their backwardness in rejecting evolutionary ideas and embracing religious dogma, he received considerable criticism. This led him to publish in 1954 the rather poorly received *Unleashing of Evolutionary Thought* and a series of much more effective articles. As an outspoken advocate of scientific, and opponent of religious, thinking, Riddle received in 1958 the Humanist of the Year Award from the American Humanist Society and a citation from the National Association of Biology Teachers, which he had founded in 1930. He served as president of the American Rationalist Federation in 1959 and 1960. The American Philosophical Society, the American Association for the Advancement of Science, and the National Academy of Sciences also elected him as member.

BIBLIOGRAPHY

I. ORIGINAL WORKS. Riddle's works are listed by Corner (see below). The most important include "What and How Much Can Be Done in Ecological and Physiological Zoology in Secondary Schools?" in *School Science and Mathematics*, **6** (1906), 212–216, 247–254; "A Study of Fundamental Bars in Feathers," in *Biological Bulletin*, **12** (1907), 165–175; "Experiments on Melanin Color Formation: Against the Current Mendelian Hypothesis of Color Development," in *Verhandlungen des VIII. Internationalen Zoologen-Kongress zu Graz* (1912), 311–319; as editor, *Posthumous Works of Charles Otis Whitman*, Carnegie Institution publication no. 257, 2 vols. (Washington, D.C., 1919); "Prolactin, a New and Third Hormone of the Anterior Pituitary," in *Anatomical Record*, **54** (1932), 25ff., written with R. W. Bates and S. W. Dykshorn; as editor, *The Teaching of Biology in Secondary Schools of the United States* (Lancaster, Pa., 1942); *Endocrines and Constitution in Doves and Pigeons*, Carnegie Institution publication no. 572 (Washington, D.C., 1947); and *The Unleashing of Evolutionary Thought* (New York, 1954).

II. SECONDARY LITERATURE. The best biography is by George Corner in *Biographical Memoirs. National Academy of Sciences*, **45** (1974), 427–465.

JANE MAIENSCHEIN

RIDEAL, ERIC KEIGHTLEY (*b.* Sydenham, England, 11 April 1890; *d.* London, England, 25 September 1974), *physical chemistry*.

Rideal was the first of four children born to a London consulting chemist, Samuel Rideal, and his Irish wife, Elizabeth Keightley. As a financially successful and leading public analyst, author of many textbooks on water and sewage purification, and a deviser of the Rideal-Walker quantitative test for disinfectant activity (1903), Samuel Rideal could afford to give his children an excellent education. After attending Farnham Grammar School in Surrey, Rideal boarded at Oundle School in Northamptonshire, a boys' secondary school that, under its brilliant headmaster, F. W. Sanderson, was unusual among English public schools for its obligatory engineering and workshop practice as part of the curriculum.

In 1907 Rideal entered Trinity Hall, Cambridge, on an open scholarship in natural science. There, although he studied formally in Sir William Pope's chemistry department, with its very strong emphasis upon inorganic and organic chemistry, it was the physics classes in the Cavendish Laboratory that excited his interest in the physical chemistry then being systematized by Wilhelm Ostwald and Walther Nernst in Germany and by James Walker in Great Britain. An even greater formative influence on Rideal at Cambridge was the stimulating lectures of the physiologist William Bate Hardy, whose interest in osmosis was to prompt Rideal's lifelong passion for surface chemistry, which he always viewed as the boundary discipline between mechanical and biological systems.

Rideal graduated with first-class honors in chemistry in 1910. Then, like most British chemists before World War I, he spent two years studying in Germany—first, at his father's suggestion, with the electrochemist A. Fischer at the Technical University in Aachen, and then with Kekulé's pupil Richard Anschütz at the University of Bonn. He obtained his doctorate, with a dissertation on the electrochemistry of uranium salts, from Bonn in June 1912.

On returning to London in 1912, Rideal spent his first two years doing electrochemical consulting in his father's office suite. He was testing water supplies in Ecuador when war broke out in Europe in 1914. After serving with the Royal Engineers in Belgium, he contracted dysentery in 1916 and spent the remainder of the war in the department of munitions inventions. Here he spent most of his time developing a catalyst for the industrial production of ammonia that used the synthetic laboratory method Fritz Haber had described in 1905. Rideal's co-worker on this project was Hugh Stott Taylor, with whom he published *Catalysis in Theory and Practice* in 1919. For his work during the war period, he was awarded the M.B.E.; he also found time to produce, with (and for) his father, four textbooks on industrial chemistry.

As visiting professor of chemistry at the University of Illinois, Urbana, from 1919 to 1920, Rideal had the opportunity to become friends with such leading American physical chemists as Gilbert N. Lewis, Richard C. Tolman, and Irving Langmuir; the influence of the latter's work proved particularly stimulating. Rideal returned to England in 1920 to take up the Humphrey Owen Jones lectureship at the University of Cambridge, where he also became a fellow of Trinity Hall.

Rideal married Peggy Jackson, sister of the American writer Schuyler Jackson, in 1921; they had one daughter. He was a devout Anglican and, but for the year in America, would probably have played an active role in the Christian Socialist campaign of the Anglo-Catholic Reverend Conrad Noel, which he joined in 1918. An internationalist in science and politics, Rideal believed fervently that Christianity should be the basis of political life.

In 1930, through Hardy's influence, Rideal was elected to the chair of colloidal physics, but within a year he moved to the Plummer chair of colloid science. Although he would undoubtedly have been elected professor of physical chemistry at Cambridge in 1937 (the post went to Ronald G. W. Norrish), a serious operation for an intestinal tumor the year before, which left him with a permanent colectomy, decided him against entering the competition.

Rideal's fears that the disability would diminish his energy for research and administration were misplaced. In 1946, following much government war work at Cambridge, Rideal was appointed Fullerian professor of chemistry and director of the Davy-Faraday Laboratory at the Royal Institution in London; he resigned in 1949 because he found the social commitments that went with the position too taxing. From 1950 to 1955 Rideal was professor of chemistry at King's College, London, where for the third time in his career he built up a surface chemistry research school from virtually nothing. He spent his long and active retirement, begun in 1955, at Imperial College, London, as senior research fellow in the chemistry department of his pupil R. M. Barrer.

Knighted for his services to chemistry in 1951, Rideal was elected a fellow of the Royal Society in 1930 and played particularly active roles in the Faraday Society (now part of the Royal Chemical Society), of which he was the president (1938–1945), the Chemical Society (president, 1950–1952), the Royal Institute of Chemistry, and the Society of Chemical Industry (president, 1945–1946), which created the Rideal Lecture in his honor. The triennial Chemisorption and Catalysis Conference, which he launched in 1962, was renamed the Rideal Conference in his honor in 1971.

Rideal, in great demand as an industrial consultant, suffered considerable financial difficulty, as well as embarrassment, in the early 1930's when he had to pay a sizable tax on previously undeclared consultancy income. His Cambridge research student C. P. Snow, who disliked Rideal, was to base the character of the lawyer Herbert Getliffe in *Strangers and Brothers* (1940) on this financial episode; earlier, Snow portrayed Rideal in *The Search* (1934) as the irrepressibly effervescent and slightly bogus Professor Desmond, "the supreme commercial traveller, the salesman of science and thermometer of scientific gossip."

Rideal published nearly 300 scientific papers in his sixty years of active research; 70 percent of them were written in collaboration with research students. Although such collaborative efforts have become normal in the twentieth century, a few of his students were disturbed by a certain casualness in his proprietorship and transmission of their intellectual and experimental creations. On the other hand, there is no doubt that Rideal was, with good students, one of the century's outstanding research supervisors. At Cambridge, the Royal Institution, and King's College, he almost single-handedly developed large and successful research schools that attracted students from overseas as well as from Great Britain. Among his pupils were R. G. W. Norrish, a future Nobel Prize winner, who began work on photolysis with Rideal in 1922; Frank P. Bowden, the Australian expert on lubrication; C. P. Snow, who pioneered infrared spectroscopy with Rideal before becoming a civil servant and successful novelist; G. van Praagh, a chemistry teacher who played an important role in the development of the heuristic Nuffield syllabi, which transformed the teaching of science in British secondary schools in the 1960's; and Daniel D. Eley, one of the fourteen fellows of the Royal Society and fifty professors of chemistry Rideal is estimated to have trained for industrial or academic careers.

Rideal was neither a good experimentalist nor a profoundly original theoretician, but he had charisma, organizing ability, good judgment on how a new technique could be exploited, and above all what he himself described as "the God within": enthusiasm. His work, although given unity by the theme of surface chemistry, was exceedingly diverse in character. The papers are uniform in style: an opening discussion of the problem, together with a thorough survey of earlier literature, a mathematical and theoretical analysis of the problem that involves experimentally determinable variables, an experimental section, and a summary of the findings. Since five or six research projects were commonly in progress simultaneously and continuously, any strictly chronological treatment would prove hopelessly complex.

Following his doctoral studies in Germany, Rideal published work on electrochemistry and was concerned with fuel cells throughout his life. His principal contribution as a physical chemist, however, was to provide an understanding of the chemistry of surfaces. Given his father's interest in disinfectants and their collaboration on the text *Chemical Disinfection and Sterilization* (1921), it is hardly surprising that Rideal's interest in surface phenomena arose from the biochemical/bacteriological problem of how germicides act on bacteria. If they were akin to Ehrlich's "magic bullets," how, exactly, did they penetrate the bacterial wall? Rideal saw that this behavior was part of the general physical phenomenon of the mechanism of adsorption by charcoal, fibers, and metal surfaces, and that a good starting point was the study of capillary penetration by liquids.

The American physical chemist Edward W. Washburn suggested in 1921, from an analysis of the forces involved, that the distance x, advanced by a liquid penetrating a capillary tube, obeyed the relationship

$$x^2 = \frac{\gamma_{\cos\theta}}{2\eta} \cdot rt,$$

where γ is the surface tension, η the viscosity, r the radius of the tube or fiber, t the time taken to reach distance x, and θ the angle of wetting (meniscus angle). In 1922 Rideal pointed out that the net forces involved varied with the velocity of flow as well as the length of the tube wetted. The time equation was therefore more accurately represented by

$$t = \frac{2\eta}{\gamma r} \cdot x^2 \cos\theta - \frac{dr^2}{8\eta} \cdot \log x + \frac{d^2 r^5}{512\eta^3 x^2} + \cdots$$

where d is the density of the liquid. For small radii, neglecting all but the first term, this reduced to the Rideal-Washburn equation, which was to be used extensively in the growing detergent industry.

Investigations of the adsorption of liquids by Irving Langmuir during World War I had shown that adsorption usually rendered the surface concentration of a solute much higher than the bulk concentration in the solvent. Rideal surmised in 1923 that if a similar effect were found for a membrane-water interface, then the germicidal efficiency of a disinfectant could be determined by its ability to lower surface tension. Experiments confirmed that the strongest bactericides were those with the highest ability to lower the surface tension of water. Both Hardy and Langmuir had shown previously that surface films are molecular monolayers, with the molecules so oriented that polar groups (such as $-OH$, $-COOH$) pointed into the water and nonpolar groups (such as hydrocarbon chains) reached above the water surface. Rideal was the first to apply this

insight to microorganisms and their destruction, pointing out that their growth could be inhibited by attaching to them a lipid-soluble molecule with heavy side chains.

Although Rideal was to return intermittently to the study of bacterial surfaces, by 1925 the more general study of surfaces had acquired its own fascination and momentum. There were, moreover, many potential industrial and commercial applications to be investigated and exploited. In 1925, for example, Rideal showed that evaporation from a water surface could be retarded by as much as 50 percent by spreading the surface with a monolayer of long-chain fatty acids. Further extension of this principle by Langmuir two years later led to important applications in the conservation of reservoirs, particularly in equatorial regions of the globe.

The state of contemporary knowledge of surface chemistry was summarized by Rideal in *An Introduction to Surface Chemistry* (1926). This text, which was rigorously presented in the formal language of chemical thermodynamics, included a discussion of colloids. Assuming that colloids could adsorb gases or liquids as monolayers analogous to the classical Langmuir surface, Rideal sought to overturn the so-called empirical Schulze-Hardy Rule (an extension by W. B. Hardy in 1900 of nineteenth-century observations by Hans Schulze), which claimed that in the coagulation of a colloid, the coagulating power of an electrolyte increased with increasing valence.

Rideal showed that these valence rules were not exact and that univalent metal ions, for example, could be made to disperse colloids differently. In joint work with J. H. Schulman in 1937, Rideal found that ions had very specific effects on colloids. Whereas a monolayer of a protein or of cholesterol could be easily penetrated by a dilute solution of saponin (a plant glycoside), in other cases the penetrating substance was trapped or "anchored" below the monolayer film. If the substance injected had the general formula $CH_3(CH_2)_{11}X$, then the degree of penetration varied as X:

$$NH_3^+ > SO_4^- > SO_3^- > COO^- > N(CH_3)_3^+$$

This demonstration of specific ion interactions had important biochemical implications for the understanding of cell chemistry as well as pharmaceutical applications.

Earlier, in 1927, following Langmuir's and Neil K. Adam's development of a trough for the investigation of surface films, Rideal and H. Mouquin measured the rigidity of monomolecular layers. By applying a torque beneath the surface, they were able to determine the displacement by the optical examination of dust particles sprinkled upon the surface. Although Rideal did not pursue such studies further, the investigation was the beginning of the quantitative surface rheology that was developed by engineers in the 1940's. The Langmuir-Adam trough was also used fruitfully with Schulman in 1931 to derive values of surface potentials for long-chain fatty acids. According to Helmholtz, the change in surface potential ΔV is given by $4\pi n\mu$, where n is the number of molecules per square centimeter of film, each molecule being credited with an average electric moment of effective vertical component μ.

The ingenious measurements, which utilized a radium bromide/air electrode technique that had been developed by Guyot and A. N. Frumkin, allowed Rideal to determine the actual orientation of adsorbed molecules and to show that the value of μ depended upon the state of aggregation of the film in the Langmuir trough. Thus, when the film surface was compressed, μ rose considerably, while below the surface monolayer Rideal could detect an ionic double layer of molecules that contributed to the interfacial potential. Information on the orientation of the surface could be obtained easily for complex proteins, and "the effects of alteration of inclination as well as of adhesion of the polar groups to the substrate were capable of quantitative measurement."

Although this technique and its results were of considerable interest to biochemists, more significant was the research program Rideal began with A. H. Hughes in 1933, in which he showed how surface potentials could be used to follow the kinetics of chemical reactions taking place on a surface film—a technique that also had bearing on Rideal's interest in catalysis. Rates of oxidation of fatty acid films were found to depend upon surface area, not thickness; and if the surface was compressed, there were marked effects of steric hindrance as preferred reaction sites were pushed above the surface. Rideal saw that what he called "a shielding or accessibility factor," ϕ, should be added to the rate equation for surface reactions:

$$K' = \phi z' p' e^{-E'}/RT,$$

where K is the rate constant, p is a function of entropy of activation, z is the collision number, and R is the gas content. This factor represented "the influence of change of molecular area on the fraction of reactive groups in the monolayer which are shielded from the reactant on compression of the film."

The study of reactions in compressed monolayers, which was the topic of Rideal's Royal Society Bak-erian Lecture in 1951, was pursued with a large number of collaborators and employing different techniques, such as infrared spectroscopy and ultraviolet irradiation of surfaces. While gaining new insights into heterogeneous catalysis from the program, Rideal also provided a model that could be used for understanding cell biology.

Rideal's fascination with surface penetration made him an ideal investigator for Imperial Chemical Industries when they wished to improve their understanding of the mechanism whereby dyestuffs adhered to fabrics. Between 1939 and 1941, Rideal and G. A. Gilbert made quantitative measurements of the adsorption of chlorine ions by woolen fibers (published in 1944). The study was premised upon a theoretical analysis of the dissociation of proteins and upon a statistical theorem developed by R. H. Fowler concerning the chemical potential μ of an uncharged adsorbed substance distributed at random among a limited number of sites,

$$\mu = \mu°(TP)\text{fibre} + RT\ln\left(\frac{\theta}{1-\theta}\right),$$

where R is the gas constant and $\mu°(TP)$ is the chemical potential of the substance at pressure P and temperature T when θ (the fraction of sites occupied) is 0.5. When the adsorbed substance was charged (ionized), the chemical potential was increased by a factor ΨF, where Ψ is the site potential and F is the Faraday constant.

This analysis led to the Rideal-Gilbert titration equation for proteins,

$$\log\left(\frac{\theta_H}{1-\theta_H}\right) = -pH - \frac{\log_e}{2RT}\left\{\Delta\mu_H + \Delta\mu_{c1}\right\},$$

where θ_H is the fraction of possible sites at which protons can be absorbed and $\Delta\mu = \mu°(TP)_{\text{fibre}} - \mu°(TP)_{\text{solution}}$. This theoretical and experimental study was to lead to further industrial understanding and applications in the postwar dyeing industry, and it is a good example of the close familiarity Rideal had with practical problems that interested chemical industrialists.

Rideal's work on ammonia synthesis during World War I stimulated a lifelong interest in catalysis, which is, of course, another problem in surface chemistry. While investigating ways of purifying hydrogen produced from water gas (a mixture of hydrogen and carbon monoxide), Rideal and Hugh Taylor found that a mixed oxide of iron and chromium catalyst would selectively oxidize carbon monoxide at a temperature of 200°C. In a detailed investigation in 1919, Rideal discovered that, of the two simultaneous reactions involved—$2CO + O_2 \rightarrow 2CO_2$ and $2H_2 + O_2 \rightarrow 2H_2O$—the former was selected by an iron-cobalt catalyst, whereas a nickel-palladium catalyst favored the latter. In a study with W. W. Hurst in 1924, Rideal used palladium as a "promoter" with copper. In this case it was found that up to 175°C there was a tendency for CO to be oxidized preferentially to H_2. This tendency could be maximized with a palladium-copper proportion of 0.2 percent. If more palladium was added, the ratio of CO/H_2 oxidized decreased, owing to the specific action of the promoter, and by 1.7 percent palladium the activity was reduced to the level of unpromoted copper.

These observations of catalytic selectivity immediately led Rideal into theoretical issues: Did the demonstrations support those, such as Paul Sabatier, who advocated a chemical, intermediate compound theory of catalysis, or a physical mechanism involving surface adsorption? In either case, what promoted or activated the reaction? In the United States between 1915 and 1917, Langmuir had shown that gaseous adsorption by monolayers varied with the pressure such that

$$\frac{x}{m} = \frac{kp}{1 + kp}$$

(Langmuir's isotherm), where x/m is the amount of substance adsorbed per gram of the adsorbent, p the pressure (or concentration), and k a constant for the system.

Following Langmuir's demonstration that the adsorption of simple gases by a series of metals depended upon the natures of the gases, the strengths of adsorption being caused by a mixture of strong valence forces and weak van der Waals forces, Rideal supposed that catalytic selectivity could be explained coherently in terms of Langmuir's isotherm if the radiation theory of activation was valid. According to this theory, which had been developed from Arrhenius' original analysis of reaction velocity by M. Trautz and Jean-Baptiste Perrin in 1909 and 1916, respectively, the active molecules in chemical reactions were triggered or "activated" by the adsorption of radiation from the walls of the reaction vessel. By showing that the combination of gases and different catalytic surfaces possessed different free energies, the progress or inhibition of selected reactions could be satisfactorily explained. Rideal was able to maintain the essential features of this explanation despite the discrediting of the radiation theory and the establishment of the collision theory of activation in the late 1920's by F. A. Lindemann and others.

In a rather intriguing collaboration with O. H. Wansborough-Jones (later chief scientist for the Advisory Council on Scientific Research and Development of the Ministry of Supply, of which Rideal was chairman from 1953 to 1958) in 1929, Rideal studied the kinetics of the oxidation of an electrically heated platinum filament and compared the results with Langmuir's studies of the oxidation of tungsten and copper. He noticed that the differences in activation energies corresponded closely to differences in the known values of the metals' work functions (free energy), and concluded that the rate-determining step in all three cases was due to collision and the transfer of an electron from the metal to an adsorbed molecule of oxygen.

Although usually well read in the current literature, Rideal seems to have been unaware that the Russian physical chemist Simon Z. Roginski had already emphasized the significance of electronic effects in surface oxidation in 1928. Postwar work on semiconductors by Nevill Mott was to lead Roginski and others to explore electronic theories of catalysis in which energy barriers are overcome by continuous changes in the chemical bonds of the reagent through the free exchange of electrons from the semiconductor surface. However, it was Rideal's pupils, rather than Rideal himself, who were to participate in these developments.

On the other hand, by the mid 1930's Rideal had developed powerful techniques that helped to establish that chemisorption (valence) rather than physical (van der Waals) forces were involved in the mechanism of catalysis, and that specific crystal lattices of surfaces were the preferred sites of reactivity. Such demonstrations were necessary preconditions for the establishment of the electron theory of catalysis. Following the spectroscopic discovery of deuterium (D_2), the isotope of hydrogen, by Harold C. Urey, G. M. Murphy, and F. G. Brickwedde in 1932, and its availability in heavy water, Rideal was one of the first to realize its usefulness in kinetic studies. In 1935 he and his collaborators studied the isotopic rate differences between hydrogen and deuterium in reducing copper oxide, hydrogenating ethylene, and the adsorption of the isotopes by charcoal.

In the same Cambridge laboratory, but working independently, J. K. Roberts showed in 1935 that in a hydrogen atmosphere a clean tungsten film was rapidly covered by a complete layer of hydrogen atoms. A theoretical analysis of the dissociation showed that adsorption of diatomic molecules by dissociation into free atoms would inevitably lead to about 8 percent empty sites at saturation.

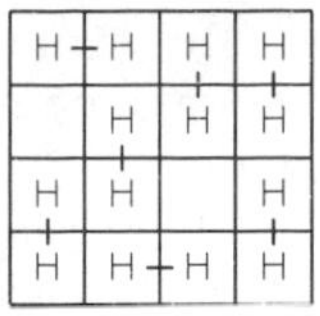

FIGURE 1. Two tungsten "holes" following surface dissociation of H₂ and adsorption of free hydrogen atoms (Rideal 1943).

Rideal saw immediately that Roberts' "Berthollide" compound model could be tested by the tungsten-promoted exchange equilibrium reaction between hydrogen and deuterium, $H + D_2 \rightleftharpoons HD + D$, and between the ortho- and para- forms of hydrogen, the mechanisms of which were revealed by the lattice deformation. As Rideal demonstrated between 1939 and 1941 with G. H. Twigg (for deuterium) and D. D. Eley (for para-hydrogen), such exchange reactions probably proceeded via "an interaction between a chemisorbed hydrogen atom and a hydrogen molecule held in the van der Waals field over the layer and in all probability of a molecule held over a 'hole' ":

In other words, the exchange $H + D_2 \rightleftharpoons HD + D$ involved three stages, with the middle, transition complex involving a "switchover" of valence. Other deuterium studies made with Twigg in 1939 showed conclusively that a very similar associative process occurred when olefins were adsorbed by nickel, the olefin opening its double bond on adsorption and thus becoming attached to two contiguous nickel surface atoms. Detailed theoretical calculations of bond lengths satisfied Rideal that such olefin adsorption could occur without distortion of the molecule.

This "Rideal mechanism," in which a molecule in a second van der Waals layer reacts with a chemisorbed atom immediately beneath it, was probably Rideal's most important contribution to catalytic and surface chemistry. The last thirty years of his life were spent exploring its ramifications, especially for an understanding of polymerization and what he called "the Mona Lisa of catalytic reactions," the industrially important hydrogenation of ethylene (ethene). Although in 1955, in joint work with G. I. Jenkins at King's College on the adsorption of ethene by nickel, Rideal rejected his own mechanism for a more complex one involving the immediate formation of triple-bond complexes, infrared investigations by R. P. Eischens in 1958 amply confirmed a Rideal mechanism. The irony here was that Rideal,

with Sir Robert Robinson, had done much to encourage the use of infrared spectroscopy, first at Cambridge in 1929 with C. P. Snow (a study of the vibration-rotation spectra of nitric oxide and carbon monoxide) and later, in 1957, at King's College with D. M. Adams (the use of infrared to map the differentiation of bacterial surfaces by species and with exposure to drugs).

BIBLIOGRAPHY

I. ORIGINAL WORKS. A comprehensive list of Rideal's dozen books and some 300 papers, based upon a privately printed (for subscribers) *List of Papers Published During 1912–46* (Cambridge, 1946), accompanies Eley's obituary of Rideal, though volume numbers and page references are sometimes inaccurate. To this should be added Rideal's admiring edition of the *Collected Papers of Sir William Bate Hardy* (Cambridge, 1936) and a paper written with J. Tadayon, "On Overturning and Anchoring of Monolayers," *Proceedings of the Royal Society*, **A225** (1954), 346–361. See also Rideal's *Sixty Years of Chemistry* (Port Sunlight, 1970), an annotated copy of which is in the Royal Institution. Rideal's few private papers that survive are at the Royal Institution, London, and are listed in the *Catalogue of the Papers of Sir Eric Keightley Rideal, FRS (1890–1974)* (Oxford, 1978), Contemporary Science Archive Centre, list 62/6/78. Snow's barbed comments on Rideal are recorded in John Halperin, *C. P. Snow. An Oral Biography* (Brighton and New York, 1983); and depicted fictionally in C. P. Snow, *The Search* (London and New York, 1934; 2nd, abridged ed., 1958), in which Rideal is Desmond; and *Strangers and Brothers* (London, 1940; repr. London and New York, 1959), in which Rideal is the lawyer Herbert Getliffe.

II. SECONDARY LITERATURE. The most comprehensive account of Rideal is given by his pupil Daniel D. Eley in *Biographical Memoirs of Fellows of the Royal Society*, **22** (1976), 381–413 (with portrait). An earlier, more anecdotal, version was given by Eley to the Rideal Memorial Symposium at Imperial College, London, on 5 June 1975 and printed as "The Life and Catalytic Work of Sir Eric K. Rideal, FRS," in *Chemistry and Industry* (4 October 1975), 800–806. See also John T. Davies, "Sir Eric Rideal and His Contribution to Surface Chemistry," *ibid.*, 806–813.

W. H. BROCK

RIESZ, MARCEL (*b.* Györ, Hungary, 16 November 1886; *d.* Lund, Sweden, 4 September 1969), *mathematics.*

Marcel Riesz, the younger brother of Frigyes Riesz and the son of Ignácz Riesz, a physician, showed his talent for mathematics early by winning the Loránd Eötvös competition in 1904. After studying at the University of Budapest, he worked on trigonometric series under the influence of Lipót (Leopold) Fejér. One of Fejér's theorems states that the first order Cesàro sums of the Fourier series of a continuous function tend to $f(x)$ at every point x. Fejér also pointed out that a trigonometric series can be $(C,1)$-summable to zero at each point $x \neq 2k\pi$ ($k = 0, \pm 1, \ldots$) without the coefficients being all zero. Riesz generalized Fejér's theorem, replacing $(C,1)$-summability with (C,α)-summability with any $\alpha > 0$. In his doctoral dissertation, "Über summierbare trigonometrische Reihen" (1912), Riesz gave a condition implying that if a trigonometric series is $(C,1)$-summable to zero everywhere, then all its coefficients are zero. This result was later sharpened by A. Rajchman, Antoni Zygmund, and S. Verblunsky.

Pierre Fatou's dissertation, "Séries trigonométriques et séries de Taylor" (1906), influenced both Riesz brothers. One of Fatou's theorems asserts that if the power series $\sum_{n=0}^{\infty} c_n z^n$ represents a holomorphic function $f(z)$ in the unit disk $|z| < 1$ and $\lim_{n \to \infty} c_n = 0$, then the power series converges at each point of the circle $|z| = 1$ where $f(z)$ is regular. Riesz improved the result in two directions: first, if $f(z)$ is regular on a closed arc, then the power series converges uniformly on the arc; second, if $\lim_{n \to \infty} (c_n/n^k) = 0$, then (C,k)-summability replaces convergence.

It was the typical means (now also called Riesz means) that made Riesz internationally known. Given a sequence $0 < \lambda_0 < \lambda_1 \ldots < \lambda_n < \ldots$, the means of type (λ_n) and order k of the series Σu_n are given by $R(\omega; \lambda, k) = \Sigma_{\lambda_j \leq \omega} \left(1 - \dfrac{\lambda_j}{\omega}\right)^k u_j$, and they are tailormade for the Dirichlet series $\sum_{n=0}^{\infty} d_n e^{-\lambda_n s}$. An exposition can be found in a Cambridge Tract written jointly with G. H. Hardy.

Like most young Hungarian mathematicians of the period, Riesz visited Göttingen regularly; he also spent the year 1910 to 1911 in Paris. There he received an invitation from Gustav Mittag-Leffler, whom he had met at the 1908 International Congress of Mathematicians in Rome, to deliver three lectures in Stockholm. Riesz accepted, and spent the rest of his life in Sweden. Some of the most distinguished Swedish mathematicians were his doctoral students.

After his arrival in Sweden, Riesz proved an interpolation formula from which S. N. Bernstein's inequality between a polynomial and its derivative follows. During World War I he wrote his only joint paper with his brother, on the boundary behavior

of an analytic function. Their theorem, with its many variants and generalizations, became central in several branches of mathematics.

In the 1920's Riesz's interests, which until then had been concentrated on classical analysis, broadened. Under the influence of his brother, he turned to functional analysis. In three notes on the moment problem of Thomas Stieltjes and Hans Hamburger, he proved and applied a result on the extension of positive linear operators similar to the Hahn-Banach theorem. He also introduced a class of orthogonal polynomials to investigate the existence and the uniqueness of the solutions of the moment problem. He never published detailed proofs because others became interested in these questions, and he did not wish to compete with them.

In 1927 Riesz published his two most often quoted results: his theorem on conjugate functions and his convexity theorem. The former states that if the function f belongs to $L^p(-\infty, \infty)$ and $1 < p < \infty$, then the conjugate

$$\bar{f}(x) = \lim_{\varepsilon \to 0+} \frac{1}{\pi} \int_{|t-x| \geq \varepsilon} \frac{f(t)}{t-x} dt$$

also belongs to $L^p(-\infty, \infty)$, and the map that associates $\bar{f}$ with f is continuous. Conjugate functions originated in the theory of Fourier series, and Riesz's theorem solved a problem that had been open for some time. The generalization of his result to several variables by A. P. Calderón and Antoni Zygmund led to singular integrals and pseudo-differential operators, which play a fundamental role in the theory of partial differential equations.

The convexity theorem asserts that if a linear map is continuous from L^{p_0} to L^{q_0} and from L^{p_1} to L^{q_1}, then it is also continuous from L^p to L^q, where $p^{-1} = (1 - \theta)p_0^{-1} + \theta p_1^{-1}$, $q^{-1} = (1 - \theta)q_0^{-1} + \theta q_1^{-1}$, $0 \leq \theta \leq 1$. The theorem has earlier results of Felix Hausdorff and William H. Young on Fourier series and integrals, and of Frigyes Riesz on orthonormal series as a consequence. A simple proof was later found by Riesz's student Olof Thorin, and the theorem is now attributed to both. It became the starting point of abstract "interpolation theorems" developed mainly by E. M. Stein, A. P. Calderón, J. L. Lions, and J. Peetre.

In 1926 Riesz obtained a professorship at the University of Lund, where he became interested in partial differential equations, mathematical physics, number theory, and (through the *Moderne algebra* of B. L. van der Waerden) abstract algebra. At the Oslo International Congress of Mathematicians in 1936 he presented four short communications: one on mixed volumes in the theory of modules, one on reciprocal modules, and two on generalizations of the Riemann-Liouville integral.

The Riemann-Liouville integral, which generalizes differentiation and integration on the real line to fractional orders, figured in the theory of typical means. Its analogue, defined by Riesz on n-dimensional Euclidean space—the Riesz potential of fractional order—has properties that, among other things, prove that the kernel of the Newtonian potential is a positive function. This observation, used in the 1935 dissertation of Riesz's student Otto Frostman, led to a renewal of potential theory by M. Brelot, H. Cartan, J. Deny, G. Choquet, and others.

The Riemann-Liouville integral defined on an n-dimensional space with the Lorentz metric $\|x\|^2 = x_1^2 - x_2^2 - \ldots - x_n^2$ yields a new approach to the Cauchy problem for the wave equation and, more generally, for hyperbolic partial differential equations with variable coefficients in which Jacques Hadamard's concept of finite parts of integrals is replaced by analytic continuation. Riesz found these results between 1933 and 1936, but his monumental paper did not appear until 1949.

Riesz was a visiting professor at the University of Chicago in 1947 and 1948. After his retirement in 1952, he spent much time in the United States, mainly at the Courant Institute in New York, the University of Washington, Stanford University, the University of Maryland, and Indiana University. In 1960 illness forced him to return to Lund. Riesz was a member of the Swedish Academy of Sciences and in 1950 received an honorary doctorate from the University of Copenhagen.

BIBLIOGRAPHY

I. ORIGINAL WORKS. Lists of Riesz's writings are in the articles by Gårding and Horváth (see below). Among his works are "Sur les séries de Dirichlet," in *Comptes rendus . . . de l'Académie des sciences*, **148** (1909), 1658–1660; "Sur la sommation des séries de Dirichlet," *ibid.*, **149** (1909), 18–21; "Sur les séries de Dirichlet et les séries entières," *ibid.*; "Une méthode de sommation équivalente à la méthode des moyennes arithmétiques," *ibid.*, **152** (1911), 1651–1654; "Über summierbare trigonometrische Reihen," in *Mathematische Annalen*, **71** (1912), 54–75; *General Theory of Dirichlet Series* (Cambridge, 1915; repr. 1952), written with G. H. Hardy; "Sur les maxima des formes bilinéaires et sur les fonctionnelles linéaires," in *Acta Mathematica*, **49** (1927), 465–497; "Sur les fonctions conjugées," in *Mathematische Zeitschrift*, **27** (1927), 218–244; and "L'intégrale de Riemann-Liouville et le problème de Cauchy," in *Acta Mathematica*, **81** (1949), 1–223.

His works have been gathered in *Collected Papers of Marcel Riesz* (Berlin and New York, 1988).

II. SECONDARY LITERATURE. See Jöran Bergh and Jörgen Löfström, *Interpolation Spaces* (Berlin, 1976); Lars Gårding, "Marcel Riesz in Memoriam," in *Acta Mathematica*, **124** (1970), i–xi; and John Horváth, "Riesz Marcel matematikai munkássága" (The mathematical works of Marcel Riesz), in *Matematikai lapok*, **26** (1975), 11–37, and **28** (1980), 65–100, French trans. in *Cahiers du Séminaire d'histoire de mathématique*, **3** (1982), 83–121, and **4** (1983), 1–59. Two writings that influenced Riesz's early work are Pierre Fatou, "Séries trigonométriques et séries de Taylor," in *Acta Mathematica*, **30** (1906), 335–400; and Lipót Fejér, "Sur les fonctions bornées et intégrables," in *Comptes rendus . . . de l'Académie des sciences*, **131** (1900), 984–987.

JOHN HORVÁTH

RITTER, WILLIAM EMERSON (*b*. Hampden, Wisconsin, 19 November 1856; *d*. Berkeley, California, 10 January 1944), *biology*.

The longest-lasting achievement of Ritter, who was recognized in his day as a philosophical biologist, was establishing a permanent marine research institution in La Jolla, California, that became the Scripps Institution of Oceanography.

Ritter was raised on the Wisconsin farm of his parents, Horatio and Leonora Eason Ritter, who had moved there from Connecticut. In 1884 he graduated from the State Normal School at Oshkosh, Wisconsin, where he found Joseph LeConte's textbook *Elements in Geology* of great interest, and determined to continue his education at the University of California under LeConte. He taught in public schools in Wisconsin to earn his college costs, and he supported himself similarly in California from 1885 while completing his B.S. (1888). After a year of graduate studies at the University of California, he was awarded a fellowship at Harvard University, where he studied for two years under Edward Laurens Mark; he earned his M.S. in 1891 and his Ph.D. in 1893 at Harvard.

Before receiving his doctorate, Ritter was appointed an instructor and simultaneously the first chairman of the newly formed department of zoology at the University of California at Berkeley in 1891. In that same year he married Mary E. Bennett, who had earned her M.D. in 1886; they had no children. At Berkeley, Ritter inaugurated several new courses, including the first laboratory courses offered there. He advanced to professor in 1902. He also determined upon a long-range goal: to survey the marine organisms of California. Ritter wrote in 1912: "Imperfectly as had any of the fields of zoology of western America been cultivated, the least studied of all had been the teeming life of the great ocean on whose margin the University [of California] is located.'' He believed that this ''practically virgin'' field of research ''would yield richly in both new problems and new light on old problems.''

From 1892 to 1903 Ritter conducted research and teaching sessions during the summers at several coastal locations in California before finding a permanent site in San Diego. There, in the community of La Jolla, he established a biological station, first in the summers and then as a year-round facility, that came under the auspices of the University of California in 1912 as the Scripps Institution for Biological Research. He cultivated local supporters, of whom the most significant were newspaper magnate Edward Willis Scripps and his half sister, Ellen Browning Scripps, who made possible the entire facility and its first endowment. The establishment of the news agency Science Service in 1921 by Edward Scripps resulted from several years of discussions with Ritter, who served as its first president until 1928.

Ritter's early research studies were morphological: on the parietal eye of lizards and on the eye and related structures of the blind goby (*Typhlogobius californiensis*). He then became interested in the taxonomy and structure of the tunicates and the hemichordate worms *Enteropneusta*. In 1899, in his capacity as president of the California Academy of Sciences, Ritter participated in the two-month Harriman Alaskan Expedition and made extensive collections of marine invertebrates. His later scientific publications were in biological philosophy, on what he called an organismal conception of life, defined thus: ''The organism in its totality is as essential to an explanation of its elements as its elements are to an explanation of the organism.''

As director of the Scripps Institution, Ritter oversaw construction of several buildings and acquired a ship, the *Alexander Agassiz*, for near-shore researches by appealing to generous benefactors. He established a staff of biologists interested especially in marine invertebrates, and he invited distinguished scientists to spend time at the facility. A dedicated researcher, he set high standards for his institution's programs and emphasized the need for studying animals in their natural environment. Ritter took keen interest in the scientific research and in the personal welfare of the staff. From the beginning he was intent upon establishing physical, chemical, and hydrographic research as well as the customary biological studies of marine stations. He appointed physicist George F. McEwen, who instituted a program in physical oceanography and began correlations of ocean temperatures with weather. Ritter

encouraged the work in marine chemistry begun by Eric G. Moberg while he was a graduate student. He also invited biologist Francis B. Sumner to join the staff to conduct studies on the inheritance of acquired characters using deer mice (*Peromyscus*), in spite of the nonmarine nature of the work, on the basis that the relation of organisms to their environment was an overall question in biology. Upon his retirement in 1923, however, Ritter urged that the institution confine itself to marine studies, and selected T. Wayland Vaughan as his successor. Ritter retired to Berkeley, where he continued writing scientific and philosophical works until his death.

BIBLIOGRAPHY

I. Original Works. A significant paper of Ritter's on *Enteropneusta* is ''Studies on the Ecology, Morphology, and Speciology of the Young of Some *Enteropneusta* of Western North America,'' in *University of California Publications in Zoology*, **1**, no. 5 (1904), 171–210, with B. M. Davis. On tunicates he wrote ''The Pelagic Tunicata of the San Diego Region, Excepting the Larvacea,'' in *University of California Publications in Zoology*, **2**, no. 3 (1905), 51–112. Some of Ritter's philosophical publications are *The Unity of the Organism, or the Organismal Conception of Life*, 2 vols. (Boston, 1919); *The Natural History of Our Conduct* (New York, 1927), with Edna Watson Bailey; and *The California Woodpecker and I* (Berkeley, 1938). A longtime project of Ritter's was published after his death as *Charles Darwin and the Golden Rule*, Edna Watson Bailey, comp. and ed. (Washington, D.C., 1954).

Articles by Ritter on the early years of the Scripps Institution of Oceanography are in the institution's archives; his most important one is ''The Marine Biological Station of San Diego: Its History, Present Conditions, Achievements, and Aims,'' in *University of California Publications in Zoology*, **9,** no. 4 (1912), 137–248.

Considerable archival material on Ritter is at the University of California, Berkeley.

II. Secondary Literature. Brief biographical accounts of Ritter are Francis B. Sumner, ''William Emerson Ritter: Naturalist and Philosopher,'' in *Science*, **99** (1944), 335–338; and Frank E. A. Thone and Edna Watson Bailey, ''William Emerson Ritter: Builder,'' in *Scientific Monthly*, **24** (1927), 256–262. Manuscript items in the Scripps Institution archives have additional material, including an eight-page typescript, ''William Emerson Ritter,'' by Tracy I. Storer. None of these has a complete bibliography of Ritter's papers. The autobiography of Mary Bennett Ritter, *More Than Gold in California* (Berkeley, 1933), provides scanty biographical information on her husband. The most valuable summary of Ritter's years as director is Helen Raitt and Beatrice Moulton, *Scripps Institution of Oceanography: First Fifty Years* (Los Angeles, 1967).

Elizabeth N. Shor

RITTHAUSEN, KARL HEINRICH (*b*. Armenruh bei Goldberg, Silesia [now Poland], 13 January 1826; *d*. Berlin, Germany, 16 October 1912), *agricultural chemistry, biochemistry.*

Little appears to be known of Ritthausen's parents and other relatives, or of his early life. After studying chemistry at Leipzig and Bonn, he began his chemical research in Liebig's institute at Giessen, and was inspired by Liebig to follow a career in agricultural chemistry. Like Liebig, Ritthausen was concerned both with the advancement of basic chemistry and with the improvement of human and animal nutrition. He made his major contributions in a long series of studies on plant proteins, in the course of which he isolated two amino acids of major importance as products of protein hydrolysis, and developed methods of purifying, and in some cases crystallizing, plant seed proteins.

After working in Liebig's laboratory, Ritthausen became assistant to Otto L. Erdmann at Leipzig (1852–1853), where he received the doctorate in 1853. From 1854 to 1856 he was director of the scientific department of the agricultural experiment station at Möckern, near Leipzig, then briefly director of the station at Ida-Marienhütte near Saarau in Silesia, not far from Breslau (now Wroclaw, Poland). In 1857 Ritthausen became professor of chemistry and physics at the Royal Agricultural Academy at Waldau, near Königsberg; in 1867 he went to Bonn as professor of chemistry at the agricultural college and director of its experiment station at Poppelsdorf. Here he married; the Ritthausens had a son and a daughter. In 1873 he became professor at the University of Königsberg (now Kaliningrad, U.S.S.R.), where he continued his work until his retirement in 1899. He was considered an outstanding teacher and a stimulating guide to his numerous research students. He moved to Berlin in 1903.

After an early period when he attempted a direct application of current chemical knowledge to the feeding of cattle, Ritthausen realized the need for further basic chemical studies and turned his attention to the study of plant proteins. In 1862 he began his studies on the proteins of wheat, which continued steadily over the next five years and led him into similar extensive work on proteins of legumes and of various oilseed proteins.

This work led to Ritthausen's discovery of two dicarboxylic amino acids in protein hydrolysates, both present in amounts large enough to represent a substantial fraction of the whole protein. With the techniques then available, separation of a pure amino acid from the complex mixture represented by a hydrolyzed protein was no easy undertaking.

Of more than twenty amino acids now known as regular constituents of proteins, only four—leucine, glycine, tyrosine, and serine—had been identified by 1865 as products of protein hydrolysis. Ritthausen was to add two more to the list. In 1866, working with proteins of wheat gluten that were soluble in alcohol-water mixtures (proteins later known collectively as gliadin), he obtained, after hydrolysis with sulfuric acid, excellent crystals of the previously unknown glutamic acid $HOOC(CH_2)_2CH(NH_2)COOH$(α-aminoglutaric acid, $C_5H_9NO_4$). His own work, and that of others, soon demonstrated the presence of this amino acid in large quantities in hydrolysates of many other proteins.[1]

Two years later Ritthausen was the first to isolate the closely related amino acid aspartic acid, $HOOC CH_2 CH(NH_2)COOH$—$C_4 H_7 NO_4$ from hydrolysates of proteins from lupines and from almonds. Unlike glutamic acid, aspartic acid was already well known. Its monoamide, asparagine, had been crystallized from asparagus juice by Nicolas Vauquelin and Pierre-Jean Robiquet in 1806. In 1827 A. Plisson had obtained crystalline aspartic acid by hydrolysis of asparagine, although controversy over the exact structure of these compounds continued for years. Ritthausen, however, was the first to demonstrate its presence in proteins.[2] He found that aspartic acid, like glutamic acid, was present in significant amounts in practically all proteins that he studied. In fact these two amino acids (or, as was realized later by Emil Fischer, their residues after elimination of water to incorporate them into peptide linkages) are almost entirely responsible for the acidic properties of proteins; thus Ritthausen's discovery represented an important step forward.

In 1872 he published a book reviewing his work of the previous decade on the proteins of cereals, legumes, and oilseed plants. To extract these proteins from powdered and defatted seed meal, he commonly used mildly alkaline solutions of dilute potassium hydroxide as solvents. He also made much use of ethyl alcohol-water mixtures (commonly around 70 percent alcohol by volume) for extraction of the class of proteins later known as prolamins from the seeds of wheat, corn, and other plants. His use of alkaline solutions, however, came under severe criticism from Felix Hoppe-Seyler and his student T. Weyl,[3] on the ground that the alkalinity of the extraction medium had irreversibly altered the character of the native protein.

Hoppe-Seyler and Weyl, like P. S. Denis and other earlier workers, preferred to use solutions of neutral salts as media for extracting proteins, and were concerned that acid and alkaline solutions would alter the proteins, perhaps irreversibly. Ritthausen considered their criticism unfair and published a detailed rebuttal. Their criticism, however, stimulated him to important studies on the use of neutral salts for extraction of plant seed proteins. He demonstrated that most of the proteins prepared by his earlier methods were still soluble in neutral salt solutions and unaltered in elementary composition. Among the proteins that he carefully described were several that could be readily obtained as well-formed crystals. In 1881 he described the preparation of a crystalline protein from hempseed, later named edestin and extensively studied by Thomas B. Osborne and others. Osborne, in his obituary of Ritthausen, noted that Ritthausen's work had been unjustly neglected after about 1880, as a result of the criticisms of Hoppe-Seyler and Weyl.

Ritthausen's work was not, however, confined to proteins. He studied many other constituents of seeds, obtaining vicin and convicin from vetch seeds, and he discovered in cottonseed the trisaccharide melitose, now known as raffinose.

Ritthausen began his work with the extremely simple concepts of protein chemistry that were current about 1850. In his long career he made substantial advances in recognizing that proteins from different sources were individually different to a far greater extent than had been realized earlier. His discovery of aspartic and glutamic acids in proteins was a major advance in a very difficult field. Other workers of a later generation, notably Osborne, director of the Connecticut Agricultural Experiment Station in New Haven, carried the study of plant proteins well beyond what Ritthausen had achieved. The techniques available to Ritthausen were very limited, compared with those of later workers, but he did more than anyone else, in the generation after Liebig, to advance the chemistry of plant proteins.

NOTES

1. An excellent description of the chemical details of the work is given by Hubert B. Vickery and Carl L. A. Schmidt in "The History of the Discovery of the Amino Acids," in *Chemical Reviews*, **9** (1931), 169–318; see 221–224 for glutamic acid.
2. The history of aspartic acid and asparagine, with a detailed discussion of Ritthausen's achievement, is given by Vickery and Schmidt (note 1), 198–207.
3. Hoppe-Seyler's criticism of Ritthausen was contained in his *Physiologische Chemie*, Pt. 1, *Allgemeine Biologie* (Berlin, 1877), 75f. The critique by Weyl, "Beiträge zur Kenntniss thierischer und pflanzlicher Eiweisskörper," is in Hoppe-Seyler's *Zeitschrift für physiologische Chemie*, **1** (1877–1878), 72–100; see esp. 84ff.

BIBLIOGRAPHY

I. ORIGINAL WORKS. Ritthausen published one book, *Die Eiweisskörper der Getreidearten, Hülsenfrüchte und Ölsamen: Beiträge zur Physiologie der Samen der Kulturgewächse, der Nahrungs- und Futtermittel* (Bonn, 1872). This gives a good survey of his earlier work, with some historical background, but for details of his major contributions one must consult his papers.

Most of Ritthausen's major work appeared in *Journal für praktische Chemie* from **53** (1851) to n.s. **30** (1884), with four papers in n.s. **59** (1899). For his initial discovery of glutamic acid in proteins, see "Über die Glutaminsäure," in *Journal für praktische Chemie*, **42** (1866), 454–462. His first report on aspartic acid is "Über die zersetzungs-Produkte des Legumins und des Proteinkörpers der Lupinen und Mandeln beim Kochen mit Schwefelsäure," *ibid.*, **103** (1868), 233–238. A further report on both these amino acids is in *ibid.*, **107** (1869), 218–240. Among his numerous later papers on protein preparation and crystallization, two of a series from the Königsberg laboratory may be cited: "Zusammensetzung der Eiweisskörper der Hanfsamen und des kristallisierten Eiweisses aus Hanf- und Ricinussamen," *ibid.*, n.s. **25** (1882), 130–137; and "Über die Zusammensetzung des kristallisierten Eiweisses aus Kürbissamen," *ibid.*, 137–141. He published several papers (1877–1880) in *Pflügers Archiv für die gesamte Physiologie*, notably "Die Eiweisskörper der Pflanzensamen," **15** (1877), 269–288, in which he replies in detail to the criticisms of Hoppe-Seyler and Weyl. Studies on proteins from various oilseeds are in *ibid.*, **21** (1880), 81–104. He reported on vicin from *Vicia sativa* in "Ueber Vicin. Bestandtheil der Samen von *Vicia sativa*," in *Berichte der Deutschen chemischen Gesellschaft*, **9** (1876), 301–304. Papers on vicin and alloxantin are in *ibid.*, **29** (1896): "Wassergelt und Reaktion des Alloxantins," 892–893; "Ueber Alloxantin als Spaltungsprodukt des Convicins aus Saubohnen (*Vicia faba minor*) und Wicken (*Vicia sativa*)," 894–896; and "Vicin ein Glycosid," 2108–2109.

II. SECONDARY LITERATURE. The best account of Ritthausen's life and work is Thomas B. Osborne, "Heinrich Ritthausen," in *Biochemical Bulletin* (Columbia University Biochemical Association), **2** (1913), 335–339, with portrait and a comprehensive bibliography by L. W. Fetzer, 339–346. There is a brief notice, signed Stutzer, also with a portrait, in *Berichte der Deutschen chemische Gesellschaft*, **47** (1914), 591–593. See also Thomas B. Osborne, *The Vegetable Proteins*, 2nd ed., rev. (New York and London, 1924).

JOHN T. EDSALL

ROBINSON, ABRAHAM (*b*. Waldenburg, Germany [now Walbrzych, Poland], 6 October 1918; *d*. New Haven, Connecticut, 11 April 1974), *mathematics, logic, aerodynamics*.

Abraham Robinson was the second son of Hedwig

Lotte Bähr and Abraham Robinsohn. His father, a scholar and secretary to the Zionist leader David Wolffsohn (and curator of the papers of Wolffsohn and Theodor Herzl), died in 1918 before Abraham was born. His mother, a teacher, moved to her parent's home in Waldenburg and later settled in Breslau, where she found work with the Keren Hayesod (the Zionist organization set up to aid the emigration and settlement of Jews in Palestine).

In 1933, as the National Socialists were beginning their attacks on Jews in all walks of life, the Robinsohns emigrated to Palestine. There, in Jerusalem, Robinson finished his secondary education and entered Hebrew University in 1936, where he studied mathematics with Abraham Fraenkel and Jakob Levitzki, as well as physics with S. Sambursky and philosophy (especially Leibniz) with L. Roth. In 1939 Robinson won a French government scholarship to the Sorbonne, where he studied in the spring of 1940 until the German invasion of France in June forced him to flee. Making his way to the coast on foot and by train, he managed to reach Bordeaux, where he embarked on one of the last boats to leave France with refugees for England.

Having resettled in London, Robinson soon changed the spelling of his name (dropping the "h" from Robinsohn). In 1940 he enlisted with the Free French Air Force, and from 1942 to 1946 served with the Royal Aircraft Establishment in Farnborough, where he was a scientific officer specializing in aircraft structures and aerodynamics, particularly in supersonic wing theory. During the war he met Renée Kopel, an actress and fashion designer from Vienna; they were married on 30 January 1944, exactly one year after they met.

In light of the success of his work in aerodynamics at Farnborough, Robinson was offered a position in 1946 as senior lecturer in mathematics at the newly founded College of Aeronautics at Cranfield. Later that year Hebrew University awarded him an M.Sc. degree, primarily for the high-level scientific research he had done during the war. By then, thanks to his technical publications, Robinson had come to be regarded as one of the world's authorities on supersonic aerodynamics and wing theory. As a result, he was invited to serve as a member of the Fluid Motion Committee of the Aeronautical Research Council of Great Britain.

Robinson returned to the study of advanced mathematics in the late 1940's, enrolling as a graduate student at Birkbeck College, University of London. Working with Roger Cooke, Paul Dienes, and others, he received his Ph.D. in 1949 for a dissertation on the metamathematics of algebraic systems (published

as a book in 1951). This was a pioneering work in model theory. Subsequently Robinson's many contributions to the study of relations between axiom systems and mathematical structures helped to provide the classic foundations for the subject.

It was largely on the strength of his work in aerodynamics that Robinson was offered a position in 1951 as associate professor of applied mathematics at the University of Toronto, where he succeeded Leopold Infeld. Increasingly, however, Robinson's research concentrated on pure mathematics. One of the most important early successes of his application of model theory to algebra was a model-theoretic solution (published in 1955) of Hilbert's seventeenth problem, for which he achieved a considerably simpler solution than the original algebraic one given by Emil Artin in 1927.

After six years in Canada, Robinson received an offer of the chair of his former professor, Abraham Fraenkel, at Hebrew University in Jerusalem. This proved irresistible, and the Robinsons left Canada for Israel in 1957. There Robinson's work was increasingly devoted to algebra and model theory. It was during this period that Robinson found a model completion for the axioms of differential fields, which then served as models of the "closure" axioms associated with this completion. Angus Macintyre said of this accomplishment, "It would be appropriate to say that he *invented* differentiably closed fields." [1]

Robinson spent the academic year 1960–1961 as a visiting professor in the department of mathematics at Princeton University, where he had the inspiration for his best-known discovery, nonstandard analysis. In the spring of 1961 he also visited the department of philosophy at the University of California at Los Angeles; a year later UCLA succeeded in negotiating a joint appointment for Robinson as professor of mathematics and philosophy, a position he held from 1962 to 1967. There the chance to build a program in logic where he could teach graduate students and interact with a large faculty having diverse interests proved extremely productive for Robinson. While he was at UCLA, he began to develop in earnest the basic features of nonstandard analysis.

The last academic move Robinson made was in 1967, when Yale University appointed him professor of mathematics; after 1971 he was Sterling professor. There the department of mathematics provided a congenial and stimulating environment where Robinson's talents as a teacher flourished, as did his publications. Late in 1973, at the height of his career, he was diagnosed as suffering from incurable cancer of the pancreas. In less than six months, at the age of fifty-five, Robinson died at Yale University Hospital.

In the course of his prematurely curtailed career, Robinson wrote more than 135 articles and 9 books. He held a number of visiting positions, including appointments at Paris, Princeton, Heidelberg, Rome, and Tübingen, as well as at the California Institute of Technology, the Weizmann Institute, and St. Catherine's College, Oxford. From 1968 to 1970 he served as president of the Association for Symbolic Logic. In 1972 Robinson was made a fellow of the American Academy of Arts and Sciences, and in 1973 he was awarded the Brouwer Medal by the Dutch Mathematical Society. The following year he was elected (posthumously) to membership in the U.S. National Academy of Sciences.

Aerodynamics. At the Royal Aircraft Establishment in Farnborough, Robinson not only tutored himself to pass examinations in aeronautical engineering but also took flying lessons in order to complement his theoretical knowledge of structures and aerodynamics with some hands-on experience. At first he dealt with fundamental problems related to structural weaknesses in aircraft design; development of the jet engine toward the end of the war, however, not only greatly increased aircraft speeds but also made questions of supersonic flow of considerable theoretical and practical interest. In the latter field Robinson made essential contributions to the understanding of delta-form wings.

After the war, having established himself as an expert on aerodynamics, Robinson was invited to join the staff of the newly founded College of Aeronautics at Cranfield, just outside London. There he taught mathematics, and by 1950 had been named deputy head of the department of aerodynamics. Although he had just begun to write a book on wing theory with a recent graduate of the college, J. A. Laurmann, Robinson left Cranfield in 1951 to accept an offer from the University of Toronto. From then on, although his interests were drawn more and more to logic and model theory, he continued to read papers at aerodynamics symposia in Canada, and to publish papers of considerable interest and sophistication on wave propagation and structural analysis. In 1956 Robinson was promoted to professor, the same year in which his book on *Wing Theory* (coauthored with Laurmann), was published.

Algebra. Robinson's career as a mathematician was typified primarily, but not exclusively, by deep research into the interconnections between algebra and symbolic logic. The first two papers he wrote (while still a student at Hebrew University) were on the independence of the axiom of definiteness in Zermelo-Fraenkel set theory and on nil-ideals in ring theory. His first book, based upon his dissertation (University of London, 1949), *On the Metamathematics of Algebra* (1951), was a pioneer in model theory and the application of mathematical logic to algebra. Many of Robinson's most important contributions to modern mathematics concern fertile hybridizations of algebra and model theory. In algebra, for example, he introduced model completeness, and in model theory he developed the idea of differentially closed fields.

Model Theory. Model theory studies the relationship between a set of axioms and various models that may satisfy the axioms in question. Among early-twentieth-century proponents of model theory, Löwenheim, Skolem, Gödel, Malcev, Tarski, and Henkin all made important contributions before Robinson's first book, *On the Metamathematics of Algebra*, appeared in 1951. This book set the tone for much of Robinson's later work, and served as a guiding force in the development of model-theoretic algebra in the decades after it was written.

One of the major tools Robinson developed was model completeness, which he introduced in 1955. This is basically an abstract form of elimination of quantifiers. It may also be regarded, in the study of algebraically closed fields, as a generalization of Hilbert's *Nullstellensatz*. Robinson's book *Complete Theories* (1956) developed the notion of the theory of algebraically closed fields and showed that real closed fields and modules over a field, among other familiar algebraic theories, are model complete. One of the most important examples of model completion in algebra is Robinson's 1959 discovery that the theory of differential fields of characteristic zero has a model completion: differentially closed fields of characteristic zero.

In 1970 Robinson developed another important method of constructing models based upon an extension of the earlier idea of model completion. This method, known as Robinson forcing, bears a close similarity to the method of forcing in set theory introduced by Paul Cohen in 1963. The paper "Model Theory as a Framework for Algebra" provided an excellent introduction to the subject of forcing. Closely related, and also influential in the work of later mathematicians, was Robinson's development of generic and existentially closed models.

Nonstandard Analysis. Robinson's best-known discovery is nonstandard analysis, which provides a means of introducing infinitesimals, or "infinitely small" quantities, rigorously into the body of mathematics. The basic idea of nonstandard analysis makes use of model-theoretic concepts that provide for the first time, 300 years after its invention by Newton and Leibniz, a rigorous foundation for the differential and integral calculus using infinitesimals. But the great interest of nonstandard analysis for mathematicians is not foundational, nor is it due to the intuitiveness with which infinitesimals can be taught to students (which is considerable). What is impressive and of great utility is the power nonstandard analysis brings to the solution of difficult and significant mathematical problems.

The source of this strength is not merely the addition of infinitesimals to mathematics but lies in Robinson's use of model theory, which makes it possible to establish a fundamental connection between the set of real numbers **R** and the nonstandard model **R*** of **R** that contains the infinitesimals (as well as infinitely large nonstandard numbers). What Robinson established is the fact that **R*** is an elementary extension of **R**. In terms of Robinson's transfer principle, this means that the infinitesimals in **R*** behave like the real numbers in **R**.

Because of the extraordinary breadth of Robinson's knowledge, he was able from the beginning to apply nonstandard analysis with impressive results in many areas of mathematics. In the years following his death, more and more mathematicians have found that nonstandard analysis can be applied to great advantage in an increasingly large number of special areas. For example, important applications have already been made to functional analysis, number theory, mathematical economics, and quantum physics. Much of this work was first done by Robinson with colleagues or graduate students, many of whom have gone on to establish significant reputations in model theory and mathematical logic, including nonstandard analysis.

Arithmetic. Class field theory and Diophantine geometry were areas in which Robinson made especially significant contributions through applications of nonstandard methods. Here "enlargements" of algebraic number fields were the key insight—"enlargements" being considered as completions in a universal sense. Thus, in terms of mathematical logic, transfer principles are extremely powerful, and consequently they prove to be of great utility, as well as of great generality, in dealing with problems of arithmetic.

In the last decade of his life Robinson became increasingly interested in these questions, especially the extent to which nonstandard methods could serve to establish new results or improve old ones. His last major work was a nonstandard treatment, developed with Peter Roquette, of the finiteness theorem on Diophantine equations of Siegel and Mahler.

Computers. Robinson spent several summers in the early 1960's at the IBM Watson Research Center in Yorktown Heights, New York. There he collaborated with Calvin C. Elgot on a paper that developed a more realistic model of a digital computer (using programming languages with semantics) for random-access stored program (RASP) machines than that provided by a Turing machine. One major result they were able to establish was a proof that particular RASP machines could compute all partial recursive functions. This work was later extended to multiple-control RASP's with the capacity for parallel processing with programs able to handle computations in partial rather than serial order. Robinson coauthored a paper on the subject of "multiple control" with Elgot and J. E. Rutledge that was a pioneering work on the subject of parallel programming when it was published in 1967. Here the problem of programming highly parallel computers was treated formally, based upon a mathematical model of a parallel computer.

Character and Influence. Again and again, those who knew Abraham Robinson remarked on his capacity for "organic growth," especially his ability to bring together vastly different areas of mathematics and respond to new ideas and techniques that united them in his mind to produce fruitful and stimulating results. As Simon Kochen put it, ". . . his viewpoint was that of an applied mathematician in the original and best sense of that phrase; that is, in the sense of the 18th and 19th century mathematicians, who used the problems and insights of the real world (that is, physics) to develop mathematical ideas."[2]

Robinson was a man of great simplicity, modesty, and charm. He loved to travel and enjoyed meeting people. He studied ancient Greek, and was fluent in French, German, Hebrew, English, and several other languages. On various occasions he lectured in Italian, Portuguese, and Spanish.

Perhaps Robinson's overall character and significance as a mathematician were best captured by the logician Kurt Gödel, who at the time of Robinson's death said that he was a mathematician "whom I valued very highly indeed, not only as a personal friend, but also as the one mathematical logician who accomplished incomparably more than anybody else in making this logic fruitful to mathematics."[3]

NOTES

1. As reported by George B. Seligman in his "Biography of Abraham Robinson," in *Selected Papers of Abraham Robinson*, H. J. Keisler *et al.*, eds. (New Haven, 1979), I, xxiv.

2. Simon Kochen, "The Pure Mathematician. On Abraham Robinson's Work in Mathematical Logic," in *Bulletin of the London Mathematical Society*, **8** (1976), 313.
3. Kurt Gödel, in a letter to Mrs. Abraham Robinson, 10 May 1974; Robinson Papers, Sterling Library, Yale University.

BIBLIOGRAPHY

I. ORIGINAL WORKS. A selection of Robinson's most important publications, including one of his earliest papers not previously published ("On Nil-ideals in General Rings," 1939), is in *Selected Papers of Abraham Robinson*, H. J. Keisler, S. Körner, W. A. J. Luxemburg, and A. D. Young, eds., 3 vols. (New Haven, 1979). Readers should also consult the special historical and critical introductions in each volume. Robinson's papers, including correspondence and lecture notes, are in the archives of Yale University, Sterling Library, New Haven.

II. SECONDARY LITERATURE. Joseph W. Dauben, "Abraham Robinson and Nonstandard Analysis: History, Philosophy, and Foundations of Mathematics," in William Aspray and Philip Kitcher, eds., *History and Philosophy of Mathematics* (Minneapolis, 1988), 177–200; Martin Davis, *Applied Nonstandard Analysis* (New York, 1977); W. A. J. Luxemburg, *Non-standard Analysis. Lectures on A. Robinson's Theory of Infinitesimals and Infinitely Large Numbers*, 2nd, rev. ed. (Pasadena, Calif. 1964), and *Introduction to the Theory of Infinitesimals* (New York, 1976), with K. D. Stroyan; Angus J. Macintyre, "Abraham Robinson, 1918–1974," in *Bulletin of the American Mathematical Society*, **83** (1977), 646–666; George B. Seligman, "Biography of Abraham Robinson," in Robinson's *Selected Papers* (see Notes); and Alec D. Young, Simon Kochen, Stephan Körner, and Peter Roquette, "Abraham Robinson," in *Bulletin of the London Mathematical Society*, **8** (1976), 307–323.

JOSEPH W. DAUBEN

ROMER, ALFRED SHERWOOD (*b.* White Plains, New York, 28 December 1894; *d.* Cambridge, Massachusetts, 5 November 1973), *paleontology, vertebrate anatomy.*

Romer was the son of Fenry Romer, a newspaper editor and owner, and of Evelyn Sherwood. A scholarship, unsupplemented by any contribution from his family, enabled Romer to get a higher education at Amherst College (1913–1917). Even though he had become fascinated by exhibits of dinosaurs and other fossil vertebrates during frequent visits to the American Museum of Natural History in New York City, he majored in history and German literature. However, when, after serving in the U.S. Army for two years, he entered graduate school at Columbia University in 1919, he switched to zoology and became a student of William K. Gregory, an outstanding comparative anatomist (particularly of mammals) and evolutionist. This was the golden age of zoology at Columbia, with other famous teachers—Thomas Hunt Morgan and Edmund B. Wilson—and a brilliant group of graduate students. Romer received his doctorate in 1921 and, after two years teaching anatomy at New York University, he went to Chicago as associate professor in 1923. There he stayed for eleven years. The university's Walker Museum had a splendid collection of Permian tetrapod fossils, to which Romer devoted thirty-seven publications. Indeed, he frequently did field-work in the Permian sediments of Texas and New Mexico. He summarized his years of experience in a detailed account of the Permian stratigraphy of Texas.

In 1934 Romer moved to Harvard, where he became professor of zoology and curator of vertebrate paleontology at the Museum of Comparative Zoology. After the death of Thomas Barbour, Romer succeeded him in 1946 as director of the museum, a position from which he retired in 1961. During the last decade of his life Romer organized and conducted a series of expeditions to the Triassic beds of Argentina, where he made major discoveries of fossil reptiles.

Romer married Ruth Hibbard in September 1924. They had three children: Sally, Robert, and James.

Romer's research objectives were in the tradition of classical comparative anatomy and phylogeny, as cultivated by Gregory's school. His chief interest was the reconstruction of vertebrate phylogeny from the lungfishes to the mammals, particularly of the primitive and intermediate amphibians and reptiles. This required a careful determination of homologies in order to be able to infer the ancestors of derived lineages. Romer clarified the taxonomic positions of numerous groups of reptiles in two outstanding monographs, *Review of the Pelycosauria* (1940), with L. I. Price, and *Review of the Labyrinthodontia* (1947). His profound knowledge was summarized in *The Osteology of the Reptiles* (1956). His principal innovation was a reorganization of the classification of the fossil amphibians. In his textbooks Romer introduced a simplified classification of the vertebrates in which he consolidated the widely scattered literature, and placed in a definite position (or in synonymy) large numbers of problematic genera and families. In addition he published more than 200 papers. His studies of Permian and Triassic fossils had made Romer a champion of transatlantic continental connections long before the theory of plate tectonics. He rarely theorized, but he did champion two major ideas. One, the freshwater origin of the vertebrates, is no longer widely accepted. The other, that the vertebrates, as descendants of an ascidian-like ancestor, have a dual nature, consisting of a somatic and a visceral component, is still under discussion. He also published ideas on the origin of the amniote egg and demonstrated the capriciousness of so-called evolutionary trends.

In none of his other activities was Romer as successful as in teaching. With his warm humor and lively presentation, he could spellbind any audience, even on the seemingly driest subjects. Not surprisingly, he was greatly in demand as a lecturer. His educational genius was also displayed in his textbooks: *Man and the Vertebrates* (1933), *Vertebrate Paleontology* (1933), and *The Vertebrate Body* (1949). For many decades (and through many editions) they were the most widely used textbooks in their respective fields. More popular were *The Vertebrate Story* (1959) and *The Procession of Life* (1968).

During his Harvard years Romer trained an outstanding cadre of vertebrate paleontologists, anatomists, and vertebrate zoologists who took up positions in universities and museums in the United States and abroad.

BIBLIOGRAPHY

I. ORIGINAL WORKS. *Man and the Vertebrates* (Chicago, 1933); *Vertebrate Paleontology* (Chicago, 1933; 3rd ed., 1966); *The Vertebrate Body* (Philadelphia, 1949; 4th ed., 1970); *Osteology of the Reptiles* (Chicago, 1956); *Bibliography of Fossil Vertebrates Exclusive of North America, 1507–1927*, 2 vols. (New York, 1962), written with Nelda E. Wright, Tilly Edinger, and Richard van Frank; *Notes and Comments on Vertebrate Paleontology* (Chicago, 1968); and *The Procession of Life* (Cleveland, Ohio, 1968).

II. SECONDARY LITERATURE. Edwin H. Colbert, "Alfred Sherwood Romer," in *Biographical Memoirs. National Academy of Sciences*, **53** (1982), 264–294, with complete bibliography; and G. E. Erickson, "Alfred Sherwood Romer 1894–1973," in *Anatomical Record*, **189** (1977), 314–324.

ERNST MAYR

ROSSITER, ROGER JAMES (*b.* Glenelg, South Australia, 24 July 1913; *d.* Helsinki, Finland, 21 February 1976), *biochemistry, neurochemistry, education.*

Rossiter was the eldest of the four children of James Leonard Rossiter and Marguerita Jacobs. His father, a Methodist schoolmaster who held a doctorate in the arts, encouraged Roger to excel aca-demically and athletically at private schools in Queensland and Western Australia. Rossiter received a B.Sc. in chemistry and mathematics from the University of Western Australia in 1934, and was awarded a Rhodes Scholarship, which he took up at Merton College, Oxford, in 1935. Before leaving Australia, he became engaged to Helen M. Randell, a medical student whom he married on 16 March 1940, just prior to her receiving a medical degree from the University of Edinburgh. They had three sons and a daughter. (Their son John, born with Down's syndrome, was never acknowledged by Rossiter.)

At Oxford, while representing his college in rowing, rugby, and field hockey, Rossiter earned a degree with first-class honors in biochemistry and physiology (1938) and set his sights on a career in medical research. To that end he sought advanced degrees in both medicine and biochemistry, receiving in a short space of time the D.Phil. (1940), bachelor's degrees in medicine and chirurgy (1941), and the M.A. (1942). Initially as a Harmsworth senior scholar and then as a Carnegie scholar, Rossiter did his graduate and postgraduate work with Rudolph Peters and Severo Ochoa. This work reaffirmed and fixed his love for academic research and resulted in the publication of several papers on the effects of vitamins and the thyroid hormone on tissue metabolism.

Upon completion of his medical studies, Rossiter was drawn into war-related research with the Medical Research Council Burns Unit at Oxford, where he initiated investigations into the toxic effects of tannic acid treatment and the metabolic response of tissues to burns. In 1943, shortly after his wife had joined the army as an anesthetist, Rossiter was commissioned as a major in the Royal Army Medical Corps. He quickly brought the techniques of experimental biochemistry to bear on medical problems exacerbated by war, first with the Army Malarial Research Unit in England, then with the British Traumatic Shock Research Unit in Italy, and finally with the Army Marasmus Research Team in India. These postings resulted in a pioneering study of the biochemical response to prolonged use of the antimalarial drug mepacrine and a comprehensive survey of the nutritional problems suffered by repatriated prisoners of war. In early 1946 Rossiter returned with his wife, with whom he had been reunited in India, to Oxford as Betty Brookes Scholar in biochemistry. In 1946 he received the D.M. degree, and in 1947 he was awarded the Radcliffe Prize.

After the war universities around the world scrambled to attract scientists freed from the war effort, and Rossiter received several offers. The most persuasive of those seeking his services was G. Edward Hall, a Canadian research physiologist who was dean of medicine and later (July 1947) became president of the University of Western Ontario. Hall wanted researchers for his medical faculty, and he found a kindred spirit in Rossiter, who accepted the invitation to move to London, Ontario, as professor and head of the department of biochemistry at the University of Western Ontario. Upon his arrival there in 1947, Rossiter threw himself into his work and began to lay the foundations for an innovative, productive, and research-oriented department. Now free to pursue the biochemical problems that most fascinated him, he focused on the chemistry of the nervous system.

Rossiter's early work helped elucidate the lipid composition of brain and peripheral nerves, as well as age-related changes during myelination. Subsequent work extended the study of myelin lipids to several animal species, with increasing emphasis on the biochemical changes associated with phosphorus-containing substances that occurred during nerve degeneration and regeneration. This work, largely carried out over the period between 1947 and 1952, yielded essential information on the lipid components of the myelin sheaths. The numerous resulting publications contributed substantially to general advances in membrane chemistry and the later construction of a molecular model for myelin.

After the completion of a hot isotope lab in 1950, Rossiter embarked on a pioneering study of the phosphorus metabolism of peripheral nerves during degeneration, and of the biosynthesis of brain lipids, using radioactively labeled phosphate as an investigative tool. These neurochemical studies proved fundamental to an emerging consensus on the mechanism of formation of glycerophosphatides and phosphoinositides.

Although neurochemical research remained at the core of Rossiter's research program, he exploited all avenues of biochemical research when the opportunity arose. He supervised studies of the metabolism of polymorphonuclear leukocytes and reticulocytes, the endocrine responses associated with cold stress, and, while on sabbatical in his native Australia, the intermediary role of O-phosphodiesters in the formation of lombricine.

Rossiter's accomplishments brought him national and international fame, and he received numerous awards and accolades. He was elected a fellow of the Royal Society of Canada in 1954 and in 1963 received its Flavelle Medal, as well as the Warner-

Chilcott Award of the Canadian Society for Clinical Chemistry. He worked diligently to promote the growth of biochemistry through his association with numerous scientific societies. He served on the editorial boards of several biochemical journals, became a member of the World Federation of Neurology's Commission on Neurochemistry in 1960, and was the first chairman of the Council of the International Society of Neurochemistry. In Canada, Rossiter was frequently a member of the national committees of medical and biochemical societies, such as the Canadian National Committee of Biochemistry, the Advisory Committee on Medical Research for the National Research Council, and the Grants Committees for Metabolism and for Clinical Investigation of the Medical Research Council.

It was inevitable that the University of Western Ontario would draw on the talents and energy of its head of biochemistry, and in 1965 Rossiter became dean of graduate studies, a position he had been instrumental in establishing in 1947. He retained the rank of professor of biochemistry, hopeful that the administrative burden would not isolate him from research. Unfortunately it did, and after 1965 Rossiter's contribution to science was primarily an administrative one. His tenure as dean lasted only three years, for in 1968 he took on the even more onerous position of academic vice president and provost. In 1974 he returned to medical science as vice president for health sciences, and he immediately embarked on a comprehensive study of national health care systems. While accumulating data in Europe, he died suddenly of heart failure.

In all his endeavors, Rossiter committed himself totally and unreservedly. To his students and colleagues his breadth of knowledge in science was rivaled only by his interest in all aspects of human accomplishment. Rossiter's scientific work figures prominently in the evolution of biochemistry into the vibrant, mature discipline it is today, and his academic career exemplifies the rise of Canadian university research after World War II.

BIBLIOGRAPHY

I. Original Works. Rossiter's publications numbered about 240, and specific titles can best be retrieved from such reference volumes as *Index Medicus* for medical topics and *Chemical Abstracts* for biochemical topics. The *Source Index* of *Science Citation Index* provides a ready entry on nearly all his scientific publications from 1955 on.

The most frequently cited of Rossiter's works include "Acid and Alkaline Phosphatase in White Cells," in *Blood*,

5 (1950), 267–277, written with W. F. Haight; "Alkaline and Acid Phosphatase in Cerebrospinal Fluid," in *Canadian Journal of Research*, E28 (1950), 56–68, written with K. G. Colling; "Phospholipid Metabolism in Rat Liver Slices," in *Canadian Journal of Biochemistry and Physiology*, 35 (1957), 143–150, written with Dorothy Kline; "Phosphorus Metabolism of the Adrenal Glands of Rats Exposed to a Cold Environment," in *Revue canadienne de biologie*, 16 (1957), 249, written with D. Nicholls; and "Discussion: Biosynthesis of Phosphatides in Brain and Nerve," in *Federation Proceedings*, 16 (1957), 853, written with W. C. McMurray and K. P. Strickland.

Chief among Rossiter's review articles are "Chemical Constituents of Brain and Nerve," 11–52, and "The Biochemistry of Demyelination," 696–714, both in Kenneth A. C. Elliott, Irvine H. Page, and J. H. Quastel, eds., *Neurochemistry: The Chemistry of Brain and Nerve* (Springfield, Ill., 1955; 2nd ed. 1962); "Lipid Metabolism," in Derek Richter, ed., *Metabolism of the Nervous System* (London, 1957), 355–380; and "The Metabolism and Function of Phosphatides," in Konrad E. Bloch, ed., *Lipide Metabolism* (New York, 1960), 69–127, written with K. P. Strickland.

II. SECONDARY LITERATURE. Obituary notices and biographical sketches by Rossiter's colleagues are in *Proceedings of the Royal Society of Canada*, 14 (1976), 110–113; *Journal of Neurochemistry*, 27 (1976), 827–828; and *Bulletin of the Canadian Biochemical Society*, 13, no. 1 (1976), 6–7, and 20, no. 2 (1983), 10–13.

Rossiter's activities as an educator and administrator are discussed in Murray Barr, *A Century of Medicine at Western* (London, Ontario, 1977), esp. 486–489; and John R. W. Gwynne-Timothy, *Western's First Century* (London, Ontario, 1978).

MELVYN C. USSELMAN

ROSTAND, JEAN CYRUS (*b*. Paris, France, 30 October 1894; *d*. Ville d'Avray, France, 4 September 1977), *biology, history of science*.

A man of science and of letters alike, Jean Rostand left a legacy of work notable for both its diversity and its content. As a biologist, he concentrated on questions having to do with the great problems of life itself: reproduction (parthenogenesis, gynogenesis), the preserving effects of glycerine on sperm subjected to hypothermia, genetics, and teratogenesis. As a popularizer of science, he disseminated scientific information in clear language: he was a much sought-after speaker, and his writings were models of French style. As a historian of science, he sought to lay the groundwork for a history of biology. Finally, in his philosophical writings he expressed and upheld an ethical approach that, though not universally accepted, remains for many a model of humanity and truth.

Rostand's father was the poet and dramatist Edmond Rostand, a member of the Académie Française and the author of *Cyrano de Bergerac* (1897) and *L'Aiglon* (1900). His mother was the poet Rosemonde Gérard. His older brother, Maurice, was a poet and novelist. His paternal grandfather, Eugène Rostand, was an economist and a member of the Academy of Moral and Political Sciences.

In 1900 the Rostand family moved to Cambo in southern France, near the Basque country. Nature was a pervasive presence in the young Jean Rostand's world, and his early fascination with natural history endured throughout his life. The work of the entomologist and writer J. H. Fabre was a revelation to him. Rostand was educated at home by private tutors, and he taught himself the life sciences as a child, reading such authors as Claude Bernard and Charles Darwin. He took his secondary-school and university-qualifying degrees in 1909 and 1911, and his bachelor of natural sciences (at the Sorbonne) in 1914.

Rostand was brought up on the works of Emile Zola, Félix Le Dantec, Eugène Bataillon, Louis Pasteur, and Jean Jaurès. During World War I he served at Val de Grâce in Paris, in the laboratory directed by Father Jean Hyacinthe Vincent, where the antityphus vaccine was developed. During the same period he did research in the laboratory of Maurice Caullery on the paedogenetic flies of the genus *Miastor*. At the end of the war, however, he abandoned his official career and conducted his research in a makeshift laboratory in his home. In 1919 he made his literary debut with the publication (under the pseudonym Jean Sokori) of *Le retour des pauvres*. By the end of his life he had published some twenty works under his own name. Among his books were *Pensées d'un biologiste* (1939), *Carnet d'un biologiste* (1959), and *Inquiétudes d'un biologiste* (1967). His published speeches include "Morale et biologie" (1962), "D'un humanisme scientifique" (1956), and "Quelques discours, 1964–1968" (1970). We find in these works a "biologiste engagé" who condemns pseudoscience, protests against the military use of the atom, condemns racism, and fights for equal rights to life and free expression for all men and women.

Rostand considered biology to be the source of knowledge indispensable in the shaping of his ethics (biological morality). "Biology," he wrote in 1963, "lies at the root of any serious contemplation of the human condition." But Rostand was above all a seeker in the most noble sense of the term. "'Seeker' is such a lovely word," he wrote in 1967, "far preferable to 'scholar!' It expresses the healthy attitude of the mind in the face of truth: absence more than acquisition, desire more than possession, appetite more than satiety."

Rostand began his career as a researcher with a 1920 study of the biology of the fly, *Sarcophaga filia,* and between that year and 1927 he published about a dozen articles on problems of the general biology of insects (embryology, grafting, and so on). He produced several works on entomology, including two articles on *Bombyx mori* (1942) and books on dragonflies and silkworms: *La vie des libellules* (1935) and *La vie des vers à soie* (1944). These books contain many original descriptions and experimental reports.

But although he continued to be fascinated by insects, the biological problems Rostand wanted to study led him to seek a different subject: the amphibians, for amphibian eggs are particularly suitable for research on fertility and embryology. The egg of the sea urchin had served as the basis for experimental embryology since the 1880's. It was therefore no accident that Rostand turned to this subject, especially since he had been influenced by Bataillon, one the masters of "the mechanics of development." In 1910 Bataillon had achieved traumatic parthenogenesis with eggs of *Rana temporaria.* His experiments had led him to delimit two stages of fertilization: activation and regulation. Whereas Bataillon concentrated on the experimental study of the phenomenon of activation, Rostand's research centered on the factors of regulation. In 1924, for instance, he showed that the "regulation factor" of frog sperm is particularly resistant to desiccation over a period of several months. Between 1924 and 1928 he did many experiments on this regulation factor in traumatic parthenogenesis.

During the 1920's Rostand forged the ideas that he was to develop throughout his life, ideas that formed a unity in his style of work and life alike. He was known first of all as a philosopher, then as a biologist whose studies of hybrids of various species and genera of amphibians led to his research on genetics and on anomalies in toads and frogs.

On 10 April 1920, Rostand married his first cousin, Andrée Mante. They had one son, François, born in 1921, who became a mathematician.

Also in the 1920's Rostand published his first work in popular science, *Les chromosomes, artisans de l'hérédité et du sexe* (1928). In his book he supported T. H. Morgan's genetics, though at the time most official "scholars" in France rejected the chromosome theory of genetics and refused to teach it in universities. In the foreword to the book Rostand wrote: "Whereas abroad, particularly in England and the United States, there is already a growing literature on the question of chromosomes, in France the general public is wholly ignorant of the matter, and even among the scientific public, only a single book (admirable though it is) is known: Professor Guyénot's *l'Hérédité.*"

Rostand was financially independent, and in 1922 he was able to move into a house in the Paris suburb of Ville D'Avray, turning a portion of the house into a laboratory. He thus enjoyed complete independence in his work. Free of institutional constraints, he undertook whatever research he desired and was able to say whatever he liked. This situation was well suited to his character, and was a necessary and sufficient condition for his pursuit of his varied intellectual activities.

In the 1930's Rostand began crossbreeding various species of amphibians, discovering the beneficial effects of refrigeration on the development of these "hybrid" eggs. On the basis of these observations, he began investigating the technique of gynogenesis (1934–1947); the diploidizing effect of cold was the most remarkable result.

Having learned the use of refrigeration in experimental biology, Rostand turned to the problem of the preservation of sperm and semen. Taking inspiration from the work of B. Luyet and E. L. Hodapp (1938), he tried saline and sugar solutions as possible protectors of frozen sperm. But unlike Luyet and Hodapp, he obtained negative results. He then thought of using glycerine, which proved to be a particularly effective protective agent (1946). This effect was independently discovered in 1949 by C. Polge, A. V. Smith, and A. S. Parkes, who were unaware of Rostand's work. But it was with the rediscovery of the "Rostand effect" that a method of preservation of sperm was established, paving the way for the practice of artificial insemination. In 1955 Rostand demonstrated the protective properties of ethyl alcohol, and in the year 1960–1961 he achieved the in vitro preservation of frog testicles. This technique permitted spermatozoa to survive beyond forty days; the testicles retained their fertility potential for about twenty days when immersed in paraffin oil.

Another question that interested Rostand was the determination of sex in toads, a problem he approached through the technique of gynogenesis. His results suggested female homozygosity (XX): all the gynogenetic toads were female. Rather surprisingly, these results contradicted those obtained in 1927 by K. Ponse, who, using a different experimental technique (fertilization of Bidder's organ [ova]), proposed male homozygosity (YY).

For these experiments the Academy of Sciences awarded Rostand the Henry de Parville Prize for 1934 and the Binoux Prize for 1941.

Continuing his research by means of the technique of gynogenesis, Rostand observed digital anomalies (ectrodactylism and polydactylism) in gynogenetic toads (1947). His attention was riveted by this discovery, and from then on, Rostand concentrated on research on amphibian genetics, demonstrating that gynogenesis was a particularly suitable method of detecting recessive mutations.

Rostand studied cases of natural polydactylism among the common toad (*Bufo bufo*), and in 1949 was the first to demonstrate genetic polydactylism in this amphibian. In 1949, during his study of polydactylous mutant frogs, Rostand discovered instances of pronounced polydactylism in the green frog (*Rana esculenta*): from six to nine toes instead of the normal five among 15 percent of the population of a pond. But this polydactylism proved not to be genetically transmissible.

Though momentarily disappointed that polydactylism in the green frog could not be incorporated into amphibian genetics, Rostand understood that "the existence of a massive, endemic somatic anomaly provoked by the action of a natural milieu was a phenomenon of great interest whose study promises to open a new chapter in teratogenesis" (1971). In 1952 he discovered unprecedented monster tadpoles. Some abnormal subjects had as many as seventeen toes on a single foot, and in most serious cases, bony outgrowths sometimes resembling tumors were observed on the limbs. Rostand even reported several cases of polymelia (an anomaly lethal among tadpoles). It was always the posterior limbs that were affected, but when the severity of the anomaly was greatest, the anterior limbs became abnormal as well. Rostand then advanced the notion of a teratogenetic gradient. For him, these unsuspected monstrous forms were an instance of the extraordinary surprises that mark the life of a naturalist.

Polydactylism in the green frog was a "teratological phenomenon" whose most serious forms among tadpoles "defied all description." Rostand called it anomaly P, for polymorphism (1952). He believed that since anomaly P was not genetic, it must have been caused by the teratogenous effect of some substance. Accordingly, in 1950 he began studying the teratogenous effects of many substances on frog larvae. He thus pioneered the field of chemoteratogenesis in amphibians, following the example of Paul Ancel, who had opened the field about a dozen years earlier, using chick embryos as experimental material. But despite his attempts to induce teratogenesis in frog larvae by chemical means, Rostand was unable to reproduce the morphological deviations observed in nature. He then advanced a new hypothesis to account for anomaly P: that it was the result of a virus in the embryo, manifested very early and only temporarily, since tadpoles affected by anomaly P regenerated normal limbs after amputation of the anomalous ones (1952). Moreover, the appearance of anomaly P in several ponds led Rostand to the "highly curious and genuinely new" notion of "monster ponds" (1971).

The ultimate cause of anomaly P remains unknown today (mid 1980's). Some of the causes were elucidated in 1969. Between 1967 and 1969 Rostand and his collaborator, P. Darré, proved that the tadpoles of a monster pond become monstrous when they are fed the excrement of certain fish (tench, eels) that live in the pond. Where the teratogenous agent has a temporary effect on the larvae of the green frog, its presence in the fish that carry it is also temporary, for the anomaly disappears from these ponds within several years. This anomaly is of interest to embryologists, teratologists, virologists, and cancer specialists, and it was for this reason that Rostand was so fascinated by anomaly P for nearly twenty-seven years.

Rostand considered himself a "loner," except on Sundays, when he was visited at home by many friends and acquaintances in quite diverse fields: painters, doctors, writers, naturalists, musicians, and the merely curious. Young and old, these visitors came to talk to a man who was known for leading discussions with passion and spirit.

Concurrently with his biological research and his popularization of the biological sciences (for which he received the Kalinga Prize for popularization of science in 1959), Rostand was interested in the history of science and published several original articles and works in this discipline, including his inaugural address to the XIIth International Congress on the History of Science, held at Paris in August 1968. Rostand considered the history of science a "slow and laborious embryogenesis of truth" and a "major chapter of thought and civilization." In its aesthetic value and speculative scope, the history of science teaches us "a lesson of confidence and modesty"— confidence in the "powers of the intellect," since the "embryogenesis of truth" is the product not of a single individual but of a collective, a fruit of the "labor of all" that does "honor to humankind."

Quite apart from the lessons the history of science teaches us, Rostand emphasized its "educational and humanist sweep" and its "emotive force." He considered the history of science to be a means of grounding his ethics in truth and a stimulant capable of arousing passion among the young. He had in mind those works that enliven and humanize science, that fill us with the "dynamism of truth discovered," such as Claude Bernard's introduction to the study of experimental medicine, Charles Nicolle's biology of invention, and J. H. Fabre's entomological memoirs—all of them writings that "awaken and provoke."

The scope of Rostand's work has not always been properly appreciated in scientific circles. Apart from the Parkes school's rediscovery of the protective effect of glycerine on frozen cells (1949), Rostand was the first to suggest that experimental gynogenesis could permit the discovery of recessive mutations, thus allowing exploration of the hereditary patrimony of animals (1950), a suggestion that was made anew by T. M. Trottier and J. B. Armstrong (1976). In an attempt to assess the relative roles of the jelly of the egg and the peculiarities of the egg itself in barriers to cross-species fertilization in amphibians, he was the first to envelop ova of a given species in the jelly of another species before attempting hybridization (1933), a technique that was later reinvented by H. W. Aplington, Jr. (1957), and employed by various others, such as R. P. Elinson (1974–1975) and R. Brun and H. R. Kobel (1977). Rostand was never cited by any of these authors.

Rostand's scientific work was notable for the diversity of subjects he studied, some repeatedly and in depth, others only in passing. This was a reflection of the breadth of his scientific curiosity. His wide knowledge of fundamental biological problems and his farsighted, synthetic spirit enabled him to grasp the totality of consequences and implications of observations and discoveries that might initially seem of limited interest. In this he was the very opposite of the "specialist" often demanded by contemporary research.

Rostand's enthusiasm for biological problems was infectious, and he preserved it to the end of his life, his words and writings inspiring many young naturalists. Nor did he lack a sense of humor, as evidenced in his "Pro Rana: Des grenouilles et des hommes," a 1963 paper delivered on the occasion of his election as honorary president of the Société Zoologique de France. In this speech Rostand responded to the mockery to which "the frog man" had often been subjected, expounding the emotional and rational reasons for his preference for amphibians.

Elected to the Edouard Herriot chair of the Académie Française on 16 April 1959, Rostand had been awarded the 1952 Grand Prix Littéraire of the city of Paris for the body of his work. In 1955 he received the Grand Prix of the Singer-Polignac Foundation, and in 1976 the Prix de l'Education of the Institut de la Vie. He was vice president of the Comité National d'Histoire et de Philosophie des Sciences and a member of the administrative council of the Centre International de Synthèse.

Rostand died at his home in Ville d'Avray after a long illness.

BIBLIOGRAPHY

I. Original Works. Tétry (see below) gives a bibliography of 390 titles, including books and articles. Rostand's principal books are *Les chromosomes, artisans de l'hérédité et du sexe* (Paris, 1928); *De la mouche à l'homme* (Paris, 1930); *La formation de l'être: Histoire des idées sur la génération* (Paris, 1930); *L'état présent du transformisme* (Paris, 1931); *L'évolution des espèces: Histoire des idées transformistes* (Paris, 1932); *L'aventure humaine*, 3 vols. (Paris, 1933–1935); *Les problèmes de l'hérédité et du sexe* (Paris, 1933); *La nouvelle biologie* (Paris, 1937); *Biologie et médecine* (Paris, 1939); *Hérédité et racisme* (Paris, 1939); *Science et génération* (Paris, 1940); *L'homme. Introduction à l'étude de la biologie humaine* (Paris, 1941); *Les idées nouvelles de la génétique* (Paris, 1941); *Hommes de vérité* (Paris, 1942); *La genèse de la vie* (Paris, 1943); *Esquisse d'une histoire de la biologie* (Paris, 1945); *L'avenir de la biologie* (Paris, 1946); *Charles Darwin* (Paris, 1947); *Hommes de vérité*, 2nd ser. (Paris, 1948); *La biologie et l'avenir humain* (Paris, 1950); *La parthénogenèse animale* (Paris, 1950); *La génétique des batraciens* (Paris, 1951); *Les grands courants de la biologie (Paris, 1951); Les origines de la biologie expérimentale et l'abbé Spallanzani* (Paris, 1951); *L'hérédité humaine* (Paris, 1952); *Instruire sur l'homme* (Nice, 1953); *Les crapauds, les grenouilles et quelques grands problèmes biologiques* (Paris, 1955); *L'atomisme en biologie* (Paris, 1956); *Peut-on modifier l'homme?* (Paris, 1956); *Anomalies des amphibiens anoures* (Paris, 1958); *Aux sources de la biologie* (Paris, 1958); *Bestiaire d'amour* (Paris, 1958); *Science fausse et fausses sciences* (Paris, 1958); *L'évolution* (Paris, 1960); *Aux frontières du surhumain* (Paris, 1962); *Le droit d'être naturaliste* (Paris, 1963); *Biologie et humanisme* (Paris, 1964); *Hommes d'autrefois et d'aujourd'hui* (Paris, 1966); *Maternité et biologie* (Paris, 1966); *Le courrier d'un biologiste* (Paris, 1970); and *Les étangs à monstres* (Paris, 1971).

II. Secondary Literature. Albert Delaunay, *Jean Rostand* (Paris, 1956); A. Dubois, "L'oeuvre scientifique de Jean Rostand (1894–1977)," in *Bulletin de la Société zoologique de France*, **102** (1977), 231–242; Jean-Louis Fischer, "Jean Rostand (30 octobre 1894–4 septembre 1977)," in *Revue d'histoire des sciences*, **31** (1978), 163–172, and "Jean Rostand, biologiste," in *Bulletin de la Société linnéenne de Lyon*, **47** (1978), 61–66; Odette Lutgen, *De père en fils* (Paris, 1965); Marcel Migeo, *Les Rostand* (Paris, 1973); and Andrée Tétry, *Jean Rostand, prophète clairvoyant et fraternel* (Paris, 1983).

JEAN-LOUIS FISCHER

ROUGHTON, FRANCIS JOHN WORSLEY (*b.* Kettering, England, 6 June 1899; *d.* Cambridge, England, 29 April 1972), *physiology, biochemistry.*

Roughton came of a line of physicians in Kettering; his father was the fifth consecutive Roughton to practice medicine there, and the family had many connections in the area. He had one sister, five years older than himself, to whom he was greatly attached. He himself might have gone into medicine, but he was subject to attacks of paroxysmal tachycardia, and his solicitous mother regarded him as a cardiac invalid. Later he came to realize that his condition was a disability, not an illness. Because of the tachycardia, Roughton was not called up for military service in World War I. He went to school at Winchester and proceeded to Cambridge in 1918. Though he planned at first to study medicine, his aptitude in basic science soon became apparent, and the inspiration and encouragement of Joseph Barcroft drew him to work on the physiology of oxygen and carbon dioxide transport in blood. Roughton's aptitude for mathematics and his training in physical chemistry enabled him to deal with problems arising from Barcroft's work concerning the respiratory function of the blood and the mechanisms involved in the absorption, transport, diffusion, and release of oxygen and carbon dioxide. Roughton could deal with these at a more advanced level than was possible for Barcroft or his contemporaries. Such problems occupied Roughton throughout his entire research career.

In 1923 Roughton became a fellow of Trinity College, a connection that he valued greatly, and took an active part in the affairs of the college. In 1925 he married Alice Hopkinson, whose father was a professor of engineering at Cambridge and whose mother was a Siemens of the German electrical firm. She herself became an active physician with numerous patients. They had a son and a daughter.

One important problem that soon concerned Roughton was the rate of uptake of oxygen by hemoglobin as the blood flows through the lung capillaries, and the release of oxygen from hemoglobin in the tissue capillaries. The time required for an individual red blood cell to pass through a capillary is on the order of one second. Was this long enough to allow these reactions to come virtually to completion, so that the blood could be considered to attain oxygen equilibrium with the lungs and tissues? Although it was known that these processes were rapid, it was not clear whether they were rapid enough to meet this requirement.

The new technique that permitted a quantitative approach to this problem was primarily the creation of another remarkable member of Barcroft's department, Hamilton Hartridge, who, as Roughton once said, was gifted with "almost diabolical technical ingenuity" in devising new approaches to difficult experimental problems. The apparatus he devised contained two large reservoirs that held two liquids that were to undergo a chemical reaction on mixing. The two liquids flowed out under pressure through tubes that led to a mixing chamber with carefully designed intake jets that achieved complete mixing within a tenth of a millisecond. The mixing chamber was Hartridge's crucial contribution. After mixing, the resultant solution moved rapidly, in turbulent flow, along an observation tube of known cross section. Knowing the rate of outflow of the liquid, one could calculate its velocity as it moved along the tube. The hemoglobin solutions under study showed strong absorption bands for visible light that shifted in position when hemoglobin combined with oxygen or carbon monoxide. Measurements of light absorption, at a suitable wavelength and at various points along the tube, permitted calculation of the extent of chemical reaction at each point as a function of distance and, therefore, of time.

Before the work of Hartridge and Roughton, accurate rate measurements of chemical reactions in solutions were possible if their times of half completion were on the order of a few minutes or more. Their new method reduced this time to about one millisecond, thus making possible the study of reactions some 50,000 times as rapid as those that could be studied before. The method, however, required large volumes of the reacting liquids in the reservoirs and was most effective for reactions, like those of hemoglobin, that could be followed spectroscopically.

Hartridge and Roughton, in the period between 1923 and 1926, showed that the reactions involving hemoglobin and oxygen were quite rapid enough to go essentially to completion in the short time required for flow through the capillaries. Roughton also showed in 1934, to the surprise of many, that carbon monoxide (CO) combines with hemoglobin some ten times as slowly as oxygen does, although at equilibrium it binds some two hundred times as strongly as oxygen. This comes about because CO, once bound, is released at a rate only about 1/2000 the rate of oxygen release.

The continuous-flow techniques of Hartridge and Roughton were forerunners of such later developments as Quentin H. Gibson's stopped-flow technique, which permitted accurate study of rapid processes with very small quantities of liquid. G. A. Millikan, who took his Ph.D. with Roughton, developed photoelectric techniques for recording rapid reactions in work published in 1936. Electronic methods of rapid recording, nonexistent in the 1920's, were essential for later developments. Britton Chance, who also took his Ph.D. with Roughton, was a major figure in these and later developments. Quentin H. Gibson, another leader in the field, also worked closely with Roughton.

Roughton soon became concerned with the kinetic problems relating to carbon dioxide (CO_2) transport in blood. Whereas oxygen is transported almost entirely in combination with hemoglobin in the red cell, CO_2 is mostly converted to bicarbonate ion; and both CO_2 and bicarbonate are distributed between the cells and the surrounding plasma, passing readily back and forth across the cell membrane. Some early authors had suggested that part of the CO_2 in the cells is directly bound to hemoglobin, but by 1920 this view was largely discredited. Lawrence J. Henderson at Harvard and Donald D. van Slyke at the Rockefeller Institute, the principal architects in the 1920's of a comprehensive picture of blood as a physicochemical system, disregarded possible CO_2 binding to hemoglobin. Roughton considered the question to be still open; moreover, he noted that no one had considered the kinetics of the uptake and discharge of CO_2 in blood. New evidence made this a crucial question. A. Thiel in 1913, and especially Carl Faurholt in 1925, had shown that the hydration of CO_2 to form carbonic acid and the reverse dehydration process were relatively slow reactions that could be accurately measured, although the ionization of H_2CO_3, and the reverse reaction, were far too rapid to be measured by techniques then available:

$$CO_2 + H_2O \overset{slow}{\rightleftharpoons} H_2CO_3 \overset{fast}{\rightleftharpoons} H^+ + HCO_3^-$$

Roughton's calculations from Faurholt's kinetic data led him to believe that the first step in the above reaction would go far too slowly, in the absence of a catalyst, for CO_2 in blood to equilibrate with its surroundings while flowing through the capillaries. Yet the physiological evidence indicated that equilibrium was in fact attained. To explain these facts there appeared to be two obvious possibilities, not mutually exclusive: the blood might

contain a catalyst to speed up the reaction, or some of the CO_2 might exist in a bound form that could be rapidly released to the lungs. O. Henriques in Copenhagen was also studying the problem, and in 1928 showed that some CO_2 was indeed rapidly released when the blood was exposed to a partial vacuum; the rest was released much more slowly. The slow release, he inferred, represented CO_2 derived from the HCO_3^- ion, whereas the rapid release could come from CO_2 bound directly to hemoglobin. Roughton, reinvestigating these findings, found that all the CO_2 released from normal blood came off rapidly; he could duplicate the phase of slow release, reported by Henriques, only by adding cyanide or some other chemical inhibitor. He concluded that there must indeed be an active catalyst in blood to accelerate the uptake and discharge of CO_2 that could be poisoned by cyanide.

With N. U. Meldrum, Roughton achieved the separation of the catalytic enzyme from mammalian red cells (there was none of it in plasma) in 1932 and 1933. The enzyme was christened carbonic anhydrase, and the amount present in the cells was shown to be far more than sufficient to produce rapid equilibration of CO_2 in the capillaries. Roughton and others later showed the presence of carbonic anhydrase in many other organs of vertebrates and invertebrates; it is also found in plants, and even in certain bacteria. In 1940 and 1941 David Keilin and Thaddeus Mann at Cambridge showed that it contained zinc, which proved to be essential for its catalytic activity. The detailed chemistry and catalytic action of carbonic anhydrase have been widely studied by many investigators, especially since 1960.

With J. K. W. Ferguson, Roughton investigated the evidence for direct binding of CO_2 to hemoglobin. There was a well-known chemical reaction that might well explain the facts: proteins contain amino groups (RNH_2) that in their basic form can bind CO_2 directly and reversibly to form carbamates: $RNH_2 + CO_2 \rightleftharpoons R \cdot NH \cdot COO^- + H^+$. Ferguson and Roughton concluded that this reaction did occur with hemoglobin, and also inferred that oxygenation of the hemoglobin must cause release of much of the CO_2 transported as carbamate, perhaps as much as 20 percent of the total CO_2 discharged in the lungs. Jeffries Wyman, a leading worker in the field, questioned the latter conclusion, arguing that a small change of blood pH in the lungs might explain the facts without assuming any change in carbamate content of the blood. Roughton was unwilling to accept Wyman's view and finally, with Luigi Rossi-Bernardi of Milan (1967), developed greatly improved methods for the study of carbamates that gave evidence for the essential validity of his earlier work. Rossi-Bernardi, with J. V. Kilmartin of Cambridge, in 1969 produced decisive evidence that the carbamate formation was located on the amino terminal α-amino groups on the four peptide chains of the hemoglobin molecule.

Over many years Roughton studied the equilibrium in the reaction of hemoglobin with oxygen (and with other gases). Hemoglobin, as Roughton's colleague G. S. Adair had shown, contains four oxygen binding sites (heme groups) and the binding is cooperative; that is, the oxygen affinity increases as binding proceeds. In 1955, following many earlier studies, Roughton and his co-workers, A. B. Otis and R. L. J. Lyster, carried out the most accurate measurements made up to that time on the successive binding constants under various conditions. They showed that the fourth oxygen bound, with all the other three sites occupied, combined with an affinity more than one hundred times as great as that for the first oxygen to be picked up. Since the hemoglobin in blood is carried in the erythrocytes, Roughton was also much concerned with the process of diffusion of oxygen across the cell membrane, which imposed an added delay on the total course of the hemoglobin-oxygen reactions. He studied this and other problems of diffusion, both experimentally and mathematically, in extensive calculations. With his considerable mathematical ability, Roughton was very much a physiologist; he was concerned with gas transport in the blood in its relation to the total functioning of the organism, not merely with the reactions of hemoglobin in solution.

At Cambridge, Roughton was lecturer in biochemistry (1923–1927) and then in physiology (1927–1947). In 1947 he succeeded E. K. Rideal as professor of colloid science, in which post he presided over a group of investigators working on diverse problems. In his personal research he continued to work on the same problems as before, and much of his most important work was done in these later years. Roughton frequently visited the United States, and during World War II he worked extensively in the Fatigue Laboratory at the Harvard Business School, with David B. Dill and his colleagues, on problems related to carbon monoxide in blood and other problems related to the war. Indeed, his work was perhaps somewhat more widely known in the United States than in England. In any case, Roughton's leading place among workers on blood and hemoglobin was clear. In May 1971 he was to have been the central figure in a conference in Copenhagen on oxygen affinity of hemoglobin and red cell acid-base status (Fourth Alfred Benzon Symposium). At

the last moment illness prevented his attendance, but four papers he coauthored were presented there. He continued his work for nearly another year, until his sudden death.

BIBLIOGRAPHY

I. ORIGINAL WORKS. Roughton published about two hundred papers. On his collaboration with Hartridge on the kinetics of hemoglobin reactions, see "Velocity with Which Oxygen Dissociates from Its Combination with Hemoglobin," in *Proceedings of the Royal Society of London*, **A104** (1923), 395–430, written with Hartridge; and "Diffusion and Chemical Reaction Velocity as Joint Factors in Determining the Rate of Uptake of Oxygen and Carbon Monoxide by the Red Blood Corpuscle," *ibid.*, **B111** (1932), 1–36. His studies on the combination of carbon monoxide with deoxyhemoglobin are in the series "The Kinetics of Hemoglobin, IV, V, and VI," in *Proceedings of the Royal Society of London*, **B115** (1934), 451–464, 464–473, 473–495. See also "The Origin of the Hartridge-Roughton Rapid Reaction Velocity Method," in Britton Chance, R. H. Eisenhardt, Q. H. Gibson, and K. K. Lonberg-Holm, eds., *International Colloquium on Rapid Mixing and Sampling Techniques in Biochemistry: Proceedings* (New York, 1964), 5–13.

For Roughton's early work on oxygen equilibrium in blood, "The Equilibrium between Oxygen and Haemoglobin. I. The Oxygen Dissociation Curve of Dilute Blood Solutions," in *Journal of Physiology*, **71** (1931), 229–260; and the later, much more advanced study, "The Determination of the Individual Equilibrium Constants of the Four Intermediate Reactions Between Oxygen and Sheep Haemoglobin," in *Proceedings of the Royal Society of London*, **B144** (1955), 29–54, written with A. B. Otis and R. L. J. Lyster. On his kinetic studies in this period, see "The Kinetics of Human Haemoglobin in Solution and in the Red Cell at 37° C," in *Journal of Physiology*, **129** (1955), 65–89, written with Q. H. Gibson, F. Kreuzer, and E. Meda; and "The Kinetics and Equilibria of the Reactions of Nitric Oxide with Sheep Haemoglobin," *ibid.*, **136** (1957), 507–526, written with Q. H. Gibson.

The discovery of carbonic anhydrase is described in "Carbonic Anhydrase. Its Preparation and Properties," in *Journal of Physiology*, **80** (1933), 113–142, written with N. U. Meldrum. His work with J. K. W. Ferguson on "carbamino-bound" CO_2 in blood is in "The Direct Chemical Estimation of Carbamino Compounds of CO_2 with Haemoglobin," in *Journal of Physiology*, **83** (1934), 68–86, and "The Chemical Relationships and Physiological Importance of Compounds of CO_2 with Haemoglobin," *ibid.*, 87–102. A survey of the field is "Recent Work on Carbon Dioxide Transport in the Blood," in *Physiological Reviews*, **15** (1935), 241–296. A major advance on earlier work is "The Specific Influence of Carbon Dioxide and Carbamate Compounds on the Buffer Power and Bohr Effects in Human Haemoglobin Solutions," in *Journal of Physiology*, **189** (1967), 1–29, written with Luigi Rossi-

Bernardi. Investigations on the Bohr effect—the oxygen-linked ionizations of hemoglobin—both by calorimetry and by the temperature variation of the ionization constants are reported in "Direct Calorimetric Studies on the Heats of Ionization of Oxygenated and Deoxygenated Haemoglobin," in *Journal of Biological Chemistry*, **242** (1967), 777–783, and "The Effect of Temperature on the Oxygen-Linked Ionization of Haemoglobin," *ibid.*, 784–792, written with Luigi Rossi-Bernardi and J. R. Chipperfield. For a view of his thinking on all these subjects near the end of his life, see Roughton's Hopkins Memorial Lecture, "Some Recent Work on the Interactions of Oxygen, Carbon Dioxide and Haemoglobin," in *Biochemical Journal*, **117** (1970), 801–812 (with portrait).

Roughton published no books, but he was coeditor with J. C. Kendrew of *Haemoglobin: Barcroft Memorial Conference* (London and New York, 1949) and with Robert E. Forster, John T. Edsall, and A. B. Otis of *Carbon Dioxide: Chemical, Biochemical and Physiological Aspects* (Washington, D.C., 1969). He contributed important papers to both these volumes.

Roughton's personal scientific papers, including correspondence, laboratory notebooks, diaries, unpublished speeches and lectures, manuscripts of published papers, reprints, and referee reports, have been deposited by Dr. Alice Roughton in the American Philosophical Society Library in Philadelphia. The collection is a large one: over three hundred boxes, with a finding aid. See D. Bearman and John T. Edsall, "Archival Sources for the History of Biochemistry and Molecular Biology" (Philadelphia, 1980), p. 84, collection 40154.

II. SECONDARY LITERATURE. The principal source of information on Roughton's life and work is Quentin H. Gibson, "Francis John Worsley Roughton (1899–1972)," in *Biographical Memoirs of Fellows of the Royal Society*, **19** (1973), 563–582, with portrait. There is also a brief, unsigned article in *Nature*, **238** (1972), 297.

JOHN T. EDSALL

RUSSELL, RICHARD JOEL (*b.* Hayward, California, 16 November 1895; *d.* Baton Rouge, Louisiana, 17 September 1971), *geomorphology, climatology*.

Russell was the son of Frederick James Russell, a lawyer and estate manager, and Nellie Potter Morril. Thanks to his determined mother, his early schooling was eclectic but effective. He enrolled at Berkeley in 1915 to study forestry but soon switched to geology. During World War I he was in the Naval Reserve. Russell returned to take a bachelor's degree in vertebrate paleontology (1920), then changed fields again to do graduate work in structural geology under George Louderback. Staff shortages in geography led him to instruct large undergraduate classes in elementary geography while learning the subject "on the fly." He used undergraduates to help compile the detailed paper "Climates of California" (1926), the first of many papers in climatology that had such considerable influence that in five successive years he was offered a senior chair of climatology in the United States. However, climatology remained a hobby he could cultivate whenever administration curtailed field activities. In later years his climatic interests were expressed mainly through work on Quaternary chronology. Russell was president of both the Association of American Geographers (1948) and the Geological Society of America (1957), the only scholar to hold both posts after World War II. He founded the Coastal Studies Institute at Louisiana State University in 1954 and remained its director until 1966. He was elected to the National Academy of Sciences in 1959. Russell married Mary D. King on 1 January 1924; they had one son. His wife died in 1936, and on 20 August 1940 he married Josephine Burke. They had four sons.

The primary scientific influences on Russell at Berkeley were George Louderback and Andrew C. Lawson in geology, and Carl O. Sauer and William Morris Davis in geography, although his acceptance of Davis's doctrines was never more than passing. Russell completed his Ph.D. in 1926 and was associate professor at Texas Technological College (Lubbock) for two overworked years until rescued by Henry Howe, a friend from graduate school at Berkeley who had established the geology department at Louisiana State University in Baton Rouge. Howe persuaded administrators that Russell should start the geography department. Russell arrived in Baton Rouge in September 1928 and never left the university staff. His primary interests became the fluvial geomorphology of large rivers and, after 1950, coastal geomorphology.

Several circumstances helped direct Russell's attention to problems in the geomorphology of large rivers, such as the Mississippi and the Rhône. After 1928 the publication of detailed topographic maps of the Mississippi Delta made possible the accurate mapping of very-low-relief alluvial terrain. In association with Fred Kniffen, Russell began to explore the morphological forms of Louisiana, searching for Indian artifacts. Prompted by a question from Davis about the straightness of the Mississippi below New Orleans, he realized that the vertical dimension of floodplains held the secret to their evolution. This work was further stimulated by the arrival of Harold Fisk in 1935, and between them they demonstrated that the Mississippi Valley had to be understood in terms of fluctuating Quaternary sea levels, isostatic sinking in the delta region, and alternating Pleistocene periods of alluviation and erosion.

Recognition of the deep significance of this work by other geomorphologists was slow, although "Physiography of the Lower Mississippi River Delta" (1936) won the first Wallace W. Atwood Award from the Association of American Geographers and was soon cited in major textbooks. The depression years of the 1930's, the years of World War II, and a postwar shift to quantitative and statistical work in fluvial geomorphology in a reaction against Davis's doctrines all conspired to mask the importance of work that tied fluvial geomorphology intimately to Quaternary history. G. K. Gilbert foresaw this trend in 1890, and Russell took it as a text for his presidential address to the Geological Society of America in 1957, well in advance of recent recognition that only by exploiting dated Quaternary successions can a historical element be added to geomorphology with a temporal control not possible within classical Davisian precepts. Russell's Mississippi work is not cited in modern texts on processes in fluvial geomorphology but is still controversial for regional geomorphology.

After World War II, Russell, through his membership of the Committee on Geography, Advisory to the Office of Naval Research (1949–1963), was led to study trafficability in Louisiana coastal marshes. A series of contracts with the Office of Naval Research led to the foundation of the Coastal Studies Institute and a worldwide study of coasts, primarily tropical, under Russell's direction. In preparation for his retirement Russell began a study of beach rock, a puzzling feature of tropical coasts, and succeeded in showing how it developed as an interaction between carbonate-rich beach sediments and fresh groundwaters seeping onto the beach face (1967).

BIBLIOGRAPHY

I. ORIGINAL WORKS. Complete bibliographies (including abstracts) are in Kniffen and in Howe (see below). Russell's professional letters, reports, papers, reprints, lectures, and other manuscripts are on deposit at the American Philosophical Society, Philadelphia. Some private sources are mentioned in Anderson (see below). Among his works are "Climates of California," in *University of California Publications in Geography*, **2**, no. 4 (1926), 73–84; "Climatic Years," in *Geographical Review*, **24** (1934), 92–103; "Physiography of the Lower Mississippi River Delta," in *Reports on the Geology of Plaquemines and St. Bernard Parishes*, Louisiana Department of Conservation, *Geological Bulletin*, no. 8 (1936), 3–193; "Geological Geo-

morphology," in *Bulletin of the Geological Society of America*, **69** (1958), 1–21; and *River Plains and Sea Coasts* (Berkeley, Cal., 1967).

II. SECONDARY LITERATURE. Charles A. Anderson, "Richard Joel Russell," in *Biographical Memoirs. National Academy of Sciences*, **46** (1975), 369–394; Henry V. Howe, "Memorial to Richard Joel Russell," in *Geological Society of America. Memorials*, **3** (1974), 165–174; Fred B. Kniffen, "Richard Joel Russell, 1895–1971," in *Annals of the Association of American Geographers*, **63** (1973), 241–249; and William G. McIntire, in *Geographical Review*, **63** (1973), 276–279.

Russell's work is cited or discussed in Charles A. Cotton, *Landscape as Developed by the Processes of Normal Erosion* (Christchurch, New Zealand, 1941; 2nd ed., rev. and enl., 1948); Armin K. Lobeck, *Geomorphology* (New York, 1939); and William D. Thornbury, *Principles of Geomorphology* (New York, 1954; 2nd ed., 1969), and *Regional Geomorphology of the United States* (New York, 1965).

KEITH J. TINKLER

RUTTEN, MARTIN GERARD (*b.* Java, Dutch East Indies [now Indonesia], 22 October 1910; *d.* Utrecht, Netherlands, 13 October 1970), *geology.*

Rutten was the son of Louis Martin Robert Rutten, a geologist, and Catharina Johanna Pekelharing, a biologist. His father, a consultant to the burgeoning oil industry, took his family to various parts of the East Indies and South America until, in 1922, he was appointed professor of geology at the University of Utrecht. Young Martin was taught by his father and, like him, became an all-round geologist and naturalist.

Rutten's health was never robust, yet he loved fieldwork and the outdoor life, and was an active conservationist long before it became fashionable. In the early 1930's, while still a student, he participated in several expeditions to the Caribbean that resulted in a series of papers and his Ph.D. dissertation (1938). Before receiving the Ph.D. he had taken a job with the Royal Dutch Oil Company and gone to work as a field geologist in Java and Sumatra, where he remained until 1940. This reinforced his early interest in the taxonomy and evolution of foraminifera.

Rutten was in Holland when the Germans invaded and occupied the country in 1940, and he was prevented from returning to the East Indies. He therefore joined the Geological Office of Mining in the Dutch coal district. After the war he taught stratigraphy and paleontology at the University of Amsterdam. When the chair of general geology at Utrecht—which his father had held until his death in 1946—became vacant, Rutten was appointed to it (1951).

Thus began the final and most fruitful part of his career. Geology was expanding rapidly in new directions, and Rutten kept abreast of them. His professional contacts were cosmopolitan. Most of his 120 publications are brief and in clear and simple language, whether he was writing in Dutch, English, French, German, or Spanish.

Rutten upheld and expanded the validity of actualism, holding that natural causes are immutable but their manifestations depend on circumstances that have changed, either cyclically or irreversibly, because of these very causes. For example, some common types of epicontinental sediment—such as chalk with flints or phosphate beds deposited in shallow shelf seas—are formed seldom or not at all today. Rutten argued that recent shelves, scarred by glaciations and changes of sea level, offer no analogy for periods when deeply peneplained continents contributed mostly dissolved, instead of clastic, material to the broad, flat shelves surrounding them. Likewise, he showed that enigmatic tuff breccias on Iceland were caused by eruptions below a thick Pleistocene ice cap. He established criteria for the distinction of ignimbrites (fluidized hot ash flows) from lava flows and airborne tuffs, and showed the former to have been frequent and extensive.

Rutten was among the first geologists to recognize the possibilities of paleomagnetism (the study of the weak remanent magnetization induced by Earth's field in rocks at the time of formation), and he promoted the foundation of a still prominent special laboratory at Utrecht. Measuring the remanent magnetic vector in rocks of various localities and ages reveals the former position and orientation of the shifting crustal plates, and reversals of polarity provide time markers for stratigraphy. On all these topics, he supervised Ph.D. dissertations in addition to his own writings.

Rutten's greatest interest was evolution and the origin of life. His inaugural address at Utrecht was titled "Actualism and Evolution" (1951). Inspired by the Russian biochemist A. I. Oparin (who postulated that life could have arisen from inorganic matter only in a virtually oxygen-free atmosphere, and that molecular oxygen was a later, biogenic product), Rutten considered the geological implications of these ideas. For example, unoxidized grains of pyrite and uraninite in ancient sandstones like the Witwatersrand, and banded silicate iron ores like those of Lake Superior, occur in various places, but all are older than 1,800 billion years.

On the other hand, strongly oxidized deposits like red beds and minette iron ores are all younger than 1,400 billion years. However, the oldest undoubted fossils are more than 2 billion years; doubtful ones are 3 billion years old. So, as Rutten argued in his influential book *The Geological Aspects of the Origin of Life on Earth* (1962), the geological record confirms that life came first and free oxygen second.

Rutten twice spent a year at the University of Michigan at Ann Arbor as a visiting professor (1957–1958, 1966–1967). He noticed that the literature on the geology of Europe, scattered and in various languages, was not easily accessible overseas. He therefore wrote an important and lucid book, *The Geology of Western Europe* (1969), giving copious references to, and illustrations from, the original publications.

In 1967, during his second stay at the University of Michigan, Rutten suffered a near-fatal rupture of the aorta; he knew he would not live much longer. Confined to his desk, he wrote a last comprehensive book on his favorite topic, *The Origin of Life by Natural Causes*. He was completing the manuscript when he died suddenly; the book appeared in 1971.

Rutten was married twice: to T. Kooistra, with whom he had three children, and after their divorce, to H. C. van Berghem, with whom he had one child.

BIBLIOGRAPHY

For a complete list of Rutten's writings, see A. A. Thiadens, "In Memoriam Prof. Dr. M. G. Rutten," in *Geologie en mijnbouw*, **49**, no. 6 (1970), 433–438. Rutten's three most important books are *The Geological Aspects of the Origin of Life on Earth* (Amsterdam and New York, 1962); *The Geology of Western Europe* (Amsterdam and New York, 1969); and *The Origin of Life by Natural Causes* (Amsterdam, London, and New York, 1971).

E. TEN HAAF

RUŽIČKA, LEOPOLD (*b*. Vukovár, Slavonia [part of eastern Croatia, now Yugoslavia], 13 September 1887; *d*. Mammern, Switzerland, 26 September 1976), *structural organic chemistry, biochemistry.*

Ružička came from a family of artisans and peasants. His father, Stjepan Ružička, a cooper, died when Leopold was four. He then moved with his mother, Amalija Sever, to Osijek, where he attended the primary school and classical gymnasium. In his youth he considered becoming a priest, but after reading Ernst Haeckel's *Welträtsel*, he turned to technical subjects. His university education was financed by a life insurance policy left by his father. Ružička was married to Anna Hausmann from 1912 to 1950; after their divorce he married Gertrud Frei Acklin in 1951. He became a Swiss citizen in 1917. Ružička was a member of numerous scientific societies, among them the Swiss Chemical Society, of which he was president from 1936 to 1938. He was a member of the editorial board of *Helvetica chimica acta*, a joint editor in chief of *Ergebnisse der Vitamin- und Hormonforschung*, and an editor of *Experientia*.

Ružička graduated in 1910 from the Technische Hochschule in Karlsruhe, earning both his engineering diploma and his doctorate under the supervision of Hermann Staudinger. From 1911 to 1916 he worked on the active constituents of the insecticidal plant *Pyrethrum cinerariifolium*. In 1912 he moved with Staudinger to the Eidgenössische Technische Hochschule (ETH) in Zurich, where he became a *Privatdozent* in 1918 and titular professor in 1923. During the late 1910's and early 1920's, Ružička began to collaborate with the Swiss chemical industry, especially M. Naef et Cie. These associations became very important in the development of his research.

Ružička was interested primarily in the relationship between the physiological properties and the molecular structure of organic natural products. He worked successively on synthetic multimembered rings, higher terpenes, and male sex hormones. He began work on odorants from the animal kingdom. The economically important musk compounds civetone and muskone proved to be macrocyclic ketones. As a result of Adolf von Baeyer's strain theory, it had been thought that only rings of up to eight members were possible. A method was soon found to synthesize ketones with nine to thirty-four members. In 1926 Ružička moved to Naef's Geneva laboratories. In that same year he accepted the chair of organic chemistry at the University of Utrecht. In 1929 he moved to the chair of organic and inorganic chemistry at the ETH, where he remained until his retirement.

In 1920 Ružička had begun working on higher terpenes. Through the technique of dehydrogenation using sulfur (and later selenium), and through application of the empirical isoprene rule (viewing terpenes as constructed of isoprene units), he and his co-workers determined the structure of sesquiterpenes, diterpenes, and triterpenes. This work led to study of the terpenoids. In 1934 Ružička and his co-workers achieved a partial synthesis of androsterone, which had been isolated in minute amounts by Adolf Butenandt, and proved its relation to the sterols. In 1935 his collaborator Albert Wettstein achieved a partial synthesis of testosterone. These events led to the production of commercial hormones, establishing the Swiss chemical industry in this field. In 1939, Ružička shared the Nobel Prize in chemistry with Butenandt.

While at the ETH, Ružička continued to collaborate with industry, both training chemists for industry and acquiring financial support for his department. During World War II he opposed the Nazi regime. Moses Wolf Goldberg and several other Jewish co-workers from his group chose to emigrate to the United States, where they played important roles in the development of the pharmaceutical industry. Ružička was founder and president of the Swiss-Yugoslav Relief Society. As he became more politically involved, the work of his laboratory became less focused on his specific interests and became many-faceted. At this time he also began to collect the seventeenth-century Dutch and Flemish paintings that now form a special collection at the Kunsthaus in Zurich.

In the 1950's Ružička began to work especially on the biogenesis of terpenes and steroids. Through elucidation of the structure of lanosterol, his co-workers under Oskar Jegar had shown a link between these groups. Ružička built on this and other contemporary work to develop the biogenetic isoprene rule, which he elaborated in 1953. After 1957, when he retired, he continued to work with his laboratory group and to consult with industry, especially Firmenich et Cie. in Geneva and Sandoz A.G. in Basel.

BIBLIOGRAPHY

I. ORIGINAL WORKS. For Ružička's Nobel lecture and biography, see *Nobel Lectures: Chemistry, 1922–1941* (New York, 1966), 466–496. His biogenetic isoprene rule appeared as "The Isoprene Rule and the Biogenesis of Terpenic Compounds," in *Experientia*, **9** (1953), 357–367; see also his Faraday Lecture, "History of the Isoprene Rule," in *Proceedings of the Chemical Society* (1959), 341–360. His reminiscences, "In the Borderland Between Bioorganic Chemistry and Biochemistry," are in *Annual Review of Biochemistry*, **42** (1973), 1–20.

II. SECONDARY LITERATURE. A comprehensive biography by Vladimir Prelog, Ružička's successor, and Oskar Jegar, head of his triterpene research group, as well as a list of Ružička's 582 publications, is in *Biographical Memoirs of Fellows of the Royal Society*, **26** (1980), 411–501. A short but very useful biography is in *Modern Men of Science*, II (New York, 1968), 468–470.

MERRILEY BORELL

SAKATA, SHOICHI (*b*. Tokyo, Japan, 18 January 1911; *d*. Nagoya, Japan, 16 October 1970), *particle physics*.

Shoichi Sakata, the most important early collaborator of Hideki Yukawa on the meson theory of nuclear forces, and the founder of the Nagoya school of builders of theoretical models of elementary particles, was the eldest of the five sons and one daughter of Mikita Sakata and Tatsue Otsuka. His father was the son of a Buddhist priest from a small village on the Inland Sea near Hiroshima, but he was educated in Tokyo. At the time of Sakata's birth, he was secretary to the prime minister of Japan, Taro Katsura, who became Sakata's godfather. Mikita Sakata rose rapidly, being twice appointed governor of a prefecture, and in 1919 was elected mayor of Takamatsu, a city on Shikoku. After retiring from political life at the age of forty, he became a successful businessman in the Kobe area. Sakata's mother was the daughter of Mitsugu Otsuka, who had served as governor of Ibaraki prefecture on Honshu.

Sakata spent three years in primary school in Takamatsu; the rest of his education, through high school, was obtained at Konan Gakuen (now Konan University) in Kobe, where he received an education that was both modern and informal. When he was sixteen, he joined an Esperanto club. There he met Tadashi Kato, who later translated Friedrich Engels' book *Dialectics of Nature*. Kato's influence, as well as Engels and Lenin's *Materialism and Empirio-Criticism*, were, according to Sakata, lifelong guides to his thinking.

He entered the course in natural science in Konan High School, where one of his teachers was Bunsaku Arakatsu, a pioneer experimental nuclear physicist in Japan and later professor at Kyoto Imperial University. Sakata's reading in high school included works on the history and philosophy of science by Max Planck, Henri Poincaré, and Jun Ishiwara. He corresponded and talked with Ishiwara, who helped him decide to become a physicist.

After graduating from high school in 1929, Sakata audited the physics course at Tokyo Imperial University and came to know Yoshio Nishina, who had returned to Japan in 1928 after eight years abroad, six of them at the Niels Bohr Institute in Copenhagen. Sakata enrolled in the physics course at Kyoto Imperial University, attended Hideki Yukawa's first course of lectures on quantum mechanics in 1932, and wrote a graduation thesis under Yukawa's direction that dealt with Werner Heisenberg's new theory of the atomic nucleus.

After graduating from the university in 1933, Sakata spent a year in Nishina's laboratory at the Institute for Physical and Chemical Research (Japanese acronym RIKEN) in Tokyo, where he collaborated with Nishina and Sin-itiro Tomonaga to produce his first scientific paper, on electron-positron pair production by gamma rays. Tomonaga, a graduate of Kyoto Imperial University who later became a Nobel laureate for his work on quantum field theory, had come to RIKEN in 1932. At RIKEN, Sakata began a lifelong association with another Kyoto graduate, Mituo Taketani.

In the early 1930's a science faculty was established at Osaka Imperial University, whose president was the venerable physicist Hantaro Nagaoka. One of the new chairs of physics was filled by the outstanding nuclear experimentalist Seishi Kikuchi. In 1934 Yukawa was appointed lecturer in physics, and Sakata became his assistant. At the end of that year, Yukawa created his meson theory of nuclear forces, which brought him the Nobel Prize in 1949. The meson theory was applied by Yukawa and Sakata in 1935 to the process of nuclear transformation with the absorption of an atomic electron, the so-called K-capture process, later experimentally confirmed in the United States by Luis Alvarez.

The closeness of the collaboration between Sakata and Yukawa can be seen from the fact that of the fifteen papers by Sakata and the seventeen by Yukawa in the 1930's, twelve of them bear both names. Among these joint papers are parts II–IV of the article "On the Interaction of Elementary Particles," part I of which is Yukawa's paper of February 1935, without collaborator, in which he proposed the existence of the meson. Part II was by Yukawa and Sakata; in part III they were joined by Taketani, who held the position of (unpaid) assistant at Osaka and Kyoto; in part IV, they added Minoru Kobayasi, who had been Yukawa's student at Kyoto. When Sakata joined Yukawa at Osaka, Kobayasi replaced Sakata in the Nishina laboratory at RIKEN.

Prior to 1937 the meson theory had been applied only to the K-capture process, and no direct experimental confirmation of its existence had been forthcoming. But at the beginning of 1937, Yukawa tried to call attention (via a letter to *Nature*, which was rejected) to some "anomalous" cloud-chamber tracks of cosmic rays, observed by Carl Anderson and Seth H. Neddermeyer on Pike's Peak, Colorado. The particles appeared to have masses between those of the electron and the proton. In the spring of 1937, Anderson and Neddermeyer identified those particles as of intermediate mass (hence the name *meson*), rather close to the mass Yukawa had predicted. That was the immediate stimulus for Yukawa

and Sakata, joined by other theorists in Europe and
the United States, to take up the theory again. The
cosmic ray observations of Anderson and Neddermeyer were quickly confirmed by other groups in
the United States and Japan.

Unpublished preliminary versions of parts II and
III of the meson article indicate that they were
worked on simultaneously. Yukawa's first paper
had been based on a meson field analogous to electromagnetism, and his meson (which he called U-
quantum or heavy quantum) was to be the quantum
of a field analogous to the electrostatic potential.
That is similar to retaining only the Coulomb field
and neglecting radiation, in the case of electromagnetism. Part II, written with Sakata, used the
theory of the relativistic scalar field, developed in
1934 by Wolfgang Pauli and Victor Weisskopf, but
not known to Yukawa when he wrote part I. Yukawa
and Sakata derived both unlike-particle and like-
particle exchange forces between nucleons (neutrons
and protons) and calculated the collision probability
of mesons with nuclei. They also speculated on the
possible existence of a neutral meson.

Parts III and IV, which appeared in 1938, introduced the meson as a particle of spin 1 (vector
meson) in a relativistic field theory of nuclear interaction. The revision gave a form of nuclear interaction that experiment seemed to require; it was
also thought to be necessary to explain the anomalous
magnetic moments of the proton and neutron. By
this time, others than the Yukawa group were exploiting meson theory, including Nicholas Kemmer,
Herbert Fröhlich, and Walter Heitler, who constructed a "charge-independent" vector meson theory that gave equal like- and unlike-particle forces.
These three were physicists from the Continent,
working in England, as was the Indian physicist
Homi J. Bhabha, who pointed out that Yukawa's
meson, which functioned as an "intermediate boson"
in beta decay, should on that account be radioactive
and have a short lifetime. Ernst C. G. Stueckelberg
worked actively on meson theory in Geneva, and
Pauli, Heisenberg, and others were greatly interested.

The lifetime of charged mesons was treated in
part III of the Yukawa group's meson article, and
a more accurate calculation was given in notes sent
to the Physico-Mathematical Society of Japan and
to Nature by Sakata and Yukawa. However, their
lifetime did not agree with that of the cosmic ray
meson, being a factor of about 100 times too short.
Sakata also estimated, with Yasutaka Tanikawa,
the lifetime of the hypothetical neutral meson.

By 1942, it had become clear that the cosmic ray
meson (mesotron) did not, aside from its mass and

charge, have the properties expected for the Yukawa
nuclear force meson. In addition to the lifetime
problem, there was no evidence that the cosmic ray
meson had any nuclear interaction. As a result,
some Japanese physicists began to suspect that the
particle observed in cosmic rays was a secondary
decay product of the Yukawa meson, the latter
being produced in nuclear collisions occurring at
higher altitudes.

On the basis of Yukawa's unpublished laboratory
diaries found in 1979, Michiji Konuma has concluded
that the idea of a two-meson theory was first advanced in May 1942. According to Sakata, the first
idea came from Tanikawa, in whose version both
mesons had integral spin, and whose suggestion
was inspired by the work of the Copenhagen physicists Christian Møller and Leon Rosenfeld, who
pointed out that a "mixed-field" theory, containing
both a vector meson and a pseudoscalar (that is
odd parity, spin 0), meson would eliminate a troublesome mathematical singularity that occurs when
only one type of meson is exchanged to make the
nuclear force. The new theory was presented by
Tanikawa and Seitaro Nakamura at a national discussion meeting held at RIKEN on 13 June 1942.
At the same meeting, Sakata and Takeshi Inoue
presented an alternative version in which the cosmic
ray meson had half-integral spin. The Japanese text
of their paper is in the Sakata Archives in Nagoya,
and a paper with this content is in the Bulletin of
the Physico-Mathematical Society of Japan.

In 1947, Robert Marshak and Hans Bethe proposed
a different two-meson theory (not knowing of the
Japanese work) in which the cosmic ray meson had
zero spin and interacted only weakly with nuclei.
They assumed that the meson first produced was
a fermion of spin 1/2 (belonging to a theory of
strong interaction that was not of the Yukawa type,
but in which pairs of mesons were exchanged by
nucleons). Unknown to them, a group studying
cosmic ray tracks in photographic emulsion at the
University of Bristol was at that time proving the
existence of two mesons. In 1950, Sakata received
the Imperial Award of the Japan Academy for the
two-meson theory.

In 1939 Sakata married Nobuko Kakiuchi, the
daughter of a biochemistry professor at the University of Tokyo, and became instructor at Kyoto
Imperial University, where Yukawa had just been
appointed to the chair of theoretical physics. Sakata
was awarded the Ph.D. degree at Kyoto in 1941.
In 1942, he was appointed professor at Nagoya University, and remained there until his death. Japanese
academic physicists (who did not engage as inten-

sively in wartime military research as did their Western counterparts) had difficulty during the war and immediately afterward with scientific research and publication. During the war, the isolation from the scientific world outside Japan was complete, except for some scientific journals received via the Soviet Union. Between 1943 and 1946 there is a gap in Sakata's publications corresponding to the suspension of scientific journals in Japan.

In March 1945, Sakata's house was burned in an air raid. In April, the theoretical physics section of Nagoya Imperial University was evacuated to a primary school in Fujimi, located near Mt. Fuji, for safety and availability of food; there Sakata was visited by Taketani. In their retreat, the Nagoya group and Taketani considered the problem of the infinities encountered in quantum electrodynamics and in meson theory from the standpoint of Taketani's methodology. Taketani argued that between the two traditionally recognized stages of development of a scientific theory—the stage of observational data and its generalization into provisional "laws" (which Taketani called phenomenological) and the stage of a formal mathematical theory (which he called essentialistic), there was an important intermediate stage (called substantialistic). Taketani supposed science to proceed in a spiral "dialectical" progression (in the Hegelian sense), passing through the three stages and emerging again in a new phenomenological stage. In the substantialistic stage, one identifies and characterizes the substances or particles that the final theory would be about. Taketani's view on the importance of the substantialistic stage was strongly reinforced by the developments of the 1930's, when the neutron, the positron, the neutrino, and Yukawa's meson provided the answers to many nuclear puzzles.

The various attempts to remove the infinities of quantum field theory by arbitrary cutoff or subtraction techniques were classified by the group at Fujimi as phenomenological. Another type of quantum theory began by modifying the underlying classical electrodynamics to be nonlinear at small distances. Gustav Mie, and Max Born and Leopold Infeld, had proposed such theories. Fritz Bopp, on the other hand, had a theory that was both linear and finite. The Nagoya group considered it substantialistic, for they could show its equivalence to a theory in which the electromagnetic field was "mixed" with a neutral vector meson field, that is, a new substance.

Sakata attributed the cancellation of the infinite self-mass of the electron in Bopp's theory to the mixing of the two fields. However, the vector meson field was not "realistic" because it had negative energy, so Sakata and Osamu Hara proposed to replace it with a neutral scalar field of positive energy. They named the new field "cohesive" and its quantum the "C meson," since it provided the cohesive force necessary to overcome the infinite electrostatic Coulomb repulsion from which the infinite self-mass arose. (An identical theory was independently proposed by Abraham Pais in Utrecht.)

Tomonaga was interested in the Sakata-Hara result and tried to apply the C-meson hypothesis to obtain higher-order corrections to the elastic scattering of electrons; again he found it successful in removing the divergence. In so doing, he learned that the troublesome infinities could be isolated by a redefinition (renormalization) of the electron's mass and charge; thus he was only a step away from the renormalization program for which he later shared the Nobel Prize. The mixed-field method was also used in a modified form by Pauli and F. Villars in their "regulator" method of charge renormalization.

In 1947, tracks in photographic emulsions exposed to cosmic rays at mountain altitudes clearly showed a charged particle (positive pion) decaying into another charged particle (positive muon). One could infer that an unobserved neutral particle (neutrino) was also a decay product. Further emulsion experiments showed that the muon decays into an electron and two neutrinos with the mean life of the cosmic ray meson. Negative pions brought to rest were usually captured by light nuclei, showing their strong interaction with nucleons, while many negative muons survived for a long time. Thus, the general picture envisaged by Sakata and Inoue in 1942 was largely confirmed.

Except for the muon, which behaved like a heavy electron and did not find a natural place in the apparent scheme of things, elementary particle physics seemed to have closed upon itself. No one suspected the astonishing multiplicity of unstable "elementary particles" that would soon appear, first in the cosmic rays and later at the large particle accelerators of the 1950's. These particles participated in the strong nuclear interaction (as judged by their copious production in high-energy collisions), but some of them, christened "strange" by Murray Gell-Mann, had relatively long lifetimes, which showed that their decays occurred via an interaction that was as weak as beta decay. It was suggested that the "strange" characteristic might relate to a new quantum number that must be conserved in strong interactions (such as the production process), but not necessarily in weak interactions (such as the decay process).

But what was the nature of the new quantum number? In 1953, Kazuhiko Nishijima in Japan and Gell-Mann in the United States independently proposed identical schemes. There is a quantity called isospin that characterizes strongly interacting particles (hadrons) and that determines the number of charge states. For example, the nucleon ($I = 1/2$) has two: the neutron and proton; the pion ($I = 1$) has three: positive, negative, and neutral. The "strangeness" was proposed as a "displacement" of the average charge of a multiplet. Thus strong interactions, which conserve both charge and isospin, can produce only a set of particles whose displacements cancel each other.

To Sakata this scheme, while phenomenologically successful, appeared to be too abstract and positivistic. It reminded him of the arguments used in his student days to explain nuclear systematics (without the elementary neutron) and beta decay (without the neutrino). He wanted "strangeness" to be the property of a particular particle, the lambda hyperon. He proposed that hadrons were made up of three particles, which he took to be the neutron, proton, and lambda, and their antiparticles. (An example of the last is the antiproton, discovered in 1955, which has negative charge.)

In 1949, Enrico Fermi and Chen Ning Yang had modeled the pion as a very strongly bound antinucleon-nucleon system. Sakata reacted favorably to this suggestion, which corresponded to his idea of "logic of matter," growing out of Taketani's methodology. He assigned research problems based on Fermi-Yang; for example, he asked Shō Tanaka to see whether strangeness could be understood as the property of an excited state in a relativistic version of the model. Sakata spent the last half of 1954 at the Niels Bohr Institute in Copenhagen, and when he returned, his discussions with Tanaka and the rest of the group convinced him that strangeness could not be a dynamical property but must be a "substantialistic" one.

Thinking along these lines, Sakata wrote (in his research notebook of 1955) sets of analogies drawn from the history of atomic and nuclear physics. He started in May and reworked and enlarged them from month to month. One of the entries is marked "new law (Sept/Oct)"; it contains the trio P, N, V_0 (V_0 being the strange particle called lambda), and directly beneath this, a second trio: $e^{\pm}$, ν, $\mu^{\pm}$. Next to it is the statement "The theory of structure is not to be found in field theory." Since he had already written "Λ: strange neutron," it is not surprising to find, a few pages later, that the muon is called "strange electron."

Finding that the known hadrons could be accommodated in a generalized Fermi-Yang scheme with the Λ hyperon as the "strange" element, Sakata gave a talk in October 1955 at the annual meeting of the Japanese Physical Society and published his model in 1956. In the same year, he visited the Soviet Union and the People's Republic of China and lectured on it.

The Sakata model was eventually replaced by the quark model, but in the interim it had powerful heuristic consequences. It gave a useful formula for hadronic masses, and it limited the type of hadronic decay possible via the weak interaction to that in which one of the "sakatons" (proton, neutron, lambda) changed into another. The model predicted a new meson, and the resulting octet of particles was identified in 1959 as a representation of the unitary symmetry group U(3) by Mineo Ikeda, Shuzo Ogawa, and Yoshiro Ohnuki (and independently by Yoshio Yamaguchi, and by Walter Thirring and Julius Wess). In 1964, Gell-Mann and Yuval Ne'eman proposed their "Eightfold Way" symmetry, in which the lowest-lying baryons were also an octet (not the Sakata triplet), and Gell-Mann and George Zweig, independently, proposed the fractionally charged quark triplet in 1964.

During the 1960's, Sakata and his associates continued to develop the "logic of matter," proposing in 1960, for example, a "unified model" in which the sakatons were to be made of the lepton triplet with the addition of positively charged "B-matter." They generalized this, in 1962, to have two neutrinos, with the physical neutrino as a "mixed field." In 1963, Sakata made his fundamental triplet "ur-baryons," quarklike but without the fractional charge of the quarks that was proposed the following year. According to Yoichiro Nambu, in his popular book *Quarks* (1985), "It may not be an exaggeration to say that particle theory has been proceeding according to Sakata's scenario."

To summarize, Sakata's main scientific achievements were work on the meson theory, including collaboration with Yukawa in the 1930's; the two-meson theory, proposed in 1942 with Takeshi Inoue; the theory of the cohesive meson in 1946; and, perhaps most important, the composite model of hadrons (particles, such as mesons, that have strong nuclear interactions). Sakata's composite model, which included the "strange particles" discovered in 1947, was the forerunner of the quark model.

In addition to his physics research, Sakata promoted science both nationally and internationally, and worked toward democratization of the university system in Japan after World War II. He also wrote on the history and philosophy of science and advocated Taketani's "three-stage methodology" of science.

BIBLIOGRAPHY

I. ORIGINAL WORKS. Almost all of Sakata's scientific papers were written in English. They are collected in his *Scientific Works* (Tokyo, 1977), together with philosophical papers and reminiscences, originally written in Japanese but presented in English translation. Most of these translations are also available in *Supplement of Progress of Theoretical Physics*, no. 50 (1971). Unpublished Sakata papers are collected at the Sakata Archival Library, Department of Physics, Nagoya University.

II. SECONDARY LITERATURE. Other material on the development of particle physics in Japan is in Shigeru Nakayama, David L. Swain, and Eri Yagi, eds., *Science and Society in Modern Japan* (Cambridge, Mass., 1974); and in articles by Satio Hayakawa and Takehiko Takabayasi in Laurie M. Brown and Lillian Hoddeson, eds., *The Birth of Particle Physics* (Cambridge, 1983).

LAURIE M. BROWN

SALEM, RAPHAËL (*b.* Saloniki, Greece, 7 November 1898; *d.* Paris, France, 20 June 1963), *mathematics.*

Salem was born to Jewish parents of Spanish origin, and the family moved to Paris when he was fifteen. His father, Emmanuel Salem, a well-known lawyer, died in 1940. His mother, Fortunée, and other members of his family died in a concentration camp.

Salem studied law at the University of Paris and mathematics at the Sorbonne, and received the *licence* in each field in 1919. He completed the engineering course at the École Centrale des Arts et Manufactures, where he studied mathematics under Jacques Hadamard, in 1921. Though he preferred mathematics, Salem went into banking. From 1921 to 1938 he worked for the Banque de Paris et des Pays-Bas, becoming a manager in 1938. He and his wife, Adriana, were married in 1923; they had two sons and a daughter.

Among Salem's avocations were music (he played the violin and liked to join quartets), fine arts, literature (mainly Italian and French), and sports (he skied and rode horseback). His main interest, however, was mathematics. He chose Fourier series, a field rather neglected in France at the time (except by Denjoy and S. Mandelbrojt), worked on special and difficult topics, and wrote a series of short papers published in *Comptes-rendus de l'Académie des sciences*. Denjoy insisted that he write a dissertation, for which Salem received the doctorate in mathematics from the Sorbonne in 1940.

Salem was mobilized in 1939, sent to England as assistant to Jean Monnet, and demobilized in June 1940. He took his family to Cambridge, Massachusetts, after a short stay in Canada. His doctorate enabled Salem to obtain a position at the Massachusetts Institute of Technology, where he taught from 1941 to 1955, achieving a full professorship by the latter year. There he met a number of mathematicians interested in Fourier series: Norbert Wiener, J. D. Tamarkin, D. C. Spencer, and Antoni Zygmund. He and Zygmund became close friends and wrote a number of joint papers.

Salem visited Paris every year after the war and gave a course at the Sorbonne from 1948 to 1955. He became professor there in 1955 and moved to Paris, where he played a major role in the renewal of interest in Fourier series.

An extraordinary teacher, Salem lectured in both English and French in his elementary and research courses. His writings contained nothing superfluous, nothing hidden; they were easy to comprehend even when they dealt with the most intricate mathematics—such as the interplay between harmonic analysis and the theory of algebraic numbers. His work is likely to remain a masterpiece of difficult mathematics and beautiful exposition.

After Salem's death his wife established an international prize, awarded every year to a young mathematician who has made an exceptional contribution to the theory of Fourier series or a related field. The list of those who have received the prize, first awarded in 1968, is impressive and testifies to the explosive activity in this area of mathematics.

Salem's works range over topics in the theory of Fourier series, number theory, geometrical set theory, and probability theory. The following two results of Salem's convey the flavor of his work. The first was discovered by him but was developed with others until the final form was achieved. The second has been the source of considerable research.

The first is related to a problem going back to Heinrich Eduard Heine and Georg Cantor (1870). Given a set E of $[0, 2\pi]$, does the convergence of a trigonometric series out of E imply that all coefficients are 0? If the answer is yes, E is called a U set (set of uniqueness); if not, an M set (set of multiplicity). The fact that the empty set is a U set is not obvious; it was proved by Cantor, together with a number of results from which set theory originated. Now consider a set E of a special type, associated with a given number ξ between 0 and $\frac{1}{2}$: E is closed, and can be decomposed into two disjoint subsets homothetic to E with a ratio ξ. The case $\xi = 1/3$ is the classic triadic Cantor set, which is obtained from a closed interval I by removing the open middle third, then repeating this dissection on the remaining intervals, and so on; what remains is E. From the works of Rajchman and Nina Bari (about 1920) it was known that E is a U set when $1/\xi$ is an integer, and an M set when $1/\xi$ is a nonintegral rational number. What Salem discovered (stated in 1943, proved with Antoni Zygmund in 1955, using a new approach developed by I. I. Piatecki-Shapiro) is a complete and surprising answer: E is a U set if and only if $1/\xi$ is an algebraic integer (that is, a root of a polynomial with integral coefficients, the leading term having the coefficient 1), such that all other roots of the polynomial lie inside the unit circle of the complex plane. This class of numbers is a closed set on the line; the numbers in question were called Pisot-Vijayaraghayan numbers by Salem, and their class was called S (for Salem) by C. Pisot.

The second problem was posed by A. Beurling and solved by Salem in 1950. Given a number α between 0 and 1, does there exist a closed set on the line whose Hausdorff dimension is α and that carries a measure μ whose Fourier transform $_\mu(u)$ is dominated by $|u|^{-\alpha/2}$? From previous results on Hausdorff dimension found by O. Frostman, it was known that $\alpha/2$ is the critical index. The answer is affirmative and the result interesting, but the proof is of greater interest because it contains the first introduction of a random measure into harmonic analysis; no measure is exhibited as an example, but almost all measures (with a convenient probability space) fit the requirement. Today the study of random measures forms an active field in its own right and has provided new proofs of Salem's theorem. Brownian images, local times, and occupation densities can be studied through the Salem approach and have yielded new results in probability theory.

BIBLIOGRAPHY

Salem's books are *Essais sur les séries trigonométriques* (Paris, 1940); *Algebraic Numbers and Fourier Series* (Belmont, Calif., 1963); *Ensembles parfaits et séries trigonométriques* (Paris, 1963), written with Jean-Pierre Kahane; and *Oeuvres mathématiques* (Paris, 1967), see especially 295–304, 311–315, 481–493, and 590–592 for problems discussed in text. The latter volume also includes a useful preface by Antoni Zygmund and an introduction by Jean-Pierre Kahane and Antoni Zygmund.

JEAN-PIERRE KAHANE

SAUNDERS, FREDERICK ALBERT (*b.* London, Ontario, Canada, 18 August 1875; *d.* South Hadley, Massachusetts, 9 June 1963), *spectroscopy, acoustics.*

Saunders was the youngest of six children born to William Saunders and Sarah Agnes Robinson Saunders, both of whom had immigrated to Canada from England. Music filled the Saunders home, and a powerful telescope and microscope provided scientific entertainment for the entire family. William Saunders, a druggist, managed a pharmaceutical company and an experimental farm near London, Ontario. In 1886 the family moved to a farm near Ottawa, from which the elder Saunders directed a system of government-sponsored experimental farms throughout Canada.

Frederick Saunders attended school in London and Ottawa. He entered the University of Toronto intending to study chemistry, but soon transferred to physics. After receiving the bachelor of arts degree in 1895, he entered the doctoral program in physics at Johns Hopkins University, where he studied under Henry A. Rowland, a leading American spectroscopist.

Spectroscopy at that time offered insights into two significant fields of research: blackbody radiation and atomic structure. When heated, perfectly absorbing blackbodies emit heat radiation at energy intensities that form a characteristic curve (at each temperature) as a function of emitted frequencies. Saunders' dissertation, completed in 1899, involved experimental tests of available expressions for this curve for temperatures below 500°C. The results, not published until 1901, showed major deviations from Wilhelm Wien's distribution law, similar to those obtained in 1900 by experimenters at the Imperial Physical-Technical Institute in Berlin who included Heinrich Rubens, Ferdinand Kurlbaum, and Ernst Pringsheim. The latter prompted Max Planck's hypothesis of the correct distribution law and the notion of energy quanta.

After receiving his doctorate Saunders taught physics at Haverford College for two years and then transferred to Syracuse University, becoming full professor in 1905. In 1900 he married Grace A. Elder, with whom he had a son and a daughter. He married Margaret Tucker in 1925.

At Syracuse, Saunders turned to atomic spectroscopy. He utilized the concave grating method developed by Rowland to obtain the spectra of the alkali metals (such as lithium, sodium, and potassium) and the alkaline earths (magnesium, calcium, barium), grouping the observed frequencies into series.

In 1904 he discovered several lines of the subsequently well-known "fundamental series."

A sabbatical year, 1913–1914, enabled Saunders to visit European laboratories. He worked at Tübingen and was greatly impressed by Friedrich Paschen, a foremost spectroscopist and a skillful administrator. After returning to the United States, Saunders was appointed professor of physics at Vassar College. He pursued refined spectroscopic analyses learned in Tübingen and examined data supplied by his former Tübingen colleagues.

U.S. entry into World War I interrupted Saunders' research. In 1917 he joined scientists at Princeton University who were developing methods of sound ranging. Among the group was his later collaborator, the Princeton astronomer Henry Norris Russell. In 1918 Saunders moved to Washington, where he tested the military feasibility of new optical devices. Following the war he served on the National Research Council committees on spectroscopy and atomic structure.

In 1919 Theodore Lyman invited Saunders to fill a vacant position in the department of physics at Harvard University. Besides modernizing the introductory physics course, which he taught until his retirement in 1941, Saunders succeeded Lyman as department chairman in 1926, a post he also held until shortly before his retirement.

Saunders is most remembered for his work with Russell. The 1922 discovery of multiplet spectra brought a new challenge to atomic physics. Russell, according to Saunders, found a theoretical account of the effect for alkaline earths, while Saunders provided most of the experimental data. During the period 1923 to 1925 Russell and Saunders extended Alfred Landé's vector atomic model by hypothesizing that the orbital angular momenta of the two valence electrons couple together to form a resultant (L) that interacts with the angular momentum of the core (the *Rumpf*) to generate complex energy levels that in turn yield the multiplet spectra. Later identification of the core momentum with the resultant electron spin (S) led to modern L-S or "Russell-Saunders" coupling.

After several studies with Lyman of noble-gas spectra, Saunders turned to teaching, administration, and the field of musical acoustics. With the formulation of quantum mechanics and the discovery of electron spin, the heyday of atomic spectroscopy had ended by 1927. With funds provided by Henry S. Shaw, a Boston philanthropist, Saunders, an accomplished violinist, used modern techniques to examine the tonal qualities of violins. The pioneering research followed three methods: the harmonic analysis of each note, using an acoustic analyzer; comparative curves of total sound intensity, using a sound meter; and electromagnetic analysis of vibrations, using an oscilloscope. The results were surprising. Comparison of the best antique and modern instruments showed little tonal difference. Any advantage of the older instruments lay in their more rapid response to movements of the bow, often essential for complicated pieces.

As a charter member and later president (1937–1939) of the Acoustical Society of America, Saunders brought his research to wider circles. Following his retirement from Harvard, he became visiting lecturer at Mt. Holyoke College, where he established an acoustics laboratory. Collaboration with A. S. Hopping, an electronics engineer, and Carleen M. Hutchins, a constructor of violas, led to more sophisticated studies of instrument construction. Beginning in 1948, at the urging of Henry Brandt, composer-in-residence at Bennington College, Hutchins and Saunders invented and constructed a new "family of fiddles," consisting of eight physically similar stringed instruments ranging between the treble violin and large bass. Although the success of the experiment is still in question, musicians remain favorably intrigued.

Saunders continued to study and play stringed instruments to the end of his life. He also pursued his interests in ornithology, becoming a recognized authority on the identification and behavior of birds. He served from 1952 until his death as an honorary vice president of the Massachusetts Audubon Society.

BIBLIOGRAPHY

I. Original Works. Saunders published most of his papers on spectroscopy in *Astrophysical Journal*; most of his work on acoustics appeared in *Journal of the Acoustical Society of America*. A bibliography of most of his publications is in Harry F. Olson, "Frederick Albert Saunders," in *Biographical Memoirs, National Academy of Sciences*, **39** (1967), 403–416. Omissions from the list include "Some Additions to the Arc Spectra of the Alkali Metals," in *Astrophysical Journal*, **20** (1904), 188–201; "On the Spectra of Neon and Argon in the Extreme Ultra-violet," in *Nature*, **116** (1925), 358, written with Theodore Lyman; and "Physics and Music," in *Scientific American*, **179** (July 1948), 32–41. Manuscript sources include Saunders' membership file for the National Academy of Sciences and the papers of committees of the National Research Council's Division of Physical Sciences, all in the archive of the National Academy of Sciences, Washington, D.C. Scattered correspondence may be located through the Inventory of Sources for Twentieth-Century Physics, University of California, Berkeley.

II. Secondary Literature. The most complete biographical notice is by Harry A. Olson, cited above. Obituaries were published in the *New York Times*, 10 June 1963, 31, and *Physics Today*, **16** (August 1963), 74. An account of the Saunders family is Elsie Pomeroy, *William Saunders and His Five Sons* (Toronto, 1956). Some details about Harvard physics may be gleaned from the annual *Harvard University Catalogue* and the annual *Harvard University, President's Report*. Historical works on spectroscopy include Paul Forman, "Alfred Landé and the Anomalous Zeeman Effect, 1919–1921," in *Historical Studies in the Physical Sciences*, **2** (1970), 153–261; Hans Kangro, *Early History of Planck's Radiation Law*, R. E. W. Maddison, trans. (London, 1976); and J. H. Van Vleck, "Quantum Principles and Line Spectra," *National Research Council Bulletin*, **10** (1926). For discussions of Saunders' acoustical research, see Carleen Maley Hutchins, "The Physics of Violins," in *Scientific American*, **206** (November 1962), 78–93; and Lothar Cremer, *The Physics of the Violin*, John S. Allen, trans. (Cambridge, Mass., 1984), 352–356.

David C. Cassidy

SAVAGE, LEONARD JIMMIE (*b*. Detroit, Michigan, 20 November 1917; *d*. New Haven, Connecticut, 1 November 1971), *statistics, mathematics, philosophy*.

Jimmie Savage was the eldest son of Louis Savage, descended from a family of orthodox Jews, and Mae Rugawitz Savage. He was educated at Central High School in Detroit, and at the University of Michigan in Ann Arbor, where he obtained a B.S. in 1938, and a Ph.D. in 1941, both in mathematics. He had studied chemistry and physics before turning to mathematics. He was married to Jane Kretschmer in 1938; they had two sons, Sam Linton and Frank Albert. The marriage ended in divorce in 1964, and Savage married Jean Strickland Pearce the same year. Savage enjoyed good health, and was a vigorous walker, swimmer, and talker, although he had poor eyesight, suffering from a combination of nystagmus and extreme myopia.

Savage's doctoral dissertation, written under the direction of S. B. Meyers of the Department of Mathematics, was in the area of metric and differential geometry. Another mathematician at Michigan who influenced Savage was R. L. Wilder. After receiving the doctorate Savage spent an academic year, 1941–1942, at the Institute for Advanced Study in Princeton, still working in pure mathematics. While there he attracted the attention of John von Neumann, who considered Savage to be a highly gifted mathematician, but recognized that his true interests lay elsewhere. In 1944 Savage joined the Statistical Research Group at Columbia University, and it was there that he first became deeply interested in statistics, an interest that continued throughout his life.

Savage was author of two historically significant books: *The Foundations of Statistics* (1954) and *How to Gamble If You Must: Inequalities for Stochastic Processes* (1965, written with Lester Dubins). He also wrote a substantial number of extremely important articles in statistics, probability, and philosophy, centering on two main themes. The first theme concerns the foundations of statistics, how to understand and justify what statistics is about. These questions necessarily led him to ask deep philosophical questions about the various approaches to statistics, the sources of human knowledge, and the process of induction. Savage's second theme concerns the theory of gambling, which he viewed as a stimulating source of problems in probability and decision theory.

Savage's crowning achievement, which grew out of the work of the greatest mathematicians and philosophers, including Blaise Pascal, James Bernoulli, Daniel Bernoulli, the Marquis de Laplace, Carl Friedrich Gauss, Henri Poincaré, Frank Ramsey, John von Neumann, and Bruno de Finetti, was his book *The Foundations of Statistics*. Partly through the influence of von Neumann, who had developed the theory of games and formulated the basic ideas of decision theory, and partly through the influence of the English logician and mathematician Ramsey and the Italian mathematician and philosopher de Finetti, Savage developed in the first five chapters of his book the most complete version of the theory of subjective probability and utility that has yet been developed.

Starting with a set of six basic axioms, each of which he carefully motivated and discussed, Savage demonstrated the existence of both a numerical subjective probability and a utility function. Nothing quite like this had been done before for probability, although there were important predecessors. Von Neumann and Morgenstern in their *Theory of Games and Economic Behavior* (1947) had developed the existence of a utility function for the case in which probability was assumed to be objectively given. De Finetti, beginning in 1937 and culminating with his *Theory of Probability* (1975), had developed a theory of coherence and subjective probability, which, although it was partly axiomatic, did not fully develop utility theory within the system. Ramsey, in his "Truth and Probability" (1926), had developed an axiomatic system with a simultaneous derivation of subjective probability and utility; in spirit his work is very close to the later work of Savage, although with a different formulation of the axioms and a different mode of derivations.

Savage's other main contribution was the book *How to Gamble If You Must*, written with L. Dubins. This is a highly innovative development of probability theory in connection with its ancient origins in gambling, and it uses the finitely additive approach to probability. Savage and de Finetti had been the primary proponents of finitely additive probability, which was all that could be logically derived within their systems of thought.

Savage's articles include extremely important contributions to statistical inference, especially the application of the Bayesian approach. There is space only to mention a few of these. The article "Bayesian Statistical Inference for Psychological Research" (1963), written with W. Edwards and H. Lindman, is possibly the best article ever written relating to serious applications of statistical inference. In particular, the authors give the fullest development of the theory of Bayesian hypothesis tests, as originated by H. Jeffreys in his *Theory of Probability* (1939; 3rd ed., 1961). The article, "Symmetric Measures on Cartesian Products (1955), written with E. Hewitt, was a highly innovative mathematical generalization of de Finetti's theorem. The monograph, *The Foundations of Statistical Inference* (1962), contains Savage's beautiful discussion of Bayesian estimation and hypothesis testing and his theory of precise or stable measurement, which clearly shows the role of so-called uninformative prior distributions. Another important article is "Elicitation of Personal Probabilities and Expectations" (1971), which contains an innovative development of the theory of scoring rules.

Savage exerted an enormous influence upon the development of statistics in the second half of the twentieth century. The resurgence of the subjective Bayesian approach, which Savage insisted was the only foundationally sound and sensible approach, thereby opposing the views of R. A. Fisher and J. Neyman, was largely due to Savage's efforts, especially in the United States. In his last years Savage wrote a number of articles on the philosophy of statistics, emphasizing the "objectivity" of the subjective Bayesian approach, as contrasted with the "subjectivity" of the so-called objectivistic approach. Savage had an intense and spirited curiosity about almost everything. He was extremely generous in dealing with younger researchers, such as myself, who crossed his path and no doubt affected us in multitudinous ways. He was uncompromising, both with himself and with others. In his honor many of his articles have been collected in *The Writings of Leonard Jimmie Savage: A Memorial Selection* (1981), along with reminiscences by several of his friends and colleagues. Savage's honors included the presidency of the Institute of Mathematical Statistics (1957–1958), the Fisher lectureship (1970), and the Wald lectureship (1972). He received an honorary degree from the University of Rochester in 1963.

BIBLIOGRAPHY

I. ORIGINAL WORKS. Savage's two most important books were *The Foundations of Statistics* (New York, 1954; 2nd rev. ed., New York, 1972), and *How to Gamble If You Must: Inequalities for Stochastic Processes* (New York, 1965), the latter written with Lester Dubins. See also *The Foundations of Statistical Inference* (London, 1962; New York, 1962). Many of his articles are collected in *The Writings of Leonard Jimmie Savage: A Memorial Selection* (Washington, D.C., 1981). See, in particular, "Symmetric Measures on Cartesian Products," in *Transactions of the American Mathematical Society*, **80** (1955), 470–501, written with E. Hewitt; "Bayesian Statistical Inference for Psychological Research," in *Psychological Review*, **70** (1963), 193–242, written with W. Edwards and H. Lindman; and "Elicitation of Personal Probabilities and Expectations," in *Journal of the American Statistical Association*, **66** (1971), 783–801, all of which are reprinted in the 1981 anthology of Savage's writings.

II. SECONDARY LITERATURE. *The Writings of Jimmie Savage: A Memorial Selection*, cited above, includes the texts of the memorial service given for Savage at Yale University on 18 March 1972 and the memorial service tributes given by W. Allen Wallis, Frederick Mosteller, William and Esther Sleator, and Francis J. Anscombe; the volume also includes a reprint of D. V. Lindley, "L.J. Savage: His Work in Probability and Statistics," originally published in *Annals of Statistics*, **8** (1980), 1–24, and a bibliography of Savage's writings. See also Lester Dubins' preface to *How to Gamble If You Must*, cited above, and the preface to Bruno de Finetti's *Probability, Induction, and Statistics* (New York, 1972), for evaluations of Savage's work. For further information on his life and work, see D. A. Berry, "Letter to the Editor," in *The American Statistician*, **26,** no. 1 (1972), 47; S. Feinberg and A. Zellner, eds., *Studies in Bayesian Econometrics and Statistics in Honor of Leonard J. Savage* (Amsterdam, 1975); W. Kruskal, "Leonard Jimmie Savage," in W. Kruskal and J. M. Tanur, eds., *Internal Encyclopedia of Statistics* (New York, 1978), 889–892; D. V. Lindley, "L. J. Savage," in *Journal of the Royal Statistical Society*, **A135** (1972), 462–463; and "Savage, Leonard Jimmie," in *International Encyclopedia of the Social Sciences, Biographical Supplement*, **18** (1979).

BRUCE M. HILL

SAX, KARL (*b*. Spokane, Washington, 2 November 1892; *d*. Media, Pennsylvania, 8 October 1873), *horticulture, chromosome studies, demography*.

Sax was the son of William L. Sax, a farmer as well as a public figure in local education and politics, and Minnie A. Morgan Sax, an artist and amateur botanist. After his early schooling in Colville, Washington, he attended Washington State College from 1912 to 1916, and then the Bussey Institution of Applied Biology at Harvard (M.S., 1917; D.Sc., 1922). In 1916 he married Dr. Hally Jolivette, with whom he had three sons.

In 1919 Sax was an instructor at the University of California, Berkeley. The following year he was a plant breeder at the Riverbank Laboratories in Geneva, Illinois. From 1920 to 1928 he worked at the Maine Agricultural Experiment Station at Orono. From 1928 to 1936 he was an associate professor of plant cytology at the Arnold Arboretum and Bussey Institution at Harvard; in 1936 he became a full professor at Harvard, where he remained until his retirement in 1959. Thereafter he served as a visiting lecturer at several universities.

Sax's interest in plants was evident early on, and remained with him throughout his active career and on into retirement. He grew up in the Palouse area of southeastern Washington, a region noted for its deep, rich soil of laval origin, and for wheat and barley production. At Washington State he was encouraged by Professor Edward Gaines, a wheat breeder at the agricultural station. Sax wrote, "Here I learned that one could have all of the pleasures of an agricultural career without the financial headaches by going into agricultural research work." From 1918 to 1936 all of his academic appointments, even at Harvard, had agricultural and applied overtones, and from 1946 to 1954 he was director of the Arnold Arboretum. His studies on the effects of X rays on chromosomes, and his demographic interest, with its emphasis on food production, arose out of these early concerns.

Sax's publications spanned a period of fifty-two years (1916–1968) and included over 150 articles and reviews, and one book. The first article appeared when he was a senior in college; the last was a contribution in response to an invitation from the Japanese Genetics Society. A number were written with his wife, who also was his collaborator for fifty-eight years. The publications fall generally into three distinct areas: horticulture, chromosome studies, and demography. The first two areas overlap considerably, since much of his cytotaxonomic and cytogenetics research was carried out on ornamental species in the Arnold Arboretum and on crops of importance to Maine agriculture.

Three of Sax's horticultural undertakings proved to be of signal importance. He shared with the Japanese cytologists Te Tsu Sakamura and Hisashi Kimura the credit for elucidating the alloploid chromosome relationships in wheat species, and in the process he played a major role in establishing the science of cytotaxonomy in the United States. In the area of plant breeding, he produced a number of excellent varieties and hybrids of *Forsythia, Malus, Magnolia,* and *Prunus* that found a place in the landscape trade. One of his *Forsythia* selections, Arnold Giant, received an award of merit from the Royal Horticultural Society of England. His favorite hybrid, however, was the result of a cross between *Prunus subhirtella* and *P. apetela;* graceful, semidwarf, but hardy, it was named Hally Jolivette after his wife.

The third area of horticultural significance arose out of Sax's dwarfing investigations. The dwarfing of fruit trees is an ancient art, but through combinations of interspecific and intergeneric root stocks and scions, and by single and double bark inversions, Sax established and simplified procedures whereby the average nurseryman could readily produce his own dwarfs with a high measure of success.

Sax has been called "the father of radiation cytology." On the basis of his cytotaxonomic collaboration with Edgar Anderson, and following the discovery of the mutagenic effects of high-energy radiations by H. J. Muller and L. J. Stadler, Sax initiated his most important studies, the effects of X rays on chromosome structure, with *Tradescantia paludosa* as his experimental organism of choice. His first publication in the area appeared in 1938, and the following three decades witnessed an extraordinary number of publications by Sax and his students that established the quantitative and qualitative bases of spontaneous and induced chromosomal aberrations. These researches also provided an understanding of the dangers of radiation exposure and a base for radiation therapy. In his later years Sax conducted similar studies that dealt with the chromosomal effects of aging, chemicals, and food additives.

Sax referred to his demographic study as an avocation, but his approach to it provided insight into his character as a man of action as well as a laboratory scientist. Sax was a gentle man, but one of great inner strength, strong convictions, and firmly held principles. He never hesitated to enter the lists when his beliefs were challenged. He argued unsuccessfully, as a director, against the dismantling by Harvard University of the Arnold Arboretum herbarium and library, even though he paid a high price in personal anguish and in the loss of position and friends. At the international level, Sax challenged Lysenkoism and all that it stood for; and he was among the first to call the attention of the scientific world to the Soviet threat to free science, and to the oppressive treatment accorded the biologists N. I. Vavilov, N. P. Dubinin, S. G. Navashin, and N. V. Timofeev-Ressovsky.

Throughout his academic career, as an integral part of his horticultural and chromosomal interests, Sax vigorously pursued a public involvement in family planning. This interest probably had its genesis in his close association with E. M. East, whose *Mankind at the Crossroads* (1926) was a Malthusian indictment of the consequences of unchecked human fecundity and limited agricultural productivity. Both East and Sax were advocates of deliberate birth control, and of wide dissemination of birth control information; Sax stated his position in his Lowell Lectures and a related book, *Standing Room Only: The Challenge to Overpopulation* (Boston, 1955). His public targets, particularly in the 1950's and 1960's, were the restrictive birth control laws of Massachusetts, actively supported by the Roman Catholic church. Sax and the Planned Parenthood League were instrumental in having these laws rescinded by popular vote. He also fought against Pollyannas of science, some of them his own colleagues at Harvard, who, through ignorance or design, duped a gullible public with glowing scenes of abundance for all. He considered foreign financial aid, unaccompanied by family planning advice and action, not only politically bad but, in terms of subsequent human misery, self-defeating and cruel as well.

Sax's love of the soil and plants, his rural upbringing, his choice of scientific investigations, and his acceptance of public responsibility were inseparable pieces of a whole man. Greatness as a scientist was not thrust upon him; it was something earned and honored in his several areas of interest. Sax received the Jackson Dawson Memorial Medal of the Massachusetts Horticultural Society (1959) and the Norman J. Coleman Award of the American Association of Nurserymen (1961). He was a Guggenheim Fellow (1961) and received honorary doctorates from the University of Massachusetts (1965), Washington State University (1966), and the University of Maine (1971). He was a Lowell Lecturer (1951), and a lecturer at the American Institute of Biological Sciences (1957) and the Society of Sigma Xi (1962). Sax belonged to the Genetics Society of America (president, 1958); the Botanical Society of America (certificate of merit, 1956); the American Genetics Association; the American Society of Horticultural Science; the Population Association of America; the Planned Parenthood League (president, Massachusetts chapter, 1958); the Radiation Research Society; and the American Academy of Political and Social Sciences. He was elected to the American Academy of Arts and Sciences (1941); the National Academy of Sciences (1941); the Japanese Genetics Society (honorary member, 1956); the French Academy of Agriculture (foreign correspondent, 1946); and Phi Beta Kappa (honorary member, 1941).

BIBLIOGRAPHY

I. ORIGINAL WORKS. A complete list of Sax's publications is in C. P. Swanson and N. H. Giles, "Karl Sax: November 2, 1892–October 8, 1973," in *Biographical Memoirs. National Academy of Sciences*, 57 (1987), 373–397. His most noteworthy articles are "Chromosome Relationships in Wheat," in *Science*, 54 (1921), 413–415; "The Relation Between Chromosome Number, Morphological Characters and Rust Resistance in Segregates of Partially Sterile Wheat Hybrids," in *Genetics*, 8 (1923), 301–321; "The Origin and Relationships of the Pomoideae," in *Journal of the Arnold Arboretum*, 12 (1931), 3–22; "The Cytological Mechanism of Crossing Over," *ibid.*, 13 (1932), 180–212; "A Cytological Monograph of the American Species of *Tradescantia*," in *Botanical Gazette*, 97 (1936), 433–476, with Edgar Anderson; "Chromosome Aberrations Induced by X-rays," in *Genetics*, 23 (1938), 494–516; "An Analysis of X-ray Induced Chromosomal Aberrations in *Tradescantia*," *ibid.*, 25 (1940), 41–68; "Population Problems of a New World Order," in *Scientific Monthly*, 58 (1944), 66–71; "Soviet Science and Political Philosophy," *ibid.*, 65 (1947), 43–47; "The Control of Tree Growth by Phloem Blocks," in *Journal of the Arnold Arboretum*, 35 (1954), 251–258; "Dwarf Ornamental and Fruit Trees," in *Proceedings of the Plant Propagators Society*, 7 (1957), 146–155; and "The World's Exploding Population," in *Perspectives in Biology and Medicine*, 7 (1964), 321–330.

II. SECONDARY LITERATURE. Alan D. Conger, "Karl Sax, 1892–1973," in *Radiation Research*, 53 (1974), 557–558; Richard A. Howard, "Karl Sax, 1892–1973," in *Journal of the Arnold Arboretum*, 55 (1974), 333–343; and an obituary in the *New York Times*, 9 October 1973.

CARL P. SWANSON

SCATCHARD, GEORGE (*b*. Oneonta, New York, 19 March 1892; *d*. Cambridge, Massachusetts, 10 December 1973), *physical chemistry*.

Scatchard was an authority on the physical chemistry of solutions. He investigated the equilibria, thermodynamics, and kinetics of aqueous and non-aqueous solutions, electrolytes and nonelectrolytes, and solutions of small and large molecules, especially proteins. Scatchard stressed the similarities that existed among solutions rather than their differences, and tried to keep his descriptions of them general and free from assumptions and restrictions. In his lifetime he published 165 papers.

Scatchard was the second son and fourth child of Elmer Ellsworth Scatchard and Fanny Lavinia Harmer. After his early education at Oneonta Normal School (1898–1909), Scatchard entered Amherst College, graduating in 1913 with a degree in chemistry. He received the Ph.D. from Columbia in 1917, having studied under the organic chemist Marston T. Bogert. After graduation Scatchard remained at Columbia, assisting Alexander Smith. But once the United States entered World War I in April 1917, he also assisted W. K. Lewis of M.I.T., who was then at Columbia doing war research. In 1918 Scatchard was drafted and commissioned a first lieutenant in the army's Sanitary Corps. He spent the war in France, at the Sorbonne, where he worked with Victor Grignard on the development of a rapid and sensitive method for detecting small airborne quantities of mustard gas.

In 1919 Scatchard received one of the newly established National Research Council fellowships but declined it in favor of a teaching position at Amherst. He stayed there for four years, investigating the hydration of sucrose from vapor pressure measurements and the reaction rate and mechanism of the sucrose inversion in concentrated solutions. This work showed the advantage of using mole fractions instead of volume concentrations. It was done prior to the introduction in 1922 of Johannes Brönsted's theories of "specific ion interactions" and "critical complex reaction rates" (today called the activated complex) and the Debye-Hückel theory of interionic attraction in 1923. Scatchard went to the Massachusetts Institute of Technology in 1923; on 28 July he married Willian Watson Beaumont. He remained there, except for the World War II years, until his death.

During the war years Scatchard spent part of each week in Boston, serving as acting director of the physical chemistry laboratory at M.I.T. and also working with Edwin Cohn of the Harvard Medical School on the fractionation of plasma proteins, and the remainder in New York, assisting Harold Urey at Columbia with the gaseous diffusion of uranium hexafluoride isotopes. In July 1946, he went to Berlin for six months to serve as scientific adviser to General Lucius D. Clay, deputy military governor in Berlin, and as the member of commissions charged with preventing the revival of German war research and liquidating its war potential.

At M.I.T., Scatchard expanded his research on solutions to include electrolytes, protein and other colloidal solutions, and the thermodynamics of non-electrolytic solutions, particularly their entropy and enthalpy of mixing. His studies on electrolytic solutions contributed significantly to the acceptance of the Debye-Hückel theory after its publication in 1923. According to their theory, the attractions among ions in a solution always produced an atmosphere of oppositely charged ions around each ion, and this atmosphere retarded the central ion's motion upon application of an electric field to the solution. In ten papers appearing between 1932 and 1936, Scatchard and co-workers carried out an extensive freezing-point study of aqueous salt solutions that strongly supported Debye and Hückel.

Of fundamental importance was Scatchard's extension of the Debye-Hückel theory to dipolar ions, large ions such as the amino acids, carrying two or more separate charges. This work became the basis for later investigations that established the dependence of a dipolar ion's activity coefficient on the solution's dielectric constant and ionic strength. His research on electrolytic solutions continued into the late 1940's and showed that the Debye-Hückel model of ion atmospheres accounted equally well for the interionic attractions of strong electrolytes.

Scatchard once said he was only a "part-time colloid chemist." But in this field he made major contributions, especially in applying thermodynamics to protein solutions. Scatchard's interest began around 1924 and grew out of his many discussions with his long-time colleague and friend Edwin Cohn on the relation of the Debye-Hückel theory to the solubility of proteins in salt solutions. But not until Scatchard had worked with Cohn on the wartime blood plasma fractionation program to produce albumin and other proteins did independent investigations begin in his own laboratory. In these studies he measured the osmotic pressure of albumin solutions at different pH values and salt and protein concentrations. This was of great importance because the albumin was responsible for maintaining osmotic equilibrium between the plasma and the cells and tissues in contact with it.

Scatchard's studies on osmotic pressures also led to protein molecular-weight determinations. Søren P. L. Sørenson in Copenhagen and G. S. Adair in Cambridge had already used osmotic pressures to calculate molecular weights of proteins, and by 1946 Scatchard extended the calculations to a broad range of protein concentrations and pH values. Further work on albumin solutions showed that albumin had a tendency to bind ions electively. To account for the binding on it and other macromolecules, Scatchard derived a simple relation for plotting the binding data, and from the plot he determined the number of binding sites on the molecule. This equation, first published in 1949, remains useful today.

Scatchard's research on the thermodynamics of nonelectrolytic solutions began in 1931 when he published an equation that successfully predicted the magnitude of the enthalpy change upon mixing different solutions. While most chemists at that time agreed that the entropy change was ideal and that the deviation of real solutions from ideal behavior resulted from an enthalpy change, they disagreed in their interpretations. Scatchard believed the enthalpy was a quadratic function of the composition and argued for the use of volume fractions rather than mole fractions. Of the several interpretations proposed, his was the simplest and most successful for predicting the enthalpy on mixing because he established it completely from a solution's physically determined properties (vapor pressure, density). In 1935 Scatchard introduced the term "excess free energy," which he defined as the difference between free energies for real and ideal solutions. Excess functions still find general application in defining a solution's thermodynamic properties.

During his career Scatchard received many awards and honors. He was a National Research Council Fellow in 1923, and in 1931–1932 a Guggenheim Fellowship enabled him to study with such European scientists as Peter Debye in Leipzig. Scatchard was active in the American Chemical Society (ACS), and held membership in the National Academy of Sciences (1946), the New York Academy of Sciences, and the American Academy of Arts and Sciences. He was a Sigma Xi national lecturer in 1951. The ACS awarded him its Theodore W. Richards Medal in 1954, and in 1962 he received the Kendall Award in Colloid Science. The unpublished manuscripts of Scatchard's texts on chemical thermodynamics and colloids have been published as *Equilibrium in Solutions and Surface and Colloid Chemistry* (1976).

BIBLIOGRAPHY

I. ORIGINAL WORKS. Scatchard's papers are in the archives of the Massachusetts Institute of Technology (two boxes, three linear feet). They contain reprints, reports, photographs, manuscripts, slides, and other material. John H. Edsall and Walter H. Stockmayer, "George Scatchard," in *Biographical Memoirs. National Academy of Sciences*, **52** (1980), 335–377, contains a complete list of Scatchard's publications. Scatchard's *Equilibrium in Solutions: Surface and Colloid Chemistry* (Cambridge, Mass., 1976) has an introductory "Autobiographical Note" with a valuable commentary on each of his 165 publications. A second autobiographical account is Scatchard's "Half a Century as a Part-Time Colloid Chemist," in K. J. Mysele, C. M. Samour, and J. M. Hollister, eds., *Twenty Years of Colloid and Surface Chemistry: The Kendall Award Addresses* (Washington, D.C., 1973).

Scatchard's important publications include "The Interaction of Electrolytes with Non-electrolytes," in *Chemical Reviews*, **3** (1927), 383–402; "Equilibria in Non-electrolyte Solutions in Relation to the Vapor Pressures and Densities of the Components," *ibid.*, **8** (1931), 321–333; "Das Verhalten von Zwitterionen und von mehrwertigen Ionen mit weit entfernten Ladungen in Elektrolytlösungen," in *Physikalische Zeitschrift*, **33** (1932), 297–300, written with John G. Kirkwood; "The Coming of Age of the Interionic Attraction Theory," in *Chemical Reviews*, **13** (1933), 7–27; "Concentrated Solutions of Strong Electrolytes," *ibid.*, **19** (1936), 309–327; chapters 3, 8 (with John T. Edsall), and 24 in Edwin J. Cohn and John T. Edsall, eds. *Proteins, Amino Acids and Peptides* (New York, 1943, repr. 1965); "Chemical, Clinical, and Immunological Studies on the Products of Human Plasma Fractionation. VI. The Osmotic Pressure of Plasma and of Serum Albumin," in *Journal of Clinical Investigation*, **23,** (1944), 458–464, written with Alan C. Batchelder and Alexander Brown; "Chemical, Clinical, and Immunological Studies on the Products of Human Plasma Fractionation. XXVI. The Properties of Solutions of Human Serum Albumin of Low Salt Content," *ibid.*, **24** (1945), 671–679, written with L. E. Strong, W. L. Hughes, Jr., J. N. Ashworth, and A. H. Sparrow; "Physical Chemistry of Protein Solutions. I. Derivation of the Equations for the Osmotic Pressure," in *Journal of the American Chemical Society*, **68** (1946), 2315–2319; "Preparation and Properties of Serum and Plasma Proteins. VI. Osmotic Equilibria in Concentrated Solutions of Serum Albumin and Sodium Chloride," *ibid.*, 2320–2329, written with Alan C. Batchelder and Alexander Brown; "Preparation and Properties of Serum and Plasma Proteins. VII. Osmotic Equilibria in Concentrated Solutions of Serum Albumin," *ibid.*, 2610–2612, written with Alan C. Batchelder, Alexander Brown, and Mary Zosa; "Physical-Chemical Characteristics of Certain of the Proteins of Normal Human Plasma," in *Journal of Physical and Colloid Chemistry*, **51** (1947), 184–198, written with J. C. Oncley and Alexander Brown; "The Attractions of Proteins for Small Molecules and Ions," in *Annals of the New York Academy of Sciences*, **51** (1949), 660–672; "Physical Chemistry of Protein Solutions. IV. The Combination of Human Serum Albumin with Chloride Ion," in *Journal of the American Chemical Society*, **72** (1950), 535–540, written with I. Herbert Scheinberg and S. Howard Armstrong, Jr.; "Physical Chemistry of Protein Solutions, V, The Combination of

Human Serum Albumin with Thiocyanate Ion," *ibid.*, 540–546, written with I. Herbert Scheinberg and S. Howard Armstrong, Jr.; "Equilibria and Reaction Rates in Dilute Electrolyte Solutions," in *National Bureau of Standards (U.S.) Circular*, no. 524 (1953), 185–192; "Physical Chemistry of Protein Solutions, X, The Binding of Small Anions by Serum Albumin," in *Journal of the American Chemical Society*, **81** (1959), 6104–6109, written with Ying Victor Wu and Amy Lin Shen; and "Solutions of Electrolytes," in *Annual Review of Physical Chemistry*, **14** (1963), 161–176.

II. SECONDARY LITERATURE. The most complete account of Scatchard is Edsall and Stockmayer's memoir. I. Herbert Scheinberg has written a shorter biographical account as an introduction to Scatchard's *Equilibrium in Solutions*. Other articles on Scatchard are "Behavior of Serum Albumin," in *Chemical and Engineering News*, **32** (24 May 1954), 2098–2099, on his receiving the ACS's Theodore Richards Medal; and **40** (2 April 1962), 100, on his receiving the Kendall Company Award in Colloid Chemistry.

ANTHONY N. STRANGES

SCHÄFER, WILHELM (*b.* Crumstadt, Hesse, Germany, 18 March 1912; *d.* Frankfurt am Main, Federal Republic of Germany, 27 July 1981), *biology, paleontology.*

The son of a liberal-minded Protestant parson, Wilhelm Schäfer, and his wife, Elizabeth, Schäfer spent his youth in the small Hessian town of Oppenheim am Rhine. From 1927 to 1931 he attended secondary school at Mainz. The lessons attracted him less than the animal life in the wooded meadows along the river. After passing the *Abitur*, he enrolled at Giessen University to study zoology, botany, geography, art history, philosophy, and pedagogy. He received a doctorate in zoology in 1937 with the dissertation "Bau, Entwicklung und Farbentstehung bei den Flitterzellen von *Sepia officinalis*." His advisers were W. J. Schmidt and W. E. Ankel.

Schäfer then worked at the Senckenberg Museum in Frankfurt, which was directed by Rudolf Richter. In May 1938 Schäfer was named director of the branch institute at Wilhelmshaven, Senckenberg am Meer. This institute, founded by the Senckenbergische Naturforschende Gesellschaft in 1928, had as its purpose the investigation of how the sediments of shallows are formed and how living forms leave traces in developing sediments (actuogeology, actuopaleontology). It proved the actualistic principle of geopaleontological research: understanding and interpreting stratified rocks and the fossils contained in them by means of a thorough knowledge of their origins. The shallows of the subsiding North German

coastline and the chain of islands offshore presented ideal opportunities for observations that could be related to fossil sediments.

In May 1939 Schäfer married the zoologist Dr. Elisabeth (Lisel) Götze, daughter of a Giessen University professor; they had four children. He soon turned his attention to marine zoological research and enlarged the range of Senckenberg am Meer through his observations as an expert in biology. Between 1938 and 1943 he published papers on sedimentological and biological topics in *Senckenbergiana* and other periodicals.

Schäfer was drafted for military service in 1939. He returned to a totally destroyed Wilhelmshaven Institute in 1947 and immediately started its reconstruction. Although he received no financial aid from the Senckenberg Museum in Frankfurt, by 1953 he could report that a new institute building was being completed and that research work had fully resumed. In his first postwar publication he observed and described the destruction by sinking of the Oberahn fields, the last remnants of a marshy island that remained after the North Sea formed Jade Bay in the fifteenth century. He also observed and described the formation of the island of Mellum from quicksands, the forms of destruction and re-formation during this process, and changes in the flora and fauna during those processes.

For years he had done research on the life of Brachyura, and with a treatise on the multiform and multifunctional Brachyura claws, he qualified in 1954 as a university teacher at Frankfurt. He collected and published much additional information on processes of marine biology and biology-actuopaleontology, and also dealt with shallow-water sedimentation processes, especially with tidal currents and rough seas. Among his co-workers were Konrad Lüders, an expert in shipping matters, and, from 1954, Hans-Erich Reineck, a sedimentologist. In 1962 Schäfer summarized the results of his research on the shallows in *Aktuo-Paläontologie nach Studien in der Nordsee*, illustrated with his own drawings. It concludes with a characterization of the essential features and of the change of biocenoses, and a systematics of biofacies, so important for the comparison of fossil sediments.

In 1961 Schäfer was appointed director of the Senckenberg Natural History Museum and Research Institute at Frankfurt. He began to remodel both, which had been destroyed during the war. In this capacity he was in charge of 140 workers and had a budget of eleven million marks, putting his artistic and didactic capacities to good use. He sought to restore the classical architecture of the old museum as well as to establish the primacy of the excellent paleontological exhibits, which were characterized by large graphic and sculptural works, as well as intelligible captions. At a time of increasingly abstract science, he revolutionized scientific illustration after having given, in *Das wissenschaftliche Tierbild* (1949), a fascinating account of zoological illustration as a mirror of the current state of knowledge. In numerous articles he dealt with the functions of a natural history museum and with questions of museology. Despite his heavy schedule, Schäfer found time to travel. In 1963 he visited the Gulf of Naples. This led to another Senckenberg branch station on the island of Ischia. In 1964 and 1965 Schäfer was a member of the first Meteor expedition and did research on the reefs of the coral island of Sarso in the Red Sea.

Schäfer retired in 1978, and during his last years became deeply alarmed by the disturbed balance of the environment, made intensive studies of the endangered ecology of the Upper Rhine, along which he had grown up, and proposed regenerative measures for the river and the land along its banks. His last book, *Fossilien Bilder und Gedanken, zur Paläontologischen Wissenschaft* (1980), tries to elucidate paleontology and to render transparent its relation to adjacent sciences and the totality of human knowledge and culture by reference to many related historical and philosophical aspects. Paleontology, according to Schäfer, can be of use to man in so far as "he can see himself as part of this organic world, of its environments and of its historicity, with which man is inescapably intertwined and show respect to this earth with all it living creatures. . . . What paleontology can tell him hits the center of all problems of our present world."

BIBLIOGRAPHY

I. ORIGINAL WORKS. Schäfer's works include "Bau, Entwicklung and Farbentstehung bei den Flitterzellen von *Sepia officinalis*," in *Z. Zellforsch. u. microskop. Anatomie*, **27** (1937), 221–245; "Fossile und rezente Bohrmuschel-Besiedlung des Jadegebietes," in *Senckenbergiana*, **21** (1939), 227–254; "Zum Untergang der Oberahneschen Felder im Jadebusen," *ibid.*, **25** (1948), 1–15; *Das wissenschaftliche Tierbild* (Frankfurt, 1949; 2nd enl. ed. 1951); "25 Jahre Forschungsanstalt für Meeresgeologie und Meeresbiologie 'Senckenberg' in Wilhelmshaven," in *Natur. u. Volk*, **83** (1953), 245–254; "Form und Funktion der Brachyuren-Schere," *Abhandlungen der Senckenbergischen naturforschenden Gesellschaft*, no. 489 (1954), 1–65; "Mellum: Inselentwicklung und Biotopwandel," in *Abh. naturwiss. Ver. Bremen*, **33** (1954), 391–406; "Fossilisations-Bedingungen der Meeressäuger

und Vögel," in *Senckenbergiana leth.*, **37** (1955), 1–25; "Gesteinsbildung im Flachseebecken, am Beispiel der Jade," in *Geologische Rundschau*, **45** (1956), 71–84; "Der kritische Raum und die kritische Situation in der tierischen Sozietät," in *Aufsätze u. Reden senckenberg. naturforsch. Ges.*, *Aktuo-paläontologie nach Studien in der Nordsee* (Frankfurt, 1962), also in English as *Ecology and Palaeoecology of Marine Environments*, Irmgard Oertel, trans., and G. Y. Craig, ed. (Chicago, 1972); "Arbeit im Mittelmeer," in *Natur. u. Museum*, **93** (1963), 384–389; "Biozönose und Biofazies in marinen Bereich," *Aufsätze u. Reden senckenberg. naturforsch. Ges.* (1963); "Forschungsanstalt für Meeresgeologie und Meeresbiologie Senckenberg in Wilhelmshaven," in *Senck. leth*, **48** (1967), 191–217; "Sarso, Modell der Biofazies-Sequenzen im Korallenriff-Bereich des Schelfs," in *Senckenbergiana maritima*, v. [1] **50** (1969), 165–188; *Fossilien. Bilder, und Gedanken zur paläontologischen Wissenschaft* (Frankfurt, 1980).

II. SECONDARY LITERATURE. Obituary notices are Emil Kuhn-Schnyder, "Wilhelm Schäfer 1912–1981," in *Paläontologische Zeitschrift*, **56** (1982), 1–4; and Siegfried Rietschel, "In memoriam Wilhelm Schäfer," in *Carolinea*, **40** (1982), 125–126.

HELMUT HÖLDER

SCHAIRER, JOHN FRANK (*b.* Rochester, New York, 13 April 1904; *d.* Point-no-Point, Maryland, 26 September 1970), *physical chemistry, mineralogy.*

Schairer's father, John George Schairer, was a master lithographer who took up farming; his mother, Josephine Marie Frank Schairer, taught school before her marriage. Frank (as he preferred to be called) was the first of seven children and the only son. He married Ruth Naylor on 20 July 1940; they had a son and a daughter.

Schairer attended elementary and high school in Rochester. He entered Yale University in 1921, with a scholarship from the Yale Alumni Association of Rochester, to study chemistry. His interest in mineralogy developed in his sophomore year as a result of an inspiring course in that subject taught by William E. Ford. He organized the Yale Mineralogical Society in 1923 and was elected its first president. Schairer graduated with the B.S. magna cum laude in 1925, and received the M.S. in mineralogy in 1926, by which time he had published five papers in mineralogy.

Schairer's main interest was still chemistry, and his doctoral dissertation was a phase-equilibrium study of the system Na_2SO_4-NaF-NaCl-H_2O at 25° and 35°C; one compound in this system, $Na_{21}(SO_4)_7F_6Cl$, was later found as a mineral at Searles Lake, California, and named schairerite by

W. F. Foshag. Schairer applied to the Geophysical Laboratory of the Carnegie Institution in Washington, D.C., for a one-year fellowship to complete his dissertation work. Arthur L. Day, director of the laboratory, recognized his potential and offered him a staff position effective 1 September 1927, although he had not yet received the doctorate. Schairer accepted, and worked at the Geophysical Laboratory for the rest of his life. He received the Ph.D. in physical chemistry from Yale in 1928.

Day told Schairer that he could do anything he chose to do, but hoped it would have something to do with iron oxides. Schairer took this mandate seriously and joined Norman L. Bowen in studies of iron-bearing silicate systems. They pioneered the iron crucible-nitrogen gas quenching technique for the investigation of solid-liquid phase relations in these systems. Initially they worked on the systems $CaO-FeO-SiO_2$ and $MgO-FeO-SiO_2$, and combined and expanded these investigations to include $CaO-FeO-MgO-SiO_2$ and $CaO-FeO-Al_2O_3-SiO_2$. These systems had wide scientific and technical applications: they elucidated the relationships of the common mineral groups of olivines and pyroxenes and contributed to a better understanding of the role of slags and refractories in metallurgical processes. Schairer and Bowen next extended their investigations to systems containing alkalies—specifically $Na_2O-K_2O-Al_2O_3-SiO_2$—which included the important mineral groups of feldspars and feldspathoids. Their work resulted in the discovery of the low-temperature ternary compositions described by Bowen as "petrogeny's residua system," and in a major contribution to the origin of granitic rocks.

World War II brought a complete reorientation of the work of the Geophysical Laboratory. Schairer was first a consultant and then a special assistant to Division 1 (Ballistics Research) of the National Defense Research Committee (1942–1945); his work led to development of remarkable alloys, ideal for high-pressure, high-temperature research vessels, that were used as gun liners. For his services Schairer was awarded the President's Certificate of Merit (1948) and His Majesty's Medal for Service in the Cause of Freedom (Great Britain, 1948). The alloys so developed proved to be instrumental in the development of high-pressure vessels for research at the Geophysical Laboratory after the war.

By 1946 most of the Geophysical Laboratory's war work had terminated, and Schairer returned to the investigation of silicate systems relevant to rock-forming minerals and processes. He concentrated on four-component systems within $K_2O-Na_2O-MgO-Al_2O_3-SiO_2$. The results elucidated the significance of an invariant point close to the composition of many granites, which could be reached either by the fractionation of basaltic liquids or by the partial melting of common sedimentary rocks. Schairer then returned to investigation of systems related to basalts, specifically those involving the crystallization of pyroxenes, pyroxcnoids, melilites, and feldspathoids. The results had direct application to the origin of both alkaline and tholeiitic basalts. All this work was carried out at one atmosphere of pressure, and was the essential base for further investigations by Schairer's colleagues on the same materials at moderate to high pressures, with and without water as a component, thereby providing critical information about the behavior of minerals in the earth's crust and mantle.

Schairer contributed greatly to his profession by service to scientific societies: Mineralogical Society of America (president, 1943; Roebling medalist, 1963); Geological Society of America (vice president, 1944; Arthur L. Day medalist, 1953); National Academy of Sciences; Geochemical Society (president, 1960); International Association of Volcanology (vice president, 1957–1960); American Geophysical Union (section president, 1956–1959).

BIBLIOGRAPHY

I. ORIGINAL WORKS. Among Schairer's writings are "The Minerals of Connecticut," in *Connecticut Geological and Natural History Survey, Bulletin*, **51** (1931); "The System $MgO-FeO-SiO_2$," in *American Journal of Science*, **229** (1935), 151–217, written with Norman L. Bowen; "The Origin of Igneous Rocks and Their Mineral Constituents," in *Scientific Monthly*, **49** (1939), 142–154; "The Ternary System Pseudowollastonite-Akermanite-Gehlenite," in *American Journal of Science*, **239** (1941), 715–763, written with E. F. Osborn; "Some Aspects of the Melting and Crystallization of Rock-Forming Minerals," in *American Mineralogist*, **29** (1944), 75–91; "The System $K_2O-MgO-Al_2O_3-SiO_2$," in *Journal of the American Ceramic Society*, **37** (1954), 501–533; "Heterogeneous Equilibria and Phase Diagrams," in *Annual Review of Physical Chemistry*, **6** (1955), 45–70; "Melting Relations of the Common Rock-Forming Oxides," in *Journal of the American Ceramic Society*, **40** (1957), 215–235; and "Phase Equilibria at One Atmosphere Related to Tholeiitic and Alkali Basalts," in *Researches in Geochemistry*, **2** (1967), 568–592.

II. SECONDARY LITERATURE. H. S. Yoder, Jr., "Presentation of Roebling Medal to J. Frank Schairer," in *American Mineralogist*, **49** (1964), 454–456, and "Memorial to John Frank Schairer," *ibid.*, **57** (1972), 657–665.

BRIAN MASON

SCHAUDER, JULIUSZ PAWEL (*b.* Lvov, Galicia, Austria-Hungary [now Ukrainian SSR], 21 September 1899; *d.* Lvov, September 1943), *mathematics.*

The son of Samuel Schauder, a Jewish lawyer, Schauder was educated in the Austro-Hungarian school system. In 1917 he was drafted into the Austro-Hungarian army, fought in Italy, and was taken prisoner. He joined the new Polish army in France and after his return to Lvov started his studies at the Jan Kazimierz University.

His university studies brought him into contact with the Polish mathematical school, of which he was to become an integral part. Zygmunt Janiszewski, who had studied in Paris under Henri Poincaré, Henri Lebesgue, and M. Fréchet, played a decisive role in the formation of this school. Schauder received his Ph.D. in 1923 and then worked in insurance and as a secondary-school teacher in Przemyślany. In 1927 he received his *venia legendi*, which entitled him to give courses at the university. In 1928 and 1929 he gave his first course on partial differential equations. He then became an assistant lecturer at the university, and for a time held two jobs, one as an assistant lecturer and one as a teacher in a secondary school. In 1929 he married Emilia Löwenthal, whose grandfather had been expelled from his small Jewish community for being an atheist.

L. E. J. Brouwer published his famous fixed point theorem for finite dimensional spaces in 1911. A fixed point x^* is a point that does not change under a transformation T, that is, for a fixed point we have $T(x^*) = x^*$. Schauder published his fixed point theorem for infinite dimensional spaces (Banach spaces) in 1930, using compactness arguments in the proof. For 1932 and 1933 he was awarded a Rockefeller Fellowship. He spent September 1932 to May 1933 with L. Lichtenstein in Leipzig and the remaining time to September 1933 with Jacques Hadamard in Paris.

With J. Leray he published a paper (1934) considered to be a landmark in topological thinking in connection with partial differential equations. In this paper what is now known as Leray-Schauder degree (a homotopy invariant) is defined. This degree is then used in an ingenious method to prove the existence of solutions to complicated partial differential equations. First the existence of solutions to a simple partial differential equation is proved and then, by deforming this simple partial differential equation in a suitable function space, the existence of solutions to the complicated partial differential equation can be established. Schauder attended conferences at Geneva and Moscow in 1935 and at

Oslo in 1936. At about the same time he tried to get an invitation to Princeton University.

Schauder's last paper was published in 1937. It includes a correction to his 1930 fixed point paper and thus completes the proof of his fixed point theorem. After 1934 his papers are mainly concerned with refining his techniques, for instance, by giving detailed estimates for the norm of the solution function for elliptic partial differential equations. In the context of hyperbolic partial differential equations, R. Courant, K. Friedrichs, and H. Lewy had investigated the connection between the original partial differential equation and discrete approximations suitable for numerical solution. Schauder generalized their approach and used inequalities of the Sobolev type to obtain estimates for hyperbolic partial differential equations. In 1938 he and Leray were awarded the Prix Internationaux de Mathématiques Malaxa.

In 1939 the Red Army entered Lvov. Schauder was made a professor at the university and became a member of the Ukrainian Academy of Sciences. This lasted until the Germans occupied Lvov in June 1941 and began the systematic extermination of Jews. A last desperate plea for help, delivered by a Polish student who escaped to Switzerland, reached the topologist Heinz Hopf. Among other things, Schauder wrote that he had many important new results but no paper to write them on. He implored the Swiss mathematicians to ask the German physicist Werner Heisenberg to intervene with the German authorities so that his life would be spared. The Swiss physicist W. Scherrer wrote a letter to Heisenberg, but to no avail. Schauder died in September 1943. According to one version he was betrayed to the Gestapo, was arrested, and disappeared; according to another (more probable) version he was shot after one of the regular roundups. His wife, Emilia, and his daughter, Eva, were hidden by the Polish underground and lived for a while in the sewers of Warsaw. Eva survived the war in a Catholic nunnery. Emilia surrendered to the police and perished in Majdanek (Lublin) concentration camp. After the war Eva went to live with her father's brother in Italy and became an English teacher.

Schauder's fixed point theorem and his skillful use of function space techniques to analyze elliptic and hyperbolic partial differential equations are contributions of lasting quality. Existence proofs for complicated nonlinear problems using his fixed point theorem have become standard. The topological method developed in the 1934 Leray-Schauder paper, known as the continuation or homotopy method, is now utilized not only to obtain qualitative results but also to solve problems numerically on computers.

BIBLIOGRAPHY

I. Original Works. Schauder's collected works are available in an excellent edition prepared by the Polish Academy of Sciences, *Oeuvres* (Warsaw, 1978). Writings specifically discussed in the article are "Der Fixpunktsatz in Funktionalräumen," in *Studia mathematica*, **2** (1930), 171–180; and "Topologie et équations fonctionelles," in *Annales scientifiques de l'École normale Supérieure*, 3rd ser., **51** (1934), 45–78, written with J. Leray.

II. Secondary Literature. Walter Forster, "J. Schauder: Fragments of a Portrait," and J. Leray, "My Friend Julius Schauder," in Walter Forster, ed., *Numerical Solution of Highly Nonlinear Problems* (Amsterdam, 1980), 417–425 and 427–439; and Kazimierz Kuratowski, *A Half Century of Polish Mathematics*, Andrzej Kirkor, trans. (Oxford, 1980).

WALTER FORSTER

SCHEFFÉ, HENRY (*b*. New York City, 11 April 1907; *d*. Berkeley, California, 5 July 1977), *mathematics, statistics*.

Scheffé was born of German parents living in New York. His father, who had for many years worked as a baker, lost his job during the Depression and was reduced to selling apples at a street corner. The memory of this injustice and of his father's suffering remained with Scheffé throughout his life.

Following some preliminary training and work in engineering, Scheffé studied mathematics at the University of Wisconsin, where he obtained his B.A. in 1931 and his Ph.D. in 1935 with a thesis on differential equations, written under R. E. Langer. After teaching mathematics at Wisconsin (1935–1937), Oregon State University (1937–1939, 1941), and Reed College (1939–1940), he decided to switch from pure mathematics to statistics, and for this purpose in 1941 joined the statistics group assembled by S. S. Wilks at Princeton. As a statistician he taught at Syracuse (1944–1945), U.C.L.A. (1946–1948), and Columbia (1948–1953), and then went to Berkeley as professor of statistics and assistant director of the Statistical Laboratory. Although he soon resigned from his administrative position, he remained in Berkeley until his retirement in 1974. At both Columbia and Berkeley he chaired the statistics department for a number of years.

Scheffé was elected fellow of the Institute of Mathematical Statistics (1944), the American Statistical Association (1952), and the International Statistical Institute (1964). He also served as president of the IMS and vice president of the ASA.

Throughout his life Scheffé enjoyed reading, music (as an adult he learned to play the recorder), and traveling. He was also physically active. At Wisconsin he was an intercollegiate wrestler, and he liked to bicycle, swim, and backpack with his family. (In 1934 he had married Miriam Kott and they had two children, Miriam and Michael.)

As he came to statistics from mathematics, it was natural for Scheffé to become interested in the more mathematical aspects of statistical theory, particularly in optimality properties of statistical procedures. In a series of papers (1942–1955) he supplemented and extended the Neyman-Pearson theory of best similar test, and eventually in joint work with Lehmann developed a general theory containing many of the earlier results as special cases. The central concepts of this approach were those of sufficiency and completeness, which led to a characterization of all similar tests (and all unbiased estimates) when the minimal sufficient statistics are complete.

Scheffé's interest in more applied aspects of statistics grew out of, and was constantly fed by, consulting activities. From 1943 to 1946 he worked as consultant and senior mathematics officer at the Office of Scientific Research and Development under a contract with Princeton University. Later, he became a consultant for Consumers' Union and Standard Oil. Nearly all of Scheffé's research during the second phase of his career, which started in the early 1950's, was concerned with various aspects of linear models, particularly the analysis of variance. By adapting the theory to new situations, he significantly extended its range of applicability. Throughout, this work is characterized by a combination of the mathematical and applied points of view. He insists on clearly defined mathematical models. However, these are not formulated on the basis of mathematical convenience but are carefully grounded in the process generating the obervations.

Perhaps the most important of Scheffé's papers from this period is the 1953 paper in which he develops his *S*-method of simultaneous confidence intervals for all contrasts (and more generally for all estimable functions in a linear subspace of the parameter space), which permits the testing and estimation of contrasts suggested by the data. While this work had forerunners in Tukey's *T*-method (and, though not known to Scheffé at the time, in the much earlier work of H. Working and H. Hotelling [1929]), this was the first general procedure, applicable to all linear models. It is an extremely elegant solution of a fundamental problem of statistical practice. That it is the only solution exhibiting certain desirable symmetry properties was shown by Wijsman (1979).

Among other analysis of variance topics treated in this rigorous yet practice-oriented way are paired comparisons with ordered categorical response (1952), mixed models (1956), experiments on mixtures (1958, 1963), and some aspects of calibration (1973). Of these, the work on mixtures initiated a new methodology, which since then has developed a substantial literature.

Scheffé's research extended into his expository writing. In 1943 he published the first comprehensive review of nonparametric statistics, which laid a foundation for the explosive development of this field during the next two decades. His most influential work, however, was his book *The Analysis of Variance* (1959). Its careful exposition of the different principal models, their analyses, and the performance of the procedures when the model assumptions do not hold is exemplary, and the book continues to be a standard text and reference. Scheffé hoped to revise it after retirement. However, a few weeks after returning to Berkeley from a three-year post-retirement position at the University of Indiana, while still in the midst of the revision, he died as the result of a bicycle accident.

BIBLIOGRAPHY

A complete list of Scheffé's publications is given at the end of the obituary by C. Daniel and E. L. Lehmann in *Annals of Statistics*, **7** (1979), 1149–1161. Optimality of Scheffé's *S*-method was proved by Robert A. Wijsman in "Constructing All Smallest Simultaneous Confidence Sets in a Given Class, with Applications to MANOVA," *ibid.*, 1003–1018. The mixture designs introduced by Scheffé constitute the foundation of the later theory, an account of which is provided by John A. Cornell, *Experiments with Mixtures* (New York, 1981).

ERICH LEHMANN

SCHERRER, PAUL HERMANN (*b.* St. Gall, Switzerland, 3 February 1890; *d.* Zurich, Switzerland, 25 September 1969), *physics, physical chemistry.*

After Scherrer completed the compulsory portion of his education, it was decided that he should have commercial training. He therefore entered the Eidgenössische Handels- und Verkehrsschule in St. Gall. He was soon attracted by the natural sciences, however, and in 1908 entered the Eidgenössische Technische Hochschule (ETH) in Zurich. At first his main field of study was botany, but after a year he changed to mathematics and physics. In 1912 Scherrer decided to become a physicist and went to the University of Königsberg for one semester. The following year he transferred to Göttingen, a famous center of mathematics and physics.

At Göttingen, Scherrer became a promising physicist under the influence of Peter Debye, Woldemar Voigt, and Hermann T. Simon. World War I forced him to interrupt his studies at Göttingen in order to do his military service in Switzerland. In early 1916 Scherrer completed his doctoral dissertation, on the Faraday effect of hydrogen molecules; it was accepted, and he received the doctorate summa cum laude.

Two years later Scherrer became a *Privatdozent* with a *Habilitationsschrift* that dealt with the determination of the size and structure of very small colloidal particles, a subject related to the colloidal research being conducted at Göttingen under the leadership of Richard A. Zsigmondy. But while Zsigmondy and other researchers investigated colloidal particles with the ultramicroscope, Scherrer applied the X-ray method that he had recently developed with Debye. In this way Scherrer contributed greatly to the new science of colloids. Investigating organic colloids with X rays, he was the first to observe the fibrous structure of cellulose and other organic compounds.

Scherrer's most important work was the invention of the X-ray technique for studying the structure of polycrystalline materials. The initiative seems to have come from Debye, who in 1915 proposed to Scherrer that they study diffraction effects of monochromatic X rays. After an unsuccessful attempt using paper and charcoal as scattering substances, Scherrer constructed a new X-ray diffraction device with a cylindrical camera. Using this apparatus, in December 1915 Debye and Scherrer found a series of sharp lines arising from X-ray diffraction in lithium fluoride powder. The result was contrary to Debye's expectations, but Debye and Scherrer soon provided the accepted interpretation: that the lines are due to diffraction from the randomly oriented microcrystals.

In subsequent experiments Debye and Scherrer saw X-ray diffraction effects in fluids. They studied benzene and cyclohexane and showed that the diffraction diagrams yield information about the molecular structure of liquids.

Other collaborative work by Scherrer and Debye dealt with the structure of graphite, diamond, and various ionic crystals. In 1918 they determined what is now called the atomic form factor of lithium fluoride. They argued from the X-ray diffraction diagram that lithium fluoride consists of singly ionized atoms (Li^+F^-), a result not obvious at the time. The Debye-Scherrer method in X-ray analysis soon developed into an important branch of physics and also proved to have industrial applications. A very similar method was independently invented in 1917 by Albert W. Hull, who worked for General Electric.

Debye was appointed professor at the ETH in 1920, and Scherrer followed him a few months later as professor of experimental physics. In 1927, when Debye went to Leipzig, Scherrer became director of the ETH Institute of Physics. First with Debye and later with Wolfgang Pauli (who in 1928 succeeded Debye), Scherrer made ETH a physics center of international reputation. He was professor at ETH until his retirement in 1960. After retiring he lectured regularly at the University of Basel.

In Zurich, Scherrer at first continued his work with X-ray analysis. In 1922 he determined the structure of various complex salts and proved they were in accordance with the ideas of Alfred Werner, which were based on chemical reasoning. Scherrer soon turned to other subjects that he found more promising. In the 1920's he dealt with ferroelectrics, magnetism, piezoelectricity, and other aspects of solid-state physics. When the atomic nucleus became a fashionable subject of study in the late 1920's, Scherrer was quick to start a research program in nuclear physics. Through his dynamic leadership and astute sense of fruitful research areas, ETH became a major center for nuclear and solid-state physics in the 1930's.

Scherrer's contribution to ETH, and to European physics in general, was not limited to his scientific discoveries. He was an excellent organizer and teacher, and devoted much of his time to these activities. One of his talents was his ability to raise funds for science. Scherrer realized that modern experimental physics was big science, and succeeded in attracting money and talent to ETH. After World War II he became interested in nuclear energy. He was active in the foundation of the European Center for Nuclear Research (CERN) and served as president of the Swiss Nuclear Energy Commission.

Scherrer put his stamp on Swiss physics not least through his teaching. He was an enthusiastic teacher with many devoted pupils. His lectures included perfected demonstration experiments and a considerable element of showmanship that made them attractive to nonphysicists.

BIBLIOGRAPHY

I. ORIGINAL WORKS. "Interferenzen an regellos orientierten Teilchen im Röntgenlicht," in *Nachrichten der Kgl. Gesellschaft der Wissenschaften zu Göttingen* (1916), 1–26, written with Peter Debye—also published under the same title in *Physikalische Zeitschrift*, **17** (1916), 277–283, and **18** (1917), 291–301; "Bestimmung der Grösse und der inneren Struktur von Kolloidteilchen mittels Röntgenstrahlen," in *Nachrichten der Kgl. Gesellschaft der Wissenschaften zu Göttingen* (1918), 98–100; "Atombau," in *Physikalische Zeitschrift*, **19** (1918), 474–483, written with Peter Debye; "Bestimmung der von Werner abgeleiteten Struktur anorganischen Verbindungen vermittelst Röntgenstrahlen," in *Zeitschrift für anorganische und allgemeine Chemie*, **121** (1922), 319–320, written with P. Stoll. See also his "Personal Reminiscences," in P. Ewald, ed., *Fifty Years of X-Ray Diffraction* (Utrecht, 1962), 641–646.

II. SECONDARY LITERATURE. Hans Frauenfelder, Oskar Huber, and Peter Stähelin, eds., *Beiträge zur Entwicklung der Physik: Festgabe zum 70. Geburtstag von Professor Paul Scherrer* (Basel, 1960). See also Hans Frauenfelder and Rolf M. Steffen, "Paul Scherrer: Directed Swiss Physics Institute," in *Physics Today*, **23** (January 1970), 129–133; P. Huber, "Prof. Dr. Paul Scherrer (1890–1969)," in *Helvetica physica acta*, **23** (1950), 5–8; and J. Weigle, introduction to the *Festheft* for Scherrer's sixtieth birthday, *ibid.*, **23** (1950), 4–5.

HELGE KRAGH

SCHIFF, LEONARD ISAAC (*b*. Fall River, Massachusetts, 29 March 1915; *d*. Stanford, California, 19 January 1971), *physics*.

Schiff's father, Edward, was a member of a Lithuanian family of rabbinical scholars. His mother, Mathilda Brodsky, also of Lithuanian descent, was a gifted pianist and composer. As a young man Schiff adopted an articulate Christian faith while staying close to his Jewish heritage: his funeral service included a striking reading, chosen by himself, from the New Testament Epistle to the Hebrews.[1] A prodigy, especially in music and mathematics, he was already well versed in calculus upon entering Ohio State University in 1929, at the age of fourteen. There, influenced by L. H. Thomas, with whom he coauthored his first paper, he took up physics. He received his bachelor's degree at eighteen and his master's degree two years later. Despite his youth he was active in student affairs, becoming, among other things, captain of the university shooting team.

After obtaining a Ph.D. from MIT (1937) under P. M. Morse for work on quantum scattering theory, Schiff spent three years at Berkeley with J. Robert Oppenheimer before transferring to the University of Pennsylvania, where he soon shone as teacher, administrator (acting chairman of physics, 1942–1945), and resourceful applied mathematician. After publishing papers on liquid helium and meson theory in nuclei, he did war work on helium purity in blimps, on crystal detectors used in radar, and on automatic control in submarine steering. While at Los Alamos in 1945 he witnessed the "Trinity" bomb test and developed a deep concern for peace. In 1941 he married Frances Ballard; they had a daughter and a son.

In 1947 Schiff joined the small physics department at Stanford University. He became chairman a year later, holding that position through eighteen turbulent years that brought W. W. Hansen's linear electron accelerator, Robert Hofstadter's pioneering work on nuclear form factors, construction of the two-mile-long Stanford Linear Accelerator Center, and much else. He also established himself as one of the most powerful figures in the university, becoming chairman of the Advisory Board and in 1968, at the time of maximum student unrest, first chairman of the newly formed Faculty Senate. That with these activities and service on national committees he could maintain a research career is a tribute to Schiff's rapidity of mind and intensely disciplined work habits. He died of a congenital heart defect, known to himself but hidden from colleagues, while on his way to a medical checkup prior to possible surgery.

Schiff's main achievements were his textbook *Quantum Mechanics* (1949) and his researches on scattering theory and general relativity. His penchant was for rapid and relevant calculation rather than deep probing of concepts. His book tells his quality. Workmanlike, with none of the elegant profundity of Dirac's treatise or the cluttered insights of Wigner's, it was nevertheless a landmark text from which generations of graduate students learned how to *do* quantum mechanics. The second (1955), and still more the third (1968), edition carried useful improvements.

The Stanford Mark III linear accelerator, first operated in 1951, gave collimated pulses of fast electrons, with beam currents of 10^{11}–10^{12} electrons/pulse and energies initially of 180 MeV, rising to 600 and then 900 MeV. Schiff was the ideal theoretical adviser, and in 1949, when the accelerator team was devastated by Hansen's early death, he wrote a masterly report,[2] still unpublished, on uses of the machine. One use concerned charge distributions in nuclei. Electrons energetic enough to have de Broglie wavelengths comparable with nuclear diameters could explore these distributions "much as lower energy electrons are now used to explore charge distributions in molecules and crystals by the technique of electron diffraction." Appropriate

energies were 100 MeV or higher, and although some data at 15.7 MeV were obtained earlier at Illinois, the Stanford machine stood alone. In 1951 Hofstadter, a friend and co-worker of Schiff's from the University of Pennsylvania, came to Stanford to lead a brilliant investigation establishing that nuclei, far from having sharp boundaries, comprise a uniform core surrounded by a region of progressively decreasing proton density. Parallel studies, also foreseen in Schiff's report, included electron scattering from protons, neutrons, and deuterons.

In this field, theory and experiment went hand in hand. Much was done elsewhere, notably by L. R. B. Elton in London and H. Feshbach at MIT, but Schiff built the dominant theory group. With M. R. Rosenbluth, D. R. Yennie, D. G. Ravenhall, V. Z. Jankus, and others he established methods of exact phase-shift analysis, multipole expansion in inelastic scattering, dispersion corrections, the use of "charge" and "magnetic" form factors—to name but a few—basic to nuclear theory. For this achievement Schiff has hardly received due credit. Colleagues' work never bore his name; only the warmth of acknowledgments tells his influence.

With Oppenheimer, Schiff in 1939 had learned general relativity to analyze a curious paradox about charge and rotation in electromagnetic theory. Not until 1958 did he return to a kindred topic: the mysterious absence of antimatter from the known universe. One proposal had been that matter and antimatter repel each other gravitationally. Schiff produced a startling counterargument. According to quantum electrodynamics, there are, even in ordinary matter, *virtual* electron-positron pairs associated with vacuum polarization. If matter also repels virtual antimatter, then gravitational and inertial mass will differ—by far more than experiment allows.

Next came experimental relativity. Of Einstein's three "classical" tests, one, the red shift, was known to have very limited significance; Schiff, in a pedagogical article of 1960,[3] went on to challenge the famous starlight deflection test. Although general relativity gives twice the Newtonian deflection (as experiment requires), it does so because of a special relativistic effect that Einstein had overlooked. Angry refutations[4] followed this claim, but so did many new ideas: "Schiff's conjecture" about metric theories of gravity and the equivalence principle,[5] the Dicke and "parameterized post-Newtonian" frameworks for gravitational theories,[6] and—not least—the gyroscope experiment.

In November 1959, a month after writing that article, Schiff, whose war work had made him familiar with gyroscope technology, began pondering the scientific applications of gyroscopes. After ideas about Mach's principle and a clock experiment, he hit upon[7] two phenomena in general relativity affecting gyroscopes in Earth orbit: a 6.6 arc-seconds/year *geodetic* precession, from the gyroscope's motion through curved space-time, and, even more profound, a 0.043 arc-second/year *frame-dragging* precession from Earth's rotation. Discussions with W. M. Fairbank and R. H. Cannon, joined in 1962 by the present writer, indicated that an experiment, though very difficult, might be feasible; in 1964 NASA began funding its development. Meanwhile, Schiff steadily widened his interests and at his death was in process of setting up a new group in relativistic astrophysics.

Schiff was a very good physicist, but he was greater as a human being than as a physicist. His touch appears in a colleague's remark: "I always thought I had a special relationship with Schiff until I discovered that everyone else did too."[8] The phrase "gentle strength" used by some is a misreading, however. His meticulous efficiency intimidated some people, and he could see through sham. He combined, most unusually, kindness, intellectual penetration, and moral force, and it was this last quality that made him so influential.

NOTES

1. Portions of Hebrews 11: 1–32 (personal recollection).
2. "Survey of Possible Experiments with Linear Electron Accelerators," [Stanford] Microwave Laboratory Report no. 102 (November 1949). Schiff, whose interest in accelerator design went back to 1938—see "On the Path of Ions in the Cyclotron," in *Physical Review*, **54** (1938), 1114–1115—had earlier collaborated with Hansen in several reports on resonant cavity theory.
3. "On Experimental Tests of the General Theory of Relativity," in *American Journal of Physics*, **28** (1960), 340–343. A similar claim had been advanced by W. Lenz in 1944; see *Arnold Sommerfeld, Lectures on Theoretical Physics*, III, *Electrodynamics* (New York, 1952), 313–314, esp. 313.
4. The principal references are supplied by C. W. F. Everitt, "The Stanford Relativity Gyroscope Experiment" (see below), 598–599, 636.
5. The Schiff conjecture, as usually stated, is that any theory of gravitation consistent with special relativity and the equivalence principle must be a "metric" theory. Schiff propounded it, in rather different form, in a concise and sharply worded footnote to his *American Journal of Physics* article (p. 343), responding to a critique by Robert H. Dicke—*American Journal of Physics*, **28** (1960), 344–347—who argued that Einstein's red shift formula does not automatically follow from equivalence and special relativity. For later treatments, see Clifford M. Will, *Theory and Experiment in Gravitational Physics* (Cambridge, 1981), 38–45, 50–53.
6. The "Dicke framework" was first spelled out in Appendix IV of Dicke's Les Houches lectures, "Experimental Relativity," in Cécile M. DeWitt and Bryce S. DeWitt, eds., *Relativity, Groups and Topology* (New York, 1964), 165–313.

The PPN framework, first sketched by Arthur S. Eddington in *The Mathematical Theory of Relativity* (Cambridge, 1923), 105, was revived by H. P. Robertson and Schiff and then systematically developed from 1968 on by K. Nordtvedt, C. M. Will, and K. S. Thorne. Nordtvedt tells me that his ideas evolved in part from discussions with Schiff between 1961 and 1963.

7. "Possible New Experimental Test of General Relativity Theory," in *Physical Review Letters*, **4** (1960), 215–217. For a conjectural retracing of Schiff's path to the gyroscope experiment, see C. W. F. Everitt, "The Stanford Relativity Gyroscope Experiment" (below), 590–595.
8. Dr. G. Henry to the writer. For similar comments by others, see William M. Fairbank in *Tributes* (below).

BIBLIOGRAPHY

I. ORIGINAL WORKS. Felix Bloch's memoir (see below) lists 2 books, 91 research papers, and 58 other articles, reviews, or conference reports. *Quantum Mechanics* appeared in three editions (New York, 1949, 1955, 1968); a fourth, with A. L. Fetter, is in preparation. The first edition was translated into Italian—*Meccanica quantistica*, L. Radicati di Brozolo, trans. (Turin, 1951)—the second, into Japanese (2 vols., Kyoto, 1957–1958) and Russian (Moscow, 1959). *Nucleon Structure* (Stanford, Calif., 1964), edited with Robert Hofstadter, is the proceedings of the International Conference on Nucleon Structure held at Stanford University, 24–27 June 1963.

Schiff's scientific and administrative papers are in the Stanford University archives; some personal material remains in Mrs. Schiff's possession.

II. SECONDARY LITERATURE. There is an obituary by Felix Bloch and J. D. Walecka in *Physics Today*, **24** (July 1971), 54–55; and a memoir by Bloch in *Biographical Memoirs. National Academy of Sciences*, **54** (1983), 301–323. The latter's version of the history of the Stanford physics department should be taken *cum grano salis*; a partial corrective is P. Galison, B. Hevly, and R. Lowen, "Controlling the Monster: Stanford and the Growth of Physics Research 1935–1962," in P. Galison and B. Hevly, eds., *Big Science: The Growth of Large Scale Research* (Stanford, Calif., in preparation). Personal impressions of Schiff by R. M. Brown, F. Bloch, R. Hofstadter, W. Stegner, B. D. Napier, and W. M. Fairbank appear in *Tributes to Leonard Isaac Schiff 1915–1971* (produced at Stanford in 1971 without editorial ascription or publication details). A sharp vignette by R. H. Cannon is in J. Fincher, "The Methusaleh Project," *Air & Space*, **1** (February/March, 1987), 96–98.

On nuclear scattering, see the reprint collection edited by Robert Hofstadter, *Electron Scattering and Nuclear and Nucleon Structure* (New York, 1963), which omits Schiff's paper "Interpretation of Electron Scattering Experiments," in *Physical Review*, **92** (1953), 988–993, published back to back with Hofstadter, Fechter, and McIntyre's first major experimental paper. Lewis R. B. Elton, *Nuclear Sizes* (London, 1961), may also be consulted.

On gravitational theory, see C. W. F. Everitt, "The Stanford Relativity Gyroscope Experiment (A): History and Overview," in J. D. Fairbank, B. S. Deaver, C. W. F. Everitt, and P. Michelson, eds., *Near Zero: New Frontiers of Physics* (New York, 1988), 587–639.

C. W. F. EVERITT

SCHMIDT, KARL PATTERSON (*b.* Lake Forest, Illinois, 19 June 1890; *d.* Chicago, Illinois, 26 September 1957), *herpetology*.

Schmidt was the paradigm of the modern naturalist. He was a superior observer, with a tremendous depth of knowledge of nature, and a deep interest in ecology, systematics, behavior, and biogeography. His greatest contributions to biology were the impact he had on numerous younger biologists and his willingness to serve science as editor (of five journals or serials), as officer of societies, as translator of German books, and as curator of museum collections. As one biographer wrote, "He made no important discoveries, expounded no important new theories, organized no school of thought and directed no vast enterprises." Nevertheless, Schmidt infected everyone he met with his enthusiasm and his common sense. Anything he published was thoroughly sound. More than anyone else, he turned herpetology, previously largely a hobby, into a branch of scientific biology.

Schmidt's father, George Washington Schmidt, was professor of German language and literature at Lake Forest College. Karl was the oldest of four children, and had all the personality traits of a firstborn. His mother, Margaret Patterson Schmidt, of Scottish descent, played a decisive role in forming his interests through her own active studies of nature, particularly botany. This was reinforced by three summers camping with his father in northern Wisconsin, and above all by six years he spent on a farm in Wisconsin after completing his freshman year at Lake Forest College. Schmidt had been a brilliant student, always at the head of the class, and turned to farming in 1907 only so that the family could live on a farm and the father could continue to teach until the farm could support them all. In his six farming years Schmidt took correspondence courses through the University of California and read voraciously.

At the age of twenty-three, Schmidt left the farm and in 1913 entered Cornell University as a sophomore. Here, living at the home of entomologist James G. Needham (who had been his biology teacher at Lake Forest College), he had more contact with graduate students and faculty than with undergraduates. While he was still undecided about his future, a chance meeting with herpetologist Mary

C. Dickerson led to an assistantship at the American Museum of National History in New York, where Schmidt worked for the next six years in the department of herpetology, first under Dickerson and then under G. K. Noble. Two major monographs on the reptiles of the Belgian Congo, prepared during this period, established his reputation as a herpetologist. It also awakened his interest in zoogeography, a subject to which he contributed many publications throughout his life. In 1919 Schmidt married Margaret Wightman; they had two sons.

In 1922 Schmidt took charge of the newly established Division of Amphibians and Reptiles at the Field Museum of Natural History in Chicago, and over the next twenty years, without assistants or clerical help, he built it into one of the foremost herpetological departments in the world. He became chief curator of zoology in 1941 and curator emeritus in 1955. While at the Field Museum, Schmidt took part in numerous expeditions to the Caribbean, Central and South America, New Zealand, and Israel, always returning with rich collections that usually covered all branches of natural history.

Schmidt received many honors. He was president of the American Society of Ichthyologists and Herpetologists from 1942 to 1946, and president of the Society for the Study of Evolution in 1954. In 1956 he was elected to the National Academy of Sciences. In 1952 Earlham College awarded him an honorary D.Sc., and in 1955 a volume of scientific papers by many of his associates was published in honor of his sixty-fifth birthday. In 1953 Schmidt led the American delegation to the Thirteenth International Congress of Zoology at Copenhagen that fought for common sense and stability in zoological nomenclature. Several of the subsequent improvements in the Code of Nomenclature were due to his influence.

Schmidt was a great lover of books and during his career acquired an extensive herpetological library. A one-year stay in Germany, when he was six years old, gave him a perfect command of German, and later in life he was indefatigable in translating important German works into English. Some of these translations were subsequently published, such as Richard Hesse's *Tiergeographie auf oekologischer Grundlage* and Willy Hennig's *Grundzüge einer Theorie der phylogenetischen Systematik* (with Rainer Zangerl); works by Hans Böker, Max Weber, and Adolf Portmann were made available to his associates in manuscript.

As a taxonomist Schmidt was very much a representative of the new systematics. More important, he was one of the taxonomists responsible for the rapprochement of systematics and general biology. In 1943 he was appointed lecturer in zoology at the University of Chicago, and in the ensuing years he collaborated with four of the professors of that university in writing *Principles of Animal Ecology* (1949). His extensive knowledge of the literature and his coverage of the geographical aspects were particularly valuable in this enterprise. Owing to his vast knowledge of the literature, Schmidt was preadapted to become a historian of herpetology (1955). He was very much interested in broadening the general interest in natural history, and he wrote two popular books on animals. To his closest friends he was known as a poet of no mean ability.

With his genial optimism, his keen sense of humor, and his willingness to place the common welfare over his personal interests, Schmidt was a much-sought-after member of boards and committees. Owing to his many-sided services and lack of time, he accumulated a considerable number of large, unfinished manuscripts. These he hoped to complete after his retirement. Unfortunately, he died only two years later, of snake poisoning, after being bitten by a South African boomslang he was attempting to identify for a zoo.

Schmidt was always ready to write a scientific report on reptiles and amphibians brought back by expeditions to the West Indies, Mexico, Central America, Arabia, the Sudan, any country in South America, New Guinea, islands in the Pacific, China, Iran, Sinai, or Southeast Asia. He was not a regional specialist but knew reptiles and amphibians from every area in the world. His major contribution to herpetology was the geographical and ecological slant he gave to his papers on the variation and distribution of reptiles and amphibians. This rather new approach had a lasting influence on the field.

BIBLIOGRAPHY

I. ORIGINAL WORKS. Schmidt's bibliography (compiled by Robert F. Inger but not yet published) has nearly 200 titles. Major publications are "Contributions to the Herpetology of the Belgian Congo . . . ," in *Bulletin of the American Museum of Natural History*, **39** (1919), 385–624, and **49** (1923), 1–146; *Amphibians and Land Reptiles of Puerto Rico, with a List of Those Reported from the Virgin Islands*, which is *New York Academy of Sciences Scientific Survey of Puerto Rico and the Virgin Islands*, X, pt. 1 (New York, 1928); "The Amphibians and Reptiles of British Honduras," in *Field Museum of Natural History Publication* no. 512, zoological ser., **22** (1941), 475–510; *A Check List of North American Amphibians and Reptiles*, 6th ed. (Chicago, 1953); "Faunal Realms, Regions, and Provinces," in *Quarterly Review of Biology*, **29** (1954), 322–331; *Ecological Animal Geography* (New York, 1937), an authorized, rewritten ed. based on Richard Hesse's *Tiergeographie auf oekologischer Grundlage*, with W. C. Allee; *Field Book of Snakes of the United States and Canada* (New York, 1941), written with D. Dwight Davis; *Principles of Animal Ecology* (Philadelphia, 1949), written with W. C. Allee, Alfred E. Emerson, Orlando Park, and Thomas Park; "Herpetology," in *A Century of Progress in the Natural Sciences 1853–1953* (1955), 591–627; and *Amphibia* (1959), written with Robert F. Inger.

II. SECONDARY LITERATURE. There is an obituary by D. Dwight Davis in *Copeia* (1959), no. 3, 189–192. *Fieldiana*, zoology ser., no. 37 (1955), is the Karl Patterson Schmidt anniversary volume.

ERNST MAYR

SCHMIEDEBERG, (JOHANN ERNST) OSWALD

(*b.* Laidsen, Russia, 10 October 1838; *d.* Baden-Baden, Germany, 12 July 1921), *pharmacology.*

Schmiedeberg was the son of a forester in the German Baltic province of Kurland (which later became a part of Latvia). He attended school in Dorpat (now Tartu, Estonian S.S.R.), an old Germanic town in the province of Livonia (later part of Estonia), and received a medical degree from the University of Dorpat, then an imperial Russian university at which the largely German faculty taught their courses in the German language.

Rudolf Buchheim, who founded the first institute of experimental pharmacology in 1847, had a profound influence on Schmiedeberg, who worked in his institute in 1866 while completing a dissertation dealing with the measurement of chloroform in blood. He continued his studies with Buchheim and two years later was appointed assistant professor in pharmacology.

Buchheim was a pioneer in a science that was not considered important by the medical profession and received little attention in the major European medical schools for many years. In 1869, when offered a professorship in pharmacology at the University of Giessen, he accepted but was hampered in developing his discipline. He left the University of Giessen in 1871 and died, disillusioned, in 1879. When he left Dorpat, Schmiedeberg was appointed to his chair.

Schmiedeberg took a year's leave in 1871 to work in Carl Ludwig's institute of physiology at Leipzig, where he sharpened his skills in medical research and made contacts with colleagues who would have important roles in future physiological investigations. While there, his study on the effect of poisons on the frog's heart greatly impressed Ludwig, who recommended Schmiedeberg for a chair at the University of Strassburg in 1872. The Germans, who had taken the city in the Franco-Prussian War, were anxious to develop an important medical school there; they brought together a distinguished faculty, including Bernhard Naunyn, von Mehring, and Oscar Minkowski in internal medicine, and Felix HoppeSeyler and Franz Hofmeister in physiological chemistry.

Almost single-handedly Schmiedeberg developed the discipline of pharmacology in a medical environment that questioned its importance. This was accomplished by a combination of significant research, effective writing, and a classroom presence that gave the subject lasting importance. Also, he had the good fortune to be placed in a university setting where the German government sought to encourage excellence.

Early in his tenure at Strassburg, the authorities decided that Schmiedeberg would have an institute of pharmacology near the medical center. The building, which was opened in 1887, was carefully planned by Schmiedeberg and provided laboratories for animal experimentation and chemical studies as well as offices, an auditorium, and a library. This institute attracted able young scientists who became the foundation of the new profession. More than 150 pharmacologists were educated by Schmiedeberg, including more than thirty from countries outside Germany. His outstanding students included John J. Abel, Max Cloëtta, Arthur R. Cushny, Hans H. Meyer, and Torald H. Sollmann, all of whom had an important role in training the next generation of pharmacologists.

Schmiedeberg's research was broad-ranging and at times dealt with purely biochemical problems. In his early years at Strassburg he demonstrated that benzoic acid is converted to hippuric acid by reaction with glycine in blood-perfused kidneys. His laboratory also demonstrated the conversion of ammonium carbonate to urea and studied the conditions under which this occurred. It was shown that acids administered to animals were neutralized by the physiological formation of ammonia but that such ammonia formation is limited in humans, a situation that leads to acidosis when the beta-hydroxybutyric acid formed in diabetics remains unneutralized.

Research on the effects of alcohol convinced Schmiedeberg that alcohol is a depressant of the central nervous system, acting on the highest centers first and finally dulling the medullary centers.

In his work on carbamic acid esters, Schmiedeberg studied the relation between chemical structure and narcotic influence. He studied the clinical action of amylene hydrate, paraldehyde, urethane, and various hypnotically active urea derivatives.

Schmiedeberg's laboratory isolated muscarine from *Amanita muscaria* and studied the nature of its physiological action. He was particularly interested in the action of chemical substances on the heart and in the pharmacological behavior of the autonomic nervous system. The staff of his institute experimentally explored the pharmacological action of the most important drugs and toxins encountered in the medicine of the time. These studies included the effect of nicotine on the heart, the physiological action of digitalis glycosides, and the toxic effects of heavy metals in organic combinations. Other work included studies on cartilaginous tissues and mucoid substances; the isolation of glucuronic acid from cartilage in the form of chondrosine; the relation of hyaluronic acid to chondroitin sulfate and collagen; and chemical studies on mucoproteins and mucopolysaccharides.

As a teacher, Schmiedeberg was at his best on a one-to-one basis in the laboratory. He was patient with beginners and enjoyed introducing them to the art of research, particularly the importance of experimental design and execution of experiments. In the lecture hall he was well organized but inclined to be authoritarian.

As a writer, Schmiedeberg was talented in the presentation of factual material and using it to reason out conclusions in rigorous fashion. His experimental studies were reported in more than two hundred papers, and his textbook was a formative one for the discipline. With Bernard Naunyn and Edwin Klebs he founded *Archiv für experimentalle Pathologie und Pharmakologie* soon after joining the Strassburg faculty. He and Naunyn continued to edit the *Archiv* for the remainder of their lives.

Schmiedeberg, who never married, remained active at his institute until late 1918, when the French took possession of the city and university. He left the university, moving across the Rhine to Baden-Baden, where he lived near Naunyn. He was in declining health for the rest of his life.

BIBLIOGRAPHY

I. ORIGINAL WORKS. Most of Schmiedeberg's research papers were published in *Archiv für experimentelle Pathologie und Pharmakologie*. The Schmiedeberg festschrift, a supplement to *Archiv*, contains a list of publications up to 1908. The list is updated by Hans H. Meyer in *Archiv*, **92** (1922), i–xvii; see also Poggendorff, III, 1202; IV, 1340; VI, 2346; and VIIA, supp., 592. His textbook, *Grundriss der Artzneimittellehre* (Leipzig, 1883), was retitled *Grundriss der Pharmakologie* from the 4th ed. on, and was translated by Thomas Dixson as *Elements of Pharmacology* (Edinburgh, 1887).

II. SECONDARY LITERATURE. Obituaries are Hans H. Meyer, in *Archiv für experimentelle Pathologie und Pharmakologie*, **92** (1922), i–xvii, and in *Naturwissenschaften*, **10** (1922), 105–107; Bernard Naunyn, in *Archiv für experimentelle Pathologie und Pharmakologie*, **90** (1921), i–vii; and *Lancet* (1921), 722. Analytical pieces dealing with his pharmacological work are Ernst R. Habermann, "Rudolf Buchheim and the Beginning of Pharmacology as a Science," in *Annual Review of Pharmacology*, **14** (1974), 1–8; Jan Koch-Weser and Paul J. Schechter, "Schmiedeberg in Strassburg 1872–1918," in *Life Sciences*, **22** (1978), 1361–1377; and Gustav Kuschinsky, "The Influence of Dorpat on the Emergence of Pharmacology as a Distinct Science," in *Journal of the History of Medicine and Allied Sciences*, **23** (1968), 258–271.

AARON J. IHDE

SCHOENHEIMER, RUDOLF (*b*. Berlin, Germany, 10 May 1898; *d*. Yonkers, New York, 11 September 1941), *biochemistry*.

The son of Hugo Schoenheimer, a physician, and of Gertrud Edel Schoenheimer, Rudolf attended school in Berlin and graduated from the Dorotheenstädtische Gymnasium in 1916. He was then drafted into the army and served in the artillery on the western front until the end of World War I. This traumatic experience affected his view of himself and of the world around him, and his forced emigration upon Hitler's rise to power further deepened his despair.

Upon returning from the war, Schoenheimer studied medicine at the University of Berlin and received his degree in 1922; his M.D. dissertation (dated 1923) was entitled "Über die experimentelle Cholesterinkrankheit der Kaninchen." He then spent a year as a pathologist at the Moabit Hospital in Berlin, where he continued research on sterol metabolism, with special reference to the production of atherosclerosis in experimental animals by the administration of cholesterol. He also worked briefly in the laboratory of Peter Rona at the Berlin Municipal Hospital am Urban. In 1924, Schoenheimer took advantage of the establishment by Karl Thomas,[1] professor of physiological chemistry at Leipzig, of a postgraduate program for young physicians who wished to improve their knowledge of chemistry. This program was supported through fellowships funded by the Rockefeller Foundation. Schoenheimer was one of the recipients.

An important component of the program was synthetic organic chemistry, in which Schoenheimer showed exceptional aptitude through a contribution to the methodology of peptide synthesis. The work of Emil Fischer from 1903 to 1909 had led to the synthesis of many peptides, but his halogen acyl halide coupling method had serious limitations. There was a recognized need for a method in which an amino-terminal blocking group could be selectively removed from a peptide by a nonhydrolytic process so as not to cleave the newly formed peptide bonds. Schoenheimer proposed such a procedure. In 1915, Max Bergmann, working in Fischer's laboratory, had found that *p*-toluenesulfonylamino acids (tosylamino acids) can be detosylated selectively by reduction with a mixture of hydriodic acid and phosphonium iodide. In 1926 Schoenheimer made several free peptides in this manner by using the azide coupling method, introduced by Theodor Curtius. Schoenheimer's procedure was superseded by the important carbobenzoxy method[2] introduced in 1932 by Bergmann and Leonidas Zervas, but the subsequent use of sodium in liquid ammonia to reduce tosylamino groups greatly enhanced the practicability of Schoenheimer's idea. In his later work, which involved the synthesis of organic compounds labeled with isotopes, Schoenheimer repeatedly demonstrated his excellent knowledge of synthetic organic chemistry.

Schoenheimer's work on sterol metabolism and especially on atherosclerosis brought him to the attention of Ludwig Aschoff, professor of pathological anatomy at Freiburg im Breisgau. A distinguished contributor to the study of many aspects of human pathology, Aschoff was particularly interested in atherosclerosis and abnormalities of the gall bladder, in which he had observed the deposition of cholesterol and its esters. In 1926, Aschoff invited Schoenheimer to become the chemist at his institute. This appointment was a significant one in Schoenheimer's scientific career. With Aschoff's encouragement, he energetically investigated several aspects of sterol metabolism by the use of chemical methods and those of experimental surgery. Among his many important results was the demonstration that cholestanol (dihydrocholesterol) is formed from cholesterol in animal tissues, thus disproving the then-current view that the conversion of dietary cholesterol occurs only by bacterial action in the intestinal tract.

Schoenheimer also extended the scope of his M.D. dissertation by examining the extent of atherosclerosis in rabbits after the administration of various sterols. He found that the absorption of cholesterol from the intestinal tract proceeds by way of the lymphatic channels and that other sterols (sitosterol, ergosterol) are not absorbed at all. Some of these studies formed the subject of his *Habilitationsschrift*, "Chemische und experimentelle Untersuchungen über die Athersklerose" (Freiburg, 1928), which gained him the title *Privatdozent*. Moreover, shortly before his forced departure from Germany, Schoenheimer made a particularly significant contribution by showing that mice are able to synthesize and degrade cholesterol in their tissues.

In 1930 Schoenheimer was called upon by Siegfried Thannhauser, recently appointed professor of medicine at Freiburg, for advice about a patient with high blood cholesterol who had been referred to him by a Chicago clinic. As a consequence Schoenheimer was invited to visit the University of Chicago as Douglas Smith Fellow in the department of surgery. During his year in the United States, he drew the interest of Ludwig Kast, president of the Josiah Macy, Jr., Foundation, which began to support Schoenheimer's research at Freiburg. Upon his return there in 1931, he was made titular head of the chemical division of Aschoff's institute. On 27 October 1932, Schoenheimer married Salome Glücksohn, an embryologist; they had no children.

Upon being obliged to leave Germany, Schoenheimer returned to the United States, where in 1933 he received a research appointment in the department of biological chemistry of the College of Physicians and Surgeons at Columbia University. His salary and research support came from the Macy Foundation. He was subsequently made assistant professor; at the time of his death he held the rank of associate professor. The head of the department was Hans Thatcher Clarke,[3] an organic chemist who had been associated with the Eastman Kodak Company for many years before his appointment at the College of Physicians and Surgeons in 1928. A man of generous tolerance and modest scientific ambition, Clarke encouraged his departmental colleagues to develop their own research programs and put his extensive knowledge of organic chemistry at the disposal of everyone who sought his help. He transformed the scientific atmosphere of his department by welcoming to its faculty, as regular or adjunct members, able young chemists and biochemists who had been trained in Germany or Austria.

Schoenheimer had been preceded by Oskar Wintersteiner and Erwin Brand; between 1933 and 1945, Erwin Chargaff, Zacharias Dische, Karl Meyer, and Heinrich Waelsch were added. As a consequence of the achievements of these men and their American students, by the 1940's Clarke's department had become one of the leading centers of biochemical research. Schoenheimer's contribution to this development cannot be overestimated.

At Columbia, Schoenheimer continued his work on sterol metabolism and completed a study begun at Freiburg on the occurrence, in the animal body, of cetyl alcohol [$CH_3(CH_2)_{14}CH_2OH$]. During 1934 and 1935 he published a series of short papers on sterol chemistry and metabolism, and (with Warren M. Sperry) developed a valuable micromethod for the determination of free and combined blood cholesterol. By the end of 1934, however, he was engaged in the isotope studies for which he became famous.

Shortly after his return to the United States, Schoenheimer learned of the discovery of deuterium, the stable hydrogen isotope of mass 2, by Harold Urey of the department of chemistry at Columbia. Urey expressed interest in the use of deuterium in biological studies, and a program was established with the aid of the Rockefeller Foundation to promote such efforts in several Columbia departments.[4] Among them was that of Clarke, who was placed in charge; David Rittenberg, one of Urey's former graduate students, joined Clarke's staff in the latter part of 1934.

The circumstances that led to Schoenheimer's entry into the isotope program are uncertain, and the question has been raised whether he fully appreciated the potential of the isotope-labeling method for metabolic studies before Rittenberg's arrival at the College of Physicians and Surgeons.[5] That Schoenheimer had been introduced to the use of isotopes for biological studies before coming to Columbia is evident from the account by György (George) Hevesy of his association with Schoenheimer at Freiburg, where Hevesy had been professor of physical chemistry from 1926 to 1934.[6] Moreover, unlike Rittenberg, Schoenheimer was thoroughly steeped in the German biochemical tradition, and was familiar with the work of Franz Knoop in 1903 on the use of phenyl-labeled fatty acids for the study of their metabolic degradation.

To this should be added the fact that, as shown by his peptide work, Schoenheimer was a skilled organic chemist (which Rittenberg was not) and could readily see how organic substances needed for metabolic studies might be labeled with deuterium. All these factors must be considered in relation to the origin of Schoenheimer's insight into the problem. In my view, his mind was prepared, and he seized the opportunity to use deuterium as a label in metabolic studies when it was made available to him. Indeed, it may be that no other scientist then at Columbia, including Urey, Clarke, or Rittenberg, was so uniquely ready to do so.

The first papers from Schoenheimer's laboratory on the isotope technique appeared in 1935. They described the methodology for generating deuterium gas from the "heavy" water supplied by Urey, for the catalytic hydrogenation of unsaturated compounds with deuterium, and for the purification of the water obtained by the combustion of organic material for deuterium analysis; these methods were considerably improved a few years later.

The first papers also described exploratory experiments on the metabolism of fatty acids and sterols. The most important initial finding was that when mice were fed linseed oil that had been partially hydrogenated with deuterium, the isotope appeared in the depot fats, whose amount had remained constant. This result indicated that the depot fats are not inert storage materials, mobilized only at times of starvation, but that they are involved in continuous metabolic processes.

The further study of fatty acid metabolism by means of the isotope technique, reported in subsequent papers, showed that some fatty acids are reversibly saturated and desaturated, and also undergo stepwise degradation in accord with Knoop's β-oxidation theory. Of particular importance (and elegance) were experiments by Schoenheimer's Ph.D. student DeWitt Stetten, Jr., reported in 1940. Rats were fed deuterium-labeled palmitic acid $[CH_3(CH_2)_{14}COOH]$, and several fatty acids were isolated from the fat tissues. Not only was the palmitic acid found to be heavily labeled, but so were its higher homologue stearic acid $[CH_3(CH_2)_{16}COOH]$ and its monounsaturated C_{16} derivative palmitoleic acid. The finding that the doubly unsaturated derivative linoleic acid was not labeled was in accord with its known requirement in the animal diet. Moreover, the C_{16} compound cetyl alcohol (mentioned above), obtained from the feces, also contained considerable isotope.

Another important set of experiments on the metabolism of fatty acids, reported in 1937 by Rittenberg and Schoenheimer, involved the injection of heavy water into groups of mice, whose drinking water also was labeled so as to maintain the deuterium content of the body fluids at a constant level. At various times some of the mice were killed, and the deuterium content of their fatty acids was determined. It rose steadily until a plateau was reached. From the rate at which the isotope was taken up, it could be estimated that the half-life of the fatty acids was five to nine days.

During the course of the experiments just mentioned, the body cholesterol was also isolated; its isotope content increased steadily, and a half-life of about twenty days was estimated. At the time these experiments were performed, little was known about the chemical steps in the biosynthesis of cholesterol, but the isotope data suggested that this process involves the condensation of many small molecules; this surmise was later shown to be correct. Schoenheimer's continued interest in the problems of sterol metabolism that he had investigated in Germany is evident from the isotope experiments of his Ph.D. student Marjorie Anchel on the possible role of cholestenone and coprastanone in the conversion of dietary cholesterol to fecal coprosterol, as well as from the work in his Columbia laboratory on other aspects of the chemistry and metabolism of sterols.

By 1937, Urey had succeeded in concentrating the stable nitrogen isotope of mass 15 (N^{15}) by a chemical exchange reaction, and some of it (in the form of ammonium salts) was made available to Schoenheimer for studies on protein metabolism. In this research, Sarah Ratner, who had received her Ph.D. shortly before with Clarke, played a major role; Schoenheimer's other collaborators, in addition to Rittenberg, included Goodwin LeBaron Foster and Albert Keston.

The first set of papers, published in 1939, dealt with methodology: the Kjeldahl procedure was used to convert organic nitrogen to ammonia, which was then oxidized to nitrogen gas (N_2) with alkaline hypochlorite. A mass spectrometer was constructed that allowed the separation of molecules of mass 29 ($N^{14}N^{15}$) from nitrogen of mass 28. Since N^{15} is a naturally occurring isotope (0.37 atom percent), the data obtained by mass-spectrometric analysis were expressed in terms of "atom percent excess" of N^{15}. Methods were described for the synthesis of amino acids labeled with N^{15}; except for glycine, the procedure involved the catalytic hydrogenation of the corresponding α-keto acid in the presence of N^{15}-ammonia (a reaction introduced by Knoop and Oesterlin in 1927). The products were racemic (DL) amino acids, and some of them were resolved into the L-form (present in proteins) and its enantiomeric D-isomer.

Exploratory experiments also were reported on the administration of N^{15}-labeled ammonium citrate to rats. Amino acids were isolated from hydrolysates of body proteins and, except for lysine, all of the amino acids contained significant amounts of the isotope. As in the studies on fatty acid metabolism with deuterium, this result indicated at once that the body proteins undergo continuous metabolic change. The finding that lysine was not labeled was consistent with its known requirement in the animal diet.

In succeeding papers, the results of feeding individual N^{15}-labeled amino acids were reported. Of special significance were experiments in which L-leucine labeled with N^{15} in its α-amino group and deuterium in its carbon chain was used, and amino acids were isolated from the proteins of various tissues (liver, intestinal wall, and others). It was found that the α-amino nitrogen of leucine had been transferred to other amino acids (not lysine); this discovery clearly indicated that the body proteins undergo continuous breakdown and regeneration. The finding also disproved the widely accepted theory of Otto Folin, who had proposed that, in the animal body, protein breakdown is of two kinds: a variable (exogenous) metabolism that yields chiefly urea and no creatinine, and a constant (endogenous) metabolism that leads to the excretion of creatinine and uric acid. According to this concept, most of the dietary N^{15} should have appeared in the urine, but the isotope data showed that more than two-thirds of the leucine-nitrogen had been retained in the tissues.

Further studies in Schoenheimer's laboratory on the metabolic utilization of individual amino acids gave valuable information about the chemical reactions they undergo in the animal body. Evidence was provided for the importance of enzyme-catalyzed transamination reactions, discovered a few years earlier by Aleksandr Evseevich Braunstein, and for the role of arginine and ornithine in the biosynthesis of urea, elucidated in 1932 by Hans Adolf Krebs. Moreover, it was shown that phenylalanine is converted directly into tyrosine, and that ornithine is a metabolic precursor of proline and glutamic acid. Also, in the study of the metabolism of the muscle constituent creatine, the isotope data supported the suggestion offered in 1926 by Bergmann and Zervas, on the basis of purely chemical data, that the metabolic synthesis of creatine involves the transfer of an amidine group (present in arginine) to glycine.

Some of Schoenheimer's papers appeared posthumously. Among them was an important study conducted in collaboration with the immunologist Michael Heidelberger, showing that the administration of N^{15}-labeled amino acids to actively immunized animals leads to the uptake of the isotope into antibodies, followed by a decline in N^{15}-content; from their data a half-life of about two weeks was estimated for the antibodies. That antibodies are made only in the presence of an antigen was evident from the finding that mere injection of an antibody (passive immunity) did not lead to its uptake of isotopic nitrogen. Other posthumous publications dealt with the utilization of N^{15}-labeled purines and pyrimidines into nucleic acids.

In the background of Schoenheimer's isotope studies were hypotheses in the biochemical literature about the chemical steps in the metabolic conversion of body constituents. That he first chose fatty acids for investigation is understandable, not only because in 1933 deuterium was the only isotope available for labeling studies, but also because he had extensive experience in the lipid field. In his studies on protein metabolism, in particular the intermediary metabolism of individual amino acids, he recognized the opportunity to test numerous hypotheses about their synthesis and degradation, as well as about the mode of the formation of the end products of their metabolism, such as urea and creatinine.

It should be noted that the most important general concept to emerge from Schoenheimer's work with N^{15}, that of the dynamic state of the cellular proteins, was questioned in 1955 by Jacques Monod, who suggested that protein degradation occurs only in dead cells. This conclusion was based on his studies with bacteria, but subsequent work by Joel Mandelstam showed that both the breakdown and the synthesis of proteins occur in living bacteria.

After World War II, radioactive isotopes (C^{14}, P^{32}, S^{35}) became available for biochemical research. Because of their greater utility for metabolic studies, compared with the stable isotopes used by Schoenheimer, they became the tracers of choice in the exploration of the pathways of intermediary metabolism, and between 1950 and 1970 there was a flood of publications that illuminated the details of many metabolic conversions.[7] Especially notable among these achievements were those of two men who had worked in the Columbia department of biological chemistry: Konrad Bloch, in the elucidation of the pathway for the biosynthesis of cholesterol, and David Shemin, in tracing the route of the biosynthesis of the porphyrins. Thus, Schoenheimer not only pioneered in the isotope technique but also left behind a progeny imbued with his organic-chemical approach to the study of biological processes.

Schoenheimer took his own life by the ingestion of potassium cyanide.

NOTES

1. Karl Thomas, "Fifty Years of Biochemistry in Germany," in *Annual Review of Biochemistry*, **23** (1954), 1–16.
2. Joseph S. Fruton, "The Carbobenzoxy Method of Peptide

Synthesis," in *Trends in Biochemical Sciences,* **7** (1982), 37–39.

3. Hans T. Clarke, "Impressions of an Organic Chemist in Biochemistry," in *Annual Review of Biochemistry,* **27** (1958), 1–14.

4. Robert E. Kohler, Jr., "Rudolf Schoenheimer, Isotopic Tracers, and Biochemistry in the 1930's," in *Historical Studies in the Physical Sciences,* **8** (1977), 257–298.

5. According to Clarke (*op. cit.,* p. 5), this came about as a consequence of a conversation between Rittenberg and Schoenheimer. As Kohler (*op. cit.,* p. 274) describes it, "Rittenberg's overture to Schoenheimer in the summer or fall of 1934 struck sparks because Schoenheimer had a pressing problem that the use of deuterated compounds could solve." This account is at variance with my recollection of the conversations I had with Schoenheimer during 1933 (I was one of Clarke's graduate students from June 1931 to May 1934), when he told me one evening that earlier in the day he had visited Urey to discuss the possible use of deuterium for his metabolic studies. Perhaps Clarke did not know of this visit, or had forgotten about it. Kohler (*op. cit.,* pp. 275–276) offers as "direct evidence" for his interpretation of the origins of Schoenheimer's insight a report submitted in 1938 by Clarke to Warren Weaver of the Rockefeller Foundation; Kohler considers the report to have been "obviously written by Schoenheimer," but no "direct evidence" is provided for this conclusion.

6. George Hevesy, "Historical Sketch of the Biological Application of Tracer Elements," in *Cold Spring Harbor Symposia on Quantitative Biology,* **13** (1948), 129–150.

7. Marcel Florkin and Elmer H. Stotz, eds., *Comprehensive Biochemistry,* sec. 6, *A History of Biochemistry,* pt. V, *The Unravelling of Biosynthetic Pathways,* 2 vols. (Amsterdam, 1979).

BIBLIOGRAPHY

I. ORIGINAL WORKS. Schoenheimer's only book, *The Dynamic State of Body Constituents* (Cambridge, Mass., 1941; 2nd ed., 1946), appeared posthumously; it was based on the Edward K. Dunham Lectures for the Promotion of the Medical Sciences at Harvard University. The lectures had been drafted by Schoenheimer and delivered by Hans Clarke, who prepared them for publication with the assistance of David Rittenberg and Sarah Ratner.

A nearly complete list of Schoenheimer's journal articles is in Poggendorff, VI, 2355–2356, and VIIA, pt. 4, 225–226. Among them are "Ein Beitrag zur Bereitung der Peptiden," in *Hoppe-Seyler's Zeitschrift für physiologische Chemie,* **154** (1926), 203–224; "New Contributions in Sterol Metabolism," in *Science,* **74** (1931), 579–584; "Synthesis and Destruction of Cholesterol in the Organism," in *Journal of Biological Chemistry,* **103** (1933), 439–448, written with Fritz Breusch; "Deuterium as an Indicator in the Study of Intermediary Metabolism," I–VI and XI, *ibid.,* **111** (1935), 163–192, **113** (1936), 505–510, **114** (1936), 381–396, and **121** (1937), 235–253, written with David Rittenberg, pt. IV also written with M. Graff; "Studies in Protein Metabolism, X, The Metabolic Activity of Body Proteins Investigated with *l*(-)-Leucine Containing Two Isotopes," *ibid.,* **130** (1939), 703–732, written with Sarah Ratner and David Rittenberg; "The Conversion of Palmitic Acid into Stearic Acid and Palmitoleic Acids in Rats," *ibid.,* **133** (1940), 329–345, written with Dewitt Stetten,

Jr.; and "The Biological Precursors of Creatine," *ibid.,* **138** (1941), 167–194, written with Konrad Bloch.

II. SECONDARY LITERATURE. Obituary notices are by Hans T. Clarke, in *Science,* **94** (1941), 553–554; and J. H. Quastel, in *Nature,* **149** (1942), 15–16. Other biographical writings include Aaron J. Ihde, in *Dictionary of American Biography,* supp. 3, 693–694; Robert E. Kohler, Jr. (see note 4); David Nachmanson, *German-Jewish Pioneers in Science* (New York, 1979), 357–360; Urs Peyer, *Rudolf Schoenheimer (1898–1941) und der Beginn der Tracer-Technik bei Stoffwechseluntersuchungen* (Zurich, 1972), with an English summary; and Dewitt Stetten, Jr., "Rudi," in *Perspectives in Biology and Medicine,* **25** (1982), 354–368.

JOSEPH S. FRUTON

SCHRADER, FRANZ [OTTO JOHANN WOLFGANG] (*b.* Magdeburg, Germany, 11 March 1891; *d.* Durham, North Carolina, 22 March 1962), *cytology.*

The only child of Franz Schrader and Hedwig Dorothea Rohde, Schrader received his early schooling in the cloister of the magnificent Magdeburg Cathedral and the Magdeburger Bürgerschule. In 1901 he came to the United States with his mother, who was divorced from his father, and her second husband, Friedrich Wille, a prosperous specialist in mining enterprises. The family lived on Staten Island (the borough of Richmond, New York City), where Schrader attended grammar and high school. Left to his own devices, on that still unspoiled island he continued the natural history pursuits that had so delighted him on vacations with his father in the Harz Mountains. That zest for fieldwork, and especially for the natural history of insects and fish, never abated; it gave a unique and significant stamp to Schrader's cytological research.

Schrader attended Columbia University: first its School of Mines (1910–1912), at his stepfather's urging; then, yielding to his own interests, Columbia College, from which he graduated (B.S., 1914). Following college and two summers (1915, 1916) as assistant in the Bureau of Fisheries at Woods Hole, Massachusetts, Schrader served in Minnesota as supervisor of fisheries for the U.S. Bureau of Fisheries (1916–1917). There he carried out investigations on the feeding behavior of mussels and on parasites of fish. In 1917 he returned to Columbia as assistant in zoology, completing his doctoral degree in 1919 under the preeminent cytologist Edmund Beecher Wilson. His dissertation, published in 1920, was a landmark contribution, for it proved for the first time that sex may be determined by haploidy or diploidy of a zygote; that fertilized females can produce male progeny parthenogenetically; and that these males, unlike their sisters, are fatherless, for their single set of chromosomes comes only from their mother.

After receiving his doctorate, Schrader was appointed chief pathologist of the U.S. Bureau of Fisheries in Washington, D.C., where he applied his cytological skills to an analysis of nuclear changes in oocytes that accompany the loss of fecundity of penned pike-perch. Though all went well in that post, he resigned in 1920—a pivotal year. That year Schrader accepted appointment as biological associate at Bryn Mawr College, and on 1 November he married Sally Peris Hughes, doctoral student under Wilson and lecturer at Barnard College of Columbia University, whose skills and interests in cytology and natural history matched his own.

At Bryn Mawr, Schrader's research was largely devoted to chromosomal problems of sex determination, an outcome of which was the comprehensive treatise *Die Geschlechtschromosomen* (1928). Remarkably, he found species of coccids that provided possible evolutionary intermediates between ordinary diploid species with sex chromosomes and haplo-diploid parthenogenetic species. In these coccids, one set of chromosomes of the diploid male undergoes heteropycnosis, leading, he surmised, to inactivity and ultimately to effective haploidy of the nominally diploid male. Schrader pointed out that all of one haploid set in these cases may be viewed as a compound X chromosome (an X chromosome consisting of more than one element), and all of the other set as a compound Y. On this basis a hypothesis for the evolutionary origins of haplo-diploid parthenogenesis was formulated (Schrader and Hughes-Schrader, 1931), a hypothesis that is still in the forefront though mistakenly attributed by some to M. J. D. White (1954).

In 1930, as had both Wilson and Thomas Hunt Morgan before him, Schrader left Bryn Mawr to become professor in the department of zoology at Columbia University, assuming the post vacated by Wilson at retirement. Again like Wilson, Schrader was named Da Costa professor (1949) in recognition of the world renown he had attained in chromosomal cytology. During his twenty-nine years at Columbia, Schrader served twice as executive officer (chairman) of the department of zoology (1937–1940, 1946–1949), as member of the National Research Council Fellowship Committee (1939–1943), as an editor of the Columbia Biological Series (1930–1962), as one of the founding editors of *Chromosoma* (1939–1962) and of *Journal of Biophysical and Biochemical Cy-*

tology (later *Journal of Cell Biology*, 1954–1961), as member of the editorial boards of *Journal of Morphology* (1932–1935) and *Biological Bulletin* (1939–1954, 1959–1962), and as trustee of the Marine Biological Laboratory at Woods Hole (1934–1951). He was elected vice president of the American Association for the Advancement of Science and chairman of the Section of Zoological Sciences (1947), president of the American Society of Zoologists (1952), and member of the National Academy of Sciences (1951) and of the American Academy of Arts and Sciences (1953).

The man who gained these distinctions was of cosmopolitan outlook and aristocratic mien. Sensitive, perceptive, intuitive, with a penchant for fine foods and wines, game fishing, Near Eastern rugs, art, classical music, literature, pre-Columbian archaeology, and travel, he had exceptional social grace and was a delightful host. His research and the trips to the tropics it entailed were pursued as most satisfying pleasures. Critical, dispassionate in judgment, with a vast range of learning, regarding continuity with the past as a necessity, and, like Wilson, keenly interested in the diversity of chromosomal behavior, Schrader's publications were never trivial or given to polemics. Like his book *Mitosis*, they stand apart with their clear, engaging, and individual style, with full consideration of the findings and ideas of his forerunners.

From the age of twenty-four Schrader was intermittently troubled by a weakened heart. Nevertheless he made many field trips with his wife to Central America for specially sought species. Those out-of-the-way organisms made his (and Sally Hughes-Schrader's) work unique, and so it remains today. The 122 different species upon which he published over the years, representing four phyla and some 64 genera, nearly all so different from the common grist of cytological research, added greatly to what is known of the diversity of chromosomal behavior in somatic and meiotic mitoses.

Schrader's research at Columbia may arbitrarily be viewed as comprising two periods of emphasis: 1932–1953, interrelations of spindles and chromosomes, and—overlapping the former—1945–1961, the diversity of meiotic systems, comparative cytochemical studies, and evolutionary considerations of DNA content of nuclei among related species and genera, all of which he interrelated.

The regular occurrence of very strange yet functional spindles at meiotic mitoses of some coccids he had investigated (monopolar spindles in *Pseudococcus*, tubular spindles within which chromosomes are aligned in single file in *Protortonia*), as well as the remarkable compound spindles discovered by Hughes-Schrader, diverted Schrader from problems of sex determination to an extensive research and review of spindles and the relations between chromosomes and spindles. One outcome of that preoccupation was his widely influential book *Mitosis* (1944; 2nd ed., 1953), which placed what was known of these subjects under searching analysis and offered new directions for research on chromosomal movements.

In 1930 it was generally believed that mitotic spindles are real entities, of short half-life, that originate independently of chromosomes yet are necessary for their movements. Since spindles of healthy, living cells appear nearly optically homogeneous, the fibrous structure that appears within spindles when cells become moribund, or are fixed, was widely regarded as artifactual, especially by physiologists. However, on the basis of his study of the consistency of paths taken by the fibrous components of spindles in fixed cells (1932), and on the results of his carefully controlled centrifugation experiments with living cells (1934), Schrader concluded that spindles in living cells do indeed have a fibrous structure, albeit an invisible one. In bipolar spindles he described these fibrous arrays as consisting of (1) those running from a spindle pole to each chromosome or chromatid, namely, chromosomal fibers or half-spindle components; (2) continuous fiber systems from pole to pole; and, in some organisms (3) interzonal fibers of quite different nature connecting the ends of separating chromatids at anaphase. Final proof of the validity of Schrader's conclusions came with Shinya Inoué's remarkable time-lapse motion pictures of cells undergoing consecutive mitoses, taken by means of Inoué's vast improvement of polarization optics. In these now classical films, first widely shown to audiences in 1949, the strikingly birefringent groups of chromosomal and continuous "fibers" stand out for all to see.

Before Schrader's studies of mitosis, most took for granted that the relation of spindles to chromosomes is fundamentally the same throughout eukaryotic organisms, and that spindles play the determining role in mitosis. However, both Schrader and Hughes-Schrader had described clear instances in which it is the chromosome that determines development of the spindle. Furthermore, Schrader had shown in *Pseudococcus* that the state of a chromosome can be critical in the formation of a spindle. In Schrader's view, nonchromosomal spindle initiators and chromosomes are clearly interactive and

may show various degrees of predominance at certain developmental stages and in certain cells.

Schrader (1935) contrasted those spindle "attachments" located at a fixed point on a chromosome, or localized kinetochores of complex morphology and common to most organisms, with holokinetic (or "diffuse") kinetochores first discovered in homopterous and heteropterous bugs. The diffuse kinetochore is of no known special morphology, the chromosome appearing to have spindle fibers normal to its entire poleward surfaces. These two sorts of kinetochores appear to be mutually exclusive, for all chromosomes of an organism's complement in a given cell have either localized or diffuse kinetochores. The properties that Schrader described imply that all, or nearly all, fragments of holokinetic chromosomes, unlike all but one of those of a chromosome having a localized kinetochore, should be capable of spindle fiber association and undergoing mitosis. That holokinetic chromosomes do indeed have that property was first proved by Hughes-Schrader and Hans Ris (1941).

The discoveries and their interpretation by Schrader are now regarded as expressions of fundamental properties of chromosomes in relation to spindles. Chromosomal "spindle fibers" have been shown to have their physical basis in ultramicroscopic microtubules, along with associated molecules, which in some cells appear to be formed first in fibrous arrays at kinetochores, and in others at future spindle poles or centrosomes. The distinctions between holokinetic and localized kinetochores are borne out by electron microscopy, but the evolutionary relationship between the two remains a Gordian knot. Finally, as Schrader predicted, the main advances in the resolution of these problems are now being made physicochemically.

Unlike the seminal contributions made by Schrader to sex determination, mitosis, and chromosome structure, his other studies have not been so readily assimilated or assimilable. Cyril D. Darlington's "precocity theory" (1932) was the prevalent cytogenetic theory, an eclectic one ingeniously constructed but not from wide-ranging comparative cytology. It imposed rules of behavior upon chromosomes, a behavior guaranteed to conform to classical genetics, which is based on few kinds of organisms. If chromosomal behavior could not be fitted to the "rules," it was ignored. Despite those cardinal inadequacies, in Schrader's time Darlington's theory dominated cytological work on meiosis, and Darlington's following among geneticists and cytologists was immense.

A chain of relations is required under Darlington's

theory for segregation at meiosis, with failure at any link automatically resulting in random assortment of chromosomes. That chain is as follows: precocious onset of prophase ⊂ synapsis ⊂ crossing-over (chiasma formation) ⊂ conjunction as bivalents ⊂ segregation. From his very early work (1923) to nearly his last (1960), Schrader had found unassailable cases in many diverse organisms in which segregation occurs despite failure of synapsis in some, of chiasmata in others, and of bivalent formation in still others. What is more, molecular geneticists proved that the first meiotic prophase is not "precocious," as Darlington's theory requires, for chromosomal DNA is doubled before synapsis; the theory in its original form has thus collapsed. However, its former adherents now hold crossing-over, which they equate with chiasmata, to be the sine qua non of conjunction and segregation, so most of Schrader's demonstrations of the remarkable diversity of meiotic phenomena among some forty organisms remain unassimilated by current cytogenetic theory, and accordingly are ignored by most.

Schrader's 1945–1960 studies of meiosis in what he called the "harlequin lobe" of the testes of twenty-one tropical or semitropical pentatomid bugs bear importantly on the complexity of meiosis. In that special lobe in each species, there occurs a species- or genus-specific, fantastic distortion of meiosis, wholly unlike the regular meioses in cells of the other testicular lobes. In all of these species highly aneuploid spermatozoa result that no longer can have an ordinary gametic function at fertilization. In some, only the sex chromosomes undergo their customary meiotic maneuvers and segregate. Autosomal behavior is exceptional in all, variously but regularly—according to species—involving combinations of asynapsis, desynapsis, chain formation, clumping, lateral displacement on the spindle, nonrandom segregation, and so on. Differentiation of the harlequin lobe in related species has evidently brought about different uncouplings of events of normal meiosis that are both numerous and complex, and regular in their consequences. The harlequin lobe phenomena therefore are highly significant, for, side by side, they present an aberrant meiosis and the normal meiosis from which it was derived.

Schrader believed that theoretical resolution of these and other problems would require painstaking comparative physicochemical investigation of the astonishing variety of cytological conformities and nonconformities. Accordingly he welcomed T. Caspersson's introduction of cytochemical tests quantifiable by photometry. With Cecile Leuchtenberger (1946–1956) and others, Schrader carried out a variety of photometric studies on DNA content of cells in relation to quantities of RNA and protein, on infertility in man and in dwarf bulls, on development of nebenkern and acrosome, and on apparent exceptions to DNA constancy.

Of this series, several studies of pentatomid bugs by Schrader and Hughes-Schrader (1956, 1958) are specially notable. A study of six species of Thyanta showed that five species, like the majority of pentatomids, have six pairs of autosomes; the sixth species, T. calceata, however, has twelve pairs. Remarkably, all six species have "a surprising uniformity in nuclear content of DNA." This unexpected state of affairs is accounted for by assuming that pentatomid chromosomes are polytenic, and that a longitudinal, equal separation of strands of each autosome doubles the number of autosomes without increasing the total amount of DNA per nucleus. Somewhat more complicated, but similar, relations among ten species of Banasa are also interpreted in terms of polyteny and "chromatid autonomy"—attributes that are suggested to have played important roles in chromosomal evolution.

The notion of polyteny of mitotic chromosomes of course flies in the face of the widespread belief that chromatids of all mitotically competent chromosomes are composed of but one bineme of DNA. The explanation given by the Schraders to these and still other cases is not the only possible one, but the chief basis today for rejecting their hypothesis lies in the fact that it is counter to widespread belief. That dogma, however, is not based on widespread investigation; rather, it depends upon analyses of chromosomes of a very limited range of organisms. In any case, the findings for Thyanta and Banasa are of such potential significance regarding both chromosome structure and evolution that it is to be hoped that these cases will be reinvestigated with molecular methods.

At retirement as Da Costa professor emeritus in 1958, Schrader was invited to Duke University as visiting professor and Hargitt Fellow, privileges he gladly accepted and much enjoyed. His last research (1960–1961) was published from Duke's laboratories, continuing with characteristic gratification his exploration of harlequin lobe meioses as well as an experimental study of the properties of holokinetic chromosomes and their fragmentation products at meiosis. In 1961 the editors and publisher of Chromosoma presented him with a festschrift. He died in the following year of renal neoplasia, and Sally Hughes-Schrader—whose last research paper was published in 1983 (at age eighty-eight)—died in 1984.

They were a remarkable pair of outstanding cytologist-naturalists.

BIBLIOGRAPHY

I. Original Works. A list of Schrader's publications is in *Journal of Cell Biology*, **16**, no. 3 (1963), xvi–xix, to which must be added a posthumously published article, translated into German by W. E. Ankle: "Edmund Beecher Wilson, 1856–1939," in *Geschichte der Mikroskopie, Leben und Werk grosser Forscher*, I, *Biologie* (Frankfurt am Main, 1963).

Those cited in the text are "Sex Determination in the White-Fly (*Trialeurodes vaporariorum*)," in *Journal of Morphology*, **34** (1920), 267–305; "A Study of the Chromosomes in Three Species of *Pseudococcus*," in *Archiv für Zellforschung*, **17** (1923), 45–62; "Haploidy in Metazoa," in *Quarterly Review of Biology*, **6** (1931), 411–438, with Sally Hughes-Schrader; *Die Geschlechtschromosomen* (Berlin, 1928); "Recent Hypothesis on the Structure of Spindles in the Light of Certain Observations in Hemiptera," in *Zeitschrift für wissenschaftliche Zoologie*, **142** (1932), 520–539; "On the Reality of Spindle Fibers," in *Biological Bulletin*, **67** (1934), 519–533; *Mitosis: The Movements of Chromosomes in Cell Division* (New York, 1944; 2nd ed., 1953); "Polyploidy and Fragmentation in the Chromosomal Evolution of Various Species of *Thyanta* (Hemiptera)," in *Chromosoma*, **7** (1956), 469–496, with Sally Hughes-Schrader; "Polyteny as a Factor in the Chromosomal Evolution of the Pentatomini (Hemiptera)," *ibid.*, **8** (1956), 135–151, with Sally Hughes-Schrader; "Chromatid Autonomy in *Banasa* (Hemiptera: Pentatomidae)," *ibid.*, **9** (1958), 195–215, with Sally Hughes-Schrader; "Cytological and Evolutionary Implications of Aberrant Chromosome Behavior in the Harlequin Lobe of Some Pentatomidae (Heteroptera)," *ibid.*, **11** (1960), 103–128; "Evolutionary Aspects of Aberrant Meiosis in Some Pentatominae (Heteroptera)," in *Evolution*, **14** (1960), 498–508.

American Men of Science, III–VI (New York, 1921–1938), VII–IX (Lancaster, Pa., 1944–1955), and X (Tempe, Ariz., 1960), lists memberships not cited here or in the 1963 account (above). Schrader was starred in the fifth (1933) through seventh editions as among the 150 most eminent zoologists. He strongly objected to starring, and the practice was dropped with the eighth edition. See his "Stars in the Biographical Directory of American Men of Science," in *Science*, **85** (1937), 360.

Insight into Schrader's values, attitudes, and personality may be gained from his "Edmund Beecher Wilson—Scientist 1856–1939," in *Columbia University Quarterly* (1939), 218–224, which, unlike his posthumous article of 1963, is addressed to a general audience.

II. Secondary Literature. On Schrader's life and work, see Kenneth W. Cooper, "Franz Schrader, 1891–1962," in *Journal of Cell Biology*, **16**, no. 3 (1963), ix–xv; and Donald E. Lancefield, "Franz Schrader," in *Biological Bulletin*, **125** (1963), 9–10. There is much of interest in Kenneth R. Manning, *Black Apollo of Science: The Life of Ernest Everett Just* (New York, 1983); the episodes and anecdotes relating to Schrader (which are indexed) came directly from Sally Hughes-Schrader or were verified by her. Schrader's "scientific pedigree" is diagrammed by A. H. Sturtevant in *A History of Genetics* (New York, 1965).

Citations in the text to authors other than Schrader are Cyril D. Darlington, *Recent Advances in Cytology* (London, 1932; 2nd ed., 1932; repr. 1965); Sally Hughes-Schrader, "Chromosomal Segregational Mechanisms in Ant-Lions (Myrmeleontidae, Neuroptera)," in *Chromosoma*, **88** (1983), 256–264, and "The Diffuse Spindle Attachment of Coccids, Verified by the Mitotic Behavior of Induced Chromosome Fragments," in *Journal of Experimental Zoology*, **87** (1941), 429–456, with Hans Ris; Shinya Inoué, "Studies of the Structure of the Mitotic Spindle in Living Cells with an Improved Polarization Microscope" (Ph.D. diss., Princeton University, 1951); for reproduction of frames from his motion picture, see Inoué's "Polarization Optical Studies of the Mitotic Spindle. I. The Demonstration of Spindle Fibers in Living Cells," in *Chromosoma*, **5** (1953), 487–500; M. J. D. White, *Animal Cytology and Evolution*, 2nd ed. (Cambridge, 1954). Festschrift articles appeared in *Chromosoma*, **12**, no. 1 (1961) and were privately presented as a bound volume entitled *Franz Schrader zum 70. Geburtstag gewidmete Arbeiten . . . .*

Kenneth W. Cooper

SCHWARZENBACH, GEROLD KARL (*b*. Horgen, Switzerland, 15 March 1904; *d*. Zurich, Switzerland, 20 May 1978), *chemistry*.

Schwarzenbach was born and raised in Horgen, a small town situated on Lake Zurich, nine miles from the city of Zurich. His father, Jean Schwarzenbach, managed a silk-dyeing factory founded by his mother's father and later sold by his cousin. The second youngest of seven children (three girls and four boys), Gerold was the only one to receive an academic education. In 1928 he received his doctorate, under Professor of Analytical Chemistry William Dupré Treadwell, from the Swiss Federal Institute of Technology (ETH) in Zurich with the dissertation "Studien über die Salzbildung von Beizenfarbstoffen" ("Studies on the Salt Formation of Mordant Dyestuffs"). Instead of accepting an industrial position in the textile industry, as his family desired, he spent a year (1928–1929) working on synthetic organic problems with William Bradley and Sir Robert Robinson in Manchester and London. His work in the United Kingdom on natural plant dyes gave him his first contact with substances capable of acting as ligands (complexing agents).

In 1929 Schwarzenbach returned to Switzerland

and married Martha Tobler, whom he had met in London. The couple had three children: Ursula, who became a children's nurse; Kurt, a Ph.D. chemist and product manager for Ciba-Geigy in Basel; and Dieter, professor of crystallography at the University of Lausanne. In 1929 he became chief assistant to Paul Karrer at the University of Zurich and was in charge of the analytical chemistry laboratory course for medical students and then the analytical chemistry training for natural scientists. With his *Habilitationsschrift*, "Die Acidität in verschiedenen Lösungsmitteln," he qualified in 1930 to teach at a university as an unsalaried lecturer on "the entire field of chemistry." He spent the year 1937 to 1938 in the United States, first with Leonor Michaelis as a Rockefeller Scholar at the Rockefeller Institute for Medical Research (now Rockefeller University) in New York City and then with Linus Pauling at the California Institute of Technology in Pasadena.

Schwarzenbach's wife died in 1940. In 1942 he married Erica Schoch, with whom he later had a daughter, Annette, who became an optometrist in Zurich and Schaffhausen. In 1942 he was appointed assistant professor of analytical chemistry at the University of Zurich. In 1947 he became full professor of analytical chemistry. In 1955 he succeeded his teacher Treadwell as full professor and director of the Laboratory for Inorganic Chemistry at the ETH, where he remained until his retirement on 1 September 1973. He died unexpectedly of heart failure on 20 May 1978.

Schwarzenbach had an international reputation as a pioneer in modern coordination chemistry, but he also made valuable contributions to inorganic, analytical, physical, and organic chemistry. He was awarded the Talanta (1963), Torbern Bergman (1967), Paul Karrer, and Paracelsus medals, the Werner (1936) and Marcel Benoist (1964) prizes, and honorary doctorates from the universities of Bern (1971) and Fribourg (1974). In 1962 he was elected a foreign member of the American Academy of Arts and Sciences.

Schwarzenbach is best known among analytical chemists for his discovery and development of the complexometric titration method whereby almost every metal can be determined in a very simple manner. A suitable indicator is added to the solution of the metal to be determined, and the solution is titrated with a standard solution of a complexing agent until the indicator changes color. This method resulted from his earlier studies, which revealed the similarity between the formation of metal coordination compounds and conventional acid-base neutralization. These physical organic studies involved modern theories of acids and bases (Brønsted-Lowry and G. N. Lewis); the electronic theories of Lewis, Sidgwick, Robinson, and Pauling; and the effects of substitution on the acidity of organic compounds. Schwarzenbach's measurements of keto-enol equilibria with a simple flow apparatus gave values that are still cited today.

During studies of the behavior of dyestuffs over a wide pH range, he found that metal cations could exert an important influence on the equilibrium and that nitrilotriacetic (NTA) and ethylenediaminetetraacetic (EDTA) acids show a decrease in pH on addition of cations of the alkaline earth elements (those of periodic group IIA). These results opened a new field, which is associated with Schwarzenbach's name, the study of metal complexes by potentiometric measurements and the potentiometric analytical determination of metals by use of specific metal indicators (Eriochrome Black T, for example).

In 1956 in a lecture on organic ligands Schwarzenbach sketched characteristics of coordination that adumbrated the theory of "hard" and "soft" acids and bases developed a decade later. He synthesized numerous compounds to establish the structural basis for the so-called chelate effect (the increased stability of compounds containing chelate rings compared with those that do not), and he determined many complex formation constants. These results exerted a great influence on problems in biochemistry, biology, limnology, and other fields. After his move to the ETH (1955), Schwarzenbach also studied biological chelating agents such as adenosine triphosphate (ATP), phosphoglyceric acid, and iron-complexing antibiotics. He studied protonation and deprotonation processes; salt cryoscopy; polynuclear coordination compounds of chromium(III), cobalt(III), and other transition metal cations; and metal sulfides and aromatic complexes of mercury. He called his coordination chemistry in solution "measuring complex chemistry" (*messende Komplexchemie*), since the identification of complexes results from the elucidation of equilibria and not from the classical preparative manner. Schwarzenbach also carried out historical studies of the development of chemical concepts such as acid-base theory and valence theory.

BIBLIOGRAPHY

I. Original Works. Schwarzenbach's more than 190 articles appeared from 1928 to 1977. Most were published in *Helvetica chimica acta*. A bibliography through 1963 appears in Walter Schneider, "From the Proton to the

Metal Ions: Outlines of the Early Papers of Gerold Schwarzenbach,'' in W. Schneider, G. Anderegg, and R. Gut, eds., *Essays in Co-ordination Chemistry* (Basel, 1964), 9–23. A complete bibliography appears in the obituary by Walter Schneider in *Helvetica chimica acta*, **61** (1978), 1949–1961. Schwarzenbach's books include *Allgemeine und anorganische Chemie: Ein einfaches Lehrbuch auf neuzeitlicher Grundlage* (Stuttgart, 1940; 4th ed., 1950); *Complexometric Titrations*, H. M. N. H. Irving, trans., 2nd English ed. (New York, 1969); *Stability Constants of Metal-Ion Complexes*, 2 vols. (London, 1957), written with Lars Gunnar Sillén.

II. SECONDARY LITERATURE. In addition to the works by Walter Schneider cited above, see Gerhard Geier, "Gerold Schwarzenbach zum Gedenken," in *Chemie* (Switzerland), **32** (1978), 269; and *McGraw-Hill Modern Scientists and Engineers*, III (New York, 1980), 86–87.

GEORGE B. KAUFFMAN

SELOUS, EDMUND (*b.* London, England, 14 August 1857; *d.* Weymouth, England, 25 March 1934), *ethology, field ornithology.*

Edmund Selous was an ardent Darwinian who insisted upon the importance of fieldwork for resolving major issues in animal behavior and evolutionary theory. His painstaking studies of what he called the "domestic habits" of birds—their behavior in courtship, mating, nest building, rearing their young, interacting with other members of the same species, and so forth—were virtually unprecedented in their approach and attention to detail. Especially significant were his observations on display behavior and on the role of female choice in sexual selection. His work provided an important model for the development of animal behavior studies in the twentieth century.

Selous, whose family name was spelled Slous at the time of his birth, was the son of Frederick Lokes Slous and Ann Holgate Sherborn Slous. His father was a stockbroker who became chairman of the board of the London Stock Exchange. His mother was a talented amateur poet and painter who impressed upon her three daughters and two sons, of whom Edmund was the youngest, a strong love of natural history. Edmund believed it was from his mother that he and his older brother, the famous big-game hunter Frederick Courteney Selous, inherited "the call of the wild" that was so important to each of them.

Selous entered Pembroke College, Cambridge, in 1877 and studied law. He was called to the bar in 1881. He married Fanny Margaret Maxwell; they had a son and two daughters. Though interested in wild animals from his youth, it appears that it was not until 1898 that Selous began to devote himself seriously to watching birds. He seems to have supported himself not through practice as a barrister but through possession of a small private income and writing articles and books on natural history (including books for children). In his writings he waged a constant battle against the zoological establishment of the day, which he regarded as being more interested in killing animals than in studying how animals lived. Selous does not appear to have belonged to any scientific societies, and when he died in 1934, no obituary notices were written for him in any British scientific journals, though two appreciative notices of his work did appear abroad.

Selous' first scientific publication was an article on the breeding habits of the nightjar (1899). In it he initiated the practice of publishing his field notes in full. Insofar as possible, he made it his practice to record his observations on the spot and as soon as the actions observed took place, noting precisely the date and time.

Selous prided himself on observing not just what was expected of animals but also how they deviated from that expectation, maintaining that such deviations were the material upon which organic evolution was based. He was attentive both to the intraspecific variations that made natural and sexual selection possible and to particular patterns that he believed represented behavior in the course of evolutionary change. He hypothesized, for example, that the frenzied motions of birds when sexually excited were the basis from which courting displays and nest-building habits gradually evolved.

Among Selous' most important papers were his studies of sexual selection in the ruff (1906–1907) and the blackcock (1909–1910). In his paper on the ruff he provided a powerful confirmation of Darwin's view of the importance of female choice in sexual selection, a view that had few proponents among the scientists of the day. Selous found that the females of this lek-breeding species play an active rather than a passive role in the mating process, that they do indeed choose among the males, and that this choice is not simply a reflection of male "vigor." His subsequent studies on the blackcock, another lek-breeder, provided further support for the role of female choice in sexual selection.

In addition to his studies of breeding behavior, Selous paid special attention to the movements of birds in flocks. He believed their synchronized movements could not be explained simply on the basis of cues from one bird to another, but instead were the result of what he called "collective thought" or "thought transference." This idea, first mentioned in *Bird Watching* (1901), was the primary subject of his later *Thought-Transference (or What?) in Birds* (1931). His conclusions about the evolution of formalized behavior patterns, nest building, sexual display, sexual selection, parental care, domestic cleanliness, and bird song, together with his thoughts on territoriality, were summed up in his final book, *Evolution of Habit in Birds* (1933).

Selous was not an easy person to deal with, and he did not endear himself to the professional zoologists of his day by characterizing them as murderers or "thanatologists." Though slated to be a major contributor to F. B. Kirkman's four-volume *British Birds* (1910–1913), Selous was dropped from the project after the first volume, when his written assaults on the collectors of birds' eggs and skins led to a quarrel between him and Kirkman. Nor did Selous make friends among contemporary field ornithologists by refraining from reading their writings, on the ground that he wanted his conclusions to be based entirely upon his own observations.

Selous' strong sense of alienation no doubt allowed him to relish the solitude that his field studies demanded, and it also enabled him to make unusually penetrating observations regarding the way that common societal assumptions about male dominance and female passivity permeated scientific thought. On the other hand, it may have prevented him from playing a larger role than he did in the reformation of biological thought and methodology at the beginning of the twentieth century. Nonetheless, his pioneering researches were read, and they did have an influence on the development of field studies of behavior.

Among the professional biologists who appreciated Selous' work were Julian Huxley in England and Jan Verwey in Holland. They in turn influenced the Dutch ethologist Nikolaas (Niko) Tinbergen, whose career demonstrated a claim Selous had made years earlier: "The habits of animals are really as scientific as their anatomies, and professors of them, when once made, would be as good as their brothers" (*Bird Life Glimpses*, pp. 49–50).

BIBLIOGRAPHY

I. ORIGINAL WORKS. No complete bibliography of Selous' scientific works has been published, but see N. Diana Giffard, "A Bibliography of the Published Writings of Edmund Selous, Ornithologist" (M.A. thesis, School of Librarianship and Archives, University College, London, 1951). An annotated catalog of Selous' publications and manuscripts is being prepared for publication by Dr. K. E. L. Simmons. A collection of Selous' manuscripts

(primarily field notes) is in the Edward Grey Library, Oxford. Selous' major scientific articles are listed below: "An Observational Diary of the Habits of Nightjars (*Caprimulgus europaeus*), Mostly of a Sitting Pair. Notes Taken at Time and on Spot," in *The Zoologist*, 4th ser., **3** (1899), 388–402, 486–505; "An Observational Diary of the Habits of the Great Plover (*Œdicnemus crepitans*) During September and October," *ibid.*, **4** (1900), 173–185, 270–277, 458–476; "An Observational Diary of the Habits—Mostly Domestic—of the Great Crested Grebe (*Podicipes cristatus*), and of the Peewit (*Vanellus vulgaris*), with Some General Remarks," *ibid.*, **5** (1901), 161–183, 339–350, 454–462, and **6** (1902), 133–144; "Variations in Colouring of *Stercorarius crepidatus*," *ibid.*, **6** (1902), 368–373; "Observations Tending to Throw Light on the Question of Sexual Selection in Birds, Including a Day-to-Day Diary on the Breeding Habits of the Ruff (*Machetes pugnax*)," *ibid.*, **10** (1906), 201–219, 285–294, 419–428, and **11** (1907), 60–65, 161–182, 367–381; "Some Notes on a Habit of the Great Spotted Woodpecker (*Dendrocopus major*) in Relation to a Similar but More Developed Habit in the Californian Woodpecker (*Melanerpes formicivorus*)," *ibid.*, **12** (1908), 81–91; "An Observational Diary on the Nuptial Habits of the Blackcock (*Tetrao tetrix*) in Scandinavia and England," *ibid.*, **13** (1909), 401–413, and **14** (1910), 23–29, 51–56, 176–182, 248–265; "An Observational Diary on the Domestic Habits of the Red-Throated Diver (*Colymbus septentrionalis*)," *ibid.*, **16** (1912), 81–96, 171–180, 210–219; "An Observational Diary on the Domestic Habits of the Carrion-Crow (*Corvus corone*)," *ibid.*, 321–337; "A Diary of Ornithological Observation Made in Iceland During June and July, 1912," *ibid.*, **17** (1913), 57–66, 92–104, 129–136, 294–313, 409–422, **18** (1914), 63–74, 213–225, **19** (1915), 58–66, 169–174, 303–307, and **20** (1916), 54–68, 139–152, 267–272.

"Ornithological Observations and Reflections in Shetland," in *The Naturalist* (1914), 355–357, 365–379, (1916), 324–326, 363–366, 384–388, (1917), 89–92, 260–269, (1918), 131–135, 158–160, 294–296, 317–320, 347–350, 381–383, and (1919), 167–168, 259–262, 357–360, 381–385; "The Earlier Breeding Habits of the Red-Throated Diver," in *Wild Life*, **3** (1914), 138–144, 206–213; "The Early Breeding Habits of the Shag," *ibid.*, **6** (1915), 151–155, 177–181; "An Observational Diary of the Domestic Habits of the Little Grebe or Dabchick," *ibid.*, **7** (1915), 29–35, 38–42, 98–99, 137–141, 175–178, 219–230; "The Spring Habits of the Stone Curlew," *ibid.*, **8** (1916), 51–54, 76–81, 112–115, 152–158; "On the Sexual Origin of the Nidificatory, Incubatory, and Courting Display Instincts in Birds: An Answer to Criticism," in *The Zoologist*, 4th ser., **20** (1916), 401–412; "Sex-Habits of the Great-Crested Grebe," in *The Naturalist* (1920), 97–102, 195–198, 325–328, and (1921), 173–176, 197–200, 301–305; "The Courting-Habits of the Heron," *ibid.* (1925), 179–182; and "Further Observations on the Nuptial Habits of the Heron," *ibid.*, 335–336.

In addition to eleven children's books and books of a popular nature, Selous wrote the following books on bird behavior: *Bird Watching* (London, 1901); *Bird Life Glimpses* (London, 1905); *The Bird Watcher in the Shetlands; with Some Notes on Seals—and Digressions* (London, 1905); *Realities of Bird Life, Being Extracts from the Diaries of a Life-Loving Naturalist* (London, 1927); *Thought-Transference (or What?) in Birds* (London, 1931); *Evolution of Habit in Birds* (London, 1933).

II. SECONDARY LITERATURE. There has been to date no extensive study of Selous' work, though such a study is being undertaken by Dr. K. E. L. Simmons. Two appreciative biographical notices appeared after Selous' death: Margaret Morse Nice, "Edmund Selous: An Appreciation," in *Bird-Banding*, **6** (1935), 90–96; and Jacques Delamain, "Edmund Selous," in *Alauda*, **6** (1934), 388–393. Additional comments on Selous' work are in John Durant, "Innate Character in Animals and Man: A Perspective on the Origins of Ethology," in Charles Webster, ed., *Biology, Medicine and Society, 1840–1940* (Cambridge, 1981), 157–192; David Lack, "Some British Pioneers in Ornithological Research, 1859–1939," in *Ibis*, **101** (1959), 71–81; and Erwin Stresemann, *Ornithology from Aristotle to the Present* (Cambridge, Mass., 1975), 342–344. The most extensive review of the details of Selous' life is K. E. L. Simmons, "Edmund Selous (1857–1934): Fragments for a Biography," in *Ibis*, **126** (1984), 595–596.

RICHARD W. BURKHARDT, JR.

SEREBROVSKII, ALEKSANDR SERGEEVICH (*b*. Tula, Russia, 18 February 1892; *d*. Moscow, U.S.S.R., 26 June 1948), *animal genetics, evolutionary theory, eugenics.*

A founder of Soviet genetics, Serebrovskii studied with Nikolai K. Kol'tsov before World War I and began his career just after the Bolshevik revolution. His scientific work, philosophical viewpoint, and political commitments paralleled those of H. J. Muller and J. B. S. Haldane. Stimulated by recent scientific developments in genetics and by the revolutionary social changes taking place around him, he developed his own Marxist philosophical approach and applied it with varying success to a wide range of genetic problems. This led to pioneering work on poultry genetics, gene structure, human heredity, mathematical biology, population genetics, evolutionary theory, agriculture, and the biological control of insect pests.

Several years before Muller, Serebrovskii proposed a socialist eugenics program based on widescale human artificial insemination, but the plan got him into political trouble during the "great break" (1929–1932) and was later invoked by Lysenkoists to discredit genetics. During the 1930's Serebrovskii emerged as a leader of Soviet animal breeding research and one of Lysenko's most outspoken critics.

He was never arrested, however, and died of natural causes in 1948, just six weeks before Lysenko's triumph.

Serebrovskii's most lasting impact on Soviet science came through his teaching career as chairman of the genetics department of Moscow University (1930–1948), where he trained two generations of Soviet geneticists, including many who would help to rebuild the discipline after Lysenko's fall from power in 1964.

Career. Serebrovskii was born into the family of a leftist architect acquainted with the prominent Bolshevik theoretician A. A. Bogdanov and the future commissar of education A. V. Lunacharskii. In 1909 he graduated from the Tula *Realschule* and entered the natural science division of the physico-mathematical faculty of Moscow University, from which he graduated in 1914. A student of N. K. Kol'tsov, Serebrovskii began working in his laboratory at the Shaniavskii Free Public University. There Kol'tsov was attempting to create the first Russian research center of experimental biology, encouraging each of his advanced students to specialize in a particular experimental field. Serebrovskii took up genetics, and in 1915 he published an article on the mutation theory of Hugo de Vries.

Shortly after the outbreak of World War I, Serebrovskii was mobilized into the Russian army and fought on several fronts until 1916, when he was injured while serving with the artillery in the Caucasus. In 1918 he returned to Moscow and worked briefly at the zoo. In 1919, with the outbreak of civil war and widespread urban famine, Kol'tsov secured a post for Serebrovskii as head of a poultry breeding station in the village of Slobodka, near his hometown of Tula. He served as assistant president of the Tula soviet from 1919 until 1921, when he returned to Moscow. There he worked for the rest of his life.

During the 1920's, thanks largely to Kol'tsov's patronage, Serebrovskii emerged as Russia's most exciting and energetic young animal geneticist. In 1917 Kol'tsov created the Institute of Experimental Biology (IEB) and became its director; in 1919 he established experimental genetics stations under the Commissariat of Agriculture; in 1920 he founded the Russian Eugenics Society and became its president. Serebrovskii worked under Kol'tsov as head of a division at the IEB (1921–1927), as director of research at the Central Genetics Station at Anikovo (1921–1926) and then at Nazarevo (1926–1928), and as a member of the governing board of the Russian Eugenics Society. He also chaired the poultry department (renamed the genetics department) of the Moscow Zootechnical Institute (1923–1930).

Serebrovskii's entrepreneurial energies and reformist temperament became engaged along a wide front. In 1921 he proposed that all mutations be renamed according to a new, "rational," decimal system of his own devising, and he reiterated the proposal at the International Congress of Genetics in 1927. In 1923 he published a popular book on nature. During the next few years, he undertook wide-ranging and innovative studies on poultry, *drosophila,* and human genetics, and elaborated synthetic theories for which he coined many new terms, among them "gene fund," "genogeography," "genetic analysis," and "step-allelomorphism." He was much taken with Marxist philosophy of science and often chastised colleagues for not thinking "dialectically."

In 1927 or 1928, perhaps because of growing political tensions with Kol'tsov, Serebrovskii left the Institute of Experimental Biology and its genetics station, and became increasingly involved in the Communist Academy and affiliated institutions, heading a genetics laboratory at the Timiriazev Biological Institute (1928–1932). He embraced the first Five-Year Plan with his characteristic enthusiasm and by 1930 had become a candidate member of the Communist Party. However, some of his philosophical and social positions proved too radical for party orthodoxy, and he never was promoted to full membership.

Nevertheless, at a time when efforts were under way to "Bolshevize" Russian scientific institutions, Serebrovskii was one of the few figures with prominence in both scientific and party circles. In 1930, following the arrest of Sergei Chetverikov and the breakup of Kol'tsov's department, Serebrovskii was appointed chairman of Moscow University's newly created department of genetics. The following year he became head of the division of genetics and selection at the All-Union Institute of Animal Breeding (VIZh) of the Lenin All-Union Academy of Agricultural Sciences (VASKhNIL). On 1 February 1933 Serebrovskii was elected corresponding member of the division of mathematical and natural sciences of the U.S.S.R. Academy of Sciences, in biology and genetics. In 1935 he was appointed a full member of VASKhNIL and became an audacious opponent of Lysenkoism. Its growth led to his separation from animal breeding research, but unlike most Soviet geneticists of comparable stature, he was never arrested. During his last decade, he was based at the department of genetics at Moscow University.

Poultry, Population Genetics, and Agriculture. From 1919 through the late 1930's, Serebrovskii was deeply involved in Soviet agricultural research. His specialty was the genetics of poultry. In the early 1920's he and his subordinates collected many breeds of chickens from central Russia and launched research to discover and map their genes. In a series of publications beginning in 1921, Serebrovskii explored the genetic basis of comb shape, feathering, coloration, weight, egg characteristics, fertility, and other traits. His poultry work was regularly published in both Russian and English, so it came to the attention of L. C. Dunn and other poultry geneticists in the West. During his career Serebrovskii published some twenty-five papers on the genetics of poultry, several of which were reprinted in 1976.

During the period 1922–1925, Sergei Chetverikov's group at the Kol'tsov institute created population genetics, formulating a modern view of the evolutionary process and launching the earliest studies of the genetics of natural *drosophila* populations. Serebrovskii occasionally attended the group's seminars and they apparently influenced his thinking: Chetverikov's group conducted studies of natural *drosophila* populations from the Moscow area in the summer of 1925, and in late 1925 Chetverikov completed a classic paper that synthesized Darwinism and genetics. In early 1926 Serebrovskii criticized Lamarckian and autogenetic theories of evolution, arguing for a synthesis of Darwinism and genetics. In the summer of 1926, when Chetverikov's group extended their studies to the wild fly populations of Dagestan, Serebrovskii began a comparable survey of the domesticated poultry of that region.

Serebrovskii first used the term *genofond* (gene fund) in a eugenic context, as part of his defense of genetics, at a meeting of the Communist Academy in early 1926. At an agricultural meeting in Leningrad in 1927, he generalized the concept in an important paper entitled "Genogeografiia i genofond sel'skokhoziaistvennykh zhivotnykh SSSR" (Genogeography and the gene fund of domesticated animals in the U.S.S.R.; 1928). Defining "gene fund" as "the sum total of hereditary assets, genes, of any group of organisms," he set forth a research program for determining "what percentage of the gametes carry the given gene and what percentage do not carry it," the former being the "concentration of the gene in the gene fund" (pp. 6–7). Serebrovskii defined "genogeography" as the "geographical distribution of the concentration of various genes" (pp. 8–9), and distinguished between *distributional* changes in the gene fund (resulting from diffusion and from human and animal migration) and *trans-*

formational changes (resulting from natural selection, artificial selection, and mutation). In Serebrovskii's view, distributional genogeography could supplement archaeology, since "the current geography of genes is the result of a lengthy historical process, and when we study what is written about history in the geographical distribution of the various genes, we will be able to reckon the detailed history not only of domestic livestock, but also of man" (p. 12). As for transformational genography, he stated categorically, "All evolution is in essence . . . the evolution of the gene fund" (p. 17).

In 1926 Serebrovskii and a group from the Moscow Zootechnical Institute conducted an extensive field study that established the frequencies of alleles at seventeen loci in poultry populations of small villages and settlements throughout the mountainous region of Dagestan. Subsequently he engaged in a follow-up study of the Dagestan populations (1929) that provided the first direct evidence of what Sewall Wright would later call genetic drift. In these and later studies, he developed and elaborated sophisticated mathematical and statistical techniques for analyzing the distribution and transformation of the gene funds of domesticated fowl.

In 1931 Serebrovskii was appointed head of the division of genetics and selection at VASKhNIL's newly created All-Union Institute of Animal Breeding. There, he built up a genetic program of animal breeding and continued his own studies of the genetics and genogeography of fowl, extending his Dagestan work in parallel studies of populations in Kabardy and Balkaria (1935), and in Armenia (1935). He also pressed for the widescale application of Il'ia I. Ivanov's techniques for the artificial insemination of horses and cattle, and worked to develop comparable techniques for poultry. The institute became VASKhNIL's major center of animal research, and Serebrovskii was appointed a full member of that academy in 1935.

Drosophila and Gene Theory. In connection with his early work on poultry genetics, Serebrovskii became well acquainted with the publications of William Bateson and his presence-absence theory. In August 1922, when H. J. Muller visited the Kol'tsov institute and its Anikovo station, he gave them many mutant strains of *Drosophila melanogaster* developed by the Morgan school. As a poultry geneticist, Serebrovskii had no research experience with flies, but he threw himself into the study of the stocks with his characteristic enthusiasm. During the summer of 1924, working at Anikovo, he completed work on his first major paper on *Drosophila,* which was published in Russian in 1926 and in English

the next year. The work analyzed the influence of different alleles of one gene on crossing-over between two other genes, noting that different map distances resulted. On this basis Serebrovskii advanced the view that the chromosomal theory of heredity was compatible with Bateson's presence-absence theory, so long as one assumed that genes could be divided. A study undertaken at Anikovo in the summer of 1925 on other genes located at the end of the X chromosome produced similar results and was published in both Russian (1928) and English (1929).

In the 1920's many Soviet Marxists felt that genetics was contrary to a materialist view of nature because of its concept of the immortal gene, subject only to rare, random, and generally harmful mutations, which rendered mankind impotent in controlling mutational change. Muller's demonstration in 1927 that X rays are mutagenic seemed to Serebrovskii a key breakthrough. He published a sensational article on the discovery in *Pravda,* "Chetyre stranitsy, kotorye vzvolnovali nauchnyi mir" (Four pages that shook the scientific world—a title that played on John Reed's famous account of the Bolshevik revolution, *Ten Days That Shook the World*). In late 1927 and early 1928 Serebrovskii replicated Muller's results in his own laboratory. As a result his laboratory attracted a group of young Marxist biologists who became involved in his *Drosophila* work. This group included V. E. Al'tschuler, N. P. Dubinin, A. E. Gaisinovich, N. I. Shapiro, and B. N. Sidorov, as well as three Communist Party members: Izrail' I. Agol, Solomon G. Levit, and Vasilii N. Slepkov.

In the period 1928–1932, on the basis of studies of the *scute* region at the end of the sex chromosome of *Drosophila melanogaster,* the group developed a theory of gene structure that they called "step-allelomorphism" (better known in Western literature as "step-allelism"). Using X rays to induce new mutations, the group discovered a series of alleles, each of which, they thought, controlled bristling in a specific region of the fly's body. In four years many *scute* [*sc*] mutants were discovered and studied by Dubinin (sc^2, sc^3, sc^7, sc^{10}), Agol (sc^4), Gaisinovich (sc^5), Serebrovskii (sc^6), Sidorov (sc^8), Levit (sc^9), and Shapiro (sc^{12}). It was originally believed that the alleles could be mapped in a linear series, but subsequent mutants mapped as overlapping segments.

On this basis, Serebrovskii developed the notion that *scute* was a divisible "basigene" containing a series of overlapping sections or "subgenes" affecting slightly different areas, and that the mutations represented deletions of small segments. This theory of gene structure attracted international attention, but it was subsequently undermined by experiments, published in 1934 and 1935, by H. J. Muller and A. A. Prokof'eva at the Institute of Genetics in Moscow. Nonetheless, step-allelism involved one of the first systematic attempts to study gene structure using a kind of complementation mapping. Serebrovskii's work on gene structure has been discussed by Carlson (1966, pp. 143–157) and Khesin (1972).

Eugenics and Human Genetics. From mid 1920 through early 1930, the Kol'tsov institute had a eugenics division that served as the organizational base for the Russian Eugenics Society, which was officially founded in November 1920. The utopian possibilities of eugenics for the human future appealed to Serebrovskii's revolutionary temperament, and, beginning in 1921, he served on the society's governing board. In the early 1920's he published a piece on the inheritance of the tendency for multiple pregnancy (1921), a genealogical study of the prominent Aksakov family (1922), and a programmatic statement entitled "O zadachakh i putiakh antropogenetiki" (On the tasks and trends of anthropogenetics; 1923) that called for the investigation of the genetics of human physical and mental traits in individuals, families, isolated human tribes, and the population at large.

In a paper presented to the natural science section of the Communist Academy on 12 January 1926, "Teoriia nasledstvennosti Morgana i Mendelia i marksisty" (Marxists and the theory of heredity of Morgan and Mendel), Serebrovskii gave special prominence to the prospects for eugenics under socialism. After arguing that modern genetics was both dialectical and materialist, he sought to depict it as a socially revolutionary science by focusing on its implications for human betterment. Urging the development of a truly socialist eugenics, he argued that "the totality of such genes, which create in human society talented outstanding individuals, or to the contrary idiots" constitute "a national treasure, a *gene fund* from which the society draws its people," even more important for the country than the genes of "wheat, cows, and horses which create the economic power of our country" (pp. 115–116).

In late 1927 Serebrovskii converted Solomon Levit (a physician and party member) from Lamarckism to genetics, and in 1928 the two formed the Office of Human Heredity and Constitution within the Biomedical Institute of the Commissariat of Public Health. Its first publication opened with a remarkable article by Serebrovskii, "Antropogenetika i evgenika v sotsialisticheskom obshchestve" (Anthropogenetics and eugenics in a socialist society; 1929). In it Serebrovskii argued that "anthropogenetics"—the science of human heredity—was objective and independent of its social setting, but "eugenics"—the application of such knowledge to social policy—would depend on economics and class structure. Criticizing Western eugenics movements as extensions of oppressive capitalist systems, Serebrovskii asserted that the positive potentials of eugenics could be achieved only under socialism.

Serebrovskii then made clear what he thought Soviet socialist eugenics should be. Chastising the architects of the first Five-Year Plan because it discussed reserves of gas, oil, and minerals but "completely left out the tabulation of the biological quality of the population of the Soviet Union" (p. 7), he commented: "If we calculate how much effort, time, and money would be freed if we succeeded in cleansing our country's population of various forms of hereditary ailments, then probably it would be possible to fulfill the Five-Year Plan in two-and-a-half years" (p. 12). He proposed "the widespread induction of conception by means of artificial insemination using recommended sperm," estimating that given "the tremendous sperm-making capacity of men," and "with the current state of artificial insemination technology (now widely used in horse and cattle breeding), one talented and valuable producer could have up to 1,000 or even up to 10,000 children. . . . In these conditions, human selection would make gigantic leaps forward. And various women and whole communes would then be proud . . . of their successes and achievements in this undoubtedly most astonishing field—the creation of new forms of human beings" (pp. 16–18).

Serebrovskii's plan drew heavy criticism and was the subject of a scathing lampoon by Dem'ian Bednyi in the 4 June 1930 issue of *Izvestiia*. In the period 1929–1932 a new ideological party line was imposed that held the "biologization" of social phenomena to be one of the several unacceptable trends pejoratively branded "Menshevizing idealism." Serebrovskii's proposal was frequently cited as evidence that he was guilty of this ideological aberration. In 1930 Serebrovskii was a candidate member of the Communist Party, but as a result of this criticism, he was never elevated to full membership.

Not all the changes taking place during these turbulent years were adverse to Serebrovskii, however. The widespread replacement of "bourgeois experts" by "Red specialists" no doubt played a role in Serebrovskii's appointment as chair of the Moscow University genetics department in 1930.

The same year Levit, a party member, was appointed director of the Biomedical Institute, and the office he had founded with Serebrovskii was elevated to the status of a genetics division. Its second volume of research papers (1930) concluded with a detailed apology by Serebrovskii for some of his remarks the previous year in its first volume. In 1930 Serebrovskii's wife, Raisa Isaakovna, joined the division's staff. As the accusations of Serebrovskii's "Menshevizing idealism" persisted, however, both he and his wife left the institute and did not contribute further to its publications.

Levit and Agol spent 1931 on Rockefeller grants in H. J. Muller's laboratory at the zoology department of the University of Texas at Austin. Levit probably informed Muller of Serebrovskii's views on socialist eugenics and human breeding at that time. In the spring of 1932, after Levit and Agol had returned home, Muller made his much-publicized break with the American eugenics movement in "The Dominance of Economics over Eugenics," which reiterated much of Serebrovskii's viewpoint and language. In the fall of 1932 Levit resumed directorship of the Biomedical Institute, which by 1935 had become the Maxim Gorky Institute of Medical Genetics.

In 1933 Muller came to Russia to head a laboratory in Vavilov's Institute of Genetics, but he played an active role in Levit's institute and consistently urged a program of positive socialist eugenics. In 1935 Muller incorporated Serebrovskii's discredited breeding scheme, without attribution, into the final chapter of his book *Out of the Night*. Against Serebrovskii's advice, Muller sent a copy of the book to Stalin in the spring of 1936, with a long letter urging him to implement a human breeding program. At the height of the purges, when genetics was under attack by Lysenkoists, this was a dangerous proposal. Muller managed to leave Russia on 9 March 1937. Agol, who had been arrested in December, was executed the next day. Levit was arrested in January 1938 and was probably shot later that spring. For reasons that are not clear, Serebrovskii was never arrested.

Lysenkoism. In 1936 Serebrovskii's earlier eugenic proposals were used by the Lysenkoists as a way of discrediting him for reasons that had little to do with eugenics. Serebrovskii had to be discredited principally because he stood directly in the way of their takeover of Soviet agricultural research. Indeed, his career was a refutation of Lysenko's central claims. In the mid 1930's, the Lysenkoists argued that theirs was the only truly Marxist approach to heredity; but Serebrovskii was an active and devoted Marxist, with an important party following, who argued tirelessly that genetics was the only truly Marxist theory of heredity. The Lysenkoists sought to depict genetics as a reactionary science committed to the idealist concept of an immortal, indivisible, immaterial, and unchanging gene; but Serebrovskii's own research on X-ray mutagenesis and gene structure had portrayed the gene as material, mutable, divisible, and ultimately controllable. Finally, Lysenkoists argued that geneticists had divorced themselves from agricultural practice and were incapable of aiding it; but Serebrovskii had been active in poultry work since 1919, had welcomed collectivization, and by the mid 1930's was fully engaged in agricultural research.

Perhaps most important, Serebrovskii was an outspoken Marxist critic of Lysenko's views and a persuasive defender of genetics who would not be intimidated. Having assailed Lamarckism in the 1920's, Serebrovskii naturally found much to criticize in Lysenko's theories and techniques. At public meetings in 1935 and 1936, he twice called Lysenko *mrakobes*—a pungent Russian expletive often translated as "obscurantist" but literally signifying "demon of darkness."

At the VASKhNIL session in December 1936, the four featured speakers were Vavilov, Muller, Lysenko, and Serebrovskii, whose presentation, "Genetika i zhivotnovodstvo" (Genetics and animal breeding), cogently presented his progress in mobilizing the animal resources of the country. Although the agenda of the meeting was designed to promote compromise between the geneticists and Lysenko's Michurinists, Serebrovskii continued his outspoken defense of genetics. His unusually candid summary put the matter directly:

> Editors are asking whether they can publish books on genetics. The same position is being taken by several people here, and some who were connected with Serebrovskii and genetics in one way or another are panicking and thinking of abandoning Serebrovskii before it is too late. Such fainthearted comrades exist, but I myself am not fainthearted and do not put my faith in people who are. I believe that we will overcome our difficult position and demonstrate that our method gives results that are better, not worse, precisely because it is based on this genetic theory, a theory that permits the maximal mobilization of hereditary elements of animals that could not be mobilized by any other method. (*Spornye voprosy*, p. 448)

However, Serebrovskii's position at the meeting was inadvertently undermined by Muller's insistent attempts to introduce human genetics into the agricultural discussion, despite direct political instructions not to do so. Once the topic had been broached, the Michurinists L. K. Greben', I. G. Eikhfel'd, I. I. Prezent, and others found Serebrovskii an especially apt target and castigated him for his earlier eugenic views. One remarked that Soviet women would never forgive him for his ideas on human breeding. On 27 December, the final day of the conference, Serebrovskii rose on a point of personal privilege and admitted that his 1929 article represented "a whole series of the crudest kind of political, anti-scientific, and anti-Marxist mistakes, which I now find painful to remember."

Beginning in 1936, the Lysenkoists sought to discredit genetics by claiming that it led logically and inevitably to eugenics and fascism. The accusation was unjust. Indeed, Serebrovskii, Muller, Levit, Levin, and others involved in Soviet human genetics had been among the first to warn of the scientific inaccuracy and social danger of Nazi race biology. Yet this Lysenkoist tactic was ironically apt in one respect. Serebrovskii had portrayed his eugenic proposals as following logically from the science of genetics, from which they derived their legitimacy. It should hardly have surprised him, then, when the Lysenkoists used those discredited proposals to make genetics itself seem illegitimate. For example, in a special discussion of genetics in 1939 published in *Under the Banner of Marxism,* the Stalinist ideologue M. B. Mitin, addressing Serebrovskii, charged, "Your whole 'gene fund,' with its Five-Year Plan in two-and-a-half years, is a reactionary notion rooted in your mistaken theoretical position." Nonetheless, despite the arrest of a number of his colleagues, the loss of his position at the VIZh, and repeated attacks on him in print, Serebrovskii continued his principled and outspoken defense of genetics and his sharp cirticism of Lysenko's theories.

The Final Decade. Separated from an active role in Soviet animal breeding by Lysenko's rise to power, Serebrovskii devoted himself to research, writing, and teaching, but he had difficulty publishing his work. In 1938 he developed a highly original method for the biological control of insect pests, using chromosomal translocations to produce sterile males for release in the wild. He managed to send a copy of a pioneering paper on this subject to Theodosius Dobzhansky in the United States, with a note explaining that the growth of Lysenkoism made it unlikely that the paper would be published in the Soviet Union. As it happened, in 1940 the paper was accepted and appeared in *Zoologicheskii zhurnal,* edited by Ivan I. Schmalhausen.

However, many other works by Serebrovskii, in-

cuding two books, were not published. In 1939 he completed a synthetic and original monograph, *Nekoforye problemy organicheskoi evoliutsii* (Some problems of organic evolution), which depicted evolution as a dialectical, populational process governed by historical laws not reducible to those of physiology or chemistry. The work might well have been regarded as a classic of the evolutionary synthesis had its publication not been thwarted by the growth of Lysenkoism; it first appeared in print only in 1973. In the period 1939–1940 Serebrovskii developed genetic applications of techniques of mathematical analysis and managed to publish brief mathematical papers on the "signal method" and the "triangle method." He also completed a mathematical book, *Geneticheskii analiz* (Genetic analysis), that analyzed qualitative and quantitative inheritance, including the foundations of population genetics, and set forth various methods of analysis, including path coefficients. However, this book was not published during his lifetime. In 1946, with the resurgence of genetics after the war, he reworked the book with the assistance of his wife Raisa, his student A. A. Malinovskii, M. V. Ignat'ev, and his former colleague M. M. Mestergazi. Serebrovskii's preface for the book was dated 1 May 1948.

Eight weeks later, on 26 June 1948, Serebrovskii died of natural causes. Following a funeral procession, he was buried in a public ceremony at Novodevichi cemetery, where his many students and supporters spoke against Lysenkoism and called for the triumph of genetics. However, six weeks later, it was Lysenko who triumphed at the infamous August session of VASKhNIL by declaring that the Central Committee of the Communist Party (and, by implication, Stalin) had approved his theory.

Thus empowered, Lysenko's supporters were free to conduct virulent attacks on Serebrovskii's legacy. At a meeting of the presidium of the U.S.S.R. Academy of Sciences on 24 August 1948, I. E. Glushchenko depicted the schools of Filipchenko and Kol'tsov (including Dobzhansky, Dubinin, and Timoféeff-Ressovsky) as fascist, paying special attention to Serebrovskii. After the sessions, the Minister of Education, S. V. Kaftanov, issued a pamphlet in an edition of 110,000 copies that quoted from Serebrovskii's 1929 article and asserted, "The propositions of Morganism-Mendelism led in our country, just as they did abroad, to eugenic ideas and the ideology of fascism" (*Za bezrazdel'noe gospodstvo michurinskoi biologicheskoi nauki* [For the undivided rule of Michurinist biological science], Moscow, 1948, p. 17). Throughout the period of Lysenko's dominance over Soviet biology (1948–

1964), Serebrovskii continued to be a favorite target of Michurinist propaganda. His wife survived this difficult time, and after 1965 she and his students arranged for the posthumous publication of many of his manuscripts.

Significance and Impact. The hallmark of Serebrovskii's career was his synthetic approach to his science and his self-conscious attempts to effect the dialectical synthesis of opposites. An enthusiastic reformer, he developed his own Marxist approach to science and applied it to a wide range of theoretical, experimental, and practical problems. Some of these efforts ultimately proved to be mistaken. His work on gene structure sought to synthesize Bateson's presence-absence theory with the chromosomal theory of the Morgan school, but it turned out to be an unsuccessful attempt at reductionism. His work on socialist eugenics sought to synthesize Morganist biological theory and Marxist social theory, but it proved out of keeping with the new ideologies and harsher realities of the 1930's.

On the other hand, some of Serebrovskii's other synthetic work was highly successful. His efforts to synthesize genetical "theory" with the social needs of "practice" led to highly original and useful work in poultry breeding, agriculture, and the biological control of insect pests whose potential applications were stymied only by the rising tide of Lysenkoism. His pioneering work in population genetics and evolutionary theory synthesized Darwinism and genetics, anticipating in important respects the evolutionary synthesis of the 1930's and 1940's and leading directly to some of Dubinin's important contributions to population genetics in the 1930's. Indeed, it is likely that the term "gene pool," introduced by Dobzhansky in 1950, was a translation of Serebrovskii's term "gene fund" (Adams, 1980). Finally, his field studies of domesticated fowl populations in isolated mountainous regions pioneered the use of biological data to supplement anthropology and archaeology in ways that are only now beginning to be realized.

Serebrovskii rose in prominence and visibility in the late 1920's because he was one of the first important Soviet scientists to embrace Marxism. At the same time, he never let ideology affect his scientific judgment, and was outspoken and uncompromising in his defense of his science and his opposition to Lysenkoism, even when that stance put his life at risk. With the advent of Stalinism, much of Serebrovskii's synthetic research program came to naught. Nonetheless, as a committed Marxist who also maintained his commitment to genetic science, he served as a model for his students and for a later generation of Soviet geneticists.

Perhaps his most lasting impact on Soviet science came through his extraordinary teaching career. During the last quarter century of his life, he helped to train a large school of geneticists, including I. I. Agol, S. I. Alikhanian, V. E. Al'tshuler, N. P. Dubinin, L. V. Ferri, S. M. Gershenson, Ia. L. Glembotskii, G. Himmel, O. A. Ivanova, R. B. Khesin, V. V. Khvostova, S. G. Levit, A. A. Malinovskii, S. G. Petrov, P. F. Rokitskii, V. V. Sakharov, N. I. Shapiro, B. N. Sidorov, V. N. Slepkov, N. B. Varshaver, and E. T. Vasina-Popova. Many of his students were responsible for keeping genetics alive in the Soviet Union during the Lysenko period and played a key role after 1965 in rebuilding the discipline.

BIBLIOGRAPHY

I. ORIGINAL WORKS. Serebrovskii published more than 120 works during his lifetime, many in English and German, and left some 30 unpublished manuscripts, including those of several books. For his earliest publications see "Vliianie temperatury na nabukhanie semian gorokha" (The influence of temperature on swelling of seeds in peas), in *Uchenye zapiski Instituta imeni Shaniavskogo, Trudy biologicheskoi laboratorii*, **1**, no. 1 (1951), 1–74; "Sovremennoe sostoianie teorii mutatsii" (The current status of the mutation theory), in *Priroda*, 1915, no. 10, 1239–1254; "Proekt desiatichnoi sistemy geneticheskoi simvoliki" (Proposal for a decimal system of genetic symbols), in *Izvestiia instituta eksperimental'noi biologii*, 1921, no. 1, 98–106; and *Biologicheskie progulki* (Biological walks; Petrograd, 1923; 2nd ed., Leningrad, 1946; 3rd ed., 1973).

For Serebrovskii's work on eugenics and human genetics, see "O mendelirovanii mnogoplodiia u cheloveka" (On Mendelizing multiple pregnancy in humans), in *Izvestiia instituta eksperimental'noi biologii*, 1921, no. 1, 114–119; "Genealogiia roda Aksakovykh" (The genealogy of the Aksakov family), in *Russkii evgenicheskii zhurnal*, **1**, no. 1 (1922), 74–81; "O zadachakh i putiakh antropogenetiki" (On the tasks and trends of anthropogenetics), *ibid.*, **1**, no. 2 (1923), 107–116; "Antropogenetika i evgenika v sotsialisticheskom obshchestve" (Anthropogenetics and eugenics in a socialist society), in S. G. Levit and A. S. Serebrovskii, eds., *Trudy kabineta nasledstvennosti i konstitutsii cheloveka pri mediko-biologicheskom institute* (Works of the Office of Human Heredity and Constitution of the Biomedical Institute), I (Leningrad, 1929) (supp. to *Mediko-biologicheskii zhurnal*, 1929, no. 5), 3–19; "Veroiatnyi sluchai nasledovaniia po tipu stseplennykh X-khromosom u cheloveka" (A likely case of inheritance of the double X-chromosome type in humans), *ibid.*, 79–82, with S. G. Levit; "K voprosu o geneticheskom analize cheloveka" (On the genetic analysis of humans), in *Mediko-biologicheskii zhurnal*, 1930, no. 4–5, 321–328, with S. G. Levit; and "Pis'mo v Redaktsiiu" (To the editor), *ibid.*, 447–448.

For Serebrovskii's work on drosophila mutations and gene structure, see "Novye mutatsii u *Drosophila melanogaster*" (New mutations in *Drosophila melanogaster*), in *Zhurnal eksperimental'noi biologii*, ser. A, **1**, no. 1–2 (1925), 75–91, with V. V. Sakharov; "Vliianie gena *purple* na krossingover mezhdu *black* i *cinnabar* u *Drosophila melanogaster*," *ibid.*, **2**, no. 1 (1926), 55–76 and no. 2–3, 77–100, published in English as "The Influence of the 'Purple' Gene on the Crossing-over Between 'Black' and 'Cinnabar' in *Drosophila melanogaster*," in *Journal of Genetics*, **18**, no. 2 (1927), 136–175; "'Chetyre stranitsy, kotorye vzvolnovali nauchnyi mir" (Four pages that shook the scientific world), in *Pravda*, 11 September 1927, p. 5; "Poluchenie novykh nasledstvennykh svoistv rentgenovymi luchami" (The creation of new hereditary material with Roentgen rays), in *Nauchnoe slovo*, 1928, no. 1, 34–48; "Poluchenie mutatsii rentgenovskimi luchami u *Drosophila melanogaster*" (The induction of mutations in *Drosophila melanogaster* with Roentgen rays), in *Zhurnal eksperimental'noi biologii*, ser. A, **4**, no. 3–4 (1928), 161–180, with N. P. Dubinin, I. I. Agol, V. N. Slepkov, and V. E. Al'tshuler; "Vliianie genov y, l_i, i N_i na krossingover v levom kontse polovoi khromosomy u *Drosophila melanogaster*," *ibid.*, **4**, no. 1 (1928), 1–29, with L. V. Ferri and O. A. Ivanova, published in English as "On the Influence of Genes y, l_i, and N_i on the Crossing-over Close to Their Loci in the Sex-Chromosome of *Drosophila melanogaster*," in *Journal of Genetics*, **21** (1929), no. 2, 287–314, with O. A. Ivanova and Leo Ferry; "Problema gena" (Problem of the gene), in *Pod znamenem marksizma*, 1928, no. 9–10, 215–228; "A General Scheme for the Origin of Mutations," in *American Naturalist*, **63** (July-August 1929), 374–378; "Iskusstvennoe poluchenie mutatsii i problema gena" (Artificial induction of mutations and the problem of the gene), in *Uspekhi eksperimental'noi biologii*, ser. B, **8**, no. 4 (1929), 235–247, with N. P. Dubinin; "Issledovanie stupenchatogo allelomorfizma. IV. Transgenatsiia scute[6] i sluchai 'neallelomorfizma' chlenov obshchei lestnitsy allelomorfov," in *Zhurnal eksperimental'noi biologii*, **6**, no. 2 (1930), 61–72, published in German as "Untersuchungen über Treppenallelomorphismus. IV. Transgenation scute-6 und ein Fall des 'Nicht-Allelomorphismus' von Gliedern einer Allelomorphenreihe bei Drosophila melanogaster," in *Wilhelm Roux' Archiv für Entwicklungsmechanik der Organismen*, **122**, no. 1 (1930), 88–104; and "X-ray Experiments with Drosophila," in *Journal of Heredity*, **21**, no. 6 (1930), 259–265, with N. P. Dubinin.

For his work on poultry genetics, see "Crossing-over Involving Three Sex-Linked Genes in Chickens," in *American Naturalist*, **56** (1922), 571–572; "Somatic Segregation in Domestic Fowl," in *Journal of Genetics*, **16**, no. 1 (1925), 33–42; "On the Topography of the Sex Chromosome in Fowls," *ibid.*, **17**, no. 2 (1927), 211–216,

with E. T. Vasin; "A Case of Close Autosomal Linkage in the Fowl," in *Journal of Heredity*, **19** (1928), 305–306, with S. G. Petrov; and "Observations on Interspecific Hybrids of the Fowl," in *Journal of Genetics*, **21** (1929), no. 3, 327–340.

For his works on evolution theory, genogeography, and population genetics, see "Khromozomy i mekhanizm evoliutsii" (Chromosomes and the mechanism of evolution), in *Zhurnal eksperimental'noi biologii*, ser. B, 1925, no. 1, 49–75; "Teoriia nasledstvennosti Morgana i Mendelia i marksisty" (Marxists and the theory of heredity of Morgan and Mendel), in *Pod znamenem marksizma*, 1926, no. 3, 98–117; "Opyt kachestvennoi kharakteristiki protsessa organicheskoi evoliutsii" (Attempt to characterize qualitatively the process of organic evolution), in *Estestvoznanie i Marksizm*, 1929, no. 2, 53–72; "Geneticheskii analiz populiatsii domashnikh kur gortsev Dagestana" (Genetic analysis of the populations of domesticated chickens in the mountains of Dagestan), in *Zhurnal eksperimental'noi biologii*, ser. A, **3** (1927), no. 1–2, 62–124 and no. 3–4, 125–146; "Genogeografiia i genofond sel'skokhoziaistvennykh zhivotnykh SSSR" (Genogeography and the gene fund of agricultural animals in the USSR), in *Nauchoe slovo*, 1928, no. 9, 3–22; "Beitrag zur genetischen Geographie des Haushuhns in USSR," in *Zeitschrift für induktiv Abstammungs- und Vererbungslehre*, **46** (1928), 71–72; "Beitrag zur geographischen Genetik des Haushuhns in Sowjet-Rußland," in *Archiv für Geflügelkunde*, 1929, no. 3, 161–169; "Geneticheskii analiz" (Genetic analysis), in *Bol'shaia sovetskaia entsiklopediia* (Great Soviet encyclopedia), XV (1929), 202–206; "Problemy i metod genogeografii" (The problems and method of genogeography), in *Trudy s"ezda po genetike, selektsii, i plemennomu zhivotnovodstvu* (Proceedings of the congress on genetics, selection, and animal breeding), pt. 2 (Moscow, 1930), 71–86; "Genogeografiia domashnykh kur Kabardy i Balkarii" (The genogeography of domesticated fowl in Kabardy and Balkaria), in *Uspekhi zootekhnicheskikh nauk*, **1** (1935), no. 1, 85–142; and "Genogeografiia kur Armenii" (Genogeography of chickens in Armenia), *ibid.*, **1**, no. 3, 317–348.

For other work in the 1930's see *Gibridizatsiia zhivotnykh* (Animal hybridization; Moscow, 1935); "Moi otvet kritikam" (My answer to the critics), in *Problemy zhivotnovodstva*, 1935, no. 6, 79–84; "Genetika i zhivotnovodstvo" (Genetics and animal husbandry), in O. M. Targul'ian, ed., *Spornye voprosy genetiki i selektsii* (Issues in genetics and selection; Moscow and Leningrad, 1937), 72–113 and 443–451; "Kafedra genetiki" (The genetics department), in *Uchenye zapiski MGU*, **53**, no. 4 (1940), *Biologiia*, 166–175; and "O novom vozmozhnom metode bor'by s vrednymi nasekomymi" (On a possible new method for fighting harmful insects), in *Zoologicheskii zhurnal*, **19**, no. 4 (1940), 618–630.

Since the 1960's a number of Serebrovskii's works have been reprinted, and some previously unpublished manuscripts have appeared. See *Klassiki sovetskoi genetiki 1920–1940* (Classics of Soviet genetics, 1920–1940; Leningrad, 1968), which reprints six of his papers. See also Serebrovskii, *Selektsiia zhivotnykh i rastenii* (The selection of animals and plants; Moscow, 1969); *Geneticheskii analiz* (Genetic analysis; Moscow, 1970); *Teoreticheskie osnovaniia translokatsionnogo metoda bor'by s vrednymi nasekomymi* (The theoretical basis of the translocation method for fighting harmful insects; Moscow, 1971); *Nekotorye problemy organicheskoi evoliutsii* (Some problems of organic evolution; Moscow, 1973); and *Izbrannye trudy po genetike i selektsii kur* (Selected works on the genetics and selection of poultry; Moscow, 1976), which includes four previously unpublished manuscripts from the archives of the U.S.S.R. Academy of Sciences.

II. SECONDARY LITERATURE. For discussions in Russian, see R. B. Khesin, "Teoriia gena v rabotakh A. S. Serebrovskogo" (The theory of the gene in the works of Serebrovskii), in *Priroda*, 1972, no. 8, 16–27; P. F. Rokitskii and E. T. Vasina-Popova, "Razvitie genetiki sel'skokhoziaistvennykh zhivotnykh SSSR" (The development of the genetics of agricultural animals in the U.S.S.R.), in *Istoriko-biologicheskie issledovaniia*, VI (Moscow, 1978), 5–27; N. I. Shapiro, "Pamiati A. S. Serebrovskogo" (In memory of A. S. Serebrovskii), in *Genetika*, 1966, no. 9, 3–17, which includes a list of his publications and papers, and "Aleksandr Sergeevich Serebrovskii," in *Vydaiushchiesia sovetskie genetiki* (Leading Soviet geneticists; Moscow, 1980), 57–68; E. T. Vasina-Popova, "Shkola genetiki zhivotnykh A. S. Serebrovskogo" (A. S. Serebrovskii's school of animal genetics), in *Genetika*, **21**, no. 9 (1985), 1576–1584; and E. T. Vasina-Popova and Z. M. Kogan, "Posleslovie" (Postscript), in Serebrovskii, *Izbrannye trudy*, 392–402. For a reevaluation of Serebrovskii's work by a Soviet Marxist philosopher, see I. T. Frolov, *Genetika i dialektika* (Genetics and dialectics; Moscow, 1968).

For discussions in English, see Mark B. Adams, "From 'Gene Fund' to 'Gene Pool': On the Evolution of Evolutionary Language," in William Coleman and Camille Limoges, eds., *Studies in History of Biology*, III (Baltimore and London, 1979), 241–285, and "Eugenics in Russia," in Mark B. Adams, ed., *The Wellborn Science* (New York, 1990), 153–216; and A. E. Gaissinovitch, "The Origins of Soviet Genetics and the Struggle with Lamarkism, 1922–1929," Mark B. Adams, trans., in *Journal of the History of Biology*, **13**, no. 1 (1980), 1–51. See also the references to Serebrovskii in Elof Axel Carlson, *The Gene: A Critical History* (Philadelphia, 1966), and *Genes, Radiation, and Society* (Ithaca, N.Y., 1981); David Joravsky, *Soviet Marxism and Natural Science, 1917–1932* (New York, 1961); and Zhores A. Medvedev, *The Rise and Fall of T. D. Lysenko*, I. M. Lerner, trans. (New York, 1969).

MARK B. ADAMS

SHELFORD, VICTOR ERNEST (*b.* Chemung, New York, 22 September 1877; *d.* Urbana, Illinois, 27 December 1968), *ecology*.

A man of boundless enthusiasm who was aggressive in promoting his ideas, Shelford was widely considered among ecologists to be the founder of the study of animal ecology in the United States. The son of Alexander Hamilton Shelford and Sarah Rumsey Shelford, he attended West Virginia University for two years, then transferred in 1901 to the University of Chicago, where he received the S.B. in 1903 and the Ph.D. in zoology in 1907. Also in 1907 he married Mary Mabel Brown; they had a son and a daughter. Mrs. Shelford died while accompanying her husband on a field trip to Panama in 1940. Shelford served in the zoology department at Chicago until 1914, then moved to the University of Illinois and built a strong academic center of ecology. Always vigorous and active, he led weekly student field trips and arduous longer surveys of natural areas all over North America. He continued an active research life from retirement in 1946 until the early 1960's. Shelford was strongly involved in the founding of the Ecological Society of America in 1915 and held many offices in it. Long interested in preserving parts of the country in their native state, he organized the Ecologists' Union with interested members of the Ecological Society of America in 1946; its purpose was land acquisition and protection. It became the Nature Conservancy in 1950.

As a student Shelford absorbed the strong new directions provided by experimental physiology and the mapping of plant distributions; such quantitative studies characterized zoology at the University of Chicago. He sought to explain ecological distribution in terms of physiological responses, creating an approach to ecology that characterized his whole career. From C. M. Childs he learned the experimental techniques of physiology, but it was Charles Benedict Davenport who had much to do with the development of Shelford's ideas of physiological ecology. Brought to Chicago in part to foster field studies, Davenport stimulated enthusiasm in both Shelford and C. C. Adams, a young staff member in zoology, with new researches on the relations between the environment and physiological responses. He saw behavior as an adjustment between the animal and its physical environment, an approach allowing a marriage of experimental zoology in the lab to distribution studies in nature.

But if Davenport gave ecological ideas to Shelford and Adams, the plant ecologist Henry C. Cowles provided the spark for fieldwork. Since 1899 Cowles had been studying the ecological succession of plants on the dunes south of Lake Michigan, and the resulting theoretical orderliness he brought to plant ecology stimulated Adams and Shelford to independent attempts to apply the same concepts to animals. Adams studied birds; Shelford chose for his dissertation the tiger beetles of sand dunes, including the dunes Cowles had described. Thus he was able to relate the distribution and abundance of the differently colored beetle species closely to the successional stage of the vegetation. Shelford's subsequent researches expanded this correspondence of animals to the plant community, always with regard to physiological responses of animals to habitat. His synthesis of field ecology and physiology was typical of the experimentalist attitudes at Chicago; out of this same school of ecology came Warder Clyde Allee, Shelford's student from 1908 to 1912 and later, at Chicago, one of the most influential modern ecologists.

Shelford's program for ecology was to replace the basic interpretive foundation; he moved in reaction from the theories and descriptions of evolutionary morphology and natural history to quantitative and experimental physiology. Like Davenport, he saw evolution and physiology as opposing attitudes, although he hoped for an eventual wedding. Succession studies provided the rationale for field analyses, with experiments determining which physicochemical factors were causal. In 1911 and 1912 Shelford published five papers in *Biological Bulletin* on succession in aquatic and dune habitats, including with his beetle results a theoretical discussion of the methods of animal geography. These papers were the core of his 1913 *Animal Communities in Temperate America*, and imparted a strong tradition of succession studies in American ecology. This book also is a landmark as a beginning of organized theoretical principles for animal ecology, such as Shelford's "law of toleration." Analogous to the physiologists' law of the minimum, this principle explained limits to the occurrence of a species with whatever physical factor exceeded its tolerance.

Shelford shifted toward aquatic habitats after his move to the University of Illinois in 1914. His work was marked by its attention to sophisticated equipment, which led him to write the textbook *Laboratory and Field Ecology* in 1929. In 1915, as a part of their studies of a wide range of physicochemical factors, he and his students began to investigate the effects of pollutants, such as coal distillation products, on stream fish. This work was a part of Shelford's adjunct appointment to the Illinois Natural History Survey, where he trained many limnologists and for which he also did population studies of insect pests in the 1920's and 1930's. In these he

developed his theory of paired factors that interact in complex ways ecologically and physiologically.

While teaching at Puget Sound Biological Station from 1914 to 1930, Shelford expanded his views about community processes to encompass land, freshwater, and seawater habitats. Soon after his 1913 book, he planned a book to describe the ecological regions of the whole continent. Preliminary work led to the editing of *Naturalist's Guide to the Americas* (1926), and after 1928 he stopped experimental work to concentrate on field studies. He assigned doctoral dissertations on unique habitats in America, traveling and collecting data in most of them himself. One of his students in this period was S. Charles Kendeigh, later an important teacher at Illinois.

Shelford's efforts were tied to his recognition of the need for considerable reorganization of community concepts, especially as plant and animal ecology had grown up separately, with separate and complex terminologies. He and Frederic Edward Clements, dean of American plant ecology, attempted to unify and simplify their fields with the textbook *Bio-Ecology* (1939), in the process creating the biome concept. As the basic unit of the landscape, the biome was a coherent, unified plant and animal community; plants and animals as co-actors formed a plant matrix with its accompanying animal species, characteristic of local environmental conditions. This biome bore theoretical similarity to earlier ideas of life zones and ecological provinces, but with more emphasis on relating animal and plant distributions to each other.

In *Bio-Ecology* and in the culmination of his surveys in *The Ecology of North America* (1963), Shelford revealed a concern with description and classification that he did not escape despite his early rejection of descriptive studies. Although this last book, like his career, emphasized dynamic relations, there still lingered bits of the cumbersome terminology typical of ecology in the first half of this century. His own research and prolific teaching contributed to the transformation of modern ecology, including the slow merging of plant and animal ecology.

BIBLIOGRAPHY

I. ORIGINAL WORKS. A bibliography of Shelford's voluminous research publications can be found in his books summarizing his group's research: *Animal Communities in Temperate America* (Chicago, 1913); *Laboratory and Field Ecology* (Baltimore, 1929); *A Laboratory Introduction to Animal Ecology and Taxonomy* (Chicago, 1939), with

Orlando Park and W. Clyde Allee; *Bio-Ecology* (New York, 1939), with F. E. Clements; and *The Ecology of North America* (Urbana, Ill., 1963).

Shelford left his papers at the University Archives, University of Illinois, Urbana. They include correspondence, reports, publications of his group from 1906 to 1946, and papers concerning his activities in the Ecological Society of America, as well as in preservation and conservation work.

II. SECONDARY LITERATURE. Shelford's contributions to ecology were recognized by colleagues during his lifetime. The Ecological Society of America published "An Appreciation" in its *Bulletin*, **36** (1955), 116–118, and gave him its "Eminent Ecologist" award shortly before his death. S. Charles Kendeigh evaluated Shelford's work in the award notice, in *Bulletin of the Ecological Society of America*, **49** (1968), 97–100. The principal scientific obituary notice is by John D. Buffington, in *Annals of the Entomological Society of America*, **63** (1970), 347. An evaluation of Shelford's historical role, discussing antecedents and the various schools of ecology, is in "First Four Decades of the Twentieth Century," in W. C. Allee *et al., Principles of Animal Ecology* (Philadelphia, 1949), 43–72. Gerald E. Gunning puts the work of Shelford and his students on aquatic succession and pollution into the context of ecological studies by the Illinois Natural History Survey in "Illinois," in David G. Frey, ed., *Limnology in North America* (Madison, Wis., 1963), 163–189.

WILLIAM C. KIMLER

SHEMIAKIN, MIKHAIL MIKHAILOVICH (*b.* Moscow, Russia, 26 July 1908; *d.* Riga, Latvian U.S.S.R., 26 June 1970), *chemistry, biochemistry.*

Shemiakin spent his childhood in Bolshevo, a suburb of Moscow, where he completed high school. In 1925 he entered the chemistry faculty of Moscow State University. Four years later, while still a student, he became a scientific worker at the Scientific Research Institute of Organic Intermediate Products and Dyes in Moscow; he continued to work there until 1935. Upon completion of his studies at the university in 1930, Shemiakin became an assistant at the Moscow Institute of Precision Chemical Technology (MIPCT). At first he devoted his attention primarily to the chemistry of synthetic pigments and intermediate products of their synthesis. However, he did not abandon his research on the chemistry of natural compounds. In the early 1930's he began work on the hydrolytic and oxidative-hydrolytic transformations of organic compounds. During this work he turned his attention to the mechanisms of reactions and the stereochemistry of these reactions.

In 1935 Shemiakin was appointed senior lecturer

at the MIPCT. He simultaneously was the senior scientist in the Laboratory of Organic Chemistry (of which he was director from 1939) of the All-Union Institute of Experimental Medicine in Moscow, where he worked until 1945. In 1937 he left MIPCT for the Moscow Textile Institute, where he was appointed senior lecturer.

Shemiakin received the candidate's degree in 1938, and in 1941 he defended his dissertation, "Research in the Area of Aldehyde Acids and on a Number of Diphenylcyclobutanedicarboxylic Acids: Hydrolysis of Carbon Bonds," at Moscow University for the doctorate in chemistry. In 1942 he became a full professor, chairing three departments at the Textile Institute: analytical chemistry, organic chemistry, and inorganic chemistry.

In 1945 Shemiakin headed a section of the All-Union Scientific Research Institute of Antibiotics and the laboratory at the Institute of Biological and Medical Chemistry of the Academy of Medical Sciences of the U.S.S.R. These two large institutes had just been organized in Moscow, and from this time, biochemical and bio-organic themes dominated Shemiakin's research. His interest in the mechanisms of oxidative-hydrolytic reactions found expression in the general theory of the processes of pyridoxal catalysis, which he created with A. E. Braunstein in the period 1952 to 1953.

At the Institute of Antibiotics, as well as at the Institute of Organic Chemistry of the Academy of Sciences of the U.S.S.R., where Shemiakin headed the Laboratory of the Chemistry of Antibiotics from 1957 to 1959, he began his research devoted to the chemical and biological study of numerous antibiotics. During the war years he had evaluated the practical role and theoretical significance of antibiotics, and in 1945 he began his work on the chemistry of penicillin. In 1962, before both Derek Barton and Robert Woodward, he synthesized tetracycline. Shemiakin's monograph *Khimiia antibiotikov* (Chemistry of antibiotic substances, 1949), written with A. S. Khokhlov, played a large role in the development of the chemistry of antibiotics in the Soviet Union and in other countries.

In 1958 Shemiakin was elected full member of the Academy of Sciences of the U.S.S.R. The next year he organized the Institute of the Chemistry of Natural Products of the Academy of Sciences of the U.S.S.R. and became its first director (today it is called the M. M. Shemiakin Institute of Bio-organic Chemistry). The chemistry and biochemistry of proteins and peptides became the most important area of Shemiakin's research. This work promoted the formation of bio-organic chemistry, a science of structural-functional interrelationships of biologically active substances. Shemiakin proposed a number of innovative ideas regarding the methodology of peptide synthesis and definition of the primary structure of peptides and proteins.

Shemiakin made a significant contribution to the chemistry of depsipeptides, a term he introduced in 1953 that became generally accepted. With Iu. A. Ovchinnikov, V. T. Ivanov, and others, he founded the chemistry of this very important class of natural compounds. On the basis of these investigations the function of cyclodepsipeptides as ionophores—the carriers of alkaline metals through the cell membrane—was clarified.

Throughout his scientific career Shemiakin worked with young scientists, founding a large scientific school and proving to be a major organizer of science. Among his students were Iu. A. Ovchinnikov, M. N. Kolosov, and V. T. Ivanov. Shemiakin participated in the work of various international organizations. He died suddenly in Riga, while serving as president of the Seventh International Symposium on the Chemistry of Natural Compounds.

In 1968 Shemiakin was elected member of the Academy Leopoldina (German Democratic Republic). His scientific and public activities were distinguished by the highest honor in the U.S.S.R., the title of Hero of Socialist Labor (1969).

BIBLIOGRAPHY

I. ORIGINAL WORKS. Shemiakin wrote some 300 papers. Among his works are *Hydrolytic Oxidation of Organic Substances* (New York, 1959), with I. A. Shchukina; *Khimiia antibiotikov* (The Chemistry of Antibiotics), 3rd ed., 2 vols. (Moscow, 1961), with A. S. Khokhlov, M. N. Kolosov, L. D. Bergelson, and V. K. Antonov; and "The Chemistry of Natural Depsipeptides," in *Recent Developments in the Chemistry of Natural Carbon Compounds*, **2** (1967), 1–46, with Iu. A. Ovchinnikov. An autobiographical account is in *McGraw-Hill Modern Men of Science*, II (New York, 1968), 492–494.

II. SECONDARY LITERATURE. *Mikhail Mikhailovich Shemiakin*, Materialy biobibliografii uchenykh SSSR, ser. khimicheskikh nauk, no. 65 (Moscow, 1978).

A. N. SHAMIN

SHEPPARD, PHILIP MACDONALD (*b*. Marlborough, Wiltshire, England, 27 July 1921; *d*. Liverpool, England, 17 October 1976), *evolution, genetics, population genetics, medicine.*

The only child of George Sheppard, a teacher of mathematics at a private school, and Alison Macdonald, Sheppard was related through his mother to the Darwins (being cousin, at one remove and by marriage, to Charles Darwin's granddaughter, the poet Frances Cornford). He was educated first at Bradfield College, his father's school, and then at Marlborough College (1935–1939). On leaving he immediately joined the Royal Air Force Volunteer Reserve and became a navigator with Bomber Command. Shot down over the North Sea on his sixteenth mission and twenty-first birthday, Sheppard spent the rest of the war as a prisoner and participated as an earth bearer in the famous "wooden horse" escape from Stalag Luft III. He returned to England after escaping from his second captors, the liberating Red Army, and entered Oxford University (Worcester College), under a dispensation that admitted returning servicemen without qualifications in Latin (he was no linguist), in 1946. Sheppard graduated in zoology in 1948 and obtained a D.Phil. under the supervision of Edmund Brisco Ford, who was a lifelong mentor and friend, for research in the ecological genetics of natural populations, in 1951.

Sheppard was then appointed as a junior research officer in the department of zoology at Oxford and spent a year (1954–1955) working with Theodosius Dobzhansky at Columbia University. His laboratory work on *Drosophila* remained unpublished, but the fieldwork on the moth *Panaxia* and the snail *Cepaea* became classics. Collaboration from 1952 with Cyril A. (Later Sir Cyril) Clarke, who was carrying out genetic work on swallowtail butterflies at Liverpool, led to Sheppard's taking a lecturing appointment in the zoology department at Liverpool University (1956), followed by rapid promotion through the career grades to professor of genetics in 1963. It was here, in collaboration with Clarke, that Sheppard carried out his work on the genetics of butterfly mimicry and the prevention of rhesus hemolytic disease. He was elected fellow of the Royal Society in 1965, was awarded the Darwin Medal of the Royal Society, and was honored by the Linnean Society of London and the Royal College of Physicians.

Sheppard died at the age of fifty-five from acute leukemia, against which he had put up something of a record-breaking fight, continuing in active research with barely diminished vigor almost to the end. He was survived by his devoted wife, Patricia Beatrice Lee, whom he had married in 1948, and by their three sons.

Like so many others, Sheppard entered evolutionary research through a boyhood interest in natural history, particularly of the Lepidoptera. His graduate work on *Panaxia* and *Cepaea* showed the effects of various kinds of natural selection in controlling the genetic composition of wild populations, most notably (in collaboration with Arthur J. Cain) that what had frequently been seen as the trivial characteristics of banding and color on snail shells adapted the snails to their background habitat. The study of *Panaxia*, a continuation of a long-term project by R. A. Fisher and Ford, was an exceptionally thorough examination of the dynamics of a gene in a natural population. This work, together with that carried out in Ford's laboratory at the same time by Bernard Kettlewell, was extremely influential in establishing the view of evolution that descended from the writings of Alfred Russel Wallace, August Weismann, and Fisher: that natural selection was the all-powerful process in generating evolutionary change. That view continued to be challenged; but there is no doubt that these experimental results, even if they did not and could not finally establish that selection did everything of significance, did succeed in demonstrating that selection could and did produce evolutionary changes, and that in the process it generated organic diversity. Before this work, it could be stated with some justice that the theory of evolution by natural selection rested largely on conjecture.

Sheppard's interests therefore centered on the experimental study of questions raised by the neo-Darwinian "modern synthesis" of genetics and evolutionary theory during the first half of the century, particularly of the action of natural selection in shaping both the organism and its genes. He summarized his views elegantly in *Natural Selection and Heredity* (1958), a work that was at once a student text and an original monograph. At Liverpool, in collaboration with Clarke, he produced a classic solution to a long-standing enigma of Darwinism, the evolution of mimicry. By anatomizing the genetics of mimetic patterns in the tropical butterflies *Papilio dardanus* and *P. memnon*, and *Heliconius melpomene* and *H. erato*, a monumental breeding project extending from 1956 until after Sheppard's death and involving international teams of collaborators, they synthesized the extremely gradualistic views of Darwin and Wallace with the theories of the old mutationist school of evolution, showing how the adjustment ("modification of gene action") of the genetic background to an existing large mutation could refine the mimetic resemblance and alter its genetic architecture, thus resurrecting the long-forgotten view that adaptations of this kind arose in two stages: mutation and modification. Particularly original was their discovery of "supergenes," tightly linked blocks of functionally independent genes, all controlling different aspects of the mimetic pattern.

Hoping to show that natural selection was still active in human populations, and aided by a large medical team, Clarke and Sheppard investigated the correlations of blood groups with disease. They had particular success with the ABO groups, and the study of such antigen-related disorders was later to become a major field of medicine. Believing also that the rhesus blood groups were controlled by a supergene similar to that found in mimetic butterflies, they then turned their attention to the chief form of natural selection known to act on these blood groups, hemolytic disease of the newborn. This led to an enduring advance in pediatrics: the prevention of this condition—a major cause of miscarriage, infant death, and brain damage—by injecting with rhesus antibody those mothers known to be at risk.

Sheppard's distinguished position in both medicine and population biology led to his being invited by the World Health Organization to investigate the population genetics of insecticide-resistant mosquitoes in Southeast Asia. He also undertook fieldwork on mimicry in South America. Since they lived in the most polluted part of Britain, the Liverpool team also carried out significant work on natural selection and industrial melanism in moths.

Sheppard had the ability to make everything he touched interesting, both as a researcher and as a teacher; all his best work was done in collaboration, his keen mind, his friendly lack of affectation, and his dedication inspiring the best in his teammates. Compromise was foreign to his scientifically acute mind, and his impatience with politically motivated action and inaction made him less effective among scientific bureaucrats at World Health Organization headquarters. Although he trained surprisingly few graduate students, his influence in English population biology was widely felt through his book, his undergraduate teaching, perhaps his teaching films for television, and his guidance of younger researchers; it was said that he had a superb facility for suggesting the next experiment. His was a wider influence than was immediately apparent because of his ethical refusal to add his name to a paper unless it was truly his.

BIBLIOGRAPHY

I. ORIGINAL WORKS. Among his 150 scientific publications, Sheppard's only book was *Natural Selection and Heredity* (London, 1958; 4th ed., 1975); he also edited a collection of exercises in *Practical Genetics* (Oxford, 1973).

The annotated Clarke-Sheppard-Turner collection of genetic broods of *Papilio* and other species in the British Museum (Natural History), London, includes correspondence from the period 1952 to 1953. At the time of writing, Sheppard's correspondence and scientific papers are in the department of zoology, University of Liverpool (Professor Arthur J. Cain), and a small collection of correspondence with John R. G. Turner is being donated to the John Innes Institute, Norwich, England.

II. SECONDARY LITERATURE. Bibliographies, not totally overlapping, are by John R. G. Turner, in *Journal of the Lepidopterists' Society*, **31**, no. 3 (1977), 205–212; and that accompanying the biography by Cyril A. Clarke in *Biographical Memoirs of Fellows of the Royal Society*, **23** (1977), 465–500, the first of these listing posthumous papers. Additional obituaries were published by Arthur J. Cain in *University of Liverpool Recorder*, **74** (1977), 4–7, and in *Heredity*, **40** (1978), 317–319; by B. C. C. [Clarke], in *Nature* **266** (1977), 201; and by Cyril A. Clarke, in *The Times* (London), 19 October 1976, p. 14. Eric E. Williams' *The Wooden Horse* (London, 1949; nonfiction ed., 1979) gives a detailed account of the famous escape, although the "Philip" who figures in the book is a different person.

JOHN R. G. TURNER

SHEWHART, WALTER ANDREW (*b.* New Canton, Illinois, 18 March 1891; *d.* Troy Hills, New Jersey, 11 March 1967), *physics, research statistics.*

Shewhart, the "father" of statistical quality control, was the son of Anton and Esta Barney Shewhart. He received an A.B. from the University of Illinois in 1913 and an A.M. in 1914. On 4 August 1914 he married Edna Hart. He received a Ph.D. in physics from the University of California in 1917, having been an assistant in physics (1914–1915) and a Whiting Fellow (1914–1916).

Following receipt of his doctorate, Shewhart was an assistant in physics at the University of Illinois (1916–1917), then head of the physics department at the Wisconsin Normal School in Lacrosse (1917–1918). The rest of his professional career was spent in the Bell System, initially with the Western Electric Company (1918–1924), then in the Bell Telephone Laboratories from their incorporation in 1925 until his retirement in 1956.

Sometime around 1920, the Western Electric Company, manufacturer of telephone equipment for the Bell Telephone System, learned from experience that repeated adjustment of a manufacturing process to compensate for observed departures from the process average can result in greater variability. (A mathematical explanation was provided by Preston C. Hammer in 1950.) On the other hand, a "large"

deviation from, or a succession of values above (or, below), the process average may indicate a need for corrective action. An answer was needed to the question of how to distinguish situations that call for corrective action from situations in which the process should be left alone. The problem of finding an answer was handed to Shewhart. He devised (1924) a new statistical tool, known today as the control chart, that signals when search for a cause of variation, and removal of this cause, will indeed reduce variation; and when search for a cause of variation, accompanied by action on the system, will only intensify the variation.

A control chart is a graph showing repeated determinations of some characteristic of a production process plotted in chronological order, with a horizontal center line corresponding to the average value of the characteristic, and upper and lower control limits such that plotted points outside these limits will tend to indicate the presence of a cause (or causes) of variation in addition to the random variation inherent in the process. Points outside these action limits are deemed to signal the need for a special investigation of the process to identify the disturbing cause(s). The plot of observed or measured values *in chronological order* is the essential feature of a control chart; and it marked an important departure from traditional statistical practice, in which observed or measured values are lumped together without regard to their chronological order to form a sample for which measures of location (average, median, mode), measures of dispersion (average deviation, standard deviation, range), and so on are then evaluated.

During the 1920's, Shewhart published a series of articles in the *Bell System Technical Journal* on the construction, application, and usefulness of control charts of various kinds, culminating in his definitive exposition of statistical quality control, *Economic Control of Quality of Manufactured Product* (1931), in which he recognized two distinct causes of variation: (a) chance causes, producing random variation intrinsic to the process, and (b) assignable causes (now sometimes called special causes), the kind that one should search for, try to identify, and eliminate. He noted that when all assignable causes have been removed, the variation of the outputs of the process will be stable, the process will be in "a state of statistical control," and its variation cannot be further reduced. Hence, if less variation is desired, this can be attained only by introducing a new process. A control chart is thus a triple-valued statistical tool: (1) it serves to define the goal of process performance that management might strive to achieve; (2) it is an instrument for attaining this goal; and (3) it is a tool for judging whether the goal of statistical control has been attained.

For action limits separating when to look from when to not look for assignable causes, Shewhart recommended "three-sigma" control limits, that is, horizontal lines at distances 3σ above and below the center line, with σ being the standard deviation of the plotted values implied by the inherent random variation of the process under study. From experience with a wide range of industrial processes, he had found that 3σ limits provided an approximate economic balance between the costs of mistakenly signaling the presence of nonexistent assignable causes and the costs of failure to signal the presence of existent assignable causes. Adopted by the American Society for Testing Materials in its *1933 A.S.T.M. Manual on Presentation of Data*, and with the coming of World War II recommended also in the American Standards Association's American War Standards Z1.1-1941, Z1.2-1941, and Z1.3-1942, 3σ limits became, and have largely remained, the standard practice in American industry.

In 1935 the British Standards Institution adopted Shewhart control chart techniques with two changes. First, instead of 3σ control limits, it recommended an outer pair of .001-probability action limits such that, when inherent chance causes alone are operative, the probability of a plotted point falling above the upper action limit (or below the lower action limit) would be .001. Second, it recommended an inner pair of .025-probability warning limits similarly determined, with the appearance of a succession of plotted values above the upper (or below the lower) inner limit to be taken as a warning, if not as a positive indication, of lack of control. The aim of the inner warning limits was to aid in identifying the onset of trouble.

Whereas the 3σ and .001-probability control limits are very nearly the same in the case of control charts for averages of successive sets of n (≥ 4) individual values, such is not the case for control charts for product variation, that is, charts for standard deviations or ranges of sets of n individual values, or for defects per unit area (or failures per unit time). The sampling distributions of these measures are skewed with the long "tail" to the right. Consequently, in these cases the upper 3σ limit will lie below the upper .001-probability limit, so that the risk of looking for assignable causes of increased product variation (or increased rate of defects or failures) will be greater than .001 when no change has occurred. The situation will be the opposite in

the case of the lower limits, but to a lesser degree. The net result of using 3σ limits will be an increased risk of looking for trouble when there is none, the actual increase depending on the degree of skewness.

Although the foregoing reasoning seems to favor the probability limits, Shewhart remained firm in support of 3σ limits on at least two grounds. First, as noted above, he had found from extensive experience that 3σ limits yielded an approximate economic balance between the costs of failure to notice real trouble when present, and the costs of crying, "Wolf! Wolf!" when there was no trouble. Second, 3σ limits are computationally defined and do not depend, as do probability limits, on the assumed mathematical form of the random variation of product characteristics (or on the assumed mathematical form of the sampling distributions of standard deviations, ranges, and so on, evaluated from small sets of measurements).

Instead of inner warning limits, Shewhart (1941) recommended looking for warnings in nonrandom patterns of the plotted points: a "long run" of, say, seven or more consecutive points above (or below) the center line would suggest the possibility of a shift up (down) of average performance; a "long run up" ("down") of, say, seven or more consecutive increases (decreases) would suggest the onset of a trend; and when there are no significantly long runs above or below the center line (or up or down), if, nonetheless, the total number (N) of runs above and below (or up and down) is exceptionally small (say $N \leq N_{.005}$), or excessively large (say, $N \geq N_{.995}$), or there are a great many short runs above and below (or up and down), these departures from randomness may be indicative of erratic or oscillatory behavior calling for investigation.

As Shewhart stressed (1939, Chap. 2), bringing a production process into a state of statistical control and keeping it in control (or restoring it to control) are necessary for prediction of performance of future product. Without statistical control, such prediction is not logically possible. For a production process that has been in control for a substantial period, he showed (*ibid.*), with the aid of empirical sampling experiments, how to construct prediction limits bounding a statistical tolerance range (or interval) within which a prescribed percentage of future product performance may be expected to fall as long as the process remains in control; he emphasized that such statistical tolerance intervals (limits) differ markedly from the statistician's confidence intervals (limits). Others promptly provided mathematical theory and tables for determining statistical tolerance limits of various kinds.

Whereas Shewhart's early writings and first book (1931) were focused on statistical control of industrial production processes, in his second book (1939) he extended the applications of statistical process control to the measurement processes of science, and stressed the importance of operational definitions of basic quantities in science, industry, and commerce.

In 1950, W. Edwards Deming, at the request of the Union of Japanese Scientists and Engineers, give a series of lectures in Japan on Shewhart's statistical quality control of industrial processes. These lectures were the catalyst that gave birth to Japan's industrial efficiency and emphasis on highest attainable quality of manufactured products.

Shewhart was a founding member and fellow of the Institute of Mathematical Statistics (president, 1937, 1944); founding member of the American Society for Quality Control (first honorary member, 1947; first Shewhart Medalist, 1948); a fellow of the American Statistical Association (president, 1945), International Statistical Institute, Royal Statistical Society (honorary fellow, 1954), Econometric Society, Royal Economic Society, American Association for the Advancement of Science (Council member, 1942–1949), and New York Academy of Science; and a member of the American Mathematical Society, Mathematical Association of America, American Physical Society, American Society for Testing Materials, Psychometric Society, Acoustical Society of America, Philosophy of Science Association, and Association for Symbolic Logic. In 1954, Shewhart was awarded the Holley Medal by the American Society of Mechanical Engineers, and in 1962 he received an honorary doctorate from the Indian Statistical Institute of Calcutta.

BIBLIOGRAPHY

I. ORIGINAL WORKS. Shewhart's most important publications are his two books: *Economic Control of Quality of Manufactured Product* (New York, 1931; repr. 1980) and *Statistical Method from the Viewpoint of Quality Control* (Washington, D.C., 1939; repr. New York, 1986). The first is a complete and thorough exposition of basic principles and techniques of quality control of manufactured products through statistical control of industrial processes. The second, based on his four lectures in March 1938 at the Graduate School of the U.S. Department of Agriculture in Washington, edited by W. Edwards Deming, has profoundly influenced statistical methods of research in the behavioral, biological, and physical sciences and in engineering by bringing his ideas and procedures to the attention of users of statistical methods. For a fuller appreciation of Shewhart's greatness, see his "Nature and Origin of Standards of Quality," in *Bell System Technical Journal*, **37** (1958), 1–22, written in 1935.

During the 1920's and early 1930's, Shewhart wrote a series of papers that reveal the evolution of his thinking and methods that jelled in his 1931 book: "On the Measurement of a Physical Quantity Whose Magnitude Is Influenced by Primary Causes Beyond the Control of the Observer and on the Method of Determining the Relation Between Two Such Quantities," in *Proceedings of the National Academy of Sciences*, **8** (1922), 248–251; "Some Applications of Statistical Methods to the Analysis of Physical and Engineering Data," in *Bell System Technical Journal*, **3** (1924), 43–87; "The Application of Statistics as an Aid in Maintaining Quality of a Manufactured Product," in *Journal of the American Statistical Association*, **20** (1925), 546–548; "Correction of Data for Errors of Measurement," in *Bell System Technical Journal*, **5** (1926), 11–26; "Correction of Data for Errors of Averages Obtained from Small Samples," *ibid.*, 308–319; "Finding Causes of Quality Variations," in *Manufacturing Industries*, **11**, no. 2 (1926), 125–128; "Quality Control Charts," in *Bell System Technical Journal*, **5** (1926), 593–603; "Quality Control," *ibid.*, **6** (1927), 722–735; "Economic Aspects of Engineering Applications of Statistical Methods," in *Journal of the Franklin Institute*, **205** (1928), 395–405; "Note on the Probability Associated with the Error of a Single Observation," in *Journal of Forestry*, **26** (1928), 600–607; "Small Samples: New Experimental Results," in *Journal of the American Statistical Association*, **23** (1928), 144–153, written with F. W. Winters; "Significance of an Observed Range," in *Journal of Forestry*, **26** (1928), 899–905; "Basis for Analysis of Test Results of Die-Casting Alloy Investigation," in *American Society for Testing Materials, Proceedings*, **29** (1929), 200–210; "Economic Quality Control of Manufactured Product," in *Bell System Technical Journal*, **9** (1930), 364–389; "Applications of Statistical Method in Engineering," in *Journal of the American Statistical Association*, **26** (1931), March supp., 214–221; "Random Sampling," in *American Mathematical Monthly*, **38** (1931), 245–270; and "Statistical Method from an Engineering Viewpoint," in *Journal of the American Statistical Association*, **26** (1931), 262–269.

After his 1931 book Shewhart published "The Rôle of Statistical Method in Economic Standardization," in *Econometrica*, **1** (1933), 23–35; "Annual Survey of Statistical Technique. Developments in Sampling Theory," *ibid.*, 225–237; "Some Aspects of Quality Control," in *Mechanical Engineering*, **56** no. 12 (1934), 725–730; "Applications of Statistical Methods to Manufacturing Problems," in *Journal of the Franklin Institute*, **226** (1938), 163–186; "The Future of Statistics in Mass Production," in *Annals of Mathematical Statistics*, **10** (1939), 88–90; "Contribution of Statistics to the Science of Engineering," in Hugh Dryden *et al.*, *Fluid Mechanics and Statistical Methods in Engineering* (Philadelphia, 1941), 97–124, in which he recommends augmenting his former control chart techniques with examination of the statistical significance of observed "runs above and below average" and "runs up and down"; "Statistical Control in Applied Science," in *Transactions of the American Society of Mechanical Engineers*, **65** (1943), 222–225; and "The Advancing Statistical Front," in *Journal of the American Statistical Association*, **41** (1946), 1–15.

II. SECONDARY LITERATURE. W. Edwards Deming, "Walter A. Shewhart, 1891–1967," in *Review of the International Statistical Institute*, **36** (1968), 372–375, a slightly abridged version of which appeared in *The American Statistician*, **21**, no. 2 (1967), 39–40, and "Shewhart, Walter A.," in *International Encyclopedia of Statistics*, II (New York, 1978), 942–944; Harold F. Dodge, obituary in *International Quality Control*, **23** (1967), 529; and L. H. C. Tippett, obituary in *Journal of the Royal Statistical Society*, **A130**, pt. 4 (1967), 593–594.

Seven articles on Shewhart and his impact on industrial production and quality control in *Industrial Quality Control*, **24** (1967) are rich sources of further information, insight, and perspective: "The First Shewhart Control Chart" (a facsimile of the chart and memorandum of transmittal dated 16 May 1924), 72; Paul S. Olmsted, "Our Debt to Walter Shewhart," 73; "The Shewhart Medal," 74; E. S. Pearson, "Some Notes on W. A. Shewhart's Influence on Application of Statistical Methods in Great Britain," 81–83; William A. Golomski, "Walter A. Shewhart, Man of Quality: His Work, Our Challenge," 83–85; "Highlights in the Life of Walter A. Shewhart," 109–110; "Tributes to Walter A. Shewhart," 111–122. A brief letter from Edna Shewhart and two more tributes are in *ibid.*, 332–333. See also Lloyd S. Nelson, "The Legacy of Walter Shewhart," in *Quality Progress*, **12**, no. 7 (1979), 26–28; and "Walter A. Shewhart, Father of Statistical Quality Control," *ibid.*, **19**, no. 1 (1986), 50–51.

For the background, philosophical basis, intent, and early history of Shewhart's control chart, see M. D. Fagen, ed., *A History of Engineering and Science in the Bell System* (New York, 1975), chap. 9, esp. sec. 5, which includes a facsimile of the first chart and accompanying memorandum (Fig. 9-6, p. 879).

See also American Society for Testing Materials, *1933 A.S.T.M. Manual on Presentation of Data* (Philadelphia, 1933; 4th rev., 1976); American Standards Association, *Guide for Quality Control*, American War Standard Z1.1-1941 (New York, 1941; also ANSI/ASQC Standard Z1.1-1985), *Control Chart Method of Analyzing Data*, American War Standard Z1.2-1941 (New York, 1941; also ANSI/ASQC Standard Z1.2-1985), and *Control Chart Method for Controlling Quality During Production*, American War Standard Z1.3-1942 (New York, 1942; also ANSI/ASQC Standard Z1.3-1985); Preston C. Hammer, "Interference with a Controlled Process," in *Journal of the American Statistical Association*, **45** (1950), 249–256; and E. S. Pearson, *The Application of Statistical Methods to Industrial Standardization and Quality Control* (London, 1935).

CHURCHILL EISENHART

SHUBNIKOV, ALEXEI VASILIEVICH (*b.* Moscow, Russia, 17 March 1887, *d.* Moscow, 27 April 1970), *crystallography.*

Shubnikov was the son of Vasilii Mikhailovich Shubnikov, a bookkeeper for a large textile company. His father died when Alexei was two years old. His mother, Anna Ivanovna Shubnikova, who was not professionally trained, raised six children. She was a very energetic woman, however, and soon found work as a seamstress. Despite great poverty she managed not only to bring up her children but also to educate them.

Shubnikov received his secondary education at the Commercial School, from which he graduated in 1906 with a silver medal. According to his own testimony, he developed an interest in crystallography while attending a popular course in crystallography at the Polytechnical Museum given by Georg (Iurii Viktorovich) Wulff. In 1908 Shubnikov enrolled in the department of natural sciences of the Physical-Mathematical Faculty of Moscow State University. He first studied under the famous naturalist, mineralogist, and geochemist Vladimir Ivanovich Vernadskii, who headed the mineralogy department at the university. Soon, however, he transferred to Wulff, who worked in the same department, becoming his devoted pupil and assistant.

In 1911 Wulff, Vernadskii, and many other professors left the university to protest the reactionary policy of Minister Lev A. Kasso. Wulff and Shubnikov began to work at the Shaniavskii People's University in Moscow. Shubnikov graduated from Moscow State University with honors in 1912 and the next year was called up to military service. In 1914, at the front near Warsaw, he was seriously wounded. After recovering he was assigned to noncombat duty as a chemist at a war plant in the Ukraine, and he worked there from 1916 to 1918. In 1916 he married Olga Mikhailovna Lebedieva; they had two daughters and a son. In 1918 Shubnikov returned to work as Wulff's assistant at the People's University in Moscow, but during the difficult years of civil war he could not do serious research work. In 1920 he therefore agreed to lecture on crystallography at the Urals Mining Institute of Ekaterinburg (now Sverdlovsk) and moved there. Despite the economic chaos of that period, he was able to create a basis for future research and teaching work at the institute.

Shubnikov, who enjoyed working with his hands, built tables and desks, made crystallographical models, and ground stones and minerals. Having made the acquaintance of a few skilled grinders from the Urals, he learned from them how to cut, grind, and polish stones. He made his first quartz wedges and laid the foundation for his later studies of quartz. His lectures on crystallography were a great success with students and were published as a textbook (1923–1925). Later he developed them, jointly with Evgenii Flint and Georgii B. Bokii, into his famous book *Osnovy kristallografii* (Fundamentals of crystallography, 1940).

In 1925 the famous mineralogist Aleksandr Evgenievich Fersman invited Shubnikov to Leningrad, where he accepted a position at the Mineralogical Museum of the Soviet Academy of Sciences. There he founded the laboratory of crystallography and organized an excellent staff of researchers with a great range of scientific interests. The main subject, however, was quartz, its processing, and the making of piezoelectric quartz plates. The results of the work were summarized in Shubnikov's book *Kvarts i ego primenenie* (1940). Shubnikov's team also carried out interesting investigations on crystal growth that were described in his popular book *Kak rastut kristally* (1935). Shubnikov also studied symmetry and its applications to science, engineering, and the arts. This work resulted in another popular book, *Simmetriia*, 1940, which went through three editions and was translated into English.

In 1933 Shubnikov was elected a corresponding member of the Soviet Academy of Sciences; he became a full member in 1953. When the academy was transferred to Moscow in 1934, Shubnikov moved there and became head of the crystallography section of the Lomonosov Institute. In 1937 the section was reorganized into the independent Laboratory of Crystallography of the Academy of Sciences, and Shubnikov was head of the laboratory from then until 1943. In Moscow, Shubnikov directed the work on the growing of large, defect-free seignette (Rochelle) salt crystals and conducted research on corundum (ruby-sapphire) synthesis.

After the Soviet Union entered World War II in 1941, the Laboratory of Crystallography was evacuated to the Sverdlovsk region in the Urals. There Shubnikov continued his intensive theoretical work. During this period he developed the idea of antisymmetry, that is, the unification of such opposite concepts as positive and negative, positron and electron, plus and minus, by means of symmetry. Unlike his predecessor in this field, the mathematician Heinrich Heesch, of whose work he was unaware, Shubnikov approached the subject from the physicist's point of view. This "abstract" field of crystallography rapidly found wide practical application in the study of magnetic and other properties of crystals.

The discovery of antisymmetry resulted in many papers on black-and-white as well as colored symmetry (finite and infinite). In 1960 Shubnikov suggested a new extension of the symmetry concepts. According to his "similarity symmetry," not only congruent but also all similar figures are considered to be equal. Nature has a great abundance of such forms, such as shells and flowers. From 1944 to 1955 Shubnikov also published papers on piezoelectrically active anisotropic media (piezoelectric structures) that he had discovered.

In 1944 the Institute of Crystallography of the Soviet Academy of Sciences was organized in Moscow and Shubnikov was appointed its first director, serving until 1962. Following his death the instituted was named for him. Shubnikov helped to organize specialized crystallography departments at Gorki University (1946) and at Moscow University (professor 1953–1968). He also was the founder and editor in chief of the journal *Kristallografia*, which was established in 1955.

Shubnikov's scientific papers are characterized by fine style, and clear and exact language. His film *Crystal Growth* (1960) was a great success.

Shubnikov was the recognized leader of Soviet crystallographers and the founder of Soviet applied crystallography. For his scientific work he was awarded two State Prizes (1947, 1950) and numerous orders and medals. He was also elected a foreign member of the mineralogical societies of Great Britain and of France.

BIBLIOGRAPHY

I. Original Works. *Kak rastut kristally* (How crystals grow; Moscow, 1935); *Kvarts i ego primenenie* ("Quartz and its applications"; Moscow, 1940); *Osnovy kristallografii* (Fundamentals of crystallography), with Evgenii Flint and Georgii B. Bokii (Moscow, 1940); *Simmetriia: Zakony simmetrii i ich primenenie v nauke, tekhnike i prikladnom iskusstve* (Moscow, 1940), 2nd ed. published as *Simmetriia v nauke i iskusstve* (Moscow, 1972), with V. A. Koptsik, trans. by G. D. Archard and ed. by David Harker as *Symmetry in Science and Art* (New York, 1974); *Piezoelektricheskie tekstury* ("Piezoelectrical Structures"; Moscow, 1946); *Simmetriia i antisimmetriia konechnykh figur* ("Symmetry and antisymmetry of finite figures"; Moscow, 1951), trans. by Jack Itzkoff and Jack Gollob in Shubnikov, N. V. Belov, et al., *Colored Symmetry* (New York, 1964); *Osnovy opticheskoi kristallografii* (Moscow, 1958), trans. as *Principles of Optical Crystallography* (New York, 1960); "Autobiographical Data and Personal Reminiscences," in Peter Paul Ewald, ed., *Fifty Years of X-Ray Diffraction* (Utrecht, 1962), 647–653; and *Izbrannye trudy po kristallografii*, B. K. Vainshtein, ed. (Moscow, 1975).

II. Secondary Literature. M. V. Belov and I. I. Shafranovskii, eds., *Aleksei Vasilievich Shubnikov* (Leningrad, 1984).

I. I. Shafranovskii

SIEGBAHN, KARL MANNE GEORG (*b.* Örebro, Sweden, 3 December 1886; *d.* Stockholm, Sweden, 24 September 1978, *physics.*

Manne Siegbahn modernized Swedish physics. He established experimental research schools at Lund, Uppsala, and Stockholm that commanded international attention; he also helped introduce the organization and methods of "big science" into Sweden. The research program that dominated most of his career and through which Swedish experimental physics was brought into the mainstream of international physics required perfecting X-ray spectroscopic instrumentation and measurement. His research problem may have been narrowly defined, but he chose it well and executed it to near perfection. His career also shows the importance for Swedish science of the Nobel Prize.

Siegbahn's father, Nils Reinhold Georg Siegbahn, a stationmaster for the Swedish state railway, came from a family with strong traditions in civil service and in high-precision work. His mother was Emma Zetterberg. Siegbahn first considered an education leading to a career as a military engineer but found military life not to his liking. After his father retired, the family moved to Lund, where in 1906 Siegbahn enrolled at the university; he received the candidate's degree in 1908, the licentiate degree in 1910, and in 1911, at the age of twenty-five, a doctorate in physics.

Siegbahn was immediately named a docent in physics; from 1915 to 1920 he assumed the duties of professor during Johannes (Janne) Rydberg's prolonged illness. In January 1920, after Rydberg's death, he was named professor. By this time he had established a research group working on X-ray spectroscopy. He also had married Karin Evelina Högbom in 1914; they had two sons.

When the professor of physics at Uppsala University, Gustaf Granqvist, died suddenly in 1922, Siegbahn was confronted with a choice: to remain in Lund, close to Copenhagen and the Continent, or move to Uppsala, then Sweden's primary university and physics department. He chose Uppsala, but within a few years recognized the importance of having both a well-staffed modern laboratory and a research position free from teaching and administrative chores.

Siegbahn finally achieved his goal in 1937, when he received a personal research professorship with which to lead the Royal Swedish Academy of Sciences' new Nobel Institute of Experimental Physics. He held the post of professor until 1952 and remained as director until he retired in 1964. Here he developed a school of nuclear physics. He joined the Nobel Physics Committee when he moved to Uppsala in 1923 and served as its chairman from 1945 to 1947. In 1925 he was awarded the previously withheld 1924 Nobel Prize in physics. (There had been no suitable candidates in 1924.) Several foreign universities and academies bestowed honors upon him. He received honorary doctorates from the universities of Freiburg, Bucharest, Oslo, and Paris; was elected member of the royal societies of London and Edinburgh, the Paris Academy of Sciences, and the U.S.S.R. Academy of Sciences; and was awarded the Hughes Medal (1934), the Rumford Medal (1940), and the Duddell Medal (1948). From 1938 to 1947 he was president of the International Union of Physics.

Siegbahn began his research career as an assistant to Rydberg but did not develop a disciple-master relationship with the rather reclusive professor. His early choice of problems reflected his technological predilections; he began with a series of electrotechnical projects. In his doctoral dissertation he treated methods for measuring magnetic fields. Siegbahn early recognized the importance of international contacts; he studied at Göttingen (1908) and Munich (1909). He made shorter study trips to Paris and Berlin (1911) and to Paris and Heidelberg (1914).

At Munich, Siegbahn met Arnold Sommerfeld, who introduced him to problems related to X radiation. In 1914 he published preliminary articles in Swedish and German defining the area that he staked out for his future endeavors: X-ray spectroscopy. Although he published six articles on electrotechnical studies immediately thereafter, in 1915 he became totally devoted to X-ray spectroscopy. Before leaving Lund in 1923, he had published more than thirty articles in this area, either alone or with his assistants.

Although laboratory facilities at Lund were meager, Siegbahn was nevertheless well placed for assuming a major position in X-ray spectroscopic studies. Rydberg, originally a mathematician, had devoted much of his career to the relations between spectra and Dmitri Mendeleev's periodic system for chemical elements. Moreover, Anders and Knut Ångström, Robert Thalén, and Bernhard Hasselberg had contributed to making spectroscopy the dominant feature of Swedish physics.

Beginning in 1906, Charles Glover Barkla had studied the polarization of X rays and discovered characteristic radiation from different elements. That is, when substances are exposed to X rays, they emit a secondary radiation with a specific penetrative power characteristic of the element concerned. Barkla distinguished two components in this secondary radiation that he called K and L. The significance of these radiations became apparent once new instruments for studying X radiation and their spectra were devised by the Braggs and Maurice de Broglie. William Henry Bragg and William Lawrence Bragg used an ordinary X-ray tube with a goniometer, in which a crystal of rock salt was mounted on the rotating table. To register the "reflected" X-ray beam, they placed an ionization chamber on a turntable arm. By devising focusing methods, they showed the distribution of the intensity as a function of the angle of incidence, in two or three orders, three broad peaks on a background of the "white" X-ray spectrum.

In France, Maurice de Broglie used a fixed photographic plate to register the X rays reflected by a carefully rotated crystal. He thereby produced X-ray spectra with sharp, well-defined lines similar to those obtained from optical spectra. These spectral lines could be identified with Barkla's K and L radiations.

Just prior to World War I, Henry Moseley showed in his studies of the K and L spectra of sets of consecutive elements that the square root of the frequencies of the lines progressed linearly with the atomic number. To record the spectra of the softer L radiation, which is easily absorbed in air, Moseley introduced a vacuum spectrometer.

The implications of the new techniques for physics and chemistry were further emphasized in 1914 when Walther Kossel offered an interpretation of the spectral lines in light of Niels Bohr's new atomic model. Because X-ray spectra are so much simpler than the thousands of lines that characterize optical spectra, they could be better instruments for identifying chemical elements. However, to fulfill X-ray spectroscopy's promise as a tool for atomic and chemical research, an increased resolution in the registered spectra would be necessary, as would an increase in the precision of wavelength measurement for both the emission spectra and the absorption discontinuities, or edges.

Starting with de Broglie's method and Moseley's program for mapping spectral lines, Siegbahn set out to perfect X-ray spectroscopy. In this research he was assisted in becoming the leading investigator by two factors. First, the war interrupted the work of most investigators in the field, including the Braggs and de Broglie, who did war-related research; Moseley, the most promising of all, was killed at Gallipoli. Second, Siegbahn possessed an extraordinary ability to improve, design, and build instruments. Although Siegbahn was in early contact with Bohr and had planned to go to Rutherford's laboratory at Manchester in 1915, he showed little interest in engaging in the theoretical implications or physical interpretation of X-ray spectra. He did, however, understand the significance of mapping the X-ray spectrum. When Siegbahn received a copy of Sommerfeld's 1916 article, in which elliptical orbits and additional quantum conditions were introduced into an atomic model, he immediately sought and found the predicted relativistic doublet K transitions. Siegbahn's continued contact with Sommerfeld, as well as with Bohr and Kossel, provided impetus to repeated improvement of the precision of wavelength measurements and to extension of these measurements to as wide a range of elements as possible.

Siegbahn began by constructing a metal X-ray tube that he and Ivar Malmer used in a study of the K series of heavy elements (zirconium to neodymium). They showed in 1915 that each of the two K lines identified by Mosely (K_α and K_β) actually consists of a doublet. Karl Wilhelm Stenström extended the K series in 1916 to lighter elements (down to sodium), using improved Siegbahn tubes. To extend Moseley's study of the L series, for which four lines had been identified, Siegbahn constructed improved vacuum spectrometers and X-ray tubes to reduce absorption by air and, especially for lighter elements, by the wall of the tube. He worked with Einar Friman (1916) in a study of the L series for zinc to uranium. They extended the longest recorded wavelength from Moseley's 6 Ångström units to 12.8 Ångström units, and increased the precision by two orders of magnitude. The surprisingly complicated line structure was systematically analyzed in Friman's 1916 doctoral dissertation.

In 1916 Siegbahn also identified a new series of lines for heavy elements that, following the Barkla system, he called the M series. Stenström then began a detailed investigation of this series, which was repeated with a still better X-ray tube and spectrograph by Elis Hjalmar for his dissertation (1923). Hjalmar also measured five N lines for uranium and thorium, and one for bismuth, after this series had been identified in 1922 by Siegbahn and V. Dolejsek (as predicted by Bohr).

Additional important discoveries by Siegbahn's Lund school included J. Bergengren's work (1920) showing that the position of the K absorption edge of phosphorus depends upon the atom's allotropic modifications. Axel Lindh continued this line of inquiry. Torsten Heurlinger commenced pioneering work on band spectra (1918) that was continued after his illness by Erik Hulthén. Dirk Coster, one of the many foreigners who came to Lund, learned the methods of X-ray spectroscopy while working there from 1920 to 1922. He made major contributions by clarifying the relation of the X-ray spectral lines to Bohr's theory of atomic structure and the periodic table of elements. Coster then joined Bohr's group in Copenhagen (1922–1923), where he and György Hevesy used Siegbahn-built equipment to identify element 72 (hafnium).

To increase substantially the accuracy in measuring wavelengths so as to meet the needs of atomic theory, Siegbahn began in 1918 to build spectrometers for different wavelength regions. These spectrometers increased precision and certainty to the point that the greatest errors in the measurements arose from uncertainty in the lattice constants of the crystals used. As long as the same crystal is used in all measurements, the relative values of the wavelengths are not influenced by this uncertainty. By measuring the angle of reflection with high accuracy, using a double-angle method, Siegbahn increased the precision about a hundredfold over the earlier wavelength determinations.

Siegbahn introduced a new unit of wavelength, the X unit, which is roughly one one-thousandth of an Ångström unit. First defined on the basis of the lattice constant of rock salt, the unit was later (1919) specified more precisely by the lattice constant of calcite for the cleavage surface (3029.04 X units at 18°C). Siegbahn used this value as the basis for his laboratory's program, beginning in the early 1920's, to remeasure the K, L, and M series and the K and L absorption edges with extreme precision.

Siegbahn was assisted in the construction of instruments first by the "old mechanic" Alfred Ahlström, who lived in a one-room work shed and charged 1.25 crowns for any repair, regardless of how much time was required. Eventually the Physics Institute hired A. L. Pedersen, a metalworker who was able to build X-ray tubes and spectrometers. Siegbahn sketched design diagrams for instruments and then discussed construction details at the workshop. At times he made modifications himself. He repeatedly improved X-ray tubes, spectrometers, and vacuum systems. He was able to increase the intensity of radiation considerably by building metal X-ray tubes with hot cathodes; Lindh perfected these in the early 1920's.

Two additional factors enabled Siegbahn to es-

tablish a vital school in Lund. After a series of reforms in intermediate schools in the early 1900's, enrollment at the university increased dramatically. At the Physics Institute the number of students taking laboratory instruction rose from about fifteen in 1906 to sixty-two in 1912. While Siegbahn was assisting Rydberg, he instilled enthusiasm for physics in many of these students. They followed Siegbahn, choosing to write doctoral dissertations under his supervision. After 1914 the number of undergraduate students dropped as dramatically as it had risen. At this point, room could be made in the modest laboratory for research projects; moreover, when Siegbahn assumed professorial duties, he broke with Rydberg's tradition of lecturing. He delegated teaching duties to an assistant while he supervised the advanced doctoral investigations.

After the war Siegbahn made study trips abroad to obtain insight into the requirements for better X-ray spectroscopic measurements and to bring his improvements and results to the attention of others. Although he did not direct his school toward theoretical problems, he believed it important for experimental physicists to follow the relevant advances in theory. Unlike most Swedish physicists, he was not hostile to the new atomic physics. In 1919 he organized a conference in Lund at which he brought Bohr and Sommerfeld together. Siegbahn participated in the third international Solvay Conference in 1921. Even as he and his group started remeasuring all the known lines and edges, he began in 1923 to prepare a compendium of his school's work; he was now the international leader in the field. The German University at Prague offered him a professorship. Siegbahn declined even though the crowded conditions in the Lund laboratory created obstacles. He could not, however, so easily decline the call to Uppsala in 1922.

In a remarkably short period of time following his move in June 1923, Siegbahn set his research program in motion at the larger, more modern physics institute at Uppsala. He brought to Uppsala not only an experimental research program that could command international attention but also a new style of leadership and a new attitude toward research. As he had done at Lund, he tried to minimize formalities, fuss, and meaningless rituals, and to squeeze as much research as possible from the relatively meager resources. Obtaining results was all that mattered. He did not hesitate to give the responsibility for an important problem to a promising doctoral student; if parts and materials were not otherwise at hand, he allowed their being scavenged from beautifully constructed older instruments.

His style of leadership enabled Siegbahn to attract a constant stream of students and assistants. The institute's tool shop manufactured remarkably accurate and innovative instruments that made possible the fruitful continuation of Siegbahn's program for remeasuring X-ray wavelengths. Machinists and precision metalworkers who constructed the instruments, such as John Amberntsson, whom Siegbahn brought from Lund, and Ernst Tingval were crucial in the continued march toward greater precision and further extensions of the spectral wavelengths.

In its drive toward ever greater precision, Siegbahn's school was helped by a number of technical facilities instituted by its leader: a recording microphotometer for registering a spectrogram's intensity, a ruling engine for obtaining gratings up to five millimeters, a machine for making gratings up to ten centimeters wide, and high-vacuum pumps. Increased intensity revealed more lines in each series; Siegbahn's school also measured the frequencies of spark lines and of "forbidden" transitions between the M and N series. Considerably greater detail in the absorption spectra was found, most notably by Edvin Jönsson. Using Siegbahn's gratings and suggestion, Bengt Edlén and others at Uppsala studied the optical spark spectra in the ultraviolet region, photographically recording down to 10 Ångström units. Siegbahn's team managed to extend the longwave limit of X-ray spectroscopic registrations in the K, L, M, and N series to 400 Ångström units. The two spectral regions were thereby bridged.

In 1924, acting on the initiative of the young Uppsala physicist Ivar Waller, Siegbahn and several co-workers demonstrated the long-sought refraction of X rays through a prism. Axel Larsson (Nordhult) continued Stenström's earlier studies of deviations from Bragg's equation, now with sufficient precision to be able to calculate the deviations, and thereby the dispersion. In this manner they could show that the expression obtained according to the theory of X-ray interference in crystals does not cover the whole deviation, and that an anomalous dispersion varying with wavelength also occurs.

This work was connected with Siegbahn's efforts toward the absolute determination of the X-ray scale. In a related effort, Erik Bäcklin used gratings to obtain absolute values for selected wavelengths that proved to be 0.15 percent lower than the corresponding values produced using crystals. This result implied that some factors used in calculating the crystal lattice constant had to be in error. Using Gunnar Kellström's new determination of the viscosity of air and Sten von Friesen's measurements of electron wavelengths, Bäcklin was able to show that Robert Millikan's determination of the electron charge, e, was too low because of an erroneous value for the coefficient of the air's inner friction. Using a new determination for e in calculating lattice constants, Bäcklin then obtained, within the calculated limits of error, the same values for X-ray wavelengths determined by crystal as by absolute measurements. Consequently, Siegbahn's earlier wavelength scale now lacked justification.

About 1930 Siegbahn recognized that his research program had reached a point of professional diminishing returns. He had brought Swedish experimental physics a long way toward internationalization and recognition; he understood that further institutional and organizational changes would be necessary to continue this process and to allow renewal as the frontiers and problems of physics changed. He was, however, frustrated over administrative burdens, teaching duties, and rather limited resources.

After receiving the Nobel Prize in physics, Siegbahn used his increased authority within the five-member Nobel Physics Committee to obtain resources for his research. Eventually he obtained a new institute, but this exercise in amassing resources and authority did not go unnoticed or unchallenged. First, his Nobel Prize was not without controversy. Siegbahn was nominated in 1923 by O. D. Khvol'son, but he withdrew his name from competition. In 1925 he was nominated by Stephan Meyer, Max von Laue, and David Starr Jordan (acting on David Locke Webster's recommendation) for his precision X-ray spectroscopic measurements. Committee members Svante Arrhenius and Vilhelm Carlheim-Gyllensköld opposed awarding the prize to Siegbahn, not because they felt his work was not significant but rather (they alleged) because the nomination did not meet the statutory requirements: a prize can be given only for a new invention or discovery (or an old one newly shown to be important). Also, since Siegbahn and his school were in the midst of remeasuring wavelengths, an award would have violated the committee's tradition of waiting for work to be completed before assessing its full significance. In fact, Arrhenius and Carlheim-Gyllensköld hoped to limit the authority of Siegbahn and Uppsala physics as well as to withhold the prize and divert the prize money to the committee's own fund. Uppsala Nobel Committee members C. W. Oseen (chair) and Allvar Gullstrand pressed successfully on behalf of their colleague.

After receiving the Nobel Prize, Siegbahn was able to claim a major portion of the committee's fund for his research. As important as these grants may have been for buying instruments or paying assistants, however, Siegbahn required considerably greater resources. Having watched with some envy how The Svedberg had used his 1926 Nobel Prize for chemistry to attract large sums of money for his ultracentrifuge and a new institute of physical chemistry, Siegbahn launched a similar plan in 1930.

The Knut and Alice Wallenberg Foundation was willing to donate half of the 3 million crowns needed if the rest could be obtained from other sources. Svedberg had been able to attract Rockefeller Foundation funding; Siegbahn could not. He hoped to establish a Nobel Institute for Experimental Physics, but the funds available to the committee were too meager. He therefore supported, partly as a substitute, the creation in 1933 of the Nobel Institute for Theoretical Physics for his colleague Oseen.

A new effort was begun in 1935; Oseen was then the Swedish Academy's president, and Henning Pleijel, another member of the Nobel Physics Committee, was the academy's secretary. With the assistance of academy member Gösta Forssell, who used X rays and radioactive substances for therapeutic purposes, they convinced the academy to petition the government to establish a personal research professorship for Siegbahn. The academy had terminated its physics institute and professorship more than a decade earlier for financial reasons; here was an opportunity to revive them.

Further, Siegbahn's supporters arranged that grants from funds at the disposal of the Nobel Physics Committee should be used for planning and building the institute. Some observers in the Swedish Academy protested that the diversion in 1935 of the money from the reserved 1934 prize to the committee and the Nobel Foundation's funds was based not on the lack of qualified candidates for the prize but on a desire by the committee and Siegbahn's supporters to funnel as much Nobel money as possible into the project. The Wallenberg Foundation agreed to pay much of the remaining costs: instruments, furnishings, and operating expenses. In 1937 the Nobel Institute for Experimental Physics was established under Siegbahn's leadership.

Interest in supporting the plan was perhaps heightened by Siegbahn's aims for the new institute: he hoped to introduce nuclear physics into Sweden. Even before the institute opened, he sent Sten von Friesen to Cornell University and the University of California at Berkeley for a four-month study of cyclotron construction. By 1939, thanks to an additional grant from the Wallenberg Foundation, they inaugurated a 7 MeV deuteron cyclotron with which

they hoped to pursue research and to produce radioactive isotopes for medical use.

Sweden's postwar commitment to atomic energy enabled Siegbahn to develop the institute into one of the major nuclear research facilities in Europe. In 1946 Hugo Atterling and Gunnar Lindström began construction of a larger cyclotron, aided by Rockefeller Foundation money; when completed in 1951, it was able to accelerate deuterons up to 30 MeV. A provisional high-tension generator capable of producing 400,000 volts was built during the war, and then transformed into a plant with 1.5 million volts. Other facilities that were added to the institute included an electromagnetic isotope separator and various nuclear spectrographs.

Although Siegbahn was increasingly becoming an administrator, both of his institute and of several national committees, he still found time to construct new instruments, including an electron microscope. He directed his group to the study of nuclear radiations, to the exact measurement of the magnetic properties of atomic nuclei, and to such other projects as Hannes Alfvén's experiments on cosmic radiation. Siegbahn's son Kai instituted a research program in β spectroscopy that eventually made Stockholm the international center for such studies.

Using his international contacts, Manne Siegbahn was able to send Swedish students and assistants to major foreign universities and laboratories; he also attracted or invited foreign researchers to Sweden. In the course of his career, and largely as a result of it, Swedish physics emerged as an important component of the international discipline.

BIBLIOGRAPHY

I. ORIGINAL WORKS. Bibliographies of Siegbahn's writings are in Åke Dintler and J. C. Sune Lindquist, eds., *Uppsala universitets Matrikel 1937–1950* (Uppsala, 1953); and in Poggendorff, V, 1162–1163, VI, 2443, and VIIb, 4857–4858. His *Spektroskopie der Röntgenstrahlen* (Berlin, 1924; 2nd, rev. ed., 1931), translated by George A. Lindsay as *The Spectroscopy of X-Rays* (Oxford, 1925; reiss. Ann Arbor, Mich., 1976), contains many of his school's results, including a chronologically arranged bibliography of these and related advances in X-ray spectroscopy.

II. SECONDARY LITERATURE. Olle Edqvist, "Manne Siegbahn," in *Kosmos* (1987), 163–176; Sten von Friesen, "Manne Siegbahn: Minnesteckning," in *Kungligka fysiografiska sällskapets i Lund årsbok* (1979), 75–81; Arvid Leide, *Fysiska institutionen vid Lunds universitet* (Lund, 1968), 136–146; Axel Lindh, "En svensk nobelpristagare," in *Kosmos* (1925–1926), 5–63 (a detailed account of the Siegbahn school's instruments and methods); and Torsten

Magnusson, "Manne Siegbahn," in *Swedish Men of Science 1650–1950* (Stockholm, 1950), 280–291, and *Manne Siegbahn 1886–3/12/1951* (Uppsala, 1951). Further historical background into early X-ray spectroscopy can be found in J. L. Heilbron, *H. G. J. Moseley: The Life and Letters of an English Physicist 1887–1915* (Berkeley, 1974); and B. R. Wheaton, *The Tiger and the Shark: Empirical Roots of Wave-Particle Dualism* (Cambridge, 1983).

ROBERT MARC FRIEDMAN

SIEGEL, CARL LUDWIG (*b*. Berlin, Germany, 31 December 1896; *d*. Göttingen, Federal Republic of Germany, 4 April 1981), *mathematics*.

The son of a postal worker, Siegel studied at the University of Berlin from 1915 to 1917, attending lectures by Georg Frobenius that introduced him to the theory of numbers. Called into military service in 1917, he could not adapt to army life and was discharged. He then went to the University of Göttingen (1919–1920), where he worked on his inaugural dissertation and *Habilitationsschrift* under the guidance of Edmund Landau, a specialist in analytic number theory. Siegel was a professor at the University of Frankfurt from 1922 to 1937 and at the University of Göttingen from 1938 to 1940.

Siegel despised the Nazi regime. After lecturing in Denmark and Norway in 1940, he left Norway for the United States just a few days before the Nazi invasion. From 1940 to 1951 he worked at the Institute for Advanced Study at Princeton, where he had spent the year 1935. In 1946 he was appointed to a permanent professorship at the institute. Five years later he returned to Göttingen, where he spent the rest of his life.

Siegel was one of the leaders in the development of the theory of numbers, but he also proved important theorems in the theory of analytic functions of several complex variables and in celestial mechanics.

Siegel's inaugurual dissertation (1920) was a landmark in the history of Diophantine approximations. Joseph Liouville had been the first to observe that algebraic numbers of degree $n > 1$ are "badly" approximated by rational numbers: for any such number ξ there is a constant $C(\xi)$ such that, for every rational number p/q with greatest common divisor $(p, q) = 1$, one has

$$\left|\xi - \frac{p}{q}\right| > C(\xi) \cdot \frac{1}{q^n}. \tag{1}$$

The proof is almost trivial, but the improved result obtained by Axel Thue in 1908 was more difficult to prove: the inequality

$$\left|\xi - \frac{p}{q}\right| \leq \frac{1}{q^2 + 1 + \epsilon} \tag{2}$$

(where $\varepsilon > 0$ is arbitrary) is possible only for a finite number of values of p/q. Siegel obtained a still better result, which was crucial for his work of 1929 on Diophantine equations: there are only a finite number of rational numbers p/q such that

$$\left|\xi - \frac{p}{q}\right| \leq \frac{1}{q^{2\sqrt{n}}}. \tag{3}$$

The proof was very ingenious. In fact, Siegel did not directly prove that (3) has only a finite number of solutions p/q, but he showed that this is true for the inequality

$$\left|\xi - \frac{p}{q}\right| \leq \frac{1}{q^\beta}, \tag{4}$$

where $\beta = \dfrac{n}{s+1} + s + \dfrac{1}{2}$, s being any integer such that $0 \leq s \leq n - 1$; from that (3) is easily deduced by a suitable choice of s. The proof was by contradiction. If it is assumed that (4) has infinitely many solutions, it is possible to choose two of them, p_1/q_1 and p_2/q_2, such that q_1 and $r = [\log q_2/\log q_1]$ are arbitrarily large.

Siegel introduced two integers:

$$p < \frac{r}{16n} + n^2 \tag{5}$$

and m, which is the integral part of

$$\left(\frac{n + \dfrac{1}{16n}}{s+1} - 1\right)r.$$

He considered the two numbers

$$E_1 = C^r q_1^{m+r} q_2^s \left|\xi - \frac{p_1}{q_1}\right|^{r-p},$$

$$E_2 = C^r q_1^{m+2} q_2^s \left|\xi - \frac{p_2}{q_2}\right|,$$

and showed that there is a constant C, depending only on ξ, such that $E_1 < 1$ and $E_2 < 1$. On the other hand, using the fact that ξ is an algebraic number of degree n, he constructed, by very intricate arguments, for each value of p satisfying (5) a polynomial $R_p(x, y)$ of degree $m + r - p$ in x, and degree s in y, with integral coefficients $\leq C''$ (with a constant C' depending only on ξ). Then, using

Gustav Dirichlet's pigeonhole principle, he could show that there is a degree p satisfying (5) for which

$$q_1^{m+r-p}q_2^s R_p\left(\frac{p_1}{q_1},\frac{p_2}{q_2}\right) \neq 0,$$ and hence an integer $\geq$

1; and that number, compared with the sum $E_1 + E_2$, implies that one of these two numbers must be ≥ 1, yielding the required contradiction.

In 1955 Siegel's result (3) was drastically improved by K. F. Roth: there are only a finite number of rational numbers p/q such that

$$\left|\xi - \frac{p}{q}\right| \leq \frac{1}{q^{2+\varepsilon}}, \qquad (6)$$

where ε is any number > 0; this result is the best possible because there is an infinity of rational numbers p/q such that

$$\left|\xi - \frac{p}{q}\right| \leq \frac{1}{q^2}.$$

In 1929 Siegel published a long paper in two parts that is probably his deepest and most original. The first part (contemporary with Aleksandr Gelfond's proof of the transcendence of e^π) contains an entirely new result on transcendental numbers: he proved that if J_0 is the Bessel function of index 0, then $J_0(\xi)$ is transcendent for any algebraic value of $\xi \neq 0$. More precisely, let $g(y, z)$ be a polynomial of total degree $p > 0$ whose coefficients are integers of absolute value $\leq G$; if ξ is an algebraic number of degree m and $\neq 0$, then

$$|g(J_0(\xi),J_0'(\xi))| \geq cG^{-123p^2m^3}, \qquad (7)$$

where c depends only on p and ξ.

Siegel's method differed from those used earlier in the theory of transcendental numbers. He starts with an analytic study, in the manner of Liouville, of the algebraic relations between x, $J_0(x)$ and $J_0'(x)$. The main result was the following: let

$$\phi(x) = \sum_\beta {}' \sum_{\alpha=0}^\beta f_{\alpha\beta}(x(J_0(x)^\alpha J_0'(x)^{\beta-\alpha}, \qquad (8)$$

where the $f_{\alpha\beta}$ are polynomials in x with real coefficients, which are $\neq 0$ for q values of the pair $(\alpha, \beta - \alpha)$; then ϕ and its derivatives up to order $q - 1$ are q linear forms in the $J_0(x)^\alpha J_0'(x)^{\beta-\alpha}$, whose determinant is a polynomial in x that is not 0.

Let $l > p$ be an integer, and $k = \frac{1}{2}(l + 1)(l + 2)$; let $n \geq 2k^2$ be an arbitrary integer and $\varepsilon > 0$ an arbitrary real number. The center of the proof consisted in constructing a function (8) with the following properties: (1) the k polynomials $f_{\alpha\beta}$ for $\beta \leq l$ have a degree $\leq 2n - 1$, with integer coefficients at most $(n!)^{2+\varepsilon}$; (2) the Maclaurin series of

ϕ begins with a term in $x^{(2k-1)n}$, and its coefficients are majorized in absolute value by those of the series

$$Cn! \sum_{\nu=(2k-1)n}^\infty \frac{|x|^\nu}{(\nu!)^{1-\varepsilon}}.$$

Let $T_j(x)$ for $1 \leq j \leq k$ be the functions $J_0(x)^\alpha J_0'(x)^{\beta-\alpha}$ for $\beta \leq l$ and $\alpha \leq \beta$, with $T_1 = 1$. As J_0 satisfies the second-order Bessel differential equation, the function ϕ and its derivatives can be written in the form

$$x^a\phi^{(a)}(x) = \sigma_{a1}T_1(x) + \cdots + \sigma_{ak}T_k(x), \qquad (9)$$

where $\sigma_{ab}(x)$ is a polynomial of degree $2n + a - 1$, with coefficients that are integers $0((n!)^{3+2\varepsilon})$ for $a < n + k^2$. The essential part of the proof involved showing that for $a \leq n + k^2 - 1$ and for every real number $\xi \neq 0$, the matrix $(\sigma_{aj}(\xi))$ has rank equal to k.

It is then possible to choose k integers

$$h_\nu \leq n + k^2 - 1$$

such that the k functions

$$\phi_\nu(x) = \sigma_{h_\nu 1}(\xi)T_1(x) + \cdots + \sigma_{h_\nu k}(\xi)T_k(x) \qquad (10)$$

are linearly independent. Let $r = l - p$, $v = (r + 1)(r + 2)/2$, and consider the v functions

$$J_0(x)^p J_0'(x)^\sigma g(J_0(x), J_0'(x)) \qquad (11)$$

for $p + \sigma \leq r$; they can be written

$$\psi_\mu(x) = c_{\mu 1}T_1(x) + \cdots + c_{\mu k}T_k(x) \qquad (12)$$

for $1 \leq \mu \leq v$, where the $c_{\mu j}$ are integers whose absolute value is $\leq G$; the v functions ψ_μ are linearly independent and can be completed by $w = k - v$ functions ϕ_ν in order to have k linearly independent linear combinations of the T_j. It can then be shown that the determinant Δ of the coefficients of these k linear forms is a polynomial in ξ of degree $w(3n + k^2 - 2)$ with integer coefficients all $0((n!)^{3w+2\varepsilon Gv})$. This finally proves that $|\Delta|$ is majorized by

$$K(n!)^{3w+2\varepsilon Gv}\left(\frac{g(J_0(\xi),J_0'(\xi))}{G} + (n!)^{1-2k}\right), \qquad (13)$$

where $K \geq 1$ is independent of n.

All this is true for any real number $\xi \neq 0$. But now suppose $\xi \neq 0$ is an algebraic number of degree m; if c is an integer such that $c\xi$ is an algebraic integer, then $c^{w(3n+k^2-2)}\Delta$ is an algebraic integer $\neq 0$. It is then enough to write that the norm of that algebraic integer is ≥ 1 to obtain (7) after having chosen conveniently n as a function of G.

Shidlovskii later generalized Siegel's transcendence theorem to what Siegel had called *E*-functions (he had introduced them as auxiliaries in his proof). They are series defined by arithmetic conditions on their coefficients.

The second part of Siegel's 1929 paper was even more startling, since it contained the first general result on Diophantine equations

$$f(x, y) = 0, \qquad (14)$$

where *f* is a polynomial with integer coefficients. Until then the best result had been Thue's theorem for the special type of equations (14), written $g(x, y) - a = 0$, where $a \neq 0$ and *g* is a homogeneous polynomial of degree ≥ 3. Thue had shown that such equations have only a finite number of solutions (x, y) consisting of integers. What Siegel showed is that the same thing may be said of all equations (14) except those for which the curve Γ having (14) for equation possesses a parametric representation by rational functions with denominators of degree 1 or 2 (this implies that Γ has genus 0 and at most two points at infinity).

The least difficult part of the proof concerned the case when Γ has genus 1. Let *L* be the field of rational functions on Γ and *F* a function in *L* of order *m*, and suppose there are infinitely many pairs $(x/z, y/z)$ with *x*, *y*, *z* integers having no common factor, such that (1) $F(x/z, y/z) = 0$; (2) $F(x/z, y/z)$ is an integer. Then one can extract from that set of pairs $(x/z, y/z)$ a sequence that converges to a point of Γ that is a pole of *F*; if *r* is the order of that pole, then for every function $\phi \in L$ that vanishes at that pole and every $\varepsilon > 0$ there is a constant $C(\phi, \varepsilon)$ such that

$$|\phi(x/z, y/z)| \leq C(\phi, \varepsilon)(|x| + |y| + |z|)^{-(m/hr) + \varepsilon} \quad (15)$$

(where *h* is the degree of *f*) for every point in the convergent sequence.

Since Γ has genus 1, there is a parameterizing of Γ by elliptic functions $x = w(s)$, $y = v(s)$. Let *r* be the number of roots of the equation $w(s) = a$ in a parallelogram of periods. Siegel made essential use of a theorem proved by Louis J. Mordell in 1922: If *M* is the *Z*-module of complex numbers *s* such that both $w(s)$ and $v(s)$ are rational numbers, then *M* has a finite basis $s_1, \ldots s_q$. Let *n* be an arbitrary integer (later allowed to be arbitrarily large); using the euclidean algorithm, one can write every element of *M* in the form

$$s = n\sigma + c, \qquad (16)$$

where $\sigma \in M$ and $c \in M$ takes only a finite number of values. The proof used contradiction (as in Thue's theorem). Suppose equation (14) has infinitely many

solutions in integers. There is therefore an infinity of these solutions for which, in the expression of the parameter *s*, the number $c \in M$ is the same. Apply inequality (15) to $F(x/z, y/z) = x$. From the addition theorem of elliptic functions, it follows that $s \mapsto w(ns + c)$ belongs to the field *L* and has order n^2m, and its n^2m poles have coordinates that are algebraic numbers of degree $\leq n^2m$.

From (14) it follows that one of these poles is the limit of a sequence of points $(\xi/\zeta, \eta/\zeta)$ of Γ, where ξ, η, and ζ are integers with no common factor. If the sequence of the numbers ξ/ζ has a finite limit *p*, it is an algebraic number of degree $\leq n^2m$, and the inequality (15) shows that

$$\left| \frac{\xi}{\zeta} - p \right| \leq C(|\xi| + |\zeta|)^{-kn^2m}, \qquad (17)$$

where $k > 0$ does not depend on *n*. On the other hand, the inequality (3) proved by Siegel in his dissertation showed that, except for a finite number of numbers ξ/ζ of the sequence, one has

$$\left| \frac{\xi}{\zeta} - p \right| \geq C'(n)(|\xi| + |\zeta|)^{-n\sqrt{m}}, \qquad (18)$$

where $C'(n)$ depends only on *n*. Comparing (17) and (18) yields

$$(|\xi| + |\zeta|)^{kn^2m - n\sqrt{m}} \leq \frac{C}{C'(n)}. \qquad (19)$$

But it is clear that, when $n > \dfrac{1}{k\sqrt{m}}$, the relation (19) can be verified only for finitely many pairs of integers (ξ, ζ), which yields the desired contradiction. The argument is similar and simpler when the sequence of the $|\xi/\zeta|$ tends to $+\infty$.

Siegel was able to construct a similar but much more intricate proof when Γ has genus ≥ 2, by making use of André Weil's generalization of Mordell's theorem. But instead of the curve Γ the Jacobian of Γ must be used, which causes complications. Until very recently Siegel's theorem remained the most powerful of its kind. In 1983, however, G. Faltings obtained a more profound result: for curves (14) of genus ≥ 2, there are only finitely many points of the curve that have rational coordinates, a theorem that had been conjectured by Mordell.

In 1934, H. Heilbronn had proved a conjecture of Carl Friedrich Gauss: if $h(-d)$ is the number of ideal classes in an imaginary quadratic field of discriminant $-d$, then $h(-d)$ tends to $+\infty$ with *d*. In 1935 Siegel, using the relation between the zeta functions of two quadratic fields and the zeta function of their "compositum," was able significantly to improve Heilbronn's theorem: when d tends to $+\infty$,

$$\log h(-d) \sim \tfrac{1}{2}\log d.$$

From 1935 on, most of Siegel's papers in the theory of numbers were concerned with the arithmetic theory of quadratic forms in an arbitrary number n of variables, with integer coefficients. The theory had been stated by Joseph Lagrange and Gauss for $n = 2$ and $n = 3$, and developed during the nineteenth century for arbitrary dimension n by Adrien-Marie Legendre, Ferdinand Eisenstein, Charles Hermite, Henry J. S. Smith, and Hermann Minkowski. The work of Siegel in this domain may be considered the crowning achievement of the theory; but at the same time, he broadened it considerably and prepared its modern versions by connecting it with the theory of Lie groups and automorphic functions.

In three long papers published between 1935 and 1937, Siegel tackled the general problem of using linear transformations with integer coefficients to transform a quadratic form Q in m variables with integer coefficients into a quadratic form R in $n \le m$ variables with integer coefficients. It is easier to express the problem in terms of matrices with integer coefficients: Given two symmetric matrices, an $m \times m$ matrix S and an $n \times n$ matrix T, one must study the $m \times n$ matrices X such that

$$'X.S.X = T. \tag{20}$$

The first paper deals with the case in which S and T are positive definite, which had been most studied by Siegel's predecessors. The number $A(S, T)$ of matrices X satisfying (20) is then finite. The number $E(S) = A(S, S)$ is the order of the subgroup of $GL(m, Z)$ leaving S invariant (called the group of "units" of S). Gauss had defined the concepts of class and of genus for binary quadratic forms. They can be extended to any number of variables. Two $n \times n$ matrices S, S_1 with integer coefficients belong to the same class if there exists an invertible $n \times n$ matrix Y with integer coefficients, such that

$$'Y.S.Y = S_1; \tag{21}$$

when $A(S, T)$ is finite, it depends only on the classes of S and T. The definition of genus was simplified by Henri Poincaré and Minkowski: S and S_1 are in the same genus if, on the one hand, there is an $n \times n$ invertible matrix Y with real terms satisfying equation (21) and, on the other hand, for every integer q, there is an $n \times n$ matrix Y_q with integer coefficients and a determinant invertible mod. q, such that

$$'Y_q.S.Y_q = S_1 \qquad (\text{mod. } q). \tag{22}$$

Hermite's reduction process showed that, for positive definite matrices, a genus contains only a finite number of classes. Suppose a genus contains h classes, and let S_j be matrices chosen in these classes ($1 \le j \le h$). Eisenstein and Smith had associated to the genus its "mass"

$$\frac{1}{E(S_1)} + \frac{1}{E(S_2)} + \cdots + \frac{1}{E(S_h)}, \tag{23}$$

and Smith (and independently Minkowski) had expressed (23) with the help of the "characters" of the genus.

Siegel's first paper on quadratic forms was concerned, more generally, with the expression

$$M(S,T) = \frac{\dfrac{A(S_1T)}{E(S_1)} + \dfrac{A(S_2,T)}{E(S_2)} + \cdots + \dfrac{A(S_h,T)}{E(S_h)}}{\dfrac{1}{E(S_1)} + \dfrac{1}{E(S_2)} + \cdots + \dfrac{1}{E(S_h)}}, \tag{24}$$

where S and T are positive definite, and $S_1, \cdots, S_h$ are representatives of the classes in the genus of S. The main result was the value of $M(S, T)$ as an infinite product

$$M(S,T) = A_\infty(S,T) \prod_p d_p(S,T). \tag{25}$$

In (25) p varies in the set of all prime numbers. Let $A_q(S, T)$ be the number of solutions mod. q of the congruence in matrices with integer coefficients

$$'X.S.X \equiv T \qquad (\text{mod. } q); \tag{26}$$

$d_p(S, T)$ is the limit of $A_q(S, T)/q^{mn - \frac{1}{2}n(n+1)}$ when, for $q = p^N$, N tends to $+\infty$ [a "p-adic mean value" of $A(S, T)$]. Finally, $A_\infty(S, T)$ is also a kind of "mean value": when $m > n$ and $m \ne 2$, consider a neighborhood V of T in the space of $n \times n$ symmetric real matrices (an open set in $R^{\frac{1}{2}n(n+1)}$); $A_\infty(S, T)$ is the limit, when V tends to T, of the ratio of the volume of the inverse image of V by $X \mapsto {}'X.S.X$ in R^{mn}, to the volume of V. The proof is by induction on m and a very subtle adaptation of the methods used by Gauss, Dirichlet, and Minkowski.

Siegel's second paper on quadratic forms dealt with "indefinite" quadratic forms of arbitrary signature. He first proved that the right-hand side of (25) is still meaningful except in two particular cases (when $m = 2$ and $-\det S$ is a square, and when $m - n = 2$ and $-\det S.\det T$ is a square). However, (23) and (24) are meaningless because the subgroup of $GL(m, Z)$ leaving S invariant is infinite. Finding what should replace the left-hand side of (25) was a problem that had been tackled by Georges Humbert only in a very particular case, the ternary forms.

Siegel was able to solve it in general: in the space of symmetric $m \times m$ matrices of given signature, let B be a neighborhood of S, and let B_1 be its inverse image in the space R^{mn} by the map $X \mapsto {}'X.S.X$. B_1 is invariant by the group of "units" of S acting by left multiplication. There is a fundamental domain D for that action on B_1. If the volume $v(B)$ is finite, then the volume $v(D)$ is also finite and the limit

$$p(S) = \lim v(D/v(B)$$

exists when B tends to S. In a genus containing S there are again only a finite number of classes. Let $S_1, \cdots, S_h$ be representatives of those classes. The number

$$\mu(S) = p(S_1) + p(S_2) + \cdots + p(S_h) \qquad (27)$$

replaces the "mass" of the genus of S. There is a similar, more complicated definition of a number $\mu(S, T)$ that replaces the numerator of (24). Finally, Siegel's formula (25) is valid when the left-hand side is replaced by $\mu(S, T)/\mu(S)$. Siegel improved that formula in 1944, showing that in some cases the terms in the expression of $\mu(S, T)$ are the same for all classes of a genus.

In the third paper (1937) on quadratic forms, Siegel considered quadratic forms in which the coefficients belong to a field of algebraic numbers, which nobody had studied before him. There are new difficulties in the theory, but he is able to overcome them.

Siegel's results on positive definite quadratic forms warrant further discussion. When a genus contains only one class, the left-hand side of (25) is $A(S, T)$; this is true for $m \leq 8$ when S is the unit matrix; if, in addition, $n = 1$, then (25) gives back the formulas of Carl C. J. Jacobi, Eisenstein, Smith, and Minkowski for the number of representations of an integer as a sum of m squares for $4 \leq m \leq 8$. Jacobi's proof relied on his study of theta functions and their relations with the modular group $SL(2, Z)$, which proceed from the formula (found independently by Gauss, Augustin-Louis Cauchy, and Siméon-Denis Poisson)

$$\theta(z) = \frac{1}{\sqrt{z}} \theta\left(\frac{1}{z}\right) \qquad (28)$$

for the simplest of theta functions

$$\theta(z) = \sum_{n=-\infty}^{+\infty} e^{-\pi n^2 z} \qquad (\text{where } \mathrm{Re}\, z \geq 0). \qquad (29)$$

In his first paper on positive definite quadratic forms, Siegel observed that (25) is equivalent to a remarkable identity between functions that generalize

modular forms. The space of the variables is what is now called "Siegel's half-space," a generalization of "Poincaré's half-plane." It consists of the symmetric complex $n \times n$ matrices Z, whose imaginary part is positive definite. For any symmetric $m \times m$ matrix S with integer coefficients, Siegel considered the following function of Z that is a generalization of theta functions—

$$f(S, Z) = \sum_C \exp(\pi i. \mathrm{Tr}({}'C.S.C.Z)- \qquad (30)$$

where C takes all values in the space Z^{mn} of $m \times n$ matrices with integer coefficients; this series is absolutely convergent when Z is in the Siegel half-space. It is easy to see that

$$f(S, Z) = \sum_T A(S, T) \exp(\pi i. \mathrm{Tr}(T.Z)) \qquad (31)$$

where T takes all values in the space of $n \times n$ symmetrical matrices with integer coefficients. Now, if

$$F(S, Z) = \frac{\dfrac{f(S_1, Z)}{E(S_1)} + \cdots + \dfrac{f(S_h, Z)}{E(S_h)}}{\dfrac{1}{E(S_1)} + \cdots + \dfrac{1}{E(S_h)}}, \qquad (32)$$

then (25) is equivalent (for large enough m) to an expression for $F(S, Z)$ as a convergent series

$$F(S, Z) = \sum_{K.L} c_{K.L} \det(KZ + L)^{-m/2} \qquad (33)$$

where K and L are $n \times n$ matrices with integer coefficients satisfying additional arithmetic conditions. The series (33) is clearly similar to the Eisenstein series (for $n = 1$); this led Siegel, in several later papers, to make a systematic study of what he called modular forms of degree n. They are holomorphic functions defined in the Siegel half-space D; the symplectic group $\mathrm{Sp}(2n, R)$, consisting of $2n \times 2n$ matrices $U = \begin{pmatrix} A & B \\ C & D \end{pmatrix}$ such that ${}'U.J.U = J$ for $J = \begin{pmatrix} 0 & I \\ -I & 0 \end{pmatrix}$, acts on D by

$$Z \mapsto (AZ + B)(CZ + D)^{-1}.$$

In a 1939 paper Siegel considered the subgroup $\mathrm{Sp}(2n, Z)$ of $\mathrm{Sp}(2n, R)$, which is the group of transformations of the systems of $2n$ periods of a linearly independent system of abelian integrals of the first kind on a Riemann surface of genus n. That subgroup acts on D in a properly discontinuous way. Siegel described a fundamental domain for that action, using Minkowski's reduction of quadratic forms. The modular forms of degree n and weight r are the holomorphic functions defined in D that transform under $Sp(2n, Z)$ according to the relation

$$\psi_r((AZ + B)(CZ + D)^{-1}) = \det(CZ + D)^r\psi_r(Z) \quad (34)$$

(for even r). Siegel could express these forms by series generalizing Eisenstein's series. He next considered modular functions, which are meromorphic in D and invariant under the action of $Sp(2n, Z)$. A quotient of two modular forms of the same weight is such a function, and in 1960 Siegel proved that all modular functions can be obtained in that way. He also showed that the set of all modular functions is a field having transcendence degree $n(n + 1)/2$ over C.

Siegel thus inaugurated the general theory of automorphic functions in any number of variables, which since Poincaré had not gone beyond the consideration of some very particular cases. In a paper of 1943, Siegel studied other subgroups of $Sp(2n, R)$ also acting in a properly discontinuous way on the Siegel half-space D. He linked this question to the theory of Lie groups, showing that D is isomorphic to a bounded domain in C^n that is a symmetric space in the sense of Élie Cartan (who had determined all bounded domains in C^n that are symmetric spaces). Since then the study of automorphic functions has been developed for groups acting in a properly discontinuous way in these domains.

In 1903 Paul Epstein had defined "zeta functions" for a positive definite quadratic form $Q(x_1, x_2, \cdots, x_n)$ with integer coefficients, the simplest of which is

$$\zeta_Q(s) = \sum (Q(x_1, x_2, \cdots, x_n))^{-s} \quad (35)$$

where the summation is over $Z^n - \{0\}$. The series converges for Re $s > n/2$, and Epstein had shown that it can be continued to a meromorphic function in the whole complex plane, satisfying a functional equation similar to those satisfied by zeta functions of number fields. Definitions such as (35) were of course meaningless for indefinite quadratic forms.

In two papers of 1938 and 1939, Siegel showed what to do in that case. Let S be the symmetric matrix of a quadratic form of signature $(n, m - n)$, and let $\Gamma(S)$ be its group of "units." It acts properly on the open subset U of the Grassmannian $G_{m,n}$ consisting of the n-dimensional subspaces of R^m in which the quadratic form is positive definite; there is in U a fundamental domain of finite volume $\mu(S)$ for that action. For a vector $a \in Z^m$, let $\Gamma(S, a)$ be the subgroup of $\Gamma(S)$ leaving a fixed; for $m \geq 3$, $\Gamma(S, a)$ has in U a fundamental domain of finite volume $\mu(S, a)$. For every integer $t > 0$ such that

the equation $'a.S.a = t$ has at least a solution $a \in Z^m$, Siegel wrote

$$M(S,t) = \sum_a \mu(S, a),$$

where the sum is extended to a set of representatives of the orbits of $\Gamma(S)$ in the set of solutions of $'a.S.a = t$. Siegel's zeta function is then

$$\zeta(S, s) = \sum_{t>0} M(S,t)t^{-s}. \quad (36)$$

He showed that the series converges for Re $s > m/2$ and is continued in the whole complex plane as a meromorphic function satisfying a functional equation. His proof is a generalization of Riemann's proof of the functional equation for the usual zeta function, using a theta function, which depends on a parameter varying in a fundamental domain in U of the group $\Gamma(S)$.

In the year 1951–1952 Siegel returned to the theta function and its transformations by the modular group, and gave an expression for its "mean value" in a fundamental domain of $\Gamma(S)$. From that he deduced another proof for his fundamental result of 1936 on indefinite quadratic forms. He also stated without proof that his mean value formula could be extended to quadratic forms in which both coefficients and variables belong to a simple algebra over the rational field Q, equipped with an involution.

A central theme in all these works is the computation of "volumes" of fundamental domains or, equivalently, of quotients of Lie groups by discrete subgroups. These computations have led to general views on "measures" on Lie groups or on p-adic groups, the outcome of which was the discovery by Tamagawa of a privileged measure on a group of "adeles" of an algebraic group defined on a number field. Tamagawa showed that the properties of that measure implied Siegel's theorems on quadratic forms; Weil similarly interpreted the mean value formula Siegel had proved in 1951 on such groups of "adeles."

In another area, in 1935 Siegel had deduced from his formula (25) the remarkable fact that the zeta function of a number field takes rational values at integers <0. Later he improved that result, using the theory of modular forms. These results form the basis of numerous papers on that subject published in recent years.

The papers we have analyzed are those which have given Siegel his eminent position in the theory of numbers. But they are far from exhausting his scientific production, which includes many results of lesser scope although none of them is trivial. They cover a wide range of topics: geometry of numbers, Pisot numbers, mean values of arithmetic functions, sums of squares and Waring's problem in number fields, zeros of Dirichlet's L-functions, iteration of holomorphic functions, meromorphic functions on a compact kählerian manifold, groups of isometries in non-euclidean geometries, abelian functions, differential equations on the torus, and calculus of variations. After the theory of numbers, Siegel's favorite subjects were celestial mechanics and analytic differential equations, particularly hamiltonian systems.

Siegel had few students working under his guidance; the perfection and thoroughness of his papers, which did not leave much room for improvement with the same technique, discouraged many research students because to do better than he required new methods. Siegel enjoying teaching, however, even elementary courses, and he published textbooks on the theory of numbers, celestial mechanics, and the theory of functions of several complex variables.

Siegel, who never married, devoted his life to research. He traveled and lectured in many countries, particularly at the Tata Institute in Bombay. His mental powers remained unabated in his old age, and he published important papers when he was in his seventies. He was the recipient of many honorary doctorates, and a member of the most renowned academies. In 1978, when the Wolf Prize for mathematics was awarded for the first time, he and Izrail Moiseevich Gelfand were selected for this honor.

BIBLIOGRAPHY

Siegel's writings are collected in *Gesammelte Abhandlungen*, K. Chandrasekharan and H. Maass, eds., 4 vols. (Berlin and New York, 1966).

Jean Dieudonné

SLATER, JOHN CLARKE (*b.* Oak Park, Illinois, 22 December 1900; *d.* Sanibel Island, Florida, 25 July 1976), *theoretical physics, quantum mechanics.*

John Slater was one of the few physicists trained in America in the 1920's to specialize in theoretical physics and to contribute to both the development of quantum mechanics and its application to a wide range of particular phenomena. The theme of his career was to explain observable phenomena using quantum-mechanical models. As a prolific writer of textbooks and research papers, as a teacher, as chairman of the physics department and later institute professor at the Massachusetts Institute of Technology (MIT), and as graduate research professor

at the University of Florida, Slater channeled large numbers of workers into the burgeoning areas of molecular and solid-state theory. He was among those responsible for the emergence of American theoretical physics between the two world wars, and for bringing American solid-state physics into a leading position in the international arena.

Slater grew up in an academically oriented home. When he was a baby his father, John Rothwell Slater, a Harvard graduate, was a doctoral student at the University of Chicago. In 1904 the family moved to Rochester, New York, where Slater's father joined the English department at the university, a department he later became the head of. In his boyhood Slater was very much interested in mathematics and in examining such devices as electrical motors and lamps. His father, whose home library included physics classics like A. A. Michelson's *Light Waves and Their Uses*, strongly encouraged his son's scientific bent and in later years would habitually enclose clippings from *Scientific American* in his letters. Slater's high school interests also included watercolor painting, architecture, and printing in his attic print shop.

Slater abandoned his plan to attend Harvard College when it became clear that the United States would enter World War I. He remained at home, entering the University of Rochester in 1917, and completed his undergraduate work in three years. Majoring in science, he took his A.B. in 1920. His research in atomic and molecular physics began during his senior year at Rochester, where, as an assistant in the physics laboratory, he conducted a special experimental honors thesis, examining the relationship between change of pressure and the intensities of the Balmer spectral lines in hydrogen, a project inspired by his reading of Niels Bohr's classic 1913 paper on atomic theory.

Slater then entered Harvard's graduate school in physics, from which he took his doctorate in June 1923. He was introduced there to the major problems at the frontiers of quantum theory in Edwin C. Kemble's course, one of the few in America then up to date in modern physics. Slater's exposure to the philosophy of pragmatism in science, as an assistant to Percy W. Bridgman, appears to have had a lasting influence on him, for in his subsequent research Slater never strayed far from observable phenomena. Bridgman, who was then pioneering the study of phenomena at high pressures, supervised Slater's doctoral thesis, an experimental investigation of the compressibility of alkali halide crystals. This research brought Slater into contact with fundamental problems of the solid state, which were to challenge him throughout his career. For example, he realized that the existing theory was incapable of explaining the repulsive forces in solids that counter electrostatic attraction.

Slater decided to spend the year following the completion of his doctorate abroad, close to the revolutionary breakthroughs then being made in quantum theory. Supported by a Sheldon traveling fellowship from Harvard, he spent the fall of 1923 at the Cavendish Laboratory at Cambridge studying the theoretical problem of the breadth of spectral lines. He explored the picture, suggested previously by W. F. G. Swann and others, of an electromagnetic field that guides the light photons emitted by atoms, the energy density of the field determining the probability of finding a photon at a particular position. In a theory Slater developed in these months at Cambridge, the source of the electromagnetic field was identified as either the atoms oscillating in excited Bohr states, emitting electromagnetic waves at all the frequencies corresponding to transitions to lower Bohr states, or the oscillations produced by the impact of external radiation on the atom. Slater's discussion of this theory with Bohr and Hans Kramers in December of that year in Copenhagen resulted in the celebrated joint Bohr-Kramers-Slater paper on the quantum theory of radiation, published in 1924. Historically this paper was to be a root of Werner Heisenberg's matrix mechanics, despite its incorrect assumption, due to Bohr and Kramers, that the laws of energy and momentum conservation have only statistical validity. Bohr and Kramers gave the name *virtual oscillators* to the oscillations of the electrons corresponding to the possible transitions, disagreeing with young Slater that the photons accompanying these transitions have a simultaneous real existence. Slater never quite forgave Bohr and Kramers for thus distorting his original theory.

After returning to Harvard in June 1924, he worked further on the radiation problem, publishing early in 1925 a more consistent picture of how the oscillators determine the emission and absorption probabilities and underlining the real existence of the emitted photons, the energy conservation in the system of the atoms and photons, and the probabilistic relation between the intensity of the field and the motion of the photons. These ideas were at that time also being clarified in the work of Louis de Broglie. In one important work in 1925 Slater correlated the width of spectral lines with the reciprocal lifetime of stationary states; in another he almost arrived at the notion of spin, which soon

afterward George Uhlenbeck and Samuel Goudsmit made explicit.

In 1926 Slater married Helen Frankenfeld, with whom he was to have three children: Louise Chapin, John Frederick, and Clarke Rothwell. The daughter of a minister in Rochester, Helen also studied at the University of Rochester. She graduated in 1925 with a major in English. After the marriage, she studied further in Boston, in a nursery training school, but she gave up her career plans when the children were born. Helen and John Slater hosted a large number of professional parties in their home. Their marriage ended in divorce in 1952.

In late 1926, studying the radiation problem in the context of the singly ionized hydrogen molecule, Slater extended Heisenberg's recent analysis of helium, which had established the existence of symmetric and antisymmetric two-electron states, developing a picture of electrons moving between potential wells equivalent to what was later named "tunneling." Addressing the problem of exchange effects in the helium atom, Slater returned to one of the questions raised by his doctoral thesis: Why are inert gas atoms relatively hard and impenetrable? The theme of accurate calculation of the wave functions and energies of many-electron atoms and molecules would be a major theme of his research for the next half-century.

Slater's next major move in physics was to "slay the *Gruppenpest*," the curse of having to use group theory to treat complex systems. In the mid-1920's several workers, including Eugene Wigner, Friedrich Hund, Walter Heitler, and Hermann Weyl, were trying to extend the Heisenberg two-electron picture to many electrons using abstruse group theoretical methods, which many physicists of that period, including Slater, disliked intensely. Stimulated by Douglas R. Hartree's 1928 work on the self-consistent field method for treating problems in atomic physics—an iterative method for calculating single-particle wave functions based on the recognition that the average fields felt by an electron depend on the states of all the other electrons, these states themselves being determined by the average field—Slater turned to a detailed examination of why the method was successful. This study culminated in Slater's major 1929 paper on the theory of complex spectra, which presented for this problem a convenient determinantal alternative to the unwieldy group approach. Building on ideas developed by Paul A. M. Dirac, Heisenberg, Wolfgang Pauli, and Hund, Slater found that by setting up a many-electron function in the form of a determinantal antisymmetric combination of one-electron wave functions, he could achieve a self-consistent field wave function with the correct symmetry. Electron spin was explicitly included in the individual terms of the determinant. Slater also noted that Hartree's expression for the potential of an atom could be derived by a variational approach, discovering independently of V. Fock what came to be called the Hartree-Fock method, a method improving the accuracy of Hartree's original self-consistent field method by including electron exchange terms.

Slater visited Europe again between June 1929 and February 1930, with support from a Guggenheim Fellowship. He worked for most of this visit at the theoretical physics institutes of Heisenberg in Leipzig and Pauli in Zurich, which by this time had become the most active European centers for theoretical study of solids. Extending to many other cases his determinantal method, Slater also worked on the problem of cohesion in metals, demonstrating the close relationship between Hund's molecular orbital method, which began with the assumption that an individual electron in a molecule moves in a potential arising from the nuclei and the average space charge of the other electrons, and the method of Heitler and Fritz London, which began by ignoring the interaction between the two electrons in the hydrogen molecule and treating their wave function as a product of two one-electron functions.

These methods Slater then applied to ferromagnetism. Heisenberg's classic 1928 treatise on ferromagnetism was not mathematically rigorous and could not explain why ferromagnetism is found only in certain elements. Slater found, as did Felix Bloch independently, that the low-lying stationary states in which all but one of the atoms have parallel electron spins correspond to spin waves—the wave-like propagation through the system of a slight disturbance of the spin orientation from its equilibrium value. In studying a preprint of Bloch's work (which already made use of the Slater determinants), Slater realized that the relation between the Heisenberg and Bloch approaches to ferromagnetism is analogous to the relation he had recently investigated between the Heitler-London and Hund molecular orbital approaches to molecular forces.

Slater's characteristic quantitative approach to physics is well illustrated by his discovery that the root of ferromagnetism lies in the electron atomic $3d$ shell. Bloch had shown that in the limit of large internuclear separations the magnetic state has a lower energy than the nonmagnetic state. Slater proceeded to seek the electrons responsible for ferromagnetism in narrow partly filled bands formed of slightly overlapping atomic wave functions. Es-

timating the sizes of various unfilled shells of atoms in the periodic system, he showed that the $3d$ shell of the iron group elements was the narrowest unfilled band, a band sufficiently small that it becomes energetically favorable for spins to be oriented parallel: the magnitude of the energy decrease owing to quantum-mechanical exchange when spins are parallel exceeds the energy that must be added to the system to excite electrons above the energy levels occupied in the nonmagnetized ground state. This imbalance between the two energies enables spontaneous magnetization to occur. For cobalt, nickel, and particularly iron, all ferromagnetic, he found the ratio of the internuclear distance to the radii of the $3d$ shell orbital to be particularly high.

Shortly after returning to Harvard in the spring of 1930, Slater accepted an offer from Karl Compton, MIT's new president, to head the MIT physics department. Under Slater's direction the department expanded rapidly and broadened its scope. By concentrating on solid-state physics at a time when most American institutions were turning to nuclear physics, Slater enabled the MIT department to achieve first rank with a distinctive emphasis on solving problems of real materials using quantum mechanics.

With his students, Slater applied the determinantal method to many problems, including valence bonds. In a seminal paper published in 1931 Slater introduced the concept of "directed valence," arrived at simultaneously by Linus Pauling; by constructing linear combinations of s and p waves he showed that wave functions could be made that project out in the direction of a bond. Not long afterward he was elected to the National Academy of Sciences, at the age of thirty-one.

The other emerging American effort in solid-state theory in the early 1930's was the small group in the Princeton physics department surrounding Wigner, consisting primarily of postdoctoral and doctoral students (including Frederick Seitz, John Bardeen, and Conyers Herring). Compton's wish that MIT and Princeton maintain close ties aided communication between these two groups in the 1930's. Slater was particularly impressed by Wigner and Seitz's classic paper in 1933 on the energy bands of sodium, laying out the first approximate method for calculating realistically the band structure of simple solids. Immediately recognizing that this work opened new paths, Slater extended the Wigner-Seitz method to the excited bands of metals, and with his students applied the technique to a series of particular solids, including copper, diamond, carbon, and sodium chloride. Slater surveyed the applications of the Wigner-

Seitz method in an important article in the 1934 *Reviews of Modern Physics*, one of several reviews on the electron theory of metals to appear circa 1933 (the most extensive being that by Hans Bethe and Arnold Sommerfeld in the 1933 *Handbuch der Physik*). With powerful new quantum-mechanical concepts developed between 1927 and 1933 (including the Fermi sea, Bloch waves, and energy bands), Pauli, Sommerfeld, Heisenberg, Bloch, Rudolf Peierls, Alan Wilson, Slater, and others had resolved the outstanding dilemmas of the classical electron theory of metals and placed the theory of ideal metals and semiconductors on a sound intellectual foundation. The reviews circa 1933 enabled this fundamental theory to enter the graduate programs at leading physics institutions, providing the basic texts for training the first generation of physicists who referred to themselves as solid-state physicists. This generation faced the challenging problem of explaining the detailed properties and behavior of real, rather than ideal, solids.

Slater was one of the few physicists (another was his Harvard colleague and close friend John Van Vleck) who worked steadily in the solid-state area through this transition. Due to various circumstances—the displacement of Jewish physicists, a feeling that most of the fundamental problems other than superconductivity were solved, and the discovery of new and exciting phenomena and techniques in nuclear and particle physics—most of the contributors to solid-state theory were by 1933 redirecting their primary attention to nuclear physics and quantum electrodynamics. Fortunately, at just this time, several new workers, including Bardeen, Herring, and Seitz in the United States and Nevill Mott in England, were entering the study of the solid state, sharing Slater's burden in establishing this new subfield of physics.

Slater students engaged in energy band calculations in the mid-1930's included Harry M. Krutter, who studied the Wigner-Seitz method in relation to the Thomas-Fermi method for metals; George Kimball, who computed energy bands in diamond; and William Shockley, who studied sodium chloride. Slater applied the Wigner-Seitz method to ferromagnetism in 1936. Other concerns of Slater's solid-state group in the late 1930's included the determination of charge densities by summing over the occupied orbitals, calculating forces and energies by applying the Feynman-Hellmann theorem, and computing the potential and kinetic energies by using the virial theorem. Slater also turned to the study of localized excitations in crystals. In 1936, with Shockley, Slater developed a framework for a theory of the exciton; and in the spring of 1937 he worked out a useful relationship between the theory of excitons and Bloch's 1929 theory of spin waves.

Slater continued to seek better methods of computing energy bands and in 1937 invented the "augmented-plane-wave method," which expands wave functions in spherical harmonics and radial solutions within spheres surrounding the atoms, and in plane waves outside. Slater's students, including Marvin Chodorow, tested this method on copper bands before World War II, but only in the 1950's, with the help of digital computers, could large-scale application of the method be made. The group also explored extensively the "orthogonalized-plane-wave-method," an alternative to the Slater augmented-plane-wave method developed by Herring in 1940 and applied first to computation of the energy bands of beryllium. In the method of orthogonalized plane waves, the wave function has been made orthogonal to the ion-core wave function so that there is no wave amplitude for ion-core levels (which are filled).

Slater's principal concern during World War II—partly at MIT and partly as a member of the technical staff of the Bell Telephone Laboratories—was microwave radar, particularly the theory of the magnetron, which drew on mathematical techniques he had developed earlier while trying to understand the Meissner effect in superconductivity and the self-consistent field in atoms. Immediately after the war, Slater turned to rebuilding MIT's physics department. Through his war work he sensed the possible physics applications of wartime technological developments, including microwaves, rapid electronics, digital computers, neutron beams, and the Collins cryostat (a compact helium liquefier enabling experiments to be conveniently carried out over long periods at temperatures as low as two degrees above absolute zero). He made a decided effort to apply these wartime advances in the postwar research program at MIT, for example in experimental studies of superconductivity and in building linear accelerators.

The invention of the first transistors in 1947 and 1948 set off a revolutionary expansion in the field of solid-state physics. Slater, stimulated by several solid-state conferences held in mid-1948, returned to active work in this field and set up MIT's Solid-State and Molecular Theory Group (which a decade later would evolve into MIT's Center for Materials Science and Engineering). The program included practical calculations employing Hartree-Fock, Wigner-Seitz, Thomas-Fermi-Dirac, and other methods, pioneering the use of digital computers in solving a variety of problems, including ferromagnetism, antiferromagnetism, binding energies, and energy bands. The MIT physics department also expanded its programs in X rays, acoustics, electronics, and optics, all fields of great interest to industry.

Attracted by the opportunity to explore neutron diffraction in the study of magnetic and other properties of the solid state, Slater accepted an appointment for the academic year 1951–1952 at Brookhaven National Laboratory. At this juncture he stepped down from the post he had held for twenty-one years as MIT's physics department chairman and was appointed MIT's first institute professor, a position which allowed him far more time for research, teaching, and travel, both in the United States and in Europe. In 1954 he married Rose Mooney, a physicist specializing in the study of crystals by X-ray diffraction.

In anticipation of his retirement in 1966 from MIT, Slater in 1964 transferred his base to the University of Florida in Gainesville, where he joined the Quantum Theory Project, set up by Per-Olov Löwdin. Until his retirement from his Florida position in June 1976, a month before his death, Slater continued, both individually and with students, to work intensively on theories of the detailed properties of real crystals. Slater particularly enjoyed these last years in Florida. He described the Florida department in his autobiography as congenial, and with its emphasis on just the problems in which he was most interested, the areas of solid-state physics and related fields, it reminded him of the MIT physics department in the years when he served as its head. He was awarded the Medal of Science in 1971. Slater wrote fourteen textbooks between 1933 and 1974—characteristically typing them himself, with little revision after the first draft—on theoretical physics, mechanics, electromagnetism, the quantum theory of atoms, molecules and solids, chemical physics, microwave transmission and electronics, energy bands, and self-consistent field methods. Slater's roles as teacher of theoretical physics, quantum mechanics, and solid-state physics and as a prolific writer of textbooks useful to both the student and practicing physicist touched most of the physicists who worked in the five decades following the invention of quantum mechanics.

BIBLIOGRAPHY

I. ORIGINAL WORKS. The most complete source for Slater's life and works is the exceptionally well cataloged collection of letters, manuscripts, and other documents in the John Clarke Slater Papers at the American Philosophical Society Library in Philadelphia, Pennsylvania. A bibliography of Slater's published works (including approximately 150 research papers and other articles, in addition to his textbooks and scientific autobiography) appears in Philip M. Morse, "John Clarke Slater, December 22, 1900–July 25, 1976," in *Biographical Memoirs National Academy of Sciences*, **53** (1982), 297–321. Slater's colorful scientific autobiography, *Solid-State and Molecular Theory: A Scientific Biography* (New York, 1975), offers his view of the developments in physics that impressed him most as he moved through his career. Partial autobiographical accounts are also included in "Quantum Physics in America Between the Wars," in *Procceedings of the International Symposium on Atomic, Molecular, and Solid-State Theory: Symposium No. 1, International Journal of Quantum Chemistry* (1967), 1–23; and "The Current State of Solid-State and Molecular Theory," *ibid.*, 37–102. Many useful reflections on Slater's career can be found in Slater's oral history interviews with Thomas Kuhn and John H. Van Vleck on 3 October 1963, with Kuhn on 8 October 1963, and with Charles Weiner on 23 February and 7 August 1970, all on file at the American Institute of Physics Center for History of Physics, New York City.

II. SECONDARY LITERATURE. In addition to the biographical memoir by Philip M. Morse listed above, see P. Hoch (with contributions from K. Szymborski), "The Development of the Band Theory of Solids, 1933–1960," in L. Hoddeson *et al.*, eds., *Out of the Crystal Maze* (New York and Oxford, 1990); L. Hoddeson, G. Baym, and M. Eckert, "The Development of the Quantum-Mechanical Electron Theory of Metals: 1928–1933," in *Reviews of Modern Physics*, **59** (1987), 287–327; Katherine Russell Sopka, *Quantum Physics in America, 1920–1935* (diss., Harvard University, 1976).

LILLIAN HODDESON

SLICHTER, LOUIS BYRNE (*b*. Madison, Wisconsin, 19 May 1896; *d*. Los Angeles, California, 25 March 1978), *geophysics*.

Slichter was the second of four sons of Mary Louise Byrne Slichter, a teacher, and Charles Sumner Slichter, a professor of mathematics and dean of the graduate school at the University of Wisconsin. Although Slichter's father is best remembered as the teacher of Max Mason and Warren Weaver, he was also an accomplished student of analytical mechanics and had a strong interest in the application of mathematics to the study of the physical properties of the earth. In 1899 the elder Slichter developed a theory that treated the motion of groundwater through porous rock as a special case of the steady flow of a perfect fluid. Later he built a successful consulting business upon his development of an electrical technique for measuring the direction and velocity of the flow of groundwater. His taste for mathematical analysis, his dual concern with the abstract and the practical, and his ability to move with equal facility in the academic and business worlds are all mirrored in the career of his son.

Louis Slichter received his education at the University of Wisconsin, Madison, where he took a B.A. in mechanical engineering in 1917 and a Ph.D. in physics in 1922. His studies were interrupted by a brief stint as a student test engineer with the General Electric Company (1917) and wartime service in the study of methods of submarine detection (1917–1919). After completing his Ph.D., Slichter worked for the Submarine Signal Company of Boston. In 1924 Slichter entered into a business partnership with Max Mason, who had taught him mathematical physics at Wisconsin and had supervised his wartime antisubmarine work. Their firm, Mason, Slichter, and Gauld, specialized in providing scientific advice to firms engaged in prospecting for ores.

In 1930 Slichter returned to academic life as a research associate at the California Institute of Technology. The following year he was appointed to the faculty of the Massachusetts Institute of Technology, where he organized a program in geophysics within the Geology Department. In 1940 Slichter resumed research on the problem of submarine detection, first for the National Academy of Sciences and later for the National Defense Research Committee. He directed the program that developed the magnetic airborne detector and later contributed both to the development of techniques for using rockets in antisubmarine warfare and to the design of torpedoes. In recognition of his contributions, Slichter was awarded a Presidential Certificate of Merit in 1947. After the war Slichter taught briefly at the University of Wisconsin (1945–1947) and then joined the faculty at the University of California, Los Angeles, where he directed the growth of the Institute of Geophysics and Planetary Physics until his retirement in 1963.

Slichter began his career when geophysical methods were first coming into widespread use in prospecting. During the 1920's demand for oil and minerals could no longer be satisfied by the exploitation of deposits lying close to the surface. At the same time, physicists had begun to develop a variety of electromagnetic and seismographic instruments that promised to be of great value in underground exploration. The conjunction of a strong industrial demand and a new set of techniques produced an era of explosive growth in geophysics.

Slichter was among the many consultants who prospered from these circumstances in the 1920's.

What set him apart, however, was his command of applied mathematics and his strong interest in the theoretical foundations of geophysical prospecting. Although he published little during the 1920's, very soon after joining the faculty at MIT he wrote a series of influential papers on the solution of inverse boundary value problems associated with the interpretation of seismological, electrical, and electromagnetic data on the earth's crust. Such problems were central to the geophysics of prospecting, where it is necessary to interpret the observed surface readings of a space field in terms of concealed geological structures—for example, in the interpretation of travel-time curves due to a seismic pulse or the interpretation of a direct-current flow from a point electrode at the surface of a half-space of varying conductivity.

Slichter never abandoned his interest in geophysical prospecting, and during the 1940's he extended his work by taking up problems relating to the earth's deeper structure and processes. His 1941 paper on the cooling of the earth was notable both for its analysis of the role of radioactivity as a source of internal heat and for its emphasis on the contribution of even small amounts of convection to heat-transfer processes. Slichter's analysis of gravimetric and seismographic evidence following the massive earthquake in Chile of 22 May 1960 constituted some of the first convincing evidence for the existence of a solid inner core, which had long been hypothesized by earth scientists.

Although Slichter was best known for his contributions to geophysical theory, he was also accomplished in the craftsmanship of experiment. In 1933 he used thirty miles of telephone circuits as lead wires in an effort to investigate the electrical conductivity of the upper crust. He succeeded in obtaining the conductivity profile to a depth of eight kilometers, a dramatic advance on what was then believed possible. During the 1930's he was also a pioneer in the use of explosive charges and portable seismographs to study the structure of the earth's crust. Later, while at UCLA, he took a strong interest in the collection of gravimetric and seismological data at the South Pole. In connection with this work, he invented a suspension system to minimize the effects of tilting of the ice platform on gravimetric measurements.

Slichter was married in 1926 to Martha Mary Buell; they had two daughters. He was awarded honorary degrees by the University of Wisconsin (1967) and UCLA (1969) and was the recipient of the Jackling Award of the American Institute of Mining and Metallurgical Engineers (1960) and the

William Bowie Medal of the American Geophysical Union (1966). In 1944 Slichter was elected to the National Academy of Sciences. Slichter Hall at UCLA and Slichter Foreland in Antarctica are named for him.

BIBLIOGRAPHY

I. Original Works. Slichter's major articles include "The Theory of the Interpretation of Seismic Travel-time Curves in Horizontal Structures," in *Physics* **3** (1932), 273–295; "The Interpretation of the Resistivity Prospecting Method for Horizontal Structures," *ibid.*, **4** (1933), 307–322; "An Inverse Boundary Value Problem in Electrodynamics," *ibid.*, 411–418; "Cooling of the Earth," in *Bulletin of the Geological Society of America*, **52** (1941), 561–600; and "The Fundamental Free Mode of the Earth's Inner Core," in *Proceedings of the National Academy of Sciences*, **47** (1961), 186–190.

II. Secondary Literature. On Slichter's family, see Mark H. Ingraham, *Charles Sumner Slichter: The Golden Vector* (Madison, Wis., 1972). A colorful biographical sketch and complete bibliography of Slichter's writings to 1974 are in Robert Rakes Shrock, *Geology at M.I.T. 1865–1965: A History of the First Hundred Years of Geology at Massachusetts Institute of Technology*, I, *The Faculty and Supporting Staff* (Cambridge, Mass., 1977), 665–678. Slichter's work during World War II is described in John Burchard, *QED: MIT in World War II* (New York, 1948, 47–51, 267–268. On his years at UCLA, see Clarence E. Palmer, "Louis Byrne Slichter: Builder of the Institute of Geophysics and Planetary Physics," in *Journal of Geophysical Research*, **68** (1963), 2867–2870. Slichter's contribution to the study of the earth's core is discussed in Stephen G. Brush, "Discovery of the Earth's Core," in *American Journal of Physics*, **48** (1980), 705–724. There is one obituary notice: L. Knopoff, R. E. Holzer, and C. F. Kennel, "Memorial to Louis Byrne Slichter, 1896–1978," in *Geological Society of America. Memorials*, **10** (1980).

John W. Servos

SNOW, CHARLES PERCY (*b.* Leicester, England, 15 October 1905; *d.* London, England, 1 July 1980), *physics, science administration, literature and criticism.*

The second of William Edward and Ada Sophia Robinson Snow's four sons, C. P. Snow grew up in England's industrial Midlands. His father, a fellow of the Royal College of Organists, secured a precarious lower-middle-class existence by giving music lessons and clerking in a shoe factory. More than the apparently abundant intellectual stimulation in the home, it was the unsteady hovering just above subsistence, punctuated by bankruptcy of his father's attempt at business, that had a decisive effect on the young Snow, who chose science as a career largely for the escape it offered from financial insecurity.

Scholarships permitted him to attend Leicester's University College, where he took first-class honors in chemistry (1927) and an M.Sc. in physics (1928); another scholarship took him as a research student to Christ's College, Cambridge, from which he secured a fellowship in 1930, the same year he obtained his Ph.D. Snow remained as a fellow until 1950. After 1935, with his career as research physicist over and that of novelist conclusively under way, his college duties consisted of tutoring, administration, and service to the university's press as editor of the Cambridge Library of Modern Science and, from 1937 until 1940, the popular science magazine *Discovery*.

During World War II, Snow was a member of the Royal Society Advisory Subcommittee on Deployment of Scientific Resources (1939–1942), becoming, upon absorption of this committee by the Ministry of Labour, the ministry's director of technical personnel. His service, which included training scientists for radar work and helping to cull the British contingent for the Manhattan Project, earned him the rank of C.B.E. (1943) and paved the way to his postwar career as a scientific adviser to the government.

Concurrently with his post as a civil service commissioner (1945–1960), where again his job was spotting scientific talent for government projects, Snow served as director (later physicist-director) of scientific personnel for the English Electric Company (1944–1964). Knighted in 1957, he became Baron Snow of Leicester in 1964 and the House of Lords' parliamentary secretary to the newly formed Ministry of Technology (1964–1966).

Snow's many honors included fellowship in the Royal Society of Literature (1951), honorary membership in the American Academy of Arts and Sciences (1962), and an appointment as extraordinary fellow of Churchill College, Cambridge (1966). In 1950 he married the English novelist and critic Pamela Hansford Johnson. They had one son.

Snow's brief career as a research physicist was devoted mainly to extensions of his doctoral work on the infrared spectra of simple diatomic molecules and to crystallographic studies of complex organic molecules. A blunder he made in one of these studies convinced him he would never be a successful scientist. Snow and a colleague, Philip Bowden, thought they had hit upon a method for synthesizing vitamin

A. However, their publication, which received excited attention, contained an obvious and critical error. The embarrassment, conjoined with the warm critical reception his third novel was just then receiving, finally determined the direction that Snow's creative energy would take.

Snow wrote (and destroyed) his first novel at twenty, while he was still a chemistry student in Leicester. During the first years of his fellowship at Christ's College, he published a detective story, *Death Under Sail* (1932); an exercise in science fiction, *New Lives for Old* (anonymous, 1933); and *The Search* (1934), a tale of the rise and fall of a young crystallographer. In 1935 he conceived a sequence of novels meant to capture (on the scale of Balzac's *Comédie humaine*) the essential variety of his time and place. The realization of his scheme, the eleven-volume *Strangers and Brothers*, absorbed him for thirty years (1940–1970).

In pronouncement and practice Snow was resolutely antimodernist, regarding the literary mainstream's experimentation and its concentration on the self as intellectually impoverished and perniciously antisocial. His intimate familiarity with the officialdoms of science, universities, and government was his stock in trade, while his unadorned prose, attention to plot, concern with the motives and moral dilemmas of the powerful, and preference for the large canvas made him, as the critic Melvin Maddocks observed, "the greatest living nineteenth-century novelist."

It was not as a novelist, however, but as a besieged publicist for the increasing importance of science in human life and as a pundit concerned with global problems of poverty, nuclear weapons, and the menacing collapse of Western civilization, that Snow became a major public figure with an international reputation. Enormous attention, much of it irritated, was paid his Rede Lectures, delivered at Cambridge in 1959 and published as *The Two Cultures and the Scientific Revolution* (1960). In them Snow claimed that lack of communication between literary and scientific intellectuals distorted understanding of the past, led to misjudgment of the present, and immobilized industrially advanced Western nations that would soon have to export applied science to the underdeveloped world. His case for science as an intrinsically moral activity, for technology as the answer to mankind's most pressing problems, and against the "natural Luddism" of traditional culture's leading exponents seemed to many a crass simplification. His archnemesis, the vituperative Cambridge literary critic F. R. Leavis, saw in Snow's assessment of the relative significance of science and the hu-

manities an example of how far real culture had deteriorated since the onset of its decline during the industrial revolution. The ensuing debate between partisans was one of the liveliest and most acerbic in the history of English literature, serving, as had the contest between the ancients and the moderns in the seventeenth century, to bring into the open, though not to bridge, the divide of suspicion and mistrust between literary and scientific intellectuals.

Snow's Godkin Lectures at Harvard in 1960, published under the title *Science and Government* (1961), used the clashes between Henry Tizard and Churchill's science adviser F. A. Lindemann during World War II over the viability of radar and strategic bombing to bring to the public's attention "the great underground domain of science and government." His purpose was to warn against the overinvestiture of power in science advisers, who function in a closed world of committee politics free from the checks and balances that might otherwise be provided by the scientific community. The same year, speaking before the American Association for the Advancement of Science on "The Moral Un-Neutrality of Science," Snow insisted on the responsibility of scientists to urge a restriction of nuclear armaments.

BIBLIOGRAPHY

I. ORIGINAL WORKS. Paul Boytinck's valuable *C. P. Snow: A Reference Guide* (Boston, 1980) is an annotated bibliography of Snow's novels, pamphlets, essays, book reviews, and open letters; coverage of his scientific output, however, is incomplete and should be supplemented with Poggendorff, VI, pt. 4, 2487, and VIIb, pt. 8, 5005–5008. The three-volume omnibus edition of *Strangers and Brothers* (London, 1972) is definitive and contains useful introductory material; *Public Affairs* (London, 1971) brings together Snow's major essays, including "The Two Cultures and the Scientific Revolution" (1959) and "Science and Government" (1962), and his afterthoughts on both. At the time of his death, Snow had finished the first draft of a highly personal memoir on modern physics; these vignettes, errors in place, were posthumously published as *The Physicists* (Boston, 1981).

The Humanities Research Center at the University of Texas in Austin possesses an extensive collection of Snow manuscripts, letters, and assorted papers.

II. SECONDARY LITERATURE. No biography ranging as widely as the subject itself has yet been written; the sketches are predominantly by those interested in Snow's fiction. John Halperin's transcription of conversations with Snow and his wife, *C. P. Snow: An Oral Biography* (Brighton, 1983), seeks its subject in his novels; Snow's brother Philip, in his *Stranger and Brother: A Portrait of C. P. Snow* (London, 1982), relies chiefly on Snow's letters. Boytinck (see above) lists biographical-critical treatments written during Snow's lifetime by English literature professors.

Boytinck also surveys the debate in the English-speaking world precipitated by F. R. Leavis' ferocious *Two Cultures? The Significance of C. P. Snow* (London, 1962), along with other work on Snow and his influence. For the tellingly large literature in non–Western European languages, the student is mostly on his or her own, though I. M. Levidova's *Charlz Persi Snou: Biobibliograficheskii ukazatel* (Moscow, 1977) gives guidance for readers of Russian.

J. G. MAY

SONNEBORN, TRACY MORTON (*b*. Baltimore, Maryland, 19 October 1905; *d*. Bloomington, Indiana, 26 January 1981), *genetics, protozoology.*

Tracy Sonneborn first received scientific recognition for his 1937 discovery of mating types in the ciliate *Paramecium*. This discovery made controlled matings in this organism possible and extended genetic analysis to microorganisms ten years prior to the discovery of genetic recombination in bacteria by Joshua Lederberg and Edward L. Tatum. Most of Sonneborn's work dealt with the interaction of nuclear Mendelian factors with various types of non-Mendelian hereditary mechanisms. The richness of non-Mendelian phenomena in ciliates is probably a consequence of the fact that the organism inherits the entire parental body when a new life cycle starts at fertilization.

Sonneborn was raised in Baltimore and did his undergraduate work at Johns Hopkins, graduating in 1926. As an undergraduate he came into contact with H. S. Jennings, who pioneered the study of heredity in protozoa. Jennings' courses and his way of thinking made a great impression on Sonneborn, and in 1926 he started graduate work with Jennings. His doctoral research dealt with the development of the turbellarian *Stenostomum* and the vegetative inheritance of an abnormal doublet biotype that was stably propagated over many cycles of vegetative fission. He received the Ph.D. from Johns Hopkins in 1928. During his postdoctoral research with Jennings, he studied the production and inheritance of a doublet phenotype in the ciliate *Colpidium*. In both of these cases Sonneborn suspected that the abnormal traits were inherited cytoplasmically, independently of the nuclear Mendelian genes. He was unable to prove this, because genetic breeding analysis was not possible with these organisms at the time.

On 6 June 1929 Sonnborn married Ruth Meyers. They had two sons, Lee and David. As academic positions were difficult to obtain following the economic collapse of 1929, Sonneborn took a position as Jennings' research associate in 1930 and began studying factors controlling conjugation in *Paramecium*, in the hope of being able to reliably carry out Mendelian breeding analyses. It was not until 1937, however, that the key factor controlling conjugation, mating types, was discovered. The central observation was that while conjugation occurred rarely among cells in clonal cultures derived from a single progenitor cell, it occurred readily in mixtures of cells pooled from several different clonal cultures. Pairwise mixture of cultures led directly to the concept of mating type: cells of one clone could mate only with certain other clones, but not among themselves.

During the next ten years Sonneborn worked out the basic genetics of *Paramecium*. This included elucidation of the nature of conjugation (cross-fertilization) and autogamy (self-fertilization) and the roles of these two processes in the life history of the organism, as well as procedures to control the transmission of cytoplasmic factors between cells during mating. Sonneborn also developed a method for transferring part of a mature macronucleus into a young cell, a procedure that was critically important in his analysis of epigenetic determination in macronuclei. His early investigations of mating also revealed that the morphological species *Paramecium aurelia* was in fact a complex of several genetically isolated sibling species, each with its own characteristic breeding strategy. In later years he created proper Linnean binomials for these biological species.

During this period Sonneborn discovered a variety of non-Mendelian hereditary phenomena that provided the basis of most of his subsequent work, almost all of which took place at Indiana University in Bloomington, where he had taken a position in 1939. His analysis revealed that these phenomena were of several different types.

These types included a hereditary symbiosis that manifested itself in the killer trait, whereby cells of one strain were able to kill cells of other strains. The inheritance of this trait proved to be remarkable, for it relied on both a normal nuclear Mendelian factor and a self-replicating, genelike cytoplasmic particle that later analysis revealed to be a symbiotic bacterium. In absence of the nuclear gene, the symbionts were unable to grow. In absence of the symbionts, the killer trait could not be produced, even in the presence of the required nuclear factor.

A second category of non-Mendelian phenomena proved to involve epigenetic differentiation of macronuclei in response to cytoplasmic or environmental factors. Sonneborn demonstrated that both mating type and cell surface antigen type were epigenetically determined in response to cytoplasmic factors inherited at fertilization with the parental cytoplasm. Through an ingenious series of experiments he was able to demonstrate the cytoplasmic nature of the determinative factors and to show that they affected only new macronuclei produced after fertilization; they had no effect on old macronuclei present in the same cytoplasm. Later, in the 1970's, Sonneborn discovered and analyzed in detail another phenomenon, trichocyst nondischarge, which showed a similar pattern of determination and inheritance. These studies are important because they provide paradigmatic examples of epigenetic differentiation and indicate that the basic machinery of epigenesis occurs in unicells as well as multicellular eucaryotes.

With the development of suitable genetic procedures, Sonneborn returned in the 1960's to the problem of the inheritance of abnormal patterns of cell organization, and demonstrated a third type of non-Mendelian phenomenon. He conclusively proved that the doublet phenotype in *Paramecium* was not controlled by Mendelian factors, but was a result of the cytoplasmic inheritance of the doublet organization. In a brilliant series of experiments with Janine Beisson he demonstrated through grafting that supernumerary longitudinal rows of basal bodies and flagella were perpetuated because the new structures produced prior to cell division were assembled in a precise geometric relationship to preexisting structures within a single longitudinal row of basal bodies.

Sonneborn received many honors during the course of his career. He was elected to the National Academy of Sciences in 1946, to the American Academy of Arts and Sciences in 1949, and to foreign membership in the Royal Society in 1964. In 1959 he received the Kimber Award for Genetics from the National Academy of Sciences, and in 1965 the Mendel Medal of the Czechoslovak Academy of Sciences. Sonneborn was awarded honorary degrees by Johns Hopkins University (1957), Northwestern University (1975), the University of Geneva (1975), Indiana University (1978), and the University of Münster (1979). He served as president of the American Society of Naturalists (1949), the Genetics Society of America (1949), the American Society of Zoologists (1956), and the American Institute of Biological Sciences (1961).

BIBLIOGRAPHY

I. ORIGINAL WORKS. A list of Sonneborn's scientific papers is included in G. H. Beale's biographical memoir (see below). A list of his major papers through 1975 was published in *Genetical Research*, **27** (1976), 349–351. Complete bibliographies and unpublished material, including an autobiographical sketch, are in the Lilly Library, Bloomington, Indiana.

II. SECONDARY LITERATURE. G. H. Beale, "Tracy Morton Sonneborn," in *Biographical Memoirs of Fellows of the Royal Society*, **28** (1982), 537–574; D. L. Nanney "T. M. Sonneborn: An Interpretation," in *Annual Review of Genetics*, **15** (1981), 1–9; "The Ciliates and the Cytoplasm," in *Journal of Heredity*, **74** (1983), 163–170; "Heredity Without Genes: Ciliate Explorations of Clonal Heredity," in *Trends in Genetics*, **1** (1985), 295–298; J. Harwood "The Erratic Career of Cytoplasmic Inheritance," in *Trends in Genetics*, **1** (1985), 298–300; Jan Sapp, "Inside the Cell: Genetic Methodology and the Case of the Cytoplasm," in J. A. Schuster and R. R. Yeo, eds., *The Politics and Rhetoric of Scientific Method* (Dordrecht, Netherlands, 1986), 167–202, and *Beyond the Gene: Cytoplasmic Inheritance and the Struggle for Authority in Genetics* (New York and Oxford, 1987).

JAMES D. BERGER

STANLEY, WENDELL MEREDITH (*b*. Ridgeville, Indiana, 16 August 1904; *d*. Salamanca, Spain, 15 June 1971), *chemistry, virology, education.*

In 1935 Wendell Stanley crystallized tobacco mosaic virus, an achievement that was awarded a Nobel Prize in 1946. This and subsequent findings demonstrated that an infectious agent could have the properties of a chemical molecule and posed the biochemical problems of the mechanisms of inheritable duplicability. The initial observations were soon confirmed in England by F. C. Bawden and N. W. Pirie, who showed also that this and other plant viruses contained ribonucleic acid (RNA). Their result, in its turn, set the problem of the structural and functional roles of the nucleic acids in viruses. The almost simultaneous discovery by M. Schlesinger of deoxyribonucleic acid (DNA) in some bacterial viruses extended this finding. Thus, in 1935 and 1936, biologists were startled to learn that some of the smallest organisms, in the group known as "filterable viruses," were isolable by methods designed for proteins and were amenable to rigorous chemical and physical characterization. The results at that time indicated that the viruses contained both protein and a distinctive but little-studied substance, a nucleic acid. Early commentators on these findings called attention to the similar reproductive capabilities of viruses and genes, and in 1937 E. Wollman added, "The possibility of 'inoculating' genes into cells does not seem to us to be excluded *a priori*."

By 1944 these events culminated in the demonstration by O. T. Avery, C. M. Macleod, and M. McCarty that the pneumococcal transforming agent was a biologically specific DNA. Thus, between 1935 and 1944, the fundamental problems of the nature of the gene, its duplication and mode of action, had been transferred to model systems of virology and microbiology. The analysis of these systems over the next thirty years determined the course of biological science by facilitating the dissection of the mechanisms of inheritance and by leading to the integrative development of numerous disciplines (biochemistry, genetics, and structural chemistry) as "molecular biology."

Wendell Stanley, an initiator of this modern era of biology, was the son of James G. Stanley and Claire Plessinger Stanley. His parents published the local newspaper, and as a boy Stanley helped to collect news, set type, and deliver the final product. He attended public schools in the little town of Ridgeville, completed the last two years of high school in Richmond, Indiana, and entered Earlham College in Richmond in 1922. In addition to academic majors in chemistry and mathematics and an active social life, Stanley played football for all four of his collegiate years and captained a winning team in his senior year. In a state known for several outstanding sports-oriented colleges, the relatively slight Stanley was selected as end on the Indiana All-State team. Nevertheless, Earlham College, which began as a Quaker school, prided itself on the quality of its liberal arts education, stressing the examination of values and moral commitments, as well as of "facts." The choice of Earlham and his life there may have contributed significantly to his later bearing and attitudes.

On graduation in 1926 Stanley aspired to be a football coach, and he visited the campus of the University of Illinois with this future in mind. While there he met Roger Adams, a doyen of organic chemistry. He learned of graduate work in chemistry and, armed with his baccalaureate from Earlham, he entered the University of Illinois. As a graduate student with Adams he worked on two types of problems, the stereochemistry of biphenyls and the synthesis and properties of compounds potentially bactericidal for *Mycobacterium leprae*. He published eleven papers on these subjects with Adams between 1927 and 1933, obtaining an M.S. in 1927 and a Ph.D. in 1929. Stanley and Adams synthesized hydnocarpylacetic acid and showed it to be identical with natural chaulmoogric acid. Also, all the bactericidal aliphatic sodium salts were found to be marked depressants of surface tension.

A paper on this subject was published in 1929 with Adams and another graduate student, Marian S. Jay, who married Stanley in that year. The couple had three daughters and a son, Wendell, Jr., who is known for work in molecular biology. It may be relevant to Stanley's later success that the single joint paper of Stanley, Jay, and Adams in the *Journal of the American Chemical Society* follows a paper by J. B. Sumner and D. B. Hand on the isoelectric point of crystalline urease, determined as the point of minimum solubility. This is a method used by Stanley in his later crystallization of tobacco mosaic virus.

Stanley was an instructor at Illinois in 1930 and won a National Research Council Fellowship in chemistry, which he took in the academic year 1930–1931 with Heinrich Wieland in Munich, Germany. His work with Wieland was on the characterization of the sterols of yeast.

The Stanleys returned to the United States during the Depression; he was appointed to a position with W. J. V. Osterhout at the Rockefeller Institute in New York City. Osterhout, who had been studying the transport and concentration of ions in plant cells such as *Valonia*, had asked Stanley to develop a model system to transport ions selectively across a membrane. Stanley, quite unfamiliar with problems of this type, read extensively in the field and in 1931 helped to devise systems for the selective accumulation of potassium and sodium. A nonaqueous medium representing the protoplasmic surface was interposed between alkaline and acidic aqueous phases. An accumulation of the cations occurs in the more acid phase, followed by an increase of osmotic pressure and of water entry. The entire system simulated accumulation in *Valonia* very well, permitting a comparison in the model and *Valonia* of the factors modifying uptake. The work with Osterhout undoubtedly sharpened Stanley's understanding of the biophysical chemistry of the time and probably introduced him to some current problems of plant physiology.

In 1932 he moved to the Department of Animal and Plant Pathology of the Rockefeller Institute, established at Princeton, New Jersey, in 1916. This branch arose in response to the principle that the

Institute could not limit itself to the study of human disease and to the proposal in 1914 to establish a department of plant pathology. The distinguished American microbiologist and comparative pathologist Theobald Smith became director. Laboratories were built on farmland on the outskirts of Princeton. Smith and the groups he assembled became active in the study of various protozoan, bacterial, and viral diseases of veterinary importance. In 1926 a group in general physiology, comprised of John Northrop and Moses Kunitz, became part of Smith's administrative domain, as had numerous other groups representing insect physiology, parasitology, genetics, and nutrition. By 1926 the size and diversity of the enterprise became excessive for Smith, who was eventually replaced by Carl TenBroek, an early collaborator knowledgeable in virus infections. Under TenBroek, who helped to sustain the work of virologists such as Richard Shope and Otto Glaser, the Division of Plant Pathology was established in 1931 with Louis O. Kunkel as its head. He moved to Princeton in 1932 and brought Stanley there shortly thereafter.

Kunkel had come from the Boyce Thompson Institute for Plant Research and had been associated with C. G. Vinson and A. W. Petre, who had obtained promising results in the chemical separation of tobacco mosaic virus. Kunkel asked his entire group to focus on mosaic diseases, principally the tobacco mosaic disease. In 1892 the Russian D. Ivanovsky had shown that this disease could be transmitted by the sap of an infected plant after filtration through porcelain. M. Beijerinck in Delft had made similar observations in 1898 and had postulated the existence of a pathogen smaller than bacteria. One virologist in Kunkel's group, Francis Holmes, had developed a method of estimating infectious virus particles by counting the localized lesions arising after inoculating the leaves of selected plants. Philip White was growing virus-susceptible tomato roots aseptically in tissue cultures in order to dilute out possible secondary invaders. Kunkel himself discovered related viruses and compared their host ranges with that of tobacco mosaic virus. He is also known for the "heat cure" of plants, including trees, thought to be infected by viruses.

Beginning with the work of H. A. Allard in 1916, various investigators had concentrated and purified the virus. Between 1925 and 1935, Vinson and Petre had used lead acetate to precipitate the virus. The fact that the virus might be handled as a chemical precipitable by protein precipitants led Stanley to explore the possibility that this virus was a protein. In 1933 and 1934 Stanley worked furiously to test the infectivity of fresh or partially purified extracts exposed to more than a hundred reagents, including some proteolytic enzymes. Such enzymes, including trypsin, had been isolated and crystallized just a few years earlier by Northrop and Kunitz at the institute in Princeton. The successes and methods of this group were a continuing source of encouragement in this early period. Stanley found that trypsin inactivated the virus but that the latter could be reactivated. The enzyme affected the plant more than the virus, and Stanley concluded that trypsin did not degrade the virus proteolytically. On the other hand, a slow inactivation by pepsin in the range of hydrogen-ion concentration (pH) in which pepsin was proteolytic was consistent with the idea that the virus was a protein. In general, infectivity was lost at extreme pHs, or in the presence of oxidizing agents or protein precipitants. Pursuing the results of Vinson and Petre, it was possible to use a low concentration of lead acetate at high pH to eliminate colored materials without reducing infectivity, and Stanley introduced such a step in his initial successful purification. During purification steps the pH was adjusted at noninactivating levels, which facilitated solubilization or precipitation, and which he had established earlier.

In this early work, published in 1935, large batches of frozen infected plants, ground in the frozen state, were thawed in a buffer containing sodium phosphate (high pH), and the filtrate was precipitated at lower pH with a high concentration of ammonium sulfate. This precipitate contained virus that was extracted and reprecipitated. Lead acetate at high pH was used to remove colored material and an asbestos powder adsorbed the virus at low pH. The virus was eluted at high pH and was then crystallized from this solution as small "needles" by the addition of acetic acid to a defined low pH in the presence of 20 percent saturated ammonium sulfate.

The initial report in 1935 described a product containing 20 percent nitrogen, but the first complete paper in 1936 reported nitrogen contents by two methods of 16.1–16.6 percent, values consistent with those of proteins and most nucleoproteins. However, Stanley did not find phosphorus or sulfur in the virus. The protein was recognized to be very large since it did not pass through membranes that did not retain smaller proteins, such as egg albumin. Numerous recrystallizations of the protein did not affect the dilution of the virus used to produce local lesions. The extracts of single lesions gave rise, in subsequent infections, to very much larger amounts of the infectious protein, indicating its multiplication. Antisera prepared against the virus in guinea pigs and rabbits reacted specifically against purified virus preparations, as well as against the juice of infected plants. Uninfected plants did not contain proteins capable of reacting with these antisera. In a later study it was shown that tobacco mosaic virus multiplied as such in tomato plants. Further, a distinctly different strain of the virus, the aucuba mosaic virus, multiplied as such in aucuba-infected tobacco.

In interpreting his results, Stanley was influenced by the results of Northrop and Kunitz, who had described the existence of pancreatic proenzymes, such as proteolytically inactive trypsinogen. This substance was converted by proteolysis to active trypsin by adding a trace of the active proteolytic enzyme. Could a plant contain a serologically inert provirus that would be converted "autocatalytically" by the active virus to a serologically active virus? Significant amounts of comparable large molecules capable of serving as provirus were not present in the juice of normal plants. It was not until the late 1940's, in work with bacteriophage systems, that it was shown that virus multiplication required extensive de novo synthesis of proteins and nucleic acids, and very much later, in the 1960's, that the processes of synthesis of nucleic acids and proteins were composed of far more complex metabolic and synthetic events than that described for the conversion of trypsinogen to trypsin. In 1935 Stanley stated, "Tobacco-mosaic virus is regarded as an autocatalytic protein which, for the present, may be assumed to require the presence of living cells for multiplication." It was shown in 1946 and 1947, in studies with bacterial viruses, that the host cells continued to supply the energy, as well as an extensive metabolic apparatus, for the multiplication of these viruses. These conclusions are applicable similarly to plant and animal viruses multiplying in their respective hosts.

In discussing the extraordinary result that an organism capable of inheritable duplication could be defined as a relatively simple substance capable of forming crystalline arrays, Stanley wondered if the virus were "alive." His conclusion that this virus was not "alive" elicited much discussion of the meaning of the term and, in particular, we can note the important essay in 1937 by N. W. Pirie entitled "The Meaninglessness of the Terms 'Life' and 'Living.'" Summarizing the attributes of the many properties of organisms and substances, Pirie noted the lack of agreement on the meaning of the word "living." He suggested that "it seems prudent to avoid the use of the word 'life' in any discussion about border-line systems," and indeed his essay squelched further discussion for about twenty-five years.

However, in later years, with the development of space programs, many individuals have had to attempt to define just which characteristics ought to be sought in the samples to be collected on Mars or elsewhere.

The first group to confirm Stanley's discovery included the English workers F. C. Bawden and N. W. Pirie, who in earlier studies of the potato X virus had concluded that this virus was comprised of proteinase-sensitive proteins. However, this flexuous virus did not easily form crystalline arrays. Turning to tobacco mosaic virus, they were able to isolate the "needles" observed by Stanley, but with the aid of the X-ray crystallographers J. D. Bernal and I. Fankuchen, it became clear that the "needles" did not possess three-dimensional regularity. The purified virus particles were relatively stiff rods of constant diameter, which were aligned during flow, and packed in hexagonal arrays to form needlelike "liquid" crystals or "paracrystals." This occurred on precipitation by salts at a pH of minimum solubility or by steric exclusion and the abstraction of water to large foreign hydrophilic molecules. Bernal and Fankuchen, in later detailed studies of the virus "paracrystals," described the open-ended needles as "tactoids." Bawden and Pirie also showed that a further purification of virus particles in concentrated suspension permitted a separation into two phases, of which the bottom phase was spontaneously birefringent in polarized light; that is, the virus had crystallized in the arrays represented by the smaller "tactoids." The top phase was now more dilute and showed anisotropy of flow, becoming birefringent in polarized light in regions of flow aligning the particles.

Although the identity of Stanley's initial product has been questioned, it should be noted that the high nitrogen content was corrected by the end of 1935, before the first paper in 1936 by the English group of Bawden, Pirie, Bernal, and Fankuchen. Furthermore, Stanley's material was analyzed by an American crystallographic group, and the data published in November 1936 was described by the English group, in a note added on 3 December 1936, as follows: "Wyckoff and Corey have published an X-ray study of the ammonium sulphate crystals of tobacco mosaic and aucuba protein. Their measurements of the intramolecular spacings obtained with unorientated material agree with ours, notably the lines they record at 11.0, 7.44, 5.44 and 3.7 A correspond to our measurement of the planes (0006, 9, 12, 18) respectively." Thus the material obtained by the English workers was identical to an early preparation of the virus obtained by Stanley, made before any publication by the former group.

In addition to the clarification by Bawden, Pirie, and their crystallographic collaborators of the degree of order found in isolated viral arrays, their earliest paper records their discovery of the presence of 5 percent RNA in this virus, a result they soon extended to related viruses. Higher percentages of RNA were discovered later by Bawden and Pirie in some spherical viruses, such as the tomato bushy stunt virus and the tobacco necrosis viruses. At first Stanley was unwilling to accept this result, which had been communicated to him by Pirie early in 1936. Stanley considered the RNA to be a disposable contaminant and disregarded the unusual ultraviolet absorption spectrum of the virus, now known to relate to the presence of nucleic acid. However, H. S. Loring, a collaborator of Stanley, found phosphorus and RNA in organic combination with protein in several viruses, and in 1938 Loring and Stanley corrected their earlier variable and confusing values. Their report was extended in 1939 by A. F. Ross and Stanley to include the presence of sulfur in the virus, exposed as sulfhydryl groups in side chains of cysteine in the native protein.

The discovery of the presence of RNA in the virus and its solubilization after denaturation of the virus protein by heat, detergents, alkali, or acid facilitated the characterization of this material. It had been suggested by P. A. Levene that RNA was comprised of four different nucleotides to form a tetranucleotide. The RNA of the virus contained the four classical nucleotides but diffused more slowly than a tetranucleotide might. In 1942 the nucleic acid, isolated after heat denaturation of the virus, was shown by S. S. Cohen and Stanley, using measurements of diffusion, sedimentation, and viscosity, to be much larger, indeed, having an average molecular weight of 300,000. The product was highly asymmetric and spontaneously birefringent, although it slowly depolymerized on standing. The size and shape of this material suggested a lengthwise orientation within the virus, which also contained linearly assembled smaller subunits of protein. The packaging of the protein around the nucleic acid presumably rendered the latter insusceptible to degradative enzymes. Although the largest weight of the product isolated at this time was only an eighth of the total RNA of a virus particle, less drastic methods have yielded RNA molecules of greater than two million daltons. Such molecules of RNA are infectious themselves, and indeed some of this size were probably among the mixture of molecules

isolated in 1942, since some fifteen years later infectious RNA was prepared after heat denaturation.

As indicated above, the criticism of Stanley's early studies had been severe. The dialogue, criticism, and competition led in many instances to stimulated efforts and new results. Before 1937 Stanley had obtained collaborative assistance from physical chemists in New York: R. W. G. Wyckoff, J. Biscoe, and G. I. Lavin. From 1937 to 1942 the work of Stanley's laboratory multiplied with the assistance of numerous younger chemists: H. S. Loring, A. F. Ross, M. A. Lauffer, G. L. Miller, C. A. Knight, and S. S. Cohen. The physical biochemist Max Lauffer was particularly important in formulating approaches to defining the molecularity of tobacco mosaic virus and of tomato bushy stunt virus, and in characterizing macromolecules generally. Bawden and Pirie asked early on if the crystalline preparations of infectious protein contained only the distinctive rodlike particles, and both groups used physical and chemical methods in developing the affirmative answer. Was the infectivity a function of a singularly sized rod? Lengthwise aggregation occurred under many biological and chemical conditions, but careful sedimentation studies by Lauffer revealed that monomeric rods were the infectious entity. Rods of shorter length were seen in electron microscopy of infectious samples, but these are now known to be derived from longer rods broken in the preparation of the sample for microscopy. How homogeneous was a population of virus particles? Lauffer, analyzing the spreading of a sedimenting boundary of tomato bush stunt virus, concluded that the diameters of the particles could deviate from the mean by no more than 1 percent. In an exuberant moment Lauffer referred to "living molecules."

Nevertheless, it is of considerable interest that neither group tested the infectivity of viral RNA before 1956. Despite the availability of appropriate viral RNA after 1936 and inactivating crystalline ribonuclease in 1940, and despite the demonstration of DNA as pneumococcal transforming agent in 1944 and the apparent infectivity of phage DNA, accepted by the community of phage workers in 1953 following the discovery of the Watson-Crick model, the thought that the viral RNA might be the genetic element of this virus was not tested before 1956.

In 1940 E. Pfankuch, G. A. Kausche, and H. Stubbe had studied X-ray–induced mutations of the virus and had attributed differences in the phosphorus contents of the parent and mutant strains to irradiation-induced alterations in the nucleic acid part of the virus. These data were not considered convincing in 1941 by C. A. Knight and Stanley, who had found differences in the amino acid compositions of various strains. The Rockefeller group had concluded that "the chemical differences between strains probably lies not in the nucleic acid but rather in the protein part of the virus molecule." Stanley's group apparently did not consider the possibility that the nucleic acid might determine the composition of the protein. Following this line of thought, Miller and Stanley modified amino acid residues with a variety of reagents but found that, although many groups could be modified without loss of biological activity, the virus propagated was normal virus. At this point in the work, with the entrance of the United States into World War II, the work of the laboratory was diverted to the isolation of influenza virus and the production of an influenza vaccine.

After the startling reports of Gierer and Schramm and of Fraenkel-Conrat in 1956, Bawden and Pirie undertook the testing of the infectivity of RNA preparations. Finding low levels of such activity in an inefficient assay by their RNA samples, they were suspicious initially of the meaning of their results. However, as the mechanisms of virus multiplication and of the roles of the nucleic acids were clarified, they eventually accepted the concept that the RNA or DNA of a particular virus can constitute its genetic element.

Although Stanley had defined the reproductive process as one requiring the participation of cells, his approach to the problems of virus multiplication, as well as that of Bawden and Pirie, focused on the nature and structure of the virus particle. This approach provided unique materials for the development of electron microscopy, and for some years the well-defined tobacco mosaic virus served as the yardstick for the standardization of the magnification in the microscope. Neither group ever attempted to analyze the multiplication of a virus in its cellular site, because it appeared too difficult to obtain tissue in which a high percentage of cells were infected. This problem had led a few workers to begin to reexplore the long-known bacteriophage systems, in which it was possible to time the initiation of infection, the duration of the multiplication process, and the yield of virus per infected cell. Furthermore, it was possible to infect all the bacteria of a population simultaneously to provide a system for the study of chemical events during bacteriophage multiplication. This type of chemical study of virus multiplication began in 1946 and was extended to animal cells infected in tissue culture in 1953 and finally to infection of separated plant protoplasts in 1967.

The exigencies of World War II altered the priorities of Stanley's laboratory, and with the participation of Miller, Lauffer, and Knight, Stanley developed an inactivated vaccine for viral influenza. A Sharples Super-centrifuge, found to be useful in sedimenting various types of particles, was applied to the study of the concentration of influenza virus grown in the allantois of the embryonated chick. The large capacity and efficiency of this equipment made this the method of choice for a large-scale preparation of virus. The size, stability, and chemical inactivation of the virus were studied, as well as its immunizing potency. The general procedure has proved to be useful in the development of several commercial vaccines. Stanley became a consultant to the secretary of war and a member of the U.S. Army Commission on Influenza. In 1948 he received a Presidential Certificate of Merit for his work in vaccine development.

The many exciting and important results from Stanley's laboratory led to his election to the American Philosophical Society and National Academy of Sciences in 1940 and 1941 respectively. He had won many prizes and academic honors, including honorary degrees from Earlham, Harvard, and Yale before the beginning of the war. A new round of awards began in 1946, including the Nichols Medal of the American Chemical Society and the Nobel Prize, shared with J. B. Sumner and John H. Northrop, for their crystallization of enzymes. Stanley also received an honorary degree from the University of California. Nevertheless, in 1947 the trustees of the Rockefeller Institute decided to close the Princeton laboratory.

In 1948 both Nobelists accepted positions at the University of California at Berkeley. Stanley joined the faculty as the founder of the Virus Laboratory and the chairman of a new department of biochemistry. Science was perceived as an enormous force in the future of the planet, and, although the development of penicillin had not solved the problem of virus infection, it was expected that the development of similarly wonderful drugs for the cure of virus disease was only a step away. Stanley began his second career as an educational administrator, in an optimistic university environment.

From 1948 to 1953 he recruited able young scientists for both departments, and in 1953 resigned as chairman of the department of biochemistry, as that developing unit was increasingly productive and independent. After that resignation Stanley focused on the tasks for which he had been recruited. The Virus Laboratory became an assembly of leaders in disciplines crucial to the development of virology. C. A. Knight reestablished study of the plant viruses. H. K. Schachman, a physical chemist who had worked for years with Lauffer, organized the laboratory concerned with the physical characterization of macromolecules. (Schachman was to become director of the Virus Laboratory after Stanley's death.) R. C. Williams, a distinguished electron microscopist, had been recruited, as had the protein chemist, H. Fraenkel-Conrat, and G. Stent, a phage worker, who had studied with M. Delbrück. H. Rubin began a study of tumor viruses, and the animal virologists F. L. Schaffer and C. E. Schwerdt, concerned with the isolation of the virus of poliomyelitis, crystallized the virus in 1955. Also in that year Fraenkel-Conrat and Williams had reassembled the RNA and protein subunits of tobacco mosaic virus to form an infectious product, and in the following year the former showed that the RNA alone was active and had been protected by its protein coat. In 1960 Stanley participated in a group that had determined the complete sequence of the amino acids in the protein subunit.

Stanley urged the university to create the department of virology, which he chaired from 1958 until 1964. In this period Stanley wrote many reviews and participated in many symposia related to viruses. In 1959 he and F. M. Burnet edited a three-volume compendium entitled *The Viruses*. Before and during this period he had become increasingly active in the affairs of national science, as chairman of the editorial board of the *Proceedings of the National Academy of Sciences*, as a director-at-large of the American Cancer Society, and as a member of the Board of Scientific Counselors of the National Cancer Institute.

He was also deeply and consistently occupied in campus life. In the period of a developing Cold War, the influence of McCarthyism had led to an imposition of loyalty oaths on the faculties of many universities, including that at Berkeley. Stanley served as chairman of the University Senate Committee on Academic Freedom. He signed the California oath himself, but publicly defended the rights of others who refused to sign oaths as a matter of conscience. He vigorously opposed this imposition as a condition of employment and participated in the work of groups of academics in resisting oaths and in bringing the legal issues to the courts. A court decision eventually declared the unconstitutionality of the oath.

Stanley was convinced of the need to communicate current advances and perspectives of science to lay and medical groups. He helped to organize a television series on viruses. His efforts in addressing the public led to his election as an honorary member of the National Association of Science Writers.

After 1964, when the department of virology was enlarged to become the department of molecular biology, Stanley was relieved of some administrative duties. In this period of the growth of the National Institutes of Health, he served as a member of the advisory committees to the director, James A. Shannon, and to the secretary of the Department of Health, Education, and Welfare. In the 1960's the work on avian and mammalian tumor viruses had increasingly created the sense that such viruses might be etiological agents of human cancer, and the feeling grew that Stanley's contributions might relate to the control of this disease as well. In addition to awards from the American Cancer Society, he was selected as president of the Tenth International Cancer Congress in 1970. The hypothesis that tumor viruses responsible for human cancer might be isolated and used in the development of immunizing vaccines was one perspective leading to the passage of the National Cancer Act in 1971. The expanded national effort, which attempted to document the concept, discovered in the next five years that this idea was much too oversimplified, but in its turn discovered new facts concerning the genetic relations of tumor viruses.

Stanley suffered several severe illnesses in his later years but continued to travel extensively. He died of a heart attack in Spain, where he had attended a scientific conference and had discussed tumor viruses. He is buried in California. The laboratory that he built at the University of California is named the Wendell M. Stanley Hall.

BIBLIOGRAPHY

I. ORIGINAL WORKS. "The Synthesis of Chaulmoogric Acid from Hydnocarpic Acid," in *Journal of the American Chemical Society*, **51** (1929), 1515–1518, written with R. Adams; "The Preparation of Certain Octadecanoic Acids and Their Bactericidal Action Toward *B. leprae*, XV," *ibid.*, 1261–1266, written with M. S. Jay and R. Adams; "Zur Kenntnis der Sterine der Hefe, III," in *Liebigs Annalen der Chemie*, **489**, no. 1 (1931), 31–42, written with H. Wieland; "The Accumulation of Electrolytes, V, Models Showing Accumulation and a Steady State," in *Journal of General Physiology*, **15** (1932), 667–689, written with W. J. V. Osterhout; "Kinetics of Penetration, VII, Molecular Versus Ionic Transport," *ibid.*, **17** (1934), 469–480, written with W. J. V. Osterhout and S. E. Kamerling; "Chemical Studies on the Virus of Tobacco Mosaic, I, Some Effects of Trypsin," in *Phytopathology*, **24** (1934), 1055–1085; "Chemical Studies of the Virus of Tobacco Mosaic, IV, Some Effects of Different Chemical

Agents on Infectivity," *ibid.*, **25** (1935), 899–921; and "Isolation of a Crystalline Protein Possessing the Properties of Tobacco-Mosaic Virus," in *Science*, **81** (1935), 644–645.

"Chemical Studies on the Virus of Tobacco Mosaic, VI, The Isolation from Diseased Turkish Tobacco Plants of a Crystalline Protein Possessing the Properties of Tobacco-mosaic Virus," in *Phytopathology*, **26** (1936), 305–320; "Isolation of Crystalline Tobacco Mosaic Virus Protein from Tomato Plants," in *Journal of Biological Chemistry*, **117** (1937), 733–754, written with H. S. Loring; "Properties of Virus Proteins," in *Cold Spring Harbor Symposia on Quantitative Biology*, **6** (1938), 341–360, written with H. S. Loring; "The Sulfur and Phosphorus Contents of Tobacco Mosaic Virus," in *Journal of the American Chemical Society*, **61** (1939), 535–540, written with A. F. Ross; "The Physical Chemistry of Tobacco Mosaic Virus Protein," in *Chemical Reviews*, **24** (1939), 303–321, written with M. A. Lauffer; "Studies on the Sedimentation Rate of Bushy Stunt Virus," in *Journal of Biological Chemistry*, **135** (1940), 463–472, written with M. A. Lauffer; "The Chemical Composition of Strains of Tobacco Mosaic Virus," in *Cold Spring Harbor Symposia on Quantitative Biology*, **9** (1941), 255–262, written with C. A. Knight; and "A Study of Purified Viruses with the Electron Microscope," in *Journal of Biological Chemistry*, **139** (1941), 325–344, written with T. F. Anderson.

"Derivatives of Tobacco Mosaic Virus, II, Carbobenzoxy, *p*-chlorobenzoyl, and Benzenesulfonyl Virus," in *Journal of Biological Chemistry*, **146** (1942), 331–338, written with G. L. Miller; "The Molecular Size and Shape of the Nucleic Acid of Tobacco Mosaic Virus," *ibid.*, **144** (1942), 589–598, written with S. S. Cohen; "The Preparation and Properties of Influenza Virus Vaccines Concentrated and Purified by Differential Centrifugation," in *Journal of Experimental Medicine*, **81** (1945), 193–218; "Biochemical Studies on Influenza Virus," in *Chemical and Engineering News*, **24** (1946), 755–758; "The Isolation and Properties of Crystalline Tobacco Mosaic Virus," in *Les prix Nobel en 1947* (Stockholm, 1949), 196–225; "Virus Composition and Structure: 25 Years Ago and Now," in *Federation of American Societies for Experimental Biology*, *Federation Proceedings*, **15** (1956), 812–818; "The Potential Significance of Nucleic Acids and Nucleoproteins of Specific Composition in Malignancy," in *Texas Reports on Biology and Medicine*, **15** (1957), 796–810; "Relationships, Established and Prospective, Between Viruses and Cancer," in *Annals of the New York Academy of Sciences*, **71** (1958), 1100–1113; and "The Complete Amino Acid Sequence of the Protein of Tobacco Mosaic Virus," in *Proceedings of the National Academy of Sciences of the United States*, **46** (1960), 1463–1469, written with A. Tsugita, D. T. Gish, J. Young, H. Fraenkel-Conrat, and C. A. Knight.

II. SECONDARY LITERATURE. G. C. Ainsworth, *Introduction to the History of Plant Pathology* (Cambridge, England, 1981); F. C. Bawden, N. W. Pirie, J. D. Bernal, and I. Fankuchen, "Liquid Crystalline Substances from Virus-infected Plants," in *Nature*, **138** (1936), 1051–1052; F. C. Bawden, *Plant Viruses and Virus Diseases*, 4th ed. (New York, 1964); S. S. Cohen, "Some Contributions of the Princeton Laboratory of the Rockefeller Institute on Proteins, Viruses, Enzymes, and Nucleic Acids," in P. R. Srinivasan *et al.*, eds., *The Origins of Modern Biochemistry* (New York, 1979), 303–306; G. W. Corner, *A History of the Rockefeller Institute, 1901–1953: Origins and Growth* (New York, 1965); and John T. Edsall, "Wendell Meredith Stanley (1904–1971)," in *American Philosophical Society, Year Book 1971* (Philadelphia, 1971), 184–190.

J. S. Fruton, *Molecules and Life* (New York, 1972); N. W. Pirie, "The Meaninglessness of the Terms 'Life' and 'Living,'" in Joseph Needham, ed., *Perspectives in Biochemistry* (Cambridge, England, 1937), 11–22; R. E. Shope, "In Honor of Wendell M. Stanley," in *Gustav Stern Symposium on Perspectives in Virology*, V (New York, 1967), xv–xxi; R. L. Shriner and V. Du Vigneaud, "The William H. Nichols Medalist for 1946," in *Chemical and Engineering News*, **24** (1946), 750–755; A. Tiselius, "The Nobel Prize for Chemistry, 1946," in *Les prix Nobel en 1946* (Stockholm, 1948), 29–32; A. P. Waterson and L. Wilkinson, *An Introduction to the History of Virology* (Cambridge, England, 1978); and "Wendell Meredith Stanley," in *Nature*, **233** (1971), 149–150.

SEYMOUR S. COHEN

STAUB, RUDOLF (*b.* Glarus, Switzerland, 29 January 1890; *d.* Fex, Graubünden, Switzerland, 25 June 1961), *geology.*

Rudolf Staub's father, who owned a small textile factory in Glarus, died soon after his son's birth. His mother took over the mill; she died when Staub was twelve years old. Nevertheless he enjoyed his boyhood, especially at the high school at Trogen. At the request of his trustees, he started to study mechanical engineering at the Swiss Federal Institute of Technology (ETH), but upon coming of age, he switched to geology at the University of Zurich, fascinated by the structure of his native mountains. He did his Ph.D. dissertation in the Bernina Mountains with the petrologist Johann Ulrich Grubenmann; during World War I he served as one of the first army geologists. Staub was married three times and had one son and four daughters.

Rudolf Staub began his career at an exciting time for an Alpine geologist. After the discovery of nappe structures by Marcel Bertrand and Hans Schardt, Maurice Lugeon had unrevelled the Helvetic nappes; Pierre Termier had presented grand views of both the Western and the Eastern Alps; and Émile Argand, greatest of these great geologists, had applied the principle of oblique axial projection to the Penninic nappes of Valais. Staub chose the Penninic and Austroalpine nappes of Graubünden and adjacent areas of Italy as his main field of research. The Graubünden section is of special importance, because a great axial flexure exposes almost all tectonic units, from the lowest in the west to the highest in the east. Staub had two advantages over his contemporaries: he was a keen mountaineer and, having independent means, he owned a car, a luxury for a young geologist at that time. This enabled him to travel widely, not only in the Alps but also in the Apennines, Corsica, Spain, and Morocco.

Staub was above all a field geologist. He mapped the rugged and complex mountains of Val Bregaglia (1921) and of the Avers (1926). But soon he started to think about general problems of Alpine geology. His first works along these lines closely follow Argand's ideas. In 1924 he published his masterpiece, *Der Bau der Alpen*. Staub produced the first modern tectonic map of the Alps and included numerous beautiful transverse sections, the latter an effort that has not been repeated since. While he relied on Argand and Termier for the Western Alps, the part on the Eastern Alps is highly original and prefigures many modern ideas.

In *Der Bewegungsmechanismus der Erde* (1928) Staub presented a resolutely mobilistic picture of the earth's structure, based partly on Wegener's and Argand's ideas, but insisting on the somewhat mythical forces of *Polflucht* and *Poldrift*. This little-known work deserves consideration as one of the early attempts at some kind of plate tectonics.

In 1928 Staub was elected professor at the ETH and at the University of Zurich and soon became the *capo* (chief) of a lively group of followers. His students worked in Graubünden, the Helvetic Alps, the Tauern window, and the Molasse Basin. Staub's interest in the Molasse was reflected in his magnificent "Grundzüge und Probleme alpiner Morphologie" (1934), a refreshing paper in which his intuitive way of reasoning and his vast knowledge of the Alps were used to reconstruct the Tertiary evolution of the chain. Papers from 1937 and 1942 on the Western Alps contain many original views on the correlation of Alpine nappes.

New tasks awaited Staub with the outbreak of World War II. As a militia captain in the Swiss army, he organized the Geological Service, where about sixty young geologists learned to cooperate with young civil engineers in building fortifications and studying water supplies. During and after the war Staub provided expert advice on the construction of large power dams in various parts of the Alps. In spite of his strong involvement in practical geology, he continued to publish on many subjects: the Southern Alps (1950), the Glarus Alps (1954, with a remarkable chapter on the history of the nappe discovery), and the origin of the Prealpine nappes (1958). The Bernina map (1946) completes the trilogy of his high-mountain geological cartography.

Staub's strength was his great experience and his intuitive feeling for rocks and their large-scale structures, rather than logical reasoning. He was at his best on a peak, sipping a glass of Valtellina or Maienfeld wine and explaining the mountains he loved. His colleagues did not always find his papers easy to read; they demand a thorough knowledge of Alpine geography. Staub was an honorary member of five geological societies and recipient of the Vienna Geological Society's Eduard Suess Medal.

BIBLIOGRAPHY

I. ORIGINAL WORKS. *Der Bau der Alpen: Versuch einer Synthese* (Bern, 1924); *Der Bewegungsmechanismus der Erde, dargelegt am Bau der irdischen Gebirgssysteme* (Berlin, 1928); "Grundzüge und Probleme alpiner Morphologie," in *Denkschriften der Schweizerischen naturforschenden Gesellschaft*, **69** (1934); "Gedanken zum Bau der Westalpen zwischen Bernina und Mittelmeer," in *Vierteljahrsschrift der Naturforschenden Gesellschaft in Zürich*, **82** (1937), 197–336, and **87** (1942), 1–138; "Betrachtungen über den Bau der Südalpen," in *Eclogae geologicae Helvetiae*, **42** (1949), 215–408; *Der Bau der Glarneralpen und seine prinzipielle Bedeutung für die Alpengeologie* (Glarus, 1954); *Klippendecke und Zentralalpenbau. Beziehungen und Probleme* (Bern, 1958).

Geological maps (scale of 1:50,000) are *Geologische Karte der Val Bregaglia* (Bern, 1921); *Geologische Karte des Avers, Piz Platta-Duan* (Bern, 1926); *Geologische Karte der Bernina-Gruppe und ihrer Umgebung im Oberengadin, Bergell, Val Malenco, Puschlav und Livigno* (Bern, 1946). A bibliography is in R. Hantke, "Verzeichnis der wissenschaftlichen Publikationen von Rudolf Staub," in *Eclogae geologicae Helvetiae*, **52** (1959), 403–406.

II. SECONDARY LITERATURE. A brief biography is by Rudolf Trümpy, in *Vierteljahrsschrift der Naturforschenden Gesellschaft in Zürich*, **104**, no. 4 (1961), 503–504.

RUDOLF TRÜMPY

STEENBOCK, HARRY (*b*. Charlestown, Wisconsin, 16 August 1886; *d*. Madison, Wisconsin, 25 December 1967), *agricultural chemistry, biochemistry, nutrition*.

Steenbock was the second child of Henry and Christine (Oesan) Steenbock, German-speaking Lutheran farmers in rural Wisconsin. He received his elementary education in a one-room schoolhouse and his high school education in the town of Chilton. In 1948 he married Evelyn Van Donk. Steenbock was an empiricist who had high personal standards and a strong sense of the Protestant work ethic. He and his wife were founders of the Madison Art Foundation and benefactors of the Wisconsin Academy of Sciences, Arts, and Letters. Steenbock was a member of numerous scientific societies, including founding member (1928) and fellow (1958) of the American Institute of Nutrition. In 1959 he received the Borden Award in Nutrition.

Steenbock earned his bachelor of science in agriculture in 1908 from the University of Wisconsin, Madison. Upon graduating he became an assistant in the department of agricultural chemistry at the University of Wisconsin, then headed by Edwin B. Hart, successor to Stephen M. Babcock. Hart strongly influenced Steenbock, especially through his interest in practical problems. Also influential was Elmer V. McCollum, who had studied with Russell H. Chittenden, Lafayette B. Mendel, and Thomas B. Osborne at Yale before joining the department in 1907. McCollum brought a strongly contrasting theoretical training to Madison. The biological method for food analysis was greatly advanced by the work of the Wisconsin group, which came to include Steenbock.

Steenbock earned his master's degree in 1910 and his Ph.D. in 1916, both at Madison. In 1912 he worked at Yale with Mendel and in 1913 in Berlin with Carl Neuberg. As a graduate student Steenbock participated in the "single grain ration experiment." This work arose out of Babcock's criticism of chemical analysis as an index of nutritional value and his belief that chemical analysis probably failed to reveal important nutritional substances. Babcock suggested formulating chemically identical feeds. Using a mixture of different parts of a single plant (in the case of corn, wheat, and oats) and a composite corn-wheat-oat ration, they found that these chemically identical mixed rations were nutritionally dissimilar. Known chemical methods could not reveal the cause of differences in vigor, appearance, and reproductive capacity of cows fed these rations. This initiated, as Howard Schneider has noted, "a methodological revolution" in the use of animal experimentation in nutrition studies.

Steenbock was appointed assistant professor in the department in 1916, associate professor in 1917, and full professor in 1920. During his career he produced more than 250 scientific papers and supervised the laboratory work of more than 135 graduate students. He was a pioneer of the new field of vitamin research. His series of forty-two papers on "Fat Soluble Vitamine" in the *Journal of Biological Chemistry* appeared from 1918 to 1934 ("Vitamine" was changed in 1923 to "Vitamins"). At a 1919 meeting of the American Society of Biological Chemists, he noted the correlation between yellow pigmentation in foods and the occurrence of vitamin A. In 1920 he crystallized carotene. The relationship between carotene and vitamin A was later solved through the work of Thomas Moore in England. The economic implications of such research led Steenbock to attempt to safeguard the Wisconsin butter industry from the competition that would be engendered by the possibility of adding vitamin A to margarine.

The fat-soluble vitamin was composed of the growth-promoting vitamin A and antirachitic vitamin D. Steenbock attempted to measure vitamin A and used ultraviolet light as an antirachitic agent. The antirachitic effect could apparently be transferred from animal to animal merely by their occupying the same space. This observation led to experimental irradiation of the feed and to the discovery that ultraviolet light produced the antirachitic agent directly in the food. This phenomenon, discovered independently by Alfred Hess, was announced in 1924 in both *Science* and *Journal of Biological Chemistry*. Here, too, Steenbock sought to patent the process. Patents were finally assigned to the Wisconsin Alumni Research Foundation, a nonprofit trust incorporated in 1925 as a result of these events. The Wisconsin response was based in part on related experiences elsewhere with patents for thyroid extract and for insulin.

Steenbock also worked on nutritional anemia, especially on the role of copper in supplementing iron, work announced in 1928 and usually credited to Hart. In addition he studied hemoglobin formation, calcification, the nutritional value of cereals, the mode of action of vitamins A and D, and the nutritional effects of lipids and vitamin E. He became professor of biochemistry in 1938 and professor emeritus in 1956.

BIBLIOGRAPHY

I. ORIGINAL WORKS. Steenbock's bibliography, compiled by Howard A. Schneider, is available on microfiche (NAPS document 02175, Microfiche Publications). Important publications include "Physiological Effect on Growth and Reproduction of Rations Balanced from Restricted Sources," in *University of Wisconsin Agricultural Experiment Station Research Bulletin*, no. 17 (1911), written with E. B. Hart, E. V. McCollum, and G. C.

Humphrey; the "Fat Soluble Vitamine" series in *Journal of Biological Chemistry*, **35–107** (1918–1934); "The Induction of Growth Promoting and Calcifying Properties in a Ration by Exposure to Light," in *Science*, n.s. **60** (1924), 224–225; and "A Review of Certain Researches Relating to the Occurrence and Chemical Nature of Vitamin A," in *Yale Journal of Biology and Medicine*, **4** (1932), 563–578. Steenbock's correspondence, research files, and notebooks are held in the Steenbock Memorial Library at the University of Wisconsin, Madison.

II. SECONDARY LITERATURE. Howard A. Schneider's vivid account of Steenbock's life and work is in *Journal of Nutrition*, **103** (1973), 1235–1247. See also E. Neige Todhunter in *Journal of the American Dietetic Association*, **54** (1969), 432.

MERRILEY BORELL

STEIN, WILLIAM HOWARD (*b*. New York City, 25 June 1911; *d*. New York City, 2 February 1980), *biochemistry*.

Stein was the second of the three children of Fred M. and Beatrice Borg Stein. His father was a businessman who retired early to devote full time to the New York Tuberculosis and Health Association, Montefiore Hospital, and other organizations concerned with the health of the community. His mother was also involved in community activities and was a pioneer in creating programs of afterschool activities for children.

Stein's elementary education was at the Lincoln School, run by Teachers College of Columbia University. At the age of sixteen he transferred to Phillips Exeter Academy, a distinguished school with a demanding college preparatory program. In 1929 he entered Harvard College, following his father and older brother. After graduating in 1933 with a major in chemistry, Stein spent an additional year at Harvard to further his training in organic chemistry. In 1934 he began graduate studies in the department of biological chemistry at the College of Physicians and Surgeons of Columbia University, at that time one of the leading departments in the field; it had an outstanding faculty and a gifted assembly of graduate students, many of whom later became leaders in biochemical research.

In 1937 Stein completed his Ph.D. dissertation, on the amino acid composition of elastin, under the supervision of Edgar G. Miller, Jr. It was this initial foray into purifying and determining the structure of elastin that formed his lifelong devotion to the study of protein chemistry. In his doctoral investigations Stein used two new precipitating agents for isolating amino acids—potassium trioxalatochromate for glycine and ammonium rhodanilate for proline—that had recently been introduced by Max Bergmann.

It was thus natural that Stein decided to pursue postdoctoral research with Bergmann, who in 1934 had come to the United States from Dresden as a refugee from Nazi Germany and was on the staff of the Rockefeller Institute for Medical Research (now Rockefeller University). Bergmann had worked with Emil Fischer, one of the great pioneers in protein chemistry, and had made many important contributions to protein research before coming to the United States. He was particularly known for his development with Leonidas Zervas of the carbobenzoxy method for peptide synthesis.

In 1937, when Stein came to the Rockefeller Institute, Bergmann's laboratory was one of the few in the United States devoted entirely to investigations of the chemistry of proteins and peptides, and to the specificity of proteolytic enzymes in hydrolyzing synthetic peptides and derivatives. As a result, over the years it attracted an outstanding group of postdoctoral fellows. When Stein joined the laboratory, he decided to investigate the use of the new precipitating agents that were being developed by Bergmann to improve quantitative gravimetric analysis of amino acids in protein hydrolysates. Stein introduced the solubility product method as a way of attempting to obtain more precise results, inasmuch as most precipitating reagents left a considerable amount of the amino acid in the mother liquor. In 1939, when Stanford Moore joined the laboratory as a postdoctoral fellow, Bergmann suggested that Stein and Moore combine their efforts to try to develop practical analytical procedures. During the next few years they were successful in developing precise methods for the analysis of glycine and leucine, two amino acids for which there had been no satisfactory analytical methods earlier. Thus began a collaboration that, except for an interval during the war years, lasted more than forty years.

In 1942, with the United States at war, research on amino acid analysis was stopped. The efforts of Bergmann's laboratory were devoted to the study of the physiological and chemical actions of mustard gas and the nitrogen mustard compounds, in the hope of finding therapeutic agents to counter the effects of these highly toxic substances. Fortunately, none of these were used during World War II. Stein was a co-author of a series of papers, published after the war, on the chemical reactions of these compounds with amino acids and peptides. These studies provided valuable experience in understanding the reactivity of amino acid side chains. At the same time Moore served with the Office of Scientific Research and Development in Washington and elsewhere for some three years.

Max Bergmann died in 1944. Stein continued in the laboratory, where Moore rejoined him in 1945. Herbert Gasser, then director of the Rockefeller Institute, offered them the opportunity to initiate a joint program in protein chemistry, with the first efforts to be devoted to development of methods for precise amino acid analysis, an essential prerequisite for any detailed study of the structure of proteins.

In the meantime there had been a renaissance in separation methods by chromatography, largely because of the work performed during the war by Archer J. P. Martin and Richard L. M. Synge in England, and the development of liquid-liquid countercurrent distribution by Lyman C. Craig at the Rockefeller Institute. These achievements brought attention to the high resolving power of multiplate separations. Stein and Moore then began to develop chromatographic methods for separation of all of the amino acids in a protein hydrolysate. Their first efforts were concerned with the use of potato starch as a supporting matrix for partition chromatography with n-butanol-water as the resolving system, a procedure already attempted by S. R. Elsden and Synge, but with limited success.

After several years of intensive effort, elution systems with starch columns were developed for the quantitative determination of all the common amino acids in protein hydrolysates. These procedures, involving the use of three separate columns, were successfully applied to the analysis of bovine β-lactoglobulin and bovine serum albumin in 1949. The analyses required less than five milligrams of protein with a standard error of less than 5 percent, a remarkable achievement for that time.

The success of these analytical procedures was due to several significant advances in methodology. First, the metal contaminants in the potato starch had to be removed by use of 8-hydroxyquinoline in order to give reproducible results for the elution of each amino acid. Second, a photoelectric drop-counting method was developed to collect equal volumes of eluate from the columns. This, together with the invention of an automatic fraction collector, facilitated the process of collection. The machine that Moore and Stein developed became the prototype of similar commercial instruments that soon were used for all types of chromatographic procedures. Third, in order to estimate quantitatively the amount of amino acid in each test tube, a reagent form of ninhydrin was devised that produced a stable color with each eluted amino acid. This novel reagent, stabilized with a reducing agent and in an organic solvent miscible with water, was used to monitor the procedure. It was important that the developed color was proportional to the amount of amino acid in each fraction.

Although the starch-column chromatography was useful and represented an important advance, the procedures were slow, requiring a few weeks for a single complete analysis. The method was soon abandoned in favor of ion-exchange chromatography. Sulfonated polystyrene resins of reproducible properties in a finely powdered form had become available at that time. As a result, one or two columns with buffers at different pH values could be used in a procedure that shortened the elution time appreciably; these methods were published in 1951.

The methods were later made completely automatic by continuous elution at high pressure. The automatic machines, described in 1958, developed in collaboration with Darrel H. Spackman, gave a continuous flow of eluate from the column with the ninhydrin color produced in the stream of liquid. The optical density was recorded potentiometrically on continuous charts. A variety of commercial machines soon became available that had further practical advances in speed, sensitivity, and automation. Thus, within a relatively short time the ability to analyze the amino acids in protein hydrolysates, in body fluids, and in other biological materials had become routine and quantitative, readily available to every investigator.

Concurrently, beginning in 1949, Stein and Moore began to apply their chromatographic methods to the isolation and then to the study of the structure of bovine pancreatic ribonuclease. With the collaboration of a group of younger investigators (C. H. Werner Hirs, J. Leggett Bailey, Darrel H. Spackman, and Derek G. Smyth), the complete sequence was described between 1958 and 1960, the first enzyme for which the primary structure was established. The methods that were employed included cleavage of the oxidized peptide chain by various proteolytic enzymes or by cyanogen bromide, followed by separation of each of the resulting peptides by chromatography on ion-exchange columns with volatile buffers as the eluting agents. The sequence of each of the peptides was determined mainly by the repetitive application of the phenylthiohydantoin method developed by Pehr Edman for identification of the amino-terminal residue simultaneously with the removal of that residue.

With Arthur Crestfield and Moore, in 1963 Stein showed that iodoacetate, a known inhibitor, could react with either of two specific histidine residues, yielding a carboxymethyl group on the 1-nitrogen of histidine-119 or on the 3-nitrogen of histidine-12, but not with both on the same polypeptide chain. With Robert Heinrikson and Moore, Stein showed that carboxymethylation of lysine-41 inhibited the enzyme. From these data it was concluded that the reactive nitrogens of the two histidine residues were approximately five Ångstrom units apart at the active site of the enzyme and that the ε amino group of lysine-41 was seven to ten Ångstrom units from the nitrogen-3 of histidine-12. These predictions, based on purely chemical information, were later confirmed by X-ray crystallographic analysis of the three-dimensional structure elucidated independently by Frederic M. Richards and Harold Wyckoff at Yale and by G. Kartha, J. Bello, and David Harker in 1967.

Two further points on the studies of ribonuclease should be noted. First, Stein, Moore, and George Stark showed that carboxymethylation of the enzyme does not occur when it is unfolded in solutions of eight-molar urea. Thus, the specific reactivity of the two histidine nitrogen atoms depends on their proximity in the native enzyme, although one of the two histidine residues is near the amino-terminal end and the other is near the carboxyl-terminal end of the polypeptide chain of 124 amino acid residues. A by-product of this study was the realization that traces of cyanate in the urea solutions had carbamylated the ε amino groups of the enzyme, thus inactivating the ribonuclease. It is noteworthy that in 1828 Friedrich Wöhler had discovered the reverse reaction—that ammonium cyanate forms urea—a discovery that laid to rest the notion that organic compounds could be formed only in living organisms.

Ribonuclease forms active dimers when it is freeze-dried from a 50 percent solution of acetic acid. With Arthur Crestfield, Stein and Moore demonstrated that dimers also form when an equal mixture of the inactive derivatives 1-carboxymethyl-His-119 and 3-carboxymethyl-His-12 ribonucleases is freeze-dried in the same manner. About 25 percent of the mixture of dimers possesses half the activity of the native enzyme. They concluded that three kinds of dimers are formed; two of them have either alkylated His-119 or alkylated His-12 at the active sites, and are inactive. However, a third dimer is formed with one productive active site and one inactive site that contains both alkylated residues. Hence, such a dimer posseses only half the normal activity. This activity is lost when the dimers are dissociated to monomers. These experiments provided the first example of an active site of an enzyme that is formed by the noncovalent binding of two polypeptide chains, a situation later encountered by other investigators of several native enzymes.

Coincident with the work of Stein and Moore and their associates, Christian B. Anfinsen and his coworkers were investigating the properties of ribonuclease at the National Institutes of Health in Bethesda, Maryland. The contributions of both laboratories were recognized by the award of the Nobel Prize for chemistry in 1972 jointly to Stein and Moore and to Anfinsen. The Nobel Lecture by Moore and Stein was devoted mainly to the chemical studies on ribonuclease and deoxyribonuclease.

After the major studies on ribonuclease with 124 residues were essentially completed, Stein and Moore began work on the much larger pancreatic deoxyribonuclease, a glycoprotein with 257 residues in a single polypeptide chain. The sequence was established in 1973 with the collaboration of several students and postdoctoral fellows—Paul Price, Teh-yung Liu, Brian Catley, Johann Salnikow, and Ta-hsiu Liao—and in later studies with Tony Hugli, Bryce Plapp, and Dalton Wang. In the purification of this enzyme, three chromatographically distinct active forms were isolated and identified. One of the forms, in minor amount, proved to contain a residue of proline for histidine at residue 118; since this form of the enzyme is fully active, His-118 is not essential. The carbohydrate side chain is attached via an aspartamidohexosamine linkage at residue 18; another active form of the enzyme possesses a shorter carbohydrate chain at the same residue. The enzyme is inactivated by nitration of tyrosine-62 and by carboxymethylation of histidine-131. In these studies, as in many others from this laboratory, the results were obtained by chromatographic isolation of highly purified fragments and careful quantitative analyses.

After the methods of ion-exchange chromatography for amino acid analysis and peptide separation were developed, they were applied to joint studies with other investigators at Rockefeller University on a variety of problems. In addition, a large number of other investigations were pursued, partly with the aim of training the many individuals who came to the laboratory to gain experience in the use of these methods. These studies included many on structure-function relationships in enzymes other than pancreatic ribonuclease and deoxyribonuclease. Among these investigations were those on bromelains (with Shoshi Ota), chymotrypsin (with Denis C. Shaw), pepsin (with T. G. Rajagopalan, T. A. A. Dopheide, and Roger Lundblad), streptococcal proteinase (with Teh-yung Liu, William Ferdinand, Brenda Gerwin, Norbert Neumann, Michael C. Lin,

Michael Bustin, and Stuart D. Elliott), ribonuclease T₁ (with Kenji Takahashi), $2',3'$-cyclic nucleotide $3'$ phosphohydrolase from the brain (with Arabinda Guha, David C. Sogin, and Robert J. Drummond), and carboxypeptidase Y (with Rikimaru Hayashi).

Concurrently with the investigations on protein structure, the methods of analysis by ion-exchange chromatography for amino acids and derivatives were modified for application to analyses of urine, blood, and extracts of animal tissues. From several studies of this sort (with Harris Tallan) came the identification of 3-methylhistidine and tyrosine-O-sulfate as normal constituents of human urine, the discovery that acetylaspartic acid and cystathionine are major constituents of human brain tissue, and the observation (with Alejandro C. Paladini and C. H. W. Hirs) that phenylacetylglutamine is a normal major metabolic product in human urine. In addition, quantitative estimates were made for many other previously known constituents of these fluids and of brain tissue. These results provided a framework for subsequent studies of this type in many laboratories devoted to investigations of human and animal metabolism, and of many clinically important metabolic disorders.

In all of the above studies, Stein and Moore continued their remarkable collaboration, one of the longest in any scientific field. It is impossible to judge which of the two was responsible for specific contributions to the work that emanated from their laboratory. Indeed, in Moore's biographical memoir of Stein, he comments: "During the early years of our cooperation, Stein and I worked out a system of collaboration which lasted for a lifetime. Stein combined an inventive mind and a deep dedication to science with great generosity. Over a period of forty years, we approached problems with somewhat different perspectives and then focused our thoughts on the common aim. If I did not think of something, he was likely to, and vice versa, and this process of frequent interchange of ideas accelerated progress in research."

Stein served on the editorial committee of the American Society of Biological Chemists from 1955 to 1961. He joined the editorial board of the *Journal of Biological Chemistry* in 1962, became an associate editor in 1964, and was named editor in 1968. He thus served during a period of great growth of the science and helped to further the progress of the *Journal* as one of the leading publications in the field.

In the summer of 1969, while attending an international symposium on proteolytic enzymes in Co-penhagen, Stein came down with a high fever. A few days later, on the way home, he became paralyzed; the disease was later diagnosed as a severe case of Guillain-Barré syndrome. He survived the acute phase of the disease but, after a year of hospitalization, he remained a quadriplegic. Despite this handicap, for eleven years he maintained his interest in science and in the activities of the laboratory. He continued to consult with his collaborators in the laboratory and to hold informal seminars in his home on current research. In all of these efforts, he was firmly supported and encouraged by his wife, Phoebe Hockstader Stein, whom he had married in 1936, and by their three sons. Stein died suddenly of heart failure at his home in New York on 2 February 1980.

In addition to the Nobel Prize, Stein received many honors and awards. He was elected to both the National Academy of Sciences and the American Academy of Arts and Sciences in 1960. With Moore he shared the American Chemical Society Award in Chromatography and Electrophoresis in 1964, the Richards Medal of the American Chemical Society in 1972, and the Kaj Linderstrøm-Lang Award in 1972. He received honorary degrees from Columbia University and the Albert Einstein College of Medicine of Yeshiva University in 1973.

Stein spent almost his entire scientific career after his doctoral training at what is now Rockefeller University. He was away for brief periods as a visiting professor at the University of Chicago in 1961 and at Harvard University in 1964. His lectures to graduate students at Rockefeller, on visits to other institutions, and at scientific meetings were characterized by the same precision and rigor as his scientific research, and conveyed an enthusiasm for the developments in biochemistry that was undiminished to the end of his life.

It is useful to recall the large changes in the field of protein chemistry that developed as a result of the pioneering work of Stein and Moore. Studies by many investigators had firmly established the general biological importance and functional properties of proteins between the years 1925 and 1940. It was already known that aside from their structural roles, proteins could be enzymes, antibodies, hormones, oxygen carriers, and a host of other things, yet little was known of their structure. Not even the exact amino acid composition could be given for any protein. It was this gap in information to which Stein and Moore first devoted their investigations, in following up their fledgling efforts in Bergmann's laboratory before the war. Their successful development of analytical procedures permitted a comprehensive attack on protein structure.

A great impetus for these efforts was provided by the work at Cambridge of Frederick Sanger, who with his co-workers was able to determine by 1952 that the hormone insulin, a small protein with two chains of thirty and twenty-one residues, has a unique amino acid sequence in a given species of animal. By 1955, the complete structure of insulin with its disulfide bridges had been ascertained. The methods used by Sanger were satisfactory for relatively small proteins but clearly would not be universally applicable for the bulk of proteins, most of them possessing polypeptide chains longer by at least an order of magnitude.

The work of Stein and Moore and their co-workers provided methods that, at least in theory, could be applied to proteins of almost any size and complexity. In itself, this provided a stimulus to the entire field. Part of the reason why their methods were adopted so rapidly and widely was the care they took to make the procedures easily reproducible even by novices. Further, they were careful to examine each minor artifact and difficulty that was encountered in order to resolve the problem. It was this meticulous attention to detail for each chemical and analytical procedure that rendered their methods so readily applicable to a host of problems in peptide and protein chemistry.

Stein and Moore's methods have been complemented by the analytical procedures for determining the sequences of the deoxyribonucleic acids (DNA) of the individual genes that determine the sequence of the polypeptide chain of a protein. For very large proteins and for those that can be isolated only in minute amounts, the methods for determining the DNA sequence coding for the protein sequence are invaluable. Nevertheless, for study of the protein itself and its reactive residues, binding sites, and so on, the pioneering methods of Stein and Moore will continue to be essential. Indeed, it was their studies on the enzyme pancreatic ribonuclease that demonstrated that detailed understanding of the mechanism of action of such catalysts could be achieved purely by the use of chemical methods, once the amino acid sequence was determined. The meticulous investigations on the reactions of inhibitors with the enzyme produced a good picture of the nature and properties of the "active site." Later, physical studies by various methods, including nuclear magnetic resonance and X-ray crystallography, served to confirm and expand knowledge of the properties of the amino acid side chains in the active site.

BIBLIOGRAPHY

I. ORIGINAL WORKS. A bibliography of Stein's works is in Moore's 1987 memoir (see below). Stein and Moore's Nobel speech, "Chemical Structures of Pancreatic Ribonuclease and Deoxyribonuclease," is in *Les prix Nobel en 1972* (Stockholm, 1973), 120–143, and in *Science*, **180** (1973), 458–464.

II. SECONDARY LITERATURE. On Stein, on Moore, and on their work, see Joseph S. Fruton, *Molecules and Life: Historical Essays on the Interplay of Chemistry and Biology* (New York, 1972), 87–179; Stanford Moore, "William H. Stein," in *Journal of Biological Chemistry*, **255** (1980), 9517–9518, "Dedication to William H. Stein," in *Chemical Synthesis and Sequencing of Peptides and Proteins: Proceedings of the International Conference Held 8–9 May 1980, at the National Institutes of Health, Bethesda, Maryland* (New York, 1981), and "William H. Stein," in *Biographical Memoirs, National Academy of Sciences*, **56** (1987), 414–440; Frederic M. Richards, "The 1972 Nobel Prize in Chemistry," in *Science*, **178** (1972), 492–493; and Emil L. Smith and C. H. W. Hirs, "Stanford Moore," in *Biographical Memoirs, National Academy of Sciences*, **56** (1987), 354–385.

EMIL L. SMITH

STEPANOV, ALEKSANDR VASIL'EVICH (*b.* St. Petersburg, Russia, 26 August 1908; *d.* Yalta, U.S.S.R., 16 May 1972), *physics.*

Stepanov's father, Vasilii Fedorovich Stepanov, was a building technician; his mother, Nadezhda Vasil'evna Bratanova, was a housewife. Stepanov graduated from the secondary school in Leningrad in 1925; a year before he had already started to work at the Leningrad Physical-Technical Institute, as an assistant in one of the radio engineering departments.

In 1925 Stepanov entered the Faculty of Physics and Mechanics at the Leningrad Polytechnical Institute, from which he graduated in 1930. Two years before graduation he joined Ivan Vasil'evich Obreimov's laboratory at the Leningrad Physical-Technical Institute, and in 1930 he moved with Obreimov to the Ukrainian Physical-Technical Institute in Kharkov. There he worked for a short time. From 1931 until his death Stepanov served as a scientific fellow at the Leningrad Physical-Technical Institute and eventually became head of the laboratory of mechanical properties of crystals. At the same time he taught at the Faculty of Physics and

Mechanics, where he also conducted experiments in the laboratory of optics directed by V. K. Fredericks. In 1937 he moved to the Pokrovskii Pedagogical Institute in Leningrad, where he lectured for the rest of his life. At this institute he founded the department of theoretical physics.

Stepanov's early work in Obreimov's laboratories was connected with optical methods of observing the stress state in crystals. He also participated in Obreimov and Lev Vasil'evich Shubnikov's elaboration of an experimental technique for growing ideal crystals.

Beginning in the early 1930's, Stepanov directed his efforts to the investigation of physical properties of crystals, especially their strength. The work of Abram Fedorovich Ioffe and his associates established the influence of surface (and internal) defects (scratches, cracks, holes) on crystal strength. Stepanov went farther, showing that the centers of brittle fracture arise within the body of the crystal because of stress due to plastic strain (shear, twinning), prior to fracture. This view of Stepanov's (now generally accepted) did not originally receive support because it was commonly held that plastic strain results only in strengthening. Stepanov formulated and showed experimentally the existence of anomalously high thermal conductivity associated with the shear of boundary layers. He established the connection between the melting heat and the strain, and described the influence of plastic strain on electrical conductivity of ionic crystals. In 1933 he discovered the effect of slip-band electrification that occurs during plastic deformation of ionic crystals (in modern terminology, "charged dislocations").

An important series of Stepanov's investigations is related to the halides of silver and thallium and to alloys based on them. Stepanov demonstrated that their plastic behavior closely resembles that of metals, and therefore called them "transparent metals" (because the crystals are transparent). He grew large monocrystals of these aggregations and examined their properties in detail. He found, in particular, that the mutual polarization of ions decreases electrical conductivity, and thus influences plastic properties. (During numerous sessions and seminars, Ioffe, the director of the Leningrad Physical-Technical Institute, would ring a bell made of silver chloride that Stepanov had presented to him.) These investigations formed the bases of Stepanov's candidate thesis (1937) and doctoral dissertation (1939).

Producing artificial damages on the surface of the examined crystals, Stepanov observed the dynamics of shear formation (using the optical polarization method for studying the stress state). He examined the transformation of microslips to macroshear and demonstrated that this process of unification starts not only with the achievement of a certain stress level but also at a certain temperature.

In the early 1960's Stepanov and his colleagues started to investigate mechanical properties of solids at liquid helium temperatures. During these pioneering experiments a number of new effects were discovered: the modifications of the character of a fracture, the time variation of a fracture diagram, and the plastic strain of ionic crystals at liquid helium temperatures. These results are important today for work in space. Stepanov's laboratory also carried out experiments with threadlike crystals (whiskers).

In the late 1940's Stepanov investigated mechnical properties of wood and bone, whose structure accounts for a sharp anisotropy of elastic and strength properties. The anisotropy impedes the growth of fracture and may form a basis for creation of highly durable materials. Stepanov's work in this field is rightly considered pioneering in the development of composite materials.

In the late 1940's Stepanov developed a method of forming solid objects immediately from the melt, known in literature as "Stepanov's method." His idea was not to use the conventional methods of forming solid objects (such as rolling, pressing, and drawing). He argued that it might be possible to obtain these objects immediately from a liquid metal, but that it would be necessary to overcome the typical property of any liquid (including metal) not to conserve its shape. He showed that under suitable conditions, the capillary forces may promote sustaining the "prescribed" shape of a liquid mass set free in space and without any mechanical support. As early as the late 1940's Stepanov obtained in this way monocrystal plates of zinc, aluminum, bismuth, and other materials. This method, a modification of the earlier Chokhralskii method, made it possible during Stepanov's life to stretch solid articles of a required shape directly from the melts of aluminum, copper, iron, halides, and semiconductor materials (first of germanium and silicon, and later of more complex semiconductor aggregations). This stretching was produced by the capillary mechanism of shape formation under specific conditions of heat and velocity. The foundations of this method and the history of its discovery and development are discussed in Stepanov's book *Budushchee metalloobrabotki* (1963). Practically each year since 1968, All-Union meetings on Stepanov's method of obtaining semiconducting materials have been held at the Leningrad Physical-Technical Institute. The proceedings of these meetings are usually published in physical journals and special collections.

In recognition of his scientific achievements, the U.S.S.R. Academy of Sciences elected Stepanov a corresponding member in 1968. Stepanov, who never married, loved music and was a skilled amateur tennis player and skier on both snow and water. Hoping to enjoy some water skiing, he took a short leave in the spring of 1972 and went to the Crimea, where he died of a heart attack.

BIBLIOGRAPHY

I. Original Works. "Über den Zusammenhang der Deformationsarbeit mit der Schmelzwärme," pt. 1, in *Physikalische Zeitschrift der Sowjetunion*, **2** (1932), 537–543, and "Über den Mechanismus des plastischen Deformation," pt. 2, *ibid.*, **5** (1935), 706–713; "Grundlagen der Theorie der praktischen Festigkeit," in *Zeitschrift für Physik*, **92**, Heft 1–2 (1934), 42–60; "Artificial Slip Formation in Crystals," in *Nature*, **140** (1937), 64; "Iavlenie iskusstvennogo sdvigoobrazovaniia" (The phenomena of artificial shearing), pt. 1, in *Zhurnal eksperimentalnoi i teoreticheskoi fiziki*, **17**, no. 7 (1947), 601, pt. 2, *ibid.*, **18** no. 8 (1948), 741–749, pt. 3, written with E. A. Mulkamanovich, *ibid.*, no. 9 (1948), 773–775, pt. 4 *ibid.*, **21**, no. 3 (1951), 401–408, pt. 5, written with E. A. Mulkamanovich, *ibid.*, 409–412, and pt. 6, written with E. A. Mulkamanovich, in *Fizika tverdogo tela*, **1**, no. 4 (1959), 666–670; "Iskusstvennaia anizotropiia kak sredstvo pridaniia izdeliiam trebuemykh mekhanicheskikh svoistv" (Artificial anisotropy as a means for giving an article required mechanical properties), in *Sbornik posviashchennyi semidesiatiletiiu akademika A. F. Ioffe* (Memorial volume dedicated to Academician A. F. Ioffe on the occasion of his seventieth birthday; Moscow, 1950), 341–354; "Ob elektrostaticheskoi teorii ionnykh kristallov" (On the electrostatic theory of ionic crystals), in *Zhurnal eksperimentalnoi i teoreticheskoi fiziki*, **34**, no. 6 (1958), 1661–1662; *Budushchee metalloobrabotki* (The future of metal treatment; Leningrad, 1963); "O vliianii sostoianiia poverkhnosti na skachkoobraznuiu deformatsiiu aluminiia pri T 1,3 K" (On the influence of the state of surface on a 'jump-type' deformation of aluminum at 1,3 K), in *Fizika metallov i metallovedenie*, **17**, no. 4 (1964), 502; "Poluchenie monokristallov opredelenoi formy" (On the formation of monocrystals of a certain form), in *Materialy pervogo soveshchaniia po polucheniiu poluprovodnikovykh monokristallov sposobom Stepanova i perspektivam ikh primeneniia v priborostroenii* (Leningrad, 1968), which contains a total of fourteen papers written by Stepanov and his colleagues; "O dlinne probega dislokatsii v kristallakh ftoristogo litiia pri gelievikh temperaturakh" (On the length of dislocation of free path in LiF crystals at helium temperatures), in *Dinamika dislokatsii* (The dynamics of dislocations; Kharkov, 1968), which contains two other papers by Stepanov on the same subject; "De-

formation of Alkali-Halide Crystals at Liquid Helium Temperatures," in *Second International Conference on the Strength of Metals and Alloys* (Metals Park, Ohio, 1970), 235; and *Osnovy prakticheskoi prochnosti kristallov* (The foundations of the practical strength of crystals; Moscow, 1974).

II. Secondary Literature. Obituaries are in *Kristallografiia*, **17**, no. 5 (1972), 1087–1088, English trans. in *Soviet Physics: Crystallography*, **17**, no. 5 (1973), 970–971; and *Izvestiia Akademii nauk, seriia fizicheskaia*, **37**, no. 11 (1973), 2250–2253. See also V. J. Frenkel, G. V. Kurdiumov, and M. V. Klassen-Nekliudova, "Aleksandr Vasilievich Stepanov," in *Materialy k biobibliografii uchenikh SSSR* (Moscow, 1976).

V. J. Frenkel

STEPHENSON, MARJORY (*b*. Burwell, near Cambridge, England, 24 January 1885; *d*. Cambridge, 12 December 1948), *microbiology, biochemistry.*

Marjory Stephenson figures in the history of science in several ways: most important, she was one of the half dozen or so people who, between the two world wars, created the new specialty of bacterial biochemistry. In so doing, she contributed to the distinctive and influential style of practice of F. G. Hopkins' school of biochemistry at Cambridge. Her papers on adaptive enzymes in the 1930's became, in the decade after her death, one of the growth points of molecular genetics. She was one of the first women to receive a D.Sc. from Cambridge, her alma mater, and with Kathleen Lonsdale was one of the first two women to be made fellows of the Royal Society (in 1945). She never married.

Stephenson was the youngest (by almost nine years) of four children born to Robert and Elizabeth Rogers Stephenson, comfortably well-to-do, public-minded, and progressive farmers and horse breeders in the fenlands of Cambridgeshire. Robert Stephenson was active in county politics and was instrumental in marshaling local support for the creation of a school of agriculture at Cambridge University. For this he received an honorary M.A. in 1903, the year that Marjory entered Newnham College, Cambridge. There she read part I of the natural science tripos in chemistry, physiology, and zoology, taking her degree (second class) in 1906. She would have liked to go on to medical school but lack of funds obliged her to earn her living by teaching.

Stephenson spent five not very happy years teaching at the Gloucester County Training College in Domestic Science and the Kings College of

Household Science in London. Nutrition and dietetics were not an uncommon career choice for women scientists at the time (the more elite academic disciplines were virtually closed to them). For most it was an occupation that offered little chance for doing science, but for a few nutrition was an entry into the developing profession of physiological chemistry. Stephenson was one of the lucky ones. In 1911 her talents caught the eye of the nutritional biochemist R. H. A. Plimmer, who offered her a job in his laboratory at University College, London. There she assisted Plimmer in advanced teaching and in his researches on lipid metabolism and metabolic disease. In 1913 a Beit Memorial Fellowship for Medical Research gave Stephenson a measure of independence, but the outbreak of war in 1914 interrupted her career. In the British Red Cross from 1914 to 1918, she put her knowledge of nutrition and diet to practical use in France and Greece.

Resuming her fellowship in 1919, Stephenson moved to the very center of British biochemistry, joining F. G. Hopkins' group at Cambridge. Hopkins' prewar paper on essential amino acids had made him the most visible exponent of research on "vitamines." Stephenson went there hoping to move from the metabolism of fats into the emerging field of fat-soluble vitamins. She was disappointed: her own research (on the possible role of vitamin A deficiency in keratomalacia) got nowhere, and Hopkins, unable to compete with better-organized and -funded research teams in London, lost interest in vitamins and threw himself into the chemistry of biological oxidation. It was in these circumstances that Stephenson turned to the decidedly more risky and less fashionable field of bacterial biochemistry.

In fact, she happened to be at the right place at the right time. Hopkins had long had a keen interest in the biochemistry of microorganisms. He envisioned "general" biochemistry much as comparative physiologists envisioned their discipline—as encompassing every kind of organism from bacteria to man. (Probably it was a strategy to keep the nascent discipline of biochemistry from being coopted by the medical physiologists.) During the war, with funds from his friend and secretary of the Medical Research Council, Walter Fletcher, Hopkins arranged for a young chemist, Harold Raistrick, to begin a line of work on the chemistry of microbes. In 1921, however, Raistrick left to take a job in industry, just as a large endowment and a new laboratory were finally enabling Hopkins to realize his dream of a comparative biochemistry. Fletcher, who had his own (medical) reasons for developing bacterial biochemistry, was eager to provide support

for a successor. Thus a strategic niche in Hopkins' group became vacant just as Stephenson's work on vitamins was coming to a dead end. She was never lacking in courage, and at that juncture she had little to lose.

Stephenson had carte blanche to develop bacterial biochemistry according to her own vision. The field had yet to be defined; space had been created for it before there was a body of certified knowledge to define it. Hopkins gave all his junior staff great freedom to develop their special fields, and Fletcher, while he hoped Stephenson would form strong connections with pathologists, shrank from pushing too hard. Stephenson's distinctive style of practice is apparent from her first publications in 1922. Whereas Raistrick had been interested in the organic chemistry of fungal metabolites, Stephenson was interested in microbes as organisms with distinctive physiologies. Her early work built upon the classical researches of Pasteur, Max Rubner, and other biologists on material and energy metabolic balance. She was always fascinated by the evolutionary meaning of the extraordinary diversity of microbial metabolism. At the same time, Stephenson was deeply influenced by the more mainstream lines of biochemical work in enzymology and oxidation, which dominated Hopkins' expanding school.

Between 1922 and 1940 Stephenson's own work and that of her students alternated between mainline enzymology and a more biological approach. In the 1920's, for example, she was greatly influenced by Juda Quastel, a young organic chemist with whom she worked on the inhibition by oxygen of the growth of anaerobic bacteria. But when Quastel delved into the chemical theory of biological oxidation, Stephenson turned to a more biological aspect of their problem, the adaptation of microbes to changes in their environment. Between about 1929 and 1935, she was preoccupied with the enzymology of a novel class of hydrogen-activating enzymes, and between 1938 and 1941 she put most of her own and her students' efforts into the enzymology of amino acid deaminases. Yet in between, with her student John Yudkin, she did important work on the puzzling phenomenon of enzyme adaptation, with its rich implications for the big questions of biologists: physiological regulation, adaptation, and evolution.

Among biochemists, Stephenson is remembered best for her discovery of a new kind of enzyme. But her most distinctive contributions to the practice of bacterial chemistry are on the biological side. Most enzymologists saw cells as convenient bags of enzymes and preferred to work in cell-free systems; Stephenson always returned to the cell and devised experimental methods to assure herself that she was not dealing with chemical artifacts. With Margaret Whetham she perfected the "resting cell" technique of studying the chemical activities of heavy suspensions of nongrowing cells in minimal medium. She took pains to learn microbiologists' techniques of isolating pure cultures and counting viable cells; she made it a standard part of every experiment to determine the proportions of viable and dead cells— to quiet biologists' doubts that her "resting" cells were not resting but dead, and their chemical activities not normal physiology but chemical artifacts. Such techniques were a hallmark of Stephenson's practice and enabled her to prove, among other things, that enzyme adaptation was the result not of selection but of a chemical change in the cell's regulation of its physiology.

Stephenson's alternation between biochemical and biological approaches to bacterial biochemistry mirrored the balance of interests within Hopkins' school. Enzymology, oxidation, and intermediary metabolism were the prestigious mainstream fields, and chemists like Malcolm Dixon and Norman Pirie formed a powerful interest group. Hopkins himself talked like a chemist half the time, yet it was his broad biological outlook that gave his school its distinctive intellectual vigor. The biochemistry lectures and practicums, for example, were organized around organisms, not kinds of compounds, as was usual everywhere else. With Joseph Needham, Margaret Whetham, and Robin Hill, Stephenson constituted a biological interest group that was able to resist pressures to bring the Cambridge style of biochemistry more into the chemical mainstream.

Stephenson's work and career can be understood only as integral to the remarkable social organism of which she was a part. She gave concrete shape to an institutional and intellectual space that had been prized open between bacteriology and biochemistry by Hopkins and Fletcher. There were many ways it could have been done: as pure enzymology, organic chemistry, medical (or agricultural) applications, bacterial nutrition. Stephenson's way was broader and more comprehensive: like Hopkins' vision of a "general" biochemistry, Stephenson's vision of a "general" microbiology was a blend of chemical technique and biological vision. She made use of the diverse resources of the Cambridge school and the Medical Research Council (MRC) network without being captured by any one of them. Enough of the political work of discipline building had been done to enable Stephenson to make effective use of her special gifts. Probably she could not have done what she did anywhere

but at Cambridge. But someone with a better chance for a career in the mainstream probably would not have used those local resources so imaginatively.

In 1929 Walter Fletcher put Stephenson on the MRC's regular payroll, as a full-time external research worker. Once again she inherited a niche created for Harold Raistrick, who had decided to return to academe, and whom Fletcher hoped to set up as director of an MRC-sponsored research unit in bacterial biochemistry. When Raistrick opted for a university chair in London, Fletcher offered Stephenson a regular position, with the prospect of support for her small group of student apprentices. It would not be a research unit, however: Fletcher, while he greatly admired and valued Stephenson's achievements in her personal research, clearly did not see her as a manager of a team of full-time researchers. No doubt Fletcher did not expect women to be entrepreneurial. In any case, Stephenson's style of leadership was essentially individual and informal; like Hopkins, she led by inspiring and setting an example.

Stephenson was a bench worker, and her enthusiasm for new lines of experiment never ran dry. Her list of publications is not long by modern standards, but there are no potboilers. She was never a good lecturer but was a generous and inspiring mentor. Her few students were unusually able. She had a deep sense of duty (a Stephenson family trait) and was active in college and professional matters, but never became a smooth operator of committees. Stephenson had a vivid and impetuous personality, and was known for occasional impulsive enthusiasms and outbursts. (She would take on, if provoked, even such strong personalities as Walter Fletcher.) She did not know how to tolerate pretension and sided instinctively with underdogs. It took her a long time—a lifetime, indeed—to develop her own capabilities, and she grew slowly but continually throughout her career.

The growing popularity of bacterial biochemistry in the 1940's drew Stephenson into more formal organizing and managing. She was a vigorous and influential member of the MRC's Committee on Chemical Microbiology, and after 1945 she devoted much of her time to organizing the MRC's Research Unit in Chemical Microbiology at Cambridge. She helped found the Society for General Microbiology (1944) and served as its second president. She organized a summer school (1946) to meet the growing demand for workers in bacterial biochemistry. Stephenson took on the duties of an official university appointment (1947), as reader in the discipline she had helped to invent. Visitors to the Dunn Institute forty years later find her photograph in offices and the memory of her warm and vivid personality still fresh.

BIBLIOGRAPHY

I. ORIGINAL WORKS. "Some Reactions of Resting Bacteria in Relation to Anaerobic Growth," in *Biochemical Journal*, **19** (1925), 304–317, with Juda H. Quastel and Margaret D. Whetham; *Bacterial Metabolism* (London, 1930; 2nd ed., 1939; 3rd. ed., 1949); "Hydrogenase: A Bacterial Enzyme Activating Molecular Hydrogen. I. The Properties of the Enzyme," in *Biochemical Journal*, **25** (1931), 205–214, with Leonard H. Strickland; "Galactozymase Considered as an Adaptive Enzyme," *ibid.*, **30** (1936), 506–514, with John Yudkin; and "The Economy of the Bacterial Cell," in Joseph Needham and David Green, eds., *Perspectives in Biochemistry* (Cambridge, 1937), 91–98.

Stephenson's papers are in the archives of the Medical Research Council, London, and the archives of Cambridge University.

II. SECONDARY LITERATURE. Robert E. Kohler, "Innovation in Normal Science: Bacterial Physiology," in *Isis*, **76** (1985), 162–181; Muriel Robertson, "Marjory Stephenson 1885–1948," in *Obituary Notices of Fellows of the Royal Society*, **6** (1949), 563–577, with full bibliography; and Donald D. Woods, "Marjory Stephenson, 1885–1948," in *Biochemical Journal*, **46** (1950), 377–383.

ROBERT E. KOHLER, JR.

STERN, CURT (*b.* Hamburg, Germany, 30 August 1902; *d.* Sacramento, California, 23 October 1981), *genetics.*

Curt Stern was the son of a businessman, Barned Stern, and his wife, Anni, a schoolteacher. He grew up in Berlin during World War I. During the war his father, a British citizen, was interned. Stern graduated from gymnasium in 1918 at the age of sixteen, which was not unusual during the war years since it enabled young men to join the army two years earlier than normal. However, since the war ended before Stern could be drafted, he went immediately on to study zoology at the University of Berlin. He did his doctoral work under the great protozoologist and general biologist Max Hartmann, who was a member of the Kaiser Wilhelm Institute (KWI) and an honorary professor at the university. Stern received his Ph.D. with a cytological thesis on the mitosis of a heliozoan in 1923, at the age of twenty-one, an unusually early age even for boys who had graduated early from gymnasium. At that time the Rockefeller Foundation started a program of international fellowships and Stern was one of the first recipients. In 1924 he went to Columbia University to work with T. H. Morgan in the famous "fly room," where the linear arrangement of genes in the chromosomes of *Drosophila* had been discovered and where work on chromosomal genetics was progressing very fast. Stern worked in this group with enthusiasm, learned the methods used in the genetics of *Drosophila*, and published his first *Drosophila* paper together with C. B. Bridges; it established the order of genes in the extreme left end of the second chromosome. *Drosophila* remained the main object of Stern's research, to which he later added human genetics.

In 1926 Stern returned to Germany and became an assistant at the KWI in the department of Richard Goldschmidt. His duties were not onerous; he mainly helped Goldschmidt in proofreading his influential book *Physiologische Theorie der Vererbung*. Otherwise he was free to pursue his own research, working out the problems he had started at Columbia. In 1931 Stern married Evelyn Sommerfield, whom he had met in 1925 while he was working in Morgan's lab. They had three daughters. In 1932 he won a second Rockefeller Fellowship and again went to Morgan's lab, which in the meantime had been moved to the California Institute of Technology at Pasadena. When Hitler came to power in 1933 Mrs. Stern, who was an American citizen and not in danger, went to Germany to find out whether it was safe for her husband to return. His friends advised against it, and Stern immediately set out to find a position in the United States.

At that time the University of Rochester in Rochester, New York, was in the process of developing from a small liberal arts college into a major university. The noted embryologist Benjamin Willier had been appointed chairman of the biology department and had started to build up the department. He appointed Stern a research associate in 1933, and in 1935 Stern joined the teaching faculty as an assistant professor. In 1940 Willier left Rochester and Stern was appointed acting chairman. In 1941 he was named chairman of the department of zoology and of the division of biological sciences and full professor. In 1947 he became professor of zoology at the University of California at Berkeley, succeeding his former boss, Richard Goldschmidt, who had just retired. In 1958 Stern was also appointed professor of genetics at Berkeley. He retired in 1970, suffering from the beginning stages of Parkinson's disease. His last public address was the presidential address at the Thirteenth International Congress of Genetics at Berkeley, which he delivered against the advice of his physicians. The address was an inspiring event, impressive in its enthusiasm and love for research. Stern died of cardiac failure.

During his stay at Columbia, Stern worked on several topics in *Drosophila* but became particularly interested in the function of the Y chromosome. He found that the X-linked gene bobbed (*bb*, short bristles) has an allele in the Y chromosome. Thus an $X^{bb}O$ male (a male carrying one X marked by the gene *bb* and no Y) is phenotypically bobbed, while a X^{bb}/Y^+ male is normal; an $X^{bb}/X^{bb}/Y^+$ female also has normal bristles. He found in addition that the Y chromosome can contain a mutated *bb* allele, so that a male X^{bb}/Y^{bb} is bobbed. XO animals are sterile males, and one fragment of the Y chromosome attached to the X chromosome does not restore fertility; but two or three fragments can do so. Stern had then proved, by a combination of genetic and cytological techniques, that the Y chromosome carries an allele of the *bb* gene and two or more genes that are needed for fertility. Previously it had been assumed that the Y chromosome is genetically empty; the demonstration of genes in the Y therefore constituted a major discovery.

The presence of *bb* alleles on the X and Y chromosomes was used for a further study of much broader implications. It permitted Stern to study the effect of different doses of alleles at the bobbed locus on bristle length. He had at his disposal five *bb* alleles: + in the X and Y chromosomes, and a standard *bb* in both chromosomes, and in addition bb^l, an extreme allele that is lethal in homozygous and hemizygous condition but in compound with a standard *bb* (bb/bb^l) results in very short, fine bristles. These five alleles could be tested in hemizygous condition (XO males) in homozygotes and heterozygotes in diploid males and females, triploid males and females, and superfemales (normal females trisomic only for the X chromosome) and tetraploid females (XXYY). The result was simple. The interaction of *bb* alleles is in all cases additive: One *bb* allele ($X^{bb}O$ male) causes shorter bristles than two alleles (X^{bb}/X^{bb} females and X^{bb}/Y^{bb} males), and still larger bristles are present in triploid females ($X^{bb}/X^{bb}/Y^{bb}$). In triploid males the bristles were even of normal length ($X^{bb}Y^{bb}Y^{bb}$). The lethal allele and a further allele that arose by mutation are weaker than standard *bb*. Thus all bobbed alleles act in an additive way toward the production of the normal phenotype.

This principle of additive action of alleles of the *bb* locus has had great importance for the theory of gene action. It was taken as supporting Goldschmidt's quantitative theory of gene structure and gene action, though it was not involved in its original conception. It has been demonstrated for other genes, but in other cases genes have been shown to act in a different direction, higher doses producing a more mutant phenotype. It later turned out that bobbed is in many respects a special type of gene. In 1968 Ritossa, Atwood, and Spiegelman showed that the bobbed locus is identical with the nucleolar organizer whose primary gene product is ribosomal RNA. The ribosomal DNA gene is a long tandem repeat, now known to consist of two alternating coding sequences and spacers. The bobbed mutations are loss mutations in which part of the ribosomal DNA is lost; thus fewer ribosomes are present and less protein is produced in *bb* cells, resulting, among other phenotypes, in short, slender bristles. Thus the bobbed mutations are true quantitative mutations, while most mutations have qualitatively different gene products as their primary effects.

Another project started at Columbia dealt with the cytological basis of genetic recombination. Morgan and his collaborators, basing their work on the chiasmatype theory of F. A. Janssens (1909), interpreted crossing-over of genes as due to physical exchange of parts of chromosomes, the breakage-and-reunion mechanism. Goldschmidt had proposed a different mechanism of crossing-over, and Stern, who as a graduate student had studied the literature on crossing-over thoroughly, wrote an unpublished critical review of Goldschmidt's ideas and decided to test the breakage-and-reunion theory directly. The way was shown in Karl Belar's 1923 paper on the meiosis of the heliozoan *Actinophrys sol*. In this paper Belar states that breakage-and-reunion can be demonstrated only if two homologous chromosomes are cytologically distinguishable from each other and from the normal chromosome.

Stern, with this idea in mind, searched, during his stay at Columbia, for such cytologically distinct chromosomes. He found one X chromosome to which the long arm of the Y chromosome had been attached at the proximal end. But he had to wait for two years until he obtained a second usable chromosome. In 1928 H. J. Muller found that X rays could induce not only mutations but also chromosomal rearrangements. He sent Stern several of these, and Stern chose for his experiments a translocation called Bar-of-Stone. In this translocation the distal third of the X chromosome is translocated to the small fourth chromosome, so that the X chromosome appears only two-thirds its normal length and is marked by the dominant gene Bar (reduced size of the eye). Another gene, the recessive eye-color gene carnation, was introduced into the X chromosome marked by the long arm of the Y chromosome, so that Stern now had two chromosomes that differed both in chromosomal structure and in genetic makeup. He looked in the progeny of females heterozygous for these two chromosomes for recombinant males, that is, males with completely normal eyes, or males that had Bar eyes of carnation color. These recombinants were investigated cytologically and found to have either normal X chromosomes or short X chromosomes carrying the arm of the Y chromosome. This correlation between genetic and cytological recombination established the breakage-and-reunion theory since crossing-over is accompanied by the exchange of chromosome parts. A similar proof was given at the same time for chromosomes of maize by Harriet Creighton and Barbara McClintock.

Even though this proof was accepted among geneticists, it was regarded as "anticlimactic" by L. C. Dunn in his *A Short History of Genetics* because the breakage-and-reunion theory appeared to be already well established by the large amount of genetic data accumulated by Morgan and his group, and Stern (1971) agreed with him. It was, however, an important contribution because alternative interpretations of recombination continued to appear. One of these was put forth at about the time of Stern's work by the botanist Hans Winkler. He proposed a mechanism called "conversion" that assumed that genes in heterozygous condition are more likely to mutate to the other allelic state than they are in homozygotes, thus producing the illusion of exchange of parts. Stern reviewed Winkler's book critically (1930) and Winkler answered with a countercritique. But the weight of Stern's experiments was so strong that breakage-and-reunion remained the established theory for twenty-five years. In 1955 Mary Mitchell obtained segregations in the fungus neurospora that were incompatible with a simple breakage-and-reunion mechanism, and that she called "conversion," but not in the sense of Winkler. While Winkler had used the analogy to mutation, Mitchell proposed an error in copying DNA, the newly synthesized copy switching from one strand of DNA to the other, the copy-choice mechanism. For some years the question of breakage-and-reunion versus copy-choice was widely debated in the genetic literature. Only thirty years after Stern's experiments was breakage-and-reunion established at the DNA level in bacteriophage lambda by Meselson and Weigle (1961). They used DNA strands labeled by heavy isotopes and differing in two genes. The experimental design is thus exactly the same as that used by Stern.

A final project started during Stern's stay in the fly room at Columbia was the demonstration of somatic crossing-over. Crossing-over was at that time well known to occur during meiotic division but was not suspected to occur in mitotic division. The work started from the observation made by Bridges (1925) that females heterozygous for an X chromosome-linked recessive gene and a dominant Minute gene, actually a small deletion causing small bristles and rough eyes, occasionally showed non-Minute recessive patches. Stern (1927) established the same phenomenon for autosomal genes and Minutes. This mosaicism was originally interpreted as being due to loss of the Minute-carrying chromosome. Stern investigated this mosaicism extensively, starting at Columbia and continuing at Dahlem, Pasadena, and Rochester.

In 1936 he published his findings and conclusions. The hypothesis of chromosome loss due to the presence of Minutes was rejected because mosaicism also occurs rarely in the absence of Minutes—Minutes only increase the frequency of mosaics—and because a Minute gene could have a similar effect if present in a chromosome other than that carrying the recessive. The decisive observation was made on females that carried the sex-linked genes yellow (bristles) and singed (bristles) on opposite chromosomes. In these the mosaics appeared sometimes in the form of twin spots containing adjacent areas where the bristles were yellow of normal shape and singed of normal color. This phenomenon was called "somatic segregation" and Stern proposed that it may be due to rare crossing-over between the homologous chromosomes at mitosis. He showed through models that crossing-over between two genes would lead to single spots, but crossing-over closer to the centromere than the more proximal gene would lead to twin spots. Stern could show that somatic crossing-over occurs between two strands at the four-strand stage. The recombination values between specific genes are different from those obtained at meiosis: somatic crossing-over is most frequent close to the centromere and becomes increasingly rare removed from it. In order to establish somatic crossing-over more convincingly, Stern carried out a number of further experiments using chromosome rearrangements together with recessive marker genes; all agreed with the expectations from the theory. Stern cautioned that the theory of mosaic formation by somatic segregation, caused by somatic crossing-over, was not yet proven. But it succeeded so well in explaining all the unexpected phenomena observed, some of which are quite complicated, that the theory was immediately accepted by all geneticists.

This acceptance has remained to the present day. Somatic segregation is routinely used in the study of developmental effects of genes. This use was actually introduced by Stern himself and is still widely employed. Another problem in which somatic crossing-over has been useful is the mapping of genes on the chromosomes, particularly in organisms that have no sexual stages and therefore no meiosis, such as the fungus *Aspergillus*.

Stern's classical paper on somatic crossing-over represents the last paper in the series of genetic-cytological investigations that had been started during his Rockefeller fellowship at Columbia. He turned now to other topics, most of which had as their goal the elucidation of gene action. This problem had already been raised in his work on the bobbed alleles. It now became the main focus of his attention. The first technique he used was organ transplantation in larvae of different genotypes. The structures the grafts form in the adult are scored for the gene-controlled characters. This technique had been introduced into genetics by Caspari in the moth *Ephestia* (1933) and had just been adapted by Beadle and Ephrussi to the study of eye pigments in *Drosophila* (1936). The technique permits the distinction between autonomous genes, in which each cell develops the character determined by its own genotype, independently of the genotype of the remainder of the organism, and "nonautonomous" genes, in which the phenotypes of host and graft influence each other. In these studies he was joined by the Swiss embryologist Ernst Hadorn, who was spending the year 1936–1937 in Rochester as a Rockefeller Fellow.

The first character investigated by the transplantation method was the sterility of XO males. It turned out to be autonomous. The next character was the pigmentation of the testes, which is suppressed in some eye color mutants. If the implanted testis remained free in the body cavity, no influence of the host was found. But if it became attached to the host's sperm ducts, which develop independently of the testis and in the pupal stage fuse with it, pigmented spots appeared on the colorless testis or sperm duct. This is due to migration of epithelial sheath cells between the testis and the sperm ducts. In a final project Stern investigated the difference in shape between different *Drosophila* species. In many *Drosophila* species the testes are coiled tubules. They arise from an elliptical larval testis that in late pupal stages grows out at the posterior end, without cell division. The outgrowth proceeds at different rates on the two sides, leading to a coiled structure. But in some species, such as *Drosophila pseudoobscura,* the testis does not grow

out strongly and remains elliptical. Transplantation between species with coiled and uncoiled testes showed that the coiling is induced by the sperm ducts that fuse with the testis and that are themselves coiled in the opposite direction. It appears that the sperm duct releases a growth-promoting substance. Also, different species may show different degrees of coiling, for example, two to three coils in *Drosophila melanogaster* as opposed to four coils in *Drosophila virilis*. This difference is also due to the genetic constitution of the inductor, the vas deferens, and not the constitution of the testis itself. This is the only example of a genetic influence on an inductor. In all other cases of differences in induction described in the literature, the differences are due to differences in the competence and norm of reaction of the reacting tissue, while the inducer is remarkably constant in evolutionary history.

When he had finished these transplantation experiments Stern embarked on a very ambitious project, the study of the position effect. The position effect was, and still is, regarded as one of the great unsolved problems of genetics. This project was associated with a change in Stern's style of research. Due to his rising reputation, Stern began to attract graduate students and postdoctoral research associates. He had had one Ph.D. student in Germany, Ursula Philip, who later went to England and worked with Haldane. In Rochester he began to attract the first in a long series of Ph.D. students. His first students were James V. Neel and Harrison Stalker, both of whom became prominent geneticists. Stern's last collaborator, C. Tokunaga, estimated that during his lifetime Stern trained about thirty Ph.D.s. Several of them made major contributions to science in their own research and perpetuated Stern's influence on the younger generation of scientists. In addition, since his collaboration with Hadorn, Stern almost continually had research associates and postdoctorals associated with him, so that he became the leader of a team. This change in the style of research was to a certain degree general, since beginning with World War II large amounts of funds for research from government sources became available.

Stern's collaborators on the position effect worked in two areas: Gertrude Heidenthal and Elizabeth W. Schaeffer participated in the genetic work, while Robert MacKnight and, after his untimely death, Masuo Kodani carried out cytological investigations on the salivary gland chromosomes to determine the position of the breaks in translocations. The project was very carefully prepared and designed. Stern chose the gene cubitus interruptus (cubitus is a vein on the wing). The gene appeared suitable because several mutants were known, its phenotypic effect could be expressed quantitatively, a position effect for this gene had been demonstrated by Dubinin and Serebrovskii, and the gene was located in the small fourth chromosome, which in single, double, and triple dose gives rise to viable animals. It was thus possible to compare mutant and wild-type alleles in homozygotes and heterozygotes in haploid, diploid, and triploid conditions; in addition, a deletion for the gene was available. The quantitative possibilities were thus parallel to the earlier work on bb.

In analogy to bb, most ci alleles were shown to act additively toward the production of a normal vein. Stern showed that different wild-type alleles could be distinguished by their effect in heterozygotes at different temperatures, a phenomenon to which the term "isoalleles" was applied. One ci allele, ci^w, is different from others in that it is more abnormal in the homozygous than in the hemizygous condition, showing that this allele does not act toward normality but toward the abnormal condition antagonistic to the wild type. Still harder to explain are the interactions of ci alleles with the fourth chromosome deficient for the ci gene: The deficient fourth chromosome also acts toward normality. These results led Stern to abandon the hypothesis of simple additivity and instead propose a more complex model: The primary reaction of a gene consists in conversion of a "substrate" to a "product." Each allele has not only a characteristic efficiency in transforming "substrate" into "product" but also a characteristic combining power for the "substrate." The different alleles in a diploid and triploid organism compete for a limited amount of substrate, so that the final amount of "product" depends not only on the efficiency of the allele itself, but also on the combining power and efficiency of the other alleles present in the same genome.

This ingenious hypothesis was, however, insufficient to interpret the position effects. Stern and his collaborators produced nineteen chromosomal rearrangements of the wild-type allele of ci and fifty-five rearrangements involving the mutant alleles. Their phenotypic effects were tested in compounds with normal and mutant alleles in their normal positions. Stern could exclude the possibility that the position effect is due to a disturbance of somatic pairing of chromosomes or to a closeness to particular chromosomal structures in their new location, but a general conclusion encompassing all observed facts remained elusive. In his last paper of the series (Stern and Kodani 1955) Stern writes, "This lack of correlation in effects points to qualitative dif-

ferences in the developmental reactions of the different $R(ci)$ alleles or their products," and "No deeper insight into the mechanism of position effect at the ci locus can be presented."

Stern was obviously disappointed in this outcome of a large and well-conceived project; he mentions it only briefly in his memoirs of his scientific career (1971, 1974) and cites only the discovery of isoalleles as a positive result. But it is still the most thorough investigation of a position effect ever attempted, and the lack of a clear-cut result may very well be due to the fact that there is no general rule for the behavior of position alleles, or that the rule cannot be seen at the chromosomal level but only at the DNA level. Attempts to analyze position effects (not the ci effect, though) at the DNA level are in progress but have not yet led to generalized models either.

Parallel with this project Stern directed a major study on the mutagenicity of X rays at low dosages. During these years the Manhattan Project was organized by the U. S. Army, and the University of Rochester was chosen to investigate all biological aspects important for the use of atomic energy for war as well as for peacetime purposes. The genetic division of this project was led by Donald R. Charles, but Stern took over the direction of the *Drosophila* work in collaboration with Warren P. Spencer, Ernst Caspari, and Delta Uphoff. Spencer and Stern demonstrated that the straight relationship between radiation dose and mutation rate was valid down to 25r. But experiments designed to test the effect of low-level radiation over an extended span of time led to contradictory results. Since the experiment involved irradiation of sperm stored in the spermatheca of a female for up to three weeks, and since it is known that aging of sperm induces mutations, it is possible that the mutagenic effect of radiation is not simply superimposed on the aging effect but is subject to a more complex interaction.

A by-product of this work was a large collection of X chromosome–linked lethal mutations, most of them spontaneous. Stern, in collaboration with Ed Novitski and others, used this collection to study a problem that was at that time much discussed by evolutionists: whether heterozygotes may be superior in fitness to the dominant, wild-type homozygotes. Stern and his collaborators tested heterozygotes for thirty-six spontaneous lethals and thirty-nine lethals derived from exposure to 50r low-intensity gamma rays for viability and found that their ability to survive varied. On the average, the viability of heterozygotes for lethals was slightly lower than that of normal homozygotes (0.965:1.000), but some heterozygotes had definitely reduced viability, up to almost half that of the wild-type homozygotes, while others were definitely superior to the normal homozygotes, a phenomenon designated as heterosis.

During his time in Rochester, Stern started yet another project, which he continued all his life: work in human genetics. This interest grew out of his teaching activities. It started out with a graduate student seminar in some problems of human genetics. There followed an undergraduate course in the subject for nonbiology majors and without prerequisites in biology. The course became known as a very valuable one and was made obligatory for sociology majors. While the course had no prerequisites, it was very exacting. Stern presented the usual contents of a genetics course—Mendelian rules, linkage, and chromosome mechanics—as facts, but he derived the foundations of population genetics, breeding patterns, human mutation rates, and inbreeding quantitatively and required students to become well acquainted with the algebraic techniques used in these problems. It must have required a great amount of work to organize this course because Stern had to study the extensive literature on human genetics and become acquainted at first hand with the mathematical methods he was using. His fresh insight enabled him to present these matters simply and clearly. For example, his derivation of the Hardy-Weinberg law is the simplest and most convincing one I have ever seen.

One difficulty for this course was the lack of a suitable textbook. There were several textbooks of human genetics, but they were restricted to presentations of factual data in the form of pedigrees, mostly of rare diseases, and in their theoretical part pointed to the importance of eugenics, a movement which was still strong at the time. Therefore, Stern published a textbook, *Principles of Human Genetics* (1949), which caught on only slowly since few biologists were prepared to teach such a course. But after a short time it became popular, went through three editions, and was translated into seven languages. It now has a special position among the books on human heredity.

Stern attacked several research programs in human genetics and became a highly respected authority on human genetics. Among his projects the subject on which he published most was an investigation of genes in the human Y chromosome, reminiscent of the *Drosophila* problem several decades earlier. The method here was different, however. He investigated several cases in which genes, on the basis of pedigrees, had been regarded as Y-linked. He found that in all cases the basis for the claim was weak, and much of the evidence was derived from stories of patients and not from direct observation. Many of the early human pedigrees had been obtained in a similar manner, and Stern emphasized that genetic hypotheses should be based only on direct observations by the investigator. One case in question concerned the occurrence of hair on the outer rim of the ear. The patient who first showed the trait claimed that all his male relatives had it, but since the man was old and mentally disturbed, and no further confirmation was offered, Stern felt safe to reject the claim. Around the same time some pedigrees from India seemed to bear out the hypothesis that hairy ears were indeed due to a gene carried in the Y chromosome. Stern went to India and together with W. R. Centerwall and S. S. Sarkar collected pedigrees himself. While the data seemed to support a Y-linked inheritance, Stern remained skeptical because difficulties of ascertainment and some other irregularities of expression made it impossible to exclude autosomal dominant inheritance. In the meantime other workers collected similar pedigrees. The results were the same but several authors interpreted them as clear evidence of Y linkage. The resulting controversy did not clear up the matter. Stern was inclined to believe that Y linkage was the most likely explanation, but he preferred to remain cautious.

In the last twenty years of his active scientific life Stern concentrated on the problem of pattern formation. In this work Aloha Hannah-Alava, Chiyoko Tokunaga, and a large number of graduate students were associated with him. He studied the pattern of bristles on the surface of *Drosophila* and the sex combs on the legs of males, and a large number of genes influencing these structures. The method involved the use of genetic mosaics produced either by loss of one X chromosome or by somatic crossing over in genetic heterozygotes. Genetically mutant patches produced in this way on a genetically wild-type background could behave in either one of two ways: they could develop autonomously so that the mutant areas show the mutant phenotype, or they could show the wild-type phenotype of the background, that is, develop in a nonautonomous way. He interpreted the data according to a model by which underlying the visible pattern is "a system of patterned singularities" or "prepattern," a term introduced by Karl Henke, on which the cuticle reacts with the formation of bristles or sex combs. Most mutant patches turned out to behave in an autonomous way, suggesting that the genes involved affect the ability of the reacting structures to respond to the prepattern. But one gene-controlled aberration, the increase in number of sex combs in males of the mutant "eyeless-dominant," behaved in a non-autonomous way and was therefore regarded as affecting the prepattern itself. In this mutant the growth pattern of the leg segment is abnormal and this seems to affect the structure of the prepattern.

The reports of his experimental research do not comprise the whole of Stern's publications. He became interested in the history of genetics and edited with Eva Sherwood a book on Gregor Mendel and the rediscovery of his work. In his systematic study of human genetics he found that the fundamental expression of population genetics, at that time known as Hardy's law, had been discovered at the same time by the German physician Wilhelm Weinberg, and he was able to change the established name to the Hardy-Weinberg law. He was concerned about public affairs and spoke out on his opinions, but always within the borders of his special competence. He was one of the first to express concern about the danger of exposure to radiation for human populations and the future of mankind. He also had an interest in philosophy and ethics and published a number of philosophical essays.

In his relations with his colleagues, students, and friends Stern was friendly, pleasant, and always ready to help with advice and action. He had the luck early in life to become closely acquainted with the present and future leaders in his field. In his year at Columbia he was associated with the leaders of genetics (Morgan, Sturtevant, and Bridges); in Germany the KWI was the center of genetic research and Stern came to know closely the leading geneticists of Germany (Correns, Goldschmidt, and Hartmann) as well as the younger group of biologists at KWI (Belar, Hämmerling, Holtfreter, and others). He formed strong and lasting friendships with many of these colleagues. Stern was therefore in the unique position of knowing both the American and the German traditions in genetics and of combining these influences in a unique and original way.

While his manner was always friendly and polite, there was a very strong character under the smooth surface. Stern was fundamentally serious, and had high expectations for himself and his fellow humans. He had much determination and willpower and pursued his goals with perseverance and a strong sense of duty. He worked constantly and with great concentration, but in an unhurried and relaxed way. To his students he was kind and tolerant of minor lapses and faults, but he was exacting as far as their work was concerned and did not tolerate sloppy work. He was highly esteemed by his colleagues and former students and therefore had an enormous

influence not only on the progress of genetics but also on the attitudes and opinions of his fellow scientists. Stern's devotion to his science and his loyalty to his friends were widely appreciated, and he was generally regarded as a wise, humane, and upright human being in addition to being an outstanding scientist.

BIBLIOGRAPHY

I. ORIGINAL WORKS. "Ein genetischer und cytologischer Beweis für Vererbung im Y-Chromosom von *Drosophila melanogaster*," in *Zeitschrift für induktive Abstammungs- und Vererbungslehre*, **44** (1927), 187–231; "Fortschritte der Chromosomentheorie der Vererbung," *Ergebnisse der Biologie*, **4** (1928), 205–359; "Über die additive Wirkung multipler Allele," in *Biologisches Zentralblatt*, **49** (1929), 261–290; "Konversionstheorie und Austauschtheorie," *ibid.*, **50** (1930), 608–624; *Multiple Allelie* (Berlin, 1930); *Faktorenkoppelung und Faktorenaustausch* (Berlin, 1933); "Somatic Crossing-Over and Segregation in *Drosophila melanogaster*," in *Genetics*, **21** (1936), 625–730; "The Determination of Sterility in *Drosophila* Males Without a Complete Y-Chromosome," in *American Naturalist*, **72** (1938), 42–52, written with Ernst Hadorn; and "The Relation Between the Color of Testes and Vasa Efferentia in *Drosophila*," in *Genetics*, **24** (1939), 162–179, written with Ernst Hadorn.

"The Growth of Testes in *Drosophila*, I, The Relation Between Vas Deferens and Testis Within Various Species" and "II, The Nature of Interspecific Differences," in *Journal of Experimental Zoology*, **87** (1941), 113–158, 159–180; "Genic Action as Studied by Means of the Effects of Different Doses and Combinations of Alleles," in *Genetics*, **28** (1943), 441–475; "The Hardy-Weinberg Law," in *Science*, **97** (1943), 137–138; "On Wild-type Iso-alleles in *Drosophila melanogaster*," in *Proceedings of the National Academy of Sciences of the United States of America*, **29** (1943), 361–367; "The Journey, Not the Goal," in *Scientific Monthly*, **58** (1944), 96–100; "The Effects of Changes in Quantity, Combination, and Position of Genes," in *Science*, **108** (1948), 615–621; "Experiments to Test the Validity of the Linear *R*-dose/Mutation Frequency Relation in *Drosophila* at Low Dosage," in *Genetics*, **33** (1948), 43–74, written with Warren P. Spencer; and "The Influence of Chronic Irradiation with Gamma-rays at Low Dosages on the Mutation Rate in *Drosophila melanogaster*," *ibid.*, 75–95, written with Ernst Caspari.

"The Genetic Effects of Low Intensity Irradiation," in *Science*, **109** (1949), 609–610, written with Delta E. Uphoff; *Principles of Human Genetics* (San Francisco, 1949; 3d ed., 1973); "The Sex Combs in Gynanders of *Drosophila melanogaster*," in *Portugaliae acta biologica*, ser. A, R. B. Goldschmidt volume (1949–1951), 798–812, written with Aloha M. Hannah; "The Viability of Heterozygotes for Lethals," in *Genetics*, **37** (1952), 413–449, written with G. Carson, M. Kinst, E. Novitski, and

D. Uphoff; "Model Estimates of the Frequency of White and Near-white Segregants in the American Negro," in *Acta genetica et statistica medica*, **4** (1953), 281–298; "Two or Three Bristles," in *American Scientist*, **42** (1954), 213–247; "Studies on the Position Effect at the Cubitus Interruptus Locus of *Drosophila melanogaster*," in *Genetics*, **40** (1955), 343–373, written with Masuo Kodani; and "The Genetic Control of Developmental Competence and Morphogenetic Tissue Interactions in Genetic Mosaics," in *Wilhelm Roux Archiv für Entwicklungsmechanik der Organismen*, **149** (1956), 1–25.

"Genetics in the Atomic Age," in *Eugenics Quarterly*, **3** (1956), 131–138; "Dosage Compensation—Development of a Concept and New Facts" (Fifth Huskins Memorial Lecture), in *Canadian Journal of Genetics and Cytology*, **2** (1960), 105–118; "New Data on the Problem of Y-linkage of Hairy Pinnae," in *American Journal of Human Genetics*, **16** (1964), 455–471, written with W. R. Centerwall and S. S. Sarkar; "The Developmental Autonomy of Extra Sex Combs in *Drosophila melanogaster*," in *Developmental Biology*, **11** (1965), 50–81, written with Chiyoko Tokunaga; *The Origin of Genetics: A Mendel Source Book* (San Francisco, 1966), edited with Eva R. Sherwood; "Nonautonomy in Differentiation of Pattern-determining Genes in Drosophila. I. The Sex Comb of Eyeless-dominant," in *Proceedings of the National Academy of Sciences of the United States of America*, **57** (1967), 658–664, written with Chiyoko Tokunaga; *Genetic Mosaics and Other Essays* (Cambridge, Mass., 1968); "From Crossing-over to Developmental Genetics," in *Stadler Genetics Symposia*, G. Kimber and G. P. Redei, eds., I/II (Columbia, Mo., 1971), 21–28; and "A Geneticist's Journey," in *Chromosomes and Cancer*, James German, ed. (New York, 1974), xii–xxv.

II. Secondary Literature. John C. Lucchesi and James V. Neel published obituaries in, respectively, *Genetics*, **103** (1983), 1–4, and *Annual Review of Genetics*, **17** (1983), 1–10.

Ernst Caspari

STEVENS, NETTIE MARIA (*b*. Cavendish, Vermont, 7 July 1861; *d*. Baltimore, Maryland, 4 May 1912), *cytology, heredity*.

Nettie Maria Stevens came from solid New England stock. The first American Stevens came from Chelmsford, England, to Boston; his eldest son went to Chelmsford, Massachusetts, in 1663. The family remained in the area for five generations; Nettie's father, Ephraim, was born on 24 March 1833. He married Julia Adams of Cavendish, Vermont, in 1854. Their first two children, both sons, died before Nettie's birth. They had one more child, Emma Julia, in 1863. The family lived in Cavendish until after Julia's death and Ephraim's remarriage, whereupon they moved to Westford, Vermont.

Nettie's father reportedly was a hardworking and reasonably successful carpenter and handyman.

Stevens' education began in the Westford public schools and continued at the Westford Academy, from which she graduated in 1880 as a college preparatory student. She and her sister both performed consistently well, achieving nearly perfect grades in all subjects. After graduating, Stevens taught high school, including zoology and physiology, in Lebanon, New Hampshire, for three terms. She then completed in two years (1881–1883), with nearly perfect grades, the four-year program at Westfield Normal School in Westfield, Massachusetts. She taught school until 1892 and again in 1895 and 1896, acquiring a reputation as an excellent teacher. In 1896 Stevens entered Stanford University, where she quickly decided to major in physiology. After the year 1897–1898, when she determined to work with Frank Mace MacFarland, she moved into histological work. She spent four summers (1897–1901) at Stanford's Hopkins Seaside Laboratory, working with marine organisms. After receiving the A.B. degree in 1899, Stevens remained at Stanford, working in experimental physiology under Oliver Peebles Jenkins. She spent 1900 in the investigator's room at the Hopkins Laboratory and completed her master's thesis (her first publication). She credited MacFarland with having assigned her to pursue cytological studies, a focus she followed in her later major work on sex determination and chromosomes.

After Stanford, Stevens went to Bryn Mawr College, where she began working under Joseph Weatherland Warren on the physiology of frog contractions and the influence of chemicals on the force of contractions. She quickly moved, however, to work with Thomas Hunt Morgan, who was then studying regeneration in various organisms. Stevens became involved in that work and in 1901 published two regeneration studies. At first she worked with material that Morgan had brought back from Naples; then she traveled to Woods Hole in 1901 to pursue cell division in regeneration of Tubularia. From 8 October 1901 to 1 April 1902, at Morgan's suggestion, she worked at the Naples Zoological Station, where she occupied the American women's table and pursued studies of cut eggs, with a particular interest in the relations of cuts to the chromosomes.

Later in 1902 Stevens went on to Würzburg, to work in the laboratory of Theodor Boveri, where she began to study ovogenesis and spermatogenesis. This contact with Boveri at a particularly productive point in his chromosome studies likely had a major directive impact on Stevens' work. She completed her Ph.D. from Bryn Mawr in 1903 and retained a professional tie with the school: as research fellow in biology (1902–1904), reader in experimental morphology (1904–1905), and associate in experimental morphology (1905–1912). She would have occupied a research professorship the next year had she not died from cancer.

In 1904 Morgan and Stevens began studying the behavior of chromosomes in aphids, work that she pursued with the support of a fellowship from the Carnegie Institution of Washington in the year 1904–1905. Several studies of germ cells in aphids appeared as a result. One paper of 1905 brought Stevens an award of $1,000 for the best scientific paper written by a woman. Another work, *Studies in Spermatogenesis*, marked her entry into the increasingly promising arena of sex-determination studies and chromosomal inheritance. In 1901 and 1902, Clarence Erwin McClung had suggested that there exists an extra, or accessory, chromosome in the male and that the presence of the accessory determines the male sex. In 1903 Morgan reported in his "Recent Theories in Regard to the Determination of Sex" the general opinion that an individual's sex is not determined by external (or environmental) factors.

But scientists were not at all sure what internal factors prevailed, Morgan concluded, nor even at what point sex is determined. McClung's suggestion had gained little support. Yet by the year 1904–1905 Stevens was actively pursuing the hypothesis that chromosomes determine sex, though not in the simple way that McClung envisioned. Both Stevens and Edmund Beecher Wilson sought to discover what role chromosomes do play. In a study that appeared as Carnegie Institution of Washington Publication 36, Stevens examined spermatogenesis in five insect species from four different groups. Two species had an extra or "accessory" chromosome in the male. But she felt that the common mealworm (*Tenebrio molitor*) proved most interesting for questions of sex determination because it exhibited a difference in size rather than in number of male and female chromosomes. Though cautious in her general conclusions, Stevens clearly felt that her work of 1905 on *Tenebrio* established that males have nineteen large chromosomes and one small one, and females twenty large ones, which implied a correlation of chromosomes with sex determination.

The period 1905 to 1908 brought a series of papers on germ cells, heterochromosomes, and the determination of sex in an attempt to elucidate the details of spermatogenesis for the unequal or "hetero" chromosomes in a range of additional species. Stevens explored what effect the different chromosomes

might have, and she suggested that the evidence supported William Castle's modified version of Mendelian heredity as well. After a leave of absence and a return research visit to Boveri's laboratory in the year 1908–1909, Stevens continued to bring her cytological concern with chromosomes, especially heterochromosomes, and their behavior in synapsis to her work on regeneration and reproduction. Her death left this series of studies uncompleted.

Nettie Stevens achieved the highest respect from the leading biologists of her time. She failed to gain a full regular university position, no doubt largely because she was a woman. Yet she achieved an admirable career of research at the leading marine stations and laboratories. Her record of at least thirty-six publications written alone and four with a coauthor includes several major contributions and a group of studies that together constitute a central addition to the emergence of ideas of chromosomal heredity.

This woman scientist from Vermont deserves recognition as one of those providing critical evidence for a Mendelian and chromosomal theory of heredity. As Morgan wrote in his obituary note, "Her single-mindedness and devotion, combined with keen powers of observation; her thoughtfulness and patience, united to a well-balanced judgment, account, in part, for her remarkable accomplishment."

BIBLIOGRAPHY

I. ORIGINAL WORKS. The most complete bibliography of Stevens' work appears in the biography by Ogilvie and Choquette (see below). Her first publication, from her master's thesis, was "Studies on Ciliate Infusoria," in *Proceedings of the California Academy of Sciences, Zoology*, **3** (1901), 1–42. Her most important works include *Studies in Spermatogenesis with Especial Reference to the "Accessory Chromosome,"* Carnegie Institution of Washington Publication no. 36, pt. I (1905); "A Study of the Germ Cells of *Aphis rosae* and *Aphis oenetherae*," in *Journal of Experimental Zoology*, **2** (1905), 313–333; *Studies in Spermatogenesis. A Comparative Study of the Heterochromosomes in Certain Species of Coleoptera, Hemiptera and Lepidoptera, with Especial Reference to Sex Determination*, Carnegie Institution of Washington Publication no. 36, pt. II (1906); *Studies on the Germ Cells of Aphids*, Carnegie Institution of Washington Publication no. 51 (1906); "A Study of the Germ Cells of Certain Diptera, with Reference to the Heterochromosomes and the Phenomena of Synapsis," in *Journal of Experimental Zoology*, **5** (1908), 359–374; and "Further Studies on Reproduction in *Sagitta*," in *Journal of Morphology*, **21** (1910), 279–319.

II. Secondary Literature. The only reliable biography of Stevens is Marilyn Bailey Ogilvie and Clifford J. Choquette, "Nettie Maria Stevens (1861–1912): Her Life and Contributions to Cytogenetics," in *Proceedings of the American Philosophical Society*, **125** (1981), 292–311, which covers material in earlier biographical sketches and surveys the archival materials available. This replaces the incomplete and sometimes inaccurate study by Hans Ris in *Notable American Women*, VIII, 372–373. In addition, Stephen G. Brush, "Nettie M. Stevens and the Discovery of Sex Determination by Chromosomes," in *Isis*, **69** (1978), 163–172, discusses her scientific work, as does Thomas Hunt Morgan, "The Scientific Work of Miss N. M. Stevens," in *Science*, **36** (1912), 468–470.

Jane Maienschein

STEVENS, STANLEY SMITH (*b*. Ogden, Utah, 4 November 1906; *d*. Vail, Colorado, 18 January 1973), *experimental psychology, psychophysics.*

Stevens was the only child in a Mormon family. After mission service abroad, he took his B.A. at Stanford in 1931. He received his doctorate under Edwin Garrigues Boring at Harvard in 1933 for experimental work on audition. As a spokesperson for "operationism" in psychology, he helped spark the "unity of science" movement in 1935.

His book *Hearing* (1938) refined Hermann von Helmholtz's place theory by incorporating the electrical response recording of E. G. Wever and C. W. Bray and the basilar membrane hypothesis of Georg von Békésy. By 1940, Stevens also had begun to replace indirect methods of defining sensation with direct scaling methods.

During World War II, Stevens was codirector of Harvard's federally funded "defense research" project to design communications systems for military applications. His Psycho-Acoustic Laboratory trained a postwar generation of sensory psychologists. He edited the authoritative *Handbook of Experimental Psychology* (1951), featuring his own classic chapter on scales of measurement. In 1953, Stevens proposed the power law to describe the growth of sensation intensity with the increase of physical intensity. Ignoring age-old criticism that sensory experience cannot be quantified, he spent two decades determining the power exponents for more than two dozen sensory continua.

Stevens' "new psychophysics" set off debates about psychological methods, data, and theory. Probabilistic choice and signal detection theory grew from radar detection and took over threshold measurement. Stevens' theory of four scales of measurement was extended into an axiomatic derivation of fundamental measurement. His program of describing power laws on all sensory continua has been extended to support the "unity of the senses" in consequence of invariant features of the environment.

Ancestry, Childhood, and Education. Stevens was raised in a family of industrious English immigrants to Utah. Smith Stevens, as he was called, graduated from high school in 1924, the same year in which his mother, Adeline, died from a lingering heart ailment and his father, Steven, was killed in an automobile accident. After a short period in the family's electrical business, he did a three-year stint (1924–1927) as a Mormon missionary in Belgium, Switzerland, and eastern France. Returning to study at the University of Utah, Stevens was introduced to behavioral psychology in a course that used J. B. Watson's *Behavior: An Introduction to Comparative Psychology*. In the summers he worked for the Idaho Power Company. Transferring in his junior year (1929) to Stanford University, he turned toward medicine after a successful anatomy laboratory course. On 28 March 1930, Stevens and Maxine Leonard of Salt Lake City were married; she joined him for his last year at Stanford.

After postgraduate summer courses in statistics (with H. E. Garrett) and the history of psychology (with J. F. Dashiell) at the University of Southern California, Stevens enrolled at Harvard in the Graduate School of Education, and Maxine studied philosophy at Radcliffe. In his first year, 1931–1932, he took statistics (with T. Kelley), systematic psychology (with E. G. Boring), and physiology (with W. J. Crozier). He switched to psychology after one semester, and took the preliminary examinations for the doctorate in the spring of 1932. Having done well, Stevens was awarded a fellowship of $900. Under the supervision of Boring, director of the psychological laboratory, he performed research on audition for his doctorate in the department of philosophy and psychology in 1933.

Psychological research and theory drew from different "schools" in the 1920's. Edward B. Titchener at Cornell had promoted "structural psychology," which emphasized systematic experimentation on the senses. Boring, Titchener's student, had sought an accommodation with behaviorism by redefining the "attributes" of sensation in terms of their physical dimensions. A former engineering student, Boring in turn encouraged his student Stevens toward "a physics of the living organism" (Boring to Stevens, 26 October 1935). Stevens and Edwin B. Newman produced sounds with an electronic oscillator that had recently been pioneered by Harvey Fletcher at

Bell Laboratories. They instructed human subjects to adjust a given sound to half or some multiple of the original sound stimulus. Despite his apocryphal account of the discovery of magnitude estimation in the 1950's, Stevens was using direct methods of adjustment, fractionation, bisection, and ratio production to generate direct sensory scales before 1940, in place of the customary Fechnerian indirect measurement by a "unit of variability" in sensory judgments.

At issue was the Weber-Fechner psychophysical law. Following Ernst Heinrich Weber, Gustav Theodor Fechner believed that the ratio of a just noticeable stimulus increment ΔR to a total stimulus R is a constant, or $\Delta R/R = k$. Fechner then made the assumption that corresponding to this fraction was a constant incremental unit of sensation ($\Delta S = c$). It follows from $\Delta S = c(\Delta R/R)$ that S, sensation magnitude, grows as a logarithmic function of stimulus magnitude, or $S = k \log R$. Another way of saying this is that sensation intensity increases arithmetically as stimulus intensity increases geometrically. In a fragment from the 1930's, Stevens incisively summed up decades of empirical criticism of Fechner's law: "In the two principal sense departments [vision and audition] it breaks down at the extremes, and in all departments the fact of the threshold interrupts its continuity. We can conclude, then, that the theoretical formulation has not been verified" (Stevens to Boring, 1932). Stevens also raised the question at this time whether Fechner's law was an empirical or a theoretical formula. Since the law did not fit the data over their entire range, he concluded that it was only theoretical. His own goal became the formulation and measurement of an empirical law, one that did not require the summation of units of variability.

Operationism and Building a Scientific Career. Boring recognized his prize student's facility with electronic equipment and public debating. He extended Stevens' assistantship of $900 through the academic year 1933–1934. He well knew that Harvard needed first-rate experimental scientists to legitimate his own rhetoric of experimentalism. At that very time, Boring's hopes for institutional legitimation of psychology had taken a propitious turn. Harvard's president, Abbott Lowell, retired in 1933, to be succeeded by a chemist, James B. Conant. In 1934, Boring's motion to separate the department of psychology from the department of philosophy was accepted by the Harvard Faculty of Arts and Sciences. The new department had Gordon Allport in social and personality psychology, C. C. Pratt in aesthetics, and J. G. Beebe-Center in emotions.

H. A. Murray directed a clinical psychology laboratory. A distinguished newcomer from Chicago, Karl S. Lashley, was housed in the biological laboratories. B. F. Skinner was sponsored as a junior fellow between 1933 and 1936 by biologists L. J. Henderson and W. J. Crozier. Stevens joined Boring on the third floor of Emerson Hall, undertaking a series of projects that promised to aid Boring's institutional ambitions and to bring a scientific career to himself. His lack of interest in classroom teaching, however, spelled trouble for his professional advancement and the fate of the department.

The aim of Boring's ambition was a physicalist positivism for psychology, and this he repeatedly conveyed to Stevens. With his *Physical Dimensions of Consciousness* (1933) in mind, Boring wrote to Stevens: "You are furnishing the justification of it and the propaganda for it. I am pleased and grateful . . ." (Boring's comments on his "tonal density" manuscript, 1933). Combining Ernst Mach's sensationism with Percy W. Bridgman's operationism, Boring and Stevens considered "the discriminatory response" to be "a step towards the operational analysis of what we mean by experience" (Stevens to Boring, 12 December 1934). While Boring traced this physicalist definition historically to Ernst Mach and R. Avenarius, Stevens couched his "operations" in terms of contemporary logical positivism as (1) a language for the physical measurement (2) of behavioral responses (3) by means of public or intersubjective statements.

Skinner, influenced by Machian positivism, remained critical of Stevens' dualistic acceptance of sensation, or consciousness. Yet there was considerable agreement between Stevens' operational epistemology and Skinner's behaviorist epistemology on all three characteristics of positivism given by Stevens. Stevens always emphasized the stimulus, and Skinner the response; but they shared a commitment to the operational description of independent and dependent variables.

Despite forays into philosophy of science, the bulk of Stevens' work was empirical. Supported in the year 1934–1935 by a National Research Council fellowship, he apprenticed at the Harvard Medical School with Hallowell Davis, whose physiological competence and electrical recording apparatus complemented Stevens' psychophysical approach. During the year 1935–1936, Stevens received financial support from the Rockefeller Foundation. He was an instructor in psychology at Harvard in the academic year 1936–1937, receiving $2,750 to teach four sections and the laboratory course for Psychology 1. In 1936 his son, Peter, was born and

Maxine was hospitalized with postpartum depression, from which she never recovered. Stevens threw himself into work on his book on hearing. His son was raised by a Mormon family in the Boston suburbs, and Stevens became a frequent guest at their dinner table.

Meanwhile, Davis urged Stevens forward, helping him to obtain a grant from the American Otological Society to look up Georg von Békésy in Budapest. Békésy's early work on the propagation of traveling waves by the basilar membrane in the cochlea earned him a Nobel Prize in 1961. In 1940, Stevens worked with John Volkmann to provide independent evidence for Békésy's neural quantum hypothesis of sensory thresholds.

During the years 1938 to 1940 Stevens became interested in William H. Sheldon's body-typing work in constitutional psychology. After satisfying himself that subjects could indeed estimate (on a seven-point scale) each of three dimensions of somatotypes from photographs, he devised a machine with which to compute correlation coefficients of seventeen measurements taken on three photographic views (front, side, back) of the nude male body. Their use of ratios of front, back, and side sections to height represented an improvement on the absolute measurements of Sheldon's chief predecessor, Ernst Kretschmer of Leipzig.

Stevens had distanced himself from physicalism and operational definition by 1939. Under the influence of C. W. Morris' pragmatic theory of signs, he endorsed a hypothetico-deductive method "to confirm by experimental observation the results of our deductions." At the Fifth International Congress for the Unity of Science in Cambridge, Massachusetts (1939), Stevens treated numerals as signs related by syntactic rules to three kinds of numerosity: ordinal, intensive ("groups showing a just noticeable difference in numerousness"), and extensive ("by determining when one group appeared half as numerous as another"). He derived this classification of scales from N. R. Campbell (1938); he revised it for the Sixth International Congress for the Unity of Science in 1941 and published it in 1946 and 1951 as four scales: nominal, ordinal, interval, and ratio. Ironically, Campbell served on the nineteen-member committee of the British Association for the Advancement of Science that in 1940 reported on Stevens' sone scale of loudness and concluded that fundamental measurement would not be possible in psychology "until a meaning can be given to the concept of addition as applied to a sensation."

Stevens ignored "the quantity objection" to "the concept of addition as applied to sensation" by simply accepting the subject's ability to "add" sensations. This faith in introspective, yet operational, measurement of subjective consciousness committed him to a dualism, although, like other positivists, he believed that his position was monistic. As Savage put it, he failed to distinguish the introspectionist interpretation of sensation as empirically real from the behaviorist interpretation of sensation as fictional. Stevens had a behaviorist's conviction that methods could define formal concepts, and that consistent formal concepts define reality. He claimed to have taken the concept of invariance from the Harvard mathematician G. D. Birkhoff, who spoke on the topic at a meeting Stevens cohosted with Rudolf Carnap. The papers Stevens wrote in the early 1940's were circulated among friends during the war and later attracted widespread acceptance in many disciplines.

The Harvard Psycho-Acoustic Laboratory. In 1940, two years after Stevens was appointed assistant professor of psychology, he undertook a project for the National Defense Research Council (NDRC) Committee on Sound Control to study the effects of noise on psychomotor efficiency. The Psycho-Acoustic Laboratory, under Stevens' direction, continued to conduct auditory research under contract with the Office of Scientific Research and Development (OSRD) throughout World War II in conjunction with the Electro-Acoustic Laboratory, directed by Harvard acoustic scientist Leo L. Beranek. Amid the turbulence of wartime priorities, Stevens demonstrated skills and leadership in a new "big science" atmosphere. He directed a laboratory that had a staff of about fifty persons, among whom were some of the outstanding talents of that generation: the senior psychologists were John Volkmann and Edwin B. Newman, who became the associate director; the administrative assistant was Geraldine Stone; Clifford T. Morgan, an instructor, was employed as liaison by the OSRD.

President Conant was not involved with the wartime Harvard NDRC-OSRD activities, and neither was Provost Paul Buck; the Psycho-Acoustic Laboratory was responsible directly to the treasurer of Harvard College, William Claflin. External support brought new institutional and scientific priorities. The 1941–1946 contract research included measurement of noise levels and their effects, intercom equipment in noisy aircraft, the control of sound in combat vehicles, cushioned earphones, insulation to take high frequencies out of aircraft engine sounds, sound amplifiers for possible tactical weapons, radar jamming devices, and an anechoic chamber to study the location, direction, and interference properties of sound. Stevens directed contract research that culminated in a joint publication with Beranek's Electro-Acoustic Laboratory, *Principles of Sound Control in Airplanes*.

Postwar Institutionalization of Psychology. Immediately after the war, Harvard psychologists foresaw the possible decline in their external funding. Stevens took the lead in counteracting this situation by writing two popular articles on his wartime research and its peacetime applications, "Machines Cannot Fight Alone" and "The Science of Noise," in 1946. He encouraged his assistants to rewrite their bimonthly technical reports into scientific articles. By this academic-political strategy, they justified the peacetime value of sensory research. Students and their instructors came to appreciate "psychometric functions" for absolute and differential thresholds along a wide spectrum of sound and light stimuli (eight or nine logarithmic units). The extension of the range of sensory stimuli, which electronics had made possible, set the stage for Stevens' revision of sensory scaling a few years later.

For his contributions to the department and the profession, Stevens was promoted to associate professor in 1944 and full professor in 1946. Gordon Allport objected, largely because of Stevens' lack of interest in undergraduate instruction.

Meanwhile, the rift between the experimental psychologists and the sociologists had reached an impasse, which Buck resolved by creating a department of social relations. Stevens' directorship of the Psycho-Acoustic Laboratory earned him and Boring a consolation prize from the administration. The Memorial Hall basement was renovated into a laboratory, library, and offices. Boring, the only person left in psychology of higher rank than Stevens, became chairman, and Beebe-Center returned to teach. Stevens directed the psychology laboratory (1949–1962), and consistently opposed cooperative teaching arrangements with the social relations group. This made difficulties for Edwin Newman, who became associate director of the laboratory and department chairman, managing the budget and teaching duties until the 1960's. Two postdoctoral researchers, J. C. R. Licklider and George A. Miller, were hired part-time. However, the department of psychology lost ground at the undergraduate level to social relations, which became one of the most popular areas of concentration on campus.

Stevens, who avoided teaching as much as possible, guided graduate student research as long as it interested him. His most effective teaching was in the laboratory or discussing a manuscript with a student or colleague. After the war, many of the postdoctoral researchers in psychoacoustics stayed on at Harvard in appointments in psychology. Stevens undertook a five-year editorial project, the *Handbook of Experimental Psychology* (1951). His eloquent introductory chapter, "Mathematics, Measurement, and Psychophysics," gave further visibility to a psychology based on operations and invariant relationships.

In 1948 Stevens bought a farmhouse in Silver Lake, New Hampshire, and renovated it with weekend assistance from his laboratory "family." He took up skiing and wrote on the dynamics of skis and skiing.

Stevens remained active in national scientific affairs after the war. He was elected to the National Academy of Sciences in 1946. He consulted in Washington for the Research and Development Board (1946–1957). He was honored by the Society of Experimental Psychologists, and was elected to the American Philosophical Society and the American Physiological Society. Stevens was a member of the Council of the Acoustical Society from 1946 to 1949. During the period 1949–1952 he was chairman of the National Research Council Division of Anthropology and Psychology. In 1960 he received the Distinguished Scientific Contribution Award of the American Psychological Association, and in 1972 he was the first recipient of the Rayleigh Gold Medal of the British Acoustical Society.

Promoting and Defending a Program of Research. In 1953 Stevens returned to the laboratory, overcoming a feeling of having "grown rusty from directing others." He was motivated by disagreement with Wendell R. Garner, who had shown that intervals produced by equisection (dividing a sensation into x equal parts) differ from ratios produced by fractionation (adjusting a stimulus to appear a fraction x as strong as a standard stimulus). In contrast with Garner's method, which constrained the subject by end points, Stevens simply allowed the subjects to assign numbers proportionate to the "subjective magnitude" of stimulus intensities. This yielded a linear relation of sensation to stimulus intensity on a log-log plot.

Soon Stevens announced "a new psychophysical law" (1957), which stated that sensation intensity increases with some expanding stimulus intensity. In other words, equal stimulus ratios produce equal sensation ratios. This law was the power function

$$\psi = k\phi^n,$$

where ψ is the sensation, ϕ is the stimulus, n is the exponent, and k is a constant. The exponent varied with the particular sensory modality, and also within a modality for different stimulus conditions, such as adaptation, inhibition, size, and duration of stimuli. This "new psychophysics" elicited controversy over method, data, and theory.

Critics questioned the validity of a method that required subjects simply to affix a number to a stimulus. They called for "convergent operations." Stevens answered by distinguishing between two kinds of sensory continua: prothetic continua, which measure "how much" (loudness, duration, apparent length, numerousness, and sensory intensity in general), and metathetic continua, which measure "what kind" (pitch, visual inclination, proportion, and sensory quality in general). Moreover, Stevens distinguished three kinds of scales—discriminability (poikilitic), category, and magnitude—that are linearly related on metathetic continua and nonlinearly related on prothetic continua.

Meanwhile, Joseph C. Stevens (no relation) performed direct matches between loudness and brightness in his dissertation under Stanley Stevens in 1957. Using Joseph Stevens' data, Stanley Stevens published "cross-modality matches" of seven prothetic continua to force of handgrip in 1959. In this work his prediction that the resulting exponents were a product of two separate modality exponents was borne out empirically.

In 1962 Stevens became professor of psychophysics and renamed his laboratory the Laboratory of Psychophysics. On 11 April 1963, he and Geraldine Stone, his administrative assistant, were married. (His first wife, Maxine, had died in October 1956.) Colleagues esteemed Geraldine (known as Didi) for the personal role she had played in the psychology department since 1940.

Reception and Further Developments. Progress in theory and experimental methods in psychophysics has continued to add to our knowledge of the sensory processes. Mathematical psychologists such as Clyde Coombs and David Krantz have axiomatized Stevens' psychophysical theories. Norman Anderson argues that the premise of functional measurement theory is that subjects do not scale sensation linearly; judgments of intensity and similarity undergo linear transformations. Hence scales must be examined simultaneously and rules for concatenating them devised. In particular, according to Lawrence Marks, ratio-scaling procedures must be distinguished from interval-scaling procedures, since they usually yield different scales of sensation. Going beyond Stevens' exclusive adherence to psychophysical relations between psychological and physical quantities, today's "new psychophysics" accepts psychosensory re-

lations between psychological attributes of sensation, as well as sensory-physical relations among physical dimensions alone. In a sense the search for the "unity of science" has thereby taken on the new goal of "unity of the senses."

Many alternatives to psychophysical scaling have grown out of critiques of Stevens' program. Signal detection methods brought probabilistic choice theory in the 1960's (see the writings of C. H. Graham, R. D. Luce, B. S. Rosner, F. Attneave, and Patrick Suppes). The nature of sensation also became a theoretical issue. Roger N. Shepard maintained that what Stevens had really shown was that equal ratios of physical magnitude are psychologically equivalent. David H. Krantz, in turn, proposed that in magnitude estimation the subject's judgments are mediated not by absolute values of sensations but by perceived relations between sensations. Behavioral psychologists such as G. E. Zuriff and William C. Stebbins have introduced the theoretical framework of "stimulus control" to deal with the issue of the subjectivity of sensation.

Despite the theoretical controversy surrounding Stevens' power law and magnitude estimation technique, his scaling methods have been fruitfully applied in sociology, criminology, and political science. Ratio scales of various nonmetric stimuli have demonstrated the applicability of scaling to, for example, degree of liberalism, social status, perception of national power, and seriousness of offenses. Stevens' approach to psychophysics thus seems certain to remain in the social and behavioral sciences. His related ambition to create a unity of systems of measurement may be seen as a qualified success.

BIBLIOGRAPHY

I. ORIGINAL WORKS. A complete bibliography of Stevens' works would be far too long. See those in Stevens' *Psychophysics*, 304–306; and in Moskowitz, Scharf, and Stevens, 447–455.

His classic works include "The Attributes of Tones," in *Proceedings of the National Academy of Sciences*, **20** (1934), 457–459; *Hearing: Its Psychology and Physiology* (New York, 1938), with Hallowell Davis; "Theory of the Neural Quantum in the Discrimination of Loudness and Pitch," in *American Journal of Psychology*, **54** (1941), 315–335; "On the Theory of Scales of Measurement," in *Science*, **103** (1946), 677–680; and "The Surprising Simplicity of Sensory Metrics," in *American Psychologist*, **17** (1962), 29–39, repr. in William S. Cain and Lawrence E. Marks, eds., *Stimulus and Sensation* (Boston, 1971).

On the philosophy of science Stevens wrote "The Operational Basis of Psychology," in *American Journal of Psychology*, **47** (1935), 323–330; "The Operational Definition of Psychological Concepts,'' in *Psychological Review*, **42** (1935), 517–527; ''Psychology: The Propaedeutic Science,'' in *Philosophy of Science*, **3** (1936), 90–103; and ''Psychology and the Science of Science,'' in *Psychological Bulletin*, **36** (1939), 221–263.

Stevens' works on measurement include ''On the Problem of Scales for the Measurement of Psychological Magnitudes,'' in *The Journal of United Science (Erkenntnis)*, **9** (1939), 94–99; ''Mathematics, Measurement, and Psychophysics,'' in S. S. Stevens, ed., *Handbook of Experimental Psychology* (New York, 1951), 1–49; ''The Quantification of Sensation,'' in *Daedalus*, **88** (1959), 606–621; and ''The Psychophysics of Sensory Function,'' in W. A. Rosenblith, ed., *Sensory Communication* (Cambridge, Mass., 1961).

Popular articles are 'Machines Cannot Fight Alone,'' in *American Scientist*, **34** (1946), 389–400; ''The Science of Noise,'' in *Atlantic Monthly*, **178**, no. 1 (1946), 96; ''The New Harvard Psychological Laboratories,'' in *American Psychologist*, **2** (1947), 239–243, with E. G. Boring; ''The NAS-NCR and Psychology,'' *ibid.*, **7** (1952), 119–124; and ''The Market for Miracles: Review of C. E. M. Hansel, *ESP: A Scientific Evaluation*,'' in *Contemporary Psychology*, **12** (1967), 1–3.

The ''new psychophysics'' is treated in ''The Direct Estimation of Sensory Magnitudes—Loudness,'' in *American Journal of Psychology*, **69** (1956), 1–25; ''On the Psychophysical Law,'' in *Psychological Review*, **64** (1957), 153–181; ''To Honor Fechner and Repeal His Law,'' in *Science*, **133** (1961), 80–86; ''Matching Functions Between Loudness and Ten Other Continua,'' in *Perception and Psychophysics*, **1** (1966), 5–8; ''Quantifying the Sensory Experience,'' in P. Feyerabend and G. Maxwell, eds., *Mind, Matter, and Method* (Minneapolis, 1966); and *Psychophysics: Introduction to Its Perceptual, Neural, and Social Prospects*, Geraldine Stevens, ed. (New York, 1975).

Autobiographical writings are ''Note for a Life Story,'' in Howard Moskowitz, Bertram Scharf, and Joseph C. Stevens, eds., *Sensation and Measurement: Papers in Honor of S. S. Stevens* (Dordrecht and Boston, 1974), 423–446; and ''S. S. Stevens,'' in G. Lindzey, ed., *History of Psychology in Autobiography*, VI (Englewood Cliffs, N.J., 1974).

The Harvard University Archives houses Stevens' personal and professional correspondence and other papers (eleven linear feet, about 1931–1973), records of the Psycho-Acoustic Laboratory (twelve linear feet, 1940–1972), and some unprocessed records of the laboratory from the war period. Additional wartime laboratory records are at the U.S. National Archives' Federal Records Center, Waltham, Mass. Material quoted in text has the call number Stevens' Papers, Harvard Archives, HUG (FP) 2.10, Correspondence and Related Documents.

II. SECONDARY LITERATURE. Biographical works include Hallowell Davis, ''S. Smith Stevens, 1906–1973,'' in *Journal of the Acoustical Society of America*, **53** (1973), 1190–1192; R. J. W. Mansfield, ''Stanley Smith Stevens,''

in *Journal of the Optical Society of America*, **63** (1973), 1022; George A. Miller, ''Stanley Smith Stevens,'' in *Biographical Memoirs, National Academy of Sciences*, **47** (1975), 425–459; and Joseph C. Stevens, ''Obituary: Professor S. S. Stevens, 1906–1973,'' in *Vision Research*, **14** (1974), 3–5.

For institutional history, see Gordon W. Allport and E. G. Boring, ''Psychology and Social Relations at Harvard University,'' in *American Psychologist*, **1** (1946), 119–122; James Phinney Baxter III, *Scientists Against Time* (Boston, 1946; repr. Cambridge, Mass., 1968); D. W. Fiske, ''Naval Aviation Psychology. III. The Special Services Group,'' in *American Psychologist*, **1** (1946), 544–548, and ''Naval Aviation Psychology. IV. The Central Research Groups,'' *ibid.*, **2** (1947), 67–72; W. S. Hunter, ''Psychology in the War,'' *ibid.*, **1** (1946), 479–492; Donald Napoli, *The Architects of Adjustment* (Port Washington, N.Y., 1981); and John M. O'Donnell, ''The Crisis of Experimentalism in the 1920s,'' in *American Psychologist*, **34** (1979), 289–295.

Intellectual history is covered in Edwin G. Boring, *A History of Experimental Psychology* (New York, 1929; 2nd ed., 1950); Kurt Danziger, ''The Positivist Repudiation of Wundt,'' in *Journal of the History of Behavioral Science*, **15** (1979), 205–230, and ''The History of Introspection Reconsidered,'' *ibid.*, **16** (1980), 241–262; Gail A. Hornstein, ''Quantifying Psychological Phenomena: Debates, Dilemmas, and Implications,'' in J. Morawski, ed., *The Rise of Experimentation in American Psychology* (New Haven, 1988), 1–34; Edwin B. Newman, ''On the Origin of 'Scales of Measurement,' '' in Howard Moskowitz, Bertram Scharf, and Joseph C. Stevens, eds., *Sensation and Measurement: Papers in Honor of S. S. Stevens* (Dordrecht and Boston, 1974), 137–145; and Laurence D. Smith, *Behaviorism and Logical Positivism: A Reassessment of the Alliance* (Stanford, Calif., 1986).

Scientific critiques are Norman H. Anderson, ''Functional Measurement and Psychophysical Judgment,'' in *Psychological Review*, **77** (1970), 153–170, and ''Crosstask Validation of Functional Measurement,'' in *Perception and Psychophysics*, **12** (1972), 389–395; N. R. Campbell, ''Symposium: Measurement and Its Importance for Philosophy,'' in *Proceedings of the Aristotelian Society*, supp. **17** (1938), 121–142; Clyde H. Coombs, *Psychology and Mathematics* (Ann Arbor, Mich., 1983); Wendell R. Garner, Harold W. Hake, and Charles W. Eriksen, ''Operationism and the Concept of Perception,'' in *Psychological Review*, **63** (1956), 149–159; Sigmund Koch, ed., *Psychology: A Study of a Science* (New York, 1959), chapters by B. Rosner, C. H. Graham and P. Ratoosh, and F. Attneave; David H. Krantz, ''A Theory of Magnitude Estimation and Cross-Modality Matching,'' in *Journal of Mathematical Psychology*, **9** (1972), 168–199; R. Duncan Luce, ''What Sort of Measurement Is Psychophysical Measurement?'' in *American Psychologist*, **27** (1972), 96–106; Lawrence E. Marks, ''On Scales of Sensation: Prolegomena to Any Future Psychophysics That Will Be Able to Come Forth as Science,'' in *Perception and Psychophysics, **16** (1974), 358–376, *Sensory Processes: The New Psychophysics* (New York, 1974), and "A Theory of Loudness and Loudness Judgments," in *Psychological Review*, **86** (1979), 256–285; Roger N. Shepard, "Psychological Relations and Psychophysical Scales: On the Status of 'Direct' Psychophysical Measurement," in *Journal of Mathematical Psychology*, **24** (1981), 21–57; William C. Stebbins, *Animal Psychophysics: The Design and Conduct of Sensory Experiments* (New York, 1970); Patrick Suppes and Joseph L. Zinnes, "Basic Measurement Theory," in R. Duncan Luce *et al.*, eds., *Handbook of Mathematical Psychology* (New York, 1963); and Richard M. Warren and Roslyn P. Warren, "A Critique of S. S. Stevens," in *Perceptual and Motor Skills*, **16** (1963), 797–810.

Philosophical critiques are Gustav Bergmann and Kenneth W. Spence, "The Logic of Psychophysical Measurement," in *Psychological Review*, **51** (1944), 1–24, repr. in Herbert Feigl and May Brodbeck, eds., *Readings in the Philosophy of Science* (New York, 1953); C. Wade Savage, *The Measurement of Sensation* (Berkeley, 1970); and G. E. Zuriff, "A Behavioral Interpretation of Psychophysical Scaling," in *Behaviorism*, **1** (1972), 118–133.

WILLIAM R. WOODWARD

STILLWELL, FRANK LESLIE (*b*. Hawthorn, near Melbourne, Australia, 27 June 1888; *d*. Melbourne, 8 February 1963), *geology*.

The seventh of eight children and youngest son of Alfred Stillwell and Mary Eliza Townsend, Stillwell came of Huguenot stock settled in Australia since 1855. Both his father and paternal grandfather were printers. Although troubled by poor health as a youth, Stillwell did well at school and entered the University of Melbourne with an exhibition in 1907 to study science and mining engineering. He graduated B.Sc. in 1911 with first-class honors in geology, advanced to M.Sc. in 1913, and in 1916 gained the D.Sc. Stillwell never married. He devoted his life largely to geological research and held no continuing appointment until he was almost forty years of age.

In 1911 Stillwell joined the Australasian Antarctic Expedition (1911–1914) led by Sir Douglas Mawson. He spent some twelve months as a geologist in Adelie Land with responsibility for a sledging party that surveyed sixty miles of coast east of Cape Denison. Relieved early in 1913, he returned to Melbourne with collections for his doctoral study. Stillwell's report on Adelie Land, published in 1918, set out what is arguably his most original contribution to geological thought, the concept of metamorphic differentiation as the means whereby during metamorphism contrasted materials arise from an initially homogeneous parent. At the time, however, his rather individual treatment of metamorphic phenomena won little support among petrologists. Eskola's critical essay of 1932, "On the Principles of Metamorphic Differentiation" (*Bulletin de la Commission Géologique de Finlande*, **16** [1932], 68–77), did not even mention Stillwell. Later writers have made some amends.

Stillwell enlisted in 1916 but was withdrawn from the army to assist the Australian Commonwealth Advisory Council of Science and Industry in a study of auriferous quartz reefs at Bendigo, Victoria. These reefs, among them the famous "saddle reefs," were then regarded as fissure fillings. Stillwell found that many had formed by replacement in favored sites and in three bulletins (1917–1919) presented detailed evidence and a revised strategy for exploration. From 1919 to 1921 Stillwell was attached to a group led by E. C. Andrews of the Geological Survey of New South Wales examining the silver-lead-zinc mining field of Broken Hill. His controversial report on the petrology of the lode and its environs appeared in Andrews' memoir of 1922.

After brief employment as a company geologist at Bendigo, Stillwell set out in 1922, at his own expense, on a tour of mining fields and universities in South Africa, Europe, and North America. He was about to go oil-prospecting in New Guinea late in 1923 when the offer of a research fellowship at the University of Melbourne gave him a chance to introduce to Australia the techniques for reflected-light microscopy of opaque minerals acquired during his travels. His discovery, for instance, that much of the silver in Broken Hill galena occurs in minute inclusions of dyscrasite belongs to the period of the 1924 fellowship. Such work showed the relevance of mineragraphic study to the Australian mineral industry and established Stillwell's reputation as both pioneer and leader in the field.

In 1927 the newly formed Council of Scientific and Industrial Research (CSIR, now CSIRO) appointed Stillwell its research petrologist but soon agreed to his secondment through 1928 to the government of Western Australia for a comprehensive study of the Kalgoorlie gold field, then in decline. Apart from its scientific value, Stillwell's work, published in 1929, led to the resurgence of exploration and mining at Kalgoorlie during the 1930's. His notable study of Kalgoorlie telluride minerals followed in 1931.

On his return to Melbourne in 1929 Stillwell assumed responsibility for the CSIR Mineragraphic Investigations Section; he remained in charge until his official retirement in June 1953. Stillwell's laboratory, housed with the geology department of

Melbourne University, where from time to time he gave courses in his fields of expertise, became a scientific service center for the Australian mineral industry. Few Australian ore deposits escaped study by Stillwell or his staff, most prominent among them being A. B. Edwards, his successor as officer-in-charge. The 540 reports issued by the section in Stillwell's time are witness to their activity.

In retirement Stillwell kept busy. He worked on at the laboratory and for some years served as a consultant to industry at Broken Hill, the subject in 1959 of his last major paper. By then syngenetic models of ore genesis were gaining favor there but Stillwell staunchly defended his epigenetic view. He was identified with the conservatives of science, of the sort who long ago thought his ideas radical. Yet throughout Stillwell remained his own man, ready to trust his observations and judgment. Many thought him diffident but no one suggested Stillwell lacked the courage of his convictions.

Stillwell received many awards and honors for his contributions to mineral science and the mining industry. In 1952 he became a correspondent of the Geological Society of America. He was made an officer of the Order of the British Empire in 1954, the year the Australian Academy of Science held its first elections and admitted him a fellow. The Australasian Institute of Mining and Metallurgy in 1958 marked his seventieth birthday by publishing the F. L. Stillwell Anniversary Volume of papers by colleagues and friends. The Stillwell Award of the Geological Society of Australia now commemorates one who was not only an active supporter of that and other societies but also their generous benefactor. Stillwell Island in Antarctica and the rare-earth borosilicate mineral stillwellite are named after him.

BIBLIOGRAPHY

Stillwell's published works are listed in the memorials by G. Baker in *Geological Society of America: Bulletin*, **75** (1964), P45–P51, and by E. S. Hills in *Records of the Australian Academy of Science*, **1** (1966), 58–66. Sir Douglas Mawson, *The Home of the Blizzard*, 2 vols. (London, 1915), provides more information about Stillwell's role in Antarctica. Unpublished letters from C. E. Tilley to W. R. Browne, in the writer's possession, have also been used in preparing this essay.

T. G. VALLANCE

STONER, EDMUND CLIFTON (*b.* East Molesey, Surrey, England, 2 October 1899; *d.* Leeds, England, 27 December 1968), *theoretical physics.*

Edmund Stoner's early years were marked by financial insecurity, since his father, Arthur Hallett Stoner, was a cricketer and later a cricket coach—a calling that assured neither regular nor long-term employment. Stoner's mother, Mary Ann Fleet, encouraged her only child in his studies and was also the principal source of his interest in music. Yet early financial problems were not the only difficulties facing Stoner: throughout his adult life, and particularly during his student days, he suffered from diabetes and related ailments. Despite these disabilities his strong will enabled him to pursue an active career in teaching and research and also to engage in a range of administrative and committee work. He was elected to the Royal Society in 1937 on the strength of his research contributions to atomic theory, the theory of magnetism, and the theory of dense stars. Stoner had mild socialist leanings and was unattached to any religious denomination. He married Jean Heather Crawford in 1951; they had no children.

After attending Bolton Grammar School, Stoner entered Emmanuel College, Cambridge, in 1918 to study for the natural sciences tripos, and three years later he accepted a research studentship at the Cavendish Laboratory under Ernest Rutherford's supervision. Although the Cavendish was a major center for experimental research and the 1920's a particularly exciting period in its history, Stoner found experimental research uncongenial and his progress frustratingly slow. Moreover, his project was interrupted by a period in the hospital, and he was also disconcerted by Rutherford's bullying manner. Partly in reaction to this inimical situation, he took an increasing interest in developments in theoretical physics, reading extensively in atomic physics and participating actively in the Kapitza Club, a select group that met regularly to discuss the latest innovations in theoretical physics. The resolution of his financial and career problems lay in turning from experimental to theoretical physics, and he achieved this transformation dramatically in 1924 when he proposed his hypothesis of the distribution of electrons in the atom. In the same year he secured a lectureship at Leeds University, where he stayed for the rest of his career, becoming professor of theoretical physics in 1939.

The problem in physics that confronted Stoner in 1924 emerged from Niels Bohr's theory of the atom, in which the elliptical orbits of electrons were described by two quantum numbers, n (indicating the length of the ellipse's major axis) and k (indicating its eccentricity), such that k could have any of the values 1, 2, . . . , n. In the early 1920's there was much disagreement about the detailed distribution of electrons and about the physical meaning of the inner quantum number j, which Sommerfeld introduced to classify multiplet spectra ($j = k - 1$, $k - 2$, $-k + 2$, $-k + 1$). Whereas Bohr had contented himself with guessing at the number of electrons in an atom having n_k orbits, Stoner tried to discriminate down to n_{k_j} levels, a task made particularly difficult by the uncertain significance of j. Stoner noticed that if the number of n_{k_j} electrons is $2j$, the number of electrons associated with a given n is $2\Sigma_1^n (2k - 1) = 2n^2$, or the length of the nth period in the table of the elements. Stoner supported this distribution by offering evidence drawn from X-ray observations and from chemical, optical, and magnetic experiments.

The publication of his paper (*Philosophical Magazine*, **48** [1924], 719–736) brought Stoner rapid recognition. His theory, however, was subsequently overshadowed by the exclusion principle of Wolfgang Pauli, who, exploiting Stoner's insight and applying it to individual electrons, transformed it into a general and powerful analytic tool.

While his paper on electron distribution represents Stoner's earliest and most spectacular success, he also worked extensively in several other problem areas. Soon after arriving in Leeds, he directed his research principally to the problem of applying quantum-theoretical ideas to explain the magnetic phenomena associated with matter, and was thereby able to adduce these explanations as further, impressive confirmations of quantum theory. Stoner played an important role in opening up this research field, with some three dozen of his papers specifically devoted to the theories of diamagnetism and paramagnetism in ionic salts and ferromagnetism in metals. Two of these papers deserve particular mention. In 1938 Stoner obtained, with Fermi-Dirac statistics based on the exclusion principle, the intrinsic magnetic properties of metals in which the electrons are in an unfilled energy band of standard form (*Proceedings of the Royal Society of London*, ser. A, **165** [1938], 372–414). Ten years later, in a paper jointly authored by E. P. Wohlfarth, he suggested that the hysteretic properties of ferromagnetics of high coercivity could be accounted for by the existence of magnetically anisotropic single domain "particles" within their matrix (*Philosophical Transactions of the Royal Society of London*, ser. A, **240** [1948], 599–642). Magnetism was also the subject of two of Stoner's books, *Magnetism and Atomic Structure* (London, 1926) and *Magnetism and Matter* (London, 1934), the latter reflecting the new quantum mechanics and theory of electron spin.

He also published a shorter introductory text, *Magnetism* (1st ed., London, 1930; 4th ed., London, 1948), in the Methuen monograph series.

Among Stoner's other research interests were the theory of specific heats and astrophysics, especially the theory of dense stars. In this and other areas, he made extensive and insightful use of Fermi-Dirac statistics. Stoner's contributions to theoretical physics are all the more impressive when it is remembered that he received little formal training in mathematical techniques. Although his published work reflects his primary research interest in theoretical physics, he believed that theoretical investigations should be combined with a close acquaintance with experimental procedures and that research should not be divorced from teaching.

BIBLIOGRAPHY

The only extensive biography of Stoner is L. F. Bates, "Edmund Clifton Stoner, 1899–1968," in *Biographical Memoirs of Fellows of the Royal Society*, **15** (1969), 201–237, which includes a bibliography of Stoner's publications. Stoner's papers are preserved in the Brotherton Library, University of Leeds, and have been cataloged by the Contemporary Scientific Archives Centre (CSAC no. 6/73); there is also a handlist (Brotherton no. 62) of additional material. Stoner's work on the distribution of electrons is discussed in J. L. Heilbron, "The Origins of the Exclusion Principle," in *Historical Studies in the Physical Sciences*, **13** (1983), 261–310.

GEOFFREY CANTOR

STRAKHOV, NIKOLAI MIKHAILOVICH (*b.* Bolkhov, Russia, 15 April 1900; *d.* Moscow, U.S.S.R., 13 July 1978), *lithology, sedimentology.*

Strakhov's father, Mikhail Vasilievich, taught at a primary school and was an accountant. His mother, Aleksandra Denisovna, a housewife, died in 1920 after a serious illness. The family then separated and settled in different cities.

Strakhov graduated with honors from the classical school in Bolkhov and in 1918 began to teach astronomy and geology at a secondary school. In 1923 he moved to Moscow and enrolled in the geological-geographical department of the Physical-Mathematical Faculty of Moscow University. He quickly distinguished himself by his talent for complex problems in geology. Soon he began to work under the guidance of Andrei Dmitrievich Arkhangelskii, studying recent Black Sea sediments. In 1928 he successfully defended his thesis on the geology and geochemistry of these sediments.

For the first seven years after graduation, Strakhov

lectured on the geology of the Soviet Union and on historical geology at the Moscow Institute of Geological Survey and the Institute of Geological Survey of Oil Fields. During these years he wrote the textbook *Zadachi i metody historicheskoy geologii* (Problems and Methods of Historical Geology, 1932), which included, together with educational materials, theoretical conclusions on general geology. This book contained the first formulation of the main principles of Strakhov's comparative lithological method. During the following years Strakhov developed these principles and established a number of laws of sedimentation.

In 1932 Strakhov and Arkhangelskii completed studies of the most recent Black Sea sediments. This work became the basis of their 1938 monograph in which they showed the distribution of three typical layers differing by age, lithological composition, and fossil remains. It was the first time that a scientific conclusion was reached about the direct dependence of composition and thickness of accumulated sediments on the relief of the drainage area.

In addition, Strakhov established that hydrogen sulfide contamination of relatively deep parts of the Black Sea favors preservation of organic matter on the sea floor.

The year 1937 was a turning point in Strakhov's life as a geologist. A serious swelling of the hip that led to nerve pressure made it difficult for him to walk, thus limiting his ability to participate in field expeditions. But this misfortune did not affect the depth of his investigations; indeed, it favored his formation as a theorist.

Strakhov's first theoretical work was an important generalization that enabled him to establish the distribution of iron ores of sedimentary origin. Strakhov found that from the Precambrian until the present there were six long and nine short epochs of intensive accumulation of sedimentary iron ores. Since he had discovered a general correlation between the peculiarities in the accumulations of iron, manganese, and aluminum, he concluded that these metals formed accumulations under similar conditions: a hot, humid climate. In addition, they were associated with the bases of transgressive deposits.

Strakhov also obtained significant results while studying the process of halogenesis. He established that the main paragenesis at the early stages of this process is later replaced by a dolomite paragenesis, and finally by a magnesite paragenesis. The significant conclusions of these investigations were presented by Strakhov in his doctoral dissertation in 1944.

In the following years Strakhov concentrated on determining general laws of sediment formation. He became convinced that the construction of lithological theory should be based on the study of recent sedimentation, on the comparative analysis of ancient sedimentary units, and on physicochemical experiments. He emphasized that only these three main areas of investigation, in combination with comparative lithology, can provide a means for the construction of a general theory of the sedimentary process.

Strakhov embarked on the complex problem of establishing laws governing lithogenesis by studying the peculiarities of recent sedimentation in continental seas and lake basins. He paid particular attention to the data obtained in studying bottom sediments of the Black Sea, the Aral Sea, and the Sea of Japan, as well as Lakes Baikal, Balkhash, and Issyk-Kul. These studies supplied hitherto unknown data and gave him the opportunity to compare the physicochemical peculiarities of recent sedimentation with sedimentary processes in the basins of the geological past. He was the first geologist to establish the decisive role of diagenesis as a mineral-forming process and to reveal the physicochemical nature of this phenomenon. He clearly proved that diagenetic transformation is a natural reaction of physicochemical imbalance and that the most important factor controlling this process under conditions of marine spillway is the burial of organic matter.

Strakhov also studied the peculiarities of carbonate accumulation. He assigned a significant role in this process in fresh water to life processes of animals, plants, and bacteria. With an increase in salinity, however, the role of living forms in carbonate accumulation sharply decreases; and in basins with high salinity purely physicochemical factors play a leading role. The pattern of the distribution of carbonates on the continents and in the oceans compiled by Strakhov showed that their distribution and mineral composition are clearly controlled by climatic and tectonic factors, with the leading role played by the former.

Strakhov's next discovery, described in *Osnovy teorii litogeneza* (1960–1962; translated as *Principles of Lithogenesis* [1967–1970]), was quite unexpected. At that time the generally accepted opinion was that chemical reactions control the process of sedimentation. Strakhov convincingly showed, after years of research, that the behavior of chemical elements is governed by a complex physical-geographical interaction between drainage areas and sea basins. By this discovery he laid the foundation of a new science, the geochemistry of sedimentary rocks and ores.

Considering the peculiarities of sedimentation in recent basins and comparing them with the most ancient sedimentary deposits, Strakhov subdivided lithogenesis into four types: humid, arid, glacial, and volcanogenic-sedimentary. These types are typical not only for recent but also for all ancient deposits up to the uppermost parts of the Proterozoic. Maps of lithogenetic types have become a basis for locating ore deposits.

The study of rock composition within different lithofacial zones enabled Strakhov to determine their contents quantitatively and, among other things, to show that the endogenetic material in them does not exceed a quarter of all the sediments accumulated for the last 550–600 million years.

Strakhov further elaborated the principles determining the formation of sedimentary ores in different zones. By comparing the regularities in distribution of rocks as indicators of lithogenesis at different stratigraphic levels, he was able to show the peculiarities in the evolution of the earth's external geospheres. This helped to reveal the directions of changes in the composition of the atmosphere, hydrosphere, and biosphere from the Archean up to the Quaternary. Analyzing the development of the biosphere, Strakhov also identified chronological boundaries in the evolution of organic matter. He elaborated in detail the effect of organisms on the processes of sedimentary rock formation.

Among other important theoretical principles proposed in this work is Strakhov's teaching on the periodicity of sedimentary processes and its relationship to epochs of global marine transgressions and regressions. He showed that transgressions are accompanied by the formation of coarse clastic rocks as well as iron, manganese, phosphorites, and some others. Deposition of clays and of carbonate and siliceous rocks takes place in the epochs of stable development of the basin. On the other hand, the periods of regression are accompanied by the accumulation of halogen rocks, copper-bearing sandstones, and siderites.

In Strakhov's theory the formation of sedimentary rock is a multistage process in which mineral accumulations in the basin area depend not only on the stage of sedimentation but also on the stage of diagenesis and catagenesis. Strakhov also emphasized that sedimentation is a complex process that involves solutions, colloids, mechanical suspensions, and biological remains. He further argued that periodicity of sedimentary rock formations is directly related to changes in the continental area, as well as to the composition of the atmosphere, hydrosphere, and biosphere.

While in *Principles of Lithogenesis* Strakhov dealt with the continental areas and the seas surrounding them, in the last years of his life he concentrated on studying ocean sediments. For this purpose he selected the most recent deposits accumulated on the floor of the Pacific Ocean and used the method of lithological facies profiles. He constructed one profile (more than 11,000 kilometers [6,875 miles] long) from the Sangar Strait via the Wake Island Atoll and the Hawaiian Islands to the Gulf of California. The data from forty-eight holes drilled approximately along the profile were available. Since each hole penetrated to a depth of seven to eight meters (about twenty-one to twenty-five feet), the data contained considerable new and interesting information. In particular they showed that for the last 100,000 years the effect of volcanism on sedimentation in the Pacific Ocean has been relatively inconsiderable. Strakhov's studies also proved that the main geochemical process controlling sedimentation in oceans was a mechanical fractionation of both autochthonous and allochthonous suspensions. These conclusions became one of the main principles of the theory of oceanic lithogenesis.

At the same time Strakhov established that the four types of lithogenesis he had identified for continental areas were not found in the ocean. Oceanic sedimentation is a single type of lithogenesis encompassing separate sedimentary rocks of volcanic origin. Strakhov therefore concluded that the rocks and ores reflecting different ways of delivering material into the area of sedimentation occur on land, in swamps and lakes, in the coastal areas of continental and marginal seas, or on the continental margins of the oceans.

The greatest amount of sedimentary deposits directly indicating the climatic environment of sedimentation is concentrated either on continents or in a transitional zone between the continent and the ocean. Strakhov established that in the deep areas of continental seas (for instance, in the Caspian and Black seas), climatic control is almost absent. The nature of sedimentation in the ocean reflects a specific dependence both on the enormous mass of water and on the climate. His studies revealed that vertical movements of air masses, as well as the change in temperature along the meridian, do not practically affect the character of sedimentation. The decisive role is played by horizontal movements of the air, which create circulating currents and form areas of constant salinity in the surface layers of oceanic waters to depths of 200–250 meters (about 600–750 feet).

Strakhov concluded that the hydrodynamic regime

created by climate in the world ocean controls the distribution of almost all components of sediments on the ocean floor, forming all their different lithological and geochemical types. The role of climatic zonation in the oceans is relatively slight; changes in the moisture and temperature regime are reflected only in the fact that there is a more intensive accumulation of magnesium calcite, and specific organisms—for example reef-building corals in the tropics and subtropics—participate in the formation of sediments.

The studies of sediments from different latitudes showed some differences between high-latitude and low-latitude modifications in the floral species content. Strakhov's hydrodynamic concept of oceanic sedimentation further included a direct correlation with processes on the continents.

Strakhov published more than 200 scientific works, including fifteen monographs, some also published in English, French, and Japanese. He was a very gifted teacher, and many prominent Soviet geologists take pride in calling themselves his disciples. A large school of lithologists carrying on the development of his theoretical ideas and methods was formed. In 1946 the U.S.S.R. Academy of Sciences elected Strakhov a corresponding member, and in 1953 a full member. He retired in 1976 but continued his scientific activities until his death. His last scientific monograph was published posthumously.

BIBLIOGRAPHY

I. ORIGINAL WORKS. Strakhov's works are listed in *Problemy litologii i geokhimii* (see below), 17–26. "Poslednie stranitsi geologicheskoy istorii Chernogo moria," in *Priroda*, 1930, no. 11–12, 1089–1108; "Geologischeskaia istoriia Chernogo moria," in *Biulleten' Moskovskogo obshchestva ispytatelei prirody, otdel geologicheskii*, **10**, no. 1 (1932), 3–104, written with Andrei D. Arkhangelskii; "K voprosy o prichinakh i vremeni serovodorotsnogo zarazheniia Chernogo moria," in *Zemlevedenie*, **34**, no. 1–2 (1932), 79–91; *Zadachi i metody istoricheskoy geologii* (Moscow and Leningrad, 1932); *Geologicheskoe stroenie i istoriia razvitiia Chernogo moria* (Geological structure and history of the Black Sea; Moscow and Leningrad, 1938), written with A. D. Arkhangelskii; *Zhelezorudnye fatsii i ikh analogi v istorii Zemli* (Iron-bearing facies and analogues in the Earth's history; Moscow, 1947); *Osnovy istoricheskoi geologii*, 3rd ed., 2 pts. (Moscow, 1948), trans. by J. Kolodny and E. Rosenthal as *Principles of Historical Geology* (Jerusalem, 1962); *Izvestkovo-dolomitovye fatsii sovremennykh i drevnikh vodoemov* (Limestone-dolomite facies in modern and ancient aqueous basins; Moscow, 1951); *Obrazovanie osadkov v sovremennykh vodoemakh* (Formation of sediments in recent water basins;

Moscow, 1954); *Osnovy teorii litogeneza*, 3 vols. (Moscow, 1960–1962), trans. by J. Paul Fitzsimmons as *Principles of Lithogenesis*, S. I. Tomkeieff and J. E. Hemingway, eds., 3 vols. (New York, 1967–1970); *Tipy litogeneza i ikh evoliutsiia v istorii Zemli* (Types of lithogenesis and their evolution in the Earth's history; Moscow, 1963); *Geokhimiia osadochnogo margon-tsevorudnogo protessa* (The geochemistry of sedimentation of manganese ores; Moscow, 1968); *Razvitie litogeneticheskikh idei v Rossii i SSSR* (The development of lithogenetic ideas in Russia and the USSR; Moscow, 1971); *Problemy geokhimii sovremennogo okeanskogo litogeneza* (Problems of geochemistry of recent oceanic lithogenesis; Moscow, 1976); *Izbrannye trudy: Obshchie problemy geologii, litologii i geokhimii* (Selected works: General problems of geology, lithology, and geochemistry; Moscow, 1983).

Strakhov's manuscripts are at the U.S.S.R. Academy of Science.

II. SECONDARY LITERATURE. *Problemy litologii i geokhimii osadochnykh porod i rud: Sbornik statei k 75-letiiu akad. N. M. Strakhova* (Problems of lithology and geochemistry of sedimentary rocks and ores: Collection of articles published on the occasion of the seventy-fifth birthday of Acad. N. M. Strakhov; Moscow, 1975).

See also "Akademik Nikolay Mikhailovich Strakhov (geolog. k 70-letiiu so dnia rozhdeniia," in *Litologiia i polezniye iskopaemiye*, 1970, no. 1, 3–10, with portrait; V. N. Kholodov, "Vklad akademika N. M. Strakhova v razvitie geokhimii osadochnykh porod," *ibid.*, 1979, no. 4, 3–15; A. I. Osipova, "Strakhov, N. M., pedagog i organizator," *ibid.*, 156–159; D. G. Sapozhnikov, "Voprosy osadochnogo rudoobrazovaniia v trudakh N. M. Strakhova," *ibid.*, 16–28; and V. I. Smirnov, P. P. Timofeev, and V. N. Kholodov, "Nauchnaia deiatel'nost akademika N. M. Strakhova," in *Problemy litologii i geokhimii osadochnykh porod i rud* (Problems of lithology and geochemistry of sedimentary rocks and ores; Moscow, 1975), 1–16.

V. V. TIKHOMIROV

STRASSMANN, FRIEDRICH WILHELM (FRITZ)

(*b*. Boppard, Germany, 22 February 1902; *d*. Mainz, Federal Republic of Germany, 22 April 1980), *nuclear chemistry*.

Fritz Strassmann was the ninth and last child of Richard Strassmann, a court clerk, and of Julie Bernsmann. His father was transferred to Cologne in 1906, and a year later to Düsseldorf, where Fritz completed elementary school in three years (1908–1911) instead of the normal four. He went on to the municipal Oberrealschule (now Leibniz-Gymnasium). Shortly before he took his final examination (*Abitur*), his father died. Because all but one of his brothers and sisters had already left home, however, Strassmann was able to pursue his desire to study chemistry.

The industrial and economic crisis of postwar Germany offered discouraging professional prospects for a chemist, but Strassmann had been captivated by the subject in school, and had already carried out chemical experiments in a corner of his mother's kitchen. Inflation and the smallness of his mother's pension made it impossible for her to finance a university education, so Strassmann chose to study at the Technische Hochschule in Hanover, where he could live nearby with his brother Arthur. After matriculating in 1920, Fritz commuted about sixteen miles (twenty-five kilometers) daily by train for three years before he obtained a room in the home of a milkman near the Technische Hochschule in return for tutoring the milkman's son. He supported himself by giving private lessons and helping students prepare for their examinations.

After attending the chemical lectures of Wilhelm Biltz, Wilhelm Geilmann (a distinguished expert in analytical chemistry, whom he later appointed to a professorship at his institute in Mainz), Friedrich Quincke, Gustav Keppeler, and Hermann Braune, Strassmann received his diploma as a chemical engineer in 1924 and obtained his doctorate in physical chemistry under the supervision of Braune in 1929. His dissertation dealt with the solubility of iodine in gaseous carbonic acid. Strassmann had been prompted to take his doctorate in physical chemistry by the great unemployment in Germany; the chemical industry had let it be known that such training would provide the best chance for employment. To improve his chances further, Strassmann became a lecture assistant to Braune. Three months later he accepted Otto Hahn's offer of a partial scholarship granted by the Notgemeinschaft der Deutschen Wissenschaft to the Kaiser Wilhelm Institute for Chemistry at Berlin. Strassmann was motivated by the possibility of learning radiochemistry, which had been introduced into Germany by Hahn. It was the main field of research at the Berlin institute, of which Hahn had become acting director in 1926 and director in 1929. The breadth of Strassmann's education and training, including practical applications, his knowledge, and above all his skill at chemical analysis, caused Hahn to offer him the scholarship—and twice to submit an application for renewal to the Notgemeinschaft.

When his scholarship expired in September 1932, Strassmann had to support himself again. But he was allowed to continue his research work on "Hahn's emanation method" (which Strassmann modified from the point of physical chemistry) in Hahn's private laboratory, without pay but also without the tuition that research students normally had to pay to the institute. In 1934 Lise Meitner, the head of the physics department of Hahn's institute, persuaded him to grant Strassmann 50 marks per month from a private fund he had at his disposal for special contingencies. After Hitler's seizure of power and the economic recovery following it, Strassmann refused the lucrative posts offered to him by the chemical industry because entering a firm would have required him to join the Nazi party or a Nazi organization—a step he consistently resisted until the collapse of the German Reich in 1945. This stand also prevented his *Habilitation*. As early as the fall of 1933 he withdrew from the German Chemical Society, then the professional organization of German chemists, because it had dropped its Jewish members. During the spring of 1943 he and his wife hid a Jewish woman for two months in their apartment, running—in consequence of the frequent bombings—the risk of disclosure, which would have cost them their lives.

After joining the special working team of Meitner and Hahn, Strassmann was employed as assistant as of January 1935 (at half pay for the first years); but the political situation forced him to remain isolated and dependent on Hahn, which prevented him from developing his own field of research, as the other members of the institute did.

Thus it was the political situation with its social consequences, on the one hand, and the liberal political attitude of Hahn as the head of the institute, on the other (on account of which Meitner, whose parents were Jewish, could remain at the institute after 1933 and Strassmann could stay and be employed there after 1935), that made possible the formation of a highly effective interdisciplinary team of these three scientists: the organic and radiochemist Hahn, the theoretical physicist Meitner, and the analytical and physical chemist Strassmann.

On 20 July 1937, Strassmann married the chemist Maria Heckter, to whom he had once given private lessons in Hannover. They had one son, Martin. Strassmann, a self-taught violinist, and Heckter had also been members of a group of young musicians in Hanover, as was a mutual friend, Irmgard Hartmann. (Maria Heckter died of cancer in 1956. Three years later, Strassmann and Irmgard Hartmann were married.)

His studies on Hahn's emanation method had already earned Strassmann a reputation outside the institute, and his knowledge and skill at chemical analysis (for which he often was consulted by Hahn and the members of the institute) made him the essential third man to join the Hahn-Meitner team when Meitner persuaded Hahn, in the autumn of

1934,[1] to embark on the joint investigation of the alleged "transuranics," which Enrico Fermi and his collaborators had found by bombarding uranium with slow (so-called thermal) neutrons. In the following years Strassmann was the only one of the three who was able to concentrate exclusively upon their common experimental investigations. It was only after Meitner's emigration to Sweden in mid July 1938 that this teamwork led to the discovery of the fission of uranium nuclei by chemical analysis of the products of neutron irradiation of uranium (and thorium) carried out by Strassmann. But Meitner had been the initiator of these joint investigations; she was the "theoretical head" of the team—as Strassmann characterized her—who kept in touch by letter after leaving Berlin, and she was the one who (together with her nephew Otto Robert Frisch) gave the first and correct theoretical explanation of fission. Nevertheless, Meitner's absence apparently enabled Strassmann to pursue the approach, based on an investigation he had carried out with her, that led to the discovery.

When she became acquainted with Fermi's transuranic elements in the autumn of 1934, Meitner wanted to make use of the experience she had acquired with Hahn in identifying radioactive substances between 1907 and the early 1920's, because Ida Noddack had advanced general objections against Fermi's chemical precipitations.[2] From the physical point of view and in conformity with the displacement laws of Ernest Rutherford (or, rather, of Frederick Soddy and Kasimir Fajans), according to which the atomic decay of an alpha-emitting radioactive isotope (such as uranium 92) leads to a daughter isotope (such as thorium 90) whose place in the periodic table is two positions below that of the parent (that is, the neutron-bombarded element), while the daughter of a beta-emitting isotope (such as proactinium 91) takes the place of the element next to the place of the parent (thorium 90), it had been obvious that Fermi's beta-emitting uranium produced by neutron irradiation led to elements beyond uranium. And because the actinides were still unknown, Strassmann's more specific operations chemically corroborated ekarhenium, ekaosmium, and so on, within the decay products of irradiated uranium, while the measurements of the half-life periods led to the certainty that the three beta-ray emitters discovered by Fermi's group produce three isomeric series of these transuranics.

The results, which were reproduced and accepted around the world, were published in several papers between 1935 and 1938. At the end of their second paper, Hahn and Meitner wrote: "Finally we would like to thank cordially . . . Dr. F. Strassmann for his exceptionally useful collaboration concerning chemical separation."[3] From the third paper on, however, Strassmann's name appeared as coauthor. Although he had taken an active and increasingly independent role in the experimentation from the beginning of the joint research, he was now acknowledged as an equal collaborator. Being the youngest, his name was mentioned last in all these papers (and in all subsequent papers) but one.

In this sole case,[4] Hahn (still the head of the institute) is listed last, indicating that he had not directly taken part in the investigations published in the paper. The paper concerned the results of experiments carried out by Strassmann since mid 1937 by order of Meitner, resuming investigations of the products of neutron-irradiated thorium published in mid 1935.[5] At that time they had assumed two decay series: one should have been induced by fast neutrons and have led after alpha decay to an isotope of radium that as a beta emitter transmuted into beta-emitting actinium and thence again into an isotope of thorium; the second series, induced by slow neutrons, should have begun with a new beta-emitting isotope of thorium produced by neutron capture. The new investigations incorporated the experience acquired with the alleged isomeric series of the transuranics. Chemical separations and measurements of the beta radiation led to the conclusion that fast neutrons had produced isomeric series in the case of thorium. Three such isotopes of radium and of actinium seemed to be proved. To separate these isotopes, Strassmann had used barium and lanthanum as the carriers homologous to radium and actinium.

These isomeric isotopes therefore seemed to be confirmed, particularly when H. Braun, Peter Preiswerk, and Paul H. Scherrer published a brief note alleging that they had detected alpha rays after neutron irradiation of thorium.[6] However, an assistant of Meitner's, assigned to demonstrate such rays, did not succeed. Only after the discovery of uranium fission could Hahn and Strassmann show that the alleged isotopes of radium and actinium had indeed been the lower homologues barium and lanthanum, produced by a splitting of the thorium nuclei in which alpha rays did not appear.

The discovery of uranium fission took place in connection with the checking of the results of Irène Joliot-Curie and Pavel Savič (Paul Savitch), who in mid 1937 had reported finding a decay product of neutron-irradiated uranium with a 3.5-hour half-life that apparently had escaped the notice of the Berlin team and did not fit into the previous isomeric series.

Joliot-Curie and Savič supposed the substance to be an isotope of thorium. But on Meitner's request, Strassmann had searched as early as 1935, without success, for such a thorium isotope within the decay products of irradiated uranium. Even though he repeated that examination with new and more precise operations, he still could not find thorium in the filtrates. Meitner communicated this negative result by letter to Joliot-Curie and Savič. Thereupon they proposed that the substance was an actinium isotope—which seemed to Meitner, after the refutation of thorium, theoretically most improbable. Thereupon she lost all interest in further investigations of this substance, which was afterward called *curiosum* in Berlin.

Joliot-Curie and Savič published a further note in mid October 1938, in which the substance now seemed to be confirmed as actinium. They claimed it was similar to the lanthanum of the potassium lanthanum sulfate they used as carrier, from which it should be separable only by fractional crystallization. Although Hahn did not take the new paper seriously, Strassmann felt sure of the reality of the substance, because the Paris scientists had communicated exact decay curves for the first time. He therefore tried to find a theoretical explanation that would encompass the results of both the Paris and the Berlin team. Based on the pattern of the decay scheme of thorium that Meitner and he had found and published, he put forth the following reflections:

1. The irradiation of uranium with neutrons leads to an alpha-radiating thorium. That would explain why the earlier measurements, carried out with beta counters, had been negative.
2. The alpha-radiating thorium has to produce a radium.
3. If these isotopes of radium were beta emitters, then the radium would decay into an actinium, and the actinium potentially into a thorium.
4. The Paris scientists had used potassium lanthanum sulfate. In this case at least some radium should be in the precipitate because of the sulfate ions. Therefore a fractionation should have produced the effects described [by Joliot-Curie and Savič].
5. Barium chloride as carrier should elude [exclude] sulfate ions.[7]

Strassmann was able to convince Hahn of the applicability of these reflections. Meitner, as well as Niels Bohr and Otto Robert Frisch, did, in fact, reject them when Hahn visited the Bohr Institute at Copenhagen for a lecture on 13 November. But Strassmann's experiments quickly seemed already to have corroborated the reflections—the paper with the first results was delivered to *Die Naturwissen-*

schaften on 8 November. Strassmann supposed that the irradiated uranium, as an alpha emitter, decays into a very short-lived thorium isotope, which could not be proved because of its short half-life but should also be an alpha emitter, so that it produces an isotope of radium, which as a beta emitter decays into an actinium isotope that also is a beta emitter, which therefore leads back to thorium, in three (later four) isomeric series. In Copenhagen, Hahn had asked for a theoretical explanation of the "double" (instead of successive) alpha decay caused by slow neutrons.

Meitner's objections caused the chemists in Berlin to test the results again and again. Strassmann struggled especially with the difficulty of separating by fractional crystallization the alleged active radium produced by the successive alpha decay from the inactive barium used as carrier. In addition, the degree of the enrichment of the radiation was not the same as what they were familiar with. Hahn therefore diluted some natural radium down to the intensity of the preparations separated by Strassmann from the neutron-irradiated uranium with barium chloride as carrier. But the enrichment in this case remained the same as usual. Therefore the artificial radium ought to display the same chemical behavior as the barium. Gradually Strassmann became persuaded that the alleged radium not only behaves like barium but *is* barium.

Such a view was entered in Strassmann's laboratory notebook for the first time on 15 December 1938. In the evening of 16 December, he started the famous indicator experiment, being in agreement with the conclusion that Hahn reported to Meitner in a letter of Monday, 19 December 1938:

> Of course, there is something about the "radium isotopes" that is so remarkable that I will tell it only to you. The half-lives of the three isotopes are rather exactly ascertained. They are separable from *all* the elements except barium. All the reactions are correct, except one . . . : The fractionation does not work. Our radium isotopes behave like barium. We do not get a clear enrichment with barium bromide or chromate etc. . . . On Saturday Strassmann and I fractionated one of our [alleged] "radium" isotopes with Msth 1 [radium 228] as indicator. The mesothorium was enriched as prescribed, our radium was not. . . . We more and more come to the terrible conclusion: Our radium isotopes do not behave like radium, but like barium. . . .[8]

The measurements were finished on 19 December: The enrichment of the radium 228 in the barium chloride had the right proportion of 6:1, whereas the enrichment of the alleged radium yielded a proportion of nearly 1.2:1. The latter therefore was radioactive barium, which could have been produced only by bursting of the uranium nuclei (later called "fission" by Frisch).

The paper that communicated these results was finished by Hahn on 22 December 1938 and delivered to *Die Naturwissenschaften* the same day. It appeared on 6 January 1939. Meitner had learned about it by letter some days earlier. The theoretical explanation, which she and her nephew Frisch found immediately, and which led to the identification of the inert gases krypton and xenon as the other products of the splitting of uranium or thorium nuclei, was made known to Hahn on 24 January. The Berlin chemists at once tried to identify these inert gases within the products of splitting uranium (and thorium). After Christmas vacation Strassmann had confirmed the fission by means of other indicator experiments. Because none of the inert gases could be used as a carrier, he now had to develop a novel experimental arrangement, in which an airstream sucks the radioactive gases into a glass tube filled with wadding (later with activated charcoal), which collects the solid decay products of the beta-radiating inert gases. The evidence of the radioactive inert gases followed from the chemically proved existence of active isotopes of strontium and cesium, which resulted from the gases.

Thereby the fission of heavy nuclei was proved, and simultaneously the previous alleged transuranic elements were rejected. Through Strassmann's revised analyses they turned out, one after the other, to be isotopes or homologues of the carrier substances—that is, products of splitting atoms of uranium or thorium—except one. This exception was the beta decay product of uranium 239, the latter called neptunium (239), which was discovered by Edwin M. McMillan and Philip Abelson in 1940 and a little later, but independently, by Kurt Starke at the Kaiser Wilhelm Institute.

Strassmann then engaged intensively in the study of the chemical nature of this transuranic element, which was of great general interest especially in regard to the problem of the continuation and/or end of the periodic system. Satisfied that element 93 was not an ekarhenium, he was rather inclined to interpret it as a beginning of the "uranides," a new series similar to the lanthanides following uranium. The puzzle of the chemical nature of the transuranics, which then was still far from being solved, demonstrates very well the difficulties in proving transuranics. Without the knowledge of the actinides and prior to the discovery of fission, Strassmann's excellent chemical analyses could hardly have led to other interpretations. But from the beginning of 1939, physicists and chemists throughout the world, including the other members of the Berlin institute, took part in clarifying the products of the splitting and decay of heavy nuclei. None of the members of Hahn's institute participated in any military investigations or applications, however; on the contrary, Strassmann, Hahn, and the others published nearly all their findings even during the war. Unlike Hahn, Strassmann was not interned after the war, but like him, he affirmed (especially in connection with the rearmament of the Federal Republic of Germany in the 1950's) his opposition to atomic weapons of every kind, feeling sure that the scientist as an expert is obligated to give publicity to his special knowledge. Moreover, he was a confirmed pacifist.

A second field of Strassmann's research was the determination of the age of minerals from the half-life of present radioactive elements and the enrichment of the products of their decay chain separated chemically. With Ernst Walling (and Hahn) he developed the rubidium-strontium method for the determination of geological age in 1936 and 1937. He resumed this research in 1942 and 1943 at the request of Josef Mattauch, Meitner's successor as head of the physics department of the Kaiser Wilhelm Institute and an expert on mass spectrography. The method has since become a cornerstone of geochronology. Age determination was also a field of activity at Strassmann's university institute in Mainz.

Because of the numerous air attacks on Berlin, the Kaiser Wilhelm Institute of Chemistry was transferred to Tailfingen in southwest Germany in early 1944. At the end of the war Hahn was taken into custody and interned in England with other prominent German atomic scientists. Released early in 1946, he was elected president of the Kaiser Wilhelm Society (in 1949 named the Max Planck Society) and went to Göttingen, where the society had been transferred from Berlin. Mattauch, deputy director since 1943, was elected director in 1946 (at the same time Strassmann was elected scientific member of the society), succeeding Hahn as appointed managing director on 1 August 1947. But he was then suffering from pulmonary tuberculosis and spent four years in sanatoria in the Black Forest and Switzerland. Thereupon Strassmann led the institute and was appointed second director in 1950.

A year before that the institute had been transferred to Mainz. Following a suggestion of Frédéric Joliot's, then high commissioner for atomic energy in the French-occupied zone of Germany and responsible for the institute, Mattauch had entered into negotiations for taking it over with the newly reestablished university and the local authorities in Mainz in May 1946. Because Strassmann had been appointed professor of inorganic and nuclear chemistry at Mainz University on 1 July 1946, he had to conduct the negotiations with the university, the occupation bureaucracy, and the provincial government. Later he had to supervise the construction work—which swallowed up all of the funds intended for the university's institutes of physics and chemistry, including Strassmann's own institute. These latter were put off from year to year with provisional arrangements. Until the Max Planck Institute was finally moved in the autumn of 1949, Strassmann had to shuttle between Tailfingen and Mainz, where he had started lecturing in the summer of 1946.

When Mattauch returned to the institute in the autumn of 1951, he demanded for his physics department the greater part of the budget that Strassmann had wrested from the provincial government in tedious negotiations. Mattauch argued that Strassmann's chemical department should be diminished radically, because Strassmann had in addition a university institute (which, however, had been postponed in favor of the Max Planck Institute). In accord with its rules, the central administration of the society and its president, Hahn, accepted the demands of Mattauch as the director of the institute. Strassmann therefore resigned his directorship and left the institute in 1953 to concentrate all his efforts upon the university Institute for Nuclear Chemistry.

Strassmann had to begin anew. His "institute" consisted of a few rooms dispersed over the campus. The university's building funds had been exhausted. But in 1954 Strassmann read in the newspaper that I. G. Farbenindustrie would be dismantled so that Badische Anilin- und Soda-Fabriken (B.A.S.F.), a part of this combine, would become independent and thereby liable to pay corporation income tax to the state of Rheinland-Pfalz. He considered that it would be in B.A.S.F.'s interest to support an institution in that state that would provide outstanding instruction and training of the rising generations of chemists. This argument convinced the chairman of the B.A.S.F. board of directors; and negotiations with the state government reached an agreement to use 5 million marks from the corporate income tax paid by B.A.S.F. (in addition to the university's funds) to build a large institute for the chemical sciences with a special division for nuclear chemistry. The construction work dragged out from 1955 to 1958. Simultaneously Strassmann was negotiating with the German federal government to obtain funds for a neutron generator, which, however, was not put in operation until 1961. But as early as 1958 he had filed an application with the federal minister of atomic energy (Siegfried Balke, an atomic scientist himself) to grant funds for a research reactor and a special institute for nuclear chemistry. These negotiations dragged through official channels until 1962. The erection of the atomic pile (TRIGA Mark II) and the buildings took a long time. The new Institute for Nuclear Chemistry with reactor was inaugurated on 3 April 1967—too late for Strassmann to use the reactor for his own research, although he postponed his retirement at the request of the minister of education until 1970.

Thus Strassmann devoted all his time and energy after the war to building up three chemical institutes in Mainz, and to training and guiding students. Giving up his personal research, he became a highly successful, beloved teacher. He took these sacrifices as a kind of return for the Berlin years he had spent almost exclusively on research. In contrast with the head of the institute at the time, Strassmann did not insist on attaching his name as co-author to the papers of his pupils and assistants. Consequently, his name was gradually forgotten outside of Mainz, even though he received the Enrico Fermi Award, together with Meitner and Hahn, in 1966. His special qualities as a teacher were recognized in 1969, when the Nuclear Chemistry Section of the Society of German Chemists established an annual Fritz Strassmann award for young nuclear chemists. By the time he retired, his Institute for Inorganic and Nuclear Chemistry had attained a worldwide reputation for developing the new methods of rapid analytical separation required to identify extremely short-lived isotopes and transuranic elements. This was the field in which Strassmann himself had specialized since the mid 1930's.

NOTES

1. See Lise Meitner, "Wege und Irrwege zur Kernenergie," in *Naturwissenschaftliche Rundschau*, **16** (1963), 167–169; and her letter to Max von Laue of 4 September 1941, quoted in K. E. Boeters and J. Lemmerich, eds., *Gedächtnisausstellung zum 100. Geburtstag von Albert Einstein, Otto Hahn, Max von Laue, Lise Meitner in der Staatsbibliothek Preussischer Kulturbesitz, Berlin, vom 1. März–12. April 1979* (Bad Honnef, 1979), 116.
2. Ida Noddack, "Über das Element 93," in *Angewandte Chemie*, **47** (1934), 653f.; against Enrico Fermi, "Possible Production of Elements of Atomic Number Higher Than 92," in *Nature*, **133** (1934), 898f.; and Enrico Fermi, Edoardo Amaldi, Oscar d'Agostino, Franco Rasetti, and Emilio Segrè, "Artificial Radioactivity Produced by Neutron Bombardment," in *Proceedings of the Royal Society*, **A146** (1934), 483–500.
3. Lise Meitner and Otto Hahn, "Neue Umwandlungsprozesse bei Bestrahlung des Urans mit Neutronen," in *Die Naturwissenschaften*, **24** (1936), 158f.; quote, 159.

4. Lise Meitner, Fritz Strassmann, and Otto Hahn, "Künstliche Umwandlungsprozesse bei Bestrahlung des Thoriums mit Neutronen; Auftreten isomerer Reihen durch Abspaltung von α-Strahlen," in *Zeitschrift für Physik*, **109** (1938), 538–552.
5. Otto Hahn and Lise Meitner, "Die künstliche Umwandlung des Thorium durch Neutronen: Bildung der bisher fehlenden radioaktiven 4n + 1-Reihe," in *Die Naturwissenschaften*, **23** (1935), 320f.; and, "with exprimental collaboration of F. Strassmann," "Künstliche radioaktive Atomarten aus Uran und Thor," in *Angewandte Chemie*, **49** (1936), 127f.
6. *Nature*, **140** (1937), 682.
7. See Strassmann, *Kernspaltung* . . . , p. 17.
8. Most of the letters by Hahn, Meitner, and Strassmann that concern the experimental investigations are included in Krafft, *Im Schatten* . . . , arranged chronologically. See also, for the correspondence 1938–1939 (with some omissions), Dietrich Hahn, ed., *Otto Hahn, Erlebnisse und Erkenntnisse* (Düsseldorf and Vienna, 1975).

BIBLIOGRAPHY

I. ORIGINAL WORKS. A bibliography of Strassmann's papers is in Krafft, *Im Schatten*. . . . They include "Über die Löslichkeit von Jod in gasförmiger Kohlensäure," in *Zeitschrift für physikalische Chemie*, A143 (1929), 225–243, his dissertation, with Hermann Braune; "Einige neue Anwendungsmöglichkeiten der 'Emaniermethode,'" in *Die Naturwissenschaften*, **19** (1931), 502–504; "Untersuchungen über Oberflächengrösse und Gitterveränderungen kristallisierter Salze nach der Emaniermethode von Hahn," in *Zeitschrift für physikalische Chemie*, B26 (1934), 353–361; "Untersuchungen über den Zusammenhang zwischen Gitterstruktur und Gasdurchlässigkeit organischer Salze nach der Emaniermethode von Hahn," *ibid.*, 362–372; seven papers with Otto Hahn and Lise Meitner on the decay chains of uranium and thorium, and alleged transuranics; "Die Abscheidung des reinen Strontium-Isotops 87 aus einem alten Rubidiumhaltigen Lepidolith und die Halbwertszeit des Rubidiums," in *Berichte der Deutschen chemischen Gesellschaft*, **71B** (1938), 1–9, with Ernst Walling; and many papers with Otto Hahn, including "Über die Entstehung von Radiumisotopen aus Uran beim Bestrahlen mit schnellen und verlangsamten Neutronen," in *Die Naturwissenschaften*, **26** (1938), 755f.; "Über den Nachweis und das Verhalten der bei der Bestrahlung des Urans mittels Neutronen entstehenden Erdalkalimetalle," *ibid.*, **27** (1939), 89–95 (includes the discovery of fission); "Nachweis der Entstehung aktiver Bariumisotope aus Uran und Thorium durch Neutronenbestrahlung; Nachweis weiterer aktiver Bruchstücke bei der Uranspaltung," *ibid.*, 89–95; "Zur Frage nach der Existenz der 'Trans-Urane.' I: Die endgültige Streichung von Eka-Platin und Eka-Iridium," *ibid.*, 451–453; "Weitere Spaltprodukte aus der Bestrahlung des Urans mit Neutronen," *ibid.*, 529–534; "Über einige Bruchstücke beim Zerplatzen des Thoriums," *ibid.*, 544–547, also with Siegfried Flügge; "Verwendung der 'Emanierfähigkeit' von Uranverbindungen zur Gewinnung von Spaltprodukten des Urans," *ibid.*, **28** (1940), 54–61; "Getrennte Abscheidung der bei der Uranspaltung entstehenden Krypton- und Xenon-Isotope," *ibid.*, 455–458;

"Über einige weitere Produkte der Uranspaltung," *ibid.*, 543–550; "Über die Isolierung und einige Eigenschaften des Elements 93," *ibid.*, **30** (1942), 256–260; "Einige weitere Spaltprodukte des Urans," *ibid.*, **31** (1943), 499–501. Other papers are "Über das Zerplatzen des Urankerns durch langsame Neutronen," in *Abhandlungen der Preussischen Akademie der Wissenschaften, Mathematisch-naturwiss. Klasse* (1939), no. 12; and "Einiges über die experimentelle Entwirrung der bei der Spaltung des Urans auftretenden Elemente und Atomarten," *ibid.* (1942), no. 3, with Hans Götte.

See also "Barium," in *Handbuch der analytischen Chemie*, pt. 3, vol. IIa (Berlin, 1940), 365–402, with Maria Strassmann-Hekter; "Die Auffüllung und Erweiterung des periodischen Systems," in *Die Naturwissenschaften*, **29** (1941), 492–496; *Friedliche Chemie der Atomkerne* (Mainz, 1949); "Über einige Strontium- und Yttriumisotope bei der Uranspaltung," in *Zeitschrift für Naturforschung*, **11a** (1956), 946–954, with Günter Hermann, his successor at Mainz; and "Abtrennung und Bestimmung kurzlebiger Isotope," in *Zeitschrift für Elektrochemie: Berichte der Bunsengesellschaft für physikalische Chemie*, **64** (1960), 1011–1014.

The laboratory notebook *Chemie II* of Hahn and Strassmann, including the experiments and measurements leading to the discovery of fission, and the original apparatus are located in the Deutsches Museum, Munich.

II. SECONDARY LITERATURE. There is a full biography, including facsimiles of the most important papers and extensive excerpts from the notebooks and the correspondence, in Fritz Krafft, *Im Schatten der Sensation: Leben und Wirken von Fritz Strassmann, dargestellt . . . nach Dokumenten und Aufzeichnungen* (Weinheim, 1981). For brief personal sketches, see Hans-Joachim Born's obituary in *Berichte und Mitteilungen der Max-Planck-Gesellschaft*, no. 3 (1981), 34–36; Gerhart Friedlander and Günter Herrmann in *Physics Today*, **34** (April 1981), 84, 86; Günter Hermann, "Ein Forscher, der Geschichte machte," in *Jogu: Universitätszeitung*, no. 68 (May 1980), 3; and Fritz Krafft, "Ein Leben im Dienste der Chemie und des akademischen Nachwuchses," in *Jahrbuch der Vereinigung "Freunde der Universität Mainz,"* **25/26** (1976/1977), 226–230. There are two autobiographical sketches by Strassmann, both published privately: *Damals: Institutsgeschichten, erzählt von Siegfried Knoke und Fritz Strassmann* (Mainz, 1976; 2nd ed., 1980), concerning the years at Hanover, and *Kernspaltung: Berlin, Dezember 1938* (Mainz, 1978), essential parts reprinted in Fritz Krafft, *Im Schatten.* . . .

For literature on the discovery of fission, see Lawrence Badash, "Otto Hahn," in *Dictionary of Scientific Biography*, VI, 14–17; and the bibliography of secondary literature in Krafft, *Im Schatten.* . . . See also Walther Gerlach, "Otto Hahn, Lise Meitner, Fritz Strassmann: Die Spaltung des Atomkerns," in Kurt Fassmann, ed., *Die Grossen der Weltgeschichte*, XI (Zurich, 1978), 50–71; Fritz Krafft, "Ein frühes Beispiel interdisziplinärer Team-Arbeit: Zur Entdeckung der Kernspaltung durch

Hahn, Meitner und Strassmann," in *Physikalische Blätter*, **36** (1980), 85–89, 113–118, and "An der Schwell des Atomzeitalters: Die Vorgeschichte der Entdeckung der Kernspaltung im Dezember 1938," in *Berichte zur Wissenschaften*, **11** (1988), 227–251; and William R. Shea, ed., *Otto Hahn and the Rise of Nuclear Physics* (Dordrecht, 1983), esp. Spencer R. Weart, "The Discovery of Fission and a Nuclear Physics Paradigm," 91–133; and Fritz Krafft, "Internal and External Conditions for the Discovery of Nuclear Fission by the Berlin Team," 135–165. For a repetition of the historical experiments, see Helmut Menke and Günter Herrmann, "Was waren die 'Transurane' der dreissiger Jahre in Wirklichkeit?" in *Radiochimica acta*, **16** (1971), 119–123.

FRITZ KRAFFT

STRATTON, SAMUEL WESLEY (*b*. Litchfield, Illinois, 18 July 1861; *d*. Boston, Massachusetts, 18 October 1931), *physics, metrology, science and engineering education.*

As founding director of the National Bureau of Standards and later as president of the Massachusetts Institute of Technology, Stratton significantly shaped the study and teaching of the physical sciences and engineering in America. He grew up on the farm of his parents, Samuel and Mary Webster Stratton, and worked his way through Illinois Industrial University (now the University of Illinois), earning a certificate in mechanical engineering in 1884 and a B.S. in 1886. His academic performance was so outstanding that the university offered him a faculty appointment in mathematics and physics, and also gave him responsibility for organizing its first course in electrical engineering.

In 1892 Stratton joined the physics department of the newly opened University of Chicago. With department chairman Albert Michelson on leave at the International Bureau of Weights and Measures, Stratton was asked to organize the physics curriculum, plan and equip the Ryerson Physical Laboratory, and offer graduate and undergraduate classes during his first year. Upon Michelson's return in 1893, they entered into a scientifically rewarding, though personally frustrating, partnership. Certainly Michelson's obsession with precision and measurement left its mark upon Stratton's subsequent career. Stratton soon discovered, however, as had other young physicists (including Robert Millikan, who joined the department in 1896), that Michelson was easier to work for than with. Stratton and Michelson collaborated on several important experiments and developed a new kind of harmonic analyzer for Michelson's spectrographic studies, but

Stratton later told close friends that he never felt Michelson had given him proper credit for his contributions. Turning his attention from research to teaching, Stratton joined Millikan in reorganizing the undergraduate curriculum and coauthoring *A College Course of Laboratory Experiments in General Physics* (1898).

Stratton's career took an unexpected turn in 1899 when he was invited by the office of the secretary of the treasury to spend a sabbatical year in Washington, D.C., evaluating the federal office of Weights and Measures. Germany had established the Physikalisch-Technische Reichsanstalt (PTR) in 1887, and Great Britain the National Physical Laboratory (NPL) in 1899. Many American political and business leaders feared that unless the United States followed suit, it would fall behind its commercial rivals, especially in the high-technology electrical and chemical industries, in which Germany was then leading the world.

After careful study Stratton drafted a proposal for a national standards laboratory modeled on the PTR; solicited endorsements for it from prominent scientific, technical, and business organizations; and lobbied key congressmen on its behalf. Thanks in large measure to Stratton's efforts, on 3 March 1901 Congress passed a bill establishing the National Bureau of Standards. A week later President McKinley appointed Stratton its first director.

Over the next two decades Stratton built the bureau into one of the world's premier laboratories in the physical sciences. Starting with a staff of fourteen and an annual budget of only $32,140 (when the PTR, by contrast, had an annual appropriation of $80,000 and the NPL $62,100), Stratton had by 1921 increased his staff to 850 and his budget to $2,209,089 while maintaining a consistently high level of scientific research on subjects ranging from basic metrology to electricity, radio, optics, and materials. He recruited top graduates from leading universities and helped some complete their doctorates under a unique cooperative education plan. Just a decade after the bureau's founding, Joseph S. Ames, head of the physics department at the Johns Hopkins University, wrote: "There is not a college or university in the United States that can give a student as much apparatus for experimental work and as much help in the theoretical field of the physical sciences as he can obtain at the Bureau of Standards." By the time Stratton left the bureau in 1923, it was perhaps the strongest department of physics in the country, boasting twenty-three physicists who had earned stars of distinction in *American Men of Science*.

Stratton always envisioned a greater role for the bureau than basic metrology. Exploiting the open-endedness of his legislative charter—"the solution of problems which arise in connection with standards"—he extended the bureau's mission well beyond the boundaries of physical constants and scientific measurement. In keeping with the commercial spirit of the bureau's founding, Stratton forged important new links between federal science and private industry. He made industrial research a significant portion of the bureau's work; formed a "research associates" program that brought corporate researchers into bureau laboratories, at company expense, to learn state-of-the-art science and engineering; and generally put science to work for industry much as the Department of Agriculture had put it to work for farming. Recognizing as well the bureau's obligations to the public interest, Stratton launched a "consumers' crusade" for fair and accurate weights and measures in the marketplace, published consumer product testing bulletins, and, to make sure that the government got what it was paying for, initiated a large-scale testing program covering everything from scientific instruments and light bulbs to concrete and the cable for the elevator in the Washington Monument.

Despite a somewhat aloof and formal manner, Stratton was long remembered by his staff for his close personal attention. Perhaps because he never married, he treated his "boys," as he called them, like family. He kept in touch with their research by means of daily walks through the laboratories and threw elaborate holiday parties. While he proved better at selling bureau programs to Congress than he had ever been at doing research himself, Stratton never gave up laboratory work entirely and always kept a small shop adjoining his office just for tinkering.

In 1923, at the age of sixty-one, Stratton left the bureau for the presidency of the Massachusetts Institute of Technology. He spent much of his seven-year tenure there refashioning MIT on the model of the National Bureau of Standards. With new programs in aeronautical and automotive engineering, building construction, and fuel studies, Stratton reemphasized MIT's commitment to cooperative research with industry. At the same time he recognized, perhaps more clearly than his predecessors, the dangers of too much reliance on applied research and corporate patronage. He tightened up MIT's freewheeling policies on sponsored research, strengthened its basic science departments, and looked to private foundations to supplement industrial funding. Although Stratton was more suc-

cessful in augmenting MIT's traditional strengths in engineering than in creating new ones in the sciences, his programs did set the stage for its dramatic transformation in the 1930's under his successor, Karl Compton, from a respected technical school into a national center for science and engineering research and education. Stratton stepped down from the presidency in July 1930 to become the first chairman of the MIT Corporation.

Stratton remained active until his death, traveling, lecturing, and serving on government commissions, including the Sacco and Vanzetti trial review board. He received half a dozen honorary degrees and many awards, including a commendation from the National Academy of Sciences for eminence in application of science to the public welfare.

BIBLIOGRAPHY

I. ORIGINAL WORKS. Stratton wrote very little. A complete list of his dozen or so publications, including transcripts of several speeches, is in A. E. Kennelly, "Samuel Wesley Stratton," in *Biographical Memoirs. National Academy of Sciences*, **17** (1937), 253–260. In addition he wrote *A College Course of Laboratory Experiments in General Physics* (Chicago, 1898) with Robert A. Millikan. Stratton's papers from his days as director of the National Bureau of Standards are held by the National Archives in Washington, D.C. The Institute Archives and Special Collections at MIT also has substantial Stratton holdings, including material gathered by one of Stratton's close friends for a biography that was never completed.

II. SECONDARY LITERATURE. Rexmond C. Cochrane, *Measures for Progress: A History of the National Bureau of Standards* (Washington, D.C., 1966; repr. New York, 1976), gives a detailed account of Stratton's career with the bureau and includes a short biography in an appendix. Samuel C. Prescott, an associate of Stratton's at MIT, published a brief appreciation in *Proceedings of the American Academy of Arts and Sciences*, **69** (February 1935), 544–547. A. Hunter Dupree, *Science in the Federal Government* (Cambridge, Mass., 1957), places Stratton's bureau career in context; and John Servos, "The Industrial Relations of Science: Chemical Engineering at MIT, 1900–1939," in *Isis*, **71** (1980), 531–549, does the same for Stratton's MIT years.

STUART W. LESLIE

STRESEMANN, ERWIN (*b.* Dresden, Germany, 22 November 1889; *d.* Berlin, Federal Republic of Germany, 20 November 1972), *ornithology, systematics.*

The son of Richard Stresemann, a well-to-do pharmacist, and of Marie Dunkelbeck, Stresemann had an excellent education in a culturally stimulating atmosphere. From his earliest youth he kept living animals in his parents' house and built up a collection of bird skins. In 1908 he began the study of medicine at the University of Jena, where he became acquainted with Ernst Haeckel. In 1909 he transferred to the University of Munich, where he prepared for an expedition to the Moluccas with the geologist K. Deninger. Since the best bird collections from that area were at the Rothschild Museum, Stresemann traveled to Tring, England, where he came under the tutelage of Ernst Hartert, then the world's leading ornithologist. They remained close friends and are buried in the same grave in a Berlin cemetery. The Moluccan expedition (second Freiburg expedition), in the field from September 1910 to April 1912, was immensely successful. Stresemann studied at Freiburg from 1912 to 1914, and his reports on the bird collections made on Ceram and Buru, published while he was there (1913, 1914), established his reputation as an ornithologist.

Stresemann married Elisabeth Deninger on 20 June 1916; they had a daughter and two sons. They were divorced in July 1939, and on 20 September 1941 Stresemann married Vesta Grote.

Stresemann's interests were extraordinarily broad, ranging from philosophy to literature and history. The anthropological and linguistic materials he had collected in the Moluccas were later published in two books (1918, 1927) that were highly praised by specialists.

World War I interrupted his studies, but in 1918 Stresemann returned to Munich and in March 1920 obtained the D.Phil. (summa cum laude) under Richard von Hertwig. The degree was only a formality, since by then he had published more than forty papers, including some very important ones. At that time he worked at the Munich Zoological Museum in association with C. E. Hellmayr. There he completed the *Avifauna Macedonica* (1920), a work in which he introduced a number of methodological innovations. He also completed the first installment of the *Aves* volume of the *Handbuch der Zoologie*. When he sent this in 1920 to Willy Georg Kükenthal, the editor of the *Handbuch*, who had just been appointed director of the Zoological Museum in Berlin, Kükenthal was so impressed by its outstanding quality that he offered Stresemann the vacant position of curator of ornithology at that museum. He accepted and held this position, the foremost in Germany, from April 1921 until 1961. Since several older, and at that time seemingly far better qualified, zoologists had applied for the vacancy, Stresemann at first encountered a good deal of envy, if not enmity. The brilliant manner in which

he filled the position of the "Berlin ornithologist," as successor to Jean Louis Cabanes and Anton Reichenow, quickly converted resentment into admiration.

The tempo of Stresemann's activity is documented by the number of papers he published annually in the years 1922 to 1926: twenty-seven, twenty-seven, fifty-nine, twenty-nine, and twenty-nine. They included taxonomic notes and the description of new subspecies from Indonesia, the New Guinea region, Eurasia, and North and South America; the history of ornithological collections; questions of nomenclature; reports on the results of expeditions; the history of aviculture and domestic races of birds; "mutation studies" (the unmasking of color varieties described as separate species); hybrids; sibling species; polytypic species; range expansions; revisions of difficult genera (*Accipiter, Collocalia, Phylloscopus, Zosterops, Spizaetus, Pitohui, Lamprocolius, Meliphaga, Cyornis*); and almost every other aspect of ornithology.

Stresemann's capacity for work is best represented by mentioning his many activities: secretary general of the German Ornithological Society (the oldest in the world), a position he held from 1922 to 1949 (also president 1949–1967 and honorary president 1967–1972); editor of two ornithological periodicals, *Journal für Ornithologie* and *Ornithologische Monatsberichte*; author of the *Aves* volume of the *Handbuch der Zoologie*; reorganizer of the bird collections and the ornithological library of the Berlin Museum; and supervisor of the work of twenty-one doctoral candidates between 1924 and 1939. Even those closely associated with him during this period could not understand how he could master so many tasks simultaneously, and so well, without an assistant and with very insufficient secretarial help. The answer was, in part, his enormous enthusiasm, an unbelievable memory, a great capacity for concentration, and, of course, superior intelligence.

The *Aves* volume (1927–1934) presented a sovereign account of everything known about birds, from morphology, physiology, and embryology to all aspects of distribution, life history, behavior, and ecology. It is the only case in the history of ornithology of a single author's succeeding in presenting total knowledge of birds in a superbly competent manner. All subsequent handbooks of birds are multiauthor productions. It was particularly through this work, but also through many of his other activities, that Stresemann succeeded in integrating ornithology into biology. There had been a tendency up to that time to consider it a hobby or a very peripheral specialty.

As early as 1919 Stresemann had published a species definition identical almost to the last word with Theodosius Dobzhansky's often quoted definition of 1936. Except for Hartert, no one applied the polytypic species concept as consistently as Stresemann. As a result, many hundreds, if not thousands, of typologically defined species were reduced to subspecies. In this period he sometimes carried the principle "geographical representative = subspecies" too far. Not a few of these "subspecies" have recently been raised to the rank of allospecies.

None of his larger works was strictly descriptive. Stresemann always followed a subject to its theoretical consequences. A report on the birds collected by G. Heinrich on Celebes culminated in a superb treatment of principles of zoogeography (including dispersal and competition).

From the beginning Stresemann had a great interest in the history of ornithology. He wrote extensively on the lives of famous and some undeservedly forgotten authors and published some of their correspondence. Through him Lazarus Roting, Johann Leonhard Frisch, Ferdinand Adam von Pernau, Friedrich Sellow, Carl Heinrich Merck, Johann Heinrich Zorn, Christian Ludwig Brehm, Johann Friedrich Naumann, Heinrich Boie, Conrad Jacobus Temminck, Martin Heinrich Lichtenstein, Johann Carl Illiger, Eduard Eversmann, Petr Simon Pallas, and several others were brought closer to our understanding. His *Die Entwicklung der Ornithologie von Aristoteles bis zur Gegenwart* (1951) is an extraordinary achievement. Not only does it contain vivid portraits of the men who had left their mark on ornithology, but it also sheds a great deal of light on the interactions between ornithology and the rest of biological science, as well as on the role of the study of birds in the total cultural life of each period.

In spite of the difficulties of working in divided Berlin and of visiting other museums, and the impossibility of receiving new material, Stresemann remained active after 1945. In addition to continuing his historical studies, he concentrated on the sequence and seasonal occurrence of the molt in the orders, families, and species of birds. In this first truly thorough analysis of the phenomenon (largely in collaboration with his second wife, Vesta) he discovered an almost bewildering diversity of molt patterns, which allowed regrettably few generalizations (such as relation between molt and migration).

Stresemann had a charismatic personality and was able to charm (and often deeply influence) anyone he encountered. His phenomenal memory, his ability to cut through complex obscurities to reach clear formulations, the elegance of his written work, and his clear vision of desirable goals had an extraordinary impact on his associates and on ornithology as a whole. In 1934 Stresemann served as president of the Eighth International Ornithological Congress (Oxford), and in the ensuing years he received numerous other honors. Active almost to the end of his life, he succumbed to a heart attack two days before his eighty-third birthday.

BIBLIOGRAPHY

I. ORIGINAL WORKS. Among Stresemann's thirteen books or major monographs are *Die Paulohisprache. Ein Beitrag zur Kenntnis der amboinischen Sprachengruppe* (The Hague, 1918); *Avifauna Macedonica* (Munich, 1920); *Die Lauterscheinung der amboinischen Sprachen* (Berlin, 1927); *Aves*, VII, pt. 2, of Willy Georg Kükenthal, ed., *Handbuch der Zoologie* (Berlin, 1934); and *Die Entwicklung der Ornithologie von Aristoteles bis zum Gegenwart* (Berlin, 1951), trans. by Hans J. Epstein and Cathleen Epstein as *Ornithology from Aristotle to the Present* (Cambridge, Mass., 1975). He also published some 600 journal articles.

II. SECONDARY LITERATURE. L. Gebhardt, "Die Ornithologen Mitteleuropas," in *Journal für Ornithologie*, **115** (spec. iss.) (1974), 83–86, including a bibliography of some twenty obituaries; Ernst Mayr and William B. Provine, eds., *The Evolutionary Synthesis* (Cambridge, Mass., 1980), 414–416; R. Nöhring, "Erwin Stresemann," in *Journal für Ornithologie*, **114** (1973), 455–500, with full bibliography by I. Jahn, titles of twenty-eight dissertations done under his guidance, titles of the periodicals he edited, and titles of four festschriften published in his honor in 1949 and 1959; and K. E. Westerskov, "Erwin Stresemann and His Contribution to Australasian Ornithology," in *Notornis*, **23** (1976), 138–167.

ERNST MAYR

TAKAGI, TEIJI (*b.* Kazuya Village, near Gifu, Japan, 21 April 1875; *d.* Tokyo, Japan [?], 29 February 1960), *mathematics.*

Teiji Takagi came from a family of landowners and government officials of a rural part of Gifu prefecture in central Japan. His mother, Tsune Takagi, was married to Mitsuzo Kinomura, of the town of Kitagata, but she returned to her family's home to bear her child and never returned to her husband, allegedly because she was repelled by the leeches on his farm. The boy's uncle, Kansuke Takagi, who was unable to have children of his own, adopted Teiji as his son, a common Japanese practice at the time for propertied families without heirs. The boy was frail and, under the severe discipline of his adoptive father, spent his childhood in study rather than in play with other children. He was an outstanding pupil, advancing through the six-year curriculum of the village school in three years, then graduating five years later, first in his class, from the middle school in Gifu. From 1891 to 1894 he attended the Third National Senior High School in Kyoto.

In 1894 Takagi entered the Imperial University in Tokyo, having already chosen mathematics as his field of study while in Kyoto. After his graduation in 1897, he began graduate study at the same university, but a prestigious government scholarship soon enabled him to go to Germany for three years; he elected to spend the first half of this period in Berlin, the second half in Göttingen.

Takagi read David Hilbert's famous report on the theory of algebraic numbers while he was in Berlin, and he developed an interest in pursuing the subject in the same direction as Hilbert himself—toward Kronecker's *Jugendtraum* ("dream of his youth") theorem on the abelian extensions of imaginary quadratic number fields. Hilbert, however, had shifted to other interests, so his direct influence on Takagi's work during Takagi's year-and-a-half stay in Göttingen was not great. Nonetheless, Takagi believed that his development was profoundly affected by Hilbert, especially by the spirit of mathematical study that Hilbert and Klein generated in turn-of-the-century Göttingen.

Soon after his return home in December 1901, Takagi married Toshi Tani, the sister-in-law of his landlord, in Tokyo on 6 April 1902. The couple had five daughters and three sons. He completed his doctorate at the Imperial University of Tokyo (26 December 1903) on the basis of a paper he had written in Göttingen on a special case of Kronecker's *Jugendtraum* theorem, namely, the case in which the imaginary quadratic field is the one obtained by adjoining i, the square root of -1. This paper and a few brief notes were published in 1902 and 1903, but there was no other published work in the following years prior to World War I. In 1904 he was made full professor at the university.

Class field theory grew out of attempts by Hilbert and Heinrich Weber, among others, to understand and prove the *Jugendtraum* theorem and other works of Leopold Kronecker. Weber gave the original definition of a "class field" (*Klassenkörper*) in terms of a rather complicated construction, the essence of which was to describe the way in which prime ideals of an algebraic number field (called the "ground field") factor in an abelian extension field (that is, a normal extension field whose Galois group over the ground field is an abelian group). Hilbert recast the theory, simplifying it by using a less general definition; Hilbert defined a class field to be what is now called an "absolute" class field, that is, a maximal abelian extension that is "unramified." (An extension is called unramified if the factorization of a prime ideal of the ground field never contains a repeated factor in the extension field.) The existence of class fields in Hilbert's sense was proved by Furtwängler in 1907.

Takagi returned to Weber's original viewpoint, but, instead of considering the way in which primes factor in an abelian extension field, considered the question of determining which ideals of the ground field are relative norms of ideals in the extension field. His main theorems were: (1) For any abelian extension, the ideals of the ground field that are relative norms of ideals of the extension field can be determined by simple multiplicative congruence conditions; (2) conversely, given a set of congruence conditions of the type Takagi describes, there is an abelian extension field in which these congruences determine the ideals that are relative norms of ideals in the extension field; (3) the prime ideals that figure in the muliplicative congruences coincide with the prime divisors of the discriminant of the extension; (4) the Galois group of the extension is isomorphic to the multiplicative group of classes of ideals of the ground field described by the multiplicative congruences; and (5) the way in which a prime ideal factors in the extension field depends only on its image in the Galois group—in particular, the prime ideals that factor into prime ideals of the first degree are precisely the ones that are relative norms (corresponding to the identity of the Galois group).

Takagi, having discovered these sweeping and unexpected theorems in isolation from his German colleagues, doubted they were correct. In fact, by his own account, he was sure they were wrong and spent a great deal of effort looking for an error in his reasoning. By the time the war was over and communication reestablished, however, he had convinced himself and had completed his theory. He set it forth in two long papers (1920, 1922) that constitute, in number of pages, half the volume of his published papers in languages other than Japanese, and contain most of his creative work.

At the International Congress of Mathematicians in Strasbourg in 1920, Takagi gave a brief presentation of his results. Whether because the German mathematicians had been excluded from participation in the congress, or because his presentation was so diffident, the significance of Takagi's work seems not to have been grasped by anyone present. Only in 1922, when C. L. Siegel persuaded Emil Artin to read the first of Takagi's two great papers, did the importance of his work begin to be recognized. A few years later, Helmut Hasse's expository treatises on class field theory made Takagi's theory known to the mathematical world, establishing it in its proper place as a revolutionary advance in algebraic number theory.

Beginning in 1930 Takagi wrote a number of textbooks in Japanese (he had also written one in 1901) dealing with algebra, analysis, the history of mathematics in the nineteenth century, and number theory. These books grew out of his long teaching career at the Imperial University and reportedly had a great effect on the education of later generations of Japanese mathematicians. In addition, he wrote a number of popular works that reached a wide audience and did much to stimulate interest in mathematics in Japan, particularly among young people.

BIBLIOGRAPHY

I. Original Works. "Über eine Theorie des relativ Abelschen Zahlkörpers," in *Journal of the College of Science, Imperial University of Tokyo*, **41** (1920), 1–133; and "Über das Reciprocitätsgesetz in einem beliebigen algebraischen Zahlkörper," *ibid.*, **44** (1922), 1–50. See also *The Collected Papers of Teiji Takagi*, S. Kuroda, ed. (Tokyo, 1973).

II. Secondary Literature. Kin-ya Honda, "Teiji Takagi: A Biography," in *Commentarii mathematici Universitatis Sancti Pauli*, **24**, no. 2 (1975), 141–167.

Harold M. Edwards

TANAKADATE, AIKITSU (*b.* Iwate, Japan, 18 September 1856; *d.* Tokyo, Japan, 21 May 1952), *physics*.

One of the most famous first-generation physicists in Japan, Tanakadate was born into a samurai family of the Nambu fief. His father, Inazo, was a teacher of the Jitsuyo school of military tactics, and his mother, Kisei, was from a family of Shinto priests. In preparation to succeed his father, Tanakadate began his education at the age of four, at age eight began training in swordsmanship, and at nine enrolled in a small private school to begin Chinese classical studies. In 1867 his life changed radically with the outbreak of the wars that ended the Tokugawa shogunate and led to the Meiji Restoration, which abolished the samurai and fiefs and set in motion the transformation of Japan to a modern state. Impoverished and no longer able to enjoy the privileges of the governing class, the Tanakadates moved to Tokyo in 1872, where the father sought to make a living as a merchant.

With Western nations increasingly encroaching on Japan, young Tanakadate realized that the survival of the country depended upon the Japanese gaining a knowledge of Western institutions and learning, and so in 1872, while continuing to study traditional Chinese and Japanese subjects privately, he entered Keio Gijuku, a private college in Tokyo, to study English. Soon financial pressures led him to prepare for entrance to a less expensive government school called Kobu Daigakko (school of engineering), which he did by studying such Western subjects as geometry and algebra on his own. When later he saw that the school's catalogue said not one word about training students to govern the country (which he, as a Confucian-trained samurai, felt to be the true aim of education) but described only courses on such subjects as building bridges and lighthouses and putting up electrical wires, he was shocked and changed his mind about entering. He studied English from 1874 to 1876 at the Gaikokugo Gakko (school of foreign languages), and in 1876 he finally entered Tokyo Kaisei Gakko, which was later to become the Imperial University.

After two years of general education courses, he chose physics as his major for the concluding four-year specialization. Several factors seem to have influenced his decision. Since childhood his samurai education had been predicated upon the assumption that his ultimate role would be to govern, and even after the abolition of his class he believed his proper role was to become a government official and serve the country. Yet Japan lacked Western studies, and so to study science could serve the country. After his first two years of general education, Tanakadate began to believe that learning could be pursued for its own sake, and not merely as moral training, an idea foreign to Confucian thought. And he became convinced that in true learning one must start with the basics and build from there, and physics seemed to constitute the basis of Western science.

From 1878 to 1882 Tanakadate studied under Kenjiro Yamagawa, the first Japanese professor of physics at the university, as well as with two visiting foreign teachers, James Alfred Ewing, from Edinburgh, who had an appointment in mechanical engineering from 1878 to 1883, and Thomas Mendenhall, an American who from 1878 to 1881 had been the university's very first professor of physics. Upon graduation in 1882 Tanakadate was made a lecturer, and in 1886, by which time the school had been renamed the Imperial University, he was made assistant professor of physics. The university sent Tanakadate abroad in 1888, and he went first to the University of Glasgow, with an introduction from Ewing, to study with William Thomson for two years. While there he published papers in English on such problems as the magnetization of soft iron bars and the thermal effects of magnetization reversals. In 1890 he went to Berlin for a year. He returned to Japan in July 1891 and was immediately promoted to full professor, a title he held until his retirement in 1916. In August 1891 he received the doctor of science degree from the Imperial University. He married Kiyoko Honjuku in 1893, but his wife died the next year due to complications arising from the birth of a daughter.

Tanakadate's scientific activity centered on four subjects: electricity and magnetism, geophysics, aeronautics, and weights and measures. He was introduced to the subject of electricity and magnetism through Ewing, who was interested in hysteresis. He got Tanakadate and others involved in the experimental investigation of this phenomenon. Mendenhall, who introduced Tanakadate to geophysics, did not limit his laboratory experiments to mere repetition of known experiments but took his students out into the city and countryside to measure, for instance, the force of gravity in Tokyo and at the top of Mt. Fuji to determine the density of the earth. After Mendenhall's departure Tanakadate became the person responsible for making such measurements at different locations in Japan. Geomagnetic measurement techniques were also studied by the Mendenhall group early on, but in 1887 Tanakadate, Cargill Knott, who was Ewing's replacement, and their students undertook an extensive geomagnetic measurement project of Japan as a whole. The Nobi earthquake of 1891 brought him a renewed interest in geomagnetism. Preliminary investigation indicated a difference between the 1887 and 1891 measurements, showing that earthquakes change the geomagnetism of an area, and in 1893 Tanakadate organized a four-year expedition sponsored by the university to make new geomagnetic measurements throughout Japan. His interest in geomagnetism gradually was replaced by aeronautics and weights and measures. His contributions in these areas were mostly governmental and administrative, but continued until well after World War II.

Although Tanakadate justified to himself his work in physics by Confucian arguments, he never confined himself inside a Confucian worldview. He saw in experimental physics something that should be pursued in its own right. He further questioned the simplistic dichotomy that was then frequently drawn between so-called Eastern spirituality and Western materialism. To Tanakadate, who traveled abroad more than twenty times during his active years, mostly on scientific missions or to international conferences, physics was his passport. The Japanese government awarded him the Bunka Kunsho (Order of Culture) in 1944 for his contribution to the modernization of Japan.

BIBLIOGRAPHY

I. ORIGINAL WORKS. "A Magnetic Survey of Japan, Carried Out by Order of the President of the Imperial University," in *Journal of the College of Science, Imperial University of Tokyo*, **2** (1888), 163–262, written with C. Knott; "Mean Intensity of Magnetization of Soft Iron Bars of Various Lengths in a Uniform Magnetic Field," in *Philosophical Magazine*, 5th ser. **26** (1888), 450–456; "The Thermal Effect Due to Reversals of Magnetization in Soft Iron," *ibid.*, 5th ser. **27** (1889), 207–218; "The Disturbance of Isomagnetics Attending the Mino-Owari Earthquake of 1891," in *Journal of the College of Science, Imperial University of Tokyo*, **5** (1892), 149–192, written with H. Nagaoka.

Tanakadate's papers are deposited at the National Science Museum in Tokyo.

II. SECONDARY LITERATURE. Kenkichiro Koizumi, "The Emergence of Japan's First Physicists: 1868–1900," in *Historical Studies in the Physical Sciences*, **6** (1975), 72–81; Seiji Nakamura, *Tanakadate Aikitsu sensei* (Tokyo, 1946), which contains a list of Tanakadate's scientific papers; Shigeru Nakayama, "Shushin saika jikoku heitenka to kagaku—Tanakadate Aikitsu o chushin to shite," in *Butsurigakushi kenkyu*, **2** (1963), 155–168.

KENKICHIRO KOIZUMI

TARSKI, ALFRED (*b*. Warsaw, Poland, 14 January 1901; *d*. Berkeley, California, 27 October 1983), *mathematical logic, set theory, algebra.*

Trained as both a mathematician and a philosopher, Tarski discovered interconnections between such diverse areas of mathematics as logic, algebra, set theory, and measure theory. He brought clarity and precision to the semantics of mathematical logic, and in so doing he legitimized semantic concepts, such as truth and definability, that had been stigmatized by the logical paradoxes. Tarski was extroverted, quick-witted, strong-willed, energetic, and sharp-tongued. He preferred his research to be collaborative—sometimes working all night with a colleague—and was very fastidious about priority. An inspiring teacher, at Berkeley he supervised the doctoral dissertations of many of the leading mathematical logicians of the next generation. Tarski's influence was especially pervasive in model theory—in forming its concepts, problems, and methodology. Although he did much research in algebra, he remained a logician first and an algebraist second. Collectively, his work can be regarded as an immensely fruitful interplay among algebra, set theory, and logic.

Tarski was the son of Ignacy Tajtelbaum, a successful shopkeeper, and his wife, Rose Prussak Tajtelbaum. (Around 1924 he changed his name from Tajtelbaum to Tarski—to protect his as yet unborn children from anti-Semitism.) He was educated in Warsaw, where he submitted his doctoral dissertation, supervised by Stanislaw Leśniewski, in 1923. His other principal teachers in logic and philosophy were Tadeusz Kotarbiński and Jan Łukasiewicz; in mathematics, Stefan Banach and Wacław Sierpiński. The University of Warsaw granted Tarski a Ph.D. in mathematics in 1924. In 1918, and again in 1920, he served briefly in the Polish army.

From 1922 to 1925 Tarski was an instructor in logic at the Polish Pedagogical Institute in Warsaw. Then he became a *Privatdozent* and an adjunct professor of mathematics and logic at the University of Warsaw. Since this was not a regular university position, in 1925 he also accepted a position as professor at Zeromski's Lycée in Warsaw, teaching there full-time and keeping both positions until 1939. On 23 June 1929 he married Maria Witkowski; they had a son and a daughter. From January to June 1935 he worked in Vienna, holding a fellowship from Karl Menger's colloquium, where he had lectured by invitation in February 1930. Shortly before the war, Tarski was a candidate for the chair of philosophy at the University of Lvov, but that position went to Leon Chwistek. Tarski's difficulty in obtaining a regular academic appointment, which some have blamed on anti-Semitism, contrasted sharply with his acknowledged role as a leading Warsaw logician. Politically, he was a socialist.

In 1939 Tarski traveled to the United States for a lecture tour. When World War II broke out, he remained there, and was naturalized as an American citizen six years later. With the influx of refugees from Europe, academic positions were scarce. Nevertheless, from 1939 to 1941 Tarski was a research associate in mathematics at Harvard, and in 1940 also served as visiting professor at the City College of New York. During the year 1941–1942 he was a member of the Institute for Advanced Study at Princeton.

Tarski did not obtain a permanent position until 1942, when the University of California at Berkeley hired him as a lecturer. There he remained for the rest of his career, becoming an associate professor in 1945 and full professor a year later. The breadth of his interests is illustrated by his establishment at Berkeley in 1958 of the Group in Logic and the Methodology of Science, bringing together mathematicians and philosophers to study foundational questions. Although Tarski was made emeritus professor in 1968, he continued to teach for five years and to supervise doctoral students and do research until his death. In 1981 he received the Berkeley Citation, the highest award that university gives to its faculty.

Tarski established ties with other academic institutions, serving as Sherman memorial lecturer at University College (London) in 1950 and again in 1966, as lecturer at the Institut Henri Poincaré (Paris) in 1955, and as Flint professor of philosophy at U.C.L.A. in 1967. In addition to his European connections, he had close ties to Latin America. He was visiting professor at the National University of Mexico in 1957, and at the Catholic University of Chile in the year 1974–1975.

Despite his early difficulties in securing a regular position, Tarski received numerous honors. In 1935 he was made a Rockefeller fellow, and a Guggenheim fellow in the year 1941–1942 (and again in the year 1955–1956). From 1958 to 1960 he served as research professor at the Miller Institute for Basic Research in Science. In 1966 he was awarded the Jurzykowski Foundation Prize. The journal *Algebra Universalis* made Tarski honorary editor for his work in universal algebra. He was awarded honorary doctorates by the Catholic University of Chile in 1975 and by the University of Marseilles in 1977.

For many years Tarski was actively involved with mathematical and scientific organizations. From 1935 to 1939 he served as vice president of the Polish Logic Society. In 1940 he was elected to the executive committee of the Association for Symbolic Logic and was the association's president from 1944 to 1946. In 1948 he became a council member of the American Mathematical Society. Tarski served as president of the International Union for the History and Philosophy of Science (1956–1957) and was chairman of the U.S. National Committee on History and Philosophy of Science (1962–1963). In 1965 he was elected to the National Academy of Sciences. In addition, he was a fellow of the American Academy of Arts and Sciences, a foreign member of the Royal Netherlands Academy of Sciences and Letters, and a corresponding fellow of the British Academy.

Tarski was more eclectic than most logicians educated in the 1920's. He drew not only from Bertrand Russell and Alfred North Whitehead's *Principia mathematica* and from David Hilbert, but also from the Peirce-Schröder tradition of algebraic logic and from the Polish logic of Leśniewski and Łukasiewicz. All four traditions repeatedly influenced his work. His dissertation examined the definability of propositional connectives in the theory of types, but his interests were already quite broad. During his career he wrote several hundred articles, as well as monographs, in French, Polish, German, and English. The extreme richness of his work makes it necessary to treat it thematically rather than chronologically.

In 1921 Tarski began publishing in set theory and continued to do so until his death. His first substantial paper (1924), on finite sets, completed several decades of research on this topic by Georg Cantor, Richard Dedekind, Ernst Zermelo, and others. His work often combined foundational concerns with mathematical results, as in the Banach-Tarski paradox (a sphere can be decomposed into a finite number of pieces and reassembled into a sphere of any larger size). Influenced by Sierpiński, Tarski investigated the role of the axiom of choice and showed many propositions (such as the proposition that $M^2 = M$ for every infinite cardinal M) to be equivalent to this axiom. By 1929 he became convinced that cardinal arithmetic divided naturally into those propositions equivalent to this axiom and those independent of it. The latter propositions, he believed, formed part of a new theory of the equivalence of sets with respect to a given class of one:one mappings, a theory intensively studied by Tarski and Banach. In 1926 Tarski established that the axiom of choice is implied by the generalized continuum hypothesis (that is, for every infinite set A, there is no cardinal between A and its power set). His concern with propositions equivalent to the axiom of choice was lifelong, as was his interest in cardinal arithmetic dispensing with that axiom.

A second theme in Tarski's set-theoretic research was large cardinals. In 1930 he introduced, jointly with Sierpiński, the notion of a strongly inaccessible cardinal, and in 1939 he put forward the axiom of inaccessible sets, a large cardinal axiom that implies the axiom of choice. In 1943, in a joint paper with Paul Erdös, he introduced the seminal notions of strongly compact cardinal and weakly compact cardinal. They observed that every strongly compact cardinal is measurable and that every measurable cardinal is weakly compact. Proofs were not published until 1961, a year after Tarski also established, by using the work of his student William Hanf on infinitary logic, that a measurable cardinal is very large among inaccessible cardinals, thus settling a thirty-year-old problem.

From 1926 to 1928 Tarski conducted a seminar on metamathematics at Warsaw University. There he investigated, in particular, the structure of complete theories in geometry and group theory. He also exploited the technique of quantifier elimination on the theory of discrete order and the theory of real closed fields, thereby establishing the decidability of these theories. The latter work, which yielded the decidability of first-order Euclidean geometry, was not published until 1948. Never published was Tarski's 1949 result that the theory of Boolean algebras is decidable. And his 1939 discovery, with his former student Andrzej Mostowski, that the first-order theory of well-orderings is decidable was published in 1978. The richness of Tarski's discoveries, and the clarity he demanded of their published form, increased the number of his unpublished results and lengthened the time between discovery and publication.

During the 1930's Tarski did much research on the metamathematical notion of deductive system, axiomatizing the notion of consequence with a generality that included all kinds of logic known at the time. He then specialized the notion of consequence to treat specific logics, such as classical propositional logic. Here he was particularly concerned with determining the number of complete extensions of a given mathematical theory. This research was connected with his desire to find purely mathematical (and especially algebraic) equivalents of metamathematical notions.

A recurring theme in Tarski's work was the role of the infinitary in logic. In 1926 he formulated the *w*-rule (an infinitary version of the principle of mathematical induction), which, by 1933, he considered to be problematical. He showed in 1939 that even in the presence of this rule there are undecidable statements. Around 1957 Tarski investigated first-order logic extended by infinitely long formulas. In 1961 the incompactness of many such languages led to very important results in set theory.

Tarski's famous work on definitions of truth in formalized languages (1933–1935) gave the notion of satisfaction of a sentence in a structure for first-order logic, second-order logic, and so on. This work had a very pronounced influence on philosophers concerned with mathematics, science, and linguistics.

During the mid 1930's Tarski started to do research in algebra, at first as a tool for studying logic and then, in the 1940's, increasingly for its own sake as well. In 1935 he investigated complete and atomic Boolean algebras, notions closely related to logic. His increasing concern in the late 1930's with ideals in Boolean algebras reflected his discovery that such ideals correspond to the metamathematical notion of a mathematical theory. He wrote several joint papers on closure algebras with J. C. C. McKinsey in the 1940's. While Tarski's original motivation for inventing closure algebras was to provide an algebraic analogue for the notion of topological space, he showed that these algebras were intimately related to modal logic and to intuitionistic logic. In 1941 he axiomatized the theory of binary relations and posed the problem of representability: Is every model of this theory isomorphic to an algebra of relations? Although in 1950 Roger Lyndon found the answer to be no, Tarski proved in 1955 that the class of all representable relation algebras is a variety. The following year he determined all complete varieties of rings and of relation algebras. Closely related to this work on varieties was his 1968 paper on equational logic.

Tarski's research on relation algebras led to his most ambitious algebraic creation, cylindrical algebras. During the period 1948–1952 he and his student Fred Thompson formulated the notion of cylindrical algebra as an algebraic analogue of first-order logic. That is, the class of cylindrical algebras was to bear the same relation to first-order logic with identity that the class of Boolean algebras bears to propositional logic. From the 1950's until his death, Tarski investigated cylindrical algebras and their representability, first with Leon Henkin and then with his former student Donald Monk as well.

Another major area of Tarski's logical research was the undecidability of theories. In 1939 he and Mostowski reduced Gödel's incompleteness theorems to a form that depended only on a finite number of first-order arithmetic axioms, and thereby were able to extend greatly the number of theories known to be undecidable. Their results were published in 1953 in the monograph *Undecidable Theories*, in which Tarski established the undecidability of the first-order theory of groups, of lattices, of abstract projective geometries, and (with Mostowski) of rings.

In his research after World War II, Tarski no longer used the theory of types as his basic logical system; instead, he used first-order logic. At most, he considered certain extensions of first-order logic, such as weak second-order logic and infinitary logics.

Tarski's immense influence cannot be properly judged on the basis of his publications alone. He influenced the many mathematicians with whom he did joint work, and he molded the perspectives of many doctoral students who became leading mathematical logicians. While still at Warsaw, he unofficially supervised Mostowski's dissertation on set theory (1939) as well as M. Presburger's master's thesis on decidability (1930). But it was during his years at Berkeley that Tarski exerted his greatest influence. Those who wrote their dissertations under him included Bjarni Jónsson (1946), Julia Robinson (1948), Robert Vaught (1954), Chen-chung Chang (1955), Solomon Feferman (1957), Robert Montague (1957), Jerome Keisler (1961), Haim Gaifman (1962), William Hanf (1963), and George McNulty (1972). Tarski also molded Dana Scott's approach to logic, although Scott received his Ph.D. at Princeton. Nor was Tarski's influence felt only in mathematics; it was also seen in J. H. Woodger's work on the axiomatic foundations of biology and in Patrick Suppes' research on the axiomatic foundations of physics.

BIBLIOGRAPHY

I. ORIGINAL WORKS. Tarski's *Collected Papers* were published in 4 vols. (1986). His *Nachlass* is in the Bancroft Library, University of California at Berkeley. A complete bibliography is in Steven Givant, "Bibliography of Alfred Tarski," in *Journal of Symbolic Logic*, **51** (1986), 913–941. A list of his Ph.D. students is in the Tarski symposium volume, *Proceedings of Symposia in Pure Mathematics*, **25** (1974), honoring his seventieth birthday and in Hodges (see below).

II. SECONDARY LITERATURE. A series of articles on Tarski's life and work appeared in *Journal of Symbolic Logic*: W. J. Blok and Don Pigozzi, "Alfred Tarski's Work on General Metamathematics," **53** (1988), 36–50; John Doner and Wilfrid Hodges, "Alfred Tarski and Decidable Theories," *ibid.*, 20–35; John Etchemendy, "Tarski on Truth and Logical Consequence," *ibid.*, 51–79; Wilfrid Hodges, "Alfred Tarski," **51** (1986), 866–868; Bjarni Jónsson, "The Contributions of Alfred Tarski to General Algebra," *ibid.*, 883–889; Azriel Levy, "Alfred Tarski's Work in Set Theory," **53** (1988), 2–6; George F. McNulty, "Alfred Tarski and Undecidable Theories," **51** (1986), 890–898; J. Donald Monk, "The Contributions of Alfred Tarski to Algebraic Logic," *ibid.*, 899–906; Patrick Suppes, "Philosophical Implications of Tarski's Work," **53** (1988), 80–91; L. W. Szczerba, "Tarski and Geometry," **51** (1986), 907–912; Lou van den Dries, "Alfred Tarski's Elimination Theory for Real Closed Fields," **53** (1988), 7–19; and Robert L. Vaught, "Alfred Tarski's Work in Model Theory," **51** (1986), 869–882. On Tarski's contributions to model theory, see C. C. Chang, "Model Theory 1945–1971," in *Proceedings of Symposia in Pure Mathematics*, **25** (1974), 173–186; and R. L. Vaught, "Model Theory Before 1945," *ibid.*, 153–172.

GREGORY H. MOORE

TAYLOR, GEOFFREY INGRAM (*b.* London, England, 7 March 1886; *d.* Cambridge, England, 27 June 1975), *applied mechanics, physics.*

Taylor's father, Edward Ingram, was an artist. His mother, Margaret Boole, came from a family with a distinguished scientific background: she was the daughter of George Boole, the mathematician and logician, and her uncle was Sir George Everest, one of the founders of geodesy. Taylor studied from 1889 to 1905 at University College School and then went to Trinity College, Cambridge. He passed the natural science tripos in 1908 with first-class honors and was given a scholarship for research at Trinity, where he stayed for the rest of his life.

In 1925 Taylor married Stephanie Ravenhill, who shared his deep love for sailing; with their yacht *Frolic* they made several adventurous voyages. They had no children. Aside from these cruises and frequent travels abroad related to his scientific activity, Taylor had a very quiet life, spent in his house, Farmfield, at the periphery of Cambridge, and his room, next to Rutherford's, at the Cavendish Laboratory. He was a rather shy man who disliked large scientific enterprises and preferred to concentrate on problems that could be formulated and managed by a single person, from the theoretical aspects to the design of the apparatus and the experimental observations.

Taylor received honorary degrees from about a dozen universities in Europe and America and was awarded honorary membership or fellowship in a number of scientific institutions. He was a member of the International Committee for the International Congresses of Applied Mechanics from their beginning in 1924.

Following a suggestion by J. J. Thompson in 1909, Taylor's first research experiment was an investigation of interference fringes formed by light waves of very small intensity. After that he turned to topics in applied mechanics, and all of his following scientific production was in this field, though he used to label himself a classical physicist. In 1911 he was appointed to a temporary readership in dynamical meteorology established at Cambridge with funds given by Arthur Schuster, and the following year he spent six months aboard HMS *Scotia*, sent on a scientific expedition in the North Atlantic. Taylor did experimental research on the mixing processes occurring in the lower layers of the atmosphere because of turbulent fluctuations of wind velocity, and on his return to Cambridge published a theoretical analysis of his data in which he put forward the idea of a "mixing length" characteristic of turbulent diffusion, allowing a rough analogy between turbulent motion of a fluid and the kinetic theory of gases.

This was Taylor's first attack on a field in which, twenty years later, he would produce what is possibly his most important contribution to science. But his activity encompassed a much wider range of subjects in applied mechanics, both in theory and in experiment. During World War I, Taylor did research for the Royal Flying Corps at the Royal Aircraft Factory, Farnborough, where a team of scientists worked on aeronautical problems. With A. A. Griffith, he investigated the problem of the stress distribution in cylindrical shafts under torsion, which had a bearing on the manufacturing of stronger propeller shafts for aircraft, and starting from this he was led to think about the physical processes that limit the strength of solid materials. This analytical investigation was the source of a line of thinking that led him to his theory of dislocations in metal crystals, published in 1934.

In 1923 Taylor was appointed to a Royal Society research professorship, relieving him from teaching duties and allowing him to concentrate on research; as Rutherford said, he was "paid provided he does no work." In the same year he published a study of the stability of steady flow between concentric circular cylinders in relative rotation. Here, as in most of his activity, he showed a peculiar ability to extract from the experimental study of a specific phenomenon general principles amenable to a thorough mathematical investigation. This ability was especially manifest in a beautiful paper on diffusion by continuous movements, published in 1921, in which the observation of pictures of the shape of the smoke plume from a chimney prompted him to introduce a correlation coefficient between velocity components at different times, regarded as random functions, to study the properties of turbulent diffusion.

In the following years an increasing familiarity with the phenomenology of turbulence, largely due to his association with the work done by B. M. Jones in wind tunnels at the Aeronautical Laboratory at Cambridge, and his interest in the mathematical work of Norbert Wiener on chaotic motion, converged to produce his famous papers on the statistical theory of turbulence (1935). In these works Taylor extended the idea first advanced in 1921 to a full description of the statistical properties of turbulence, introducing the concept of isotropic turbulence and showing that in this case the theoretical treatment on the basis of the correlation coefficient between the random fluctuating velocities led to results that could be tested, and were in fact confirmed, by data obtained in wind-tunnel experimental research. He crowned this line of research three years later, introducing the idea of the energy spectrum of turbulence with the use of Fourier's transform analysis, a radically new approach in the field of fluid dynamics, dominated up to that time by semiempirical methods. Here again he made use of Wiener's highly sophisticated mathematical work on harmonic analysis, translating it into a formulation that could be used for his specific problem and applied to obtain definite results.

During World War II Taylor was engaged in several fields as scientific consultant for war-related projects, mainly as an expert on blasts and shock waves. He was involved with the Manhattan Project, and he saw the first nuclear explosion in the desert at Alamogordo. He retired from the professorship in 1952, but kept doing research until 1972, when he suffered a severe stroke from which he never recovered.

BIBLIOGRAPHY

I. ORIGINAL WORKS. His papers, published and unpublished, have been collected in G. I. Taylor, *Scientific Papers*, G. K. Batchelor, ed., 4 vols. (Cambridge, 1958–1971). His papers have been collected by G. K. Batchelor and deposited in the library of Trinity College, Cambridge. A catalog, compiled by Jeannine Alton, Harriot Weiskittel, and Julia Latham-Jackson, has been published by the Contemporary Scientific Archives Centre (Cambridge, 1979).

II. SECONDARY LITERATURE. An authoritative biography by G. K. Batchelor appeared in *Biographical Memoirs of Fellows of the Royal Society*, **22** (1976), 565–633, with a list of honors and a complete bibliography. More information about Taylor's scientific activity is in G. K. Batchelor, "An Unfinished Dialogue with G. I. Taylor," in *Journal of Fluid Mechanics*, **70** (1975), 625–638; and D. B. Spalding, "An Interview with Sir Geoffrey Taylor," in *Chartered Mechanical Engineer*, **9** (1962), 186–191.

GIOVANNI BATTIMELLI

TAYLOR, HUGH STOTT (*b.* St. Helens, Lancashire, England, 6 February 1890; *d.* Princeton, New Jersey, 17 April 1974), *physical chemistry.*

Hugh Stott Taylor was the third of the eight children of James and Ellen Stott Taylor. His father was a glass technologist and his mother a schoolteacher. Like his parents, Taylor was a devout Roman Catholic. After school in St. Helens, Taylor attended Liverpool University (1906–1912), where he received the B.Sc. (1909), the M.Sc. (1910), and, on the evidence of published researches, the D.Sc. (1914). Acting on the advice of F. G. Donnan, professor of physical chemistry at Liverpool, Taylor went to study with Svante Arrhenius at Stockholm

(1912–1913) and then with Max Bodenstein at Hannover (1913–1914). He was appointed instructor in chemistry at Princeton University in 1914, partly on the recommendation of James Kendall, a fellow Stockholm student. Taylor remained at Princeton for the rest of his life. In 1919 he married Elizabeth Sawyer from Southport, England. They had two daughters.

His academic advancement was rapid. Taylor became associate professor (1921), full professor (1922), chairman of the chemistry department (1926–1951), and dean of the graduate school (1945–1958). In 1953 he was knighted (K.B.E.). Finally, Taylor became the first president of the Woodrow Wilson National Fellowship Foundation (1958–1969).

Taylor was an industrious, well-organized chemist whose judgment was both well respected and sought after. He wrote over three hundred scientific papers and articles and undertook valuable editorial work. His research began in inorganic chemistry and phase equilibria under Donnan's pupil, Henry Bassett, Jr., at Liverpool. At Stockholm, under Arrhenius, he examined the influence of neutral salts on the acid-catalyzed hydrolysis of esters. The catalytic activity of hydrochloric acid was increased when he added potassium chloride. From his results Taylor derived a relationship between the catalytic constant and the acid-dissociation constant that to some extent anticipated the Brönsted-Pederson equation for general acid catalysis.

In Bodenstein's laboratory Taylor gained important experience in high-vacuum techniques through an investigation of the effect of alpha particles on a mixture of hydrogen and chlorine gases. Large numbers of hydrogen chloride molecules were produced for each ion pair formed. His results were comparable with those obtained in 1913 by Bodenstein and Dux from the same reaction with photochemical initiation. Bodenstein originally interpreted this reaction as an ionic chain sequence. In 1918 H. W. Nernst suggested that it was an atomic chain sequence, a view that is now generally accepted.

At Princeton, Taylor was encouraged by his professor, G. A. Hulett, to determine thermochemical data and to test the Nernst heat theorem using electrical cells. His major studies, however, were devoted to gas adsorption and heterogeneous catalysis. Taylor's research during World War I may have stimulated his interest in catalysis. In 1917 he rejoined Donnan for two years at University College, London. Working with E. K. Rideal, Taylor manufactured synthesis gas (CO_2 and H_2) in order to prepare hydrogen for ammonia synthesis. This was achieved by the water-gas shift reaction $CO + H_2O \rightleftarrows CO_2 + H_2$, for which they developed a coprecipitated iron oxide/chromium oxide catalyst.

In the 1920's Taylor and his co-workers at Princeton investigated the adsorption of gases on metals in order to elucidate the action of catalysts. The specific nature of adsorption was revealed by measurements of the heat of adsorption of hydrogen on both nickel and copper. Adsorption depended on both the gas and the metal used in experiments. It was not a simple liquefaction process. Catalysts were also revealed to be quite specific in their action. They were markedly sensitive to heat treatment, sintering, and poisons. In a notable paper of 1925, Taylor emphasized that catalyst surfaces were heterogeneous and that only a fraction of the surface available for gas adsorption might be active. The catalytic action was connected with exposed atoms on the corners, edges, or surfaces of metal crystals. He called these sites "active centers." In an extension of Irving Langmuir's views on adsorption, Taylor suggested that several gas molecules might be adsorbed on one site, and there they might react with one another.

Further insight into the mechanism of heterogeneous catalysis came in 1930 and 1931; Taylor suggested that adsorption of gases by solids might be a very slow process. He distinguished between two kinds of adsorption of diatomic gas molecules. First, there was weak but rapid molecular adsorption involving van der Waals forces. This was physical adsorption. Second, there was a stronger dissociative adsorption that produced gaseous atoms on the catalyst surface. This was chemisorption, and it required a certain activation energy comparable with that of chemical reactions. He emphasized that activated adsorption was fundamental to any understanding of the mechanism of heterogeneous catalysis. In 1931 Taylor and A. T. Williamson obtained evidence for different kinds of activated adsorption of hydrogen on manganous oxide/chromic oxide surfaces. Taylor found further support for activated adsorption in the 1930's by isotope-exchange reactions with hydrogen and deuterium.

During the same period Taylor continued to investigate homogeneous gas reactions and photochemistry. By using photosensitization to excite mercury atoms, Taylor and A. L. Marshall dissociated hydrogen molecules into atoms and examined their reactions. In 1925 Taylor showed that ethylene reacted rapidly with a hydrogen atom to give an ethyl radical: $C_2H_4 + H \rightarrow C_2H_5$. This ethyl radical then reacted with a hydrogen molecule to make both the product ethane and a hydrogen atom to

repeat the whole process: $C_2H_5 + H_2 \rightarrow C_2H_6 + H$. This was one of the earliest examples of organic free radicals acting as chain carriers in chemical reactions. Taylor and Marshall also demonstrated free radical chain reactions between hydrogen and carbon monoxide to produce formaldehyde, and in 1926 Taylor and J. R. Bates converted ethylene into liquid polyethylene, a forerunner of industrial polyethylene production. A commercially useful reaction studied by Taylor and J. Turkevich in 1935 was the dehydrogenation and ring closure of heptane to make toluene, using a chromium oxide gel catalyst.

In the 1930's Taylor was one of the first chemists to produce heavy water on a reasonable scale. This experience was valuable in 1941 and 1942, when he worked on the large-scale production of water for the Manhattan Project. From 1943 to 1945 he again assisted with the project by statistically testing new nickel barriers for the separation of uranium 235 from uranium 238 by fractional diffusion of uranium hexafluoride.

BIBLIOGRAPHY

I. ORIGINAL WORKS. *Catalysis in Theory and Practice* (London, 1919; 2nd ed., London and New York, 1926), written with E. K. Rideal; *Fuel Production and Utilization* (London and New York, 1920); *Industrial Hydrogen* (New York, 1921; 2nd ed., New York, 1931); *A Treatise on Physical Chemistry* (editor and contributor), 2 vols. (New York, 1924; 3rd ed., edited with S. Glasstone, 1942–1951); "Photosensitization and the Mechanism of Chemical Reactions," in *Transactions of the Faraday Society*, **21** (1925), 560–568; *Elementary Physical Chemistry* (New York, 1927; 3rd ed., written with H. A. Taylor, New York, 1942); "Fundamental Science from Phlogiston to Cyclotron," in *Molecular Films, Cyclotron and the New Biology* (New Brunswick, N.J., 1942, repr. 1946), written with Irving Langmuir and Ernest O. Lawrence; *Physical Measurements in Gas Dynamics and Combustion*, ed. with B. Lewis and R. N. Pease (Princeton, 1954); *Science in Progress*, editor of the 10th and 11th series (New Haven, 1957–1960).

II. SECONDARY LITERATURE. C. M. Kemball, "Hugh Stott Taylor," in *Biographical Memoirs of Fellows of the Royal Society*, **21** (1975), 517–547, includes a complete bibliography. Obituaries appeared in *Nature*, **251** (1974), 266; and *Chemistry in Britain*, **11** (1975), 370–371.

MICHAEL STANLEY

TEICHMÜLLER, PAUL JULIUS OSWALD (*b.* Nordhausen im Harz, Germany, 18 June 1913; *d.* Dnieper region, U.S.S.R., September 1943 [?]), *mathematics.*

Oswald Teichmüller was the only child of Julius Adolf Paul Teichmüller, an independent weaver by trade, and his wife, Gertrud Dinse. He grew up in the provincial Harz region around St. Andreasberg and Nordhausen. In the spring of 1931 he enrolled to study mathematics and physics at Göttingen University. Only a few months later, he joined the Nazi Party and the SA (Storm Troopers). Although he was a brilliant student of mathematics, he supported the expulsion of most of Göttingen's mathematicians by the Nazi regime in 1933.

After Helmut Hasse's call to a vacant chair at Göttingen in the early summer of 1934, Teichmüller engaged in algebraic investigations (nos. 2, 3, 4, and 11 of his collected works) while also preparing a doctoral dissertation on spectral theory in quaternionic Hilbert space (no. 1), finished in 1935. After a short period of postdoctoral work at Göttingen, during which E. Ullrich and R. Nevanlinna introduced him to function theory (nos. 8 and 9), he transferred to the University of Berlin in April 1937, where a group of Nazi mathematicians had gathered around Ludwig Bieberbach and the journal *Deutsche Mathematik*. Teichmüller qualified as university lecturer in March 1938 with a good, though not spectacular, thesis on function theory (no. 13). One of the technical devices used there, quasi-conformal mappings, provided a clue to his main contribution to the theory of Riemann surfaces, the program of which he sketched in 1938 and 1939 while continuing work at Berlin, supported by a modest fellowship (no. 20).

Teichmüller was drafted into the army in the early summer of 1939, just before World War II, but continued his research, first as a soldier in Norway (no. 24), then in Berlin from 1941 to early 1943, working on decoding for the army high command (nos. 29 and 32). In early 1943, however, after the first successes of the Soviet army against the Germans, Teichmüller was sent to the eastern front. He disappeared in September 1943 at the Dnieper and very likely died in the same month, sharing the fate of a great majority of young men in his unit.

Teichmüller's early algebraic investigations dealt with the valuation theory of fields and the structure of algebras. In valuation theory he introduced multiplicative systems of representatives of the residue field of valuation rings (no. 2), which, in a joint effort with E. Witt, led to a characterization of the structure of the whole field in terms of the residue field (no. 11). In the theory of algebras he started to generalize Emmy Noether's concept of crossed products from fields to certain kind of algebras (*Normalringe*, no. 3), gaining new insights, for example, into the structure of p-algebras (algebra of rank p^n over a field of characteristic p; no. 4).

Although from 1937 on, his main interests shifted to function theory, Teichmüller did not give up algebra. In a paper published in 1940, he explored further steps toward a Galois theory of algebras, resulting in the introduction of a group that was later recognized as a third Galois cohomology group (no. 22).

After his *Habilitation*, Teichmüller turned energetically to questions in the variation of conformal structures on surfaces, raised earlier by G. F. B. Riemann, H. Poincaré, C. F. Klein, and R. Fricke. His most important innovation was the introduction of quasi-conformal mappings to this field, using ideas first developed by H. Grötzsch and L. Ahlfors in different contexts. That is, considering marked surfaces S of type (g, n), for example (that is, S orientable, closed of genus g with n distinct distinguished points, each S endowed with a homotopy class of sufficiently regular maps $\phi: S_o \to S$, where S_o is fixed of the same type), he concentrated on sufficiently regular homeomorphisms ϕ such that for z varying in S_o the dilatation dil $\phi(z)$ (ratio of maximal and minimal diameters of the image of a circle in the tangent plane $T_z S_o$ with respect to conformal metrics on S_o and S) is bounded. Moreover, he analyzed the close relationship between such quasi-conformal ϕ and reciprocal Beltrami differentials q on S_o ($q = \mathrm{H}\dfrac{dz}{dz}$; z is the local parameter, H is the complex-valued function on S_o) as invariants of the conformal metrics pulled back by ϕ.

Teichmüller's main conjecture (I) may be stated as follows: In any homotopy class there is exactly one extremal quasi-conformal mapping ϕ_o—that is, a mapping with dilatation bounded from above by $\inf_{\phi} \sup_{z}$ dil (z). That means variation of conformal structure can be realized uniquely by extremal quasi-conformal mappings (no. 20, secs. 46, 52, 122).

Teichmüller established a connection between extremal quasi-conformal mappings and regular quadratic differentials on S_o using a class of related reciprocal Beltrami differentials. That led him to another conjecture (II) proclaiming the existence of a bicontinuous bijective correspondence Φ between a space T_1 of real parts of certain reciprocal Beltrami differentials and $M_{g,n}$, the moduli space of all conformal structures considered. (T_1 consists of all expressions $c\,\mathrm{Re}\{''/''\}$, where $''$ is a regular quadratic differential on S_o and $0 < c < 1$.) In fact, he proved existence and injectivity of Φ (theorem A; no. 20, secs. 132–140).

Teichmüller attacked surjectivity along different lines. In his 1939 paper (no. 20) he analyzed infinitesimal deformations of conformal structures on S heuristically, looking upon them as forming the tangent spaces of $M_{g,n}$. After the introduction of an appropriate norm, $M_{g,n}$ was endowed with a Finsler space structure. On that basis he speculated about a possible path to a kind of continuity proof of surjectivity in another central conjecture (III): After appropriate change of norms, T_1 coincides with $T_S M_{g,n}$ and the exponential map of the Finsler metric coincides with Φ of theorem A; thus a Rinow-Hopf type argument can be used to show geodetical completeness of the Finsler space $M_{g,n}$ and the surjectivity of Φ (20, secs. 115–123).

Because his heuristic arguments met with severe criticism, Teichmüller next showed existence of extremal quasi-conformal mappings in the special case of certain simply connected plane regions (pentagons; no. 24). Back in Berlin and working under slightly better conditions, he then gave an existence proof (theorem B) for surfaces of type $(g,0)$ by a classical continuity argument from uniformization theory, avoiding infinitesimal deformations and Finsler metrics (no. 29). But theorem B was also intended as a first step toward a deeper investigation of moduli spaces. In one of his last papers, Teichmüller sketched an idea of how to endow the moduli space $M_{g,o}$ with an analytic structure and how to construct an analytic fiber space of Riemann surfaces parametrized by the points of $M_{g,o}$ (no. 32).

Owing to his being sent to the front and his early death, Teichmüller could not work out most of his ideas. They became seminal, however, for later work.

BIBLIOGRAPHY

I. ORIGINAL WORKS. Teichmüller's works are collected in his *Gesammelte Abhandlungen,* Lars V. Alfors and Frederick W. Gehring, eds. (Berlin, Heidelberg, and New York, 1982), with a complete bibliography on 747–749.

II. SECONDARY LITERATURE. Reference to some of Teichmüller's algebraic work is made in Saunders MacLane, "Topology and Logic as a Source of Algebra," in *Bulletin of the American Mathematical Society,* **82** (1976), 1–40. On his function theoretical contributions, see L. Bers, "Quasiconformal Mappings with Applications to Differential Equations, Function Theory and Topology," in *Bulletin of the American Mathematical Society,* **83** (1977), 1083–1100. For the broader context, see L. Furtmüller and M. Pinl, "Mathematicians Under Hitler," in *Leo Baeck Yearbook,* XVIII (London, Jerusalem, and New York, 1973), 129–182; H. Mehrtens, "Ludwig Bieberbach and 'Deutsche Mathematik,'" in E. Phillips, ed., *History of Mathematics* (1987); and Norbert Schappacher, "Das Mathematische Institut der Universität Göttingen 1929–1950," in Heinrich Becker, Hans-Joachim Dahms, and Cornelia Wegeler, eds., *Die Universität Göttingen in Nazionalsozialismus* (Munich, 1987), 345–373. See also William Abikoff, "Oswald Teichmüller," in *Mathematical Intelligencer,* **8,** no. 3 (1986), 8–16, 33.

ERHARD SCHOLZ

TEISSIER, GEORGES (*b.* Paris, France, 19 February 1900; *d.* Roscoff, France, 7 January 1972), *zoology, population genetics.*

A field naturalist from childhood, Teissier took an early interest in mathematics. When he was admitted to the École Normale Supérieure in 1919, he was accepted in the mathematics section, not that of natural sciences. Throughout his life there were three aspects to his scientific activity: zoology, biometrics, and population genetics. These interests are shown not only in his scientific articles but also in the orientations of his students. In 1945 he was appointed professor of zoology at the Sorbonne and director of the Biological Center at Roscoff in Brittany. He hated scientific meetings and traveling and spent most of his time in Paris and Roscoff. Characterized by an inexorable logical rigor and a notable erudition, he was very abrupt and rarely encouraging; nevertheless, he succeeded in training many young scientists who are now internationally known. This rigor, which was expressed in his public life as well as in his scientific activity, had family roots. His parents, who were schoolteachers, belonged to the rigidly moral Calvinist community of southern France, a group that had been persecuted in the seventeenth and eighteenth centuries. Although an agnostic, Teissier possessed many Calvinist attitudes.

During World War II Teissier was a member of the French Resistance from 1941 and organized resistance activities at the Sorbonne. He then joined the Francs Tireurs et Partisans resistance group, succeeding Marcel Prenant (a fellow professor) at headquarters when Prenant was arrested and deported by the Nazis. In 1945 after the liberation of France, Teissier contributed to the development of scientific research and to the training of young scientists as deputy director, and then director, of the newly formed Centre National de la Recherche Scientifique (CNRS), where he succeeded Frédéric Joliot-Curie. It was at this time that he set up the Laboratoire de Génétique Evolutive at Gif-sur-Yvette (director, 1951–1965). He was obliged to leave his post at the CNRS in 1950 for political reasons. Throughout this period he played an important role, together with Boris Ephrussi and Philippe L'Héritier, in establishing a genetics course at the Sorbonne.

Author of more than 175 publications and a member of the Académie des Sciences, Teissier's main interests were Cnidaria, growth, and population genetics.

Cnidaria. From 1920 on, Teissier had a particular interest in marine biology. He wrote several articles on the growth of hydrozoans and other Cnidaria. He showed that the eggs of hydroids are anisotropic and described their early polarity and the persisting polarity of embryo fragments during regulation following experimental fragmentation (1931). With Bertil Swedmark he published descriptions of several Cnidaria of the littoral interstitial meiofauna and established the order Actinulida for these newly described organisms (1966).

Growth and Biometrics. In 1927 Teissier began his studies of animal growth. He rapidly became aware that quantitative methods were necessary, a view not widely accepted at the time. He increasingly adopted biometrical methods and became a statistician.

His dissertation (1931) was devoted to insects, in particular the flour beetle, *Tenebrio molitor,* and the honeycomb moth, *Galleria mellonella.* The size of an arthropod increases at each molt. At each step, the form and structure change. These changes can be expressed quantitatively by comparing the growth rate of the organ under study at each molt with an overall logarithmic body measure used as a reference. The relative growth rates of the different organs are represented by curves: if the studied organ grows more rapidly than the overall measure, the slope is greater than 1. If growth takes place less rapidly in the organ under investigation, the slope is less than 1. The same mathematical relationship was discovered independently by J. S. Huxley. The two men agreed to describe this phenomenon as an "allometric relationship" (1936). The practical importance of this law and its general applicability were quickly shown for both crustaceans and insects.

In the crustacean *Maia squinado,* growth consists of three distinct stages separated by two critical molts. These are clearly shown in Figure 1. The laws of growth, shown for the first time in this study, are applicable to both animals and plants. Their general applicability has made them particularly useful in the study of chemical embryology and in endocrinology. For example, by studying changes in the slope of curves on this kind of graph, Hélène Charniaux-Cotton was able to show the existence

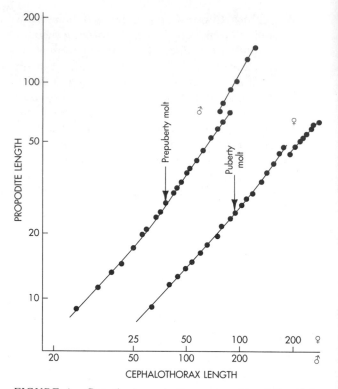

FIGURE 1. Growth stages in the protopodite of the *Maia squinado* claw. Locomotor appendages, which first grow in the same way in the two sexes, grow more rapidly in males after the pubertal molt, producing important discontinuities. Because of the difference between males and females, these appendages are called sexual variants.

of a gland responsible for secondary sexual characters in crustaceans.

A more intensive study of sexual variants enabled Teissier to develop a method for correlational factor analysis and for analysis of principal components (1938). Along with experimental studies of growth, he carried out a series of theoretical studies with René Lambert that revealed the existence of a "biological similarity" and showed the variation of a number of biological rhythms with size (1927).

Evolutionary Genetics. Teissier's interest in mathematics led him to population genetics. In 1932, at a time when Darwinism was of only peripheral interest in France, he began a series of studies on *Drosophila* populations with Philippe L'Héritier. At this stage, population genetics—which had originated a dozen years before under the inspiration of J. B. S. Haldane and R. A. Fisher in England and Sewall Wright in America—was still largely theoretical. The main project of population geneticists was to give a mathematical expression to the changes in allelic and genotypic frequencies from one generation to another, given the existence of certain parameters. But no experimental study had yet been carried out.

Drosophila melanogaster, whose genetics were already well known, seemed to be the ideal subject. L'Héritier and Teissier set up population cages that allowed populations of 2,000 to 3,000 flies to be followed over a period of months or years, under conditions of severe food competition (1933). These cages, which are still used throughout the world, enabled many discoveries to be made.

By placing two isogenic strains that differed by only one mutation (such as *Bar* and *Wild-type* or *Sepia* and *Wild-type*) in a cage, they were able to make direct measurements of changes in allelic and genotypic frequencies during competition and to calculate the selective value of the different genotypes. The experimental model could then be used to test various theoretical models for reliability and to suggest possible modifications.

Whichever gene is studied, the replacement of normal mutant individuals by normal flies initially takes place very rapidly. However, the rate of change soon declines, and after several months, changes in the proportions of the two alleles take place extremely slowly. The frequency of the mutant gene may be so low that it can disappear completely, by chance; for other mutations a quasi-stable situation may be reached while the mutation is still relatively frequent (1937). In such cases it seems that natural selection, resulting from food competition, tends to maintain the two alleles in stable proportions.

The genetic basis of the situation described by Darwin for natural populations was thus established. Such balanced polymorphisms, described in natural populations of *Drosophila pseudoobscura* by Theodosius Dobzhansky, are now universally considered to be an indispensable condition for the evolutionary process. The maintenance of such polymorphisms despite the existence of selection may seem somewhat paradoxical. This problem led to a series of studies to explain the manner in which polymorphisms are maintained. The most straightforward hypothesis suggests that the three genotypes do not have the same adaptive value, with heterozygotic individuals producing more offspring on average than the two homozygotic types. This hypothesis is difficult to test when one of the alleles is completely recessive and the heterozygotes cannot be distinguished from the dominant homozygotes. Where only two genotypes are involved and one of the homozygotes is inviable, such a study is clear-cut. Using this procedure, Teissier showed the possibility of maintaining a lethal gene and a viable allele in high, stable frequencies in an experimental population (1942). The observed equilibrium occurs at exactly the level predicted theoretically, given experimental differences in fecundity between strains. These results led to an exhaustive theoretical study of the equilibria shown by lethal genes (1944).

Another way in which polymorphisms may be maintained was revealed in a study of competition between *Bar* and *Sepia* mutants and their wild-type alleles. An abnormally slow decline in the elimination of the mutant strains was coupled with an increase in the selective value of *Bar* mutants when they were only in competition with normal larvae (1934). This phenomenon, which had been predicted theoretically but never shown to exist, has since been studied by a number of authors and probably plays an important role in maintaining polymorphisms.

Another line of research was opened up by the discovery of a fixed mutant—later discovered to be *Sepia*—in a natural population. This strain had a consistent frequency of around 0.22 (1943). Given that mutations are normally eliminated, this discovery was of obvious interest. Its presence suggested that the adaptive value of a mutant depends not only upon the mutation itself but also upon the genetic background in which it is found. This hypothesis was confirmed by a series of experimental results (1947). Although this conclusion may seem obvious today, at the time it was revolutionary, raising the problem of interactions within the individual's genome, which has been the subject of much study since Teissier's discovery. Besides these particularly original studies, Teissier carried out a series of important collaborative investigations into genetic polymorphisms in natural populations of the crustacean *Spaheroma serratum* (1960).

Teissier was an important early figure in the field of biometrics and population genetics. However, the isolation of France during World War II—at a time when these subjects were really beginning to take off—together with the fact that although Teissier wrote many articles, he did not produce any book synthesizing his ideas and approach, limited his scientific impact, despite the importance of many of his discoveries.

BIBLIOGRAPHY

I. ORIGINAL WORKS. "Théorie de la similitude biologique," in *Annales de physique et de physico chimie biologique*, **3** (1927), 212–246, written with René Lambert; "Étude expériementale du développement de quelques Hydraires," in *Annales de science naturelle*, sér. zoologique, 10th ser., **14** (1931), 5–59; "Recherches morphologiques et physiologiques sur la croissance des Insectes," in *Travaux de la station biologique de Roscoff*, **9** (1931), 29–238; "Étude d'une population de Drosophiles en équilibre," in *Comptes rendus de l'Académie des sciences*, **197** (1933), 1765–1767, written with Philippe L'Héritier; "Une expérience de sélection naturelle. Courbe d'élimination du gène 'bar' dans une population de Drosophiles en équilibre," in *Comptes rendus de la Société de biologie*, **117** (1934), 1049–1051, written with Philippe L'Héritier; "Croissance des variants sexuels chez *Maia squinado*," in *Travaux de la station biologique de Roscoff*, **13** (1935), 91–130; "Terminologie et notation dans la description de la croissance relative," in *Comptes rendus de la Société de biologie*, **121** (1936), 934–936, written with J. S. Huxley; "Elimination des formes mutantes dans les populations de Drosophiles. I. Cas des Drosophiles 'bar,'" *ibid.*, **124** (1937), 882–884, written with Philippe L'Héritier; "Elimination des formes mutantes dans les populations de Drosophiles. II. Cas des Drosophiles 'ebony,'" *ibid.*, 884–886, written with Philippe L'Héritier; "Un essai d'analyse factorielle. Les variants sexuels de *Maia squinado*," in *Bio-typologie*, **7** (1938), 73–96; "Persistance d'un gène léthal dans une population de Drosophiles," in *Comptes rendus de l'Académie des sciences*, **214** (1942), 261–263; "Apparition et fixation d'un gène mutant dans une population stationnaire de Drosophiles," *ibid.*, **216** (1943), 88–90; "Équilibre des gènes léthaux dans les populations stationnaires panmictiques," in *Revue scientifique*, **82** (1944), 145–159; "Mécanismes de l'évolution," in *La pensée*, **2** (1945), 5–19 and **3** (1945), 15–31; "Variation de la fréquence du gène *ebony* dans une population stationnaire de Drosophiles," in *Comptes rendus de l'Académie des sciences*, **224** (1947), 1788–1789; "L'évolution du patrimoine héréditaire dans les populations naturelles," in *La progenèse* (Centre International de l'Enfance, Travaux et Documents), **8** (1955), 57–85; "Génétique des populations de *Sphaeroma serratum* (F.)," in *Cahiers de biologie marine*, **1** (1960), 103–111, 221–230, 279–293, and **6** (1965), 195–200, written with Charles Bocquet and Robert Lejuez; and "The Actinulida and Their Evolutionary Significance," in *The Cnidaria and Their Evolution. Symposia of the Zoological Society of London*, **16** (London, 1966), 119–134, written with Bertil Swedmark.

CLAUDINE PETIT

THIERFELDER, HANS (*b.* Rostock, Germany, 22 February 1858; *d.* Tübingen, Germany, 11 November 1930), *physiological chemistry*.

Thierfelder, best known for his isolation of the brain substance cerebron (phrenosin) and for his chemical studies of this and other cerebrosides, was born into a medical family. His father, Theodor Thierfelder, was a university professor and director of a medical clinic in Rostock. After graduating from Rostock Gymnasium, Thierfelder studied medicine (1876–1881) at Rostock, Tübingen, Heidelberg, Munich, and Freiburg. His instructors in physiology included Carl von Voit at Munich and Wilhelm Kühne at Heidelberg, both of whom were influential teachers with special interests in physiological chemistry. After passing his state examinations in Freiburg, Thierfelder worked for a year with Otto Nasse at the latter's Institute for Pharmacology and Physiological Chemistry in Rostock. Under Nasse's direction Thierfelder took his M.D. in 1883 with a dissertation on the chemical processes involved in the formation of milk sugar and casein, a study that became the basis of his first publication.

Drawn to science rather than to medical practice, Thierfelder applied to Felix Hoppe-Seyler at Strassburg and in 1884 was appointed assistant in Hoppe-Seyler's Institute for Physiological Chemistry. Later Thierfelder's student and collaborator Ernst Klenk would describe him as "one of the last outstanding physiological chemists to come out of the old Hoppe-Seyler school," and there is no doubt that the more than six years that Thierfelder spent in Strassburg left an impression on his subsequent work. In Hoppe-Seyler's institute, where he habilitated in 1887, Thierfelder continued his training in the problems and methods of physiological chemistry, the chemical analysis of body substances, and the study of the changes these substances undergo in the body. Here he also absorbed Hoppe-Seyler's view that physiological chemistry constituted a field of research distinguishable from the anatomical and physical aspects of physiology, a field that could best be pursued in an institutionally distinct setting. One expression of that view was Hoppe-Seyler's *Zeitschrift für physiologische Chemie*, founded in 1877. Most of Thierfelder's work was published in this journal, and he served for the greater part of his career as one of its editorial consultants. Another indication both of the identity of the field and of the continuity of Thierfelder's work with that of his teacher was Hoppe-Seyler's *Handbuch der physiologisch und pathologisch-chemischen Analyse*. Thierfelder collaborated with Hoppe-Seyler in preparing the sixth edition (1893) and kept the classic text up to date after the latter's death with editions in 1903, 1909, and 1924.

Another effect of Thierfelder's time in Strassburg was his association with several young workers in physiological chemistry. Among them was Joseph von Mering, with whom Thierfelder collaborated in a study of the behavior of a series of tertiary alcohols in the animal organism. They found that administration of the alcohols, like other substances previously studied, could lead to the appearance of paired glucuronic acids in the urine, but that the outcome varied depending on the species of animal used. This work led Thierfelder into further investigations on the formation of glucuronic acid in the fasting animal and on the constitution of that acid. In the latter studies he was able to give evidence of the aldehyde nature of the acid and of its close relationship to glucose. Prompted in part by Hoppe-Seyler's interest in brain chemistry, Thierfelder undertook other research at Strassburg that resulted in the identification of brain sugar with galactose.

In 1891 Thierfelder left Strassburg to join the physiologist Max Rubner at the Hygiene Institute at the University of Berlin. The new setting encouraged different kinds of investigations. Thierfelder resumed his study of milk and its constituents. With Carl Günther he showed that, contrary to prevailing opinion, the milk acid isolated from sour milk was not always the optically inactive acid but frequently the dextrorotatory form. Günther and Thierfelder were able to isolate a substance that, inoculated into sterilized milk, always produced dextrolactic acid.

With George H. F. Nuttall, Thierfelder began to address experimentally Pasteur's view that the microorganisms of the intestinal canal played an important role in the life of the organism. In technically difficult studies, Nuttall and Thierfelder kept guinea pigs born by cesarean section completely sterile. When the animals remained healthy and behaved normally, the two investigators concluded against Pasteur. While at the Hygiene Institute, Thierfelder met Emil Fischer, and with him conducted tests on the behavior of a series of natural and synthetic sugars in relation to purebred varieties of yeast.

In 1895 Thierfelder was named director of the chemical department of the Physiological Institute at the University of Berlin, as successor of Albrecht Kossel. In 1896 he became extraordinary professor at the institute. He held both positions until 1909. Shortly after the first appointment, in 1895, Thierfelder married Luise von Beseler; they had two sons and two daughters.

On two occasions Thierfelder was offered a chair of physiology, first at Marburg in 1901, as successor of Albrecht Kossel, then at Göttingen in 1905, as successor of Georg Meissner. He declined both offers, on the grounds that physiological chemistry, as a field with its own research problems and methods, required its own institutional locale. This requirement was met when, in 1909, Thierfelder was called to the chair of physiological chemistry at the University of Tübingen, vacated by the death of Carl Gustav von Hüfner. He remained at Tübingen, as director of the Physiological-Chemical Institute, for the rest of his career.

In 1900 Thierfelder and his collaborator Emil Wörner reported the isolation of cerebron (later called phrenosin), the first of a group of substances known as cerebrosides to be obtained in unequivocally pure form. This work marked a breakthrough in the sense that it opened the way to determination of the chemical nature of these compounds and their relationships to other substances found in the brain. In taking over leadership of this field, Thierfelder carried forward Hoppe-Seyler's interest in brain chemistry and his own earlier studies on brain sugar and its sources.

Except for the decade between 1913 and 1923, Thierfelder's work on the cerebrosides and related problems occupied him for the rest of his life. Working with several collaborators, he established reliable methods for preparing cerebron and cerasin, the second cerebroside to be isolated, and obtained more exact descriptions of decomposition products of these two substances. Thierfelder showed that cerebronic acid, obtained from cerebron, is an α-hydroxy acid, and that the fatty acid of cerasin is not a hydroxy acid but another acid of formula $C_{24}H_{48}O_2$, later identified as lignoceric acid by Phoebus A. Levene and Clarence J. West. On the basis of studies of the acetyl products of cerebron and cerasin, Thierfelder advanced structural formulas for these compounds that were accepted with minor modifications by the time of his death. In the course of his work on the cerebrosides, Thierfelder repeatedly encountered phosphatides, fatty substances that could hinder the purification of cerebrosides because of their chemical and physical similarities to the latter. Several studies on the phosphatides were carried out by Thierfelder, his collaborators, and his students; and in the last years of his life he turned to research on the group of phosphatides closest to the cerebrosides, the sphingomyelins.

The slow, painstaking nature of the work in brain chemistry called forth Thierfelder's finest qualities as an investigator. Not only capable of, but also preferring, long hours in the laboratory, he worked with great intensity on the problems he chose to pursue. A skillful experimenter, he demanded of himself the greatest exactitude, and of his results the highest possible reliability. To the recalcitrance of his research problems Thierfelder opposed what his collaborator Ernst Klenk called an "iron diligence and tough perseverance," and the conviction that his work was necessary if new knowledge was to be gained of the brain, which he regarded as one of the most obscure areas of physiological chemistry.

The same qualities may be observed in Thierfelder's studies of the fate of several foreign substances in the animal body, problems to which he turned between 1913 and 1923. In one set of investigations he showed that after administration of phenylacetic acid and related substances to humans, phenylacetylglutamine appeared in the urine. This finding led Thierfelder to try to determine whether glutamine is present in protein and to conduct a study of the constitution of glutamine. In other research he examined the behavior of aliphatic-aromatic ketones and of hydrocarbons in the animal body, and was able to propose rules for the oxidative decomposition of these substances.

After an illness and operation in 1927, Thierfelder returned to his work with difficulty, but before his death he was able, with Ernst Klenk, to finish a monograph on the cerebrosides and phosphatides. Serious, kindly, and modest, Thierfelder was a conscientious teacher and a valued colleague. As a physiological chemist he made his influence felt not only through his own publications but also through his work on Hoppe-Seyler's *Handbuch*, his service to the *Zeitschrift für physiologische Chemie*, and his association with numerous collaborators and students.

BIBLIOGRAPHY

I. ORIGINAL WORKS. There is no single comprehensive bibliography of Thierfelder's publications. A nearly complete list may be compiled by consulting *Index Medicus*, 5 (1883)–21 (1898–1899); *Bibliographia Medica* [*Index Medicus*], 1 (1900)–3 (1903); *Index Medicus*, 2nd ser., 1 (1903)–5 (1907); *Royal Society Catalogue of Scientific Papers* (*1884–1900*), XIX (Cambridge, 1925), 75–76; and *Chemical Abstracts* 1 (1907)–19 (1925), with decennial indexes for 1907–1916, 1917–1926, and 1927–1936.

Thierfelder's dissertation was "Beiträge zur Kenntniss der Entstehung einiger Milchbestandtheile" (Rostock, 1883). An abbreviated version was published as "Zur Physiologie der Milchbildung," in *Pflüger's Archiv für die gesamte Physiologie*, 32 (1883), 619–625. The study with Joseph von Mering appeared as "Das Verhalten tertiärer Alkohole im Organismus," in *Hoppe-Seyler's Zeitschrift für physiologische Chemie*, 9 (1885), 511–517. Among Thierfelder's papers on glucuronic acid are "Über die Bildung von Glykuronsäure beim Hungerthier," *ibid.*, 10 (1886), 163–169; and "Untersuchungen über die Glykuronsäure," *ibid.*, 11 (1887), 388–409, and 13 (1889), 275–284. His early publication on brain sugar was "Über die Identität des Gehirnzuckers mit Galactose," *ibid.*, 14 (1889), 209–216. With Carl Günther, Thierfelder published "Bacteriologische und chemische Untersuchungen über die spontane Milchgerinnung," in *Archiv für Hygiene und Bakteriologie*, 25 (1895), 164–195. Thierfelder's research with George H. F. Nuttall appeared as "Thierisches Leben ohne Bakterien in Verdauungskanal," in *Hoppe-Seyler's Zeitschrift für physiologische Chemie*, 21 (1895), 109–

121, 22 (1896), 62–73, and 23 (1897), 231–235. His work with Emil Fischer was published as "Verhalten der verschiedenen Zucker gegen reine Hefen," in *Berichte der Deutschen chemischen Gesellschaft*, 27 (1894), 2031–2037.

Thierfelder's isolation of cerebron was announced in his paper with Emil Wörner, "Untersuchungen über die chemische Zusammensetzung des Gehirns," in *Hoppe-Seyler's Zeitschrift für physiologische Chemie*, 30 (1900), 542–551. Other publications with various collaborators in the same field include "Über das Cerebron," *ibid.*, 43 (1904), 21–31, 44 (1905), 366–370, 49 (1906), 286–292 (with F. Kitagawa), 68 (1910), 464–470 (with H. Loening), and 77 (1912), 511–515 (with K. Thomas); "Phrenosin und Cerebron," *ibid.*, 46 (1905), 518–522; and "Untersuchungen über die Cerebroside des Gehirns," *ibid.*, 74 (1911), 282–289, 77 (1912), 202–217 (with H. Loening), 85 (1913), 35–58, 89 (1914), 236–247, 248–250, and 91 (1914), 107–114. With Ernst Klenk, Thierfelder published the monograph *Die Chemie der Cerebroside und Phosphatide* (Berlin, 1930).

His publications related to foreign substances in the body include "Phenylacetylglutamin und seine Bildung im menschlichen Körper nach Eingabe von Phenylessigsäure," in *Hoppe-Seyler's Zeitschrift für physiologische Chemie*, 94 (1915), 1–9; "Über glutaminhaltige Polypeptide und zur Frage ihres Vorkommens im Eiweiss," *ibid.*, 105 (1919), 58–82, with E. von Cramm; and "Die Konstitution des Glutamins," *ibid.*, 114 (1921), 192–198.

Thierfelder published two appreciations of his teacher: "Zur Erinnerung an Felix Hoppe-Seyler," in *Berliner klinische Wochenschrift*, 32 (1895), 928–930; and "Felix Hoppe-Seyler" (Stuttgart, 1926), an address to the Natural Science Faculty of the University of Tübingen, 17 December 1925.

II. SECONDARY LITERATURE. Two notices on Thierfelder, which appeared at the time of his death, are Ernst Klenk, "Hans Thierfelder†," in *Hoppe-Seyler's Zeitschrift für physiologische Chemie*, 203 (1931), 1–9; and Percy Brigl, in *Berichte der Deutschen chemischen Gesellschaft* 63, pt. A (1930), 176–177.

JOHN E. LESCH

THOMAS, KARL (*b.* Freiburg im Breisgau, Germany, 28 November 1883; *d.* Göttingen, Germany, 6 September 1969), *physiological chemistry*.

Thomas's father, Ludwig, was professor of internal medicine and pediatrics at the University of Freiburg; as a youth he met his father's associates, and almost from the beginning he planned to attend medical school. In 1896, when Ludwig Zehnder, an associate of Wilhelm Röntgen, gave a lecture on the newly discovered X rays at Freiburg, father and son were in attendance. Zehnder asked Karl to stand before a screen, on which he saw the beating of his own heart. On another occasion his father introduced him to Eugen Baumann, who soon afterward detected the presence of iodine in the thyroid gland. Iodine therapy as a substitute for surgery was a frequent topic of discussion in the home.

As a medical student at Freiburg, Thomas attended the chemistry lectures of Heinrich Kiliani and Ludwig Gatterman even though chemistry was not a part of the medical curriculum at that time. Although he completed the medical requirements in 1906, Thomas's objectives were deflected from medical practice and toward the physiological and chemical side of medical research. As a senior in medicine he completed a thesis titled "Urobilinogen, seine klinische Bedeutung, seine chemische Eigenschaften und seine Farbenreaktionen," using the Hellige colorimeter developed by his teacher of analytical chemistry, Johann von Autenrieth.

Soon thereafter Thomas joined the Hygiene Institute of the University of Berlin, where he worked under Max Rubner on nutritional problems, particularly the metabolism of nitrogen. By experimenting on himself, he sought to determine the minimal intake of nitrogen necessary for satisfactory health. His methodology was followed in other laboratories where work was being done on nitrogen balance; H. H. Mitchell at the University of Illinois pursued such work, adapting Thomas's methods to rats. Thomas soon realized, however, that the problem of nitrogen balance was more subtle than comparing protein intake with nitrogen elimination. The structure of the amino acids provided by specific proteins was of greater significance.

Thomas had to abandon laboratory work in 1910 in order to complete his compulsory year of military service by working in a medical unit. He then asked Rubner for a two-year leave of absence to study chemistry at Tübingen, where he was soon made an assistant to Hans Thierfelder and studied the amino acids in blood plasma proteins. Upon returning to Rubner's laboratory in Berlin (1913), he was placed in charge of the Institute for Work Physiology, an appendage of the recently created Kaiser Wilhelm Society. By the time Thomas's carefully planned laboratory was completed in 1914, Germany was at war and Thomas left to serve as an army physician. His military service ended late in 1915, after he was seriously wounded. A year later he was sufficiently recovered to resume research at the institute, but his work was hampered by the instabilities associated with Germany's loss of the war, the subsequent political unrest, and the monetary inflation that followed.

Thomas accepted an invitation to become professor of physiological chemistry at the University of Leipzig in 1921, spending more than two fruitful

decades there. During the period he declined attractive offers from Freiburg and Basel. A grateful Saxon government showed its appreciation by building a fine new laboratory that was completed according to his plans in 1939. Very soon thereafter Germany was at war, and the laboratory was forced to undertake research relevant to the war effort. Thomas chose to study the nutritive value of the synthetic fats being produced from coal to supplement the shortage of natural food fats. Considerable progress had been made in the research before the laboratory was destroyed during a bombing raid in 1943.

When the war ended, American troops removed Thomas and some of his associates to the West when Saxony was turned over to the Soviet occupation forces in accord with the Potsdam Agreement. In 1946 Thomas became director of the Institute for Physiological Chemistry in Erlangen, but in 1948 he moved to Göttingen to become director of the Medical Research Institute set up there by the Kaiser Wilhelm Society. Although he retired as director in 1958, at age seventy-five, for another ten years he continued his research there as leader of the group working on silicosis.

Thomas's leadership qualities are exemplified by the fact that he built up facilities and staff at laboratories in Berlin, Leipzig, and Göttingen despite financial, political, and military obstacles. Much of his career was plagued with personal financial problems, but through simple living he managed to pursue his scientific objectives. He never married but had strong relationships with his scientific associates. He was noted for a rich sense of humor that helped him face many obstacles. Although not sympathetic to the Nazi movement, he managed to survive because of his apolitical stance.

Thomas's early work on nitrogen metabolism, and later on metabolism of fatty substances, was clearly influenced by the work of Franz Knoop, who clarified the pathway of fatty acid breakdown in his concept of beta-oxidation and further recognized the conversion of keto acids into optically active amino acids. Thomas utilized Knoop's practice of labeling organic acids (as fatty acids with terminal phenyl groups) to study metabolic changes. He made effective use of methyl groups in studying the breakdown of amino and fatty acids and, after his former student Rudolf Schoenheimer developed the technique of labeling metabolic compounds with isotopic markers, was a pioneer in the use of radioactive tracers in research.

When Thomas chose to study the metabolism of synthetic fats during World War II, he was utilizing research tools he had been developing throughout his career. The fats being synthesized from coal contained all of the fatty acids present in the natural animal fats and vegetable oils but with a difference—they were diluted with fatty acids not normally present in natural glycerides. Whereas food fats normally contain only straight-chain acids with an even number of carbon atoms, the synthetic fats contained not only straight-chain acids with an uneven number of carbon atoms but also acids with branched chains, particularly with methyl groups.

Early feeding experiments with dogs revealed that the synthetic fats were absorbed to a significant degree and, therefore, available as a source of calories. It was also observed that the fatty acids were not oxidized completely, and some strange residues appeared in the urine. Dicarboxylic acids of chain length C_6 to C_{10} were identified, but the bulk of the oily residue defied characterization. A problem appeared in the form of methylated acids, compounds considered not normally present in normal fats. However, study of the preen glands of birds showed the wax to be rich in such compounds. With the return to peace, coupled with destruction of the laboratory, the urgency of such research was lost and Thomas's later research was concentrated primarily on silicosis.

Although Thomas was strongly motivated toward research, he did not neglect basic teaching, and felt that research and teaching constituted the dual responsibility of a university professor. While at Leipzig he organized a program in which medical school graduates might spend two years developing their research talents as an adjunct to their medical work.

BIBLIOGRAPHY

I. ORIGINAL WORKS. See Poggendorff, VI, 2649, and VIIa (pt. 5), 670–671, for listings of Thomas's periodical publications. He wrote an autobiographical piece, "Fifty Years of Biochemistry in Germany," in *Annual Review of Biochemistry*, **23** (1954), 1–16, which covers much of his own career and includes a selected list of more than fifty principal publications by various authors, arranged according to subject area.

II. SECONDARY LITERATURE. Ernst Schutte, "Karl Thomas zum 80. Geburtstag," in *Die Naturwissenschaften*, **50** (1963), 701–702. Also see the following obituaries: *Chemischer Zeitung*, **93** (1969), 788–789; Hans Fisher, in *Journal of Nutrition*, **101** (1971), 1109–1115; and Günther Weitzel, in *Hoppe-Seyler's Zeitschrift für physiologische Chemie*, **351** (1970), 1–14. Both Fisher and Weitzel include bibliographies.

AARON J. IHDE

THOMSON, GEORGE PAGET (*b*. Cambridge, England, 3 May 1892; *d*. Cambridge, England, 10 September 1975), *physics*.

George Paget Thomson, widely known as "G. P.," was born and bred a Cambridge physicist. His father was the famous physicist Sir J. J. Thomson ("J. J."), Cavendish Professor of Physics from 1884 to 1919 and subsequently master of Trinity College. His mother was Rose Paget, daughter of the Cambridge Regius Professor of Physic Sir George Paget, and herself a physics student of J. J.'s at the Cavendish Laboratory. G. P. grew up effectively an only child (his sister Joan was not born until he was eleven years old) in the privileged environment of the Cambridge elite. He attended King's College Choir School and the Perse School, where he won a scholarship to Trinity College. At Trinity he gained a double first in mathematics and physics, and after a year's postgraduate work at the Cavendish Laboratory, he was elected a fellow and mathematical lecturer at Corpus Christi College in 1914. During the war, from 1914 to 1918, he served first with the Queen's Regiment in France and then, from 1915, with the Royal Flying Corps at the Royal Aircraft Factory at Farnborough.

After a brief spell in the aircraft manufacturing company, Thomson returned to Cambridge and to Corpus Christi in 1919. In 1922 he was appointed professor of natural philosophy at Aberdeen University, and while there he married Kathleen Smith, the daughter of the principal of the university. They had four children, the youngest of whom was only two when, in 1941, after a severe illness, Kathleen died. G. P. did not remarry. Meanwhile, in 1931, he had been appointed professor of physics at Imperial College, London, and he remained there apart from wartime assignments until 1952. He then returned to Cambridge as master of Corpus Christi College, retiring from this position in 1962. Apart from a period of illness in the late 1930's, he enjoyed generally good health and remained active into his eighties.

Thomson was elected a fellow of the Royal Society in 1930, and served as a vice president in 1950 and 1951. He received the Hughes (1939) and Royal (1949) medals of the society, together with the Faraday Medal of the Institution of Electrical Engineers (1960) and a number of other honors and awards. He shared the 1937 Nobel Prize in physics with C. J. Davisson and was knighted in 1943. From the beginning of World War II onward he served on a range of government committees. Among many other activities he was president of the Society for Freedom in Science, and a vice president of the Atomic Scientists Association. Outside science and public service his main interest was in the Voluntary Euthanasia Society, of which he was a vice president.

Thomson's early scientific work fell into two classes. Under his father's supervision he worked at the Cavendish Laboratory and later at Aberdeen on a range of gas discharge phenomena, in particular those involving positive rays. During and immediately after World War I, he devoted himself to aerodynamics.

Thomson's work on aerodynamics did not incorporate any great breakthroughs but was of considerable practical value. Combining the skills of mathematician, engineer, and pilot, he concentrated on the application of aerodynamic theory to practical problems of flight, achieving a degree of coherence and completeness that the subject had not previously had. After the war, encouraged by Henry Tizard, he wrote up his own and other people's work in the form of a comprehensive textbook, *Applied Aerodynamics*. Having outlined the basic physical theory and experimental methods, he applied these to the aerodynamic performance of each part of an airplane's structure, and then to the airplane as a whole. In the second part of the book, he gave a thorough mathematical analysis of aircraft stability.

For Thomson himself the work on aerodynamics provided an opportunity to hone his skills in mathematics and develop those in theoretical engineering; in later life his work drew heavily on this combination of abilities. For the interwar period, however, it was his apprenticeship in gas discharge physics, dating from before the war and leading to a series of publications from 1920 onward, that proved most relevant. In one of his earliest publications, he provided experimental confirmation of Johannes Stark's suggestion that the observed secondary spectrum of hydrogen was to be attributed to hydrogen molecules rather than to the atoms responsible for the primary spectrum. In another investigation he developed a technique for extracting "anode rays" (secondary emissions from the surface of the anode in a discharge tube, consisting of charged metallic atoms) as beams from discharge tubes. Coating the anodes with salts of different metals, he was able, by analyzing these beams, to determine the isotopic content of lithium and other metals. In another investigation, studying the scattering of slow positive rays (protons), he found a significant discrepancy from the established theory, suggesting the existence of a strong field of force within the hydrogen molecule. More precise experiments a few years later (1925–1926) seemed to suggest an inverse cube force

law between the protons and electrons in a molecule. Meanwhile, picking up on his father's interest in the development of mechanical models of light-quanta as structures in the ether, Thomson provided experimental support for the fully localized light-quantum hypothesis as opposed to that of an elongated "light-dart." Then in 1925, prompted by his reading of Louis-César-Victoir-Maurice de Broglie's theory of matter waves, he worked out a theory of the Bohr atom in which the constituent particles were described by de Broglie's theory and the emitted and absorbed radiation by J. J. Thomson's theory of light-quanta.

By 1926 Thomson had accumulated a good body of research, but with nothing spectacular to show for it. In the course of that year, however, his experimental work on positive rays and his theoretical work on the quantum theory began to come together. On the theoretical side he was greatly impressed by the work of de Broglie, and in the summer of 1926 he used de Broglie's theory to compare the broadening of spectral lines owing to pressure on the classical and quantum theories. (He had not yet encountered Erwin Schrödinger's wave mechanics, though he did so shortly afterward, and had either not encountered or not taken up the matrix mechanics of Werner Heisenberg and others.) Meanwhile, pursuit of the discrepancy between observation and theory in the scattering of slow positive rays led him to compare the observed phenomena with those noted earlier by Carl Wilhelm Ramsauer, in which slow electrons appeared to pass unhindered straight through an atomic nucleus.

Ramsauer's results dated from the early 1920's and were quite widely regarded as problematic, but with the quantum theory of the atom itself in a state of ferment, it had seemed difficult and premature to draw any conclusions from them. A few physicists had however linked these results with others obtained by Davisson and his collaborators, Lester H. Germer and Charles H. Kunsman, at the laboratories of General Electric in America. In work stemming originally from a patent suit, Davisson and Kunsman in 1923 had found distinctive patterns in the scattering of slow electrons by metallic surfaces, principally platinum. And in 1925 Davisson and Germer found a rather different but still more distinctive set of patterns for scattering from single crystals. Meanwhile, in the spring of 1925, in the course of an investigation of de Broglie's theory in Max Born's physics seminar at Göttingen, Walter Elsasser had suggested that the Ramsauer and Davisson and Kunsman results might be interpreted as evidence of the wave nature of electrons, the scattering patterns corresponding to those to be expected from wave diffraction.

Thomson did not know, in 1926, of Elsasser's speculation. But he may have known through his father (who was however skeptical) of the Davisson and Kunsman results. And in September 1926, on his way back from a meeting of the British Association for the Advancement of Science at Oxford (at which Davisson was also present, but at which they apparently did not meet), he discussed with Dymond in Cambridge the latter's work on the energy distribution of electrons after collisions with helium molecules. In the course of this work, Dymond, who had read Elsasser's paper, had observed some patterns that suggested to him a wavelike diffraction of the electrons by the helium. Strangely enough Elsasser's speculation does not seem to have been discussed by Dymond and G. P. Thomson—at least Thomson did not later recall it having been so.

But the idea of a wave theory of the electron based on de Broglie's theory was discussed, and Thomson, already deeply interested in de Broglie's work himself, saw how his work with positive rays might be adapted to test the idea. Reasoning that the effect should be easier to analyze with a solid than with a gaseous target, and that some of the positive ray apparatus at Aberdeen could be readily adapted for such an experiment, he asked Alexander Reid to look at the scattering of electrons through thin celluloid films (3.10^{-6} cms) onto photographic plates. The result was clear pictures of "halos" much as one would expect from a diffraction effect, and in a joint paper with Reid, published in May 1927, Thomson wrote of celluloid as a "diffracting system" and of the electrons as having "wavelengths" given by de Broglie's theory. Since the structure of celluloid was unknown, the experiment was not conclusive. So Thomson next turned to metallic films of the same thickness, for which the crystal structure was known, and repeated the experiment for scattering from aluminum, gold, and platinum. He found that the dimensions of the observed diffraction patterns agreed in all cases, to within 5 percent, with those predicted by de Broglie's wave theory of matter. These results were published in brief in December 1927 and in detail two months later. Suggestions that the phenomenon might be owing to classical X-ray effects were refuted in a subsequent paper.

Meanwhile Davisson, whose visit to England had introduced him to de Broglie's theory, and Germer had pursued their own analysis, and in a paper published in April 1927 (before that by Thomson and Reid), they had interpreted their own results on the scattering of slow electrons by single crystals in terms of de Broglie's theory. But the two investigations were essentially independent. Credit for them should probably be shared not only between Thomson and Davisson (who shared the Nobel Prize) but also between de Broglie, Elsasser, and Dymond. Davisson, it would seem, had de Broglie's theory thrust upon him in England, and given Elsasser's speculation it required no great imagination to test the theory on his own, already existing experiments. Thomson's work was perhaps more original in this respect, but he too was essentially developing someone else's suggestion, in his case Dymond's, which was itself influenced by Elsasser's speculation.

That G. P. Thomson should have demonstrated the wave nature of the electron was perhaps ironic, in view of the fact that it had been his father who had first demonstrated its particulate nature. But it was also fitting, in that the son's interests had followed closely those of the father. In the 1920's they were separated by hundreds of miles, but the two components of G. P.'s electron diffraction work, quantum theory and gas discharge phenomena, were precisely the subjects in which J. J. himself was most interested. And while the electron diffraction work was going on, the two Thomsons were in fact collaborating on a new edition of J. J.'s classic work *Conduction of Electricity Through Gases*, published in 1928 under both their names.

As an experimental confirmation of the quantum theory, the demonstration of electron diffraction was of the utmost importance. But by the time it occurred, quantum theory itself, in the form of the new quantum mechanics, was already making rapid progress. Thomson followed the more straightforward developments of the new theory, writing the textbook *Wave Theory of the Free Electron* (1930) and treating Schrödinger's wave mechanics in his popular book *The Atom*, published in the same year. But there was no natural development of Thomson's work at the forefront of that research. Instead he turned to the exploration of the potential of electron diffraction as an investigative tool. First at Aberdeen and then at Imperial College, he studied such phenomena as electron diffraction by single crystals, and used high-voltage diffraction techniques to study the microscopic structure of surfaces. A significant part of the work of the Department of Physics at Imperial College was focused on the practical improvement of diffraction techniques, and although Thomson himself contributed relatively little directly to the enormous strides made in this respect, mainly by his students, he did supervise and direct this work and he did prepare with W. Cochrane the definitive account of the subject, *Theory and Practice of Electron Diffraction*, published in 1939.

While Thomson maintained his interest in electron diffraction, he also devoted increasing attention to the dramatic developments of nuclear physics in the 1930's. A significant aspect of the attraction that electron diffraction had held for him had been related to its significance in the context of the developing quantum theory, which aroused his theoretical as well as his experimental interest. With the discovery of the neutron and the positron, and the splitting of the atom, in 1932, followed by the discovery of artificial radioactivity two years later, the leading edge of physics moved from the mathematically obscure realm of quantum mechanics and quantum field theory to the equally taxing but more readily approachable area of nuclear physics, and Thomson's interest soon moved with it. With J. A. Saxton he looked for artificial radioactivity from positron bombardment. And following Enrico Fermi's work on the effects of slow neutrons, he led a team of researchers, including P. B. Moon and C. E. Wynn-Williams, in a study of the velocity distribution of slow neutrons. A deuteron beam was used to bombard a target of frozen heavy water, and the neutrons produced in the resulting deuteron-deuteron reactions were slowed down in paraffin. Time-of-flight techniques were then used to measure the velocity distribution and absorption coefficients of the neutrons. Then in 1939, following the discovery of uranium fission, Thomson led another team in a measurement of the neutron yield from fission reactions.

Apart from two postwar papers on effects produced by cosmic ray collisions, Thomson's fission paper and another joint paper of the same year with a student, Moses Blackman, who was working on the theory of electron diffraction, were his last significant original scientific publications. But there was one major unpublished piece of work to come, and his contributions through science, which were just beginning, were in some ways as significant as his contributions to science.

Thomson's experiments on the neutron yield from fission reactions gave results roughly the same as those announced a few weeks earlier by Hans von Halban, Frédéric Joliot, and Lew Kowarski in Paris ($3 \cdot 5 \pm 0 \cdot 7$, an overestimate), and pointed clearly to the possibility of a self-sustaining chain reaction within a body of fissionable material. And seeing at once the possible implications of this result, Thomson was, more than anyone, instrumental in the establishment of the wartime British atomic energy project. Through Tizard, who was both rector

of Imperial College and chairman of the Committee for the Scientific Study of Air Defence (the principal organization for mobilizing scientific effort for the anticipated war), he persuaded the government to purchase a ton of uranium oxide for his own experiments. With this material he made both a solid pile, with blocks of paraffin as moderator, and a liquid pile of uranium oxide in water. There was no sign of either system even approaching a chain reaction (any neutrons emitted were quickly absorbed); satisfied that a uranium oxide bomb was out of the question and that the separation even of metallic uranium would be a massive and impracticable operation in wartime, Thomson gave up his experiments. In April 1940, however, he read a copy of the O. R. Frisch–R. F. Peierls memorandum, in which these two refugee physicists offered a theoretical analysis leading to the conclusion that a bomb composed purely of the isotope uranium 235 might be possible using only a few pounds of material. Thomson promptly consulted his scientific and government colleagues, and despite continuing skepticism as to the feasibility of a fission bomb—the calculations were far from conclusive and the problem of isotope separation seemed to many people practically insuperable—a uranium subcommittee was set up under Tizard's committee, with Thomson in the chair. By the summer, his subcommittee had become the MAUD committee of the Ministry of Aircraft Production, and a report on the prospects of a uranium bomb, drafted by Thomson, had reached the prime minister. The wartime project was under way.

Although he had from the first taken the initiative in respect to fission, Thomson soon stepped down. He had been ill himself, and his wife was critically ill in America. In the autumn of 1941 he was appointed to Ottawa as scientific liaison officer to explore the possibility of a team of British and French scientists transferring their nuclear reactor research from Britain to Canada, a move that duly took place. Returning to England in 1942 after his wife's death, Thomson acted as deputy chairman of the Radio Board (supervising radar research) and scientific adviser to the Air Ministry. Later, in 1946, he also acted as adviser to the British delegation to the United Nations Atomic Energy Commission. But by that time he had become interested in a new topic, the peaceful application of thermonuclear fusion.

The possibility of a controlled thermonuclear fusion device was already in the air by the late 1930's. There was by then a clear prima facie possibility of net energy production from the fusion of deuterium ions (deuterons), and it was in particular possible to envisage such energy production taking place in a toroidal gas discharge tube, not unlike a circular particle accelerator, the plasma or ionized gas in which would be isolated from the walls of the tube by the "pinch effect" owing to its own self-magnetic field. A number of people, including Leo Szilard and Peter Thonemann, apparently discussed this possibility before and during the war, and in 1946 a group of leading Los Alamos physicists turned their attention temporarily to an informal study of the problem. But the first detailed, documented proposal for a controlled fusion device appears to be that of Thomson. As an authority on both gas discharge physics (he knew his father's experiments on toroidal discharge tubes) and nuclear physics (in which he had used the deuteron-deuteron fusion reaction to produce neutrons), Thomson was particularly well placed to see and explore the possibilities of controlled fusion. And early in 1946 he sketched out a proposal in which deuterium gas would be confined in a toroidal solenoid in a strong magnetic field.

He proposed to ionize the gas using an external source and then to heat up the resulting plasma using a high-frequency alternating current applied through pairs of wave guides to feed a unidirectional wave into the torus. This would accelerate the electrons in the plasma, which would then transfer their energy to the positive deuterons carried around with them. Beginning with a gas density of around 10^{15} molecules/cm^3, Thomson suggested, the deuterons could within a few minutes be heated to about 100keV, at which point fusion energy would be generated. With the help of Moses Blackman, and following helpful criticisms from Peierls, he then developed this idea, with solenoid containment being replaced by reliance on the pinch effect, and made it the subject of a secret provisional patent specification lodged in May 1946. The torus proposed was of 3m diameter (increased in the final specification of 1947 to 4m) and 60cm bore.

Thomson's proposed torus was never constructed, and the main development of controlled fusion devices in Britain, leading in 1957 to the operation of the ZETA torus, followed instead the ideas of Thonemann. But Thomson's proposal and subsequent lobbying were instrumental in establishing the British fusion program as the first in the world, and many of Thomson's ideas were developed by smaller teams at Imperial College and later at the AEI laboratories at Aldermaston Court. Thomson himself remained active in the field through the 1950's, and maintained a strong interest thereafter.

In his later years Thomson's scientific activities were dominated by his popular articles and books, including *The Inspiration of Science* (1961) and *The Foreseeable Future* (1955). He was a prolific writer and speaker on such subjects as science and religion, the education of scientists, and the place of scientists in society, with all of which he was passionately concerned.

BIBLIOGRAPHY

The principal published account of Thomson's work is the Royal Society obituary by P. B. Moon, in *Biographical Memoirs of Fellows of the Royal Society*, **23** (1977), 528–556. Thomson also wrote an unpublished autobiography (see below), and there is an interview with him in the *Sources for History of Quantum Physics* archive, copies at the American Philosophical Society, the American Institute of Physics, the University of California at Berkeley, the Niels Bohr Institute in Copenhagen, and the Science Museum in London. There are several published reminiscences by Thomson, including *Nuclear Energy in Britain during the Last War: The Cherwell-Simon Lecture . . . 1960* (Oxford, 1962), and "The Early History of Electron Diffraction," in *Contemporary Physics*, **9** (1968), 1–15. There are no other historical accounts of his work on electron diffraction, attention having been focused more on the work of Davisson, but see R. K. Gehrenbeck, "C. J. Davisson, L. H. Germer, and the Discovery of Electron Diffraction," Ph.D. dissertation, University of Minnesota, 1973. For Thomson's work on fusion, see J. Hendry, "The Scientific Origins of Controlled Fusion Technology," forthcoming.

The Royal Society obituary cited above contains a select bibliography of Thomson's scientific articles and books, with many omissions and some misprints. His principal papers on electron diffraction are "Diffraction of Cathode Rays by a Thin Film," in *Nature*, **119** (1927), 890, written with A. Reid; "The Diffraction of Cathode Rays by Thin Films of Platinum," in *Nature*, **120** (1927), 802; and "Experiments on the Diffraction of Cathode Rays," in *Proceedings of the Royal Society* (A), **117** (1928), 600–609. For Thomson's fusion device see British Patent no. 13963/46.

Thomson's papers are archived at Trinity College, Cambridge, and have been catalogued by the Contemporary Scientific Archives Centre, catalog no. 75. The collection includes Thomson's unpublished autobiography, a substantial collection of correspondence, and many drafts of papers, some eventually published, others not.

JOHN HENDRY

TIETZE, HEINRICH FRANZ FRIEDRICH (*b.* Schleinz, Austria, 31 August 1880; *d.* Munich, Germany, 17 February 1964), *mathematics*.

Tietze was the son of Emil Tietze, director of the Geological Institute at the University of Vienna, and of Rosa von Hauer, daughter of the geologist Franz Ritter von Hauer. He was married in 1907 to Leontine Petraschek; they had no children.

Tietze began the study of mathematics at Vienna in 1898. Following the advice of his friend Gustav Herglotz, in 1902 he went for a year to Munich and then returned to Vienna. Gustav von Escherich was his adviser, and for the dissertation "Über Funktionalgleichungen, deren Lösungen keiner algebraischen Differentialgleichung genügen können" Tietze was awarded the Ph.D. in 1904. Through Wilhelm Wirtinger's lectures on algebraic functions and their integrals, Tietze became interested in topological problems, thereafter the focus of his most important mathematical work. In 1908 he qualified as lecturer at Vienna with the *Habilitationsschrift* "Über die topologischen Invarianten mehrdimensionaler Mannigfaltigkeiten." Topology—at this time still in a rudimentary stage—involved studying the properties of geometrical objects, which are invariant with respect to bijective and bicontinous mappings. Today it is one of the most important foundations of mathematics. In his *Habilitationsschrift*, Tietze made essential contributions to combinatory topology, inspired by results of Henri Poincaré. He accepted a position as associate professor of mathematics at the Technical College of Brünn (today Brno) in 1910, and was promoted to full professor in 1913.

Drafted into the Austrian army during World War I, Tietze was forced to interrupt his academic activities. He returned to Brünn after the war, and in 1919 he accepted a full professorship at the University of Erlangen. While at Erlangen he wrote his three-part "Beiträge zur allgemeinen Topologie." Part I is concerned with axioms for different versions of the concept of neighborhood; today one of them bears his name. In 1925 Tietze accepted an offer from the University of Munich, where Constantin Carathéodory and Oskar Perron were colleagues. Most of his some 120 publications were produced during his tenure at Munich. He retired in 1950 but continued his research until a short time before his death in 1964.

As a topologist Tietze did pioneering work. In addition to the papers previously mentioned, his first publication, "Über das Problem der Nachbargebiete im Raum" (1905), should be noted. Whereas in the plane there are at most four domains touching one another along a line, it was already known that in three-dimensional space there exist any number of solids touching one another along a surface. Tietze showed that this can occur even in convex domains. In a further publication, "Einige Bemerkungen über

das Problem des Kartenfärbens auf einseitigen Flächen" (1910), he proved that six is the minimum number of colors needed to color any map on the Möbius band or on the projective plane.

In 1914 Tietze stated the important theorem, which now bears his name, that any function bounded and continous on a closed set can be continously extended to the whole space. With his friend Leopold Vietoris, he published an article in the *Encyklopädie der mathematischen Wissenschaften* ("Beziehungen zwischen den verschiedenen Zweigen der Topologie," 1930), which discusses the relationship between combinatorial topology and set theoretic topology. This work also was crucially important in clarifying the terminology, which was not yet standardized. Tietze's other papers on topology deal with the theory of knots, Jordan curves, and continous mappings of areas, among other subjects.

In addition to topology, Tietze worked in many other fields of mathematics. In 1909 he noticed that the usual criterion for the possibility of constructing a geometrical figure with only compass and ruler as instruments is not sufficient. The arrangement of the constructed points also plays an important role that must be considered. For the theory of continued fractions Tietze developed a decisive criterion of convergence based on geometrical ideas. Further papers involved the theory of convex domains and the fundamental theorem of symmetrical functions, which he proved in a new manner, extending it to the case of an infinite number of variables. In analysis, Tietze gave a new demonstration for J. B. J. Fourier and F. F. D. Budan's rules of signs, generalizing these rules to nonrational holomorphic functions. Tietze's "Über das Schicksal gemischter Populationen nach den Mendelschen Vererbungsgesetzen" (1923) treats a problem belonging to an area of what today is called biomathematics. Between 1940 and 1944 Tietze wrote a series of papers on systems of lattice points and partitions, on the distribution of prime numbers, and on questions of differential geometry.

Tietze's publications mentioned above were addressed to the specialist, but Tietze took great pains to make mathematical problems clear to the general public as well. For this purpose he wrote the two-volume *Gelöste und ungelöste mathematische Probleme aus alter und neuer Zeit* (1949; translated into English and Dutch). It shows his gift for representing even difficult mathematical questions in a very clear and impressive manner for interested people.

In 1929 Tietze was elected a member of the Bavarian Academy of Sciences, and in the years 1934–

1942 and 1946–1951 he was secretary of its Mathematical-Natural Sciences Division. He also was a corresponding member of the Austrian Academy of Sciences (elected 1959) and received the Bavarian Verdienstorden (1959).

BIBLIOGRAPHY

I. ORIGINAL WORKS. Complete bibliographies of Tietze's works are with the obituaries by Perron, Seebach and Jacobs, and Vietoris. His works include "Über das Problem der Nachbargebiete im Raum," in *Monatshefte für Mathematik und Physik*, **16** (1905), 211–216; "Über Funktionalgleichungen, deren Lösungen keiner algebraischen Differentialgleichung genügen können," *ibid.*, 329–364, his dissertation; "Über die topologischen Invarianten mehrdimensionaler Mannigfaltigkeiten," *ibid.*, **19** (1908), 1–118; "Einige Bemerkungen über das Problem des Kartenfärbens auf einseitigen Flächen," in *Jahresberichte der Deutschen Mathematiker-Vereinigung*, **19** (1910), 155–159; "Über Funktionen, die auf einer abgeschlossenen Menge stetig sind," in *Journal für die reine und angewandte Mathematik*, **145** (1915), 9–14; "Beiträge zur allgemeine Topologie," pt. 1 in *Mathematische Annalen*, **88** (1923), 290–312, pt. 2, *ibid.*, **91** (1924), 210–224, pt. 3 in *Monatshefte für Mathematik und Physik*, **33** (1923), 15–17; "Über das Schicksal gemischter Populationen nach den Mendelschen Vererbungsgesetzen," in *Zeitschrift für angewandte Mathematik und Mechanik*, **3** (1923); "Beziehungen zwischen den verschiedenen Zweigen der Topologie," in *Encyklopädie der Mathematischen Wissenschaften*, III, 1.2, art. AB 13 (Leipzig, 1930), 141–237, written with Leopold Vietoris; "Systeme von Partitionen und Glitterpunktfiguren I–IX," in *Sitzungsberichte der Bayerischen Akademie der Wissenschaften* (1940), 23–54, 69–166, and (1941), 1–55, 165–191; and *Gelöste und ungelöste mathematische Probleme aus alter und neuer Zeit* (Munich, 1949; 4th ed., 1965).

II. SECONDARY LITERATURE. G. Aumann, "Heinrich Tietze, 31.8.1880–17.2.1964," in *Jahrbuch der Bayerischen Akademie der Wissenschaften (1964), 197–201*; O. Perron, "Heinrich Tietze, 31.8.1880–17.2.1964," in *Jahresberichte der Deutschen Mathematiker-Vereinigung*, **83** (1981), 182–185; K. Seebach and K. Jacobs, "Verzeichnis der unter H. Tietze angefertigten Dissertationen und Verzeichnis der Veröffentlichungen," *ibid.*, 186–191; and Leopold Vietoris, "Heinrich Tietze," in *Almanach der Österreichischen Akademie der Wissenschaften*, **114** (1964), 360–377.

KARL SEEBACH

TILLEY, CECIL EDGAR (*b.* Adelaide, South Australia, 14 May 1894; *d.* Cambridge, England, 24 January 1973), *mineralogy, petrology.*

Tilley was the son of a civil engineer in the South Australian State Service and so spent his early years in various parts of South Australia and at Darwin in the Northern Territory of Australia, where his father was concerned with harbor construction. The family was very musical, and as a boy he was a proficient pianist and organist. When Tilley entered the University of Adelaide in 1911, his enthusiasm for science had already developed and displaced, much to his subsequent regret, his musical interests. The events that directed his scientific interest toward geology and petrology are unrecorded. The geology department at Adelaide was small but distinguished; Walter Howchin was a stratigrapher of some eminence, and Douglas Mawson, a petrologist, was away leading the Australian Antarctic Expedition (1909–1913), which quickly earned him a knighthood. In his second year, 1912, Tilley accepted the post of cadet in the geology department; his fees were remitted in exchange for his performing several minor duties, including making thin sections. During Mawson's absence his locum tenens was W. R. Browne, who quickly recognized Tilley's ability.

Having completed the B.Sc. course in November 1914, he transferred to Sydney University, to which Browne had returned in 1913, and took the final year B.Sc. courses in chemistry and geology; he was awarded medals in both subjects and was appointed a junior demonstrator in geology and mineralogy. He held the post for only one year and then, at the end of 1916, made his first voyage to Britain to work as a chemist for the Department of Explosives Supply at Queensferry, near Chester, where, in charge of a chemical plant at the early age of twenty-three, he had his first taste of being in command. After the Armistice he returned to Sydney to resume his demonstratorship in geology and mineralogy. After a year he was on his way back to Britain with a 1851 Exhibition Scholarship to do petrological research under Alfred Harker in Cambridge.

Physically Tilley was a large man, tall and broadshouldered. In youth he was shy and did not make friends easily. In middle life his manner was reserved in his own department, but outside it he relaxed and at parties his great voice could be heard booming above the general hum of conversation. After his marriage in 1928 to Irene Doris Marshall, he kept his private and professional lives separate. He was a man of regular habits, arriving early at his laboratory and staying late into the night with breaks only for afternoon tea at home with his wife and daughter Anne and for dinner in Emmanuel College. He was dedicated to his work from an early age and had no hobbies. He appeared to have a photographic memory, never forgetting anything he had read or any mineral he had once seen. He traveled widely, exclusively in connection with his work.

After acting as Browne's field assistant in early 1913, Tilley went to investigate the granites of Cape Willoughby on Kangaroo Island. The results, his first published petrological work, appeared in two papers in 1919. After Browne's return to Sydney in 1913, pupil and teacher began a correspondence that lasted for over a decade; fragments survive in the possession of T. G. Vallance. Browne exercised a strong formative influence on the first decade of his pupil's career.

On 5 February 1920 Tilley first set foot in Cambridge. He was taken into the "august presence of Harker," who, as he wrote to Browne, "had none of the severity with which I had associated the name." At this time Harker was reader in petrology in the Sedgwick Museum of Geology and had lately transferred the attention of his original and rigorous mind from igneous to metamorphic petrology. He was to provide the second major influence on the development of Tilley's career. Tilley had brought to Cambridge an extensive collection of metamorphic rocks from Southern Eyre Peninsula, South Australia, on which he based five papers (1920–1921), which brought him to the notice of the geological world; these were followed by a wealth of publications over the next thirty years that established his leadership in metamorphic petrology.

Tilley's dissertation was approved for the Ph.D. degree on 15 June 1922, and later that year his 1851 Exhibition Scholarship was converted to a senior scholarship. In 1921 he had made his first visit to the classic Norwegian localities, and to V. M. Goldschmidt's superbly equipped laboratory in Oslo, which made a lasting impression on him. His Norwegian experience clearly influenced his seminal work on contact metamorphism in the Comrie area of Perthshire, Scotland (1924). Tilley's important contribution here was the derivation of the possible assemblages of silica-poor hornfelses from the corresponding classes of Goldschmidt's free silica hornfelses. Tilley showed that all the hornfelses could have formed from mixtures of sericite, chlorite, and quartz, the dominant minerals of the sediments from which they were derived. This was the most comprehensive study of a British thermal aureole yet made. Further papers followed on contact metamorphism, in one of which, in 1926, he recognized the significance of manganese in promoting the formation of garnet.

At the same time Tilley was working on the regionally metamorphosed rocks of the Start area of South Devon, England (1923). Here he discovered that the so-called Green Schists could be divided petrographically into two types, both having the chemical composition of basalt and representing different grades of metamorphism. He recorded for the first time that in the presence of a notable content of manganese, garnet develops before biotite in regional metamorphism.

In 1923 Tilley had met N. L. Bowen while on a field trip with Harker in Skye; Bowen became a close friend who was greatly to influence Tilley's thinking. On 31 December 1923 he was appointed demonstrator in petrology for five years. At this time Tilley's research was mainly concerned with regional metamorphism in the Scottish Highlands. G. Barrow's pioneer map of the metamorphic zones of the Southeastern Highlands (1912) had been largely neglected, but Tilley extended it by publishing in 1925 a preliminary survey of the metamorphic zones of the Southern Highlands and in 1926 a discussion of the genesis of biotite, almandine, and staurolite in regional metamorphism. This was pioneer work on which little advance was made until the advent of the electron microprobe some thirty years later. Several summers were then devoted to detailed mapping with G. L. Elles in the attempt to demonstrate tectonic inversion of the metamorphic zonation; this work, published in 1930, has not found general acceptance. During this period he delineated the mineral assemblages developed in the Loch Tay limestone with progressive metamorphism through the chlorite, biotite, and almandine zones of the associated pelites (1927).

In 1926 Tilley undertook to prepare accounts of Australian igneous rocks for inclusion in T. W. E. David's projected "Geology of the Commonwealth of Australia," a monumental work that was never published. This work, as well as seven papers between 1923 and 1940 on Antarctic petrology, represent his continuing contact with and interest in his native Australia.

In the late 1920's Tilley began his great work on the dolerite-chalk contact at Scawt Hill, Larne, Northern Ireland. Following his by now established practice, he made an extensive collection and published preliminary papers on melilite as a product of interaction of limestone and basaltic liquid (1929) and on the new minerals larnite (1929) and scawtite (1930). The substantive work appeared in 1931. Tilley identified an exogenous contact zone of silicates grading outward into a coarse marble and then into normal chalk. The contact zone was unique in its mineralogy with spurrite rock, larnite ($\pm$ spurrite) rock, spurrite-larnite-gehlenite rock, and spurrite-gehlenite-merwinite-spinel (± larnite) rock. He concluded from the evidence of these assemblages that solutions emanating from the dolerite had enriched the contact zone in silicon and some other elements and had raised the temperature of the limestone envelope more rapidly than could have been achieved by conduction alone. Equally remarkable was the endogenous contact zone where the olivine dolerite magma had been contaminated by lime to yield, in the first stage, pyroxene-rich rocks and a residual magma enriched by plagioclase and lime; in the next stage, titanaugite rocks; then titanaugite-melilite-nepheline rocks; and, in the final stage, a melilite rock by interaction of lime with an alkali magma having the composition of a titanaugite-nepheline rock.

The importance of this work was that it showed in detail for the first time how a basic alkali residuum could be produced from a doleritic liquid by absorption of lime. This was the mechanism proposed earlier by Daly for the normal production of basic alkali rocks; Tilley, however, drew attention to the very limited zone of contamination at Scawt Hill and to the dominance within it of pyroxene-rich dolerite and pyroxenite, forcing him to the correct conclusion that limestone assimilation has a restricted potential to generate alkali magmas. Detailed work on the mineralogy of Scawt Hill led to the discovery of six new minerals: larnite, Ca_2SiO_4 (1929); scawtite, $Ca_7Si_6O_{16}CO_3(OH)_4$ (1929); portlandite, $Ca(OH)_2$ (1933); hydrocalumite, $Ca_2Al(OH)_7 \cdot 3H_2O$ (with H. D. Megaw and M. H. Hey, 1934); rankinite, $Ca_3Si_2O_7$ (1942); and bredigite, $\alpha'\text{-}Ca_2SiO_4$ (with H. C. G. Vincent, 1948). This was not only a study of signal significance in thermal metamorphism, it was also extraordinary in its wealth of fine detail. Later, in 1948, Tilley described the similar gabbro-limestone contact at Camus Mor, Muck, Scotland. In the light of these two examples, he discussed (1952) the trends of basaltic magma in limestone syntexis, showing that extreme iron enrichment is characteristic.

His appointment as lecturer in petrology in 1928 and his marriage settled Tilley in Cambridge. At this time a wind of change was beginning to blow through the Cambridge geology department. The Woodwardian professorship of geology, founded in 1727, had increasingly become identified with stratigraphy and paleontology. The professorship of mineralogy, founded in 1808, had gradually become identified with crystallography. The imminence of the simultaneous retirements of Hutchinson, professor of mineralogy, and of Harker, reader in pe-

trology, prompted the university to consider establishing a department of minerology and petrology. Tilley took sabbatical leave while these proposals were being considered and worked at the Geophysical Laboratory in Washington, D.C., with J. F. Schairer on the system $Na_2SiO_3\text{-}Na_2Si_2O_5\text{-}NaAlSiO_4$, accomplishing also a formidable program of travel and fieldwork. Thus began a happy and lasting association with the Geophysical Laboratory. It was also his introduction to the United States, which he saw as a land of promise, where he was always stimulated, relaxed, and happy.

Tilley returned to Cambridge in late 1931 as the professor of mineralogy and petrology. Simultaneously his college, Emmanuel, elected him to a fellowship, which was to become an important factor in his life. A laboratory, built largely to his own design, was ready for occupation in 1933. His aim was to produce a laboratory of the first rank in teaching and research; in that he succeeded, with total dedication and some ruthlessness. He made it clear to his research students that the excellent optical, chemical, and X-ray crystallographic facilities that he had assembled were there to be used all of every weekday. He drove himself hard and expected his students to do likewise. He was never happier than when he was alone in the laboratory late at night or on weekends, sitting at his old Swift microscope, cigarette in his mouth and a towel over his left shoulder ready for wiping the dust and ash from his slides. In the first decade a flood of papers came from Tilley and his students and, apart from the war years, that was to be the pattern for the future. He was elected a fellow of the Royal Society in 1938.

Once the laboratory was built, Tilley returned to a problem in contact metamorphism on which he had worked earlier with Sir John Flett. In 1930 they had concluded that the cordierite-anthophyllite hornfelses of Kenidjack, Cornwall, England, had been produced from the original greenstones with considerable loss of lime due to intensive weathering prior to metamorphism. In his new study (1935) Tilley advocated the hypothesis that the hornfelses had been produced by the metasomatic effect of solutions emanating from the nearby granite. In 1937 he showed that cordierite-anthophyllite granulites had been produced at the Lizard, Cornwall, variously by metasomatism of hornblende schists with introduction of silica and loss of lime during folding at high temperature and by isochemical metamorphism of sediments. The Lizard and Kenidjack rocks provide a splendid illustration of metamorphic convergence.

Work was continuing in Scotland: the rare rock eulysite (1936) and the rare mineral pyroxmangite (1937) were discovered at Glenelg, and manganiferous rocks were found at Gairloch (1938). There were two general papers on the paragenesis of kyanite-eclogites (1936) and kyanite-amphibolites (1937). These were all brief but significant papers.

Tilley's last two papers on contact metamorphism, both of considerable importance, were published in 1951. The first, on the progressive thermal metamorphism of siliceous limestones and dolomites, extended the thirteen stages and ten mineral indicators of Bowen (1940) to seventeen stages and thirteen mineral indicators; tilleyite and rankinite were placed in the sequence and talc became the indicator of the first stage. The second paper concerned the zoned contact-skarns of Broadford, Skye, Scotland, which occur at the contact of granite with dolomite horizons of the Durness limestone and which have locally been affected by boron-fluorine metasomatism. A wealth of rare minerals occurs in the complex skarns, and Tilley discovered here a new mineral that he named harkerite. The parageneses of skarn zones are explored in detail and this paper, like those on Scawt Hill, illustrates Tilley's remarkable eye for minerals, his great skill in identifying the rarer minerals, and his flair for discovering new minerals. Since much of Tilley's work on contact metamorphism had concerned carbonate rocks, it was appropriate that a new mineral found in metamorphosed limestones at Crestmore, California, should have been named tilleyite in his honor in 1933.

Tilley's Presidential Address to the Geological Society of London in 1950, "Some Aspects of Magmatic Evolution," represented a change of course from metamorphic to igneous petrology that was to be permanent. Among those who knew him only from his publications, it evoked surprise; to his friends, colleagues and students it had long been evident from his lectures that his interests embraced all of petrology. The concept of magma types had been a principal result of the work of the Geological Survey on the Tertiary Igneous Rocks in Mull (1924) and in Ardnamurchan (1930). Subsequently the nature and genetic relations of primary and derivative basic and intermediate magma were widely discussed, but usually in a restricted context or in diffuse generalizations. "Olivine basalt" and "tholeiitic basalt" were terms in common use but there was little consensus as to their precise definitions. An authoritative and comprehensive survey was needed; it was provided brilliantly by the presidential address.

Few, if any, could match Tilley's knowledge of the literature, his analytical power, or his ability to point the way forward. His definition of tholeiite and concept of the tholeiitic series gained general acceptance. His plea for more precise definitions and more quantitative chemical and mineralogical studies bore fruit; 1950 marked the start of a new and systematic approach in igneous petrology. Some of the questions posed had to wait many years for the development of high-pressure and high-temperature experimental techniques before they could be answered. Over the years the lucid, elegant style in which his early papers were written had given way, especially after Harker's death in 1939, to a compact style making unusual demands of knowledge and acuity in the reader; the presidential address is a particularly difficult example of this new style.

Thirty years of driving himself to the limit in his research, coupled with the exacting duties in London necessitated by the coincidence of his presidency of the Geological Society (1949–1950), his presidency of the Mineralogical Society (1948–1951), and his vice presidency of the Royal Society (1949) took their toll in 1950. The preparation of a fitting presidential address to the Geological Society worried Tilley greatly and appears to have been the final factor in the nervous exhaustion that rendered him unable to deliver the address in person.

A brief convalescence in Canada, spent in fieldwork among the Haliburton-Bancroft alkaline gneisses, restored his health and started him on another significant problem, the petrogenesis of alkaline rocks. Characteristically he began with a close study of the critical mineral nepheline, made a global survey of the environmental controls on its composition in a wide variety of rocks, and concluded that whereas in the volcanic environment the composition of the nepheline reflects that of the host rock, in metamorphic and plutonic occurrences the nepheline composition is restricted to the Morozewicz-Buerger convergence field. Tilley paid particular attention to nepheline-feldspar associations and showed that in the heteromorphic pair phonolite and nepheline gneiss, the feldspar phases become more sodic and the nepheline more potassic in the nepheline gneiss in response to changing temperature. In his paper on nepheline associations (1956) he advocated further experimental work; that was provided by the experimental hydrothermal study of the nepheline-kalsilite-SiO_2 system by his former pupil W. S. Mackenzie and his associates at Manchester, which yielded a surer guide to the crystallization history of the undersaturated rocks.

917

The alkaline rocks provided him with another new mineral, latiumite (with N. F. M. Henry, 1953).

Some seven years after his presidential address Tilley delivered the William Smith Lecture to the Geological Society of London in November 1957. He took as his subject "Problems of Alkali Rock Genesis," was naturally very nervous about the quality of the lecture, and achieved another instant triumph. Some of the new data presented in the lecture related to a drill core from the Haliburton-Bancroft area of Ontario, Canada, which he had obtained with a view to investigating the problem of nephelinization; that he had had cut and examined 1,500 thin sections from the core is yet another reminder of the enthusiasm, energy, and stamina that he brought to each successive undertaking. Tilley demonstrated conclusively that the nephelinized rocks were original crystalline schists and gneisses converted to a subsolvus feldspathoidal assemblage by the action of metasomatic fluids derived from a feldspathoidal magma. Subsequently he showed with J. Gittins (1961) that the ultimate sources of the agents of nephelinization that had converted Grenville sediments into nepheline gneisses were hypersolvus nepheline syenites.

Tilley retired from the professorship of mineralogy and petrology at Cambridge on 31 September 1961 and was succeeded by W. A. Deer, a former pupil who had explored and interpreted the Skaergaard intrusion in east Greenland and was to be the principal author of a five-volume work on rock-forming minerals. Tilley's final service to the laboratory he had created and equipped so well was the provision of electron-microprobe analysis by the appointment of J. V. P. Long in 1959. The year following his retirement was spent at the Geophysical Laboratory, where he had been appointed a research associate in 1956.

A visit to Hawaii had renewed Tilley's interest in basalts, and he had started a program of experimental work with H. S. Yoder, Jr. (subsequently director of the Geophysical Laboratory), a remarkable collaboration between the supreme mineralogist-petrologist and the leading experimentalist. In 1962 they published a paper of almost 200 pages, "The Origin of Basalt Magma: An Experimental Study of Natural and Synthetic Rock Systems," which was a triumph of interpretative petrology and experimental skill. The basis of their approach was to treat natural basalts and their chemical equivalent, eclogites, as bulk compositions in a multicomponent system the crystallization trends of which could be followed by the quenching method. They established clearly that the two basalt series could form in the region of magma generation from the same parental source, a garnet peridotite. They showed also that under hydrothermal conditions the stability field of basalt is drastically reduced by the development of amphibolite and were able to conclude that amphibole settling and resorption not only may operate to convert tholeiitic to alkali basalt liquids but also may effect the reverse change, depending on the composition of the amphibole at the liquidus. As a by-product they demonstrated that for all basalt compositions plagioclase is the first mineral to disappear completely with rising temperature at pressures above 1.5 kbar, suggesting a possible mode of genesis of certain types of anorthosite.

Between 1961 and 1967 Tilley was engaged not only in experimental work with Yoder in Washington, but also in detailed petrological studies of the differentiation of basalts and related rocks with I. D. Muir in Cambridge, in the course of which much new chemical data was presented in eight papers.

Tilley's last visit to the Geophysical Laboratory in 1967 did not end his active interest in experimental petrology; for Washington he substituted Manchester. In five papers with R. N. Thompson, he described and explained the melting relations of lavas from Kilauea, Snake River, Réunion, the mid-Atlantic ridge, and Nyiragongo. The style of these papers is terse even for Tilley's later period. These were the basic data papers, which, following his usual practice, were to be followed by a significant work of synthesis and review. But that was never to happen. He had suffered a mild thrombosis in 1970; such attacks occurred with increasing frequency over the next three years. He knew that he was slowing down but was determined to keep going to the very end. He had been invited as guest of honor to a dinner on 20 January 1973 in Emmanuel College that was to celebrate the centenary of the last day in the life of Adam Sedgwick, but felt too tired to attend. He died quietly by his fireside four days later.

Tilley was much honored in his lifetime. The Geological Society of London awarded him its Wollaston Fund in 1924, its Bigsby Medal in 1937, and its highest award, the Wollaston Medal, in 1960; he was president during the year 1949–1950 and William Smith Lecturer in 1957. He was president of the Mineralogical Society of Great Britain between 1948 and 1951 and, unprecedentedly, again between 1957 and 1960. He was an honorary fellow of the Mineralogical Society of America, which awarded him its Roebling Medal in 1954. The Royal Society of London elected him to its fellowship in 1938, appointed him a vice president in 1949, and awarded him a Royal Medal in 1967. He was president of the International Mineralogical Association between 1964 and 1970, presiding over meetings in Cambridge in 1966 and in Tokyo and Kyoto in 1970. He received honorary doctorates from the universities of Manchester, England, and Sydney, Australia, and he was vice master of Emmanuel College, Cambridge, between 1952 and 1958.

The naming of the mineral tilleyite in his honor in 1933 was a particular source of pleasure to him. A source of even greater pleasure was the dedication of a special volume of *Mineralogical Magazine*, with papers by colleagues and former students, to mark his seventieth birthday; a copy sumptuously bound by Sydney Cockerell was presented to him at a dinner attended by many of the contributors at St. John's College on 30 September 1965. A posthumous honor was the naming of the lecture theater in the department of mineralogy and petrology, where his softly booming voice had so often instructed and enthralled his audience over a span of thirty years, as the Tilley Lecture Theatre, a commemorative plaque of orbicular diorite being unveiled by H. S. Yoder, Jr., on 17 January 1981.

No petrologist of his generation ranged over so wide a field as Tilley; to significant contributions to the study of both contact and regional metamorphism must be added seminal works on the genesis of both basaltic and alkaline igneous rocks as well as substantial contributions to mineralogy and effective application of experimental petrology. He never published until he was satisfied that he could go no further toward the solution of the problem in hand or had solved it. Thorough collection in the field (by himself or by the few whose ability he trusted) was followed by exhaustive petrographic investigation and chemical analysis of selected rocks and of significant minerals (however difficult it might be to obtain the separations necessary before the advent of electron microprobe analysis) and supplemented by his comprehensive knowledge of the literature. His style of research and his obliteration of any demarcation between mineralogy and petrology were passed on to his many students and by them to a generation of petrologists worldwide. Passed on too was his aesthetic appreciation of rocks seen in thin section under the polarizing microscope.

BIBLIOGRAPHY

I. ORIGINAL WORKS. Tilley wrote more than 120 original papers, of which the most significant are "The Petrology of the Metamorphosed Rocks of the Start Area," in *Quarterly Journal of the Geological Society*, **79** (1923), 171–204; "Contact Metamorphism in the Comrie Area of the Perthshire Highlands," *ibid.*, **80** (1924), 21–71; "A Preliminary Survey of Metamorphic Zones in the Southern Highlands of Scotland," *ibid.*, **81** (1925), 100–112; "Some Mineralogical Transformations in Crystalline Schists," in *Mineralogical Magazine*, **21** (1926), 34–36; "The Dolerite-Chalk Contact at Scawt Hill, Co. Antrim. The Production of Basic Alkali Rocks by the Assimilation of Limestone by Basaltic Magma," *ibid.*, **22** (1931), 439–468; "Metasomatism Associated with the Greenstone-Hornfelses of Kenidjack and Botallack, Cornwall," *ibid.*, **24** (1935), 181–202; "Some Aspects of Magmatic Evolution," in *Quarterly Journal of the Geological Society*, **106** (1950), 37–61; "A Note on the Progressive Metamorphism of Siliceous Limestones and Dolomites," in *Geological Magazine*, **87** (1951), 175–178; "The Zoned Contact-Skarns of the Broadford Area, Skye: A Study of Boron-Fluorine Metasomatism in Dolomites," in *Mineralogical Magazine*, **29** (1951), 621–666; "Nepheline Associations," in *Verhandlingen van het Koninklijk Nederlands geologisch mijnbouwkundig genootschap*, **16** (1956), 1–11; "Problems of Alkali Rock Genesis," in *Quarterly Journal of the Geological Society*, **113** (1958), 323–360; and "Origin of Basalt Magmas: An Experimental Study of Natural and Synthetic Rock Systems," in *Journal of Petrology*, **3** (1962), 342–532, written with H. S. Yoder, Jr.

II. SECONDARY LITERATURE. The obituary notices by G. A. Chinner in *American Mineralogist*, **59** (1974), 427–437, and by W. A. Deer and S. R. Nockolds in *Biographical Memoirs of Fellows of the Royal Society*, **20** (1974), 380–400, provide critical appraisals, bibliographies, and reminiscences.

DUNCAN MCKIE

TIMOFEEFF-RESSOVSKY, NIKOLAI VLADIMIROVICH (*b.* Kaluga district, Russia, 7 September 1900; *d.* Obninsk, USSR, 28 March 1981), *genetics.*

Little of Timofeeff's early life can be ascertained at present. According to Zhores Medvedev, Timofeeff was of the Kaluga nobility in origin and as a youth took part in the Civil War. Before he graduated from Moscow State University in 1925, he had already (in 1922) commenced work in genetics under S. S. Chetverikov at the Kol'tsov Institute of Experimental Biology. After Lenin's death in 1924, the Kaiser-Wilhelm Institut für Hirnforschung (KWI), located at Berlin-Buch, helped to organize a laboratory in Moscow for the study of Lenin's brain. In exchange, Oscar Vogt, director of the KWI, requested that someone be sent to his institute to organize a department of genetics, which Vogt considered to be an important adjunct to an institute of neurobiology and psychiatry. Although he had not yet received his doctoral degree, Timofeeff already had a good grounding in the genetics of *Drosophila,* including population genetics and systematics, so his superiors recommended him for this appointment. In 1925, with his young wife, Helena (Elena) Aleksandrovna, also a geneticist, he went to Berlin for a projected stay of possibly six years.

Timofeeff-Ressovsky evidently had a gift for languages, for he quickly became a master of spoken and written German; and by 1932, when he attended the Sixth International Congress of Genetics, held in Ithaca, New York, he had mastered English sufficiently to converse readily and to deliver a major address in that language. His memorable, widely consulted reviews, "The Experimental Production of Mutations" (1934) and "Mutations and Geographical Variation" (1940), reveal a fluent control of the English language that enabled him to make difficult concepts and novel developments extremely clear. Timofeeff's mastery of German style was also evident, and his addresses were delivered with enthusiasm and vigor.

By 1927 the new department at the KWI was well established, and Timofeeff entered upon a period of amazing scientific productivity that lasted through the troublous 1930's until the outbreak of World War II. Essentially, all of his contributions to genetics were accomplished in the fifteen years from 1925 to 1940. Timofeeff managed quite successfully to stay out of Nazi politics. Even when Oscar Vogt retired in 1937, and Timofeeff succeeded him as director of the KWI, he managed to limit his relationships with the political authorities to perfunctory appearances on public occasions, when he summarized in sober tones the gravity of the genetic load borne by human populations. His statements, from 1935 to 1938, to that effect in no way altered his conclusions, based on his own work, that it is unsafe to consider the effects of a harmful gene apart from its total "genetic milieu," that is, the entire genotype with its many significant modifiers of the action of any gene. Timofeeff also believed that it is unsafe to judge the effects of a harmful gene apart from the "environmental milieu," including both the internal physiological system of an organism and the external environment, either or both of which can totally change the relative detrimental status of the gene in question. Timofeeff never endorsed the racial policies of the Nazi Party and its eugenicists, or any particular eugenic measures.

Nevertheless, the time was an unhappy one for Timofeeff. As the terror and political pressure on science increased, he began to search for ways to leave Germany. Although he could have accepted certain tentative offers from the United States, he did not wish to leave Europe; and in 1937 he wrote to Kol'tsov about the possibility of returning to the Soviet Union. Not even the rise to power over genetics and agriculture of T. D. Lysenko and I. I. Prezent, and their persecution of any geneticists who upheld the condemned Mendelian-Morganian theories accepted in the West, dissuaded him, nor did the arrests of two of his own brothers as well as many of their friends and many relatives of his wife. Nikolai I. Vavilov, president of the Academy of Agricultural Sciences, sent a message to Timofeeff by the American geneticist H. J. Muller, who at this time escaped from Moscow to Spain and thence to Edinburgh, to warn him that only disaster could await him were he to return to his native land; Kol'tsov smuggled a letter to Timofeeff through the Swedish embassy. He wrote, according to Medvedev, "Of all the methods of suicide, you have chosen the most agonizing and difficult. And this not only for yourself, but also for your family. . . . If you do decide to come back, though, then book your ticket straight through to Siberia!" Timofeeff stayed on in Berlin.

Explicitly or implicitly, all of Timofeeff's genetic studies addressed the major questions of the time concerning the relation of genes and mutations to the processes of evolution. The first were experiments begun before Timofeeff left Moscow and extended through 1933. These were studies of the reversibility of gene mutations; for if, he reasoned, mutations were the basis of evolutionary change, they must not always be completely destructive. If a mutant gene could mutate back to a state restoring the original wild phenotype, the original mutation must not have been a total loss of substance, as many eminent scientists skeptical about the role of gene mutations in evolution supposed. Timofeeff's investigations of reverse mutation were concerned principally with the white eye-color locus of *Drosophila melanogaster*. His first reverse mutations were spontaneous occurrences; but after Muller's discovery of the induction of mutations at vastly increased frequencies by exposure of the flies to X rays, Timofeeff quickly made use of the new technique.

Although subsequent investigations have revealed that this locus is not really a simple single gene but a compound of several pseudoalleles, Timofeeff established several generalizations that have not yet been challenged. First, he confirmed the earlier reports relating to other genetic loci that, by means of exposure to X rays, reverse mutations, as well as forward mutations, can be obtained. That is, not only could the gene at the selected locus, which is necessary for the production of red eye color in the flies, be made to mutate to an allele that resulted in white eye color or an intermediate shade, but the less effective or impotent alleles could be made to mutate back to the red eye color allele.

Next Timofeeff demonstrated that the mutation rates in opposed directions are different and depend upon what particular allele is mutating. He showed that some reverse mutations cannot be secured in a single step but may be obtained in two or more successive steps. He also discovered isoalleles (W^A and W^R) that are distinguishable only on the basis of their mutation rates. He proved that the recurrence of the original alleles was demonstrable on a pleiotropic basis, that is, of several types of phenotypic effects, not only the eye color but also the form of the spermatheca, color of testes, viability of males, and fertility of females.

Timofeeff was probably the first geneticist to realize that in studies of reverse mutation it is essential to exclude the possibility that the reversion is actually not at the site of the original forward mutation but that a mutation at a suppressor locus elsewhere might be involved. His techniques for excluding that possibility in interpreting his own results were inadequate but represented a significant development of technique at the time.

Significant studies in the analysis of the relationships between X-ray dose and mutation rate formed a second major part of Timofeeff's contributions. He was among the early workers to conform the linear dose relationship for sex-linked lethals. He demonstrated that the proportions between sex-linked lethals and visibles did not change with dose; that neither the fractionation of the dose nor the dose rate affected the mutation frequency; that the mutation frequency for a given dose was independent of the hardness of the rays; and that within the limits of 10° and 35°C the temperature during radiation has no effect. Some of these generalizations are now considered to be more limited because they were applicable only to mutations induced in mature spermatozoa; but in general Timofeeff's studies in this area were among the most important and fundamental in early mutation work, second in importance only to those of H. J. Muller and L. J. Stadler.

An entirely different type of study, and one of classic value to this day, was Timofeeff's investigation of the influence of the residual genotype and of selected environmental conditions on the expression of particular mutant genes. This work utilized especially the mutant venae transversae incompletae

(vti) of Drosophila funebris. It led Timofeeff to a distinction between the penetrance, expressivity, and specificity of the mutant gene. Of particular importance was the discovery that each of these parameters of gene expression can to a certain degree vary independently. The modifying genes in the rest of the genotype provide a "genotypic milieu" that, together with the "external milieu" of environmental variables and the "internal milieu" (the physiological variables), determines the expression in the organism of the primary gene alleles. It was demonstrated that the genotypic milieu present in different geographic strains of a species varies in respect to its effect upon the expression of vti.

Another classic series of investigations performed by Timofeeff related to "viability mutations." From the standpoint of interest in the evolutionary process and especially of the action of natural selection, it was of critical importance in the 1930's to show whether recessive lethal mutations—on which most studies of mutation rates had been based—were indeed the commonest kind of mutations, or whether in fact there were many more mutations with less drastic effects upon viability, defined as the ability of the organism to survive to the age of reproduction. In a program involving a stupendous amount of work, Timofeeff succeeded in showing that X rays induce about twice as many mutations without visible effects but detrimental in some measure to viability as they induce lethal and sublethal mutations combined, from the same dose of X rays. He also detected a single radiation-induced mutation with increased viability. For this mutant and the others, the measured viability was different at different temperatures.

A further important contribution to an understanding of the evolutionary significance of mutations was derived from the analysis of the viability of different mutations in Drosophila funebris when placed in different combinations with other mutants. Timofeeff demonstrated that the standard viability of a particular mutant at a given temperature offered a scant basis for predicting what the viability would be under the same conditions when it was combined with other mutants. Thus a combination of ev and sn, rated individually at viabilities of 104 percent and 79–88 percent of normal (wildtype), proved to be 103 percent, whereas ev with Va (rated at 89 percent) turned out to be 84 percent. In other words, the viability of the compound was sometimes as good as the higher of the component mutants taken singly, sometimes as poor as the poorer of the component mutants. Sometimes it was intermediate. It could even exceed the better, or fall below the poorer, of the component mutants taken alone. From the standpoint of clarifying the selective process upon the raw material of evolution, the mutations, this investigation is one of the most important ever made by anyone.

Timofeeff's later work on the nature of mutation and deductions regarding the nature of the gene itself was highly stimulating to geneticists the world over. The primary contribution was one made jointly with K. G. Zimmer and Max Delbrück (published in 1935). It represented the debut in genetics of the young physicist Delbrück, whose conversion to biology would alone have constituted a major achievement by Timofeeff, for after leaving Germany for America, Delbrück pioneered with Salvador Luria in the study of mutations in bacteria and virtually founded bacterial genetics; then went on to play an equally significant role in establishing bacteriophage genetics; and became a Nobel laureate and a father of molecular genetics of vast influence. He warmly attributed his early training in genetics and his insight into the problems of mutation to Timofeeff-Ressovsky.

In the paper with Zimmer and Delbrück, Timofeeff led off with a masterly summation of all the existent data on mutation, both radiation-induced and spontaneous. He deduced that the dependence of the latter on temperature (corrected for the altered length of the generations at different temperatures) revealed a Q_{10} of about 5, which throws it far outside the range of ordinary chemical reactions. He analyzed the spectrum of mutability of different loci, and the relation of mutation rate to dose of radiation, and with Zimmer and Delbrück concluded that a mutation is a molecular rearrangement within a particular molecule, and the gene a union of atoms within which a mutation, in the sense of a molecular rearrangement or dissociation of bonds, can occur. The actual calculations of the size of the gene, deduced from calculations on the assumption of a spherical target, were not cogent, as Delbrück wryly admitted in his Nobel Prize lecture, but the entire approach to the problem of mutation and the gene adopted by the three collaborators was highly stimulating to other investigations.

Later, Timofeeff wrote a book, *Das Trefferprinzip in der Biologie,* with K. G. Zimmer as coauthor. Its publication was delayed, however, until after World War II (1947), at which time it was principally of historical interest. It contained a full, masterly summary of the data on radiation-induced mutation up to 1940, and, in spite of the fact that later work by other investigators showed that mutation may be induced indirectly through the production of free radicals in the medium or inner milieu surrounding the chromosomes, Timofeeff's deductions are still valid for the considerable proportion of mutations that are induced by direct hits rather than indirect effects.

Timofeeff was well aware of the dimensions of the problem, and one of his last papers before the war (published in 1937) was an investigation of the direct versus indirect influence of irradiation on the mutation process. In this study he compared the effects of direct irradiation of the chromosomes in the spermatozoa of *Drosophila* with the effects of irradiating the plasma of the eggs and then introducing unirradiated chromosomes from the sperm into it. Finding no increase in mutation in the latter case, in contrast with the former, he concluded that there is no indirect effect of radiation on mutation. This was a valid conclusion for the circumstances, for the indirect effects later demonstrated by other geneticists do not endure for the length of time required for the fertilization of eggs by untreated spermatozoa. Indirect effects produced by the formation in the medium of chemical mutagens of a semipermanent character are of course a different phenomenon, the ignorance of which Timofeeff could not avoid, since chemical mutagenicity was discovered only during and after World War II, and Germany was shut off from knowledge of these developments until the 1950's.

When it became evident in the spring of 1945 that Germany would soon fall to the combined pressure of the Western and the Russian armies, Timofeeff's friends urged him to escape from Berlin to the West before he was captured by the Soviet troops. I was personally informed by his good friend Boris Rashevsky, director of the Max-Planck Institut für Biophysik in Frankfurt, that at considerable personal risk Rashevsky made a special trip to Berlin in the winter or spring of 1945 to urge Timofeeff to make his way to the West while there was still a possibility of getting out of Berlin. Timofeeff, however, refused to leave the institute in Berlin-Buch, for which he had by then assumed principal responsibility. Although his oldest son had been captured by the Nazis in underground activity and sent to a concentration camp, where he subsequently died, Timofeeff did not fear personal reprisals from the German government; and he spoke with conviction of his belief that no one else could talk to the Russian commanders when they arrived and save the institute and its personnel from damage and disruption except himself.

From this point on, we must rely on the writings of Zhores Medvedev to tell us the sequel. When the Russian forces did arrive in Berlin-Buch, Timofeeff was confirmed in the post of director of the Hirnforschungs-Institut and indeed temporarily saved both the equipment and the personnel from destruction. Soon, however, a new high command replaced the original field commanders. Most of the equipment was taken away and sent to Russia, and Timofeeff was arrested and sent to Moscow. After a period of imprisonment and investigation in the Lubianka prison, on a charge of being a German spy, Timofeeff was transferred to the Butyrka prison. He stayed there for some months, with his characteristic energy organizing a Scientific and Technical Society, with lectures by members who included physicists, electronic engineers, and a chemist in addition to the geneticist. Here Timofeeff made the acquaintance of Aleksandr Solzhenitsyn, who has described life in this prison so graphically.

Next Timofeeff was sent to a special labor camp in northern Kazakhstan and condemned to "general labor only." Again he organized a scientific society to save himself and his fellow scientists from intellectual death. He was not so fortunate physically and began to suffer badly from malnutrition and avitaminosis. The lack of vitamin A in the prison diet was responsible for a swift decline in his vision, verging on blindness. Fortunately, he was saved by the need in the Soviet Union for scientists knowledgeable in radiobiology and radiation genetics, as the Soviet program to develop first a nuclear bomb and then a hydrogen bomb got under way. He was shipped back to Moscow in a crowded prison wagon, forced to stand crushed together with others most of the time, and arrived unconscious. In the Central Prison Hospital strenuous efforts saved his life, but his vision, although improving, remained permanently impaired. According to Medvedev, he was never again able to use a microscope and could read only with a large magnifying glass and a brightly lighted page.

After his recovery, Timofeeff was transferred to a laboratory in the Ural atomic establishment. For the first time in two years, he was able to write to his wife in Germany, who thereupon hastened to be reunited with him, together with their younger son, who had remained with his mother in Berlin. They were of course all virtually imprisoned and closely guarded. There was also trouble from the archenemies of genetics in Russia, the Lysenkoists. I. E. Glushchenko, a follower of Lysenko, singled him out as a "sworn enemy" of the people, and orders went out from Moscow to ban genetic research in all institutes; the classic subject of genetic research, the laboratory stocks of *Drosophila* flies, were to

be destroyed. At this juncture, Timofeeff virtually created a new science for himself. He called it "radiation biogeocenology," defined as the science of the radiation aspects of total ecology, the complete living community of organisms, earth, air, and waters in their fullest interdependence.

In 1955, two years after the death of Stalin, Timofeeff was released from imprisonment. He had already become scientific director of the laboratory in the Urals where he worked. He now began to form a biophysics section within the Ural branch of the U.S.S.R. Academy of Sciences, and it soon "became the most productive biological establishment in the Urals and Siberia" (Medvedev, p. 99). At Miassovo, near Sverdlovsk, Timofeeff also founded a summer seminar on genetics and theoretical biology, the first such center in existence in the Soviet Union since 1948. It was very popular with scientists and, like the dozens of papers and monographs he issued through the Ural branch of the U.S.S.R. Academy of Sciences, it exerted a profound effect on the renaissance of biology after the demise of Lysenkoism.

On the occasion of the centenary of Charles Darwin's publication of the *Origin of Species,* the Deutsche Akademie der Naturforscher Leopoldina (East Germany) decided to confer four Darwin Prizes on Russian geneticists and evolutionists. Of these persons, S. S. Chetverikov, Timofeeff's first teacher of genetics and a founder of population genetics, was one, and N. V. Timofeeff-Ressovsky was another. The other two were I. I. Schmalhausen and N. P. Dubinin. The four distinguished scientists were invited to Berlin to receive the honors to be conferred upon them, but in 1959 none of the four was permitted to go. Instead, the medals and diplomas were forwarded to them by mail. Chetverikov died before receiving his medal. Schmalhausen had been dismissed from his posts in 1948, and his books destroyed. Timofeeff was in the Urals, and received his medal while at the summer institute of genetics he had founded at Miassovo. Even Dubinin, who was already a corresponding member of the U.S.S.R. Academy of Sciences, was disgraced and dismissed from his post as director of the Institute of Genetics and Cytology in Novosibirsk, at the special direction of Nikita Khrushchev. The Soviet Union was clearly not yet ready for a renaissance of genetics and evolution.

By 1962 Timofeeff had been convinced by his friends that he should defend a thesis and acquire a doctoral degree, for in the Soviet Union every administrator in science must possess such a degree, regardless of the eminence of his scientific contributions and the distinction with which he is regarded outside the country. Timofeeff did so, and was awarded the degree of doctor of biological sciences by the Ural branch of the U.S.S.R. Academy of Sciences. This academic standing had to be confirmed by a commission in Moscow, which was still controlled by Lysenko, and the commission balked. Not until October 1964, after Timofeeff had moved to Obninsk to become head of a section of genetics and radiobiology, and after Khrushchev had resigned, was Lysenko's power curbed. Timofeeff was finally confirmed in the possession of his doctorate, became the recognized leader of research in radiation biology and genetics at the Obninsk Institute of Medical Radiology of the Academy of Medical Sciences, and began to give many lectures and courses, write popular books in the fields in which he was an authority, and, as in Miassovo, to organize a summer institute.

Even so, Timofeeff's difficulties were not at an end. In 1965, on the occasion of the centennial of Mendel's discovery of the laws of heredity, the Czechoslovak Academy of Sciences planned an international celebration to be held in Brno. Timofeeff was invited to be one of twenty noted geneticists to receive the newly established Mendel Medal and to present a paper at the memorial symposium. He was, however, not permitted to go. The necessary exit dossiers required to go abroad were blocked by deliberate delays, first in the Academy of Medical Sciences and later in the Kaluga Provincial Committee of the Communist Party of the Soviet Union. Timofeeff's medal was eventually delivered to him in Moscow by a Czechoslovak embassy official in December 1965.

Only a few days had elapsed when a similar experience began. In the fall of 1965 the committee of the National Academy of Sciences of the United States, appointed to nominate recipients of the Kimber Gold Medal and Award in genetics, and of which the author of this article was a member, had chosen Timofeeff-Ressovsky to be the thirteenth recipient of the medal. I had personally prepared the nomination, and a good portion of the foregoing summation of Timofeeff's contributions to genetics is based on the unpublished memoir I circulated to the other members of the Kimber Award Committee. The medal itself and the monetary award of $2,000 constitute, in the eyes of geneticists throughout the world, possibly the highest honor a geneticist could receive, outranking even the Nobel Prize in esteem. Only one other non-American had previously been awarded the medal (J. B. S. Haldane), and Timo-

feeff's own recruit for genetics, Max Delbrück, had been a previous recipient.

The unanimous nomination of Timofeeff by the committee was confirmed by the council of the academy, whose president wrote to Timofeeff in December 1965 to inform him of the honor. A special letter was also sent by President Seitz to the president of the U.S.S.R. Academy of Sciences, expressing the hope that Timofeeff would be permitted to attend the annual meeting of the U.S. Academy of Sciences in Washington in April 1966 to receive the medal and award.

Again the matter was referred to the Academy of Medical Sciences, within which Timofeeff's laboratory and section were located; and again the matter dropped out of sight. In the opinion of the authorities, the award to Timofeeff was simply a political provocation by the Americans. Eventually, as in the case of the Mendel Medal, the Kimber Gold Medal and Award had to be presented to Timofeeff in Moscow, on an occasion when the vice president of the U.S. Academy of Sciences was there for an official visit.

In 1969, while I was president of the American Association for the Advancement of Science, I made an official visit to the Soviet Union as a return courtesy for a visit to the AAAS by the officers of Znaniye, a very large, popular scientific association in Russia. When I spoke of my friendship with Timofeeff, in whose laboratory at Berlin-Buch I had worked in the spring and summer of 1933, I was shown with pride several popular books on genetics and evolution written for the organization by Timofeeff. Yet when I expressed the hope that I might meet with him, either at Obninsk or in Moscow, my suggestion met with a blank response. Upon inquiry, he was "away," or "not available." From Medvedev's book *The Medvedev Papers,* I later learned why (pp. 107–112).

Timofeeff was expectably excluded from attendance at the International Congress of Genetics held in Tokyo in 1967, where I had hoped to see him. He became a candidate for election to the U.S.S.R. Academy of Sciences in 1968, having in the previous five years published, according to Medvedev, more than fifty papers and a monograph. (These works still remain unknown in the West.) Nevertheless, Timofeeff's candidacy was turned down through the combined opposition of the Michurinists and of Lysenko himself. Favorable publicity in the press did not help Timofeeff's candidacy in the least. A dossier on his supposed political anti-Russian activities was compiled, and later it was used to put pressure on Timofeeff to resign a year before reaching the compulsory age of retirement for administrators (seventy years). For Timofeeff, this was a severe penalty, since his pension could not be based on any of the years he spent in Germany or while imprisoned. The denial of even one additional year was therefore serious.

The ultimate sequel is more pleasant to relate. Photographs are in the possession of the Library of the American Philosophical Society (Collection Caspari) sent by Timofeeff's friend, the plant geneticist Georg Melchers of Tübingen (West Germany). These photographs show participants at the meeting of the N. I. Vavilov All-Union Society of Geneticists and Selectionists at Lomonosov University in 1972. Especially revealing is a merry supper party at which Timofeeff and his wife are happily conversing with their old friends Georg Melchers and Hans Stubbe, the latter the leader of genetics in East Germany. In the meantime Timofeeff had been elected a member of the Leopoldina Academy and received its Mendel Medal in 1970. When the Thirteenth International Congress of Genetics met in Moscow in the summer of 1978, Timofeeff was a greatly honored senior member and at last met many of his friends and admirers from the Western countries. He died in Obninsk on 28 March 1981, in his eighty-second year, his wife having predeceased him. It seems possible that, like Vavilov, he will ultimately be posthumously rehabilitated and honored in his own country as its greatest geneticist, even though he was never elected to membership in the U.S.S.R. Academy of Sciences.

BIBLIOGRAPHY

I. ORIGINAL WORKS. "Rückgenovariationen und die Genovariabilität in verschiedenen Richtungen. I," in *Wilhelm Roux' Archiv für Entwicklungsmechanik der Organismen*, **115** (1929), 625–635; "Reverse Genovariations and Gene Mutations in Different Directions. II," in *Journal of Heredity*, **22** (1931), 67–70; "Verschiedenheit der 'normalen' Allele der White-Serie aus zwei geographisch getrennten Populationen von *Drosophila melanogaster*," in *Biologische Zentralblatt*, **52** (1932), 468–476; "Rückmutationen und die Genmutabilität in verschiedenen Richtungen. III," in *Zeitschrift für induktive Abstammungs- und Vererbungslehre*, **64** (1933), 173–175; "Rückgenmutationen und die Genmutabilität in verschiedenen Richtungen. IV. Röntgenmutationen in verschiedenen Richtungen am white-Locus von *Drosophila melanogaster*," ibid., **65** (1933), 278–292; "Rückmutationen und die Mutabilität in verschiedenen Richtungen. V. Gibt es ein wiederholtes Auftreten identischer Allele innerhalb der white-Allelenreihe von *Drosophila melanogaster?*" ibid., **66** (1933), 165–179; "Einige Versuche an *Drosophila melanogaster* über die Beziehungen zwischen Dosis und Art der Röntgenbestrahlung und der dadurch ausgelösten Mutationsrate," in *Strahlentherapie*, **49** (1934), 463–478; "The Experimental Production of Mutations," in *Biological Reviews* (Cambridge), **9** (1934), 411–457; "Über den Einfluss des genotypischen Milieus und der Aussenbedingungen auf die Realisation des Genotyps," in *Nachrichten von der Gesellschaft der Wissenschaften zu Göttingen, Mathematische-physikalische Klasse*, VI, Biol., n.s. **1** (1934), 53–106; "Über die Vitalität einiger Genmutationen und ihrer Kombinationen bei *Drosophila funebris* und ihre Abhängigkeit vom 'genotypsichen' und vom äusseren Milieu," in *Zeitschrift für induktive Abstammungs- und Vererbungslehre*, **66** (1934), 319–344.

"Auslösung von Vitalitätsmutationen durch Röntgenbestrahlung bei *Drosophila melanogaster*," in *Nachrichten von der Gesellschaft der Wissenschaften zu Göttingen, Mathematisch-physikalische Klasse*, VI, Biol., n.s. **1** (1935), 163–180; "Über die Natur der Genmutation und der Genstruktur," ibid., 189–245, written with K. G. Zimmer and Max Delbrück; "Zur Frage über einen 'direkten' oder 'indirekten' Einfluss der Bestrahlung auf den Mutationenvorgang," in *Biologische Zentralblatt*, **57** (1937), 233–248; *Experimentelle Mutationsforschung in der Vererbungslehre* (Dresden and Leipzig, 1937); "Mutations and Geographical Variation," in Julian Huxley, ed., *The New Systematics* (Oxford, 1940), 73–136; "Populationsgenetische Versuche an *Drosophila*. I–III," in *Zeitschrift für induktive Abstammungs- und Vererbungslehre*, **79** (1940), 28–34, 35–43, 44–49, written with E. A. Timofeeff-Ressovsky; *Das Trefferprinzip in der Biologie* (Leipzig, 1947), written with K. G. Zimmer; *Primenenie printsipa popadaniia v radiobiologii* (Principles of target theory in radiobiology; Moscow, 1968), written with V. I. Ivanov and V. I. Korogodin; *Kratkii ocherk teorii evoliutsii* (Brief sketch of the theory of evolution; Moscow, 1969), written with N. N. Vorontsov and A. V. Iablokov; and *Ocherk ucheniia o populiatsii* (Sketch of population theory; Moscow, 1973), written with A. V. Iablokov and N. V. Glotov.

Photographs of Timofeeff-Ressovsky are in the Ernst Caspari Collection at the Library of the American Philosophical Society, Philadelphia.

II. SECONDARY LITERATURE. B. L. Astaurov, "Za vydaiushchiisia nauchnyi vklad v genetiku: Kimberovskaia premiia—sovetskomu uchenomu" (For the excellent scientific contribution to genetics: The Kimber Gold Medal to a Soviet scientist), in *Priroda*, 1967, no. 6; Bentley Glass, "Nomination of N. W. Timofeeff-Ressovsky for the Kimber Gold Medal and Award of the National Academy of Sciences, USA," unpublished manuscript in the Library of the American Philosophical Society (1965); Zhores Medvedev, *The Medvedev Papers* (New York, 1971), chap. 5; Robert Proctor, *Racial Hygiene: Medicine Under the Nazis* (Cambridge, Mass., 1988), 34–35, 85, 105, 362 n. 38; Karl Heinz Roth, "Schöner neuer Mensch," in Heidrun Kaupen-Haas, ed., *Der Griff nach der Bevölkerung* (Nördlingen, 1986), 11–63; and N. N. Vorontsov and A. V. Iablokov, "K 70-letiu N. V. Timofeeva-Re-sovskogo" (On the 70th Birthday of N. V. Timofeeff-Ressovsky), in *Biulleten Moskovskogo obshchestva is-pytatelei prirody, Otdel biologicheskii*, 1970, no. 5, 144–158, with bibliography.

BENTLEY GLASS

TIMOSHENKO, STEPAN [STEPHEN] PRO-KOF'EVICH (*b*. Shpotovka, Chernigovskaia *gub-erniia* [now Sumyskaia oblast, Ukrainian S.S.R.], Russia, 22 December 1878; *d*. Wuppertal, Federal Republic of Germany, 25 May 1972), *mechanics*.

Timoshenko's father, Prokofii Stepanovich, was a land surveyor; his mother, Josefina Iakovlevna Sarnovskaia, was a housewife.

In 1889 Timoshenko entered the Practical School in Romny, where one of his classmates was Abram Fedorovich Ioffe. In 1896 Timoshenko enrolled in the Institute of Railroad Transport in St. Petersburg, from which he graduated in 1901. The next year he started teaching there. In August of that year he married Aleksandra Arkhangelskaia, a medical student. They had three children.

In 1903 Timoshenko moved to the department of strength of materials at the St. Petersburg Poly-technical Institute. Three years later he won the competition for the chair in the department of strength of materials at the Kiev Polytechnical In-stitute, but in 1911 he was dismissed from the institute because of his opposition to the Ministry of Edu-cation's quotas for the admission of Jews.

Timoshenko then returned to St. Petersburg, where he taught as a nonstaff instructor at the Polytechnical Institute and the Electrotechnical Institute. In 1913 he was reinstated in the state service (as the result of a public petition that he had initiated) and resumed his work at the Institute of Railroad Transport as the head of the department of theoretical mechanics. During World War I, Timoshenko served as a con-sultant on materials strength at military plants as well as at the Ministry of Communications. From 1918 to 1920 he was again at the Kiev Polytechnical Institute. At the same time he took part in the organization of the Ukrainian Academy of Sciences and became the head of its Institute of Mechanics.

In 1920 Timoshenko emigrated to Yugoslavia, where for two years he taught at the Zagreb Poly-technical Institute. Then he moved to the United States. He first worked in research departments of several engineering companies in Philadelphia and Pittsburgh (including Westinghouse from 1923 to 1927), and then lectured at a number of universities. During 1927–1936 Timoshenko was a professor at

the University of Michigan, and from 1936 until 1955 at Stanford University.

As a scholar Timoshenko was greatly influenced by Ivan Grigorievich Bubnov, Viktor Lvovich Kir-pichev, and Aleksei Nikolaevich Krylov in Russia, and by August Föppl, Woldemar Voigt, Felix Klein, and Ludwig Prandtl in Germany. He traveled to Europe practically every year (except during the two world wars), and he maintained scientific con-tacts with colleagues all over the world.

Timoshenko always did research along with his teaching. Despite his long experience as a lecturer, he firmly believed that his lectures could be suc-cessful only if he had previously treated the subject in written form. Because of this belief and of his great productivity, he left an enormous number of courses published and republished in Russian and in English (dating from 1908) and covering practically all areas of pure and applied mechanics. These courses are remarkable not only for their detailed exposition of material but also for their inclusion of the author's scientific researches and results.

Timoshenko's first paper (1905) was devoted to resonance in shafts. A group of his papers concerning the theory of stability of flange beams, bars, plates, and shells was gathered in *Collection of Problems in Strength of Materials* (1910). The book was awarded the D. I. Zhuravskii Gold Medal and Prize by the Institute of Railroad Transport.

Another group of Timoshenko's papers dealt with the classical theory of elasticity. He developed an approximative method of solving the plane problem of elasticity and a method of calculating stresses in plates with holes, in circular rings, and in rods subject to bending and torsion. He also investigated circular and rectangular plates and, as was typical for him, paid much attention to effective approximative procedures.

Being interested in the immediate applications of his investigations in mechanics, Timoshenko was involved in the design of bridges, including sus-pension bridges. During World War I he advised the government on the practical problems of the strength of rails (which were especially critical in view of the overloaded railroads), as well as of shafts and turbines. He was concerned with the fatigue of materials associated with the concentration of stress near holes. In addition to the theory of the strength of materials, Timoshenko worked out experimental methods of investigating stress, and carried out experiments on stability, strength, and buckling of beams and plates. He made an extraor-dinary contribution to the organization of training laboratories at all the educational institutions where he taught for more than half a century.

Timoshenko also published works on the mechanical properties of materials, on shock loads, on applications of the theory of vibrations to engineering, and on the history of mechanics (particularly the strength of materials).

In 1919 Timoshenko was elected full member of the Ukrainian Academy of Sciences; in 1928 he became corresponding member, and in 1964 full member, of the Soviet Academy of Sciences. He was a corresponding, full, or honorary member of the academies of science of the United States, Poland, France, and Italy, and of the Royal Society of London, and held honorary doctorates from a number of universities. His works were awarded medals in Britain and the United States. The American Society of Mechanical Engineers established two medals named for him, and in 1957 he was the first recipient of one of them, "for an extraordinary contribution to creation of a new era in applied mechanics, for the personal example and leadership in work."

Timoshenko's hobby was travel. He traveled throughout Europe, and after World War II twice went to the Soviet Union, where he visited his birthplace, as well as Kiev, Leningrad, and Moscow. He loved music and literature, and was a gifted writer. In 1963 he published his memoirs (parts of which were used for the preparation of this article).

After his retirement in 1944, Timoshenko became professor emeritus at Stanford University (though he continued to teach on a limited basis until 1955). He remained in the United States until 1960, when he moved to the Federal Republic of Germany, where his daughter lived.

BIBLIOGRAPHY

I. Original Works. Timoshenko wrote more than 120 papers, the most important of which were published in *The Collected Papers* (New York, 1953) and in *Ustoichivost sterzhnei, plastin i obolochek: Izbrannye trudy* ("Stability of Strings, Plates, and Shells: Selected Works"; Moscow, 1971). To these should be added the first and the last of Timoshenko's papers: "K voprosu o iavleniiakh rezonansa v valakh" ("On the Problem of Resonance Phenomena in Shafts"), in *Vestnik obshchestva tekhnologov*, **19**, no. 7 (1905), 266; and "Deflexion of Strings and Beams," in *Miscellany Dedicated to the Memory of the Late Academician J. M. Klitcheff* (Belgrade, 1970).

Timoshenko's books include *Advanced Dynamics* (New York, 1948), written with D. H. Young; *History of Strength of Materials* (New York, 1953); *Vibration Problems in Engineering*, 3rd ed. (New York, 1955), written with D. H. Young; *Engineering Mechanics*, 4th ed., 2 vols. (New York, 1956), written with D. H. Young; *Strength of Materials*, pt. II, *Advanced Theory and Problems*, 3rd ed., 2 vols. (New York, 1956); *Theory of Structures*, 2nd ed. (New York, 1965), written with D. H. Young; *Theory of Plates and Shells*, 2nd ed. (New York, 1959), written with S. Woinowski-Krieger; *Theory of Elasticity*, 3rd ed. (New York, 1970), written with J. N. Goodier. His memoirs are *Vospominaniia* (Paris, 1963), trans. by Robert Addisas *As I Remember* (New York, 1968).

II. Secondary Literature. E. I. Grigoluik, "Scientific Works of S. P. Timoshenko," in *Issledovaniia po teorii plastin i obolochek* (Kazan, 1972), 3–54; and J. M. Lessels, ———, in *Contributions to the Mechanics of Solids Dedicated to Stephen Timoshenko by His Friends on the Occasion of His Sixtieth Birthday* (New York, 1938).

V. J. Frenkel

TOMONAGA, SIN-ITIRO (*b.* Tokyo, Japan, 31 March 1906; *d.* Tokyo, 8 July 1979), *physics.*

Sin-itiro Tomonaga, who shared the 1965 Nobel Prize with Richard P. Feynman and Julian Schwinger for "fundamental work in quantum electrodynamics," was the son of Hide and Sanjuro Tomonaga. When Sin-itiro was born, his father, Sanjuro, was a professor at Shinshu University in Tokyo. In 1907 he accepted a chair in philosophy at Kyoto Imperial University. From 1909 to 1913 he studied abroad, mostly in Germany, and his family moved to Tokyo to live with relatives. Sin-itiro spent his first year in primary school there; after the family was reunited in 1913, he attended school in Kyoto. He was frequently ill, and in 1918 he missed the first semester of middle school. Hideki Yukawa, who was also to become a Nobel laureate in physics, entered the same school one year after Tomonaga; they became classmates as a result of the latter's illness and continued to be, at the Third High School and at Kyoto Imperial University.

Tomonaga's reminiscences, "My Teachers, My Friends," describe his university experience as so distasteful that he became pessimistic about his future. About the instruction he said, "I thought the level of the lectures was low and was greatly disappointed as I had high expectations, especially for physics."

Tomonaga's interest in physics had been stimulated by a well-publicized visit to Japan by Albert Einstein in 1922 and by reading a book on relativity theory by Jun Ishiwara. In high school Niels Bohr's atomic theory had been discussed, with stress on its abstruse and revolutionary character. Tomonaga's last year at high school was 1925–1926, the year of the new quantum mechanics of Werner Heisenberg, Erwin

Schrödinger, and Paul A. M. Dirac. His physics teacher, Takeo Hori, who had just graduated from Kyoto Imperial University, presented material on matrix mechanics and wave mechanics.

Tomonaga was therefore disappointed with the old-fashioned physics being taught at the university. The theory lectures were tedious and had too many dry formulas; the laboratories were dark, dirty, and old-fashioned. He did, however, find the mathematics instruction interesting and challenging; the instructors were active in research and conveyed their own excitement to the students.

During their final year at the university (1928–1929), Tomonaga, Yukawa, and several other ambitious students studied quantum mechanics together from original journal articles and without a professor. After graduation Tomonaga and Yukawa stayed on in Kyoto as unpaid assistants to Kajuro Tamaki.

In September 1929, Heisenberg and Dirac came to Japan from America, where they had spent the summer, at the invitation of Yoshio Nishina. Tomonaga went to Tokyo to hear their lectures, given in English (published two years later in Japanese). The visitors spoke on their own latest works: Heisenberg on ferromagnetism and Dirac on his relativistic electron theory. Tomonaga was deeply impressed but, being shy, took a rear seat at the lectures and did not meet Nishina or either of the visitors.

However, in 1931 Nishina lectured at Kyoto for a month, and Tomonaga established a good rapport with him. Nishina had returned to Japan in December 1928, after seven years of study in Europe, six of them at Bohr's institute in Copenhagen, where he had done important theoretical research with Oskar Klein. In Tokyo, at the Institute for Physical and Chemical Research (Riken), the organization he had joined in 1918 and that had financed his stay abroad, Nishina formed a group to do research in both theoretical and experimental nuclear physics. Nishina's lectures at Kyoto conveyed to Tomonaga and Yukawa the spirit of the Copenhagen approach to quantum mechanics.

Tomonaga joined Nishina's laboratory at Riken in April 1932 to do theoretical research and began a fruitful scientific collaboration with Nishina. His first five papers, through 1935, are on the creation and annihilation of positrons, and the sixth is on the neutron-proton interaction; all have Nishina as coauthor. Other collaborators of this period were H. Tamaki and two of Yukawa's students from Kyoto, Shoichi Sakata and Minoru Kobayashi.

In the summer of 1933, Nishina, Sakata, and Tomonaga worked together at Gotemba, near Mt. Fuji. Two years later Kobayashi, Tamaki, and Tomonaga

rented a villa in Karuizawa, Nagano Prefecture, and translated Dirac's *Principles of Quantum Mechanics* into Japanese. A 1935 paper with Nishina and Kobayashi, "On the Creation of Positive and Negative Electrons by Heavy Charged Particles," is a comprehensive work that complements theoretical studies of this problem by E. J. Williams, J. R. Oppenheimer, L. Landau and E. Lifshitz, E. C. G. Stueckelberg, and other well-known physicists.

Tomonaga's next three papers, dealing with nuclear structure, are in German. An English paper of 1937 (with Tamaki) treats, for the first time, the collision of a very-high-energy neutrino with a neutron. It is an outgrowth of Heisenberg's discussion of "explosive showers" produced by cosmic rays and emphasizes the rapid rise, with increased energy, of the probability of neutrino interaction. According to Rudolf Peierls, it "foreshadowed the present role of high-energy neutrinos as practical projectiles."

At the end of 1937, Tomonaga went to Leipzig to work with Heisenberg and remained there until just before the outbreak of war in Europe in 1939. On his arrival, he found there was a great interest in Yukawa's meson theory, which attracted worldwide attention at this time because of the discovery of the cosmic-ray meson in 1937, but Heisenberg suggested to Tomonaga that he should work first on a less speculative subject. In fact, Tomonaga wanted to improve the compound nucleus model advanced by Bohr in 1936 and 1937. In that model, a nuclear collision results in an excited nucleus (regarded as analogous to a drop of liquid), which then evaporates one or more nucleons. Tomonaga's idea was to treat the nuclear matter as a degenerate Fermi gas and to study the process by which it reaches its equilibrium temperature, taking into account its viscosity and thermal conductivity. His paper was published in *Zeitschrift für Physik*, and he submitted it to Tokyo Imperial University in 1939 to obtain the D.Sc. degree.

In an interview in 1978, Tomonaga recalled his second research project in Leipzig: to modify Yukawa's picture of meson decay. It was occasioned by an analysis of cosmic-ray data by Heisenberg and Hans Euler that showed an unexpectedly long mean life of the cosmic-ray meson. Yukawa had postulated a direct decay into an electron and a neutrino, but Tomonaga's model had the meson decaying (virtually) into a nucleon pair, which was then annihilated to produce the electron and neutrino through the four-fermion beta-decay interaction. The calculation led to an integral that was infinite.

Heisenberg agreed with Tomonaga's negative conclusion and stated that the perturbation techniques that had yielded useful results for electromagnetic and weak interactions (in spite of difficulties of principle) would be totally inapplicable in meson theory. He handed Tomonaga proof sheets of a paper containing a semiclassical approach to meson interaction, and Tomonaga decided that he would produce a quantum theoretical version of it.

Tomonaga wanted to extend his stay in Leipzig but was dissuaded by the threat of war in Europe. In mid August 1939, Yukawa visited Tomonaga in Leipzig. He was making his first trip out of Japan, having been invited to attend the Eighth Solvay Conference at Brussels in October (later canceled because of the outbreak of war in September) and to lecture to the German Physical Society, which was to meet in September. However, on 25 August they were urgently advised by the Japanese embassy in Berlin to proceed to Hamburg and to board the ship *Yasukuni Maru*.

The ship took them first to Bergen, Norway, and then to New York, where they visited the World's Fair. Yukawa traveled overland to the West Coast, while Tomonaga, happy to be in a Japanese setting, remained on the ship as it passed through the Panama Canal, stopped in San Francisco, and continued to Japan.

On 27 October 1940, Tomonaga married Ryoko Sekiguchi, daughter of Koikichi Sekiguchi, director of the Tokyo Astronomical Observatory and a professor at Tokyo Imperial University; they had three children. He continued his association with Riken, and in 1941 was also appointed professor at Tokyo Bunrika Daigaku (Tokyo University of Literature and Science, which became Tokyo University of Education in 1949, and University of Tsukuba in 1973). In 1944 he became part-time lecturer at Tokyo Imperial University and was also required to do research for the navy.

Like Schwinger, with whom he shared the Nobel Prize, Tomonaga did war work on the theory of microwave circuits and wave guides, especially on the theory of the magnetron oscillator used to generate short radio waves for radar. In a sense, the work was pure engineering, but the physicist's approach, starting from first principles and applying techniques such as that of the "scattering matrix" used in nuclear physics (a theory extended by Heisenberg in the 1940's) proved to be very powerful. With Masao Kotani, Tomonaga was awarded the Japan Academy Prize in 1948 for his work on the magnetron.

Aside from military research, Tomonaga's work in the 1940's was mainly on the theory of mesons and on quantum electrodynamics, with many of his ideas stemming from what he had done at Leipzig. The first work he did after returning from Germany led to his writing a letter to *Physical Review* with Gentaro Araki that emphasized the differences between the nuclear capture rates of slow positive and negative mesons. They pointed out that "the competition between nuclear capture rates and spontaneous disintegration must in this way be different for mesons of different signs." Checking of the Tomonaga-Araki predictions by the Rome group of M. Conversi, E. Pancini, and O. Piccioni, in experiments begun in 1943 and completed in 1946, showed conclusively that the cosmic-ray meson observed at sea level could *not* be the Yukawa nuclear-force meson, because it interacted only weakly with nucleons.

A second line of research led to a unique "intermediate coupling" approximation for meson theory. The strength of an elementary electromagnetic interaction (between, say, an electron and a photon) is measured by a dimensionless quantity called the fine-structure constant. It is equal to the square of the electron's charge multiplied by 2π and divided by the product of Planck's constant and the velocity of light, its value being about $1/137$. The analogous quantity in the meson theory, obtained by substituting the meson "coupling constant" g for the electronic charge e, has a value near 1. Consequently, the method usually used to obtain results in quantum electrodynamics—the expansion of the interaction probability in powers of the fine-structure constant (the so-called perturbation method)—cannot be used effectively in meson theory.

In 1940, Gregor Wentzel at Zurich introduced the "strong-coupling" approximation, in which an expansion is made in powers of the inverse of the coupling constant. Wentzel's treatment gave new predictions not obtainable by perturbation theory, such as strongly bound states of the nucleon with one or more mesons (isobars). In his paper of 1941, "Zur Theorie des Mesons, I," Tomonaga points out that the meson coupling is effectively near unity, so that one anticipates a "poor convergence for both [that is, strong and weak coupling] approximations." Thus a third procedure is called for, one that is useful for an intermediate coupling.

The method invented by Tomonaga and developed in a series of papers (some with Tatsuoki Miyazima and others) resembles the so-called Hartree approximation, often used in the treatment of multiparticle systems such as atoms or nuclei, but differs from it in that the number of particles (mesons) is not fixed.

Unquestionably, though, the most important work

of Tomonaga is based upon his paper "On a Relativistically Invariant Formulation of the Quantum Theory of Wave Fields." The English version, in the first issue of *Progress of Theoretical Physics*, a journal that Yukawa started in 1946, is a translation of a paper that appeared in 1943 in the Riken journal (*Riken-iho*).

Tomonaga's paper is a generalization to quantum field theory of a prophetic work by Dirac, done in 1932, in which each of a set of particles carries its own time variable as well as a spatial label, Dirac's "many-time" theory. The equal treatment of time and space, in contrast with the usual Hamiltonian treatment that singles out the time variable, makes possible a fully relativistic treatment of the many-particle problem. Tomonaga's Nobel address begins by discussing his generalization of Dirac's theory to an infinite number of degrees of freedom (that is, to a quantum field), the super-many-time theory: "This paper of Dirac's attracted my interest because of the novelty of its philosophy and the beauty of its form."

The essential point was the description of the field on a succession of arbitrary spacelike surfaces. As Julian Schwinger put it in 1980:

> All of space at a common time is but a particular coordinate description of a plane spacelike surface. Therefore the Schrödinger equation, in which time advances by a common amount everywhere in space, should be regarded as describing the normal displacement of a plane spacelike surface. Its immediate generalization is to the change from one arbitrary spacelike surface to an infinitesimally neighboring one, which change can be localized in the neighborhood of a given space-time point. Such is the nature of the generalized Schrödinger equation that Tomonaga constructed in 1943, and to which I came toward the end of 1947 (*Birth of Particle Physics*, p. 364).

Because of the intense bombing of Tokyo, in April 1944 Tomonaga sent his family to live in the country while he remained in the city. By September several physicists without their families were sharing his house. He went sometimes to the Shimada Naval Research Laboratory to work on radar. However, Tomonaga's health became bad once again, and in December he was obliged to take to bed on account of eye trouble and infected teeth. On 13 April 1945, the area of professors' houses near Tokyo University was completely burned out, including the houses of Tomonaga and Nishina, as was Riken.

During this period Satio Hayakawa kept a notebook that he used in writing an article (1988) that describes Tomonaga as "a great teacher." Released

from military service in November 1944, he had returned to the University of Tokyo and, together with fellow students Hiroshi Fukuda, Ziro Koba, and Yoneji Miyamoto, enrolled in a seminar course taught by Tomonaga. All of them, as well as Takao Tati, Daisuke Ito, and Suteo Kanesawa, were subsequently coauthors with Tomonaga of one or more of the nearly two dozen papers on cosmic-ray phenomena, quantum theory, and renormalization theory that he wrote during the next few years.

In April 1946 Tomonaga described to the students his ambitious program: to develop a completely covariant quantum electrodynamics to the point where it could be applied to realistic problems. First it would be necessary to modify the so-called auxiliary (or subsidiary) condition that is imposed on the four-vector potential in the classical Hamiltonian theory of the electromagnetic field to obtain Maxwell's equations. The analogous procedure in the quantum field theory results in the separation of the instantaneous Coulomb interaction from the retarded transverse radiation field. While that is convenient for treating many problems, it destroys the relativistic covariance of the theory.

Once a covariant formulation for the electromagnetic field had been obtained, it was combined with Dirac's electron theory and tested by solving problems in the framework of many-time theory. Then they turned to Tomonaga's more general super-many-time theory and applied it to the electromagnetic interactions of electrons, did the same for mesons, and then attacked the meson-nucleon interaction.

By 1 June 1946 the formulation of quantum electrodynamics in super-many-time theory was nearly completed, with Koba, Hayakawa, and Miyamoto doing significant work; then, with Kanesawa, Tomonaga began to consider the electromagnetic interactions of the vector meson. By early August, Tomonaga decided it was time to prepare a series of papers for publication. The whole group would contribute to these, with authorship assigned to subsets of the members in a somewhat arbitrary manner. At a meeting of the Physical Society at Kyoto University on 21 and 22 November 1946, no fewer than twenty-three papers were presented by Tomonaga and his associates.

At the same meeting, Sakata presented a theory of mixed fields, which, as he and Osamu Hara showed, gave no electromagnetic self-energy correction to the mass of the electron; in the standard theory, the result was infinity. Sakata's theory was similar to one proposed by Fritz Bopp in Germany, which canceled the electromagnetic self-energy of the electron by assuming that this particle also interacted with a neutral vector field of negative energy. The Sakata-Hara work replaced Bopp's vector field with a neutral scalar meson field, with positive energy, and accordingly could be considered "realistic" rather than a mathematical artifice. Sakata called the scalar field that stabilized the electron the "cohesive field" and named its quantum the C-meson. Tomonaga, struck by Sakata's suggestion, wondered whether the removal of the self-energy divergence would work in a higher order of approximation.

In 1947 the Tomonaga group began to recalculate the radiative corrections to the elastic scattering of an electron in a Coulomb field (calculated in 1939 by Sydney M. Dancoff in the United States), using the idea of the cohesive field. At first their result was negative; an infinite term appeared in the scattering probability (in addition to another infinity, due to the polarization of the vacuum, against which the cohesive field was known to be powerless). However, in the course of the calculation Tomonaga developed a new calculational method, much more transparent, and with its aid they discovered an error in Dancoff's work; the final answer was then finite. Dancoff had introduced the word "renormalization" and had tried to express the infinities in the scattering problem in terms of mass and charge renormalization; except for his calculational error, he would have succeeded.

Renormalization means a redefinition of the theoretical mass and charge of the electron, which are inserted at the starting point of the theory of quantum electrodynamics as "bare" nonphysical quantities. The observable mass and charge are defined to be the sum of the "bare" quantities and their radiative corrections (which involve the virtual creation and annihilation of photons and electron-positron pairs). Stated thus, the idea may appear self-evident, but since the "corrections" are infinite, the "bare" mass and charge are also infinite and of opposite sign. The scheme thus involves a delicate mathematical cancellation.

Communication with the West was still a problem in Japan, but gradually news filtered through that similar developments were taking place in the United States. On 26 April 1947, Willis E. Lamb, Jr. and Robert C. Retherford discovered an anomaly in the hydrogen spectrum. Lamb reported it in June at a small private conference on Shelter Island, New York, attended by both Feynman and Schwinger. Soon afterward, Hans Bethe explained the main part of the effect by a nonrelativistic application of the renormalization method. Tomonaga read about these exciting developments in *Time* and *Newsweek*.

The shift of energy separating the first and second excited levels of the hydrogen atom, the Lamb shift, was the first testing ground of the new quantum electrodynamics, which was rapidly applied to extend Bethe's calculation to the relativistic region. Besides the calculations of Feynman and Schwinger, of Tomonaga (with Fukuda and Miyamoto), and of Lamb (with Norman M. Knoll), the same calculations were independently done by J. Bruce French and Victor F. Weisskopf and by Yoichiro Nambu.

In the years 1948 and 1949 Yukawa was at the Institute for Advanced Study in Princeton, after which he accepted a chair at Columbia University (1949–1953). His letters to colleagues in Japan helped to keep them in touch with developments in the West. In the years 1949 to 1950 Tomonaga was a member of the Institute for Advanced Study, and he wrote letters that were published in the informal journal *Soryushiron Kenkyu*. At Princeton he worked on the properties of nuclear matter.

After his return to Japan in 1950, Tomonaga continued to do physics research but was increasingly involved in scientific administration, becoming a member (later president) of the Science Council of Japan, succeeding Nishina in 1951. In 1956 he was elected president of Tokyo University of Education. From 1957 on, he was active in movements against the deployment of nuclear weapons, such as the Pugwash conferences.

Besides the Nobel Prize (1965) and the Japan Academy Prize (1948), Tomonaga received numerous other honors. They included Japan's highest award, the Cultural Medal (1952) and the Lomonosov Medal of the Academy of Sciences of the U.S.S.R. (1964). He was a member of the Japan Academy, the Royal Swedish Academy of Sciences, the (U.S.) National Academy of Sciences, and the American Philosophical Society.

BIBLIOGRAPHY

I. ORIGINAL WORKS. Most of Tomonaga's original scientific work is in his *Scientific Papers of Tomonaga*, T. Miyazima, ed., 2 vols. (Tokyo, 1971–1976). Volume I contains the physics papers, in English and German, and Tomonaga's Nobel lecture. Volume II contains articles on ultrashort wave circuits and the magnetron, review articles in Japanese on nuclear and elementary particle physics, and letters written from America to Japanese colleagues. Tomonaga's textbook *Quantum Mechanics*, Masatoshi Koshiba, trans., 2 vols. (Amsterdam, 1962–1966), has a historical plan. Eighteen volumes of his essays, letters, and diaries have been published in Japanese. His papers are at Riken (Tokyo) and at Tsukuba University.

II. SECONDARY LITERATURE. Several articles on Japanese elementary particle physics are in Shigeru Naka-yama, David L. Swain, and Eri Yagi, eds., *Science and Society in Modern Japan* (Cambridge, Mass., 1974). "Nuclear Research at Riken," a "dialogue" with To-monaga, is in L. M. Brown, M. Konuma, and Z. Maki, eds., *Particle Physics in Japan, 1930–1950,* II (Kyoto, 1980). See also Julian Schwinger, "Two Shakers of Physics: Memorial Lecture for Sin-itiro Tomonaga," in Laurie M. Brown and Lillian Hoddeson, eds., *The Birth of Particle Physics* (Cambridge, 1983), 354–375. A group of papers on Tomonaga (including Satio Hayakawa's) is in L. M. Brown, R. Kawabe, M. Konuma, and Z. Maki, eds., *Proceedings of the Japan–USA Collaborative Workshops on the History of Particle Theory in Japan, 1935–1960* (Kyoto, 1988), 43–84.

LAURIE M. BROWN

TRÉFOUËL, JACQUES GUSTAVE MARIE (*b*. Le Raincy, France, 9 November 1897; *d*. Paris, France, 11 July 1977), *therapeutic chemistry*.

Jacques's father, Eugène Tréfouël, a former teacher of mathematics at the Collège Chaptal in Paris, earned his living in the textile trade. Through his mother, Jeanne Pottiez, he was a grandnephew of the famous actors Constant and Ernest Coquelin, who belonged to the Comédie-Française. Jacques received a Catholic education and remained a re-ligious believer. His family wanted him to become an actor like his uncles, but he preferred to study chemistry at the Sorbonne. In 1917 he courageously took part in World War I and received the Croix de Guerre.

Tréfouël entered Ernest Fourneau's laboratory of therapeutic chemistry at the Pasteur Institute in 1920 and married a colleague, Thérèse Boyer, a young chemist he had met at the Sorbonne. Almost all his scientific writings were done with his wife and signed by both. The couple worked on chemo-therapy, physiology, and chemistry. Their most fa-mous contribution was the discovery in 1935 of the therapeutic properties of sulphanilamide against bacterial infections.

Tréfouël became *chef de service* at the Pasteur Institute in 1938 and became director general in December 1940, a duty he carried out through difficult times until his retirement in December 1964. He was a modest, extremely courteous, brilliant, and witty man. He was a member, and became president of, both the French Academy of Sciences and the National Academy of Medicine. He belonged to numerous foreign societies, including the American Chemical Society and the Association of American Physicians.

Tréfouël's master, Ernest Fourneau, a leading figure in chemotherapy, was a former student of Emil Fischer and Richard Willstaetter, and a follower of Paul Ehrlich, and he made every effort to surpass German research in that new field. When Tréfouël entered his laboratory, Fourneau was engaged in a systematic study of the therapeutic properties of arsenical derivatives against protozoa infections. Ehrlich had studied the properties of trivalent ar-senical derivatives, but Fourneau preferred to study the properties of simpler pentavalent derivatives. In a first series of experiments, published between 1923 and 1927, the Tréfouëls and Fourneau syn-thesized hundreds of different derivatives and their isomers and discovered that two of the ten isomers of acetylaminohydroxyphenylarsonic acid were ac-tive against protozoa. The first isomer, stovarsol, was active against syphilis. The second, orsanine, was active against trypanosomal infections. Two position isomers had very different and specific ac-tions. It was the first time that such specificity was shown in chemotherapy.

Another successful line of thinking was provided by the therapeutic properties of azo dyes against trypanosomes. The study of these dyes led in 1920 to the discovery of a new drug, germanine, whose activity was considerably more effective than any previous drug in this field. The German chemists at Bayers kept its formula secret. Fourneau studied the German patents from 1912 and made several guesses about the molecular structure. Working for nine months in 1924, the Tréfouëls synthesized hundreds of different derivatives, one of which, moranyl, showed the same impressive therapeutic activity as the German product. A position isomer of this derivative showed no activity. This was another example of the specificity principle in chemotherapy.

Between 1930 and 1933 the Tréfouëls, together with Daniel Bovet, Ernest Fourneau's pharmacol-ogist and later a Nobel Prize recipient (1957), in-vestigated the properties of different classes of compounds against paludism. In 1926 the German company I. G. Farben had released a new drug, plasmoquin, which belongs to the quinolines. The Tréfouëls performed a systematic study of quinoline derivatives and found several active drugs. One of them, rhodoquine, was less toxic and slightly more active than plasmoquine.

But the most fundamental contribution of the Tréfouëls was in antibacterial chemotherapy. The problem of killing the bacteria inside the organism without affecting the host remained unsolved for years, until preliminary results were obtained in 1933 with an azo dye synthesized by the I. G. Farben chemists F. Mietzsch and J. Klarer. The active substance carried a sulphanilamide group on one of the benzene rings. In 1935 Gerhard Domagk reported that this substance was active against streptococcal infections in mice.

The Tréfouëls, together with Bovet and bacteriologist Frederico Nitti, took a new route and tried several modifications to the active molecule, prontosil. All the modifications affecting the benzene ring that did not carry the sulphanilamide group left the therapeutic activity constant. Following the specificity principle, it meant that this part of the molecule did not participate in the therapeutic activity. This led the Pasteur group to postulate that the sulphanilamide half was the really active part and that the azo function $-N = N-$ of the prontosil was reduced within the organism, thus splitting the molecule into one active and colorless part and another inactive and colored. In November 1935 they tested the therapeutic properties of the sulphanilamide on infectious mice and rabbits, Sulphanilamide was at least as active as prontosil. The hypothesis of a metabolic reduction of the prontosil within the organism was later proved to be true.

The discovery of sulphanilamide was a major breakthrough in therapeutic medicine. In 1937 physicians at the Pasteur Hospital reported two cases of spectacular recoveries of children with streptococcal meningitis following administration of sulphanilamide. This very simple molecule, and hundreds of its derivatives, could be easily synthesized, and tons of these products soon became available from the pharmaceutical industry. The Pasteur group went on with the study of sulphanilamide and established its bacteriostatic activity. Other sulfur derivatives were tried, among them the sulfones, which were especially useful against leprosy.

In December 1940 Tréfouël was nominated director of the Pasteur Institute. Paris was occupied by the Nazis, but despite countless obstacles, he kept the institute working and began to reorganize it. He was at the same time an active member of the Resistance. Tréfouël arranged that no worker at the institute would be taken for compulsory work service in Germany. In the cellars of the institute he hid pharmaceutical reserves that had been parachuted in for the Resistance. Tréfouël also prevented the Nazis from obtaining the vaccines produced by the institute. He was on a deportation list when Paris was liberated in August 1944. He was awarded the Resistance Medal and in 1963 received from Général de Gaulle the cross of Grand Officer of the Légion of Honor. After the war Tréfouël began to turn the Pasteur Institute into a modern research institution. He modernized and extended it without affecting its financial autonomy. Tréfouël showed insight in his choice of new researchers, and his activity is undoubtedly one of the main reasons for the institute's major achievements in such fields as molecular biology, immunology, and virology. In Ernst Chain's opinion, "the Pasteur Institute never had a more dedicated and successful director than Jacques Tréfouël."

BIBLIOGRAPHY

I. ORIGINAL WORKS. The library of the Pasteur Institute owns a bound, five-volume collection of the publications, notes, and manuscripts of Jacques and Thérèse Tréfouël. See also "Activité du p-aminophénylsulfamide sur les infections expérimentales de la souris et du lapin," in *Comptes-rendus des séances de la Société de biologie*, **120** (1935), 756–758, written with Thérèse Tréfouël, Frederico Nitti, and Daniel Bovet; and "Les débuts de la sulfamidothérapie," in *Médecine et hygiène*, **17** (1959), 459–460.

II. SECONDARY LITERATURE. Obituaries are by Louis Aublant in *Bulletin de l'Académie nationale de médecine*, **161** (1977), 517–524; by Paul Bordet in *Bulletin et mémoires, Académie royale de médecine de Belgique*, **133** (1978), 201–210; and by Ernst Chain in *Nature*, **270** (1977), 647–648.

On sulfonamides and their discovery, see Gerhard Domagk, "Le dévelopement de la sulfamido-thérapie moderne," in *Terre d'Europe*, **7** (1958), 52–53; H. A. Feldman, "The Beginning of Antimicrobial Therapy: Introduction of Sulfonamides and Penicillins," in *Journal of Infectious Diseases*, **125** (March 1972, suppl.), 22–46; J. Kimmig, "Gerhard Domagk, 1895–1964. Ein Beitrag zur Chemotherapie der bakteriellen Infektionen," in *Internist*, **10** (1969), 116–120; and W. Schreiber, "Vor 50 Jahren: Entdeckung der Chemotherapie mit Sulfonamiden," in *Deutsche medizinische Wochenschrift*, **110** (1985), 1138–1142.

CLAUDE DEBRU

TURÁN, PAUL (*b*. Budapest, Hungary, 28 August 1910; *d*. Budapest, 26 September 1976), *mathematics*.

Turán was the eldest son of Aranha Beck and Béla Turán. He had two brothers and a sister, none of whom survived World War II. While in high school he showed considerable mathematical ability. Turán received his teaching diploma in 1933 and his Ph.D. (under Lipót Féjer) at Pázmány Péter University, Budapest, in 1935. Because of the semifascist conditions in Hungary, Turán, who was Jewish, could not obtain a post even as a high school teacher, and had to support himself by private tutoring. In 1938, when he was an internationally known mathematician, he finally became a teacher in the Budapest rabbinical high school.

After thirty-two months in a Nazi labor camp in Hungary in the years 1941–1944, Turán was liberated. He became a *Privatdozent* at the University of Budapest. In 1947 he went to Denmark for about six months and then spent six months at the Institute for Advanced Study at Princeton (during this period he completed two papers on polynomials and number theory). In 1948 he was elected corresponding member of the Hungarian Academy of Sciences, and became a full member in 1953. In 1948 and 1952 he received the Kossuth Prize, the highest scientific award in Hungary at that time. He became a full professor at the University of Budapest in 1949 and was the head of the department of algebra and number theory at the university and the head of the department of the theory of functions at the Mathematical Institute of the Hungarian Academy of Sciences.

Turán's first major result, produced when he was twenty-four, was his simple proof of the Hardy-Ramanujan result that the number of prime factors of almost all integers is $(1 + 0(1))$loglog n. Further developments led to the Turán-Kubilius inequality, one of the starting points of probabilistic number theory.

By 1938 Turán had developed the basic ideas of his most important work, the power-sum method, on which he published some fifty papers, both alone and with collaborators (Stanislav Knapowski, Vera T. Sós [his wife], János Pintz, Gabor Halász, and Istvàn Dancs, among others). Turán worked on the power-sum method until his death (his last paper was a survey of the application of the method in explicit formulas for prime numbers). The method has its most significant applications in analytic number theory, but it also led to many important applications in the theory of differential equations, complex function theory, numerical algebra (approximative solution of algebraic equations), and theory of trigonometric series. Turán devoted three books (with the same title but different—increasingly rich—contents) to this subject. The last and most comprehensive one, *On a New Method in Analysis and Its Applications*, was published in 1984.

The essence of the method is to show that the power sum of n arbitrary complex numbers $z_1, \cdots, z_n$—that is, the sum $g(\nu) = \sum_{j=1}^{n} z_j^{\nu}$—cannot be small for all ν (compared with the maximal or minimal term, say). In fact, to cite just one (perhaps the most important) result of this theory, choosing ν suitably from any interval of length n, we have

$$\nu = m + 1, \overset{max}{\cdots}, m + n \, \frac{|g(\nu)|}{\max_{1 \le j \le n}|z_i|^{\nu}} \ge \left(\frac{n}{4e(m + n)} \right)^{n}.$$

In order to understand this estimate, it should be noted that $g(m + 1) = g(m + 2) = \cdots g(m + n - 1) = 0$ is certainly possible—for instance, the z_j's are nth roots of unity. Similar results can be proved if we consider generalized power sums of the type $\sum_{j=1}^{n} b_j z_j^{\nu}$, supposing very general conditions on the coefficients b_j.

To give an idea of the connection between the theory and its applications, it should be noted that these oscillatory results concerning power sums of complex numbers lead directly to oscillatory results on the solutions of some differential equations; but through a rather sophisticated technique (developed by Turán and Knapowski), via the connection of zeros of Riemann's zeta function and primes, it is also possible to detect irregularities in the distribution of primes using these results. The variety of known applications is so rich that it is difficult to mention any area of classical analysis where the method would have no possible applications.

In 1952 Turán wrote a book in Hungarian and German on the power-sum method. A Chinese translation with some new results of this work appeared in 1954. An English version, *On a New Method of Analysis and Application*, completed by Halász and Pintz, appeared in 1984.

Besides his power-sum method, Turán did work in comparative prime number theory, analytic and quasi-analytic functions, differential equations, and other areas of analysis. In comparative prime number theory inequalities about the distribution of primes in different arithmetic progressions are studied. The subject goes back to Pafnuty Chebyshev and Edmund Landau, but Turán and Knapowski (his student and collaborator, who died young) developed it into a systematic theory.

An elementary power-sum problem posed by Turán in 1938 is the following:

Let $|z_1| = 1$, $|z_i| \le 1$ $(1 < i < n)$ be n complex numbers.

Let $s_k = \sum_{i=1}^{n} z_i^k$ where $\max_{1 < k < n} |s_k| = f(z_1, \ldots, z_n)$.

Let $f(n) = \min_{z_1, \cdots, z_n} f(z_1, \cdots, z_n)$.

Turán conjectured first of all that $f(n) > c$ for all n. This was proved by F. V. Atkinson in 1960.

Turán further conjectured that lim $f(n) = 1$. This
problem is still open. $n \to \infty$

Extremal graph theory was begun by Turán while
he was in a labor camp. He wrote the first paper
on this subject, and several more followed. Finally
he gave birth to statistical group theory, in which
he wrote seven fairly substantial papers with the
author of this essay.

PAUL ERDÖS

TURESSON, GÖTE WILHELM (*b.* Malmö, Sweden, 6 April 1892; *d.* Uppsala, Sweden, 30 December
1970), *plant systematics, genetics.*

Turesson is remembered by botanists as a pioneer
in the use of experimental methods to detect genetic
differences between races of plant species that adapt
them to different habitats. He coined two terms,
ecotype and *agamospecies*, that are currently used
widely by ecological geneticists and evolutionary
botanists.

The son of Jöns and Sophie Nilsson Turesson,
both of whom were teachers, Göte acquired his
strong interest in natural history from his parents,
who often took him on excursions on which they
collected plants and butterflies. His international
outlook on genecology began in 1912 when, at the
age of twenty, he went to live with his Aunt Anna
in Spokane, Washington, and enrolled in the University of Washington at Seattle. He received the
B.S. in 1914 and the M.S. in 1915, in plant systematics and physiology.

Turesson then returned to Sweden and became
a student at the University of Lund. He passed the
examination for the doctoral candidacy in 1920 and
the following year became docent in botany and
genetics.

Turesson's interest in physiological ecology began
while he was a student in Washington, where he
published papers on plant distribution, with special
emphasis on the Douglas fir and a comprehensive
biological-ecological investigation of skunk cabbage
(*Lysichiton camstschatcense*). A second interest,
begun in Washington and continued at Lund, was
the culture of fungi, particularly *Penicillium*. This
led to his expert knowledge of fungal diseases of
bees.

In 1916 Turesson began his investigations of prostrate races of strand plants, designed to find out
whether their distinctive growth habit is purely a
physiological response or is based upon genetic differences. He found that within a single species, the
common orache (*Atriplex patulum*), the prostrate
growth habit could result from either environmental
influence or the action of genes, depending upon
the particular race of the species. This discovery
caused Turesson to perform the extensive transplantation experiments that led to his theory of the
genotypical response of the species to the habitat.
This theory, published in 1922, was a milestone in
the progress of botanists' understanding of the adaptation of species to their surroundings. Based not
only upon Turesson's own research but also upon
his careful review of published information, it firmly
established the principle that all widespread plant
species include diverse populations, each of which
has genetic properties that adapt it to the climatic
zone and type of soil it occupies. With his research
the discipline of plant genecology, or ecological genetics, was born. With respect to both his dividing
a single plant into clonal divisions and planting each
division, under controlled conditions, in different
habitats, and his interpreting his results after a comprehensive synthesis, Turesson was without doubt
a pioneer who gave a new direction to evolutionary
botany.

The first of these research efforts, published in
1922, earned Turesson the Ph.D. from the University
of Lund. During the following five years he expanded
his program and engaged in constant, intensive research that included collecting live plants for genecological investigations from Norway, the Färoe
Islands, the Siberian Altai, Britain, the Netherlands,
the United States, and Canada.

In 1927, Turesson left the University of Lund for
the plant breeding station at Weibullsholm, where
he directed a program of improvement, using his
methods, for oats, rye, and potatoes. Four years
later he returned to Lund, where he hoped to be
appointed to a professorship that had become vacant.
For three years he and a botanist from Uppsala,
Nils Heribert-Nilsson, competed for this position.
Heribert-Nilsson was finally appointed, and Turesson
had to settle for the much less prestigious position
at the Agricultural College of Uppsala University
left vacant by his rival's departure.

This move caused a serious interruption in Turesson's research, since he had to build anew the necessary transplant gardens and gather another cadre
of co-workers. Moreover, since he was a highly
competitive and contentious person, the loss of the
expected professorship was a blow from which he
never fully recovered. During the subsequent years
Turesson turned his attention to the genetic structure
of apomictic species, those that produce seed without

the sexual union of egg and pollen, by virtue of several mechanisms that eliminate reduction division (meiosis) from their life cycles. He discovered that all the principal species investigated—sheep fescue (*Festuca ovina*), ladies' mantle (*Alchemilla alpina*), and hawkweed (*Hieracium pilosella*)—consist of clusters of genetically different races, or "ecotypes," as do sexual species. This research, although it was thoroughly sound, added little to previously acquired knowledge of asexually reproducing flowering plants. For all intents and purposes, Turesson's pioneering research was compressed into the eight years between 1919 and 1927.

In 1924, Turesson married Benedicte Lehmann, his constant companion in research, who after his death did much to further recognition of him by botanists. They had one son, Per Jördan.

Turesson was dynamic, vigorous, aggressive, and contentious. He was, moreover, deeply committed to experimentation in a discipline that had previously known only description. These traits not only made possible his pioneering in experimentation and synthesis of theory, they also were responsible for his shortcomings. Since his experiments had led him to conceive of species as clusters of "ecotypes," or distinct races, he rejected the results of other botanists who were showing during the same period that species such as Scotch pine (*Pinus sylvestris*) are systems of intergrading populations, of which Turesson's ecotypes represent only easily recognized modes of variation. He also actively opposed their theoretical conclusions. Although he can be honored for leading the way toward the now flourishing discipline of plant ecological genetics, he can by no means be given credit for solving its major problems.

BIBLIOGRAPHY

I. ORIGINAL WORKS. "The Genotypical Response of the Plant Species to the Habitat," in *Hereditas*, **3** (1922), 211–350; "The Species and the Variety as Ecological Units," *ibid.*, 100–113; "The Plant Species in Relation to Habitat and Climate. Contributions to the Knowledge of Genecological Units," *ibid.*, **6** (1925), 147–236; "Contributions to the Genecology of Glacial Relics," *ibid.*, **9** (1927), 81–101; "Zur Natur und Begrenzung der Arteinheiten," *ibid.*, **12** (1929), 323–333; "Studien über *Festuca ovina*. L. II. Chromosomenzahl und Viviparie," *ibid.*, **13** (1930), 177–184; "The Selective Effect of Climate upon the Plant Species," *ibid.*, **14** (1931), 99–152; "Studien über *Festuca ovina* L. III. Weitere Beiträge zur Kenntnis der Chromosomenzahlen viviparer Formen," *ibid.*, **15** (1931), 13–16; "Die Genenzentrumtheorie und das Entwicklungszentrum der Pflanzenart," in *Kungliga fisiografiska sällskapets i Lund förhandlingar*, **2**, no. 6 (1932),

1–11; and "Variation in the Apomictic Microspecies of *Alchemilla vulgaris* L.," in *Botaniska notiser* (Lund) (1943), 413–427.

II. SECONDARY LITERATURE. A. Muntzing, "Göte Wilhelm Turesson," in *Fisiografiska sällskapets årsbok* (1972), 62–70; and "Turesson, Göte Wilhelm," in Källa, *Nordisk familjebok* (Malmö, 1955), 483.

G. LEDYARD STEBBINS

TUVE, MERLE ANTONY (*b*. Canton, South Dakota, 27 June 1901; *d*. Bethesda, Maryland, 20 May 1982), *physics*.

All of Tuve's grandparents immigrated to the United States from Norway in the mid nineteenth century. His parents—Anthony G. Tuve and Ida Marie Larsen—came to Canton in order to teach at Augustana College, a school supported by a Norwegian-Lutheran church group (and a precursor of Augustana College at Sioux Falls); and from 1890 to 1916 his father was its president. Tuve's siblings also pursued learned professions: his older brother, George Lewis, in mechanical engineering; his younger sister, Rosemond, in English literary criticism; and his younger brother, Richard Larsen, in physical chemistry. On 27 October 1927 Tuve married Winifred Gray Whitman, who received her M.D. degree from the University of Minnesota and practiced psychiatry and psychoanalysis. They had two children, Trygve Whitman and Lucy Winifred, both of whom earned doctorates in the sciences.

As a boy, Tuve became interested in electrical devices. He and his friend Ernest O. Lawrence rejuvenated cast-off telephone dry cells and used them for electrical projects, including a telegraph line between their houses. As teenagers they turned their attention to wireless telegraphy. Their first set was one that the local Boy Scout troop had acquired. Later, each built his own vacuum-tube set.[1]

After a year at the public high school, Tuve transferred to the secondary-school program at Augustana. While there, he took a course in physics. Under the influence of the school's new president, P. M. Glasoe, however, he decided to major in chemistry when he entered the University of Minnesota in the spring of 1919.

Not long after moving to Minneapolis, Tuve changed his major to electrical engineering, the field in which he received his B.S. degree in 1922. The engineering curriculum included a required sequence of physics courses, and that—plus John T. Tate's sequence on theoretical physics—clinched his interest in the subject. As a result, he stayed for another year to work on a master's degree in physics.

Under Tate's direction he sought to determine whether bombardment by positive mercury ions could ionize mercury gas, but he observed no effect.

After leaving Minnesota, Tuve went to Princeton as an instructor, hoping to continue his work with positive ions as the basis for his doctorate under the direction of Karl T. Compton. The department, however, did not have sufficient funds to keep him for more than a year. Accordingly, after spending the summer of 1924 at Western Electric (working under the direction of Clinton J. Davisson), he went to Johns Hopkins University as an instructor and a graduate student.

In Baltimore, Tuve discussed a new project with Gregory Breit, whom he had met at Minnesota. Now at the Department of Terrestrial Magnetism (DTM) of the Carnegie Institution of Washington (CIW), Breit proposed building a large parabolic transmitter to direct a beam of very short radio waves at the ionosphere (then known as the "conducting layer" or the "Kennelly-Heaviside layer" of the earth's atmosphere). As his part in the project, Tuve was to man a mobile receiver to determine where the beam returned to earth.

Drawing on an approach described by W. F. G. Swann at Minnesota, Tuve proposed instead that they broadcast pulses of conventional-length radio waves and compare two sets of signals: one arriving from the transmitter directly and the other arriving via the ionosphere. The amount by which one train was offset from the other would serve as a measure of the time difference between the two routes—from which the height of the conducting layer could be established. Using the Naval Research Laboratory's transmitter, Tuve and Breit performed the experiment during the summer of 1925.

Prior to the mid 1920's, the existence of the ionosphere had been accepted on theoretical and practical grounds but had not been conclusively demonstrated by experiment. The first such demonstration came in December 1924. Working in England, E. V. Appleton and M. A. F. Barnett employed a different method. (Specifically, they observed the interference effects between the ground wave and the sky wave as the transmitter frequency was slowly varied.) In the years that followed, however, it was the method of Breit and Tuve that came into widespread use of ionospheric studies.[2]

In 1926 Tuve received his Ph.D. for his work on the ionosphere and thereupon joined Breit at the DTM—in part to continue the radio work. With Odd Dahl he developed a technique for sending out sharply peaked, widely spaced pulses, and with Lawrence R. Hafstad he developed a technique for leaking a portion of the signal from the transmitter to the receiver and using it for direct comparisons with the incoming sky wave. So sensitive were these techniques that their ionospheric measurements were disturbed by aircraft landing and taking off nearby— observations that played a role in the development of radar a few years later.[3]

Meanwhile, Tuve initiated a second line of research, one in which he had been interested since his Minnesota days.[4] Knowing that the repulsive electrical force between two particles of like charge had to break down in the atomic nucleus, he wanted to accelerate positively charged particles to high velocities. Directing the accelerated beam on atomic nuclei would then enable him to study the short-range attractive force that keeps the nuclear particles together.

Working at the DTM, Tuve and Breit were among the earliest researchers to develop particle accelerators as useful experimental devices. When they initiated the project in 1926, their first task was to develop a suitable high-voltage source. They found that by submerging a Tesla coil in a tank filled with transformer oil under pressure, they could produce 5 million volts. Their next step was to build vacuum tubes that could withstand such voltages. Breit's departure in 1928 to study in Europe left the task of tube development largely in Tuve's hands. Adopting the approach of W. D. Coolidge, he used a multisection tube—each section carrying only a portion of the high voltage. By the summer of 1929, Tuve, Hafstad, and Dahl had developed a multisection "cascade" tube that could withstand nearly 1.5 million volts. The third step was to use the apparatus to accelerate electrons and protons. Success with electrons led to a prize from the American Association for the Advancement of Science for the best paper presented at the annual meeting of 1930. But difficulties with protons led Tuve to seek a new type of high-voltage source.

The solution came in the form of the generator that R. J. Van de Graaff was developing at Princeton. Moving as quickly as they could as the field of nuclear physics took shape, Tuve and his DTM coworkers in 1933 used a one-meter Van de Graaff accelerator (which produced 0.4 million volts) to identify contamination effects in results reported by J. D. Cockcroft and E. T. S. Walton at the Cavendish Laboratory in England. In 1934 they used a two-meter Van de Graaff accelerator (which produced 1.2 million volts) to disconfirm results that Lawrence had obtained with his cyclotron at Berkeley. Subsequently they studied resonances in the proton bombardment of lithium and other elements.

Tuve then turned his attention to proton-proton scattering. Having arranged to make precise measurements of the accelerating voltage, he, Hafstad, and Norman P. Heydenburg initiated the studies in late 1935 and early 1936. Breit and two of his colleagues interpreted the results as demonstrating that the force at work in the proton-proton interaction is the same as the force at work in the proton-neutron interaction.[5] Subsequent refinements supported the conclusion that the nucleons are held together by a strong, charge-independent force.

As the decade progressed, the DTM emerged as one of the world's leading centers of nuclear physics. Along with using the two-meter machine, Tuve prepared plans for building an even larger Van de Graaff accelerator. Housed inside a pressurized steel container, it became operational (with a capability of accelerating protons to energies upward of 3 million volts) in late 1938. After Vannevar Bush succeeded John C. Merriam as CIW president in 1939, Tuve won approval for a sixty-inch cyclotron at the DTM—largely for producing radioactive isotopes—and much of his time that year was devoted to the new facility.

Meanwhile, Tuve did not neglect to strengthen his group's ties with theoretical physicists. In particular, he encouraged the CIW to initiate a series of annual conferences—the first of which was held in 1935—sponsored jointly with George Washington University and known as the Washington Conferences on Theoretical Physics. At the Fifth Washington Conference in January 1939, Tuve and his coworkers learned of uranium fission from Niels Bohr, and on the last day of the meeting, they verified the occurrence of the reaction, using their new Van de Graaff accelerator. Later in the year, when President Roosevelt authorized creation of the Uranium Committee (headed by L. J. Briggs), Tuve was chosen as one of its members. Not being optimistic about the rapid development of atomic bombs, however, he withdrew when others pressed for a large-scale program.

In the summer of 1940, Tuve agreed to head the National Defense Research Committee's (NDRC) efforts to devise ways of replacing contact fuses and timed fuses with influence fuses. Although his "Section T"[6] explored a variety of approaches (for example, a fuse triggered by light reflected from the target), he decided in the spring of 1941 to concentrate on radio proximity fuses. Once in flight, a tiny transmitter in the nose of an explosive projectile would send out a continuous signal. The fuse would detonate the charge when it received the Doppler-shifted reflection from the target.

Section T oversaw the development of vacuum tubes, batteries, and other components small enough to fit into artillery shells, rugged enough to withstand being shot from a gun (and spun rapidly in flight), and safe enough to be stored and handled readily. Moreover, Section T tested the mass-produced components to ensure that they were of sufficiently high quality, and it helped the military to introduce the fuses into field operations. First employed against Japanese aircraft in early 1943, they were later used to bring down V-1 buzz bombs over England and Belgium and to stem German advances in the Battle of the Bulge.[7] By the end of the war, more than 22 million fuses had been manufactured at a total cost of about a billion dollars.

Tuve's presence was felt throughout the vast enterprise. He assembled the personnel of Section T, set out the general lines along which they worked, and established their operating procedures (expressed in a series of aphoristic "running orders," such as "I don't want any damn fool in this laboratory to save money. I only want him to save *time*"[8]). Moreover, throughout the war he maintained effective liaison with military, industrial, and civilian research leaders. The result was an approach that became known as "the Section-T pattern of research organization."[9]

Although the NDRC and the more comprehensive Office of Scientific Research and Development (OSRD) were slated for termination at the war's end, the successful wartime projects demonstrated the importance of continuing similar efforts in peacetime. Tuve considered the problem of what to do after the war while serving on the Committee on Postwar Research (the Wilson Committee), formed in mid 1944. The committee proposed the creation of the Research Board for National Security, a stillborn precursor to the National Science Foundation (which was not authorized until 1950).[10]

More immediately successful were Tuve's efforts to establish the Applied Physics Laboratory (APL). In 1942, as the proximity-fuse work shifted from laboratory development to full-scale manufacturing, Johns Hopkins agreed to continue the project under an OSRD contract. Accordingly, the technical work was transferred from the DTM to quarters in Silver Spring, Maryland, and the APL was born. Tuve became its first director and remained in charge when, in 1944, the OSRD contract was replaced by a contract between Johns Hopkins and the Navy Bureau of Ordnance. He also participated centrally in discussions that led in early 1946 to the continuation of the APL as a postwar organization administered by Johns Hopkins.

After the war Tuve returned to the DTM, and in

mid 1946 Bush appointed him to succeed John A. Fleming as its director. Seeking to transform the DTM into a physics research laboratory, Tuve supported using the Van de Graaff accelerators for nuclear physics and the cyclotron for biophysics; but his own research efforts centered on seismic studies of the earth's crust using conventional explosives and investigations of radio emissions from hydrogen gas in space. These choices reflected not only "his skill in applying electronics to almost any given job"[11] but also his belief that the DTM should pursue projects in which the work of small groups could have a decisive impact on the development of entire fields.

Researchers in the years between the world wars had expanded Andrija Mohorovičič's use of earthquake-generated seismic waves for studies of the earth's interior, but there had been little systematic use of explosion-generated seismic waves.[12] Obtaining surplus explosives from the Navy and working in the Washington area, Tuve and his DTM coworkers (including Howard E. Tatel) sought to develop recording techniques that would enable them to map out the details of the earth's crustal structure. But as they extended their studies into the Appalachian highlands, their seismograms proved harder to interpret than they had expected. After tests in California in 1949 verified the similarity between waves produced through explosions and waves produced through earthquakes, they undertook reconnaissance studies in a variety of geological regions, searching for marked differences in the depths and velocities of the waves. These field strips took them to the Mesabi Range and to Puget Sound in 1951, to the Wasatch and Uinta Mountains and to the Colorado Plateau in 1954, and to Alaska and the Yukon Territory in 1955.

Meanwhile, Tuve served as a member of the executive committee of the United States national committee for the International Geophysical Year (IGY) of 1957 and 1958. As part of the CIW's participation in IGY, he led an expedition to the Andes and altiplano of South America in 1957.[13] For several years thereafter, one of his main activities was the fostering of cooperative geophysical studies with his South American colleagues.

In the 1960's Tuve's geophysical activities shifted from annual summer field trips to high-level committee work. In particular, he served as chairman of the Geophysics Research Board (GRB). Formed in 1960 under the aegis of the National Academy of Sciences, one of the GRB's first tasks was to examine what developments could be expected in solid-earth studies.[14] The GRB also oversaw the nation's participation in the international efforts arising in the wake of IGY—including the International Upper Mantle Project (throughout the decade) and the International Years of the Quiet Sun (1964–1965).

Tuve was not an early proponent of the theory of plate tectonics, which rose to prominence in the 1960's. Even though studies of paleomagnetism (which provided much of the evidence for the theory) formed an important part of the DTM's postwar research program, he discouraged the continuation of John W. Graham's work on it there in the mid 1950's.[15] Nevertheless, Tuve's seismic studies demonstrated that the earth's crustal structure was far more complex than was expected on the basis of the reigning geosynclinal view. Moreover, the center of his interest—"the earth beneath the continents"[16]—was a topic that is difficult to approach solely on the basis of the theory of plate tectonics.

Tuve's second major line of research was radio astronomy. Although the DTM pursued a variety of radio-astronomy projects in the 1950's (for example, the study of planetary radio emissions, which were first observed [from Jupiter] in 1955 using the DTM's Mills Cross[17]), his personal efforts focused mainly on observing radio emissions from interstellar hydrogen clouds. Within a year after H. I. Ewen and E. M. Purcell experimentally verified the occurrence of twenty-one-cm radiation from atomic hydrogen in 1951, Tuve and his coworkers were making similar observations using a twenty-six-foot Wurzburg parabolic antenna mounted on the DTM grounds. In the late 1950's they developed a multichannel recorder for their work and constructed a sixty-foot parabolic antenna at the DTM's Derwood field station. As a result, they were able to continue mapping the densities and velocities of the hydrogen clouds, their aim being a better understanding of galactic structure.

Meanwhile, Tuve actively promoted radio astronomy within the American scientific community. He helped to plan several important conferences, he contributed to the development of the facilities for the National Radio Astronomy Observatory (NRAO),[18] and his group was one of the primary users of the NRAO's 300-foot transit telescope at Green Bank, West Virginia. Like his geophysical work, his radio astronomy gave rise to cooperative efforts with colleagues in South America, including the construction of a 100-foot parabolic antenna near La Plata, Argentina, for studying the hydrogen clouds of the southern sky.

During the postwar era, Tuve chaired the physics section of the National Research Council's Committee on Growth and the CIW's Committee on Image Tubes for Telescopes, served as a member of the U.S. National Commission for UNESCO and as a trustee for the Johns Hopkins University, and edited *Journal of Geophysical Research*. Concerned by the prospects of a continuing arms race, he was one of twelve petitioners in early 1950 asking President Truman to renounce the first use of hydrogen bombs.

Tuve was elected a member of the American Philosophical Society in 1943 and of the National Academy of Sciences in 1946. His awards include the Presidential Medal of Merit (1946), Honorary Commander of the Order of the British Empire (awarded in 1948), the National Academy of Sciences' Comstock Prize (1948), the American Geophysical Union's Bowie Medal (1963), and the Cosmos Club Award (1966). Notable among his honorary doctorates was one from Carleton College (1961), awarded in a ceremony that similarly recognized his sister and brothers.

In late 1965 Tuve succeeded Hugh L. Dryden as home secretary of the National Academy of Sciences. At about the same time, however, he began reducing the level of his professional activities. He retired as DTM director in 1966, resigned from the GRB in 1969, and stepped down as home secretary after his term expired in 1971. As a distinguished service member of the CIW, however, he continued his work with the sixty-foot dish at Derwood into the mid 1970's.

Although Tuve ranks as one of his generation's notable research directors, he was a vocal critic of postwar trends. In an era of massive funding and complex organizations, he insisted on the importance of creative individuals using relatively modest means. In an era of narrow specialization, he insisted on the unity of knowledge—not only within the sciences but also between the sciences and the humanities. Finally, in an era of rapid-paced, high-pressure activity, he insisted on the value of quiet scholarship.

One objection to Tuve's views was "that the ideals Tuve championed were out of step with the world of 1956";[19] another was that Tuve's DTM had "much in common with a nineteenth-century Utopian community."[20] But Tuve saw things differently. In an era dominated by "big science" he chose to act as a spokesman for "Her Majesty's Loyal Opposition"[21] and to present the research of the DTM as "a good old-fashioned example of the real thing."[22]

NOTES

1. Herbert Childs, *An American Genius: The Life of Ernest Orlando Lawrence* (New York, 1968), 32, 37–42.

2. C. Stewart Gillmor, "Threshold to Space: Early Studies of the Ionosphere," in Paul A. Hanle and Von Del Chamberlain, eds., *Space Science Comes of Age: Perspectives in the History of the Space Sciences* (Washington, D.C., 1981), 103–104.

3. David K. Allison, *New Eye for the Navy: The Origin Of Radar at the Naval Research Laboratory* (Washington, D.C., 1981), 57–59.

4. Thomas D. Cornell, "Merle Antony Tuve: Pioneer Nuclear Physicist," in *Physics Today*, **41** (January 1988), 57–64.

5. Abraham Pais, *Inward Bound: Of Matter and Forces in the Physical World* (Oxford, 1986), 416–417, 424.

6. The "T" stood for "Tuve." Other DTM staff members who played notable roles were Hafstad and Richard B. Roberts. The project was established at the request of the Navy through an NDRC contract with the CIW.

7. Section T also developed better gun directors, and in early 1945 it initiated an entirely new project, developing ramjet engines for guided missiles (the "Bumblebee" project).

8. Ralph B. Baldwin, *The Deadly Fuze: The Secret Weapon of World War II* (San Rafael, Calif., 1980), 80.

9. M. A. Tuve, "Development of the Section T Pattern of Research Organization," in George P. Bush and Lowell H. Hattery, eds., *Teamwork in Research* (Washington, D.C., 1953), 135–142.

10. Daniel J. Kevles, "Scientists, the Military, and the Control of Postwar Defense Research: The Case of the Research Board for National Security, 1944–46," in *Technology and Culture*, **16** (January 1975), 20–47.

11. Maurice Ewing, "Twenty-fifth Award of the William Bowie Medal: Citation," in *Transactions of the American Geophysical Union*, **44** (June 1963), 287.

12. John S. Steinhart and Robert P. Meyer, *Explosion Studies of Continental Structure* (Washington, D.C., 1961), 16–18.

13. Walter Sullivan, *Assault on the Unknown: The International Geophysical Year* (New York, 1961), 379–382.

14. Panel on Solid-Earth Problems of the Geophysics Research Board and Division of Earth Sciences, NAS-NRC, *Solid-Earth Geophysics: Survey and Outlook* (Washington, D.C., 1964).

15. William Glen, *The Road to Jaramillo: Critical Years of the Revolution in Earth Science* (Stanford, Calif., 1982), 119n.

16. John S. Steinhart and T. Jefferson Smith, eds., *The Earth Beneath the Continents: A Volume of Geophysical Studies in Honor of Merle A. Tuve* (Washington, D.C., 1966).

17. David O. Edge and Michael J. Mulkay, *Astronomy Transformed: The Emergence of Radio Astronomy in Britain* (New York, 1976), 35, 226–227.

18. Allan A. Needell, "Lloyd Berkner, Merle Tuve, and the Federal Role in Radio Astronomy," in *Osiris*, 2nd ser., **3** (1987), 261–288.

19. *Ibid.*, 283.

20. Spencer Klaw, *The New Brahmins: Scientific Life in America* (New York, 1968), 159.

21. M. A. Tuve, "Physics and the Humanities—The Verification of Complementarity" (acceptance speech, Cosmos Club Award, 9 May 1966), Tuve Papers, box 366.

22. M. A. Tuve, "Basic Research in Private Research Institutes," in Dael Wolfe, ed., *Symposium on Basic Research* (Washington, D.C., 1959), 177.

BIBLIOGRAPHY

I. ORIGINAL WORKS. The Library of Congress holds Tuve's papers (in more than four hundred archival boxes). A year-by-year listing of his publications (and year-by-year accounts of his research) can be found in *Yearbook of the Carnegie Institution of Washington*. The oral history collection of the Center for History of Physics of the

American Institute of Physics includes tapes and transcripts of several interviews with Tuve.

His publications include "Impact Ionization by Low Speed Positive Ions" (abstract), *Physical Review*, **23** (Jan. 1924), 111; "A Test of the Existence of the Conducting Layer," *Physical Review*, **28** (Sept. 1926), 554–575, written with G. Breit; "A Transmitter Modulating Device for the Study of the Kennelly-Heaviside Layer by the Echo Method," *Proceedings of the Institute of Radio Engineers*, **16** (June 1928), 794–798, written with O. Dahl; "An Echo Interference Method for the Study of Radio Wave Paths," *ibid.*, **17** (Oct. 1929), 1786–1792, written with L. R. Hafstad; "A Laboratory Method of Producing High Potentials," *Physical Review*, **35** (1 Jan. 1930), 51–65, written with Breit and Dahl; "The Application of High Potentials to Vacuum-Tubes," *ibid.*, **35** (1 Jan. 1930), 66–71, written with Breit and Hafstad.

"Experiments with High-Voltage Tubes" (abstract), *ibid.*, **37** (15 Feb. 1931), 469, written with Hafstad and Dahl; "Disintegration-Experiments on Elements of Medium Atomic Number," *ibid.*, **43** (1 June 1933), 942, written with Hafstad and Dahl; "The Atomic Nucleus and High Voltages," *Journal of the Franklin Institute*, **216** (July 1933), 1–38; "The Emission of Disintegration-Particles from Targets Bombarded by Protons and by Deuterium Ions at 1200 Kilovolts," *Physical Review*, **45** (1 May 1934), 651–653, written with Hafstad; "High Voltage Technique for Nuclear Physics Studies," *ibid.*, **48** (15 Aug. 1935), 315–337, written with Hafstad and Dahl; "Excitation-Curves for Fluorine and Lithium," *ibid.*, **50** (15 Sept. 1936), 504–514, written with Hafstad and N. P. Heydenburg.

"The Scattering of Protons by Protons," *ibid.*, **50** (1 Nov. 1936), 806–825, written with Heydenburg and Hafstad; "The Scattering of Protons by Protons," *ibid.*, **53** (1 Feb. 1938), 239–246, written with Hafstad and Heydenburg; "The Forces Which Govern the Atomic Nucleus," *Scientific Monthly*, **47** (Oct. 1938), 344–363; "The Fifth Washington Conference on Theoretical Physics," *Science*, **89** (24 Feb. 1939), 180–182, written with C. F. Squire, F. G. Brickwedde, and E. Teller; "The Scattering of Protons by Protons. III," *Physical Review*, **56** (1 Dec. 1939), 1078–1091, written with Heydenburg and Hafstad; "Technology and National Research Policy," in *Bulletin of the Atomic Scientists*, **9** (Oct. 1953), 250–293; "Studies of the Earth's Crust Using Waves from Explosions," *Proceedings of the American Philosophical Society*, **97** (Dec. 1953), 658–669, written with H. E. Tatel and L. H. Adams; "Development of the Section T Pattern of Research Organization," in G. P. Bush and L. H. Hattery, eds., *Teamwork in Research* (Washington, D.C., 1953), 135–142.

"Seismic Exploration of a Continental Crust," in A. Poldervaart, ed., *Crust of the Earth (A Symposium)* (New York, 1955), 35–50, written with Tatel. "Basic Research in Private Research Institutes," in Dael Wolfe, ed., *Symposium on Basic Research* (Washington, D.C., 1959), 169–184; "Science and the Humanities," in G. W. Elbers

and P. Duncan, eds., *The Scientific Revolution: Challenge and Promise* (Washington, D.C., 1959), 215–226; "Atomic Hydrogen Survey Near the Galactic Plane," in R. N. Bracewell, ed., *Paris Symposium on Radio Astronomy* (Stanford, Cal., 1959), 374–389, written with B. F. Burke, E. T. Ecklund, J. W. Firor, and Tatel; "Cooperative Geophysics in the Andes," in *Transactions of the American Geophysical Union*, **44** (June 1963), 290–300; "A High-Resolution Study of M31," in F. J. Kerr and A. W. Rodgers, eds., *The Galaxy and the Magellanic Clouds*, (Canberra, 1964), 99–102, written with Burke and K. C. Turner; "A High-Resolution Study of the Outer Parts of the Galaxy," *ibid.*, 131–134, written with Burke and Turner; "Hydrogen Motions in the Central Region of the Galaxy," *ibid.*, 183–186, written with Burke; "Solid-Earth Geophysics," in *Transactions of the American Geophysical Union*, **46** (Mar. 1965), 203–204; "Symposium on the Years of the Quiet Sun—IQSY: Introductory Remarks," in *Proceedings of the National Academy of Sciences*, **58** (15 Dec. 1967), 2131–2135; "Radio Ranging and Nuclear Physics at the Carnegie Institution," in D. A. Bromley and V. W. Hughes, eds., *Facets of Physics* (New York, 1970), 163–177; *Velocity Structures in Hydrogen Profiles: A Sky Atlas of Neutral Hydrogen Emission* (Washington, D.C., 1973), written with S. Lundsager; and "Early Days of Pulse Radio at the Carnegie Institution," in *Journal of Atmospheric and Terrestrial Physics*, **36** (Dec. 1974), 2079–2083.

II. SECONDARY LITERATURE. Biographical sketches by professional colleagues include P. H. Abelson, "Merle Antony Tuve (1901–1982)," in *American Philosophical Society Year Book 1982* (1983), 521–529; and L. T. Aldrich et al., "Merle A. Tuve: 1901–1982," in *EOS*, **63** (13 July 1982), 569. In addition to the sources cited in the footnotes, see Thomas D. Cornell, "Merle A. Tuve and His Program of Nuclear Studies at the Department of Terrestrial Magnetism: The Early Career of a Modern American Physicist" (Ph.D. diss., Johns Hopkins University, 1986).

THOMAS DAVID CORNELL

UMOV, NIKOLAI ALEXEEVICH (*b.* Simbirsk [now Ul'ianovsk], Russia, 4 February 1846; *d.* Moscow, Russia, 28 January 1915), *physics.*

Umov's father, Alexei Pavlovich Umov, was a physician who achieved a reputation as an entomologist; his mother, whose maiden name was Susokolova, was a housewife. The family moved in 1858 to Moscow, where in 1863 Nikolai graduated from the gymnasium with a gold medal and then entered the division of mathematics of the Faculty of Physics and Mathematics at Moscow University. He graduated in 1867 and remained at the university to prepare for an academic career; at the same time he taught physics in a secondary school.

Umov passed his M.Sc. examinations in 1870,

and the following year was appointed docent at Novorossiia University in Odessa. In 1872 he defended his M.Sc. thesis, and two years later his doctoral dissertation. From 1875 to 1893 Umov was a professor at Novorossiia University. During that time he came into close contact with two outstanding Russian scholars—I. I. Mechnikov and I. M. Sechenov—whom he greatly admired.

In 1893 Umov moved to Moscow as professor of physics at Moscow University. He succeeded A. G. Stoletov as department head in 1896. In 1911 he was among a group (including P. N. Lebedev) who left the university to protest the reactionary policy of the Ministry of Education. Umov then concentrated his efforts at the Moscow Society of Natural Philosophy (of which he was president from 1897 to 1914) and on publishing the journal *Vremennik*.

Umov began his career as a theoretician, but he also did much experimental work (especially during the second Moscow period of his life). In his M.Sc. thesis he investigated thermomechanical phenomena in elastic bodies. He solved the general problem of distribution of the elastic stresses within a solid body placed in a nonuniform temperature field; the problem generalized that formulated by William Thomson (1857). Umov's dissertation was devoted to the problems of energy transfer in bodies. In it he put forward the idea of localization of energy and of its density, and introduced the concept of energy flux (Umov's vector). The theory was constructed in close analogy to the theory of heat conduction. In recognition of Umov's contribution to the problem of energy propagation (independently developed in 1884 by J. H. Poynting for the transfer of electromagnetic energy), the corresponding vector has been named the Umov-Poynting vector.

Umov's most fundamental experiments are associated with the optics of turbid media and with the problem of polarization and depolarization of light falling on various surfaces. In the course of the necessary research, Umov developed a spectral apparatus that has become widely used not only in the laboratory but also in industry (analysis of dyestuffs in textile production).

Early in his Moscow professorship, Umov lectured at the Faculty of Medicine of the university on the mechanics of bones and on physiological optics and acoustics. He was a sharp critic of vitalism.

Being a progressive physicist, Umov reacted positively to the theories of relativity and the quantum. He developed transformation formulas that included Lorentz's as a special case (the same way was chosen by Max von Laue in 1911). Umov also wrote some interesting papers on the quantum theory of radiation, one of which contains a formula identical to the uncertainty relation for time and energy.

Umov married Elena Leonardovna Novitskaya in 1872; they had a daughter.

Umov was involved in the work of the Pedagogical Society and the Kh. S. Ledentsov Society for Advancement of Experimental Science and Applications. The fairly large means of the latter were directed on Umov's initiative, to support the work of P. N. Lebedev and I. P. Pavlov, and to establish the society's library.

Umov was a brilliant lecturer. His university and popular lectures were illustrated by carefully prepared demonstrations.

During his free time (of which he had little) Umov drew and also painted landscapes.

BIBLIOGRAPHY

I. ORIGINAL WORKS. *Teoria termomekhanicheskikh iavlenii v tverdikh uprugikh telakh* (Theory of thermomechanical phenomena in solid elastic bodies; Moscow, 1871); "Abteilung der Bewegungsgleichungen der Energie in kontinuierlichen Körpern," in *Zeitschrift für Mathematik und Physik*, **19** (1874), 418–431; "Diffuzia vodnogo zastvoza povazennoi soli" (Diffusion of water solution of a salt), in *Zapiski Novorossiiskogo Obshchestva estestvoispitatelei*, **14**, no. 1 (1889), 1–67; "Interprétation géométrique des intégrales de Fresnel," in *Séances de la Société physique de Paris*, **14**, no. 1 (1896), 322; "Ueber eine Methode objektiver Darstellung der Eigenschaften des polarisierten Lichtes," in *Annalen der Physik*, 4th ser., **2** (1900), 72–77; "Die Konstruktion des geometrischen Bildes des Gauss'schen Potentials, als Methode zur Erforschung der Gesetze des Erdmagnetismus," in *Terrestrial Magnetism and Atmospheric Electricity*, **9** (1904), 105–112; "Einheitliche Abteilung der Transformationen, die mit dem Relativitätsprinzip verträglich sind," in *Physikalische Zeitschrift*, **11** (1910), 905–908; "Die Bedingungen der Invarianz der Wellengleichung," ibid., **13** (1912), 292–293; "Eine spektropolariskopische Methode zur Erforschung der Lichtabsorption und der Natur der Farbstoffe," ibid., 962–971; "Ein möglicher Sinn der Quantentheorie," ibid., **15** (1914), 380–382; and "Avtobiograficheskii ocherk" (Autobiographical sketch), in N. A. Umov, *Izbrannie sochineniia* (Collected works; Moscow, 1950), 9–28. Umov's papers and letters are in the U.S.S.R. Academy of Sciences Archive, Leningrad.

II. SECONDARY LITERATURE. D. D. Gulo, *Nikolai Alekseevich Umov* (Moscow, 1971); P. P. Lazarev, N. A. Umov, in *Ocherki istorii russkoi nauki* (Moscow and Leningrad, 1950); and E. V. Shpolskii, "Nikolai Alekseevich Umov," in *Uspekhi fizicheskikh nauk*, **31**, no. 1 (1947), 129.

UREY, HAROLD CLAYTON (*b*. Walkerton, Indiana, 29 April 1893; *d*. La Jolla, California, 5 January 1981), *chemistry, geophysics, planetary science.*

Harold Clayton Urey was born to Samuel Clayton and Cora (Reinoehl) Urey. His father, a schoolteacher and minister of the Brethren church, died when Harold was six, and his mother later married another clergyman. Urey was heavily influenced by the pacifism of the Brethren church and refused to do defense research except during wartime. He studied zoology and chemistry at Montana State College, and later took his Ph.D. in physical chemistry under G. N. Lewis at the University of California at Berkeley. He was a pioneer in the application of quantum mechanics to chemistry. Urey was awarded the 1934 Nobel Prize in chemistry for the discovery of deuterium in 1931, and he and his group at Columbia University established isotopic chemistry and explored its application to biology and medicine. Urey applied his knowledge and experience to the war effort, directing the Manhattan Project's separation of uranium for the atomic bomb. After the war Urey moved to the University of Chicago and turned his efforts to problems of geophysics, cosmogony, and the origin of life, attempting to understand the evolution of the earth, moon, and planets from chemical and isotopic evidence, especially in meteorites. From 1958 until his death he carried on this work at the University of California at La Jolla. He was a friendly, if at times severely critical, adviser to the space program, especially the lunar exploration program. Urey often collaborated with colleagues and students, and although he could be fiercely independent and even volatile, he inspired deep admiration and affection. Harold Urey married Frieda Daum in 1926 while teaching at Johns Hopkins University, and treasured his stable family life, which came to include three daughters and one son.

After graduating from high school Urey taught in country schools in his native Indiana and later in Montana. "Money was tight for him as a college student," reported his colleague Ferdinand G. Brickwedde. "During the academic year he slept and studied in a tent. During his summers he worked on a road gang laying railroad track in the Northwest." In his later life Urey raised parsimony and efficiency in the conduct of scientific work to a prime value. Urey graduated from Montana State University in 1917 with a B.Sc. in zoology and a minor in chemistry. His first research project was on protozoa of the Missoula River, and his interest in biology remained with him all his life.

When the United States entered World War I,

Urey went to work in an industrial chemical laboratory in Philadelphia making munitions. He later said, when accepting the Nobel Prize, that exposure to industrial chemistry helped him realize that academia was the proper place for him. After the war Urey returned to Montana State, where he resumed teaching chemistry until 1921.

In 1921 Urey began graduate work in chemistry and thermodynamics with G. N. Lewis at Berkeley, receiving a Ph.D. in physical chemistry in 1923. His doctoral research on rotational contributions to the heat capacities and entropies of gases showed Urey's talent in both theoretical calculations and empirical work. Urey was able to calculate entropies of diatomic gases that agreed with experimental data, and his method led directly to the current methods of calculating thermodynamic functions from spectroscopic data.

Urey spent the academic year 1923–1924 as an American-Scandinavian Fellow at the Institute for Theoretical Physics in Copenhagen studying atomic physics with Niels Bohr. He brought his considerable knowledge of quantum mechanics to Johns Hopkins University as an instructor in the chemistry department from 1925 to 1929. He joined Columbia University in 1929 as an associate professor of chemistry, and intensified his experimental and theoretical work in spectroscopy and quantum mechanics. He advanced to full professor in 1934.

At this time he collaborated with A. E. Ruark on the influential *Atoms, Molecules, and Quanta*, an outgrowth of his teaching of quantum mechanics at Johns Hopkins. The book was the first comprehensive English language textbook on atomic structure and a major bridge between the new quantum physics and the field of chemistry.

In 1931 Urey discovered a heavy isotope of hydrogen, later named deuterium, with his colleagues Ferdinand Brickwedde and George Murphy, through spectroscopy of the product of fractional distillation of hydrogen near its triple point. The discovery had a significant influence on chemistry, physics, and medicine (first tracer used to study physiological changes in the human body). That he was led to the discovery through two previous independent errors helped reinforce a characteristic tentativeness concerning scientific hypotheses.

During the thirties Urey's group separated isotopes of oxygen, carbon, nitrogen, and sulphur. Under Urey's direction the group worked on medical and biological applications of isotopes of all the elements basic to biological processes. He served as first editor of the *Journal of Chemical Physics* (1933–

1940), during which time it became the leading journal of the field.

Urey's work was again interrupted by war in 1940 when he joined the Uranium Committee of the Manhattan Project. He became director of the Substitute Alloys Materials Laboratory established at Columbia for separation of uranium isotopes, one of three main branches of the Manhattan Project. His ability to be equally at home in theoretical research as well as practical laboratory activity showed itself again as he directed the transformation of laboratory apparatus into massive industrial plants built at Oak Ridge, Tennessee and elsewhere to separate uranium isotopes by gaseous diffusion.

In 1945 Urey joined the Fermi Institute for Nuclear Studies at the University of Chicago, where the reactor program had its headquarters. University of Chicago president Robert Hutchins later recalled that he had tried to recruit Urey before the war: "It seems to me, as I look back on it, that I spent most of my time at the University of Chicago trying to persuade Harold Urey to join the faculty. I think it's too bad that I owe my eventual success in this high endeavor to General Groves." Urey organized a series of nuclear institutes and helped to arrange for major corporate funding.

Having aided in the development of atomic weapons out of a sense of duty, Urey's sense of social and scientific responsibility equally moved him to lead a group at Chicago that actively opposed dropping the atomic bomb on the Japanese. He worked with other scientists to defeat a bill that would have put control of future atomic research into the hands of the military, and in 1950 he resigned from the Atomic Energy Commission. He opposed Joseph McCarthy and made an appeal to save Julius and Ethel Rosenberg, accused of betraying atomic secrets, from execution. He devoted much time in his last years to the peaceful uses of atomic energy and to the exploration of alternative sources of energy. As a member of the Union of Concerned Scientists he joined in a 1975 petition to the White House to decrease the production of nuclear power plants.

In his postwar career Harold Urey turned almost fully to geochemistry and cosmic chemistry, which had already been a minor theme of his research of the 1930's. Alfred Nier at Minnesota had developed an extraordinarily precise mass spectrometer. Urey increased the precision of the instrument and used it to determine temperatures of Cretaceous seas by measuring isotopic oxygen fractionation between ocean water and carbonate precipitated by belemnites that had inhabited the seas. With his student Cesare Emiliani he reported the research in "The Thermodynamic Properties of Isotopic Substances," a paper that laid much of the foundation for the emerging discipline of isotopic geochemistry.

At Chicago, Urey, Willard Libby, Hans Seuss, Harrison Brown, Mark Inghram, Claire C. Patterson, Gerald Wasserburg, and others were forging the new discipline of cosmochemistry. The abundance tables that Urey and Seuss established at that time have since been revised, but are still in use. Urey's concentration on isotopic and general chemical abundances as they occur and develop in nature led him to consider more deeply questions of the origin of the sun and solar system. This led him to study the composition of meteorites. Urey and Craig established that there were two distinct classes of meteorites, implying descent from parent bodies formed under very different conditions in the early solar system. Their analysis forms the basis of the present classification system.

During the summer of 1950 Urey read Ralph Baldwin's *The Face of the Moon*, in which Baldwin argued that lava flows and cratering processes could explain the morphology of lunar features. Urey's interests in the chemistry of the development of the earth, in meteorites as evidence-bearing relics of the early solar system, and in the moon all converged into a creative synthesis presented first during his Silliman lectures at Yale and later published in 1952 as *The Planets: Their Origin and Development*.

In this work Urey proposed bold hypotheses about the origin of the solar system, arguing that the planets had formed at relatively low temperatures where chemical and molecular processes rather than atomic processes would dominate. The postwar revival by C. F. von Weizsäcker and others of the nebular hypothesis was everyone's starting point for theories of the origin of the solar system; but there was great latitude for discussing the specific sequence of events. The fission theory of the moon's formation, popular since the nineteenth century, held that the moon split off from the earth. Urey believed that the moon accreted independently of the earth, perhaps even elsewhere in the solar system, after which it had been captured into earth orbit. The particulars of the debate, which continued throughout Urey's career, concerned the precise chemical, physical, and dynamic nature of the population of intermediate objects from which the earth and moon had presumably formed, as well as the complicated sequence of events describing the physical and chemical processing of this material to produce the observed state of the earth and moon.

The Planets also drew others into the study of

the solar system. As his student Carl Sagan asserted, "The mere fact that a scientist of Urey's eminence considered a full-scale treatment of planetary cosmogony possible was a major contribution to the field, quite apart from his specific conclusions," a sentiment echoed by many others.

Urey had a long-standing interest in astronomy and astrophysics. Just after the war he collaborated with astronomer Gerard P. Kuiper on lunar studies, in a relationship that began in admiration and fell into intense acrimony that lasted the rest of their lives. This uncharacteristic episode was played out in the *Proceedings of the National Academy of Sciences*, at meetings, and in correspondence. Yet Urey was able to subdue his intense feelings and collaborate with Kuiper as coinvestigator on the Ranger series of lunar impacting spacecraft in the early 1960's.

Urey's interests in biology, elemental abundances, and the origin of the solar system came together in a classic work published in 1951 with his student Stanley Miller. They sent electric discharges through an atmosphere of chemically pure methane, ammonia, and steam in a sealed container. After a week the container's walls became red and turbid from amino acids produced therein. Urey's starting point was the novel conclusion that cosmic abundances of elements implied an early reducing atmosphere for the earth. Carl Sagan reports that when Urey was asked what organic compounds he expected to be produced in such an environment, he replied "Beilstein," alluding to the large published compendium on all organic compounds then known.

In 1958 Urey became professor-at-large at the University of California at La Jolla. From this base he embarked on yet another career, as a participant in and scientific counselor and adviser to the space program. Always vigilant, ever irascible with what he considered to be foolish decisions, Urey served as a scientific conscience, campaigning and arguing for the most economical and scientifically sound method of conducting space research. He firmly believed that every experiment carried into space at great expense should be designed to test a particular well-conceived hypothesis.

As a founding member of the prestigious National Academy of Sciences' Space Science Board in the summer of 1958, Urey chaired the Committee on Chemistry of Space and Exploration of the Moon and Planets. When NASA was established later that year its director, Robert Jastrow, consulted with Urey about the research the space agency should undertake. Urey convinced Jastrow of the importance of the moon as the Rosetta stone of the solar system, preserving in its cratered face and unseen interior a record of the conditions under which the solar system formed. As Homer Newell, then NASA's chief of space science, later recalled, "This was a powerful argument for including the Moon in the space science program. I, personally, did not need persuading, and Urey's story provided good ammunition for moving the proposal on up the line. The persuasiveness of the argument carried the day at each stage, within NASA, in the Administration, and finally in Congress." Urey, Jastrow, former colleagues from the Chicago Institute for Nuclear Studies, and others formed a planning committee out of which came the series of automated lunar exploration spacecraft that preceded the Apollo landings of the astronauts. Urey was involved in planning and selection of instruments to be carried, landing site selection, analysis of returned data, and a host of other issues. His influence culminated in the preparations made for the analysis of lunar samples returned to earth. The returned samples, ironically, bore evidence that contradicted Urey's theory that the moon was a primordial object formed under relatively cold conditions and later captured by the earth.

Harold Urey received numerous awards and honors, including the Research Institute of America Silver Medal (1935 and 1960), Franklin Institute Medal (1943), Medal of Merit from President Truman for his Manhattan Project work, National Medal of Science (1964) from President Johnson for his space program work, and the Priestley Medal (1973).

BIBLIOGRAPHY

I. ORIGINAL WORKS. Urey's papers, comprising 61 cubic feet, are at the University of California, San Diego, Central University Library. They include a 44-page typescript autobiography, apparently dictated and transcribed, with a few corrections in Urey's own hand. There is a transcript of an oral history interview by E. M. Emme and R. C. Hall, 18 October 1976, at the NASA History Office, Washington, D.C.

There is no available comprehensive bibliography of Urey's publications. However, a letter, William Anders to Harold Urey, 14 October 1964, A. G. W. Cameron Papers, Harvard University, includes a tally of 956 papers then under consideration for reprinting in whole or in summary under four headings: Solar System (836); Abundance of Elements (61); Life (44); Tektites (15).

Urey's first application of quantum mechanics to physical and chemical problems is in "The Distribution of Electrons in the Various Orbits of the Hydrogen Atom," *Astrophysical Journal*, **59**, no. 1 (Jan. 1924), 1–10; a full treatment is found in A. Ruark and Harold Urey, *Atoms, Molecules, and Quanta* (New York, 1930).

The thinking that led Urey to the discovery of deuterium is presented in "Natural System of Atomic Nuclei," *Journal of the American Chemical Society*, **53** (1931), 2872; and in H. C. Urey and Charles A. Bradley, Jr., "On the Relative Abundances of Isotopes," *Physical Review*, **38** (1931), 718–724. The discovery was presented first in a letter to the editor, *Physical Review*, **39** (1932), 164, and then in a full article, "A Hydrogen Isotope of Mass 2 and its Concentration," *Physical Review*, **40** (1932), 1–15, written with C. F. G. Brickwedde and G. M. Murphy. Urey's Nobel Prize lecture is printed in "Some Thermodynamic Properties of Hydrogen Deuterium," *Angewandte Chemie*, **48** (1935), 315–320. The application of deuterium is presented in "Deuterium and Its Compounds in Relation to Biology," *Cold Spring Harbor Symposium*, **2** (1934), 47–56.

Urey's thinking concerning the warming of the earth and its cosmogonical implications are in "A Hypothesis Regarding the Origin of the Movements of the Earth's Crust," *Science*, **110** (28 Oct. 1949), 445–446; "The origin and development of the earth and other terrestrial planets," *Geochimica et Cosmochimica Acta*, **1** (1951), 207–277; "The origin and development of the earth and other terrestrial planets: A correction," *Geochimica et Cosmochimica Acta*, **2** (1952), 263–268; "On the Origin of Continents and Mantles," *Proceedings of the National Academy of Sciences*, **39** (1953), 933–946; "On the Concentration of Certain Elements at the Earth's Surface," *Proceedings of the Royal Society of London*, **A 219** (1953), 281–292; "Chemical Evidence Regarding the Earth's Origin," *International Union of Applied Chemistry, XII Congress, Plenary Lectures* (Stockholm, 1953), 188–214, "The Origin of the Earth," in Henry Faul, ed., *Nuclear Geology* (New York, 1954), 355–371; "Boundary Conditions for Theories of the Origin of the Solar System," in L. H. Ahrens, et. al., eds., *Physics and Chemistry of the Earth*, **2** (1957), 46–76; "Evidence Regarding the Origin of the Earth," *Geochimica et Cosmochimica Acta*, **26** (1962), 1–13. Applications of the same thinking to other astronomical bodies is in H. C. Urey and Bertram Donn, "Chemical Heating for Meteorites," *Astrophysical Journal*, **124** (1956), 307–310; and Bertram Donn and H. C. Urey, "Chemical Heating Processes in Astronomical Objects," *Memoires de la Société Royale des Sciences de Liege*, **4**, no. 18 (1957), 124–132.

Urey's early attempts to derive the chemical evolution of the solar system can be traced in "The Abundance of the Elements," *Physical Review*, **88** (1952), 248–252; "Chemical fractionation in the meteorites and the abundance of the elements," *Geochimica et Cosmochimica Acta*, **2** (1952), 269–282; "On the Early Chemical History of the Earth and the Origin of Life," *Proceedings of the National Academy of Sciences*, **38** (1952), 351–363. The arguments are synthesized in *The Planets: Their Origin and Development* (New Haven, 1952).

Urey's later thinking on this subject and his reaction to the criticisms of others can be traced in "On the Dissipation of Gas and Volatized Elements from Proto-

planets," *Astrophysical Journal Supplement*, **1**, no. 6 (1954), 147–173; "The Cosmic Abundance of Potassium, Uranium, and Thorium and the Heat Balances of the Earth, the Moon, and Mars," *Proceedings of the National Academy of Sciences*, **41** (1955), 127–144, and a correction note in *ibid.*, **42** (1956), 889–891; "The Problem of Elemental Abundances," in L. H. Ahrens, ed., *Origin and Distribution of the Elements* (Oxford, 1968), 247–254.

The significance of the earth's moon and Urey's thought concerning its origin and evolution are in "Some Criticisms of 'On the Origin of the Lunar Surface Features' by G. P. Kuiper," *Proceedings of the National Academy of Sciences*, **41**, no. 7 (1955), 423–428; "The Moon's Surface Features," *Observatory*, **76**, no. 895 (1956), 232–235; "The Origin and Significance of the Moon's Surface," *Vistas in Astronomy*, **2** (1956), 1667–1680; "Composition of the Moon's Surface," *Z. physiche Chem. Neue Folge*, **16** (1958), 346–357; H. C. Urey, W. M. Elsasser, and M. G. Rochester, "Note on the Internal Structure of the Moon," *Astrophysical Journal*, **129** (1959), 842–848; "Duration of the Intense Bombardment Processes on the Moon," *Astrophysical Journal*, **132** (1960), 502–503; "Lines of Evidence in Regard to the Composition of the Moon," *Proceedings of the First International Space Science Symposium* (Amsterdam, 1960); "The Origin and Nature of the Moon," *Endeavor*, **19** (1960), 87–99; "The Moon," in L. V. Berkner and H. Odishaw, eds., *Science in Space* (NY: 1961), 185–197; "Earth's Daughter, Sister, or Uncle?" in W. Sullivan, ed., *America's Race for the Moon* (New York, 1962), 97–102; "Origin and History of the Moon," in Z. Kopal, ed., *Physics and Astronomy of the Moon* (New York, 1962), 481–523; "Meteorites and the Moon," *Science*, **147** (1965), 1262–1265; "The Capture Hypothesis of the Origin of the Moon," in B. G. Marsden and A. G. W. Cameron, eds., *The Earth-Moon System* (New York, 1966), 210–212); "Water on the Moon," *Nature*, **216** (16 December 1967), 1094–1095; H. C. Urey and Kurt Marti, "Surveyor Results and the Composition of the Moon," *Science*, **161** (6 September 1968), 1030–1032; "Origin and History of the Moon," in E. Rabinowitch and R. S. Lewis, eds., *Man on the Moon* (New York, 1969); H. C. Urey, K. Marti, J. W. Hawkins, and M. K. Liu, "Model History of the Lunar Surface," *Proceedings of the Second Lunar Science Conference*, vol. 2 (Cambridge, Mass., 1971), 987–998; "The Origin of the Moon and Solar System," in K. Runcorn and H. Urey, eds., *The Moon*, (Dordrecht: Reidel, 1972), 429–448; H. C. Urey and K. Marti, "Lunar Basalts," *Science*, **164** (1972), 117–119; "Evidence for Objects of Lunar Mass in the Early Solar System and for Capture as a General Process for the Origin of Satellites," *Astrophysics and Space Science*, **16** (1972), 311–323; "The Moon and Its Origin," *Science and Public Affairs* (November 1973), 5–10; S. K. Runcorn and H. C. Urey, "A New Theory of Lunar Magnetism," *Science*, **180** (11 May 1973), 636–638.

Urey's work on meteorites and cosmic abundances can be traced in H. C. Urey and H. Craig, "The Composition of the Stone Meteorites and the Origin of the Meteorites," *Geochimica et Cosmochimica Acta*, **4** (1953), 36–82; Bertram Donn and H. C. Urey, "On the Mechanism of Comet Outbursts and the Chemical Composition of Comets," *Astrophysical Journal*, **123** (1956), 339–342; H. C. Urey and V. R. Murphy, "Isotopic Abundance Variations in Meteorites," *Science*, **140** (1963), 385; "A Review of Atomic Abundances in Chondrites and the Origin of Meteorites," *Reviews of Geophysics*, **2**, no. 1 (Feb. 1964), 1–34; "Biological Material in Meteorites—A Review," *Science*, **151** (1966), 157–166; G. Edwards and H. C. Urey, "Determination of Alkali Metals in Meteorites by a Distillation Process," *Geochimica et Cosmochimica Acta*, **7** (1955), 154–168; "Diamonds, Meteorites, and the Origin of the Solar System," *Astrophysical Journal*, **124** (1956), 523–637; H. C. Urey, A. Mele, and T. Mayeda, "Diamonds in Stone Meteorites," *Geochimica et Cosmochimica Acta*, **13** (1957), 1–4; "Comments on Two Papers by John F. Lovering Concerning a Typical Parent Meteorite Body," *Geochimica et Cosmochimica Acta*, **13** (1957), 335–338; "Meteorites and the Origin of the Solar System," *Yearbook of Physical Society* (1957), 14–29; "The Early History of the Solar System as Indicated by the Meteorites," *Proceedings of the Chemical Society of London* (1958), 7–67; H. Seuss and H. C. Urey, "Abundances of the Elements in Planets and Meteorites," *Handbuch der Physik*, **52** (1958), 296–323; "Criticism of Dr. B. Mason's Paper on 'The Origin of Meteorites,'" *Journal of Geophysical Research*, **66**, no. 6 (June 1961), 1988–1991; H. C. Urey et al., "Life-Forms in Meteorites," *Nature*, **193** (1962), 1119–1133; "Lifelike Forms in Meteorites," *Science*, **137** (1962), 623–628; "Parent Bodies of the Meteorites and the Origin of Chondrules," *Icarus*, **7** (1967), 350–360.

Review articles and summaries of Urey's thinking on the evolution of the solar system include "Primary and Secondary Objects," *Journal of Geophysical Research*, **64** (November 1959), 1721–1737; "Atmospheres of the Planets," *Handbuch der Physik*, **53** (1959); "On the Chemical Evolution and Densities of the Planets," *Geochimica et Cosmochimica Acta*, **18** (1960), 151–153; "The Planets," in L. V. Barkner and H. Odishaw, eds., *Science in Space* (New York, 1961), 119–217; "The Origin and Evolution of the Solar System," in Donald P. LeGalley, ed., *Space Sciences* (New York, 1963), 123–168; "Chemical Evidence Relative to the Origin of the Solar System," *Monthly Notices of the Royal Astronomical Society*, **131** (1966), 199–223.

Urey's reflections on the space program and the direction it should take can be found in "Statement of Dr. Harold C. Urey, Professor-at-Large, University of California, San Diego, La Jolla, Calif.," in *Scientists' Testimony on Space Goals*, Hearings before the Committee on Aeronautical and Space Sciences, United States Senate, 88th Congress, 1st Session, June 10–11, 1963 (Washington, DC: U.S. Government Printing Office, 1963), 50–62, General reflections on his own life and work can be found in "As I See It," *Forbes*, **104**, no. 2 (15 July 1969), 44–48; "Acceptance Speech by Dr. Harold C. Urey for the V. M. Goldschmidt Medal," *Geochimica et Cosmochimica Acta*, **40** (1976), 570.

II. SECONDARY LITERATURE. Urey's collaborators describe the discovery of deuterium in George M. Murphy, "The Discovery of Deuterium," in H. Craig *et al.*, eds., *Isotopic and Cosmic Chemistry* (Amsterdam, 1964), 1–7, and Ferdinand G. Brickwedde, "Harold Urey and the Discovery of Deuterium," in *Physics Today*, **35** (September 1982), 34–39. Robert E. Kohler, Jr., describes the application of isotopes to biochemical and biomedical research in "Rudolf Schoenheimer, Isotopic Tracers, and Biochemistry in the 1930's," in *Historical Studies in the Physical Sciences*, **8** (1977), 257–298. Other works of interest are Roger M. Stuewer, "The Naming of the Deuteron," in *Am. Jrnl. of Physics*, **54** (1986), 206–218; and Richard G. Hewlett and Oscar E. Anderson, Jr., *The New World, 1939/1946*, vol. 1 of *A History of the United States Atomic Energy Commission* (University Park, Pennsylvania, 1962).

John G. Burke assesses the contributions of Urey and his collaborators in *Cosmic Debris: Meteorites in History* (Berkeley, 1986). Stephen G. Brush treats Urey's interest in the moon and the evolution of the solar system in "Nickel for Your Thoughts: Urey and the Origin of the Moon," in *Science*, **217** (1982), 891–898; "From Bump to Clump: Theories of the Origin of the Solar System, 1900–1960," in Paul A. Hanle and Von Del Chamberlain, eds., *Space Science Comes of Age: Perspectives in the History of the Space Sciences* (Washington, D.C., 1981), 78–100; and "Harold Urey and the Origin of the Moon: The Interaction of Science and the Apollo Program," in *Proceedings of the Twentieth Goddard Memorial Symposium* (17–19 March, 1982), 437–470. Urey's role in the Apollo program is treated in passing in R. Cargill Hall, *Lunar Impact: A History of Project Ranger* (Washington, D.C., 1977); Henry S. F. Cooper, *Moon Rocks* (New York, 1970); and Courtney G. Brooks, James M. Grimwood, and Loyd S. Swenson, Jr., *Chariots for Apollo: A History of Manned Lunar Spacecraft* (Washington, D.C., 1979). A sociological perspective is provided by Ian I. Mitroff, *The Subjective Side of Science: A Philosophical Inquiry into the Psychology of the Apollo Moon Scientists* (Amsterdam, 1974).

Robert Jastrow provides a personal account of his and Urey's work at NASA in "Exploring the Moon," in Paul A. Hanle and Von Del Chamberlain, eds., *Space Science Comes of Age: Perspectives in the History of the Space Sciences* (Washington, D.C., 1981), 45–50. Homer Newell does the same in "Harold Urey and the Moon," in *Moon*, **7** (1973), 1–5, and *Beyond the Atmosphere: Early Years of Space Science* (Washington, D.C., 1980), especially 237–239.

Appreciations and obituaries include Richard Fifield, "A Doughty Chemist," in *New Scientist*, **89** (15 January 1981), 167–168; Eugene Garfield, "A Tribute to Harold Urey," in *Current Comments*, **49** (3 December 1979), 5–9; Cyril Ponnamperuma, "Harold Clayton Urey: Chemist of the Cosmos," in *Sky and Telescope*, **61** (May 1981), 397; Carl Sagan, "Obituary, Harold Clayton Urey: 1893–1981," in *Icarus*, **48** (1981), 348–352; J. Y. Smith, "Harold Urey Dies: Nobel Prize Chemist Helped Develop A-

Bomb,'' in *Washington Post* (7 Jan. 1981), C8; H. G. Thode and Hannes Alfvén, ''Obituary, Harold C. Urey,'' in *Physics Today*, **34** (April 1981), 82–84; G. J. Wasserburg, ''Introduction of Harold Clayton Urey for the V. M. Goldschmidt Medal,'' in *Geochimica et cosmochimica acta*, **40** (1976), 569–570.

JOSEPH N. TATAREWICZ

VAN LECKWIJCK, WILLIAM (*b*. Antwerp, Belgium, 16 November 1902; *d*. Wilryck, Belgium, 19 June 1975), *geology*.

Van Leckwijck, a highly skilled and highly cultivated gentleman in the Flemish style, dedicated himself to geology for more than fifty years. At the beginning of World War I, he went with his family to England, where he completed grammar school and studied at the Clifton College in Bristol. In 1926 he graduated in mining engineering at the University of Liège in Belgium, following which he devoted himself to geological field studies, especially in coal geology, in Canada, England, and Scotland.

Between 1930 and 1936 Van Leckwijck finished a geological map of the eastern part of the Northern Atlas, and before 1940 he had completed several geological investigations in Greece—on Crete, Chios, and Lesbos (minerals); in Bulgaria (iron and manganese); in Finland (iron); in France and Italy (asbestos); and in Tunisia (lignite fields, iron, phosphorus, and lead). During the war (1940–1946) Van Leckwijck was involved with the Société Ougrée Maribaye, a Belgian company doing mineral research in Belgium, France, and Luxembourg. In the same period he studied paleontology at the University of Liège.

After the war Van Leckwijck became director of the Association pour l'Étude de la Paléontologie et Stratigraphie Houillère/Vereniging voor de Studie van de Paleontologie en de Stratigrafie van de Steenkoolformaties, a kind of advisory board on coal resources in Belgium. In 1964, at the age of sixty-two, he succeeded Theo Sorgenfrei of Denmark as secretary-general of the International Union of Geological Sciences. During his term (1964–1968) the International Geological Correlation Program was developed in cooperation with UNESCO. Also in 1964 Van Leckwijck became professor of paleontology at the Catholic University of Louvain, where he developed a laboratory of micropaleontology.

Van Leckwijck published almost 150 papers on studies conducted in Africa and Europe. He was honored by governments and learned societies all over the world. In 1958 he was elected to the Royal Belgian Academy of Sciences, Literature, and Arts. He was also a member of the Permanent Commission for the History of Sciences, the National Council of Scientific Unions, the Subcommission for Geodynamic Projects, and the National Commission of Geological Sciences.

In 1952 Van Leckwijck was named an officer of the Ordre du Oeissam Alaoeit in Morocco. In 1956 he was awarded the Prijs Baron van Ertborn of the Académie Royale de Belgique; in 1964, the Waterschoot van der Gracht Medal of the Nederlandse Vereniging voor Geologie en Mijnbouw; in 1968, the Leopold von Buch Medal of the Deutsche Geologische Gesellschaft; and in 1969, the Memorial Medal for the Centenary of the Hungarian Geological Institute. He received honorary doctorates from the University of Witwatersrand in South Africa (1970) and the University of Southampton in England (1972). He also held honorary membership in the Académie Lorraine des Sciences and the Geological Society of Sweden.

Van Leckwijck was fluent in Flemish, French, English, Spanish, German, and Arabic (he was an authority on the Koran). He was, moreover, an excellent violinist. He had a quiet and gentle sense of humor; for instance, during fieldwork in North Africa, he used his resemblance to the French movie star Jean Gabin to satisfy fans with autographs. In 1974 he married Rolande Soetens.

Van Leckwijck was above all a geologist rather than a mining engineer. Interpretation problems and the correct geometry of sedimentary layers having economical value led to his interest in the entire stratigraphical column, from the Lower Paleozoic to the Quaternary. He therefore turned his attention to paleontology and sedimentology, a new tool in development during his earlier career. His work on cyclic sedimentation as a tool for long-distance correlations within the Upper Carboniferous (Pennsylvanian) strata was particularly remarkable.

Van Leckwijck was not only a highly skilled interpreter of geological features but also a keen observer. He was the first to describe the occurrence of dissolution phenomena at the Visean-Namurian (Mississippian-Pennsylvanian) boundary beds, which resulted in the presence of an important cave network containing remobilized mineralizations or brines at high temperatures (100° C at a depth of about 2,000 m). Today these hot brines are used for geothermal purposes, and if positive closed structures occur, the cavities, filled artificially with gaseous hydrocarbons, play the role of a reservoir.

VAN LECKWIJCK

BIBLIOGRAPHY

A bibliography of Leckwijck's writings follows an obituary in Koninklijke Akademie voor Wetenschappen, Letteren en Schone Kunsten van België, *Jaarboek 1975*. They include "Le Canada et ses richesses minérales," in *Revue universelle des mines*, 7th ser., **18**, no. 5 (1928), 208–225; "Les houillères britanniques," in *La documentation industrielle* (1930), no. 13, 109–110, and no. 14, 121–122; "Sur la géologie et les gisements de lignite de la plaine de Guercif (Maroc oriental)," in *Publications du VIIe Congrès international des mines, métallurgie, et géologie appliquée, section de géologie appliquée*, I (Paris, 1935), 289–299, with J. Marçais; "Sur des phénomènes de dissolution au contact des terrains viséens et namuriens dans la région de Samson," in *Annales de la Société géologique de Belgique*, **65** (1941), B41–B46; "Les gisements de fluorine, belges et français, du bord méridional du synclinorium de Dinant," *ibid.*, B64–B75, with L. Calembert; "Les gisements belges de fluorine et leur intérêt industriel," in *Revue universelle des mines*, 8th ser., **18**, no. 2 (1942), 41–43; "Découverte d'une faune namurienne dans la vallée de la Berwinne," in *Bulletin de l'Académie royale de Belgique, classe des sciences*, 5th ser., **28**, no. 12 (1942), 889–903, with C. Ancion; "Sur l'âge famennien des grès du Val Dieu et l'existence d'une lacune stratigraphique entre Namurien et Famennien dans la vallée de la Berwinne," *ibid.*, **29**, nos. 4–6 (1943), 488–492, with C. Ancion and G. Ubaghs; "Les gisements de fluorine des Ardennes françaises et belges," in *Comptes rendus de la Société géologique de France* (1946), no. 13, 250–251, with L. Calembert; "Phénomènes pseudotectoniques, la plupart d'origine périglaciaire, dans les dépôts sablo-graveleux dits 'Onx' et les terrasses fluviales de la région liégeoise," in *Annales de la Société géologique de Belgique*, **73** (1949), M3–M78, with P. Macar (there is a 3-page English summary).

"Sur la sédimentation dans le terrain houiller de la Campine belge à l'époque du Westphalien B inférieur (zone d'Asch)," in *Annales de la Société géologique de Belgique*, **72** (1949), B439–B468; "Le fer. Géologie des gîtes minéraux marocains (zone française du Maroc)," in *Notes et mémoires du Service géologique du Maroc*, no. 87 (1952), 103–132, with J. Agard and J. Destombes; "Sur un gisement de manganèse d'âge quaternaire au N de la vallée du Dadès entre Ouarzazate et Skoura (Anti-Atlas)," *ibid.*, no. 122 (1954), 95–100, with R. Van Tassel; "Travaux publiés en Belgique depuis 1948 sur des questions de sédimentologie," in *Revue de l'Institut français du pétrole*, **10** (1955), supp., 13–21; "Contribution à la stratigraphie des terrains ordoviciens et gothlandiens de l'anticlinorium de Khouribga-Oulmes (Maroc central)," in *Notes et mémoires du Service géologique de Maroc*, no. 123 (1955), 9–44, with G. Suter, G. Termier, and H. Termier; "Découverte d'une faune strunienne au toit de la couche d'oligiste oolithique dite famennienne de Couthuin (bord nord du synclinal de Namur)," in *Bulletin de l'Académie royale de Belgique, classe des sciences*, 5th ser., **42**, no. 4 (1956), 506–514, with C. Ancion and F. Demanet.

"Problèmes relatifs à la datation de puissantes séries complexes, formées uniquement de roches volcaniques ou continentales; exemple du Mexique central," in *Annales de la Société géologique de Belgique*, **80** (1957), B175–B189; "Belgique. Carbonifère supérieur: Terrain houiller, namurien, westphalien et premien," *Lexique stratigraphique international*, vol. *Europe*, fasc. 4–11 (Paris, 1957); "Le Strunien de la vallée de la Méhaigne," in *Annales de la Société géologique de Belgique*, **81** (1958), B507–B520; *Stratigraphie et paléontologie du gisement de la concession Grande et Petite Bacnure*, Centre National de Géologie Houillère (Brussels) (1969), document no. 1, with B. M. Aderca, C. Ancion, A. Pastiels, and Y. Willière; "Les structures périglaciaires antérieures au Wurm en Belgique . . . ," in *Biuletyn peryglacjalny* (1960), no. 9, 47–59; *Étude géologique du bassin houiller de Liège. La concession Gosson-Kessales. Notes sur la paléontologie et la stratigraphie du Westphalien au nord de la faille St.-Gilles*, Centre National de Géologie Houillère (Brussels) (1961), document no. 5, with L. Lambrecht, C. Ancion, A. Pastiels, and Y. Willière; "Vertical and Lateral Variations in the Lithology and the Fauna of the Petit Buisson Marine Band in the Borinage Coalfield, Southern Belgium," in *Paläontologische Zeitschrift*, issue honoring H. Schmidt (1962), 140–153, with C. H. Chesaux; "Étude de cyclycité dans la sédimentation namurienne et accessoirement westphalienne," *6e Congrès international de sédimentologie de Belgique et Pays-Bas*, *Livret guide excursions* E/F, pt. 2 (1963); "Le développement stratinomique du Namurien A et B en Belgique méridionale," in *Comptes rendus du Ve Congrès de stratigraphie et de géologie carbonifère*, I (Paris, 1964), 415–430, with K. Fiege.

Études paléontologiques, stratigraphiques et tectoniques dans le Westphalien B du massif dit des Dressants d'Anderlues du district de Charleroi, Centre National de Géologie Houillère (Brussels) (1965), publication no. 10, with B. M. Aderca *et al.*; "Cyclic Sedimentation in the Marsdenian Stage (Namurian B) of Southern Belgium," in *Papers Published by the 7th International Sedimentological Congress* (Reading, 1967), with K. Fiege; "Les minéraux argileux et leurs altérations dans le Namurien inférieur de Belgique (Syndical de Namur)," in *Annales de la Société géologique de Belgique*, **90** (1967), B329–B380, with J. Thorez (with English summary); "Ton-Mergel-Kalk-Zyklen im südbelgischen Namur (Clay-Marl-Limestone Cycles in the Namurian of Southern Belgium)," in *Sedimentary Geology*, **2**, no. 4 (1968), 321–365, with K. Fiege; and "Précisions sur la succession stratigraphique du Mesozoïque dans le Massif Terni-Masgout (Maroc oriental)," in *Notes et mémoires du Service géologique du Maroc*, no. 213 (1969), 11–13, with M. Benzaquen, C. Hamel, and J. Marçais.

J. P. C. O. BOUCKAERT

VAN VLECK, JOHN HASBROUCK (*b.* Middletown, Connecticut, 13 March 1899; *d.* Cambridge, Massachusetts, 27 October 1980), *magnetism, quantum theory of solids, spectroscopy, chemical physics.*

Van Vleck was the only child of a wealthy family.

Of Dutch extraction, the Van Vlecks had settled in America early in the 1600's. Van Vleck's paternal grandfather, John Monroe Van Vleck, was a professor of astronomy at Wesleyan College, and his father, Edward Burr Van Vleck, a professor of mathematics there when John Hasbrouck was born. Van Vleck's mother, Hester Laurence Raymond, was from Lyme, Connecticut; the Raymonds had come to America about 1700. Both parents were domineering individuals, and as a boy their son (known to the family as Hasbrouck) had a retiring personality.

In 1906 Edward Van Vleck took a position at the University of Wisconsin, where he taught for the remainder of his career. That same year Hasbrouck took up a hobby that occupied him for the rest of his life. While sick in bed during a trip to Europe that summer, he was given an Italian railway timetable to study. He memorized it, and subsequently memorized railway passenger schedules for all of Europe and the United States. His impressive memory served him throughout his life.

Van Vleck attended public schools in Madison and lived with his parents until his graduation from the University of Wisconsin (a semester early) in 1920. He majored in physics, but it was only when he enrolled as a graduate student at Harvard University in the spring semester of 1920 that he decided to make a career of science. Having so made up his mind, Van Vleck was able to complete his Ph.D. degree in the spring of 1922. During these years at Harvard he acquired the sobriquet "Van," by which he was known thereafter.

Van Vleck's doctoral dissertation topic was to calculate the ionization energy of the "crossed-orbit" model of the helium atom, a model suggested by his adviser, E. C. Kemble, and also by Niels Bohr. The dissertation was the first in the United States to deal with a purely theoretical topic in the (old) quantum theory. Kemble supposed that the helium atom consisted of two electrons orbiting the nucleus in quantized Keplerian orbits of the same size, but in planes that crossed one another. The solution of the problem required calculating the energy arising from the mutual repulsion of the electrons. Van Vleck developed an approximation technique that allowed him to calculate this energy as a function of the inclination of the orbits with respect to one another. The ionization energy that he obtained agreed with one calculated in a similar fashion by Bohr's assistant H. A. Kramers, but it exceeded the empirical value.

Although it did not agree with experiment, Van Vleck's work did earn him his doctorate, and was published in *Philosophical Magazine*, then the leading English-language journal for physics. In addition, a brief report he gave on it at a meeting of the American Physical Society drew the attention of physicists at the University of Minnesota. After spending the year 1922–1923 as an instructor at Harvard, he taught at Minnesota from 1923 until 1928.

In the fall of 1923 Gregory Breit joined Van Vleck as an assistant professor, and the two enjoyed the privilege of teaching only graduate courses in theoretical physics. Breit left Minnesota after one year but did not overburden Van Vleck with teaching duties. Van Vleck found sufficient time during the years he spent at Minnesota for the research that established him as a physicist; he "came of age" a few years ahead of the physics profession in America.

Van Vleck made his greatest contribution to the old quantum theory in 1924, when he conceived his correspondence principle for absorption. He demonstrated that in the limit of high quantum numbers there would be a correspondence between absorption by classical, multiply periodic systems, and by their quantum analogues. His proof depended on interpreting net absorption in the quantum theory as the difference between gross absorption and stimulated emission of radiation (an interpretation prompted by a remark of Breit's). Van Vleck was particularly pleased that his classical theory reproduced the quantum result without the need for stimulated emission, which he referred to as "negative absorption."

Van Vleck's theory of absorption by multiply periodic systems was consistent with the newly derived Kramers theory of dispersion, and it convinced Bohr that his correspondence principle applied not only to emission but also to absorption. Further, Van Vleck's 1924 calculation made use of several of the ideas that Werner Heisenberg used in his matrix mechanics a year later. Van Vleck's work, however, did not lead in the direction of matrix mechanics. His intent was to explain quantum phenomena (especially "negative absorption") in classical terms rather than to devise an internally consistent quantum theory.

A larger project that Van Vleck completed while at Minnesota was his report for the National Research Council, *Quantum Principles and Line Spectra*. Both matrix and wave mechanics had appeared by the time of its publication in April 1926, so in a narrow sense it was obsolete. However, it was not so regarded at the time. It quickly sold out its initial printing of 1,000 copies, and an additional 300 copies were printed in 1928. Its success no doubt helped to bring Van Vleck two promotions at the University of Minnesota, and the offer of permanent positions at three other universities in 1926 and 1927.

The success of *Quantum Principles and Line Spectra* contrasted with Van Vleck's original research in 1926. While he quickly learned the techniques of matrix mechanics that spring, others were ahead of him; four or five of the original calculations that he worked out between May and December 1926 were duplicated by other theorists. (He withheld much of that duplicated work from publication.) Overlap was to be expected in theoretical work in 1926, for many old problems could be solved in a relatively short time by anyone familiar with the new developments. Nonetheless, the situation was particularly frustrating for Van Vleck. He had begun a three-year term as an editor of *Physical Review* in January 1926, and thus he was abreast of American work, but he could not stay ahead of the Europeans, even with the help of a stay in Europe during the summer of 1926.

Early in 1927 Van Vleck at last found a line of inquiry in which his work was not duplicated. In January of that year he discovered a way to generalize the theory of susceptibilities of simple dipolar gases that he had written about the previous August. His analysis depends on a division between "normal," or closely spaced, energy levels (atomic or molecular energy levels that differ by energies small compared with the thermal energy kT) and "excited," or widely spaced, energy levels. This division applies to most free molecules. The sum of contributions to the electric or magnetic polarization from the closely spaced levels gives a susceptibility that is inversely proportional to the temperature of the gas. Contributions to the polarization from widely spaced levels yield a quantity independent of temperature. The electric or magnetic susceptibility of a gas can therefore be represented by the simple formula

$$X = \frac{1}{3}\frac{N\mu^2}{kT} + N\alpha,$$

in which N is the number of molecules per unit volume, μ is the electric or magnetic moment of the molecule, and α is a constant. This result had been known in the classical theory of susceptibilities, and Van Vleck's note of August 1926 had demonstrated that the factor 1/3 could be carried over from the classical to the quantum theory. What had not previously been realized was that there is always a positive contribution to α from the excited states.

This term is now known as Van Vleck paramagnetism.

Not all molecules fit Van Vleck's narrow-wide dichotomy. One that does not is the nitric oxide molecule (NO), which has two states of electronic angular momentum separated by an energy that (at room temperature) is comparable with kT. Consequently its magnetic moment appears to vary with temperature. Van Vleck's theory predicted the form of variation, which was not known in 1927. Experimental results that appeared in 1929 confirmed his predictions, establishing the validity of his general theory.

Four further points about Van Vleck's theory of susceptibilities deserve mention. First, he calculated entirely with the matrix formalism, which he always preferred to the wave formalism. Second, a sum rule called the principle of spectroscopic stability played a major part in his analysis. Mentioned in Van Vleck's August 1926 note on dipolar gases, the rule establishes that the sums of certain matrix elements are independent of the way in which the system is quantized. Throughout the rest of his career, Van Vleck displayed a fondness for rules involving invariant sums. Third, Van Vleck derived his summation over closely spaced levels (which produces the $1/T$ susceptibility) by a direct analogy with an integration in the analysis of susceptibility in classical (multiply periodic) systems. In other words, Van Vleck turned around his procedure of 1924 and derived a quantum formalism from the classical formalism. He was thus able to use his experience with the correspondence principle to explore a new area of the quantum theory. Finally, this general theory of susceptibilities (rather than the calculations he had made in 1926) established his lasting interest in magnetism.

If Van Vleck was discouraged with his progress at the close of 1926, the discovery of his general theory of susceptibilities restored his spirits in 1927. When he accepted an appointment to lecture at Stanford University during the summer, he took the opportunity to make the trip his honeymoon. He and Abigail June Pearson were married in Minneapolis on 10 June. Soon after, Van Vleck was promoted to the rank of professor at the University of Minnesota. He was twenty-eight years old.

Several phenomena besides magnetism attracted Van Vleck's interest in the 1920's, among them molecular spectroscopy. One result of his early calculations was the discovery of what is now called lambda-doubling. In the lowest approximation, the energy of a diatomic molecule depends on the square of Λ, Λ being the component of electronic angular momentum perpendicular to the axis of the molecule. Hence there is a degeneracy in energy for each value of Λ. In higher approximations, states with positive and negative values of Λ couple differently to the rotational angular momentum of the molecule, and so the energy degeneracy is broken. The degeneracy disappears only in the second order of the perturbation calculation, however, and to treat this situation Van Vleck developed what is now known as Van Vleck degenerate perturbation theory. In the words of Robert Mulliken, Van Vleck's theoretical description of diatomic spectra fitted the experimental data "like a glove."

Beginning in the summer of 1927, Van Vleck had negotiated for a professorship with the University of Wisconsin, which he finally accepted early in 1928. The principal attraction was that a foreign theorist was to visit Wisconsin for a semester each year. Van Vleck had supervised three graduate students at Minnesota (two of whom were Elmer Hutchisson and Vladimir Rojansky), but there had been no other experienced theorist at the university since Breit's departure in 1924. Hence, while he remained an editor through 1928, Van Vleck was willing to distance himself somewhat from the *Physical Review* (edited by John T. Tate at Minnesota) to teach at Wisconsin. The first visiting theorist at Madison (in the spring of 1929) was P. A. M. Dirac. He and Van Vleck enjoyed hiking around Madison (and later in the Rocky Mountains), but they did not collaborate on any calculations.

At the University of Wisconsin, Van Vleck supervised several more graduate students than he had at Minnesota (nine in all, between 1928 and 1934). Two of these students were J. V. Atanasoff and Robert Serber. He also had five postdoctoral students during those years.

Soon after Van Vleck began teaching at Wisconsin, he undertook the writing of his second book, *The Theory of Electric and Magnetic Susceptibilities*. He wrote a large portion during a leave of absence in Europe in 1930. Also during that leave he attended the sixth Solvay Congress (on magnetism); he was the only American invited.

The new text was published in the spring of 1932. Early chapters discussed the classical theory of electric susceptibilities and gave considerable attention to current problems in understanding experimental data. The middle chapters principally concerned Van Vleck's general theory of gas susceptibilities. There appeared a discussion of the gas nitric oxide along with experimental data confirming the theoretical description of its susceptibility. Later

chapters sketched out subjects that Van Vleck (and his students) subsequently explored.

In one of those chapters Van Vleck explicated Heisenberg's fundamental theory of ferromagnetism in terms of Dirac's vector model of spins. By characterizing spin Hamiltonians as scalar products of vectors, rather than simply as antisymmetric wave functions, he made the alignment of atomic magnetic moments that occurs in ferromagnetism more easily visualized. The vector model has become common in textbook discussions of ferromagnetism, and Van Vleck subsequently found other uses for it. He and his students at Madison applied the Dirac model to calculations of complex spectra of atoms.

In another chapter of *Susceptibilities*, Van Vleck gave a qualitative discussion of how the paramagnetism of transition-metal ions in salts would be altered from what appeared in free atoms; he and his students William Penney, Robert Schlapp, and Olaf Jordahl soon explored the field quantitatively, and in so doing developed the crystal field theory.

The calculations done at Madison dealt with hydrated salts of elements in the rare earth and transition metal groups. These salts were supposed to contain water molecules of hydration that surround the paramagnetic ions in a roughly cubic array. The incomplete inner shells of these ions (the $4f$ shell in rare earths, and $3d$ shell in the transition metals) are largely shielded from bonding with other ions in the crystal, but they do feel electrostatic repulsion from the electrically polar water molecules. Orbitals with differing spatial arrangements feel different amounts of repulsion, and so their energies are altered by different amounts. The crystal field theory is a method for evaluating this electrostatic perturbation. The mathematical apparatus of the crystal field theory, which includes the use of the rotation group, and of trace-invariance arguments, marks the scheme clearly as Van Vleck's.

Penney, Schlapp, and Jordahl were able to match current data on susceptibilities in their early calculations. This success is less of an achievement than it might seem, however. Crystal field theory does not work ab initio, but sets the symmetry and strength of the crystalline field according to experimental data (on susceptibilities, in the case of this early work). Subsequent experimental results cast doubt on some of the fundamental assumptions of Penney, Schlapp, and Jordahl. The roughly cubic fields supposed for the salts of the rare earths probably do not exist, although cubic fields may exist in salts of the transition metals.

In 1932 Van Vleck wrote his first paper on the

crystal field theory. It explained the results of Schlapp's calculations, which seemed to demand that salts containing nickel and cobalt (adjacent elements in the periodic table) have radically different crystal structures. Using a brief argument with trace invariances, Van Vleck showed that the inversion of energy levels found by Schlapp arose in the mathematics of the calculations rather than in an inversion of the crystal structure. This calculation, he pointed out years later, was the favorite of his entire career.

In 1935 Van Vleck extended the crystal field theory to the case where covalent bonding of the paramagnetic ion to the surrounding crystal is strong enough to overcome the usual Russell-Saunders coupling of orbital angular momentum of individual electrons in the ions. The result is abnormally low magnetic moments. Van Vleck's handling of this "strong field" case has since developed into ligand field theory. Crystal field theory and ligand field theory did not mature, however, until after World War II, when the technology of microwave spectroscopy became available to explore the structure of paramagnetic crystals.

In 1932 and 1933, while his students worked on magnetic salts, the major part of Van Vleck's efforts was devoted to three-part study of the methane molecule, both on the basis of localized bonds (the method of Linus Pauling) and on the basis of molecular orbitals (the method of Robert Mulliken). In the first part he presented a general contrast of the two methods. Van Vleck found the molecular orbital approach had too "ionic" a character (electrons were too mobile), and too much charge tended to accumulate on individual atoms. Treatment by localized bonds specifically excluded the highly ionic terms from consideration. However, the symmetry of wave functions was then inappropriate to the tetrahedral structure of methane.

In a later part of the study Van Vleck demonstrated that, for four mathematically tractable cases, the tetrahedral structure is the most stable. None of these cases is a close representation of the methane molecule, but they circumscribe the mathematically intractable real case.

Van Vleck wrote two other notable papers on molecular physics, in 1935. The first, a long review article on valence theory written with Albert Sherman, concerned the connections (and contrasts) between localized bonds and molecular orbitals. Its general conclusion was that only results obtainable by both methods were trustworthy.

In his second paper of 1935, Van Vleck demonstrated that the localized bond scheme could be obtained from molecular orbitals by transforming from an irreducible to a reducible representation of the symmetry group appropriate to the molecule in question. Hence, he proved formally what he had suggested in his previous papers: The two approaches were simply different starting points for perturbation calculations. Both were approximations, and adding higher-order corrections would eventually merge the two.

By 1935 Van Vleck had moved from Wisconsin to Harvard University. He had at first balked at the Harvard offer (a joint appointment in the physics and the mathematics departments) because it was an associate professorship, and when he received it in 1934 he had already been a full professor for nearly seven years. Only when he was assured that he would soon be promoted did he accept the offer. He became a full professor at Harvard in 1935 and taught there until his retirement in 1969.

In his early years at Harvard, Van Vleck continued to explore dielectric phenomena and molecular spectra, and ventured into nuclear physics. In May 1939 he delivered a series of lectures at the Institut Henri Poincaré, on current theories of magnetism. (Publication of these lectures, delivered in French, was delayed until 1947 by World War II.) Van Vleck also considered new areas in the theory of magnetism, two of which will be described here.

Experimental work carried out in the late 1930's in the Netherlands showed that the relaxation times for various paramagnetic crystals (the time required, roughly, for a system of spins to reach temperature equilibrium with the surrounding crystal lattice) were one to four orders of magnitude less than could be explained by theory. In 1939 Van Vleck traced this behavior (in alums of titanium, chromium, and iron) to a direct interaction between spins and the lattice. At temperatures near 80 degrees absolute, this strong interaction between spins and the lattice could be explained by means of the Jahn-Teller effect.

The Jahn-Teller effect arises from degeneracy in the energy levels of an atom within a crystal. As a consequence of this degeneracy, the spatial coordinates of the water molecules of hydration enter the perturbation calculation in the first, rather than in the second, order. The presence of first-order terms indicates a strong interaction of spins and lattice, and hence a short relaxation time.

The strong interaction of spins and lattice that occurs for salt crystals near 80 degrees absolute does not occur at lower temperatures. Van Vleck demonstrated in 1941 that for the alums he had considered, there should actually be a phonon bottleneck; relaxation of a single spin moment will release only a small quantum of energy, and lattice modes of oscillation with such small energies are too few to carry the available energy. To put it another way, the speed of sound is too small to allow the requisite number of phonons to flow to the walls of the container of the crystal. Hence Van Vleck could not explain the short paramagnetic relaxation times observed at low temperatures. In spite of its validity, Van Vleck's idea of the phonon bottleneck was not pursued until the 1950's.

Antiferromagnetism drew Van Vleck's attention in 1940. In an antiferromagnet, atoms that are nearest neighbors have spins that align antiparallel, rather than parallel (as in a ferromagnet). The resultant moment for the crystal as a whole is therefore quite small. An antiferromagnetic susceptibility increases with temperature to the Néel point (the temperature above which magnetic ordering vanishes) and then falls with further increases in temperature.

Van Vleck did not attempt to explain why nearest neighbors should have antiparallel spins; he assumed it to be the case, and applied the Dirac vector model to a calculation of susceptibility. By combining two previously derived results, he found that the susceptibility at zero temperature should be two-thirds the susceptibility at the Néel temperature. This relation often agrees well with experimental data.

In 1941 Van Vleck and R. Finkelstein considered the excited states of the chromium ion in chrome alum. They found that (for a predominantly cubic field within the crystal) there was a doublet state about 2.25 eV above the ground level, which was consistent with recent experimental data. The energy of the doublet was fairly low, due to the contributions of matrix elements nondiagonal in the quantum number L. Van Vleck and his students in 1932 had developed the crystal field theory to deal with the ground state of atoms in crystals, and in 1937 he had considered excited states qualitatively. The quantitative calculation of the energy of an excited state of an atom in a crystal was novel, however. More than twenty years later the equivalent excited state in the ruby crystal became important in the development of the ruby laser.

In the summer of 1942 Van Vleck joined a theoretical study group (headed by J. Robert Oppenheimer, and including Hans Bethe, Felix Bloch, Robert Serber, and Edward Teller) that concluded that a fission bomb was technically feasible. Van Vleck's work in this study group was his greatest contribution to the atomic bomb, although he had occasional contact with the project in 1942 and 1943.

From the fall of 1942 Van Vleck spent most of his time on radar research in Cambridge, Massachusetts. He became director of the Theory Group at the Radio Research Laboratory at Harvard in 1943. This laboratory was associated with the MIT Radiation Laboratory but dealt with radar countermeasures rather than radar development. Two of the other members of the Theory Group were Felix Bloch and Julian Schwinger.

Several reports that Van Vleck wrote during the war were subsequently published in the open literature. One of them, by Van Vleck and his assistant at the Radio Research Laboratory, David Middleton, established that for both visual and aural detection of repeated pulsed signals in the presence of noise, the best filter to apply to the incoming signal is the Fourier transform of the pulse being sought.

A second report concerned the absorption of radiation by water vapor. Van Vleck concluded that there would be a transition between two rotational states of the water molecule corresponding to a wavelength of about 1.3 cm, and consequently that there would be strong absorption of radiation near that wavelength. Late in the war, radar apparatus operating near 1.3 cm was developed. It proved useless because of the strong absorption predicted by Van Vleck.

As the war neared its end, Van Vleck returned to pure research and entered a new field. He and Victor Weisskopf developed a quantum theory of the collision broadening of spectral lines based on the classical theory of H. A. Lorentz. The derivation of the quantum theory from the classical employed, in essence, the correspondence principle. It was Van Vleck's last major use of the concept.

In a further study of line breadths (1948), Van Vleck calculated broadening by dipole-dipole coupling between electronic or nuclear magnetic moments. Exact expressions for the shapes of lines are difficult to derive, but Van Vleck obtained moments (the root mean square and root mean fourth power) of the frequency distribution. He proved (as he had noted in an earlier paper with C. J. Gorter) that exchange effects for electronic moments can appreciably narrow a spectral line.

Van Vleck's exploration of line shapes was a major contribution to the theoretical understanding of nuclear magnetic resonance and of the other magnetic resonance spectroscopies developed after the war. Philip Anderson (a student of Van Vleck's in the late 1940's) points out that Van Vleck maintained close ties to relevant experimental work, such as the research of Edward Purcell at Harvard on nuclear magnetic resonance that earned Purcell the Nobel Prize.

Anderson argues that Van Vleck was a pivotal

figure in early developments in the area now known as quantum electronics. He was an expert in atomic and molecular spectra (being, for instance, one of the few theorists to note the detection of the 1.25 cm inversion line of the ammonia molecule), and his work on line breadths was crucial to the invention of the maser and the laser.

In another field, about 1950 Van Vleck and his student Thomas Kuhn developed the quantum defect method for calculating cohesive energies of alkali metals. Rather than constructing a potential for an ion in a crystal lattice and integrating Schrödinger's equation through it to obtain the binding energy, they made use of the known energy levels of free alkali atoms. The few lowest energy states of the atom define its behavior, and the energies of those states (which are the quantum defects) can be used to construct a wave function for the outer region of an atom in a crystal. The potential in the outer regions of the atom is hydrogenic. The wave function is therefore a combination of confluent hypergeometric functions, similar to the wave function of a hydrogen atom. With boundary conditions appropriate to a crystal, rather than a free atom, the hydrogenic wave function determines the cohesive energy of the crystal.

Old concerns continued to interest Van Vleck; in the late 1940's and early 1950's he wrote about an "intermediate" model of ferromagnetism. In it he supposed each atom in a metal to be in one of two states of ionization. Electrons are thus less mobile than they are in band theory (where each atom can take on several states of ionization) but are more mobile than in Heisenberg's first model of ferromagnetism (where each atom has a fixed complement of electrons). As in his earlier work on valence theory, Van Vleck took pleasure in constructing a bridge between two distinct theoretical descriptions of a phenomenon. His "intermediate" model of ferromagnetism was, however, quite difficult to use for calculations.

Although Van Vleck had returned to research at the end of the war, administrative and professional work took a great deal of his time from 1945 through 1957. As chairman of the physics department at Harvard from 1945 to 1949, his principal concern was to build up the faculty. There were many able young physicists available in the postwar period. Among those hired during Van Vleck's chairmanship were the future Nobel laureates Edward Purcell and Julian Schwinger.

In 1951 Van Vleck was appointed Hollis professor of mathematics and natural philosophy and, somewhat reluctantly, first dean of the Division of En-

gineering and Applied Physics (created by the merger of the Engineering School and the department of engineering science and applied physics). Funds bequeathed by the industrialist Gordon McKay made possible the equipping of the McKay Laboratory and the hiring of new faculty. One of the first appointments during Van Vleck's tenure as dean was Nicolaas Bloembergen, also a future Nobel laureate.

In 1952 and 1953 Van Vleck served as president of the American Physical Society. By the early 1950's it had established divisions that met separately. Van Vleck had opposed this balkanization of the society, a consequence of its postwar growth, but by 1953 the trend could not be reversed.

From 1951 to 1956 Van Vleck was a member of the Visiting Committee of the National Bureau of Standards. He was vice president of the American Academy of Arts and Sciences (1956–1957) and vice president of the International Union of Pure and Applied Physics (1958–1960).

Van Vleck resigned his deanship at Harvard in 1957 and was again able to enjoy extended travel abroad. In 1960 he was Lorentz professor at the University of Leiden, and in the year 1961–1962, Eastman professor at Oxford University.

Van Vleck published about fifty papers between 1957 and his retirement in 1969, and about fifteen more in the decade after he retired. He continued to explore the spectroscopic and magnetic properties of the rare earths. A new concern was the magnetism of garnets (ferrimagnetic silicate crystals containing cations of two chemical elements). In his later years Van Vleck frequently lectured on the half-century of physics he had taken part in. The one project that he never completed was a second edition of his *Susceptibilities*, which had achieved the status of a classic, but was outdated. The field of susceptibilities had grown too large for a single author, and Van Vleck could find no one willing to collaborate with him.

In his later years nearly a score of medals and awards found their way to Van Vleck. In 1963 he was the first recipient of the Michelson Award of the Case Institute of Technology; in 1970 he was made a chevalier of the Legion of Honor; in 1974 he won the Lorentz Medal of the Royal Netherlands Academy of Arts and Sciences; and in 1977 he shared the Nobel Prize with Philip Anderson and N. F. Mott.

Van Vleck's mathematical talent was considerable, and his physical intuition impressive, but he was not an arrogant or distant man; quite the contrary: he was approachable, and also exceedingly generous with his talents. Typical of his generosity is the fact that many of his ideas were first published by his students, without his name attached. The papers of Jordahl, Penney, and Schlapp on the crystal field theory are the best examples.

Other aspects of Van Vleck's character are not evident in his scientific work. As a young man he played the flute, and while he was unathletic, he enjoyed watching football (particularly when Wisconsin or Harvard was playing). He shared his parents' taste for art, and from them he inherited a collection of several thousand Japanese prints, which he in turn gave to the University of Wisconsin. Van Vleck also had a dry wit.

Van Vleck remained active until his death from heart failure. With funds that he bequeathed, the John Hasbrouck Van Vleck chair of pure and applied physics was established at Harvard University.

BIBLIOGRAPHY

I. ORIGINAL WORKS. Van Vleck published more than 180 papers in his lifetime. Consult the following complete bibliographies: Philip W. Anderson, "John Hasbrouck Van Vleck," in *Biographical Memoirs, National Academy of Sciences*, **56** (1987), 501–540; "Bibliography of J. H. Van Vleck," in *International Journal of Quantum Chemistry, Symposium*, no. 5 (1971), vi–xi; and Brebis Bleaney, "John Hasbrouck Van Vleck," in *Biographical Memoirs of Fellows of the Royal Society*, **28** (1982), 627–665.

Works concerning the old quantum theory include "The Normal Helium Atom and Its Relation to the Quantum Theory," in *Philosophical Magazine*, **44** (1922) 842–869; "The Absorption of Radiation by Multiple Periodic Orbits, and Its Relation to the Correspondence Principle and the Rayleigh-Jeans Law," in *Physical Review*, **24** (1924), 330–365 ("Part I, Some Extensions of the Correspondence Principle," was reprinted in B. L. van der Waerden, ed., *Sources of Quantum Mechanics* [Amsterdam, 1967; repr. New York, 1968]); "Absorption, Emission, and Line-breadths: A Semihistorical Perspective," in *Reviews of Modern Physics*, **49** (1977), 939–959, with David L. Huber; and *Quantum Principles and Line Spectra*, Bulletin of the National Research Council, no. 54 (1926).

Early calculations in the quantum theory, on susceptibilities, and molecular spectroscopy: "Magnetic Susceptibilities and Dielectric Constants in the New Quantum Mechanics," in *Nature*, **118** (1926), 226–227; "The Dielectric Constant and Diamagnetism of Hydrogen and Helium in the New Quantum Mechanics," in *Proceedings of the National Academy of Sciences*, **12** (1926), 662–670; "On Dielectric Constants and Magnetic Susceptibilities in the New Quantum Mechanics. I. A General Proof of the Langevin-Debye Formula," in *Physical Review*, **29** (1927), 727–744; "On Dielectric Constants and Magnetic Susceptibilities in the New Quantum Mechanics. II. Application to Dielectric Constants," *ibid.*, **30** (1927), 31–54; "On Dielectric Constants and Magnetic Suscep-

tibilities in the New Quantum Mechanics, III, Application to Dia- and Paramagnetism," *ibid.*, **31** (1928), 587–613; and "On Λ-Type Doubling and Electron Spin in the Spectra of Diatomic Molecules," *ibid.*, **33** (1929), 467–506.

In the early 1930's Van Vleck (or his students) wrote the following works on susceptibilities: *The Theory of Electric and Magnetic Susceptibilities* (Oxford, 1932); "The Influence of Crystalline Fields on the Susceptibilities of Salts of Paramagnetic Ions, I, The Rare Earths, Especially Pr and Nd," by William Penney and Robert Schlapp, in *Physical Review*, **41** (1932), 194–207; "Influence of Crystalline Fields on the Susceptibilities of Salts of Paramagnetic Ions, II, The Iron Group, Especially Ni, Cr, and Co," by Robert Schlapp and William Penney, *ibid.*, **42** (1932), 666–686; "Theory of the Variations in Paramagnetic Anisotropy Among Different Salts of the Iron Group," *ibid.*, **41** (1932), 208–215; "The Effect of Crystalline Electric Fields on the Paramagnetic Susceptibility of Cupric Salts," by Olaf M. Jordahl, *ibid.*, **45** (1934), 87–97; and "Valence Strength and the Magnetism of Complex Salts," in *Journal of Chemical Physics*, **3** (1935), 807–813. Papers on chemical physics include "On the Theory of the Structure of CH_4 and Related Molecules, Part I," *Journal of Chemical Physics*, **1** (1933), 177–182; "On the Theory of the Structure of CH_4 and Related Molecules, Part II," *ibid.*, 219–238; "On the Theory of the Structure of CH_4 and Related Molecules, Part III," *ibid.*, **2** (1934), 20–30; "Note on the Sp^3 Configuration of Carbon, and Correction to Part III on CH_4," *ibid.*, 297–298; "The Quantum Theory of Valence," in *Reviews of Modern Physics*, **7** (1935), 167–228, with Albert Sherman; "The Group Relation Between the Mulliken and Slater-Pauling Theories of Valence," *Journal of Chemical Physics*, **3** (1935), 803–806.

Works from the late 1930's and early 1940's on magnetism and spectroscopy: "Quelques aspects de la théorie du magnétisme," in *Annales de l'Institut Henri Poincaré*, **10** (1947), 57–187; "On the Magnetic Behavior of Vanadium, Titanium, and Chrome Alum," in *Journal of Chemical Physics*, **7** (1939), 61–71; "The Jahn-Teller Effect and Crystalline Stark Splitting for Clusters of the Form XY_6," *ibid.*, 72–84; "Paramagnetic Relaxation Times for Titanium and Chrome Alum," in *Physical Review*, **57** (1940), 426–447; "Errata: Paramagnetic Relaxation Times for Titanium and Chrome Alum," *ibid.*, 1052; "Paramagnetic Relaxation and the Equilibrium of Lattice Oscillators," *ibid.*, **59** (1941), 724–729; "Calculation of Energy Exchange Between Lattice Oscillators," *ibid.*, 730–736; "On the Theory of Antiferromagnetism," in *Journal of Chemical Physics*, **9** (1941), 85–90; "The Puzzle of Rare-Earth Spectra in Solids," in *Journal of Physical Chemistry*, **41** (1937), 67–80; and "On the Energy Levels of Chrome Alum," in *Journal of Chemical Physics*, **8** (1940), 790–797, with R. Finkelstein.

Radar-related papers: "A Theoretical Comparison of the Visual, Aural, and Meter Reception of Pulsed Signals in the Presence of Noise," in *Journal of Applied Physics*, **17** (1946), 940–971, with David Middleton; and "The

Absorption of Microwaves by Uncondensed Water Vapour," in *Physical Review*, **71** (1947), 425–433.

Calculations on line shapes: "On the Shape of Collision-Broadened Lines," in *Reviews of Modern Physics*, **17** (1945), 227–236, with Victor F. Weisskopf; "The Role of Exchange Interaction in Paramagnetic Absorption," in *Physical Review*, **72** (1947), 1128–1129, with C. J. Gorter; and "The Dipolar Broadening of Magnetic Resonance Lines in Crystals," *ibid.*, **74** (1948), 1168–1183.

Discussions of the quantum defect method, and of ferromagnetism: "A Simplified Method of Computing the Cohesive Energies of Monovalent Metals," in *Physical Review*, **79** (1950), 382–388, with T. S. Kuhn; "The Cohesive Energies of Alkali Metals," in *Proceedings of the International Conference of Theoretical Physics, Kyoto and Tokyo, September 1953* (1954), 640–649; "A Survey of the Theory of Ferromagnetism," in *Reviews of Modern Physics*, **17** (1945), 27–47; and "Models of Exchange Coupling in Ferromagnetic Media," *ibid.*, **25** (1953), 220–227.

The bulk of Van Vleck's papers are held by the American Institute of Physics' Center for History of Physics; papers relating to the administration of Harvard University are retained by the Harvard University Archives. Van Vleck was interviewed by Thomas Kuhn (in 1963) as a part of the Archive for History of Quantum Physics, and by Charles Weiner and Gloria Lubkin (in 1966 and 1973) for the AIP Center for History of Physics. Van Vleck's excellent memory made him a reliable historical source.

The best overview of Van Vleck's early career is presented in his address, "The First Decade of Quantum Mechanics," in *International Journal of Quantum Chemistry, Symposium*, no. 5 (1971), 3–20.

SECONDARY LITERATURE. The biographical memoirs by Anderson and Bleaney (cited above) discuss his entire career. Van Vleck's career to 1934 is treated in depth in Frederick Fellows, "J. H. Van Vleck: The Early Life and Work of a Mathematical Physicist" (Ph.D. diss., University of Minnesota, 1985).

H. A. Kramers' research in the old quantum theory is discussed at length by Max Dresden in his *H. A. Kramers: Between Tradition and Revolution* (New York, 1987). Katherine Sopka explores the growth of the American physics profession in *Quantum Physics in America, 1920–1935* (New York, 1980). Spencer Weart recounts the division of the American Physical Society in "The Birth of the Solid-State Physics Community," in *Physics Today*, **41** (July 1988), 38–45. The International Project in the History of Solid State Physics has produced a history of the emergence of the discipline: Lillian Hoddeson, Ernest Braun, Jürgen Teichmann, and Spencer Weart, eds., *Out of the Crystal Maze: Chapters from the History of Solid State Physics* (New York, 1990).

FREDERICK FELLOWS

VANDIVER, HARRY SCHULTZ (*b.* Philadelphia, Pennsylvania, 21 October 1882; *d.* Austin, Texas, 9 January 1973), *mathematics*.

Harry Schultz Vandiver was the son of John Lyon and Ida Everett Vandiver. At an early age he developed an antagonism to public education that was to last the rest of his life. He dropped out of Central High School and went to work for twelve years as a customshouse broker for his father's firm. He was very much interested in the theory of numbers, and at the age of eighteen began his publishing career in the problem section of the *American Mathematical Monthly*. From 1904 to 1905 he attended some graduate courses in mathematics and made extensive use of the library at the University of Pennsylvania. In 1904 he collaborated with George David Birkhoff on a first-rate paper on the prime factors of $a^n - b^n$ that appeared in the *Annals of Mathematics*.

Vandiver continued to publish three or four papers a year until the end of World War I, during which he served in the U.S. Naval Reserve as a yeoman first class. Then, at the urging of Birkhoff, he turned professional by accepting an instructorship in mathematics at Cornell University in 1919, a position he held until 1924. Vandiver spent his summers at the University of Chicago, working with L. E. Dickson on the latter's monumental *History of the Theory of Numbers* (3 vols., Washington, D.C., 1919–1923) and on the *Report of the Committee on Algebraic Numbers of the National Research Council* (2 vols., Washington, D.C., 1923–1928).

In 1924 Vandiver accepted an associate professorship at the University of Texas at Austin, where he remained until his retirement in 1966. He also continually accepted visiting professorships and lectureships. He was in Princeton in 1934 when he was elected a member of the National Academy of Sciences. More than half of the one hundred papers he wrote thereafter appeared in the *Proceedings* of the academy.

In the summer of 1952 Vandiver visited the National Bureau of Standards Institute at Los Angeles to see what the high-speed computer SWAC could do with Fermat's last theorem. The problem is to show that the equation $x^p + y^p + z^p = 0$ is not solvable in nonzero integers x, y, z, p when p is a prime greater than 2. Vandiver and others had determined various criteria that p has to meet in order for the above equation to hold. He and his students over the years had shown $p > 600$. When the criteria were presented to the SWAC, it eliminated every $p < 2000$ in a couple of hours. (Later the limit of p was set at $p < 4002$ and more recently at $p < 125000$.)

In 1923 Vandiver married Maude Folmsbee. They had one son, Frank Vandiver, who became president of Texas A&M. In accordance with his father's views on public education, Frank was privately tutored for his secondary school and undergraduate college education.

Vandiver was awarded the F. N. Cole Prize in Number Theory by the American Mathematical Society in 1931, and in 1946 the University of Pennsylvania bestowed on him the honorary degree of doctor of science. He was a Guggenheim fellow in the academic year 1927–1928, and his work until 1961 was supported by the National Science Foundation (grants in 1955 and 1957–1961) and the American Philosophical Society (grants in 1934 and 1939).

The Vandivers never owned a home in Austin. For many years they occupied a permanent suite at the Alamo Hotel, where they had a large collection of classical recordings. When he was not doing research or refereeing or reviewing the work of others, Vandiver would relax by listening to Mozart or Beethoven or, on occasion, by attending a campus baseball game. At the age of eighty-four Vandiver gave up research and went into a rest home.

Vandiver's bibliography extends from 1900 to 1963 and contains 173 titles, of which 50 are directly concerned with Fermat's last theorem; the others are mainly on properties of Bernoulli numbers and on cyclotomy and commutative algebra. There are also half a dozen expository papers on Fermat's last theorem and one entitled "On the Desirability of Publishing Classified Bibliographies of the Mathematics Literature" (1960), no doubt inspired by his early work with Dickson's *History*. He also prepared a twenty-two-page bibliography of articles on Bernoulli and Euler numbers for the years 1869–1940, which he never published.

The Fermat problem of showing the nonexistence of integers x, y, z, none zero, such that $x^p + y^p = z^p$ holds for p a prime greater than 2, has long been separated into two cases. Case I is subject to the condition that p fails to divide xyz and is much simpler than case II, in which p may divide xyz. In case I we have Weiferich's criterion that 2^{p-1} is divisible by p^2. This condition is met by $p = 1093$ and $p = 3511$, but for no other prime less than six billion. However, these two primes fail to satisfy the Mirimanoff criterion that p^2 divides $3^{p-1} 1$, so that case I is proved for $p < 6 \cdot 10^9$. Many times Vandiver expressed the conviction that case I would be disposed of in the near future.

His approach to case II was along the lines of the early German algebraic number theorist E. E. Kummer, who founded the arithmetic of numbers of the form

$$a_0 + a_1 w + a_2 w^2 + \ldots + a_{p-1} w^{p-1},$$

where $w^p = 1$, $w \neq 1$, and the a's are ordinary integers.

The Fermat equation can be written

$$x^p = z^p - y^p = (z - y)(z - wy) \ldots (z - w^{p-1} y).$$

Vandiver sought conditions on p alone to make this product a perfect of p. The criteria he derived had to do with the divisibility by p of the Bernoulli numbers $B_2, B_4, B_6, \ldots, B_{p-3}$ and the class number h of the cyclotomic field generated by w. Then there is the problem of combining the criteria to form a condition that should be impossible. Throughout this process one has to try to discover properties of the integers x, y, z, p, which one hopes do not exist after all. This sort of situation was commonplace in the scientific life of H. S. Vandiver.

BIBLIOGRAPHY

I. ORIGINAL WORKS. "On the Integral Divisors of $a^n - b^n$," in *Annals of Mathematics*, 2nd ser., **5** (1904), 173–180, written with G. D. Birkhoff; "Proof of Fermat's Last Theorem for All Prime Exponents Less Than 4002," in *Proceedings of the National Academy of Sciences*, **41** (1955), 970–973, written with C. A. Nicol and J. L. Selfridge; and "On the Desirability of Publishing Classified Bibliographies of the Mathematics Literature," *American Mathematical Monthly*, **67** (1960), 47–50.

II. SECONDARY LITERATURE. An obituary by D. H. Lehmer is in *Bulletin of the American Mathematical Society*, **80** (1974), 817–818. See also D. H. Lehmer, "On Fermat's Quotient, Base Two," in *Mathematics of Computation*, **36** (1981), 289–290; and S. Wagstaff, "The Irregular Primes to 125000," *ibid.*, **32** (1978), 583–591.

D. H. LEHMER

VEGARD, LARS (*b.* Vegorshei, Norway, 3 February 1880; *d.* Oslo, Norway, 21 December 1963), *physics, cosmic geophysics.*

Lars Vegard, who introduced modern experimental physics into Norway, grew up in southern Norway on the farm of his parents, Nils Gundersen Grasaasen and Anne Grundesdatter Espeland. Although his father was a farmer and his own early schooling was irregular, Vegard moved to Christiania (now Oslo) to attend the gymnasium. In 1899 he enrolled at Royal Frederik University (now University of Oslo), where he majored in physics. Upon receiving his bachelor's degree in 1905, he was asked to become an assistant to Kristian Birkeland, whose research on northern lights was to influence Vegard's career.

Upon receiving a university fellowship in 1908, Vegard left for Cambridge, where he learned experimental techniques from J. J. Thomson and worked on problems involving cathode rays. In 1910 he became instructor in physics at Royal Frederik University, but he soon received a fellowship that allowed him to spend the academic year 1911–1912 in Wilhelm Wien's laboratory at Würzburg. Here Vegard worked with canal (positive) rays, beginning an experimental study of their light emission that became the basis for his doctoral dissertation at Royal Frederik University, "Über die Lichterzeugung in Glimmlicht und Kanalstrahlen." After receiving his doctorate in 1913 he was named docent, and in 1918, after Birkeland's death, professor of physics. In addition to his pioneering work on the spectral analysis of northern lights, Vergard introduced the ideas and organizational forms of modern physics into Norway.

In 1915 he married Inger Hervora Petersen; they had a daughter, Anne Lise. Although he spent his adult life in Oslo, Vegard never lost the strong attachment to nature developed during his childhood. He went moose hunting every autumn until he was seventy years old, he skied until the end of his life, and among German physicists he acquired a reputation as an extraordinary sportsman.

Vegard's research career owed much to his first experiences in science. Birkeland had proposed in 1896 that northern lights arose from the effects of cathode rays emitted by the sun that are caught in the earth's magnetic field. In the university's cellar he built a model to produce analogies to northern lights and related cosmic-geophysical phenomena. Birkeland used private funds to hire assistants, which allowed him to recruit some of the brightest young natural science students for his projects; Vegard was one of them.

Vegard first analyzed data that Birkeland had obtained on expeditions to northern Norway in an effort to find relations between magnetic storms and northern lights. Subsequently his doctoral research on canal rays enabled him to open new avenues of inquiry for understanding northern lights. Vegard reasoned that the solar emissions must be electrically neutral, and therefore must consist of both negative and positive particles. Moreover, he associated the fact that northern lights often display a sharp lower boundary with similar experimental results exhibited by α-particles passing through air. If positively charged particles were indeed responsible for north-

ern lights, then the frequencies of their spectral lines should shift with their speed.

Vegard decided to make spectral photographs of northern lights, a task that required considerable experimental skill, great patience, and physical endurance. Hour after hour, night after night, he had to stand in intense cold, holding specially constructed spectrographs toward the ever-moving northern lights. In 1939 he finally identified hydrogen lines in the lights' spectrum, and in 1948 he could show the Doppler effect in the "proton" northern lights.

While constantly improving the spectral techniques, Vegard was able to provide the first realistic models of the atmosphere's composition and structure between 80 and 1,000 kilometers. One feature, however, seemed to defy explanation: the bright "green northern light line." No known atmospheric gas could account for its appearance. In the early 1920's Vegard published a theory of the physical conditions in the upper atmosphere in which he assumed that in the extreme cold, oxygen and nitrogen occurred in frozen crystalline forms. The bright green spectral line, he thought, might well be the result of frozen nitrogen.

Vegard visited Heike Kamerlingh-Onnes's cryogenics laboratory in Leiden, where he made spectral analyses of the light emitted by frozen nitrogen stimulated by electrons. In these experiments he discovered phosphorescence of solid nitrogen and the spectral band that now is called the Vegard-Kaplan band. This discovery paved the way to studies of "trapped radicals." Vegard's conclusion on the origin of the green line, however, was mistaken. It arises from a form of oxygen occurring only in the special conditions of the upper atmosphere.

Although most of his research was circumscribed by his interest in northern lights, Vegard's interest in modern physics brought him into contact with other areas to which he made contributions. Upon learning of X-ray diffraction, he traveled to Cambridge and to Leeds, where W. H. Bragg was professor, to learn the new technique. In 1916 he and a number of assistants began a series of studies on crystal structure using X-ray diffraction. This work also brought him into contact with the Bohr-Sommerfeld atomic model; he published several articles on the relation between X-ray spectra and the periodic system.

Throughout his career Vegard endeavored to obtain better facilities and opportunities for physics research and education in Norway. He initiated plans and obtained funding from the Rockefeller Foundation for a northern lights observatory at Tromsø, northern Norway's major city. This facility, opened in 1930, paved the way for the founding of the Norwegian Institute for Cosmic Physics, of which Vegard served as chairman and major inspirational force until he retired in 1955. Vegard also played a role in selecting Blindern as the site for the new university campus in Oslo and helped plan the new physics and chemistry building, which opened in 1935. He was a major figure in obtaining a nuclear physics laboratory for the physics institute; he also was twice rector of the Faculty of Mathematics and Natural Sciences in the 1930's.

BIBLIOGRAPHY

I. ORIGINAL WORKS. Vegard's writings are listed in Poggendorff, V, 1303; VI, 2740–2741. Vegard's autobiographic essays are in *Studentene fra 1899* (1924), 333–335, (1949), 210–212.

II. SECONDARY LITERATURE. J. Holtsmark, "Minnetale over professor dr. Lars Vegard," in *Det Norske videnskaps-akademi i Oslo, Arsbok 1966*, 53–58; Gotfred Kvifte, "Lars Vegard," in *Fra fysikens verden*, **26** (1964), 1–4; and J. Holtsmark, "Lars Vegard," in *Norsk biografisk leksikon*, XVII (Oslo, 1975), 524–529.

ROBERT MARC FRIEDMAN

VERNEY, ERNEST BASIL (*b*. Cardiff, Wales, 22 August 1894; *d*. Cambridge, England, 19 August 1967), *physiology, pharmacology*.

Verney, an important figure in renal physiology from the 1920's through the 1950's, was the fourth son and fifth child of Frederick Palmer Verney and Mary Ann Burch Verney. Part of his childhood was spent on his parents' farm at Hever, Kent. From 1904 to 1910 he attended Judd School, Tonbridge, and from 1910 to 1913, Tonbridge School, studying first classics and then science. Encouraged to pursue a career in medicine by science teachers at Tonbridge, he competed for and won an exhibition in science at Downing College, Cambridge, in 1913. At Cambridge, Verney studied anatomy, physiology, physics, and chemistry, and in 1916 obtained a first class in part I of the natural science tripos. Also in 1916 he entered St. Bartholomew's Hospital, London, with a scholarship, clerking under J. H. Drysdale. After receiving his M.R.C.S. and L.R.C.P. in April 1918, Verney joined the British Army as a medical officer, and served until October 1919. From demobilization until March 1921, he was house physician, first under Drysdale at St. Bartholomew's, then under Geoffrey Bourne at the East London Hospital for Children (Shadwell). At Shadwell he

met Ruth Eden Conway, a resident medical officer. They were married on 10 April 1923, and had two sons and a daughter.

The year 1921 was one of decision for Verney. He was drawn to clinical medicine, but still more strongly to experimental medical science, which held out the possibility of understanding the processes underlying health and disease. While serving as house physician to Drysdale (1919–1920), Verney had seen two boys on the wards die in uremic coma. That experience prompted an interest in renal function that took him first into the existing literature and then into a career of research in the field. Verney's decision for research was sealed by his meeting in the summer of 1921 with Ernest Henry Starling, professor of physiology at University College, London, and his appointment as assistant at Starling's Institute of Physiology.

In the congenial, energetic, and intellectually intense atmosphere of Starling's department, where he worked from 1921 to 1924, Verney gained invaluable laboratory experience and conducted research that issued in his first publications. He later described Starling as "the lineal scientific descendant of Claude Bernard," in the sense that both men recognized that functions could not be understood apart from their integration in organism and environment. Verney took as his own the aim that he ascribed to Bernard and Starling: "to detect and to measure the precise means whereby that coordinated interplay of function which we dimly perceive in the living animal is effected." To that end he made use, whenever possible, of the whole, conscious, and contented animal, and attempted to minimize the disturbances of experimental intervention.

A superbly skilled surgeon, Verney achieved experimental controls by manual operations and the use of simple mechanical devices that he often designed and constructed himself. These traits are well exemplified in the work on renal physiology that he began under Starling and that occupied most of his career. By using the heart-lung preparation invented by Starling to perfuse the kidney with blood, Verney took a major step beyond earlier reliance on isolated kidneys perfused with saline solutions. By successfully exteriorizing the renal artery and placing the kidney subcutaneously, Verney was able to control the renal blood supply and measure variations in length of the kidney without hindrance to his experimental animals. He could measure and regulate blood pressure and flow to the kidney by means of flow meters and compression units placed around the renal artery, and devised ways of adjusting these units, again so as to minimize disturbances to his animals. Starling's laboratory no doubt reinforced other qualities that informed all of Verney's subsequent scientific work, including meticulous planning of experiments, high standards, stamina for many consecutive hours in the laboratory, and familiarity with the writings of earlier physiologists.

In his work with Starling, Verney used the heart-lung-kidney preparation to study the relationship of the physiological excretory response of the kidney to the rate of blood flow through, and blood pressure in, the perfused organ. Verney and Starling also examined, among other things, the effects of asphyxia and cyanide in stopping tubular activity. In 1902 Starling had coined the term "hormone" to denote function-controlling substances released within the body. One of the results of Verney's work with Starling was their suggestion that a pituitary principle or principles control water excretion by the kidney. In Verney's first independent paper, published in 1926, he showed that the perfused kidney could be made to excrete concentrated urine if the intact head of a dog was included in the circuit. If the pituitary was then removed, polyuria (excessive passage of urine) developed. He concluded with the then novel suggestion that the secretion of the pituitary is continuous, and that the kidneys depend on this substance for normal physiological function.

In 1923, while still at Starling's institute, Verney began collaborative research on cardiovascular reflexes with Ivan de Burgh Daly. Their aim was to study the relations of heart rate, aortic pressure, atrial pressure, and nervous reflexes. As an extension of this work, which continued at intervals until 1937, they tried to determine whether reflex effects on the heart and systemic circulation could be attributed to receptors in the pulmonary vascular bed.

In 1924 Verney was appointed assistant in the Medical Unit at University College Hospital, London, under T. R. Elliott, and in 1926 he accepted the chair of pharmacology at University College, London. In 1934 he became reader in pharmacology at Cambridge University. He remained at Cambridge for the rest of his career, becoming the first Sheild professor of pharmacology in 1946 and emeritus in 1961.

Apart from the early work with Daly on cardiovascular reflexes, Verney devoted himself almost entirely to study of renal function. In work that extended from the 1920's through the 1950's, he and his collaborators clarified important ways in which water balance is controlled and modified, and described several aspects of renal hypertension.

Among other things, Verney showed the importance of the pressure of the blood supply to the kidney. He compared water diuresis, diabetes insipidus, and the behavior of the isolated kidney, and showed that nervous control of the kidney did not play a significant role in water excretion. In research published between 1938 and 1945, he investigated the inhibition of water diuresis by exercise and emotional stress, showed that small doses of pituitary extract could inhibit water diuresis, and calculated the quantity of the pituitary substance (called pituitrin, later antidiuretic hormone) that had to be released to maintain a low rate of urine flow.

With Marthe Vogt, Verney published research in 1938 and 1943 in which the effects of renal ischemia (deficiency of blood due to constriction or obstruction of a blood vessel) were investigated by experimental production of hypertension. One conclusion of this work was that the rise in blood pressure was due to a substance formed in the kidney and released into the bloodstream. In 1945 Verney published a study of the role of the sympathetic nervous system in the inhibition of the release of pituitrin, and in 1955 a detailed account of intrarenal events following oral intake of water or saline solution by dogs.

In 1957 Verney published the results of work, spanning some fourteen years, on the existence and location of osmoreceptors. This research originated in the suggestion that in water diuresis, secretion of the antidiuretic substance by the neurohypophysis (posterior lobe of the pituitary) was inhibited. This implied that the secretion was governed by some other factor, probably the osmotic pressure of the carotid artery plasma. Experiments confirmed the idea. Verney called the entities sensitive to changes in the osmotic pressure of the plasma "osmoreceptors," and said that they must have a nervous connection with the pituitary. After a great deal of preliminary work on cerebral blood distribution in the dog, Verney attempted to localize the osmoreceptors by intracranially ligating branches of the internal carotid artery. He concluded that the osmoreceptors were in the anterior hypothalamus.

On two occasions Verney transferred his research to the University of Melbourne, for six months in 1957 as a visiting professor, and for three years after his retirement in 1961 as the holder of a personal chair. He was much appreciated by colleagues in both Britain and Australia, not only for his superlative qualities in the laboratory but also for his remarkable memory and erudition, vivid imagination, keen sense of humor, and lively hospitality.

Formal academic honors came Verney's way. Elected fellow of the Royal Society in 1936, he held invited lectureships in the 1940's and 1950's at the universities of Edinburgh, Birmingham, Harvard, and Dublin, and at the Royal College of Physicians of London and the American College of Surgeons. In 1957 he was awarded the Baly Medal of the Royal College of Physicians. In 1967, the year of his death, Verney was elected honorary member of the British Physiological Society, and was awarded the Schmiedeberg Plakette of the Deutsche Pharmakologische Gesellschaft.

BIBLIOGRAPHY

I. ORIGINAL WORKS. A list of Verney's published works is given by I. de Burgh Daly and L. Mary Pickford (see below). The following selection is meant to represent the aspects of Verney's research discussed in this article. For the early work on renal function, see "The Secretion of Urine as Studied on the Isolated Kidney," in *Proceedings of the Royal Society*, **B97** (1925), 321–363, with E. H. Starling; and "On Secretion of Pituitrin in Mammals, as Shown by Perfusion of the Isolated Kidney of the Dog," *ibid.*, **B99** (1926), 487–517. For Verney's collaboration with Ivan de Burgh Daly, see "The Localisation of Receptors Involved in the Reflex Regulation of the Heart Rate," in *Journal of Physiology*, **62** (1927), 330–340, with I. de Burgh Daly; and "Sensory Receptors in the Pulmonary Vascular Bed," in *Quarterly Journal of Experimental Physiology*, **27** (1937), 123–146, with I. de Burgh Daly, G. Ludány, and Alison Todd. The later work on renal function is represented by "Goulstonian Lectures on Polyuria," in *Lancet*, (1929), **1**, 539–546, 645–651, 751–756; "The Absorption and Secretion of Water by the Mammal," in *Proceedings of the Royal Society*, **B112** (1933), 496–547, with A. Klisiecki, Mary Pickford, and P. Rothschild; and "The Antidiuretic Hormone and the Factors Which Determine Its Release: Croonian Lecture," in *Proceedings of the Royal Society*, **B135** (1947), 25–106. The latter paper is a classic summary of Verney's work on the subject.

Verney's publications with Marthe Vogt on renal hypertension include "An Experimental Investigation into Hypertension of Renal Origin, with Some Observations on Convulsive 'Uraemia,'" in *Quarterly Journal of Experimental Physiology*, **28** (1938), 253–303; and "Observations on the Effects of Renal Ischaemia upon Arterial Pressure and Urine Flow in the Dog," *ibid.*, **32** (1943), 35–65. The search for osmoreceptors culminated in Verney's publication with P. A. Jewell of "An Experimental Attempt to Determine the Site of the Neurohypophyseal Osmoreceptors in the Dog," in *Philosophical Transactions of the Royal Society*, **B240** (1957), 197–324. Verney published an appreciation of his teacher and collaborator that includes a description of the heart-lung preparation: "Some Aspects of the Work of Ernest Henry Starling," in *Annals of Science*, **12** (1956), 30–47.

Verney's collected papers, including laboratory note-books, photographs, drawings, and artifacts, are at the Physiological Laboratory, Cambridge University.

II. SECONDARY LITERATURE. The most extensive treatment of Verney's career and scientific work is I. de Burgh Daly and L. Mary Pickford, "Ernest Basil Verney 1894–1967," in *Biographical Memoirs of Fellows of the Royal Society*, **16** (1970), 523–542. Daly published a short (unsigned) version of this article in *Lancet* (1967), **2**, 518–519. Brief notices on Verney's life were published by Geoffrey Bourne in *British Medical Journal* (1967), **3**, 686, and in *St. Bart's Hospital Journal*, **72** (1968), 119–121; A. S. V. Burgen, in *British Medical Journal* (1967), **3**, 621–622; and Mary Pickford in *Nature*, **215** (1967), 415. An appreciation of Verney's work in renal physiology is J. T. Fitzsimons and W. J. O'Connor, "E. B. Verney's Demonstration of 'The Antidiuretic Hormone and the Factors Which Determine Its Release,'" in *Journal of Physiology*, **263** (1976), 92P–93P. Verney's work on osmoreceptors is discussed in Carl W. Gottschalk, Robert W. Berliner, and Gerhard H. Giebisch, eds., *Renal Physiology: People and Ideas* (Bethesda, Md., 1987), 290–298.

JOHN E. LESCH

VERNOV, SERGEĬ NIKOLAEVICH (*b.* Sestroretsk, Russia, 11 July 1910; *d.* Moscow, U.S.S.R., 26 September 1982), *physics.*

Vernov's father, Nikolai Stepanovich, was a postal clerk, and his mother, Antonina Mikhailovna, taught mathematics at a secondary school.

In 1931 Vernov graduated from the Faculty of Physics and Mechanics of Leningrad Polytechnic Institute. He then began a fellowship at the Radium Institute in Leningrad; at the same time he was working in the Physico-Technical Institute. In 1936 Vernov defended his master's thesis and began a doctoral fellowship at the P. N. Lebedev Physics Institute in Moscow. In 1939 he defended his doctoral dissertation and in 1944 he became a professor at Moscow University. In 1946 Vernov moved to the Scientific Research Institute of Nuclear Physics of Moscow University, where, from 1960 until his death, he served as a director (a position that was previously occupied by D. V. Skobeltsyn, one of his teachers).

Vernov's first paper on cosmic rays appeared in 1934. It was followed by more than three hundred published papers, most of them written in collaboration with his pupils and colleagues, and all of them devoted to cosmic rays. He began his research at the aerological observatory in Pavlovsk (near Leningrad). In order to reduce the influence of atmosphere on the observations of cosmic rays, Vernov, following A. L. Wegener and others, suggested conducting investigations beyond the atmosphere:

he used radiosondes (earlier used by P. A. Molchanov for meteorological measurements) for his research in the stratosphere. In the spring of 1935 Vernov carried out his first experiments with spherical sondes filled with hydrogen, which carried the measuring equipment over eight miles (thirteen kilometers) high; the measurements were transmitted and received throughout the flight.

In later investigations in Armenia, an altitude of almost fourteen miles (twenty-two kilometers) was reached. In the late 1930's, somewhat later than similar work by R. A. Millikan and A. H. Compton, Vernov investigated the dependence of the flux of cosmic rays in the stratosphere on the latitude. His experiments with radiosondes launched at various latitudes showed that about 90 percent of the initial component of cosmic radiation consists of the charged particles whose energy spectrum Vernov had been measuring. Vernov (and, independently, Marcel Schein) suggested that these particles are protons.

During World War II, Vernov was involved in defense research and did not publish any work. Immediately after the war, however, his research work on cosmic rays was renewed. With the aid of complex equipment, Vernov examined the east-west asymmetry of cosmic ray flux and confirmed that the primary component consists of protons. In the late 1940's Vernov and his colleagues carried out important experiments on geophysical rockets, and in the 1950's they started investigations on space rockets. In 1958 Vernov, together with A. E. Chudakov, N. V. Pushkov, and S. Sh. Dolginov, discovered the earth's outer radiation belt at the altitude of about 12,500–37,500 miles (about 20,000–60,000 kilometers) from the center of the earth. (The inner radiation belt at an altitude of about 625 miles [1,000 kilometers] was discovered by Van Allen in the same year.) The measurements were made on the Electron and Cosmos satellites, and the results were confirmed by American investigators. Vernov suggested that the earth's magnetic trap captures the electrons generated in the course of neutron decay during nuclear reactions caused by cosmic rays in the atmosphere; he and his colleagues investigated the energy spectrum of these electrons.

In the late 1950's Vernov and his collaborators built apparatus for investigation of cosmic-ray particles of ultrahigh energy (up to 10^{17} eV); a break in the spectrum was discovered at energies of 10^{15} eV on their spectral intensity graph. According to Vernov this point is associated with the transition from the cosmic particles originating in our galaxy to the most energetic particles coming from the metagalaxy. On Vernov's initiative a group of observatories was created in the Soviet Union to continuously register cosmic radiation. He also established a correlation between the intensity of cosmic radiation and the eleven- and twenty-two-year cycles of solar activity.

In 1970 Vernov and his colleagues built a detector (20 sq km in area) to investigate extended atmospheric showers; they also examined particles whose energies reached 10^{20} eV.

Vernov initiated research on radiation safety during manned space flights. He also planned and carried out the first experiments on cosmic material technology in space.

Vernov was active in the U.S.S.R. Academy of Sciences, which elected him a corresponding member in 1953 and a full member in 1968. He served as a deputy secretary of the Division of Nuclear Physics of the Academy of Sciences and head of the council on cosmic rays. In 1949 he was awarded the State Prize and in 1960, the Lenin Prize. He also received the title Hero of Socialist Labor.

BIBLIOGRAPHY

I. ORIGINAL WORKS. "On the Study of Cosmic Rays at Great Altitudes," in *Physical Review*, **46** (1934), 822; "Radio-transmission of Cosmic Ray Data from the Stratosphere," in *Nature*, **135** (1935), 1072–1073; "Analysis of the Latitude Effect of Cosmic Rays in the Stratosphere," in *Doklady Akademii nauk SSSR*, n.s. **23** (1939), 140–142; "Opredeleniye znaka zaryada pervichnikh chastic kosmicheskikh luchei po izmereniyam azimutalnoi assimetrii v stratosphere v raiyone ekvatora" (Determination of the cosmic ray particles), *ibid.*, n.s. **68** (1949), 253–255, written with N. A. Dobrotin *et al.*; "The Study of Primary Cosmic Radiation with the Aid of Satellites," in *Proceedings of the Eighth International Astronautical Congress, Barcelona, 1957* (1958), written with V. L. Ginzburg *et al.*; "Investigations of Cosmic Radiation and of the Terrestrial Corpuscular Radiation by Means of Rockets and Satellites," in *Soviet Physics Uspekhi*, **3** (1960), 230–250, written with A. E. Chudakov; "Earth's Radiation Belt," in *Proceedings of the Ninth International Conference on Cosmic Rays, London, 1965*, I (London, 1966), 40–49, written with E. V. Gortchakov *et al.*; *Radiycionniye poaysa zemli i kosmicheskiye luchi* (Earth's radiation belts and cosmic rays; Moscow, 1970), written with N. V. Vakulov *et al.*

II. SECONDARY LITERATURE. N. L. Grigorov *et al.*, "Sergei Nikolaevich Vernov (on His Seventieth Birthday)," in *Soviet Physics Uspekhi*, **23** (1980), 426–428; *Spisok pechatnikh rabot akad. S. N. Vernova* (List of S. N. Vernov's papers; Moscow, 1980).

V. J. FRENKEL

VICKERY, HUBERT BRADFORD (*b*. Yarmouth, Nova Scotia, Canada, 28 February 1893; *d*. New Haven, Connecticut, 27 September 1978), *biochemistry*.

Vickery was the second son of Edgar Jenkins Vickery, owner of a book and stationery shop, and of Mary Katherine Dudman. He spent his entire career at the Connecticut Agricultural Experiment Station as an investigator of the chemicals present in plants, particularly organic acids and amino acids, and their role in plant metabolism. His interest in chemistry began in the seventh grade, when his father presented him with a copy of Steele's *Fourteen Weeks in Chemistry*. During his years at Yarmouth Academy he took all the science courses offered there and decided to become a chemist. At Dalhousie University he completed the rigorous honors course in chemistry in three years and became a high school science teacher in Halifax. That period came to an abrupt end in December 1917, when a munitions ship exploded in the harbor, damaging the school so badly that no teaching was possible for many weeks. In the meantime Vickery took an analytical position with Imperial Oil Company (1917–1919), doing commercial analyses.

Vickery obtained a science teaching position in the Provincial Normal School at Truro in 1919 while also doing research on water resources that earned him an M.S. at Dalhousie (1920). About this time Dalhousie called on him for emergency teaching when both of its chemistry teachers became incapacitated. His services were rewarded by an 1851 Exhibition scholarship that enabled him to undertake graduate studies in organic chemistry at Yale under Treat B. Johnson.

Through somewhat accidental circumstances Johnson loaned Vickery to Thomas B. Osborne of the Connecticut Agricultural Experiment Station for some chemical studies on proteins, particularly the distinction between peptide and amide nitrogen in protein hydrolysis. The report on this work was accepted as a dissertation for the Yale Ph.D., awarded by the chemistry department in 1922. Osborne then offered Vickery an assistant chemist position in the experiment station laboratory.

Since Osborne had been deeply involved for the last decade with nutrition studies in association with Yale's Lafayette B. Mendel, studies that were shedding light on the role of trace organic materials (vitamins) in animal nutrition, Vickery's first assignment was to isolate vitamin B from alfalfa leaves, known to be a rich source of the nutrient. Because of the rudimentary state of vitamin chemistry, the search was unproductive of its primary goal but initiated Vickery into a lifetime study of the chemistry of plant leaves.

During Vickery's first two years in the station laboratory, he was associated with A. C. Chibnall, who was on a two-year leave from Imperial College in London. The two men, both interested in leaf proteins, learned techniques from each other and established a lifelong friendship. Methods of separating and purifying nitrogenous organic materials were still primitive and depended on use of heavy metal salts (mercury, lead, silver) and phosphotungstic acid as precipitants. By improving and refining prior techniques, Chibnall and Vickery made substantial progress in isolating and studying proteins, smaller nitrogenous compounds, and organic acids in leaves. Although both men soon went their separate ways, each became a recognized leader in plant chemistry, Chibnall in the field of waxes and Vickery in the area of nitrogenous intermediates in plant metabolism.

In his work on protein-free plant extracts in the 1920's, Vickery showed free amino acids to be present in significant quantities, with asparagine generally dominant. Amino acids were also present as simple peptides. Other compounds of importance included purines, particularly adenine, in free form and as methylated bases such as stachydrine in alfalfa, choline in yeast, and nicotine in tobacco.

By 1928, when Osborne retired, it was decided that the alfalfa leaf had severe limitations and a decision was made to study tobacco, a plant with large leaves that were easily harvested without including masses of stems (as was the case with alfalfa). The leaf of the tobacco plant was the subject of intensive study during the next thirty years with the collaboration of Alfred J. Wakeman, Charles Leavenworth, George W. Pucher, and others at the station. An important aspect of the tobacco studies involved the development, with the aid of Chester Bliss, station statistician, of a statistically sound procedure for the sampling of leaves.

Vickery's laboratory also made extensive studies on the metabolism, in leaves, of organic acids: citric, isocitric, malic, succinic, fumaric, and glycolic. Several of his associates developed new analytical methods for measurement of these acids, which were studied not only in illuminated plants but also in plants cultured partly in darkness.

Attention was also directed to nomenclature of amino acids, particularly the standardization of symbols used in the representation of the configuration of groups on asymmetric carbon atoms and the direction of optical rotation.

Still another area of activity was the history of

chemistry, where Vickery contributed several studies of significance. The first was an investigation, with Osborne, of the succession of hypotheses dealing with the structure of proteins. This was followed by a study, with Carl Schmidt of the University of California, of the discovery of the several amino acids present in proteins.

From 1925 until his retirement in 1963, Vickery held an appointment on the Yale faculty and, each year, offered a course on the chemistry of proteins and amino acids. After retirement he remained involved in the activities of the Connecticut Agricultural Experiment Station, particularly in preservation of the historical specimens and records of the laboratory.

During World War II, Vickery was associated with the work of Edwin J. Cohn's Plasma Fractionation Laboratory at Harvard. In 1946 he was one of the scientists invited by the U.S. Navy to observe the atomic bomb explosion at Bikini. He was a member of numerous scientific committees and received many honors, including election to the National Academy of Sciences (1943) and the American Academy of Arts and Sciences (1948).

Vickery was married three times: in 1916 to Vera Claire Heustis, who died in 1936; in 1938 to Mildred Raye Hobbs, who died in 1968; and in 1971 to Jeanette Opsahl.

BIBLIOGRAPHY

I. ORIGINAL WORKS. Much of Vickery's research on plant chemistry was published in *Journal of Biological Chemistry* between 1922 and 1962. Works not published there include "A Review of Hypotheses of the Structure of Proteins," in *Physiological Review*, **8** (1928), 395–446, with T. B. Osborne; "The History of the Discovery of the Amino Acids," in *Chemical Review*, **9** (1931), 169–318, with C. L. A. Schmidt; "The Early Years of the Kjeldahl Method to Determine Nitrogen," in *Yale Journal of Biology and Medicine*, **18** (1946), 473–516; "The Origin of the Word 'Protein,'" *ibid.*, **22** (1950), 387–393; and "A Chemist Among Plants," in *Annual Review of Plant Physiology*, **23** (1972), 1–28, a scientific autobiography.

II. SECONDARY LITERATURE. Israel Zelitch, "Hubert Bradford Vickery," in *Biographical Memoirs, National Academy of Sciences*, **55** (1985), 473–504, includes a full bibliography of Vickery's publications. See also *McGraw-Hill Modern Men of Science*, II (New York, 1968), 567–569.

AARON J. IHDE

VINOGRAD, JEROME RUBEN (*b.* Milwaukee, Wisconsin, 9 February 1913; *d.* Pasadena, California, 3 July 1976), *physical biochemistry, molecular biology.*

Like many scientists who undertake research in interdisciplinary fields, Jerome Vinograd enjoyed a diverse education. Son of Oscar and Bertha Bernstein Vinograd, he attended the University of Minnesota for two years before leaving in 1931 to study colloid chemistry under Herbert Freundlich at the University of Berlin. After Freundlich emigrated to London in 1933, Vinograd continued his apprenticeship with him at University College for two more years. He then returned to the United States, where in 1937 he obtained an M.A. in organic chemistry under W. G. Young at the University of California at Los Angeles. The same year he married Sherna Shalett, with whom he had two daughters. Vinograd completed his graduate work at Stanford University, receiving a Ph.D. in physical chemistry in 1940 under J. W. McBain. He remained active all his life, despite major heart attacks in 1954 and 1969. He was elected to the National Academy of Sciences in 1968. Following the dissolution of his first marriage, he wed Dorothy Colodny in 1975.

Vinograd's early career (1941–1949) was spent as a research chemist for the Shell Development Company in Emeryville, California. As in his work with McBain, this period involved research in colloid chemistry: the behavior of detergents, the structure of micelles, and aspects of catalysis related to petroleum chemistry. Following a year with Shell's British subsidiary, Vinograd returned to academe in 1951 as a senior research fellow under Linus Pauling at the California Institute of Technology. There he continued his research on colloids, publishing a series of papers on the mechanism of gelation, but increasingly he focused his attention on the structure and properties of biological molecules, especially hemoglobin, myxomyosin, and microsomal nucleoprotein. In extending the scope of his research to proteins (and later to nucleic acids), Vinograd employed his training in physical and colloid chemistry to relate properties of viscosity and sedimentation to the molecular structure of biological components.

Vinograd remained on the faculty of Caltech until his death, receiving an appointment as professor of biology and chemistry in 1965 and subsequently being named to the Ethel Wilson Bowles and Robert Bowles chair in 1975. The bulk of his research was concerned with the theory and applications of the ultracentrifuge in biochemical research. In 1957, with Matthew Meselson and Franklin W. Stahl, Vinograd published a seminal paper on "density gradient centrifugation," in which gradations in the density of a cesium chloride solution subjected to a high centrifugal force could be used to resolve mixtures of components with small differences in molecular weight. This technique provided the first experimental verification of James D. Watson and Francis Crick's proposal that the process of DNA replication was semiconservative: Meselson and Stahl used ^{15}N-labeled DNA to show that the sedimentation rate of the daughter DNA duplex required that it contain one polynucleotide strand from the parent molecule. The buoyant density method quickly found widespread application in the characterization of nucleic acids and other macromolecules.

Vinograd continued to seek improved techniques for the ultracentrifuge. In 1959, with Meselson and Eugene Robkin, he developed an optical system for photographing the sedimentation bands in a rotating ultracentrifuge cell. He also introduced in 1963 the technique of "band sedimentation in self-generating density gradients," in which the material to be sedimented was layered as a thin band on top of the salt medium rather than initially being dispersed within the bulk solution; such an approach required smaller quantities of material and gave better results than the moving-boundary technique he had previously developed.

In addition to advancing separation technology, Vinograd contributed extensively to the understanding of the topological properties of the nucleic acids. In 1963, simultaneously with Renato Dulbecco and Marguerite Vogt, he and Roger Weil published the first report of closed circular DNA, isolated from the polyoma virus. From the change in sedimentation rate of viral DNA after it underwent one or more strand scissions, Vinograd subsequently deduced that the DNA must possess a locked-in, twisted structure, that is, the molecule exists as a "superhelix" with extra turns that cause it to be especially compact. In 1966, from a study of the unwinding of the supercoil in the presence of ethidium bromide, which intercalates between the bases, Vinograd formulated a relationship for describing the structure of circular DNA: the "topological winding number" is the sum of the "duplex winding number" and the "superhelix winding number" ($\alpha = \beta + \gamma$). Vinograd continued to focus on the properties and occurrence of circular DNA until his death. The terminology he developed became the standard nomenclature for describing the topology of nucleic acids.

Vinograd's career, like that of many pioneers in molecular biology, illustrates the intellectual and geographical migrations that often brought physical scientists into the province of biology. His studies of DNA, begun when he was more than forty years old and working in a subordinate position as a research fellow and later as a research associate at Caltech, reveal a senior scientist undertaking a radically different direction in his professional life. Vinograd's contributions to the technique and theory of nucleic acids bear witness to the success with which he applied his physicochemical background to the understanding of biological macromolecules.

BIBLIOGRAPHY

I. ORIGINAL WORKS. Vinograd published over one hundred research papers in journals such as *Proceedings of the National Academy of Sciences, Journal of Molecular Biology*, and *Journal of the American Chemical Society*. In particular, see "Equilibrium Sedimentation of Macromolecules in Density Gradients," in *Proceedings of the National Academy of Sciences*, **43** (1957), 581–588, written with M. Meselson and F. W. Stahl, and "The Cyclic Helix and Cyclic Coil Forms of Polyoma Viral DNA," *ibid.*, **50** (1963), 730–738, written with R. Weil. An autobiographical summary and a set of selected references are in "Centrifuges, Circles, and Cancer," in K. J. Mysels, C. M. Samour, and J. H. Hollister, eds., *Twenty Years of Colloid and Surface Chemistry: The Kendall Award Addresses* (Washington, D.C., 1973), 247–255. The Vinograd collection at the California Institute of Technology archives contains twenty-seven boxes of personal and scientific papers dealing primarily with his professional activities during the last twenty-five years of his life.

II. SECONDARY LITERATURE. For obituaries, see William R. Bauer in *Engineering and Science*, **40** (1976), 26–27; and Norman Davidson in *Nature*, **263** (1976), 178. A brief biography is in *McGraw-Hill Modern Scientists and Engineers*, III (New York, 1980), 256–257. A memorial issue of *Nucleic Acids Research*, **4**, no. 5 (1977), includes contributions from many former students and collaborators. For a more detailed discussion of Vinograd's contributions to the study of nucleic acids, see V. A. Bloomfield, D. M. Crothers, and I. Tinoco, Jr., *Physical Chemistry of Nucleic Acids* (New York, 1977).

WILLIAM J. HAGAN, JR.

VLERK, ISAÄK MARTINUS VAN DER (*b.* Utrecht, Netherlands, 31 January 1892; *d.* Leiden, Netherlands, 29 June 1974), *stratigraphy, paleontology.*

After completing primary and secondary education in his birthplace, Van der Vlerk studied geology at the University of Groningen (Netherlands) from 1914 to 1918 and continued his studies at the University of Basel (Switzerland). It was August Tobler, then in charge of the East Indian collections of the Basel

Natural History Museum, who determined Van der Vlerk's lifelong scientific interest. Guided by Tobler, a retired oil geologist, Van der Vlerk acquainted himself with foraminiferid paleontology. He returned to Groningen in 1920 to pass his final examination. He accepted a teaching position in biology at a grammar school, meanwhile continuing his work on the foraminifera in a collection of rock samples from Sumbawa (one of the Lesser Sunda Islands) lent to him by the Basel Museum. The results earned him a Ph.D. from the University of Leiden in 1922, with K. Martin as supervisor. His thesis clearly shows the feature that would characterize his work in the years to come: stratigraphical conclusions based on careful faunal analysis.

In the same year Van der Vlerk joined the Netherlands East Indies Mining Survey as a paleontologist in the exploration department. There he continued his studies of foraminiferid faunas, particularly aimed at establishing a stratigraphical scheme for the thick Tertiary succession. Eventually this led to the introduction, together with J. H. F. Umbgrove, of the letter classification. In its original form the letter classification was no more than an expedient to meet the needs of field geologists engaged in the systematic survey of the isles of Java and Sumatra. Six subdivisions based on larger foraminifera were distinguished, Tertiary a–f. In 1931 two additional units were introduced: Tertiary g and h, the latter roughly corresponding to Pliocene. A further refinement was reached with additional numbers (Tertiary a_1, a_2, and so on). As long as correlations with the European series and stages were not satisfactorily established, the letter classification fulfilled its purposes very well and remained widely used even after long-distance correlations based on planktonic foraminifera became available. Adams (1970) extended the letter classification to cover the entire tropical and subtropical Indo-West Pacific region.

In 1928 Van der Vlerk went to the University of Leiden as a curator of its geological collections and to lecture on paleontology and historical geology. His abilities were recognized by his promotion to a personal readership in 1931, to professor extraordinary in 1938, and finally to full professor in 1947.

During his early years in Leiden, Van der Vlerk's interest remained in Tertiary larger foraminifera, although its scope widened to include the other end of the Tethyan realm, resulting in several publications on Central America and northern South America, mostly by his pupils. The finds of fossil mammalian remains at excavation sites for large construction works turned his interest to the thick Pleistocene succession of the Netherlands. His 1938 inaugural

address as professor extraordinary on the Netherlands in the glacial epoch reflects this new interest. At first Van der Vlerk followed the classical subdivision of Penck and Brückner but soon became convinced that this scheme was unsatisfactory. In close collaboration with the paleobotanist F. Florschütz, he developed a regional subdivision in paleontologically characterized "stages" (1953). The principle of a regional classification, independent of any preconceived system of glacial-interglacial alternations, proved extremely fertile when it was later shown that the number of paleontologically recognizable climatic oscillations was much larger than originally assumed by Van der Vlerk and Florschütz.

The fourteenth William Smith lecture, delivered to the Geological Society of London in 1959, marks another shift in Van der Vlerk's scientific activity. In 1955 he had been charged with the directorship of the National Museum of Geology and Mineralogy at Leiden when it became a separate institution alongside the university's geology department. Although retaining his chair, he left his teaching duties to a reader in the department and divided his time between making the museum a national institution and a renewed study of Tertiary foraminifera.

From then on, Van der Vlerk's emphasis was upon detailed morphogenetic analysis of foraminifera. He retired early in 1961 from his chair and from the directorship in order to devote his remaining time and energy to this aspect of foraminiferid paleontology. In spite of failing health, he pursued his research, which led to the introduction of the "grade of enclosure" (1963), later replaced by the "degree of curvature" (1968). The latter is a more easily measured parameter of the same phenomenon, namely, the extent to which the second embryonic chamber (deuteroconch) encloses the first (protoconch) in the foraminiferid test. After comparing his results with those obtained with planktonic foraminifera, Van der Vlerk considered the "degree of curvature" as a yardstick against which the geologic age of specimens could be measured. He illustrated this in a series of papers, the last one published only a few months before his death.

Apart from his original contributions to science, which were recognized by his election to membership in the Royal Netherlands Academy of Sciences in 1950, Van der Vlerk wrote books for a larger public and contributed a number of articles to encyclopedias. Although unpretentious and kindhearted, he demonstrated the courage of his convictions, as is shown by his uncompromising attitude toward the German occupiers during World War II. As a university teacher he disliked formal lecture courses to large audiences and was at his best in the more informal contact with small groups of graduate students.

BIBLIOGRAPHY

I. ORIGINAL WORKS. Van der Vlerk's scientific papers through 1961 are listed in *Evolutionary Trends in Foraminifera: A Collection of Papers Dedicated to I. M. van der Vlerk on the Occasion of His 70th Birthday*, G. H. R. von Koenigswald *et al.*, eds. (Amsterdam, 1963), 5–8. His later papers are given in Thomas van der Hammen, "In Memoriam Prof. Dr. I. M. van der Vlerk," in *Geologie en mijnbouw*, **53** (1974), 241–243. His most significant papers include "Tertiaire gidsforaminiferen van Nederlandsch-Oost-Indië," in *Wetenschappelijke mededeelingen van de dienst van de mijnbouw in Nederlandsch-Oost-Indië*, **6** (1927), 1–35, written with J. H. F. Umbgrove; "The Tertiary," in *Leidsche geologische mededeelingen*, **5** (1931), 611–648, written with W. Leupold; "The Palaeontological Base of the Subdivision of the Pleistocene in the Netherlands," in *Verhandelingen der Koninklijke Nederlandsche akademie van wetenschappen*, Afdeeling natuurkunde, eerste reeks, **20**, no. 2 (1953), 1–58, written with F. Florschütz; "Problems and Principles of Tertiary and Quaternary Stratigraphy" (fourteenth William Smith lecture), in *Quarterly Journal of the Geological Society of London*, **115** (1959), 49–63; "Biometric Research on Lepidocyclina," in *Micropaleontology*, **9** (1963), 425–426; "Stratigraphie du Tertiaire des domaines indo-pacifique et mesogéen, essai de correlation," in *Proceedings of the Koninklijke Nederlandse Akademie van Wetenschappen*, ser. B, **69** (1966), 336–344; "Oligo-Miocene Lepidocyclinas and Planktonic Foraminifera from East Java and Madura, Indonesia," *ibid.*, ser. B, **70** (1967), 391–398, written with J. A. Postuma; "Two Methods of Worldwide Correlation," in *Micropaleontology*, **14** (1968), 334–338; "Evolution of an Embryo," in *Genetica*, **39** (1968), 45–63, written with H. Gloor; "An Improved Method for Biometrical Research," in *Proceedings of the Koninklijke Nederlandse Akademie van Wetenschappen*, ser. B, **76** (1973), 245–259.

II. SECONDARY LITERATURE. In addition to the obituary by Thomas van der Hammen listed above, see R. Lagaaij, "Professor Van der Vlerk: An Appreciation," in *Evolutionary Trends in Foraminifera: A Collection of Papers Dedicated to I. M. van der Vlerk on the Occasion of His 70th Birthday*, G. H. R von Koenigswald *et al.*, eds. (Amsterdam, 1963), 1–4; E. den Tex, "Levensbericht van Isaäk Martinus van der Vlerk," in *Akademie van wetenschappen, Jaarboek 1974* (1975), 190–195. An account of Van der Vlerk's role in the National Museum of Geology and Mineralogy is in G. E. de Groot, "Rijksmuseum van Geologie en Mineralogie 1878–1978, A Retrospect," in *Scripta geologica*, **48** (1978), 3–25. A review of the origin and subsequent development of the letter classification is given by C. G. Adams, "A Reconsideration of the East Indian Letter Classification of the Tertiary," in *Bulletin of the British Museum (Natural History), Geology*, **19** (1970), 85–137.

AART BROUWER

WAGER, LAURENCE RICKARD (*b.* Batley, Yorkshire, England, 5 February 1904; *d.* London, England, 20 November 1965), *geology, geochemistry.*

L. R. Wager's parents were from the south of England although he himself was born in Batley, Yorkshire, and always thought of himself as a Yorkshireman. His father, Morton Ethelred Wager, was Cornish and his mother, Adelina Wager, née Rickard, came from Surrey. His father was headmaster of the Hebden Bridge Secondary School, which Wager attended until he was sixteen. From 1920 to 1923 he attended grammar school in Leeds, and then went to Pembroke College, Cambridge, on an open scholarship. In 1934 Wager married Phyllis Margaret Worthington, who gave him every support in his scientific work and took part in the overwintering expedition in East Greenland, during which his most important fieldwork was carried out. The Wagers had two sons and three daughters. Wager was a fellow of the Geological Society of London and a recipient of its Lyell Fund in 1939, Bigsby Medal in 1945, and Lyell Medal in 1962. He served as a vice president of the society in the years 1951–1953 and was elected to the Royal Society in 1946. In addition, he was awarded the Spendiarov Prize at the Eighteenth International Geological Congress in London in 1948, was president of the Mineralogical Society in the years 1960–1963, and was awarded the Polar Medal in 1933 and the Mungo Park Medal of the Royal Geographical Society in 1936. He was instrumental in starting *Geochimica et cosmochimica acta* in 1950 and *Journal of Petrology* in 1960, both of which are regarded as the leading journals in their respective fields.

Wager began his scientific career after graduation from Cambridge in 1926, where he obtained first-class honors in geology. At that time the geology department included Alfred Harker, the reader in petrology, and C. E. Tilley, both of whom undoubtedly had a major influence on Wager's subsequent scientific interests. It also seems clear that another important ingredient in the shaping of his latter life was his boyhood in the Yorkshire dales and the fact that while at school in Leeds he lived with his uncle, who was a botanist and a fellow of the Royal Society.

Wager's early work concerned metasomatism at the margin of a basic sill, joint patterns and tectonics in the limestones of northern England, and the beginnings of a regional study near Galway in Eire, but it was while employed at Reading University that he joined the British Arctic Air Route Expedition, which spent 1930 and 1931 in the Angmagssalik area of East Greenland. On this expedition he made important geological observations of regional interest, took part in some epic sledge journeys into the interior, and attempted to climb the area's highest peak. On this expedition the basis of his most significant research was laid and he returned to the area four times subsequently: in 1932 as part of the Scoresby Sound Committee's Second East Greenland Expedition, in 1934 on board the ship *Pourquoi Pas?*, and in the years 1935–1936 and 1953 as leader of his own expeditions. During the 1935–1936 overwintering expedition, fieldwork was carried out on the Skaergaard intrusion, with which his name (along with that of W. A. Deer) has become inextricably associated for subsequent generations of geologists.

East Greenland has an incomparably rugged terrain, extremely demanding of those who conduct fieldwork there without the benefit of powerful ships and helicopters, such as are available today. Wager was unusually well equipped to operate in such an area, having been a leading figure in the Cambridge University Mountaineering Club and having taken part in the attempt on Everest in 1933, when he and Wynn Harris reached a height only surpassed twenty years later by Hillary and Tenzing, who used oxygen, as Wager and Wynn Harris had not.

The Everest interlude demonstrates two features of Wager's personality that permeated his scientific career: he was capable of immense persistence and his mind never ceased to question the origins of the landscapes about him. He subsequently published a paper on the Yo Ri and Arun gorges and the uplift of the Himalayas that has become a classic. His love of mountaineering was doubtless also a powerful factor in determining his continued interest in East Greenland geology.

Wager is most well known for his work on layered igneous intrusions. The memoir on the Skaergaard igneous intrusion published in 1939 by Wager and Deer was based on fieldwork conducted during the 1935–1936 expedition, fieldwork which has stood the test of time and has proved to be essentially correct. In this work one of the fundamental problems of igneous petrology, the question of how a basaltic magma differentiates in nature under closed system conditions, was addressed. Detailed studies by N. L.

Bowen at Princeton had earlier established how basaltic magmas fractionated under experimental conditions. Wager and Deer's study was the first detailed field investigation and was eagerly received because of the light it threw on the origin of granites, a long-standing controversy. This memoir also awakened much interest in similar layered bodies, such as Bushveld in South Africa, Stillwater in Montana, and Muskox in Canada. Skaergaard has remained the best investigated of these bodies and is a standard subject in all igneous petrology texts.

During this period (1929 to 1939) Wager was a lecturer at Reading University, but shortly after the outbreak of World War II in 1939 he was commissioned into the Royal Air Force, serving in the United Kingdom, the Middle East, and Arctic Russia, and was mentioned in dispatches. In 1944 he was released from the R.A.F. and took the chair of geology at Durham University, a post which he held until 1950, when he was made professor of geology at Oxford and fellow of University College.

Wager conducted other important pieces of research in East Greenland and in the Hebrides of northwest Scotland, but subsequent to his active service during the war years, he embarked on extensive geochemical studies and introduced radiometric dating methods into the department at Oxford. This work actually was begun before the war in collaboration with R. L. Mitchell, who used emission spectroscopy for the determination of trace elements. Wager and his coworkers subsequently used neutron activation and isotope dilution in an attempt to document in the very greatest detail and highest precision the behavior of a host of trace elements during magmatic crystallization. Also under Wager's leadership, Oxford began to date rocks using radiometric methods. While Wager sought to understand the processes going on in magmas, others have used the same methods to understand the ocean floor and the moon, samples of both becoming available during the 1960's and in 1970. The earlier work of Wager and his co-workers thus paved the way for later explosive growth in trace element and isotope geochemistry.

Wager always resisted the temptation to go into experimental studies, which in the 1950's were popular among igneous petrologists. He always considered himself an observer of nature and found enough to occupy himself in this role. His perseverance as a mountain climber reflects itself in his scientific work in his single-minded pursuit of specific goals to be achieved using specific methods. In this way, although he was a man of wide interests, he avoided the temptation to spread his efforts too widely and became a leader in his chosen field.

BIBLIOGRAPHY

More extensive treatment of Wager's life and scientific contributions and a list of publications are given by C. K. Brooks in "Geologists and Ideas," in E. T. Drake and W. M. Jordan, eds., *Geological Society of America, Centennial Special Volume*, I (1985), 237–250; and W. A. Deer in *Biographical Memoirs of Fellows of the Royal Society*, **13** (1967), 359–385.

C. K. BROOKS

WAKSMAN, SELMAN ABRAHAM (*b.* Novaya Priluka, Russia, 22 July 1888; *d.* Woods Hole, Massachusetts, 16 August 1973), *microbiology, soil science, pharmacology.*

The Early Years. Selman Abraham Waksman, winner of the 1952 Nobel Prize in physiology and medicine, spent his childhood and early youth in Novaya Priluka, in the Kiev region of the Ukraine. Novaya Priluka was a small Jewish town resembling many others in the so-called pale of settlement, located twenty miles from Vinnitsa (population four thousand) and two hundred miles from Kiev. It was surrounded by Ukrainian peasant hamlets in a black soil (chernozem) steppe devoted to the cultivation of wheat, rye, barley, and oats. The area was owned by Polish and Russian landlords (*pomiestchiki*) and Russians served as teachers, inspectors, and police (the cossacks). The town was annihilated during the German invasion of the Ukraine in World War II.

Waksman was brought up in a matriarchate dominated by his grandmother, Eva London; his mother, Fradia; and seven aunts. His father, Jacob, a weaver of fiber chair coverings, spent time in the prayer house and taught him about the Bible and the Talmud. In what came as a severe shock to the impressionable youngster, his little sister, Miriam, died of diphtheria when he was nine years old, well after the discovery of diphtheria antitoxin. He was schooled in a traditional Hebrew heder until age nine, had private tutors from that age on, and became bar mitzvah at thirteen. He then attended gymnasium (a government Latin school) in Zhitomir, the capital of Volhynia, and later in Odessa, finally passing the examinations in 1910.

Waksman's qualities as a teacher and socially responsible individual were expressed early. With three like-minded youngsters between the ages of twelve and sixteen, he organized a school for underprivileged children, teaching Hebrew and Russian grammar, writing, arithmetic, and history. He also formed a group of boys to care for the sick. Later Waksman belonged to chess, literary, and other clubs. Finally, during the Russo-Japanese War (1904–1905) and the accompanying 1905 Revolution, when the police and cossacks were responsible for repeated pogroms and many towns were pillaged, he helped organize a Jewish youth defense group and learned the use of weapons.

Waksman left Russia after his mother's death in 1909 and his passing of the final gymnasium examinations. The choices that the young emigrant was considering included Switzerland, the United States, and South America. He chose the United States, where he had relatives. Accompanied by Peisi Mitnik, the most important companion of his youth, he landed in Philadelphia on 2 November 1910 and went to live in Metuchen, New Jersey, on a farm owned by a cousin, Mendel Cornblatt, originally a bookbinder, from whom he learned scientific farming (Waksman, 1954).

Waksman attended Rutgers College from 1911 to 1915, receiving a B.S. in 1915 and an M.S. in 1916. The crucial decision to enter an agricultural rather than a medical course was guided by Dr. Jacob G. Lipman, a bacteriologist who was dean of the College of Agriculture and himself an immigrant from Russia (Waksman, 1966). Courses in bacteriology with Lipman and summer projects with Dr. Byron David Halsted, a plant nutritionist and geneticist, helped to define Waksman's future career. He carried out his master's project at the New Jersey Agricultural Experiment Station, the institution where he spent essentially his entire scientific life, studying soil fungi and especially soil actinomycetes, organisms almost entirely neglected by others that became a mainstay of his subsequent work. His first public presentation, with R. E. Curtis, another graduate student, was "Bacteria, Actinomycetes, and Fungi of the Soil," to the Society of American Bacteriologists at Urbana, Illinois, in December 1915.

Waksman obtained a Ph.D. in biochemistry in two years, working with T. Brailsford Robertson at the University of California at Berkeley, and returned to Rutgers as a lecturer in soil microbiology in 1918.

Throughout his college and graduate studies, Waksman supported himself by scholarships and by a series of jobs: as a Sunday caretaker and night watchman, as a tutor of English and various scientific subjects, later as head of the biochemistry department at the Cutter Laboratories, and even by summer work on a ranch near Sacramento. During his first two years as an instructor at Rutgers, he worked one day a week at the experiment station and five days a week at the Takamine Laboratory in Clifton, New Jersey (producing fungal diastatic and proteolytic enzymes and running toxicity tests on Salvarsan).

Waksman married his childhood sweetheart, Bertha Deborah Mitnik (Bobili), on 4 August 1916. She went with him to California, and they returned to live in New York for two years before settling permanently in New Brunswick, New Jersey, close to Rutgers, in 1921. Their only child, Byron Halsted, was born 15 September 1919. Bobili accompanied her increasingly famous husband on his many trips. Byron attended the University of Pennsylvania Medical School and later pursued an academic career as a research immunologist and teacher.

Humus, Enzymes, and Soil Microbiology. The first phase of Waksman's research as a full-fledged university scientist dealt with the extension of his work on actinomycetes and with organisms involved in sulfur oxidation. He regarded the isolation of *Thiobacillus thiooxidans* (Waksman and Joffe, 1922) during that period as his most important scientific discovery before the antibiotics.

Waksman's early work on actinomycetes and sulfur transformations was carried out with Jacob S. Joffe and later continued with Robert L. Starkey, who became a lifelong associate and friend, and with an ever-changing group of graduate students and postdoctoral fellows.

Waksman and his colleagues developed standardized methods of evaluating microbial populations in soil samples and initiated studies of the decomposition of organic residues in soils and composts to form humus. The study of the nature, distribution, and properties of the microorganisms, and their effects on the structure and the physical and chemical properties of the soils they inhabit, dominated research in his laboratory for the next twenty years.

During this period Waksman developed a worldwide network of friends, prominent among them Sergei N. Winogradsky of the Pasteur Institute; Sir John Russell and Marjorie Stephenson of the Rothamsted Experiment Station, from whom he received his first exchange student in 1924; and Martinus Willem Beijerinck of Holland. He also began a consultative relationship with many industrial concerns that produced enzymes, vitamins, and other products from fungal and bacterial sources. This led to cooperative interactions that contributed significantly to Waksman's antibiotic work after 1940.

His first book, *Enzymes*, dates from work done during this early period (Waksman and Davison, 1926).

In 1924 Waksman and his family made a prolonged trip to Europe, with attendance at the International Conference on Soil Science in Rome and a grand tour of microbiological and soil laboratories in many countries, as well as his first return visit to Russia, now the Soviet Union. On his return home, he wrote a comprehensive review, "Soil Microbiology in 1924," a precursor of his famous book *Principles of Soil Microbiology* (1927).

Scientific research in the Waksman laboratory continued after 1924 at an accelerated pace, as his group of graduate students and postdoctoral fellows grew larger and became more cosmopolitan. Waksman now devoted himself more and more to the organizational aspects of science, as represented by editorial and society activities and a variety of national and international meetings. He made trips to Europe in 1929, 1930, 1933, 1935, and 1938 and to the Holy Land in 1938, and carried out systematic studies of peat bogs and composts throughout the United States, Europe, and the Middle East. Among the results of this activity were *The Soil and the Microbe* (1931), *Humus* (1936), and several other books. He also became an adviser on the commercial development of composts, particularly for mushroom growers.

In 1931 Waksman developed a laboratory for the study of marine microbiology at the newly constructed Oceanographic Institute in Woods Hole, Massachusetts (WHOI), where he and some of his students worked each summer over the next twelve years. Waksman became a WHOI trustee in 1945. In the last several years of Waksman's summer work there, in collaboration with the United States Navy, the laboratory studied the fouling of ship bottoms. This project, a contribution to the war effort, was terminated after World War II. Other projects sought to develop means of protecting materials against tropical deterioration owing to microbial action and to find substitutes for agar for use in microbiology laboratories. Waksman's last and most important prewar contribution to have a profound and lasting influence on human affairs was the development of simplified methods for obtaining antibiotics and the discovery of streptomycin (Waksman, 1975).

The Antibiotics. In 1939 Waksman and his colleagues undertook a systematic effort to identify soil organisms producing soluble substances that might be useful in the control of infectious disease. In 1941 he proposed to restrict the meaning of the word "antibiotics" to microbial products with antimicrobial properties. Together with the sulfonamide drugs, antibiotics have effectively eliminated the threat of fatal bacterial infections from the developed world.

The reasons that led Waksman to initiate this program included the discovery of tyrothricin by his former student René Dubos in 1939; his own profound knowledge of all classes of soil microbes and the biochemical and manipulative skills acquired over the previous quarter century; his great familiarity with the actinomycetes, the microorganisms that proved to be the producers of most antibiotics later isolated; and the threat of World War II.

Working with few resources, guiding graduate students and postdoctoral fellows, Waksman developed and applied simple screening techniques to a variety of samples of soil and other natural materials. Within a decade ten antibiotics were isolated and characterized, three of them with important clinical applications: actinomycin (Waksman and Woodruff, 1940); streptomycin (Schatz, Bugie, and Waksman, 1944); and neomycin (Waksman and Lechevalier, 1949). Eighteen antibiotics were discovered under his general direction (Lechevalier, 1980).

Merck and Company, located in Rahway, New Jersey, supported Waksman's laboratory in its study of microbial antagonisms; in exchange it had the right to patent discoveries in this field coming from his laboratory. It was agreed that Merck would pay Rutgers University 2.5 percent royalties on the sales of bulk products that might be derived from such inventions. When it became obvious that streptomycin was a most important product, Merck generously agreed to transfer its rights to Rutgers University, which licensed a number of companies to manufacture the antibiotic. By 1946 two investigators at the Mayo Clinic, H. Corwin Hinshaw and William H. Feldman, established its curative activity in guinea pig tuberculosis (Hinshaw, 1954). The first clinical trials in human tuberculosis began in 1945. Waksman, as a nonmedical scientist, was overwhelmed by the medical implications of his discovery, particularly in tuberculous meningitis of children (Waksman, 1965; Comroe, 1978).

The Postwar Period. At the end of World War II, Waksman traveled to the Soviet Union with the double purpose of trying to establish effective mechanisms of scientific exchange and of helping establish methods of producing antibiotics. There were numerous later trips and meetings with well-wishers of every description, from Pope Pius XI and Emperor Hirohito of Japan to Marshal Tito of Yugoslavia and General Franco of Spain. The crowning event among all these was his trip to Sweden in 1952 to receive the Nobel Prize in physiology and medicine for the discovery of streptomycin.

Another accomplishment of the postwar period was, following the wishes of Waksman, the assignment in 1951 by the Rutgers Research Educational Foundation of most of the royalties received from the sale of streptomycin and neomycin to the creation and support of the Institute of Microbiology at Rutgers University. This institute provided research facilities for over 100 scientists and technicians, and Waksman became its first director. Today it is known as the Waksman Institute of Microbiology, and it remains a thriving establishment (Lechevalier, 1982). Part of the royalty funds were used in setting up the Foundation for Microbiology, which since its inception in 1951 has supported courses, lectureships, exchange programs, minority fellowships, and prizes in microbiologic and related research areas. In France and Japan similar Waksman Foundations, also funded from industrial royalties, began to support research in microbiology.

Waksman as a Scientist. While research on antibiotics, started in 1939, became the dominant theme of Waksman's later scientific career and the source of his fame for the world at large, his earlier work as a soil microbiologist had made him a towering figure among scientists well before that time. The successive phases of his research culminated in a series of classic volumes or papers on enzymes, humus, peats, and soil microorganisms, and finally on the antibiotics, streptomycin and neomycin in particular (Waksman, 1945). His scholarship as a scientist and teacher was embodied in a massive compendium, the second edition of his *Principles of Soil Microbiology,* published in 1932. This book, refused by many publishers who could not believe that it had a market, became a best-seller and dominated the field for several decades. He later wrote biographies of two of his scientific heroes: Winogradsky, a lifelong friend he regarded as the true founder of soil microbiology (Waksman, 1953), and W. M. W. Haffkine, a Jewish scientist whose contributions some decades earlier were turned into tragedy by bigotry and persecution (Waksman, 1964).

Academic recognition came to Waksman first with his promotion to associate professor in 1925 and to professor in 1929. Professional recognition also came in other forms. In 1927 he was made responsible for organizing the program of the first International Congress of Soil Science in Washington (ten days followed by a one-month excursion throughout the

United States and Canada), and he helped establish the Commission on Soil Microbiology, of which he soon became president. Additional congresses took place in Leningrad and Moscow (1930) and Great Britain (1935), and he played a central role in each, as he did in the International Congress of Microbiology at New York (1939). Waksman shortly afterward became chairman of the War Committee on Bacteriology, under the aegis of the Society of American Bacteriologists (now the American Society for Microbiology). He was elected president of this society in 1941.

Only one prize came Waksman's way in the early years: the Nitrate of Soda Nitrogen Research Award in 1929. However, after 1940 awards and honors were showered on him, including honorary degrees ranging from law to medicine, from some twenty universities throughout the world; honorary memberships in a variety of organizations; and medals of scientific societies all over the world, culminating with the Nobel Prize and the Star of the Rising Sun, bestowed on him by the emperor of Japan. Other notable honors included membership in the U.S. National Academy of Sciences; the Legion of Honor (Commander) of France; the Order of the Southern Cross (Commendatore) of Brazil; the Grand Cross of Public Health of Spain; corresponding membership (later foreign associate) of the French Academy of Sciences; the Lasker Award; the Amory Award of the American Academy of Arts and Sciences; and the Trudeau Medal of the (U.S.) National Tuberculosis Association (Woodruff, 1968).

Waksman was an extraordinary scholar and bibliophile. Not only was he author or coauthor of over 400 scientific papers and various obituaries and reviews, as well as twenty-eight books, but he was also an inveterate collector of books. He became a specialist in Judaica, in books of autobiography and personal philosophy by leading scientists, and in political and other forms of caricature over the last two centuries. After his death these collections became major holdings at Brandeis University, the Burndy Science Library, and the Sterling Library of Yale University, respectively. In his professional life Waksman played many roles. He was an experimental scientist, a theoretician, an applied scientist, a popularizer, a scholar, and a teacher.

In his autobiography, *My Life with the Microbes* (1954), Waksman pays tribute to the microorganisms that remained his consuming passion for six decades, literally until the day of his death. He spoke often of the "teeming earth," with its soil organisms growing in root nodules and in dead residues to form humus. He noted the beneficent role of mi-

croorganisms in the production of cheese, wine, vinegar, enzymes, vitamins, and a variety of industrial products—as well as their nefarious role in destroying clothing, contaminating water and foods, and infecting man, other animals, and plants. Waksman contrasted the suffering during mass migrations, such as the Irish potato famine, resulting from the action of microbes, with the welfare associated with the positive "chemical warfare" made possible by the antibiotics. He studied soils, manure piles, and the sea, and he investigated all the forms of microbial life in these environments: bacteria, actinomycetes, molds (fungi), and even protozoa, both as isolated pure cultures and in the mixed populations occurring naturally. Perhaps his most famous remark, to a student, was "Young man, there is romance even in a manure pile!"

Waksman manufactured a quasi-biblical quotation, "Out of the earth shall come thy salvation," that scholars have identified as an abbreviated form of "The Lord created medicines out of the earth, and he that is wise shall not abhor them" (Apocrypha). His idiosyncratic version of the quotation appears on the simple stone that marks his grave in a churchyard in Woods Hole where many of his scientific peers are buried.

BIBLIOGRAPHY

I. ORIGINAL WORKS. "*Thiobacillus thiooxidans*, a New Sulfur-Oxidizing Organism Isolated from the Soil," in *Journal of Bacteriology*, **7** (1922), 239–256, with J. S. Joffe; *Enzymes: Properties, Distribution, Methods and Applications* (Baltimore, 1926), with W. C. Davison; *Principles of Soil Microbiology* (Baltimore, 1927; 2nd ed., 1932); *The Soil and the Microbe* (New York, 1931), with R. L. Starkey; *Humus: Origin, Chemical Composition and Importance in Nature* (Baltimore, 1936; 2nd ed., 1938; Russian trans., 1938); "Bacteriostatic and Bactericidal Substances Produced by a Soil Actinomyces," in *Proceedings of the Society of Experimental Biological Medicine*, **45** (1940), 609–614, with H. B. Woodruff; "Streptomycin, a Substance Exhibiting Antibiotic Activity Against Gram-Positive and Gram-Negative Bacteria," *ibid.*, **55** (1944), 66–69, with A. Schatz and E. Bugie; *Microbial Antagonisms and Antibiotic Substances* (New York, 1945); "Neomycin, a New Antibiotic Active Against Streptomycin-Resistant Bacteria, Including Tuberculosis Organisms," in *Science*, **109** (1949), 305–307, with H. A. Lechevalier; *Sergei Nikolaevitch Winogradsky: The Story of a Great Bacteriologist* (New Brunswick, N.J., 1953); *My Life with the Microbes* (New York, 1954); *The Brilliant and Tragic Life of Waldemar Haffkine* (New Brunswick, N.J., 1964); *The Conquest of Tuberculosis* (Berkeley, Calif., 1965); *Jacob G. Lipman, Agricultural Scientist and Humanitarian* (New Brunswick, N.J., 1966); and *The*

Antibiotic Era: A History of Antibiotics and of Their Role in the Conquest of Infectious Diseases . . . (Tokyo, 1975).

II. SECONDARY LITERATURE. V. Bryson, "Selman A. Waksman (1888–1973)," in *ASM News*, **40** (1974), 651–658; J. H. J. Comroe, "Pay Dirt: The Story of Streptomycin," in *American Review of Respiratory Disease*, **117** (1978), 773–781, 957–968; H. C. Hinshaw, "Historical Notes on Earliest Use of Streptomycin in Clinical Tuberculosis," in *American Review of Tuberculosis*, **70** (1954), 9–14; Hubert A. Lechevalier, "The Search for Antibiotics at Rutgers University," in John Parascandola, ed., *The History of Antibiotics: A Symposium* (Madison, Wis., 1980), and *The Development of Applied Microbiology at Rutgers Waksman Institute of Microbiology* (New Brunswick, N.J., 1982); A. Sakula, "Selman Waksman (1888–1973), Discoverer of Streptomycin: A Centenary Review," in *British Journal of Diseases of the Chest*, **82** (1988), 23–31; "Selman Abraham Waksman," in *Nature*, **246** (1973), 367; and H. B. Woodruff, *Scientific Contributions of Selman A. Waksman* (New Brunswick, N.J., 1968).

BYRON H. WAKSMAN
HUBERT A. LECHEVALIER

WALTHER, JOHANNES (*b*. Neustadt-Orla, Germany, 20 July 1860; *d*. Hofgastein, Germany, 4 May 1937), *geology*.

Walther was the son of Kuno Walther, an evangelical clergyman, and his wife, Marianne Louise Schwabe Walther. He was educated in Dermbach-Rhön and in Eisenach. In 1879 he entered the University of Jena, where he studied biology and anatomy with E. A. Strasburger, Ernst Stahl, and Oscar and Richard Hertwig. His studies were much influenced by Ernst Haeckel. In 1882 he received the doctorate with a dissertation titled "Die Entwicklung der Deckknochen am Kopfskelett des Hechtes." He then studied geology at the universities of Leipzig (with Hermann Credner and Ferdinand Zirkel) and Munich (with Wilhelm von Gümbel and Karl von Zittel). One of his mentors was Ferdinand von Richthofen. In 1886 Walther qualified as *Privatdozent* at Jena, where he was named Ernst Haeckel professor of geology and paleontology (1894). The nomination for the chair of geology and paleontology at the University of Halle followed in 1906. He retired in 1929 and spent his last years in Halle. His ashes were buried in the Walther family vault at Eisenach (Thuringia).

Walther, who belonged to the tradition of scientific travelers, created the bases of his biofacial and sedimentological investigations during his numerous journeys. During his first stay at the Zoological Station of Naples in 1883, he studied the habits of sea creatures by examining the sediments of their habitats. He realized the importance of observing the origin of recent sediments in order to understand fossil rocks. Walther continued his studies of recent biotopes in the Bay of Naples (1885), in southern Sweden (1886), on the shores of the Red Sea (1887), and on the coasts of Ceylon (1888–1889). These and other observations, including the results of the *Challenger* expedition (which he studied at Edinburgh in 1888), prepared him to write his books *Allgemeine Meereskunde* (1893) and *Einleitung in die Geologie als historische Wissenschaft* (1893–1894).

Walther was one of the founders of dynamic sedimentology, which he called lithogenesis. As author of the law of correlation of facies, he was one of the first geologists to present a thorough discussion of the concept of facies. He also formulated the modern concept of diagenesis and was one of the founders of paleoecology. Walther claimed that the most satisfying explanations of the genesis of ancient phenomena were analogies to modern geological processes, calling this actualistic assertion the ontological method. He wrote: "I persist in trying to investigate the events of the past through modern phenomena. From existence we explain genesis" (*Einleitung*, p. xii). His synthesis of marine ecology contained a clearly enunciated law of correlation of biotopes, a parallel to the law of correlation of facies. These laws mean that only those biotopes, facies, or sediments can follow each other in time which adjoin one another in space at the present time.

Walther was also one of the first geologists to study fossil deserts, having become interested in them through Georg Schweinfurth, with whom he traversed the Nubian Desert in 1887. Later, Walther traveled in the arid regions of Arizona and southern California (1891), the Central Asian deserts of Turkestan (1897), the Libyan Desert (1911), and the Western Australian Desert (1914). He described his experiences and observations in, for example, *Das Gesetz der Wüstenbildung in Gegenwart und Vorzeit* (1900).

Although Walther was artistically talented and an excellent orator, his scientific publications were not in the style of his time and thus were little known abroad. He was highly esteemed by the public, however, often lecturing on his numerous expeditions. He was able to present facts clearly and convincingly, and he was an excellent teacher. He was actively involved in training teachers of geology and wrote popular books, including *Geologie Deutschlands* (1910), *Geologie der Heimat* (1918), and *Das deutsche Landschaftsbild im Wandel der Zeiten* (1933). Walther also dealt with the scientific work of Geothe, editing the monograph *Goethe als Seher und Erforscher der Natur* (1930). His last publication was *Mediterranis: Geobiologische Untersuchungen über Gestaltung und Besiedlung des mediterranen Lebensraumes* (1936).

Walther was honored in his day, although his name is not well known to later generations of stratigraphers and sedimentologists. He became a member of the Leopoldina in 1892, a corresponding fellow of the Geological Society of London in 1896, a member of the Royal Society of Scientists of Moscow in 1897, an honorary member of the Hungarian Geographical Society in 1922, and an honorary member of the Geological Society of Vienna in 1923. He received honorary doctorates from the University of Melbourne in 1914 and from the Medical Faculty of the University of Halle in 1925. In 1924 he was elected president of the Leopoldina.

BIBLIOGRAPHY

I. ORIGINAL WORKS. *Allgemeine Meereskunde* (Jena, 1893); *Einleitung in die Geologie als historische Wissenschaft*, 3 vols. (Jena, 1893–1894); *Das Gesetz der Wüstenbildung in Gegenwart und Vorzeit* (Berlin, 1900; 4th ed., Leipzig, 1924); *Geologie Deutschlands: Eine Einführung in die erklärende Landschaftskunde für Lehrende und Lernende* (Leipzig, 1910; 4th ed., 1923); *Geologie der Heimat: Grundlinien geologischer Anschauung* (Leipzig, 1918; 3rd ed., 1926); *Bau und Bildung der Erde. Ein Grundriss der Geologie und ihre Anwendung im heimatkundlichen Unterricht* (Leipzig, 1925); *Allgemeine Paläontologie, Geologische Fragen in biologischer Betrachtung* (Berlin, 1919; 2nd ed., Berlin, 1927); as editor, *Goethe als Seher und Erforscher der Natur* (Halle, 1930); *Das deutsche Landschaftsbild im Wandel der Zeiten: Eine Einführung in die Geologie Deutschlands* (Lepzig, 1933); and *Mediterranis: Geobiologische Untersuchungen über Gestaltung und Besiedlung des mediterranen Lebensraumes* (Gotha, 1936).

II. SECONDARY LITERATURE. K. Beurlen, "Die Bedeutung der organischen Entwicklung für die Erdgeschichte," in *Nova acta Leopoldina*, 5 (1938), 369–391; K. von Bülow, "Johannes Walther, der Begründer der Biogeologie," in *Berichte der geologischen Gesellschaft der DDR*, 6 (1962), 373–382, with portrait and bibliography; E. Grumbt, "Johannes Walther, ein Begründer der modernen Sedimentforschung," in *Zeitschrift für geologische Wissenschaften*, 3 (1975), 1255–1263; Gerard V. Middleton, "Johannes Walther's Law of the Correlation of Facies," in *Geological Society of America, Bulletin*, 84 (1973), 979–988; E. C. Quereau, "Review of *Einleitung in die Geologie als historische Wissenschaft* by Johannes Walther," in *Journal of Geology*, 2 (1894), 856–860;

I. Seibold, "Anfänge der deutschen Meeresgeologie: Johannes Walther zum Gedächtnis," in *Zeitschrift der geologischen Gesellschaft*, 138 (1987), 1–12; G. I. Sokratov, "Histoire de la loi dite de Walther: Sur la formation des structures litées des couches sédimentaires," in *Doklady Akademii nauk SSSR*, 52 (1948), 517–519; B. P. Twenhofel, "Memorial to Johannes Walther," in *Proceedings of the Geological Society of America, 1937* (1938), 221–230, with bibliography; B. P. Vyssotzki, *Iogannes Val'ter i ego rol' v razvitii geologii* (Johannes Walther and his role in the progress of geology; Moscow, 1965); and J. Weigelt, "Johannes Walther," in *Zeitschrift der deutschen geologischen Gesellschaft*, 89 (1937), 645–656, with portrait and bibliography; "Zum Tode von Johannes Walther," in *Geologie der Meere und Binnengewässer*, 2 (1938), 323–333, with bibliography; and "Dem Andenken an Johannes Walther," in *Jahrbuch des Halleschen Verbandes für die Erforschung der mitteldeutschen Bodenschätze und ihrer Verwertung*, 16 (1938), 7–12, with portrait and bibliography.

M. SCHWAB

WANG, HSIEN CHUNG (*b.* Peking [Beijing], China, 18 April 1918; *d.* New York City, 25 June 1978), *mathematics.*

H. C. Wang was a distinguished and versatile mathematician who made important contributions to algebraic topology, Lie groups and their homogeneous spaces, and discrete subgroups of Lie groups. Wang came from a family with an impressive intellectual and scholarly tradition. His great-grandfather, Wang I Rong (1845–1900), was a famous archaeologist and president of the Imperial Academy who, with his wife, committed a glorious suicide, that is, suicide as a protest, when foreign troops entered Peking during the Boxer Rebellion. His eldest brother, Wang Xian Jun, became a professor of philosophy and logic at Peking University. Another elder brother, Wang Xian Zhao, is a well-known meteorologist, and his elder sister, Wang Xian Tian, is a professor at the Institute of Psychology of the Academia Sinica (PRC).

Upon graduation from Nankai High School in Tientsin, Wang entered Tsing Hua University in Peking in 1936 as a student of physics. After the Japanese invasion in July 1937 the university fled to Kunming in southwest China and merged with Nankai and Peking universities. After a difficult journey of almost a year, Wang rejoined the university and resumed his studies, changing his field to mathematics. He graduated in 1941 and began graduate work under Shiing Shen Chern, one of the leading differential geometers of the twentieth century. By 1944 he had obtained an M.A. degree and written his first research paper. After a year of high school teaching he won a British Council scholarship and set sail for England, where he studied first at Sheffield, and then at Manchester under M. H. A. Newman. By this time Wang was a productive research mathematician and had written about a dozen papers, including two of his most important ones. In the first of these he discovered an important exact sequence (the Wang sequence) involving the homology groups associated with fiber bundles over spheres. It was used in Leray's work on spectral sequences. In the second he gave an essentially complete solution to a problem arising from the work of Hopf and Samelson: determine the closed subgroups of maximum rank of a compact Lie group G.

After receiving a Ph.D. from Manchester in 1948, Wang returned to China as a research fellow of the Institute of Mathematics of the Academia Sinica (Chinese National Academy of Science), and followed the institute to Taiwan shortly thereafter. In the fall of 1949 he became a lecturer at Louisiana State University and began a long, fruitful career in the United States.

During his two years at Baton Rouge he wrote several more papers, among them his beautiful paper on two-point homogeneous spaces. In this paper he showed that a connected, compact metric space E, whose group of isometries carries a pair of points (p, q) to any pair (p', q') the same distance apart, is, in fact, a homogeneous space of a compact Lie group. Using this information he was able to enumerate all such spaces. Even in the noncompact case he obtained some results, later completed by J. Tits.

In the fall of 1951 he was invited for his first one-year appointment to the Institute for Advanced Study in Princeton, New Jersey, after which he was appointed for two years at Alabama Polytechnic Institute, followed again by a year (1954–1955) at the Institute for Advanced Study. It was during this period that he wrote a basic and important paper characterizing and classifying homogeneous complex manifolds, one of his works most often cited.

This was a very difficult time to secure employment in mathematics, especially for immigrants. Although this changed drastically by the late 1950's, it was still several years before Wang obtained a permanent position. The years from 1955 to 1957 were spent at the University of Washington in Seattle and then at Columbia University in New York. In 1956 he married Lung Hsien (Lucy) Kuan. His first tenured position, at Northwestern University, came in 1957;

he was made a full professor there the following year.

In 1958, in recognition of the importance of his work, Wang was invited to address the quadrennial International Mathematical Congress at Edinburgh, and in 1960 he was awarded a Guggenheim Fellowship to spend another year at the Institute for Advanced Study. At about this time he broke new ground in his research with an important study of transformation groups of $n-$ spheres with an orbit of dimension $n - 1$. This paper involves some clever and original ideas, as well as some formidable computations, and is a major departure from his earlier work.

As early as 1955 Wang had become interested in discrete subgroups of Lie groups, and in 1956 he published his first paper on this subject. This now became his major research area until the end of his career, resulting in several further important articles.

In 1965 and 1966 Wang spent a fourth year at the Institute for Advanced Study and then accepted a position at Cornell University, which he held until his death. During his tenure there, as a result of the rapprochement between the United States and the People's Republic of China, he was at last able to visit his family and friends. He went to China again in 1973 after a sabbatical year in England at the University of Warwick, this time with his wife and three daughters, and he returned for a third time in 1977. A fourth visit was being planned at the time of his death.

Wang's last paper was published in 1973, after which his research was much curtailed because of his anxiety for his wife, who had developed cancer. His teaching and other mathematical and administrative activities continued unabated, however, and he played an important role in the department at Cornell. He was very much liked there, as everywhere, for his modesty, generosity, kindness, and courtesy. He was a fine teacher and lecturer, and he guided several students to Ph.D.s and subsequent productive careers. He enjoyed excellent health until he was suddenly stricken with leukemia in June 1978. He succumbed within weeks, to be survived for only a few months by his wife.

BIBLIOGRAPHY

I. ORIGINAL WORKS. "The Homology Groups of the Fibre Bundles over a Sphere," in *Duke Mathematical Journal,* **16** (1949), 33–38; "Homogeneous Space with Non-vanishing Euler Characteristics," in *Annals of Mathematics,* **50** (1949), 925–953; "Two-point Homogeneous Spaces," *ibid.,* **55** (1952), 177–191; "Closed

Manifolds with Homogeneous Complex Structure," in *American Journal of Mathematics*, **76** (1954), 1–32; "Compact Transformation Groups of S^n with an $(n - 1)$-Dimensional Orbit," *ibid.*, **82** (1960), 698–748; "Topics on Totally Discontinuous Groups," in W. M. Boothby and G. Weiss, eds., *Symmetric Spaces* (New York, 1972), 459–487.

II. Secondary Literature. A memorial volume of the *Bulletin of the Institute of Mathematics, Academia Sinica*, **8** (1980), contains a discussion of Wang's life by S. T. Hu and of his work by W. M. Boothby, S. S. Chern, and S. P. Wang.

WILLIAM M. BOOTHBY

WATSON-WATT, ROBERT ALEXANDER (*b*. Brechin, Aberdeenshire, Scotland, 13 April 1892; *d*. Inverness, Inverness-shire, Scotland, 5 December 1973), *radio engineering, meteorological physics*.

R. A. W. Watt (the hyphen came with knighthood) was the son of Patrick and Mary (Matthew) Watt. He attended local schools in Brechin and University College, Dundee, then affiliated with the University of St. Andrews, from which he received the B.Sc. in electrical engineering with distinction in 1912; in 1919 he also qualified for the B.Sc. in physics from the University of London. In 1912 he became an assistant professor of physics at University College, Dundee. During World War I he served in the government Meteorological Office, where he attempted to use radio direction-finding methods to locate thunderstorms. His wartime suggestion that two or more intersecting bearings displayed on a cathode-ray oscilloscope could solve the problem of catching the characteristically short bursts of atmospherics generated by thunderstorms was not realized until 1923, when reliable cathode-ray tubes were developed in the United States. The work was continued at the Radio Research Station at Slough (under Watson-Watt as the superintendent) and in 1927 was assigned to the Department of Scientific and Industrial Research (D.S.I.R.), under whose auspices considerable success was achieved in locating not only thunderstorms but also naval signals. Watson-Watt's radio research laboratory also investigated the ionosphere (a term he coined), not by the frequency-shift method used by Appleton but by the pulse method developed in the United States by Breit and Tuve. In that way Watson-Watt gained expertise in radio direction finding, cathode-ray displays, and pulse techniques.

That knowledge made him the obvious person to be consulted when H. E. Wimperis, the research director at the Air Ministry, wanted to know whether enough energy could be concentrated in a radio beam to disable an enemy aircraft or pilot. The answer, based on a calculation made by Watson-Watt's assistant A. F. Wilkins at Slough, was negative, but the two men went on to calculate the feasibility of locating an aircraft from the reflected signal, this time with a positive result. Their calculation was contained in a secret memorandum dated 12 February 1935.

In his autobiography, *Three Steps to Victory* (1957), Watson-Watt asserted that this memorandum must be regarded "as marking the birth of radar and as being in fact the invention of radar," despite the fact that earlier work toward locating objects by electromagnetic waves had been done in several countries, including Britain. Moreover, when he published his autobiography, he was engaged in a struggle for reward and recognition, so his assertion could be interpreted as self-serving. Nevertheless, he was right, for several reasons. The earlier trials had been done with continuous-wave transmissions at metric and longer wavelengths, without any thought being given to translation of the results into operational commands. Watson-Watt, however, stressed the importance of pulsed signals at decimetric and shorter wavelengths and sketched a man-machine system that would back up the equipment with a team of operators who would produce a display of information on the basis of which tactical decisions could be made. That model grew into the mainstream of the subsequent development of radar, with immediate important consequences. The British government authorized the construction of the "Chain Home" (CH) radar stations, first around the approaches to London and later along the entire south and east coasts of Britain, together with a system of control rooms whose command of the tactical situation is generally acknowledged to have tipped the balance against German attackers during the Battle of Britain in 1940.

Developments in other countries lagged behind those in Britain, both technically and operationally. Among data that may be cited in that connection is the failure of American radar during the Japanese attack at Pearl Harbor in 1941 (sixteen months after the Battle of Britain): the attackers were detected, though not unequivocally, but no system for utilizing this information was in place, and no defense could be organized. Thus, it is not too much to say that Watson-Watt did indeed invent radar.

Watson-Watt's research team was transferred to the Air Ministry in 1936, and he directed it until 1938, when he handed it over to A. P. Rowe and went on to a succession of advisory posts at the ministry. After the war he went into private practice as a consultant, served as adviser to the government and leader of delegations to international meetings, and (after 1952) lived in Canada and the United States as a free-lance technical consultant. That year he and Margaret Robertson (whom he had married in 1916) were divorced; he later married Jean Smith, who died in 1964. In 1966 he married Katherine Jane Trefusis-Forbes. There were no children.

He was elected fellow of the Royal Society of London in 1941 and was knighted in 1942. He received the U.S. Medal for Merit, the Hughes Medal of the Royal Society, and the Elliott Cresson Medal of the Franklin Institute.

BIBLIOGRAPHY

I. ORIGINAL WORKS. The autobiography *Three Steps to Victory: A Personal Account by Radar's Greatest Pioneer* . . . (London, 1957) was reissued in the United States in a substantially abbreviated version, *The Pulse of Radar* (New York, 1959). Both contain the full text of the 1935 memorandum "Detection and Location of Aircraft by Radio Methods." Of special historical interest is a speech made by Watson-Watt at the postwar conference on radiolocation called by the Institution of Electrical Engineers, in which he paid tribute to the wartime contributions of American colleagues, in *Journal of the Institution of Electrical Engineers*, **93**, IIIA (1946), 11.

II. SECONDARY LITERATURE. A portrait and a biography (with a list of publications) by J. A. Ratcliffe appears in *Biographical Memoirs of Fellows of the Royal Society*, **21** (1975), 549–568. On the question of priority in the invention of radar, see Charles Süsskind, "Who Invented Radar?" in *Endeavour*, n.s. **9** (1985), 92–96; and R. W. Burns, ed., *The History of Radar Development to 1945* (London, 1988). The last two references also contain the text of the 1935 memorandum.

CHARLES SÜSSKIND

WEBER, HANS HERMANN JULIUS WILHELM

(*b*. Berlin-Charlottenburg, Germany, 17 June 1896; *d*. Heidelberg, Federal Republic of Germany, 12 June 1974), *physiology, biochemistry.*

Weber was the son of Hermann Weber, a physician who, as *Geheimrat* and professor, was head of the medical department in several Berlin hospitals, and of Annemarie Becher Weber. After attending a private preparatory school, he entered the Mommsen Gymnasium in Berlin-Charlottenburg. In August 1914, immediately after the final graduation examination, he was called up for military service,

which lasted until 1919. Weber was wounded in 1916, which gave him the opportunity to study medicine for a semester in Berlin (although artistic interests might have suggested training as a painter or sculptor). In 1919 he was able to resume his medical studies, first at Greifswald, then at Rostock and Heidelberg.

At Rostock, Weber studied with the physiologist Hans Winterstein, under whom he wrote a doctoral dissertation that brought him into contact with the physiology and biochemistry of the muscle, the area of his lifework. Winterstein gave Weber the task of experimentally investigating the role of lactic acid in the formation and relaxation of rigor mortis of the muscle. Winterstein had already studied this question. In the meantime the work of Otto Meyerhof at Kiel had drawn attention to the role of lactic acid in the energetics of the muscle.

At the end of 1921 Weber was awarded the M.D. degree. He approached Meyerhof, who was then *professor extraordinarius* at the Physiological Institute of Kiel University, and asked to be allowed to work in his laboratory. Weber spent half a year in Meyerhof's laboratory—a short time that had a lasting influence on him and his scientific approach. Through Meyerhof, Weber's interest was directed to "molecular energetics," and Weber took it upon himself to establish the physicochemical foundations for Meyerhof's energetics of the muscle.

In the autumn of 1922 Weber became an assistant to Winterstein at Rostock, a post Winterstein had promised him while he was still a student. That October he married Marga Oltmanns, a student of philosophy and history with artistic talent and interests; they had two daughters and a son. In 1924 he lost the assistantship because of financial constraints but received a Rockefeller Foundation grant that enabled him to finish his work to qualify as a lecturer.

At Rostock, Weber did work in the physical chemistry of muscle proteins because he regarded knowledge of muscle proteins as a precondition for understanding muscle contraction. In 1895 Otto von Fürth had studied the separation of muscle proteins into myogen and myosin. Weber took up these studies and developed methods for isolation of those substances. He examined their physicochemical characteristics, in particular the isoelectric point and the buffer action curve. From his investigation Weber concluded that myosin was a protein sui generis and probably represented the shortening substance of the muscle. At the same time he proved, on the basis of the isoelectric point, that neither the acid swelling theory of muscle contraction, for years an object of discussion, nor the deionization theory, suggested by Meyerhof, was supported by his data. In 1925 Weber qualified as *Privatdozent* in physiology at Rostock University.

That same year Weber went to Berlin, where he obtained a position as auxiliary assistant under Peter Rona in the chemistry department of the Pathological Institute. In the 1920's Berlin offered a wealth of inspiration for a young natural scientist, particularly through the institutes of the Kaiser Wilhelm Institute. Important to Weber was the contact with researchers using physical and physicochemical methods in the biological sciences. Besides Rona they included Leonor Michaelis, Otto Warburg, and Kurt Hans Meyer. Meyerhof also was working at the Kaiser Wilhelm Institute. Rona allowed Weber to work in his chosen field of muscle proteins, continuing his studies done at Rostock. About 1925 the research on proteins experienced a crisis. The chemical interpretation of the structure of proteins as macromolecules strictly in accordance with the laws of stoichiometry was confronted with the colloid chemistry interpretation of proteins as aggregates of smaller molecules with a bonding of small molecules or ions described as adsorption. Weber decided to investigate some basic questions of the physical chemistry of proteins and chose the muscle proteins as his subject.

With a theoretical study titled "Massenwirkungsgesetz und Kolloide" (1927), Weber embraced the "chemical" view of proteins. Working from the strict validity of the law of mass action in protein reactions, he derived equations for the dissociation of multivalent ampholytes that explained the known titration curves of proteins. In a 1929 study with David Nachmannsohn (later he spelled it Nachmansohn), who was also working with Rona, the hydration of protein ions was investigated. The work is theoretically related to Weber's studies of muscle physiology, since in 1912 Wolfgang Pauli had amplified the acid swelling theory of muscle contraction with the hypothesis that the swelling is due to an intensified water bonding of the protein ions. Weber and Nachmannsohn furnished evidence that there is no connection between protein ionization and hydration.

In 1927 Weber became an assistant at the Physiological Institute of Münster University under Rudolf Rosemann. Here he was able to continue his studies on a larger scale. In order to explain the results of the Berlin study of the hydration of proteins, Weber had taken up the dipolar ion (*Zwitterionen*) theory of proteins. In 1923 Niels Bjerrum had comprehensively and theoretically substantiated the presence of dipolar ions in ampholytes. It was presumed that under certain conditions proteins could also be present as such dipolar ions. Weber proved experimentally, using various methods, that proteins are present as dipolar ions at their isoelectric point.

Weber's outstanding accomplishment while at Münster was the discovery and careful investigation of the oriented myosin thread (which today would be described as actomyosin thread). In 1928 Alexander von Muralt and John Tileston Edsall at the Harvard Medical School had developed a method for isolating myosin based on Weber's 1925 study (muscle physiologists still speak today of "Weber-Edsall myosin"). Weber obtained the myosin thread from such a myosin solution, about which he said:

> It is indeed possible by a sort of stretch spinning method to produce from myosin solutions structures that behave mechanically, optically, and X-ray optically similarly to muscle fibrils. The method consists in injecting myosin solutions of very high purity from a capillary into distilled water in which they instantaneously solidify to a thread that can be flowingly stretched to about twice the original length. . . . These stretched myosin threads . . . represent . . . a sort of muscle model on which possibly also mechanical-thermal characteristics and perhaps some other forms of contractures can be investigated. . . . The research methods of the chemistry of fibers are applicable to the threads. ("Das Röntgendiagramm von gedehnten Myosinfäden," p. 269.)

Weber investigated this thread model, using all available methods. With Gundo Boehm he was able to show that the fiber diagram obtained with short exposure to X rays is identical to that of the freshly stretched muscle. Weber also used mechanical and polarization optical methods. The birefringence of the muscle fiber had been known for a long time. The discovery of the flow birefringence in myosin solutions by von Muralt and Edsall in 1930 had shown the myosin to be composed of rod-shaped molecules and a probable source of the birefringence of the muscle. From his polarization optical and radiographic measurements Weber derived the first data on the probable size of the myosin molecule. He summarized the results for muscle proteins in the classic paper "Die Muskeleiweisskörper und der Feinbau des Skelettmuskels" (1934). Weber did experiments in which he added creatinin, for instance, to the myosin thread—without effect. He did not, however, use the newly discovered adenosine triphosphate (ATP), so he missed the key discovery made by Albert Szent-Györgyi in 1942.

In the meantime, Weber had been appointed extraordinary professor of physiology in 1931. At

Münster, as at other German universities, after much hesitation efforts were being made to separate biochemistry (then called physiological chemistry in Germany) from physiology and to create separate chairs for them. In May 1933 an associate professorship of physiological chemistry was created that Weber, as unofficial extraordinary professor, occupied as a deputy. It was not until 1938 that he became a regular extraordinary professor of physiological chemistry, a delay that he attributed to the fact that the National Socialists considered him politically unreliable. An important recognition of Weber's studies of protein was an invitation from the Royal Society of London to a symposium titled "Discussion on the Protein Molecule" in November 1938.

In April 1939 Weber was offered the chair of physiology and physiological chemistry at Königsberg University. A few months later World War II broke out. Two outstanding studies emerged under the restricted working conditions during the war; in both of them Weber cooperated with recognized specialists. In 1941 Manfred von Ardenne in Berlin and Weber succeeded in representing for the first time thread-shaped structures from myosin solutions in photographs taken by means of the electron microscope. In 1942 Gerhard Schramm and Weber examined myosin solutions with the ultracentrifuge at the Kaiser Wilhelm Institute in Berlin-Dahlem. They found two monodisperse fractions, a discovery that shortly afterward was explained in the discovery of actomyosin.

At Königsberg, parallel to the investigations on muscle proteins, Weber had continued his work on the general physical chemistry of proteins. Outstanding was an experimental study with Ingeborg Lichtenstein of the various ionogenic groups of protein molecules. Previously information on this question came from calculations on the basis of amino acid analyses and was partly wrong. Weber summarized his studies in this field in "Eiweisskörper als Riesenionen" (1942).

In 1944 the *Oberkommando* of the army awarded Weber a research contract to study the use of animal serum albumin as a substitute for blood. This gave him the opportunity to leave Königsberg in January 1945, shortly before Soviet troops entered the city. (His family had already been evacuated to western Germany.) In 1946 Weber was offered chairs of physiology at Berlin, Erlangen, Mainz, and Tübingen. He chose Tübingen, where, due mainly to the Kaiser Wilhelm Institute, evacuated from Berlin, an extraordinarily stimulating atmosphere was developing for the life sciences. In addition, the university had

not been destroyed in the war, and therefore working conditions improved more quickly than at other universities.

While Weber was at Königsberg, research into muscle contraction had been directed into new channels by two important discoveries. At Moscow in 1939, Vladimir Aleksandrovich Engelhardt and M. N. Liubimova had observed the ATP-splitting effect of the Weber-Edsall myosin, and in 1942 Albert Szent-Györgyi at Szeged (Hungary) had determined that addition of ATP to myosin threads leads to shrinkage, which he interpreted as contraction. In spite of the war, Weber was able to visit Szent-Györgyi's laboratory and to obtain information about his discoveries, and thus started investigations while still at Königsberg. As soon as the institute directed by Weber at Tübingen was functioning, he and his colleagues began systematically to examine ATP's effects on the muscle proteins. Preparative methods were devised for the isolation of myosin and actomyosin, the latter having been recognized as a complex of myosin and actin by Brunò F. Straub at Szeged. The proteins were characterized extensively by measuring physical and physicochemical properties. Using a new extraction method, Weber's co-worker Wilhelm Hasselbach provided information on the quantity ratios of myosin and actin in the muscle.

One of Weber's basic ideas in the investigation of muscle contraction was the possibility of using suitable models to break down the complex physiological process into simple elements. The thread model discovered at Münster, which now turned out to be an oriented actomyosin thread model, offered one possibility, especially since it appeared to exhibit contraction on addition of ATP. A second model, the fiber model (more precisely, the single-fiber model), was developed by Weber's daughter Annemarie, who wrote her dissertation for the M.D. degree under her father in 1950 and became an assistant in his institute. In continuation of Szent-Györgyi's experiments, she produced glycerol-extracted individual fibers of such thinness that ATP could penetrate by diffusion into the interior of the fibers in adequate concentration.

In the following years the basic processes of the contraction cycle, the transformation of chemical energy from ATP hydrolysis to mechanical work, were individually investigated in these models and explained step by step, a considerable amount of this work being done in Weber's laboratory. First, the modulus of elasticity was measured with newly developed precision instruments. It was particularly important to block the ATP-hydrolyzing effect of actomyosin by poisoning—for instance, by SH-group blocking agents. This makes a double effect of ATP apparent: hydrolysis of ATP by actomyosin leads to contraction, and the binding of ATP on actomyosin when hydrolysis of ATP is blocked results in a plasticizing effect. The time analysis of the contraction cycle showed that ATP is the direct energy source for contraction of the muscle and that this energy is liberated at the beginning of contraction. It was now also possible to settle the question of the cause of rigor mortis, which had been the subject of Weber's doctoral dissertation more than twenty years earlier: when all the hydrolyzable ATP is used up, the plasticizing effect is eliminated and the muscle becomes rigid.

However, the living muscle and the models differ in one important way. The living muscle exhibits a state of rest in which ATP is present but not hydrolyzed. On the other hand, in the models ATP, if its hydrolysis is not blocked, is always split and initiates the contraction. The models helped to clarify this situation. Weber's colleague Hasselbach discovered an inhibiting influence of large concentrations of calcium ions on the contraction model, and it was possible to study this in the model. Shortly afterward it became apparent that there was a relationship to the relaxing factor, which B. B. Marsh and J. R. Bendall had discovered independently of each other. This factor is missing in Weber's muscle models. Weber recognized the importance of this discovery, and in the following years extensive investigations of this factor were carried out in his laboratory. Among other things they led to the discovery of the calcium pump by Hasselbach.

In spite of the great progress in the explanation of the mechanism of muscle contraction that numerous groups of workers had made in many countries, the actual molecular mechanism of the contraction was still unknown. Time and again researchers discussed the obvious idea that a folding and coiling of the thread molecules of the myosin causes the shortening, the energy needed for the relaxation. Weber also considered this. However, after investigations on the models had clearly shown that the contraction process governed by ATP hydrolysis is the energy-consuming part of the cycle, and not the relaxation, Weber dismissed the thermokinetic theories (1951).

The state of knowledge in 1954, indicated here only in quite broad outlines, was presented by Weber and Hildegard Portzehl in a brilliant summary titled "The Transference of the Muscle Energy in the Contraction Cycle" (1954). This again showed Weber's exceptional ability to analyze critically the important results of a field of research that was rapidly changing and to describe it in a synopsis.

In April 1954 Weber was appointed director of the Institute for Physiology of the Max Planck Institute for Medical Research at Heidelberg. This institute, which was founded in 1929 as the Kaiser Wilhelm Institute for Medical Research on the initiative of Ludolf von Krehl, and at which Otto Meyerhof was employed until his emigration in 1938, was headed by Weber until his retirement in 1966.

At Heidelberg it was possible for Weber to continue his previous work more extensively and with the aid of a greater number of co-workers, who included Wilhelm Hasselbach, Erich Heinz, Hartmut Hoffmann-Berling, Ingeborg Lichtenstein, Madoka Makinose, Hildegard Portzehl, Johann-Caspar Rüegg, Friedrich Tonner, Gerhard Ulbrecht, and Weber's daughter Annemarie. An ever-increasing number of study groups were formed, and under the guidance of experienced colleagues of Weber's they investigated the complex questions of muscle contraction. The experimental studies of this period were published to an increasing degree by Weber's colleagues without his coauthorship. Two particularly interesting areas of research will be mentioned briefly. While examining the relaxation factor, Hildegard Portzehl discovered that it is not an enzyme, as first assumed, but consists of ultramicroscopic particles. This cleared the way for a new field of study that connects the membrane activation of the muscle with the contraction process. (After Weber retired, his successor, Hasselbach, made this field a main area of research.) Hartmut Hoffmann-Berling added a further interesting contraction model to the thread model and the fiber model. He was able to prove the presence of ATP-dependent contractile substances in cells. On this basis the cell model was created (which cannot be discussed in any detail here).

At the beginning of the 1950's findings on the structure of myofibrils were obtained by the research groups of Hugh E. Huxley and Jean Hanson in London, as well as of A. F. Huxley in Cambridge, using microscopic and radiographic methods. These findings led in 1955 to postulation of the sliding filament theory of muscle contraction, which is generally accepted today. This theory, which came as a surprise to Weber (he had discussed the possibility of a dislocation of length-constant elements in 1942 but rejected this idea), was included by him in a lecture concerning a chemical theory of the whole process of contraction (1956). Weber thus once again provided an exceptional example of his ability to establish theories of complex processes.

At the International Congress of Biochemistry at Brussels in 1955, Weber lectured on the basic ideas of a new chemical contraction theory, which assumed a high-energy binding of a phosphate group of ATP to the contraction protein (phosphorylation). In 1956 he modified his theory and adapted it to the sliding filament mechanism. The importance of his descriptive theory lay in the assistance it offered for the understanding of the essential role of ATP and its relationship to the mechanical processes in muscle contraction, although the phosphorylation of the actomyosin assumed by Weber could not be confirmed.

At first Weber's scientific achievements found recognition abroad rather than in Germany. His physical-chemistry-oriented research was at first strange to many physiologists in Germany. He was elected a member of the Leopoldinische Akademie der Naturforscher in Halle (1955) and served as its vice president from 1963 to 1971. The Leopoldina honored him with its Carus Medal (1955) and its honorary presidentship (1971). It possesses a bronze bust of Weber created by his son, Jürgen. Weber was an honorary member of the Harvey Society (1953) and of the American Physiological Society (1959), and held honorary doctorates from Munich and Halle universities.

Weber's scientific importance lies in the fact that at an early date he directed modern muscle physiology along the path of molecular biological research. The outstanding contribution of his scientific approach through the analysis of suitable models was the explanation of the relationship between ATP hydrolysis and mechanical muscle contraction.

BIBLIOGRAPHY

I. Original Works. There is a partial bibliography of Weber's writings, drawn from an incomplete typescript, in Archiv für die Geschichte der Max-Planck-Gesellschaft in Berlin, sec. 3, Rep. 32, which also contains autograph curricula vitae and other scientific items. Besides the book *The Motility of Muscle and Cells* (Cambridge, Mass., 1958), Weber published some 100 shorter pieces.

Weber's articles include "Das kolloidale Verthalten der Muskeleiweisskörper. I. Isoelektrischer Punkt und Stabilitätsbedingungen des Myogens," in *Biochemische Zeitschrift*, **158** (1925), 443–472; "Das kolloidale Verhalten der Muskeleiweisskörper. II. Isoelektrischer Punkt und Löslichkeit des Myosins," *ibid.*, 473–490; "Massenwirkungsgesetz und Kolloide," *ibid.*, **189** (1927), 381–406; "Die Unabhängigkeit der Eiweisshydratation von der Eiweissionisation," *ibid.*, **204** (1929), 215–252, written with David Nachmannsohn; "Die Bjerrumsche Zwitterionen-

theorie und die Hydratation der Eiweisskörper," *ibid.*, **218** (1930), 1–29; "Das Röntgendiagramm von gedehnten Myosinfäden," in *Kolloid-Zeitschrift*, **61** (1932), 296–270, written with Gundo Boehm; "Der Feinbau und die mechanischen Eigenschaften des Myosinfadens," in *Archiv für Physiologie*, **235** (1934), 205–233; "Die Muskeleiweisskörper und der Feinbau des Skelettmuskels," in *Ergebnisse der Physiologie*, **36** (1934), 109–150; "Polarisationsoptik und molekularer Feinbau der Q-Abschnitte des Froschmuskels," in *Archiv für Physiologie*, **235** (1934), 234–246, written with D. Noll; "Elektronenmikroskopische Untersuchung des Muskeleiweisskörpers 'Myosin,'" in *Kolloid-Zeitschrift*, **97** (1941), 322–325, written with Manfred von Ardenne; "Über monodisperse Myosinlösungen," *ibid.*, **100** (1942), 242–247, written with Gerhard Schramm; "Eiweisskörper als Riesenionen," in *Schriften der Königsberger gelehrten Gesellschaft*, Naturwissenschaftliche Klasse, **18**, no. 4 (1942), 45–59.

"Aktomyosin und seine Komponenten, I. Mitteilung," in *Zeitschrift für Naturforschung*, **5b** (1950), 61–74, written with Hildegard Portzehl and Gerhard Schramm; "Die Aktomyosinmodelle und der Kontraktionszyklus des Muskels," in *Zeitschrift für Elektrochemie und angewandte physikalische Chemie*, **55** (1951), 511–518; "Kontraktion, ATP-Cyclus und fibrilläre Proteine des Muskels," in *Ergebnisse der Physiologie*, **47** (1952), 369–468, written with Hildegard Portzehl; "The Transference of the Muscle Energy in the Contraction Cycle," Marga Weber, trans., in *Progress in Biophysics and Biophysical Chemistry*, **4** (1954), 60–111; "Adenosine Triphosphate and Motility of Living Systems," in *The Harvey Lectures*, **49** (1955), 37–56; "Die molekularen Vorgänge bei der tierischen Bewegung," in *Verhandlungen der Deutschen orthopädischen Gesellschaft*, **44** (1957), 13–27; and "The Relaxation of the Contracted Actomyosin System," in *Annals of the New York Academy of Sciences*, **81** (1959), 409–421.

On Weber's institute at Heidelberg, see "Max-Planck-Institut für medizinische Forschung," in *Jahrbuch der Max-Planck-Gesellschaft für Förderung der Wissenschaften e.V.* (1961), pt. 2, 535–556, written with R. Kuhn. A short autobiographical note is in W. E. Böhm and G. Paehlke, eds., *Forscher und Gelehrte* (Stuttgart, 1966), 65.

II. Secondary Literature. Obituaries by Wilhelm Hasselbach include "Hans Hermann Weber," in *Mitteilungen aus der Max-Planck-Gesellschaft*, **4** (1974), 229–232, "Hans Hermann Weber, 1896–1974," in *Ergebnisse der Physiologie*, **73** (1975), 1–7, and "Hans Hermann Weber in Memoriam," in L. M. G. Heilmeyer, Jr., J. C. Rüegg, and T. Wieland, eds., *Molecular Basis of Motility* (Berlin and New York, 1976), 3–6. Also of value is "Physiologie und Biochemie der Muskelkontraktion. Akademische Gedenkfeier für H. H. Weber," *Nova acta Leopoldina*, n.s. **48**, no. 229 (1977).

A comprehensive account of the history of muscle contraction research, including Weber's work, is Dorothy

M. Needham, *Machina Carnis: The Biochemistry of Muscular Contraction in Its Historical Development* (Cambridge, 1971).

JOHANNES BÜTTNER

WEBSTER, ARTHUR GORDON (*b.* Brookline, Massachusetts, 28 November 1863; *d.* Worcester, Massachusetts, 15 May 1923), *physics.*

Webster was born into a prosperous and established New England family, the only son of William Edward Webster and Mary Shannon Davis Webster. He attended Newton High School and in 1881 went on to Harvard College, where he excelled in mathematics and physics, graduating at the head of his class in 1885. After a year as an instructor at Harvard, and with the support of a Parker Fellowship, he continued his study of physics at the University of Berlin. Webster also briefly attended the universities of Paris and Stockholm before receiving his Ph.D. from Berlin in 1890 with a dissertation written under the direction of August Kundt. While in Berlin, he met Elizabeth Munroe Townsend, the daughter of a U.S. Navy officer; they were married on 8 October 1889 in Syracuse, New York, and had two daughters and one son.

After completing his European studies, Webster began a lifelong affiliation with Clark University, the graduate institute founded a few years earlier in Worcester, Massachusetts. He spent his first two years there as a docent in physics, working under Albert A. Michelson. Following Michelson's move in 1892 to the University of Chicago, Clark administrators promoted Webster to assistant professor and placed him in charge of the physics department and laboratory. He held the rank of full professor from 1900 until his death.

Webster displayed a prodigious range of interests and skills. Besides his primary talents in physics and mathematics, he was proficient as a linguist, public speaker, musician, artist, and popular writer. He was also active in politics, once running for Congress. His election to the National Academy of Sciences in 1903, at the relatively young age of thirty-nine, was only one of many honors bestowed on him at home and abroad by his colleagues.

Although Webster made his most important contributions to science by writing advanced textbooks on mathematical physics and by helping to establish a professional organization for physicists in the United States, he also made a creditable contribution to basic research. His research encompassed a wide scope of experimental and theoretical topics; never-

theless, essentially all of his investigations were grounded in a mechanical view of nature as formulated mathematically by such nineteenth-century physicists as James Clerk Maxwell and Hermann von Helmholtz. Webster's two most enduring research interests were acoustics and mathematics as applied to classical physics. He spent over two decades (especially the years 1897 to 1919) refining a phonometer, an instrument for measuring the intensity of sound. Drawing on his mathematical and experimental skills, he also originated the concept of acoustic impedance in analogy to electric impedance.

Early in his career, Webster concentrated more explicitly on electricity and magnetism. His doctoral dissertation contained a new method for determining the ratio of the electromagnetic to the electrostatic unit of charge. In a subsequent experiment having implications for the ratio, he verified an important theoretical formula for the period of electrical oscillations in a discharging condenser. Recognizing the significance of this research, an international committee awarded him the Elihu Thomson Prize in 1895. Webster's appointment to the Naval Consulting Board during World War I brought with it a final major research project, in ballistics. During the years around 1920, he published numerous experimental and theoretical studies of rifles and cannons.

Webster's greatest strength was as an educator. Through his teaching at Clark and especially through three notable textbooks, he helped introduce a generation of advanced students to the mathematical structure of classical mechanical physics. He felt that physicists in the United States lacked adequate training in mathematics, and he designed his graduate courses at Clark to alleviate this deficiency. A skilled lecturer with a comprehensive grasp of mathematical physics, he stretched the modest facilities at Clark and successfully trained twenty-seven doctoral students. In addition, he built on knowledge acquired through preparing lectures at Clark to publish *The Theory of Electricity and Magnetism* (1897). This was a mathematical digest of the ideas of Maxwell, Helmholtz, Heinrich Hertz, and Oliver Heaviside. During the same year, he accepted an invitation from the prestigious Lowell Institute of Boston to present a series of public talks on electricity. In 1904, again drawing on his classroom lectures, he published his most influential textbook, *The Dynamics of Particles and of Rigid, Elastic, and Fluid Bodies.* This work, which went through several editions, was a mathematical compendium of the principal ideas of Lord Kelvin, Peter G. Tait, Maxwell, Helmholtz, and other masters of classical dynamics. Webster's final textbook, *Partial Differential Equations of Mathematical Physics*, appeared posthumously in 1927 through the editorial efforts of Samuel J. Plimpton. Widely adopted by physicists, the book demonstrated the mathematical unity of seemingly divergent branches of classical physics.

Whereas Webster's contemporaries knew him mainly as an expositor of the mathematical aspects of physics, subsequent generations remembered him primarily as the founder of the American Physical Society. In 1899 Webster took the lead in convening and structuring the first professional organization in the United States devoted solely to physics. He also served as the third president of the American Physical Society (1903–1904), succeeding the two foremost physicists in the country, Henry A. Rowland and Albert A. Michelson. By the time of his 1904 presidential address, Webster was able to report that the organization embraced nearly every practicing physicist in the nation. He remained an active participant in the society's regular meetings; his frequent and spirited comments on the papers read during these meetings helped establish his reputation as a loquacious and candid polymath.

Webster's self-confidence, wit, vitality, and good health combined to give the impression of a man pleased with his professional success. Thus it came as a shock to his colleagues and the public when, in 1923, he committed suicide by shooting himself in the head. Actually, he had become increasingly troubled and depressed during his final years. This appears to have been partially due to personal economic pressures, Clark's diminishing commitment to research, frustration in establishing a major ballistics program, and a sense of self-doubt about the worth of his accoustical studies.

BIBLIOGRAPHY

I. ORIGINAL WORKS. A bibliography of Webster's published writings appears in a memorial volume that was issued following a special meeting held at Clark University in Webster's honor; see Edith M. Baker, comp., "Bibliography," in Louis N. Wilson, ed., *Arthur Gordon Webster, November 28, 1863–May 15, 1923: In Memoriam* (Worcester, Mass., 1924), 55–62. The same bibliography is appended to Joseph S. Ames, "Biographical Memoir of Arthur Gordon Webster, 1863–1923," in *Biographical Memoirs, National Academy of Sciences*, **18** (1937), 342–347.

There are two main repositories of Webster's unpublished letters and manuscripts: the Clark University Archives in Worcester, Massachusetts, and the University of Illinois Archives at Urbana-Champaign. Clark also holds a number of photographs, newspaper obituaries, biographical essays, and Webster's published books and articles.

II. SECONDARY LITERATURE. The fullest biographical sketch is A. Wilmer Duff, "Arthur Gordon Webster: Physicist, Mathematician, Linguist, and Orator," in *The American Physics Teacher*, **6** (1938), 181–194. See also Ames, "Biographical Memoir," 334–341; G. S. Fletcher, "Arthur Gordon Webster, 1864 [sic]–1923," in *The Physical Review*, 2nd ser., **21** (1923), 585–586; Edwin H. Hall, "Arthur Gordon Webster," in *Science*, **58** (1923), 37–39, and "Arthur Gordon Webster, 1863–1923," in *Proceedings of the American Academy of Arts and Sciences*, **62** (1926–1927), 285–286; and Alexander G. McAdie, "Arthur Gordon Webster," *Class of 1885, Harvard College: Secretary's Report*, **9** (1925), 173–180; and Melba Phillips, "Arthur Gordon Webster, Founder of the APS," in *Physics Today*, **40**, no. 6 (1987), 48–52. For informative reminiscences by Webster's colleagues, see also *Webster: In Memoriam*, 1–54.

ALBERT E. MOYER

WEBSTER, DAVID LOCKE (*b*. Boston, Massachusetts, 6 November 1888; *d*. Palo Alto, California, 17 December 1976), *physics*.

David Locke Webster exemplified the generation of experimental physicists trained in the United States before World War I. He developed X-ray techniques as tools for atomic physics, beginning while a Harvard graduate student and continuing while chairman of the Stanford physics department. Although Webster's most important research was done before World War II, his scientific publications appeared from 1912 to 1973. He was a member of the National Academy of Sciences (elected in 1923), the American Association for the Advancement of Science (vice president and chairman of the Section of Physics, 1932), and the American Association of Physics Teachers (vice president 1933–1934 and president 1935–1936), and an editorial board member for the first twenty volumes of *Reviews of Modern Physics* (1929–1948).

Webster was the younger son of Andrew Gerrish Webster, a leather manufacturer, and of Lizzie Florence Briggs, the daughter of a banker. In their upper-class household, he was exposed to Episcopalianism, Swedenborgianism, and Irish Catholicism, and became an avid sailor. As an adult he professed agnosticism, remained devoted to sailing, and took up flying. He was married twice: to Anna Cutler Woodman on 12 June 1912—they had two sons and two daughters and were divorced in 1951—and to Olive Ross on 18 September 1951. In addition to his academic activities, service as an army researcher in both world wars influenced his life and scientific work.

Webster entered Harvard College in 1906, received his S.B. degree in 1910, and continued his studies under the spectroscopist Theodore Lyman. Since Harvard would not accept a dissertation in theoretical physics, he did experimental work on the pressure dependence of light absorption in chlorine gas. Webster's dissertation, completed in 1913, included theoretical sections on gravitation, the ether, and X-ray scattering, the latter a topic he pursued as a Harvard instructor. Also in 1913, Henry G. J. Moseley used an X-ray spectrometer to link X-ray spectra to atomic numbers, demonstrating the kinds of techniques that physicists might exploit to learn about atomic structure. In 1915 Webster, drawing on descriptions of William H. Bragg's crystal spectrometer and his own training in conventional optics, built an X-ray spectrometer on an optical mount from the freshman laboratory and began to examine the tungsten spectrum.

Harvard's leader in X-ray research was the physicist William Duane. Out of his laboratory came several experiments critical for the development of X-ray physics and quantum theory; Webster's contributions were vital but somewhat clouded by his relationship to Duane. The senior scientist had already begun to study the relationship between incident cathode-ray energy and the frequency of an X-ray tube's output when Webster began measuring spectra. Using Webster's apparatus, Duane and Franklin L. Hunt performed the experiments codified as the Duane-Hunt law: There is a definite limiting frequency for X rays produced by electrons of a given energy, the product of energy and maximum frequency being very nearly Planck's constant.

According to his notebooks and his recollections in a 1964 oral history interview, Webster made the same tests before turning his spectrometer over to Duane and Hunt, found the frequency limit, and experimentally determined the value of h. Webster realized that his results amounted to an effective argument for the quantum theory of X rays and against the pulse theory. A pulse treated by Fourier analysis, he noted, would have no maximum frequency, yet the experiments showed a sharp cutoff, which pointed to the quantum nature of the radiation.

In September 1917, Webster began a brief tenure as physics professor at the University of Michigan. Already at work on submarine detection for the Naval Consulting Board, in November he left Ann Arbor to join the Science and Research Division of the Army Signal Corps Air Service Reserve. In February 1918, he was the first man nominated for training as a "scientific pilot" to help design and test flying instruments. He flew over 215 hours on active duty, most of them at Langley Field, Virginia, and remained a member of the Air Service Reserve until 1924.

Webster returned to Michigan for only a semester, then was assistant professor in 1919 and 1920 at MIT. Dissatisfied there, he weighed an offer from General Electric but accepted the post of professor and chairman of the Stanford University physics department. At Stanford he replaced retiring professors with younger men, who joined him in X-ray studies and improved and expanded graduate education. To secure support within the university, Webster's department emphasized physics education for engineering and premedical students. But heavy teaching loads and and a paucity of funds impeded research and discouraged prominent physicists from joining the department. Professor George R. Harrison, an alumnus, left for well-heeled MIT, and Webster was unable to secure a leading theorist for the staff until 1934, when Rockefeller Foundation support brought the émigré Felix Bloch.

Still, Webster was able to make progress with the apparatus he could afford. He and P. A. Ross collaborated in 1924 and 1925 to test the possible sources of the "tertiary radiation" reported by Duane and George L. Clark, who disputed the existence of the Compton effect. Webster and Ross verified Compton's position—an important result because it was the first to come from neither Compton nor Duane.

During the late 1920's and early 1930's, Webster and his students concentrated on measuring K-lines in X-ray spectra (the discrete radiations emitted by atoms when an electron is removed from an interior orbital), using them as clues to atomic structure and processes. They specialized in observing the characteristic radiations of moderately heavy elements, such as gold and silver, produced by electron bombardment of thin foils. Without intervening matter, the energy of the cathode ray as it reached the affected atom could be known precisely, and in 1933 the Stanford group published a nonrelativistic quantum theory treatment of the ionization cross section of interior electrons that took into account nuclear attraction.

With this success behind him, and Bloch at Stanford, in 1935 Webster hoped to go on to heavier elements and higher energies. He and the physics faculty considered building a 102-foot X-ray tube; unable to find support for it, they turned their attention to the resonance methods for accelerating electrons in a conducting sphere developed by their Stanford colleague William W. Hansen, Webster's former student. With war on the horizon, though, Webster and Hansen soon joined Sigurd and Russell Varian to develop the klystron, a source of microwave power for aircraft detection and instrument landing systems.

Klystron research meant sharing laboratory space with engineers from the sponsoring Sperry Gyroscope Company, an arrangement Webster found intolerable. He left the project, after contributing a mathematical analysis of the klystron's workings, and in 1941 found a new role in the preparedness effort as an author of pilot training manuals for the Civil Aeronautics Authority. From 1942 to 1945, Webster worked on bazookas and aircraft rockets at Aberdeen Proving Ground. During his absence, plans were laid at Stanford for a special laboratory where microwave research could continue under Hansen after the war. After his experience with Sperry, Webster opposed the project, and it was finally agreed that he would give up the department chair for his final years before retirement.

Physics education took up most of Webster's time after World War II. He served on the Coulomb's Law Committee of the American Association of Physics Teachers, charged with rationalizing instruction in electromagnetism, and wrote a long entry on electricity for the *Encyclopaedia Britannica*. After retirement in 1954, he joined the University of Hawaii's tsunami research project, helping to model the diffraction of tidal waves around small islands as he had once contemplated the dispersion of X rays by crystals. In 1962 he became a consulting physicist at NASA's Ames Research Center, where he contributed to the calculation of electromagnetic fields in space. Suffering from uremic poisoning, Webster finally left NASA in 1975, and died the following year.

BIBLIOGRAPHY

I. ORIGINAL WORKS. Webster's papers are held in the Stanford University Archives; they include laboratory notebooks and teaching notes from his Harvard days until his death, journals and records saved during army service in World War I, records and correspondence from twenty years as chairman of the Stanford physics department, an autobiographical essay, and materials from postwar activities on behalf of the AAPT Coulomb's Law Committee, *Encyclopaedia Britannica*, tsunami research, and NASA. In addition, two oral history interviews with Webster are on file at the Center for the History of Physics, American Physical Society. His publications are listed in the memoir by Kirkpatrick (see below), including his *General Physics for Colleges*, (New York, 1923), with Herman W. Farwell and Elmer Reginald Drew.

II. SECONDARY LITERATURE. Paul Kirkpatrick, "David Locke Webster," in *Biographical Memoirs. National Academy of Sciences*, **53** (1982), 367–400, gives much information on Webster's personality and family background, as well as his scientific work. Kirkpatrick also makes the case for Webster's anticipation of Duane and Hunt, based on Webster's research notebooks, in "Confirming the Plank-Einstein Equation $hv = (1/2)mv^2$," in *American Journal of Physics*, **48** (1980), 803–806. For Webster's Harvard education and role in the elaboration of the old quantum theory, see Katherine Russell Sopka, *Quantum Physics in America, 1920–1935* (New York, 1980; repr. Los Angeles, 1988). Arthur Holly Compton and Samuel K. Allison, *X-Rays in Theory and Experiment* (New York, 1935), summarizes Webster's most important work and integrates it with contemporary X-ray physics. On the dispute between pulse and wave theories in the early years of X-ray physics, and Webster's argument against the pulse theory, see Bruce R. Wheaton, *The Tiger and the Shark* (Cambridge, 1983); and on his involvement in the Duane-Compton controversy of the 1920's, see Roger H. Stuewer, *The Compton Effect: Turning Point in Physics* (New York, 1975). On building up the Stanford physics department, in competition with Berkeley and CalTech, see Robert Wayne Seidel, "Physics Research in California: The Rise of a Leading Sector in American Physics" (Ph.D. diss., University of California, Berkeley, 1978); and on the difficult transition to postwar research, see Stuart W. Leslie and Bruce Hevly, "Steeple Building at Stanford: Electrical Engineering, Physics, and Microwave Research," in *Proceedings of the IEEE*, **73** (1985), 1169–1180.

BRUCE HEVLY

WENTZEL, GREGOR (*b*. Düsseldorf, Germany, 17 February 1898; *d*. Ascona, Switzerland, 12 August 1978), *theoretical physics*.

Wentzel's father, Josef Wentzel, was a lawyer who held a quasi-governmental administrative position at a state bank in one of the provinces of Prussia. He was a man of broad intellect with many and varied interests, among which music and literature were particularly prominent. Wentzel's mother, Anna Joesten, came from an intellectual family whose male members were usually either physicians or priests. The family's strong cultural interests contrasted with a rather conservative attitude in matters of religion (Catholic).

On 5 December 1929, having succeeded Schrödinger at the University of Zurich a year earlier, Wentzel married Anna L. Wielich. With their son, Donat, who was born in 1934, the Wentzels became

Swiss citizens in 1940. Wentzel was president of the Schweizerische Physikalische Gesellschaft from 1945 to 1947. In 1948 he joined the faculty of the University of Chicago, remaining as professor of physics until 1969; he became a U.S. citizen in 1955. Wentzel was elected to numerous learned societies, including the National Academy of Sciences. A final recognition of his achievements was the award of the Max Planck Medal in 1975.

Wentzel was an eminent teacher both in the classroom and as a dissertation adviser. Among his Ph.D. students were Nicolas Kemmer, Markus Fierz, Valya Bargmann, Res Jost, and Felix Villars. His fame as a teacher and as a researcher is reflected in the temporary appointments he held: in 1930, visiting professor at the University of Wisconsin; in 1947, at Purdue University; in 1949, at Stanford University; in 1951 and 1956, at the Tata Institute, Bombay, India; in 1954, at the University of California; and in 1958, at the European Center for Nuclear Research (CERN).

Wentzel's education was relatively standard. He attended a gymnasium that emphasized Latin, modern languages, the natural sciences, and mathematics. When he was fourteen, Wentzel had as his physics teacher a candidate for a teaching credential who was particularly enthusiastic about the science of astronomy. He got Wentzel to build a telescope and to observe the planets and the stars. It was this stimulus that aroused his interest in science, an interest that had scarcely existed before. Wentzel went to the University of Freiburg in 1916 with the idea of becoming an astronomer. Since a scientific career usually implied accepting a high school teaching position, and such employment meant less status than the family had enjoyed, his parents did not support his decision.

Wentzel's university career was interrupted by military service after he had been at Freiburg for a semester and a half. Wentzel served in the German Army from 1917 through 1918. Thereafter he returned to Freiburg and spent another semester and a half there. In the autumn of 1919, Wentzel went to Greifswald. Both at Freiburg and at Greifswald, he studied mostly mathematics. At Freiburg he studied with Alfred Loewy and Oskar Bolza, specializing in analysis and complex variables. At Greifswald he was introduced to "mathematician's mathematics": set theory with Felix Hausdorff. Although he liked the course, he was not enthusiastic about this sort of mathematics. He studied physics primarily on his own. His reading of Hermann Weyl's *Raum, Zeit und Materie* made a deep impression on him. The one physics course that Wentzel did take at Greifswald was a seminar with Johannes Stark, who was assisted by Rudolf Seeliger. Impressed by Wentzel's performance, Seeliger suggested to him that he study with the theoretical physicist Arnold Sommerfeld at the University of Munich.

Wentzel arrived at Munich in November 1920 and was admitted to Sommerfeld's seminar. His first presentation there consisted of a novel derivation of Peter Debye's work on the dispersion of light by permanent dipoles. Sommerfeld was impressed and accepted him as a Ph.D. student. When Wentzel asked him for a doctoral problem, Sommerfeld indicated to him that X-ray spectroscopy was in a "mess" that he was unable to straighten out. "I am prejudiced," Sommerfeld told him, "and cannot do anything with it. Perhaps you as a younger man may find a clue, and may be able to make sense out of all these lines that increasing experimental work has produced." Wentzel succeeded in disentangling the wealth of extant spectroscopic data and clarified the structure of X-ray spectra. He obtained a set of rules governing the level scheme of X-ray line spectra, and much of the terminology still used is due to him. The analysis was in terms of two quantum numbers—later interpreted as orbital (ℓ) and total (j) angular momentum—with the selection rules $\Delta\ell = \pm 1$, $\Delta j = \pm 1$ and 0. This work became Wentzel's doctoral dissertation.

It was at Munich that Wentzel met Wolfgang Pauli and Werner Heisenberg, who also were students in Sommerfeld's seminar. He saw a good deal of Pauli, and they were very close friends until Pauli's death.

In the fall of 1921, having received the Ph.D., Wentzel became an assistant at the Munich Institute, where his main duty was the correction of the problems Sommerfeld assigned in his large lecture course. He simultaneously began work on his *Habilitationsschrift*, for which he chose the problem of β-scattering. In this work he gave an important criterion for distinguishing single from multiple scattering by successive atoms. His researches between 1922 and 1925, during which time he was an assistant to Sommerfeld and a *Privatdozent*, were primarily concerned with the interpretation of atomic spectra, in particular the fine structure of hydrogen-like atoms. His accomplishments were highly regarded, and Wentzel spent the fall semester (November 1925–February 1926) in Hamburg, replacing Wilhelm Lenz, who had fallen ill.

After the advent of the new quantum mechanics in 1925, Wentzel's researches had as their object the attempt to discover how far the familiar methods of the "old" quantum theory could be recaptured or rederived within the new matrix and wave mechanics. In the course of these investigations, he developed what later became known as the WKB (Wentzel-Kramers-Brillouin) method in wave mechanics.

After becoming extraordinary professor at the University of Leipzig in 1926, Wentzel worked on the formulation of the wave mechanical theory of radiation-induced and nonradiative transitions. He gave the first wave mechanical treatment of the photoelectric effect in atoms. This paper contains the $i\varepsilon$ prescription for the separation of outgoing waves by complex integration along suitable paths. His paper on radiationless scattering contains a formula (independently derived by Dirac, using time-dependent perturbation theory) for the transition rate in terms of the interaction matrix elements that is often referred to as the "Golden Rule." In 1928, Wentzel succeeded Erwin Schrödinger at the University of Zurich. At the same time, Pauli was called to the Eidgenössische Technische Hochschule, and they made Zurich a world center of theoretical physics.

From 1928 to 1933, a good deal of Wentzel's efforts were invested in the preparation of the course of lectures he gave at the university. His major production during that period was his masterful review of scattering theory and the application of quantum electrodynamics to radiation processes, which appeared in the 1933 edition of the *Handbuch der Physik*.

In 1933, Wentzel began attacking the divergence problems plaguing quantum field theory. In a series of important papers he formulated the equations of motion of a classical point electron interacting with its own and external fields in such a way that a finite reaction force resulted; but the extension of these methods to quantum electrodynamics proved unsuccessful. After Hideki Yukawa introduced his meson theory of nuclear forces in 1935, perturbation theory became the customary tool for studying nucleon-nucleon and meson-nucleon interactions. However, these results were of dubious value because these interactions are not weak.

Wentzel devoted most of his researches after 1935 to the question of how to avoid weak coupling perturbation methods in the quantum theory of fields. In 1940 he obtained a strong coupling method for handling mesonic interactions and discovered that in several meson theories, mesons could be bound to nucleons to form isobaric states. Later, a more general version of this strong coupling theory provided a useful model that helped to promote understanding of certain phenomena in meson physics (in particular, the 3-3 resonance in pion-nucleon scattering) as caused by the presence of an isobaric state.

In 1941 Wentzel wrote *Einführung in die Quantentheorie der Wellenfelder* (published in 1943). It was the text from which an entire generation of post–World War II physicists learned quantum field theory and has become a classic. After he joined the University of Chicago faculty, Wentzel's researches centered on meson field theory and related problems of high-energy physics. His main interest shifted after 1957 to solid-state physics, particularly the problem of superconductivity. Upon retiring from the University of Chicago in 1970, Wentzel settled in Ascona, Switzerland, where he died.

BIBLIOGRAPHY

I. ORIGINAL WORKS. Wentzel's writings include "Zur Systematik der Roentgenspektren," in *Zeitschrift für Physik*, **6** (1921), 84–99, his dissertation; "Eine Schwierigkeit für die Theorie des Kreiselektrons," *ibid.*, **37** (1926), 911–917; "Zur Theorie des photoelektrischen Effekts," *ibid.*, **40** (1926), 574–589; "Über strahlungslose Quantensprünge," *ibid.*, **43** (1927), 524–530; "Über die Eigenkräfte der Elementarteilchen," *ibid.*, **86** (1933), 479–494 and 635–645, and 87 (1934), 726–733; "Wellenmechanik der Stoss- und Strahlungsvorgänge," in H. Geiger and Karl Scheel, eds., *Handbuch der Physik*, XXIV (Berlin, 1933), 695–784; "Zum Problem des statistischen Mesonfeldes," in *Helvetica acta physica*, **13** (1940), 269–308; "Zur Hypothese der höheren Proton-Isobaren," *ibid.*, **14** (1941), 3–20; *Einführung in die Quantentheorie der Wellenfelder* (Vienna, 1943; repr. Ann Arbor, Mich., 1946), trans. by Charlotte Houtermans and J. M. Jauch as *Quantum Theory of Fields* (New York, 1949); "Recent Research in Meson Physics," in *Review of Modern Physics*, **19** (1947), 1–18; and "Quantum Theory of Fields (Until 1947)," in Markus Fierz and V. F. Weisskopf, eds., *Theoretical Physics in the Twentieth Century* (New York, 1960), 48–77.

According to his wife, most of Wentzel's papers were destroyed. A list of his publications is at the Center for the History of Physics at the American Institute of Physics, New York City. An oral interview of Wentzel, by Thomas S. Kuhn, took place 3–5 February 1964; a record of the minutes of this interview is on microfilm in *Sources for the History of Quantum Physics*.

II. SECONDARY LITERATURE. An obituary by V. L. Telegdi is in *Physics Today*, **31**, no. 11 (1978), 85–86. A collection of essays dedicated to Wentzel on his retirement from Chicago is P. G. O. Freund, C. J. Goebel, and Y. Nambu, eds., *quanta* (Chicago, 1970).

S. S. SCHWEBER

WHITTARD, WALTER FREDERICK (*b*. London, England, 26 October 1902; *d*. Westbury-on-Trym, Bristol, England, 2 March 1966), *paleontology, stratigraphy.*

Walter Frederick Whittard (known as Fred) was the youngest of four children of Thomas W. and Sarah Whittard, who lived in the Battersea district of London. His father was a prosperous and successful proprietor of a grocery store in Clapham. Fred entered the County Secondary School in Battersea and was one of the founding members of the school's Natural History Society. At that time he was interested primarily in zoology, but an interest in geology was roused by a family friend, Tom Eastwood, who worked for the Geological Survey. At Eastwood's behest young Whittard was allowed to enroll in evening classes in geology at Chelsea Polytechnic (now part of the University of London). As an enthusiastic amateur the boy made many collecting excursions around London and the Home Counties, even reaching the West Country. On leaving school, Whittard enrolled as a day student at Chelsea Polytechnic and in 1922 entered the geology department at Imperial College of Science and Technology, where he studied under W. W. Watts. Two years later he graduated with first-class honors in geology and zoology in his ARCS (Associate of the Royal College of Science) examinations, and in geology he gained the external London B.Sc. degree. Such prowess won him a place as a graduate student in the college, in company with Cyril J. Stubblefield, O. M. B. Bulman, and Howel and David Williams. There he began to map the Lower Silurian of south Shropshire and to study Lower Paleozoic paleontology. He even engaged in work on fossil amphibians with Bulman, supervised by Donald M. S. Watson. He received a Ph.D. from Imperial College in 1926.

A senior government scholarship made possible Whittard's attendance of Sidney Sussex College, Cambridge, which led to a Cambridge Ph.D. in 1928. This highly formative period for Whittard included an introduction to arctic geology on the Cambridge expedition to East Greenland, led by J. M. Wordie, in 1929.

That same year Whittard was back at Imperial College with an 1851 senior studentship, and in 1931 an assistant lectureship. By then P. G. H. Boswell had succeeded Watts as professor. In 1935 Whittard accepted a full lectureship. Two years later he moved to the Chaning Wills chair of geology at the University of Bristol, succeeding A. E. Trueman, and remained there for the rest of his professional life.

In 1930 Whittard married Caroline Margaret Sheppard; they had one son, Lawrence. Whittard was devoted to his wife and son, and to serving the university, as well as to fostering his research and many other interests. He was a man of considerable energies and robust health; this was nowhere more evident than when he conducted field mapping classes with students or when he organized and ran research cruises.

In his early years of professional work, Whittard published papers on the Precambrian, Ordovician, and Silurian formations of south Shropshire. His paleoenvironmental reconstructions of the Silurian transgressions in south Shropshire have stood as a model for many years. After this, he devoted much of his time in the field to mapping the Ordovician sequence in the Shelve area, a difficult task to which he added the monographic description of the Ordovician trilobites of the region. This work was posthumously completed by a former student of his, W. T. Dean. Other paleontological studies included one on a Cambrian wormlike fossil, *Palaeoscolex piscatorum*, and a presidential address to the Bristol Naturalists Society titled "Enigma of the Earliest Fossils" (1953).

Whittard's early foray with Bulman, in 1926, into vertebrate paleontology and the reconstruction of the amphibian *Branchiosaurus* was followed by papers on fossil amphibians (1928) and a compilation on vertebrates from the Lower Cretaceous Weald (1927). Whittard's extensive knowledge of Paleozoic stratigraphy led to his assuming the joint editorship of fascicle 3a of *Lexique stratigraphique international* with Scott Simpson, contributing largely to the volumes on the Ordovician and Silurian.

During World War II, Whittard served as adviser on many local geological matters, including water supply and the use of underground quarries for wartime factories and storage. Later he advised on the siting of the Severn Bridge and of the nuclear power station at Berkeley, in Gloucestershire. Throughout this time he was an active fellow of the Geological Society of London and a member of the Geologists Association. Locally, he had joined the Bristol Naturalists Society in 1938 and was president from 1938 to 1940 and from 1952 to 1953.

Whittard of necessity devoted much time to the administration, growth, and rehousing of his department. It became well known for its balance, esprit de corps, and well-being, as well as for its impressive research output. He was dean of the Faculty of Science during the period 1945 to 1948.

In 1955 Whittard took over from W. B. R. King of Cambridge the latter's work on the geology of the English Channel, extending it to the Western

Approaches. At Bristol he built up a small team to investigate the Cretaceous and Tertiary rocks and the marine superficial deposits between Britain and France, and to continue with some of the geophysical survey. This work was carried out from the research vessel *Sarsia*, owned by the Marine Biological Association at Plymouth, and involved two cruises per year for almost ten years. A program of heavy dredging and coring was supplemented by one of acoustic survey involving the Woods Hole research vessel *Chain*. Several major publications resulted directly from this work, and the involvement of a Bristol team in marine geological studies across the continental shelf adjacent to Britain has continued to this day. The results of these voyages have been incorporated into the British Geological Survey maps of the Channel area. Less than a year before he died, Whittard organized the International Symposium on Submarine Geology and Geophysics for the Colston Research Society that was held in Bristol.

In addition to his university work, Whittard served on the councils of the Geological Society, the Palaeontological Society, and the National Committees for Geology and for Geodesy and Geophysics. He was vice president of the Palaeontological Association in 1961 and 1962. He gained his London D.Sc. and was elected a fellow of the Royal Society in 1957. The award of the Murchison Medal of the Geological Society, in 1965, a year before his death, served as a substantial recognition of his services to the study of geology.

As relaxation from his work, Whittard became an enthusiastic gardener and a skilled bookbinder, enjoyed music, and later took up watercolor painting. On a visit to Canada in 1965 he contracted a virus infection of his lungs that led to his death from heart failure early the following year.

BIBLIOGRAPHY

I. Original Works. A complete bibliography of Whittard's works is in Bulman (see below). His more important works include "The Stratigraphy of the Valentian Rocks of Shropshire: The Main Outcrop," in *Quarterly Journal of the Geological Society of London*, **83** (1928), 739–759; "The Geology of the Ordovician and Valentian Rocks of the Shelve Country, Shropshire," in *Proceedings of the Geological Association*, **42** (1931), 322–339; "The Stratigraphy of the Valentian Rocks of Shropshire: The Longmynd Shelve and Breidden Outcrops," in *Quarterly Journal of the Geological Society of London*, **88** (1932), 859–902; "A Geology of South Shropshire," in *Proceedings of the Geological Association*, **63** (1952), 143–197; "The Ordovician Trilobites of the Shelve Inlier, West Shropshire," *Palaeontological Society Monograph*, pts. I–VIII

(1955–1956), 1–306; "The Geology of the Western Approaches of the English Channel, I. Chalky Rocks from the Upper Reaches of the Continental Slope," in *Philosophical Transactions of the Royal Society of London*, **B245** (1962), 267–290, written with D. Curry, E. Martini, and A. J. Smith; "The Geology of the Western Approaches of the English Channel. II. Geological Interpretation Aided by Boomer and Sparker Records," *ibid.*, **B248** (1965), 315–351, written with D. Curry, J. B. Hersey, and E. Martini; and "The Geology of the Western Approaches of the English Channel. III. The *Globigerina* Silts and Associated Rocks," in *Colston Papers*, **17** (1965), 239–261.

II. Secondary Literature. A memoir is O. M. B. Bulman, "Walter Frederick Whittard," in *Biographical Memoirs of Fellows of the Royal Society*, **12** (1966), 531–542. See also Bernard E. Leake, "Whittard, Walter Frederick," in *Dictionary of National Biography, 1961–1970* (Oxford, 1981), 1073–1074.

D. L. Dineley

WILHELM, RICHARD HERMAN (*b.* New York City, 10 January 1909; *d.* Center Harbor, New Hampshire, 6 August 1968), *chemical engineering.*

Richard Wilhelm was the son of Ernst Richard Wilhelm, a cabinetmaker originally from Germany, and Ida Emma Krebs Wilhelm. He attended New York City schools for all of his early education. He received the B.S. degree from Columbia University in 1931 and a degree in chemical engineering in 1932. In 1934, while he was completing doctoral work at Columbia, he was hired as an instructor in the chemical engineering department at Princeton, where he remained until his death. In 1935 he received the Ph.D. from Columbia, and in 1937 he married Rachel Marjorie Hixson. They had three children: David, Joan, and Karen. Wilhelm rose through the academic ranks at Princeton to the position of professor of chemical engineering in 1946 and chairman of the department in 1954. During World War II he was involved in several programs of the National Defense Research Committee, first as a consultant for the Chemical Warfare Panel and later as codirector of a research project carried out at Princeton for the Office of Rubber Director. His association with that committee continued until 1953.

Although primarily an academician, Wilhelm served as an engineering consultant on reactor design for several chemical manufacturers. He was an active member of many professional and scientific societies and was a recipient of the William H. Walker Award in 1951, the Professional Progress Award in 1952, the Warren K. Lewis Award (all of the American Institute of Chemical Engineers), and the Industrial and Engineering Chemistry Award of the American Chemical Society. He was also a fellow of the American Academy of Arts and Sciences.

In 1964 Wilhelm's wife died. Two years later he married Sarah Kollock Strayer, the widow of Princeton economics professor Paul J. Strayer.

Wilhelm's contribution to the field of chemical engineering was strongest as a theoretician in chemical reactor design and as an educator and mentor of chemical engineers. In the early years of the chemical industry, as in many other areas of applied science, the design of large-scale manufacturing technology was mainly an empirical process. The 1930's was a period of rapid expansion in the chemical industry, particularly in petroleum refining; accompanying this sudden growth was an increased interest in the theoretical and mathematical modeling of chemical reactor systems. The ability to create such models was facilitated by a growing body of knowledge about fluid mechanics and heat and mass transfer. Wilhelm's theoretical work lay in the realm of fluid transport through chemical reactor systems, specifically in maintaining a stable set of reactor conditions in spite of the continued flow of reactants and products through a high-temperature environment.

Wilhelm's earliest papers, published in 1939, dealt with fluid flow and viscometry. In the 1940's and 1950's his work centered on the modeling of particle flow through packed and fluidized catalytic beds. For packed-bed reactors he was able to develop a mathematical model for dispersion processes that proved useful in predicting regions of abnormally high temperature. To deal with fluidized beds, in which the reactants flow through a loosely packed catalyst, producing a boiling effect, Wilhelm studied heat and mass transfer phenomena in systems of turbulent flow; he was the originator of much of the standard terminology in this field. However, he was hampered by the fact that the whole area of turbulent flow, because of the complexity of the fluid dynamics involved, was beyond the reach of simple mathematical modeling at that time. It was not until the last years of his life, when his attention had turned elsewhere, that the sufficiently sophisticated computer technology was developed that could have simplified his task.

In the mid 1960's Wilhelm's activity centered on a method of separating liquid mixtures that he had originated and named parametric pumping; upon it his remaining research was concentrated. This method consisted of pumping a solution through a column of fixed solid adsorbent while varying two of the system's parameters, such as temperature

and direction of flow, synchronously. Wilhelm was able to provide a mathematical description for this process. He felt that the process might have explanatory power outside the realm of engineering and suggested that parametric pumping might prove to be a model for active transport of ions through cell membranes, where pH would replace temperature as a variable parameter. In the years following his death, parametric pumping theory has not proved to have either the industrial applications or the explanatory power that Wilhelm hoped for.

Equal in importance to his contribution to the theory of reactor engineering was Wilhelm's role as an educator of chemical engineers. As chairman of Princeton's chemical engineering department for fourteen years, he brought that department to national prominence. (In 1966 the American Council on Education cited Princeton's chemical engineering graduate program as the second most attractive in the nation.) Wilhelm's doctoral students rose to prominence in university engineering departments as well as in the chemical industry. His educational philosophy held that the primary function of the university is to teach, and the undergraduate student should be its primary focus. He was exceptionally active in academic life and unceasingly concerned with the articulation of engineering and other disciplines, especially the life sciences.

Wilhelm had intended to resign the chair of chemical engineering in 1969 in order to give more time to research, especially to the application of parametric pumping theory. In April 1968 he was elected to the National Academy of Engineering, and in June, Princeton made him Henry Putnam university professor, an endowed chair recognizing scholarship of extraordinary ability. On 6 August of that year, while vacationing with his family at the seashore, Wilhelm died of a heart attack. In his memory the American Institute of Chemical Engineers established the R. H. Wilhelm Award in chemical reactor engineering in 1973. Princeton instituted the Wilhelm Lectureships in 1974.

BIBLIOGRAPHY

I. ORIGINAL WORKS. A complete bibliography of Wilhelm's published papers (forty-eight in all) is in Rutherford Aris, "R. H. Wilhelm's Influence on the Development of Chemical Reaction Engineering," in *Chemical Engineering Education*, **17** (Winter 1983), 10–15, 38–41. His doctoral dissertation is "Vapor Phase Nitration of Benzene" (Columbia University, 1935). Key papers on his research include "Fluidization of Solid Particles," in *Chemical Engineering Progress*, **44** (1948), 201–218, with

Mooson Kwauk, an early paper on fluidized beds; "Progress Towards the A Priori Design of Chemical Reactors," in *Pure and Applied Chemistry*, **5** (1962), 403–420, in which he discusses the difficulty of modeling industrial reactor systems, and his successes in doing so for packed-bed reactors; "Parametric Pumping: A Model for Active Transport," in Katherine Brehme Warren, ed., *Intracellular Transport* (New York, 1966), 199–220; and "Parametric Pumping: A Dynamic Principle for Separating Fluid Mixtures," in *Industrial and Engineering Chemistry Fundamentals*, **7** (1968), 337–349, with Alan W. Rice, Roger W. Rolke, and Norman H. Sweed.

II. SECONDARY LITERATURE. Aris's article, cited above, is a good summary of Wilhelm's contributions to chemical reactor theory. An assessment of his success as an educator is in "Dick Wilhelm of Princeton" in *Chemical Engineering Education*, **2** (1968), 60–61. An autobiographical sketch of his contributions to chemical engineering theory is in *McGraw-Hill Modern Men of Science*, II (New York, 1968), 600. His colleague at Princeton, R. K. Toner, summarized his career in the Wilhelm memorial issue of *Industrial and Engineering Chemistry Fundamentals*, **8** (1969), 178–179.

MARGARET JACKSON CLARKE

WILSON, HAROLD ALBERT (*b*. York, England, 1 December 1874; *d*. Houston, Texas, 13 October 1964), *physics*.

Harold Albert Wilson was the only son of a North Eastern Railway clerk who later became a district manager, and Anne Gill, daughter of a local farmer and innkeeper. He had one sister, Lilian, who married Owen Willans Richardson, a physicist and Nobel Prize winner whose work was closely related to Wilson's. Wilson attended a private boys' school and later, when he was about twelve, entered a private preparatory school called St. Olave's, at which he stayed until he was nineteen, the last two years as an assistant mathematics master. At school he took lessons in chemistry and got some practical knowledge of machines such as railway engines and steam rollers, but his passion for science was stimulated more by his home than his schools. Wilson's father was an enlightened man who studied mathematics and philosophy, and encouraged the development of his son's scientific interests. By the time he left St. Olave's, Wilson had done chemical experiments in his home lab and taken evening classes in chemistry at the Railway Institute in York, receiving the advanced certificate in elementary inorganic chemistry.

In 1893 Wilson entered Victoria University College at Leeds, where he studied mathematics, physics, chemistry, and biology. It was at Leeds that he started, with Professor Arthur Smithells, research on the electrical conductivity of flames that he continued, with varying intensity, for more than thirty years. After receiving B.Sc. degrees in physics and chemistry, in September 1897 Wilson arrived at Cambridge to work at the Cavendish Laboratory with J. J. Thomson.

This was an exciting time for Cavendish physics. Thomson and Rutherford had just published their fundamental paper on conduction by gaseous ions produced by X rays, and the concept of the electron was taking concrete shape; C. T. R. Wilson (unrelated to Harold) had invented his cloud chamber, making it possible to observe trajectories of single charged particles; Paul Langevin was studying the properties of the ions produced in gases by X rays, and shared his laboratory with Rutherford and H. A. Wilson. The years at the Cavendish, interrupted by an eight-month visit at Jacobus Van't Hoff's laboratory in Berlin in 1899, were among the most productive in Wilson's scientific career. He investigated the mobility of ions in flames, studied electric discharge in rarefied gases, measured the Hall effect in gases, and, following J. J. Thomson, made an attempt to determine the charge of the electron by using the cloud chamber. The experiment, in which he observed the fall of the condensation drops in the vertical electric field and in its absence, was a forerunner of the more precise technique developed by Robert Millikan. Wilson, however, used water instead of oil droplets and observed the top edge of the condensation cloud instead of individual droplets. His result was about 35 percent too small, mostly owing to the effect of evaporation during the experiment.

In 1904 Wilson joined the faculty of King's College, London, and in the following year was named professor and head of the department of physics. In 1906 he was elected a fellow of the Royal Society. Three years later he left England for Canada, to accept a professorship at McGill University; and in 1912, when the Rice Institute (now Rice University) was established in Houston, Texas, Wilson became one of its eleven original professors. In the same year he married Marjorie Patterson Smyth, a former gold medalist in physics at McGill. He remained at Rice for the rest of his academic career, leaving it for only one year (1924) for the chair of natural philosophy at Glasgow, once occupied by Kelvin. He gained a reputation as an excellent teacher and developed an active research center.

Wilson's professional interests ranged from practical problems such as oil cracking and sound perception (during World War I he designed an underwater sound receiver, later developed by General

Electric for use in antisubmarine warfare) to the theory of relativity and the structure of the nucleus. He was best known for his research on the conductivity of flames, but after 1932 nuclear physics became his primary focus. During World War II, Wilson did research for the Manhattan Project.

Although an experimentalist, Wilson had well-developed mathematical skills. He used them mostly in a semiempirical manner for interpretation of his experimental results. He belonged to the last generation of classical physicists who witnessed the full triumph of the modern, quantum-relativistic vision of the world. Like many others he did not immediately embrace revolutionary ideas. As late as 1928 he believed that atoms could be viewed as absorbing light like simple damped oscillators; in 1910 he tried to explain the results of the Michelson-Morley experiment without resorting to relativity; and in 1921 he still referred to ether in discussing electromagnetism. However, Wilson later accepted the relativity and quantum theories. Upon his retirement he chose relativity as a subject of his teaching to a small class of Rice students who met at his home.

Wilson was naturalized as an American citizen in 1931. In 1947 he was named professor emeritus but continued to teach part-time until 1964. He died six weeks before he would have become ninety years old. He was survived by his wife, two sons, and two daughters.

BIBLIOGRAPHY

I. ORIGINAL WORKS. Thomson's article (see below) includes a bibliography of Wilson's works. It consists of ninety-nine research papers and four books: *The Electrical Properties of Flames* (London, 1912); *Experimental Physics* (Cambridge, 1915); *Modern Physics* (London and Glasgow, 1928); and *The Mysteries of the Atom* (New York, 1934).

Archival materials held at the American Institute of Physics in New York include undated *Biographical Notes of H. A. Wilson* (21 pp.) and a transcript of an interview conducted with Wilson by G. Phillips and W. J. King on March 3, 1964 (28 pp.).

II. SECONDARY LITERATURE. G. P. Thomson, "Harold Albert Wilson, 1874–1964," in *Biographical Memoirs of Fellows of the Royal Society,* **11** (1965), 187–201, is the only published biography of Wilson. A brief obituary is in *Physics Today,* **18,** no. 1 (1965), 154.

KRIS SZYMBORSKI

WINKLER, HELMUT GUSTAV FRANZ (*b.* Kiel, Germany, 3 April 1915; *d.* Göttingen, Federal Republic of Germany, 10 November 1980), *mineralogy, petrology.*

The son of Paul Arthur Aloysius Winkler, a canal pilot, and Martha Auguste Hedwig Rhinow, Winkler became interested in geology during his last few years in high school. In 1934 he entered the University of Rostock, where he studied mineralogy, geology, and chemistry, with mineralogy as his major subject. While there, he met C. W. Correns, who exerted a considerable, possibly decisive, influence on Winkler's scientific development. For a time he studied at Tübingen (1935–1936) and at the University of St. Andrews (1937). His dissertation, on the thixotropy of mineral powders of microscopic size, inspired by Correns, earned him the doctorate in 1938. He was married to Ursula Wichmann on 4 May 1942; they had two daughters and a son.

After an interruption of nearly six years (1939–1944), during World War II, Winkler continued his scientific work at the University of Göttingen with Correns. At first he worked on crystallographic problems, in particular on the crystal analysis of eucryptite and related compounds. As a result of these and other studies, Winkler became the first chairman of the department of crystallography at the University of Göttingen in 1949. During this period he concentrated on finding or deriving quantitative relations between the structures and the physical properties of crystals. His conception of these relations is documented in his book *Struktur und Eigenschaften der Kristalle* (1950).

In 1951 Winkler was simultaneously offered professorships at the University of Marburg, the University of Saarbrücken, and the Technical University of Munich. He accepted the chair at Marburg, where he continued his studies in crystallography. In addition, he did work in the applied mineralogy of ceramic clay.

Winkler's instinct for discerning promising future developments in research made him change fields in 1955. During a lecture tour in the United States, Winkler became acquainted with recently developed high-pressure apparatus that made it possible to simulate in the laboratory the pressures and temperatures deep within the earth's crust. Fascinated with these developments and foreseeing the future success and the new opportunities of experimental petrology, he turned to that new field. His works on the experimental metamorphism of sediments (1957) show that he was a pioneer of experimental petrology in Europe. In the late 1950's he proved experimentally the assumed relation between high-grade metamorphism and the formation of anatectic granitic magmas in the earth's crust. In order to achieve as close to natural conditions as possible in his experiments, Winkler used common, naturally formed sediments, clays, and graywackes. He studied their metamorphic change under the pressure and temperature conditions of the earth's crust up to the emergence of anatectic melts. The discussion of the origin and formation of granitic magmas, which had been controversial for a long time, was thus given a new and sound base.

In 1962 Winkler accepted a chair at the Georg-August University of Göttingen. With his assistants and graduate students, he continued the petrological work that had begun in Marburg, experimentally investigating many metamorphic mineral reactions. It was his aim to establish a systematic order in the diversity of metamorphic rocks on the basis of petrographically observed and experimentally calibrated mineral reactions. In this he followed the concept of metamorphic facies introduced by P. E. Eskola in 1914 and 1939, making it the starting point of further intensive studies. In the late 1960's, simultaneously with other scientists, he recognized the limits of this concept and developed a new division into four metamorphic grades subdivided by zones, which are defined by specific, experimentally calibrated mineral reactions.

At the same time, he sought to find general laws determining the formation and crystallization of granitic magmas. The results and the general ideas of his petrological research were published in many essays and in his book *Die Genese der metamorphen Gesteine*, of which five editions in six languages appeared between 1965 and 1986.

Winkler's life was characterized by an extraordinary enthusiasm for mineralogical and geological problems. The wide range of his scientific achievement was unusual even for his time. Winkler's work brought him international recognition and many honors. He was a member of the German Mineralogical Society, the Academy of Science of Göttingen, the Academy of Sciences of Austria, and the Geological Society of Finland; an honorary member of the Geological Society of America, the Geological Society of Belgium, and the Geological Society of London; an associate member of the Geological Society of France; and a fellow of the Mineralogical Society of America.

BIBLIOGRAPHY

Winkler's books include *Struktur und Eigenschaften der Kristalle* (Berlin, 1950; 2nd ed., 1955); and *Die Genese der metamorphen Gesteine* (Berlin, 1965), trans. from 2nd rev. ed. by N. D. Chatterjee and E. Froesl as *Petrogenesis of Metamorphic Rocks* (New York, 1967). Among his papers are "Synthese und Kristallstruktur des Eu-cryptits," in *Acta Crystallographica* (London), **1** (1948), 27–34; "Die Struktur des Tief-$K_2Li(AlF_6)$ und ihre Beziehung zu elpasolith . . . und anderen Strukturen," in *Heidelberger Beiträge zur Mineralogie und Petrographie*, **3** (1952), 297–306; "Bedeutung der Korngrössenverteilung und des Mineralbestandes von Tonen für die Herstellung grobkeramischer Erzeugnisse," in *Berichte der Deutschen Keramischen Gesellschaft*, **31** (1954), 337–343; "Hydrothermale Metamorphose karbonatfreier Tone," in *Geochimica et Cosmochimica Acta* **13** (1957), 42–69; "Experimentelle Gesteinmetamorphose, II, Bildung von anatektischen granitischen Schmelzen bei der Metamorphose von NaCl-führenden kalkfreien Tonen," *ibid.*, **15** (1958), 91–112, with Hilmar von Platen; "Ultrametamorphose kalkhaltiger Tone," *ibid.*, **18** (1960), 294–316; "Bildung anatektischer Schmelzen aus metamorphisierten Grauwacken," *ibid.*, **24** (1961), 48–69; "Experimentelle anatektische Schmelzen und ihre petrogenetische Bedeutung," *ibid.*, **24**, 250–259; "Genesen von Graniten und Migmatiten auf Grund neuer Experimente," in *Geologische Rundschau*, **51** (1961), 347–361; "Das T-P Feld der Diagenese und niedrigtemperierte Metamorphose aufgrund von Mineralreaktionen," in *Beiträge zur Mineralogie und Petrographie*, **10** (1964), 70–93; "Abolition of Metamorphic Facies, Introduction of the Four Divisions of Metamorphic Stage, and of a Classification Based on Isograds in Common Rocks," in *Neues Jahrbuch für Mineralogie: Monatshefte* (1970), 189–248; "Temperaturen und Drucke bei der regionalen Metamorphose: Prinzipielle und praktische Hinweise," in *Geologische Rundschau*, **65** (1976), 874–885; "Low Temperature Granitic Melts," in *Neues Jahrbuch für Mineralogie. Monatshefte* (1975), 245–268, with Manfred Boese and Theodor Marcopoulos; and "New Aspects of Granitic Magmas," *ibid.* (1978), 463–480, with Reinhard Breitbart.

Some of Winkler's papers are at the Mineralogical and Petrological Institute, University of Göttingen, and some are in the possession of his widow.

KARL-HEINZ G. NITSCH

WINSTEIN, SAUL (*b*. Montreal, Quebec, Canada, 8 October 1912; *d*. Los Angeles, California, 23 November 1969), *chemistry*.

In 1923 Louis and Anne Dick Winstein moved to the United States. Their son, naturalized in 1929, attended Los Angeles public schools before enrolling in the University of California at Los Angeles (B.A., 1934; M.A., 1935) and the California Institute of Technology (Ph.D., 1938). On 3 September 1937 he married Sylvia V. Levin; they had a son and a daughter.

Winstein was a National Research Council fellow under Paul D. Bartlett at Harvard (1939–1940) and instructor at the Illinois Institute of Technology (1940–1941). In 1941 he became instructor of chemistry at UCLA, where he remained, becoming full professor in 1947. His many honors include election to the National Academy of Sciences (1955), UCLA Alumnus of the Year (1958), California Scientist of the Year (1962), and the National Medal of Science (posthumous). UCLA recognized his excellence with its Distinguished Teaching Award (1963). Winstein was active in the Academic Senate, the Alumni Association, and the UCLA Art Council and Friends of Music. He was at the peak of his career and influence at the time of his sudden death following a heart attack.

One of the leading figures in physical organic chemistry, Winstein started his career during the infancy of the field. In his undergraduate years E. D. Hughes and C. K. Ingold were making the first detailed kinetic studies of nucleophilic substitution reactions. At UCLA, William G. Young introduced him to the subject, an introduction that resulted in eight publications on allylic rearrangements and Grignard reagents by the time he had his M. A. Winstein's love for the field deepened when he moved to Caltech to work with Howard Lucas, the American pioneer of physical organic chemistry. Lucas, at Caltech since 1913, was among the first organic chemists to explore electronic interpretations of organic reactions.

In 1939 Lucas and Winstein published an important paper on the stereochemical role of neighboring bromine in displacement reactions, providing an elegant proof that the bromine on the carbon atom adjacent to the reactive center formed a cyclic bromonium ion intermediate. Winstein was to be the foremost creator of these bridged ions. Except for research on antimalarials during World War II, most of Winstein's work can be traced to the studies with Young and Lucas, the major interest always being the nature of the cationic intermediates in organic reactions.

A 1948 paper demonstrated that a great acceleration of the ionization process often accompanied neighboring group participation. Winstein originated the concept of driving force and developed means to determine its quantitative value. This concept first appeared in the context of the discovery of the homoallylic cholesteryl ion. Winstein studied the cholesteryl system as an extension of his work on allylic compounds, since the 5,6-double bond in cholesteryl derivatives should act as a neighboring group. The solvolysis of cholesteryl-*p*-toluene sulfonate was 100 times faster than expected, which suggested the formation of an abnormally stable intermediate due to the driving force toward ionization in the displacement reaction. The product

was a derivative of *i*-cholesterol, but an abnormally rapid conversion of this to the normal derivative meant that the intermediate was an electronically resonating ion. Winstein formulated it thus, as the common intermediate for the forward and reverse rearrangements:

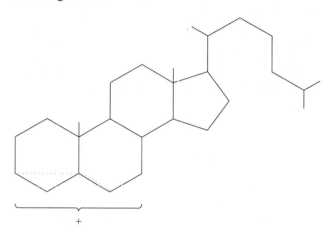

FIGURE 1.   The homoallylic cholesteryl ion.

In subsequent publications Winstein developed the subject of "nonclassical" ions, defined as carbonium ion intermediates with an electron pair delocalized and binding three centers. Such ions, formed by participation of the electron cloud associated with neighboring groups, were important in understanding the kinetics, stereochemistry, and mechanism of many substitution and rearrangement reactions. Winstein's studies on bridged carbonium ions took continually new directions through the 1950's and 1960's, though not without controversy. Herbert C. Brown, in particular, strongly opposed the postulation of such entities.

For the remainder of his life Winstein synthesized new substances, many of considerable structural beauty, to show the importance of neighboring groups. Whether they involved the *pi* participation of a double bond or the *sigma* participation of a saturated group, all were aspects of the principle of optimal charge delocalization through the most favorable overlap of atomic orbitals. Winstein justified his structural creations with molecular orbital calculations showing that the stabilization is due to electron delocalization.

Winstein's studies in the 1950's included the discerning of various kinds of ionic intermediates, from intimate ion pairs and solvent-separated ion pairs to dissociated ions. A reaction product may not derive from a carbonium ion but from ion pairs with varying degrees of tightness. He extended his kinetic analyses to the point where all rate constants were related to the various intermediates present.

During the 1960's Winstein became fascinated with the similarities between a double bond and a three-membered ring. His inventiveness peaked with his creation of a series of "homoaromatic" compounds having all or part of the double bonds replaced by cyclopropane rings. Winstein prepared cations, radicals, and anions of enhanced stability owing to homoaromatic properties and developed this area into an active one taken up by many investigators. The unfolding of homoaromaticity provided a good example of his role as a trailblazer and innovator. The development of nuclear magnetic resonance in the last five years of his life enabled Winstein to directly observe a variety of such species, all of which existed because of cyclic electron delocalization and the induced ring current.

From Winstein's creations and discoveries flowed new types of structures, syntheses, rearrangements, and concepts. His terms and concepts entered into the language and textbooks of organic chemistry, and were so common and familiar by the mid 1970's that their recent origin was unknown to the current generation of students.

BIBLIOGRAPHY

I. ORIGINAL WORKS. Paul Bartlett collected Winstein's most important papers in his *Nonclassical Ions* (New York, 1965), which is a reprint of papers on the subject with commentary by Bartlett. Winstein himself provided two valuable reviews of his work, the first in George R. Robertson, ed., *Modern Chemistry for the Engineer and Scientist* (New York, 1957), 146–167; and the second as British Chemical Society centenary lecturer, "Nonclassical Ions and Homoaromaticity," in *Quarterly Reviews,* **23** (1969), 141–176.

II. SECONDARY LITERATURE. Appreciations and analyses of Winstein's work by his colleagues appeared shortly after his death. William G. Young and Donald J. Cram wrote the biography for *Biographical Memoirs, National Academy of Sciences,* **43** (1973), 321–353. Paul D. Bartlett's study, "The Scientific Work of Saul Winstein," is in *Journal of the American Chemical Society,* **94** (1972), 2161–2170; that of Andrew Streitwieser is in *Progress in Physical Organic Chemistry,* **9** (1972), 1–24. Each of these articles provides a bibliography of his publications.

ALBERT B. COSTA

WOLFOWITZ, JACOB (*b.* Warsaw, Russian Poland, 19 March 1910; *d.* Tampa, Florida, 16 July 1981), *mathematical statistics, information theory.*

Jacob Wolfowitz was born into a Jewish family, the son of Samuel and Chaya Wolfowitz. Samuel emigrated to the United States shortly before the outbreak of World War I, planning to have his family join him after a brief period. The outbreak of the war prevented this, and the family was not able to join Samuel in New York City until 1920. The war years were particularly difficult times for the family. Jacob Wolfowitz was educated in the public schools of Brooklyn, New York, and graduated from the College of the City of New York with the degree of bachelor of science in 1931. This was during the Great Depression, and Wolfowitz secured whatever employment he could, including high-school teaching, while continuing his education part-time. He obtained the M.A. degree from Columbia University in 1933, and the Ph.D. in mathematics from New York University in 1942. In 1934 he married Lillian Dundes. Their children, Laura Mary and Paul Dundes, were born in 1941 and 1943, respectively.

In 1942 Wolfowitz joined the Statistical Research Group of Columbia University, doing war-related research. In 1945 he became associate professor of statistics at the University of North Carolina. In 1946 he joined the newly formed Department of Mathematical Statistics at Columbia University. In 1951 he became professor of mathematics at Cornell University, and in 1970 he joined the Department of Mathematics at the University of Illinois. After retiring from Illinois in 1978, he became distinguished professor of mathematics at the University of South Florida, a position he held until his death. He also held visiting professorships at the universities of Paris, Heidelberg, and California at Los Angeles, and the Technion (Israel Institute of Technology).

His research accomplishments were recognized by a long list of honors, including an honorary doctorate from the Technion; election to the U.S. National Academy of Sciences and to the American Academy of Arts and Sciences; election as fellow of the International Statistics Institute, the Econometric Society, the American Statistical Association, and the Institute of Mathematical Statistics; a term as president of the Institute of Mathematical Statistics; and selection as Shannon Lecturer of the Institute of Electrical and Electronic Engineers and as the Wald and the Rietz lecturer of the Institute of Mathematical Statistics. He was an excellent lecturer, with a remarkable ability to clarify some very complicated mathematics. Wolfowitz was a physically vigorous man who played handball while he lived in New York City and took long, brisk walks when he moved away from the city. He was an omnivorous reader, with a remarkable knowledge of political, social, and economic conditions in all of the large countries and many of the small countries of the world. He was a lifelong and committed Zionist and was active in organizing protests against Soviet repression of dissidents, intellectuals, and minorities.

Wolfowitz met Abraham Wald soon after Wald arrived in New York City in the autumn of 1938. Wald was well known for his research on geometry and econometrics in Vienna, and the two men quickly became close friends and collaborators. Their earliest joint work was in the area of nonparametric statistical inference, their first paper appearing in 1939. Nonparametric statistical inference is necessary when the statistician is unable to assume that he is sampling from a population whose form is known, and that the only unknowns are a finite number of parameters. The first appearance of the word "nonparametric" was in a 1942 paper by Wolfowitz. Wald and Wolfowitz constructed confidence bands for a completely unknown distribution function and constructed a test to determine whether two samples come from the same population, without making any assumptions about the form of the populations.

Another important subject on which Wald and Wolfowitz collaborated was sequential analysis. While working with the Columbia University Statistical Research Group, Wald had developed what he called the "sequential probability ratio test." This test decides which of two populations is being sampled by taking observations one at a time and determining after each observation whether another observation should be taken or whether sampling should be terminated and a final choice made. The conventional technique was to take a predetermined number of observations. Wald conjectured that the sequential probability ratio test minimizes the average number of observations required, but no rigorous proof existed until Wald and Wolfowitz published one in 1948. This 1948 paper may have been the paper of which Wolfowitz was proudest. Wolfowitz published many other papers on sequential methods, including several that constructed estimators of unknown parameters using sequential sampling.

Wald died in 1950, and his death removed the strongest tie binding Wolfowitz to Columbia University. He moved to Cornell University in 1951. Jack Kiefer, who was just completing his doctorate at Columbia, moved to Cornell at the same time, and Wolfowitz and Kiefer started a long and fruitful collaboration. One important area they explored was the optimal design of experiments, which is the theory specifying where to take observations in order to estimate unknown parameters with the smallest possible error. Kiefer and Wolfowitz also made important contributions to the mathematical theory describing the properties of queues. In col-

laboration with A. Dvoretzky they published fundamental research on the inventory problem, which is the problem of deciding how much inventory to hold in each of a sequence of intervals when there are penalties for holding too much or too little inventory and demand is random. This research was an early example of what came to be known as dynamic programming.

Starting in 1957 Wolfowitz devoted an increasing proportion of his research to information theory. Information theory describes how rapidly information can be sent over a channel when random errors occur in the transmission and the probability of correct decipherment must be at least equal to a preassigned value. Wolfowitz gave various limits on the rate at which information can be sent for various types of channels. His monograph *Coding Theorems of Information Theory* contains most of these results.

BIBLIOGRAPHY

Wolfowitz's research covered all of the major areas in mathematical statistics. *Jacob Wolfowitz: Selected Papers* (New York, 1980) contains a complete list of his 120 publications, the complete text of 49 papers he chose as among his most important, a brief biography, and a detailed discussion of his research. See also *Coding Theorems of Information Theory*, 3rd ed. (New York, 1978). An obituary by Rudolph Ahlswede, with bibliography, appeared in *IEEE Transactions on Information Theory*, **28** (1982), 687–690.

LIONEL WEISS

WOLFROM, MELVILLE LAWRENCE (*b.* Bellevue, Ohio, 2 April 1900; *d.* Columbus, Ohio, 20 June 1969), *carbohydrate chemistry.*

Wolfrom was the ninth and last child born to Frederick and Maria Louisa Sutter Wolfrom. His father died in 1907; his mother, a minister's daughter, raised him in a strict Lutheran tradition. Lacking the financial means to continue his education beyond high school, he became a quality control chemist in 1917 for the National Carbon Company in Fremont, Ohio. In 1918 he moved to Cleveland, joining the Students' Army Training Corps and taking courses at Western Reserve University, which he found unsatisfactory. A second attempt at higher education, at Washington Square College in New York, also ended in failure. After several odd jobs in Bellevue, Wolfrom entered Ohio State in 1920. He became an assistant to the carbohydrate chemist William Lloyd Evans and graduated cum laude in

1924. He enrolled at Northwestern to work with another carbohydrate chemist, Winford Lee Lewis, receiving the M.S. in 1925 and the Ph.D. in 1927. He married a Northwestern music student, Agnes Louise Thompson, on 1 June 1926. They had five children.

A National Research Council fellowship for 1927 to 1929 enabled Wolfrom to work with two eminent scientists, Claude Hudson at the National Bureau of Standards and Phoebus Levene at the Rockefeller Institute. They exposed him to the enormous challenge of the structural chemistry of complex natural products. His work with Levene led to the publication of three papers on the linkage positions in disaccharides and the ring structures of sugar derivatives.

In 1929 Wolfrom became an instructor in chemistry at Ohio State, advancing to professor in 1940, research professor in 1960, and regents' professor in 1965. He belonged to the leading chemical societies in America and Europe and was a member of the National Academy of Sciences and the American Academy of Arts and Sciences. His interest in human personality and the motivations of scientists led him to publish several biographical memoirs, notably those of his mentors, Evans, Lewis, Hudson, and Levene.

Wolfrom's researches were almost entirely devoted to the problems of the structure and reactivity of carbohydrates. His first important work was a contribution to the debate on whether simple sugars have chain or ring structures. By the 1920's the cyclic structures of monosaccharides were well established, but in 1929 Wolfrom synthesized an acyclic free aldehyde form of *D*-glucose acetate, which he subsequently extended to other simple sugars. The disclosure that acyclic structures exist, either as reactive intermediates or, in many instances, as stable entities, rests largely on his work.

His studies on structural forms of sugars involved the development of several important synthetic methods. These methods enabled him to establish configurational relationships, including the correlation in 1949 between the configurations of *D*-glyceraldehyde and *L*-serine, the configurational standards for the sugar and amino acid series, respectively.

Wolfrom elucidated the structural and configurational nature of the antibiotic streptomycin. Following its discovery by Waksman in the 1940's, he isolated and characterized its streptose and streptidine components. He also synthesized many amino sugars, including the complete series of 2-amino-2-deoxypentose stereoisomers. Much of his research after 1950 was on the synthesis of the nucleosides of 2-deoxysugars.

His most challenging task was the elucidation of the structure of heparin, the anticoagulant polysaccharide in animal tissue. By 1950 he had revealed the presence of a repeating unit of D-glucuronic acid and D-glucosamine. These investigations required all of the resources of organic chemistry in order to find derivatives amenable to fragmentation analysis and structural characterization.

Wolfrom continually sought to apply new chemical methods to his field. He made the first major applications of thin-layer and extrusive column chromatography as well as ion-exchange resins to carbohydrate chemistry, and greatly facilitated research efforts by the ease and rapidity with which carbohydrate mixtures could be separated and identified.

For the last twenty-five years of his life, Wolfrom engaged in editorial work and tackled the problems of documentation in his chosen field. He, as much as anyone, helped make carbohydrate chemistry one of the best-documented chemical disciplines. He was responsible for the formation of an international committee to develop acceptable rules of nomenclature. In 1963 the committee published these rules and submitted them to the International Union of Pure and Applied Chemistry for adoption. The importance of this project lay in the fact that decades of carbohydrate research had been accumulating without any fully recognized and agreed-upon principles of nomenclature.

Simultaneous with his nomenclature work, Wolfrom served as editor of newly created publications. He was the prime mover in the creation of *Advances in Carbohydrate Chemistry* in 1945 and its coeditor for twenty-two volumes. This annual series had the purpose of providing review articles on important developments in the field and became one of the best-known and most highly regarded of all annual reviews in chemistry. In 1962 Wolfrom became coeditor of the series *Methods in Carbohydrate Chemistry*, an invaluable collection of experimental procedures in the field. In 1965 the international journal *Carbohydrate Research* appeared with Wolfrom on the editorial advisory board. His work as editor, carrying on the concern for accuracy and high standards that characterized his research, made him an indispensable figure within the community of carbohydrate chemists.

BIBLIOGRAPHY

I. ORIGINAL WORKS. Wolfrom published more than five hundred research articles, review articles, and chapters in books. Bibliographies are included in the obituaries by Derek Horton and W. Z. Hassid in *Biographical Memoirs, National Academy of Sciences*, **47** (1975), 487–549; and by Derek Horton in *Advances in Carbohydrate Chemistry and Biochemistry*, **26** (1971), 1–47.

Important articles by Wolfrom include "The Acetate of the Free Aldehyde Form of Glucose," in *Journal of the American Chemical Society*, **51** (1929), 2188–2193; "A New Synthesis of Aldehydo Sugar Acetates," *ibid.*, **56** (1934), 1794–1797, written with L. W. Georges and S. Soltzberg; "Degradative Studies on Streptomycin," *ibid.*, **69** (1947), 1052–1056, written with I. R. Hooper, L. H. Klemm, and W. J. Polglase; "A Synthesis of Streptidine," *ibid.*, **72** (1950), 1724–1729, written with S. M. Olin and W. J. Polglase; "Synthesis of Amino Sugars by Reduction of Hydrazine Derivatives," in *Journal of Organic Chemistry*, **27** (1962), 4505–4509, written with J. Bernsmann and D. Horton; "Thin-layer Chromatography on Microcrystalline Cellulose," in *Journal of Chromatography*, **17** (1965), 488–494, written with D. L. Patin and Rosa M. de Lederkremer; and "Extrusion Column Chromatography on Cellulose," *ibid.*, **18** (1965), 42–46, written with D. H. Busch, Rosa M. de Lederkremer, Sharon C. Vergez, and J. R. Vercellotti.

II. Secondary Literature. In addition to the obituaries listed above, see *McGraw-Hill Modern Men of Science*, II (New York, 1968), 614–616. Wolfrom's contributions to chemical documentation are discussed in "Patterson Award Honors Wolfrom," in *Chemical and Engineering News*, **45** (3 July 1967), 59.

Albert B. Costa

YUKAWA, HIDEKI (*b*. Tokyo, Japan, 23 January 1907; *d*. Kyoto, Japan, 8 September 1981), *physics*.

Hideki Yukawa, inventor of the meson theory of nuclear forces, was the fifth of seven children born to Takuji and Koyuki Ogawa. Both parents came from scholarly families of the samurai tradition. At the time of Hideki's birth, Takuji Ogawa was a geologist on the staff of the Geological Survey Bureau in Tokyo. In 1908 he became professor of geography at Kyoto Imperial University, and Hideki received all of his formal education in Kyoto, which he regarded as his home. The Ogawa children were strongly influenced by their father's broad cultural interests, which extended well beyond his scientific profession. Four sons became university professors: of metallurgy, of Chinese history, of Chinese literature, and (Hideki) of physics. The youngest son, Masuki, died in World War II.

In 1923 Yukawa enrolled at the Third High School in Kyoto. The future physicist Sin-itiro Tomonaga was his classmate there and also at Kyoto Imperial University (now Kyoto University), which both entered in 1926. After graduating in 1929, they stayed on at Kyoto until 1932, in which year Yukawa was appointed lecturer at Kyoto and Tomonaga moved to Tokyo. In the same year, Hideki married Sumi Yukawa, assumed her family name, and went to live with the Yukawa family in Osaka. In 1933 Yukawa became a lecturer at Osaka Imperial University while continuing to lecture at Kyoto. He proposed the meson theory in his first published scientific paper (January 1935) and was appointed associate professor at Osaka in 1936. He received the Ph.D. at Osaka in 1938.

In the fall of 1939 Yukawa returned to Kyoto Imperial University as professor (a position he retained until his retirement) and also made his first journey abroad. During the war he played a minor consulting role in military research while continuing his scientific work. In the year 1948–1949 he was visiting professor at the Institute for Advanced Study in Princeton, then went to Columbia University, where, after receiving the Nobel Prize for physics for 1949, he became professor of physics. To honor him (and to bring him back to Japan), the Japanese government in 1953 established the Research Institute for Fundamental Physics at Kyoto University, with Yukawa as its first director. After his retirement in 1970, he remained active, writing essays, editing *Progress of Theoretical Physics*, a Western-language journal he founded in 1946, and working in international movements for peace and world federation.

The paper in which Yukawa proposed the meson theory was written in English and published in *Proceedings of the Physico-Mathematical Society of Japan*. The article attracted little attention for about two years, although it turned out to define a watershed in nuclear and elementary particle physics and proved to be a powerful influence on the development of the Japanese physics community. The most striking feature of the new theory was the prediction that new particles, serving as the "heavy quanta" of the nuclear force field, would be produced in high-energy nuclear collisions, such as those that occur naturally when cosmic rays enter the earth's atmosphere. Particles that appeared to meet Yukawa's requirements were actually observed in 1937, and as a result Yukawa immediately acquired a worldwide reputation.

In 1949 Yukawa received the first Nobel Prize in physics to be awarded to a citizen of Japan, "for his prediction of the existence of mesons." Coming so soon after their disastrous defeat in World War II, Yukawa's international recognition gave the Japanese particular pride and encouragement.

With regard to the delay in the acceptance of Yukawa's theory, Nicolas Kemmer, one of the first

Western physicists to work on the meson theory, wrote in 1965 that "Yukawa in 1935 was ahead of his time and found the key to the problem of nuclear forces when no other theoretical physicist in the world was ready to accept it." In his introduction to Yukawa's *Scientific Works*, Yasutaka Tanikawa calls the meson theory "a miracle in the history of Japanese physics." But upon closer examination we can see that this "miracle" was preceded by arduous and intensive personal preparation. By examining the unpublished record and Yukawa's own account, we can follow the internal and external influences on his scientific thinking.

An account of Yukawa's intellectual development up to 1935 is given in his popular autobiography *Tabibito* (*The Traveler*). In it he describes how he grew up in a large household that included the children, three grandparents, an affectionate mother, and a father who appeared to the young Yukawa as a cold and humorless intellectual. The grandparents were warmly attentive; his maternal grandfather, Komakitsu Ogawa, who had been a samurai teacher at the Tokugawa castle in Wakayama until the Meiji regime abolished the samurai class, taught him to read *kanji* (Chinese characters) before he entered school. Although he showed an early talent for mathematics, Yukawa had no interest in science until he reached high school, when he began to consider a scientific career.

Yukawa matriculated at Kyoto Imperial University in 1926, the year after Werner Heisenberg's quantum mechanics and the year of Erwin Schrödinger's wave mechanics. By his second year Yukawa was spending all his spare time reading Schrödinger's papers in the physics library. He had already read some of Max Planck's and Niels Bohr's writings with profit; on the other hand, he found Heisenberg difficult to understand. Yukawa's graduation thesis in 1929 was based upon Paul A. M. Dirac's relativistic electron theory of 1928.

For three years following graduation, Yukawa was an unpaid assistant of Kajuro Tamaki. From 1929 to 1931, the Japanese physicists Bunsaku Arikatsu, Yoshikatsu Sugiura, and Yoshio Nishina, all of whom had studied in Europe, lectured on quantum mechanics at Kyoto. Through them, especially Nishina, Yukawa became acquainted with the Copenhagen spirit. Nevertheless, he remained determinedly independent and resolved to seek out his own problems and their solutions, unlike the more practical-minded Tomonaga, who began to work on molecular problems suggested by Sugiura.

Two great and evident problems remained: the atomic nucleus and quantum electrodynamics. The latter, the quantum theory of the electromagnetic field, was introduced by Dirac in 1927. It was formulated in a relativistically covariant manner in a 1929 paper by Heisenberg and Wolfgang Pauli that has become a classic of physics. This careful work exposed a terrible defect in the quantum theory of fields, that of the so-called divergences, which meant that some measurable physical quantities, such as the electron mass, were predicted by the theory to be infinite when electromagnetic corrections were taken into account. Yukawa's view agreed with the consensus that the divergence problems were related to the behavior of the fields near their source—or, to put it otherwise, to the singularity of the point charge.

In Yukawa's introduction to an unpublished work of early 1933, "On the Problem of Nuclear Electrons, I," he wrote [with our minor grammatical editing]:

> The problems of the atomic nucleus, especially the problems of nuclear electrons, are so intimately related with the problems of the relativistic formulation of quantum mechanics that when they are solved, if they ever be solved at all, they will be solved together. But meanwhile, we can only attempt to solve one or the other problem on rather arbitrary assumptions, insofar as they do not contradict our experimental knowledge.

By "relativistic formulation of quantum mechanics," Yukawa meant the problem of consistently quantizing the combined electromagnetic field and Dirac electron-positron field. He considered that to be a deeper problem than that of the nucleus, and he returned to it throughout his lifetime. Ironically, it was Yukawa who provided the key to the nuclear force problem but Tomonaga who, a decade later, showed how one could deal with the divergence problem of quantum fields.

Yukawa began to approach the nuclear force problem by studying (in his words) "what was probably the only organized book on the theory of the nucleus at that time," George Gamow's *Constitution of Atomic Nuclei and Radioactivity* (1931). Gamow's book presented the then standard view that the nucleus was composed of protons and electrons. In that unified picture all matter, including nuclear matter, was considered to be electrical in nature, and the fundamental forces in nature were thought to be exclusively electromagnetic and gravitational. To explain the detailed behavior of specific nuclei— for instance, the radioactivity of heavy elements— certain nuclear substructures were introduced, such as the alpha particle and the "neutron" (proposed by Ernest Rutherford); but these, too, were considered to be composites of protons and electrons.

Systems composed of electrons and nuclei held together by electrical forces, such as atoms, molecules, and crystals, were being successfully treated by quantum mechanics. These systems are characterized by distances of the order of the Bohr radius, about 10^{-8} cm. Relativistic quantum dynamics, as shown by the success of the Klein-Nishina formula for Compton scattering, appeared to be successful at least down to the scale of the Compton wavelength, about 10^{-11} cm. Nuclei, however, are about 100 times smaller than that, and there were serious doubts (originating with the electron theories at the beginning of the century and never finally laid to rest) that the ordinary laws of physics, even the modern relativistic quantum electrodynamics, would apply at such short distances.

It was clear to many physicists that the presence of electrons within the nucleus would imply a failure of quantum mechanics. Gamow set forth the reasons in his textbook of 1931: violation of the uncertainty principle of Heisenberg; contradiction of observed nuclear spin angular momentum and statistical behavior; and nuclear magnetism as it affected atomic spectra. (The latter problem, the so-called hyperfine structure, was treated by Yukawa while he was a member of Tamaki's research group in Kyoto. That work was never published, as it was similar to a paper by Enrico Fermi that appeared at about that time.)

After James Chadwick's discovery of the neutron in 1932, the situation did not at first seem different, since the neutron was thought to be a composite of a proton and an electron. It occurred to some physicists (notably Dmitri Ivanenko) that the neutron could be an elementary particle and not a composite, but several physical processes seemed to demand that nuclei contain electrons. Perhaps the most compelling example was beta-decay, in which electrons appear to emerge from the nucleus, but other processes also seemed to demand them. Heisenberg wrote in 1932:

> Such phenomena are the Meitner-Hupfeld effect, the scattering of γ-rays on nuclei; further all experiments which split neutrons into protons and electrons (an example is the stopping of cosmic ray electrons on their passage through nuclei).

This sentence is from the article in which Heisenberg proposed his neutron-proton model of the nucleus ("Über den Bau der Atomkerne," in *Zeitschrift für Physik*, **77** [1932], 1–11). In that work the neutron is treated (as regards nuclear structure) as an electrically neutral proton. In particular, it is assigned the same spin angular momentum as the proton. Such particles (fermions) obey Fermi-Dirac statistics, while particles of zero or integer spin (bosons) obey Bose-Einstein statistics, as do identical systems that contain even numbers of fermions. That meant the neutron could not be a proton-electron composite, *unless* the laws of quantum mechanics did not apply to such a small system; that was indeed what Heisenberg concluded. At the same time, he proposed his mechanism for the neutron-proton force: a neutron emits a negative electron, thus turning into a proton; that electron is absorbed by another proton, which is transformed into a neutron. Heisenberg also assumed a similar charge-exchange mechanism, analogous to homopolar chemical binding, to provide an attractive force between neutrons. Between protons he allowed only the repulsive electric Coulomb force. Thus he regarded the neutron as composite but the proton as elementary, even though at the same time he introduced a formalism that treated proton and neutron symmetrically (later known as the isospin formalism).

Besides violating the principles of quantum statistics, Heisenberg's picture violated the conservation of angular momentum in the elementary process of neutron breakup and formation, which he supposed also provided the mechanism for beta-decay; in the latter case it also violated the conservation of energy.

All that was not strange at the time, for many phenomena at high energy and small distances seemed unexplainable without either new dynamics or new particles. The former was favored by the Copenhagen school, to which Heisenberg belonged, but the explanation turned out to be new particles. These particles were the neutron (an elementary particle) and the positive electron (positron), both discovered in 1932, and the neutrino, proposed in print by Pauli for the first time in 1933.

Heisenberg's article appeared in three parts in *Zeitschrift für Physik* during 1932 and early 1933. Yukawa read them eagerly and prepared a summary in Japanese of the first two parts, which he published together with his own critical introduction in *Journal of the Physico-Mathematical Society of Japan* (his first publication). On 3 April 1933, Yukawa read a paper entitled "A Comment on the Problem of Electrons in the Nucleus" at the annual meeting of the Physico-Mathematical Society at Tohoku Imperial University, Sendai; in it he tried to make a fundamental quantum field theory of Heisenberg's phenomenological charge-exchange force.

Meanwhile, Ettore Majorana in Rome and Eugene Wigner in Princeton had pointed out that Heisenberg's forces, in their original form, did not lead to good agreement with the known properties of the lightest nuclei. For example, if only the Heisenberg forces acted, then the deuteron spin would be given incorrectly, and the small binding energy of the deuteron would be incompatible with the large binding energy of He^4. Majorana and Wigner each proposed different modifications of Heisenberg's nuclear forces and both, especially Majorana, stressed the essentially phenomenological nature of theories of the Heisenberg type.

Yukawa, on the other hand, wanted to construct a formalism analogous to the Heisenberg-Pauli quantum electrodynamics of 1929, which is an intrinsic expression of the wave-particle duality, since in it field and particle are simply different representations of the same physical entity. He wanted the electron to play a role analogous to the light quantum, while the source, analogous to the electric current, was to be composed of proton and neutron, which he regarded as the charged and neutral components of a single field (today called the nucleon).

Among the Yukawa papers in Kyoto, there are four sets of calculations along these lines and three unfinished manuscripts from 1933, including (in English) "On the Problem of Nuclear Electrons, I," the opening sentence of which was quoted above. In the abstract published in advance of Yukawa's talk at the Sendai meeting in 1933, he says that a nuclear electron acts "as a kind of field inside the nucleus." Its equation of motion, however, is not derivable from any Hamiltonian function, so that "we may not apply the concept of energy in the usual sense." Since Yukawa, like Heisenberg, wanted electron emission to account for beta-decay as well as for nuclear binding, and since beta-decay appeared to violate the energy principle, the lack of energy conservation in the theory might have been seen as a boon, not a defect.

Yukawa writes further in the Sendai abstract: "From the fact that the electron has a finite rest mass, we expect the interaction energy to decrease rapidly as the distance between neutron and proton becomes large in comparison with $h/2\pi mc$." (Here h, m, and c are, respectively, Planck's constant, the electron mass, and the velocity of light.) That combination is a distance about 200 times the range of nuclear forces. Nevertheless, the statement has a prophetic ring, for a more massive electron would produce a suitably short range.

In reminiscences, Yukawa recalled that at the Sendai talk, Nishina asked him why he did not just assume that the nuclear electron, unlike the atomic one, obeyed Bose-Einstein statistics and had zero or integer spin. In his recorded recollections, Yukawa failed to note that on that occasion, he had already

expressed the key relationship between the range of a force field and the rest mass of its quantum. Perhaps his memory lapse occurred because in the lecture he delivered, he withdrew the statement in the abstract about the range of the force. On the back of one page of his lecture notes, Yukawa wrote the wave equation satisfied by the electron field, and next to it, an exponentially decreasing (damped) solution. But beside that he wrote "mistaken conjecture," and in a colloquium he gave a bit later at Osaka Imperial University, the solution he presented was propagating and undamped.

Up to that point, Yukawa was not aware that Pauli, as early as 1930, had suggested that the electron in beta-decay might be accompanied by a light (perhaps massless) neutral particle of spin 1/2, eventually called the neutrino. Such a particle, for which there was no direct experimental evidence, would allow all conservation laws to be satisfied. Pauli's first publication of the idea was as a comment to the report "Structure of the Nucleus," given by Heisenberg at the Solvay Conference held at Brussels in October 1933. Enrico Fermi, who was present at that conference, returned to Rome, where he incorporated Pauli's neutrino idea in a new field theory of beta-decay.

Sometime in 1934, Yukawa saw Fermi's paper and considered the possibility that the strong nuclear binding force could be mediated by the exchange of the electron and neutrino as a pair, to give a unified treatment of binding force and beta-decay. That idea, called the Fermi field, was taken up by others as well, including Heisenberg. In particular, the Russians Igor Tamm and Ivanenko each published a letter in *Nature*, in which they gave the results of calculating the force of the Fermi field and claimed it was impossible to reconcile the strength and the range of the nuclear force with the strength of the beta-decay interaction. When Yukawa saw this work (as he says in *Tabibito*), he resolved not to look among the known particles, including the neutrino, to find the quantum of the nuclear force field. The result was the meson theory of nuclear forces.

Yukawa's theory was proposed at meetings in Osaka and Tokyo in October and November 1934, and described in the article "On the Interaction of Elementary Particles, I," published in February 1935. Its characteristic features are retained in current theory, although certain additions and alternative forms have been considered from time to time. The presentation of the theory begins thus: "In analogy with the scalar potential of the electromagnetic field, a function $U(x,y,z,t)$ is introduced to describe the field between the neutron and the proton.'' The paper then develops the properties of the U-field in a compelling manner, using electromagnetism as a model.

The full theory of electromagnetism requires a vector potential in addition to the scalar one, but the U-field is primarily intended to describe the forces in nuclei, where the nearly nonrelativistic motion of the source particles (neutrons and protons) allows their description by nonrelativistic wave functions and also implies the dominance of the scalar potential over the vector. When the classical U-field is quantized, it is represented by U-quanta that are analogous to electromagnetic light quanta; later the U-quanta were called by many names and eventually became known as mesons. Like light quanta, U-quanta obey Bose-Einstein statistics, but unlike them, they are massive (their mass being inversely proportional to the range of the nuclear force) and have zero spin. The source of the U-field, analogous to electric charge and current, is the neutron-proton transition current, which had appeared in the articles of Heisenberg and Fermi to which Yukawa refers. The strength of the interaction is described by a new coupling constant, g, the analogue of the electronic charge.

The exchange of U-quanta is intended to provide a theoretical basis for Heisenberg's phenomenological charge-exchange force, so the U-quanta carry electric charge, either plus or minus, in addition to g. Thus the U-field is complex, as opposed to the electromagnetic field, which is real. In order to incorporate the beta-decay process in a unified way, Yukawa gives the U-quanta an additional (weak) interaction with the electron-neutrino interaction current, its strength characterized by a second chargelike constant, g'. In this way he distinguishes clearly, and for the first time, two nuclear forces, one strong and one weak. The U-quantum is the carrier for both the strong and weak interactions.

The meson theory replaced Heisenberg's phenomenological exchange potential, $J(r)$, with an explicit function,

$$J(r) = + \text{ or } - (g/r)\exp(-ar),$$

with $a = Mc/h$, M being the mass of the U-quantum. (The reciprocal of a is the range of the nuclear force.) Heisenberg's $J(r)$ was an arbitrary function, and he chose the plus sign to give the deuteron zero spin. But by 1934 the spin of the deuteron was known to be 1, leading Yukawa to prefer the minus sign. (Since his theory is a fundamental one, it actually fixes the sign. With later and more elaborate versions of meson theory, the deuteron spin is shown to be given correctly.)

From an estimate of the range of the nuclear force, Yukawa calculated the mass M to be about 200 times that of the electron. To explain why such particles had not yet been observed, he noted that they could not be produced in ''ordinary nuclear transformations,'' where the energy available was insufficient, but that they might be present in the cosmic rays. Curiously, he did not at first realize the relevant fact that the U-quantum's weak interaction would make it radioactive, with a short mean life, so that it could not be found in ordinary matter. After the Indian physicist H. J. Bhabha pointed out that the meson should decay, Yukawa and Shoichi Sakata calculated its lifetime and found it to be about one hundred-millionth of a second.

For two years the impact of Yukawa's meson theory, both in Japan and abroad, was nil. Yukawa pursued other scientific activities, publishing ten papers in English, most of them in collaboration with Sakata, including an important calculation of the inverse beta-decay process: the absorption of an orbital electron by a nucleus with the emission of a neutrino. That article (submitted in July 1935) was noteworthy, not only because it was the first to call attention to a new effect but also because it was the first additional application of the meson theory and thus showed that Yukawa and Sakata had faith in it. Although that is the only published reference to the meson during those two years, the Yukawa archive in Kyoto contains a number of incomplete versions of a second meson paper begun in 1936, as well as a letter submitted to *Nature* on 18 January 1937, calling attention to the theory of the U-field. The latter was probably stimulated by a paper in *Physical Review* of 15 August 1936 by Carl D. Anderson and Seth H. Neddermeyer, reporting anomalous cosmic-ray tracks, observed in a cloud chamber exposed in a magnetic field atop Pike's Peak, that were not easily classifiable as either electrons or protons; Yukawa's letter to *Nature* states that ''it is not altogether impossible'' that they were mesons.

Yukawa's letter was rejected, but in July 1937 he published a note in *Proceedings of the Physico-Mathematical Society of Japan* entitled ''On a Possible Interpretation of the Penetrating Component of the Cosmic Rays.'' It had the same opening paragraph and essentially the same content as the rejected *Nature* letter. However, during the first half of 1937, several cloud-chamber groups had confirmed the existence of anomalous tracks, and while interpretations differed, Neddermeyer and Anderson (and also J. C. Street and E. C. Stevenson) asserted that they had observed positive and negative particles intermediate in mass between the electron and the proton. A clear example was also given by a Japanese cloud-chamber group led by Nishina. In June, E. C. G. Stueckelberg from Geneva and J. R. Oppenheimer and R. Serber from Pasadena sent letters to *Physical Review* that called attention to the meson theory. From that point on, Yukawa's international fame was assured.

With his students at Osaka University, Yukawa completed three additional parts of the series entitled "On the Interaction of Elementary Particles," part I being the original paper on the U-quantum. With Sakata as co-author, part II was submitted in November 1937; it includes the material in Yukawa's unpublished manuscript of 1936, subtitled "Generalization of the Mathematical Scheme," and it reformulates meson theory as that of a relativistic scalar field, using a method developed by Pauli and V. F. Weisskopf in 1934. Forces between neutrons or between protons required the exchange of two oppositely charged mesons. By 1937, however, the equality of like-particle and unlike-particle nuclear forces (charge independence) had been inferred from nuclear scattering experiments, and a corresponding "field theory" (of Fermi-field, not meson, type) had been proposed by Nicolas Kemmer. For that reason, part II contains a speculation on the possible existence of an additional electrically neutral "heavy quantum."

Part III of the series added Mituo Taketani as a third author, and part IV had Minoru Kobayashi as a fourth. Both of these papers, worked on simultaneously with part II, appeared in 1938; both used a quantized generalization of Maxwell's electromagnetic theory involving "two four vectors and two six vectors, which are complex conjugate to each other respectively." Neither of the two previous formulations was judged to be "ample enough" for the description of the broad spectrum of processes to which the theory was to be applied: nuclear forces and nuclear scattering, meson-nuclear scattering, magnetic moments of the neutron and proton, and weak interactions, among others. At the same time, essentially the same problems were being attacked by similar methods by Stueckelberg, Bhabha, Kemmer, H. Fröhlich, and W. H. Heitler. The last two theorists, refugees from the Nazis, were in England at that time; together with Kemmer, they produced the first charge-independent meson theory of nuclear forces.

The publications of Yukawa and his school from 1939 until after World War II became increasingly concerned with resolving a disturbing discrepancy between the meson regarded as the carrier of nuclear forces and the "meson" observed in the cosmic rays. For example, in 1943 Sakata and Takesi Inoue wrote "On the Correlations Between Mesons and Yukawa Particles." At issue were the mean lifetime, where there was a discrepancy of a factor of about 100, and the apparent lack of strong nuclear interaction of the cosmic-ray meson, evidenced by its very small absorption in matter. Both of these problems were resolved by the discovery of the existence of two mesons, the cosmic-ray meson being the daughter arising from decay of the short-lived nuclear-force meson. This solution was proposed theoretically as early as 1942 by Sakata and Inoue and by Yasutaka Tanikawa, and it was experimentally confirmed after the war.

Although meson theory was Yukawa's greatest accomplishment, throughout his scientific career he regarded the nuclear force problem as of less importance than that of formulating a mathematically consistent relativistic quantum theory, free of "infinities" like those brought to light in the Heisenberg-Pauli quantum electrodynamics of 1929. One of Yukawa's earliest unpublished manuscripts (1934) approached the problem of a relativistic quantum theory from the standpoint of the theory of measurement. He continued to examine epistemological questions, such as the nonseparability of cause and effect in quantum mechanics, and fundamental issues of the theory of quantum fields, even while he was working most actively on meson theory. Around 1940 he introduced the idea he called "*maru*" (circle), representing a finite region of an elementary particle within which relativistic causality is not valid.

Beginning in 1950, Yukawa developed the idea of nonlocal quantum fields, an idea strongly influenced by Heisenberg's concept of a fundamental universal length. Like some older physicists, notably Heisenberg and Dirac, Yukawa never fully accepted the renormalization method of quantum electrodynamics, regarding it as a mere calculational device, a door that concealed the difficulty but at the same time blocked the road to progress.

The idea of nonlocal fields (which is to be distinguished from the idea of local fields having nonlocal interaction) gradually became a theory of elementary particles with internal structure. By the late 1960's it was superseded by Yukawa's concept of "elementary domain," based upon the quantization of the classical continuously deformable body. These fundamental ideas do not play a major role in current theoretical physics but may well be vindicated in a future physics.

Yukawa's emphasis in the early 1940's on the importance of formulating quantum field theory in a closed space-time region helped Tomonaga to develop his covariant quantum electrodynamics, according to the latter's testimony. It is not possible to discuss here Yukawa's original ideas on creativity, history and philosophy of science, and the differences between Eastern and Western modes of thought. These ideas, carefully presented and ranging over subjects as diverse as Epicurus, Taoism, *The Tale of Genji*, and the nature of creative scientific thought, have been influential in Japan as well as (in translations) on the international level.

BIBLIOGRAPHY

I. ORIGINAL WORKS. *Scientific Works*, Yasutaka Tanikawa, ed. (Tokyo, 1979), contains all of Yukawa's scientific papers not in Japanese as well as English translations of some of his scientific papers and essays in Japanese. His books include *Creativity and Intuition*, John Bester, trans. (Tokyo, 1973); and *Tabibito* (*The Traveler*), L. Brown and R. Yoshida, trans. (Singapore, 1982). There are many works in Japanese only.

The bulk of Yukawa's extensive unpublished notes, manuscripts, and letters are in the Yukawa Hall Archival Library, Kyoto University, Kyoto 606, Japan; parts have been cataloged. Unpublished manuscripts, trans. Rokuo Kawabe, and other material on Yukawa, are in L. M. Brown, R. Kawabe, M. Konuma, and Z. Maki, eds., *Proceedings of the Japan–USA Collaborative Workshops on the History of Particle Theory in Japan, 1935–1960* (Kyoto, 1988).

II. SECONDARY LITERATURE. Laurie M. Brown, "Yukawa's Prediction of the Meson," in *Centaurus*, **25** (1981), 71–132; L. M. Brown, M. Konuma, and Z. Maki, eds., *Particle Physics in Japan, 1930–1950* (Kyoto, 1980), I and II; Satio Hayakawa, "The Development of Meson Physics in Japan," in Laurie M. Brown and Lillian Hoddeson, eds., *Birth of Particle Physics* (Cambridge, 1983), 82–107; N. Kemmer, "Hideki Yukawa," in *Biographical Memoirs of Fellows of the Royal Society*, **29** (1983), 661–676; Viśvapriya Mukherji, "History of the Meson Theory of Nuclear Forces from 1935 to 1952," in *Archive for History of Exact Sciences*, **13** (1974), 27–102; and Shigeru Nakayama, David L. Swain, and Eri Yagi, eds., *Science and Society in Modern Japan* (Cambridge, Mass., 1974).

LAURIE M. BROWN

ZACHARIASEN, (FREDRIK) WILLIAM HOULDER (*b.* Langesund, Norway, 5 February 1906; *d.* Los Alamos, New Mexico, 24 December 1979), *chemical crystallography, X-ray diffraction.*

Zachariasen was born near Brevik, Norway, the center of the now classic nepheline-syenitic and foyaitic rock occurrences that have yielded over thirty new mineral species. Many of these mineral species contain essential light elements (such as hydrogen, beryllium, and boron) and the heavy lanthanides (lanthanum through lutetium) and natural actinides (actinium through uranium). These elements and their chemical crystallography occupied much of Zachariasen's thoughts in later years, and one suspects that the environs of his youth left a permanent imprint.

Zachariasen's father, Johannes, a ship captain, and his mother, Vissa, had three sons (of whom Fredrik was the youngest) and a daughter. Fredrik early dropped his first name and was thereafter called William or Willie. He received the Ph.D. in 1928 under Victor Moritz Goldschmidt at the University of Oslo, then did further study on crystal structures of minerals with Sir Lawrence Bragg at Manchester. In 1930 Zachariasen married Ragni ("Mossa") Durban-Hansen, granddaughter of Waldemar Christopher Brøgger, a leading authority on nepheline-syenite mineralogy, especially of Langesundfjord. They had a daughter, Ellen, and a son, Fredrik, who is a physicist. That same year Zachariasen joined the department of physics at the University of Chicago, where he went on to serve as chairman (1945–1949, 1956–1959) and dean of the Division of Physical Sciences (1959–1962). He was the Ernest DeWitt Burton Distinguished Service professor from 1962 to 1974. An intense, outspoken man with strong convictions, he always sought excellence and high qualities in candidates, thereby furthering a strong scientific foundation at the university. He became professor emeritus in 1974.

Zachariasen's more than two hundred scientific publications cover crystal structures of inorganic substances (mostly minerals), anionic groups, the glassy state, actinide crystal chemistry, and X-ray diffraction theory. Crystal structure determinations before vector set techniques (especially the Patterson function) and the advent of artificial intelligence, that is, before World War II, was largely simply algebraic, intuitive, and trial-and-error in its approach. Zachariasen solved many structures, especially between 1930 and 1950, by these relatively tedious methods, and it is a credit to his genius that these structure solutions stand to this day as basically correct. Structures and mineral chemistries during this period include hambergite, meliphanite, titanite (sphene), eudidymite, epididymite, and eudialyte, phases characteristic of the Langesundfjord nepheline-syenite paragenesis.

Anionic groups (such as borates, carbonates, sulfates, and sulfites) occupied Zachariasen's attention during the early 1930's. He deciphered and interpreted a large body of crystal structures. We should recall that at that time neither reliable atomic coordinate parameters nor bond distances were known for most groups or radicals. Zachariasen undertook a series of studies on sulfur-oxygen groups, and he established sulfate $[SO_4]^{2-}$, sulfite $[SO_3\psi]^{2-}$,

pyrosulfite $\begin{bmatrix} O & & O \\ O \searrow S & - S & - O \\ O & & \psi \end{bmatrix}^{2-}$ or $[S_2O_5]^{2-}$,

trithionate $\begin{bmatrix} O & \psi & O \\ O \searrow S & - S & - S \swarrow O \\ O & \psi & O \end{bmatrix}^{2-}$ or $[S_3O_6]^{2-}$

(ψ = lone pair; present author's designation), and others. These studies culminated in a 1931 paper in which Zachariasen discussed two classes of XO_3 "groups" in crystals: Class 1 included $(NO_3)^{1-}$, $(CO_3)^{2-}$, and $(BO_3)^{3-}$; Class 2 included $(PO_3)^{3-}$, $(SO_3)^{2-}$, $(ClO_3)^{1-}$, $(AsO_3)^{3-}$, $(SeO_3)^{2-}$, $(BrO_3)^{1-}$, and $(SbO_3)^{3-}$. Class 1 possessed oxygens coplanar to the central cation, while in Class 2 the oxygens are pyramidally displaced above the central cation. Zachariasen recognized the duality of two different explanations, the one of shared electron pairs (the quantum mechanical treatment), the other of ions and their deformation in the field of surrounding ions. Today we would probably refer to Zachariasen's "(3 × 8 + 2) electron rule" of Class 2 as groups that possess a lone pair of electrons on the cations. Along with G. N. Lewis and his evolution of the rule of octets in the first decade of the twentieth century, it appears that Zachariasen anticipated our modern notion of lone electron pairs in crystal structures by about six years.

Speculations on the glassy state can be dated to the Old Testament, but a scientifically sensible model was achieved relatively recently, in the form of the famous Zachariasen glass model. Zachariasen was the first scientist to advance a model for the atomic arrangement in glassy substances that agreed with all the observations at hand. He argued that a small difference in energy between a symmetry-repeating crystalline substance and its glassy counterpart could be observed for cations in triangular, trigonal pyramidal, or tetrahedral coordination by oxygens such as B^{3+}, Si^{4+}, P^{3+}, P^{5+}, As^{3+}, As^{5+}, and Ge^{4+}, which tend to form glassy oxides from a quenched liquid. He further noted that the need for maximal separation of like ions owing to electrostatic repulsion forced arrangements based on sheets or networks composed of structural rings or loops of varying sizes. Large cations of low charge would fill the spaces in the loops. Where an equal number of cations are surrounded by anions, and vice versa, a glass would not form because its energy content would be about the same as or identical to that of a crystal. Zachariasen proposed a general formula A_mB_nO, where B is the cations in triangular, pyramidal, or tetrahedral coordination by oxygen that define the framework, and A is the large cations of low charge. The condition for most favorable glass formation is $n \sim 0.4–0.5$. The ultimate condition for a glass is the formation of an extended three-dimensional network that lacks periodicity and has energy content comparable with but not equal to the corresponding crystal network.

In 1943 Zachariasen was senior physicist on the Manhattan Project. Elucidating the nature and chemistry of the synthesized actinides is among his most celebrated work. From 1943 to 1948 Zachariasen characterized the crystal chemistries of over 150 discrete compounds of Group $5f$ elements, and elevated the tool of X-ray crystallography to the level of ultramicrochemical analysis where microgram quantities could be studied. His technique proved far more reliable than any chemical analytical technique at that time. In 1925 Goldschmidt had demonstrated lanthanide contraction of the ionic radii for the Group $4f$ elements by techniques of X-ray diffraction. Zachariasen demonstrated the same effect for the Group $5f$ elements. In addition, he solved numerous crystal structures and showed that formal valences vary from 2^+ to 6^+, with uneven charge distributions, from actinium to americium. He attributed this to mixing between the closely spaced $5f$-$6d$ electronic shells. Detailed accounts of these studies appeared after 1948, when such studies were declassified.

In 1931, Zachariasen published a set of empirical crystal radii for ions with inert gas configuration. Such crystal radii form the basis of crystal chemistry because bond distances, problems in radius ratio and solid solution, and variation of bond lengths with variation in formal charge for some given ion all are derived from these radii. Today reliable tables of effective ionic radii exist because a large number of precisely refined crystal structures became available after 1950. In 1931 the problem was far more difficult because only the data of simple oxides and fluorides, with few, if any, variable atomic parameters, were available.

An X-ray diffraction experiment allows only the determination of a diffracted intensity from some crystallographic plane. Since the intensity is a product of a structure factor amplitude and its complex conjugate, the associated phase information is lost. This is the famous phase problem in X-ray crystallography. Zachariasen (1952) utilized an identity from which the Schwarz inequality follows. In a metaboric acid crystal, $12HBO_2$, the coordinates of nine unique atoms, each with three degrees of freedom, were determined by this direct method. Today many kinds of "direct methods" have been studied and tested; most of them involve inequalities between and among sets of reflections with strong relative intensity and usually proceed with the assistance of artificial intelligence.

In 1945 Zachariasen published *Theory of X-ray Diffraction in Crystals*. Although many books of varying depth have recently been published on crystals and X-ray diffraction, this self-consistent and rigorous work is still eminently suitable. Dyadics (second-order tensors) and group theory play a central role in this tome. From crystal symmetry and X-ray diffraction in ideal crystals, there follow more contemporary problems in real crystals, such as disordered crystal structures, temperature diffuse scattering, and crystal mosaicity. Several papers published between 1960 and 1965, including the problem of power loss during the course of diffraction in mosaic crystals (secondary extinction) and multiple diffraction in imperfect crystals, round out Zachariasen's studies in X-ray diffraction theory.

BIBLIOGRAPHY

I. ORIGINAL WORKS. Zachariasen's writings include "A Set of Empirical Crystal Radii for Ions with Inert Gas Configuration," in *Zeitschrift für Kristallographie*, **80** (1931), 137–153; "The Structure of Groups XO_3 in Crystals," in *Journal of the American Chemical Society*, **53** (1931), 2123–2130; "The Atomic Arrangement in Glass," *ibid.*, **54** (1932), 3841–3851; *Theory of X-ray Diffraction in Crystals* (New York, 1945); "The Crystal Chemistry of the 5f-Series of Elements," in *Record of Chemical Progress*, **10** (1949), 47–51; "A New Analytical Method for Solving Complex Crystal Structures," in *Acta Crystallographica*, **5** (1952), 68–73.

A bibliography of Zachariasen's professional papers and his books, on microfiche, is available as Document AM-81-177 from the Business Office, Mineralogical Society of America, 2000 Florida Avenue, N.W., Washington, D.C. 20009.

II. SECONDARY LITERATURE. A short and more personal account is Paul B. Moore, "Memorial of Fredrik William Houlder Zachariasen, February 5, 1906–December 24, 1979," in *American Mineralogist*, **66** (1981), 1097–1098. For a longer tribute, see Robert A. Penneman, "Chapter 2: William H. Zachariasen," in D. McLachlan, Jr., and J. P. Glusker, eds., *Crystallography in North America* (1983), 108–111. An extended memorial concluding with over 200 titles has been submitted to the National Academy of Sciences by Mark G. Inghram.

PAUL BRIAN MOORE

ZERVAS, LEONIDAS (*b.* Megalopolis, Greece, 21 May 1902; *d.* Athens, Greece, 10 July 1980), *organic chemistry*.

After completing secondary school in Kalamata in 1918, Zervas spent two years as a student of chemistry at the University of Athens. In 1921 he moved to Germany and continued his studies at the University of Berlin, where he received his D.Phil. degree in 1926 for the dissertation *Über die Aldehydverbindungen der Aminosäuren*. It was based on work he did at the Kaiser Wilhelm Institute for Leather Research in Dresden, under the supervision of Max Bergmann, its director.

Zervas then became a research associate at the Dresden institute, and in 1929 was appointed its deputy director and head of the organic chemistry section. In 1933 the Nazis forced Bergmann to resign as director; after finding a haven at the Rockefeller Institute for Medical Research in New York, he secured the help of the Rockefeller Foundation in bringing Zervas to his new laboratory. Zervas resigned his post in Dresden, remained in New York for two years (1934–1936), and then returned to Greece. In 1937 he was appointed professor of organic chemistry and biochemistry at the University of Thessaloniki. Two years later he became professor of organic chemistry at the University of Athens; he reached emeritus status in 1968. In 1930 Zervas married Hildegard Lange.

The outbreak of World War II, the German occupation of Greece, and the civil war that followed liberation prevented Zervas from fully developing his research program until about 1950. Despite an interruption during the rule of the Greek military junta, when Zervas was dismissed from his professorship, he organized an outstanding laboratory from which there came not only important chemical contributions but also able young men and women who later gained recognition for their independent work. Zervas' research career is therefore marked by two productive phases: the period 1926 to 1936, when he was associated with Bergmann in Dresden and New York, and that after about 1950, when he directed his laboratory in Athens.

Most of Zervas' papers of the first period appeared with Bergmann's name as the first author, but there can be little doubt that from the beginning of their association, Zervas made numerous original contributions. Initially his research dealt with the chemistry of amino acids. For example, in 1927 he demonstrated the chemical transfer of the amidine group of arginine to glycine; this "transamidination" reaction was later shown by others to be an enzyme-catalyzed process in biological systems. In 1930 Zervas turned to sugar chemistry. One of his contributions was the synthesis of 1-benzoylglucose by the hydrogenolysis of its 4,6-benzylidene derivative with palladium black as the catalyst. This procedure for the gentle removal of benzyl groups had been introduced during the 1920's, and its use in Bergmann's laboratory led to the invention of an important new method for the synthesis of peptides. The method involved the protection of reactive groups in amino acids (amino, carboxyl, hydroxyl) by means of the "carbobenzoxy" group (more accurately, benzyloxycarbonyl group; abbreviated Z). Selective removal of the Z-group after the assembly of the protected amino acid units had been completed gave the desired free peptides.

The publication in 1932 of the Bergmann-Zervas paper "Über ein allgemeines Verfahren der Peptidsynthese" marked a new stage in the development of peptide chemistry, a field first explored systematically by Emil Fischer from 1901 to 1909. Fischer's procedure for the synthesis of peptides had many limitations, which were overcome by the introduction of the carbobenzoxy method. In rapid succession, from 1933 to 1934, there appeared a series of papers from the Dresden institute describing the synthesis of many hitherto inaccessible peptides containing amino acid units (aspartic acid, glutamic acid, lysine, arginine) with reactive side-chain groups, thus showing the general applicability of the method. Moreover, an important advantage of the use of Z-amino acids was that they were relatively resistant to racemization.

After his return to Greece in 1936, Zervas worked on the synthesis of phosphorylated amino and hydroxy compounds, a subject he had begun to explore in Dresden through the use of derivatives of dibenzylphosphoric acid. However, this promising approach was developed elsewhere from 1939 to 1950, a time when conditions in Greece prevented Zervas from continuing his research. After he was able to resume work, he published several papers on the use of dibenzylphosphorochloridate in synthetic reactions, but in succeeding years the main efforts in his laboratory were directed to the development of new methods in the peptide field.

During the 1950's peptide chemistry gained wider interest as a consequence of the discovery that many antibiotics and hormones are peptides. Moreover, the elucidation of the amino-acid sequence of insulin by Frederick Sanger offered a challenge to peptide chemists to synthesize this protein hormone. Of particular interest was Sanger's finding that insulin consists of two peptide chains joined by disulfide bridges involving cysteinyl units of the separate chains. Zervas undertook a systematic study of the synthesis of such structures and developed methods for making asymmetric cystine peptides. New protecting groups for the sulfhydryl group were introduced, among them the trityl (triphenylmethyl), diphenylmethyl, and benzoyl groups; the selective removal of these groups permitted the formation of the desired disulfide bridges. Also, Zervas developed the use of o-nitrophenylsulfenyl chloride (NPS-Cl) for the protection of amino groups; the lability of the NPS group under mildly acidic conditions made it a valuable adjunct to the available tools of peptide synthesis.

Except when the political situation in Greece prevented it, Zervas was active in the general development of science in his country. He served as chairman of the Greek Commission for Atomic Energy (1964–1965) and later helped to organize the Greek National Research Foundation, of which he was president from 1974 to 1979.

BIBLIOGRAPHY

I. ORIGINAL WORKS. A list of Zervas' scientific papers before 1972 is given with the biographical article by P. G. Katsoyannis, in *The Chemistry of Polypeptides* (New York, 1972), 1–20.

II. SECONDARY LITERATURE. Only brief accounts of Zervas' life have appeared. Especially noteworthy is the one by P. G. Katsoyannis (see above). An excellent summary of the contributions of the Zervas group to the synthesis of asymmetric cystine peptides is provided by his collaborator Iphigenia Photaki on pages 59–85 of that volume.

JOSEPH S. FRUTON

ZIEGLER, KARL WALDEMAR (*b.* Helsa, near Kassel, Germany, 26 November 1898; *d.* Mülheim (Ruhr), Federal Republic of Germany, 11 August 1973), *organic chemistry, organometallic chemistry.*

Karl was the youngest son of Carl August Ziegler, a Protestant minister, and Caroline Helene Louise, née Rall. In 1910 the family moved to Marburg, where he attended the *Realgymnasium*. In 1916 he began studying chemistry at the University of Marburg. Due to previous private chemical experimentation, Ziegler soon proved to be so well advanced that he was allowed to forgo the first two semesters.

In 1920 he received his Ph.D. under the direction of Karl von Auwers, an organic chemist noted for his use of physical methods in determining molecular constitution. As Auwers' assistant from 1919 through 1926, Ziegler first studied Grignard reactions, but soon turned to another and more promising field, namely, the theory of valency and the study of organic radicals. His starting points were a paper of 1919 by Hans Meerwein on the pinacol-pinacolone rearrangement and Johannes Thiele's theory of partial valencies, which aimed at explaining the reactivity of unsaturated bonds by assuming localized affinity residues. At this time the most controversially discussed example of partial valency was Moses Gomberg's triphenylmethyl radical, discovered in 1900 as a dissociation product of hexaphenylethane. The existence of a stable, trisubstituted carbon compound was a serious threat to the firmly estalished doctrine of the tetravalent carbon atom. In 1923 Ziegler began to study the steric and electronic factors that influence the dissociation into, and the stability of, such free radicals. In a series of papers ("Zur Kenntnis des 'dreiwertigen' Kohlenstoffs") published over a period of twenty-seven years, the first of which qualified him as *Privatdozent* at Marburg in December 1923, he determined activation energies and dissociation kinetics of various hexasubstituted ethanes that he had synthesized. Among them, 1, 2, 4, 5-tetraphenylallyl and pentaphenylcyclopentadienyl, prepared in 1923 and 1925, proved to be almost entirely dissociated into free radicals.

In 1922 Ziegler married Maria Kurtz of Marburg, with whom he had two children. In 1925 the young family had to move, since Ziegler was given leave from his assistantship to fill a vacancy at the University of Frankfurt. The following year Karl Freudenberg offered him an assistantship at Heidelberg's Chemical Institute; Ziegler became a professor there in 1927. In 1924 Ziegler observed that phenylisopropylpotassium, prepared by his "ether method," easily added to substituted olefines such as stilbene. This first example of an organometallic synthesis opened an entirely new field of research and provided the key to subsequent studies on the mechanism of sodium-induced butadiene polymerization. Ziegler's inquiry into the chemistry of alkali organic compounds was extended to include the organolithium compounds in 1930, when the metal became

easily available. In 1933, while studying butadiene polymerization, he investigated the relationship between intermolecular polymerization and intramolecular cyclization. Expanding on observations made by Paul Ruggli twenty-one years earlier, he introduced his "dilution principle" as a means of obtaining large-ringed alicyclic compounds.

In 1936 he left Heidelberg to become, for a short time, visiting professor at the University of Chicago, and, later in that year, full professor and director of the Chemical Institute at the University of Halle, a position awarded to him despite his reserved attitude toward the Nazi regime. In Halle, Ziegler continued studying alkali organic compounds, free radicals, polymerization mechanisms, and ring syntheses, which he successfully applied to some naturally occurring polycyclic substances.

The political and economic situation made fundamental research of this type increasingly difficult. Eventually, in 1943, the Kaiser Wilhelm Institute offered Ziegler the opportunity to succeed Franz Fischer as director of the society's Institute for Coal Research at Mülheim, in Germany's coal mining region. Ziegler accepted under the condition that his research would not be bound to coal chemistry and its industrial use but would be allowed to deal with the chemistry of carbon compounds in general. After a two-year period of divided responsibility for Halle and Mülheim, he finally moved permanently from Halle to Mülheim, to the Kaiser Wilhelm Institute, which after the war became the Max Planck Institute.

Ziegler's initial research in Mülheim continued his earlier studies of organometallic syntheses with alkyllithium and opened up the way to organoaluminium compounds, now easily accessible through his direct synthesis of aluminum trialkyls and lithium aluminum hydride in 1949. One year later Ziegler's stepwise addition of aluminium alkyls to olefines resulted in a new method of preparing hydrocarbons of any desired molecular size, which immediately was adopted for the industrial synthesis of straight-chain primary alcohols; the corresponding displacement reaction yielded a technically important intermediate for isoprene, the basis of synthetic rubber.

The breakthrough for industrial application came in 1953, when Ziegler unexpectedly observed that traces of nickel influence the relationship of growth-to-displacement reactions. He soon realized that combinations of trialkyl aluminum with transition elements worked as extremely active catalysts that polymerize ethylene at atmospheric pressure, as opposed to the widely accepted belief that high pressures and high temperatures were required for producing polyethylene. The impact on industrial chemistry was rapid and revolutionary. Giulio Natta, a consultant for an Italian chemical company, extended the use of "Ziegler catalysts" to stereospecific polymerization in order to obtain polymers with defined molecular structures and properties. Within a few years after the public announcement of Ziegler's method in 1955, various industrial polymerization processes using his invention were in operation all over the world. In 1963 Ziegler and Natta shared the Nobel Prize for this discovery.

A great many honors and awards followed, including foreign membership in the Royal Society (London). Meanwhile the Mülheim institute had developed into one of Germany's leading research institutions for applied chemistry. There Ziegler continued his research on organometallic, especially alkyl aluminum, compounds and explored a new approach to metal alkyls by electrolysis of complex organometal compounds. He retired in July 1969. Almost two hundred publications, with about the same number of coauthors, in journals and handbooks, numerous patents, and about 150 doctoral theses completed under his supervision document the breadth of his research interests.

BIBLIOGRAPHY

I. Original Works. Full bibliographies are included in the obituaries by Günther Wilke in *Justus Liebigs Annalen der Chemie* (1975), 804–833; and C. E. H. Bawn in *Biographical Memoirs of Fellows of the Royal Society*, **21** (1975), 569–584. Ziegler's personal recollections include his Noble lecture, "Folgen und Werdegang einer Erfindung," in *Angewandte Chemie*, **76** (1964), 545–553, translated in *Rubber Chemistry and Technology*, **38** (1965), xxiii–xxxvi; and "A Forty Years' Stroll Through the Realms of Organometallic Chemistry," in *Advances in Organometallic Chemistry*, **6** (1968), 1–17. For a report on the Mülheim institute, see his "Max-Planck-Institut für Kohlenforschung," in *Jahrbuch der Max-Planck-Gesellschaft, 1961* (Göttingen, 1962), pt. 2, 492–510. This institute holds Ziegler's scientific papers and correspondence.

II. Secondary Literature. John J. Eisch, "Karl Ziegler, Master Advocate for the Unity of Pure and Applied Research," in *Journal of Chemical Education*, **60** (1983), 1009–1014; Christoph Meinel, *Die Chemie an der Universität Marburg seit Beginn des 19. Jahrhunderts* (Marburg, 1978), 304–311.

Christoph Meinel

ZIMMERMANN, WALTER (*b*. Walldürn, Baden, Germany, 9 May 1892; *d*. Tübingen, Federal Republic of Germany, 30 June 1980), *botany*.

Walter Zimmermann, the son of Emil Zimmermann, a lawyer, and of his wife, Maria Welte, attended the classical gymnasium in Karlsruhe and studied science at the Karlsruhe Technical University as well as at the universities of Berlin and Freiburg. At the latter, studying under Friedrich Oltmann, he received the doctorate in natural sciences (1921). From 1919 to 1925 Zimmermann was an assistant at the Freiburg Botanical Institute. In 1925 he qualified as a lecturer at Tübingen, where he was appointed extraordinary professor in 1930, and full professor and professor emeritus in 1960. He fought as a front-line soldier in both world wars. In 1921 he married Anna Schleiermacher; they had two daughters and a son. Anna died in 1950, and in 1960 Zimmermann married Karin Krause.

Zimmermann's scientific life's work was in three main fields: algae, kinetic physiology, and phylogeny (evolution). His first scientific publications were on algae. In his dissertation on *Volvox* he clarified important points in cytology and the history of evolution. He discovered several new taxa, one of which was the genus *Oltmannsiella* (the link between Volvocales and Ulotrichales), and studied the polarity of various marine algae.

Zimmermann began his studies of plants' kinetic physiology in Freiburg and continued them in Tübingen. He investigated a very complex phenomenon, plagiotropism, which occurs in horizontally growing shoots and offshoots, and proved that it has three components: epinasty, negative geotropism, and positive geotropism. Zimmermann also strove to analyze the movement of blossoms. In 1927 he wrote a critical summary of the knowledge of georeactions.

The majority of Zimmermann's scientific publications, which established his high standing outside Germany, concern plant phylogeny. The first was *Die Phylogenie der Pflanzen* (1930), in which he describes the course of plant evolution on a paleobotanical basis and discusses the factors of development. The second, completely revised edition of *Phylogenie* (1959) is a standard work that has no equal in international literature. Zimmermann based his work on fossil plants and treated various problems of evolution in numerous publications. He strove especially to clarify the methodological fundamentals of phylogeny (1931, 1967). He elaborated on the differences between idealistic and phylogenetic morphology, explained the epistemological and methodological foundation, and showed the meaning of "phylogenetic tree" as well as how to construct it. Zimmermann also dedicated (1953) an extensive work to the history of the concept of evolution as well as to research on evolution. He chose several problems from the seemingly inexhaustible material of plant phylogeny proper: the phylogeny of trees, of leaf arrangements, of steles, of the *Ophioglossum* leaf, of sporophylls, of blossoms, and of inflorescences. He also discussed the phylogeny of individual groups within the plant kingdom, such as bryophytes, pteridophytes, and psilophytes. The last group led Zimmermann to develop his "telome theory," that the oldest cormophytes are built from undifferentiated single organs (telomes). The great morphological diversity of cormophytes has developed from these original structures through a few "elementary processes" (overtopping, planation, fusion, incurvation, and reduction). In *Vererbung "erworbener Eigenschaften" und Auslese* (1938, 1969), Zimmermann discussed the factors of evolution and shed a critical light on ambiguous concepts like mutation, purpose, adaptation, orthogenesis, and selection. Since man, too, is a link in evolution and subject to its laws, there are many complex implications for our world view and what should constitute ethical behavior. In *Evolution und Naturphilosophie* (1968) Zimmermann offers a well-rounded synopsis of these complex issues.

Phylogeny lets us trace the course of transformation, as observed when adult stages are compared. In nature transformation occurs in a chain of consecutive ontogenies. Zimmermann called this entire process "*Hologenie.*" In order to trace the evolutionary process, he chose the living example of the genus *Pulsatilla,* which, with its numerous primitive characteristics and subspecific taxa, seems to be especially suitable for this purpose. The results of these taxonomical and genetic studies, which he conducted over three decades, have been recorded in numerous publications and are evaluated in his book on the telome theory (1965), as well as in Hegi's *Illustrierte Flora von Mittel-Europa.*

Zimmermann's works are characterized by the clarity of the descriptions and the definitions, the sharp formulation of problems, and the discussion of differing opinions.

Besides being active as a researcher and academic teacher, Zimmermann was an energetic advocate in word and deed for the conservation of nature and the countryside.

BIBLIOGRAPHY

I. ORIGINAL WORKS. "Die Georeaktionen der Pflanze," in *Ergebnisse der Biologie, 2* (1927), 113–256; *Die Phylogenie der Pflanzen* (Jena, 1930; 2nd, rev. ed., 1959); "Arbeitsweise der botanischen Phylogenetik" in Emil Abderhalden, ed., *Handbuch der biologischen Arbeits-* *methoden* (Berlin and Vienna, 1931), Abt. 9, teil 3.2, 941–1053; *Vererbung "erworbener Eigenschaften" und Auslese* (Jena, 1938; 2nd ed., 1969); *Grundfragen der Evolution* (Frankfurt, 1948); *Geschichte der Pflanzen* (Stuttgart, 1949; 2nd ed., 1969), also in Spanish, *Evolución vegetal* (Barcelona, 1976); *Evolution: Die Geschichte ihrer Probleme und Erkenntnisse* (Freiburg and Munich, 1953); *Die Telomtheorie* (Stuttgart, 1965); "Methoden der Evolutionswissenschaft (-Phylogenetik)," in Gerhard Heberer, ed., *Die Evolution der Organismen,* 3rd ed., I (Stuttgart, 1967), 61–160; *Evolution und Naturphilosophie* (Berlin, 1968); "Magnoliaceae, Paeoniaceae, Ranunculaceae," in Gustav Hegi, ed., *Illustrierte Flora von Mittel-Europa,* III. 3 (Munich, 1974), 36–356.

II. SECONDARY LITERATURE. K. Mägdefrau, "Walter Zimmermann's botanisches Werk," in *Veröffentlichungen der Landesstelle für Naturschutz Baden-Württemberg,* **30** (1962), 10–18 (listing works 1921–1962); and W. Weber, "Walter Zimmermann, Botaniker, Phylogenetiker, Naturschützer," in *Jahreshefte der Gesellschaft für Naturkunde in Württemberg,* **137** (1982), 166–171, with a portrait and a list of selected publications.

KARL MÄGDEFRAU

ZWICKY, FRITZ (*b*. Varna, Bulgaria, 14 February 1898; *d*. Pasadena, California, 8 February 1974), *physics, astrophysics, rocketry.*

An irascible maverick, Fritz Zwicky had a penchant for investigating extreme phenomena, speculating outside the confines of prevailing theory, and undertaking ambitious observational programs. His most significant work was in astrophysics, where he initiated research on supernovas and coordinated the preparation of important catalogs of galaxies.

At the age of six, Zwicky—the eldest of the three children of Fridolin Zwicky, a Swiss merchant, and his Czech wife, Franziska Wrcek Zwicky—was sent for schooling to his ancestral district in Glarus, Switzerland. In his teens he did so well in science courses that upon the urging of his teachers, his father allowed him to train for engineering rather than commerce. Accordingly, in 1914 he went to Zurich, where he attended the Oberrealschule and then the Eidgenössische Technische Hochschule (ETH). Midway through the ETH, Zwicky displayed characteristic independence by transferring from mechanical engineering to mathematics.

In 1920, having passed examinations in experimental physics and mathematics, and having written an acceptable essay for Hermann Weyl on reflection in an inhomogeneous stratum, Zwicky received his teaching diploma. Two years later he took a doctorate in theoretical physics at the ETH with a dissertation on the theory of ionic crystals, written under Paul

Scherrer and Peter Debye. He remained at Debye's Physical Institute until mid 1925, when he went to the California Institute of Technology as an International Education Board fellow to work with Robert A. Millikan and Paul Epstein. Thenceforth, despite his steadfast loyalty to and frequent stays in Switzerland, Zwicky operated out of Pasadena. From 1927 to 1968 he was a faculty member at Caltech; from 1943 to 1961, the research director and then a research consultant at Aerojet Engineering in Pasadena; and from 1948, an astronomer at the Mount Wilson and Palomar observatories.

Zwicky married twice. On 25 March 1932 he married Dorothy Vernon Gates, whose father had long been a California state senator; they were divorced in 1941. On 15 October 1947 he married Anna Margarita Zürcher, whose father was a prominent Bernese hotel owner. He had three daughters by his second wife. Zwicky enjoyed mountaineering, making many first ascents in the Alps. He also devoted much time to charitable activities, especially to helping rebuild scientific libraries destroyed during World War II and to participating in the Pestalozzi Foundation of America's program of aid to orphanages.

During the decade following his doctorate, Zwicky worked mainly on the equations of state for gases, liquids, and solids. However, his papers on such subjects as the specific heat of electrolytes and cooperative effects in imperfect crystals attracted little attention. Meanwhile, inspired by Millikan's research on cosmic rays, Edwin P. Hubble's discovery of the distance–red shift relation, and George E. Hale's success in raising funds for a two-hundred-inch telescope on Mount Palomar, Zwicky began thinking about astrophysical questions. In 1928 he maintained that the entire chain of reactions linking radiation to galaxies must be considered when analyzing the postulate that the universe is in thermodynamic equilibrium. The following year, before Arthur S. Eddington and others began using Hubble's relation to argue that the universe is expanding, Zwicky proposed that the light from distant galaxies is redshifted because of a gravitational drag. And in 1933 he and Walter Baade, who in 1931 had joined the Mount Wilson staff, began teaching astrophysics at Caltech. This enabled Zwicky to acquire a more systematic command of the field.

Zwicky and Baade were evidently led by Zwicky's continuing interest in Hubble's relation to consider whether exceptionally bright novas, which had been distinguished from ordinary novas by K. Lundmark in 1919, might be used as distance indicators for far-off galaxies. In late 1933, pursuing this idea as well as Zwicky's interest in the origin of cosmic rays, they concluded that these bright novas, which they named "supernovas," were of great intrinsic interest. They proposed that supernovas occur once a millennium in typical galaxies, that they signal the transformation of ordinary stars into "neutron stars," and that they give rise to cosmic rays. Zwicky followed up on these speculations by searching the Virgo cluster of galaxies for supernovas with a Wollensack 3.25-inch-lens camera. Frustrated by his inferior equipment, he persuaded Caltech's Observatory Council to install an eighteen-inch, large-field Schmidt telescope at Palomar.

In early 1936, before the Schmidt was completed, Zwicky was scooped by Hubble and G. Moore, who, using a ten-inch refractor at Mt. Wilson, found a supernova in one of the Virgo galaxies. A year later, as the first observer to work at Palomar, he began finding supernovas. Over the next few years, Zwicky, Baade, and Rudolph Minkowski used Zwicky's first twelve supernovas to establish their infrequency, spectra, and light curves. After this flurry of work, Zwicky did not resume his study of supernovas until the mid 1950's, when he began a successful campaign for an international supernova patrol. Finally, in the late 1960's, thanks mainly to the radio astronomers, he had the satisfaction of seeing his hypothesis that supernovas result in neutron stars enter the mainstream of astronomy.

In 1937, as he was finding his first supernovas, Zwicky was beginning a long-term program of cataloging galaxies and clusters of galaxies with the Schmidt telescope. His goal was to amass data that not only would facilitate his supernova search but also would allow statistical calculations of mean galactic mass. After the war he and his collaborators continued this project, eventually producing catalogs of galaxies (1961–1968) and compact galaxies (1971).

Despite the skepticism with which astronomers regarded much of Zwicky's interpretive work, his research on supernovas and galaxies was of such importance that he was invited to give Oxford University's Halley lecture in 1948 and was awarded the Royal Astronomical Society's Gold Medal in 1972. In his Halley lecture he broke with the tradition of discussing a celestial phenomenon, focusing instead on his "morphological" method and its applications in astronomy. The lecture must have struck much of Zwicky's audience as rather impenetrable. But his basic point—that astronomers should be more resolute about considering all the options when designing equipment and interpreting phenomena—reflected his abiding concern that his colleagues were too set in their ways.

Besides his astronomical research, Zwicky played a role in the development of jet propulsion and rocketry during and after World War II. He evidently helped Theodore von Kármán raise the capital for Aerojet Engineering Corporation, a firm established in 1942 to stimulate as well as serve the military's interest in jet aircraft and rockets. Appraisals of his performance as Aerojet's director of research, though vague, indicate that he was exceptionally energetic and inventive. Perhaps more important than his work at Aerojet was his leadership in 1945 and 1946 of U.S. Air Force teams that went first to Germany and then to Japan to evaluate wartime research on jet propulsion in these countries and to promote the effective transfer of their best technology to the United States. In 1949 Harry Truman recognized this contribution by awarding Zwicky the Presidential Medal of Freedom.

In late 1946 Zwicky attempted to use an early V-2 shot at White Sands, New Mexico, to launch some "artificial meteors." His apparatus failed, and because those coordinating upper atmospheric research regarded his idea as no more than a stunt, he did not get a second chance until October 1957. Then, in a U.S. Air Force Aerobee launching that was planned before Sputnik but carried out twelve days later, Zwicky made a second try. If, as he repeatedly claimed, he was successful, his tiny pellets were the first interplanetary objects launched from Earth. In subsequent years he was a tireless proponent of space exploration and space law, eventually becoming a vice president of the International Academy of Astronautics.

BIBLIOGRAPHY

I. ORIGINAL WORKS. Zwicky's earliest astrophysical papers are "On the Thermodynamic Equilibrium in the Universe," in *Proceedings of the National Academy of Sciences*, **14** (1928), 592–597; and "On the Red Shift of Spectral Lines Through Interstellar Space," *ibid.*, **15** (1929), 773–779. His most important papers on supernovas and neutron stars are "On Super-Novae" and "Cosmic Rays from Super-Novae," *ibid.*, **20** (1934), 254–263, both written with Walter Baade; "Photographic Light-Curves of the Two Supernovae in IC 4182 and NGC 1003," in *Astrophysical Journal*, **88** (1938), 411–421, written with Baade; "Types of Novae," in *Reviews of Modern Physics*, **12** (1940), 66–85; and "On the Frequency of Supernovae. II," in *Astrophysical Journal*, **96** (1942), 28–36. His publications on galaxies include "On the Masses of Nebulae and Clusters of Nebulae," in *Astrophysical Journal*, **86** (1937), 217–246; *Catalogue of Galaxies and of Clusters of Galaxies*, with E. Herzog, P. Wild, *et al.*, 6 vols. (Pasadena, 1961–1968); and *Catalogue of Selected Compact Galaxies and of Post-Eruptive Galaxies*, with Margrit A. Zwicky (Gümligen, Switzerland, 1971).

Zwicky's methodological works include "Morphological Astronomy," in *Observatory*, **68** (1948), 121–143; and *Morphological Astronomy* (Berlin, 1957). A copy of his "Report on Certain Phases of War Research in Germany" (1 October 1945) is in the California Institute of Technology's Archives. His most informative autobiographical writings are the "Lebenslauf" in his dissertation, *Zur Theorie der heteropolaren Kristalle* (Leipzig, 1922), 17; "Review of the Research on Supernovae," in Cristiano B. Cosmovici, ed., *Supernovae and Supernova Remnants* (Dordrecht and Boston, 1974), 1–16; and "A Stone's Throw into the Universe: A Memoir," in *Essays on the History of Rocketry and Astronautics*, II, NASA Conference Publication 2014 (Washington, D.C., 1977), 325–337.

A complete listing of Zwicky's 559 publications is in the California Institute of Technology's Astrophysics Library. His papers, which include more than 10,000 letters to and from some 2,000 correspondents, are at the Landesbibliothek, 8750 Glarus, Switzerland. Materials bearing on Zwicky's IEB fellowship and his early years at Caltech are in the Rockefeller Archive Center, North Tarrytown, New York. The University of Zurich's Archives hold an interesting set of papers connected with the decision to offer him Erwin Schrödinger's former chair in 1928. For materials bearing on his research and his relations with his Caltech and Mount Wilson colleagues, see the Millikan, von Kármán, DuBridge, and Greenstein papers in the Caltech Archives. A copy of Zwicky's interview with R. C. Hall (17 May 1971) is also there.

II. SECONDARY LITERATURE. A useful early biography is "Zwicky, Fritz," in *Current Biography*, **14** (1953), 677–678. For an appraisal of Zwicky's astronomical work by another maverick, see Fred Hoyle, "Presidential Addresses on the Society's Awards," in *Quarterly Journal of the Royal Astronomical Society*, **13** (1972), 483–484. The best obituaries are Jesse L. Greenstein and Albert G. Wilson, "Remembering Zwicky," in *Engineering and Science*, **37** (March–April 1974), 15–19; Cecilia Payne-Gaposchkin, "A Special Kind of Astronomer," in *Sky and Telescope*, **47** (1974), 311–313; and Albert G. Wilson, "Fritz Zwicky," in *Quarterly Journal of the Royal Astronomical Society*, **16** (1975), 106–108. For insights on Zwicky's relations with his students circa 1930, see "Caltech's Perfect Student: Helmar Scieite," in *Engineering and Science*, **37** (February 1974), 29–31. For Zwicky's role in Aerojet and the review of German rocket work, see Theodore von Kármán, *The Wind and Beyond* (Boston, 1967). The first book-length biography is Roland Müller, *Fritz Zwicky: Leben und Werk des Glarner Astrophysikers, Raketenforschers und Morphologen (1898–1974)* (Glarus, Switzerland, 1986).

KARL HUFBAUER

DICTIONARY
OF
SCIENTIFIC BIOGRAPHY

NOTE

This index covers material in Supplement II (Volumes XVII and XVIII) of the *Dictionary of Scientific Biography*. An index for Volumes I–XV appears in Volume XVI, together with "A Note on the Index," which provides a discussion of the criteria followed in compiling both indexes.

DICTIONARY OF SCIENTIFIC BIOGRAPHY

INDEX

B

atomic weight calculations in, 84a
biological
　see Biochemistry
colloid, 515a, 622a, 777b–778a, 784b–785a
crystallographic, 1005b–1007a
electro, 322a–323b
and geology, 48b
historiography of, 184a
industrial, 390a–391a, 661a–662b
inorganic, 183b
macromolecular, 661b–662b
marine, 746b
and microbiology, 296a–b
mineralogical, 67a–68a, 183a–184b, 582b–585a
nuclear, 285a–b, 878b–885b
organic
　see Organic chemistry
physical
　see Physical chemistry
physiological
　see Biochemistry
popular writings on, 619a
and quantum mechanics, 606a–610a, 943a–945b
and quantum theory, 280a, 280b
stereochemistry, 729a
structural, 412a, 998a–b
surface,
　Rideal mechanism, 743a
theoretical, 691b–694b
see also Biochemistry; Colloids; Compounds; Cosmochemistry; Elements, chemical; Industrial research; Neurochemistry; Reactions, chemical; Thermodynamics
Chemoteratogenesis, 757a–b
Chemotherapy
antibacterial, 588a, 932a–933b, 971a, 971b–972a
arsenicals, 473b–474a
see also Drugs; Pharmacology; *specific drugs*
Chen Jing-run, 733b
Chen Ning Yang, 482a, 769a–b
Chen-chung Chang, 896b
Cherry, R.O., 599b
Chetverikov, Sergei Sergeevich (1880–1959), 155–165, 35b, 36a, 36b, 38b, 804b, 919b, 923b
　"On Certain Aspects of the Evolutionary Process from the Viewpoint of Modern Genetics," 158b–160a, 162b, 163a
Chiasma, 205a–207b, 208a
Chibnall, A.C., 966b
Chicago, University of
ecology at, 17a, 17b, 18a, 811b, 812a
genetics and evolution at, 668b
Institute for Nuclear Studies, 24b, 25a, 607b–610a, 610b, 944a–b, 947b
mathematics at, 6b
Metallurgical Laboratory
　Manhattan Project, 24a–b
physics at, 887a–b
zoology at, 665b–666a
Chick, Harriette (1875–1977), 165–166
The Present State of Knowledge Concerning Accessory Food Factors (Vitamins), 165b
Chickens and chicks
　see Poultry
Child, Charles Manning, 213b, 442a, 665b, 811b
Chimpanzee
　see Apes
China
geology in, 553a–554a
Chittenden, Russell, 734b
Chlorites, 700a–701a

Chlorophyll
chemistry of, 177a
genetics and, 732a
Chodorow, Marvin, 835b
Choice, axiom of
　see Axiomatization, Axiom of Choice
Cholestanol
formation of, 791a, 792b
Cholesterol
biosynthesis of, 793b, 794b
dietary absorption of, 791b–792a
and gallstones, 199b
metabolism of, 196a–197a
structure of, 391a, 474a
Cholesteryl ion
discovery of, 995a–b
Choline, 378a
physiological action of, 439b–440a
Chondrites, 701a
Choquet, Gustave, 220b, 745a
Chovnick, A., 375a–b
Christensen, L. Korsgaard, 560a
Christiansen, Jens A., 557a
Christiansen, Johanne, 92b
Christie, Roger, 143a
Christofilos, Nicholas C. (1916–1972), 166–168
Chromatids, 206a–b
Chromatin, 634b, 635a
Chromatography, 390b, 998b
ion exchange, 852b, 853b–854a
starch-column, 852a–b
Chromium
spectrum of, 954a
Chromosoma
founding of, 797a
Chromosomes
arrangement
　in hybridizations, 170b–171a
　variations in, 236b–237a, 237b–238a
DNA behavior, 798a–b
and heredity, 805b
isolation of, 634b
mapping of, 10a, 238a
mutation of
　see Mutations
number of
　in differing species, 710a
pairing of, 205b, 206a–b
and plant hybridization, 26a
radiation effects on
　see Mutations
reduction of, 43a, 204b–205a
role of, 756a–b
segmental interchange of, 205b–206a
sex determining, 709b, 795b–797a, 868a
spindle interrelations, 796b–797b
theories of
　chiasma vs. classical, 205a–207b
　X, 238a
　lethal mutations of, 864b–865a
　Y, function of, 861a, 865a–b
see also Cytogenetics; Cytology; DNA; Genetics; Heredity; Linkage, genetic; Mitosis; Mutations
Chudakov, A.E., 965a
Church, Alonzo, 353b
Chwistek, Leon, 894a
Chymotrypsin, 515a, 853b
Ciliates
conjugation of, 840a–841a
Citric acid cycle, 502a–504a
Civil rights movement (U.S.), 456a, 603b, 604b
Claflin, William, 871b
Claisen, Ludwig, 488b
Clark, George L., 23b, 987b
Clark, William Mansfield, 296a, 623b, 624a
Clark University
Graduate School of Geography, 40a
physics at, 983a–984a

Clarke, Cyril A., 814b, 815a–b
Clarke, F.W., 676a
Clarke, Hans Thatcher, 792a, 793b
Clarke, John M., 358a
Class field theory (math.), 751b, 891a–892a
revision of, 386b
Classical linear groups (math.), 98b–99a
Classification
fossil, 702a–b, 752b
geosynclines, 466b
natural history, 21b, 22b
specifies, 442b
stratigraphic, 479a, 727b, 967a–b
Clausen, Jens Christen (1891–1969), 168–170
Stages in the Evolution of Plant Species, 169a
Clausen, Roy E., 359b
Genetics in Relation to Agriculture, 42b
Clausius, Rudolf, 339a
Clay, Jacob, 587a
Clay, Lucius D., 777b
Clayton, J.O., 339a
Clebsch, Rudolf, 260a
Cleland, Ralph Erskine (1892–1971), 170–171, 205b–206a, 208a, 732a
Oenothera: Cytogenetics and Evolution, 171a
Clement, John K., 19a
Clementel, E., 482a
Clements, Frederic Edward, 150b
Bio-Ecology, 812b
Cleve, Per, 184a–b
Climate
and sedimentation, 880a
and species variation, 22a–b
Climatology, 762b
　see also Meteorology; Weather
Cloëtta, Max, 790a
Cloos, Hans, 116b
Closure axioms (math.), 749b
Clotting
　see Blood, coagulation of; Milk, clotting of
Cloud chamber, 766b–767a, 992b, 1003b–1004a
Club of Rome
founding of, 324b, 327b
Cnidaria, 904a
Coacervates, 697b, 698a
Coagulation
　see Blood, coagulation of
Coal
gasification of, 661b
paleonbotany, 727b–728a
tar analysis, 616b, 617b–618a
Coastal Studies Institute (U.S.)
founding of, 763a
Coastlines
geomorphography, 763a
Coccidia
life cycle, 262a
Cochlea (ear)
and sensory inhibition study, 63a–64a
Cochran, William Gemmell (1909–1980), 171–173
Cochran's theorem, 171b
Experimental Designs, 172a
Sampling Techniques, 172a, 172b
Statistical Methods, 172b
Cochrane, W.
Theory and Practice of Electron Diffraction, 910b–912a
Cockayne, A.E., 470b
Cockcroft, J.D., 541a, 939b
Cockrill, J.R., 9a
Coe, Conway, 136a
Coefficients
Denjoy, 220a–b
of trigonometric series, 220a–b
Coen-Aubert, Marie, 307a

D

Dancs, István, 934a
Daniels, Farrington (1889–1972), 200–202, 279b, 280a
Dantzig, David Van (1900–1959), 202–203
Dapples, E.C., 465a
Darbyshire, J.A., 584a
Darlington, Cyril Dean (1903–1981), 203–209
   The Evolution of Man and Society, 204a
   meiosis theory, 20a–207b
   precocity theory, 797b–798a
   Recent Advances in Cytology, 203b
Darré, P., 757b
Darwin, Charles
   acquaintances of, 617a, 681b
   influence of, 297b, 355a, 371b, 372a, 814b, 815a
   natural selection theory, 314b–315a
   Origin of Species centennial, 470b, 925b
Darwin, Charles Galton, 23b, 143b, 284b, 327b
Darwinism
   contradictions to, 31b
   critics of, 668b
   and genetic theory, 804b
   and Mendelism, 159b, 235b–236a, 238b
   natural selection
      support for, 372a–373a
   sexual selection theory, 802b
   support for
      British, 722a–726b
      Soviet Union, 156a, 159b, 162b
   see also Natural selection; Neo-Darwinism
Dastre, Albert, 33a, 410b, 411b
Dasypus novemcinctus texanus
   see Armadillo
Data base
   communal concept, 277b
Datura stramonium, 170b
Daumer, Karl, 315b
Davenport, Charles Benedict, 738b, 811b
Davenport, Harold (1907–1969), 209–211, 386b, 392a, 656b
   The Higher Arithmetic, 211a
David, Tannatt William Edgeworth, 115a, 115b, 917b
Davidsohn, Heinrich, 622a–b
Davidson, E., 635a
Davies, David, 130a
Davies, R.O., 78a
Davis, B.M., 170a, 170b
Davis, D. (Delbert) Dwight (1908–1965), 211–213
   The Giant Panda, 212a
Davis, Hallowell, 870b
Davis, William Morris, 357b, 762a, 763a
Davisson, Clinton J., 908b, 909b, 910a–b, 937a
Davitashvili, L. Sh., 576a
Dawkins, Richard
   The Selfish Gene, 208b
Dawson, Martin Henry, 588a
Day, Arthur L., 18b, 19b, 20a, 781a
DDT, 390b
Dean, B., 187a
Dean, W.T., 991b
De Beer, Gavin Rylands (1899–1972), 213–214
   Charles Darwin, 214a
   The Development of the Vertebrate Skull, 214a
   The Elements of Experimental Embryology, 213b
   Embryology and Evolution, 213a–b
Deborin, A.M., 3b, 4a
Debye, Peter, 341a, 397b, 399b, 411b, 412a, 989b
Debye-Hückel theory, 557a, 690b, 777a–b
Debye-Scherrer method, 785a

influence of, 784b
and Onsager, 690a–691a
quantum theory, 105a
students of, 778a, 1014a
Decamethonium iodide, 474a
Decision theory, 773b–774a
Decompression sickness, 384b
Dedekind, Richard, 895a
Deduction, logical
   notion of consequence, 895b
Dee, Philip, 146b
Deegener, P., 17b
Deer, W.A., 918a, 969a, 970a
Defense, U.S. Department of
   Advanced Projects Research Agency, 167b
   Office of Research and Engineering, 74a
Deficiency diseases
   see Nutrition, deficiency effects; Vitamins
De Finetti, Bruno
   Theory of Probability, 773b–774a
Deformation, physical
   kinetics of, 283a
De Groot, Johannes (1914–1972), 214–215
Dehn, Max, 659a, 689a
Delbrück, Max, 451b, 637b, 847a, 922a, 924b
Delone, L.N., 550b
Delsarte, Jean Frédéric Auguste (1903–1968), 215–217
Demagnetization
   cooling by, 337b, 340b–342b
Demerec, Milislav (1895–1966), 217–219, 249b
   Drosophila Guide, 218a
Deming, W. Edwards, 84b, 672a, 818a
Demography
   see Population
Deninger, K., 889a
Denis, P.S., 747b–748a
Denjoy, Arnaud (1884–1974), 219–220, 770a–b
   Leçons sur le calcul des coefficients d'une série trigonométrique, 220b
Denmark
   biochemistry, 196a–199b
   chemistry, 555b–561a
   respiratory physiology, 92a–93b
   see also Institute for Theoretical Physics (Copenhagen)
Dennison, David Mathias (1900–1976), 220–222
Density
   currents
      see Turbidity currents
   distribution in Earth's layers, 125b, 127b–128b
   and geometric properties of small sets, 79a
Dentition
   see Teeth
Deny, J., 745a
Deoxyribonuclease
   structure of, 853b
Deoxyribonucleic acid
   see DNA
Depéret, Charles, 344b
Depressants, physiological, 790a
Depsipeptides
   chemistry of, 814a
Derick, Clarence, 601b
Deryagin, B.V., 323a
De Salvio, Alfonso, 189b
Desarques, Girard
   theorem of, 659b
Deserts
   fossil, 974b
Dessauer, Friedrich, 529a
Determinism, biological, 208b
Deuterium

in biological studies, 792b–794b
discovery of, 84a, 792a, 943a, 943b
in kinetic studies, 742b–743a
nuclear energy from, 911b–912a
nuclear reactions of, 146b
Deuterons
   electron scattering from, 786a
   spin, 1002a
Deutsche Gesellschaft für Vererbungswissenschaft
   founding of, 54b
Deutsches Entomologisches Institut (Berlin), 407b
Developmental Biology
   founding of, 376b
Devonian period
   paleontological boundaries, 358a, 358b
   paleontology, 369b
   stratigraphy, 306b–307a
De Vries, Hugh, 731a, 732a, 803b
Dewar, James, 341a
Diabetes
   and metabolic rate, 567b–569a, 590a
   pancreatic
      discovery of, 628a–631a, 631b
   treatment of
      alkali therapy, 627b
      insulin, 80a–81a, 348a
      pancreatic extract experiments, 630a–b
Diagenesis, 878b, 974b
D'iakonov, Dmitrii M., 300a, 300b
Dialectical materialism, 3b
   and science, 3b, 697b–698a, 804a
   see also Communism
Diamagnetism, 877a
Diamagnetism, 877a
Dickerson, Mary C., 788a–b
Dickson, L.E., 99b, 100a, 651b
   History of the Theory of Numbers, 957b
Didymium, 184a
Dieke, Gerhardt, 84a, 607b
Dielectric constant
   of polar liquids, 690a–b
Diener, Carl, 514a
Dienert, Frédéric, 640b
Dienes, Paul, 749a
Diet
   see Nutrition; Vitamins
Dietrich, Wilhelm Otto (1881–1964), 222–224
Dietz, Robert, 418b
Dieudonné, Jean
   History of Functional Analysis, 310a
Differentiably closed fields (math.), 749b
Differential (math.)
   analyzer, 136a
   of function, 310a
   manifold
      topological properties, 259b–260a
Differential equations
   see Equations, differential; Equations, partial differential
Diffraction
   of electrons, 910b–911a
   theories of, 304a
   of X rays
      see X rays, diffraction of
Diffusion
   of oxygen across cell membrane, 761a
   pump, 328b, 329b–330a
Digital computer
   RASP, 751b
Dihydroxyacetone, 533b
Dijkman, J.G., 421a
Dill, David B., 761a
Dimension
   theory of, 440b, 506b, 521a
   see also Measure theory
Ding Wenjiang, 553b
Dinosaurs
   classification of, 435b–436a

E

G

1039

I

J

K

N

W

Lists of Scientists by Field

ASTRONOMY

Bowen, I. S.

LeMaître

Zwicky

CHEMISTRY

Allen, E. T.

Badger
Belozerskii
Brode
Bury

Cameron
Chain
Chick
Conant
Cossa

Dakin
Dam
Daniels

Eyring

Fajans
Fieser

Freudenberg
Frumkin

Giauque

Halliburton
Heilbron
Hofmeister, F.
Hunt, R.

Jones, W. J.
Julian

Kargin
King, H.
Klenk
Knorr, L.
Krebs
Kunitz

Laves
Lebedev, A. N.
Linderstrøm-Lang

Machatschki
Marrack
Marvel
Mehl
Meldola

Natta

Onsager

Purdie

Richards, A. N.
Rideal
Ritthausen
Ružička

Scatchard
Schairer
Schmiedeberg
Schoenheimer
Schwarzenbach
Shemiakin

Steenbock
Stein, W. H.
Strassman

Taylor, H. S.
Thierfelder
Thomas, K.
Tréfouël

Urey

Vickery
Vinograd

Winstein
Wolfrom

Zachariasen
Zervas
Ziegler

EARTH SCIENCES

Adams, L. H.
Allen, E. T.
Arambourg
Atwood, W. W.

Bandy
Barrabé

Bateman, A. M.
Belov
Bentz
Bianchi, A.
Bjerknes, J. A. B.
Bogdanov, A. A. (*d.* 1971)
Brouwer, H. A.
Browne, W. R.
Bubnoff, von
Buddington

Bullard
Bullen

Campbell, I.
Chapman, S.
Correns, C. W.
Cossa

Dal Piaz
Dietrich
Dunbar

Edelman
Edinger
Edwards, A. B.

Lists of Scientists by Field

Ertel
Escher
Ewing, W. M.

Huene, von
Hurewicz

Leverett
Li Siguang

Ramsdell
Russell, R. J.
Rutten

Illing

Fedorov
Foshag
Fourmarier

Jepsen

Mather, K. F.
Moore, R. C.
Moret

Shubnikov
Slichter
Staub
Stillwell
Strakhov

Gignoux
Gilluly
Goldring
Gortani
Gross

Kay, M.
King, W. B. R.
Knight, S. H.
Knopf
Kuenen, P. H.
Kühn, O.
Kuno

Nieuwenkamp
Nikolaev

Tilley

Orcel

Van Leckwijck
Van Der Vlerk

Häntzschel
Heezen
Heiskanen
Helland-Hansen
Hess, H. H.
Hill, M. N.

Lane, A. C.
Lehman

Pfannenstiel
Pruvost

Wager
Walther
Whittard
Winkler, H. G. F.

LIFE SCIENCES

Agol
Albright
Allee
Allen, J. A.
Anderson, E.
Arthus
Astaurov

Dobzhansky
Dubois, R.-H.
Dunn

Jordan, K.

Oparin
Orlov, Y. A.
Osterhout

Eimer

Karpechenko
Kettlewell
King, H. D.
Köhler, W.
Krebs

Palladin, A. V.
Patterson
Payne
Peyer, B.
Poulton

Babcock, E. B.
Bates, M.
Baur
Bawden
Békésy, von
Bělař
Belozerskii
Best
Bohr, C. H. L. P. E.
Bronk
Bumpus

Fenn
Fildes
Filipchenko
Frisch

Lack
Lancefield
Levit
Levitskii
Little
Long
Lysenko

Renner
Riddle
Romer, A. S.
Rossiter
Rostand
Roughton

Carson
Chaney
Chapman, F. M.
Chetverikov
Clausen, J. C.
Cleland
Cole, L. J.
Crampton
Cunningham

Garrod
Garstang
Gley
Goodspeed
Gregory, W. K.
Gulick

MacArthur
McAtee
MacLeod
Magnus-Levy
Marrack
Martin, C. J.
Michaelis, L.
Michaelis, P.
Minkowski, O.
Mirsky
Monod

Sax
Schäfer
Schmidt, K. P.
Schmiedeberg
Schrader
Selous
Serebrovskii
Shelford
Sheppard
Sonneborn
Stanley
Stephenson
Stern, C.

Hadorn
Halliburton
Harington
Harvey, E. N.
Heinroth
Hennig
Herbst
Höber
Hubbs
Huene, von
Hyman

Dahlberg
Darlington, C. D.
Davis, D. D.
De Beer
Demerec

Neubauer
Newman
Noble

Stevens, N. M.
Stevens, S. S.
Stresemann

Teissier
Timofeeff-Ressovsky
Turesson

Verney

Waksman
Weber, H. H. J. W.

Zimmerman

MATHEMATICS

Akhiezer
Albert, A. A.
Aleksandrov

Ehresmann
Erdélyi
Evans, G. C.

Krull
Kuratowski

Rényi
Riesz, M.
Robinson

Bergman, S.
Bernays
Besicovitch
Bochner
Borsuk
Bowen, R.
Brauer

Feller
Fréchet

Gödel

Lefschetz
Levinson
Linnik
Littlewood
Löwenheim

Salem
Savage
Schauder
Scheffé
Shewhart
Siegel

Cochran

Harish-Chandra
Hasse
Heilbronn
Helly
Heyting
Hodge

Montel
Moore, R. L.
Mordell
Mostowski
Moufang

Takagi
Tarski
Teichmüller
Tietze
Turán

Vandiver

Dantzig
Davenport, H.
de Groot, J.
Delsarte
Denjoy

Kalmár
Koebe

Naimark
Nevanlinna
Neyman
Novikov

Wang, H. C.
Wolfowitz

HISTORY, PHILOSOPHY, DISSEMINATION of KNOWLEDGE

Berkner
Briggs, L. J.
Bumpus
Bush

Harington

Kowarski

Pegram
Polányi

Savage
Snow, C. P.
Stanley
Stratton, S. W.

Gödel

Marsden

Ritter, W. E.
Rostand

PHYSICS

Adams, L. H.
Alikhanov
Allison
Andreev

Chadwick
Chapman, S.
Christofilos
Coolidge, W. D.
Corbino
Cotton
Crew

Ehrenhaft
Epstein
Ewald

Giauque
Goudsmit

Barnes
Bates, L. F.
Becquerel, J. A. E. M.
Berkner
Birge, R. T.
Bowen, I. S.
Briggs, L. J.
Brillouin, L. N.
Bullard

Dennison
Dirac
Dorgelo
Dryden
Dumond

Fok
Frisch, O. R.

Gabor
Gaede
Garbasso

Heisenberg
Henri
Hunt, F. V.

Jordan, E. P.

Khokhlov
Klein, O. B.
Knudsen, V. O.
Kowarski
Kravets
Krutkov

Mayer, M. G.
Meissner, W.

Nishina

Schiff, L. I.
Siegbahn
Slater
Stepanov, A. V.
Stoner

Van Vleck
Vegard
Vernov

Webster, A. G.
Webster, D. L.
Wentzel
Wilson, H. A.

Lark-Horovitz
Laub
Leipunskii
LeMaître
Lifshits
Lukirskii

Papaleksi
Placzek
Pohl
Pomeranchuk

Tanakadate
Taylor, G. I.
Thomson, G. P.
Tomonaga
Tuve

Yukawa

McLennan
Martyn

Sakata
Saunders
Scherrer

Umov

Zwicky

TECHNOLOGY, ENGINEERING

Ayrton

Gabor
Gaede

Papaleksi

Watson-Watt
Wilhelm, R. H.

Bush

Marvel

Timoshenko